PURCHASING AND SUPPLY CHAIN MANAGEMENT

Fourth Edition

Robert M. Monczka
Arizona State University and
CAPS Research

Robert B. Handfield
North Carolina State University

Larry C. Giunipero
Florida State University

James L. Patterson
Western Illinois University

Australia • Brazil • Japan • Korea • Mexico • Singapore • Spain • United Kingdom • United States

Purchasing and Supply Chain Management, 4e

Robert M. Monczka, Robert B. Handfield, Larry C. Giunipero, James L. Patterson

VP/Editorial Director: Jack W. Calhoun

VP/Editor-in-Chief: Alex von Rosenberg

Sr. Acquisitions Editor: Charles McCormick, Jr.

Developmental Editor: Bryn Lathrop

Marketing Comm. Manager: Libby Shipp

Marketing Manager: Kristen Hurd

Marketing Coordinator: Gretchen Wildauer

Content Project Manager: Scott Dillon

Manager of Technology: John Barans

Technology Project Manager: John Rich

Prod. Technology Analyst: Adam Grafa

Sr. Manufacturing Coordinator: Diane Gibbons

Production Service: Newgen–Austin

Art Director: Stacy Jenkins Shirley

Cover Designer: Joseph Pagliaro

Library of Congress Control Number: 2008926725

Student Edition ISBN-13: 978-0-324-38134-4
Student Edition ISBN-10: 0-324-38134-4

South-Western Cengage Learning
5191 Natorp Boulevard
Mason, OH 45040
USA

Cengage Learning products are represented in Canada by Nelson Education, Ltd.

For your course and learning solutions, visit **academic.cengage.com**

Purchase any of our products at your local college store or at our preferred online store **www.ichapters.com**

Printed in the United States of America
3 4 5 6 7 12 11 10

To Shirley, Kathleen, Thomas, and Elliana

Robert M. Monczka

To Sandi, Simone, and Luc

Robert B. Handfield

To Tressa, Jan, Matthew, Michael, and Amanda

Larry C. Giunipero

To Diane, Lindsay, Karl, Drew, and Seth

James L. Patterson

Brief Contents

Contents

Preface

The Fourth Edition of *Purchasing and Supply Chain Management* is the culmination of ongoing discussions and research with purchasing and supply chain executives and managers across many industries from around the world. In this edition, we have combined our experience and research to further enhance a managerial perspective of the core tasks and challenges required to effectively manage the purchasing function within the context of an integrated supply chain. Although prior editions have dealt with many components of obtaining goods and services, we have created an integrated text that helps managers develop purchasing and supply chain strategies that contribute to overall business objectives. This new edition includes a number of innovative subjects that have been developed as a result of recent research projects undertaken by the authors.

Some of the subjects that are newly introduced or expanded upon in this edition include:

- Cross-functional teaming
- Purchasing and supply performance measurement
- Supplier integration into new product development
- Digitizing purchasing through electronic procurement systems and full e-sourcing and supply
- Supplier development
- Strategic cost management and total cost of ownership
- B2B electronic commerce and e-reverse auctions
- Enterprise resource planning
- Third-party logistics
- Price analysis tools and techniques
- Negotiation simulations
- Contracting and Internet law
- Creating the lead supply chain
- Emerging strategies and practices
- Expanded and comprehensive cases

We are proud of this new edition and believe that it reflects many new themes that are only beginning to emerge in industries worldwide.

Course Description

Purchasing and Supply Chain Management is intended for college and university courses that are variously entitled purchasing, materials management, supply chain management, sourcing management, and other similar titles. The text is also well suited for training seminars for buyers, and portions of it have been used in executive education forums. Chapters have been used in both undergraduate and M.B.A. classes in purchasing, e-commerce, operations management, and logistics. Some instructors may also elect to use sections of the book for a class in operations management or logistics.

The text is appropriate for either an elective or a required course that fulfills the American Assembly of Collegiate Schools of Business (AACSB) requirements for coverage of materials management issues. Most of the cases included in the book are based on actual companies and have all been used and modified through classroom use by the authors.

Course Objectives

Depending on the placement of a course in the curriculum or the individual instructor's philosophy, this book can be used to satisfy a variety of objectives:

1. Students should be made aware of the demands placed on purchasing and supply chain managers by business stakeholders.
2. As prospective managers, students need to understand the impact of purchasing and supply chain management on the competitive success and profitability of modern organizations.
3. Students should appreciate the ethical, contractual, and legal issues faced by purchasing and supply chain professionals.
4. Students must understand the increasingly strategic nature of purchasing, especially the fact that purchasing is much more than simply buying goods and services.
5. Students entering or currently in the workforce must understand the influence of purchasing on other major functional activities, including product design, information system design, e-commerce, manufacturing planning and control, inventory management, human resource development, financial planning, forecasting, sales, quality management, as well as many other areas.

Unique to This Edition

Many of the insights and topics presented throughout this book are based on examples developed through discussions with top purchasing executives and from various research initiatives, including research published by CAPS Research, work at the North Carolina State University Supply Chain Resource Consortium, and a project on supplier integration funded by the National Science Foundation. In addition, the text has a chapter format that includes an opening vignette, a set of sourcing snapshots, and a concluding good practice example that illustrates and integrates each chapter's topics. These new case studies and examples provide up-to-date illustrations of the concepts presented throughout each chapter.

The concept of teaming is emphasized throughout this book. Many of the case exercises require a team effort on the part of students. We recommend that the instructor have students work in teams for such projects to prepare them for the team environment found in most organizations.

Structure of the Book

This book is subdivided into six parts and 20 chapters that provide thorough coverage of purchasing and supply chain management.

Part 1: Introduction

Chapter 1 introduces the reader to purchasing and supply chain management. This chapter defines procurement and sourcing, introduces the notion of the supply chain, and summarizes the evolution of purchasing and supply chain management as an organizational activity.

Part 2: Purchasing Operations and Structure

The chapters in Part 2 provide an in-depth understanding of the fundamentals surrounding the operational activity called purchasing. These chapters focus primarily on the fundamentals of purchasing as a functional activity. Without a solid understanding of purchasing basics, appreciating the important role that purchasing can play becomes difficult.

Chapter 2 provides an overview of the purchasing process by presenting the objectives of world-class purchasing organizations, the responsibilities of professional purchasers, the purchasing cycle, and various types of purchasing documents and types of purchases. Chapter 3 examines various categories and types of purchasing policy and procedure. Most firms have a set of policies outlining the directives of executive management. These directives guide behavior and decision making and place boundaries on the behavior of personnel. Chapter 4 examines purchasing as a boundary-spanning function. Much of what purchasing involves requires interacting and working with other functional areas and suppliers. This chapter examines the intra-firm linkages between purchasing and other groups, including suppliers. Chapter 5 focuses on purchasing and supply chain organization. This includes a discussion of purchasing in the organizational hierarchy, how the purchasing function is organized, and the placement of purchasing authority. The chapter also describes the team approach as part of the organizational structure.

Part 3: Strategic Sourcing

A major premise underlying this book is that purchasing is a critical process and makes as important a contribution as manufacturing, marketing, or engineering to the pursuit of a firm's strategic objectives. Progressive firms have little doubt about purchasing's impact on total quality, cost, delivery, technology, and responsiveness to the needs of external customers. Part 3 addresses what firms must do to achieve a competitive advantage from their procurement and sourcing processes. Realizing these advantages requires shifting our view of purchasing from a tactical or clerically oriented activity to one focusing on strategic supply management. Strategic supply management involves developing the strategies, approaches, and methods for realizing a competitive advantage and improvement from the procurement and sourcing process, particularly through direct involvement and interaction with suppliers.

Chapter 6 develops an understanding of how firms set purchasing strategies. This process should include a vision and plan of what a firm must do in its purchasing/sourcing efforts to support achieving corporate goals and objectives. Clearly, the strategic planning process should be the starting point for any discussion of strategic supply management. Purchasing and commodity strategy development processes are discussed. Chapter 7 focuses on one of the most important processes performed by firms today—that is, supplier evaluation, selection, and measurement. Selecting the right suppliers helps ensure that buyers receive the right inputs to satisfy their quality, cost, delivery, and technology requirements. Selecting the right suppliers also creates the foundation for working closely with suppliers, when required, to further improve performance. Chapter 8 describes how a progressive firm manages and improves supplier quality once it selects its suppliers. Improving supplier quality may also create advantages that are not available to competing firms. Six Sigma applications are discussed. Chapter 9 describes what firms must do to manage and develop world-class supply-base performance. Supplier development is a focus. Finally, Chapter 10 focuses on worldwide sourcing, which is an important part of strategic supply management as firms search worldwide for the best resources.

Part 4: Strategic Sourcing Process

Chapter 11 focuses on strategic cost management and cost/price analysis. Progressive firms focus on cost control and reduction with suppliers as a way to improve (i.e., reduce) purchase price over time. Understanding cost fundamentals and appreciating how and when to use advanced costing techniques is critical for purchasers. This chapter details various types of costs, presents cost analysis techniques, and discusses the factors that affect a supplier's price. The chapter also discusses total cost analysis, cost-based pricing, and other innovative techniques designed to provide accurate and timely cost data.

Purchasing professionals rely on an assortment of tools, techniques, and approaches for managing the procurement and supply chain process. Chapter 12 presents various tools and techniques that purchasers use when problem solving and pursuing performance improvements. The use of these tools and techniques can help purchasers achieve specific outcomes such as reducing cost/price, improving quality, reducing time, or improving delivery performance from suppliers.

Chapter 13 deals with purchase negotiation. Effective purchasers know how to plan for and negotiate contracts that create value within a buyer-seller relationship. Increasingly, purchase contracts emphasize more than simply purchase price. Buyers and sellers may negotiate cost reductions, delivery requirements, quality levels, payment terms, or anything else important to the parties. Purchase negotiation will become increasingly important as firms focus on non-price issues and longer-term, complex purchase agreements.

Chapter 14 addresses the fundamentals of contracting. The formal contracting process creates the framework for conducting business between two or more firms. As such, an understanding of contracting is essential when attempting to manage costs within a buyer-seller relationship. Chapter 15 addresses the major legal considerations in purchasing, including the legal authority of the purchasing manager. The chapter also discusses sources of U.S. law, warranties, purchase order contracts, breaches of contract, and patent and intellectual property rights. Because contracting is a part of the legal process, this chapter naturally follows the contracting chapter.

Part 5: Critical Supply Chain Elements

Part 5 describes the major activities that relate to or directly support supply chain management. Some of these activities involve specific disciplines, such as inventory management or transportation; other activities relate to the development of supply chain support systems. These systems include performance measurement systems and computerized information technology systems. The activities presented in this part may or may not be a formal part of the purchasing organization. These activities and systems, however, are key elements of purchasing and supply chain management.

Without them, purchasing probably cannot effectively pursue its goals and objectives. Therefore, purchasing students must be familiar with a range of supply chain activities.

Chapter 16 focuses on a topic of increasing interest—the management of a firm's inventory investment. The money that a firm commits to inventory usually involves a significant commitment of financial resources. This chapter discusses the function of inventory within a firm, factors leading to inventory waste, creating a lean supply chain, approaches for managing a firm's inventory investment, and future trends related to managing inventory. At some firms, purchasing is responsible for the day-to-day management of inventory.

Another area of interest involves the purchase of transportation and other services. We have witnessed major changes in transportation over the last 15 years, many of which have affected purchasing. Since Congress deregulated the transportation industry in the early 1980s, the role of the buyer has changed dramatically. More than ever, purchasing is involving itself in the evaluation, selection, and management of transportation carriers. Even if a buyer does not get involved directly with transportation, having a working knowledge of this dynamic area is critical. Chapter 17 highlights purchasing's role in transportation and service buying, presents a decision-making framework for developing transportation strategy, discusses ways to control and influence inbound transportation, and evaluates trends affecting the purchase of transportation services such as performance-based logistics. In addition, insights into how other services are purchased are discussed.

Information technology systems are changing business. Purchasing, too, can benefit from the development of current information technology systems. Chapter 18 examines the role of supply chain information systems and electronic commerce. The chapter also addresses the electronic linkage between firms through electronic data interchange (EDI) and Internet capability. Finally, this chapter discusses some advanced and future e-purchasing and supply systems' applications. The availability of information technology systems greatly enhances purchasing's ability to operate at the highest levels of efficiency and effectiveness.

Chapter 19 focuses on performance measurement and evaluation. Increasingly, firms must develop valid measurement systems that reveal how well a firm is performing, including the performance of its purchasing and supply chain management efforts. These systems need to be clearly linked to overall company objectives. Measurement systems support procurement and sourcing decision making by providing accurate and timely performance data. This chapter examines why firms measure performance, defines various purchasing performance measurement categories, and discusses how to develop a purchasing performance measurement system, including a balanced scorecard.

Part 6: Future Directions

Chapter 20 focuses on what purchasing and supply chain management will look like in the 21st century. These trends, which are adapted directly from recent surveys and studies of key executive managers from a variety of global organizations, can help students identify how the field of purchasing and sourcing management is changing, and what skills they will need to develop in view of these changes. The latest predictions are included from CAPS Research Project 10X EA and a joint CAPS Research, AT Kearney, and ISM study focused on supply strategies for the decade ahead.

Case Studies and Instructor's Resources

Purchasing and Supply Chain Management contains new and revised cases featured within the book. These cases have been classroom tested and used within the industry. A test bank, PowerPoint® presentation, and other ancillary materials are available on CD-ROM (ISBN: 0-324-38135-2) to help instructors identify how best to use and interpret the text and cases. Of particular interest are the negotiation and supplier selection cases, which allow students to experience the purchasing decision-making process in real time. The Instructor's Resource CD is available to adopters of the Fourth Edition by calling the Academic Resource Center at 1-800-423-0563. More information about this text can be found at the product website, http://monczka.swlearning.com.

Acknowledgments

We very much appreciate the work of Bryn Lathrop, Developmental Editor, and Scott Dillon, Content Project Manager, both of South-Western Cengage Learning, in making this Fourth Edition possible. In addition, we thank Fran Andersen, Project Manager at Newgen–Austin, for her excellent editorial work and content review.

Robert M. Monczka
Robert B. Handfield
Larry C. Giunipero
James L. Patterson

About the Authors

Robert M. Monczka, Ph.D., is Distinguished Research Professor of Supply Chain Management in the W. P. Carey School of Business at Arizona State University. He is also Director of Strategic Sourcing and Supply Chain Strategy Research at CAPS Research, where he leads initiatives focused on sourcing and supply strategy innovation, development, and implementation. He has published more than 200 books and articles. He has also consulted worldwide with leading companies in the Fortune 100 and is a frequent speaker at professional meetings. He has also been the recipient of two National Science Foundation grants to study supply strategy.

Robert B. Handfield is Bank of America University Distinguished Professor of Supply Chain Management in the College of Management at North Carolina State University. He is also Co-Director of the Supply Chain Resource Cooperative (http://scrc.ncsu.edu). He is Consulting Editor of the *Journal of Operations Management* and on the editorial board of several leading academic journals. His research focuses on strategic sourcing, supply market intelligence, supplier relationship management, and sourcing overseas. He has served in consulting and executive education roles for more than 20 Fortune 500 companies.

Larry C. Giunipero, Ph.D., C.P.M., is Professor of Marketing and Supply Chain Management at Florida State University. He has published more than 50 articles in various academic journals. His research interests are in the areas of e-purchasing, supply chain sourcing strategies, and supply management skills and competencies. He has served as a consultant and or executive trainer to more than 20 Fortune 1000 organizations both domestically and globally. He holds a Ph.D. from Michigan State University.

James L. Patterson, Ph.D., is Associate Professor of Operations and Supply Chain Management for the College of Business and Technology at Western Illinois University and served as founding director of WIU's Quad Cities Executive Studies Center. Patterson also holds the ISM C.P.M. and A.P.P. lifetime designations. He has been recognized as WIU's Outstanding Teacher of the Year and also listed four times in *Who's Who Among America's Teachers.* He has served on the board of directors for CAPS Research, the Three Rivers Manufacturing Technology Consortium, and the Quad City Manufacturing Laboratory. His research interests include buyer-supplier relationships, negotiation and conflict resolution, and sourcing strategy.

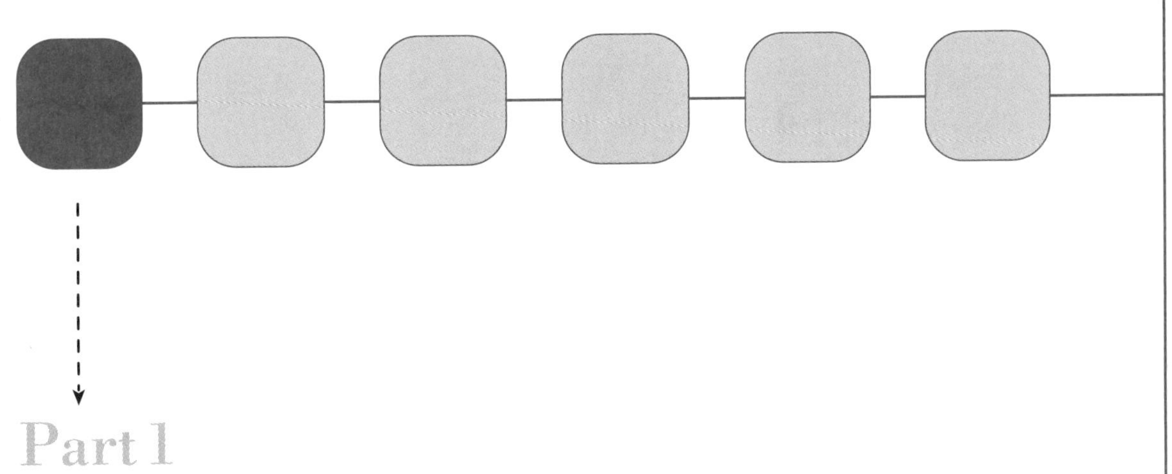

Part 1

Introduction

Chapter 1

INTRODUCTION TO PURCHASING AND SUPPLY CHAIN MANAGEMENT

Learning Objectives

After completing this chapter, you should be able to

- Understand the differences between purchasing and supply management
- Understand the differences between supply chains and value chains
- Identify the activities that are part of supply chain management
- Appreciate the importance of supply chain enablers
- Identify the historical stages of purchasing's evolution

Chapter Outline

Putting the "ROAR" Back in CSX Purchasing

Fran Chinnici, a Penn State University engineering graduate, knows all about the Nittany Lion "roar" from his days in State College (a.k.a. Happy Valley). When Chinnici was named vice president of purchasing and materials at CSX Transportation just over three years ago, he felt that a major change was needed to get his sourcing team on a new track. Since his appointment to the job, he has put the purchasing function on the global track to 21st-century excellence.

CSX is one of four Class 1 Railroads in the United States. In 2007 the company had sales of over $10 billion and earnings of $2.99/share. With a barrel of crude oil fluctuating in the $90 to $100 range and fuel prices at close to $3 a gallon, the railroads have become a favorite of many shippers. The railroads' low cost-per-ton-mile allows them to compete very favorably with other transportation modes.

Supporting this business growth and sustaining high levels of service, while controlling materials costs, posed major challenges for the CSX Purchasing and Materials Department. Meeting the challenge was compounded by a changing supply base. Chinnici states that "a reduction in the number of railroads and the subsequent consolidation of purchases resulted in a downsizing of our domestic supply base." With the growth in shipments experienced by the U.S. Class 1 Railroads, the lack of domestic suppliers is a major concern. This is especially true considering that Chinnici and his team are responsible for $4 billion in purchases. This money is spent on over 100,000 items necessary to keep 21,000 route miles of track, about 100,000 freight cars, and over 4,300 locomotives moving freight to the thousands of localities and customers served by CSX. "Based on the demands of our operating environment, the shrinking supply base, and the need to continuously add value to the company from a supply perspective, it was a no-brainer that we had to develop a more global perspective," says Chinnici.

His goal was to raise the skill levels of his organization to meet the global as well as other challenges required of a 21st-century supply function. Toward that end, he made it a requirement for all current employees and new hires to further develop their skill sets and attain the status of Certified Purchasing Manager (C.P.M.). Leading by example, Chinnici attended C.P.M. training along with his staff members and successfully passed the necessary exams. He proudly displays his C.P.M. certificate in his office overlooking Jacksonville's growing skyline. "Attending classes with my people was a way of visibly demonstrating my commitment to raising our level of professionalism," he says, "and the C.P.M. is just a start." After three years he is proud to say that over 95% of his supply management professionals are C.P.M. certified.

"The journey from a domestic to a global supply base is not always smooth and it requires both time and effort to make a significant impact," Chinnici states. Without adding headcount, Chinnici reorganized his resources and formed a team focused on developing current suppliers and growing the supply base. Led by Rod Keefe, the Purchasing Strategy and Supplier Development team was formed to develop suppliers and create a process to begin sourcing railroad materials globally. An early success was the sourcing of rail from Eastern Europe. So now, in addition to two domestic rail mills and mills in Japan, CSX sources rail from the Czech Republic. Then, 25-year purchasing veteran Jim Fronckoski, manager of Locomotive Purchasing, began scouring the globe for rail wheels, brake shoes, and coupler parts. "Many of the commodities in the marketplace where we play are becoming global," states Fronckoski. So in order to move the skill set of his purchasing team to yet another level of professionalism in global awareness, Chinnici had his key managers and staff attend a series of global sourcing workshops. "The customized workshops provided my staff with a much deeper understanding of global sourcing issues and required relationships," he states. To date, the department has several global sourcing initiatives in the pipeline. Some are pending approval from the American Association of Railroads standards board; others require extensive laboratory and field testing to ensure their integrity for service use.

"We won't cut corners," says Chinnici. As evidence of that, the Penn State engineer recently huddled resources from around CSX to expand the supplier quality efforts for purchased materials, and it's no surprise he gave them a global perspective on launch day. With the cooperation and vision of Rich Regan, vice president of Mechanical Operations, Chinnici centralized this technical group in Purchasing, added additional resources, and expanded the focus to include all critical materials from around the globe.

Complementing the global push is CSX's extensive involvement in e-commerce. The railroads have a long history of doing business electronically, beginning with their pioneering efforts in using EDI with their customers. CSX continues the use of electronic tools to facilitate sourcing. "98.6% of our purchasing expenditures are now transmitted electronically," states Stan Hefley, director of Process Improvement. Hefley further states, "On an average month we run about 2,000 items a day over our Oracle system." Another major e-commerce initiative is the association with Railmarketplace.com, where the four major railroads meet to discuss potential purchases of nonstrategic items. Elaine Mosley, manager of Supplier Development, says, "The consortium gives CSX and the other major railroads an opportunity to leverage their smaller nondirect purchases to provide savings for all the participants."

Putting the right structure in place to achieve these results is no easy task. "I felt my direct reporting staff was somewhat disjointed and hindered the ability to make rapid decisions," states Chinnici. "We needed to streamline our organization and become able to identify and seize market opportunities quickly." Chinnici's vision is to have a lean, responsive supply management organization that anticipates and meets the needs of CSX. "I want to be like Wal-Mart . . . by having a quality product available, at a convenient place and at the right cost, while working with both our suppliers and internal customers to provide a very high level of cooperation and service."

Chinnici is pushing his procurement team to work at a much higher strategic level in the industry, providing even more value-added service to CSX. To that end the supply group is starting to become a player in areas often described as nontraditional, because these areas of spend were traditionally purchased by functional groups outside of purchasing. Becoming involved in these new service areas, such as audit, legal, and advertising, allows the CSX supply function to apply professional supply management and contracting practices to areas that were previously the domain of users in other functional areas. Chinnici sums it up by stating that "in today's rapidly changing environment we need skilled, open-minded supply professionals who can deliver results to our organization regardless of economic conditions and in any area of spend." Oscar Munoz, CSX executive vice president and chief financial officer, concurs. "I view our purchasing and supply area as a major contributor to the bottom line and critical to the service capabilities of our railroad company," says Munoz. Accomplishing their mission requires a staff of dedicated professionals who can ensure availability of the locomotives, cars, track, and maintenance parts needed to keep CSX trains running at a very demanding operating capacity. Chinnici and Munoz both are optimistic that their sourcing group will continue to build on their string of recent successes. The ROAR is back . . . at least at CSX Purchasing and Materials.

Source: L. Giunipero, Interview with Fran Chinnici and CSX supply management personnel, February 2008.

As the CSX story illustrates, the development of progressive purchasing approaches and strategies can help a company maintain or improve its competitive position. In reality, it is only recently that managers would even place the words "progressive" and "purchasing" in the same sentence. Not so long ago, the life of a purchasing professional was comfortable and predictable. When someone required something, a buyer sent a request to suppliers for competitive bids, awarded short-term contracts based on price, enjoyed a free lunch or ball game with salespeople, and figured out how to meet not-too-demanding performance measures. Although the buying position did not carry much prestige, it was a good way to earn a pension.

This model worked relatively well until new competitors from around the world showed there was a better way to manage purchasing and the supply base. New and better methods helped these competitors achieve dramatic reductions in cost, exponential improvements in quality, and unheard-of reductions in the time it takes to develop new products. This new model featured closer relationships with important suppliers, performing due diligence on suppliers before awarding long-term contracts, conducting worldwide Internet searches for the best sources of supply, and participating with suppliers during product and process development. Furthermore, executive managers began to require purchasing professionals to achieve demanding performance improvements. What really changed the purchasers' comfortable world, and ended the era of free lunches, was global competition. Borrowing a phrase from Thomas Friedman, the world is flat and competition is now 24/7, anywhere and anytime.[1]

As is illustrated in the CSX story, global sourcing is a requirement and no longer a luxury for most firms. This chapter introduces the reader to the changing world of purchasing and supply chain management. It is a world that has changed more during the last 15 years than the previous 150 years combined. The first section of this chapter describes the new competitive environment where we now operate—an environment that affects every major industry. We next present the reasons why purchasing has taken on increased importance. Third, we clarify the confusing terminology that surrounds purchasing and supply chain management. The next sections present the activities that are part of supply chain management, discuss the four enablers of purchasing and supply chain excellence, and review the historic evolution of purchasing and supply chain management. The last section outlines the contents of this book.

A New Competitive Environment

The new millennium features increasing numbers of world-class competitors, domestically and internationally, that are forcing organizations to improve their internal processes to stay competitive. Sophisticated customers, both industrial and consumer, no longer talk about price increases—they demand price reductions! Information that is available over the Internet will continue to alter the balance of power between buyers and sellers. An abundance of competitors and choices have conditioned customers to want higher quality, faster delivery, and products and services tailored to their individual needs at a lower total cost. If a company cannot meet these requirements, the customer will find someone who is more accommodating.

Throughout the 1960s and 1970s, companies began to develop detailed market strategies that focused on creating and capturing customer loyalty. Before long, organizations also realized that this required a strong engineering, design, and manufacturing function to support these market requirements. Design engineers had to translate customer requirements into product and service specifications, which then had to be produced at a high level of quality at a reasonable cost. As the demand for new products increased throughout the 1980s, organizations had to become flexible and responsive to modify existing products, services, and processes, or to develop new ones to meet ever-changing customer needs.

As organizational capabilities improved further in the 1990s, managers began to realize that material and service inputs from suppliers had a major impact on their ability to meet customer needs. This led to an increased focus on the supply base and the responsibilities of purchasing. Managers also realized that producing a quality product was not enough. Getting the right products and services to customers at the right time, cost, place, condition, and quantity constituted an entirely new type of challenge. More recently, new technology has spawned a whole set of time-reducing information technologies and logistics networks aimed at meeting these new challenges. The availability of low-cost alternatives has led to unprecedented shifts toward outsourcing and offshoring. The impact of China as a major world competitor poses tremendous challenges for U.S. firms in both the manufacturing and services sectors. Because the services sector now accounts for over 70% of the Gross Domestic Product, new strategies are required for effective supply management in this sector.

All these changes have made 21st-century organizations realize how important it is to manage their supply base. They must be involved in the management of (or at least take a serious interest in) the suppliers that provide materials and services. They must also be concerned with the network of downstream firms responsible for delivery and aftermarket service of the product to the end customer. From this realization emerged the concept of the supply chain and supply chain management.

Several factors are driving an emphasis on supply chain management. First, the *cost and availability of information resources* between entities in the supply chain allow easy linkages that eliminate time delays in the network. Second, the *level of competition* in both domestic and international markets requires organizations to be fast, agile, and flexible. Third, *customer expectations and requirements* are becoming much more demanding. Fourth, the *ability of an organization's supply chain to react rapidly* to major disruptions in both supply and downstream product or services will lessen the impact on lost sales. As demands increase, organizations and their suppliers must be responsive or face the prospect of losing market share. Competition today is no longer between firms, it is between the supply chains of those firms. The companies that configure the best supply chains will be the market winners and gain competitive advantage.

Why Purchasing Is Important

As companies struggle to increase customer value by improving performance, many companies are turning their attention to purchasing and supply management. Consider, for example, CSX, the company featured at the beginning of this chapter. Over 40% of the total sales of CSX is expended with suppliers for the purchase of materials and services. It does not take a financial genius to realize the impact that suppliers can have on a firm's total cost. Furthermore, many features that make their way into final products originate with suppliers. The supply base is an important part of the supply chain. Supplier capabilities can help differentiate a producer's final good or service.

In the manufacturing sector the percentage of purchases to sales averages 55%. This means that for every dollar of revenue collected on goods and services sales, more than half goes back to suppliers. It is not difficult to see why purchasing is clearly a major area for cost savings. However, savings come in different forms; the traditional approach is to bargain hard for price reductions. A newer approach is to build relations with suppliers to jointly pull costs out of the product or service.

A three-year study within the automobile industry studied the extent to which major producers emphasized relationships. The results showed a clear difference in the approach taken to managing suppliers. When suppliers were asked to rate their automobile customers, the Japanese transplants Toyota, Honda, and Nissan were all above the median on their "Supplier Relations Working Index" score, whereas Chrysler, Ford, and General Motors were rated below the median. This says something about how suppliers perceive the dominant purchasing philosophy of these large automobile companies. The 17-category index measured key supplier relationship parameters including relationship development and communications. Out of a maximum score of 500, Toyota was first with an index score of 399, while General Motors was last with a score of 144. The superior management of supplier relationships has helped give Japanese automobile producers a cost advantage over Detroit's Big Three.[2]

Purchasing and supply management also has a major impact on product and service quality. In many cases, companies are seeking to increase the proportion of parts, components, and services they outsource in order to concentrate on their own areas of specialization and competence. This further increases the importance of the relationships between purchasing, external suppliers, and quality.

The following example illustrates this important link between supplier quality and product quality. Heparin is a main ingredient in products for patients requiring dialysis and medicines that prevent blood clots during surgery and thin the blood. Heparin has recently come under suspicion in the deaths of four Americans and allergic reactions from another 350 patients who obtained heparin from Baxter International. Interestingly, more than half of the world's heparin comes from China. The recent deaths have highlighted the need to control sourcing accountability. One of the key ingredients in the process of making heparin is pulp extracted from pig intestines, which is then heated in large vats. This key ingredient is widely sourced in small, poorly regulated Chinese factories. For example, one Chinese firm, Yuan Intestine and Casing Factory, also manufactures sausage casings. Baxter buys its heparin from Scientific Protein. The president of Scientific Protein says it can't trace its supplies in China as well as it can in the United States. The example illustrates the importance of the supplier selection process and its role in the entire supply chain, from raw material to finished product. This example further illustrates how lapses in managing supplier quality can potentially tarnish a firm's reputation.[3]

Purchasing, acting as the liaison between suppliers and engineers, can also help improve product and process designs. For example, companies that involve suppliers early, compared to companies that do not involve suppliers, achieve an average 20% reduction in materials cost, 20% improvement in material quality, and 20% reduction in product development time. Development teams that include suppliers as members also report they receive more improvement suggestions from suppliers than teams that do not involve suppliers. Thus involving suppliers early in the design process is a way purchasing can begin to add new value and contribute to increasing their competitiveness.

Many executives will agree that a focus on effective purchasing has become a critical way to gain competitive advantage. An indication of this enhanced reputation and recognition is the higher salaries that are being paid to purchasing professionals. The most recent *Purchasing* magazine salary survey showed an average annual income of $84,611. Interestingly, those with responsibility for sourcing services are among the highest earners in the profession, with an average annual compensation of $104,110. Purchasers who buy IT goods and services make $101,104, and those purchasing logistics services are compensated $97,802. Additionally, the survey found that purchasers continue to make more when compared to their colleagues in other related fields, such as logistics and engineering. Eighty percent of purchasing executives made over $100,000, with bonuses averaging over 13% of base salaries.[4]

Understanding the Language of Purchasing and Supply Chain Management

Anyone who has written about purchasing and supply chain management has defined the various terms associated with these concepts one way or another, making confusion about the subjects a real possibility. How, for example, is purchasing different from supply management? Are supply chains and value chains the same? What is supply chain management? What is an extended enterprise? It is essential to define various terms before proceeding with this book.

Purchasing and Supply Management

We need to recognize the differences between purchasing and supply management. **Purchasing** is a functional group (i.e., a formal entity on the organizational chart) as well as a functional activity (i.e., buying goods and services). The purchasing group performs many activities to ensure it delivers maximum value to the organization. Examples include supplier identification and selection, buying, negotiation and contracting, supply market research, supplier measurement and improvement, and purchasing systems development. Purchasing has been referred to as doing "the five rights": getting the right quality, in the right quantity, at the right time, for the right price, from the right source. In this text we will interchange the terms "purchasing" and "procurement."

Supply management is not just a new name for purchasing but a more inclusive concept. We feel **supply management** is a *strategic approach to planning for and acquiring the organization's current and future needs through effectively managing the supply base, utilizing a process orientation in conjunction with cross-functional teams (CFTs) to achieve the organizational mission.* Similar to our definition, the Institute for Supply Management defines supply management *as the identification, acquisition, access, positioning, and management of resources and related capabilities an organization needs or potentially needs in the attainment of its strategic objectives.*[5] Exhibit 1.1 depicts the key elements in our definition of supply management.

Exhibit 1.1 Defining Supply Management

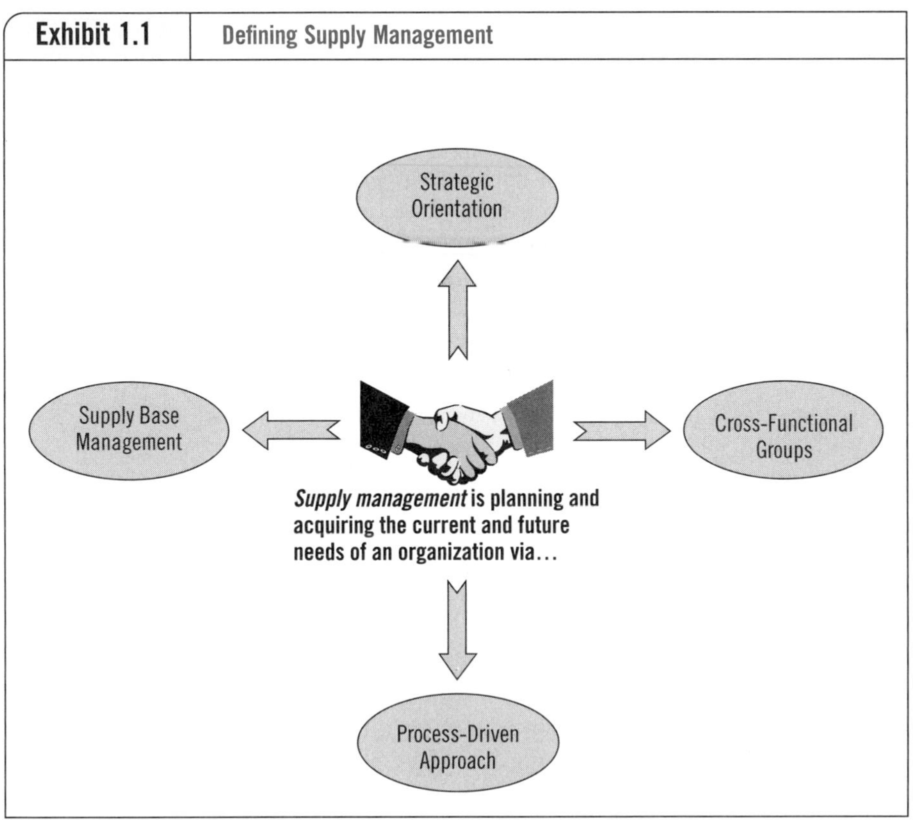

Supply management requires pursuing **strategic responsibilities**, which are those activities that have a major impact on longer-term performance of the organization. These longer-term responsibilities are not pursued in isolation, but should be aligned with the overall mission and strategies of the organization. These strategies exclude routine, simple, or day-to-day decisions that may be part of traditional purchasing responsibilities. The routine ordering and follow-up of basic operational supplies is not a strategic responsibility. The development of the systems that enable internal users to order routine supplies, however, is considerably more important.

Supply management is a broader concept than purchasing. Supply management is a progressive approach to **managing the supply base** that differs from a traditional arm's-length or adversarial approach with sellers. It requires purchasing professionals to work directly with those suppliers that are capable of providing world-class performance and advantages to the buyer. Think of supply management as a progressive and supercharged version of basic purchasing.

Supply management often takes a **process approach** to obtaining required goods and services. We can describe supply management as the process of identifying, evaluating, selecting, managing, and developing suppliers to realize supply chain performance that is better than that of competitors. We will interchange the terms "supply management" and "strategic sourcing" throughout this book.

Supply management is **cross-functional**, meaning it involves purchasing, engineering, supplier quality assurance, the supplier, and other related functions working together as one team, early on, to further mutual goals.[6] Instead of adversarial relationships, which characterize traditional purchasing, supply management features a long-term win-win relationship between a buying company and specially selected suppliers. Except for ownership, the supplier almost becomes an extension of the buying company. Supply management also involves concrete, on-site, and frequent help to suppliers in exchange for dramatic and continuous performance improvements, including steady price reductions. In short, supply management is a new way of operating, involving internal operations and external suppliers to achieve advances in cost management, product development, cycle times, and total quality control.

Organizationally, leading and coordinating strategic supply management activities has largely become the responsibility of the functional group called purchasing. Practicing professionals often use the terms "supply management" and "purchasing" interchangeably. Through the above discussion we have sought to clarify some of the differences while recognizing that good purchasing and supply management practices can have significant impact on the organization's overall performance.

Supply Chains and Value Chains

Over time, researchers and practitioners have developed dozens of definitions to describe supply chains and supply chain management. One group of researchers has indicated that defining supply chain management both as a philosophy and as a set of operational activities[7] creates confusion. These researchers break down the concept into three areas and separate supply chain orientation from supply chains and from supply chain management.

A **supply chain orientation** is a higher-level recognition of the strategic value of managing operational activities and flows within and across a supply chain. A **supply chain** is a set of three or more organizations linked directly by one or more of the upstream or downstream flows of products, services, finances, and information from a source to a customer. **Supply chain management**, then, endorses a supply chain orientation and involves proactively managing the two-way movement and coordination of goods, services, information, and funds (i.e., the various flows) from raw material through end user. According to this definition, supply chain management requires the coordination of activities and flows that extend across boundaries. Organizations that endorse a supply chain orientation are likely to emphasize supply chain management.[8]

Regardless of the definition or supply chain perspective used, we should recognize that supply chains are composed of interrelated activities that are internal and external to a firm. These activities are diverse in their scope; the participants who support them are often located across geographic boundaries and often come from diverse cultures.

Although many activities are part of supply chain management (which a later section discusses), an improved perspective visualizes supply chains as composed of processes rather than discrete, often poorly aligned activities and tasks. A process consists of a set of interrelated tasks or activities designed to achieve a specific objective or outcome. New-product development (NPD), customer-order fulfillment, supplier evaluation and selection, and demand and supply planning are examples of critical organizational processes that are part of supply chain management. Recent product recalls of consumer products such as toys, peanut butter, and dog food have placed increasing emphasis on a new supply chain concept: the reverse supply chain; its goal is to rapidly identify and return these tainted products back through the supply chain.

Conceiving of supply chains as a series of systematic processes makes sense for a number of reasons. Almost by definition, processes usually move across functional boundaries, which aligns well with a supply management and supply chain orientation. Well-communicated processes also accelerate learning as participants become familiar with a defined process. Furthermore, formal supply chain processes can "build in" best practices and knowledge that enhance the likelihood of success. Perhaps most importantly, organizations can document, measure, and improve their supply chain processes.

A question that often arises, and one that has no definite answer, involves the difference between a value chain and a supply chain. Michael Porter, who first articulated the value chain concept in the 1980s, argues that a firm's **value chain** is composed of primary and support activities that can lead to competitive advantage when configured properly. Exhibit 1.2 presents a modified version of Porter's value chain model. This exhibit also defines some important supply chain–related terms and places them in their proper context.

One way to think about the difference between a value chain and supply chain is to conceptualize the supply chain as a subset of the value chain. All personnel within an organization are part of a value chain. The same is not true about supply chains. The primary activities, or the horizontal flow across Exhibit 1.2, represent the operational part of the value chain, or what some refer to as the supply chain. At an organizational level, the value chain is broader than the supply chain, because it includes all

Exhibit 1.2 The Extended Value Chain

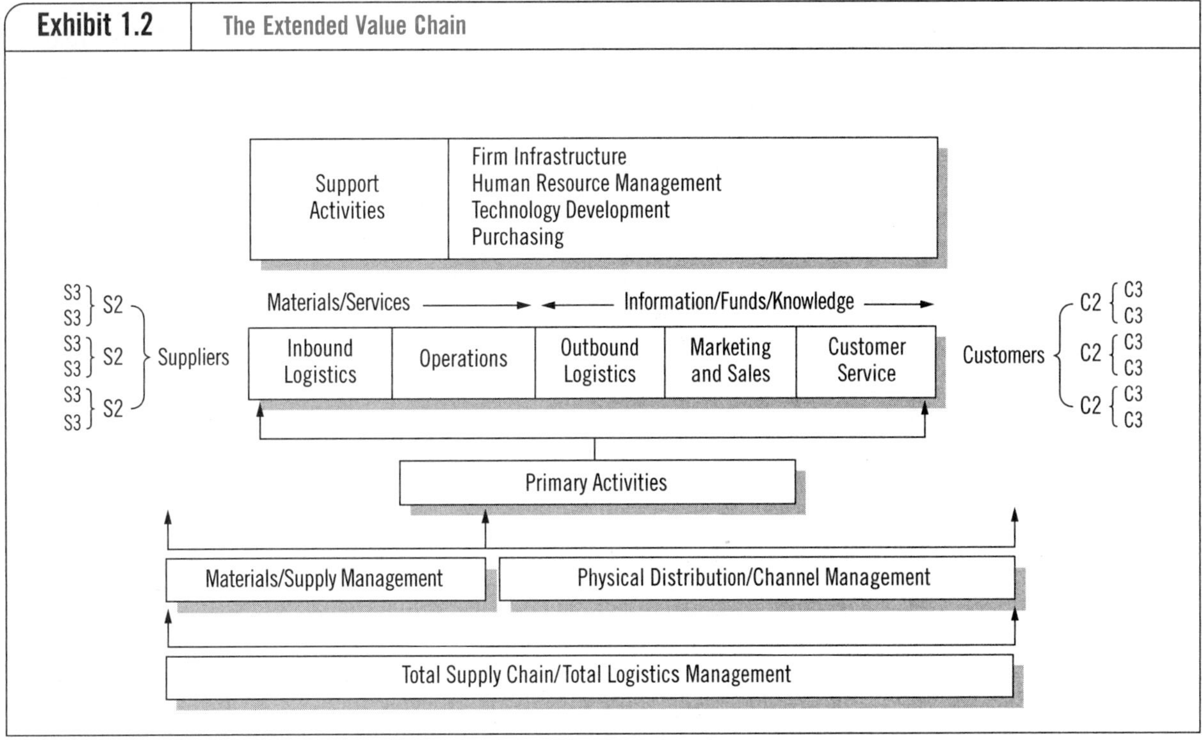

activities in the form of primary and support activities. Furthermore, the original value chain concept focused primarily on internal participants, whereas a supply chain, by definition, is both internally and externally focused.

To reflect current thinking, we must expand the original value chain model, which focused primarily on internal participants, to include suppliers and customers who reside well upstream and downstream from the focal organization. Multiple levels of suppliers and customers form the foundation for the **extended value chain** or the **extended enterprise** concept, which states that success is a function of effectively managing a linked group of firms past first-level suppliers or customers. In fact, progressive firms understand that managing cost, quality, and delivery requires attention to suppliers that reside several tiers from the producer. The extended enterprise concept recognizes explicitly that competition is no longer between firms but rather between coordinated supply chains or networks of firms.

Notice that Exhibit 1.2 identifies purchasing as a support activity. This means that purchasing provides a service to internal customers. Although purchasing is the central link with suppliers that provide direct materials, which is the upstream or left-hand side of Exhibit 1.2, purchasing can support the materials and service requirements of any internal group. (Direct materials are those items provided by suppliers and used directly during production or service delivery.) Purchasing is becoming increasingly responsible for sourcing indirect goods and services required by internal groups. Examples of indirect items include personal computers, office and janitorial supplies, health care contracts, transportation services, advertising and media, and travel. Although indirect items are not required for production, they are still vital to the effective running of an organization. The right-hand side of the model illustrates the customer, or downstream, portion of the supply chain. Because meeting or exceeding customer expectations is the lifeblood of any organization, it should become the focal point of supply chain activities. Exhibit 1.2 presents a relatively straightforward and linear view of the value and supply chain, which is often not the case. First, the flows of materials, information, funds, and knowledge across a supply chain are often fragmented and uncoordinated. The "hand-off" points from one group to the next or from one organization to the next usually provide opportunity for improvements. Second, the value chain model shows suppliers linking with inbound logistics and then operations. Although this is usually the case with direct materials, indirect items and finished goods sourced externally can result in suppliers delivering to any part of the supply chain.

Supply Chains Illustrated

The increasing importance of supply chain management is forcing organizations to rethink how their purchasing and sourcing strategies fit with and support broader business and supply chain objectives. Supply chains involve multiple organizations as we move toward the raw material suppliers or downstream toward the ultimate customer. Simple supply chains pull materials directly from their origin, process them, package them, and ship them to consumers.

A good example of a simple supply chain involves cereal producers (see Exhibit 1.3). A cereal company purchases the grain from a farmer and processes it into cereal. The cereal company also purchases the paperboard from a paper manufacturer, which purchased the trees to make the paper, and labels from a label manufacturer, which purchased semifinished label stock to make the labels. The cereal is then packaged and sent to a distributor, which in turn ships the material to a grocer, who then

Exhibit 1.3 A Cereal Manufacturer's Supply Chain

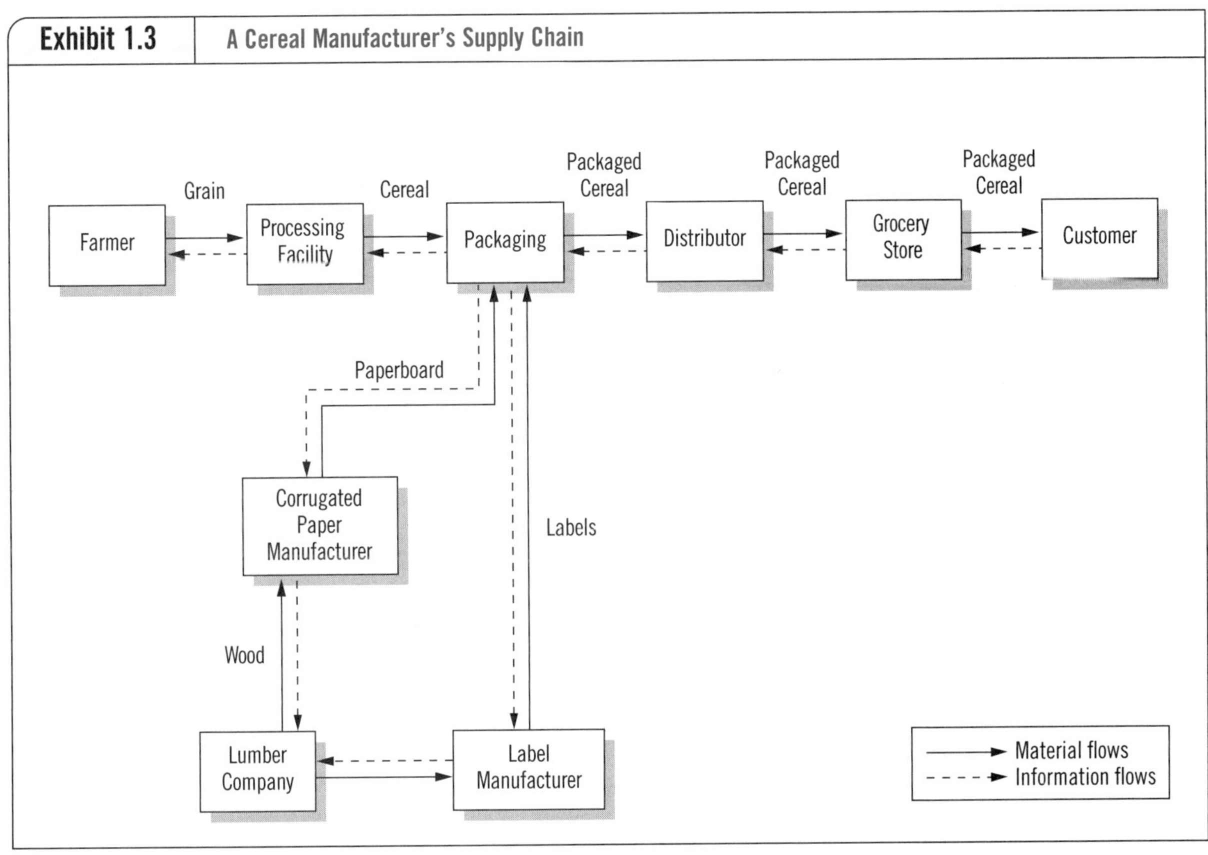

sells it to an end customer. Even for a simple product such as cereal, the number of transactions and of material and information flows can be considerable.

The supply chain for the cereal manufacturer features an extensive distribution network that is involved in getting the packaged cereal to the final customer. Within the downstream portion of the supply chain, logistics managers are responsible for the actual movement of materials between locations. One major part of logistics is transportation management, involving the selection and management of external carriers (trucking companies, airlines, railroads, shipping companies) or the management of internal private fleets of carriers. Distribution management involves the management of packaging, storing, and handling of materials at receiving docks, warehouses, and retail outlets.

For products such as automobiles, which feature multiple products, technologies, and processes, the supply chain becomes more complicated. The materials, planning, and logistics supply chain for an automotive company is shown in Exhibit 1.4 on p. 14, which illustrates the complexity of the chain, spanning from automotive dealers back through multiple levels or tiers of suppliers. The automotive company's supplier network includes the thousands of firms that provide items ranging from raw materials, such as steel and plastics, to complex assemblies and subassemblies, such as transmissions, brakes, and engines.

Participants in a supply chain are willing to share such information only when there is trust between members. Thus, the management of relationships with other

Exhibit 1.4 An Automotive Supply Chain: The Role of Materials Planning and Logistics in the Production and Delivery System

Car Dealers
CARS
Sales Operations
Allocated Buildable Orders
19 Plants

Assembly Material Planning
- Vehicle scheduling
- Pre-production planning
- Components scheduling
- Planning/sequencing

Shipping
Assembly Line
Warehousing
Receiving

Product Engineering
New Products and Engineering Changes
Ship Release
PARTS
PARTS
Request to Buy
Ship Releases Engineering Changes
Request to Buy

Manufacturing — 57 Plants

		Stampings
Engines	Transmissions	Castings
Electrical/Fuel Handling Devices	Components Group	Electronics
Glass	Plastics/Trim Products	Climate Control

PURCHASING
Sourcing
MATERIALS
SUPPLIERS (Hundreds)
Advance Ship Notice
Engineering Changes and Ship Release

Information
Parts

parties in the chain becomes paramount. Organizations are effectively forming new types of relationships (sometimes called "partnerships" or "alliances") that require shared resources. For instance, organizations may provide dedicated capacity, specific information, technological capabilities, or even direct financial support to other members of their supply chain so that the entire chain can benefit.

Achieving Purchasing and Supply Chain Benefits

When the pieces come together, can assuming a supply chain orientation with the right kinds of activities really produce the results envisioned by proponents? Consider the rebirth of Apple Computer, which had *BusinessWeek* asking in 1997, "Is Apple mincemeat?" Apple made a great comeback through an impressive, steady stream of new and innovative products such as the iPod, iPod Nano, and iPhone. Apple has re-engineered itself from being considered "mincemeat" to now once again being the "darling of Wall Street."[9] Facilitating this turnaround was Apple's pursuit of an impressive array of purchasing and supply chain activities to manage product demand, inventory investment, channel distribution, and supply chain relationships. The company reduced its product line by almost half, forecasted sales weekly instead of monthly with daily adjustments to production, and relied on suppliers to manage inventory for standard parts and components. Apple also formalized a partnership with a supplier to build components close to Apple facilities with just-in-time (JIT) delivery, created a direct ship distribution network through the Web, and simplified its finished goods distribution channel. Because of these activities, Apple now rivals, and sometimes exceeds, Dell Computer in terms of supply chain performance.

The Supply Chain Umbrella

A large set of activities besides purchasing is part of supply chain management. Each of these seemingly diverse activities has one important feature in common—it is part of a network that will define how efficiently and effectively goods and information flow across a supply chain. Although the need to perform supply chain–related activities has been present for many years, it is an organization's willingness to align, coordinate, integrate, and synchronize these activities and flows that is relatively new. What are the activities that are part of this concept called supply chain management?

Management Activities

Purchasing

Most organizations include purchasing as a major supply chain activity. Because purchasing is the central focus of this book, there is no need to provide more detail here.

Inbound Transportation

Larger organizations usually have a specialized traffic and transportation function to manage the physical and informational links between the supplier and the buyer. For some organizations, transportation is the single largest category of single costs, especially for highly diversified organizations. Although a firm may have minimal common purchase requirements among its operating units, there usually are opportunities to coordinate the purchase of transportation services.

Quality Control

Quality control has taken on increased importance during the last 15 years. Almost all organizations recognize the importance of supplier quality and the need to prevent, rather than simply detect, quality problems. The emphasis has shifted from detecting defects at the time of receipt or use to prevention early in the materials-sourcing process. Progressive organizations work directly with suppliers to develop proper quality control procedures and processes.

Demand and Supply Planning

Demand planning identifies all the claims (or demand) on output. This includes forecasts of anticipated demand, inventory adjustments, orders taken but not filled, and spare-part and aftermarket requirements. Supply planning is the process of taking demand data and developing a supply, production, and logistics network capable of satisfying demand requirements.

Receiving, Materials Handling, and Storage

All inbound material must be physically received as it moves from a supplier to a purchaser. In a non-just-in-time environment, material must also be stored or staged. Receiving, materials handling, and storage are usually part of the materials management function because of the need to control the physical processing and handling of inventory. Receipts from users indicating that services have been performed are also run through receiving to trigger invoice payment.

Materials or Inventory Control

The terms "materials control" and "inventory control" are sometimes used interchangeably. Within some organizations, however, these terms have different meanings. The materials control group is often responsible for determining the appropriate quantity to order based on projected demand and then managing materials releases to suppliers. This includes generating the materials release, contacting a supplier directly concerning changes, and monitoring the status of inbound shipments. Materials control activities are sometimes the responsibility of the purchasing department, particularly in smaller organizations.

The inventory control group is often responsible for determining the inventory level of finished goods required to support customer requirements, which emphasizes the physical distribution (i.e., outbound or downstream) side of the supply chain. Integrated supply chain management requires that the materials and inventory control groups coordinate their efforts to ensure a smooth and uninterrupted flow to customers.

Order Processing

Order processing helps ensure that customers receive material when and where they require it. Problems with order processing have involved accepting orders before determining if adequate production capacity is available, not coordinating order processing with order scheduling, and using internal production dates rather than the customer's preferred date to schedule the order. Order processing is an important part of supply chain management—it represents a link between the producer and the external customer.

Production Planning, Scheduling, and Control

These activities involve determining a time-phased schedule of production, developing short-term production schedules, and controlling work-in-process production. The production plan often relies on forecasts from marketing to estimate the volume of materials that are required over the near term. Because operations is responsible for carrying out the production plan and meeting customer order due dates, order processing, production planning, and operations must work together closely.

Warehousing/Distribution

Before a product heads to the customer, it may be stored for a period in a warehouse or distribution center. This is particularly true for companies that produce according to a forecast in anticipation of future sales. Increasingly, as companies attempt to make a product only after receiving a customer order, this part of the supply chain may become less important.

Shipping

This activity involves physically getting a product ready for distribution to the customer. This requires packing to prevent damage, completing any special labeling requirements, completing the required shipping documents, and/or arranging transportation with an approved carrier. For obvious reasons, shipping and outbound transportation must work together closely.

Outbound Transportation

Fewer organizations "own" the transportation link to their customers, compared with just a few years ago. Increasingly, full-service transportation providers are designing and managing entire distribution networks for their clients.

Customer Service

Customer service includes a wide set of activities that attempt to keep a customer satisfied with a product or service. The three primary elements of customer service are pre-transaction, transaction, and post-transaction activities.

Four Enablers of Purchasing and Supply Chain Management

Now that we have a better understanding of the terminology surrounding purchasing and supply chain management, we must recognize that excellence in these areas does not just happen. What separates firms that achieve real benefits from those that fail to reap any benefits is a commitment to the four enablers of purchasing and supply chain excellence. These enablers provide the support that makes the development of progressive strategies and approaches possible. Later chapters present these four areas in detail.

Exhibit 1.5 Four Pillars of Purchasing and Supply Chain Excellence

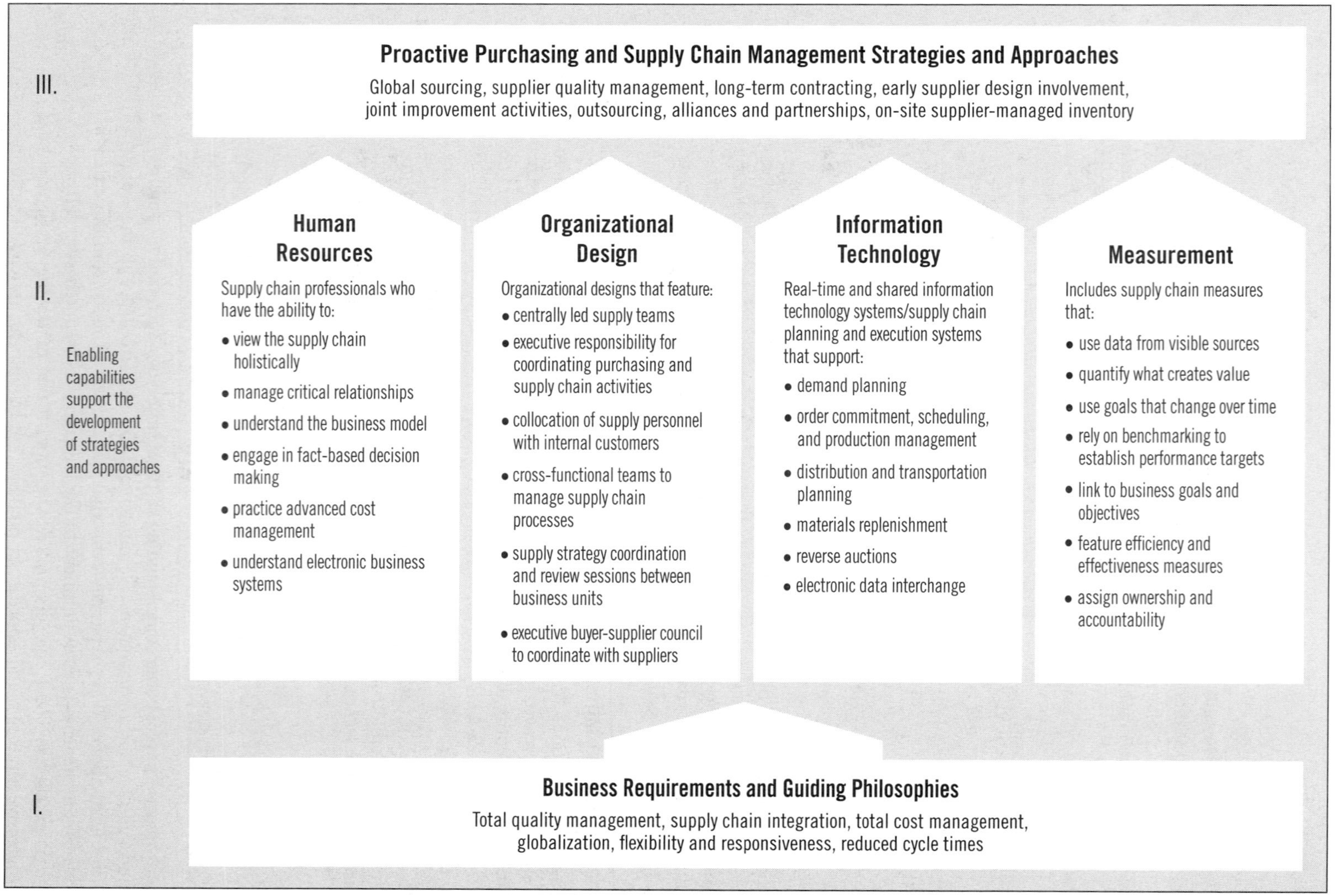

III. Proactive Purchasing and Supply Chain Management Strategies and Approaches

Global sourcing, supplier quality management, long-term contracting, early supplier design involvement, joint improvement activities, outsourcing, alliances and partnerships, on-site supplier-managed inventory

II. Enabling capabilities support the development of strategies and approaches

Human Resources

Supply chain professionals who have the ability to:

- view the supply chain holistically
- manage critical relationships
- understand the business model
- engage in fact-based decision making
- practice advanced cost management
- understand electronic business systems

Organizational Design

Organizational designs that feature:

- centrally led supply teams
- executive responsibility for coordinating purchasing and supply chain activities
- collocation of supply personnel with internal customers
- cross-functional teams to manage supply chain processes
- supply strategy coordination and review sessions between business units
- executive buyer-supplier council to coordinate with suppliers

Information Technology

Real-time and shared information technology systems/supply chain planning and execution systems that support:

- demand planning
- order commitment, scheduling, and production management
- distribution and transportation planning
- materials replenishment
- reverse auctions
- electronic data interchange

Measurement

Includes supply chain measures that:

- use data from visible sources
- quantify what creates value
- use goals that change over time
- rely on benchmarking to establish performance targets
- link to business goals and objectives
- feature efficiency and effectiveness measures
- assign ownership and accountability

I. Business Requirements and Guiding Philosophies

Total quality management, supply chain integration, total cost management, globalization, flexibility and responsiveness, reduced cycle times

Exhibit 1.5 presents the four enablers of purchasing and supply chain excellence. This model shows that firms have certain guiding philosophies and business requirements that are the foundation of all supply chain activities. These guiding philosophies and requirements may relate to areas such as globalization, customer responsiveness, or supply chain integration. The four enablers, in turn, support the development of strategies and approaches that not only align with an organization's philosophies and requirements but also support the attainment of purchasing, supply chain, and organizational objectives and strategies.

Capable Human Resources

The key to the success of any company is the quality of its employees. This is certainly true for purchasing. Exhibit 1.5 identifies, from focus group research, the various kinds of knowledge and skills demanded of today's supply chain professional. The knowledge and skills that purchasing and supply chain professionals require are different from just a few years ago. Recent research indicated that the top five knowledge areas for purchasers of the future were (1) supplier relationship management, (2) total cost analysis, (3) purchasing strategies, (4) supplier analysis, and (5) competitive market analysis.[10] Effective supply chain management requires close collaboration with suppliers as well as internal coordination with engineering, procurement, logistics, customers, and marketing to coordinate activities and material flows across the supply chain. These relationships with key suppliers become the basis for purchasing strategies. The Babson College Good Practice Example illustrates how suppliers and the college benefit from developing these strong ties. Developing strong ties often requires purchasers to take a more entrepreneurial approach to running their business.

Cost-management skills are becoming more important. With an inability to raise prices to customers, cost management becomes essential to longer-term success. Purchasing specialists at a major U.S. chemical company, for example, evaluate major supply decisions using total cost models with data provided by suppliers and other sources. Another company requires its teams to identify upstream cost drivers past immediate suppliers, which the teams then target for improvement. Cost management has become an integral part of purchasing and supply chain management. These analyses of total cost are then imposed upon the market situation and analysis of supplier capabilities to arrive at an overall purchasing strategy.

Gaining access to the right skills will require a sound human-resources strategy that includes internal development of high-potential individuals, recruiting talent from other functional groups or companies, and hiring promising college graduates. This occurs to satisfy one primary objective—ensuring that qualified participants are available to support purchasing and supply chain requirements.

Proper Organizational Design

Organizational design refers to the process of assessing and selecting the structure and formal system of communication, division of labor, coordination, control, authority, and responsibility required to achieve organizational goals and objectives, including supply chain objectives.[11] Although formal charts illustrate an organization's formal design, they also present an incomplete picture. Organizational design is much more than a series of lines and boxes across a chart.[12] Exhibit 1.5 highlights the more important features that promote the achievement of purchasing objectives.[13]

The use of teams as part of supply chain design will continue to be important. However, managers should use teams selectively. Few studies have established a clear connection between teaming and higher performance, and even fewer have quantitatively assessed the impact of teaming on corporate performance. The use of organizational work teams to support purchasing and supply chain objectives does not guarantee greater effectiveness.

Real-Time and Shared Information Technology Capabilities

The development of information technology (IT) software and platforms that support an end-to-end supply chain have grown rapidly in the 21st century, as have identification technologies such as radio frequency identification (RFID). These technologies allow enhanced collaboration between the parties in the supply chain. One example of this is highlighted by the mission of e-supply chain company EPIC: "EPIC delivers a comprehensive product line that enhances enterprise profit margins through collaboration and real-time connectivity."[14] Software packages that are gaining the attention of purchasers include e-purchasing suites (see Chapter 18), which have become popular with firms. Two primary supply chain applications involved in supply chain collaboration that involve purchasing are supply chain planning and supply chain execution. Planning software seeks to improve forecast accuracy, optimize production scheduling, reduce working capital costs, shorten cycle times, cut transportation costs, and improve customer service. Execution software helps obtain materials and manage physical flows from suppliers through downstream distribution to ensure that customers receive the right products at the right location, time, and cost.

Regardless of the type of information technology platform or software used, supply chain systems should capture and share information across functional groups and organizational boundaries on a real-time or near-real-time basis. This may involve transmitting the location of transportation vehicles using global positioning systems (GPSs), using Internet-based systems to transmit material requirements to suppliers, or using bar code technology to monitor the timeliness of receipts from suppliers. RFID tags are being used in more applications to capture real-time data about material and product movement across the supply chain.

Examples regarding the relationship between information technology and supply chain excellence are not hard to find. TaylorMade adidas has led the golf industry's technological revolution since its founding in 1979. TaylorMade uses supply chain planning and execution software from i2 to optimize its end-to-end supply chain activities. It all starts with demand planning, which is needed to manage TaylorMade's strong yet unpredictable product sales. For example, when a competitor dropped its prices on a new line of titanium drivers, demand spiked much higher than the company anticipated. This resulted in multiple suppliers being required to meet the extra demand at a premium cost. The new system enables improved visibility into demand, which can then be immediately seen by the purchasing function, permitting a more integrated approach to sourcing and reduced inventory. Demand from retail customers is now collected on wireless devices by sales representatives, who then transmit it to the warehouse. If stock is not available at the warehouse, then another wireless transmission is made to the TaylorMade facility. This may require purchasing action to obtain the desired components to complete the order. By sharing demand forecasts with suppliers, every member of the chain now has demand visibility, allowing better planning on all fronts. Suppliers now can look ahead and improve their schedules and TaylorMade gets shipments of items that are needed to satisfy customer requirements with less inventory. One of TaylorMade's executives sums it up: "In the past we never really knew how much we were going to sell in one period; as a result we built up inventory to guard against placing customers on backorder."[15]

Right Measures and Measurement Systems

The right measures and measurement systems represent the fourth pillar supporting purchasing and supply chain excellence. Unfortunately, there are many roadblocks between measurement and improved performance. Some of these include (1) too many metrics, (2) debate over the correct metrics, (3) constantly changing metrics, and (4) old data.[16] Overcoming these roadblocks requires that the organization know what it wants to measure, has a process in place to measure it, and has accessibility to the right data. The next step involves taking action on the measurement data.[17] Finally, as with any planning system, the targets are revised to reflect the realities of the marketplace, competition, and changing goals of the organization.

Why is measurement so important? First, objective measurement supports fact-based rather than subjective decision making. Secondly, measurement is also an ideal way to communicate requirements to other supply chain members and to promote continuous improvement and change. When suppliers know their performance is being monitored, they are likely to perform better. Many firms use the measurement system not only to improve future supplier performance but also to recognize outstanding performance. For example, United Technologies awarded two suppliers its "General Procurement Key Supplier Award."[18] Measurement also conveys what is important by linking critical measures to desired business outcomes. The measurement process also helps determine if new initiatives are producing the desired results. Finally, measurement may be the single best tool to control purchasing and supply chain activities and processes.

Although there is no definitive or prescriptive set of supply chain measures, and there certainly is no one best way to measure supply chain performance, we do know that effective measures and measurement systems satisfy certain criteria. These criteria, which Exhibit 1.5 summarizes, provide a set of principles with which to assess supply chain measures and measurement systems.

These four enablers support the pursuit of progressive approaches and strategies that begin to define purchasing and supply chain excellence. If organizations ignore these areas, they will see their ability to develop progressive practices and approaches fall short of competitors that have stressed these enabling areas.

The Evolution of Purchasing and Supply Chain Management

There have been more changes affecting purchasing over the last 15 years than over the previous 125 years. To appreciate how we arrived at where we are today requires a brief understanding of the evolution of purchasing and supply chain management, although some might argue the last 15 years resembled a revolution. This evolution covers seven periods spanning the last 150 years.

Period 1: The Early Years (1850–1900)

Some observers define the early years of purchasing history as beginning after 1850. There is evidence, however, that the purchasing function received attention before this date. Charles Babbage's book on the economy of machinery and manufacturers, published in 1832, referred to the importance of the purchasing function. Babbage also alluded to a "materials man" responsible for several different functions. Babbage wrote that a central officer responsible for operating mines was "a materials man who selects, purchases, receives, and delivers all articles required."[19]

In the textile industry, the selling agent often handled purchasing and was also responsible for the output, quality, and style of the cloth. The selling agent was responsible for all purchasing decisions, because the grade of cotton purchased was a factor in determining the quality of the cloth produced. Customer orders were transformed into purchase orders (POs) for cotton and subsequently into planned production.[20]

The greatest interest in and development of purchasing during the early years occurred after the 1850s. During this period, the growth of American railroads made them one of the major forces in the economy. Railroads were vital to the country's ability to move goods from the more developed Eastern and Midwestern markets to less developed Southern and Western markets. By 1866, the Pennsylvania Railroad had given the purchasing function departmental status, under the title of Supplying Department. A few years later, the head purchasing agent at the Pennsylvania Railroad reported directly to the president of the railroad. The purchasing function was such a major contributor to the performance of the organization that the chief purchasing manager had top managerial status.[21]

The comptroller of the Chicago and Northwestern Railroad wrote the first book exclusively about the purchasing function, *The Handling of Railway Supplies—Their Purchase and Disposition,* in 1887. He discussed purchasing issues that are still critical today, including the need for technical expertise in purchasing agents along with the need to centralize the purchasing department under one individual. The author also commented on the lack of attention given to the selection of personnel to fill the position of purchasing agent.

The growth of the railroad industry dominated the early years of purchasing development. Major contributions to purchasing history during this period consisted of early recognition of the purchasing process and its contribution to overall company profitability. The late 1800s signaled the beginning of organizing purchasing as a separate corporate function requiring specialized expertise. Before this period, this separation did not exist.

Period 2: Growth of Purchasing Fundamentals (1900–1939)

The second period of purchasing evolution began around the turn of the 20th century and lasted until the beginning of World War II. Articles specifically addressing the industrial purchasing function began appearing with increasing regularity outside the railroad trade journals. Engineering magazines in particular focused attention on the need for qualified purchasing personnel and the development of materials specifications.

This era also witnessed the development of basic purchasing procedures and ideas. In 1905 the second book devoted to purchasing—and the first nonrailroad purchasing book—was published. *The Book on Buying* contained 18 chapters, each written by a different author.[22] The editors devoted the first section of the book to the "principles" of buying. The second section described the forms and procedures used in various company purchasing systems.

Purchasing gained importance during World War I because of its role in obtaining vital war materials. Purchasing's central focus during this period was on the procurement of raw material versus buying finished or semifinished goods. Ironically, the years during World War I featured no publication of any major purchasing books. Harold T. Lewis, a respected purchasing professional during the 1930s through the 1950s, noted that there was considerable doubt about the existence of any general recognition of purchasing as being important to a company. Lewis noted that from World War I to 1945, at least a gradual if uneven recognition developed of the importance of sound procurement to company operation.

Period 3: The War Years (1940–1946)

World War II introduced a new period in purchasing history. The emphasis on obtaining required (and scarce) materials during the war influenced a growth in purchasing interest. In 1933, only nine colleges offered courses related to purchasing. By 1945, this number had increased to 49 colleges. The membership of the National Association of Purchasing Agents increased from 3,400 in 1934 to 5,500 in 1940 to 9,400 in the autumn of 1945. A study conducted during this period revealed that 76% of all purchase requisitions contained no specifications or stipulation of brand. This suggested that other departments within the firm recognized the role of the purchasing agent in determining sources of supply.[23]

Period 4: The Quiet Years (1947–Mid-1960s)

The heightened awareness of purchasing that existed during World War II did not carry over to the postwar years. John A. Hill, a noted purchasing professional, commented about the state of purchasing during this period: "For many firms, purchases were simply an inescapable cost of doing business which no one could do much about. So far as the length and breadth of American industry is concerned, the purchasing function has not yet received in full measure the attention and emphasis it deserves."[24]

Another respected purchasing professional, Bruce D. Henderson, also commented about the state of affairs facing purchasing. In his words, "Procurement is regarded as a negative function—it can handicap the company if not done well but can make little positive contribution."[25] He noted that purchasing was a neglected function in most organizations because it was not important to mainstream problems. He went on to say that some executives found it hard to visualize a company becoming more successful than its competitors because of its superior procurement.

Articles began appearing during this period describing the practices of various companies using staff members to collect, analyze, and present data for purchasing decisions. Ford Motor Company was one of the first private organizations to establish a commodity research department to provide short- and long-term commodity information.[26] Ford also created a purchase analysis department to give buyers assistance on product and price analysis.

The postwar period saw the development of the value analysis (VA) technique, pioneered by General Electric in 1947. GE's approach concentrated on the evaluation of which materials or changes in specifications and design would reduce overall product costs. Although important internal purchasing developments occurred during this era, there was no denying that other disciplines such as marketing and finance overshadowed purchasing. The emphasis during the postwar years and throughout the 1960s was on satisfying consumer demand and the needs of a growing industrial market. Furthermore, firms faced stable competition and had access to abundant material —conditions that historically have diminished the overall importance of purchasing. The elements that would normally cause an increase in the importance of purchasing were not present during these quiet years of purchasing history.

Period 5: Materials Management Comes of Age (Mid-1960s–Late 1970s)

The mid-1960s witnessed a dramatic growth of the materials management concept. Although interest in materials management grew during this period, the concept's historical origins date to the 1800s, when U.S. railroads organized under the materials management concept during the latter half of the 19th century. They combined related functions such as purchasing, inventory control, receiving, and stores under the authority of one individual.

External events directly affected the operation of the typical firm. The Vietnam War, for example, resulted in upward price and materials availability pressures. During the 1970s, firms experienced materials problems related to oil "shortages" and embargoes. The logical response of industry was to become more efficient, particularly in the purchase and control of materials.

There was widespread agreement about the primary objective of the materials concept and the functions that might fall under the materials umbrella. The overall objective of materials management was to solve materials problems from a total system viewpoint rather than the viewpoint of individual functions or activities. The various functions that might fall under the materials umbrella included materials planning and control, inventory planning and control, materials and procurement research, purchasing, incoming traffic, receiving, incoming quality control, stores, materials movement, and scrap and surplus disposal.

The behavior of purchasing during this period was notable. Purchasing managers emphasized multiple sourcing through competitive bid pricing and rarely viewed the supplier as a value-added partner. Buyers maintained arm's-length relationships with suppliers. Price competition was the major factor determining supply contracts. The purchasing strategies and behaviors that evolved over the last half century were inadequate when the severe economic recession of the early 1980s and the emergence of foreign global competitors occurred. Overall, the function was relegated to secondary status in many companies. Dean Ammer's classic 1974 article in the *Harvard Business Review* categorized top management's view of purchasing as passive, risk averse, and a dead-end job. Ammer felt overcoming this perception could be accomplished by active purchasing, which is measured in terms of meeting overall company objectives and contributing to bottom-line profitability.[27] He argued that the purchasing executive should be part of non-purchasing decisions, for the entire organization loses when purchasing is not part of the organization's consensus on major decisions.[28] Finally, Ammer suggested that the function should have sufficient stature to report to top management or a division manager. However, this happened in only 37% of his responding firms.[29]

Period 6: The Global Era (Late 1970s–1999)

The global era, and its effect on the importance, structure, and behavior of purchasing, has already proved different from other historical periods. These differences include the following:

- Never in our industrial history has competition become so intense so quickly.
- Global firms increasingly captured world market share and emphasized different strategies, organizational structures, and management techniques compared with their American counterparts.
- The spread and rate of technology change during this period was unprecedented, with product life cycles becoming shorter.
- The ability to coordinate worldwide purchasing activity by using international data networks and the World Wide Web (via intranets) emerged.

This intensely competitive period witnessed the growth of supply chain management. Now, more than ever, firms began to take a more coordinated view of managing the flow of goods, services, funds, and information from suppliers through end customers. Managers began to view supply chain management as a way to satisfy intense cost and other improvement pressures.

Period 7: Integrated Supply Chain Management (Beyond 2000)

Purchasing and supply chain management today reflects a growing emphasis concerning the importance of suppliers. Supplier relationships are shifting from an adversarial approach to a more cooperative approach with selected suppliers. The activities that the modern purchasing organization must put in place are quite different from just a few years ago. Supplier development, supplier design involvement, the use of full-service suppliers, total cost supplier selection, long-term supplier relationships, strategic cost management, enterprisewide systems (enterprise resource planning, or ERP) and integrated Internet linkages and shared databases are now seen as ways to create new value within the supply chain. Purchasing behavior is shifting dramatically to support the performance requirements of the new era.

It is possible to reach three conclusions about 21st-century purchasing. First, the reshaping of purchasing's role in the emerging global economy is under way, in response to the challenges presented by worldwide competition and rapidly changing technology and customer expectations. Second, the overall importance of the purchasing function is increasing, particularly for firms that compete in industries characterized by worldwide competition and rapid change. Third, purchasing must continue to become more integrated with customer requirements, as well as with operations, logistics, human resources, finance, accounting, marketing, and information systems. This evolution will take time to occur fully, but the integration is inevitable.

The history and evolution of purchasing and supply chain management provides an appreciation for the growth, development, and increased stature of the profession over the last 150 years. Each historical period has contributed something unique to the development of purchasing, including the events that have shaped today's emphasis on integrated supply chain management.

Looking Ahead

This book comprises 20 chapters, divided into six parts including this introduction. The remainder of this book addresses the major tasks and challenges facing the modern purchasing professional operating within the context of a dynamic supply chain.

Part 2, *Purchasing Operations and Structure,* Chapters 2 through 5, provides a basic understanding of the functional activity called purchasing. Without a solid understanding of basic purchasing processes and organization, appreciating the important role that purchasing has within a supply chain is difficult.

With this understanding, Part 3, *Strategic Sourcing,* considers how purchasing evaluates, selects, manages, and improves supplier performance. Chapters 6 through 10 present strategic sourcing activities, which are activities that can affect the competitiveness of a firm. The ability to realize advantages from our purchasing and supply efforts requires shifting our view of purchasing from a tactical or clerically oriented activity to one that focuses on strategic supply management.

Part 4, *Strategic Sourcing Process,* recognizes that purchasing professionals must play a major role in improving supply chain performance. Chapters 11 through 15 present an assortment of tools, techniques, and approaches for managing the procurement and sourcing process, including an understanding of contracting and legal issues.

Part 5, *Critical Supply Chain Elements,* deals extensively with the critical elements of integrated supply chains from supplier through customer. The activities and topics presented in Chapters 16 through 19 may or may not be a formal part of the purchasing organization. They are, however, integral stepping stones to effective supply chain management.

The last part, *Future Directions,* contains a single chapter that presents future directions identified during research and experience with many organizations. The trends identified in Chapter 20 help us identify how the field of purchasing and supply chain management is changing, what is behind these changes, and how best to respond. As we move further into the 21st century, this section must change on a continuous basis to reflect the dynamic changes occurring in purchasing and supply chain management.

Good Practice Example — *Taking an Entrepreneurial Approach to Purchasing at Babson College*

MEET A PURCHASING ENTREPRENEUR

Peter Russo has been an entrepreneur for more than 20 years. His hands-on experience is diverse—everything from founding start-ups in his basement, to serving as chairman of a venture-owned turnaround, to licensing products to billion-dollar companies. He has opened design, sales, and distribution offices in both China and Japan, overseeing the transition of production and materials supply from the United States to China. Russo has also created production methods that are proprietary to the United States, successfully defending them against competitors with overseas sourcing. He's set up direct consumer selling systems and has developed and sold hundreds of products to America's largest big-box retailers, such as Wal-Mart, Toys "R" Us, and Petco.

So what could entice this serial entrepreneur to leave his own business and become the director of purchasing at Babson College? Considering that Babson has the premier entrepreneurship program in the country, according to *U.S. News and World Report,* it's a perfect partnership. The academic world has traditionally been characterized as somewhat rigid and bureaucratic, following traditional rules and regulations engrained by decades of use or imposed by state legislators, boards of regents, or other governing boards. Purchasing is no exception. It, too, operates in a clerical, paper-intense atmosphere. But true to the very definition of an entrepreneur, Russo believes there is always the ability to innovate, so he decided to come to Babson.

"I undertook the challenge only because Babson encouraged me to take a fresh view," says Russo. "They recognize that providing superior service and value can only be achieved by thinking of supply management as an entrepreneurial business." Russo's approach was to evaluate college purchasing in the same way he evaluated consumer products. "Buying can usually be segmented into buying processes and customer groups," says Russo.

In this discussion, Russo focuses on three buying processes and their associated customers:

1. *Automated buying.* This empowers the customer to independently purchase and manage material from a defined inventory. Office supplies are the best example of this type of purchase.
2. *Competitively bidded buying.* This requires the research and evaluation of multiple options to determine needs, best price, and service levels and is sent to multiple suppliers soliciting their bids. Examples in this category include desktop printers, kitchen equipment, software, and construction materials.
3. *Contracted services.* This buying process involves using the expertise of suppliers that team with the college to provide products used on a daily, ongoing basis, such as dining services and books.

"Our purchasing department is no different from most companies in the private sector," says Russo. As he sees it, today's challenge is twofold:

1. Leverage technology to simplify and automate repetitive activities while capturing and disseminating information/knowledge.
2. Maximize strategic alliances for best practices and supply management in areas that are outside its expertise.

Russo goes on to explain how Babson's purchasing group plans to address these challenges.

PREPARING FOR CHANGE

Among Russo's first endeavors was to reinforce the idea and benefit of centralized purchasing, operating on a foundation of service. "Creating an effective, efficient process requires consistent campuswide use," says Russo. "To achieve this goal, our purchasing department would have to be recognized by our customers as capable of reducing complexity and adding value, knowledge, and skill to the process."

In the past, the typical purchasing process was initiated with the customer coming to the purchasing department with a product and supplier already selected. Overall, the process was fairly manual, with hand-completed paper forms and little use of technology. Everyone knew that before a purchase order was placed for any significant buy, policy required three bids to be received by the purchasing department. Some thought this process turned the purchasing department into the "purchasing police"—a mindset that Russo feels can be avoided with the proper buying processes. "We want to be viewed as fast and flexible, with creative solutions to sourcing," he says.

Russo inherited an experienced team, led by two veteran staffers with extensive college purchasing experience. "I'm very fortunate," he says, "to have a staff that's not just talented and experienced, but service-minded."

Russo and his team evaluated and modified the buying process to meet the desired format of the customers, but he felt it would also be critical to increase the campus awareness of each new service. Russo also wanted to communicate the staff's knowledge and professionalism. He and two key staff members are currently taking certification training to become Certified Purchasing Managers. Raising the bar higher, Russo has set his sights on attaining the new Certified Professional in Supply Management (CPSM) designation.

"Many of our customers have advanced degrees," says Russo. (It should be added that Russo considers everyone on campus a customer.) "We are obviously in an environment that values expertise," he continues, "but it takes more than education. It takes motivation to enhance credibility. We need to continually increase our level of knowledge, professionalism and service."

TAKING CHARGE OF PROCESS IMPROVEMENTS

In his first few weeks at Babson, Russo realized that his purchasing manager, Anne, and his buyer, Kerrie, were very good at administering the process that was in place. "More importantly, they were well respected by the customers on our campus," he adds. "But I realized that the antiquated, paper-based system they were using needed updating. It was too labor intensive and dependent on the staff's personal knowledge."

The system was weighed down by lengthy procedures and minimal automation, with no capabilities to assimilate current technology-driven processes, thereby creating two obstacles. First, Russo's team was prevented from fully leveraging group buying efficiencies or maximizing product knowledge. Second, Russo was concerned with "what if?" Should one of the purchasing team leave for another job, a major setback would be inevitable.

Speaking with his team, Russo discovered that day-to-day operations required 100% of their attention, leaving little time to enhance the purchasing process. He quickly learned that his talented staff was drowning in paperwork and telephone calls.

The inspiration came in the form of a question: What would you do to fix what isn't working? "My staff really had knowledge of which processes were effective and which needed changes. In many instances they had started to lay out solutions; however, limited time and resources kept the realization of these improvements on perpetual hold," says Russo. "I also believe," Russo continues, "that an effective purchasing process is built upon the customers' desired buying behavior. We realized it was not effective to force customers to change their behavior to meet a purchasing process. Our first steps were to prioritize our objectives, establish our strategies and timelines, and outline measurable goals. Next, we quickly determined what actions could reduce their current workload without risking service levels, so my team could focus on enhancing the process. Then we went into action."

Russo empowered his staffers to get the job done, then let them be. After just six months, their progress was impressive!

AUTOMATING THE EVERYDAY

Kerrie focused on the automated buying processes. She spent many hours at the computer, creating an interactive purchasing website for both internal customers and suppliers. When it's up and running, a new era will begin. Gone will be manual entries and multiple data inputs. POs being faxed across campus and then re-entered by hand into the system will finally be a thing of the past. Customer-friendly, user-driven resource pages will also be in place. The campus will have a master supplier list with links to company websites, eliminating the time-consuming search for basic products and suppliers.

The suppliers will also benefit, with access to complete information on how to do business with Babson and forms for each online process. Best of all, every aspect of the website can be continually refined, adapting to the appropriate circumstances. As their workload is reduced by automation, both the purchasing and accounts payable departments will be able to explore new, improved ways to serve customers.

CLOSING THE BACK DOOR

The underside, if you will, of Babson's entrepreneurial culture is the action-oriented independence of its internal customers. Supply management channels are often overlooked by those who believe "we know what we want, so why do we need central purchasing?" The result has been multiple purchasing of single-need items, lack of safeguards, inconsistent pricing, and contracts. Russo's goal? "To maximize our department's ability to leverage campuswide buying power, benchmark resources, negotiate better terms, eliminate duplicate spending, and manage contract services." He adds, "We haven't forgotten that faculty and staff want maximum freedom in sourcing, so our challenge is to preserve their independence—and still improve the way we manage the $145 million in college spending every year."

Anne put her efforts behind improving the competitively bidded buying process. She started evaluating current campuswide strategies for products and services that were previously made on a single-purchase basis. A great example of this is the snack vending machines. Around the Babson campus, there are many snack vending machines. Each of these machines was purchased on an individual, as-needed basis. The result was a total of six machines, bought at six different times. More importantly, Babson received no financial incentives, such as a percentage of sales for allowing the suppliers to put the machines on campus. Often the machines had malfunctioning card readers—a problem Babson seemed powerless to impact with so little supplier leverage.

Taking a strategic approach, Anne re-evaluated the customer need for campuswide snack vending. She started with a survey of the customers' buying needs. To develop a new strategy, Anne also evaluated headcounts of residents and office staff, studied traffic flow, and benchmarked her findings against other schools. This effort culminated in a request for quote (RFQ).

An RFQ is a document provided to bidding suppliers which details exacting parameters of the goods or services being requested. For example, an RFQ from snack suppliers might include details like number, kind, and location of vending machines; snack prices; method and timing for refills—even issues regarding potential vandalism are covered. This provides the suppliers with all the specifics on which to base their bids and, later, the contracts.

The result is that now, Babson will have just one supplier that will manage approximately 22 machines, and a comprehensive card payment system. Babson will enjoy shared profits—and online live tracking of snack purchases by machine!

In another effort Anne developed a travel portal to help faculty, staff, and alumni access discounted flight deals, hotel rates, and special promotions.

Anne is also preparing the launch of a beta test for a new procurement card system, allowing customers to make adjustments to a general ledger prior to posting online expenditures. Not only will this allow users to better manage their budgets, but the time spent by the purchasing department making adjustments will be reduced by over 20 hours a month.

DEVELOPING NEW RELATIONSHIPS

Although the traditional college purchasing process presents both challenges and rewards, Russo's enthusiasm peaks when he talks about contract services. He draws from his pre-Babson decades and recalls that finding the right partner was crucial. Leveraging a supplier's expertise, whether it's in raw materials testing or third-party fulfillment and distribution, was a major tool in realizing success. The common perception is that outsourcing reduces supply options and service management flexibility. Russo feels differently. "It actually increases capabilities," he says, "as I can leverage the talent, skills, and assets of both Babson and the supplier."

As a modestly funded entrepreneur, Russo often called on suppliers to perform functions that would traditionally go to a key department in a larger company. In order to make this "outsourced/in-house operation" effective, a cultural shift must take place. Suppliers need freedoms and restrictions, as well as incentives and guidelines that are similar to those of an internal department.

"I try never to fall into the trap of thinking that the customer is always right, or that the supplier is holding out and can always do better," says Russo. "Once you replace 'us' and 'them' with 'we,' the returns come in multiples!"

Russo's relationship-building philosophy is practical and powerful:

- Get a tight contract agreement, stating even the most basic terms. Who gets what, as well as when, where, and how they get it. When facts like this are unclear, the relationship can suffer.
- Set a tone of collaboration and teamwork. When suppliers realize we're all on the same team, they provide revolutionary new products, enhance production methods, and even reduce their prices—voluntarily!
- Fight for supplier rights, protect them in company-driven experiments, help to train their employees, and collaborate on improving their companies! In short, make sure you understand and respect their company's mission, goals, and objectives.
- Together create goals, measurements for success and a communication system that assures clear and constant understanding of action steps and timing.

Establishing such strong relationships with suppliers has often resulted in lifelong friendships for Russo. Ironically, these friendships have made it easy to terminate professional ties if and when the alliance is no longer working. "Cooperation and communication at that level insures that there's no mystery about performance requirements," Russo adds.

WHAT'S IN STORE FOR BABSON?

"At Babson, we aren't experts in every field. Take dining and book sales, for example," says Russo. "In these areas, contracted service companies like Sodexo and Barnes & Noble have done a great job working with student affairs and other such departments."

"These campus departments know their particular customer—the students in this case—and they interface with suppliers as what I call 'Use Managers,' " continues Russo. "They identify the need based on their observations and student comments on use. They then request the service and challenge the supplier to propose a creative solution."

Russo likes the Use Manager model and feels it complements his role. "My intention is to enhance the Use Manager model by working with the contracted service companies as a business partner of sorts—as if we had a stake in their success, which we do!

"In my role I review detailed elements on the operational side, such as tracking equipment life and monitoring the associated repair process and capital planning for replacement."

Russo also gets to look at the Babson customer from an operator's point of view. "The great part," he says, "is the information these contracted service suppliers possess. They provide access to statistical data that adds to the observation-based information we get from the Use Managers. For example, Sodexo dining tracks how many students are served during 15-minute intervals of each day and how much of each entrée is consumed per day. My goal is to add this type of data to information provided by our Use Managers and additional consumer surveys and research to assure that we are providing the best food product, when, where, and how the student desires. I can also work with suppliers to determine the benefits, risks, and effects of various staffing options, service and materials changes, merchandising, advertising, and promotion plans that they may be considering."

Russo believes that once a team approach is truly in place at Babson, "safety positions," otherwise known as "sandbagging," will be abandoned. "When our goals and those of our suppliers are aligned, it follows that mutual benefits are at a maximum, and risk is at a minimum," he says. Another benefit is that Use Managers' operational demands are reduced allowing them to focus energies on their customers. "And that," he adds, "is a definite win/win!"

Peter Russo's 20-plus years of experience are hard at work in his new position at Babson. But it might be argued that his best qualifications are his three children. Two are in college now, and a third is set to begin soon. And so the father, entrepreneur, and director of purchasing wryly sums up his professional philosophy: "Nobody understands how crucial it is to maximize the buying power of every tuition dollar more than I do!"

Source: L. Giunipero, Personal interview with Peter Russo, February 2008.

KEY TERMS

cross-functional, 10
extended enterprise, 12
extended value chain, 12
managing the supply base, 9
organizational design, 19
process approach, 9
purchasing, 8
strategic responsibilities, 9
supply chain, 10
supply chain management, 10
supply chain orientation, 10
supply management, 8
value chain, 11

DISCUSSION QUESTIONS

1. Why are more top managers recognizing the importance of purchasing/supply management?
2. What is the difference between purchasing and supply management? What is the difference between a supply chain orientation and supply chain management?
3. What is the difference between a supply chain and a value chain?
4. Do you think organizational purchasers should behave like entrepreneurs? Why or why not?
5. What are some of the factors that might influence how important purchasing is to the success of an organization?
6. What knowledge and skills do you feel are required for a purchasing professional?
7. What challenges do organizations face as they attempt to integrate different activities and organizations across the supply chain?
8. What performance areas do you think will benefit most from purchasing involvement in the future?
9. Discuss the four enablers of purchasing and supply chain excellence.
10. What is the relationship between the growth in worldwide competition and the evolution of the supply chain concept?
11. Briefly discuss each of the seven periods in the evolution of purchasing and supply management. What do you forecast for the future?

ADDITIONAL READINGS

Anderson, M. G. (1998), "Strategic Sourcing," *International Journal of Logistics Management,* 9(1), 1–13.

Bhote, K. R. (1989), *Strategic Supply Management: A Blueprint for Revitalizing the Manufacturing-Supplier Partnership,* New York: American Management Association, p. 13.

Ellram, L. M., and Carr, A. (1994), "Strategic Purchasing: A History and Review of the Literature," *International Journal of Purchasing and Material Management,* 30(2), 10–20.

Fearon, H. (1965), "The Purchasing Function within 19th Century Railroad Organization," *Journal of Purchasing,* 1–7.

Giunipero, L., Handfield, R., and El Tantawy, R. (2006), "Supply Management's Evolution: Key Skill Sets for the Purchaser of the Future," *International Journal of Production and Operations Management,* 26(7), 822–844.

Gonzalez-Benito, J. (2007), "A Theory of Purchasing's Contribution to Business Performance," *Journal of Operations Management,* 25(4), 901–917.

Handfield, R., and Onitsuka, M. (1995), "Process and Supply Chain Management Evolution in the American Cotton Textile Industry," *St. Andrew's University Economic and Business Review,* December, 1–35.

Henderson, B. D. (1975), "The Coming Revolution in Purchasing," *Journal of Purchasing and Materials Management,* Summer, 44–50.

Hill, J. A. (1975), "The Purchasing Revolution," *Journal of Purchasing Management,* Summer, 18–19.

Larson, P. D. (2002), "What Is SCM? And Where Is It?" *Journal of Supply Chain Management,* 38(4), 36–44.

Rozemeijer, F. A., van Weele, A., and Weggeman, M. (2003), "Creating Corporate Advantage through Purchasing: Toward a Contingency Model," *Journal of Supply Chain Management,* 39(1), 4–13.

Sprague, L. G. (2007), "Evolution of the Field of Operations Management," *Journal of Operations Management,* 25(2), 219–238.

ENDNOTES

1. Friedman, T. L. (2005), *The World Is Flat,* New York: Farrar, Straus, and Giroux, p. 6.

2. Verespej, M. (2005), "Detroit Needs a Different Driver," *Purchasing,* April 7.

3. Fairclough, G., and Burton, T. M. (2008), "In China, Gaps Found in Drug Supply Chain," *Wall Street Journal,* February 21, pp. A1, A14.

4. Avery, S. (2007), "Purchasing 2007 Salary Survey: Purchasing Salaries Continue Their Climb," *Purchasing,* December 13.

5. Flynn, A., Harding, M. L., Lallatin, C. S., Pohlig, H. M., and Sturzl, S. R. (Eds.) (2006), *ISM Glossary of Key Supply Management Terms* (4th ed.), Tempe, AZ: Institute for Supply Management.

6. Bhote, K. R. (1989), *Strategic Supply Management: A Blueprint for Revitalizing the Manufacturing-Supplier Partnership,* New York: American Management Association, p. 13.

7. Mentzer, J., DeWitt, W., Keebler, J., Min, S., Nix, N., Smith, C., and Zacharia, Z. (2001), "Defining Supply Chain Management," *Journal of Business Logistics,* 22(2), 1–25.

8. Mentzer et al., pp. 3, 11, 17.

9. "1997–2007: The Ten-Year Apple Comeback," October 15, 2007, 9rules.com/apple/notes/8244/.

10. Giunipero, L., and Handfield, R. (2004), *Purchasing Education and Training II,* Tempe, AZ: CAPS Research, p. 74.

11. Hamel, G., and Pralahad, C. K. (1994), *Competing for the Future,* Cambridge, MA: Harvard Business School Press, as reported in Hellriegel, D., Slocum, J. W., and Woodman, R. W. (2001), *Organizational Behavior,* Cincinnati: South-Western, p. 474.

12. Champoux, J. E. (2000), *Organizational Behavior: Essential Tenets for a New Millennium,* Cincinnati: South-Western, p. 325.

13. Trent, R. J. (2003), *Supply Management Organizational Design Effectiveness Study,* Working paper, Lehigh University, Bethlehem, PA. For an electronic copy of study results, please send an e-mail request to rjt2@lehigh.edu.

14. EPIC website www.epiqtech.com/corp/products/index_products/index.htm.

15. From www.i2.com/customers.

16. Hofman, D. (2006), "Getting to World-Class Supply Chain Measurement," *Purchasing,* October 1, from www.purchasing.com/article/CA6389475.html?ref=nbra&q=+World+Class+supply +chain+Measurement+systems+2007+.

17. Hofman.

18. Avery, S. (2007), "UTC General Procurement Presents Key Supplier of the Year Awards," *Purchasing,* March 15.

19. Babbage, C. (1968), *On the Economy of Machinery and Manufacturers* (2nd ed.), London: Charles Knight Publishing, p. 202, as reported in Fearon, H. (1968), "History of Purchasing," *Journal of Purchasing,* February, 44.

20. Handfield, R., and Onitsuka, M. (1995), "Process and Supply Chain Management Evolution in the American Cotton Textile Industry," *St. Andrew's University Economic and Business Review,* December, 1–35.

21. Fearon, H. (1968), "History of Purchasing," *Journal of Purchasing,* February, 44–50, reprinted in Journal of Purchasing and Materials Management, 1989, 71–81.

22. Fearon, p. 47.

23. Fearon, p. 48.

24. Hill, J. A. (1975), "The Purchasing Revolution," *Journal of Purchasing Management,* Summer, 18–19. (Note: This is a reprint of a speech given by John Hill in 1953.)

25. Henderson, B. D. (1975), "The Coming Revolution in Purchasing," *Journal of Purchasing and Materials Management,* Summer, 44. (Note: This is a reprint of an article first appearing in 1964.)

26. Browning, A. J. (1947), "Purchasing—A Challenge and an Opportunity," *Purchasing,* December, 99–101.

27. Ammer, D. S. (1974), "Is Your Purchasing Department a Good Buy?" *Harvard Business Review,* March–April, 136–158.

28. Ammer, p. 158.

29. Ammer, p. 158.

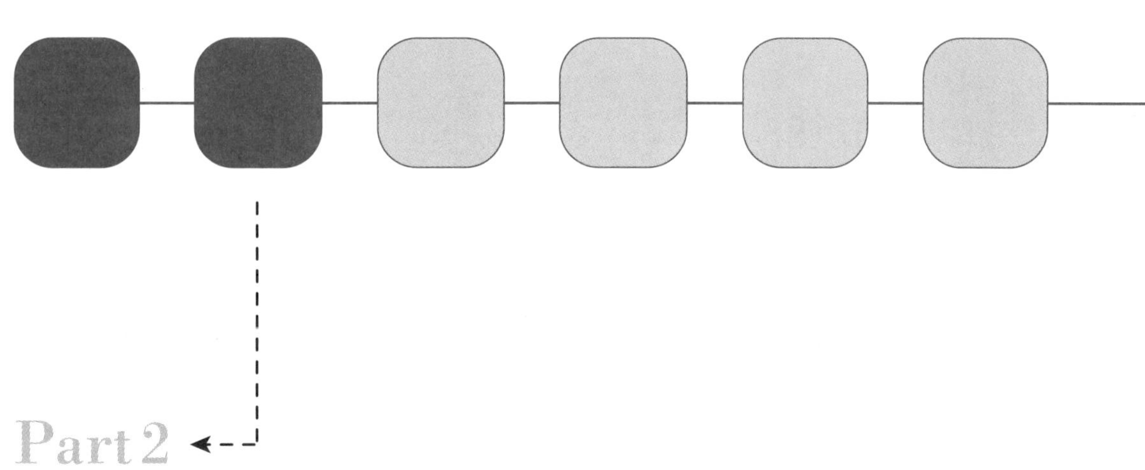

Part 2

Purchasing Operations and Structure

Chapter 2

THE PURCHASING PROCESS

Learning Objectives

After completing this chapter, you should be able to

- Understand the key objectives of any purchasing function
- Understand the responsibilities of the purchasing function
- Understand the purchasing process and the role of e-procurement tools in the process
- Understand the different types of purchases made by organizations
- Understand how organizations are seeking to improve the purchasing process

Chapter Outline

A Supplier's View of the P2P Process at a Large Chemical Company

A large chemical company was seeking to build and extend relational capital with suppliers, by building trust and becoming the "Customer of Choice." The capital gained through this approach can result in preferred supplier delivery priorities, information sharing, participation on supplier councils, and other important rewards. Some important elements in becoming a "Customer of Choice" are to enable rapid payment, provide equitable and ethical treatment of suppliers, and focus on improving the procure to pay (P2P) process.

To address some of the major problems identified by suppliers, the company interviewed suppliers to identify their experiences with the current procure to pay process with some of their major customers. The most common symptoms experienced by suppliers involve high manual workarounds required to address problems, long cycle times for payment, no central point of contact, and a problem with matching the **purchase order (PO)** and invoice.

Suppliers interviewed also noted a number of root causes associated with the P2P problems. The most common root causes were associated with the lack of a formally designed P2P process, the lack of a central relationship management, and problems associated with supplier interfaces with their enterprise resource planning (ERP) system. Other reasons included the increased complexity associated with ERP catalog and line items, and the lack of a forecasting process.

Suppliers believed that the fundamental root causes are the lack of a process with designated roles and specific processes; in association, different internal and external functions are not defined. Maintenance people, buyers, planners, schedulers, accounts payable, project planners, and others are not in synch. Further, the system is not designed to be able to withstand the various approaches in which people enter data and request information. When too many people are not using the system in a unified manner, it is no wonder that the system rejects the input and causes problems! This points to a choice: either the tolerances of such systems must be changed, or the manner in which the system is used must be changed.

RECOMMENDED SOLUTIONS

Suppliers recommended that their customers explore the following solutions: redesigning the P2P process, developing a dedicated relationship manager to work with suppliers on key areas of interface, exploring the use of a vendor portal using the CATS interface in SAP, and reducing catalog items through a spend analysis to reduce the inherent complexity of entering information into the SAP system.

These responses by and large provide significant insights into the problems and complexities associated with improving the P2P cycle from a supplier's perspective. Unfortunately, these issues also translate into significant problems for the purchasing company, which is often lost in translation when the need for P2P improvement is communicated to a senior management team.

Late payment and excessive workaround to obtain payment in a timely manner will definitely increase the cost to serve for companies with a broken P2P process. Some of the typical problems that can occur when a malfunctioning P2P process is not fixed include the following events (adapted from Handfield 2006):

- Deteriorating response time from suppliers, which have no motivation to improve performance and respond quickly to a customer that fails to pay them for 90 days or more

- Lower service levels from suppliers, which may choose to service their more profitable customers first in their Cost to Serve Model
- Deterioration as the "Customer of Choice" in the minds of suppliers' senior management, which further breaks down trust and strategic alignment
- Delivery delays
- Higher pricing due to the cost of money that is attributed to late payment and excessive personnel allocated to the account
- Increased personnel on non-value-added activities (e.g., chasing payments) to the detriment of other value-added activities that can improve customer service
- Loss of the supplier as a critical link in the supply chain
- Higher costs internally for the purchasing company, which must also dedicate AP people and buyers to non-value-added activities

A world-class purchasing staff must continuously work to improve the efficiency and effectiveness of what we call the **purchasing process**. This is the process used to identify user requirements, evaluate the need effectively and efficiently, identify suppliers, ensure payment occurs promptly, ascertain that the need was effectively met, and drive continuous improvement. The challenges in ensuring that this process occurs effectively and efficiently are the theme of this chapter. Until an organization can streamline the day-to-day purchasing process, it will continually delay implementing other important strategic activities that help their organization become more competitive. This chapter introduces the following topics and ideas associated with purchasing in multiple industries:

- Purchasing objectives
- Purchasing responsibilities
- E-procurement and the procure to pay process
- Types of purchases
- Purchasing process improvements
- Good practice example at Federal Express

Purchasing Objectives

The objectives of a world-class purchasing organization move far beyond the traditional belief that purchasing's primary role is to obtain goods and services in response to internal needs. To understand how this role is changing, we must understand what purchasing is all about, starting with the primary objectives of a world-class purchasing organization.

Objective 1: Supply Continuity

Purchasing must perform a number of activities to satisfy the operational requirements of internal customers, which is the traditional role of the purchasing function. More often than not, purchasing supports the needs of operations through the purchase of raw materials, components, subassemblies, repair and maintenance items, and services. Purchasing may also support the requirements of physical distribution centers responsible for storing and delivering replacement parts or finished products to end customers. Purchasing also supports engineering and technical groups, particularly during new-product development and outsourcing of key processes.

With the dramatic increase in outsourcing, enterprises are relying increasingly on external suppliers to provide not just materials and products, but information technology, services, and design activities. As a greater proportion of the responsibility for managing key business processes shifts to suppliers, purchasing must support this strategy by providing an uninterrupted flow of high-quality goods and services that internal customers require. Supporting this flow requires purchasing to do the following:

1. Buy products and services at the right price
2. Buy them from the right source
3. Buy them at the right specification that meets users' needs
4. Buy them in the right quantity
5. Arrange for delivery at the right time
6. Require delivery to the right internal customer

Purchasing must be responsive to the materials and support needs of its internal users (sometimes also called **internal customers**). Failing to respond to the needs of internal customers will diminish the confidence these users have in purchasing, and they may try to negotiate contracts themselves (a practice known as **backdoor buying**).

Objective 2: Manage the Purchasing Process Efficiently and Effectively

Purchasing must manage its internal operations efficiently and effectively, by performing the following:

- Determining staffing levels
- Developing and adhering to administrative budgets
- Providing professional training and growth opportunities for employees
- Introducing procure to pay systems that lead to improved spending visibility, efficient invoicing and payment, and user satisfaction

Purchasing management has limited resources available to manage the purchasing process and must continuously work toward improved utilization of these resources. Limited resources include employees working within the department, budgeted funds, time, information, and knowledge. Organizations are therefore constantly looking for people who have developed the skills necessary to deal with the wide variety of tasks faced by purchasing. Procurement people must be focused on continuously improving transactional-level work through efficient purchasing systems that keep suppliers satisfied, which makes life easier for internal users.

Objective 3: Develop Supply Base Management

One of the most important objectives of the purchasing function is the selection, development, and maintenance of supply, a process that is sometimes described as **supply base management**. Purchasing must keep abreast of current conditions in supply markets to ensure that purchasing (1) selects suppliers that are competitive, (2) identifies new suppliers that have the potential for excellent performance and develops closer relationships with these suppliers, (3) improves existing suppliers, and (4) develops new suppliers that are not competitive. In so doing, purchasing can select and manage a supply base capable of providing performance advantages in product cost, quality, technology, delivery, and new-product development.

Supply base management requires that purchasing pursue better relationships with external suppliers and develop reliable, high-quality supply sources. This objective also requires that purchasing work directly with suppliers to improve existing capabilities and develop new capabilities. A good part of this text focuses on how purchasing can effectively meet this objective.

Objective 4: Develop Aligned Goals with Internal Functional Stakeholders

U.S. industry has traditionally maintained organizational structures that have resulted in limited cross-functional interaction and cross-boundary communication. During the 1990s, the need for closer relationships between functions became clear. Purchasing must communicate closely with other functional groups, which are purchasing's internal customers. These are sometimes called **stakeholders**, in that they have a significant stake in the effectiveness of purchasing performance! If a supplier's components are defective and causing problems for manufacturing, then purchasing must work closely with the supplier to improve its quality. Similarly, marketing may spend a great deal on advertising and promotion, so purchasing must ensure that the pricing is competitive and that service-level agreements are being met. In order to achieve this objective, purchasing must develop positive relationships and interact closely with other functional groups, including marketing, manufacturing, engineering, technology, and finance.

Objective 5: Support Organizational Goals and Objectives

Perhaps the single most important purchasing objective is to support organizational goals and objectives. Although this sounds easy, it is not always the case that purchasing goals match organizational goals. This objective implies that purchasing can directly affect (positively or negatively) total performance and that purchasing must concern themselves with organizational directives. For example, let's assume an organization has an objective of reducing the amount of inventory across its supply chain. Purchasing can work with suppliers to deliver smaller quantities more frequently, leading to inventory reductions. Such policies will show up as improved performance on the firm's balance sheet and income statements. In so doing, purchasing can be recognized as a strategic asset that provides a powerful competitive advantage in the marketplace.

Objective 6: Develop Integrated Purchasing Strategies That Support Organizational Strategies

Far too often the purchasing function fails to develop strategies and plans that align with or support organizational strategies or the plans of other business functions. There are a number of reasons why purchasing may fail to integrate their plans with company plans. First, purchasing personnel have not historically participated in senior-level corporate planning meetings, because they were often viewed as providing a tactical support function. Second, executive management has often been slow to recognize the benefits that a world-class purchasing function can provide. As these two conditions are rapidly changing, purchasing is being integrated within the strategic planning process in multiple industries. A purchasing department actively involved within the corporate planning process can provide supply market intelligence that contributes to strategic planning. Effective supply market intelligence involves the following:

- Monitoring supply markets and trends (e.g., material price increases, shortages, changes in suppliers) and interpreting the impact of these trends on company strategies
- Identifying the critical materials and services required to support company strategies in key performance areas, particularly during new-product development
- Developing supply options and contingency plans that support company plans
- Supporting the organization's need for a diverse and globally competitive supply base

Purchasing Responsibilities

Functional groups carry out certain duties on behalf of the organization. We refer to this as a function's responsibility or **span of control**. Purchasing must have the legitimate authority to make decisions that fall within their span of control. Span of control is established through senior management policies and support. Although internal customers influence many important decisions, final authority for certain matters must ultimately be assigned to the purchasing department. This section details those decision areas that are rightfully part of purchasing's operating authority in most organizations. (Further details on the factors that influence how senior management determines purchasing's span of control are discussed in Chapter 5.)

Evaluate and Select Suppliers

Perhaps the most important duty of purchasing is the right to evaluate and select suppliers—this is what purchasing personnel are trained to do. It is important to retain this right to avoid **maverick** buying and selling—a situation that occurs when sellers contact and attempt to sell directly to end users (purchasing's internal customers). Of course, this right does not mean that purchasing should not request assistance when identifying or evaluating potential suppliers. Engineering, for example, can support supplier selection by evaluating supplier product and process performance capabilities. The right to evaluate and select suppliers also does not mean that sales representatives are not allowed to talk with non-purchasing personnel. However, non-purchasing personnel cannot make commitments to the seller or enter into contractual agreements without purchasing's involvement. A trend that is affecting purchasing's right to select suppliers is the use of sourcing teams with purchasing and non-purchasing representation. The selection decision in sourcing teams requires that the members reach a consensus in selecting suppliers.

Review Specifications

The authority to review material specifications is also within purchasing's span of control, although engineering sometimes disputes this right. Purchasing personnel work hard to develop knowledge and expertise about a wide variety of materials but must also make this knowledge work to an organization's benefit. The right to question allows purchasing to review specifications where required. For example, purchasing may question whether a lower-cost material can still meet an engineer's stress tolerances. The right to question material specifications also helps avoid developing material specifications that only a user's favorite supplier can satisfy. A review of different requisitions may also reveal that different users actually require the same material. By combining purchase requirements, purchasing can often achieve a lower total cost.

Act as the Primary Contact with Suppliers

Purchasing departments historically have maintained a policy that suppliers have contact only with purchasing personnel. Although this makes sense from a control standpoint, some firms today are beginning to relax this policy. Today, we recognize that purchasing must act as the primary contact with suppliers, but that other functions should be able to interact directly with suppliers as needed. Involving multiple people enables the communication process between internal customers, purchasing, sales, and the suppliers' internal functions to be more efficient and accurate. Although purchasing must retain the right to be the primary contact with suppliers, involving other people can improve the transfer of information and knowledge between buying and selling organizations.

Determine the Method of Awarding Purchase Contracts

An important area of control is that purchasing has the right to determine how to award purchase contracts. Will purchasing award a contract based on competitive bidding, negotiation, or a combination of the two approaches? If purchasing takes a competitive bidding approach, how many suppliers will it request to bid? Purchasing should also lead or coordinate negotiations with suppliers. Again, this does not mean that purchasing should not use personnel from other functions to support the negotiation process. It means that purchasing retains the right to control the overall process, act as an agent to commit an organization to a legal agreement, and negotiate a purchase price.

E-Procurement and the Procure to Pay Process

In this section, we examine in detail the purchasing process, which includes all the steps that must be completed when someone within the organization requires some product, material, or service. As stated in the chapter introduction, purchasing is a process made up of all activities associated with identifying needs, locating and selecting suppliers, negotiating terms, and following up to ensure supplier performance. These activities, or steps, are highlighted in Exhibit 2.1; this is often referred to as the procure to pay cycle. This term includes all of the steps required, from the initial identification of requirements, to the procurement/purchasing of the item, through the receipt of the goods, and finally, to the payment of the supplier once the goods are received.

Exhibit 2.1 The Purchasing Process

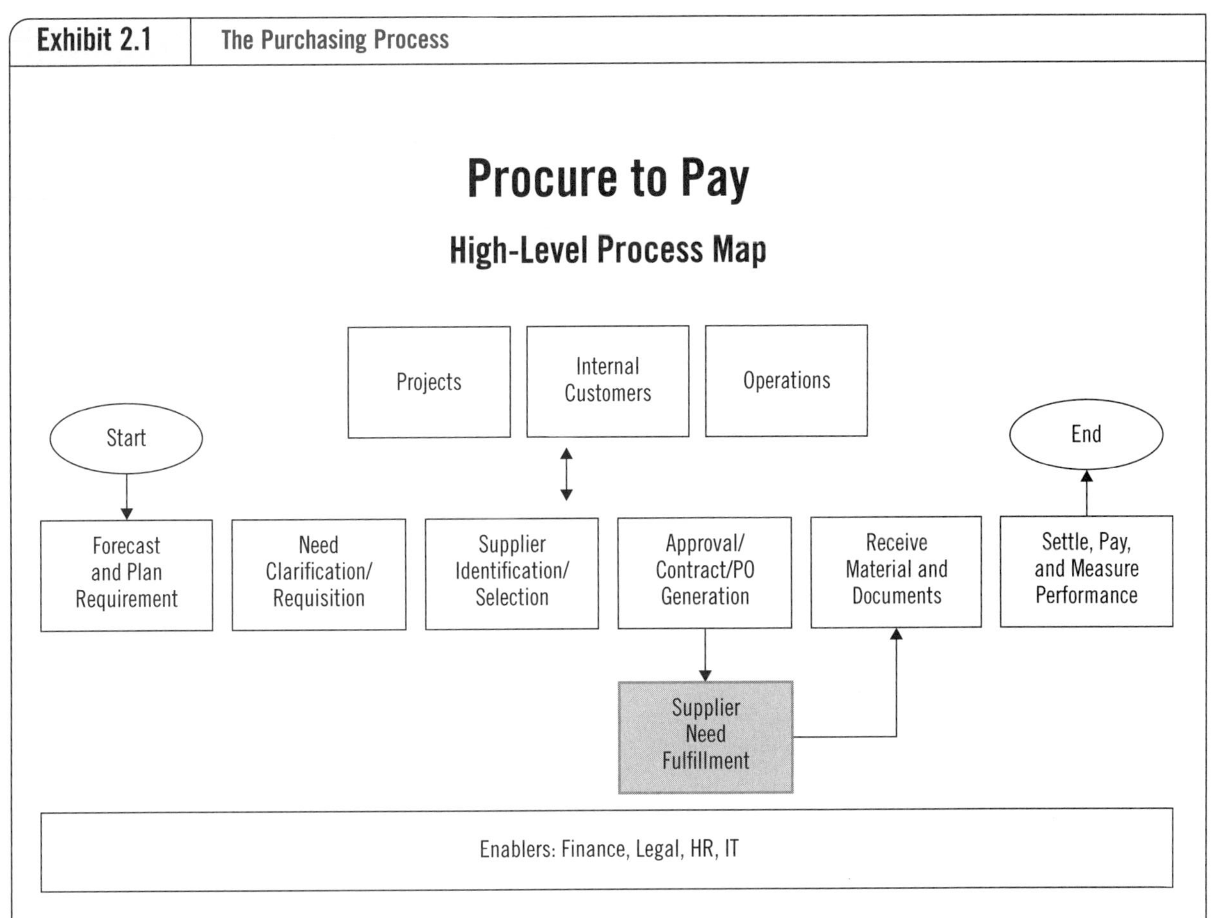

There are two things to keep in mind as we describe the purchasing process. First, how much effort a company spends on these activities will differ greatly from one situation to the next. The purchasing process leading to a $30 billion contract for military jets is very different from that for a routine purchase of office supplies!

Second, as you look at the steps in the procure to pay cycle shown in Exhibit 2.1, recognize that companies can often gain a competitive advantage by performing these activities better than their competitors. Many organizations, for example, use information systems to automate routine purchase order preparation, whereas others use sourcing management teams to improve the outcome of supplier evaluation and selection efforts.

This section presents the purchasing process as a cycle consisting of six major stages:

1. Forecast and plan requirement
2. Need clarification (requisition)
3. Supplier identification/selection
4. Contract/purchase order generation
5. Receipt of material or service and documents
6. Settlement, payment, and measurement of performance

These stages may vary in different organizations, depending on whether purchasing is sourcing a new or a repetitively purchased item, and also whether there is a detailed approval process for purchases that exceed a specific dollar amount. New items require that purchasing spend much more time up front evaluating potential sources. Repeat items usually have approved sources already available. Exhibit 2.1 illustrates a typical purchasing process used in many enterprises, with some typical contingency elements shown.

The process flow shown in Exhibit 2.1 is often called the procure to pay process, as it documents all of the stages from the initiation of a need, through to the payment element. A document flow accompanies the movement of orders and material throughout the procure to pay process. Historically, preparing and managing the proper purchasing documents has been a time-consuming process. Most firms have streamlined the document flow process to reduce the paperwork and handling required for each purchase. The suite of tools used to achieve efficiency in purchasing transactions is broadly defined as **e-procurement**. Companies are using e-procurement tools to manage the flow of documents by (1) automating the document generation process and (2) electronically transmitting purchase documents to suppliers. The benefits of electronically generating and transmitting purchasing-related documents include the following:

1. A virtual elimination of paperwork and paperwork handling
2. A reduction in the time between need recognition and the release and receipt of an order
3. Improved communication both within the company and with suppliers
4. A reduction in errors
5. A reduction in overhead costs in the purchasing area
6. A reduction in the time spent by purchasing personnel on processing purchase orders and invoices, and more time spent on strategic value-added purchasing activities

The electronic documents often used in the process are represented in Exhibit 2.1 by boxes, which we shall now discuss.

Forecast and Plan Requirement

The purchasing cycle begins with the identification of a need (a requirement). In most cases, procurement personnel have an annual or biannual planning process, whereby they will review the spending pattern for the organization (through a spend analysis, discussed later in the chapter), and prepare a forecast of what will be purchased. In some cases, there may be a whole set of new requirements that have not been planned for (such as for new product introductions). In such cases, purchasing personnel meet with internal customers to discuss their needs for the coming year. In many firms today, purchasing is the primary vehicle for obtaining external inputs (products or services) from suppliers, so that means that purchasing personnel have to work with a large number of internal customers, which will often include marketing, operations, finance, information technology, and other internal customers. Through a structured dialogue, purchasing will understand and plan for what these customers will be buying and translate this into a forecast that is shared with suppliers. (In the next chapter, we will discuss the sourcing process that takes place to identify which suppliers are to receive the business associated with fulfilling this need.)

Sourcing Snapshot *Honeywell: Understanding Future Demand*

Many spend analysis systems capture data only after the money is gone. Honeywell's OneSource, by contrast, is like an expanding universe, covering both backward- and forward-looking spend data. It gives the company's commodity managers a way to spot strategic sourcing and spend management opportunities in real time.

Powered by an i2 Technologies SRM, Strategic Sourcing platform, OneSource automatically gathers procurement data from 107 (eventually 152) Honeywell locations. Data available for analysis and decision supports span two previous years plus the current year. Each site provides six discrete data feeds: open purchase orders, receipts, rejects, unplaced demand or forecast (demand from MRP system but not yet purchased), supplier master, and accounts payable spend, including off-purchase order MRO spend. The seventh and eighth data feeds capture contract manufacture bill of materials (part list) and component part approved vendor list for businesses doing subcontract spend analysis.

OneSource is technology agnostic, meaning Honeywell's business units don't need to change the way they capture and store their spend data. "Data in a specified format is taken from the systems the site has—from Excel spreadsheets to a vast array of ERP and MRP systems, including Avalon, BPICS, Cullinet, JD Edwards, MacPac, Oracle, SAP as well as some homegrown versions," says Dennis Lemon, corporate director of supplier quality and health management. That's important for a diversified company like Honeywell, where procurement is decentralized.

Data classification and cleansing is done as part of project rollout and continues using data maintenance applications administered by designated sites or business resources. "As deployment has continued," Lemon says, "data cleansing has identified up to 25% overlap with other sites as new sites are added. Global supplier rationalization has allowed Honeywell to realize supply base reductions in the 40–50% range."

Typically, according to Lemon, it takes about three months to bring a new site on board with OneSource. A key factor has been the development of a formal process for doing this. "We use a defined process that specifies who we work with and how. We involve their sourcing, IT, and quality people. We help them create data feeds, test, and validate their data, and we train them to use the system. We really nurture them as they begin to use OneSource."

Source: "Purchasing Honors Seven Companies in 2004 for Their Leading-Edge Practices in Spend Analysis," *Purchasing,* March 18, 2004.

A projected need may take the form of a component (e.g., a set of fasteners), raw material (e.g., resins), subassembly (e.g., a motor), or even a completely finished item (e.g., a computer). In other cases, the need may be a service, such as the need to contract with an ad agency for a new marketing campaign, or a food service to provide lunches at the company cafeteria. Because purchasing is responsible for acquiring products and services for the entire organization, the information flows between the purchasing function and other areas of the organization can be extensive.

Of course, not all needs can be forecasted ahead of time. There are situations that arise when an internal customer has a need that comes up suddenly, which is not planned for and for which there is no pre-existing supplier identified to provide the product or service required. Such needs are often handled through a **spot buy** approach, which is also discussed within the context of the P2P process. For example, marketing may need to purchase a set of pens and cups for a special promotion and may alert purchasing on sudden notice of this need. If it was not planned for, then purchasing must work with marketing to quickly identify a supplier to provide these products on short notice at the lowest possible cost with an acceptable level of quality and delivery time.

When creating a forecast for a needed product or service, internal customers may not always be able to express exactly what it is they will need at a single point in time. For example, a chemical plant maintenance group may say that they will need replacement parts for their equipment, but they might not be able to provide details on the exact nature of the specific parts they will need, nor the exact time they will need them. In such cases, purchasing may negotiate agreements with distributors of parts that can provide a whole different set of products that can meet that need. In other cases, an internal customer may say that they need to work with a specific service provider for temp services, consulting services, or software programming, but they cannot express exactly what type of service they will need in advance. Purchasing will then go off and attempt to secure a contract with predefined costs for different classes of workers who can provide these services on short notice.

Needs Clarification: Requisitioning

At some point, however, internal customers identify their need for a product or service and communicate to purchasing exactly what it is they need and when it is required.

Internal users communicate their needs to purchasing in a variety of ways including purchase requisitions from internal users, forecasts and customer orders, routine reordering systems, stock checks, and material requirements identified during new-product development. Let's take a closer look at these electronic (or paper) documents that communicate internal customer requirements to purchasing.

Purchase Requisitions/Statement of Work

The most common method of informing purchasing of material needs is through a **purchase requisition**. (An example is shown in Exhibit 2.2.) Users may also transmit their needs by phone, by word of mouth, or through a computer-generated method. Although there are a variety of purchase requisition formats, every requisition should contain the following:

- Description of required material or service
- Quantity and date required
- Estimated unit cost
- Operating account to be charged
- Date of requisition (this starts the tracking cycle)
- Date required
- Authorized signature

Although varieties of formats exist, at a minimum a purchase requisition should include a detailed description of the material or service, the quantity, date required, estimated cost, and authorization. This form of communication for a specific need is called a requisition. A requisition is an electronic or paper form that provides some

Exhibit 2.2 The Purchasing Requisition

AnyCompany

TO: PURCHASING DEPARTMENT, PLEASE FURNISH THE FOLLOWING

REQUISITION

			OUR P.O. NUMBER	No. 36010
ACCOUNT CODE NO./A.F.E. NO./A.F.M. NO./W.O. NO./EQUIP. NO.			REQUESTED BY	VENDOR NO.
DATE	DATE DELIVERY REQ'D.	F.O.B.	DEPARTMENT OR LOCATION	TERMS
TO BE USED FOR			COST ESTIMATE	APPROVAL
			APPROVAL REQUIRED BY	

SUGGESTED SUPPLIER	SHIPPING INSTRUCTIONS
	☐ TAXABLE ☐ TAX EXEMPT

ITEM NO.	QUANTITY	PART NO.	DESCRIPTION	PRICE

DELIVER TO			INSPECTION REQUIRED	
☐ CONFIRMING ORDER	TO	DATE	BY	METHOD
COPIES OF PURCHASE ORDER TO			☐ ACKNOWLEDGMENT COPY	☐ PURCHASING APPROVAL OF INVOICE REQUIRED

REASON FOR AWARD

- ❑ Low Bid
- ❑ Only Bid
- ❑ Only Available Source
- ❑ National Account/Contract Supplier
- ❑ Blanket Order
- ❑ Only Approved Source
- ❑ Emergency
- ❑ Small Purchase
- ❑ Priority Source
- ❑ Commitment made outside of Purchasing Department
- ❑ Low Bidder not acceptable (explanation attached)
- ❑ Other – or additional comments

CORPORATE FORMS MANAGEMENT

Exhibit 2.3 Purchase Requisition Flow

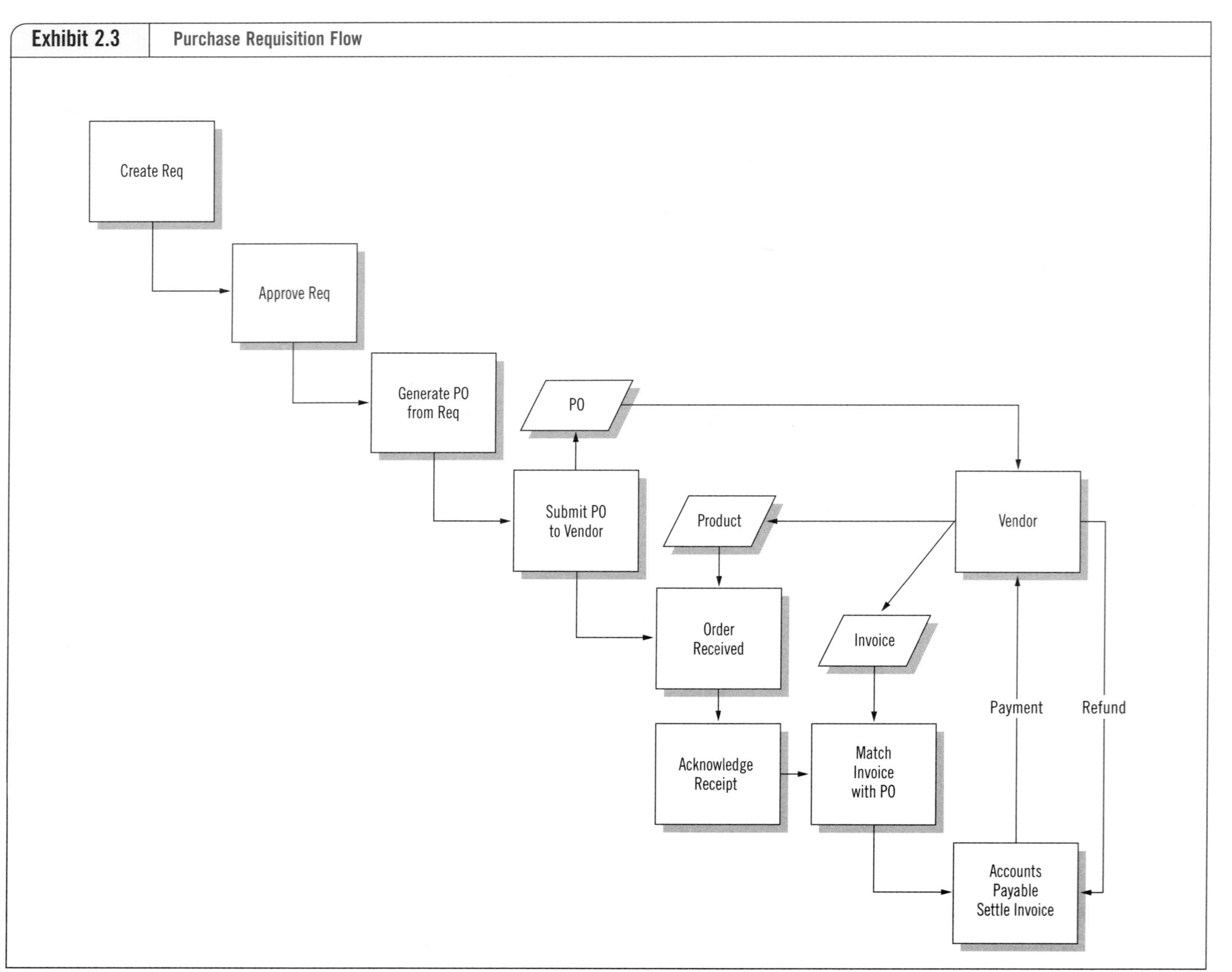

critical information about the need. A typical requisition will provide a description of the product (e.g., a valve), the material and color (brass, red valve), the quantity required (20 red brass valves), the intended purpose (20 red brass valves to be used in a maintenance project for equipment XYZ), and the required date for delivery (three weeks).

Sometimes a service is required. For instance, marketing may want to purchase an advertising campaign, R&D may need a clinical trial, or human resources may need to print a brochure. In this case, the user will complete a **statement of work (SOW)** that specifies the work that is to be completed, when it is needed, and what type of service provider is required.

A standard purchase requisition or SOW is used most often for routine, noncomplex items that are increasingly being transmitted through online requisitioning systems linking users with purchasing. An online requisition system is an internal system designed primarily to save time through efficient communication and tracking of material requests. Users should use these systems only if they require purchasing involvement. It is possible that users have access to other systems that will allow them to purchase an item directly from a supplier, such as a corporate procurement card. In that case requisitions forwarded to purchasing are unnecessary.

There are wide differences across organizations in the quality and use of electronic purchase requisition systems. A system that simply requires users to submit to purchasing what they require for electronic transmission is similar to electronic mail. This type of system provides little added value except to speed the request to purchasing. Conversely, one system studied was so complex that users were afraid to use it. They bypassed online requisitioning and relied instead on the phone or intracompany mail.

Exhibit 2.3 provides further details regarding how a purchase requisition is approved, converted into a purchase order, and ultimately prepared for delivery and payment. Although the user may suggest a supplier, purchasing has final selection authority. For routine, off-the-shelf items, the requisition may contain all the information that purchasing requires. However, for technically complex or nonstandard items, purchasing may require additional information or specifications with the requisition. Examples of such specifications include the grade of material, method of manufacture, and detailed measurements and tolerances. Purchasing may send an acknowledgment of the receipt of the purchase requisition to the requestor. This acknowledgment often takes the form of a confirming order requisition. The acknowledgment may be a separate form notifying the user that purchasing has received and is processing the requisition, or it may be a copy of the original requisition. The confirmation verifies the accuracy of the user's material request.

Traveling Purchase Requisitions/Bar Codes

Material needs are also communicated through a traveling purchase requisition—a form consisting of a printed card or a bar code with information about whom the item is purchased from. This method is used primarily for very small companies that have not automated their purchasing or inventory management processes. Information on the card or the database entry associated with the bar code can include the following:

- Description of item
- List of approved suppliers

- Prices paid to suppliers
- Reorder point
- Record of usage

A traveling requisition can be helpful because it can conserve time when reordering routine materials and supplies. When stock levels reach a specified reorder point, an employee notifies purchasing by forwarding the traveling requisition maintained with the inventory, or by electronically scanning the bar code into the ordering system. The employee notes the current stock level and desired delivery date. To eliminate the need to research information, the traveling requisition includes information required by a buyer to process an order. This system saves time because it provides information for the item on the card (or in the database) that otherwise would require research by a buyer. For example, the traveling requisition can include a list of approved suppliers, prices, a history of usage and ordering, and lead-time information. Historical ordering information is noted directly on the record over a period of time. As inventory systems continue to become computerized (even at smaller companies), traveling requisitions are used less frequently. With an automated system, clerks simply enter the order requirement and the system generates a purchase requisition or automatically places an order.

Forecasts and Customer Orders

Customer orders can trigger a need for material requirements, particularly when changes to existing products require new components. Customer orders can also signal the need to obtain existing materials. As companies increasingly customize products to meet the needs of individual customers, purchasing must be ready to support new material requirements. Market forecasts can also signal the need for material. An increasing product forecast, for example, may signal the need for additional or new material. If a supplier is already selected to provide that material, then an automated ordering system such as a material requirements planning (MRP) system may forward the material request to suppliers automatically.

Reorder Point System

A reorder point system is a widely used way to identify purchase needs. Such a system uses information regarding order quantity and demand forecasts unique to each item or part number maintained in inventory. Each item in a reorder point system, which is usually computerized, has a predetermined order point and order quantity. When inventory is depleted to a given level, the system notifies the materials control department (or the buyer, in some organizations) to issue a request to a supplier for inventory replenishment. This signal might be a blinking light on a screen, a message sent to the materials control department's e-mail address, or a computer report. Most reorder point systems are automated using predetermined ordering parameters (such as an economic order quantity, which considers inventory holding and ordering costs). Electronic systems (such as material requirements planning systems) can instantly calculate reorder point parameters. Most systems can also calculate the cost tradeoffs between inventory holding costs, ordering costs, and forecast demand requirements. Reorder point systems are used for production and nonproduction items.

An automated reorder point system efficiently identifies purchase requirements. This type of system can routinely provide visibility to current inventory levels and requirements of thousands of part numbers. The reorder point system is the most common method for transmitting routine material order requests today, particularly for companies that maintain spare-part distribution centers.

Stock Checks

Stock checks (or cycle counts) involve the physical checking of inventory to verify that system records (also called the **record on hand**, or **ROH**) match actual on-hand inventory levels—also called the **physical on-hand (POH)** levels. If the physical inventory for an item is below the system amount, an adjustment to that part's record can trigger a reorder request for additional inventory. Why might physical inventory be less than what the computerized system indicates should be on hand? Placing material in an incorrect location, damage that is not properly recorded, theft, and short shipments from the supplier that receiving did not notice all can contribute to the POH being less than the ROH. For example, at one major hardware retailer, missing inventory on the shelf may be located in another area of the store, or may simply be missing because of a problem with the incorrect item being entered into the system.

Smaller firms that rely on standard, easy-to-obtain items often use stock checks to determine material ordering requirements. In this environment, the stock check consists of physically visiting a part location to determine if there is enough inventory to satisfy user requirements. No purchase reorder is necessary if there is enough inventory to cover expected requirements.

Cross-Functional New-Product Development Teams

When users contact purchasing with a specific need, we say that purchasing is operating in a *reactive* manner. When purchasing works directly with internal customers to anticipate future requirements, such as during new-product development, purchasing is being *proactive*. What does it mean to anticipate a requirement? If purchasing is part of new-product development teams, then the opportunity exists to see product designs at early stages of the process. Purchasing can begin to identify potential suppliers for expected requirements rather than reacting to an engineering requirement at a later date. Anticipating requirements can contribute to faster product development cycle times and better supplier evaluation and selection. As firms continue to be forced to reduce the time required to develop new products, cross-functional interaction will increasingly be the means through which organizations identify, and hopefully anticipate, material requirements in the purchasing process cycle.

However the need is clarified, the point here is that a requisition document is completed by a requisitioner. A requisitioner is someone who is authorized by purchasing to complete the needs clarification process. In some cases, the person who expresses the need can also be the requisitioner. This occurs in cases where the supplier has already been qualified, and the individual who has the need can go to a supplier's online catalog, order the product or service directly (e.g., through Amazon), and pay for the item using a company purchasing credit card. In such cases, the item is typically low cost, and it is not worth the expense and trouble of completing an entire requisition and going through the entire P2P cycle.

Description

Within the requisitioning process, it is important to include a description of what is to be sourced. Why? If the time is not spent to describe the product or service, purchasing will have no idea of what to go out and purchase! How purchasing accomplishes this will differ dramatically from one situation to the next. There are a variety of methods for communicating the user's requirements. **Description by market grade** or **industry standard** might be the best choice for standard items, where the requirements are well understood and there is common agreement between supply chain partners about what certain terms mean. **Description by brand** is used when a product or service is proprietary, or when there is a perceived advantage to using a particular supplier's products or services. A builder of residential communities, for example, might tell the purchasing staff to purchase R21 insulation, an industry standard, for walls, and to buy finish-grade lumber, a market grade, for the trim and fireplace mantels. In addition, it might also specify brands such as Georgia-Pacific's Catawba® hardboard siding, Kohler® faucets, and TruGreen-Chemlawn® lawn treatment for all the homes. As you can see, brand names, market grades, and industry standards provide purchasing with an effective and accurate shortcut for relaying the user's needs to potential suppliers.

More detailed and expensive methods of description will be needed when the items or services to be purchased are more complex, when standards do not exist, or when the user's needs are harder to communicate. Three common methods include description by specification, description by performance characteristics, and prototypes or samples.

In some cases, an organization may need to provide very detailed descriptions of the characteristics of an item or service. We refer to such efforts as **description by specification**. Specifications can cover such characteristics as the materials used, the manufacturing or service steps required, and even the physical dimensions of the product. Consider one extreme example: the special heat shield tiles used on NASA's space shuttles. Each tile has a unique shape and location on the space shuttle. Furthermore, each shield must be able to protect the space shuttle from heat generated by re-entry into the Earth's atmosphere. In providing a description of these tiles, NASA almost certainly includes specifications regarding the exact dimensions of the tiles and the composite materials to be used in making them. Such information might be relayed in the form of detailed blueprints and supporting documentation. Furthermore, NASA likely specifies the precise manufacturing steps and quality checks to be performed during the manufacture of the tiles.

In contrast, **description by performance characteristics** focuses attention on the *outcomes* the customer wants, not on the precise configuration of the product or service. The assumption is that the supplier will know the best way to meet the customer's needs. A company purchasing hundreds of PCs from Dell Computer might demand (1) 24-hour support available by computer or phone, and (2) 48-hour turn-around time on defective units. How Dell chooses to meet these performance characteristics is its choice.

Firms often develop prototypes or samples to share with their suppliers. Prototypes can provide critical information on the look or feel of a product or service. Such information is often difficult to convey in drawings or written descriptions. Note that prototypes or samples are not limited to physical products. An excellent example is a prototype information system that a company might share with potential software vendors. The prototype may include sample output screens and reports. Through the prototype, the company can give its software vendors a clearer idea of how the company expects its users to interact with the system.

Sourcing Snapshot *Subject Matter Expert Insights into P2P Processes*

As part of a research study, a number of senior procurement executives from a variety of different industries were interviewed to get their responses to the same problems associated with the P2P cycle. Each of these individuals provided a different perspective on how to improve the P2P process, but some common themes validated many of the vendors' suggested recommendations as well.

ROBUST PROCESSES AND TRAINING

A critical element identified by all of the subject-matter experts was the need to develop standardized processes and training around the P2P process. Specifically, roles and duties of the different people involved in the process must be clearly defined, training should emphasize how invoices and requests should be processed, and the reasons why deviation from the process is unacceptable and what consequences are involved with deviating from the process should be explained. This ensures that everyone not only is compliant, but understands the need and rationale behind the compliance. Part of the process redesign effort should also focus on simplifying processes to reduce complexity. If there is no need for a specific channel for purchasing, then eliminate it.

ON-SITE RELATIONSHIP MANAGERS

An important point that many respondents noted was the need to establish dedicated roles around on-site relationship managers from procurement who were on site to manage invoices, service entries, and the like. The simple fact is that many maintenance and project managers do not think in terms of procurement, but rather are focused on people, equipment, and schedules; they do not have the time or patience required to ensure that the correct entries are put into a P2P system. The relationship manager can also act as the liaison between the supplier and the maintenance organization, to ensure prompt payment, resolution of issues, and improvement of processes.

SIMPLIFIED ONLINE PORTALS TO MINIMIZE HUMAN INTERVENTION

A number of SMEs described the need to eliminate the manual intervention of multiple untrained individuals in entering information into systems such as SAP. Many ERP systems have modules for purchasing and plant maintenance, but they all require significant configuration. On the other hand, a number of bolt-on packages are also available, but our SMEs advise against these because of the high probability of interface issues associated with deployment.

IMPROVE FORECASTING FOR MAINTENANCE AND PLANNING FOR EMERGENCIES THAT CAN FLEX WITH DIFFERENT SITUATIONS THAT ARISE

The need to improve forecasting processes is a critical element in ensuring that maintenance needs are met. Although maintenance is often an emergency, there are many scheduled maintenance activities that can be planned and communicated to suppliers. Even in emergency situations, having a plan in place with a designated supplier can avoid many of the problems that occur downstream in the P2P cycle. Too often, data, invoices, service entries, and other key elements are entered incorrectly as a result of a fundamental lack of planning and forecasting. These elements need to be incorporated into the design of new P2P systems.

REDUCE COMPLEXITY IN CATALOGS AND BUYING CHANNELS TO STREAMLINE PROCUREMENT

Many of the experts also emphasized that the need to reduce complexity in the interface systems through pre-defined procurement buying channels is critical to improving the entire P2P cycle. There is no need for users to have multiple channels for procurement. However, establishing the credibility for users to only be able to use these channels also requires significant management support.

Source: R. Handfield, "Best Practices in the Procure to Pay Cycle," *Practix,* March 2006, Center for Advanced Purchasing Management, http://www.caps.org.

Supplier Identification and Selection

Once the need and the description of the need are identified, one of two things can happen: (1) The need is fulfilled by a supplier that has an existing contractual relationship with the buying company. (2) The need is fulfilled by a new supplier that is not currently qualified to provide products and services to the firm.

In the first case, the P2P process moves quite smoothly. Through the need forecasting process, purchasing personnel have already identified which suppliers will be used to source the need, and they have already taken steps to evaluate and prequalify the supplier. Qualification is important, as the purchasing firm must ascertain that the supplier meets several criteria and evaluate whether it is qualified to do business and meet the needs of their internal customers in a satisfactory manner. This evaluation process is described in some detail in the next chapter.

In the second case, where a supplier is not identified, or when the internal customer requests that the need be fulfilled by a specific supplier of their choosing, purchasing face a more difficult challenge. Because there is no existing contract with the supplier, they may balk at approving the need fulfillment from this supplier. When internal customers purchase directly from nonqualified suppliers and try to bypass purchasing in the process, this is known as maverick spending. That is, customers are acting as a maverick, in that they do not wish to use suppliers already deemed by purchasing as qualified to fulfill the need. Although some level of maverick spending is always going to occur in an organization, there are significant risks that can occur when it reaches high proportions. We will discuss some of these risks later in the chapter.

Maverick spending is acceptable when there is little risk associated with the purchase. For example, if someone needs to purchase a box of copy paper, there is little risk when an internal customer goes to the local Staples store and purchases a box using the company procurement card. In fact, purchasing will often encourage them to do so, as this does not represent a productive use of their time in managing these types of expenses. However, when high levels of maverick spending occur repeatedly throughout the company, it can result in major lost opportunities to control cost and also expose the firm to undue risk and loss of control over the purchasing process.

Let's assume for the moment that a qualified supplier is able to provide the product or service, and that the supplier has been through the evaluation process. For some items, firms may maintain a list of **preferred suppliers** that receive the first opportunity for new business. A preferred supplier has demonstrated its performance capabilities through previous purchase contracts and therefore receives preference during the supplier selection process. By maintaining a preferred supplier list, purchasing personnel can quickly identify suppliers with proven performance capabilities.

In cases when there is not a preferred supplier available, purchasing must get involved in selecting a supplier to fulfill that need.

Final supplier selection occurs once purchasing completes the activities required during the supplier evaluation process. Selecting suppliers is perhaps one of the most important activities performed by companies. Errors made during this part of the purchasing cycle can be damaging and long-lasting. Competitive bidding and negotiation are two methods commonly used for final supplier selection when there is not a preferred supplier.

Bidding or Negotiating?

Identifying potential suppliers is different from reaching a contract or agreement with suppliers. Competitive bidding and negotiation are two methods commonly used when selecting a supplier. Competitive bidding in private industry involves a request for bids from suppliers with whom the buyer is willing to do business. This process is typically initiated when the purchasing manager sends a **request for quotation (RFQ)** form to the supplier. The objective is to award business to the most qualified bidder. Purchasers often evaluate the bids based on price. If the lowest bidder does not receive the purchase contract, the buyer has an obligation to inform that supplier why it did not receive the contract. Competitive bidding is effective under certain conditions:

- Volume is high enough to justify this method of business.
- The specifications or requirements are clear to the seller. The seller must know or have the ability to estimate accurately the cost of producing the item.
- The marketplace is competitive, which means it has an adequate number of qualified sellers that want the business.
- Buyers ask for bids only from technically qualified suppliers that want the contract, which in turn means they will price competitively.
- Adequate time is available for suppliers to evaluate the requests for quotation.
- The buyer does not have a preferred supplier for that item. If a preferred supplier exists, the buyer may simply choose to negotiate the final details of the purchase contract with that supplier.

Buyers use competitive bidding when price is a dominant criterion and the required item (or service) has straightforward material specifications. In addition, competitive bidding is often used in the defense industry and for large projects (e.g., construction projects and information system development). If major nonprice variables exist, then the buyer and seller usually enter into direct negotiation. Competitive bidding can also be used to narrow the list of suppliers before entering contract negotiation.

Negotiation is logical when competitive bidding is not an appropriate method for supplier selection. Face-to-face negotiation is the best approach in the following cases:

- When any of the previously mentioned criteria for competitive bidding are missing. For example, the item may be a new or technically complex item with only vague specifications.
- When the purchase requires agreement about a wide range of performance factors, such as price, quality, delivery, risk sharing, and product support.
- When the buyer requires early supplier involvement.
- When the supplier cannot determine risks and costs.
- When the supplier requires a long period of time to develop and produce the items purchased. This often makes estimating purchase costs on the part of the supplier difficult.

As firms continue to develop closer relationships with selected suppliers, the negotiation process becomes one of reaching agreement on items in a cooperative mode. One thing is certain: The process that buyers use to select suppliers can vary widely depending on the required item and the relationship that a buyer has with its suppliers. For some items, a buyer may know which supplier to use before the development of final material specifications. For standard items, the competitive bid process will remain an efficient method to purchase relatively straightforward requirements. The bid process can also reduce the list of potential suppliers before a buyer begins time-consuming and costly negotiation. Chapter 14 discusses negotiation in detail.

After bids have been received or the negotiation has taken place, the sourcing team will select a supplier and then move on to authorize the purchase through the purchase approval process.

Request for Quotation

If the requisition requests an item for a higher dollar amount with no existing supplier, then purchasing may obtain quotes or bids from potential suppliers. Purchasing forwards a request for quotation to suppliers inviting them to submit a bid for a purchase contract. Exhibit 2.4 presents an example of a request for quotation form. The form provides space for the information that suppliers require to develop an accurate quotation, including the description of the item, quantity required, date needed, delivery location, and whether the buyer will consider substitute offers. Purchasing can also indicate the date by which it must receive the supplier's quotation. The supplier completes the form by providing name, contact person, unit cost, net amount, and any appropriate payment terms. The supplier then forwards the request for quotation to the buyer for comparison against other quotations. The normal practice is for a buyer to request at least three quotations. Purchasing evaluates the quotations and selects the supplier most qualified to provide the item.

Specifications or Blueprints

If the requested item is complex or requires an untested or new production process, purchasing can include additional information or attachments to assist the supplier. This might include detailed blueprints, samples, or technical drawings. In addition, buyers can use requests for quotation as a preliminary approach to determine if a potential supplier even has the capability to produce a new or technically complex item. A buyer must identify suppliers with the required production capability before requesting detailed competitive bids. Further quotation and evaluation can then occur to identify the best supplier.

Exhibit 2.4 Request for Quotation

USE ONLY 3 LINES FOR VENDORS 1 & 3
USE ONLY 4 LINES FOR VENDOR 2. NOTE SMALL NUMBERS 1 2 & 3 FOR FOLDING TO FIT STD. NO. 10 ENVELOPE

CORPORATE FORMS MANAGEMENT

SEPARATE BETWEEN PLIES 2 & 3 – RETAIN 1 & 2 INTACT WITH CARBON IN FOR LATER ENTRIES. DISTRIBUTE 3 - 4 - 5 TO VENDORS & PLY 6 TO REQUISITIONER.

AnyCompany

REQUEST FOR QUOTATION

THIS IS NOT A PURCHASE ORDER

DATE

SUMMARY OF QUOTATIONS QUOTATION NO.

NO. 1

NO. 2

NO. 3

QUANTITY	NO. 1	NO. 2	NO. 3
DELIVERY DATE			
F.O.B.			
FREIGHT COST			
TERMS			

PLEASE QUOTE ON THE FOLLOWING ITEMS: WE WILL ☐ WE WILL NOT ☐ CONSIDER SUBSTITUTE OFFERS.

FOR SHIPMENT TO	DELIVERY REQUIRED BY	REPLY MUST BE IN BY:
F.O.B.	TERMS	ADDRESS REPLY TO:

ITEM NO	QUANTITY	DESCRIPTION	UNIT COST	DISCOUNT	NET AMOUNT

AnyCompany PURCHASING DEPARTMENT BY

IN COMPLIANCE WITH THE ABOVE AND SUBJECT TO ALL THE CONDITIONS STATED, THE UNDERSIGNED OFFERS AND AGREES, THAT IF HIS QUOTATION OR PART OF QUOTATION BE ACCEPTED, THAT HE WILL FURNISH AND DELIVER THE ARTICLES OR SERVICES SO LISTED ABOVE, AT THE PRICES QUOTED, TO THE DESIGNATED POINT, AND WITHIN THE TIME SPECIFIED.

QUOTATION DATE ____________ FIRM NAME ____________ BY ____________

QUOTATION MUST BE SUBMITTED ON THIS FORM

PURCHASING DEPT. COPY

If the purchase contract requires negotiation between the buyer and seller (rather than competitive bidding), purchasing sends a **request for proposal (RFP)** to a supplier. In many firms, RFQs and RFPs are synonymous. However, in the latter case, the item's complexity requires that a number of issues besides price need to be included in the supplier's response.

Evaluate Suppliers

As shown in Exhibit 2.1, when the size of the purchase dictates that a detailed evaluation is required for a new purchase, supplier evaluation may be required. The potential evaluation of suppliers begins after determining that a purchase need exists (or is likely to exist) and the development of material specifications occurs. For routine or standard product requirements with established or selected suppliers, further supplier evaluation and selection is not necessary, and the approval process may be generated. However, potential sources for new items, especially those of a complex nature, require thorough investigation to be sure that purchasing evaluate only qualified suppliers.

The source evaluation process requires the development of a list of potential suppliers. This list may be generated from a variety of sources, including market representatives, known suppliers, information databases, and trade journals. For some items, companies may maintain a list of preferred suppliers that receive the first opportunity for new business. A preferred supplier has demonstrated capability through past performance. Relying on a list of preferred suppliers can reduce the time and resources required for evaluating and selecting suppliers.

Buyers use different performance criteria when evaluating potential suppliers. These criteria are likely to include a supplier's capabilities and past performance in product design, commitment to quality, management capability and commitment, technical ability, cost performance, delivery performance, and the ability to develop process and product technology. These factors are weighted in the supplier evaluation process. Specific examples of such weighting schemes appear in Chapter 8 on supplier evaluation. Final evaluation often requires visits to supplier plants and facilities. Because the resources to conduct such visits are limited, the purchaser must take great care in deciding which suppliers to visit.

In recent years, firms have also begun to utilize an electronic competitive bidding tool called a **reverse auction** or an **e-auction**. These mechanisms work exactly like an auction, but in reverse. That is, the buyer identifies potential qualified suppliers to go online to a specific website at a designated time and bid to get the business. In such cases, the lowest bid will often occur as suppliers see what other suppliers are bidding for the business and, in an effort to win the contract, bid it lower. Although they are somewhat ruthless, reverse auctions have been found to drive costs much lower when there is adequate competition in a market.

Approval, Contract, and Purchase Order Preparation

After the supplier is selected or a requisition for a standard item is received, purchasing grant an approval to purchase the product or service. This is accomplished through several different approaches, depending on the type of system in place.

Exhibit 2.5 Purchase Order

CORPORATE FORMS MANAGEMENT

ACCOUNT CODE NUMBER/A.F.E. NO./A/F/M/ NO.	REQUESTED BY	REQUISITION NO.	VENDOR NO.

AnyCompany

PURCHASE ORDER

No.

PURCHASE ORDER NUMBER MUST BE SHOWN ON ALL DOCUMENTS, ACKNOWLEDGEMENTS, SHIPPING PAPERS, PACKING SLIPS, PACKAGES, INVOICES AND CORRESPONDENCE.

INVOICE IN TRIPLICATE
ATTN: ACCOUNTS PAYABLE

DATE WRITTEN	DATE DELIVERY REQUIRED	F.O.B.	DEPARTMENT OR LOCATION	TERMS

TO

SHIPPING INSTRUCTIONS

THIS ORDER SUBJECT TO CONDITIONS ON REVERSE SIDE

☐ TAXABLE ☐ TAX EXEMPT

ITEM NO	QUANTITY	DESCRIPTION	PRICE

– IMPORTANT –
IF YOU CANNOT DELIVER THIS MATERIAL OR SERVICE BEFORE DATE REQUIRED PLEASE NOTIFY US **IMMEDIATELY**

AnyCompany

PURCHASING AGENT ☐ ASST ☐ BUYER

NOTICE:
EQUIPMENT, MATERIALS AND/OR SERVICE UNDER THIS CONTRACT MUST COMPLY WITH ALL APPLICABLE STATE AND FEDERAL SAFETY CODES FOR PLACES OF EMPLOYMENT, INCLUDING OSHA.

AN EQUAL EMPLOYMENT OPPORTUNITY EMPLOYER

Purchase Order

The drafting of a purchase order, sometimes called a **purchase agreement**, takes place after supplier selection is complete. Purchasing must take great care when wording a purchase agreement because it is a legally binding document. Almost all purchase orders include on the reverse side of the agreement the standard legal conditions that the order (i.e., the contract) is subject to. The purchase order details critical information about the purchase: quantity, material specification, quality requirements, price, delivery date, method of delivery, ship-to address, purchase order number, and order due date. This information, plus the name and address of the purchasing company, appears on the front side of the order. Exhibit 2.5 on p. 59 presents an example of a purchase order, and Exhibit 2.6 illustrates a typical set of conditions and instructions.

Companies with an older paper system have a cumbersome process (see Exhibit 2.3). Approximately seven to nine copies typically accompany the purchase order. In computerized environments, a file containing a copy of the PO is sent to each department's computer mailbox. The supplier receives the original copy of the purchase order along with a file copy. The supplier signs the original and sends it back to the buyer. This acknowledges that the supplier has received the purchase order and agrees with its contents. In legal terms, the transmittal of the purchase order constitutes a contractual offer, whereas the acknowledgment by the supplier constitutes a

Exhibit 2.6 A Typical Set of Conditions and Instructions for a Purchase Order

1. Any different or additional terms or conditions in Seller's (Contractor's) acknowledgment of this order are not binding unless accepted in writing by Buyer.
2. Seller shall comply with all applicable state, federal, and local laws, rules, and regulations.
3. Seller expressly covenants that all goods and services supplied will conform to Buyer's order; will be merchantable, fit, and sufficient for the particular purpose intended; and will be free from defects, liens, and patent infringements. Seller agrees to protect and hold harmless Buyer from any loss or claim arising out of the failure of Seller to comply with the above, and Buyer may inspect and reject nonconforming goods and may, at Buyer's option, either return such rejected goods at Seller's expense, or hold them pending Seller's reasonable instructions.
4. The obligation of Seller to meet the delivery dates, specifications, and quantities, as set forth herein, is of the essence of this order, and Buyer may cancel this order and Seller shall be responsible for any loss to or claim against Buyer arising out of Seller's failure to meet the same.
5. Buyer reserves the right to cancel all or any part of this order which has not actually been shipped by Seller, in the event Buyer's business is interrupted because of strikes, labor disturbances, lockout, riot, fire, act of God or the public enemy, or any other cause, whether like or unlike the foregoing, if beyond the reasonable efforts of the Buyer to control.
6. The remedies herein reserved shall be cumulative, and additional to any other or further remedies provided in law or equity. No waiver of a breach of any provision of this contract shall constitute a waiver of any other breach, or of such provisions.
7. The provisions of this purchase order shall be construed in accordance with the Uniform Commercial Code as enacted in the State of Georgia.
8. Government Regulations:
   (1) Seller's and Buyer's obligations hereunder shall be subject to all applicable governmental laws, rules, regulations, executive orders, priorities, ordinances, and restrictions now or hereafter in force, including but not limited to (a) the Fair Labor Standards Act of 1938, as amended; (b) Title VII of the Civil Rights Act of 1964, as amended; (c) the Age Discrimination in Employment Act of 1967; (d) Section 503 of the Rehabilitation Act of 1973; (e) Executive Order 11246; (f) the Vietnam Era Veteran's Readjustment Assistance Act of 1974; and the rules, regulations, and orders pertaining to the above.
   (2) Seller agrees that (a) the Equal Opportunity Clause; (b) the Certification of Nonsegregated Facilities required by Paragraph (7) of Executive Order 11246; (c) the Utilization of Minority Business Enterprises and the Minority Business Enterprises Subcontracting Program Clauses; (d) the Affirmative Action for Handicapped Worker's Clause; and (e) the Affirmative Action for Disabled Veterans and Veterans of the Vietnam Era Clause are, by this reference, incorporated herein and made a part hereof.
   (3) Seller agrees (a) to file annually a complete, timely, and accurate report on Standard Form 100 (EEO-1) and (b) to develop and maintain for each of its establishments a written affirmative action compliance program which fulfills the requirements of 41 C.F.R. 60-1.40 and Revised Order No. 4 (41 C.F.R. 60-2.1 et seq.).

contractual acceptance. Offer and acceptance are two critical elements of a legally binding agreement.

Purchasing forwards a copy of the purchase order (either electronically or manually) to accounting (accounts payable), the requesting department, receiving, and traffic. Purchasing usually keeps several copies for its records. There are good reasons for allowing other departments to view purchase orders and incoming receipts:

- The accounting department gains visibility to future accounts payable obligations. It also has an order against which to match a receipt for payment when the material arrives.
- The purchase order provides the requesting department with an order number to include in its records.
- The requestor can refer to the purchase order number when inquiring into the status of an order.
- Receiving has a record of the order to match against the receipt of the material. Receiving also can use outstanding purchase orders to help forecast its inbound workload.
- Traffic becomes aware of inbound delivery requirements and can make arrangements with carriers or use the company's own vehicles to schedule material delivery.
- Purchasing use their copies of the purchase order for follow-up and monitoring open orders.
- Orders remain active in all departments until the buying company acknowledges receipt of the order and that it meets quantity and quality requirements.

Note that firms are increasingly using computerized databases to perform these processes and are moving toward a paperless office.

Blanket Purchase Order

For an item or group of items ordered repetitively from a supplier, purchasing may issue a **blanket purchase order**—an open order, usually effective for one year, covering repeated purchases of an item or family of items. Exhibit 2.7 on p. 62 provides an example of such a form. Blanket orders eliminate the need to issue a purchase order whenever there is a need for material. After a buyer establishes a blanket order with a supplier, the ordering of an item simply requires a routine order release. The buyer and seller have already negotiated or agreed upon the terms of the purchase contract. With a blanket purchase order, the release of material becomes a routine matter between the buyer and seller.

Almost all firms establish blanket purchase orders with their suppliers. In fact, blanket orders have historically been the preferred method for making the purchasing process more efficient and user friendly. Buyers usually prefer a purchase order for initial purchases or a one-time purchase, which purchasing professionals may also call a "spot buy." Blanket purchase orders are common for production items ordered on a regular basis or for the routine supplies required to operate. A maintenance supplies distributor, for example, may have a purchase order covering hundreds of items. It is not unusual for the buyer or seller to modify a purchase order to reflect new prices, new quantity discount schedules, or the adding or deleting of items.

Exhibit 2.7 Blanket Purchase Order

CORPORATE FORMS MANAGEMENT

ACCOUNT CODE NUMBER/A.F.E. NO./A.F.M. NO.	REQUESTED BY	REQUISITION NO.	VENDOR NO.
Refer to Blanket Order Release	J. M. Smith	20659	02867

AnyCompany
Corporate Purchasing
Street Address
Any City, State 00000
Telephone

PURCHASE ORDER
No. 34833

SEND INVOICE TO:
ATTN: ACCOUNTS PAYABLE

PURCHASE ORDER NUMBER MUST BE SHOWN ON ALL DOCUMENTS, ACKNOWLEDGEMENTS, SHIPPING PAPERS, PACKING SLIPS, PACKAGES, INVOICES AND CORRESPONDENCE.

DATE WRITTEN	DATE DELIVERY REQUIRED	F.O.B.	DEPARTMENT OR LOCATION	TERMS
1/ 3/ 04	As Requested	Our Plant	Various	2% 10, Net 30

TO
Miller Plumbing Supply Company
1616 S. E. 3rd Avenue
Anytown, Any State 90641

SHIPPING INSTRUCTIONS
☑ ATTN: SUPPLY ROOM
☐
☑ TAXABLE ☐ TAX EXEMPT

ITEM NO.	QUANTITY	DESCRIPTION	PRICE

BLANKET PURCHASE ORDER

This Blanket Purchase Order is issued to cover our purchases of valves, pipe and fittings from you for the period 1/3/04 through 6/30/04. Prices are not to exceed your proposal dated 12/15/03 for the period of this order.

This order is not a commitment for any material until actual releases are made on our standard Blanket Order Release form #GP-3809 by an authorized AnyCompany employee whose name appears below.

All shipments, deliveries, and pick-ups will be accompanied by a delivery ticket or packing slip.

All packing slips, delivery tickets, invoices and any other documents relating to this order must reference this Blanket Purchase Order number and the applicable Blanket Order Release number.

AnyCompany reserves the right to cancel this order at any time without cost or obligation for any items not released against this order.

Personnel authorized to make releases against this Blanket Purchase Order:

THIS PURCHASE ORDER SUPERSEDES PURCHASE ORDER #40019, DATED JULY 1, 2002.

– IMPORTANT –
IF YOU CANNOT DELIVER THIS MATERIAL OR SERVICE BEFORE DATE REQUIRED PLEASE NOTIFY US **IMMEDIATELY.**

AnyCompany
John M. Doe
PURCHASING AGENT ☐ ASST ☐ BUYER

THIS ORDER SUBJECT TO CONDITIONS ON REVERSE SIDE

NOTICE: EQUIPMENT, MATERIALS AND/OR SERVICE UNDER THIS CONTRACT MUST COMPLY WITH ALL APPLICABLE STATE AND FEDERAL SAFETY CODES FOR PLACES OF EMPLOYMENT, INCLUDING OSHA.

AN EQUAL EMPLOYMENT OPPORTUNITY EMPLOYER

The blanket purchase order is similar to the purchase order in general content and is distributed to the same departments that receive a copy of a purchase order. The major difference between a purchase order and a blanket purchase order is the delivery date and the receiving department. This information on the blanket order remains open because it often differs from order to order.

When negotiating a blanket purchase order, the buyer and supplier evaluate the anticipated demand over time for an item or family of items. The two parties agree on the terms of an agreement, including quantity discounts, required quality levels, delivery lead times, and any other important terms or conditions. The blanket purchase order remains in effect during the time specified on the agreement. This time period is often, but not always, six months to a year. Longer-term agreements covering several years are becoming increasingly common with U.S. firms. Most buyers reserve the right to cancel the blanket order at any time, particularly in the event of poor supplier performance. This requires an **escape clause** that allows the buyer to terminate the contract in the event of persistently poor quality, delivery problems, and so on.

Material Purchase Release

Buyers use material purchase releases to order items covered by blanket purchase orders. Purchasing specifies the required part number(s), quantity, unit price, required receipt date, using department, ship-to address, and method of shipment and forwards this to the supplier. Purchasing forwards copies of this form to the supplier, accounting, receiving, and traffic. Purchasing retains several copies for its records. The copy to the supplier serves as a notification of a required item or items. Accounting receives a copy so it can match the quantity received against the quantity ordered for payment purposes. Receiving must have visibility of incoming orders so it can compare ordered quantities with received quantities. As with other forms, this part of the process is increasingly becoming electronic.

Different types of material releases exist. Organizations often use the material release as a means to provide visibility to the supplier about forecasted material requirements as well as actual material requirements. One U.S. automobile producer provides suppliers with an 18-month forecast for replacement parts. The first three months of the release are actual orders. The remaining nine months represent forecasted requirements that help the supplier plan.

In other cases, a more detailed contract is required above and beyond a simple purchase order. A contract is typically required if the size of the purchase exceeds a predetermined monetary value (e.g., $1,000), or if there are risks associated with doing business with a supplier where the potential for conflict and problems is not negotiated prior to the purchase. Because purchasing professionals buy products and services as a career, it is not surprising that they deal regularly with contracts. It is therefore critical that purchasing managers understand the underlying legal aspects of business transactions and develop the skills to manage those contracts and agreements on a day-to-day basis. Once a contract has been negotiated and signed, the real work begins. From the moment of signing, it is the purchasing manager's responsibility to ensure that all of the terms and conditions of the agreement are fulfilled. If the terms and conditions of a contract are breached, purchasing personnel are also responsible for resolving the conflict. In a perfect world, there would be no need for a contract, and all deals would be sealed with a handshake. However, contracts are an important part of managing buyer-supplier relationships as they explicitly define the roles and responsibilities of both parties, as well as how conflicts will be resolved if they occur (which they almost always do).

Purchasing contracts can be classified into different categories based on their characteristics and purpose. Almost all purchasing contracts are based on some form of pricing mechanism and can be categorized as a variation on two basic types: fixed-price and cost-based contracts. The differences in contracts will be discussed later in Chapter 14.

Fixed-Price Contracts

Firm Fixed Price

The most basic contractual pricing mechanism is called a firm fixed price. In this type of purchase contract, the price stated in the agreement does not change, regardless of fluctuations in general overall economic conditions, industry competition, levels of supply, market prices, or other environmental changes. This contract price can be obtained through a number of pricing mechanisms: price quotations, supplier responses to the buying organization's requests for proposal, negotiations, and other methods. Fixed-price contracts are the simplest and easiest for purchasing to manage because there is no need for extensive auditing or additional input from the purchasing side.

If market prices for a purchased good or service rise above the stated contract price, the seller bears the brunt of the financial loss. However, if the market price falls below the stated contract price because of outside factors such as competition, changes in technology, or raw material prices, the purchaser assumes the risk or financial loss. If there is a high level of uncertainty from the supplying organization's point of view regarding its ability to make a reasonable profit under competitive fixed-price conditions, then the supplier may add to its price to cover potential increases in component, raw material, or labor prices. If the supplier increases its contract price in anticipation of rising costs, and the anticipated conditions do not occur, then the purchaser has paid too high a price for the good or service. For this reason, it is very important for the purchasing organization to adequately understand existing market conditions prior to signing a fixed-price contract to prevent contingency pricing from adversely affecting the total cost of the purchase over the life of the contract.

Cost-Based Contracts

Cost-based contracts are appropriate for situations in which there is a risk that a large contingency fee might be included using a fixed-price contract. Cost-based contracts typically represent a lower level of risk of economic loss for suppliers, but they can also result in lower overall costs to the purchaser through careful contract management. It is important for the purchaser to include contractual terms and conditions that require the supplier to carefully monitor and control costs. The two parties to the agreement must agree on what costs are to be included in the calculation of the price of the goods or services procured.

Cost-based contracts are generally applicable when the goods or services procured are expensive, complex, and important to the purchasing party or when there is a high degree of uncertainty regarding labor and material costs. Cost-based contracts are generally less favorable to the purchasing party because the threat of financial risk is transferred from the seller to the buyer. There is also a low incentive for the supplier to strive to improve its operations and lower its costs (and hence the price to the purchaser). In fact there is an incentive, at least in the short run, for suppliers to be inefficient in cost-based contracts because they are rewarded with higher prices.

Receipt and Inspection

This phase of the purchasing cycle involves the physical transmittal of purchase requirements (see Exhibit 2.1 with further details in Exhibit 2.8). This should be a fairly routine, although not necessarily the most efficient, part of the purchasing cycle. Some organizations transmit orders electronically, whereas others send material releases through the mail or by fax. Purchasing or materials planning must minimize the time required to release and receive material. **Electronic data interchange (EDI)**, which involves the electronic transfer of purchase documents between the buyer and seller, can help shorten order cycle time. EDI transactions, particularly through the Internet, will increase over the next several years. Also, better relationships with suppliers can support a just-in-time (JIT) ordering system. In some companies, once a contract is negotiated, internal end users may be directly responsible for releasing material orders covered under the terms of the contract, and purchasing personnel are no longer involved until the contract is renewed. Exhibit 2.9 on p. 66 shows the trend in how organizations are moving toward automating the different portions of the procurement process.

Purchasing or a materials control group must monitor the status of open purchase orders. There may be times when a purchaser has to expedite an order or work with a supplier to avoid a delayed shipment. A buyer can minimize order follow-up by selecting only the best suppliers and developing stable forecasting and efficient ordering systems. The receiving process should also be made as efficient as possible by using bar code technology to receive and place supplier deliveries in inventory.

Exhibit 2.8 Receiving Process

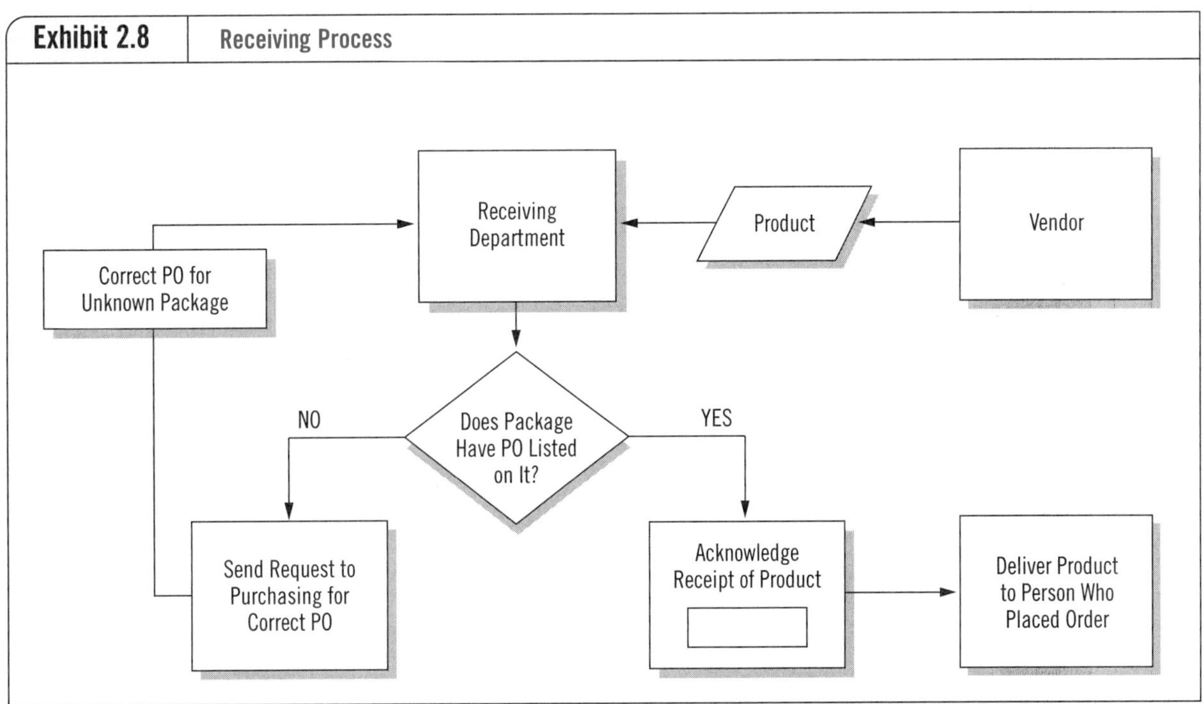

Exhibit 2.9 Methods or Approaches Organizations Expect to Emphasize to Reduce the Effort or Transactions Required to Process Low-Value Purchases

METHOD OR APPROACH	TOTAL SAMPLE	INDUSTRIAL	NONINDUSTRIAL
Online requisitioning systems from users to purchasing	66.3%*	64.9%	67.4%
Procurement cards issued to users	65.1	59.7	69.6
Electronic purchasing commerce through the Internet	60.9	68.8	54.3
Blanket purchase order agreements	57.4	63.7	52.2
Longer-term purchase agreements	54.4	58.4	51.1
Purchasing online ordering systems to suppliers	61.0	46.7	53.3
Purchasing process redesign	53.3	50.7	55.4
Electronic data interchange	52.7	58.4	47.8
Online ordering through electronic catalogs	51.5	49.4	53.3
Allowing users to contact suppliers directly	49.7	54.5	45.7
User online ordering systems to suppliers	49.1	51.9	46.7
	$N = 169$	$N = 77$	$N = 92$

*Represents the percentage of total respondents expecting to emphasize a method or approach.
Source: Trent and Kolchin, 1999.

The shipping and receiving processes require several other important documents that also can be electronic, including the material packing slip, the bill of lading, and the receiving discrepancy report.

Material Packing Slip

The **material packing slip**, which the supplier provides, details the contents of a shipment. It contains the description and quantity of the items in a shipment. It also references a specific purchase order and material release number for tracking and auditing purposes. A packing slip is a critical document when receiving material at a buyer's facility. The receiving clerk uses the packing slip to compare the supplier packing slip quantity against the actual physical receipt quantity. Furthermore, the packing slip quantity should match the material release quantity. The comparison between material release quantity and packing slip quantity is critical. It determines if suppliers have over- or undershipped.

Bill of Lading

Transportation carriers use a **bill of lading** to record the quantity of goods delivered to a facility. For example, the bill of lading may state that ABC carrier delivered three boxes to a buyer on a certain date. This prevents the purchaser from stating a week later that it received only two boxes. The bill of lading details only the number of boxes or containers delivered. Detailing the actual contents of each container is the supplier's responsibility; that information appears on the packing slip.

The bill of lading helps protect the carrier against wrongful allegations that the carrier somehow damaged, lost, or otherwise tampered with a shipment. This document does not necessarily protect the carrier against charges of concealed damage, however. A user may discover concealed damages after opening a shipping container. Responsibility for concealed damage is often difficult to establish. The receiving company may blame the carrier. The carrier may blame the supplier or maintain that the damage occurred after delivery of the material. The supplier may maintain total innocence and implicate the carrier. While all this goes on, the buyer must reorder the material as a rush order. This can affect customer service or commitments.

Receiving Discrepancy Report

A **receiving discrepancy report** details any shipping or receiving discrepancies noted by the receiving department. It is often the job of purchasing or material control to investigate and resolve material discrepancies. Material discrepancies usually result from incorrect quantity shipments. They can also result from receiving an incorrect part number or a part number incorrectly labeled.

Just-in-Time Purchasing

Just-in-time purchasing and manufacturing allows firms to eliminate most receiving forms. Honda of America, for example, assumes that if its production line does not shut down it must have received its scheduled shipments from its suppliers. The accounts payable department makes payment unless informed otherwise. Honda's JIT system eliminates the need for packing slips and inbound material inspection. The system also eliminates the need to examine, file, and forward multiple copies of each packing slip to various departments. If a receipt does not arrive on time or is not damage free, Honda realizes this within minutes. With this system, no news means the shipment arrived and is production ready.

Black & Decker employs a similar system called **backflush accounting**. In this system, suppliers are paid only for the quantity of components that are used in each week's production runs. In the event that parts are tossed aside on the production line because of defects, Black & Decker does not pay for them.

Someone (typically purchasing or materials personnel) must monitor the status of open purchase orders. There may be times when the buying firm has to expedite an order or work with a supplier to avoid a delay in a shipment. A company can minimize order follow-up by selecting only the best suppliers and developing internally stable forecasting and ordering systems. When the order for a physical good arrives at the buyer's location, it is received and inspected to ensure that the right quantity was shipped and that it was not damaged in transit. Assuming that the product or service was delivered on time, it will be entered into the company's purchasing transaction system. Physical products delivered by suppliers then become part of the company's working inventory.

In the case of services, the buyer must ensure that the service is being performed according to the terms and conditions stated in the purchase order. For services, the user will typically sign off on a supplier time sheet or other document to signal purchasing that the service was delivered as promised, on time, and according to the conditions stated in the initial SOW. That may mean checking with the actual users within the organization who requested the service in the first place and ensuring that all is going as planned. Deviations from the statement of work must be noted and passed on to the supplier, which in some cases may require modifications to the original PO or contracted SOW (often called a **change notice** when this occurs).

Invoice Settlement and Payment

Once the item or service is delivered, the buying firm will issue an authorization for payment to the supplier. Payment is then made through the organization's accounts payable department. This is increasingly being accomplished through electronic means. Suppliers are more often being paid through **electronic funds transfer (EFT)**, which is the automatic transfer of payment from the buyer's bank account to the supplier's bank account. More and more organizations are moving to integrated systems where all purchase orders, receipts, and payments are made electronically.

Records Maintenance

After the product or service has been delivered and the supplier paid, a record of critical events associated with the purchase is entered into a supplier performance database. The supplier performance database accumulates critical performance data over an extended period, helping purchasing identify trends or patterns in supplier performance.

Why is it important to capture the transaction-level data associated with all purchasing processes? This answer is discussed in the next section. Specifically, from time to time the firm must identify opportunities for savings through a process known as a spend analysis. Spend analysis becomes a critical input into building sourcing strategies—the topic of the next section.

Continuously Measure and Manage Supplier Performance

One way to identify the best suppliers is to track performance after awarding a contract. Supplier measurement and management is a key part of the purchasing cycle. As shown in Exhibit 2.1, buyers should not assume that the purchasing cycle ends with the receipt of an ordered item or the selection of a supplier. Continuous measurement is necessary to identify improvement opportunities or supplier nonperformance. A later chapter discusses purchasing measurement and evaluation tools. This section simply summarizes the key points about this phase of the purchasing cycle.

A desired outcome from performance measurement is improved supplier performance. If no formal evaluation takes place, a buyer has little insight into supplier performance over time, and tracking any performance improvement that results from supplier development efforts is not possible. Without a measurement and evaluation system, a buyer lacks the quantitative data necessary to support future purchase decisions.

A major issue when evaluating supplier performance is the frequency of evaluation and feedback. For example, should a buyer receive a supplier quality performance report on a daily, weekly, monthly, or quarterly basis? Although most firms recognize the need to notify suppliers immediately when a problem arises, there is little consensus about the frequency for conducting routine or scheduled supplier evaluations. For many firms, this overall evaluation may occur only one or two times a year. Regardless of the reporting frequency, supplier performance measurement is an important part of the purchasing process cycle.

Re-engineering the Procure to Pay Process

Many companies have P2P processes that are in disrepair and are focused on improving the P2P cycle. In re-engineering the procure to pay process, suppliers and experts recommend that executives apply the following approach:

1. Secure top management support for the initiative and budgeting for the project. Develop a list of key benefits and deliverables that will occur as a result of

the improvements. Document the cost of leaving the system "broken" in its current state.

2. Map existing processes and problems with the P2P cycle. Identify where the breakdowns are occurring and why they are occurring.
3. Understand the needs and requirements of the user groups. Many of the people involved—maintenance, planning, project management, supplier's accounts payable, buyers, and so on—have specific issues that prevent them from using the existing system. Also, many of the specific sites may have issues that need to be considered in designing the new system.
4. Team redesign workshops should be used to bring together key subject matter experts (SMEs) from each of the business units. Suppliers should also be invited to attend and participate, as they may have solutions they have adopted with other customers that may prove to be efficient and simple to use ("why reinvent the wheel?").
5. Explore existing technology solutions with ERP systems, as well as bolt-on applications. Map out the business requirements and ensure they are aligned with the technology solutions that are available. Begin to estimate cost of deployment, and ensure that adequate planning and due diligence is taken at this step.
6. Following the workshops, define the new process, and begin to pilot using a planned technology. Ensure that it takes place in a real environment, with actual nontrained users involved in the pilot before cutting over to the next process.
7. Train and deploy other users based on the new processes and systems. Be sure to make the training appropriate to the specific functional unit and user groups.
8. Monitor, update, and improve the system, ensuring that catalogs are kept up to date. Hold periodic meetings with suppliers and user groups to solicit input and identify problems with the systems.

As technology and business requirements evolve, the P2P cycle will probably need to be revisited from time to time to ensure it is meeting the needs of internal customers and that suppliers are satisfied with the system.

Types of Purchases

Organizations buy many different goods and services. All purchases represent a tradeoff between what an organization can make itself versus what it must buy externally. For many items, the make-or-buy decision is actually quite simple. Few firms could manufacture their own production equipment, computers, or pencils. However, all firms require these items to support continued operations. The challenge is deciding which suppliers offer the best opportunity for items an organization must purchase externally. The following sections outline the variety of goods and services a typical purchasing department is responsible for buying. Please note that for each category, organizations should establish measures that track the amount of goods in physical inventory.

Raw Materials

The raw materials purchase category includes items such as petroleum, coal, and lumber, and metals such as copper and zinc. It can also include agricultural raw materials such as soybeans and cotton. A key characteristic of a raw material is a lack of processing by the supplier into a newly formed product. Any processing that occurs makes the raw material saleable. For example, copper requires refining to remove impurities from the metal. Another key characteristic is that raw materials are not of equal quality. Different types of coal, for example, can differ by sulfur content. Raw materials often receive a grade indicating the quality level. This allows raw materials purchases based on the required grade.

Semifinished Products and Components

Semifinished products and components include all the items purchased from suppliers required to support an organization's final production. This includes single-part number components, subassemblies, assemblies, subsystems, and systems. Semifinished products and components purchased by an automobile producer include tires, seat assemblies, wheel bearings, and car frames.

Managing the purchase of semifinished components is a critical purchasing responsibility because components affect product quality and cost. Hewlett-Packard buys its laser jet printer engines, which are a critical part of the finished product, from Canon. HP must manage the purchase of these engines carefully and work closely with the supplier. Outsourcing product requirements increases the burden on purchasing to select qualified suppliers, not only for basic components, but also for complex assemblies and systems.

Finished Products

All organizations purchase finished items from external suppliers for internal use. This category also includes purchased items that require no major processing before resale to the end customers. An organization may market under its own brand name an item produced by another manufacturer. Why would a company purchase finished items for resale? Some companies have excellent design capability but have outsourced all production capability or capacity. Examples include IBM, Hewlett-Packard, Sun, Cisco, General Motors (Geo), and others. The purchase of finished products also allows a company to offer a full range of products. Purchasing (or engineering) must work closely with the producer of a finished product to develop material specifications. Even though the buying company does not produce the final product, it must make sure the product meets the technical and quality specifications demanded by engineering and the end customer.

Maintenance, Repair, and Operating Items

Maintenance, repair, and operating (MRO) items include anything that does not go directly into an organization's product. However, these items are essential for running a business. This includes spare machine parts, office and computer supplies, and cleaning supplies. The way these items are typically dispersed throughout an organization makes monitoring MRO inventory difficult. The only way that most purchasing departments know when to order MRO inventory is when a user forwards a purchase requisition. Because all departments and locations use MRO items, a typical purchasing department can receive thousands of small-volume purchase requisitions. Some purchasers refer to MRO items as nuisance items.

Historically, most organizations have paid minimal attention to MRO items. Consequently, (1) they have not tracked their MRO inventory investment with the same concern with which they track production buying, (2) they have too many MRO suppliers, and (3) they commit a disproportionate amount of time to small orders. With the development of computerized inventory systems and the realization that MRO purchase dollar volume is often quite high, firms have begun to take an active interest in controlling MRO inventory. At FedEx, an agreement with Staples allows purchasing to be free of the burden of tracking office supply requests. Instead, Staples provides a website listing all supplies with prices; users can point and click on the items they need, and the supplier will deliver to the user's location the next business day.

Production Support Items

Production support items include the materials required to pack and ship final products, such as pallets, boxes, master shipping containers, tape, bags, wrapping, inserts, and other packaging material. Production support items directly support an organization's production operation; this is a key distinction separating production support and MRO items. The DaimlerChrysler sourcing snapshot in Chapter 19 provides a good example of how this activity can be managed.

Services

All firms rely on external contractors for certain activities or services. An organization may hire a lawn care service to maintain the grounds around a facility or a heating and cooling specialist to handle repairs that the maintenance staff cannot perform. Other common services include machine repair, snow removal, data entry, consultants, and the management of cafeteria services. Like MRO items, the purchase of services occurs throughout an organization. Therefore, there has been a tendency to pay limited attention to them and to manage the service purchases at the facility or department level. A study by AT&T several years ago revealed that the company was spending over a billion dollars a year on consultants. As with any purchase category, careful and specialized attention can result in achieving the best service at the lowest total cost. More and more, companies are negotiating longer-term contracts with service providers just as they would with other high-dollar purchase categories.

Capital Equipment

Capital equipment purchasing involves buying assets intended for use over one year. There are several categories of capital equipment purchases. The first includes standard general equipment that involves no special design requirements. Examples include general-purpose material-handling equipment, computer systems, and furniture. A second category includes capital equipment designed specifically to meet the requirements of the purchaser. Examples include specialized production machinery, new manufacturing plants, specialized machine tools, and power-generating equipment. The purchase of these latter items requires close technical involvement between the buyer and seller.

Several features separate capital equipment purchases from other purchases. First, capital equipment purchases do not occur with regular frequency. A production machine, for example, may remain in use for 10 to 20 years. A new plant or power

Sourcing Snapshot — *Microsoft: 100% Visibility on Indirect Spend*

Few companies have as good a handle on their indirect spending as Microsoft. In February 2003, the software giant began using MS Spend, a tool it developed to link data from MS Market, its e-procurement system, with other information on the company's purchasing activities generated by its MS Vendor and MS Invoice technologies. Now Microsoft has 100% visibility of both its global direct and indirect spends at the commodity code level. Microsoft's annual purchasing tab is about $11.5 billion.

Using the latest versions of its own software, Microsoft developed a series of web-based tools to provide a user-friendly interface to its SAP ERP system. MS Market is the company's electronic ordering system that creates and tracks purchase orders and captures United Nations Standard Products and Services Code (UNSPSC) categorization for purchases. MS Invoice is its electronic invoice-processing system that allows suppliers to invoice Microsoft electronically and track the status of invoices submitted. MS Inquire allows suppliers and internal users to pose queries about orders.

MS Spend integrates information captured using MS Market and MS Invoice to provide comprehensive procurement reporting on the corporate intranet. Users access the tools via Internet Explorer. Although Microsoft does not sell the tools, they are available through such company partners as Accenture and EDS.

At Microsoft, procurement has been completely paperless since 1997. Under its distributed procurement model, all the company's employees are buyers of goods and services. As such, they can purchase directly from suppliers as well as use the online procurement tools.

Once the corporate procurement group slashed transaction costs to about $5 through use of the tools, it turned its focus to strategic sourcing. "Our goal has been to leverage more cost-effective sourcing strategies to increase value and efficiency," says Don Jones, general manager, corporate procurement. "Spend analysis is our cornerstone." On the spend analysis team with Jones are John Stevens and Jana Shull of Microsoft Corporate Procurement and Mike Huber of Microsoft Corporate Services.

After benchmarking other companies, Microsoft selected the UNSPSC as its standard commodity classification system. The procurement team was looking for a coding system that it could use not only to classify spend, but also to communicate with its trading partners. Developing an internal system, Jones says, "would hamper our ability to communicate through our e-procurement system with our supply base." The company's hardware suppliers, for instance, all use the same version of the UNSPSC code.

To ensure accurate reporting of spend data, Microsoft invested in additional technology that guides buyers to select proper codes for goods and services they purchase through MS Market. After more benchmarking, the corporate procurement team learned that other UNSPSC users said requisitioners typically don't make the effort to ensure they are using correct codes when placing orders, typically selecting one of the first codes appearing on a list. In UNSPSC code, one of the first codes is for sheep. Once procurement teams ran reports on spend, they learned only that requisitioners in their companies were purchasing a lot of sheep.

Jones was determined that this would not be the case with buyers at Microsoft. As such, the team incorporated a logical selection into its ordering system. The system is designed to host a subset of UNSPSC codes based on the supplier selected by the buyer. As part of the ordering process, the buyer discretely identifies the good or service at the transaction level. The buyer is given a targeted selection to choose from based on supplier selected. "This information is integrated for our analysis as well as passed to our reporting tools," Jones says. Although the team has a process to randomly check codes, it doesn't cleanse the data; "no one knows better what they are ordering than the buyers themselves," he adds. Corporate procurement uses an online video to train buyers not only on how to use the codes, but also to explain the benefits gained by Microsoft by their doing so.

Source: "Purchasing Honors Seven Companies in 2004 for Their Leading-Edge Practices in Spend Analysis," *Purchasing,* March 18, 2004.

substation may remain in operation over 30 years. Even office furniture may last over 10 years. A second feature is that capital equipment investment requires large sums of money. This can range from several thousand dollars to hundreds of millions of dollars. High-dollar contracts will require finance and executive approvals. For accounting purposes, most capital equipment is depreciable over the life of the item. Finally, capital equipment purchasing is highly sensitive to general economic conditions.

Buyers can rarely switch suppliers in the middle of a large-scale project or dispose of capital equipment after delivery because of dissatisfaction. Furthermore, the relationship between the buyer and supplier may last many years, so the buyer should also consider the supplier's ability to service the equipment. The consequences of selecting a poorly qualified supplier of capital equipment can last for many years. The reverse is also true. The benefit of selecting a highly qualified capital equipment provider can last many years.

Transportation and Third-Party Purchasing

Transportation is a specialized and important type of service buying. Few purchasing departments involved themselves with transportation issues before the early 1980s. However, legislation passed during the late 1970s and early 1980s deregulated the air, trucking, and railroad industries. This legislation allowed buyers to negotiate service agreements and rate discounts directly with individual transportation carriers. Previously, the U.S. government, through the Interstate Commerce Commission, established the rate (referred to as a **tariff**) that a transportation carrier charged. It was common for suppliers to arrange shipment to a purchaser and simply include the transportation cost as part of the purchase cost.

Purchasing personnel have become involved with transportation buying and the management of inbound and outbound material flows. It is now common for purchasing personnel to evaluate and select logistics providers the same way they evaluate and select suppliers of production items. Buyers are also selecting suppliers that are capable of providing coordinated transportation and logistics services for an entire company, including warehousing, packaging, and even assembly. Because many carriers now provide service throughout the United States, a buyer can rely on fewer transportation carriers. The cost savings available from controlling and managing logistics are significant.

Improving the Purchasing Process

Most companies spend too much time and too many resources managing the ordering of goods and service, particularly lower-value items. Some purchasing departments spend 80% of their time managing 20% of their total purchase dollars. Recent research on maintenance, repair, and operating purchases reported that while the average MRO invoice was $50, the total cost of processing an MRO transaction was $150.[1] In another example, a U.S. government agency reported that in a single year it processed 1.1 million transactions at an estimated cost of $300 per transaction! How can organizations create value through their purchasing process when they spend more time processing orders than what the orders are worth?

A recent study by Trent and Kolchin[2] addressed how organizations are improving the purchasing process by reducing the time and effort associated with obtaining lower-value goods and services. The study involved 169 randomly selected organizations, of which 77 are industrial companies and 92 are nonindustrial companies or organizations. Exhibit 2.9 identifies the methods or approaches that organizations expect to emphasize over the next several years to improve the low-value purchasing process. The following sections summarize the approaches and methods presented in the exhibit.

Online Requisitioning Systems from Users to Purchasing

Online requisitioning systems are internal systems designed primarily to save time through efficient and rapid communication. Users should use these systems only if they require purchasing involvement to support a material or service need. If users do not require assistance, they should have access to other low-dollar systems that do not require purchasing involvement.

Advanced organizations are much more likely to allow users to request low-value purchases through internal electronic systems when the need requires purchasing involvement. Organizations that have made less progress managing low-value purchasing use company mail or the phone to receive user requests. Users should rely on efficient requisitioning systems for items that require purchasing involvement. A longer-term focus should be to create systems and processes that empower users to obtain low-value items directly from suppliers rather than involving purchasing.

Procurement Cards Issued to Users

One tool or system that most organizations agree is central to improving the purchasing process is the use of the procurement card, which is essentially a credit card provided to internal users. When users have a lower-value requirement, they simply contact a supplier and use the card to make the purchase. Cards work well for items that do not have established suppliers or are not covered by some other purchasing system. The users make the buying decisions (the money for which comes out of their department's budget) and bypass purchasing completely. The dollar value of the items covered by procurement cards is relatively low. The cost to involve purchasing or engage in a comprehensive supplier search would likely outweigh the cost of the item.

The study by Trent and Kolchin found that the average cost per transaction due to procurement card use decreased from over $80 to under $30. The primary benefits from using cards include faster response to user needs, reduced transaction costs, and reduced total transaction time. In most organizations, purchasing is responsible for introducing and maintaining the card program.

Electronic Purchasing Commerce through the Internet

Electronic purchasing commerce through the Internet refers to a broad and diverse set of activities. Using the Internet to conduct purchasing business is not extensive today, although commercial Internet usage by purchasers should increase dramatically over the next several years. The highest expected growth areas in e-commerce purchasing include the following:

- Transmitting purchase orders to suppliers
- Following up on the status of orders
- Submitting requests for quotes to suppliers
- Placing orders with suppliers
- Making electronic funds transfer payments
- Establishing electronic data interchange capability

Longer-Term Purchase Agreements

Longer-term purchase agreements usually cover a period of one to five years, with renewal based on a supplier's ability to satisfy performance expectations. These agreements can reduce the transactions costs associated with lower-value purchases by eliminating the need for time-consuming annual renewal. Furthermore, once a purchaser and a supplier reach agreement, material releasing responsibility should shift to user groups. Ideally, material releasing becomes electronic rather than manual, even for lower-value items.

Although the two approaches are conceptually similar, differences exist between a blanket purchase order, which purchasers routinely use, and longer-term purchase agreements. Both approaches rely on a contractual agreement to cover specific items or services; they may be for extended periods; they are legal agreements; and they are highly emphasized ways to manage lower-value purchases. However, blanket purchase orders are typically used more often for lower-value items than for longer-term agreements. Longer-term agreements are usually more detailed in the contractual areas they address compared with blanket purchase orders.

Online Ordering Systems to Suppliers

Online ordering systems involve direct electronic links from a purchaser's system to a supplier's system, often through a modem or other web-enabled technologies. A major feature of online ordering systems is that suppliers often bear the responsibility for developing the software required to link with a customer's system. Online ordering is a logical approach once an organization has established a blanket purchase agreement or longer-term contract with a supplier. The strategic part of the sourcing process involves identifying, evaluating, and selecting suppliers. Online ordering systems allow purchasing or users to place orders directly into a supplier's order-entry system. Advantages of online ordering systems include the following:

- Immediate visibility to back-ordered items
- Faster order input time, which contributes to reduced order cycle times
- Reduced ordering errors
- Order tracking capabilities

Sourcing Snapshot — *IBM: Closing the Loop on Spend*

The real strength in IBM's spend-analysis system lies with its cyclical—as opposed to linear—approach to strategic planning and sourcing. It lies also with IBM's organizational and corporate governance structures.

Through governance, IBM limits the ways in which people can spend money. External commitment requires a PO, and old spending loopholes—like check requests, wire transfers, and expense accounts—are closely controlled, according to Bill Fanning, director of procurement finance, who reports directly to IBM's finance organization and indirectly to chief procurement officer John Paterson.

"There's no escape route," Fanning says. "Our system detects and reports anyone who bypasses the procurement system every time they do it. If a person comes to us with an invoice in hand, we say, 'Okay, we'll pay, but we have to set up a PO.' That creates an immediate report to their manager. If they do it a second time, they receive an official reprimand. If they do it a third time, they're subject to dismissal. People have been fired."

IBM captures spend data in real time at two different points: when money is committed (often 30–60 days before it is paid out) and again when money goes out the door. Planned refinements to the system will capture even more forward-looking demand data earlier in the decision cycle.

After capturing its spend data, IBM classifies it automatically using a proprietary, highly granular taxonomy and closes the procurement-to-finance loop by mapping corporate spend data—which is organized by commodity, supplier, etc.—to the various brands' and business-units' accounting ledgers. "Financial folks are not really interested in how a commodity is defined," explains Fanning. "They understand the ledger. By building a bridge between procurement's taxonomy and the ledger's taxonomy, we have created an ability to really manage spend and to affect our business units' profit and loss (P&L) statements."

But IBM doesn't stop there. The company also has the ability to associate spend data with other procurement information such as competitive cost (IBM's historical cost curve compared to an industry benchmark cost curve), absolute lowest cost, and other competitive commodity market intelligence gathered routinely by its 31 sourcing councils. "Fundamentally, the only reason procurement has a reason to exist is to develop a competitive advantage, but you have to be able to measure that," Fanning says.

IBM's spend analysis structure allows the procurement organization to do the following:

- Forecast what the company will spend over the coming year and how the spend will break down by business unit
- Provide an outlook as to what is likely to happen with commodity market pricing
- Report how sourcing councils will deliver savings to specific IBM brands or business units
- Plan with brand managers or business units how they will deploy expected savings (either "take down" or invest elsewhere) in their P&Ls
- Close the loop by measuring performance to plans

"Spend data is used in tracking monthly performance of all (31) commodity councils and the global procurement organization," says Fanning. "The data provides a direct link to the profit and loss metrics of each brand and group within IBM."

Source: "Purchasing Honors Seven Companies in 2004 for Their Leading-Edge Practices in Spend Analysis." *Purchasing,* March 18, 2004.

- Order acknowledgment from the supplier, often with shipping commitment dates
- Ability to batch multiple items from multiple users on a single online order
- Faster order cycle time from input to delivery

Suppliers establish online ordering systems so purchasers can have dedicated access to the supplier's order-entry system. The system creates a seamless tie-in or linkage between organizations. Third-party software providers such as Ariba provide turnkey solutions that will help to further this development in the future.

Purchasing Process Redesign

Most organizations recognize that purchasing process redesign efforts often precede the development of low-dollar purchase systems. Properly executed redesign efforts should lead to faster cycle times and simplified processes that result in reduced transactions costs.

The purchasing process is composed of many subprocesses, which means it can benefit from process mapping and redesign. The low-value purchase process affects hundreds or even thousands of individuals throughout a typical organization—users in every department, office, plant, and facility; accounts payable; receiving and handling; purchasing; systems; and of course, suppliers. Anyone with a need for low-value goods or services is part of the low-value purchase process.

Electronic Data Interchange

Electronic data interchange involves a communications standard that supports interorganizational electronic exchange of common business documents and information. It is a cooperative effort between a buyer and seller to become more efficient by streamlining communication processes. When used by buyers and suppliers, EDI can help eliminate some steps involved in traditional communication flows, which reduces time and cost.

Although actual volumes through EDI have increased through the 1990s, actual EDI volume does not match the expected volume that was projected by companies. In 1993, for example, purchasing professionals estimated that 60% of the supply base, 70% of total purchase dollars, and 65 percent of total purchasing transactions would flow through EDI systems. Actual 1997 volume was 28% of suppliers, 38% of total purchase dollars, and 32% of total purchasing transactions flowing through EDI systems.[3] Part of this shortfall is due to the introduction of auto fax technology. For many organizations, especially smaller organizations, auto fax is a quicker and less expensive method of communicating with suppliers. Auto fax systems automatically fax requirements to suppliers once those requirements are known by the buyer. The Internet also captures electronic volume that formerly would have passed through third-party EDI providers. Chapter 19 discusses this important topic in greater detail.

Online Ordering through Electronic Catalogs

Purchasers are increasingly using this approach in conjunction with other low-dollar purchase systems. For example, one organization allows its user to identify supply sources through the Internet and then use a procurement card to process the order. The key benefit of using electronic catalogs is their powerful low-cost search capability and, if users order directly instead of relying on purchasing, reduced total cycle time and ordering costs. Perhaps the greatest drawback to online ordering is the limited number of suppliers that offer electronic catalogs, along with questions about security of electronic ordering and control issues.

Allowing Users to Contact Suppliers Directly

This general method or approach involves different kinds of low-dollar systems. Procurement cards technically qualify as a system that allows users to contact suppliers directly. Online ordering systems also allow users to contact suppliers directly, or the system may involve nothing more than a multiple part form, such as a limited purchase order, that users complete as they initiate an order. FedEx refers to its "pick up the phone" system, which allows users to contact suppliers directly, as its **convenience ordering system**.

Approaches that allow users to contact suppliers directly shift responsibility for the transaction from purchasing to the user. Even for items with no established supplier, purchasing still may have limited or no involvement unless the requirement reaches a predetermined dollar or activity level. If an item becomes a repetitive purchase, then purchasing may determine if the item warrants a blanket purchase order. Blanket purchase orders usually allow users to contact suppliers directly when a need arises for material. The following Good Practice Example describes a system that allows users to contact suppliers directly below some dollar threshold level.

Why is it important to capture the transaction-level data associated with all elements of the P2P process? This answer is discussed in Chapter 6 on sourcing strategy. Specifically, from time to time the firm must identify opportunities for savings through a process known as a spend analysis. A spend analysis becomes a critical input into building sourcing strategies, the topic of Chapter 6.

Good Practice Example — *Sourcing Process at Federal Express*

FedEx Corporation is a $20 billion market leader in transportation, information, and logistics solutions, providing strategic direction to six main operating companies. These are FedEx Express, FedEx Ground, FedEx Freight, FedEx Custom Critical, FedEx Trade Networks, and FedEx Services.

THE FEDEX CENTER-LED INITIATIVE

Prior to the purchase of the Ground, Freight, and other non-express-based services, Federal Express had reorganized all of its major indirect spend in information technology, aircraft, facilities/business services, vehicles/fuel/ground service equipment, and supply chain logistics groups under the Strategic Sourcing and Supply group, led by Edith Kelly-Green. After the purchase of these different businesses, the supply management function was reorganized into a Center-led supply chain management (SCM) sourcing model. ("Center" refers to a Center of Excellence that focuses on centralizing sourcing strategy teams.) Over the last two years, FedEx Supply Chain Management has been focusing on leveraging sourcing and contracting for all of the FedEx family of companies. For office supplies, instead of having each company run a contract, SCM has a single corporate contract for all of the negotiation effort that allows for different transactional approaches. It has been a gradual migration to a centralized view of how procurement happens. It is central for the larger spend areas and different policy requirements.

THE SOURCING PROCESS

FedEx established a seven-step sourcing process, shown in Exhibit 2.10 on p. 81.

Step 1: A user provides a requisition for an item. When the user provides the requisition, the sourcing specialist or team must establish whether it is worth putting a strategy around it. This is typically done using a return-on-investment criterion: Is the spend large enough to put a significant amount of time into sourcing the product through a full-blown supplier evaluation? For example, if the requisition is for something that turns out to be a $200,000 per year spend, the payback on it may not be worth the resources required to do a full supplier evaluation and selection process. However, if the spend is large enough, the team will conduct an assessment of the category that profiles that industry and commodity. This assessment involves researching the nature of existing purchasing activity: How much is it, who is it with, and what are the issues with existing suppliers? If it is not large enough, the user may be directed to a simple purchase order and invoice through the Ariba system.

Step 2: Assuming a large spend, based on research conducted in Step 1, the team goes into a process to select the sourcing strategy, in essence taking all of the information it has and deciding how it will approach that marketplace. Is a request for proposal appropriate? Does it need to maintain existing relationships or revisit negotiation and develop a strategy regarding the sourcing strategy?

Step 3: Assuming it is going beyond a negotiation, the team must conduct in-depth research with suppliers in that area, including qualification of the suppliers. Can the suppliers satisfy user requirements, service aspects, and so on? The end goal is to develop a list of suppliers to send RFPs to. The team conducts a supplier portfolio analysis.

Step 4: Another phase of this implementation pass is to revisit this strategy and have the team take another look at it. Has it uncovered something that will cause it to change negotiation? The team develops a strategy for negotiation; does it want to use a reverse auction or use a conventional RFP, as well as criteria for supplier evaluation? Is this still something it wants to do? If so, it proceeds with the RFP to the selected suppliers.

Step 5: After receiving RFPs, the team conducts the supplier selection and negotiation process.

Step 6: Once the team has made the selection, it needs to do the integration. This is done by applying the Ariba toolset with the supplier and identifying integration conflicts to be resolved to make the contract workable.

Step 7: The final stage in this process is to benchmark the supply market by monitoring the supplier(s) through the FedEx Supplier Scorecard system.

E-procurement tools through the Ariba Buyer system play a big role in the process. For example, users who need a PC can select one online and requisition it. Depending on the business rules governing authority threshold, the user may need a supervisor's authorization and may need higher-level approval as well. If the spend goes into the capital range, there is another set of approval rules to ensure that people who oversee capital purchases also approve it. It also draws on the business rules from the IT group, which may be a different set of rules. Business rules are established within Ariba Buyer depending on the category of spend taking place. The types of controls made on purchases will vary. Once those approvals are completed, it releases out to the supplier.

In Ariba, users have an online catalog for contracts that are in place; several thousand office supplies are set up on the catalog. Requisitioners can find what they want, and once submitted, the requisition is bounced against a purchase approval policy. Requisitioners can also use an RFP before they initiate the sourcing process. One of the first things they will do is get a handle on accounts payable information using Ariba to identify the largest suppliers and establish prior sales to FedEx with information on line items. Ariba Buyer also tracks receipts. Because FedEx receives products and services at many different locations around the globe, all employees have an obligation to enter a receipt into the system when the shipment arrives or the service is performed, which generates an acknowledgment and a matching invoice on the system. If an individual does not receive the product or service, Ariba will develop e-mail reminders that will eventually escalate to senior management if left unattended.

The value of using a single e-procurement system is that if FedEx supply management decides to implement a change on the control levels, it is easy to do across the company using the system. For example, if the CEO mandates a spending freeze (no PCs without VP-level approval), SCM can change the business rules on the system. FedEx also uses ELAMS, another information system for temp labor contract programmers. The ELAMS system allows online requisitions for contract programmers or temp labor based on contracts that are in place—it controls the rate and type of individual sent out by that company and can approve the invoices online. It can also ensure that the skill level of temp labor FedEx is paying for is matched to the skill level of the individual actually doing the work. This enables FedEx to control the type of person that it actually pays for, delivering both value and cost savings to the bottom line.

This example illustrates that improving the purchasing process in terms of efficiency *and* effectiveness requires more than one single system or approach. Purchasing, accounts payable, user groups or departments, and those responsible for handling inventory and material can all benefit from a systematic approach to improving how goods and services flow into an organization.

Questions

1. What steps in the purchasing process are done electronically versus on paper?
2. What types of controls can be used as a result of e-procurement in the sourcing process?
3. What do you think are the challenges associated with implementing e-procurement in this example?

Exhibit 2.10 FedEx Strategic Sourcing Process

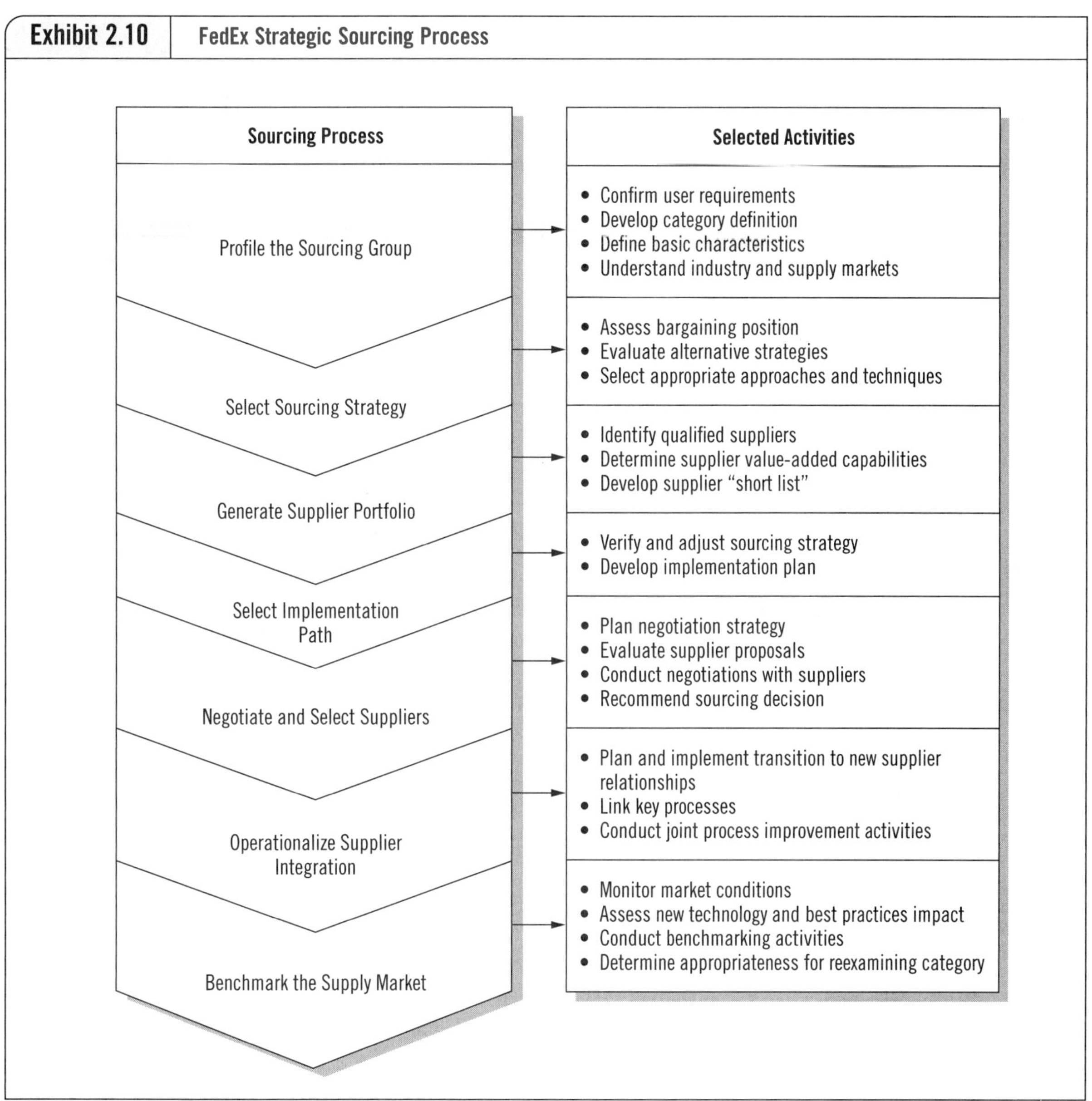

CONCLUSION

This chapter provides an overview of purchasing and the purchasing process, including the objectives of a world-class purchasing function, purchasing's span of control, the purchasing cycle, and the documents used to manage the purchasing process. These topics provide the foundation from which to introduce the tools, techniques, and strategies used by purchasing organizations in a competitive market.

This chapter also points out the many different categories of purchases. In addition to buying production material and items, purchasing can be responsible for buying transportation, services, packing supplies, MRO items, capital equipment, and even the corporate jet! There is no one system or approach that applies to all purchase situations. Purchases can vary according to type, importance, impact on quality, time frame for delivery, and dollar volume. We rarely find purchasing personnel who are experts in all the different types of purchases, which is why so many purchasing departments have specialized personnel. These personnel all have one thing in common, however: the opportunity to manage large amounts of resources through the purchasing process. By utilizing e-procurement tools, purchasing can achieve the goals of satisfying user requirements, minimizing non-value-added time, and focusing on deployment of sourcing strategies that can provide tangible value to their enterprise.

KEY TERMS

backdoor buying, 39
backflush accounting, 67
bill of lading, 66
blanket purchase order, 61
change notice, 67
convenience ordering system, 78
description by brand, 52
description by industry standard, 52
description by market grade, 52
description by performance characteristics, 52
description by specification, 52
e-auction, 58
e-procurement, 44
electronic data interchange (EDI), 65
electronic funds transfer (EFT), 68
escape clause, 63
internal customers, 39
material packing slip, 66
maverick, 41
physical on-hand (POH), 51
preferred suppliers, 54
purchase agreement, 60
purchase requisition, 46
purchasing process, 38
receiving discrepancy report, 67
record on hand (ROH), 51
request for proposal (RFP), 58
request for quotation (RFQ), 55
reverse auction, 58
span of control, 41
spot buy, 46
stakeholders, 40
statement of work (SOW), 49
supply base management, 39
tariff, 73

DISCUSSION QUESTIONS

1. How can an effective purchasing department affect organizational performance?
2. Discuss the concept of the internal customer. Who are purchasing's internal customers?
3. Discuss the contributions a purchasing department can make to the corporate strategic planning process.

4. List the areas typically considered within purchasing's span of control. Explain why it is important that purchasing have authority over each of these areas.
5. Describe how purchasing become aware of purchase requirements.
6. How is anticipating a material requirement or need through purchasing's involvement on a new-product development team different from reacting to a purchase need?
7. Why do some firms no longer rely only on competitive bidding when awarding purchase contracts?
8. Provide a list of the major documents that are covered in a suite of e-procurement software tools.
9. Discuss the advantages of electronically transmitting and receiving purchasing documents between a buyer and seller. What are the challenges involved in implementing e-procurement tools?
10. Why is it important to measure and monitor supplier performance improvement over time?
11. How does a just-in-time purchasing and production system reduce the need for certain purchasing documents?
12. Why is purchasing becoming increasingly involved in the purchase of transportation services and other nontraditional purchasing areas?
13. Discuss how the purchase of capital equipment differs from the purchase of routine supplies.
14. Develop a list of topics that non-purchasing personnel should be allowed to talk about with their counterparts at suppliers. Develop a list of topics that only purchasing should be allowed to talk about with suppliers.
15. What is the difference between a purchase order and a blanket purchase order? What are the advantages of using blanket purchase orders?

ADDITIONAL READINGS

Antonette, G., Sawchuk, C., and Giunipero, L. (2002), *E-Purchasing Plus* (2nd ed.), New York: JGC Enterprises.

Carborne, J. (1999), "Reinventing Purchasing Wins the Medal for Big Blue," *Purchasing,* 127(4), 38–41.

Croom, S. (2001), "Restructuring Supply Chains through Information Channel Innovation," *International Journal of Operations and Production Management,* 21(4), 504–515.

Handfield, R. (March 2006), "Best Practices in the Procure to Pay Cycle," *Practix.*

Martinson, B. (2002), "The Power of the P-Card," *Strategic Finance,* 83(8), 30–36.

Neef, D. (2001), *E-Procurement: From Strategy to Implementation,* Saddle River, NJ: Prentice Hall.

Palmer, R. J., Gupta, M., and Davila, A. (2003), "Transforming the Procure-to-Pay Process: How Fortune 500 Corporations Use Purchasing Cards," *Management Accounting Quarterly,* 4(4), 14–22.

Sabri, E., Gupta, A., and Beitler, M. (2006), *Purchase Order Management Best Practices: Process, Technology, and Change Management,* J. Ross Publishing.

Trent, R. J., and Kolchin, M. G. (1999), *Reducing the Transaction Costs of Purchasing Low-Value Goods and Services,* Tempe, AZ: Center for Advanced Purchasing Studies.

ENDNOTES

1. Antonette, G., Sawchuk, C., and Giunipero, L. (2002), *E-Purchasing Plus* (2nd ed.), New York: JGC Enterprises.

2. Trent, R. J., and Kolchin, M. G. (1999), *Reducing the Transaction Costs of Purchasing Low-Value Goods and Services,* Tempe, AZ: Center for Advanced Purchasing Studies.

3. Trent and Kolchin.

Chapter 3

PURCHASING POLICY AND PROCEDURES

Learning Objectives

After completing this chapter, you should be able to

- Understand why purchasing policies are important
- Understand the different types of purchasing policies
- Understand the different types of purchasing procedures

Chapter Outline

Developing a Policies and Procedures Manual in a Decentralized Cement Company

A U.S.-based cement company that is a global leader in cement, building materials, related technologies, and research recently decided to redesign its procurement organization and recognized that policies and procedures were an important part of this process. The company consists of several cement operations located in one region of the United States. Each operation had established decentralized procurement processes. Although the basic manufacturing processes are not dissimilar, there existed a variety of supply strategies, approved suppliers, and procurement channel strategies.

In 1999, the company developed a purchasing policies and procedures manual to define guidelines by which the purchasing function would be practiced at the company.

In January 2007, an external team of experts completed a procure to pay (P2P) assessment of the company, focusing on the requisition to payment process. The key objective was to identify opportunities to improve user satisfaction and transactional efficiency such that the procurement staff could shift their efforts from pushing transactions through the system to strategic sourcing and contracting activities.

The study was concluded and presented in early February 2007. One of the recommendations made by the team was to enhance the current process; improvements were needed to eliminate or reduce current issues and reduce the purchase order cycle time for a tighter distribution, thus reducing the mean cycle time and the effort to achieve this.

In order to begin the multiple improvement efforts needed to accomplish this, the senior executive team, composed of IT, procurement, maintenance, and operations departments, recognized that it was necessary to first re-establish a common and consistent baseline of beliefs, methods, and behaviors across all of the company's facilities. The purchasing policies and procedures manual was a good start, but the manual had not been updated since the time of publication. There was a strong need to educate, train, and monitor compliance with policies and procedures. The eight-year-old manual was also in need of review and revision to capture changes in organizational structure from a decentralized environment to a centralized procurement environment and to reflect the changing set of strategies and practices that impacted the currently accepted business practices.

In addition to the much-needed update, two additional purposes for a policies overhaul were recognized. The first was to set the stage for a concentrated effort to educate employees so that they would comply with policies and procedures. Second, the new policies and procedures manual would serve as the basis for development of a worldwide corporate procurement governance model.

In order to successfully accomplish these goals, a team was chartered to review and update the present documents and address current pain points. The stated goal was the following:

- To revise the current procurement policies and procedures documents to reflect current practices and to relieve pain points and areas of confusion
- To develop a document management strategy, including centralized location, easy accessibility to stakeholders and users, regular review of documents for necessary changes/updates, and a notification method for new or revised documents
- To establish ownership within Central Procurement and establish processes to ensure companywide compliance

The end deliverable will be an updated policies and procedures manual that is accessible online, in compliance with global directives, and available in a common web-based policies and procedures template.

The opening vignette illustrates an important point about purchasing policies: From time to time, it is important to review them and update them as required! Because the company's environment is constantly changing, there is a need to keep up with these changes and provide guidelines and directions to employees regarding how these changes will impact their ways of working. Policies provide the basis for action on the part of sourcing professionals, as well as a set of guidelines for the appropriate way to deal with new situations. As the purchasing and technology environment changes, policies and procedures must be kept up to date with these changes.

Most organizations have a set of policies outlining or detailing the directives of executive management across a range of topics. These directives provide guidance while at the same time placing operating constraints on personal behavior. This chapter, divided into three major sections, discusses the role of purchasing policy and procedures in today's business environment. The first section provides a general overview and discussion of policy. This includes defining policy, the characteristics of an effective policy, the advantages and disadvantages of policy, and the policy hierarchy. The second section focuses on specific categories of purchasing policies, with a special emphasis on one area known as maverick spending. The third section presents purchasing procedures, which are operating instructions detailing functional duties and tasks.

Policy Overview

The term **policy** includes all the directives, both explicit and implied, that designate the aims and ends of an organization and the appropriate means used in their accomplishment.

Policy refers to the set of purposes, principles, and rules of action that guide an organization.[1] Rules of action refer to standard operating procedures along with any rules and regulations. Although policies are usually documented in writing, unwritten or informal policies can also exist. Informal policies are understood over time and eventually become part of an organization's culture.

What Are the Advantages and Disadvantages of Policies?

Having written and implied policies is an opportunity to define and clarify top management objectives. Policy statements are a means for executive management to communicate its leadership and views. Executive management should develop a series of high-level policy statements that provide guidance to employees at all levels.

Another advantage is that policies provide a framework for consistent decision making and action. In fact, one of the primary objectives of a policy is to ensure that personnel act in a manner consistent with executive or functional management's expectations. Finally, an effective policy provides an additional advantage by defining the rules and procedures that apply to all employees.

There are also potential disadvantages to policy development. First, a policy is often difficult to communicate throughout large organizations. Second, employees might view policies as a substitute for effective management. Policy statements are guidelines that outline management's belief or position on a topic. They are not a set of how-to instructions designed to provide specific answers for every business decision. Third, policy development can also restrict innovation and flexibility. Too many policies accompanied by cumbersome procedures can become an organization's worst enemy.

What Makes for an Effective Policy?

Several characteristics of a policy render it effective. Effective policies are action-oriented guidelines that provide guidance. They provide enough detail to direct behavior toward a specific goal or objective but are not so detailed that they discourage personnel from following the policy.

An effective policy is relevant (avoiding trivial or unimportant issues) and concise (stating a position with a minimum number of words). An effective policy is unambiguous, allowing personnel little doubt as to how to interpret the policy's intent and direction. Policies that are subject to different interpretations will, over a period of time, result in several possible outcomes. This can lead to inconsistent behavior, as people will simply ignore the policy because it is so difficult to interpret.

Sourcing Snapshot

Supplier Relationship Policies Apply to Everyone at Wal-Mart!

Wal-Mart Stores Inc. Chief Executive H. Lee Scott, who recently was accused by a fired marketing executive of accepting sweetheart deals from suppliers, purchased a diamond ring from a Wal-Mart vendor, according to that vendor's officials.

Mr. Scott purchased the ring for his wife in April 2003 from The Aaron Group, a wholesale supplier of jewelry to Wal-Mart, said Robert Kempler, president of the New York–based company. Mr. Kempler declined to discuss the terms of the diamond sale other than to say Mr. Scott hadn't received preferential pricing.

Wal-Mart has a famously strict ethics code that prohibits employees from receiving anything free from suppliers. It has pursued even senior executives who violate these policies. Last week, Julie Roehm, a former Wal-Mart marketing executive who was fired in December for allegedly violating the retailer's ethics rules, claimed in a federal court filing that Mr. Scott obtained "a number of yachts" and "a large pink diamond" at preferential prices.

The lawsuit didn't identify the specifics of the diamond sale, other than to say that Mr. Scott had purchased the stone through a relationship with Irwin Jacobs, a financier who has numerous business relationships with Wal-Mart. It isn't clear whether the diamond ring purchased from The Aaron Group is the same one referred to in Ms. Roehm's suit.

Mr. Kempler said he'd never heard of Mr. Jacobs, and he said everything about the transaction was "above board." Mr. Jacobs said the allegations were without any substance and denied knowing anything about any diamond purchase by the Wal-Mart CEO.

A Wal-Mart spokeswoman declined to comment specifically on the diamond purchase or Wal-Mart's policies on employee purchases from suppliers. Mr. Scott "is subject to the same ethics policy as any other associate and has not violated either the spirit or the letter of Wal-Mart's ethical standards," the spokeswoman said. She characterized the allegations in Ms. Roehm's court filing as "old news. No facts have been presented to back them up."

Source: J. Bandler and G. McWilliams, "Wal-Mart Chief Bought Ring from Firm's Vendor," *Wall Street Journal,* May 30, 2007, p. A4.

Another characteristic of effective policies is that they are timely and current, which assumes that they are periodically reviewed for clarity and conformance. A policy is ineffective or counterproductive if it is confusing, ignored, or outdated. For example, in the opening vignette, each cement plant was operating under a different set of rules, and everyone was essentially ignoring the fact that a common set of policies or procedures existed! Policy formation and review should be a dynamic activity undertaken at least once every year or so. A policy may be timely and correct but not properly enforced by management. In this case, it is management's responsibility to re-educate the workforce about the policy's intent. There is no other substitute for detailed training on policies, to ensure that everyone understands how to do their jobs.

The following characteristics apply to effective policies:

- Action oriented
- Relevant
- Concise
- Unambiguous/well understood
- Timely and current
- Guide problem solving and behavior

Purchasing Policies—Providing Guidance and Direction

Purchasing management develops policies to provide guidance and support to the professional purchasing and support staff. These policies are general outlines clarifying purchasing management's position on a subject. Although many purchasing policies exist, most fall into one of five categories:

- Policies defining the role of purchasing
- Policies defining the conduct of purchasing personnel
- Policies defining social and minority business objectives
- Policies defining buyer-seller relationships
- Policies defining operational issues

The following discussion does not include all possible purchasing policies. Organizations will also develop policies to meet unique operational requirements.

Policies Defining the Role of Purchasing

This set of policies defines purchasing's authority. It usually addresses the objectives of the purchasing function and defines the responsibilities of the various buying levels. These policies often serve as a general or broad policy statement from which more detailed or specific policies evolve.

Origin and Scope of Purchasing Authority

Personnel at all levels must be aware of purchasing's authority to conduct business and to represent organizational interests. An executive committee usually grants this authority and develops this policy. This policy may also detail the authority of purchasing to delegate certain tasks or assignments to other departments or functions.

An important section of this policy describes the areas where purchasing authority does or does not exist. The policy may exclude the purchasing function from any responsibility for purchasing real estate, medical insurance policies, or other areas where purchasing may not have direct expertise. (However, purchasing is increasingly becoming involved in all types of purchases, including these nontraditional areas.) This policy outlines the overall authority of purchasing as granted by the executive committee while describing the limits to that authority.

Objectives of the Purchasing Function

As noted in Chapter 2, purchasing generally has the final authority over a certain spending area. This is typically set forth in a policy describing the general objectives or principles guiding the purchasing process. The following describes one company's purchasing objectives or principles:

- To select suppliers that meet purchase and performance requirements
- To purchase materials and services that comply with engineering and quality standards
- To promote buyer-seller relations and to encourage supplier contribution
- To treat all suppliers fairly and ethically
- To work closely with other departments
- To conduct purchasing operations so they enhance community and employee relations
- To support all corporate objectives and policies
- To maintain a qualified purchasing staff and to develop the professional capabilities of that staff

Although these objectives or principles appear broad, they are important because they set forth, in writing, management's commitment to achieving a professional level of purchasing behavior. These principles are also important because they give rise to other policies that directly support purchasing activities.

Corporate Purchasing Office Responsibilities

It is also useful to understand the duties and responsibilities of the central or corporate purchasing office (if a central office exists). This policy may also detail the relationship of the corporate office to purchasing centers located at the divisional, business unit, or plant level. The corporate purchasing office is usually a staff position directing, supporting, and coordinating the purchasing effort. This policy can provide guidance concerning the role of the corporate purchasing staff in the following areas:

- Carry out executive policies
- Develop and publish functional purchasing and material policies and procedures to support efficient and effective purchasing operations at all levels
- Coordinate strategy development between purchasing departments or centers to maximize purchasing leverage of critical commodities
- Evaluate the effectiveness of purchasing operations

- Provide expert support to purchasing departments (e.g., international sourcing assistance, contract negotiations, systems development)
- Perform other tasks typically associated with a corporate support staff

Exhibit 3.1 illustrates a policy detailing corporate purchasing office responsibilities.

Policies Defining the Conduct of Purchasing Personnel

These policies outline management's commitment to ethical and honest behavior while guiding personnel who are confronted with difficult situations. Some business practices are technically not illegal but are potentially unethical or questionable.

Because of this, purchasing management must develop policies that provide guidance in these gray areas. Because purchasing personnel act as legal agents and

Exhibit 3.1 Example of a Functional Purchasing Policy

ABC Technologies
Purchasing Policy

Policy Number: 2 Applies to: Corporate Staff
Divisional Purchasing
Plant Buyers

Date: 1-1-04

Subject: Corporate Purchasing Office Responsibilities

This policy outlines the responsibilities and authority of the Corporate Purchasing office and staff and its relationship to Division Purchasing and Buying Units.

Executive policy E-7 sets forth the principles supporting the organization and management of ABC Technologies and its operating Divisions:

ABC Technologies, by executive policy, is organized on a line and staff basis, with divisional operations largely decentralized. It is corporate policy to assign responsibility and delegate authority concerning operational matters to executive divisional management. All responsibilities not delegated to divisional management remain as official responsibilities of the corporate staff.

The Corporate Purchasing staff is one of the corporate staffs referred to in executive policy E-7. As such, it retains responsibility for the following functions, activities, and duties:

- Responsibility for carrying out and ensuring that each division and buying unit adheres to each corporate policy as stated by executive management.
- Responsibility for developing and publishing functional purchasing and material policies and procedures. The purpose of this is to support efficient and effective purchasing operations throughout the company.
- Coordinate strategy development between divisional purchasing and other buying units to support companywide efficiencies and reduced duplication of effort.
- Develop systems to evaluate companywide purchasing performance and operations.
- Provide expert support to purchasing departments and buying units throughout the company.
- Assume responsibility for (1) tasks typically associated with a corporate support staff and (2) tasks not directly assigned to divisional or plant purchasing.

This policy reaffirms the autonomy of the divisions and other buying centers to conduct operational purchasing duties and functions. It also reaffirms the company's commitment to efficient companywide purchasing operations through a strong corporate support staff.

representatives, they must uphold the highest standards as defined by executive policy and the law.

Ethics Policy

Most organizations, particularly medium- and larger-sized ones, have a written policy describing management's commitment to ethical purchasing behavior. Chapter 15 discusses purchasing ethics in considerable detail.

Reciprocity Policy

A formal policy often exists detailing management's opposition to reciprocal purchase agreements. **Reciprocity**, discussed in the purchasing ethics section of Chapter 15, occurs when suppliers are pressured to purchase the buyer's products or services as a condition of securing a purchase contract. A reciprocity policy usually describes management's opposition to the practice and lists the type of behavior to avoid. Personnel must not engage in behavior that suggests any of the following:

- A buyer gives preference to suppliers that purchase from the buyer's organization.
- A buyer expects suppliers to purchase the buying company's products as a condition for securing a purchase contract.
- A buyer looks favorably on competitive bids from suppliers that purchase the buyer's products.

This area requires an executive management policy because disagreement occurs regarding this topic. Reciprocity is relatively easy to control once management issues a policy on the subject.

Contacts and Visits to Suppliers

An understanding must exist regarding direct visits or other communication contacts with suppliers or potential suppliers. This policy should address not only purchasing personnel but also other departments or functions that visit or contact suppliers. Purchasing wants to control unauthorized or excessive contacts or visits because these can impose an unnecessary burden on suppliers.

Also, unauthorized supplier visits or contacts by non-purchasing personnel undermine purchasing's legitimate authority as the principal commercial contact with suppliers. Purchasing wants to avoid situations where suppliers might interpret statements and opinions offered by non-purchasing personnel as commitments.

Former Employees Representing Suppliers

Occasionally, an employee may leave to work for a supplier. This is a concern because the former employee probably has knowledge about business plans or other confidential information that might provide an unfair advantage over other suppliers. One way to address this issue is to establish a policy prohibiting business transactions with suppliers that employ former employees known to have inside or confidential information. This exclusion can range from a period of a few months to several years, depending on the employee and the situation. Another possibility involves including a clause in the employee's original employment contract prohibiting employment with a competitor or a supplier for a specified time. This can offset the advantage a former employee may have from his or her previous employment.

Sourcing Snapshot — *Gap Cracks Down on Suppliers with Labor Abuses*

Gap's Factory Inspections Continue to Uncover Abuses, Such As Excessive Overtime

Gap Inc.'s continuing crackdown on labor abuses at the overseas factories making the retailer's clothes identified hundreds of plants engaged in a wide range of unsavory practices, including excessive overtime, paltry wages, and fining workers who wanted to quit their jobs.

The San Francisco–based company listed the transgressions Wednesday in a report summarizing the findings of 92 inspectors, who scrutinized all but a handful of the 2,672 supplier factories approved to manufacture clothes for Gap last year.

Spurred by the most terrible violations cited, Gap severed ties with 70 factories last year, down from 136 in 2003. The company rejected 15% of the new factories seeking to make its clothes in 2004 compared with 16% in 2003.

But the owner of Gap, Old Navy, and Banana Republic stores continued to contract with hundreds of overseas factories that mistreated its workers, according to the company's second annual social responsibility report—a document that represents an unusual bit of self-flagellation in corporate America.

The abuses are most prevalent in China, where Gap products are made at 423 factories. Between 25 and 50% of those Chinese companies don't fully comply with local labor laws, Gap said, and 10 to 25% of them pay below the minimum wage. The company ended its business relationship with 18 Chinese factories last year—less than 5% of its suppliers in that country.

The Persian Gulf, where Gap contracts with 29 factories, caused another major headache. More than half the factories inspected there imposed work weeks of more than 60 hours per week. In three cases in Egypt, Morocco, and Vietnam, Gap flagged factories that required their workers to pay them if they resigned before a contract ended. Gap required all three factories to stop the practice.

By publicly acknowledging its role in the recurring labor problems at factories often derided as "sweatshops," Gap hopes to prod its entire industry to embrace reforms and establish more rigorous standards to improve the working conditions.

"To quote U.S. Supreme Court Justice Louis Brandeis, we believe that a 'bright light is the best disinfectant,' " Gap wrote in the 58-page report. "The more open and honest we can be about conditions and challenges, the more helpful we can be in addressing them."

Since Gap first owned up to the troubles at its overseas factories last year, shoe manufacturer Nike Inc. also has launched a similar social responsibility report examining the conduct in its overseas factories. The increased attention will likely make it appear as if things are getting worse before they get better, Gap warned, simply because its inspectors are likely to become progressively better at rooting out violations as time goes on.

Gap acknowledged it has contributed to some of the labor problems by making last-minute production demands that prod overseas contractors into exploiting their workers. The company has vowed to phase out its "inefficient purchasing practices." Bob Jeffcott, policy analyst for the Maquila Solidarity Network, a workers' rights group in Toronto, said he believes Gap and other retailers that rely on overseas factories could make a huge difference by agreeing to pay more for their products—a daunting commitment to make because it could erode profits or result in price increases that alienate customers. "No one is dealing with the fundamental question on how much you should be paying these suppliers so they can afford to pay their workers better wages," Jeffcott said.

Source: M. Liedtke, "Gap's Factory Inspections Uncover Abuses," Associated Press, July 13, 2005.

Reporting of Irregular Business Dealings with Suppliers

This policy may establish a reporting mechanism for buyers or other employees to report irregular business dealings. Examples of irregular dealings include accepting bribes from suppliers, cronyism, accepting late bids, owning a stake in a supplier's company, and other types of behavior that are not considered part of the normal course of business. The policy can specify the proper office to which to report the irregularity, the safeguards in place to protect the reporting party, and the need to report suspected irregularities as soon as possible. This policy sends the message that management will not tolerate irregular business transactions involving employees.

Policies Defining Social and Minority Business Objectives

In the long run it is likely in a purchaser's best interest to use its power to support social and minority business objectives. This may include supporting and developing local sources of supply or awarding business to qualified minority suppliers.

Purchasing's actions help shape a perception of good corporate citizenship. Pursuing social objectives may require the development of policies specifically defining management's position. A list of the top companies engaged in minority supplier development is shown in Sourcing Snapshot: The Best Companies for Minority Supplier Contracting.

Supporting Minority Business Suppliers

Supporting minority suppliers is not only the right thing to do, it is also the smart thing to do. As the nature of America's demographics and workforce continually changes, organizations will need to hire and train people with multicultural backgrounds and promote relationships with suppliers and customers from diverse backgrounds. At the same time, it is important to recognize that minority suppliers are a special class of supplier. As such, they face many problems that are unique to their special status, while also facing many of the same problems that confront nonminority suppliers. Several factors lie at the core of these problems: lack of access to capital; large firms' efforts to optimize their supply bases; inability to attract qualified managers and other professionals; and minority suppliers' relatively small size, which may lead to over-reliance on large customer firms.

Management's position concerning transactions with minority business suppliers provides guidance to buyers. A minority business supplier is a business that is run or partially owned by an individual classified as a minority by the U.S. government. Such policies typically state that these suppliers should receive a fair and equal opportunity to participate in the purchasing process. The policy may outline a number of steps to achieve the policy's objectives, including the following:

Sourcing Snapshot

The Best Companies for Minority Supplier Contracting

Many companies often deploy supplier diversity programs that are aimed at increasing the representation of minority-owned suppliers in their supply base. For some companies, supplier diversity programs are based on social considerations. However, an increasing number of companies have focused on supplier diversity simply because it is good business. Minorities now represent the largest sales growth markets, especially in consumer goods, and companies realize that increasing the amount of business with minority businesses may mean increased sales for their own firm over the long term.

A list of "America's Top Organizations for Multicultural Business Opportunities" was developed as a result of a poll sponsored by DIV2000.com, an organization that provides business connections and resources for small businesses and large organizational buyers. Over 525,000 women- and minority-owned businesses had the opportunity to vote in the online election. The election was conducted in a secure Internet environment utilizing the latest technology available. Fortune 500 companies and government agencies were selected for the awards based on business opportunities they provide to minority-owned businesses. The best companies for 2005 are shown in the following table.

RANK	TOP 50 CORPORATIONS	RANK	TOP 50 CORPORATIONS
1	Lockheed Martin	28	ExxonMobil
2	Bank of America Corp.	29	Walt Disney Co.
3	BellSouth Corp.	30	Pitney Bowes
4	Dell Computer	31	Fannie Mae
5	Wal-Mart Stores Inc.	32	American Express
6	OfficeMax	32	Chevron
7	IBM	33	Starbucks Corp.
8	Procter & Gamble Co.	34	JC Penney Co.
9	Boeing Co.	34	Verizon Wireless
10	The Coca-Cola Co.	35	Cisco Systems Inc.
11	Time Warner Inc.	36	General Dynamics Corp.
12	Raytheon Co.	36	Bristol-Myers Squibb Co.
12	General Mills	37	McDonald's Corp.
13	SBC Communications/AT&T	38	Ford Motor Co.
14	Office Depot Inc.	39	Verizon
15	General Motors Corp.	40	General Electric Co.
16	Toyota	41	Citigroup Inc.
17	Northrop Grumman Corp.	42	Comcast Corp.
18	United Parcel Service	42	Wells Fargo & Co.
19	Xerox	43	Major League Baseball
20	DaimlerChrysler	44	Merrill Lynch & Co. Inc.
21	Avon Products	45	Corporate Express
21	Pepsico Inc.	46	Pfizer Inc.
22	Altria Group	47	Progress Energy Inc.
23	Home Depot Inc.	47	Cardinal Health
24	Sprint/Nextel	48	Sempra Energy
25	Johnson & Johnson	49	United Technologies
26	Microsoft Corp.	50	Waste Management

Source: http://www.diversitybusiness.com/Resources/DivLists/2007/.

- Set forth management's commitment on this subject
- Evaluate the performance potential of small and disadvantaged suppliers to identify those qualifying for supplier assistance
- Invite small and disadvantaged suppliers to bid on purchase contracts
- Establish a minimum percentage of business to award to qualified small and disadvantaged suppliers
- Outline a training program to educate buyers regarding the needs of the small and disadvantaged suppliers

Policies supporting disadvantaged suppliers are common in contracts with the U.S. government, which encourages awarding subcontracts to small and disadvantaged suppliers. Other companies have formal procedures for including minority business suppliers. For instance, one large pharmaceutical company has developed a process for identifying minority suppliers, which includes the following questions:

- Is the supplier fully qualified?
- Does the supplier satisfy U.S. government criteria defining a minority business?
- Does the supplier meet our standard performance requirements?
- Is the supplier price competitive?
- How much business can we give the supplier given its capacity?

Links and information having to do with minority business development can be found at http://www.mbda.gov.

A recent study on best practices conducted by the Supply Chain Resource Cooperative at NC State University emphasized that companies in many industries are making great improvements in minority supplier development programs. However, until organizations can devote more resources to actively improving minority suppliers through focused supplier development programs, growth of minority suppliers in the supply base will remain problematic.

The research also suggested that almost all industries have limited resources for supplier diversity programs. One interesting observation regarding resource allocation is that industries that are rife with financial difficulties do not have the luxury to dedicate additional resources for these programs. However, in industries that are not experiencing financial difficulties, the research found that there was often a lack of executive sponsorship, which led to the same outcome: Diversity does not get enough attention or budget allocation for its progress. Two important features of any supplier development initiative were identified: process improvement and leadership/corporate commitment. These elements were viewed by many executives as critical foundational elements for any minority supplier development initiative. The industry-specific best practices in how organizations developed their policies and procedures include the following:

- Mandate Tier 1 suppliers to have a Tier 2 diversity spend goal and incorporate the terms in the contracts. Tier 1 suppliers should be able to record their diversity spend online through the customer's website. Increasing Tier 2 diversity spend offsets to some extent the effect of diminishing opportunities for minority suppliers due to increased global sourcing and offshore contracting. Online tracking of minority spend in Tier 2 suppliers also increases visibility and compliance.

- Include minority suppliers in all RFQs, without exception. Policies may be defined on the basis of mutually agreed-upon terms between business units and the organization's Supplier Diversity Council. Awarding of RFQs should in all circumstances be tied to performance.
- Tie the goals and objectives of the supplier diversity program (SDP) to supply chain management strategies and supply chain job functions. Business units should also have diversity goals tied to performance to increase participation and commitment to the program.
- Incorporate supplier diversity programs within the corporate procurement organization and assign supplier diversity advocates to specific business units. These advocates can provide training and support to buyers and drive compliance. This approach also enables consolidation of spend with the minority suppliers that are being developed by the corporate supplier diversity programs.
- Incorporate all corporate functions in which suppliers are selected and procurement commitments are made. Corporate supplier diversity committees should include management representatives from all such cross-functional areas: Advertising, Public Relations, Finance, Legal, R&D, Human Resources, Engineering, Real Estate, Traffic and Distribution, Sales, and Corporate Office Administration. This is in recognition of the fact that SDP should be a supply chain accountability and not just a corporate accountability.

Environmental Issues

A set of policies outlining a position related to environmental issues is becoming increasingly important. Moreover, governments are now requiring such policies by law. These policies include the use of recycled material; strict compliance with local, state, and federal regulations; and proper disposal of waste material. The Clean Air Act of 1990 imposes large fines on producers of ozone-depleting substances and foul-smelling gases. As a result, buyers must consider a supplier's ability to comply with environmental regulations as a condition for selection. This includes, but is not limited to, the proper disposal of hazardous waste.

A good example of environmental policy involves the chemical industry, which traditionally has been a major source of industrial pollution. This industry knows that if it does not adopt a set of environmental policies, then government regulators will initiate strict regulations. Dow Chemical, for example, considers environmental concerns a critical feature of its policies and procedures.[2] As a member of the Chemical Manufacturers Association, Dow is a participant in Responsible Care, a program initiative that addresses a community's concerns regarding chemicals, including their manufacture, transportation, use, and safe disposal; health and safety issues; prompt reporting of environmental accidents; and counseling of customers. Supplier evaluation involves assessing the environmental policies of suppliers (primarily other major chemical companies). A key element of evaluation involves understanding and assessing the environmental risk associated with the particular chemical being purchased. Dow searches for suppliers that are green, according to industry standards.

Policies Defining Buyer-Seller Relationships

The policies that are part of buyer-seller relationships cover a wide range of topics. Each topic, however, relates to some issue involving the supply base.

Supplier Relations

The principles that guide relations with suppliers are often contained in a policy stating that buyer-seller relationships are essential for economic success. Furthermore, relationships based on mutual trust and respect must underlie the purchasing effort. This policy often describes a number of principles that support positive relationships, including the following:

- Treating suppliers fairly and with integrity
- Supporting and developing those suppliers that work to improve quality, delivery, cost, or other performance criteria
- Providing prompt payment to suppliers
- Encouraging suppliers to submit innovative ideas with joint sharing of benefits
- Developing open communication channels
- Informing suppliers as to why they did not receive a purchase contract
- Establishing a fair process to award purchase contracts

Qualification and Supplier Selection

Buyers may require guidance regarding the performance criteria used to evaluate potential sources of supply or to evaluate an existing supplier for an item not traditionally provided by suppliers. Management wants to make sure that supplier selection occurs only after purchasing thoroughly reviews all criteria. Supplier selection criteria include the following:

- Price/cost competitiveness
- Product quality
- Delivery performance
- Financial condition
- Engineering and manufacturing technical competence
- Management of its own suppliers
- Management capability
- Ability to work with the customer
- Potential for innovation

This policy may also outline management's position on single and multiple sourcing or the use of longer-term purchase agreements. It may also acknowledge purchasing's need to rely on non-purchasing personnel to evaluate technical or financial criteria during the supplier selection process.

Principles and Guidelines for Awarding Purchase Contracts

The process for selecting and awarding purchase contracts is central to effective purchasing. This policy covers a number of critical topics:

- Buyer's authority to award a contract within a certain dollar limit
- Conditions where the competitive bid process is and is not acceptable

- Conditions outlining the use of competitive bids
- Process of analyzing sealed competitive bids
- Conditions prompting the sourcing of an item to other than the lowest bid supplier
- Conditions prompting a rebid
- Operating guidelines that pertain to the negotiation of contracts with suppliers

Although there is a trend toward less reliance on competitive bids and more on negotiated longer-term agreements, many contracts are still awarded through the competitive bid process. Routine items available from many different sources are generally purchased through competitive bidding. It is important for purchasing to have a standard set of guidelines for awarding purchase contracts to suppliers. These guidelines provide assurances that purchasing awards contracts based on a fair set of principles.

Labor or Other Difficulties at Suppliers

Management's position concerning supply or labor disruptions as well as possible courses of action provides guidelines during supplier strikes or other labor problems. One issue this policy can address is the legal removal of company-owned tooling from suppliers during a strike so that the buyer can establish an additional source during the interruption. The policy can provide details about this issue, which can be part of the contract with the supplier, to suspend temporarily any purchase contracts or outstanding orders with a striking supplier. Since 9/11, emergency policies must be established to deal with sudden disruptions in the supply chain. In one case, a single-source supplier to Toyota had a supplying plant burn down; there was no official policy to deal with this issue. Other major automotive companies including Honda and Nissan ended up working with Toyota to help it obtain parts during this crisis.

Other Policies Dealing with Buyer-Seller Relations

Organizations must be cautious about liabilities associated with accepting and using ideas provided by suppliers interested in doing business with a purchaser. A policy may state that the buyer accepts unsolicited proposals from interested suppliers only on a nonconfidential basis with no obligation or liability to the provider. Suppliers may even have to sign a waiver releasing the purchaser from liabilities in this area.

Another policy can clarify management's position on financial obligations to suppliers that provide early product design involvement. A buyer may request that suppliers submit cost-reduction ideas during the early phases of new-product design. This policy can provide guidance about the extent of financial obligation to suppliers, particularly to suppliers whose ideas were not accepted.

In cases where purchasing is attempting to integrate suppliers into the new-product development process, many companies have established a policy manual written by engineering, marketing, manufacturing, and purchasing. This manual specifies the steps in developing a new product and the triggers in the process that identify when and how suppliers should be part of the process. The policy may also specify the types of nondisclosure agreements used, the criteria for sharing patents, and other joint product development policies.

Sourcing Snapshot

Conflict of Interest Issues Becoming Front-Page Materials

Consider the following examples described in the *Wall Street Journal*:[3]

- At Lear Corp., a large Southfield, Mich.–based auto-parts supplier, 17 relatives of senior officials are employed by or have business ties to the company, a group of family ties that the company failed to report until late last year despite a federal requirement to do so.
- Apple Computer Inc. paid Chief Executive Steven Jobs nearly $1.2 million to reimburse him for costs he incurred using his personal Gulfstream V jet on company business in 2001 and 2002. Apple is one of many companies with side deals involving the private planes of their executives.
- Ford Motor Co. paid two of its directors, William Clay Ford and Edsel B. Ford II, hundreds of thousands of dollars in consulting fees. The two members of the auto giant's founding family also receive directors' pay and millions of dollars of dividends on their Ford stock.
- Sam Nunn has served on the board of seven public companies since he left the Senate in 1996. All those companies have done business with his law firm, King & Spalding, while he was serving on the boards.

In the wake of Enron and other corporate scandals, these types of transactions—generally defined as a business deal involving an outside director, senior executive, significant shareholder, or a relative of one of those people—are attracting new attention from government officials and business and labor leaders. New legislation curtails certain deals. Other rules are in the works aimed at increasing the independence and accountability of corporate officers and directors. But related-party transactions remain legal and deeply entwined in the corporate culture. This is an increasingly important area for purchasing policy making to consider.

Policies Defining Operational Issues

The broadest of the five purchasing policy categories involves policies that provide guidance for operational issues that confront buyers during the normal performance of duties.

Hazardous Materials

Purchasers must take an active role controlling hazardous waste. During the last 10 years, new regulations and policies outlined the proper handling of toxic and hazardous material. In the period from 1899 to 1950, the U.S. government passed seven laws that involved environmental protection. From 1976 to 1978, Congress passed nine environmental laws. More recent legislation has further emphasized the need for business to have a carefully considered response to environmental initiatives. Another important trend is the requirement for an organization to be ISO 14000 certified to engage in global business transactions. ISO 14000 certification requires companies to establish an environmental management system (EMS) to deal with environmental issues.[4] An EMS requires a company to do the following:

- Create an environmental policy
- Set appropriate objectives and targets

- Help design and implement a program aimed at achieving these objectives
- Monitor and measure the effectiveness of these programs
- Monitor and measure the effectiveness of general environmental management activities within the firm

Involvement in developing an EMS is a critical responsibility for purchasing, because the purchase of waste disposal services is often a purchasing task. For companies that routinely use or produce hazardous materials, the law requires a policy that outlines in detail the legal requirements and conditions for the handling of toxic waste. Failure to have such a policy is considered a federal offense. This policy details the responsibility of purchasing to select only those contractors that conform to local, state, and federal laws. Before awarding a contract for the hauling and disposing of dangerous materials, some policies require that the contractor provide the following detailed information:

- Evidence of valid permits and licenses
- Specification of the types of disposal services the contractor is licensed to provide
- Evidence of safeguards to prevent accidents along with contingency plans and preparations if a hazardous spill occurs
- Details of the specific process used to control hazardous material once it exits a buyer's facilities
- Evidence of adequate liability insurance on the part of the contractor
- Evidence that the waste transporter uses properly certified disposal sites

Selecting a qualified hazardous waste contractor is critical. On a larger scale, this requires an environmental policy that is clearly expressed. Increased government and public awareness of environmental concerns is driving this issue.

Supplier Responsibility for Defective Material

This policy outlines supplier responsibility for defective material shipments or other types of nonperformance. It usually details the various charge-back costs for which suppliers are liable in the event of nonperformance. These costs can include the cost of material rework, repackaging for return shipment, additional material-handling costs, return shipping costs, or costs associated with lost or delayed production. Purchasers operating in a just-in-time environment are usually quite strict about the charges associated with supplier-caused material problems. A single defective shipment in a just-in-time production environment can shut down an entire production process, resulting in some cases in fines of up to $10,000 per minute (in automotive OEMs).

Defective material policies may also outline purchasing's authority to negotiate and settle claims against suppliers. This requires purchasing to carefully review each nonperformance to determine a fair settlement. This policy provides protection for the purchaser in the case of supplier-caused problems.

Purchased Item Comparisons

Another policy may outline management's position concerning the continued evaluation of purchased items. This evaluation may require buyers to periodically review purchased items or services to determine if existing suppliers still maintain market leadership. This evaluation can include cost, quality, delivery, and technological comparisons.

Sourcing Snapshot — *Caterpillar's Code of Conduct*

Caterpillar is almost a century old. The company, based in Peoria, IL, has grown from a Midwest manufacturer of farm equipment into a global construction equipment powerhouse. With this growth into different countries, cultures, and markets, the company has also struggled at times to maintain the Midwest homegrown culture of integrity associated with its early roots. To that end, Jim Owens, CEO, has put forth a code of conduct that applies to all associates, based on the code that "integrity is the foundation of all we do." An additional set of implied statements were developed that have direct implications for purchasing policy and actions of purchasing associates. In particular, the following elements stand out:

- We align our actions with our words and deliver what we promise. We build and strengthen our reputation through trust. We do not improperly influence others or let them improperly influence us. In short, the reputation of the enterprise reflects the ethical performance of the people who work here.
- We are honest and we act with integrity. We hold ourselves to the highest standard of integrity. We strive to keep our commitments. Our company's shareholders, customers, dealers, those with whom we do business (suppliers), and our fellow employees must be able to trust what we say and to believe that we will always keep our word.
- We compete fairly. Caterpillar believes that fair competition is fundamental to free enterprise. In relationships with competitors, dealers, suppliers, and customers, we avoid arrangements or understandings with competitors affecting prices, terms upon which products are sold, or the number and type of products manufactured or sold.
- We ensure accuracy and completeness of our financial reports and accounting reports. The same standards of integrity that apply to external financial reporting apply to the financial statements that we use as internal management tools.
- We are fair, honest, and open in our communications. We keep investors, creditors, securities trading markets, employees, dealers, suppliers, and the general public informed on a timely basis through public release of relevant and understandable financial and other information about our company. In releasing information about Caterpillar, we make every effort to ensure that full disclosure is made to everyone without preference or favoritism to any individual or group.
- We handle "inside information" appropriately and lawfully. A Caterpillar employee who has undisclosed information about a supplier, customer, or competitor should not trade in that company's stock, nor should an employee advise others to do so.
- We refuse to make improper payments. In dealing with public officials, other corporations, suppliers, and private citizens, we firmly adhere to ethical business practices.
- We will not seek to influence others, either directly or indirectly, by paying bribes or kickbacks, or by any other measure that is unethical or that will tarnish our reputation for honesty and integrity. Even the appearance of such conduct must be avoided.

Source: Caterpillar Code of Conduct, http://www.cat.com.

For items purchased through the competitive bid process, purchased item comparisons often mean requesting new bids for an item from qualified suppliers. This policy usually states how often management expects competitive comparisons and the general procedure for conducting a comparison. For items on longer-term purchase contracts, purchased item comparisons may involve benchmarking or comparing cost performance against leading competitors.

Other Operating Policies

Many other operating policies guide purchasing. Additional examples include policies that outline the following:

- Compliance with U.S. laws and regulations
- Restrictions on source selection outside of the purchasing function
- The proper disposal of material assets
- Purchasing's legal right to terminate a purchase contract or order
- Supplier responsibility for premium transportation costs
- Supplier-requested changes in contractual terms and conditions
- Supplier use of trademarks or logos

All of the policies just listed have something in common: They clarify management's position on a topic while providing guidance to the personnel responsible for carrying out the policy. The outcome of these policies should be consistent actions on the part of personnel at different locations or organizational levels. A basic set of policy statements outlining management's position on different topic areas should be readily available and distributed. All policies should be regularly reviewed and updated. Increasingly, progressive companies are posting their policies on their intranet.

Purchasing Procedures

Procedures are the operating instructions detailing functional duties or tasks, and a procedure manual is really a how-to manual. A large purchasing department may have hundreds of procedures detailing the accepted practice for carrying out an activity.

It is beyond the scope of this discussion to present more than a brief overview of purchasing procedures, particularly because there is no uniform set of principles to guide the development of purchasing procedures. Every organization develops a unique set of operating instructions to meet its own specific requirements.

A procedure manual serves a number of important purposes. First, the manual is a reference guide for purchasing personnel and is especially valuable to new employees who require explanation about how to accomplish different activities or assignments. For experienced personnel, the manual provides clarification or simply reinforces knowledge about different topics. Second, the manual provides consistency and order by documenting the steps and activities required to perform a task. A well-documented procedure manual supports efficient operations and is usually more extensive and detailed than the policy manual. The procedure manual may also specify industry best practices to follow that are identified through benchmarking comparisons with leading firms.

Exhibit 3.2 Examples of a Functional Purchasing Procedure

ABC Technologies
Purchasing Procedure

Procedure Number: 4.3 Date: 10/1/00

Subject: Sourcing Requests from Engineering

I. INTRODUCTION

This procedure outlines the steps to follow when purchasing receives a material request from engineering with a Specified Source form attached (form SS-1). Processing a specified source request differs from processing a suggested supplier source listing. The purpose of this procedure is to evaluate engineering source requests in a fair, timely, and thorough manner.

II. RELATED POLICY

Executive policy grants purchasing the authority to obtain materials, components, and other items that meet the delivery, quality, lowest total cost, and other competitive requirements of the company. Restriction of this authority can have a serious impact on purchasing's ability to perform its required duties and assignments. Certain conditions, however, may warrant the specification of sources by departments other than purchasing.

III. RESPONSIBILITY

It is the responsibility of the direct supervisor or manager of the buyer that receives the Specified Source form to evaluate and determine the final disposition of the specified source request in accordance with the following procedure.

IV. PROCEDURE

A. Upon receipt of an SS-1 form submitted by engineering, purchasing departmental management verifies that each section of the form is properly completed.

B. Purchasing management must verify that the requested item is not currently an actively purchased item. If the item is currently purchased, purchasing must inform engineering of this.

C. For items not currently purchased, purchasing management must evaluate engineering's reasons for specifying a source for the required item. It is also within purchasing's authority to identify and evaluate equally qualified sources if the reasons for the specified source are found not to reflect acceptable purchasing or market principles.

D. If engineering's source request is accepted, purchasing management signs the Specified Source form and promptly processes the purchase order.

E. Rejected requests are sent back to engineering with reasons. In order to promote close working relations between purchasing and engineering, purchasing will respond to specified source requests within a reasonable amount of time. Furthermore, purchasing agrees to work with engineering to identify sources that satisfy engineering's technical requirements while meeting the commercial requirements of the company.

Simplifying procedures should be a goal whenever possible. A primary emphasis should be on the development of a concise, accurate, and complete set of operating instructions. A word of caution is in order here. A procedure is ineffective if it specifies too many steps to carry out or presents unnecessary detail. Many companies have found that the traditional procedure for developing new products does not support cooperation between departments. Existing procedures are being replaced by streamlined procedures that encourage timeliness and responsiveness. As with a policy, management must review and evaluate its procedures to make sure that they are timely and accurate and that they contribute to rather than hinder performance.

Exhibit 3.2 shows a purchasing procedure for a large high-technology company. This procedure, which establishes purchasing's authority to select sources of supply, includes the different sections just discussed. As with all procedures, this procedure will require future review to verify its timeliness and effectiveness. Increasingly, engineering and purchasing are located closer together to reduce product development cycle times. When this occurs, the determination of source selection often is made by a team rather than an individual. Existing procedures may no longer apply when well-established processes are changed.

Purchasing Procedural Areas

There are procedures to cover just about any subject involving purchasing. Most purchasing procedures correspond to one of the following areas.

The Purchasing Cycle

Existing procedures usually document the proper steps to follow during each stage of the purchasing cycle or process. The purchasing process is described in Chapter 2.

The Proper Use of Purchasing Forms

A typical purchasing function relies on many forms to conduct its business. Recall that Chapter 2 provided examples of commonly used purchasing documents and forms. The procedure manual is a valuable source that includes a description of the proper use of each form, the detailed meaning of each information field on the form, and a description of the proper handling and storage of each form. For the latter point, this usually includes information about where, and for how long, to store each copy of the form along with required signatures or approvals. Storage can be manual or electronic. The movement toward electronic storage of forms requires major revisions to procedures relating to this subject.

The Development of Legal Contracts

The development of legal purchase contracts can require dozens of pages and address many topics. Most organizations have specific procedures for contracting with outside suppliers and individuals for goods and services. It is the purchasing employee's responsibility to become familiar with and follow the procedures covering legal contracts. Some of the topics discussed in legal contract procedures include the following:

- Basic features of the standard purchase contract
- Basic contract principles
- Execution and administration of agreements
- Essential elements of the contract
- Compliance with contract terms and performance assessment
- Formal competitive contracting procedures
- Contract development process

- Examples of sample agreements
- Legal definitions
- Use of formal contract clauses

The procedures covering the development, execution, and enforcement of legal purchase agreements and contracts are usually quite detailed (much like the contracts themselves!). A purchaser may rely on a specialized staff to provide assistance in this complex procedural area.

Operational Procedures

Operational procedures provide instruction and detail across a broad range of topics. A procedure can be developed for any operational topic that benefits from following a specific set of steps, requires consistent action to promote efficiency and consistency, or carries out the directives of functional or executive policies. The following procedure topics appear in the material manual of a Fortune 500 company:

- Control of material furnished to suppliers
- Storage of purchasing documents
- Process of supplier qualification
- Use of purchasing computerized systems
- Analysis of competitive quotations
- Use of single source selection
- Requirements for order pricing and analysis
- Procedures for cost analysis
- Acceptable cost reduction techniques and documentation
- Intracompany transactions
- Processing and handling of overshipments
- Supplier acknowledgment of purchase orders
- Disposition of nonconforming purchased material
- Removal of company-owned tooling from supplier

This is a small sample of the different operational topics that often require documented procedures. The topic of purchasing procedures is broad and sometimes mundane. However, an effective set of procedures can result in the efficient use of a purchasing professional's time. Procedures serve as a ready reference covering a host of questions. They also ensure that employees follow the same basic steps when performing similar tasks.

Good Practice Example — *Best Practices in Diverse Supplier Development*

The research on minority supplier development conducted by the Supply Chain Resource Cooperative (http://scrc.ncsu.edu) found that leadership was one of the critical success factors differentiating successful from unsuccessful diverse supplier programs.

Leadership support of diversity goals involves establishing specific strategic objectives and performance goals that ensure that the initiative is taken seriously. Leaders lead by example, and this applies to diversity goals as well. A number of best practices, identified through interviews with executives, are listed below. In each case, the company ensured that senior executives were motivated to include diverse suppliers in their sourcing decisions and that efforts were used to promote the policy across business functions. Consider the following:

- An executive diversity council was instituted in one company to review and guide the supplier diversity program. This council ensured that top management were involved and participated in the program. One of the pharmaceutical health care companies cited an example where the CFO took the lead as the program champion, with active sponsorship of the CEO. This sent a message to the organization that the leadership team was serious about diversity.
- The CEO and other higher-ranking officers should demonstrate personal commitment to the supplier diversity program through participating in SDP events, meeting with the diversity council members and with minority suppliers, and spreading success stories and personal commitment through formal communication with the organization.
- Supplier diversity goals should be included in executive performance plans. In one of the leading aerospace companies, implementing the plan has resulted in active executive leadership at the top and has triggered initiatives such as outreach events, support of advocacy groups, and travel around the country to find suppliers and make investments to help promote diverse suppliers.
- Performance reviews of managers involved in buying activities in various departments in the organization should include supplier diversity program goals. Developing the supplier diversity program should not be thought of as a responsibility of the procurement department or the supplier diversity advocates, but should be the responsibility of all buyers in the organization.

In view of the fact that every industry is unique and has its own challenges and opportunities, the best practices identified in the SCRC report may need to be synthesized as is appropriate on a case-by-case basis. The research points to the fact that supplier development is the weakest link in most companies' supplier diversity programs. Supply managers need to dedicate more time and resources toward helping minority suppliers grow and become more capable of serving the needs of the customers. It is also essential to form a critical mass with competitors and suppliers to support the supplier development efforts. The new mantra is quickly becoming "Help your partners to serve you better."

Questions

1. Why do you believe supply management leaders are not inherently motivated to pursue minority suppliers unless such measures are taken?
2. What are some specific ways that the CEO and other senior executives can demonstrate commitment to supplier diversity objectives?
3. What are the tangible benefits that differentiate the firms in Sourcing Snapshot: The Best Companies for Minority Supplier Contracting from others? How do they benefit from being on this list versus others that are not?

Source: R. Handfield and S. Edwards, "Best Practices in Minority Supplier Development," http://scrc.ncsu.edu.

CONCLUSION

Understanding policies and procedures is essential for understanding how organizations operate and work. Policy is based on the idea that guidelines are documented and applicable to all the internal and external relations of an organization. A policy prescribes methods of accomplishment in terms broad enough for decision makers to exercise discretion while allowing employees to render judgment on an issue. Well-formulated policies and procedures support efficient, effective, and consistent purchasing operations. On the other hand, policies and procedures that are out of date, require unnecessary actions, or do not address current issues or topics will not support effective purchasing operations. As organizations expand their global sourcing activity, they are increasingly revisiting their purchasing policies and procedures, to ensure that they are keeping up with the rapid set of changes their professional associates are facing in their work lives.

KEY TERMS

policy, 87 **procedures,** 103 **reciprocity,** 92

DISCUSSION QUESTIONS

1. Write a brief policy statement that presents a position on the need for utilizing more diverse suppliers. What are the features or characteristics that your policy statement should have?
2. Why is it important to include a policy that outlines the origin and scope of purchasing authority? What might happen if such a policy did not exist?
3. Why should management periodically review its purchasing policies and procedures? What are the potential consequences if management does not review policies and procedures? How often do you think it should go through a minor or major set of rewrites?
4. What are the benefits associated with a comprehensive policy and procedure manual? Is there a downside to the manual's being too comprehensive?
5. Discuss the concept of ethics. Why is the purchasing profession particularly sensitive to this topic?
6. Describe a potential ethical dilemma that a purchasing professional might encounter in day-to-day activities.
7. Describe a potential situation in which a purchasing professional might be guilty of conflict of interest.
8. What are the risks associated with backdoor (maverick) buying and selling? Why is purchasing interested in controlling this business practice?
9. Consider the elements of the code of conduct developed by Caterpillar in Sourcing Snapshot: Caterpillar's Code of Conduct. What are some specific examples of purchasing behavior that would violate elements of this code of conduct?
10. This chapter listed a number of different operational procedures. Describe and discuss three additional topic areas that might benefit from written procedures.

ADDITIONAL READINGS

Baumer, D. L., and Poindexter, J. C. (2002), *Cyberlaw and E-Commerce,* New York: McGraw-Hill.

Baumer, D. L., and Poindexter, J. C. (2004), *Legal Environment of Business in the Information Age,* New York: McGraw-Hill.

Center for Advanced Purchasing Studies (1999), *ISO 14000: Assessing Its Impact on Corporate Effectiveness and Efficiencies,* Tempe, AZ: National Association of Purchasing Management.

Duerden, J. (1995), "'Walking the Walk' on Global Ethics," *Directors and Boards,* 19(3), 42–45.

Forker, L. B., and Janson, R. L. (1990), "Ethical Practices in Purchasing," *Journal of Purchasing and Materials Management,* 26(1), 19–26.

Handfield, R., and Baumer, D. (2006), "Conflict of Interest in Purchasing Management," *Journal of Supply Chain Management,* 42(3), 41–50.

Handfield, R., and Edwards, S. (2006), "Minority Supplier Development: We're Not There Yet," *Inside Supply Management,* 17(5), 20–21.

Ireland, J. (1998), "Purchasing Policies and Procedures," *Supply Management,* May 21.

Maignan, I. (2002), "Managing Socially-Responsible Buying: How to Integrate Non-economic Criteria into the Purchasing Process," *European Management Journal,* 20(6), 641–648.

Murray, J. E. (2003), "When You Get What You Bargained For—But Don't," *Purchasing,* 132(4), 26–27.

National Association of Purchasing Management (1995), "Ethics Policy Statements for Purchasing, Supply, and Material Management: Examples of Policies and Procedures," Tempe, AZ: National Association of Purchasing Management.

Quayle, M. (2002), "Purchasing Policy in Switzerland: An Empirical Study of Sourcing Decisions," *Thunderbird International Business Review,* 44(2), 205–236.

ENDNOTES

1. Klein, W. H., and Murphy, D. C. (1973), *Policy: Concepts in Organizational Guidance,* Boston: Little Brown, p. 2.

2. Additional information on the responsible care program and Dow Chemical's commitment to the environment can be found at http://www.dow.com.

3. Emshwiller, J. (2003), "Many Companies Report Transactions with Top Officers," *Wall Street Journal,* December 29.

4. Center for Advanced Purchasing Studies (1999), *ISO 14000: Assessing Its Impact on Corporate Effectiveness and Efficiencies,* Tempe, AZ: National Association of Purchasing Management.

Chapter 4

SUPPLY MANAGEMENT INTEGRATION FOR COMPETITIVE ADVANTAGE

Learning Objectives

After completing this chapter, you should be able to

- Understand why integration is important and the role that supply management plays in internal and external integration
- Understand the role of cross-functional teams in promoting integration
- Understand how supply management can work with engineering and suppliers to develop new products and services

Chapter Outline

The Critical Role of Purchasing at Manitowoc

Once lowly bureaucrats, purchasing managers are shifting onto the front lines. Robert Ward is one of them and is in charge of purchasing for Manitowoc Co., one of the world's biggest crane makers. His job is to ensure an unbroken flow of parts and materials from around the globe, hunting industrial tires in China and scouring the Midwest for giant bearings. And he has broad discretion over Manitowoc's operations to make sure critical supplies aren't held up.

"Buyers are the ones with the checkbook—and there's a huge power in that," says Mr. Ward. Recently, he was in France, agitated, and meeting with two Polish suppliers that weren't delivering all of the metal chassis they had promised to Manitowoc's big crane factory in Germany. No chassis means no cranes.

The president of one of the suppliers—who had just driven 16 hours from Poland to meet with Mr. Ward and other managers—announced unexpectedly that deliveries could actually slow further in coming months. "I have a lot of angry customers, because I have not been able to deliver cranes," said Mr. Ward, gazing at the Pole over the top of his half-glasses.

Mr. Ward is one of a new breed of purchasing gurus who have become a hot commodity in recent years. As more companies globalize and outsource production, they need a top-level point person who can manage these complex relationships, navigate various foreign cultures, and be willing to travel constantly.

Nothing is worse for a buyer's reputation than throwing business to a low-ball supplier that then has trouble delivering. Mr. Ward has had his share of problems. For example, he has been working recently with a new supplier in China to develop it as a low-cost alternative for a U.S.-made part used in Manitowoc's refrigeration equipment, called a "copper accumulator."

"The supplier told us he was UL qualified," says Mr. Ward, referring to the Underwriters Laboratories certification that is often required on manufactured goods. Manitowoc did its own due diligence, conducting engineering and quality studies of samples sent by the Chinese outfit and visiting the supplier's factory in China.

But on a recent trip, the supplier admitted to Mr. Ward he wasn't UL approved after all. "So now we're back to square one," he says. In another case, he thought he had found a good low-cost Chinese supplier for the electric horns used on cranes. Horns are a very basic item and finding a cheaper source than the company's current U.S. supplier seemed like it would be a no-brainer, he says. But, he has tested two shipments of samples thus far—and the horns keep failing Manitowoc's quality tests.

"The thing you have to realize is that if you're going to buy so much from outside the company, you'd better be very good at it," says Glen Tellock, Manitowoc's chief executive, noting that in the crane business alone the percentage of the total cost of products made up of outsourced components has doubled to 60% in the past decade. "If you're not good at buying in today's world, it's a big competitive disadvantage."

Mr. Tellock says it's crucial to have someone like Mr. Ward, who reports to him, guiding the system. And it helps, he adds, that he comes from outside the company—and the industry—because he brings new ideas. That was critical because the crane business is Manitowoc's most global and also the one that has faced the biggest problems with suppliers.

Mr. Ward has been through this situation before and finds that power is constantly shifting from buyers to sellers and back again. Last year it was tires. Manitowoc's factories kept running short of the large sizes of tires used on mobile cranes.

But no matter how many times Mr. Ward pressed his longtime suppliers, they refused to produce more for him. So he called an outside consulting firm, which sent him a list of 97 tire factories from Brazil to Bulgaria that could potentially make the tires. He eventually found one in China.

"And now, wouldn't you know it, my old tire suppliers are saying they can make more for me after all," says Mr. Ward. "It's amazing what a little competition can do."

Source: T. Aeppel, "Global Scramble for Goods Gives Corporate Buyers a Lift," *Wall Street Journal,* October 2, 2007, p. A1.

The opening vignette illustrates how important supply management is in determining firm performance. The area of supply delivery and availability is becoming an increasingly important element in the global supply chain. A single glitch in the supply chain, such as the earthquake described in Sourcing Snapshot: Apple's I-Pod Supply Chain at Risk, can shut down multiple assembly plants and impact customer delivery and sales around the globe. In this new environment of global sourcing, the need for supply management to work closely with businesses to drive cost savings, reduce disruptions and risk, and deliver innovation and value to customers becomes more important than ever.

Sourcing Snapshot — *Apple's I-Pod Supply Chain at Risk*

Could a typhoon in Manila affect what teenagers in Minneapolis find in their Christmas stockings?

A lot of high-tech gadgets are made in the Philippine Islands, including parts of Apple Computer's iPod music player. Apple depends on that Philippine link in its supply chain: In the third quarter of 2007 (July through September), Apple sold almost 9 million iPods, an average of just under 100,000 per day.

In September, researcher Nathaniel Forbes reviewed the contingency planning at a Philippines factory that assembles 1.8-inch disk drives that go into iPods. I'll call the factory "Pod Parts."

Pod Parts is located in Laguna Technopark (LTI), about 50 kilometers (30 miles) south of the capital city of Manila. Pod Parts ships 20,000+ disk drives each day from this factory. It employs 6,000 people and runs 24 hours a day. To give you a sense of the human logistics involved, Pod Parts contracts a fleet of 80 buses to bring those employees to and from work (most employees don't own cars).

In the review, it was discovered that Pod Parts has only one factory making iPod disk drives—this one in the Philippines. If it were destroyed, it would take months, and several hundred million dollars, to build a new assembly line from scratch for 1.8-inch drives.

Apple needs at least 50,000 drives a day to make iPods, and probably more, assuming that flash memory iPods don't need disk drives. What would be the business impact (on Apple, and on Pod Parts' relationship with Apple) if Pod Parts couldn't deliver those drives?

Sure they could—the other supplier is just down the street in Laguna Technopark—about 1 kilometer away. In fact, there are four other manufacturers in Laguna Technopark that supply Pod Parts with components for disk drives. For manufacturing efficiency, the proximity of these factories to one another is an obvious advantage. Their proximity is, however, a potential risk to the continuity of the supply chain. It's hard to imagine a natural catastrophe that would affect just one manufacturer in LTI; it's likely they'd all be affected at the same time.

Is a calamity likely? Pod Parts has a documented and tested emergency-response system, an active emergency team, and a visible and active security force. There is a municipal fire department in LTI. There are fire extinguishers all over the plant. Pod Parts is reasonably prepared for a fire or a plant-specific event. But what if a widespread national catastrophe occurred? Consider the following data:

1. The Taal volcano, 30 kilometers (18 miles) from Pod Parts, is one of 16 "Decade Volcanoes" identified as a serious potential hazard to population centers by the International Association of Volcanology and Chemistry of the Earth's Interior. (Manila is the sixth largest city in the world with a population of 10 million people.) The Taal volcano recorded 29 volcanic earthquakes in one day in September 2006, according to the Philippine Institute of Volcanology and Seismology (PHIVOLCS). The Philippine Islands are in the Pacific Ring of Fire, which includes 75% of the world's active volcanoes.
2. There were four earthquakes in the Philippines in one weekend in October 2006, one felt in Laguna that measured 4.7 on the Richter scale. The Philippines experiences up to 10 earthquakes a day, according to PHIVOLCS.
3. Tropical storms and typhoons are a regular occurrence in the Philippines. Just two weeks after Forbes visited, Typhoon Xangsane (means "elephant") killed 80 people in Manila, left as many missing, and blew over so many gigantic billboards that the government is changing regulations to prohibit them.

Typhoon Xangsane also went directly over Laguna. Another serious typhoon was also headed toward the Philippines in October.

The area around Laguna Technopark is subject to regular flooding from storm water, blocking logistics in and out of the area. Pod Parts even sends people home early when a serious storm is forecast, because of the risk that the roads will be impassable.

Pod Parts has about two days of finished product stored on-site, waiting for shipment. The drives are just too valuable to keep around in inventory. Construction of an alternative production line is excruciatingly expensive and would raise the cost of production, putting Pod Parts at a competitive disadvantage to its competitor.

A disruption at Pod Parts could have a direct and serious impact on Apple's ability to produce iPods; any effects would be felt within about 48 hours of its occurrence.

If that interruption happened in October, it could drastically reduce the supply of iPods available at retail for Christmas. Two years ago, in late October 2006, LTI experienced the most destructive typhoon in the last decade.

Source: N. Forbes, "Tuning Out Supply Chain Risk," October 28, 2006, http://www.zdnetasia.com/blog/bcp/0,39056819,61963177,00.htm.

Purchasing offices were once corporate backwaters, filled with people who didn't dream of advancing to the top rungs of their organizations. Many buyers saw themselves as industrial bureaucrats, filing purchase orders with the same short list of familiar, mostly nearby suppliers. When possible, they avoided the complex process of assessing potential new suppliers, especially those overseas.

Top supply managers today need different skills and often have higher aspirations. Sometimes they're engineers or others with operating experience that gives them more intimate knowledge of how their company's products are made.

Today's transformation in buying was made possible by a technological breakthrough more than a decade ago, when companies began installing computer systems that record their every transaction. This often revealed startling weaknesses. For instance, many companies found that different divisions—or even different offices down the hall from one another—were sometimes paying different prices for the same product bought from outside suppliers.

Purchasing managers play a role as highly effective cost cutters, though that part of their job has some surprising nuance. To be sure, buyers save companies huge amounts by trolling the world for new, lower-cost sources, and this is certainly a big reason for their growing stature at many multinationals. But in an era of scarce commodities and the risks of disruptions to supply lines posed by terrorist attacks or striking dockworkers, they also have to make sure they pick dependable sources—which might mean choosing the more expensive source just to ensure no disruptions.

Different functions or groups within any organization must work together to achieve a wide range of common goals—from the reduction of product cost and improved product quality and delivery to the development of innovative new products. Supply management plays an active role in supporting such performance objectives, interacting with and supporting the needs of groups within the organization and outside of it. How does supply management achieve this? **Supply integration** involves professionally managing suppliers and developing close working relationships with different internal groups. The central theme of this chapter is that supply management must become closely integrated with other internal and external functions in order to develop the capabilities that will lead to improved competitive performance. Integration spans a number of areas, including finance, engineering, logistics, service operations, production, new-product development, and customer service.

The first section of the chapter defines what we mean by integration. Next we address supply management's critical internal and external linkages with various groups. The third section discusses the need to develop closer and more collaborative buyer-seller relationships to achieve improved external integration. The fourth section discusses the cross-functional sourcing team—an increasingly important approach taken to achieve supply management integration. The final section focuses on supply management's involvement in developing new products and order fulfillment.

Integration: What Is It?

Integration, a term often heard in the popular press, is in many cases not well defined. In this text, we define **integration** as "the process of incorporating or bringing together different groups, functions, or organizations, either formally or informally, physically or by information technology, to work jointly and often concurrently on a common business-related assignment or purpose." Although this is a very broad definition, it implies certain elements. First, that people are coming together to work together on a problem. It is no surprise that "two heads are better than one" when it comes to solving problems, but many enterprises do not apply the idea of bringing together people with a different point of view to solve a common problem. This is especially true in a global environment, with team members located all over the world. Thus, another caveat to this definition involves doing so either formally or informally, through physical methods or by information technology. Finally, integration requires that people create a common understanding of the end goal or purpose; as we will see, this is an important aspect of the success of integration strategies.

A recent study of senior executives in the United States and Europe indicated that integration is at the top of these executives' minds, in terms of what will be required in the future.[1] Moreover, when asked about the most critical skills required for supply management managers in the year 2010, executives did not list some of the more common elements such as process focus, financial analysis, or efficiency. The single most important element that senior executives look for is **relationship management (RM) skills**, defined as the ability to act ethically, listen effectively, communicate, and use creative problem solving. The ability to drive relationships is critical for firms seeking to build strong integration with internal business functions, as well as with external suppliers.

Integration can occur in many forms. It can occur through functions, such as in sourcing or new-product development teams. It can also occur through cross-location teams, where people from different business units are brought together. Finally, the most difficult and challenging form is cross-organizational teams, which involves working with suppliers, customers, or even both concurrently! Bringing different people to the table to work on a problem can provide significant benefits. People will generally provide input in the form of the following:

- Information
  - About their markets
  - About their own plans and requirements
- Knowledge and expertise
  - Product and service knowledge and technology
  - Process knowledge and understanding of how to make it work
- Business advantages
  - Favorable cost structures that can benefit customers
  - Economies of scale, which can also help reduce costs
- Different perspective on an issue, which may drive a team to look at the problem from a new perspective that they hadn't thought of before

Some of the different methods that supply management will apply to achieve integration include the following:

- Cross-functional or cross-organizational committees and teams
- Information systems such as videoconferencing and webmail
- Integrated performance objectives and measures that drive a common goal
- Process-focused organizations that are dedicated to certain processes
- Co-location of suppliers and customers
- Buyer or supplier councils that provide input and guidance to a steering committee

Paradoxically, the very elements of sound supply chain business practice that are the cornerstones of mature spend management cultures—and a crucial foundation for supplier relationship management (SRM)—can also serve as an anchor holding back progression to the higher levels of success.

One part of breaking through is tied to the personal effectiveness of the supply chain professionals charged with doing the work. Supply management professionals must begin to work with their internal functions, not against them! This means that the key building blocks for integration (team-building, communication, and relationship management) will become more important than ever! Let's discuss the first of these integration elements: internal integration with the functional entities in their own enterprise!

Internal Integration

Supply management must maintain a number of communication flows and linkages. Exhibit 4.1 illustrates the two-way linkages between supply management and other key groups along with a sample of the information exchanged between these groups. The linkages between supply management and other groups will become even stronger and more important as the role of supply management continues to develop and evolve.

Supply Management's Internal Linkages

To facilitate integration with other internal functions, a number of critical communication linkages or interfaces have evolved between supply management and other departments. This need for internal integration has increased exponentially in the last five years. Many organizations have actively moved toward an outsourced environment, and in some cases are sourcing all products through low-cost-country sourcing environments or contract manufacturers. These environments are very different from North American buyer-seller situations, and supply management must play a critical role in establishing these agreements and identifying global requirements for success. Supply management must often work to become part of the global negotiations teams and become involved in supplier qualification, contract management, and logistics, working with multiple internal parties in the firm including finance, legal, logistics, marketing, and operations.

Operations

Supply management has always been a major supporter of the operations group. Because the links between operations and supply management have been so close, it has not been unusual for supply management to report directly to operations. A major link between operations and supply management is through the development of global operations strategy. Because supply management directly supports operations, it must develop insights into production or service strategic plans. One area in which supply management has critical input to operations (and marketing) is through the sales and operations plan, which identifies the level of production and sales for six months to one year, as well as the required input to execute the plan. Clearly, supply management's strategies and plans must be aligned with the sales and operations plan. For example, supply management must be aware of the components and services needed by operations as they plan to fulfill customer requirements for products

Exhibit 4.1 Purchasing's Communications Flows and Linkages

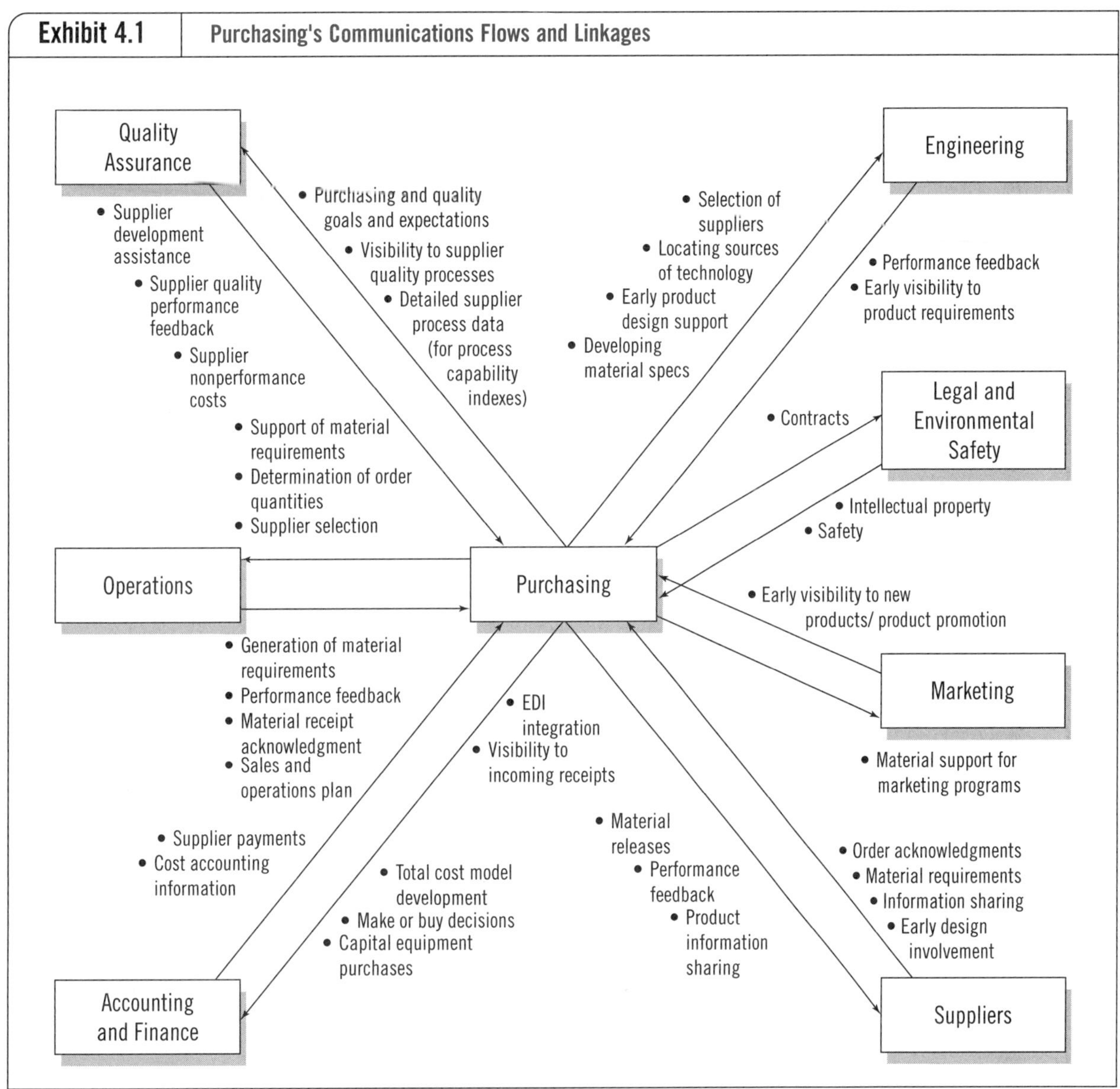

or services. This could include materials, software, services, travel, hotel, information technology, and outsourced labor. Because supply management is responsible for sourcing the inputs to support operation's plans, supply management managers must work with operations to coordinate the execution to plan.

Supply management and operations also maintain communication linkages through direct personnel contact. Many firms are now co-locating supply management personnel directly at operating locations so supply management can respond quickly to operation's needs. For example, in many financial institutions, supply managers are co-located within the strategic business units and provide supplier relationship managers to act as a primary single point of contact between suppliers and the organization. These managers can work to identify problems, create problem resolution strategies, and act as a liaison for discussions of service management expectations.

Quality Assurance

The supply management–quality linkage has increased in importance during the last 10 years. As firms externally source a larger percentage of finished product requirements, supply management and quality assurance must work together closely to ensure that suppliers perform as expected. Joint projects involving these two groups include supplier quality training, process capability studies, and corrective action planning. This linkage has become so important that some firms have placed the responsibility for supplier quality management directly with supply management. Many firms now have a dedicated supplier quality management function with a dual reporting element to both quality and supply management.

Engineering

Perhaps the most important and challenging linkages exist between supply management and engineering. The need to develop quality products in less time has drawn supply management and engineering closer over time. There are still opportunities, however, to improve the level of interaction between these two groups.

Firms can create stronger communication linkages and flows between supply management and engineering in several ways. Engineers and buyers can develop open communication by working together on product development or supplier selection teams. Supply management can also co-locate a buyer within the engineering group. The buyer can maintain direct contact with product and process engineers to respond quickly to their needs. A firm can also appoint a liaison that coordinates interdepartmental communications and makes sure that each group is aware of the other group's activities. The two departments can hold regular meetings to report on items of mutual concern. Finally, many supply management groups are recruiting commodity managers with very strong technical backgrounds, who are able to talk the talk and walk the walk alongside their engineering counterparts. The key to a successful relationship between supply management and engineering is open and direct communication, which in turn should lead to increased teamwork and trust.

Engineering looks to supply management to perform certain tasks to support engineering's efforts. For example, engineering expects supply management to identify the most technically and financially capable supplier for an item and to make sure each supplier meets engineering's quality and delivery targets. In addition, engineering expects supply management to assess a supplier's production capabilities, actively involve suppliers early in the design process, and develop relationships that encourage a supplier to offer innovative ideas. Engineering also expects supply management to identify sources of new technology that can be integrated into new products and services. It is also important to note that supply and engineering must work closely together to deal with quality risks that may arise in new products, such as the example shown in Sourcing Snapshot: Ensuring Quality Requirements: Batteries from Sony.

Finally, manufacturing and process engineering will want to ensure ongoing technical support and service during product launch and ongoing customer order fulfillment, as problems inevitably arise during this phase of the product life cycle as well.

Sourcing Snapshot — *Ensuring Quality Requirements: Batteries from Sony*

Outsourcing has its risks. Suppliers may misstate their capabilities, their process technology may be obsolete, or their performance may not meet the buyer's expectations. In other cases, the supplier may not have the capability to produce the product at the level of quality required. The most obvious example of this is the Sony battery catastrophe. Major manufacturers such as Dell, Apple, and IBM outsourced the power supply for their laptops to Sony. However, it quickly became apparent that the batteries were defective. When the batteries were made, the metal case of the cell was crimped, and microscopic shards of metal could be released into the battery, causing a short circuit that triggered overheating and in some cases a fire! After several of these incidents, Dell recalled 4.1 million batteries and Apple recalled 1.9 million batteries. The supplier, in this case Sony, had to recall over 9.6 million laptop batteries, a problem that has rattled confidence in the company's image. Sony announced that the recalls of lithium-ion batteries will boost its costs by $429 million between July and September 2006, which doesn't include provisions for possible lawsuits!

Accounting and Finance

Supply management also maintains linkages with the accounting and finance department. These linkages are not as strong, however, as the linkages with operations, engineering, and quality control. In fact, much of the communication linkage between supply management and accounting today is electronic. For example, as supply management transmits material releases to suppliers, it also provides information concerning inbound material requirements to the accounting department. Upon receipt of the ordered material, the material control system updates the supply management files from on-order or in-transit to a received status. The accounts payable system then receives the receipt information and compares the amount received to the amount ordered for payment.

Supply management may require data from the cost accounting system. For example, supply management must know handling and material rework costs for an item resulting from poor supplier performance. Supply management usually does not maintain data about individual activity costs that can increase total cost. The supply management performance measurement system relies on input from cost accountants to help calculate the total cost of an item, which is also important in make-or-buy decisions. Finally, supply management must work closely with finance when making capital acquisition decisions.

Marketing/Sales

Supply management maintains indirect linkages with marketing. Many new-product ideas that supply management must support start with marketing personnel, who are the voice of a firm's end customers. Marketing also develops sales forecasts that convert into production plans. Supply management must select suppliers and request material to support both marketing and production plans.

Legal

Supply management often confers with the legal department to seek counsel on specific elements of contracts. Issues that may arise include patent ownership terms

Sourcing Snapshot — *The New Role for Supply Management in Contracts*

In April 2007, more than 300 delegates joined together at the International Association of Commercial and Contract Managers (IACCM) Americas Conference (www.iaccm.com/americas) to debate issues related to contract management and to work together in creating a framework for the future. Representatives from top universities and business schools around the world explored cooperation in learning and research.

The emerging business environment demands increased global awareness and capabilities, better integration across business functions and external suppliers, and a more collaborative approach to relationship management. What is the role of the procurement or negotiations professional? What is the organizational model that will best equip companies for success? How do we integrate technology, skills, and organizational design to create a winning mix?

These issues were debated at this conference. Tim Cummins, CEO of IACCM, emphasized the dynamics of the new global contract management environment:

> The leaders in the community must raise their sights above logistics and purchasing savings, risk, and compliance, to understand the full value chain implications of the global networked economy. They must avoid being obsessed with tinkering with the mechanics and instead engage in the overall design of the vehicle. And to do this, they should engage with IACCM and the wider community it represents. One problem in developing professional status is that today we are an apparently random mix of job roles and titles—no one really thinks of us as a "professional community." Yet research shows we possess very similar skills and knowledge and there is more in common about the roles we perform than there is that divides us. Indeed, lawyers or doctors probably have greater differences within their ranks than we do—yet they have a composite status. One of the steps we have taken to address this is to adopt the term "commitment management" as an overarching title for the work we perform. Our community identifies, negotiates, documents, and manages the commitments required for successful realization of corporate goals from its external relationships (supplier, customer, distribution channel, strategic alliance, etc.).
>
> Another key problem is to escape from the constraining transactional focus of our work (which creates limited executive interest and results in low visibility) and instead to be visible in driving strategic performance. That means we must start collecting more data and accepting greater accountability for business outcomes. What process do we own, what results will we commit to monitoring, who will we challenge to change their process, rules, capabilities to ensure greater competitiveness, quality, or efficiency?
>
> In the end, the market will decide who survives. Our focus must be to drive the competitiveness of our business through greater speed, innovation, creativity. We must manage risks, but that means finding new and better ways to do things so they become less risky, not avoiding doing things because history or experience tells us they might be risky.

in new-product development, intellectual property, product liability claims, antitrust, long-term contracts containing escape clauses, and other legal issues. Electronic commerce also raises many legal issues that require supply management to consult with the legal department. Later chapters discuss legal issues in greater detail. Sourcing Snapshot: The New Role for Supply Management in Contracts illustrates some of the major challenges that lie ahead, specifically with respect to the role of procurement on contract management and legal overlapping responsibilities.

Environmental Management, Health, and Safety

Supply management may also confer with personnel from the environmental, health, and safety departments to ensure that suppliers are employing safe methods of transportation and are complying with Occupational Safety and Health Administration and safety regulations.

External Integration

Supply management represents the external face of the organization and also serves as the primary vehicle by which to integrate external suppliers and other entities into the organization. This is done by creating and maintaining linkages with groups external to the firm—these linkages are in some respects more important than supply management's internal linkages.

Supply Management's External Linkages

Supply management acts as a liaison with external parties on multiple fronts, including materials, new technology, information, and services. These parties include suppliers, government, and local communities.

Suppliers

Supply management's primary external linkages are with its suppliers. Supply management's primary responsibility is to maintain open communications with suppliers and select the suppliers with which to do business. Supply management should be the primary communication linkage with suppliers, although non–supply management personnel may contact a supplier about a particular item or question.

Supply management has the responsibility to select suppliers and to remain the primary commercial linkage with the buying firm, including any matter involving the conditions of the purchase agreement or other issues of importance. Non–supply management departments should not select, independently work with, or directly negotiate with potential suppliers for items for which the supply management department is responsible.

Government

Supply management sometimes maintains communication linkages with governments at different levels and locations. For example, supply management has an active role in international countertrade and often negotiates directly with foreign governments when establishing countertrade agreements. Supply management may also need to consult with federal government agencies on various matters, including the Environmental Protection Agency, the Department of Defense, the Department of External Affairs, and other agencies that have authority over issues governed by public policy.

Local Communities

Supply management may have contact with local communities and leaders. Because supply management controls a large budget, it has the potential to affect certain social goals. These goals include sourcing from local suppliers, awarding a certain percentage of business to qualified minority suppliers, and establishing ethical business practices in all dealings.

Collaborative Buyer-Seller Relationships

Most purchasers and sellers now recognize a need for joint cooperation to achieve cost, quality, delivery, and time improvements. During the 1980s, progressive purchasers eliminated poor or marginal suppliers from their supply base. They then developed collaborative relationships or alliances with many of the remaining suppliers.

Collaboration is defined as the process by which two or more parties adopt a high level of purposeful cooperation to maintain a trading relationship over time. The relationship is bilateral; both parties have the power to shape its nature and future direction over time. Mutual commitment to the future and a balanced power relationship are essential to the process. Although collaborative relationships are not devoid of conflict, they build mechanisms into the relationship for managing conflict.[2]

The following characteristics define a collaborative buyer-seller relationship:

- One or a limited number of suppliers for each purchased item or family of items. Remaining suppliers often provide material under long-term contracts with agreed-upon performance improvement targets.
- A win-win approach to reward sharing.
- Joint efforts to improve supplier performance across all critical performance areas.
- Joint efforts to resolve disputes.
- Open exchange of information. This includes information about new products, supplier cost data, and production schedules and forecasts for purchased items.
- A credible commitment to work together during difficult times. In other words, a purchaser does not return to old practices at the first sign of trouble.
- A commitment to quality, defect-free products having design specifications that are manufacturable and that the supplier's process is capable of producing.

Exhibit 4.2 compares the characteristics of traditional and collaborative buyer-seller relationships. Although not all relationships between purchasers and suppliers should be collaborative, the trend is toward greater use of the collaborative approach.

Advantages of Closer Buyer-Seller Relationships

A firm can gain many advantages by pursuing closer relationships with suppliers. The first is the development of mutual trust, which is the foundation of all strong relationships.

Exhibit 4.2 Characteristics of the Buyer-Seller Relationship

	TRADITIONAL APPROACH		COLLABORATIVE APPROACH
Suppliers	Multiple sources played off against each other	→	One of a few preferred suppliers for each major item
Cost sharing	Buyer takes all cost savings; supplier hides cost savings	→	Win-win shared rewards
Joint improvement efforts	Little or none	→	Joint improvement driven by mutual interdependence
Dispute resolution	Buyer unilaterally resolves disputes	→	Existence of conflict-resolution mechanisms
Communication	Minimal or no two-way exchange of information	→	Open and complete exchange of information
Marketplace adjustments	Buyer determines response to changing conditions	→	Buyer and seller work together to adapt to a changing marketplace
Quality	Buyer inspects at receipt	→	Designed into the product

Trust

Although trust seems intangible, it refers to the belief in the character, ability, strength, and truthfulness of another party. Trust makes it possible, for example, for the seller to share cost data with a buyer, which can result in a joint effort to reduce a supplier's cost through a mutual sharing of ideas. Trust can also result in a supplier working with a purchaser early in the design of a new product.

Long-Term Contracts

Another advantage of closer buyer-seller relationships is the opportunity to evaluate which suppliers should receive longer-term contracts. Purchaser and seller both realize benefits from longer-term contracts. A long-term contract provides an incentive for a supplier to invest in new plants and equipment. This investment can make a supplier more efficient and result in lower costs to the purchaser. Longer-term contracts can also lead to the joint development of technology, risk sharing, and supplier capabilities (see Sourcing Snapshot: Suncor Energy Partners with Drilling Suppliers).

Obstacles to Closer Buyer-Seller Relationships

A number of obstacles can prevent the development of closer relationships between a purchaser and a seller. A firm must evaluate whether these obstacles are present and identify ways to overcome them if the goal is to pursue closer interfirm cooperation.

Confidentiality

The need for confidentiality regarding financial, product, and process information is the most frequently cited reason for not developing closer supplier relationships. Supply management managers are sometimes reluctant to share critical information with suppliers that may also sell to competitors. There is also the possibility that a supplier is a direct competitor or may become one in the future.

Limited Interest by Suppliers

Closer relationships may not interest all suppliers. A supplier may have the leverage or power in some relationships, particularly when it is in a monopolistic or

Sourcing Snapshot

Suncor Energy Partners with Drilling Suppliers

In the oil and gas exploration business, a successful exploration and development drilling program requires strong performance from a multidisciplinary team, as well as active participation and support from many suppliers and contractors. Suncor Energy is a diversified oil and gas company based in Calgary, Alberta. As part of its strategic supplier relationship program, the Suncor Foothills Drilling-Asset Team was formed; it includes people from the drilling department and the Foothills Asset Team, as well as contractors and suppliers. This team drills mainly in the foothills of the Canadian Rocky Mountains.

The drilling business is traditionally very cyclical and somewhat secretive, with most of the actual drilling being outsourced to groups of specialized service suppliers. The on-again, off-again nature of the work can significantly damage service quality and expertise. Often the staffing of a drilling effort is determined by who is available, not by who is the best fit. The secretive nature of the business amplifies the difficulties of the service suppliers by the lack of information available for planning, forecasting, and workload leveling. To drill a well, materials and services are required from approximately 20 different suppliers. Often the information used by the service supplier is subject to change and can oftentimes be incorrect. Changes in timing or design can impact each of these suppliers significantly.

In addition to the coordination issues listed above, the technical issues related to drilling deep sour gas wells are also highly significant. Suncor has drilled wells as deep as 6400 m, with horizontal sections close to 2000 m in length. In the last five years the Foothills Drilling-Asset Team has drilled approximately 50 wells throughout the Alberta Foothills. In mountainous regions, expertise and extensive area experience go hand-in-hand with successfully drilling wells. Drilling techniques downhole have to be adapted to very challenging mountainous-type conditions. Poor drilling execution can result in safety concerns, increased costs, and lower capital returns. Even when drilling techniques are well executed, the Foothills challenges can result in significant timing fluctuations that can affect the entire supply chain network.

In order to overcome these challenges, a total integration of objectives was initiated to create greater influence on the factors affecting drilling performance. In essence, a greater team concept was created with one common center and full alignment. Team integration between the drilling group and the Foothills Drilling-Asset Team has extended further than previously documented for the industry. This integration has also been extended to a number of contractor services. The greater team concept has created a high trust environment that allows for accelerated learning and has enhanced integrated expertise. As a result, the key service suppliers and the different groups from Suncor work together as though they were one company with one set of objectives.

The implementation of this unified philosophy in all phases of the life cycle, as well as the creation of an environment of openness, trust, and mutual success, has resulted in substantial improvements. Based on a 2003 cost study, the team has achieved the following: (1) drilling costs reduced by 18% ($1.4 million/well), (2) planning times reduced by 42% (five months), (3) drilling times reduced by 20% on average, and (4) 80%-plus success rate on wells drilled. In addition, Foothills production volumes have tripled over the past five years. These results have been accomplished against a backdrop of 5% inflation. Suncor's Foothills Drilling-Asset Team has become one of the preferred employers from the service supplier perspective within its operating region. This position continues to strengthen.

Source: K. McCormack, P. H. Cavanagh, and R. Handfield, Foothills Drilling Team White Paper, Suncor Energy, 2003.

oligopolistic industry position. In such cases, the purchaser may be unable to pursue a closer relationship simply because of the relative sizes or power positions of the two firms.

Legal Barriers

In some industries, legal antitrust concerns may act as barriers or obstacles to closer buyer-seller relationships (covered in greater detail in Chapter 16, which discusses the legal aspects of supply management).

Resistance to Change

Entire generations of supply management professionals grew up using an arm's-length approach. A shift toward a more trusting approach is not easy. Resistance to change is a powerful force that takes time, patience, and training to overcome. Also, firms that practice traditional supply chain management may not have the skills or knowledge in their workforce to evolve toward closer supplier relationships.

An example of how buyer-supplier teams can work together, despite the odds, to create mutually beneficial outcomes is described in Sourcing Snapshot: Suncor Energy Partners with Drilling Suppliers.

Critical Elements for Supplier Relationship Management

Recent research conducted by Ward, Handfield, and Cousins based on interviews with executives revealed the following critical elements for building effective supply relationships.[3]

Focus on deliverables at the level of the product or service, not the centralized relationship that occurs at an abstract level and fails to get into the details of the business performance metrics. Too often, thoughts about SRM start with discussions about global contracts or broad-based partnering marketing initiatives. Although these can be seductive, they rarely produce sufficient short-term payoff to sustain the level of effort required to maintain focus on the initiative. Instead, as one group-level category manager said, "You need to provide short-term payoff on the basics before leaping into the other neat stuff. Our job is to make it a pull, not a push."[4]

- Start with the business outcome at the business unit level. This means defining a specific measurable performance indicator that means something to the business stakeholder (e.g., operational cost savings, supply continuity, process improvement suggestions, access to new technology, or process innovation).
- Let the business outcome drive the relationship process, course of action, and level of investment through initiation of projects focused on achieving the outcome.
- The overall relationship (Big R) then becomes an outcome of various relationships with different products and services that meet different business outcomes (little r's).
- Program management (Big R) drives incongruity resolution, aggregation of benefits, and opportunity analysis across lines of business.

Business cases must be clearly understood and compelling at all levels. Although well-intentioned efforts sometimes get off the ground because the business case is intuitively obvious, these efforts often are the first to founder in tougher times. Explicit documentation of time, efforts, and investments against projected payoffs is an essential component of success. A site-level procurement person who managed the little r at his location put it this way: "You've got to understand their strategic priorities and day-to-day pressures, make sure there is a direct line of sight between what we are asking them to do and how it will support their performance objectives."[5]

- Specific benefits to supplier and buyer need to be outlined with clear criteria for success and a realistic timeline for assessing leading and lagging indicator metrics.
- Benefits need to be weighed against a realistic assessment of costs of adopting a different way of working and the time and resource investment required to realize the benefits.
- Soft benefits should be rolled up to believable metrics that are meaningful to business units. Metrics need not always be financial, but need to be compelling and strategically important.
- Metrics should conform to existing available data; gathering the data should not be an additional hardship

External RM starts with internal RM; internal alignment is key. SRM will expose and even magnify the fault lines in an organization's structure and alignment. Although governance models for SRM have been much discussed, they are often used to mask fundamental conflicts or gaps in accountabilities and responsibilities. In today's heavily matrixed environments, perfect alignment is neither possible nor desirable. Instead, procurement executives need to be conscious of the hot spots and tensions and have plans in place to manage through them.

An exasperated category manager discussing his company's SRM failings noted, "Do you have an appetite for the culture change this requires? Planning, sharing, having real dialogue, and investing the time and resources to engage at each level with real teams, and open communication? In our case the answer was no."[6] To avoid this type of negative outcome, SRM initiatives should consider the following approach:

- Start with how a firm interacts with itself; where are the functional silos, and who are the key decision makers at each level who determine the course of action?
- Once identified, internal conflicts between stakeholder needs within different functional silos need to be resolved before trying to change or refocus externally.
- Once established, procurement should become the initial point of contact to make and deliver on supplier commitments, but then it needs to drive the relationship into each business and transition into a facilitator role.
- Relationship management governance needs engaged relationship managers. Ideally, the business line sponsors focus on the achievement of little r business outcomes, with dedicated procurement resource leaders and senior business executive sponsors focused on Big R enterprisewide coordination.

Engineer change into the process; keep structure and key performance indicators (KPIs) dynamic. SRM is by definition a multiyear, long-horizon effort, at least at the

Big R level. But businesses rarely have the discipline to manage beyond pressures for short-term results. Rather than try to swim against the tide, SRM advocates would do well to remember that for most business executives, "if it doesn't work in the short term, there may be no long term." The need to meet short-term goals is an important component of successful program management; each relationship must be tuned to emerging and shifting business priorities.

Otherwise, as one procurement executive said, "The big guys stop showing up at the meetings, you keep measuring things nobody cares about anymore, and it becomes just another piece of work."[7]

In managing both internal and external relationships, some of the key points to keep in mind include the following:

- Different stages of SRM require different people and skills and levels of investment and attention; the people needed to jump-start the effort may not be the best ones to nurture, manage, and sustain it.
- Recruit from the business. The best supplier relationship managers are those who have worked in the business, understand the day-to-day pressures, and speak the same technical vernacular. These individuals can align the business realities for stakeholders and suppliers with the opportunities.
- Monitor internal and external shifts, and establish mechanisms that facilitate readjustment in roles, metrics, and project deliverables.
- Schedule regular site-level meetings with suppliers and stakeholders to reevaluate and revise KPIs to reflect current business priorities.
- Drive people to insight and to commitment; as one executive noted, "It's a business relationship, not a marriage." Be willing to cut bait on people or directions that aren't in alignment with strategy.

The Critical Role of Cross-Functional Sourcing Teams

The pressure to improve, already intense, is expected to increase even more in the years ahead. Many firms are responding to this pressure by creating organizational structures that promote cross-functional and cross-organizational communication, coordination, and collaboration. In support of this effort, cross-functional sourcing teams have become increasingly important as firms pursue leading-edge supply management strategies and practices.

Cross-functional sourcing teams consist of personnel from different functions and, increasingly, suppliers, brought together to achieve supply management or supply chain–related tasks. This includes specific tasks such as product design or supplier selection, or broader tasks such as responsibility for reducing purchased item cost or improving quality.

When executed properly, the cross-functional sourcing team approach can bring together the knowledge and resources required for responding to new sourcing demands, something that rigid organizational structures are often incapable of doing. Prior researchers on team-building, such as Likert, have noted that groups and teams can accomplish much that is good, or they can do great harm. There is nothing

Exhibit 4.3 Purchasing at Different Organizational Levels

Personal Commitment	Time Frame: Finite	Time Frame: Continuous
Full-Time	Move from project to project	Assigned permanently to specific team with evolving or changing responsibilities
Part-Time	Support a specific team assignment in addition to regular responsibilities Disband after completion	Ongoing support of team assignments in addition to regular responsibilities

implicitly good or bad, weak or strong, about teams, regardless of where an organization uses them.

Exhibit 4.3 segments cross-functional sourcing teams by the team's assignment (finite or continuous) and the member's personal commitment to the team (full or part time). Although some progressive firms are creating full-time sourcing team assignments, in most cases sourcing team assignments are still part time. The lower half of this matrix (finite or continuous team assignments supported by part-time members) presents a special challenge. It is often a struggle to obtain the commitment of members who have other professional responsibilities. Experience reveals that cross-functional sourcing teams are usually part-time/continuous assignments, making the use of sourcing teams a challenging way to work.

The following discussion of sourcing teams examines the benefits and potential drawbacks to team interaction, identifies when to form a cross-functional team (CFT), and concludes with a set of questions and answers that will explain how to make sourcing teams effective.

Benefits Sought from the Cross-Functional Team Approach

Firms commit the energy needed to form teams to realize specific performance benefits. When cross-functional teams meet their performance objectives, the benefits can far outweigh the cost of using teams. The following highlights some of the benefits that organizations hope to realize from cross-functional sourcing teams.

Reduced Time to Complete a Task

Individuals working as a team can often reduce the time required to solve a problem or complete an assigned task. The traditional approach to completing organizational tasks often requires duplication of effort between groups, and the individual sign-off of different functional groups may take an extended period of time. The team approach supports members reaching agreement together, which can result in reduced rework and the time required to execute a decision.

Increased Innovation

Firms look to teams to develop innovative products and processes to maintain an advantage over competitors. Innovation is critical to long-term success. Research has revealed that lower levels of formal rules and procedures along with informal organizational structures support increased levels of innovation.[8]

The team approach should require fewer formal rules and qualifies as a less formal organizational structure. Teams can be a means to encourage increased innovation among members.

Joint Ownership of Decisions

The team approach requires joint agreement and ownership of decisions among different members. Through team interaction, members begin to understand each other's requirements or limitations and develop solutions that different departments can support. Perhaps the greatest benefit of team interaction is that once a team makes a decision, implementing the decision often becomes easier due to group buy-in. The stakeholders involved in carrying out the decision are more likely to do so efficiently and effectively, because the team has established cross-functional agreement and ownership regarding the change or decision.

Enhanced Communication between Functions or Organizations

Those who have worked in an organization with rigidly separated departments know the inefficiencies associated with interdepartmental communication. The problems are even worse as parties attempt to communicate across organizations. The cross-functional team approach can help reduce communication barriers because members are in direct contact with each other (either face to face or by electronic communication). For example, the team approach can help reduce design or material changes during product development because the team works together when developing product specifications. This cross-functional team approach, by design, encourages open and timely exchange of information between members.

Realizing Synergies by Combining Individuals and Functions

A primary objective of using teams is to bring together individuals with different perspectives and expertise to perform better on a task compared to individuals or departments acting alone. The synergistic effect of team interaction can help generate new and creative ways to look at a problem or approach a task. Ideally, a team works together to solve problems that individuals could not solve as well acting alone, to create new ways to perform routine (though time-consuming) tasks, and to develop ideas that only a diverse group could develop.

Better Identification and Resolution of Problems

Teams with diverse knowledge and skills have an opportunity to quickly identify causes of problems that may affect the team or the organization. Early problem identification and correction minimizes or even prevents a problem's total impact. Furthermore, a team should assume joint ownership of problems and accept the responsibility for problem correction, which helps prevent finger-pointing for blame between departments.

The Need to Build Internal Relationships through Teams

Research[9] suggests that supply management professionals may, indeed, be placed in some of the most interpersonally demanding situations of any occupational group studied. Success depends upon the ability to navigate organizational fault lines with facility and interpersonal sophistication akin to that of the best general managers—without the organizational clout to back it up. Some of the comments below from supply management senior executives reflect the recognition of this need to create a tighter bridge between procurement professionals and business stakeholders.[10]

- "A number of our people have the perception that once the contract is done, you put it in the drawer. . . . We have no culture of continuous management and measurement, so this level of engagement is new for us."
- "They've got to believe that we know we are only in service to the business. There's a credibility gap and we've got to change the quality of the conversation, change the way we present information."
- "Don't give us procurement SRM tools without investing the time and money to help us adapt it to our business and make sure we know how to use it. And you can't even use the tools until you can earn a seat at the table! How're we supposed to do that?"

Critically, SRM means learning to exercise a new kind of power, one not grounded in the ability to force compliance with procurement procedures and contracting processes. Instead, procurement executives need to learn to build relationship capital that inspires trust and commitment from stakeholders and suppliers. Relationship capital is a function of the professional's ability to translate supply market data into compelling insights that solve business problems and to enable organizational connections and networking that accelerate business success.

Potential Drawbacks to the Cross-Functional Team Approach

The use of cross-functional sourcing teams does not guarantee a successful outcome to a project or assignment. The team approach requires careful management, open exchange of information between members, motivated team members, clearly understood team goals, effective team leaders, and adequate resources. There are potential drawbacks to the team approach when conditions do not support an effective team effort. Supply management managers must be willing to address these drawbacks if they begin to affect team performance.

Team Process Loss

Process loss occurs when a team does not complete its task in the best or most efficient manner or members are not motivated to employ their resources to create a successful outcome.[11] When process loss is present, the total group effort is less than the expected sum of the individual parts. There is a potential drawback if the benefits resulting from team interaction do not outweigh team process loss. For example, a supplier selection team with 12 members, 5 of whom are active on the team, would experience a loss and waste from a lack of team interaction and participation.

Negative Effects on Individual Members

Membership on a team can have negative effects on individuals. Teams can exert pressure to conform to a decision or position that the member does not support. An example might involve a materials engineer who is pressured by other team members to select the lowest-price supplier, even though he or she knows that a higher-priced supplier will provide better quality.

A team may also pressure an individual to support or conform to a lower productivity norm than the individual's personal norm. Also, some individuals may feel stifled in a team setting or may not interact well with other team members. When this occurs, individual performance suffers.

Poor Team Decisions

Although it seems counter to what we popularly believe, cross-functional teams can arrive at poor decisions. **Groupthink**—the tendency of a rational group or team to arrive at a bad decision when other information is available —may become a problem for individuals in a cohesive group. By striving for group uniformity and consensus, they may suppress their motivation to appraise alternative courses of action.[12] The team may arrive at a decision that careful evaluation of all available information or critical discussion normally would not support.

When to Form a Cross-Functional Team

All organizations face resource constraints that affect the number of cross-functional teams, including sourcing teams, they can establish. Clearly, a firm cannot use the team approach for every business decision. Certain business decisions simply do not require a team approach. A team approach is useful when the task at hand satisfies certain characteristics.

A firm faced with a complex or large-scale business decision should consider the cross-functional team approach. Examples include new-product development, locating a new production facility, developing a commodity or purchase family strategy, or establishing a new business unit. These tasks are so large or complex that one person or function cannot effectively accomplish the assignment. A firm can also use the team approach when a team is likely to arrive at a better solution than a person or department acting individually. For example, supply management may be able to handle the evaluation and selection of suppliers but may benefit from a team with diverse experience whose members are better equipped to evaluate suppliers from a number of perspectives. Engineering can provide technical specifications, marketing can provide details on the features required, accounting can provide material and labor cost data estimates, and so on. In these situations, selecting a better supplier(s) for the situation at hand is more likely as better information becomes available and is analyzed by team members.

An assignment that directly affects a firm's competitive position, such as negotiation with a joint venture partner, might also benefit from the team approach. The cross-functional team approach is also useful when no single function has the resources to solve a problem that affects more than one department or function.

Improving Sourcing Team Effectiveness

The remainder of our team discussion presents a set of questions that require students and managers to think about various issues that affect the quality of sourcing team interaction and performance. Each question includes a brief discussion of major points and insights related to that question.

Question 1: Does Our Organization Consider Cross-Functional Team Planning Issues When Establishing Sourcing Teams?

Successfully using teams requires extensive planning before a team should be allowed to pursue an assignment. Ignoring these issues or the needs of team members during team formation increases the risk of team failure. The following summarizes several sourcing team planning issues.

Selecting a Task

Organizations should use teams selectively due to limited resource availability. Sourcing teams should work only on tasks that are important to an organization's success. One expert recommends selecting tasks that are meaningful. A **meaningful task** is one that requires members to use a variety of higher-level skills, supports giving members regular feedback about performance, results in an outcome with a significant affect on the organization and others outside the team, and provides members autonomy for deciding how they will do the work. For example, reducing purchase cost is an example of a broad performance objective.

Selecting Team Members and Leaders

Perhaps one of the most critical planning issues involves selecting the right members and leader. An effective team member is one who meets the following requirements:

- Understands the team's task—the member has task-relevant knowledge
- Has the time to commit to the team
- Has the ability to work with others in a group
- Can assume an organizational rather than strict functional perspective

Training Requirements

Interacting as a team requires a set of skills different from the skills required for traditional work. Organizations must consider carefully the training requirements of sourcing team members. Members may require training in project management, conflict resolution, consensus decision making, group problem solving, goal setting, and effective communication and listening skills.

Resource Support

An earlier study of cross-functional sourcing teams by Monczka and Trent revealed that the types of resources that cross-functional sourcing teams had access to made a major difference in team performance.[13] Adapted from work by Peters and O'Connor, we can identify 10 categories of team resources, as presented in Exhibit 4.4.[14] The resources that correlate the highest, on average, with effective sourcing teams (in order of importance) are supplier participation, required services and help from others, time availability, and budgetary support. Budgetary support is especially

Exhibit 4.4 Organizational Resource Requirements

1. **Supplier Participation**
   The degree to which suppliers directly support completion of the team's task assignments when supplier involvement is required
2. **Required Services and Help from Others**
   The services and help required from others external to the team to perform the team's assignment
3. **Time Availability**
   The amount of time that can be devoted by all team members to the team's assignment
4. **Budgetary Support**
   The financial resources needed to perform the team's assigned tasks
5. **Materials and Supplies**
   The routine items that are required to perform the team's assignment
6. **Team Member Task Preparation**
   The personal preparation and experience of team members, through previous education, formal company training, and relevant job experience, required to perform the team's assignment
7. **Work Environment**
   The physical aspects of the immediate work environment needed to perform the team's assignment—characteristics that facilitate rather than interfere with team performance
8. **Executive Management Commitment**
   The overall level of support that executive management exhibits toward the cross-functional team process
9. **Job-Related Information**
   The information, including data and reports, from multiple sources required to support team performance. Examples include data on costs, technical issues, suppliers, supply market, performance targets, and requirements.
10. **Tools and Equipment**
    The specific tools, equipment, and technology required to perform the team's assignment

Source: Adapted from L. H. Peters and J. O. O'Connor, "Situational Constraints and Work Outcomes: The Influences of a Frequently Overlooked Construct," *Academy of Management Review*, March 1980, 3, 391–397.

critical for teams whose members must travel from different geographical areas or for teams that must visit suppliers during the course of their assignment.

Other planning issues not addressed here include determining the level of sourcing team authority, the types and frequency of team evaluations and rewards, and the physical location of team members. This list of planning issues reveals that organizations must give serious attention to some important considerations before allowing sourcing teams to begin work.

Question 2: Does Executive Management Practice Subtle Control over Sourcing Teams?

A major issue involves management's willingness to exert subtle control over cross-functional sourcing teams, a process that does not mean that management dictates or supervises team activities. Instead, subtle control involves activities undertaken by management to increase the probability of team success. There are several ways that management can practice subtle control over sourcing teams:

- Authorizing the creation of the sourcing team
- Selecting the team's task
- Establishing broad objectives (with the team later establishing specific performance targets or goals)
- Selecting the team leader and members
- Requiring performance updates at regular intervals or at key milestones (What team wants to report to executive management that they have made no progress?)
- Conducting performance reviews and holding teams accountable for performance outcomes

Although management does not involve itself in a team's day-to-day activities, management must concern itself with moving the sourcing team process forward.

Question 3: Does Our Organization Recognize and Reward Team Member Participation and Team Performance?

A direct link exists between rewards and team member effort, and also between rewards and team performance. Unfortunately, many organizations still fail to recognize the time and effort members must commit to sourcing teams, particularly members of part-time teams. This lack of recognition often causes team members to commit their time to non-team work activities.

How should organizations recognize and reward team member participation and team performance? Although no single answer exists, there are some guidelines that will help in this area. First, team membership should be part of an individual's performance review. This sends a message that team participation is valued and recognized by the organization, just like an individual's other work responsibilities. Second, along with an evaluation of the entire team's performance, management should consider assessing each individual's contribution to the team. This helps ensure that nonparticipating members do not benefit unfairly from the efforts of other team members.

Rewards and recognition that organizations offer teams cluster into four broad categories:

- Executive recognition, including plaques or mention in the company newsletter
- Monetary bonuses and other one-time cash awards
- Nonmonetary rewards, including dinners or sports and theater tickets
- Merit raises awarded during the team member's annual performance review

Rewards offer an opportunity to reinforce desired activity and behavior. It is well understood that what gets rewarded gets done. If team members are positively reinforced for high performance, they will likely exert even greater effort. Furthermore, if members receive immediate reinforcement, they will exert greater effort than if the reinforcement is delayed. If positive work is never recognized or reinforced through rewards, the positive effort will likely be extinguished.

Question 4: Do We Have the Right Individuals Selected as the Sourcing Team Leader?

The previously mentioned research by Monczka and Trent found that the effectiveness of the sourcing team leader is one of the strongest predictors of team success. An additional finding from that research was that most sourcing teams had formally designated leaders who usually were selected by management (see Question 3 on subtle control). Zenger and his colleagues, in extensive research with teams, found the following to be true:[15]

- Most organizations report they should give more attention, training, and support to their team leaders.
- Within days of taking a leadership role, team leaders usually realize they need a new set of skills.
- Even when shared team leadership among members is the goal, the team as a whole still reports to someone who might need advanced team-leadership skills.
- Overly structured team leaders who see themselves as "top sergeants with a few extra duties" greatly increase the chance of team failure.

We may conclude that selecting and training an effective team leader is critical to team success. Being an effective team leader means satisfying a demanding set of essential operating responsibilities and requirements while still promoting the creativity, leadership ability, and cohesiveness of team members. Unfortunately, relatively few individuals have the qualifications, experience, or training to immediately assume such a demanding leadership position.

Organizations should (1) evaluate team leader strengths and weaknesses; (2) rank team leaders, which is valuable when considering future leadership responsibilities; (3) provide feedback regarding improvement opportunities, which can lead to training that is targeted to the specific needs of the leader; and (4) allow individual leaders, teams, and organizations to take corrective action as required. A failure to select a qualified individual as team leader greatly reduces the probability of sourcing team effectiveness.

Question 5: Do Our Sourcing Teams Effectively Establish Performance Goals?

One of the most important activities relating to sourcing team interaction is the ability of teams to establish quantified goals that focus on end results (rather than desired activities). For example, a sourcing team that establishes a goal of 2% cost reduction for the first quarter of 2005 has likely established a more effective goal than one that establishes a goal of holding three team meetings in the first quarter.

Establishing sourcing team goals is important for several reasons. Teams with established goals often use those goals as a basis for evaluating how well the team is performing. The goals provide a benchmark for assessing progress, providing feedback, and allocating performance rewards for superior effort and results. Teams will also establish, on average, challenging rather than easy goals. Furthermore, external pressure on a team to set goals usually results in the setting of more challenging goals (recall our discussion of subtle control). We also know that teams with goals perform better, on average, than teams that are asked simply to perform their best without explicit end goals. Goal setting is a critical cross-functional team requirement.

Sourcing teams should develop goals for which they will be held accountable. This is a three-part process. The first part of the process requires a team to describe its task. For example, a team may be responsible for managing suppliers that provide a certain commodity. The second part of the process requires the team to assess its ability to achieve certain outcomes on a scale ranging from 1 (no potential) to 7 (high potential). Finally, the team identifies those areas offering the highest performance potential (usually the items within the 5–7 range) and develops quantified or specific objectives relating to that item. If the team believes it has the potential to improve material delivery, then it should develop an objective goal that relates to material delivery.

Question 6: Are Key Suppliers Part of the Sourcing Team Process?

The potential benefit of closer buyer-seller relationships is well understood by most organizations. Cross-functional sourcing teams are an ideal way to promote cross-organizational cooperation. Research reveals that relying on supplier involvement and input (when a team's assignment warrants involvement) demonstrates, on average, the following positive characteristics compared with teams that do not involve suppliers:[16]

- They are rated as more effective than teams that do not involve suppliers.
- They are rated as putting forth greater effort on team assignments than teams that do not involve suppliers.
- They report greater satisfaction concerning the quality of key information exchanged between the team and key suppliers.
- They report greater reliance on suppliers to directly support the team's goals, thus making the supplier a resource.
- They report fewer problems coordinating work activity between the team and key suppliers.
- They report receiving greater supplier contribution across many performance areas, including cost-reduction and quality improvement ideas, process improvement suggestions, and material-ordering and delivery cycle time reductions.

An integrated approach to supply chain management should also begin to identify key customers that should be part of sourcing teams (at least on an informal basis). Sourcing teams, with supplier involvement, can work to incorporate customer needs directly into sourcing strategies and practices.

Cross-functional sourcing teams offer all types of organizations, not just manufacturing firms, the opportunity to realize advantages across many performance areas. Underlying the development and use of sourcing teams must be a recognition that sourcing increasingly affects a firm's overall competitiveness along with the realization that cross-functional integration among supply management, manufacturing, marketing, and technical groups can improve a firm's sourcing effectiveness.

Integrating Supply Management, Engineering, and Suppliers to Develop New Products and Services

In forward-thinking enterprises, supply management plays a key role in the development of new products and services. As the main contact with suppliers, supply management is in a unique position to include suppliers early in the design process as well as to perform early evaluation of supplier capabilities. This is a task that engineering team members are not trained to do. Think about how much easier it is for supply management to support new-product development teams than for engineering to do it alone! As a team member, supply management has early visibility to new-product requirements, which allows managers to contribute directly during the design and specification of material requirements. With a more traditional approach, supply management plays a reactive role after other functions have completed their tasks. Because supply management knows more about supplier capabilities, it is a valuable resource for engineering staff faced with understanding the capabilities of suppliers, as well as the new and emerging technologies that lie on the horizon and are within reach of current or new suppliers.

Common Themes of Successful Supplier Integration Efforts

A recent study[17] funded by the National Science Foundation (NSF) identified the key factors that distinguished successful from unsuccessful attempts at involving suppliers in new-product development. The following key attributes of successful supplier integration initiatives were common among all of the companies studied, as shown in Exhibit 4.5 on p. 138.

1. Formalized Process for Selecting Items for Supplier Integration

Supply management's involvement enables it to determine at an earlier point the materials or service requirements for a new product and provide input during the design phase based on its knowledge of materials supply markets. Supply management can recommend substitutes for high-cost or volatile materials, suggest standard items wherever possible, and evaluate longer-term materials trends. However, as we noted in Chapter 3, the right to make this decision must be formally authorized in the new-product development process, with supply management given the appropriate level of authority.

Supply management should always monitor and anticipate activity in its supply markets. For example, supply management should forecast long-term supply and prices for its basic commodities. It should monitor technological innovations that impact its primary materials or make substitute materials economically attractive. It should evaluate not only its existing suppliers but other potential suppliers. Because team participation provides timely visibility to new-product requirements, supply management can monitor and forecast change on a continuous basis.

2. Use of Cross-Functional Team for Supplier Evaluation and Selection

The evaluation and selection of suppliers requires a major time commitment by supply management, the group that must evaluate and select suppliers regardless of the new-product development approach used. The team approach allows supply

Exhibit 4.5 Practices That Separate the "Best" from the Rest

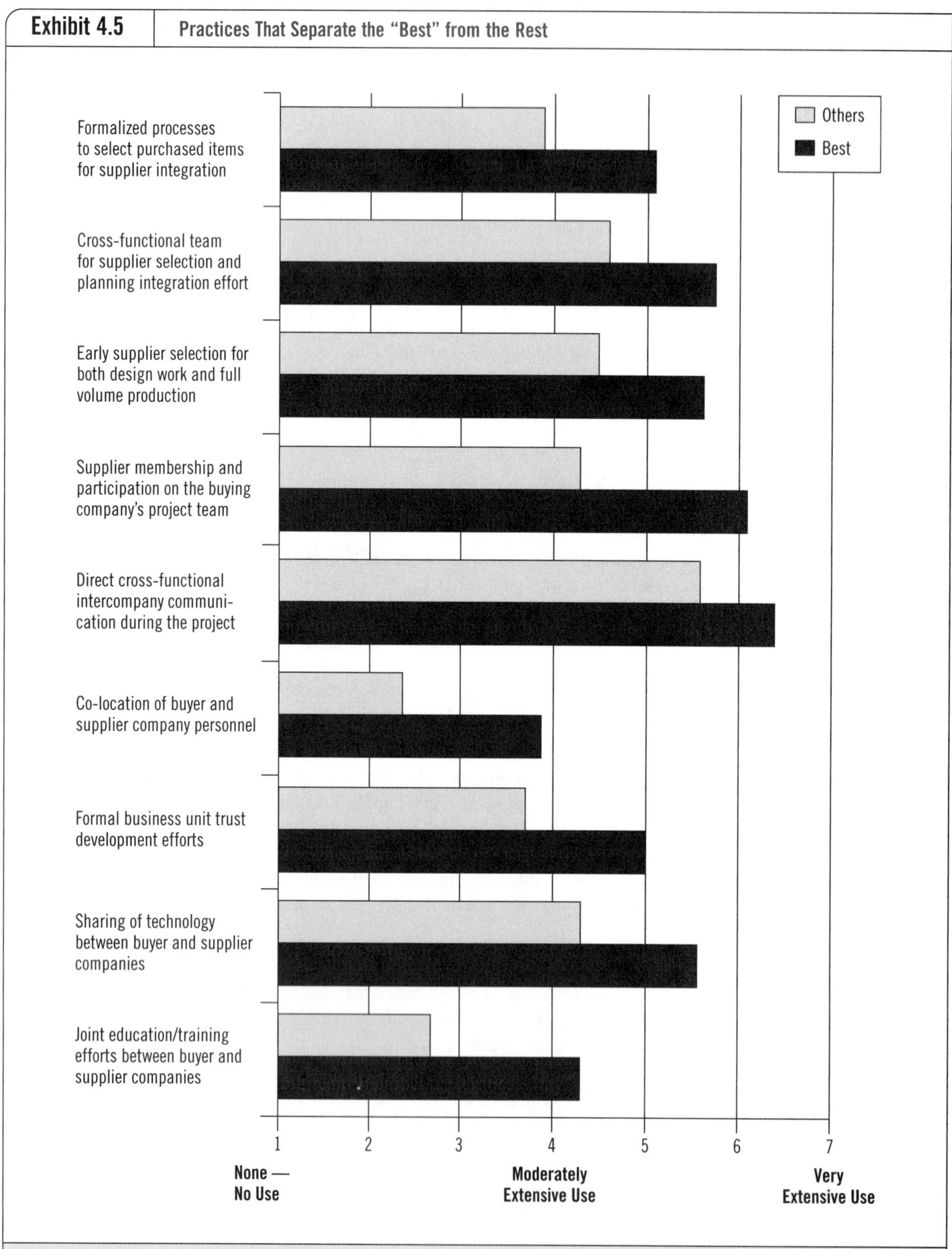

Source: R. Monczka, D. Frayer, R. Handfield, G. Ragatz, and T. Scannell, *Supplier Integration into New Product/Process Development: Best Practices,* Milwaukee, WI: ASQ Quality Press, 2000.

management to anticipate product requirements earlier so it can identify the most capable suppliers.

The supplier assessment should be systematically carried out, based on hard performance data, by a cross-functional team of technical and non-technical personnel who conduct subjective evaluations. Performance data should be weighted in such a manner that they are aligned with customer performance requirements. All of the above criteria must be tied into the evaluation/measurement system in order to develop a comprehensive risk assessment that answers the following questions:

- What is the likelihood that this supplier has the ability to bring the product to market?
- How does this risk assessment compare to other potential suppliers (if there are others)?
- At what point are we willing to reverse this decision if we proceed, and what are the criteria and measures for doing so?
- What is the contingency plan that takes effect in the event of reversing our decision?

3. Early Supplier Selection for Design and Volume Work

Supplier selection can occur before a new part is actually designed or reaches production. The team approach helps eliminate a source of frustration for supply management—a lack of time to evaluate, select, and develop suppliers to support new-product requirements. With the team approach, supplier selection can begin earlier in the development process, which allows supply management to perform this critical task earlier in the process and with better information.

The following elements are important in considering new or existing suppliers for integration:

- *Targets.* Is the supplier capable of hitting affordable targets regarding cost, quality, conductivity, weight, and other performance criteria?
- *Timing.* Will the supplier be able to meet product introduction deadlines?
- *Ramp-up.* Will the supplier be able to increase capacity and production fast enough to meet our market share requirements?
- *Innovation and technical.* Does the supplier have the required engineering expertise and physical facilities to develop an adequate design, manufacture it, and solve problems when they occur?
- *Training.* Do the supplier's key personnel have the required training to start up required processes and debug them?
- *Resource commitment.* If the supplier is deficient in any of the above areas, is management willing to commit resources to remedy the problem?

4. Supplier Membership and Participation on the Team

Bringing suppliers into the product development process is different from simply sharing information, and it can involve including important suppliers early in the design process of a new product, perhaps even as part of the new-product team. The benefits of early supplier involvement include gaining a supplier's insight into the design process, allowing comparisons of proposed production requirements against a supplier's existing capabilities, and allowing a supplier to begin preproduction work early. A supplier can bring a fresh perspective and new ideas to the development process.

Exhibit 4.6 Extent of Design Responsibility

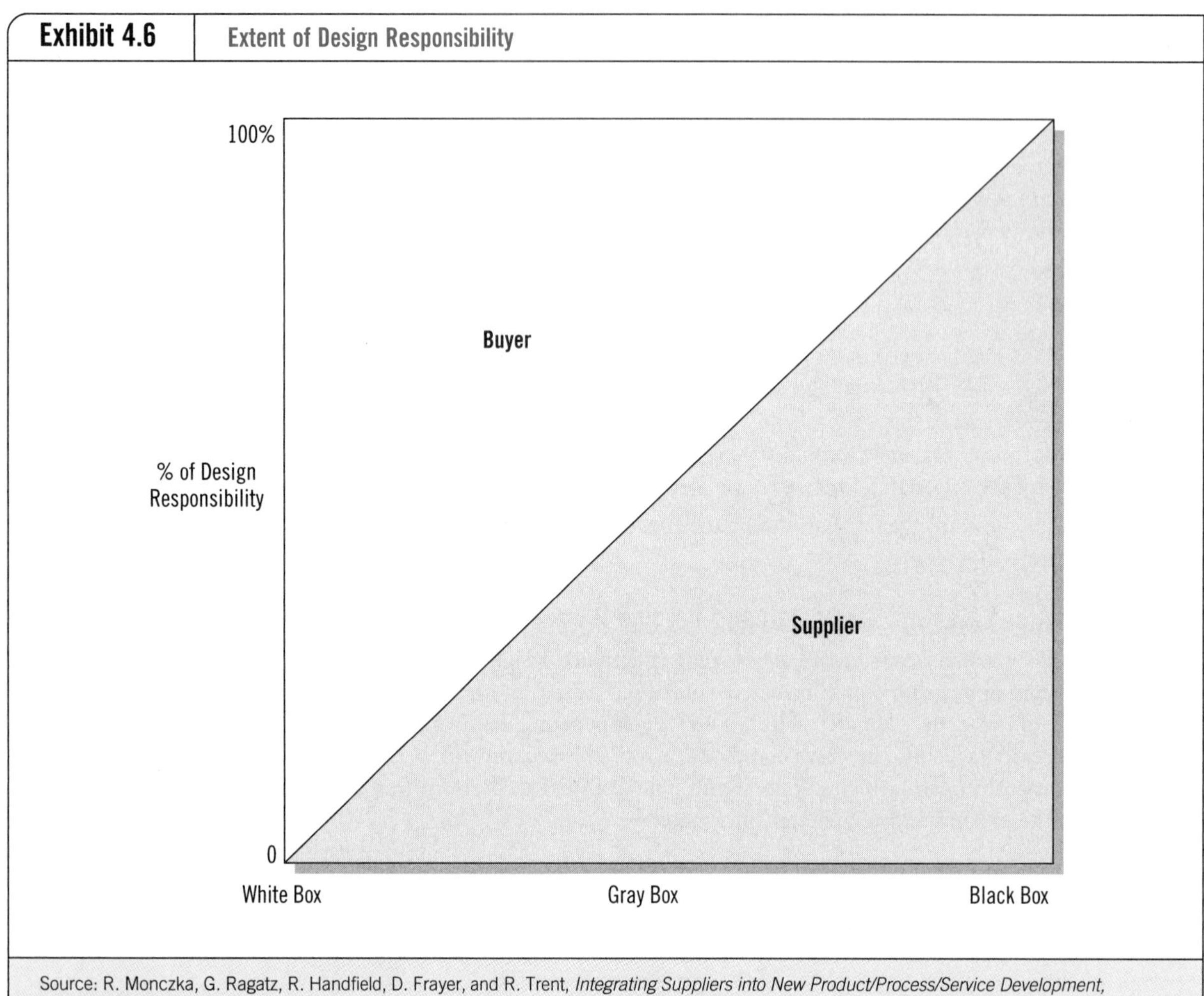

Source: R. Monczka, G. Ragatz, R. Handfield, D. Frayer, and R. Trent, *Integrating Suppliers into New Product/Process/Service Development*, Milwaukee, WI: ASQ Quality Press.

If given the opportunity, suppliers can have a major impact on the overall timing and success of a new product. The type of involvement can also vary (see Exhibit 4.6). At one extreme, called **white box design**, the supplier is given blueprints and told to make the product from them. At a more involved level, often called **gray box design**, the supplier's engineers work cooperatively with the buying company's engineers to jointly design the product. At the highest level of supplier involvement, **black box design**, suppliers are provided with functional specifications and are asked to complete all technical specifications, including materials to be used, blueprints, and so on. Depending on the level of involvement, the supplier may need to be a full-time member of the team, working alongside supply management, engineering, and manufacturing to bring the project to fruition.

5. Direct Cross-Functional Intercompany Communication during the Project

In the study of supplier integration, a variety of information-sharing mechanisms were employed to assess the alignment of technology roadmaps with potential suppliers. In most cases, no specific product or project was discussed at initial meetings, only the potential for a meeting of the minds. The sharing of technology roadmaps often strongly influenced the type of buyer-supplier relationship that resulted in the integration process. Very often, the buyer or supplier decided that this was not a company they were interested in doing business with due to a diverging technology roadmap. In cases when the supplier's current technology could be used but its long-term technology roadmap diverged, companies often exploited the technology for the current product or process but returned to the supply pool for future product cycles.

Team participation allows supply management to evaluate the timing of each phase of the product development project. Supply management can assess whether project timing is realistic as it applies to a new part's sourcing requirements. If the timing is not realistic, supply management should have enough visibility to re-evaluate the timing requirements or come up with plans to meet the proposed time frame. In addition, an ongoing set of milestones should be established to ensure that communication with the supplier is ongoing and occurs at regular intervals. This can prevent the occurrence of nasty surprises if the supplier falls behind schedule in completing the project.

Sourcing Snapshot: Suncor Energy Partners with Drilling Suppliers illustrates how one company worked to closely integrate suppliers with its engineering and sourcing teams, resulting in a competitive advantage in the industry.

6. Co-Location of Buyer and Supplier Personnel

The physical co-location of a supplier engineer at a buying company is increasingly becoming a part of the normal product development process structure. One company in the study operates what it calls a "guest engineer" program through which it invites key suppliers to place an engineer in the buying company's facility for a short period of time (two to three weeks) in the very early stages of product development. During this period, the firms develop product and design specifications and assign responsibilities for development. Another buying company co-locates its personnel and the supplier's personnel at a neutral site due to union rules. The result is the same: a focused and closely integrated team who work together throughout the duration or just during critical stages of the development project. As discussed in Sourcing Snapshot: Toyota Is Shut Down by a Supplier Problem, the importance of being close to suppliers is particularly apparent during periods of supply chain disruption.

The NSF study suggested that certain types of suppliers are more likely to be integrated earlier and may need to be physically co-located with the development team. For instance, at a Japanese computer manufacturer, the extent of interaction that takes place between product development engineers and suppliers appears to depend on the volatility of the commodity technology. Suppliers of critical nonstandard commodities are involved much earlier in the product development initiative. These suppliers are involved in face-to-face discussions with engineers on a regular basis. On the other hand, suppliers of noncritical, standard items are not integrated until the final stages of the development cycle, and communication appears to occur more in the form of computerization (e.g., computer-aided design, or CAD, is used with noncritical items such as PCBs, keyboards, and chassis). In general, face-to-face discussions are quicker, and information can be exchanged more effectively. However, in cases when suppliers are located within a day's travel of the operating divisions, co-location is often unnecessary.

Sourcing Snapshot — *Toyota Is Shut Down by a Supplier Problem*

On July 19, 2007, financial markets worldwide learned of Toyota's production shutdown in Japan, which was due entirely to the damage caused by the shutdown of one of its suppliers, Tokyo-based Riken Corp. This supplier supplies engine parts to a host of global OEMs. Toyota said it would cease production at all 12 of its domestic plants after a 6.8-magnitude earthquake damaged the main production facilities of Riken Corp. Japan's No. 1 car maker by sales had to stop production for at least three shifts. Despite applying lean inventory management practices, the plants had a supply of parts that kept them running during the first few days after the quake hit.

Most important of all, this one supply disruption impacted several other car makers, which also said their production also was affected. Mitsubishi Motors Corp., Japan's No. 4 car maker, said it suspended production for at least three days at three of its major assembly plants. The company sent 40 of its engineers to the Riken plant to help get it up and running again. Suzuki Motor Corp. said it suffered from a production loss of about 10,000 cars and 5,000 motorcycles because of a temporary shutdown at five domestic plants. Fuji Heavy Industries Ltd., which makes the Subaru brand of vehicles, also halted production at five plants. Honda Motor Co. and Nissan Motor Co., which also depend on Riken for engine parts, were impacted.

The widespread impact highlights how auto companies are relying on a common parts maker for a crucial part of their product. Riken is Japan's biggest maker of piston rings for engines and of seal rings, which prevent leaks in transmissions. It provides parts for more than half the cars built in Japan and about 20% of cars worldwide, according to the company, including vehicles from Ford Motor Co., BMW AG, and Volkswagen AG. A Volkswagen spokesperson in Germany said the company's production hadn't been affected. A BMW spokesperson couldn't say whether production would be affected. Ford couldn't be reached.

Riken has plants in and around Kashiwazaki, the city most severely struck by the quake. The earthquake killed nine and destroyed hundreds of homes.

Source: A. Chozick, "Japan's Car Makers Stall after Quake Hits Supplier," *Wall Street Journal,* July 19, 2007, p. A3.

7. Formal Business Unit Trust Development Efforts

A major responsibility of supply management is to provide information to suppliers involved in a new-product development project. Sharing of information can help avoid unwelcome surprises throughout the life of a project, particularly if suppliers are brought in early in the concept stage to design parts. If supply management selects capable and trustworthy suppliers, it should be able to share product information early in the development process. For example, if a component for a new part requires a specific production process, it is important to make sure the supplier has the required process capability. Early visibility to product requirements allows supply management to share critical information with suppliers that can help avoid delays. In turn, suppliers will be expected to share their information with the new-product development team. To build this level of trust may require that parties sign appropriate nondisclosure or confidentiality agreements prior to meeting. These types of agreements are covered in Chapter 16.

8. Sharing of Technology between Buyer and Supplier Companies

Supply management must work closely with engineering to determine whether there is a common convergence in technology strategies with the supplier. The most common reference to this concept is a **technology roadmap**, which refers to the set of performance criteria and products and processes an organization intends to develop or manufacture. Many companies define their technology roadmaps in terms of the next decade, whereas others employ a horizon of 50 years or even a century! Although the exact form of a technology roadmap is somewhat industry specific, it typically is defined in the following terms:

- Projected performance specifications for a class of products or processes (e.g., memory size, speed, electrical resistance, temperature, or pressure)
- An intention to integrate a new material or component (e.g., a new form of molecule or chemical)
- Development of a product to meet customer requirements that is currently unavailable in the market (e.g., new television screen technology)
- Integration of multiple complementary technologies that results in a radical new product (e.g., a combined fax/phone/modem/copier, or combining television, cable, and computer technology)
- A combination of the above as well as other possible variations

9. Joint Education and Training Efforts

Achieving this level of involvement, however, may prove difficult for personnel on both sides of the fence. Some of the typical concerns that arise in these scenarios include the following:

- Unwillingness of internal design personnel to relinquish responsibility
- Concerns over sharing proprietary information—both buyer and supplier
- Lack of business processes to support integration
- Lack of cultural alignment

To overcome these problems, personnel at both the buyer and supplier may need to be educated regarding the benefits of the integration effort, as well as be assured that the proper confidentiality agreements have been completed. In addition, engineering staff may require further education to ensure that they realize that they are not relinquishing their authority over design; another member is simply coming in to provide additional insights that will lead to a better product and a more satisfied customer.

Supplier Integration into Customer Order Fulfillment

Many companies are continuing to integrate suppliers not just in the product development phase, but also in the order fulfillment phase of the product life cycle. Suppliers can provide significant benefits in the form of lower costs, improved delivery, lower inventory, and problem-solving capabilities during the fulfillment stage of production. Supplier integration takes place in various forms, including supplier suggestion programs, buyer-seller improvement teams, and on-site supplier representatives.

Supplier Suggestion Programs

Suppliers can be an invaluable source of ideas for process improvement. They bring with them a different expertise, a different point of view, and a greater volume of ideas. Supply management groups are missing out on a great source of expertise when they do not tap into suppliers' suggestions. Suppliers may submit suggestions through an Internet site, at a formal meeting, or during supplier conferences. Typically, a supplier will submit a proposal using a standard form that identifies the nature of the improvement, impact areas, estimated savings, and business unit or functional area of application. The suggestion is assigned a tracking number, to ensure that the idea is not lost in the cracks! The suggestion then goes through a formal internal review, which may consist of multiple stages. The review team will use the following criteria in assessing the suggestion:

- Feasibility
- Resources required
- Potential savings
- Go/no-go decision
- Feedback to supplier

As a result of this review, the implementation team accepts or rejects the suggestion. Accepted suggestions may go through further refinement, and the supplier may be formally involved and given the go-ahead to proceed. Results from the suggestion will then be tracked.

Successful supplier suggestion programs tend to have several elements in common. First, the savings from the suggestion are often shared 50/50, not kept solely by the buying company. This encourages the supplier to provide further suggestions. Second, the program focuses on cost improvement, not simply cutting the supplier's margins. Third, successful buying companies provide prompt feedback to the supplier on its suggestion and also implement good suggestions promptly. This sends a clear message that the supplier's idea is being taken seriously. It is important to do more than just put the focus on suppliers' problems. Other opportunities for improvement may include those in the buying company, in intercompany communication and processes, and even within second-tier suppliers. Finally, it is critical to acknowledge the supplier's suggestion, through an awards program, newsletter, or announcement at a supplier conference.

Buyer-Seller Improvement Teams

More and more companies are involving suppliers on improvement teams in a variety of different areas. Why? Research reveals that teams that relied on supplier input and involvement (when the task warranted involvement) were more effective in their task, on average, than teams that did not involve suppliers.[18] Teams that include suppliers as participants report positive outcomes and great supplier contributions across many performance areas, including the following:

- Providing cost reduction ideas
- Providing quality improvement ideas
- Supporting actions to improve material delivery
- Offering process technology suggestions
- Supporting material-ordering cycle time reductions

Also, teams that included suppliers as participants reported other important outcomes:

- Greater satisfaction concerning the quality of information exchange between the team and key suppliers
- Higher reliance on suppliers to directly support the team's goals—the supplier is a resource
- Fewer problems coordinating work activity between the team and key suppliers
- Greater effort put forth on team assignment

A manager at Honeywell described the advantages of working on a buyer-seller improvement team when it came time to quickly identify and solve a quality problem with a major customer.[19] He noted: "Customers came to us with a product quality problem, and eventually we traced it back to the supplier. We had problems with the supplier's product, and we identified the problem as occurring because their process had shifted. Initially, we went to process quality assurance with the problem and confronted them. At first, the supplier refused to believe that it was their fault, and claimed that we were not using the material correctly. Our group leader for the product team found it difficult to coordinate with the supplier and therefore requested an in-house person from their facility to work with us. The problem was resolved through many teleconferences, meetings at their facility, checking their processes, supplier teams coming to our plant, and many exchanges on specifications via e-mail, fax, etc. They identified the problem in their process, and since then they are performing very well. There was clearly a learning phase in transitioning from a traditional relationship, but resolving this problem clearly showed how to work together to strengthen our relationship."

On-Site Supplier Representative

Many companies are encouraging suppliers to provide a permanent on-site representative who can aid the company in improving customer order fulfillment processes. The idea behind this initiative (called **vendor-managed inventory** in some circles) is to have the representative assist in managing the inventory of materials or services, provide technical support, and in some cases even aid in assembling and producing the product or service! On-site suppliers are established when the purchaser empowers a supplier representative to work on-site to perform various tasks. The supplier assumes administrative costs and assigns a full-time or part-time representative to be physically co-located on-site.

There are a number of purchase categories where an on-site supplier representative can be used, including the following:

- Waste management
- Printing services
- Spare parts inventory and other MRO items
- Computer equipment and software
- Office furniture
- Uniforms and protective equipment

- Process control equipment
- Production parts
- Transportation services
- Production maintenance

On-site representatives can be used in a number of functional areas as well.

Supply Management

An on-site supplier representative can process purchase transactions between customer and supplier using the customer's supply management system and purchase orders. In addition, the on-site rep can work cooperatively with the customer's planner to ensure timely and efficient delivery of materials. In some cases, the on-site representative can also assume a buyer-planner role and coordinate multiple facilities. It should be noted that the on-site rep places orders only at the established price and only with the supplier company involved.

Sales

An on-site supplier rep may perform the routine responsibilities of a traditional sales representative. The supplier is empowered to sell directly to internal units from an on-site location. This can often result in a reduction in the supplier's overhead cost structure for this particular customer, because a good portion of overhead goes to budgeting for a sales force.

Engineering

Preferred suppliers can reside on-site and are empowered to provide design support under the supervision of customer engineers. These full-time, on-site supplier representatives act as resident information resources. The customer can thus utilize supplier ideas and expertise at the earliest stages of product and process development.

Transportation

Overseas transportation modes (surface, air, ocean, foreign brokerage) may be combined into one location controlled at the customer's site. Suppliers of freight services provide professional on-site support to the using location and can create a command center for coordination of all inbound and outbound transportation within the supply chain.

Potential Benefits of On-Site Supplier Representatives

A number of benefits can occur for both parties in a supplier representative situation. These are also summarized in the form of a win-win proposition shown in Exhibit 4.7.

- Customer-supplier coordination and integration are increased.
- Supplier personnel work on-site to support the purchaser.
- Supply management staff are increased.
- Supplier in-plant personnel perform various buying and planning activities, allowing supply management staff to pursue other value-added activities.

Exhibit 4.7 Win-Win Elements of On-Site Supplier Representatives

Customer Wins with:

Supplier Wins with:	Consignment Inventory	Direct-Floor Stocking	Releases from Rolling Forecast	Resident at Customer
More Business	X	X		X
Access to New Designs				X
Stabilized Production	X	X	X	
Fewer Transactions	X	X	X	
Quicker Payments	X			
Less Selling Expense	X	X		X
Assured Sales		X	X	X
Access to Information Earlier			X	X

The supplier also wins with the following:

- Increased supplier insight into customer needs and access to new designs
- Daily interface with customer personnel concerning current and future customer needs
- Increased supplier production efficiency
- Increased insight, leading to fewer schedule changes and surprises
- Reduced transaction costs
- Reduced inventory
- On-site material plan development using a customer's systems in a real-time mode

Although doing business in this mode is very new for most companies, more and more companies are exploring the benefits of increased supplier integration in customer order fulfillment processes, as shown in Exhibit 4.8 on p. 148.

Exhibit 4.8 Good Practice: ESI at MRD

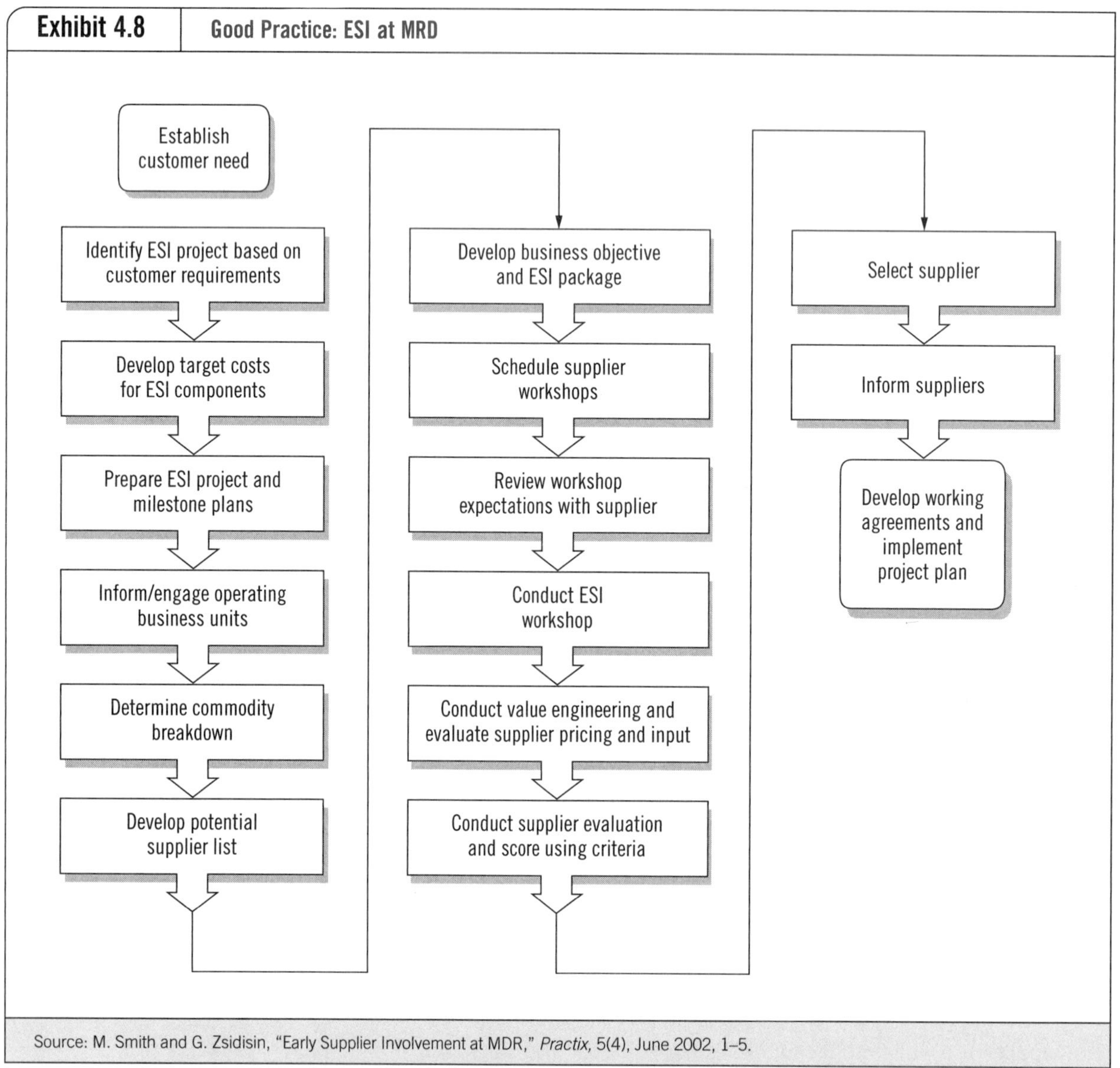

Source: M. Smith and G. Zsidisin, "Early Supplier Involvement at MDR," *Practix,* 5(4), June 2002, 1–5.

Good Practice Example

Caterpillar Works with Delco to Achieve Mutually Beneficial Outcomes

Over the last decade, Caterpillar Inc. has worked closely with Delco Electronics (now known as Delphi) to create a highly integrated relationship. It first approached Delco Electronics in 1997 with the opportunity to compete for the strategic position as its electronics supplier. Two factors were driving this opportunity. The first was that Caterpillar was dissatisfied with its current supplier. The second was that it wanted to reduce its in-house electronics capability to allow it to focus more on its core business. In the case of Caterpillar, the buyer has had two distinct roles.

As a participant in the strategic supplier selection, the buyer was involved in an extensive process to evaluate suppliers and ultimately recommend to senior management a supplier to assume the role of strategic supplier. This process lasted six to eight months. It involved numerous visits by the team to Delco Electronics' headquarters, engineering facilities, and manufacturing facilities. It included quoting several different scenarios ranging from build-to-print to design-and-build. Quoting was a benchmarking exercise to understand capability and not an exercise to set pricing. The evaluation included several Delco Electronics visits to meet with Caterpillar's engineering groups and present its execution, quality, and cost reduction plans in the event of being selected. It included several rounds of discussions.

Delco Electronics received word through the buyer that it had been selected to be the strategic supplier of electronics to Caterpillar. It was at this point that the buyer's role switched to that of executor of the strategy. At this point, Delco Electronics had not yet been awarded any business. Shortly after the announcement, the buyer presented a preliminary draft of an agreement that started something like this: "Delco Electronics has agreed to supply Caterpillar 100% of its electronics requirements for the next five years. . . . " He also restated the strategy outlined during the selection process. This consisted of Delco Electronics starting immediately to supply existing products on a build-to-print basis and evolving to a design-and-build basis. He also explained the Caterpillar business model for pricing.

From that point forward, the buyer's role was to ensure successful execution of the strategy. The buyer spent his time ensuring that the two companies were developing the right working relationship. He had weekly meetings with all team members, ensured that deliverables were met, and escalated issues in both Delco Electronics and Caterpillar. He and other Caterpillar participants attended prototype builds at the Delco Electronics manufacturing site. When new programs were identified, he would attend the Sanctioning Body Approval event, the first formal gate in the Delco Electronics Product Development Process. His attendance was focused on ensuring that Delco Electronics was ready to start the development of the new program. Did it have resources in place? Did it understand the technical requirements? Was it linked up with the correct Caterpillar technical resources? Early in the relationship the team established a regular cadence of management meetings. The buyer always attended and assumed the prime Caterpillar lead role. On pricing there was no competitive bidding. There were discussions pertaining to volume and recovery of engineering content.

Much of this activity continues today at a much higher level of maturity as both companies have nourished the relationship. Throughout, Caterpillar never lost any sleep over the success of Delco Electronics as a supplier. The buyer clearly felt responsibility for the outcome. There was no hand-off to others in the organization or to other organizations. Today, Delphi is involved in more than 20 electronics programs with Caterpillar worth millions of dollars. As the business has grown, the buyer's office has expanded to include a senior buyer, two buyers, and a person involved in quality and readiness issues. Although there have been changes in personnel over the years, clarity of ownership has not changed 10 years later!

Questions

1. Review Caterpillar's process for early supplier involvement. What was critical to the success of the relationship?
2. How important was the role of specific individuals involved in the discussion? What does this say about the importance of trust in managing buyer-supplier relationships in such an environment, and the role of individuals in the relationship?
3. How were the risks minimized? Do you believe the benefits in this case outweighed these potential risks?

Source: Interviews with Caterpillar and Delphi executives, 2007.

CONCLUSION

This chapter discussed the need for supply management to develop closer relations with internal and external groups. To accomplish this, supply management professionals must develop a working knowledge of the principles of engineering, manufacturing, cost-based accounting, quality assurance, and team dynamics. The days are over when supply management could operate in a confined area with only an occasional visit to a supplier.

Firms are using the team approach to streamline and improve the product development process. This directly affects firms that rely on innovative new products for their continued success. Supply management has a key role to play on these teams. In its role, supply management helps select suppliers for inclusion in the process, advises engineering personnel of suppliers' capabilities, and helps negotiate contracts once the product team has selected a supplier. Supply management also acts as a liaison throughout this process, in facilitating supplier participation at team meetings and helping to resolve conflicts between the supplier and the team when they occur. Supply management may also be involved in developing a target price for the supplier to aim at while planning the component or system, and helping the supplier to analyze costs and identify ways of meeting this target price. Finally, supply management may also be involved in developing nondisclosure and confidentiality agreements in cases where technology sharing occurs.

Part of the increased interaction between supply management and other functions is due to the need to compete in an environment driven by reduced product cycle times. Supply management supports this effort by developing closer internal and external relationships and by participating on cross-functional teams. Those interested in the supply management profession should learn as much as they can about what it takes to compete in today's markets, including expanding their knowledge about the team approach as well as understanding how firms compete on cost, quality, and time. The need to interact effectively with different groups plays a major role in how well supply management can accomplish its tasks.

KEY TERMS

black box design, 140
collaboration, 122
cross-functional sourcing teams, 127
gray box design, 140
groupthink, 131
integration, 114
meaningful task, 132
process loss, 130
relationship management (RM) skills, 115
supply integration, 114
technology roadmap, 143
vendor-managed inventory, 145
white box design, 140

DISCUSSION QUESTIONS

1. Describe the different types of integration that supply management should become actively involved in.
2. Describe the types of information and data that supply management may share with different internal and external functions.
3. What are the barriers to integration? How can they be overcome?
4. Research with cross-functional sourcing teams revealed that teams that included suppliers as active team participants put forth greater effort, on average, than

teams that did not include suppliers. Discuss why the involvement of external suppliers can positively affect a team's effort.

5. Why is goal setting so important to the success of the sourcing team process? What is the role of the team leader when setting team goals?
6. Relatively few individuals have the qualifications, experience, and training to immediately assume demanding sourcing team leadership positions. Do you agree or disagree with this statement? Why?
7. Describe the traditional model of buyer-seller relationships. How is the traditional model different from the collaborative model? What are the major characteristics of the collaborative model?
8. Describe a typical technology roadmap for a manufacturer of PCs. How does this affect supply management's activities in the new-product development cycle?
9. Discuss the most important elements that characterize the most successful efforts at integrating suppliers in new-product development. How do these factors contribute to success?
10. What types of information can a supplier provide that are useful during new-product development?
11. What is the difference between a gray box and a black box approach to early supplier involvement? Under what circumstances might each approach be appropriate?
12. What criteria are most important when considering whether a supplier should be involved in a new-product development effort?

ADDITIONAL READINGS

Cousins, P., Handfield, R., Lawson, B., and Peterson, K. (2006), "Creating Supply Chain Relational Capital: The Impact of Formal and Informal Socialization Processes," *Journal of Operations Management,* 24(6), 851–864.

Handfield, R., and Bechtel, C. (2001), "The Role of Trust and Relationship Structure in Improving Supply Chain Responsiveness," *Industrial Marketing Management,* 31, 1–16.

Handfield, R., Ragatz, G., Monczka, R., and Peterson, K. (1999), "Involving Suppliers in New Product Development," *California Management Review,* 42(1), 59–82.

Handfield, R., Ragatz, G., and Peterson, K. (2003), "A Model of Supplier Integration into New Product Development," *Journal of Product Innovation Management,* 20(4), 284–299.

Monczka, R., Frayer, D., Handfield, R., Ragatz, G., and Scannell, T. (2000), *Supplier Integration into New Product/Process Development: Best Practices,* Milwaukee, WI: ASQ Quality Press.

Monczka, R. M., and Trent, R. J. (1993), *Cross-Functional Sourcing Team Effectiveness,* Tempe, AZ: Center for Advanced Supply Management Studies.

Monczka, R. M., and Trent, R. J. (1994), "Cross-Functional Sourcing Team Effectiveness: Critical Success Factors," *International Journal of Supply Management and Materials Management,* Fall, 2–11.

Trent, R. J. (1996), "Understanding and Evaluating Cross-Functional Sourcing Team Leadership," *International Journal of Supply Management and Materials Management,* Fall, 29–36.

Trent, R. J. (1998), "Individual and Collective Team Effort: A Vital Part of Sourcing Team Success," *International Journal of Supply Management and Materials Management,* Fall, 46–54.

Ward, N., Handfield, R., and Cousins, P. (2007), "Stepping Up on SRM," *CPO Agenda,* Summer, 42–47.

ENDNOTES

1. Giunipero, L. (2004), *Purchasing Education and Training Part II,* Tempe, AZ: Center for Advanced Purchasing Studies.
2. Spekman, R. E. (1988), "Strategic Supplier Selection: Understanding Long-Term Buyer Relationships," *Business Horizons,* 31(4), 76.
3. Ward, N., Handfield, R., and Cousins, P. "Stepping Up on SRM," *CPO Agenda,* Summer, 42–47.
4. Ward et al.
5. Ward et al.
6. Ward et al.
7. Ward et al.
8. Russell, R. D. (1990), "Innovation in Organizations: Toward an Integrated Model," *Review of Business,* 12(2), 19.
9. Ward et al.
10. Ward et al.
11. Steiner, I. D. (1972), *Group Process and Productivity,* New York: Academic Press, p. 88.
12. Janis, I. L. (1982), *Groupthink: Psychological Studies of Policy Decisions and Fiascoes,* Boston: Houghton Mifflin, p. 9.
13. Monczka, R. M., and Trent, R. J. (1993), *Cross-Functional Sourcing Team Effectiveness,* Tempe, AZ: Center for Advanced Supply Management Studies.
14. Peters, L. H., and O'Connor, E. J. (1980), "Situational Constraints and Work Outcomes: The Influences of a Frequently Overlooked Construct," *Academy of Management Review,* 5(3), 391–397.
15. Zenger, J., et al. (1994), *Leading Teams: Mastering the New Role,* Homewood, IL: Irwin, pp. 14–15.
16. Monczka, R. M., and Trent, R. J. (1994), "Effective Cross-Functional Sourcing Teams: Critical Success Factors," *International Journal of Supply Management and Materials Management,* 30(4), 7–8.
17. Monczka, R., Handfield, R., Ragatz, G., Frayer, D., and Scannell, T. (2000), *Supplier Integration into New Product/Process Development: Best Practices,* Milwaukee, WI: ASQ Press.
18. Monczka and Trent.
19. Monczka et al.

Chapter 5

PURCHASING AND SUPPLY CHAIN ORGANIZATION

Learning Objectives

After completing this chapter, you should be able to

- Recognize the role of organizational design in enabling purchasing and supply chain success
- Understand the factors that influence organizational design in purchasing and supply chain
- Recognize the differences between centralized, decentralized, and hybrid forms of the purchasing organization
- Understand the team concept and its influence and roadblocks to adoption in purchasing and supply chain
- Identify features of the supply organization of the future

Chapter Outline

Harley-Davidson Creates a High-Powered Purchasing Organization

Harley-Davidson, a pre-eminent maker of heavy motorcycles, learned the hard way about the need for a high-powered purchasing organization. Faced with declining sales, poor quality, and once-loyal customers switching to Japanese motorcycles, managers at this once-proud company knew they had to reinvent how they did business if they expected to rejuvenate the Harley-Davidson brand. Creating the right supply organization became a central feature of this reinvention. The results today speak for themselves. The saying at the company is that it "began as the motor company, it became a family" by realizing that every member of the family has a stake in the company's success. The financial results indicate the company's philosophy is working. In 2006 total revenue grew by 8.6% to $5.8 billion. Net income also rose to $1.04 billion, an increase of 8.7%. Part of this success is due to the successful re-engineering of the purchasing function.

For many years, Harley-Davidson maintained a traditional approach to purchasing. The company haphazardly selected suppliers and evaluated purchase costs, kept suppliers at a distance, and positioned purchasing as a lower-level function where engineers made crucial buying decisions. This approach mirrored the company's financial performance, which declined to the point that its very survival was in question.

Today's Harley-Davidson is nothing like the Harley of the mid-1980s and early 1990s. Quality is strong, new products are introduced on a regular basis, demand is outpacing supply, and customer loyalty has never been higher. And at the center of this resurgence is a purchasing organization that has become the benchmark for others to study.

While Harley-Davidson has taken many steps to restore its luster, some of the more important changes center on creating the right purchasing organization. One of the company's more important changes involved creating a higher-level position to lead the charge in supply management. A new vice president of materials and product costs brought a vision to help articulate company objectives through materials management strategies, elevate the visibility of the purchasing organization, encourage suppliers to work directly with Harley, and help the company adopt a unique Internet-based strategy to make communication with suppliers more efficient.

The new vice president wasted no time in creating an on-site residency program for suppliers to participate in during the development of new products. Fifty full-time resident (i.e., on-site) suppliers and 80 part-time residents take part in new-product design. Suppliers participate in design meetings to help Harley-Davidson's engineering teams improve quality while reducing costs. This interaction takes place at the company's Product Development Center in Milwaukee and brings together design, engineering, manufacturing, and suppliers in an atmosphere that promotes supply chain collaboration.

The vice president also recognized the importance of having purchasing personnel work directly with engineers. He created the position of purchasing engineer, which requires a combination of commercial and technical knowledge and skills. Purchasing engineers support product design and manufacturing teams and have responsibility for integrating suppliers into Harley-Davidson's processes. Purchasing professionals are also co-located with engineers so purchasing can work side-by-side with engineering, providing that group with a better feel for cost issues at the early stages of product design. Purchasing brings knowledge of sourcing, alternative materials, and information on new technology. Because of purchasing's involvement, engineering, a group that traditionally did not consider costs a top priority, now considers costs more closely when designing new products.

Another part of Harley-Davidson's organizational design is the company's Supplier Advisory Council. This council, which meets on a regular basis, features executive-to-executive interaction between Harley-Davidson and a rotating group of critical suppliers. In general, these councils share product development plans and supply chain information, create joint measures of success, create a co-destiny and trust between members, and work to align long-range goals and technology development.

The purchasing organization is structured in a center-led philosophy with four major categories. The categories are listed below, and one can see there are differences in the focus that individual suppliers need to address to be successful in selling to Harley-Davidson:

1. General Merchandise—Much of the focus and energy is spent in the area of new-product development due to the shorter product life cycles.
2. Maintenance, Repair, and Operating (MRO)—Suppliers are critical to the success of Harley-Davidson in that the products and services they provide ensure continual production and acquisition of quality products.
3. Original Equipment—A supplier's initial involvement with Harley-Davidson is likely to be with a purchasing engineer from the Product Development Centers. Purchasing leads a cross-functional group of stakeholders in the supplier selection process.
4. Parts and Accessories—Because of their shorter life cycles, much of the focus and energy of this group is spent in the area of new-product development. Suppliers must recognize that due to this shorter product life cycle, much emphasis is placed upon a shorter product development cycle. Failure to address this requirement can lead to a missed opportunity in the market. Service parts usually have longer life cycles than accessories.

Over the last several years, income has grown faster than sales, and purchased costs have shrunk by $37 million. This compares with the $40 million increase that would have occurred if purchasing had continued to let costs increase at the historical level of 1.5 to 2%. And, most suppliers now supply materials on a just-in-time basis, further reducing inventory-carrying costs. So, has Harley-Davidson's purchasing organization helped the company? You be the judge!

Source: Harley-Davidson website (www.hdsn.com/genbus/PublicDocServlet?docID=19&docExt=pdf); and B. Milligan, "Harley-Davidson Wins by Getting Suppliers on Board," *Purchasing*, September 21, 2000, pp. 52–60.

When considering the many ways to create competitive advantage through supply management efforts, we often hear about exciting initiatives involving information technology, outsourcing, cost management techniques, or strategic relationships. Rarely discussed, however, is how the more mundane topic of organizational design can promote or impede the attainment of procurement and supply objectives. Except perhaps for cross-functional teaming, organizational design does not receive much attention within supply management.

Organizational design refers to the process of assessing and selecting the structure and formal system of communication, division of labor, coordination, control, authority, and responsibility required to achieve organizational goals and objectives, including supply management objectives. Although charts may illustrate the formal design of an organization, they present an incomplete picture. The design of an organization is much more than a series of lines and boxes on an organizational chart.[1]

An effective (or ineffective) organizational design affects the success of purchasing and inevitably the entire organization. This chapter explores purchasing within the context of a formal organization, which requires the presentation of certain topics:

- Purchasing's position within the organizational structure
- Organizing the purchasing function
- Placement of purchasing authority
- Organizing for supply chain management
- Using teams as part of the organizational structure
- Creating the organization of the future

Purchasing's Position within the Organizational Structure

A formal organizational structure serves several purposes. First, it shows the assignment of work along with the authority that accompanies those responsibilities. Second, a formal structure helps define how a firm communicates and integrates decision making across the groups comprising the organization (a process also referred to as **coordination**).[2]

Our concern here is with the physical position or placement of purchasing in the organizational hierarchy or reporting structure. Why is purchasing's position or placement in an organizational structure important? Basically, the physical placement and reporting relationship of a function usually indicate its organizational status and influence. A function whose highest responsible executive is a manager (or even several managers) lacks the organizational importance of a function whose highest responsible executive is a senior vice president. In some organizations, the highest purchasing professional's reporting status is on a par with other major functions. In others, we have to search before finding an individual executive responsible for purchasing. The trends shown in recent research support the fact that purchasing is gaining more visibility in the corporate hierarchy. The results of a study covering 16 years indicated that in both manufacturing and services, chief purchasing officers (CPOs) have greater responsibilities, report higher in the organization, and carry more significant titles than their predecessors.[3] This section presents some of the factors influencing purchasing's position or placement in the formal organizational structure.

Factors Affecting Purchasing's Position in the Organizational Hierarchy

History

Perhaps the most important factor contributing to purchasing's position in the organizational hierarchy is history. For established organizations, early purchasing history emphasized the gradual development of the policies and procedures defining proper purchasing from an operational perspective. For many years, many viewed an assignment in purchasing as a career with few prospects for promotion or increased decision making. In recent years, however, this trend has been reversing. Purchasing is slowly but surely receiving greater attention from executive management.

Type of Industry

Some industries are not as driven by materials or external technological change as others. The need to constantly innovate and improve often places materials-related activities at a higher level compared with mature industries or those with a history of treating purchasing as a lower-level function. In rapidly changing industries or those where purchased goods and services comprise a larger portion of product or service costs, management usually recognizes the need to place purchasing in a higher position within the organizational hierarchy.

Total Value of Goods and Services

Companies such as John Deere, Honda, and DaimlerChrysler spend 60 to 70% of their sales dollars on purchased goods and services. In the computer and telecommunications industries, companies such as Nortel Networks, Solectron, IBM, Cisco, Hewlett-Packard, and Sun rely on suppliers for parts as well as new technology—which means that purchasing plays a critical role. A service organization spending 10 to 20% of its sales dollar for purchased goods and services will, on average, view purchasing differently compared with a firm spending over 60%.

Other Factors

The philosophy of the founder (particularly when the founder still plays an active role) exerts a strong influence on an organization's formal design. This is especially true in high-technology organizations started during the last 25 years. If the founder is marketing oriented, the firm usually has a strong marketing perspective. If the founder is engineering oriented, the emphasis is usually on product and process development. The founder of Herman Miller Inc., a producer of industrial office furniture, believed that organizations should be the "stewards" of the environment. Consequently, purchasing plays a strong role at that company in emphasizing environmental responsibility.

The type of purchased materials affects organizational position. The purchase of routine items is quite different from the purchase of leading-edge high technology. Purchasing departments confronted with fast-paced change usually have closer contact with other functional groups and a higher organizational reporting level.

The ability to influence a company's performance is another factor affecting purchasing's position. When purchasing can strongly affect competitiveness, purchasing assumes a higher position in the organizational structure. The ability to influence performance is such a critical factor that it often overrides any other factor that previously supported a lower purchasing profile.

To Whom Does Purchasing Report?

A clear trend during the last 25 years is that the level of executive to whom purchasing reports has increased. Bloom and Nardone reported that "during the 1950s and early 1960s, a high percentage of the purchasing departments reported in a second-level capacity to the functional managers, most commonly production and operations."[4]

A study by the Center for Advanced Purchasing Studies (CAPS) revealed a change in the reporting level of purchasing during the 1980s.[5] The study found that in almost 35% of the organizations surveyed, the highest purchasing executive reported to a senior or group vice president or higher. The percentage of CPOs reporting to a top-five executive position category has continued to increase. One research study indicated that in 2003, 70% of the responding CPOs reported to a top-five executive, up from 61% in 1995 and 44% in 1987.[6] Another study indicated this was higher in smaller firms, which, because of their simplified structures, tend to have their highest purchasing or supply manager report to higher organizational levels. Purchasing reports to the highest executive or one level from the highest executive in almost 90% of smaller firms. Purchasing reports to the highest executive or one level from the highest executive in almost 65% of medium and large firms (based on sales).[7]

Exhibit 5.1 illustrates three possible placements of purchasing in the organizational hierarchy. In (a), purchasing is an upper-level function reporting directly to the executive vice president. In (b), purchasing is a mid-level function reporting to an executive one level below the executive vice president, which is a common reporting level today. In (c), purchasing reports at least two reporting levels from the executive vice president.

Is the reporting level of purchasing important? One research study found that having a higher-level procurement officer who makes regular presentations to the president or chief executive officer (CEO) is the design feature that correlates highest with the achievement of procurement and supply objectives.[8] In general, the higher that purchasing is in the corporate structure, the greater the role it plays in supporting organizational objectives.

Organizing the Purchasing Function

Each functional group, and even department, has its own organizational structure. Exhibit 5.2 on p. 160, for example, presents the organizational structure for a high-tech company's sourcing office in China. With this chart, we begin to see the division of duties and the formal reporting structure among the participants. This section discusses the organization of the functional activity called purchasing into specialized subgroups.

Specialization within Purchasing

Purchasing departments in larger organizations usually structure themselves to support specialized purchasing activities, which are grouped into four major areas: (1) sourcing and negotiating; (2) purchasing research; (3) operational support and order follow-up; and (4) administration and support. It is not efficient or practical to have all purchasing personnel responsible for every task located within each group. Instead, most purchasing departments organize into specialized subgroups.

Sourcing and Negotiating

This group identifies potential suppliers, negotiates with selected suppliers, and performs the buying of goods and services. Buyers are usually responsible for a specific range or type of item(s), which may be grouped into commodities or services categories. For example, plastic injected parts are an example of a purchase commodity. Trash removal and security are examples of services. Other buyers may specialize in raw materials and are responsible for steel, copper, packaging supplies, and so on. Regardless of the commodity or service, higher-dollar items will involve extensive negotiations with suppliers. Very often, buyers will work in teams that have responsibility for negotiating contracts for the entire organization.

Exhibit 5.1 Purchasing at Different Organizational Levels

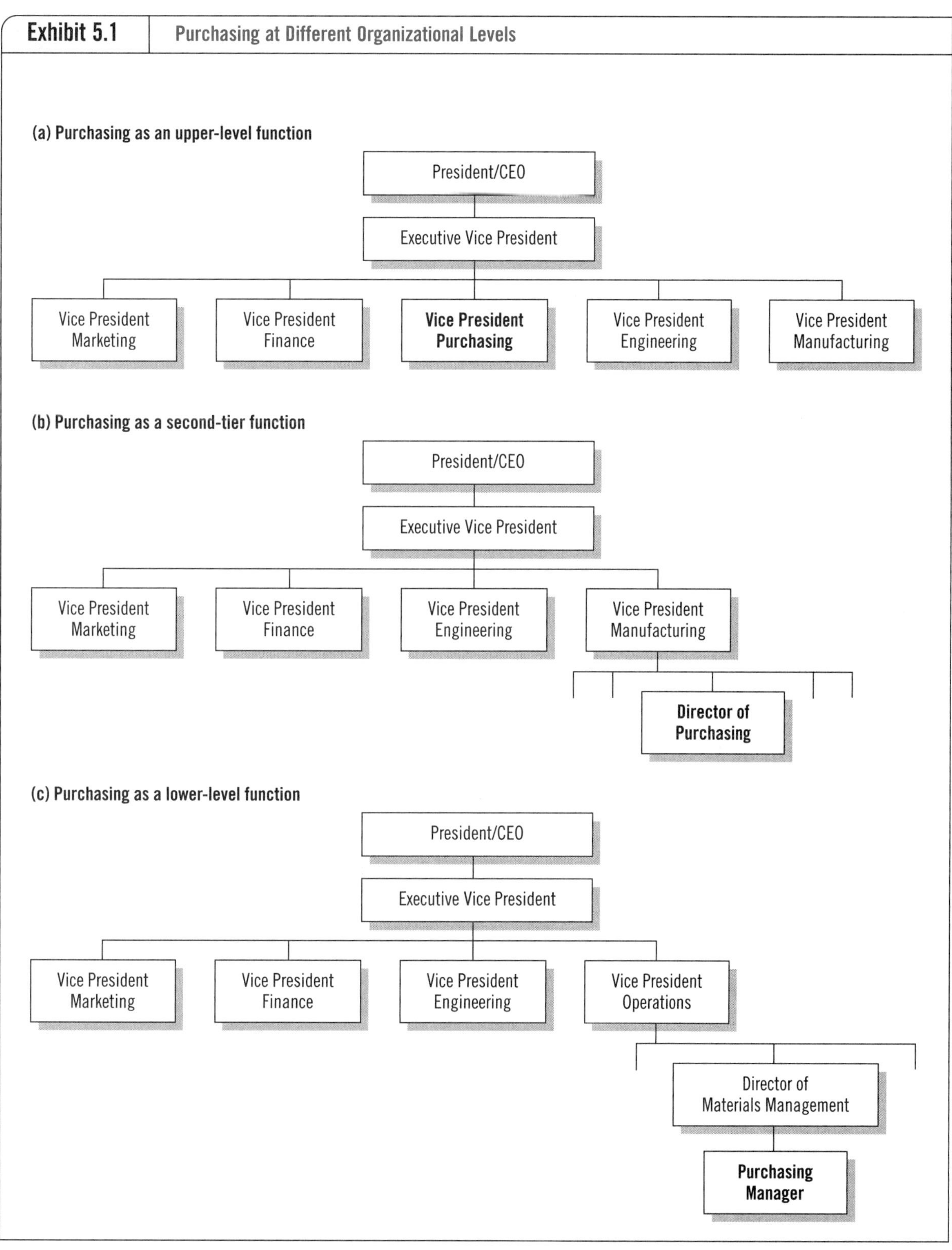
(a) Purchasing as an upper-level function
President/CEO
Executive Vice President
Vice President Marketing
Vice President Finance
Vice President Purchasing
Vice President Engineering
Vice President Manufacturing
(b) Purchasing as a second-tier function
President/CEO
Executive Vice President
Vice President Marketing
Vice President Finance
Vice President Engineering
Vice President Manufacturing
Director of Purchasing
(c) Purchasing as a lower-level function
President/CEO
Executive Vice President
Vice President Marketing
Vice President Finance
Vice President Engineering
Vice President Operations
Director of Materials Management
Purchasing Manager

Exhibit 5.2 Organizational Chart for International Purchasing Office

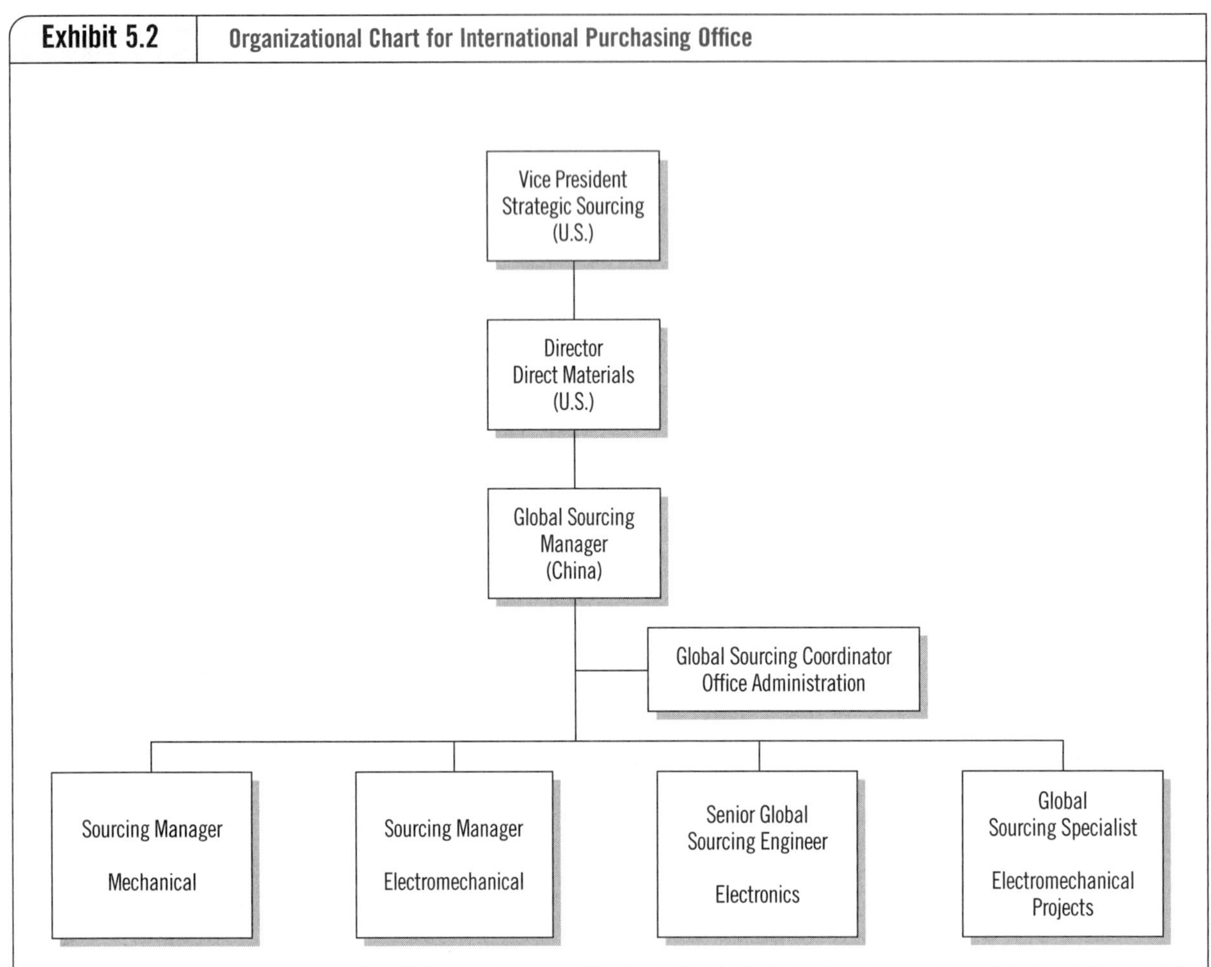

Purchasing Research

Purchasing research involves developing long-range materials forecasts, conducting value analysis programs, assessing supplier capabilities, and analyzing the cost structure of suppliers. Although some of these specialized tasks are the responsibility of individual buyers, more and more organizations recognize the benefit of having specialized research personnel. The development of product and material plans requires detailed and accurate research.

Operational Support and Order Follow-Up

This group includes the activities supporting the day-to-day operations of the purchasing or materials function. Order expediters and follow-up personnel are part of this group. The preparation and transfer of material releases to suppliers is also part of the operational support process. Many of the tasks that qualify as operational support are being streamlined or automated, especially with the advent of business-to-business (B2B) e-commerce technologies. As a result, the number of purchasing personnel committed to these types of tasks is declining. Because operational support activities represent a poor use of a buyer's time, organizations are increasingly developing two categories of purchasers: strategically oriented and tactical. Strategically oriented buyers focus on the company and industry future by managing total cost, enhancing value, and minimizing risks, whereas tactical buyers focus more on the day-to-day challenges required to meet the organization's current needs.[9]

Administration and Support

This group is responsible for developing the policies and procedures that purchasing personnel follow, administering and maintaining the purchasing information system and database, determining required staffing levels, developing department plans, organizing training and seminars for buyers, and developing measurement systems to evaluate purchasing performance. This group concerns itself with making sure the purchasing department runs smoothly and meets its targeted goals within budget, and fulfills its responsibilities to both internal and external customers.

Purchasing Department Activities

Today's purchasing department does much more than the traditional buying of materials, parts, and services. The role of purchasing is expanding to reflect the growing importance of purchasing and the performance contribution of suppliers. The following responsibilities are commonly performed tasks performed by a modern purchasing group. Not all departments perform every one of these tasks. The trend, however, is for more of these assignments to become purchasing's responsibility.

Buying

By definition, a primary responsibility of the purchasing function involves buying—a broad term describing the purchase of raw materials, components, finished goods, or services from suppliers, some of whom can be another operating unit within the organization. The purchase can be a one-time requirement or the release for materials against an established purchase order. The buying process requires supplier evaluation, negotiation, and selection.

Expediting

Expediting is the process of personally or electronically contacting suppliers to determine the status of past-due or near-past-due shipments. In smaller organizations, expediting is often part of the purchasing function. In larger organizations, expediters often report to a separate materials control department. The actual expediting process rarely provides new value within the purchasing process. Unfortunately, expediters are an accepted overhead cost at some organizations.

Progressive organizations recognize that a need for expediters indicates that suppliers are not performing as required or that suppliers are not receiving realistic or stable material release schedules. It is also possible that the buying organization is making frequent and demanding schedule changes. To prevent this situation, more companies are reducing their use of expediting by developing realistic material release schedules and doing business with suppliers capable of meeting material shipment schedules.

Increasingly, purchasing is becoming less involved with expediting and inventory control. The increased sophistication and usability of enterprise systems such as ERP allow many of the traditional expediting and inventory-control decisions to be put into the hands of users. Chapter 18 provides in-depth coverage of ERP systems.

Inventory Control

The inventory control function monitors the day-to-day management of purchased and in-process inventory at each using location. This activity often relies on sophisticated equations or algorithms to facilitate balancing the product or service demand requirements with the required purchase inputs for each location. In many larger companies, the individual responsible for sourcing an item is often not responsible for the maintenance or routine release of purchase requirements.

Transportation

The U.S. government deregulated transportation services in the early 1980s. Since that time, purchasing has taken an active role in the evaluation, negotiation, and final selection of transportation services and carriers. Transportation is a highly specialized activity with its own set of requirements. Chapter 17 discusses the purchase of transportation services.

Managing Countertrade Arrangements

Purchasing may have responsibility for managing countertrade—international or domestic trade where goods are exchanged for goods as payment—although at some companies it is a specialized activity separate from purchasing. Because countertrade involves the purchase of foreign goods, purchasing may involve itself with this specialized form of international trade. Chapter 10 discusses countertrade.

Insourcing/Outsourcing

Purchasing often analyzes whether a new or existing purchase requirement should be internally or externally sourced. Certain items or services, such as standard or routine items, do not require insourcing/outsourcing evaluations. For other items, however, the analysis takes on strategic importance involving more than simple cost comparisons. Purchasing's role in make-or-buy analyses is an important one. Regarding outsourcing, purchasing must identify whether qualified suppliers exist in the marketplace. Further requirements may include supplier visits, negotiation, and monitoring supplier performance.

Value Analysis

Value analysis, a continuous improvement methodology developed by Larry Miles at General Electric during the late 1940s, is the organized study of an item's function as it relates to value and cost. Value represents the relationship between function and cost. The objective of value analysis is to enhance value by reducing the cost of a good or service without sacrificing quality, enhancing functionality without increasing cost, or providing greater functionality to the user above and beyond any increase in cost. Purchasing actively involves itself with value analysis through the study of materials, specifications, and suppliers. Chapter 12 discusses this methodology further.

Purchasing Research/Materials Forecasting

Purchasing often has responsibility for anticipating short- and long-term changes in material and supply markets. Research and forecasting are critical for any organization that sources raw materials or components. Detailed short- and long-term purchasing plans are required for items subject to technological, economic, or political change. These plans should include the historical and projected future usage of the purchased item, purchase objectives, assessment of the supply market, cost/price analysis, supplier evaluation, and the recommended procurement strategy.

Supply Management

As discussed in the first chapter, supply management is a progressive approach to managing the supply base that differs from a traditional arm's-length or adversarial approach with sellers. It requires purchasing professionals to work directly with those suppliers that are capable of providing superior performance to the buyer.

Supply management involves purchasing, engineering, supplier quality assurance, the supplier, and other related functions working together to further mutual goals. Instead of adversarial relationships, supply management features closer relationships with specially selected suppliers. It involves frequent help to suppliers in exchange for dramatic and continuous performance improvements, including steady price reductions.

Other Responsibilities

Purchasing can also assume a variety of other responsibilities such as receiving and warehousing, managing company travel arrangements, production planning and control, commodity futures trading, global transportation and materials management, economic forecasting, and subcontracting.

Separating Strategic and Operational Purchasing

Managing day-to-day operations is quite different from managing longer-term responsibilities. Can the personnel who must manage the uninterrupted flow of materials also find time to practice strategic supply management? Do these personnel even have the right skills to shift from operational to strategic purchasing? When pressed for time, strategic responsibilities take second place to the immediate needs presented by operational issues. Strategic responsibilities lack the immediacy of tactical duties and, as a result, are often ignored.

One way to ensure that both types of assignments receive adequate attention is to separate the staff according to tactical and strategic job assignments. Separation does not mean one group or area is more important than another. Both types of assignments are important and require specialized attention. Often the group responsible for strategic activities is part of a centrally led sourcing group at a headquarters or regional location. The operational purchasing group is often located at buying centers, sites, or plants.

Exhibit 5.3 on p. 164 highlights the characteristics of tactical and strategic buying. Both positions require buyers to work closely with internal groups while displaying the ability to think creatively. The skills required for a strategic focus, however, will be different from the skills required for an operational focus. The separation of professional duties will become increasingly common as a means to satisfy operational and strategic performance objectives. Larger firms, compared with smaller and medium-size firms, rate the formal separation of strategic and tactical responsibilities, personnel, positions, and structure quite highly as an expected design feature over the next five years.[10]

Exhibit 5.3 Separating Strategic and Operational Activities

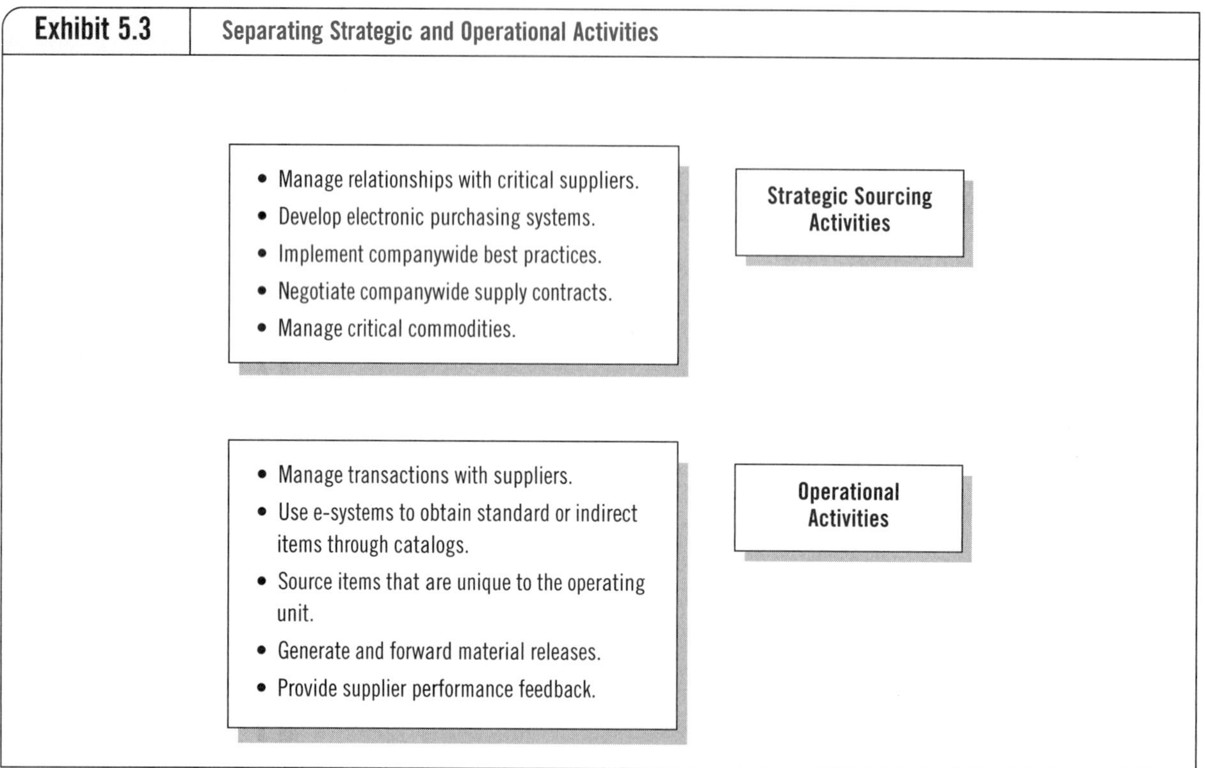

• Manage relationships with critical suppliers.
• Develop electronic purchasing systems.
• Implement companywide best practices.
• Negotiate companywide supply contracts.
• Manage critical commodities.
Strategic Sourcing Activities
• Manage transactions with suppliers.
• Use e-systems to obtain standard or indirect items through catalogs.
• Source items that are unique to the operating unit.
• Generate and forward material releases.
• Provide supplier performance feedback.
Operational Activities

Placement of Purchasing Authority

Placement of purchasing authority refers to where an organization locates its decision-making authority. If a supply executive at corporate headquarters has the authority for the majority of the organization's purchase expenditures, then a firm maintains a **centralized** authority structure. If purchasing authority for the majority of purchase expenditures is at the divisional, business unit, or site level, then a firm has a more **decentralized** decision-making authority.

We can envision different purchasing organizations in terms of authority as existing on a continuum, with complete centralization at one end and complete decentralization at the other. Few organizations lie at these polar extremes; rather, most organizations lie somewhere toward one end or the other. Certain decisions or tasks, such as the evaluation and selection of suppliers that will support an entire organization, may be centrally led. The actual generation of individual purchase orders or contract releases can be located with local buyers. Different items may be subject to different authority levels. For example, a firm might centralize the authority for capital expenditure purchases over a specified dollar amount while lower-dollar decisions are made at a facility level.

The one thing that is certain regarding organizational structure is that it will change. The 1970s and 1980s' version of centralized purchasing authority often resulted in complete purchasing control, along with a large staff, placed at the corporate level. This additional layer of decision making quickly became unresponsive to the fast-paced needs of global competitors, leading to a push for more decentralized purchasing structures. Moreover, bloated organizational charts represented a major barrier to a flexible and responsive approach to supply chain management. The impact of mergers, consolidations, and downsizing coupled with global competition and increased information systems visibility pushed organizations to a more centralized stance in the 1990s. Today's version of centralized or centrally led purchasing should emphasize support, integration, and coordination of different tasks that are common across a business rather than strict control over all the activities within the purchasing process. The challenge today is to know which activities, processes, and tasks to control or coordinate centrally and which to assign to operating units. This type of organizational structure, which combines a centralized approach for purchased items common to several business units and a decentralized approach to unique requirements, is termed **hybrid**. A recent study indicated that the hybrid structure was the most used among large firms (54% using) and that it would remain the most popular until 2010 (44% forecasted using) but would lose some popularity to more centralized organizations (42% forecasted using).[11] Tyco's experience in the Sourcing Snapshot: Tyco Customizes Its Sourcing Organization to Fit Business Needs provides a good example of developing a centrally led structure in a large conglomerate.

Sourcing Snapshot — *Tyco Customizes Its Sourcing Organization to Fit Business Needs*

The structure of many global sourcing organizations starts at the top and moves downward through an organizational chart. Although this traditional model works well for companies with one business, it can be somewhat limiting to diversified companies with multiple business units. And worse, it fails to capitalize on the individual strengths that each division or business unit can bring to the table.

Tyco International, of Princeton, NJ, has developed a custom-designed procurement organizational strategy that gives its individual business units the flexibility they need while centralizing certain functions or aspects when that makes sense.

Tyco is a large conglomerate that has been developed through numerous corporate acquisitions. "There was a time when Tyco was acquiring four to five companies a week, but it wasn't devoting a lot of resources to integrating those companies," says Russ Davis, senior director of corporate sourcing at Tyco. Because of that, clearly integrating all these segments and divisions became a challenge. When Davis and Shelley Stewart, senior vice president of operational excellence and CPO, joined Tyco four years ago, there was no real corporate sourcing organization in place—each of the very diverse business segments did its own sourcing.

When Stewart and Davis began to set up a number of sourcing initiatives, though, the differences between Tyco's many business units and companies began to show themselves. One difference that became clear was that some of Tyco's companies had well-integrated sourcing teams, whereas others did not. In addition, each company had a number of divisions, some of which had multiple locations. This meant that getting to the actual stakeholders was a challenge. For these reasons, running center-led corporatewide initiatives became very challenging.

"We realized what we really needed to do first was to create a team that could work in this environment, so that we could begin to leverage our spend," Davis explains. This led to looking at the concepts of visibility, stakeholder mapping, and team development.

Gaining spend visibility meant mapping how products were sourced and how decisions were made. From this evolved a standardized strategic sourcing process that involves seven steps. These are (1) understand internal spend and external markets; (2) create a go-to-market approach; (3) open the supply base and identify all viable suppliers; (4) decide the most appropriate execution strategy; (5) conduct aggressive negotiations and select suppliers; (6) operationalize supplier agreements; and (7) monitor the market and supplier performance.

Once the standardized process was in place, Tyco worked to customize the process to each segment. Tyco refers to this as stakeholder mapping. Stakeholder mapping is a six-step process: (1) determine who the stakeholders are and what their needs and concerns are; (2) identify the key decision makers and methodologies; (3) review the measurement and reporting structure; (4) assess the maturity of the existing team, activities, and structure; (5) address the team's skill and resource gaps and identify the best team players; and (6) drive synergistic opportunities.

The next stage centered on development of customized sourcing teams based on the information gained during the previous processes. "There was no standard formula," says Davis. "Each and every team requires the appropriate amount of analysis, stakeholder mapping, and identification of spend. This led to the creation of a number of different types of teams." Although Tyco worked to create a standard process for its reporting, it was very flexible with team creation, and the company ended up with a number of different types of successful teams.

For example, in the IT spend, "We created a team using a model that allows the stakeholders, who are the subject matter experts, to coordinate and run the sourcing activities with minimal sourcing support," reports Davis. Stakeholder mapping showed that the stakeholder base was very knowledgeable and engaged. Four subteams were created: hardware, telecom, software, and resellers. Subsequently, the first initiatives designed to harvest the low-hanging fruit proved the team's ability to be successful. The results of the center-led team approach have been very fruitful; the company's custom-designed energy sourcing team completed bids and projects that will achieve $17.5 million in savings over a four-year period.

Source: Adapted from W. Atkinson, "Tyco Customizes Its Sourcing Organization to Fit Business Needs," *Purchasing*, April 5, 2007.

Factors Influencing Centralized/Centrally Led or Decentralized Structures

The correlation between purchase dollar expenditures and purchasing staff size varies widely according to (1) the type of company; (2) the nature or complexity of the product or service produced; (3) the physical number of items that must be purchased; and (4) the scope of the purchasing responsibility, including involvement in activities such as strategic sourcing and market research and analysis, and the extent of involvement in services. The corporate purchasing group is headed by a chief purchasing officer, who reports directly to a top executive. In multifacility organizations the purchasing manager reports directly to an executive at the facility and often has a dotted-line connection to a corporate CPO. Thus, in larger corporations with multiple locations there are local purchasing personnel plus a corporate purchasing department. In more centralized purchasing organizations, the corporate purchasing department may commit a majority of the spend. Alternatively, in primarily decentralized purchasing organizations the corporate purchasing department serves the entire organization in a staff or support role.

Several factors determine the degree of centralization or decentralization that an organization considers when implementing its supply structure. These interaction factors must be considered in total because decisions should not just focus on one factor. Oftentimes one of the more dominating factors will move the organization to a more hybrid form of organization.

The Firm's Overall Business Strategy

If the organization's strategy is to be responsive to individual customers in different markets, then a more decentralized approach is likely. Conversely, if the organization builds its competitive advantage by being more efficient than the competition, then a more centralized approach to supply will be favored.

Similarity of Purchases

When purchases are fairly similar across the organization, they can be combined for leverage; a more centralized approach is favored. Conversely, if purchases are very different across business units, an argument could be made for decentralization.

Total Purchase Dollar Expenditures

As the physical size of the purchase expenditure increases, the pressure to centralize becomes more pronounced. There is a perceived opportunity to garner savings on and better manage these large purchase expenditures on a centralized basis; historically, geographic dispersion resulted in more decentralized structures, whereas geographic concentration permitted easier centralization. However, technology has leveled the geography variable. It enables increased spend visibility regardless of location.

The Overall Philosophy of Management

If upper management is committed to operating in a decentralized mode, then oftentimes the purchasing function will be decentralized. If the management philosophy is more to control the operations from a central location, then a more centralized approach to supply will likely follow.

Advantages of Centralized/Centrally Led Purchasing Structures

A centrally led purchasing effort can provide some definite advantages, particularly when an organization has purchase expenditures at more than one business unit, division, or facility. The mission of the central group is to facilitate the consolidation of similar buying requirements and standardize buying processes at the various facilities. Fulfilling this mission involves many tasks, including the selection of suppliers and negotiation of purchase contracts on a corporatewide basis. Although there are many potential benefits to centrally led purchasing, the following highlights the more important advantages.

Consolidate Purchase Volumes

Historically, the primary advantage of centralized purchasing has been to realize a favorable price due to accumulated volumes. Spend analysis involves using systems technology to identify items purchased in common among divisions or business units. These items are then consolidated, and a purchasing strategy is developed as to how to obtain the best value for the entire organization. Depending on the items, business unit or facility purchasing personnel provide their input to the centralized sourcing team. Local supply managers also retain the authority to generate orders directly to a supplier. A firm can achieve material cost reductions by combining purchase volumes while still meeting the operating requirements of division or plant buyers.

Centrally led buying can also enhance service requirements. For example, a companywide transportation contract results in not only cost reductions but also more uniform, consistent performance standards across all locations. General Electric established a central executive transportation committee comprised of divisional transportation managers. This committee acts as a central body to evaluate carriers for corporate transportation contracts, award corporate contracts to the best carriers, and establish uniform carrier performance standards for all divisions. By combining transportation volumes, GE realizes cost and service improvements that benefit the entire corporation.

Reduced Duplication of Purchasing Effort

Another reason for centrally controlling purchasing authority is to reduce duplication of effort. Consider an organization with 10 locations and a completely decentralized purchasing structure. This company may find itself with 10 sets of material release forms, 10 supplier quality standards, 10 supplier performance evaluation systems, 10 purchasing training manuals, and 10 different ERP systems with different communications protocols to the same suppliers. Duplication adds costs but very little in the way of unique value. It is costly and inefficient, and it creates a lack of consistency between operating units.

Ability to Coordinate Purchasing Plans and Strategy

Several strategy development trends are occurring today. First, purchasing is becoming less of a tactical function and more of a strategic function. Second, organizations are linking corporate, operations, and purchasing plans into an overall strategic plan. These two trends require a centrally led group responsible for developing purchasing strategy at the highest levels of an organization. Without this group, an organization cannot coordinate its purchasing strategy. Chapter 6 describes the strategy development process in detail.

Ability to Coordinate and Manage Companywide Purchasing Systems

Sophisticated ERP systems, e-purchasing systems, and data warehouses are increasingly important. The design and coordination of these systems should not be the responsibility of individual units. If each division or unit is responsible for developing its own e-purchasing system or data gathering and part-numbering system, the result will be a mixture of incompatible systems.

Hewlett-Packard, historically a decentralized company, relies on a centrally led procurement group to develop and manage companywide databases. This results in visibility to common items between HP's dozens of divisions as well as the ability to evaluate supplier performance at the corporate level. The system also supports the development of companywide materials forecasts.

Developing Expertise

Purchasing personnel cannot become experts in all areas of purchasing, especially as the purchasing function becomes more complex and sophisticated. The ability to develop specialized purchasing knowledge and to support individual buying units is another advantage of a centrally led purchasing group. The following list, although not exhaustive, presents some of the areas where a central group either develops specialized expertise or provides training and support to divisional or business unit personnel:

- Purchase negotiations
- Global sourcing
- Legal aspects
- Quality/Six Sigma programs (e.g., TQM, ISO)
- Supplier relationship management
- Competitive market analysis
- Lean process improvement techniques
- Supplier development
- Total cost analysis
- Team building
- Data analysis and information systems

The Institute for Supply Management (http://www.ism.org) provides information on training seminars and online learning.

Managing Companywide Change

Faced with the need to continually anticipate or adapt to changing competitive environments, firms restructure to meet these new demands. Purchasing is not spared from these structural challenges. Although no structure is perfect, there are better structures at certain points in the firm's life cycle. Often top management philosophy will dictate the predominant form of organization; however, CPOs must insure that the form of their organization best meets the overall corporate goals. The example below compares two firms with different organizational approaches to sourcing.

The first firm had a strong central focus to its major functional activities while the second had over 80 highly decentralized operating companies. The decentralized company struggled to initiate change because support or compliance with corporatewide global purchasing processes was voluntary or not a priority. The centrally focused company experienced few problems getting participants around the world to support centrally led initiatives, such as the use of companywide suppliers selected through its global sourcing process. This example shows that managing the change process is often easier in a centrally controlled or coordinated purchasing environment.

Advantages of Decentralized Purchasing

With all the advantages that centrally led or coordinated purchasing appears to offer, why would any organization support a decentralized structure? Although competitive pressures encourage a more centralized approach to certain tasks, these same pressures also support the decentralized placement of authority for other purchasing tasks. A firm can gain an advantage from placing purchasing personnel with sourcing authority directly "where the action is." So what are the potential benefits of decentralizing purchasing authority?

Speed and Responsiveness

The ability to respond quickly to user and customer requirements has always been a major justification for decentralized purchasing authority. Most purchasing professionals agree that decentralized purchasing authority often contributes to greater responsiveness and support. Organizations may resist a stronger centralized purchasing group simply because of previous negative experiences with centralized management. Some organizations fear that any centralization of authority results in slower response times.

Understanding Unique Operational Requirements

Decentralized purchasing personnel should gain a greater understanding and appreciation of local operating requirements. These personnel become familiar with the products, processes, business practices, and customers the division or plant serves. Increased familiarity allows a buyer to anticipate the needs of the departments it supports while developing solid relationships with local suppliers. This is especially important for global companies such as Colgate-Palmolive, which has facilities on every populated continent.[12]

Product Development Support

In organizations where new-product development occurs at the divisional or business unit level, a decentralized purchasing structure can support new-product development at earlier stages. Purchasing can support new-product development in a number of ways. First, purchasers can involve suppliers early in the product design process. They can also evaluate longer-term material product requirements, develop strategic plans, determine if substitute materials are available, and anticipate product requirements.

Ownership

Organizations may prefer decentralized purchasing authority for an intangible reason called ownership. In essence, **ownership** refers to the assumption that local personnel understand and support the objectives of the business unit or division and feel a personal commitment to a particular operation. Business unit managers are responsible for the profitability of the unit. They should have jurisdiction over purchasing because a large part of the costs and efficiency of the operation are represented in procurement.

A Hybrid Purchasing Structure

Exhibit 5.4 presents the results of a study on the decision-making process that best describes the current and expected placement of procurement and supply management authority for a sample of 172 manufacturing companies.[13] This exhibit reveals an expected shift toward greater centralization over the next five years. This agrees with another research study that indicated that, whereas the predominant form of organization in purchasing would be hybrid, it would be accompanied by an increase in centralized structures.[14]

Intense global competition requires firms to develop organizational designs that capture the advantages of centrally led and decentralized purchasing. Most companies will likely evolve toward a hybrid organizational structure. A hybrid structure is one that is neither totally centralized nor totally decentralized. In a hybrid structure, the authority for some tasks lies with a centrally led group whereas the authority for other tasks remains at the operating level.

Exhibit 5.4 Placement of Purchasing Authority

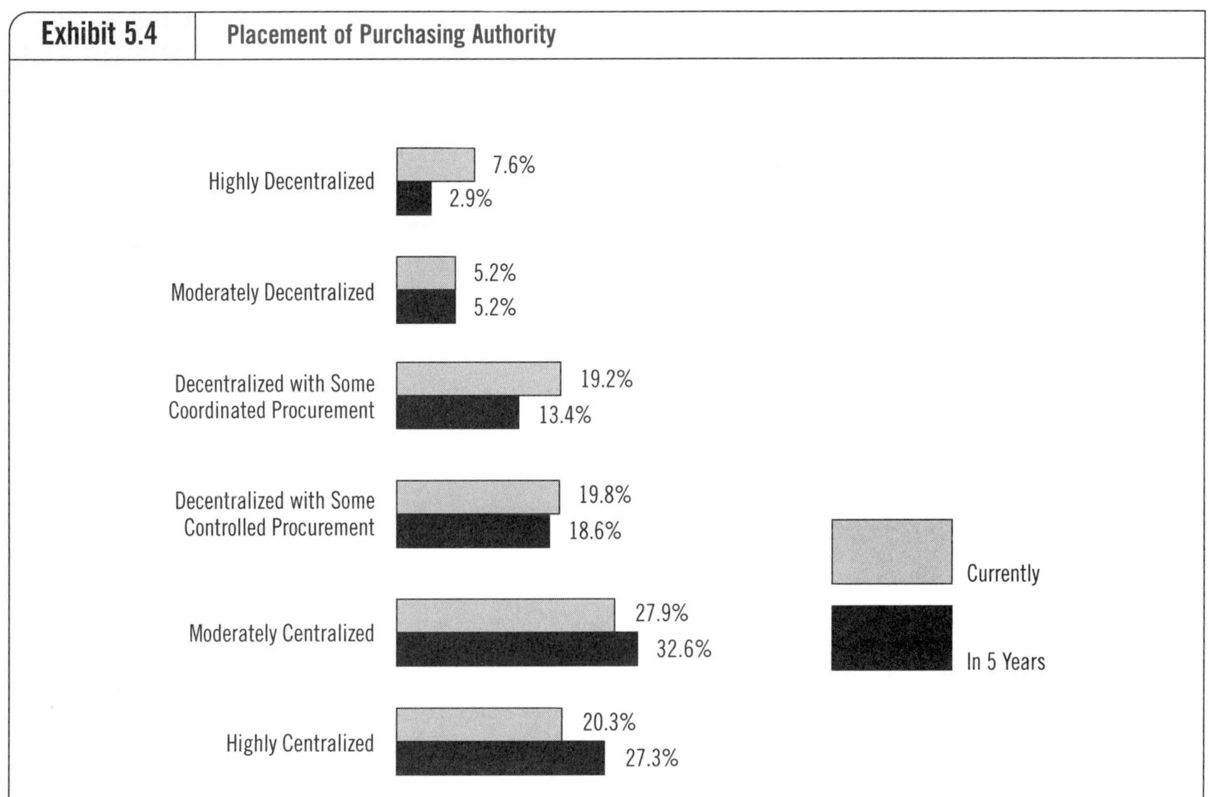

Most organizations should benefit from a structure that retains the advantages and expertise of a centrally led purchasing group but also is responsive to plant and divisional purchasing requirements. Hybrid organizations can take many forms and be called by many different names. Some of the more common structures include (1) lead division buying, (2) regional buying groups, (3) global buying committees, (4) corporate purchasing councils, and (5) corporate steering committees.

Lead Division Buying

In **lead division buying**, a group of operating units buy common items, typically because they produce common products. For example, one firm combined the efforts of several plants that produced transformers and distribution equipment for utility firms. The group first identified common commodities and then appointed a lead negotiator. The lead negotiator was the buyer at the facility having the largest expenditure or having expertise in the commodity or item purchased.

Regional Buying Groups

Regional buying groups are most advantageous where geographic concentration exists within a company. Various facilities within the particular geographic region (e.g., Pacific Northwest, the Southeast) join forces to negotiate with local and regional sources of common commodities. They generally are responsible for the purchase of large-volume items common to all facilities. They also assist individual locations that may or may not have in-house purchasing personnel to handle local purchases. Regional buying groups are useful in many service organizations (e.g., banks and insurance companies), given that they are structured on a regional basis. Regional groups also facilitate implementation of joint inventory sharing and vendor-managed inventory arrangements with suppliers.

Global Buying Committees

When a key commodity is purchased by many major business units, a joint global strategy is beneficial. For example, one large diversified firm with interests in the defense and automobile parts industry has a worldwide steel-buying committee. The central corporate headquarters leads the committee, and every major steel-buying location has a representative on the committee. Demand forecasts, strategic supplier purchase plans, and negotiation strategies are established at committee meetings.

Corporate Purchasing Councils

With smaller centrally led corporate staffs and fewer personnel at the business unit level, purchasing councils provide a way to share expertise and develop common sourcing strategies. A purchasing council is comprised of a group of buyers who purchase similar items at various facilities. A conglomerate organization had been acquiring firms at the rate of one per month for the past 10 years and was left with an organization of 280 factories. It was decided a center-led form of structure with purchasing councils was needed to reduce the firm's 60,000 suppliers to a manageable number. As another example, a chemical firm created an MRO council that meets as needed and members divide up the work. The corporate representative oversees and coordinates the council members' activities. Members are given responsibility for purchases of companywide requirements for which their division is the biggest user. National contracts are negotiated and awarded by the center-led corporate group.

Corporate Steering Committees

Steering committees are quite similar to councils except that they tend to be more advisory in nature. These committees will meet periodically and discuss strategies on the company's major purchased commodities. Steering committees will also invite large suppliers in for discussions, negotiations, performance assessments, and forecasts of purchase volumes for the coming year. They provide an opportunity for various operating-unit personnel to meet and discuss buying plans in decentralized environments.

Sourcing Snapshot

Con-way Appoints Its First Chief Purchasing Officer and Becomes More Centralized

Con-way Inc. was named *Fortune* magazine's "Most Admired Company" in transportation and logistics for 2007. The company is a $4.7 billion freight transportation and logistics services company, with over 30,000 employees with decades of transportation experience. However, it was not until February of 2006 that it named Mitch Plaat as its first chief procurement officer (CPO). His charge: improve efficiency, identify savings opportunities, and make changes to help Con-way be a more successful company.

Until January 2006, Con-way followed a hybrid purchasing model, with some centralized sourcing and some decentralized buying. Purchasing was focused on three silos: fleet (trucks and trailers), IT (computer hardware, software, and services), and indirect goods and services. There were central processes for sourcing fleet and IT, both considered strategic to the transportation and logistics company. But for indirect purchases, the company's 500 locations did much of the buying, managing relationships with some 35,000 suppliers.

There was no real oversight or system used by all three groups. Management has approved Plaat's strategy to restructure supply and backed this up with investments. Such executive support is helping to break down hurdles that come when centralizing the purchasing function. "The executive team has a vision for procurement," he says. "They've allowed us to restructure, and they are willing to invest in tools and resources in order to achieve goals we've set forth. In the past, most investments were for customer-driven systems. Now, we're investing in procurement and procurement's ability to deliver competitive value and bottom-line impact."

In the past year, Plaat and his team have worked to attract talented purchasing professionals to the new operation, tripling the number of people there to more than 100. Nine individuals are dedicated to strategic sourcing. They have also invested in sourcing software provided by Emptoris, providing improved visibility over Con-way's spend.

"As we started to view procurement differently, we saw that our ultimate goal is not only to deliver bottom-line savings to the corporation, but to become world class," he says. "And to do that, we need to have visibility into our spending. If our CFO asked about our spending on fuel, we could get to that information, but it wasn't something we had at our fingertips. We wanted tools to provide that insight."

Plaat states, "Even though we thought we were doing a good job, it wasn't until we went through the process and really used the tools and negotiation tactics that we saw we really hadn't been doing the best we could. We know there's potential for improvement, especially in areas that we hadn't been involved in, such as HR services. For instance, we've never had a national contract for temporary labor services." Other spend areas ripe for consolidation: computer hardware, corporate cards, hotels, and rental cars. When the company changed its name, it negotiated a new contract on driver uniforms with a savings of 26% over the previous contract. Waste disposal is another big area that is currently being studied by Plaat's team. "We're looking at various options—whether or not there's a single supplier that can provide coverage over 500 locations—but we definitely think there's leverage to be had by consolidating the spend with a fixed number of suppliers."

The move to a more centralized structure should allow further savings on Con-way's total spend of about $500 million annually. This spend covers a wide range of goods and services, from heavy-duty tractors, trucks, and trailers to fuel, tires, computers, and office supplies. Currently, savings on these purchases average 20% and are due mainly to consolidating the buy with fewer suppliers. Further savings are likely in areas such as human resources, marketing, and legal services categories, which purchasing has not traditionally been involved in.

Another phase in Con-way's centralization initiative toward becoming a world-class purchasing operation: developing processes for managing contracts and measuring supplier performance.

Source: Adapted from N. Hitchcock, "Mitch Plaat Tells of Challenges, Opportunities and Successes He's Experienced in His First Year at the Helm of the Purchasing Operation at Logistics Giant Con-way," *Purchasing,* February 15, 2007. Other information obtained from the company website: con-way.com.

Organizing for Supply Chain Management

The need to coordinate and share information across organizations and functional groups has resulted in the development of higher-level positions designed to oversee various supply chain activities. Chapter 1 identifies the activities that fall under the supply chain umbrella.

A structure that coordinates the diverse activities within a supply chain contrasts greatly with one where separate supply chain groups or activities report to different executive managers. The latter model can result in each function or activity pursuing conflicting organizational goals and objectives. Organizing as an integrated supply chain structure requires traditionally separate activities to report to an executive responsible for coordinating the flow of goods, services, and information from supplier through customer.

Most large organizations have materials or supply chain executives responsible for coordinating separate supply chain activities. Historically, the concept of supply chain management evolved from earlier organizational forms called materials management and physical distribution. In fact, some organizations still maintain these as organizational functions. Materials management was a consolidation of functions required to purchase, manage inbound transportation for, receive, store, inventory, and schedule material flows. Physical distribution then took the finished product to market either directly or through warehouses. Earlier research revealed that 70% of U.S. operations organizations used the materials concept (i.e., the predecessor to supply chain management) to some extent, a figure that was consistent across all sizes of organizations.[15] Historically, the greatest growth of the materials management concept occurred during the mid-1960s to late 1970s.

In the 1980s and through the mid-1990s, many firms combined these two functions into logistics. From the mid-1990s and continuing through the current period, firms realized that other factors such as information and process flows were as important as (if not more so than) the physical flow of goods. Hence many adopted the moniker of "supply chain management" to indicate this complex web of relationships, processes, and information flows from the supplier to the final customer. Perhaps one of the best comments that captured this new philosophy was made by Frederick W. Smith, the chairman and CEO of FedEx, who stated that the "information about the package is more important than the package itself."

Organizations that develop a coordinated approach to materials and supply chain management show a greater interest in the control of material costs. This can only increase the importance of purchasing within the organizational hierarchy because of purchasing's influence on cost and quality.

It is easy to see why organizations have endorsed the concepts of materials management, physical distribution, logistics, and now supply chain management. All these organizational approaches can lead to some tangible benefits:

- Controlling material costs while improving customer service
- Developing an awareness of supply chain total cost tradeoffs
- Opening channels of communication that promote the sharing of ideas across organizations and functional groups
- Supporting the career paths of talented personnel by providing the means to develop multifunctional expertise

- Developing operating efficiencies across various supply chain activities to streamline material processes, coordinate procedures, and improve movement of materials and data
- Creating a direct link from the customer back to external suppliers

Advances in software and systems have enabled visibility across the supply chain that allow multiple participants to coordinate and schedule more efficient material information and processes. Ideally, there is increased access to demand forecasts, production requirements, and inventory levels at any point within the supply chain. Each party could now plan its own production and distribution requirements with greater accuracy. The result of this integration will be lower inventories, shorter cycle times, an improved ability to plan, and lower costs.

A Supply Chain Management Structure

The first chapter of this book identified the various activities that fall under the supply chain umbrella. Key processes found in an integrated supply chain include (1) customer relationship management; (2) customer service management; (3) demand management; (4) order fulfillment; (5) manufacturing flow management; (6) sourcing; (7) product development and commercialization; and (8) return channel processes.[16] Exhibit 5.5 on p. 176 illustrates one possible way to structure around supply chain management.

The actual groups under the supply chain umbrella can vary widely among organizations. The reporting level of the supply chain executive can also be higher or lower than shown here. In this exhibit, patterned after a high-tech company in Massachusetts, the vice president of supply chain management is responsible for materials sourcing, production planning and scheduling, logistics, operations, and customer service. The director of materials is responsible for receiving and storage, inventory control, and inbound transportation. This shows only one of many possible ways to integrate supply chain management through the formal organizational structure.

Using Teams as Part of the Organizational Structure

We have witnessed an increased reliance on teams over the last 25 years. In purchasing and supply chain management, teams are used to evaluate and select suppliers, develop global commodity strategies, perform demand and supply planning, and carry out supplier development activities.

Not all observers agree that the use of teams is a guarantee of greater effectiveness. Although teams can yield the benefits envisioned by their use, they often have a less-than-desirable side. They can waste the time and energy of members, enforce lower performance norms, create destructive conflict within and between teams, and make notoriously bad decisions. Teams can also exploit, stress, and frustrate members—sometimes all at the same time.[17]

If we believe that making teams a major part of the formal organizational structure does not guarantee success, then the challenge becomes one of creating an environment where teams will be successful. Much of the success or failure of teams rests on an organization's ability to ask the right questions about using teams. Exhibit 5.6 on p. 177 identifies the kinds of questions that supply managers should ask when they are planning to use teams.

Exhibit 5.5 Reporting Relationships in a Supply Chain Reporting Structure

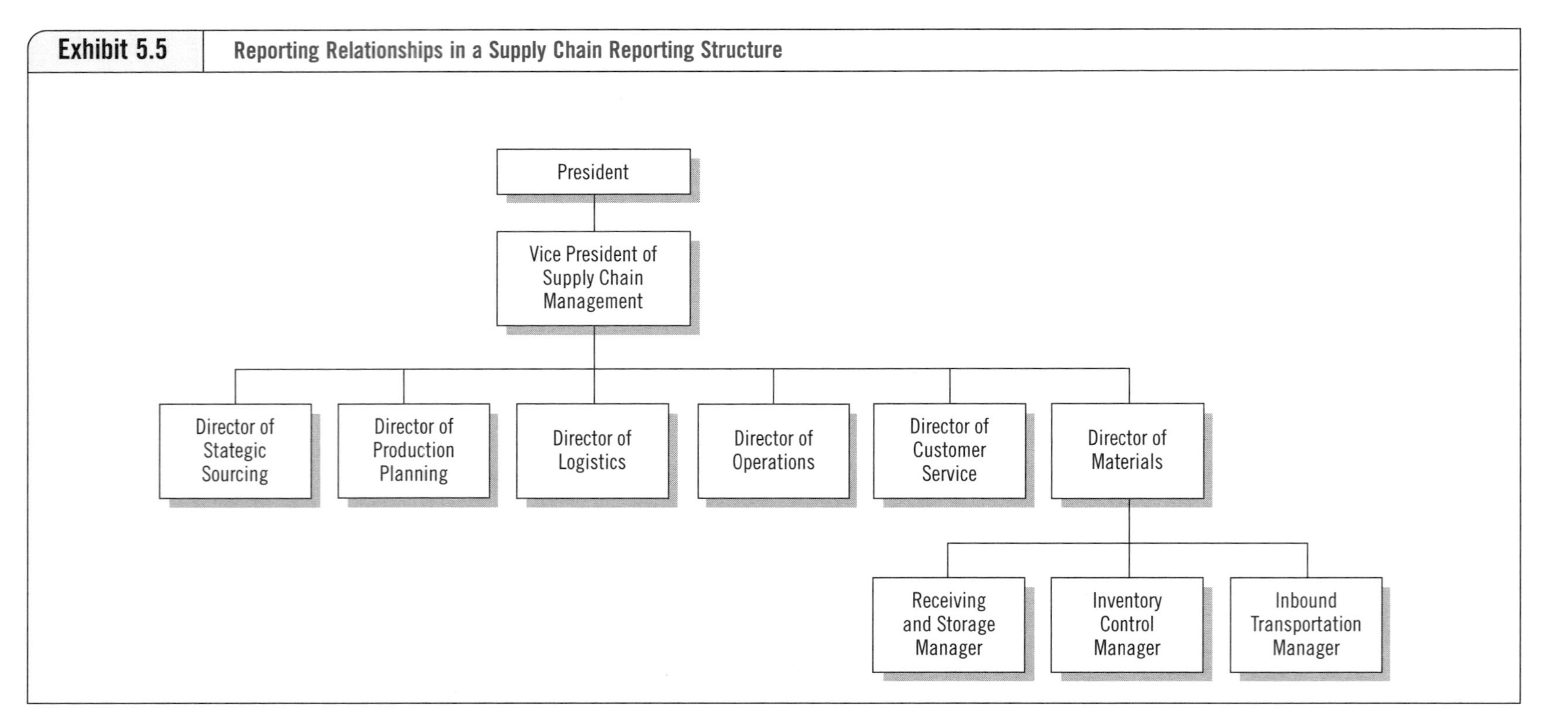

Exhibit 5.6 Work Team Planning Guide

Identify Appropriate Team Assignments

Do assignments justify the use of teams?
Has the proper team model been identified (i.e., part-time versus full-time assignments)?
Does executive and functional management support the use of a team?

Form Work Team and Select Qualified Members and Leader

Have core versus as-needed members been identified?
Do members have the proper skills, time, and commitment to support the team?
Have team sponsors identified and selected a qualified team leader?
Are customers or suppliers part of the team if required?
Do members understand their formal team roles?

Determine Member Training Requirements

Have team member training requirements been assessed?
Is required training available on a timely basis?

Identify Resource Requirements

Are resources provided or available to support the team's task?

Determine Team Authority Levels

Have team authority levels for the team been determined?
Have team authority levels been communicated across the organization?

Establish Team Performance Goals

Has the team established objective performance goals?

Determine How to Measure and Reward Participation and Performance

Are approaches and systems in place that assess team performance and member contribution?
Are there reporting linkages to team or executive sponsors?
Is team performance effectively linked to performance reward systems?

Develop Team Charters

Has a formal charter been developed that details team mission, tasks, broad objectives, etc.?
Has the charter been communicated across the organization?

Although most supply managers endorse the use of teams, the reality is that there are major hurdles or challenges that can affect how well an organization uses them. First, many organizations form teams using part-time members. Although some organizations create teams staffed by full-time members, teams staffed by part-time members are popular within purchasing and supply chain management. Organizations that rely on part-time teams typically maintain their existing functional structure while adding additional team-related duties. It can be difficult to obtain commitment from members who face conflicting demands on their time.

A second hurdle that still confronts too many organizations is a failure to recognize and reward the effort team members put forth toward their assignments. In fact, many recognition and reward systems today encourage members not to participate on teams. Members who receive inadequate recognition for their efforts will likely direct their energy toward those areas that are recognized and rewarded. Participation may present a personal risk and create conflict once members realize that supporting a team takes time away from activities that are recognized and rewarded. Unfortunately, many companies still do not grasp the importance of this issue.

A third hurdle relates to our individualistic national culture. It is simply not our nature, except perhaps for sporting events, to be group or team focused, especially when compared to other countries. In his study of culture, Hofstede concluded that the United States was the most individualistic nation of any studied.[18] Although some cultures place group needs above individual needs, this is usually not the case within the United States. Team participants may perceive that group assignments will stifle individual creativity and personal recognition. We value individualism and find that a shift away from it is often uncomfortable and threatening.

Although these barriers are important, they certainly do not represent an exhaustive list of what can affect purchasing and supply chain teams. In fact, a host of barriers may affect a specific team at a given point in time. Supply leaders must understand how to use this demanding but often difficult way to perform work.

Creating the Organization of the Future

A major debate today continues to be about determining the best organizational structure, including the structure for purchasing and integrated supply chain management. The trend today is to move away from a vertical focus, where work and information are managed up and down within functional groups, toward a horizontal focus, where work and information are managed across groups and between organizations. The horizontal organization largely eliminates hierarchy and functional or departmental boundaries. Although there will always be a need for functional groups, increasingly parts of the organization will work together horizontally in teams or groups to perform core processes. Exhibit 5.7 compares the vertical and horizontal approaches to structuring organizations. It is easy to see how a horizontal focus applies to purchasing and supply chain management.

There is some evidence that purchasing is beginning to assume a horizontal rather than strictly vertical focus. Almost 80% of companies surveyed use cross-functional teams to manage some part of the purchasing and supply chain management process. We have also witnessed a shift over the last 15 years from a commodity focus to one that is end-item or process focused. In 1990, purchasing was organized around commodities in almost 80% of firms surveyed. By 1999, purchasing was organized by commodities less than 65% of the time.[19] A shift has occurred toward organizing around end items (which supports new-product development efforts) and hybrid structures, such as organizing around processes. Of course, few organizations will choose to be purely vertical or purely horizontal. Most will create structures that attempt to capture the best that vertical and horizontal alignments have to offer.

The ideal procurement organizational model in the 21st century should have certain broad features. These include flattened hierarchies for faster decision making and freer flow of ideas along with joint ventures and alliances with key supply chain members. Future organizational designs should also feature cross-functional teams to pursue new opportunities and cross-fertilize ideas across organizations. Greater decentralization of buying activity along with centrally led coordination of major spending

Exhibit 5.7 Shifting from a Vertical to a Horizontal Organization

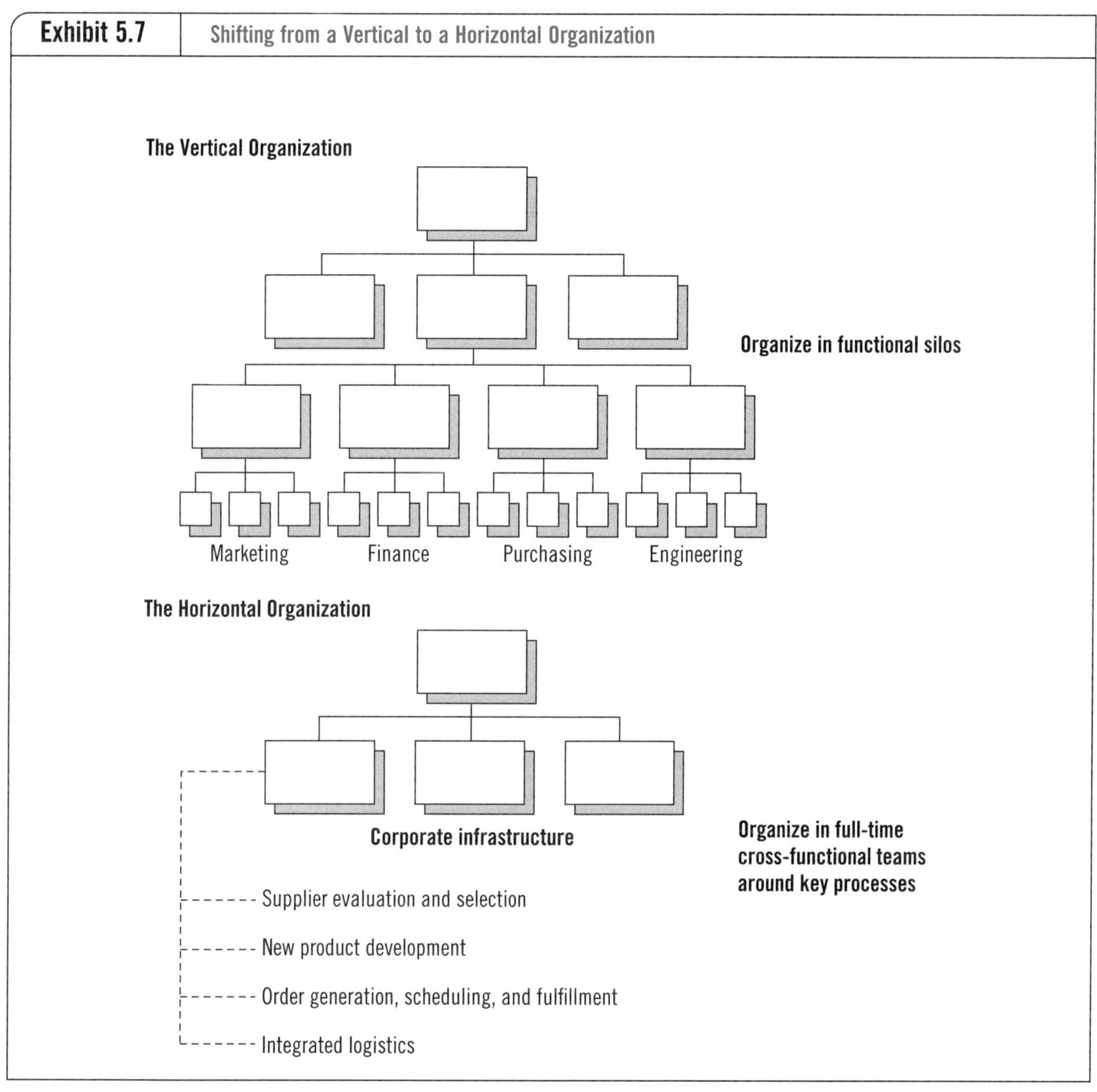

categories should provide the best that centralization and decentralization have to offer. Open information channels—the Internet, intranets, and information technology systems that make information widely available across the supply chain—will help coordinate activities across the organizational chart. Finally, rotation of managers across business units and functional groups will support the development of broad knowledge and expertise. Thriving in a fast-paced environment requires new kinds of leadership and organizational designs. A design with the right features can help a company meet the challenges of the 21st century.

What specific design features will organizations put in place over the next five years? Exhibit 5.8 on p. 180 presents the top 12 expected purchasing organizational design features from a list of 30 future design features. This study included data from

Exhibit 5.8 Expected Purchasing Organizational Design Features

Feature	Rating
Specific individuals assigned responsibility for managing supplier relationships	5.06
Physical co-location between procurement and key internal customers	4.78
Centrally coordinated commodity teams that develop companywide supply strategies	4.62
Formal procurement and supply strategy coordination and review sessions between functional groups	4.61
New-product teams that include procurement representatives	4.61
Lead buyers to manage noncommodity items or services	4.53
Physical co-location between procurement and technical personnel	4.51
Regular strategy/performance review presentations by the chief procurement officer to the president or CEO	4.50
New-product teams that include suppliers as members or participants	4.49
A higher-level chief procurement officer who has a procurement and supply-related title	4.46
Formal procurement and supply strategy coordination and review sessions between business units	4.42
Cross-functional teams that manage some or all of the procurement and supply process	4.27

Scale: 1 = Do not expect to rely on; 4 = Expect to rely on somewhat; 7 = Expect to rely on extensively

Source: R. Trent, *Procurement and Supply Management Organizational Design Survey,* 2003.

172 manufacturing firms. From this list we see a number of themes emerge that begin to define the purchasing organization of the future. First, companies expect to rely extensively on the use of teams to support the attainment of procurement objectives. This includes commodity teams, teams that manage some or all of the procurement and supply process, and new-product development teams. Next, new-product development teams will feature the active involvement of purchasing and supplier representatives. Third, because purchasing is a support activity, the co-location of purchasing personnel with internal customers is an important way to be responsive to internal customer needs. Exhibit 5.9 presents the kinds of insights that purchasing personnel should gain from closer interaction with internal customers.

Strategy development and the need for procurement leadership are also evident from the top 12 list. One highly rated feature is a higher-level chief procurement officer who makes regular strategy and performance review presentations to the president or CEO. The need to coordinate procurement strategy with other functional groups and between business units also reflects a growing reliance on purchasing to demonstrate leadership, to support corporate objectives, and to work cross-functionally.

Exhibit 5.8 also notes the importance of relying on lead buyers to manage noncommodity goods and services along with the importance of having specific individuals responsible for managing supplier relationships. These features combine to help create a picture of what the purchasing organization of the future will resemble.

The supply chain organization of the future will rely much more on systems capability to enable the efficient and effective management of the flow of goods information and processes from suppliers to final customers. These technology-enabled supply chains will permit several advantages. Perhaps one of the greatest advantages will be viewing the process as circular rather than linear. This feature will allow any members, regardless of their position in the chain, to access activities either upstream or downstream. Thus, a final customer will have visibility into the shipment activity of a key supplier. Another key activity is the ability to bring together a firm's expertise in the form of a virtual team to address a problem, provide alternatives and recommended solutions, and then disband.

Exhibit 5.9 Co-locating Purchasing with Internal Customers

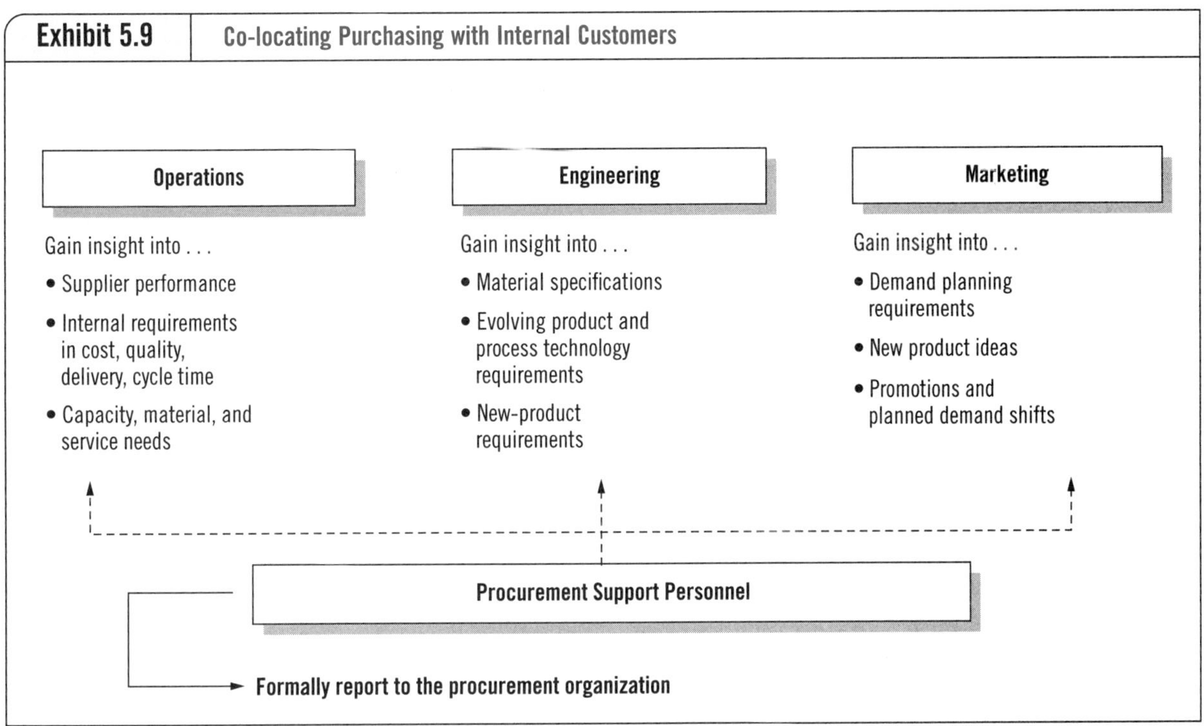

Sourcing Snapshot

Johnson & Johnson Uses Organizational Design to Integrate Marketing and Purchasing

Johnson & Johnson, a global company known for high-quality products and brands, is showing how the creative use of organizational design can promote integration between some important supply chain groups. Supply management professionals, who are part of the support activity called procurement, have a wide range of internal customers. One internal customer group is marketing, which is responsible for activities that could benefit from the involvement of professional supply managers.

Executive managers have assigned a sourcing manager to J&J's corporate marketing and promotion strategy team to support their efforts when developing contracts. Examples of service areas where the marketing team requires contract support include printing, convention and meeting space, media purchases, promotional displays and tradeshows, marketing research, and advertising and promotion. For example, sourcing involvement resulted in a reduction of companywide printing suppliers from 600 to 5.

By being part of the marketing strategy team, the sourcing professional adds value to the marketing and promotion process. She verifies that every unit within the corporation is charged the same best rate from suppliers and reserves the right to audit advertising "job jackets" and costs. She controls the buying of advertising and media support while working to gain most-favored-customer status with media suppliers. In short, she assumes a major part of the contracting process that marketing simply does not want. This allows marketing professionals to focus on those areas where they can make the greatest contribution. Although this sourcing manager currently supports only U.S. marketing, her business plan calls for providing support to worldwide marketing units over the next several years.

Source: Company interviews.

Good Practice Example

Air Products and Chemicals Organizes to Meet Global Challenges

Air Products and Chemicals, an industrial producer of gases and chemicals headquartered in the eastern United States, designs and operates production facilities worldwide. Unfortunately, industrial buyers are increasingly viewing the company's products as commodity items, which, along with intense global competition from China and other countries, has created extensive downward price pressures. This has created the primary challenge that Air Products faces—margins are under pressure, yet the company has made strong performance commitments to shareholders.

Air Products has operated historically as an engineer-to-order company, which implies a great deal of engineering and design work customized to each new facility and project. Engineers traditionally design new facilities without considering previous designs or leveraging commonality across design and procurement centers. Management now recognizes the company must pursue standard-design and off-the-shelf-product-based thinking. The company's objective is to enter the global marketplace as a global rather than regional company. Achieving that objective demanded the development of a globally integrated engineering and procurement process.

GLOBAL ENGINEERING AND PROCUREMENT PROCESS

Responding to the call to globalize engineering and procurement, the director of project and logistics supply assembled a leadership team to develop, sell internally, and launch the company's global process. The process that Air Products developed involves an extensive analysis between the U.S. and European design centers to determine areas of commonality and synergy. Although the process began with focused commodities, projects became broader in scope once the cost-saving possibilities became obvious.

ORGANIZATIONAL SUPPORT MECHANISMS

Perhaps the major reason Air Products has enjoyed success with its global engineering and procurement process is due to the organizational design features the company has put in place. These features include two steering committees, a globalization manager, and extensive use of cross-functional/cross-locational teams.

Steering Committees

Two steering committees support the global process—an executive steering committee and an operating steering committee. The executive steering committee consists of senior managers from engineering, procurement, and operations. Financial representatives support the group as required. This committee brings higher-level commitment and exposure to the global process. The committee also allocates the budget that supports a globalization manager and staff along with travel and living expenses for team members.

A globalization manager, a project procurement manager, and the director of Asian sourcing (who commits a part of his effort to the global process) comprise the core operating steering committee. The steering committee, working with the globalization manager, assumes some important responsibilities. This committee identifies and prioritizes global opportunities, establishes cross-functional teams, and identifies savings targets. Committee members also work to remove any hurdles that affect the process. The operating steering committee also has responsibility for maintaining online support documents, updating the status of projects on the company's intranet, and conducting lessons-learned sessions with teams at the end of each project.

Globalization Manager

Consensus exists among managers concerning the importance of the globalization manager, a position created specifically to oversee the global engineering and procurement process. This manager, who is also the operating steering committee leader, is a well-respected engineer with 25 years of experience. He reports to the vice presidents of engineering in Europe and the United States. This is an important consideration because the two design centers must work together during global projects. He has located his office with the procurement group at U.S. headquarters, which facilitates teamwork and trust between engineering and procurement.

The globalization manager commits 100% of his time to supporting the global process. His responsibilities include working with the operating steering committee to identify future projects, monitoring the status and progress of current projects, and determining where to spend budgeted funds. He also approves all operating steering committee expenditures and identifies team members for project teams, including working with other managers to gain support and member time. The globalization manager also plays an important role in helping teams establish project milestones.

CROSS-FUNCTIONAL/CROSS-LOCATIONAL TEAMS

Air Products relies extensively on cross-functional/cross-locational teams to support global engineering and procurement. These teams, which typically have four to six members, are responsible for developing and proposing global sourcing strategies. The steering committee selects members on the basis of experience and confidence in an individual's ability to support the team. Each team has representatives from the United States and Europe participating.

Project teams follow a nine-step global process, which includes regular reporting of progress to the operating steering committee. Perhaps the most important responsibility performed by these project teams is the development of a hypothetical material cost that identifies where savings can be realized. Savings occur primarily in three areas: (1) material savings, (2) currency savings, and (3) savings due to opening a purchase requirement to competition.

Has Air Products been successful? With over 100 projects completed, the company is averaging 20% cost savings compared with previous agreements. Executive management considers the global process to be one of the more important internal processes in place at Air Products today. Success would not be possible, however, without careful attention to the right organizational design—a design that recognizes the importance of leadership, coordination, communication, and resource support.

CONCLUSION

Just as having the right people, systems, and performance measures in place is critical to purchasing success, so too is having a properly designed organizational structure. Careful attention to assessing and selecting the structure and formal systems of communication, division of labor, coordination, control, authority, and responsibility will make the attainment of supply management objectives more likely.

Without question, the kinds of organizational design features that a firm selects often relate to the size of the firm. Larger firms differ from smaller firms in terms of scope, complexity, and available resources. They tend to have operations that are worldwide (scope), more organizational levels covering a wider array of businesses and product lines (complexity), and more resources that support the use of certain design features. As firm size increases, many of the design features put in place help coordinate and integrate a globally diverse and large organization. Whatever the size of the firm, progressive supply managers recognize the important relationship between organizational design and supply management effectiveness. Future organizational structures will need to be more flexible and responsive regardless of whether they are centralized, decentralized, or hybrid.

KEY TERMS

centralized, 164
decentralized, 164
lead division buying, 171
coordination, 156
hybrid, 165
ownership, 170

DISCUSSION QUESTIONS

1. Do you feel that choosing an organizational design is simple? If so, explain why firms would change their supply management organization structure.
2. Why is a function's placement in the organizational hierarchy important?
3. What factors contribute to the increasing importance of purchasing within the organizational hierarchy?
4. Why would you believe that the importance of purchasing diminishes when a firm organizes under a supply chain management structure?
5. Discuss the two or three most important benefits to centralized purchasing authority. Justify your choices. Discuss the two most important benefits to decentralized purchasing authority. Justify your choices.
6. What are some of the factors that would influence whether a firm centralizes or decentralizes its supply management organization?
7. Why was purchasing not a higher-level function during the early industrial years in the United States?
8. What is the difference between strategic and operational purchasing? Provide some examples of strategic and operational tasks.
9. Discuss the logic behind physically separating strategic and operational buyers.
10. Discuss the role of a purchasing research staff.
11. You are the chief purchasing officer for a company with worldwide production and buying locations. Design an organizational structure that allows you to compete

effectively. Describe the reporting structure, the physical placement of personnel, the placement of purchasing authority, and the coordination of activities with other functional groups.

12. Discuss the advantages of using a cross-functional team to evaluate and select suppliers.
13. Compare a vertical and horizontal organizational structure. What is the logic behind a vertical structure? What is the logic behind a horizontal structure?
14. What are some of the barriers to using teams in purchasing and supply chain management?
15. What is the logic behind co-locating purchasing personnel with internal customers?

ADDITIONAL READINGS

Anderson, J. A. (2002), "Organizational Design: Two Lessons to Learn before Reorganizing," *International Journal of Organization Theory and Behavior,* 5(3–4), 343.

Fearon, H., and Leenders, M. (1996), *Purchasing's Organizational Roles and Responsibilities,* Tempe, AZ: Center for Advanced Purchasing Studies.

Johnson, P. F., Klassen, R. D., Leenders, M. R., and Fearon, H. E. (2002), "Determinants of Purchasing Team Usage in the Supply Chain," *Journal of Operations Management,* 20(1), 77–89.

Johnson, P. F., Leenders, M., and Fearon, H. (2006), "Supply's Growing Status and Influence," *Journal of Supply Chain Management,* 42, 38–48.

Leenders, M. R., and Johnson, P. F. (2000), *Major Structural Changes in Supply Organizations,* Tempe, AZ: Center for Advanced Purchasing Studies.

Leenders, M. R., and Johnson, P. F. (2002), *Major Changes in Supply Chain Responsibilities,* Tempe, AZ: Center for Advanced Purchasing Studies.

McDonough, E. F. (2000), "An Investigation of Factors Contributing to the Success of Cross-Functional Teams," *Journal of Product Innovation Management,* 17(3), 221.

Walter, D., and Buchanan, J. (2001), "The New Economy, New Opportunities, and New Structures," *Management Decision,* 39(10), 818–834.

ENDNOTES

1. Champoux, J. (1999), *Organization Behavior: Essential Tenets for a New Millennium,* Cincinnati: South-Western, p. 325.
2. Gordon, J. R. (1987), *A Diagnostic Approach to Organizational Behavior,* Boston: Allyn and Bacon, pp. 522–526.
3. Johnson, F., Leenders, M., and Fearon, H. (2006), "Supply's Growing Status and Influence: A Sixteen-Year Perspective," *Journal of Supply Chain Management,* 42(2), 33.
4. Bloom, H., and Nardone, J. (1984), "Organizational Level of the Purchasing Function," *International Journal of Purchasing and Materials Management,* 20(2), 16.
5. Fearon, H. (1988), "Organizational Relationships in Purchasing," *Journal of Purchasing and Materials Management,* 24(4), 7.
6. Johnson, F., and Leenders, M. (2007), *Supply Leadership Changes,* Tempe, AZ: CAPS Research.
7. Trent, R. J. (2003), "Procurement and Supply Management Organizational Design Survey," research white paper. For a copy of study results, contact rjt2@lehigh.edu.
8. Trent (2003).

9. Giunipero, L., and Handfield, R. (2004), *Purchasing Education and Training II,* Tempe, AZ: CAPS Research, pp. 40–41.

10. Trent, R. J. (2004), "The Use of Organizational Design Features in Purchasing and Supply Management," *Journal of Supply Chain Management,* 40(3), 4.

11. Giunipero and Handfield, pp. 77–79.

12. "Global Purchasing at Colgate" (1997), *Purchasing,* 40–45.

13. Trent (2003).

14. Giunipero and Handfield.

15. Fearon, pp. 2–12.

16. Lambert, D., Giunipero, L., and Ridenhower, G. (2000), "Supply Chain Management: The Key to Achieving Business Excellence in the 21st Century," working paper.

17. Hackman, R. (1987), "The Design of Work Teams," in *Handbook of Organizational Behavior,* Englewood Cliffs, NJ: Prentice Hall, pp. 315–342.

18. Hofstede, G. H. (1984), *Culture's Consequences: Differences in Work-Related Values,* Newbury Park, CA: Sage, p. 158.

19. From data collected at the 1999 Executive Purchasing and Supply Chain Management Seminar, Michigan State University, East Lansing.

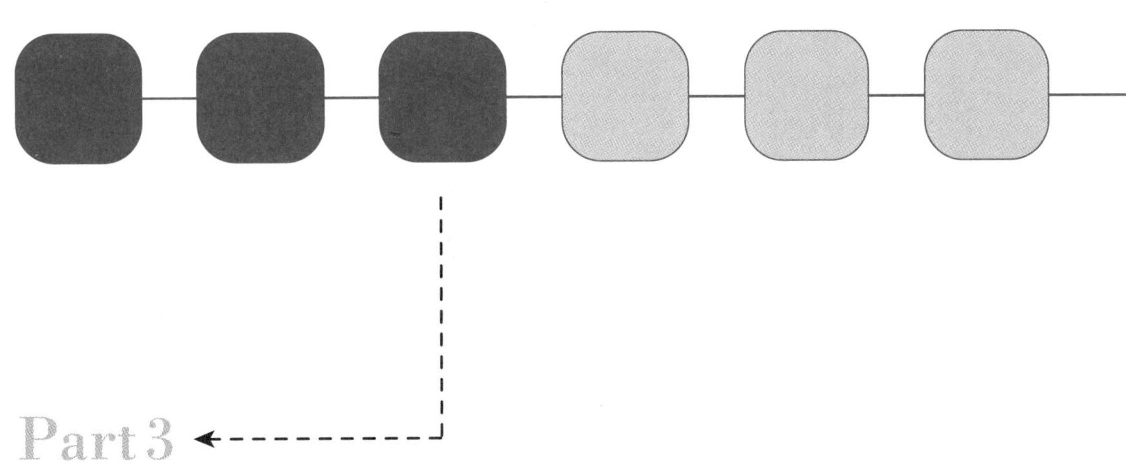

Part 3

Strategic Sourcing

Chapter 6

SUPPLY MANAGEMENT AND COMMODITY STRATEGY DEVELOPMENT

Learning Objectives

After completing this chapter, you should be able to

- Align the supply management and enterprise objectives
- Recognize a category strategy
- Understand category strategy development
- Identify the types of supply management strategies
- Understand e-reverse auctions
- Develop sourcing strategies

Chapter Outline

Building the 787 Dreamliner: The Critical Role of Supply Management

Boeing Co. recently announced that its new wide-body jet, the 787 Dreamliner, will be delayed by at least six months, a blow for the company's ambitious plan to revamp how it builds airplanes by having suppliers take on a greater role. Jim McNerney, their CEO, noted that "notwithstanding the challenges that we are experiencing in bringing forward this game-changing product, we remain confident in the design of the 787, and in the fundamental innovation and technologies that underpin it." This strategy indeed represents an entirely new approach to building airplanes that relies much more on sourcing strategy. In planning for the 787, Boeing remade its production process to rely heavily on major suppliers as risk-sharing partners. In return for investing more up front and taking on a share of the development costs, suppliers have been given major sections of the airplane to build. The wing sections are made in Japan, whereas factories in Italy, South Carolina, and Wichita, Kansas, assemble the bulk of the fuselage. The parts are flown aboard modified 757 cargo planes to Everett, Washington, for final assembly.

Boeing says that when the system is up and running, it will eventually be able to snap together Dreamliners in as little as three days, not unlike how plastic model airplanes are assembled. Further, Boeing officials say the system has reduced the company's upfront development costs by billions of dollars. The downside? Boeing has less control over the day-to-day progress of the Dreamliner program than it has had for any new airliner in its history.

However, unlike the delays that have plagued Airbus, which has delayed its A380 jetliner by two years, Boeing says the problems don't point to a fundamental flaw in its design, but rather involve difficulties in the supply chain. For example, since the summer of 2007, the industry has been beset by a shortage in titanium and aluminum fasteners used to hold airplanes together. Boeing's problems were exacerbated because suppliers are working with composite materials instead of the more familiar aluminum. After a major ceremony on July 8 when the first Dreamliner was unveiled before a crowd of more than 15,000 guests, the plane actually had to be largely disassembled by unfastening the thousands of fasteners on the body. Suppliers hadn't preinstalled wiring or other major components needed to make the system work smoothly. Once engineers got inside, it became evident that it would take more time to put the plane back together than anticipated.

Outsourcing design to suppliers has definitely proven to increase the risk associated with developing new products. For more than a year, teams of Boeing experts have lived on the road, troubleshooting problems at factories all over the globe, and making sure they have enough raw materials to do their work. In some cases, such as with a factory that was erected in Charleston, South Carolina, by Italy's Alenia Aeronautica SpA and Bought Aircraft Industries Inc. of Dallas, relatively inexperienced workers were hired from the local area to begin building an airplane that is technically more advanced than any commercial airplane in history! "If there's a lesson learned, you'd start earlier and do a little more training with our people there," said Scott Carson, chief executive of Boeing's Commercial Airplanes unit. Carson noted that unlike the previous schedule, the new delivery schedule has a margin built in for unexpected problems that might arise during flight testing, which gives Boeing "much more confidence in our ability to deliver this plane on time."

Source: J. L. Lunsford, "Boeing Delays 787 by Six Months as Suppliers in New Role Fall Behind," *Wall Street Journal,* October 11, 2007, p. A1.

Remaining competitive means that supply management must contribute to profitability by focusing on not only cost savings, but contributions to top-line growth and innovation. World-class supply management requires that leaders align with business unit stakeholders, understand their direct and indirect requirements for success, develop a deep insight into the global supply market's ability to meet these requirements, and negotiate contracts and manage supplier relationships that create a competitive advantage. This is a dynamic and difficult task, given the complexity and challenges that exist under current market conditions.

This chapter focuses on the contribution that supply management can make to a firm's competitive position and how this contribution should filter down to category management teams. A **category** refers to a specific family of products or services that are used in delivering value to the end customer. We begin by discussing how supply management executives can contribute to the strategic plan at the companywide level. In order to contribute to corporate strategy, supply management must be able to translate corporate objectives into specific supply management goals. Supply management goals serve as the driver for both strategic supply management processes and detailed commodity strategies—specific action plans that detail how goals are achieved through relationships with suppliers. To illustrate this, we provide a step-by-step process employed by category teams that is used to define business requirements, research the supply market, and develop a plan to source the product or services. We conclude with some specific examples of category strategies that best-in-class firms are deploying to cope with an increasingly challenging set of circumstances in today's supply market.

Aligning Supply Management and Enterprise Objectives

A company's leadership team, in defining how the firm will compete and succeed in the global environment, must clearly and succinctly communicate the following to their executive team:

- What markets will the firm compete in, and on what basis?
- What are the long-term and short-term business goals the company seeks to achieve?
- What are the budgetary and economic resource constraints, and how will these be allocated to functional groups and business units?

When faced with these challenges, business unit functions must then work together to define their functional strategies, which are a set of short-term and long-term plans that will support the enterprise strategy.

The first part of this process requires that the leadership team understand its key markets and economic forecasts, and provide a clear vision of how the enterprise will differentiate itself from its competitors, achieve growth objectives, manage costs, achieve customer satisfaction, and maintain continued profitability in order to meet or exceed the expectations of stakeholders.

Although it is beyond the scope of this chapter to go into detail regarding corporate strategies, the economics associated with corporate strategy are fairly straightforward. An organization must take in more revenues than it spends on operating costs

Exhibit 6.1 How Companies Create Shareholder Value

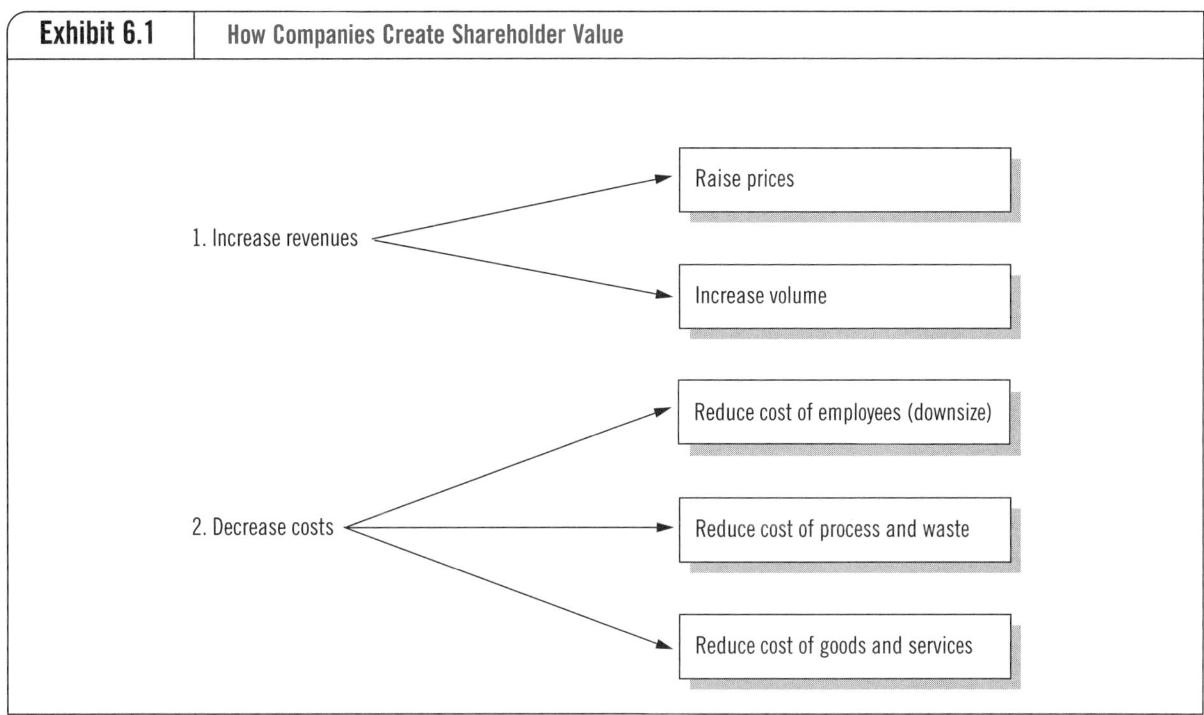

in the long term to grow and increase profits. As shown in Exhibit 6.1, there are two fundamental ways of balancing this equation: increase revenues or decrease costs.

Increasing revenues involves either raising prices or keeping prices stable and increasing volume. Simultaneously, costs must be held steady or must increase at a rate smaller than the rate of increasing revenues. However, this option has become increasingly more difficult to realize over the last several years. Since 2004, prices for commodities such as nickel, steel, oil and gas, coal, resin feedstocks, and copper have doubled or tripled. To combat these trends, many firms have sought new suppliers in China, India, and Asia, to counteract these higher costs with lower labor costs. As a result, inflation has been largely kept at bay, and the number of competitively priced, higher-quality products has increased. Today, there are only a few markets in which a seller can increase or even hold prices steady. For example, the price of automobiles has remained largely stable, even as the cost of materials going into these cars has increased dramatically.

Reducing costs has become an area of intense interest. Faced with global competition, companies are constantly searching for ways to reduce costs and pass the savings on to customers while preserving their profit margins and maintaining a return to shareholders.

Reducing the cost of materials and services has remained an important enterprise objective. Another is innovation. Firms are constantly seeking to find the next new technology that will create new markets and capture a share of consumers' wallets. Consider the iPod and the massive market for online music that followed this innovation.

Integrative Strategy Development

The process of aligning supply management goals with corporate objectives is especially important for supply management and supply chain managers. These managers often face some very broad directives from corporate management—for example, to reduce costs or to improve quality. The strategy development process takes place on four levels:

- Corporate Strategies: These strategies are concerned with (1) the definition of businesses in which the corporation wishes to participate and (2) the acquisition and allocation of resources to these business units.
- Business Unit Strategies: These strategies are concerned with (1) the scope or boundaries of each business and the links with corporate strategy and (2) the basis on which the business unit will achieve and maintain a competitive advantage within an industry.
- Supply Management Strategies: These strategies, which are part of a level of strategy development called functional strategies, specify how supply management will (1) support the desired competitive business-level strategy and (2) complement other functional strategies (such as marketing and operations).
- Commodity Strategies: These strategies specify how a group tasked with developing the strategy for the specific commodity being purchased will achieve goals that in turn will support the supply management–, business unit–, and ultimately corporate-level strategies.

Companies that are successful in deploying supply chain strategies do so because the strategy development process is **integrative**. This means that the strategy is drafted by (or has significant input from) those people responsible for implementation.

Exhibit 6.2 Components of Integrative Strategy Development

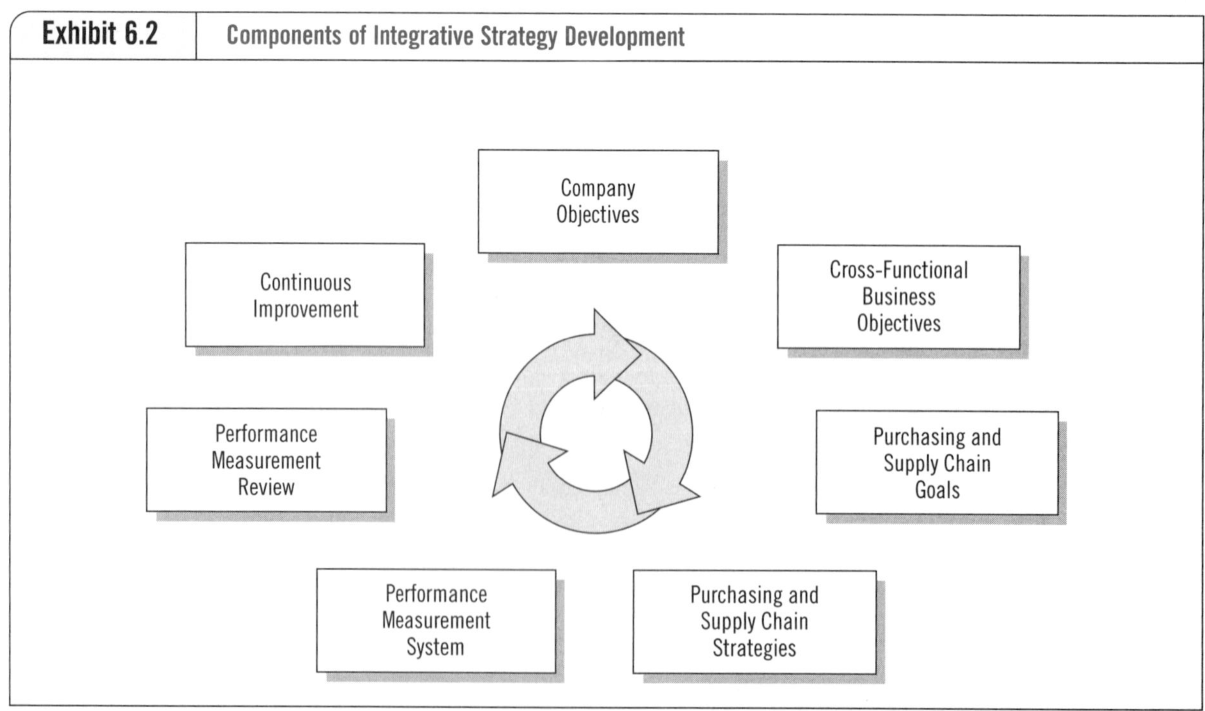

Integrative supply chain strategies occur when corporate strategic plans are effectively "cascaded" into specific supply management and commodity goals, through a series of iterative planning stages (shown in Exhibit 6.2). Corporate strategy evolves from corporate objectives, which effectively evolve from a corporate mission statement drafted by the chief executive officer (CEO), functional executives, and the board of directors. Corporate strategies are crafted by the CEO, taking into consideration the organization's competitive strengths, business unit and functional capabilities, market objectives, competitive pressures and customer requirements, and macroeconomic trends. What distinguishes an integrative strategy development process is that business unit executives, as well as corporate supply management executives, provide direct input during the development of corporate strategy.

Translating Supply Management Objectives into Supply Management Goals

A major output of the strategy development process is a set of functional strategic objectives, including supply management strategic objectives. As supply management managers interact with other members within their business, as well as with corporate executives, a major set of strategic directives should begin to emerge. These strategic objectives may or may not provide details concerning how they are to be achieved. However, the process is not yet complete. Unless supply management executives can effectively translate broad-level objectives into specific supply management goals, these strategies will never be realized.

Supply management must couple each objective with a specific goal that it can measure and act upon. These specific goals become the initial step for a detailed commodity strategy formulation process. Remember—objectives drive goals, whether at the highest levels of an organization or at the functional or department level. The following are examples of corporatewide supply management goals associated with various supply management objectives.

Cost-Reduction Objective

- Be the low-cost producer within our industry. (Goal: Reduce material costs by 15% in one year.)
- Reduce the levels of inventory required to supply internal customers. (Goal: Reduce raw material inventory to 20 days' supply or less.)

Technology/New-Product Development Objective

- Outsource non-core-competency activities. (Goal: Qualify two new suppliers for all major services by end of the fiscal year.)
- Reduce product development time. (Goal: Develop a formal supplier integration process manual by the end of the fiscal year.)

Supply Base Reduction Objective

- Reduce the number of suppliers used. (Goal: Reduce the total supply base by 30% over the next six months.)
- Joint problem-solve with remaining suppliers. (Goal: Identify $300,000 in potential cost savings opportunities with two suppliers by the end of the fiscal year.)

Sourcing Snapshot

Ford Rebuilds Its Supply Base

In the latest sign of how U.S. automakers are rethinking their business, Ford Motor Co. plans to overhaul its $90-billion-a-year global purchasing process to offer larger, long-term contracts to a smaller group of suppliers on future models, a switch that could save billions of dollars a year. In particular, Ford will tap seven major suppliers in its initial effort to streamline parts purchasing (see table below as compiled from company sources).

COMPANY (LOCATION)	SOME KEY PRODUCTS
Autoliv (Stockholm)	Safety systems such as seat belts and airbags
Delphi (Troy, Michigan)	Steering systems; remote keyless entry systems
Johnson Controls (Milwaukee)	Seats; instrument panels; batteries
Lear (Southfield, Michigan)	Seats; instrument panels; acoustics
Magna International (Aurora, Ontario)	Center consoles; interior mirrors; transmission parts
Visteon (Van Buren Township, Michigan)	Heating and cooling systems; lighting
Yazaki (Tokyo)	Wire harnesses; advanced electronics

The initial phase of the plan covers more than $35 billion in Ford purchasing for 20 key parts such as seats, tires, and bumpers. Ford will cut by more than half the number of suppliers from whom it buys these parts, starting with vehicles that will be built in 2008–2009 and beyond, Ford officials said.

That effort in turn promises a shake-up in the beleaguered auto-parts industry, a key part of the nation's manufacturing base. In recent months, several auto suppliers have filed for Chapter 11 bankruptcy protection amid broader pressure on the industry from the rising price of oil, steel, and other commodities and their inability to raise prices as car companies maintain steep consumer discounts.

Globally, there are an estimated 5,000 direct suppliers of parts to the auto industry, with combined sales in excess of $500 billion, according to CSM, a Farmington Hills, Michigan–based auto research and production firm.

Ford's move to revamp how it buys everything from paint to health care is the latest stage in the efforts of Chairman and Chief Executive Officer William Clay Ford Jr. to turn around the nation's No. 2 automaker, whose automotive business reported a $1.1 billion operating loss in the second quarter and whose debt recently was downgraded to junk-bond status. It comes at a time when the big U.S. automakers are facing profit-margin squeezes from steep discounting, rising gasoline prices, and fierce competition from Asian rivals.

Source: J. McCracken, "Ford Seeks Big Savings by Overhauling Supply System: No. 2 Automaker Will Offer Larger and Longer Contracts but Use Fewer Companies," *Wall Street Journal,* September 29, 2005, p. A1.

Supply Assurance Objective

- Assure uninterrupted supply from those suppliers best suited to filling specific needs. (Goal: Reduce cycle time on key parts to one week or less within six months.)

Quality Objective

- Increase quality of services and products. (Goal: Reduce average defects by 200 ppm on all material receipts within one year.)

The next level of detail requires translating companywide supply management goals into specific commodity-level goals.

What Is a Category Strategy?

Although not always the case, companies often use commodity teams to develop supply management strategies. Supply management strategies often apply to categories—general families of purchased products or services. Examples of major commodity classifications across different industries include body side moldings (automotive), microprocessors (computer), steel (metalworking), cotton (apparel), wood (pulp and paper), petroleum products (chemicals), outsourced business processes (IT programming, call centers), and office supplies (all industries). A category team is often composed of personnel from the operational group, product design, process engineering, marketing, finance, and supply management. The personnel involved should be familiar with the commodity being evaluated.

For instance, if the team is tasked with supply management computers, then users from information systems should be included. If the team purchases vehicles and vehicle parts, then it would be a good idea to include maintenance managers who are familiar with the characteristics of these commodities. In general, the more important the commodity, the more likely that cross-functional members and user groups will be involved. Together, the commodity team will develop a commodity strategy that provides the specific details and outlines the actions to follow in managing the commodity.

As noted in previous sections and shown in Exhibit 6.2, supply management derives its strategic direction from corporate objectives and the business unit strategy development process.

The business unit functional strategy acts as the driver for the cross-organizational supply management strategies that emerge for the major products and services purchased by the business unit. These in turn translate into supply management goals. Once supply management has identified a set of broad-level goals that it must achieve, another set of more detailed strategies should emerge at the commodity/service/product family level. The process of supply management strategy deployment effectively begins at the commodity/product family level.

Before initiating any category strategy, there must be buy-in from the key stakeholders, especially at the senior leadership level. Without executive commitment, strategic sourcing results are unlikely to be successful. To ensure buy-in of the corporate team, supply management must clearly define the "prize" or carrot at the end of the stick, to obtain the go-ahead to pursue the strategy. To enable an effective category strategy, the team must:

1. Spend money on resources initially, including assessment of current spend, data collection, market research, training, and people.
2. Validate the savings or contribution to other company objectives achieved by supply management and drive them to the bottom line.

3. Sustain the initiative through presentations to senior executives who support the move toward an integrated supply management function with other functional groups in the supply chain, including marketing, research and development, and accounting.

The individual who will ensure that this can happen will often report to the chief financial officer (CFO)—so making a solid business case is an important element in building support for category strategies in most firms.

A study[1] conducted by Accenture, Stanford, and INSEAD found that 89% of senior executives at leading companies view supply chains as critical or very important to their company and industry, and 89% also agreed investments in supply chain capabilities have increased in the last three years. Chief financial officers are especially interested. Driven by cost-cutting needs and general dissatisfaction with supply chain performance, CFOs are adding supply chain management to the financial levers they already control.[2] They see this activity as integral to meeting their strategic goals and view the supply chain as having a large or very important effect on their ability to achieve corporate objectives. Above all else, CFOs consider reducing operating costs as a key goal of their supply chain, with improving customer service coming in a close second. This suggests that CFOs are not just obsessed with financial rigor but also appreciate the importance of customer-relationship management to the future of their organizations.

According to the survey, 34% of CFOs have taken more of a leadership role in supply chain management, and 49% believe that they will be playing such a role in two years. And CFOs see themselves as suited to the task; they wield significant corporate power, yet have no ax to grind in a supply chain sense because they are not bound by the traditional political and organizational ties that anchor this discipline within companies. CFOs can bring "a certain degree of coherence to what may be a fragmented reporting structure," said Gene Long, president of UPS Consulting. Because they are already charged with managing cash and capital allocations, in a supply chain sense they "probably are in a critical position to be able to manage the tradeoffs that should be made," Long said. Also, he said CFOs are adept at quantifying value, something that supply management can benefit from. In many cases this is already happening; 20% of respondents said that senior supply chain professionals already report to the CFO, but the survey indicates that this will become more widespread, enabling financial executives to take a more proactive role.

The most common approach for building a business case is through an annual process review of where the company is spending its money: the "spend analysis."

Conducting a Spend Analysis

As we discussed in Chapter 2, a robust procure to pay process is critical, in order to facilitate an accurate spend analysis. Why is it important to capture the transaction-level data associated with all purchasing processes? Because from time to time the firm must identify opportunities for savings through a process known as a spend analysis. A spend analysis becomes a critical input into building category strategies.

A **spend analysis** is an annual review of a firm's entire set of purchases. This review provides answers to the following questions:

- What did the business spend its money on over the past year? (This value is an important component in calculating the cost of goods sold in the financial statement. Purchased goods and materials are often more than 50% of the total cost of goods sold.)

- Did the business receive the right amount of products and services given what it paid for them? (This is an important requirement to meet the legal requirements of the Sarbanes Oxley Act, which requires accountability and correct reporting of financial statements to the SEC.)
- What suppliers received the majority of the business, and did they charge an accurate price across all the divisions in comparison to the requirements in the POs, contracts, and statements of work? (This is an important component to ensure contract compliance.)
- Which divisions of the business spent their money on products and services that were correctly budgeted for? (This is an important component for planning annual budgets for spending in the coming year.)
- Are there opportunities to combine volumes of spending from different businesses, and standardize product requirements, reduce the number of suppliers providing these products, or exploit market conditions to receive better pricing? (This is an important input into strategic sourcing planning, the topic of the next chapter in the book.)

Moreover, a spend analysis provides insights and clarity into these questions and becomes an important planning document for senior executives in finance, operations,

Exhibit 6.3 **Best Practices in Spend Analysis**

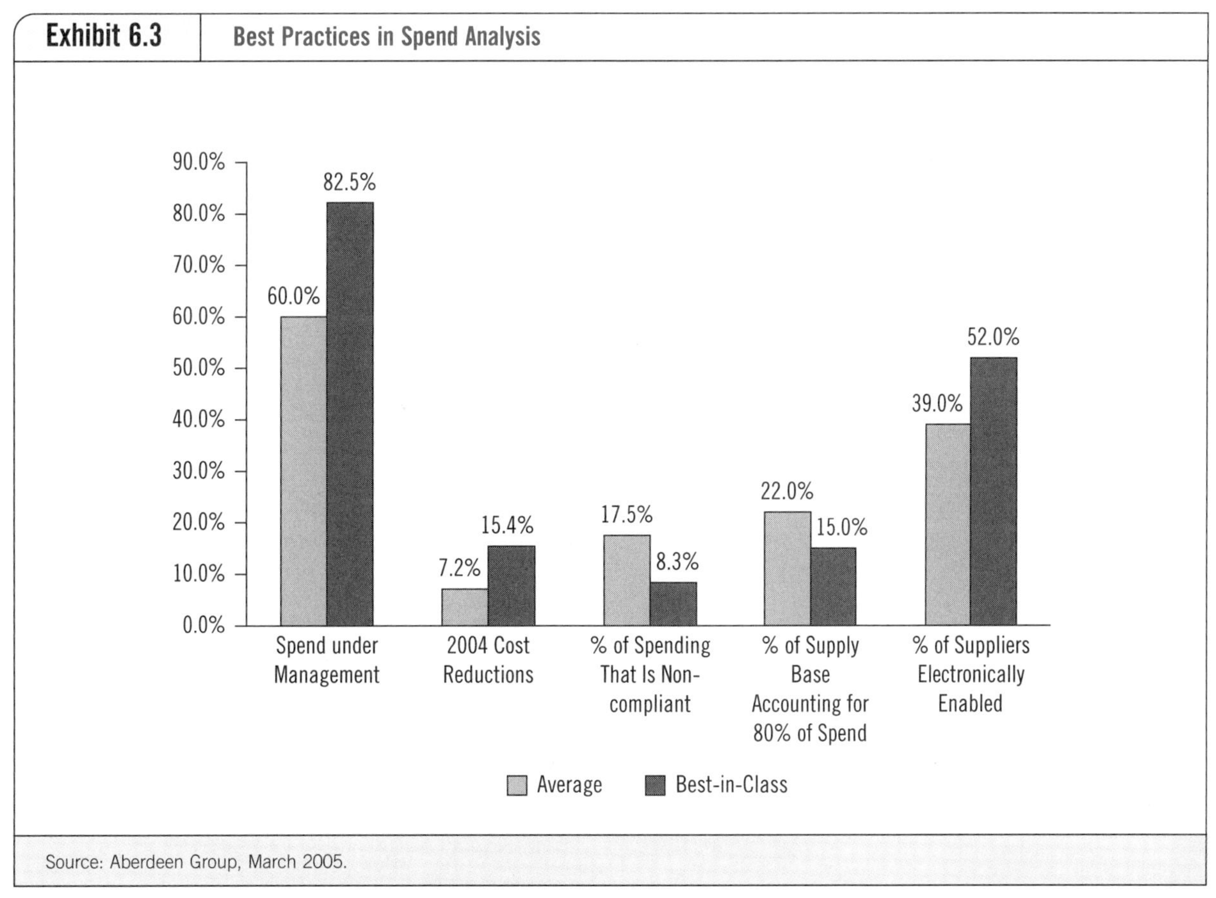

Source: Aberdeen Group, March 2005.

marketing, purchasing, and accounting. Despite the importance of this element, many firms struggle to develop a comprehensive and accurate spend analysis report. This is because purchasing was for many years a paper-based system, and figures were not entered correctly into accounting systems. Even with the evolution of sophisticated enterprise systems such as SAP and Oracle, purchasing transactions are often entered incorrectly, which elicits the old phrase "garbage in, garbage out." Another problem is that many enterprises have grown through mergers and acquisitions. When a new division is acquired, they may be using a different system from the acquiring company, and so the data is not easily translatable. For this reason, many firms are undergoing major initiatives to streamline procurement through electronic procurement systems that will revamp the purchase to pay process and automate different portions to capture transactions more effectively. Indeed, the research shown by Aberdeen Research in Exhibit 6.3 on p. 197 suggests that "best in class" firms are more likely to have a higher proportion of their spend under management, which has led to important improvements such as cost reductions, reduction of noncompliant purchases, supply base reduction, and electronically enabled suppliers.

Spend Analysis Spreadsheet

Assuming that a spend database is available and is reasonably accurate, how do firms produce a spend analysis? The best way to illustrate is to go through a specific example of a spend analysis and identify the requirements at each stage.

Exhibit 6.4 Example of Spend Analysis

SUPPLIER	COMMODITY	ANNUAL SPEND
REBATE CO	Rebate Fulfillment & Call Center	$329,873,663
INVEST CO	Investments	$130,328,512
ADVERT CO	Advertising	$ 56,134,490
REPAIR CO	Service Repairs	$ 49,339,218
BENEFITS CO	Benefits	$ 48,969,149
HARDWARE CO	Hardware	$ 40,572,450
PARTCO	Service Parts	$ 39,910,372
TELECOM	Telecommunications	$ 31,055,599
DISPLAY CO	Store Displays	$ 30,020,969
PENPAPER CO	Paper	$ 29,175,843
LABOR CO	Contract Labor	$ 27,880,363
SUPPLY CO	Paper	$ 23,844,707
CONTRACT CO	General Contracting	$ 22,579,113
OFFICE CO	Paper	$ 22,257,690
GRAPHICS CO	Graphic Design	$ 21,966,989
PAYMENT CO	Business & Management Services	$ 20,380,275
FREIGHT CO	Surface Freight	$ 19,369,010
PAPER CO	Paper	$ 15,603,682
SERVICE PLAN CO	Service Plan	$ 15,478,827
SERVICE CO	Service Parts	$ 14,868,023
CONSUMER CO	Consumer Financing	$ 14,833,333
ENERGY CO	Energy	$ 14,087,177

Exhibit 6.4 shows spend data sorted by descending dollar. Note that the dataset contains information on the general classification or "commodity," the primary supplier for that category, and the dollar amount spent with that supplier in that commodity. It is important to note that there may be multiple suppliers that supply a single commodity, and vice versa (multiple commodity classifications supplied by a single supplier). The entire spreadsheet is NOT shown in this case; in fact, the spreadsheet has over 2,500 lines in it, and this would be considered a simple spend analysis. Many datasets have literally millions of transactions in them. With this information in hand, you can proceed as follows:

1. The first step is to take this information and sort the data by commodity. In this case, a commodity is a "category" of spending.
2. From the commodity sort, find the total spend by commodity. (Hint: The subtotal or pivot table functions in Excel can help.) Calculate the total spend by commodity.
3. Make a chart of the top 10 commodities by descending $ spend. A Pareto chart is used to show the total value of spend that occurs within each category. As shown in Exhibit 6.5, the top 10 categories of spending are rebate fulfillment and call center spending, advertising, general contracting, hardware, investments, paper, service parts, business and management services, contract labor, and telecommunications. These areas represent the highest level of spend and, therefore, the biggest opportunity for sourcing analysis and opportunities for cost savings and price reductions. But we aren't done yet!
4. From the commodity sort, find the number of suppliers by commodity. (Hint: The pivot table function in Excel can help.) Perform a descending sort of number of suppliers by commodity.

Exhibit 6.5 Pareto Chart of Spend by Commodity Category

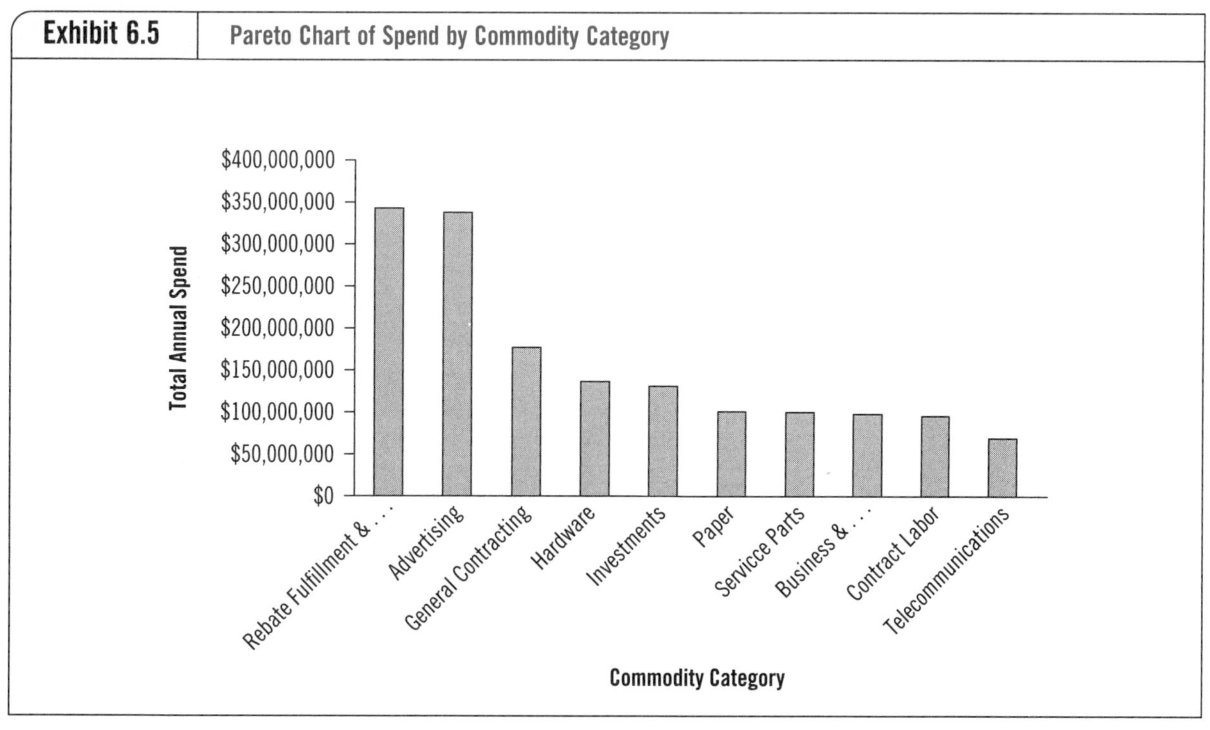

5. Make a chart of the top ten commodities by descending number of suppliers. As shown in Exhibit 6.6, the advertising category has the highest number of suppliers within it, followed by other miscellaneous small dollar suppliers (who might be supplying office products or other noncritical items), energy, security, general contracting, and business and management services. It is amazing that this firm is using almost 2,500 different suppliers of advertising! However, this is not uncommon, as business units will often use their own local preferred supplier, because they are nearby and they know them. Although this is appropriate in some cases, it may also be an opportunity for supply base reduction and further cost savings.
6. From the commodity sort, find the average spend per supplier by commodity. Perform an ascending sort of average spend per supplier. Exhibit 6.7 shows the categories that have the lowest volume of spending by supplier. A low spend per supplier figure is indicative that there are too many suppliers in that category, as the volume per supplier should be increased. It is interesting that none of these parameters show up in the other two charts, suggesting that there may or may not be an opportunity worth pursuing in the categories shown in these charts.
7. Applying the concept of Pareto analysis to the chart of top 10 commodities by descending $ spend, what are the recommendations for savings opportunities?

From Exhibit 6.5, the areas of Rebate Fulfillment and Advertising are clear areas for savings opportunities. As shown in Exhibit 6.8, total spend for this company is $2,449,428,985, of which 14% ($342M) and 13.8% ($336M) are in these two areas alone. Note that overall, these 10 categories constitute 65% of the company's total spend. Further analysis shows that rebate fulfillment only has eight suppliers, although

Exhibit 6.6 Pareto Chart of Spend Analysis of Suppliers by Commodity Group

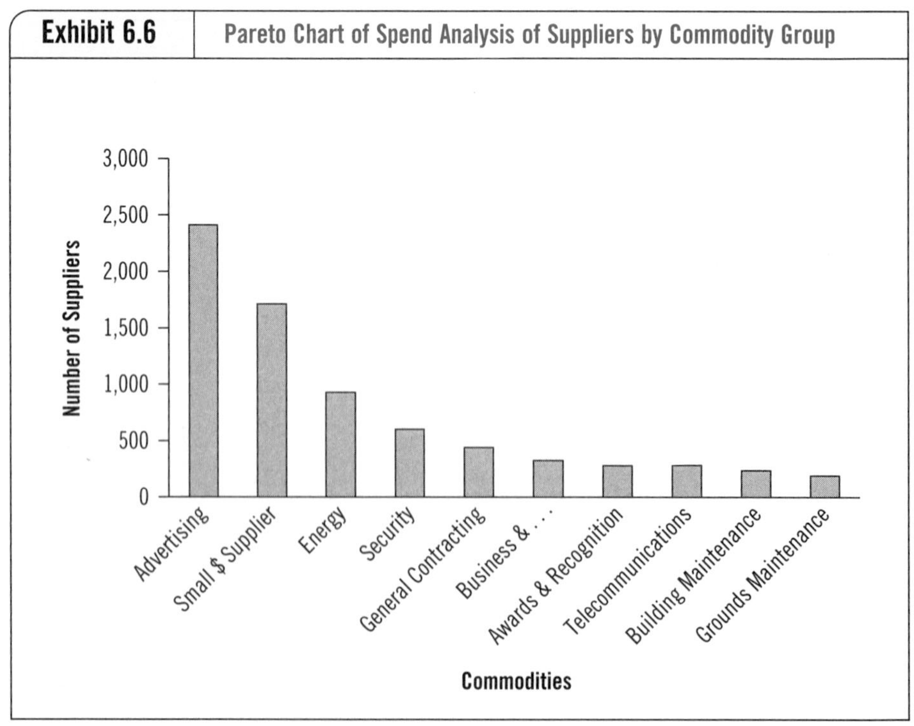

Exhibit 6.7 Pareto Chart of Spend per Supplier by Commodity

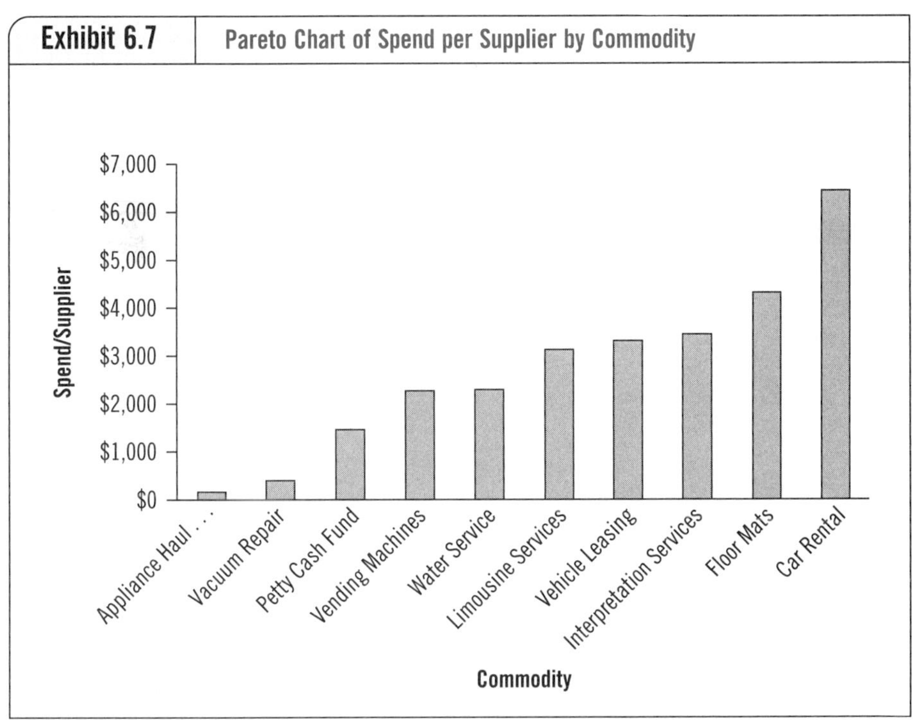

Exhibit 6.8 Pareto Chart by Percentage of Total Spend by Category

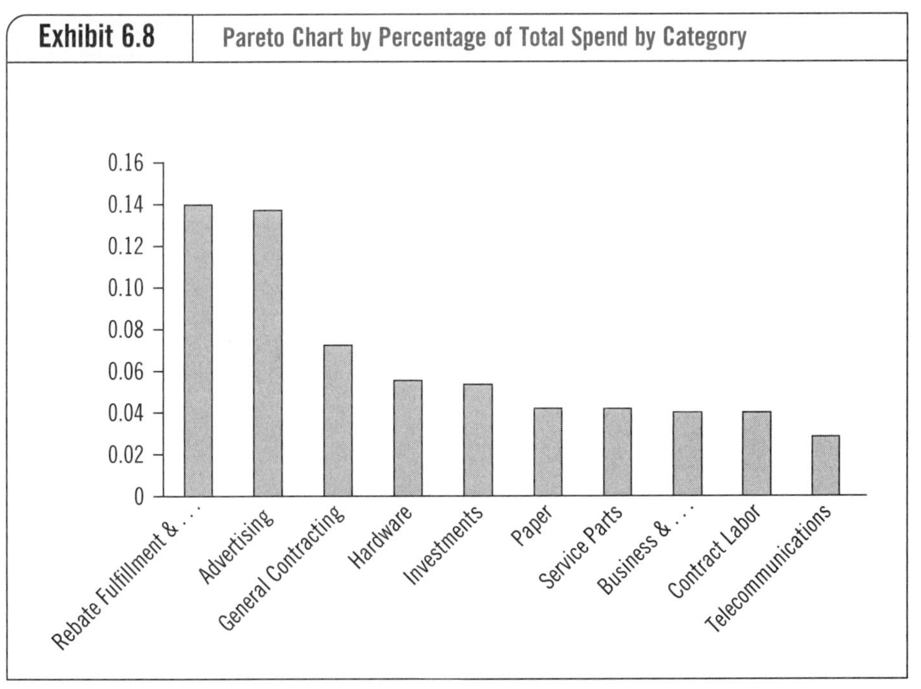

advertising has close to 2,400! Clearly, by reducing the number of suppliers in the advertising sector, spend volumes can be leveraged and more favorable pricing can be achieved, leading to a significant cost savings (perhaps on the order of 5–10%), which could lead to a net bottom line contribution of between $17M and $33M!

The same logic applies to general contracting, although the size of this opportunity is not as great. With close to 500 suppliers of this service, and the third highest spend ($175M), further negotiation and supply base reduction could lead to additional savings of $8–$17M. Combined, these two initiatives alone could contribute up to $50M of net savings to this enterprise, which could either be utilized in other investments, or passed on to shareholders in the form of increased profitability and shareholder value.

Not bad for a day's work!

From this analysis, the supply management team might approach the senior leadership team and ask for resources to deploy two category management teams: one in the rebate fulfillment services area, and another in the advertising sector. If approved, the deliverables might be, say, a 5% savings on current spend in these two areas.

Sourcing Snapshot — *Shipping Shortages Drive Raw Material Costs*

Category strategies do not just focus on commodities and goods, but also on services such as transportation. For many commodities, raw material costs are increasingly being driven by the cost of shipping. The cost of shipping raw materials across the world's oceans has reached an all-time high in October 2007, pushing up prices of grain, iron ore, coal, and other commodities. The average price of renting a ship to carry raw materials from Brazil to China has nearly tripled to $180,000 from $65,000 a year ago. In some cases, ocean shipping can be more expensive than the cargo itself. Iron ore, for example, costs about $60 a ton, but ship owners are charging about $88 a ton to carry it from Brazil to Asia. The trend is forcing many manufacturers to pay more for basic ingredients, which will probably be passed on to consumers, affecting everything from automobiles to washing machines and bread. The main reason for these shipping rates escalating is that there are not enough bulk ships. The shortage is related to the fact that explosive growth in China, India, and other developing nations is driving a need for importing of raw materials, such as iron ore from Brazil. Experts believe that shipping rates are not through escalating, either. New batches of bulk freighters are not expected to come online until 2010. "All of the ship owners are making a lot of money because these are numbers the market has never seen," said John P. Dragnis, commercial director of Goldenport Inc., one of the largest providers of ships to commodity sellers. And even when ships are available, bottlenecks at port facilities can cause delays, driving up the costs of shipments. At many ports in Brazil, Australia, and elsewhere, wait times have increased by 35%. The Baltic Exchange Dry Index, which reflects rates to transport bulk commodities such as coal, iron ore, and grains in vessels of typical sizes, is up from 4000 in October of 2006 to 11,000 in October 2007. Don't expect it to go away soon, as Chinese and Indian manufacturers tie up more ships in their hunger for more raw materials to drive their economies.

Source: R. G. Matthews, "Ship Shortage Pushes Up Prices of Raw Materials," *Wall Street Journal*, November 12, 2007, p. A1.

Category Strategy Development (Strategic Sourcing)

Once the decision has been made to outsource a product or service, firms will typically use a process known as strategic sourcing to decide to whom to outsource the product or service, as well as the structure and type of relationship that should be established. A sourcing strategy is typically focused on a category of products or services, and for that reason, the strategy is sometimes called a category strategy. A category strategy is a decision process used to identify which suppliers should provide a group of products or services, the form of the contract, the performance measures used to measure supplier performance, and the appropriate level of price, quality, and delivery arrangements that should be negotiated. A typical category may include many smaller subcategories. For example, a category around information technology may include subcategories such as laptops, desktops, servers, and keyboards. If a firm outsources accounting services, the category strategy may include tax accountants and managerial accountants. The strategic sourcing decision is typically made by a cross-functional team, composed of sourcing professionals, operations managers, finance, or other stakeholders for the product or service. A stakeholder is someone who is impacted by the sourcing decision. They have a stake in the game, so to speak, so their input in the sourcing decision is critical to reaching a successful sourcing decision. The sourcing process is described below and is shown in Exhibit 6.9.

Exhibit 6.9 Strategic Sourcing Process

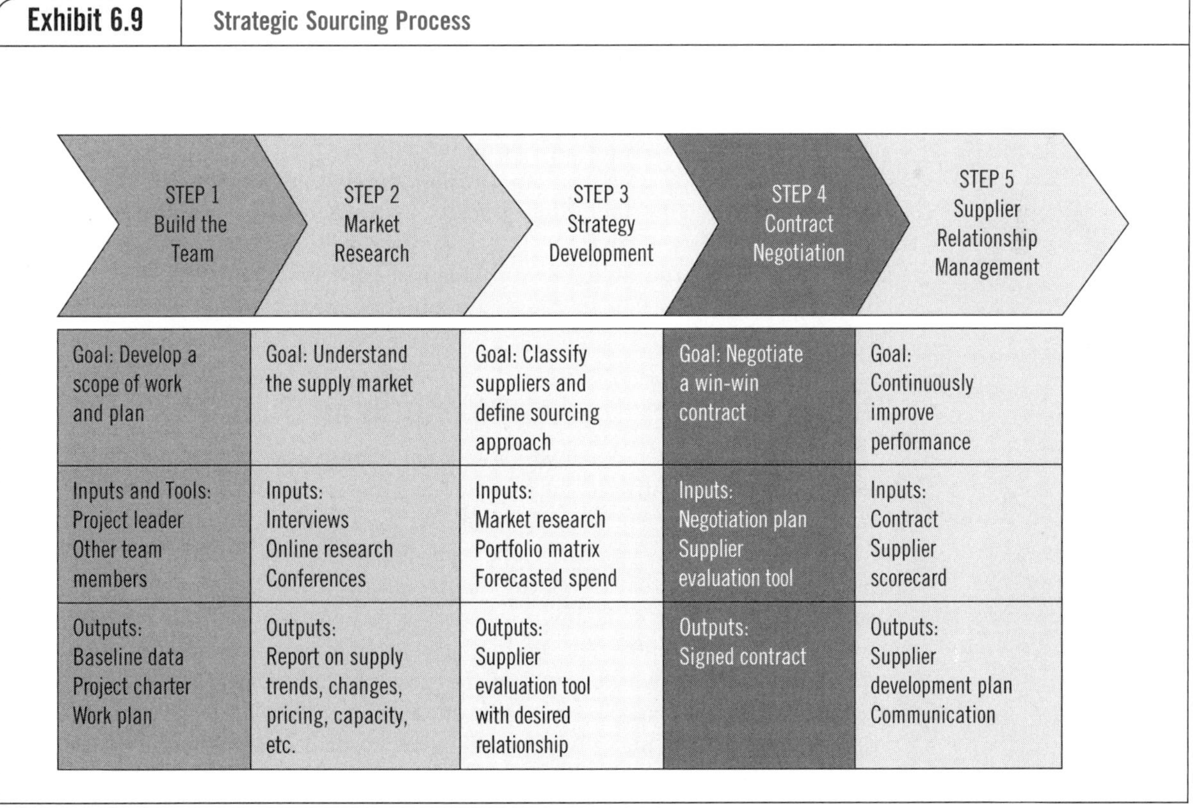

Step 1: Build the Team and the Project Charter

Companies are increasingly using a team approach to sourcing decision making by bringing together personnel from multiple functions who are familiar with the product to be purchased. Part of the first phase of the category management process is to identify the people who should be involved, as well as the key subject matter experts who may be part of the extended team. Once developed, the team should then define the scope of the category strategy, publish a project charter, and develop a work plan and communication plan. These steps help to define the purpose, boundaries, and goals of the process; identify the tasks involved; and provide a plan for communicating the results to the primary stakeholders.

A category team can be composed of personnel from operations, product design, process engineering, marketing, finance, and purchasing. The personnel involved should be familiar with the commodity being evaluated. For instance, if the team is tasked with purchasing computers, then users from information systems should be included. If the team purchases vehicles and vehicle parts, then it would be a good idea to include maintenance managers who are familiar with the characteristics of these commodities. In general, the more important the commodity, the more likely that cross-functional members and user groups will be involved. Together, the commodity team will develop a commodity strategy that provides the specific details and outlines the actions to follow in managing the commodity. Strong skills in team building and leadership, decision making, influencing internal users and suppliers, and compromising in reaching a team consensus are therefore critical skills found in individuals who will succeed in these roles.

Every sourcing team should begin by assigning a project lead, who will coordinate meetings, project deliverables, and requirements. The project lead will assemble a group of subject matter experts from various stakeholder groups in the team to provide feedback and assist with delivering the project charter. The project charter is a clear statement of the goals and objectives of the sourcing project, which is officially announced shortly after the team's first few meetings. The project charter can be issued before or after the cross-functional sourcing team has been formed, and in fact, it can be used to garner interest from potential participants in the process. The purpose of a project charter is to demonstrate management support for the project and its manager.

Step 2: Conduct Market Research on Suppliers

The second step when developing a sourcing strategy is to fully understand the purchase requirement relative to the business unit objectives. Also involved in this step is a thorough supplier spend analysis to determine past expenditures for each commodity and supplier, as well as the total expenditures for the commodity as a percentage of the total. Note that the spend analysis identified in the prior section looked at spending for the entire company. A category spend analysis will drill down to a more granular level and identify the specific business units that are purchasing the products or services, and which suppliers they are currently using. Generally, this produces a Pareto chart as shown before; often one or a handful of suppliers are the primary sources of the majority of spending in a particular category. After understanding the spend, the category team should also educate themselves as to what is happening in the marketplace, as well as what their internal customer requirements are. Just as you would perform research before buying a car (e.g., going online, reading reviews of vehicles, looking into gas mileage, and looking at warranty history reports at

Consumer Reports), teams perform the same type of market research on the supply base. This is critical in building and understanding the key suppliers, their capabilities, and their capacity to perform and meet the stakeholders' requirements.

To make an informed decision about sourcing, several pieces of information are needed. These include the following:

- Information on total annual purchase volumes. This is often an important element from the spend analysis. This analysis should show how much was spent on the category of goods or services by supplier, by business unit, and by subgroups.
- Interviews with stakeholders to determine their forecasted requirements. For example, if the annual purchase volume last year was $10 million, is this figure expected to go up or down next year based on the predicted amount of work? Stakeholders should also be interviewed to determine any new sourcing elements that may not have been included in last year's figure.
- External market research identifying information on key suppliers, available capacity, technology trends, price and cost data and trends, technical requirements, environmental and regulatory issues, and any other data that is available. In effect the team must educate themselves through a detailed analysis of the marketplace and identify how best to meet the forecasted demand (generated by the spend analysis and interviews with stakeholders) given the market conditions that will occur in the next year.

The data can be collected in a number of ways. For example, the team might elect to meet with a supplier that is an expert on the marketplace, or an external consultant who specializes in studying certain markets (e.g., chemicals, resins, IT providers). These interviews are often the best source of information and are not published. Secondary data sources are published available databases, reports, websites, and so on. Examples might be a "state of the industry" report purchased from a consulting company or a publicly available database such as the Census of U.S. Manufacturers or the U.S. Department of Labor Statistics. The problem with secondary data such as these is that they are often outdated and may not provide the specific information the team is looking for.

When conducting market research, the team may use an outsourced provider such as Beroe (www.beroe-inc.com), ICE, or Global Outlook. However the data are collected, the team must also process and integrate the data to ensure that they are relevant and can be effectively communicated to stakeholders. The whole point of conducting market research is to understand the prevailing market conditions and the ability of current or potential new suppliers to effectively deliver the product or service. In that respect, supply market intelligence becomes one of the most important and critical stepping stones for an effective category strategy. As one manager noted, "Supply market intelligence may be the only competitive advantage of the future!"

Where do most firms go to find good market intelligence? There are multiple sources of market and supplier information available. The key here is to **triangulate**, which means that you need to explore, compare, and contrast data from multiple sources before you can validate it. Triangulation is part of the scientific method and requires that you establish corroborating data to validate a given hypothesis. The more data points you have supporting the hypothesis, the greater the likelihood that the hypothesis is correct. Your job is to go through these sources and identify key elements that support your hypothesis.

- Trade journals are a great place to start. These journals provide good leads and recent updates to what is happening in the industry.
- Start also with annual reports for supplier companies, as well as other customers, and make sure you read the notes to investors.
- The Internet is great and provides a ton of leads.
- Don't forget the power of books. Many people just start by using Google, which leads you to a massive set of links that may or may not be useful. A visit to a university library can lead you to some great reference books and trade journals, with multiple leads for further information.
- The power of snowball sampling is important. This means finding experts in a particular category, who can refer you to other experts whom you can also talk to.
- There are trade consultants who can provide information, but they are very often costly.
- Category managers will also visit trade association conferences and trade websites. These conferences offer a great opportunity to network and learn more from other people who know a lot about what is going on in the industry.
- You've got to be scanning the headlines.
- Suppliers are about the best sources. Don't just talk to salespeople. Talk to the line and their purchasing people.
- Investment analyst reports, as well as interviews, can provide very good information on what is happening in certain industries where they are investing.

Collecting the data is just the first part of the job. To effectively represent and communicate the market conditions, category teams may employ a number of different data representation tools to portray and explain the current situation. Three tools we will discuss here are Porter Five Forces analysis, SWOT analysis, and supplier analysis.

Porter Five Forces

Porter Five Forces was created to describe competitive forces in a market economy. Porter Five Forces is a heavy-hitting strategy development tool that is used widely for business strategy development and sales and marketing strategies. The five forces are the forces that shape an industry (see Exhibit 6.10).

Michael Porter's industry analysis methodology was introduced in his book *Competitive Strategy,* first published in 1980 and now in its 60th printing. The powerful tool provides understanding of an industry with a simple framework.

Data for creation of a Five Forces analysis requires a review of all of the different data sources described to date in this section. It may also involve deep market intelligence through focused discussions with key stakeholders and subject matter experts. The tool helps to predict supplier and buyer behavior in the marketplace and is a critical element in shaping supply strategy. Five Forces analysis is close to a crystal ball and can be used to predict the future. It is also a helpful educational tool to lead stakeholders to understand current supply market conditions. When you understand your supplier's needs, you can figure out how you can help them help you.

Exhibit 6.10 Porter's Five Forces Analysis

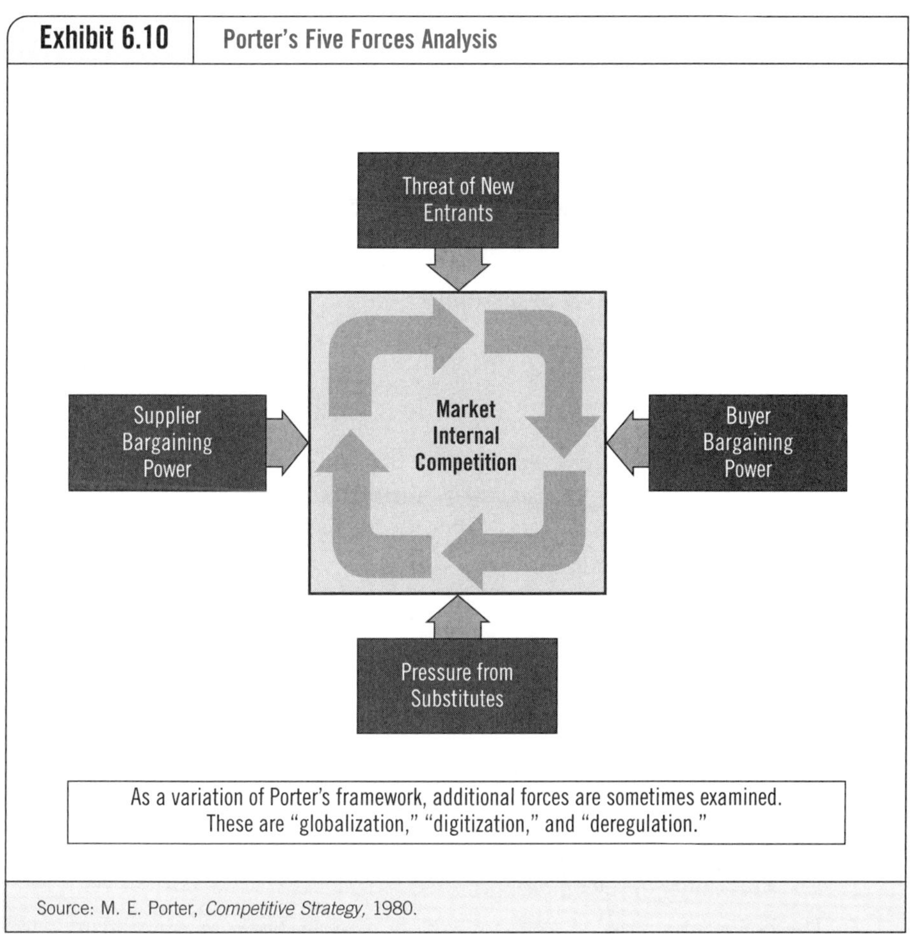

As a variation of Porter's framework, additional forces are sometimes examined. These are "globalization," "digitization," and "deregulation."

Source: M. E. Porter, *Competitive Strategy,* 1980.

The following are the five forces:

1. Higher levels of competition create more options for buyers and suppliers. Factors include the following:
   - Speed of industry growth
   - Capacity utilization
   - Exit barriers
   - Product differences
   - Switching costs
   - Diversity of competitors
2. The threat of new entrants. Examples here might be the new set of Chinese and other low-cost-country manufacturers that are entering many of the traditional U.S. manufacturing strongholds such as electronics and automobiles. Factors include the following:
   - Capital markets
   - Availability of skilled workers
   - Access to critical technologies, inputs, or distribution
   - Product life cycles

- Brand equity/customer loyalty
- Government deregulation
- Risk of switching
- Economies of scale

3. The threat of substitute products and services. For example, there are a new set of growing composites, thermosets, and carbon fibers that are replacing traditional elements such as steel. Factors influencing this include the following:
   - Relative performance of substitutes
   - Relative price of substitutes
   - Switching costs
   - Buyer propensity to substitute
4. The power of buyers. For example, as buyers begin to consolidate specifications and develop industry standards, increasing power is created over suppliers in the marketplace. Factors include the following:
   - Buyer concentration
   - Buyer volume
   - Buyer switching costs
   - Price sensitivity
   - Product differences
   - Brand identity
   - Impact on quality or performance
   - Buyer profits
   - Availability of substitutes
5. The power of suppliers. As many supply markets begin to consolidate, fewer suppliers means that a greater amount of supplier power exists in markets. Factors include the following:
   - Prices of major inputs
   - Ability to pass on price increases
   - Availability of key technologies or other resources
   - Threat of forward or backward integration
   - Industry capacity utilization
   - Supplier concentration
   - Importance of volume to supplier

Generally speaking, summarizing these elements requires that participants take a high-level view of the marketplace and begin to brainstorm and review the implications of these changes in the marketplace.

SWOT Analysis

An analysis that examines strengths, weaknesses, opportunities, and threats (SWOT) can provide insight even with limited data. (It is often a good way to figure out what data you have and where there are gaps.) As a strategic planning tool, the goal is to minimize weakness and threats, and exploit strengths and opportunities (see Exhibit 6.11).

Exhibit 6.11 SWOT Analysis

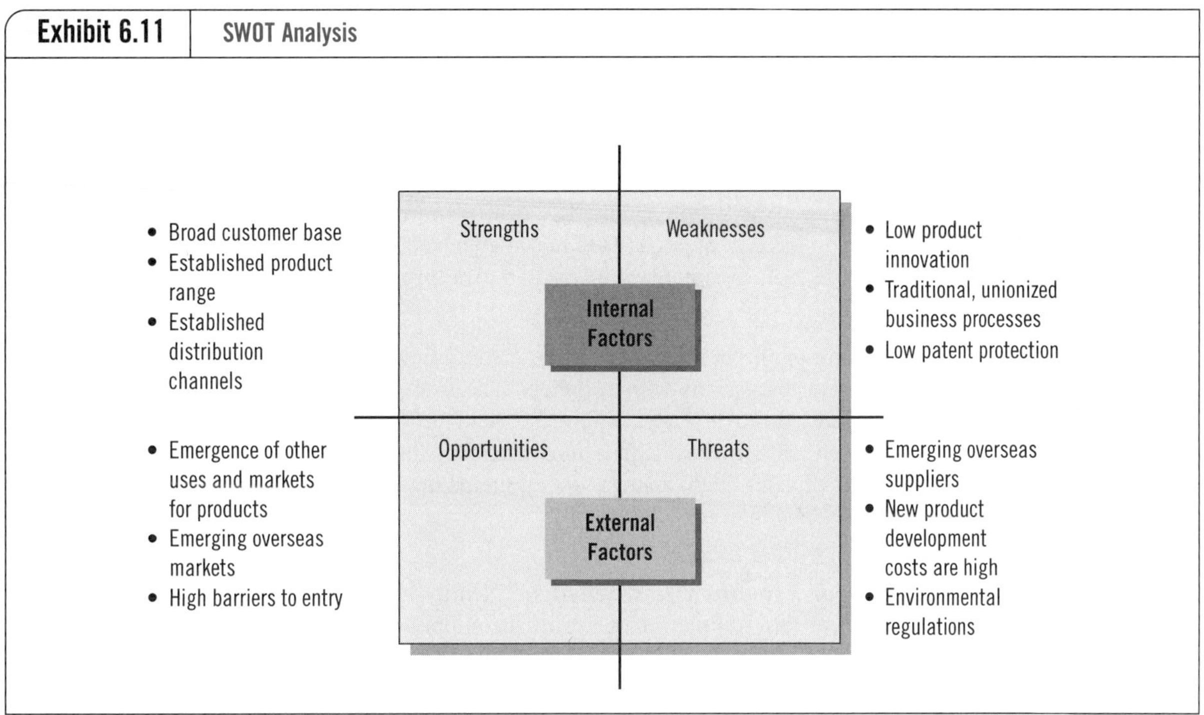

Supplier Analysis

Establish Benchmarks through Industry Databases

Benchmarking is an important element in building competitive strategy. Benchmarking requires identifying the critical performance criteria that are being benchmarked and identifying relative competitive performance. Industry benchmarks involve comparisons of performance with firms in the same industry, whereas external benchmarks involve best practices and performance levels achieved by firms that are not within the same industry.

The Center for Advanced Supply Management Studies has a number of supply management benchmark reports that can provide comparative insights into supply management performance. A number of reports on various components of supply strategy can also be found through consulting organizations, such as Aberdeen Group, Gartner, Procurement Strategy Council, Hackett Group, and other firms.

Requests for Information

A request for information (RFI) is generally used before a specific requisition of an item is issued. Most organizations will issue an RFI if they have determined that there are several potential suppliers. The RFI is a solicitation document that is used by organizations to obtain general information about services, products, or suppliers. This document does not constitute a binding agreement by either the supplier or the purchaser. The information gathered from an RFI can be disseminated throughout the organization or to specific departments.

This procedure is generally used when a large or complicated purchase is being considered and the potential pool of suppliers must be prequalified. In this case an

RFI is a questionnaire or inquiry into the supplier's background. This is used to determine if the supplier meets the minimum standards needed to successfully bid on the project and, if awarded, successfully complete the project

Value Chain Analysis

Value chain analysis is used to help identify the cost savings opportunities that exist within the supply chain. The goal is to be able to understand, identify, and exploit cost savings opportunities that may have been overlooked by business unit managers or even by suppliers in bringing the products and services to the appropriate location.

Some of the best data for value chain analysis comes from books, industry journals, and discussions with suppliers. The tool provides insights into where products originate (from dirt) and where they end up (cradle to grave). A good value chain analysis can provide insights into where in the market you need to be buying. Examples of value chain analysis are discussed in Chapter 12.

Supplier Research

Supplier research is required to identify the specific capabilities and financial health of key suppliers that are in the supply base or that may not currently be in the supply base. Some of the key elements that should be documented and included in a comprehensive supplier analysis study include the following:

- Cost structure
- Financial status
- Customer satisfaction levels
- Support capabilities
- Relative strengths and weakness
- How the buying company fits in their business
- How the company is viewed
- Core capabilities
- Strategy/future direction
- Culture

Identifying the major suppliers in a market is an important first step of any supplier analysis, especially when you are talking about global market share. This tells you who the world prefers, who the world is buying from! It is also critical to understand global capacity versus global demand and trends.

Step 3: Strategy Development

Once the team have educated themselves to the point that they feel they know enough about the supply market conditions, the forecasted spend, and the user stakeholder requirements, they are faced with a different challenge. The team must convert all of this data into meaningful knowledge and apply some meaningful tools to structure the information so that it will render an effective decision. Two tools are most often used in this process: a portfolio analysis matrix (sometimes called the strategic sourcing matrix), and the supplier evaluation scorecard.

Exhibit 6.12 Strategy Portfolio Matrix for Category Management

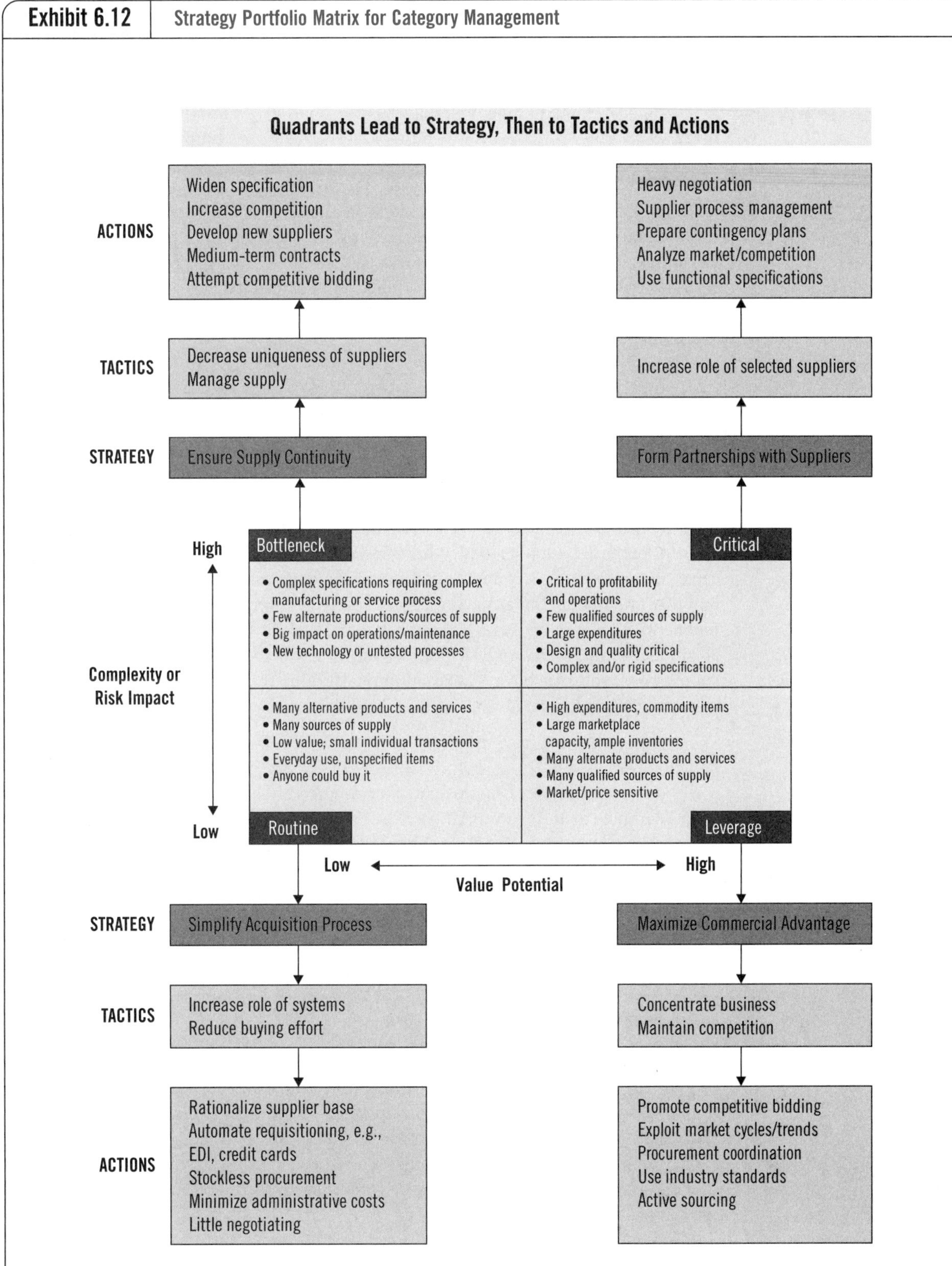

Portfolio Analysis

Portfolio analysis is a tool to structure and segment the supply base, and is used as a means of classifying suppliers into one of four types. The objective is to categorize every purchase or family of purchases into one of four categories. The premise of portfolio analysis is that every purchase or family of purchases can be classified into one of four categories or quadrants: (1) Critical, (2) Routine, (3) Leverage, and (4) Bottleneck.[3] By effectively classifying the goods and services being purchased into one of these categories, those responsible for proposing a strategy are able to comprehend the strategic importance of the item to the business. The results of this analysis can then be compared to the current sourcing strategy for the category group, and tactics and actions defined for moving forward. Exhibit 6.12 on p. 211 summarizes the essential elements of strategy, tactics, and actions associated with managing categories that fall into each of the different quadrants in the matrix, and these are described in greater detail below.

Critical Commodity—Strategic Supplier

Generally speaking, the goals for a strategic commodity are to develop a competitive advantage, support and leverage the supplier's core competencies, develop best-in-class suppliers, support the company's overall strategy, and improve value-added services beyond a simple purchasing agreement. If the annual spend on the item is high, then it also makes sense for the company to establish a strategic preferred supplier. A preferred supplier designation indicates that the selected supplier should receive the business under most conditions. Formally designating a supplier as strategic builds a foundation for achieving higher levels of information sharing and improvement. In the words of Dave Nelson, a guru in supply management who has worked at Honda, John Deere, and Delphi, "If you develop the right relationship with your supply base, you can have 10,000 additional brains thinking about ways to improve your product and generate cost savings. And that is very powerful!"[4]

Routine Commodity

Products and services in this category are readily available and often are low in cost. Examples include janitorial services, facilities management, and office suppliers. The goal for the team is to reduce the number of items in this category through substitution, elimination of small-volume spend, elimination of duplicate SKUs, rationalization of the number of units to control costs, and simplification of the procurement process using electronic tools (e.g., electronic data interchange, auto-order systems, online vendor catalogs, and purchasing cards). For example, at GlaxoSmithKline, a pharmaceutical company, the chief procurement officer discovered that the R&D group was using 50 different types of Bunsen burners and beakers simply because scientists have particular preferences that they acquired in graduate school.

The team will also try to find suppliers that can automate the purchasing process to the greatest extent possible. For example, companies such as Staples and Office-Depot will consolidate a company's purchases of paper and office supplies, and enable users to order supplies directly from their online catalog. A supplier catalog allows users to order directly through the Internet using a company procurement card (just like a credit card), with the delivery made directly to the site the next day.

Leverage Commodity—Preferred Supplier

As in the case of a common commodity, a leverage commodity also provides the opportunity for savings. These items or services have a high volume of internal consumption, are readily available, are important to the business, and represent a significant portion of spend. Because of their importance to the business, the need to maintain a high level of quality and compliance with corporate objectives is paramount. Preferred suppliers are awarded the business under these conditions with the understanding that they will be expected to significantly reduce the cost of supplying these items or services over time, in return for a significant volume of business and possible multiyear agreements. A high level of service is also expected, which may include supplier capabilities such as management of on-site inventory, e-purchasing capabilities, and ability to quickly respond to customer requirements. In so doing, the supplier will also be expected to maintain a high level of quality and to reduce the total cost to the business of managing this commodity.

One of the tools often used for this category of spend is an e-reverse auction (e-RA), an online auction that awards the business to the lowest bidder (as opposed to the highest bidder, as in a traditional auction, hence the terminology "reverse auction").

Bottleneck Commodity—Transactional Supplier

The final combination often found in developing sourcing strategy is for bottleneck commodities, which have unique requirements or niche suppliers yet are significant to the business. Such items tend to be expensive, due to the exclusive market position maintained by the supplier. The goal of the team is to not run out and to ensure continuity of supply. In such cases, an optimal strategy might be to scan the marketplace and develop an agreement with a supplier to enable a streamlined accounts payable and receiving process. If the supplier is relatively small, this may involve sending an IT team to establish this capability at the supplier's location, with some minimal technology investment required. After a competitive bid, a detailed negotiation should take place that establishes high levels of service as critical to the business, with specific service level agreements detailed. The supplier must be validated to ensure that it can deliver in a responsive manner, is capable of handling orders from multiple locations, and is responsible for managing inventory of the item. In service agreements, the supplier must be led to understand the specific requirements around providing the service.

Supplier Evaluation

Once the portfolio analysis is completed, the team must then dive into the category and evaluate individual suppliers as to their suitability, narrowing the list down to a critical few. The ultimate result of this step is to make supplier recommendations, so the team must first identify current and potential suppliers, determine any information technology requirements, and identify opportunities to leverage the commodity expenditures with similar commodities.

Some of the criteria used to evaluate suppliers, as well as the tools that can be used to do so, are discussed in the next chapter, which describes weighted point supplier evaluation systems. Here we limit ourselves to a brief description of the different criteria that a company may use to assess potential suppliers, which include the following capabilities:

- Process and design capabilities
- Management capability
- Financial condition and cost structure
- Planning and control systems
- Environmental regulation compliance
- Longer-term relationship potential
- Supplier selection scorecards

These criteria are worth talking about in more detail. Although it may not be possible to obtain all the relevant information, data that can be obtained will help the buying firm assess the potential for a successful match.

Process and Design Capabilities

Because different manufacturing and service processes have various strengths and weaknesses, the buying firm must be aware of these characteristics upfront. When the buying firm expects suppliers to perform component design and production, it should also assess the supplier's design capability. One way to reduce the time required to develop new products is to use qualified suppliers that are able to perform product design activities.

Management Capability

Assessing a potential supplier's management capability is a complicated, but important, step. Different aspects of management capability include management's commitment to continuous process and quality improvement, its overall professional ability and experience, its ability to maintain positive relationships with its workforce, and its willingness to develop a closer working relationship with the buyer.

Financial Condition and Cost Structure

An assessment of a potential partner's financial condition usually occurs during the evaluation process. Evaluation teams will typically evaluate the different financial ratios that determine whether a supplier can invest in resources, pay its suppliers and its workforce, and continue to meet its debt and financial obligations. These elements are important in determining whether the supplier will continue to be a reliable source of supply, and that supply will not be disrupted.

Planning and Control Systems

Planning and control systems include those systems that release, schedule, and control the flow of work in an organization. As we shall see in later chapters, the sophistication of such systems can have a major impact on supply chain performance.

Environmental Regulation Compliance

The 1990s brought about a renewed awareness of the impact that industry has on the environment. The Clean Air Act of 1990 imposes large fines on producers of ozone-depleting substances and foul-smelling gases, and governments have introduced laws regarding recycling content in industrial materials. As a result, a supplier's ability to comply with environmental regulations is becoming an important criterion for supply chain alliances. This includes, but is not limited to, the proper disposal of hazardous waste. (This is discussed in a later chapter.)

Longer-Term Relationship Potential

In some cases, a firm may be looking to develop a long-term relationship with a potential supplier. This is particularly true if the supplier is in the "Critical" quadrant, and the category of spend is high volume and critical to the company's business. This approach requires that the parties share their mutual goals, establish metrics to guide the relationship, and develop a series of ongoing discussions on how issues and conflicts can be resolved in a mutually beneficial manner. These relationships may also involve joint cost-savings projects and new-product development efforts, which are also described in a later chapter on integration.

This is not a complete list of criteria that can be applied when evaluating the possibility of a closer, longer-term relationship. This list does provide, however, a framework concerning the types of issues that are important in this area.

Supplier Selection Scorecards

During the selection stage, oftentimes companies need a structured way to evaluate alternative suppliers. This can be particularly hard when the criteria include not just quantitative measures (such as costs and on-time delivery rates), but other, more qualitative factors, such as management stability or trustworthiness. A supplier selection scorecard may be used as a decision support tool. The team will assign a weight to the different categories and develop a numerical score for each supplier in each category, thereby developing a final performance score.

The need for assessment does not end with the selection decision, however. After the buyer-supplier relationship has been established, buyers also must track supplier performance over time. The ability to rank suppliers across multiple criteria can be especially helpful in identifying which suppliers are providing superior performance, and which are in need of some work.

After making the selection using some of the different supplier evaluation tools, the team must reach consensus on the strategy. The team may even take the suppliers short list and hold meetings with the selected suppliers to enable an effective decision. Finally, the suppliers are chosen that best fit the commodity strategy to be employed, based on their performance in the supplier analysis.

Step 4: Contract Negotiation

After the sourcing strategy has been determined and suppliers have been recommended, it is time to implement the strategy and negotiate the contract. Effective implementation of the strategy includes establishing tasks and time lines, assigning accountabilities and process ownership, and ensuring adequate resources are made available to the process owners. The strategy should also be communicated to all stakeholders, including suppliers and internal customers, in order to obtain buy-in and participation.

Before entering into contract negotiations, the commodity team should perform an analysis of market and pricing issues so that a fair price for both parties can be agreed upon. This analysis attempts to define the marketplace, including best price, average price, and the business unit's price, and determines expected trends in pricing. In preparation for negotiations, the buyer should develop a negotiation plan and an ideal contract. There should also be a contingency plan in case negotiations with the recommended suppliers do not go as expected. Finally, the negotiation is conducted, and a contract is signed.

For some items, firms may maintain a list of preferred suppliers that receive the first opportunity for new business. A **preferred supplier** has demonstrated its performance capabilities through previous purchase contracts and, therefore, receives preference during the supplier selection process. By maintaining a preferred supplier list, purchasing personnel can quickly identify suppliers with proven performance capabilities. Competitive bidding and negotiation are two methods commonly used for final supplier selection when there is not a preferred supplier.

Competitive Bidding

Competitive bidding in private industry entails a request for bids from suppliers with whom the buyer is willing to do business. This process is typically initiated when the purchasing manager sends a request for quotation (RFQ) to qualified suppliers. The RFQ is a formal request for the suppliers to prepare bids, based on the terms and conditions set by the buyer. Purchasers often evaluate the resulting bids based on price. If the lowest bidder does not receive the purchase contract, the buyer has an obligation to inform that supplier why it did not receive the contract. Competitive bidding is most effective when the following conditions apply:[5]

- The buying firm can provide qualified suppliers with clear descriptions of the items or services to be purchased.
- Volume is high enough to justify the cost and effort.
- The firm does not have a preferred supplier.

Buying firms use competitive bidding when price is a dominant criterion and the required items or services have straightforward specifications. In addition, government agencies often require competitive bidding. If there are major nonprice variables, then the buyer and seller usually enter into direct negotiation. Competitive bidding can also be used to identify a short list of suppliers with whom the firm will begin detailed purchase contract negotiation.

More advanced online tools are becoming available that feature the ability to negotiate issues beyond price with multiple suppliers. With these tools, e-procurement managers no longer have to spend hours in face-to-face meetings arguing over details with suppliers. A buyer simply fills out an RFQ template and forwards the document electronically to suppliers.[6] Suppliers can respond electronically with online proposals detailing price, payment terms, shipping methods, or any other issue relevant to the buyer. These tools enable a buyer to negotiate the process simultaneously with more than one supplier, which leads to efficiencies and lower prices due to increased competition (similar to reverse auctions).

Negotiation

Negotiation is a more costly, interactive approach to final supplier selection. Face-to-face negotiation is best when the following conditions apply:

- The item is a new or technically complex item with only vague specifications.
- The purchase requires agreement about a wide range of performance factors.
- The buyer requires the supplier to participate in the development effort.
- The supplier cannot determine risks and costs without additional input from the buyer.

Negotiations with a supplier should occur only when a purchaser feels confident about the level of planning and preparation put forth. However, planning is not an open-ended process; buyers must usually meet deadlines that satisfy the needs of internal customers within the purchaser's firm. Thus, the buyer faces pressure to conduct the negotiation within a reasonable amount of time.

Step 5: Supplier Relationship Management

The strategic sourcing process does not end when a contract is signed with a supplier. Although the sourcing team may disband and go their separate ways once the contract is signed, typically one member of the team will continue to work with the supplier in the role of supplier relationship manager. This individual must continuously monitor the performance of the sourcing strategy, as well as the supplier. The buying firm should revisit the sourcing strategy at predetermined intervals, to ensure that it is achieving its stated objectives, and may need to make modifications to the strategy if it is not working as planned or if there are changes in the market. The buying firm should also continuously monitor the performance of suppliers based on predetermined and agreed-upon criteria such as quality, delivery performance, and continuous cost improvement. And there should be a plan in place to manage any conflicts that occur with suppliers.

One of the most important tools used to monitor supplier performance is the supplier scorecard. Just like the supplier evaluation matrix, the scorecard often reflects the same set of categories used during the evaluation process, but the scores are updated typically once a quarter, and reviewed with the supplier. Over time, the nature of the classifications used in the scorecard may also change, as the stakeholders' requirements and their requests may change. Scorecards typically include the categories of price, quality, and delivery reliability used in the evaluation process, but the team may also choose to add categories such as "Responsiveness" (how quickly does the supplier return a call when there is a problem?). These scorecards are used in regularly scheduled review meetings with suppliers, so that deficiencies in performance can be noted, discussed, and acted upon.

Regular reviews must be held to determine if the strategy is successful or whether it requires modification. The review may include feedback and input from key suppliers. In any case, all suppliers should be advised of results along with future expectations. Supply management personnel play a key role in this review because they are often the primary contact for the supplier with responsibility for supplier performance measurement. Earlier decisions may have to be revisited and re-evaluated if suppliers do not perform as expected.

The key goals defined in Step 2 must be revisited periodically to identify modifications to the original strategy. Key elements of the results-monitoring process include the following:

- Conduct regular review meetings (at least annually) to determine if the strategy is well aligned with an organization's objectives.
- Share results with top management to provide additional momentum to the strategy; be sure to report the performance improvements achieved through the strategy.

- Assess internal customers' and suppliers' perceptions. Are they satisfied with what has happened? If not, why not, and can the strategy be altered to improve the situation?
- Determine whether key goals are being achieved. If they are not being achieved, what is the contingency plan? If the goals are being achieved, are there any lessons to be learned?
- Provide feedback to those involved.

These strategy development steps are relatively general—they describe the steps to follow only when proposing and executing a strategy. However, the actual outcomes of the commodity strategy development process may vary considerably, depending on the specific commodity and the supply market.

Types of Supply Management Strategies

Organizations can employ a variety of different strategies that may be unique to each commodity. Although we cannot cover all of the possible variations of strategies that may emerge, we will briefly review some of the most common and important supply management strategies. As we will see later, certain strategies are used more often than others, depending on how advanced an organization is at the supply management strategy development process. Each of these strategies or supply management approaches is covered in greater detail in other chapters throughout the book.

Supply Base Optimization

Supply base optimization is the process of determining the appropriate number and mix of suppliers to maintain. Although this has also been referred to as **rightsizing**, it usually refers to reducing the number of suppliers used. Moreover, suppliers that are not capable of achieving world-class performance, either currently or in the near future, may be eliminated from the supply base. This process is continuous because the needs of the business unit are always changing. Optimization requires an analysis of the number of suppliers required currently and in the future for each purchased item. For example, General Motors was ready to eliminate 160 suppliers worldwide that it considered poor performers in 2003 and 2004. Chapter 9 discusses supply base optimization in detail.

Supply Risk Management

Events in 2005 such as Hurricane Katrina and corresponding escalating commodity prices have highlighted more than ever the impact of disruptions on supply chain operations and global competition. Although many events are not easily predicted, there are many other sources of supply chain disruption that have the potential to be better managed, thereby reducing the impact on firm agility and profitability.

As firms outsource a greater proportion of products and services from China, India, and other low-cost countries, the hidden perils of these approaches are often not considered, especially within the context of enterprise risk management (ERM). Global outsourcing affords many benefits in the form of lower prices and expanded market access, but only recently have senior executives begun to recognize the increased risk attributed to the higher probability of product and service flow disruptions in global sourcing networks. A major disruption in the offshore supply chain can shut down a company and have dire consequences for profitability. This was felt most drastically in the last few years, when such events as 9/11, the war in Iraq, the West Coast port workers' strike, and increased regulatory and customs delays brought supply chain operations to a standstill. Recently, the impact of Hurricane Katrina was felt by companies relying on supplies of critical commodities produced on the Gulf Coast such as fuel, natural gas, chemicals, and resins. Other, less serious events that can also impact customer service include fire and theft, poor communication of customer requirements, part shortages, and quality problems.

The impact of supply chain disruptions, although difficult to quantify, can be costly. A study investigated stock market reactions when firms publicly announced that they were experiencing supply chain glitches or disruptions causing production or shipping delays.[7] Results of the study of 519 supply chain problem announcements showed that stock market reactions decrease shareholder value by 10.28%. A follow-up study assessed the effect 827 publicly announced disruptions had on long-run stock price (one year before the disruption and two years after) and found a mean abnormal return of nearly –40% along with significant increases in equity risk.[8] Their results also showed that the majority of supply chain disruptions involved parts shortages, lack of response to customer-requested changes, production problems, ramp-up problems, and quality problems.

Many recent events illustrate this phenomenon. For example, Boeing experienced supplier delivery failure of two critical parts with an estimated loss to the company of $2.6 billion. In 2002, less than 100 workers in the longshoremen's union strike disrupted West Coast port operations. As a result, it took six months for some containers to be delivered and schedules to return to normal. Finally, Hurricane Katrina resulted in billions of dollars of lost revenue to major retailers such as British Petroleum, Shell, Conoco Phillips, and Lyondell, as well as causing gasoline shortages in many parts of the United States, resulting in lost economic activity. Given these and other events, it is not surprising that supply chain disruptions have caught the attention of executives.

In a survey of *BusinessWeek* Global 1000 companies, supply chain disruptions were perceived to be the single biggest threat to their companies' revenue streams. Although senior executives now recognize that supply chain disruptions can be devastating to an enterprise's bottom line, strategies to mitigate supply chain disruptions are typically not well developed or even initiated. A troubling statistic is that only between 5 and 25% of Fortune 500 companies are estimated to be prepared to handle a major supply chain crisis or disruption.

One factor that is increasing the risk exposure to supply chain disruption is the increasing propensity of companies to outsource processes to global suppliers. The complexity associated with multiple hand-offs in global supply chains increases the probability of disruptions. As the number of hand-offs required to ship products through multiple carriers, multiple ports, and multiple government checkpoints increases, so does the probability of poor communication, human error, and missed shipments. One executive we interviewed from a major electronics company noted: "We have successfully outsourced production of our products to China. Unfortunately, we now recognize that we do not have the processes in place to manage risk associated with this supply chain effectively!"[9] In this environment, questions arise such as, What steps can an organization take to design its supply chains to ensure uninterrupted material availability? Is it possible to respond in an agile manner to customer requirements in a global sourcing environment? These are issues that supply chain managers must think through in the future, to build effective contingency plans before these disruptions occur, so that there is a plan when they do occur.

Global Sourcing

Global sourcing is an approach that requires supply management to view the entire world as a potential source for components, services, and finished goods. It can be used to access new markets or to gain access to the same suppliers that are helping global companies become more competitive. Although true global sourcing is somewhat limited in most industries, more and more companies are beginning to view the world as both a market and a source of supply.

The major objective of global sourcing is to provide immediate and dramatic improvements in cost and quality as determined through the commodity research process. Global sourcing is also an opportunity to gain exposure to product and process technology, increase the number of available sources, satisfy countertrade requirements, and establish a presence in foreign markets. This strategy is not contradictory to supply base optimization because it involves locating the worldwide best-in-class suppliers for a given commodity. Some buyers also source globally to introduce competition to domestic suppliers.

There are several major barriers to global sourcing that must be overcome. Some serious issues are that some firms are inexperienced with global business processes and practices, and there are few personnel qualified to develop and negotiate with global suppliers or manage long material pipelines. In addition, more complex logistics and currency fluctuations require measuring all relevant costs before committing to a worldwide source.

Finally, organizations may not be prepared to deal with the different negotiating styles practiced by different cultures, and they may have to work through a foreign host national in order to establish contacts and an agreement. Chapter 10 addresses global sourcing in detail.

Longer-Term Supplier Relationships

Longer-term supplier relationships involve the selection of and continuous involvement with suppliers viewed as critical over an extended period of time (e.g., three years and beyond). In general, the use of longer-term supplier relationships is growing in importance, and there will probably be greater pursuit of these relationships through longer-term contracts. Some purchasers are familiar with the practice, whereas for others it represents a radical departure from traditional short-term approaches to supply base management.

Longer-term relationships are sought with suppliers that have exceptional performance or unique technological expertise. Within the portfolio matrix described earlier, this would involve the few suppliers that provide items and services that are critical or of higher value. A longer-term relationship may include a joint product development relationship with shared development costs and intellectual property. In other cases, it may simply be an informal process of identifying suppliers that receive preferential treatment. Chapter 14 discusses longer-term relationships and contracts.

Early Supplier Design Involvement

Early supplier design involvement and selection requires key suppliers to participate at the concept or predesign stage of new-product development. Supplier involvement may be informal, although the supplier may already have a purchase contract for the production of an existing item. Early involvement will increasingly take place through participation on cross-functional product development teams. This strategy recognizes that qualified suppliers have more to offer than simply the basic production of items that meet engineering specifications. Early supplier design involvement is a simultaneous engineering approach that occurs between buyer and seller, and seeks to maximize the benefits received by taking advantage of the supplier's design capabilities. This strategy is discussed in detail in Chapter 4; the Good Practice Example at the end of this chapter also highlights how one company has successfully employed early involvement.

Supplier Development

In some cases, purchasers may find that suppliers' capabilities are not high enough to meet current or future expectations, yet they do not want to eliminate the supplier from the supply base. (Switching costs may be high or the supplier has performance potential.) A solution in such cases is to work directly with a supplier to facilitate improvement in a designated functional or activity area. Buyer-seller consulting teams working jointly may accelerate overall supplier improvement at a faster rate than will actions taken independently by the supplier. The basic motivation behind this strategy is that supplier improvement and success lead to longer-term benefits to both buyer and seller. This approach supports the development of world-class suppliers in new areas of product and process technology. Chapter 9 discusses supplier development in detail.

Total Cost of Ownership

Total cost of ownership (TCO) is the process of identifying cost considerations beyond unit price, transport, and tooling. It requires the business unit to define and measure the various cost components associated with a purchased item. In many cases, this includes costs associated with late delivery, poor quality, or other forms of supplier nonperformance. Total cost of ownership can lead to better decision making because it identifies all costs associated with a supply management decision and the costs associated with supplier nonperformance. Cost variances from planned results can be analyzed to determine the cause of the variance. Corrective action can then prevent further problems. TCO is discussed in detail in Chapters 10 and 11.

E-Reverse Auctions

An e-RA is an online, real-time dynamic auction between a buying organization and a group of pre-qualified suppliers who compete against each other to win the business to supply goods or services that have clearly defined specifications for design, quantity, quality, delivery, and related terms and conditions. These suppliers compete by bidding against each other online over the Internet using specialized software by submitting successively lower-priced bids during a scheduled time period. This time period is

Sourcing Snapshot *Reverse Auctions*

Reverse auctions can be used for one specific product/service in a spot buy or for contracts to provide the products or services over the course of a year. The goal of reverse auctions is to bring buyers and sellers together to expose prices on a dynamic and real-time basis. A reverse auction involves suppliers bidding on a clearly specified buyer requirement. All activity takes place online. The majority of reverse auctions are completed in 30 minutes or less (although some have been stretched out over 12 hours). A recent auction carried out by a large engineering project construction firm for a large commodity group included multiple suppliers from Japan, Korea, and the United States. The pricing behaviors that were evidenced in the auction stunned the buying company executives who witnessed them. The price paid for the commodity was well below the group's expectation of market price. One executive who participated said, "It showed us just how little we really knew about what the market was doing." Reverse auctions can provide some deep insights into true market pricing, especially in situations when there is available capacity in a supply marketplace.

Source: Interview with executive, Supply Chain Resource Cooperative executive meeting, North Carolina State University, Raleigh, April 2004.

usually only about an hour, but multiple, brief extensions are usually allowed if bidders are still active at the end of the initial time period.

The use of e-RAs has been facilitated by a number of company internal and external developments including the following:

- Buyers' and suppliers' ability to communicate in real time, worldwide, via the Internet.
- Development of robust, user-friendly Internet-based software systems to support worldwide e-RAs hosted by a third party or conducted by the buying company with little or no outside assistance.
- Significant improvements in goods and service quality and cycle-time reductions have resulted in buying companies requiring superior quality and service. Therefore, buyers have emphasized low price as a major sourcing-decision variable.

E-RAs are discussed in Chapter 13.

Evolving Sourcing Strategies

If we compare the level of supply management strategy evolution to the strategies available, there is clearly an implementation sequence that emerges. Exhibit 6.13 presents the sequence of supply management strategy execution based on research from multiple studies and interviews with many executives. Organizations tend to evolve through four phases as they become mature and sophisticated in their supply management strategy development.

Exhibit 6.13 Stages of Supply Management Strategy Evolution

1. BASIC BEGINNINGS	2. MODERATE DEVELOPMENT	3. LIMITED INTEGRATION	4. FULLY INTEGRATED SUPPLY CHAINS
• Quality/cost teams • Longer-term contracts • Volume leveraging • Supply-base consolidation • Supplier quality focus	• E-RAs • Ad hoc supplier alliances • Cross-functional sourcing teams • Supply-base optimization • International sourcing • Cross-location sourcing teams	• Global sourcing • Strategic supplier alliances • Supplier TQM development • Total cost of ownership • Nontraditional purchase focus • Parts/service standardization • Early supplier involvement • Dock to stock pull systems	• Global supply chains with external customer focus • Cross-enterprise decision making • Full-service suppliers • Early sourcing • Insourcing/outsourcing to maximize core competencies of firms throughout the supply chain • E-systems

Phase 1: Basic Beginnings

In the initial stages of supply management strategy development, supply management is often characterized as a lower-level support function. Supply management adopts essentially a short-term approach and reacts to complaints from its internal customers when deliveries are late, quality is poor, or costs are too high. The only impetus for change here is the demand for change by management. The primary role of supply management managers is to ensure that enough supply capacity exists, which usually means that suppliers are viewed in an adversarial manner. However, the amount of resources for improvement is limited, usually because the highest-ranking supply management manager likely reports to manufacturing or materials management. Performance measures focus on efficiency-related measures and price reduction. Information systems are location or facility focused and primarily transaction based.

In Phase 1, supply management often focuses on supply base optimization, and more attention is paid to total quality management than to other progressive supply management strategies. In a sense, these two strategies represent the building blocks from which to pursue increasingly sophisticated strategies. A reduced supply base is necessary because of the increased two-way communication and interaction necessary for successful execution of more complicated strategies. TQM also provides the fundamental focus on process that is required to implement supply management strategies.

Phase 2: Moderate Development

The second phase of the strategy progression usually occurs as an organization begins to centrally coordinate or control some part of the supply management function across regional or even worldwide locations. Supply management councils or lead buyers may be responsible for entire classes of commodities, and companywide databases by region may be developed to facilitate this coordination. The primary purpose of this coordination is to establish companywide agreements in order to leverage volumes to obtain lower costs from volume discounts. Single sourcing with long-term agreements may eventually emerge as a policy for leveraged or consolidated purchase families. At this stage, limited cross-functional integration is occurring. In addition, e-RAs have recently been selectively used to leverage purchases and improve goods and service pricing by between 15 and 30%.

The approaches in Phases 1 and 2—supply base optimization, TQM, and long-term contracting—have the potential, over time, to effect a steady increase in supplier contributions and improvements, but the performance change rate may not be dramatic.

Purchasers must now begin to pursue strategic supplier relationships that focus on customer needs and the organization's competitive strategy. In Phase 2, buyers may begin to establish better relationships with critical suppliers while continuing to optimize the supply base. The supply management department may now be evaluated on the achievement of competitive objectives, and suppliers are viewed as a resource. As such, there may be some informal channels of functional integration developing between supply management, engineering, manufacturing, marketing, and accounting. Some of this may occur through infrequent cross-functional team decision making. The execution of supply management strategy still takes place primarily at the business unit or local level.

Phase 3: Limited Integration

A number of supply management initiatives discussed in this book, including concurrent engineering, supplier development, lead-time reduction, and early supplier involvement, characterize this phase. In this environment, supply management strategies are established and integrated early into the product and process design stage, and first- and second-tier suppliers are becoming actively involved in these decisions. Supply management is evaluated on the basis of strategic contribution, and resources are made available according to strategic requirements. Extensive functional integration occurs through design and sourcing teams that focus on product development, building a competitive advantage, and total cost analysis for new and existing products and services. Supply management is viewed as a key part of the organizational structure with a strong external customer focus. As such, multiple customer-oriented measurements are used to identify performance improvements. Information systems include global databases, historical price and cost information, joint strategy development efforts with other functional groups, and the beginning of total cost modeling.

Phase 4: Fully Integrated Supply Chains

In the final and most advanced phase, supply management has assumed a strategic orientation, with reporting directly to executive management and a strong external, rather than simply internal, customer focus. Non-value-added activities such as purchase order follow-up and expediting have been automated, allowing purchasers to focus their attention on strategic objectives and activities. Organizations demand a higher performance standard from suppliers. Executives take aggressive actions that will directly improve supplier capability and accelerate supplier performance contributions.

Examples of aggressive actions include developing global supplier capabilities, developing full-service suppliers, and adopting a systems thinking perspective that encompasses the entire supply chain. In such a mode, insourcing core activities add the greatest value, whereas components of the value chain are often outsourced to upstream or downstream parties that are more capable.

Such a system can directly affect the ability of the supply base to meet world-class expectations and often involves direct intervention in the supplier's operating systems and processes.

Relatively few organizations have evolved to this phase. However, for those that succeed, a number of tangible and intangible benefits accrue from the progression of supply management from a supportive role to an integrated activity. These include price reductions across all product lines ranging from 5 to 25%; improved quality, cost, and delivery performance in the range of 75 to 98% in six to eight months; and a supply base that is better than the competition's. Supply management is now in a position to influence rather than react to the supply base, and it can actually develop key suppliers in cases where a weak link exists. Moreover, all of these processes help establish the critical capabilities required of a global leader.

Observations on Supply Management Strategy Evolution

It is important that the supply management student recognize an important point about the sequence shown in Exhibit 6.13 and the phases just discussed: Few organizations have fully executed the more complex strategies found in Phases 3 and 4. This is due to a variety of factors including the relative complexity of higher-level strategies, the resources and commitment necessary to execute the strategy, a lack of a supply base optimization effort, and personnel who lack the skills and capabilities necessary for developing advanced sourcing strategies. However, those that successfully execute more sophisticated and comprehensive sourcing strategies should realize greater performance improvement over time. The following Good Practice Example illustrates how one company developed a higher-level commodity strategy. This strategy may be considered to be within the Phase 3–4 category of maturity.

Good Practice Example

Commodities Forecasting: It's All in Your Head

Strong global growth has pushed industrial commodity prices to new heights in 2006 and 2007. This has wreaked havoc with procurement budgets and created a quandary for buyers trying to forecast pricing trends in the second half of 2007 and into 2008. In a nutshell, forecasting has been muddled by supplier consolidations, pricing volatility, economic uncertainties, monetary unpredictability, and geopolitical concerns.

But forecasts are critical in business. Estimated prices are the core of product-development budgets. Those estimates are also the basis for evaluating buying strategies, planning quarterly cash flows, making forward pricing decisions, and implementing such risk-management plans as hedges.

So what's a buyer to do in the face of all the economic uncertainty? Use his or her head.

Of the three types of commodity price forecasts—those based on personal judgment, those relying exclusively on historical price data, and those incorporating commodity futures prices at the time of the forecast together with historical price data—the judgmental forecasts have the best record of accuracy.

According to Aasim Husain, of the International Monetary Fund's research department in Washington, analysis indicates that "judgmental forecasts tend to outperform the model-based forecasts over short horizons of one quarter for several commodities." They're also the most popular, he says.

Purchasing surveys show that many buying groups tend to use homegrown projections or forecasts developed for them by various research organizations. Academicians explain that's because statistical models can be short-circuited by the volatility of energy, metals, chemicals, plastic resins, wood products, and other production materials.

But if you're going to use personal judgment in commodities forecasting, you have to base it on the right factors. Analysts and buyers alike agree that the most critical data to review are the following:

- Market intelligence
- Global economic trends
- Supplier safeguards against volatility
- Your own company's selling strategies

Even in calm economic times, those tools are critical. With the current volatility in commodities, they're essential. "The commodity markets are crazy these days," says Peter Connelly, CPO at diversified manufacturer Leggett & Platt in Carthage, Missouri, which buys $3.7 billion annually in production and packaging materials. "Prices are affected by local and world demand and supply trends, global currency movements, the economic policies of such developing economies as Brazil, Russia, India, and China—and even today's instant communications."

The latest demand boom for base metals is in its third year and has elevated nonferrous metals pricing to record highs. Steel prices are reflecting iron ore, scrap, ferroalloy, and energy costs—rather than demand trends—probably for the first time.

"Pricing cycles for commodities are shrinking," says the global procurement manager at a Detroit-area auto parts company. "The steel cycle used to be 7 to 10 years in length from peak to valley in prices. Nowadays, it's more like 18 months due to the rapid change in delivery of information."

Atop all that, says Leggett & Platt's Connelly, "supplier consolidation and pricing volatility is making forecasting difficult and, actually, past a 90-day window very inaccurate." Rather than a sign of the top for commodity prices, analysts worry that the deal making could help put a lid on supply and put even more pressure on a host of commodity prices.

This view is supported by research director Anirvan Banerji at the Economic Cycle Research Institute in New York. Most forecasters have a dismal record of predicting the timing of cyclical turns in economic growth, jobs, and inflation, Banerji writes, "because most people and forecasting models expect recent patterns to persist in the near future." This is "a sure recipe for being surprised on prices by the next turn in the global industrial cycle."

And then, there is nature. The late-summer hurricanes of 2005 taught energy and petrochemical buyers just how fast supply can be disrupted and prices can explode.

"It's all about energy and raw materials these days," says Dan DiMicco, CEO of Nucor Corp., the Charlotte, North Carolina–based steelmaker. "With the volatility in and high level of materials pricing nowadays, nobody wants to carry inventory—whether it's in the raw materials at my mills or the finished products we ship to our customers."

INTELLIGENCE IS KING

Stating that "in a commodity market today, intelligence is king," DiMicco tells a recent steel industry conference that "to run as efficiently as we can, mills and service centers will have to start at the customer—and talk to buyers about what they really need and what they expect they will be paying. Only then can we take some volatility out of the metals market—and come to some equitable long-term arrangements on price and supply."

So, the foundation for any successful commodity forecasting program must be based on detailed market knowledge that can smooth out current volatility and help ensure against disrupted flow of raw materials, says Mike Burns, global business director for polyethylene at supply chain consultancy Resin Technology Inc. in Fort Worth, Texas.

Burns insists that buyers "emerge from their comfortable silos" and get knowledgeable about global economics, supply, demand, and sourcing alternatives—"whatever they need to know to become expert about their company, their industry, and their regional and global supply chain." Solid market facts are needed to develop effective buying plans, and that includes accurate price forecasting, says Burns in an interview.

IT'S A SMALL WORLD

A key piece of advice from this purchasing coach and several top-level buyers interviewed: Whatever the commodity, watch the international marketplace to determine supply, demand, pricing, and trading trends. That's because economic conditions that affect supply and prices are changeable—and usually global. "Buyers have got to know demand, as best as they can, but not just demand in North America—demand globally," says Burns.

Today's lean and highly outsourced supply chains leave procurement teams with little visibility to anticipate and react to global risks, complain some analysts. That's why they suggest that buyers learn as much as possible about global supply chains and determine what safeguards their world supplier organizations are putting in place to maintain continuous supply and honor agreed-upon future pricing.

"The days of going out with an RFQ and a spreadsheet of needed materials are over," agrees the commodities buyer for a Chicago-based multinational corporation. "Past-paid price averages are just the start of what we'll expect to pay in the future. We have to work closely with materials engineering and quality folks on the materials specifications and then we

	2005		2006		2007	
	FORECAST	ACTUAL	FORECAST	ACTUAL	FORECAST	ACTUAL*
Aluminum	80	85	104	116	91	127
Copper	156	167	279	305	237	269
Nickel	625	666	945	1102	870	1878
Lead	41	44	51	60	44	81
Tin	314	335	345	397	278	577
Zinc	59	64	130	148	119	164

*First quarter 2007

Forecast: World Bank; Actual: London Metal Exchange

have to find out what's available. Remember, you can't buy all over the world for the same price—ever."

Yet another essential weapon in the commodities-forecasting wars is knowledge of your own company's strategies. "The key to future pricing is to remember that the company's sourcing strategy is there to support the company's business," says Dan Ronchetto, vice president of global direct materials for Greif in Delaware, Ohio. "So, the purchasing organization has to know how the company sells into the market—what the competitive dynamics are and how competitors are competing."

In an interview, Ronchetto says the sourcing strategy has to be in line with the company's sales strategy. If a company's sales are on an annual fixed basis, then purchasing arrangements should be on an annual fixed-prices basis. "The bottom line is the key issue! Wall Street doesn't like surprises or volatility," he says. And it's not just for public companies. Sourcing strategy has to be aligned with overall business strategy and how end customers are served. "If you sell monthly, buy monthly," Ronchetto advises. Fixed two-year or three-year contracts are disappearing into indexing to adjust quarterly market changes, he says.

Some analysts suggest that futures prices on commodity exchanges in London and New York may be the best measure of imminent sales price trends. The various commodity futures exchange markets do provide a mechanism for price discovery on an aggregate level through arbitrage between multiple buyers and sellers.

To many buyers, though, futures trading is just one of several possible tools to guesstimate future pricing—and only for certain raw materials. Although nonferrous metals are traded globally, other materials—such as resins and lumber products—have limited regional exchange liquidity, and other materials, such as steel, have yet to find a trading floor. Also, price discovery at any given location—whether that is New York, Chicago, Winnipeg, London, Tokyo, or Shanghai—is not necessarily definitive because supply and demand relationships are murky.

Nevertheless, buyers are the ones expected to navigate the terrain. Says Greif's Ronchetto, "My CFO and other chief financial officers also are putting more and more pressure on manufacturing and purchasing colleagues to reduce corporate costs." And forecasts, however unscientific, are an important tool in that effort.

TEN FORECASTING TIPS FOR BUYERS

1. Determine corporate price goals; if necessary, adjust them to economic realities.
2. Reduce purchasing pricing strategies to 30, 60, or 90 days.

3. Adjust actual timing of buys to weekly, monthly, or quarterly events.
4. Analyze and, if necessary, adjust the structure of supply-contract agreements.
5. Pay attention to inventory levels to determine comfort of spot versus contract buys.
6. Ensure true supply tie-in with buying company's operational action plans.
7. Study global pricing and sourcing trends of commodities—and their feedstocks.
8. Survey primary suppliers' operating rates, inventory, and costs.
9. Analyze the secondary sourcing market for alternative suppliers.
10. Determine potential alternatives of supply and prices of commodity products.

Source: T. Stundza, "Resin Technology Inc.," *Purchasing* online, www.purchasing.com, May 14, 2007.

CONCLUSION

Category management is perhaps one of the most important ways that supply managers create value for their stakeholders. Category teams must effectively scan the market environment, conduct research on suppliers and cost drivers, analyze internal spend characteristics, and establish appropriate strategies for managing these relationships. In doing so, supply managers depict and create insights for stakeholders on key elements of their supply environment that shape their operational, financial, and market planning decisions. Effective category strategies also create the foundation for cost management, contract frameworks, and ongoing supplier performance management metrics and relationships. These elements will be discussed in greater detail in later chapters, but it is important for students to understand how to conduct research and analysis leading to these actions.

KEY TERMS

category, 190

integrative, 192

preferred supplier, 216

rightsizing, 218

spend analysis, 196

supply base optimization, 218

triangulate, 205

DISCUSSION QUESTIONS

1. Select a commodity that you believe might be chosen for a strategic commodity analysis in the industries listed below. Describe the factors impacting each commodity, using a Porter Five Forces analysis. Justify why you believe the commodity is strategic to that industry, and the approach to be used in developing a commodity strategy.
    - Oil (West Texas intermediate) versus gasoline (discuss differential)
    - Metals
    - Chemicals
    - Plastic resins
    - Shipping
    - Wood products and other production materials
    - Aeronautical equipment
    - Machine tools
    - Telecommunications
    - Paper
2. Why has supply management traditionally not been involved in the corporate strategic planning function?
3. Describe a set of supply management goals that might be aligned with the following corporate objective made by an automotive manufacturer: "To be the number one in customer satisfaction."
4. Describe where you think the following commodities—paper clips, machine tools, castings, personal computers, fuel, computer chips, printers, styrofoam cups, paper, custom-designed networks—might fall within the portfolio matrix. Under what circumstances might one of these items fall into more than one quadrant of the matrix, or evolve from one quadrant to another?

5. Under what conditions might you consider single-sourcing an item in the leveraging category of the portfolio matrix?
6. When conducting research, what are some advantages and disadvantages of the different types of information you might obtain from the Internet? Which types of Internet sites are likely to be more reliable as compared with personal interviews?
7. Why is it important to establish a document explaining the commodity strategy and share it with others? What are the possible consequences of not doing so?
8. Why must organizations develop suppliers? Is supplier development a long-term trend or just a fad? Explain.
9. Supply base optimization must occur before long-term agreements can be put into place. What are the implications of this statement?
10. How long do you believe it takes a company to move from a Stage 1 phase to a Stage 4 phase of supply management strategy development? In providing your response, consider all of the changes that must take place.
11. Provide a list of companies that, based on your reading of recent articles in the popular press, fit into the category of Stage 1 companies. What companies can you think of that might fall into the category of Stage 3 or 4? Provide some justification for your lists.
12. What do you think are the reasons why there are so few companies classified as Stage 4 companies? Do you think this is likely to change?

ADDITIONAL READINGS

Craighead, C. W., Blackhurst, J., Rungtusanatham, M. J., and Handfield, R. B. (2007), "The Severity of Supply Chain Disruptions: Design Characteristics and Mitigation Capabilities," *Decision Sciences,* 38(1), 131–156.

D'Avanzo, R., et al. (2003), "The Link between Supply Chain and Financial Performance," *Supply Chain Management Review,* 27(6), 40–47.

Handfield, R. (2006), *Supplier Market Intelligence,* Boca Raton, FL: Auerbach Publications.

Handfield, R., Elkins, D., Blackhurst, J., and Craighead, C. (2005), "18 Ways to Guard against Disruption," *Supply Chain Management Review,* 9(1), 46–53.

Handfield, R., and Krause, D. (1999), "Think Globally, Source Locally," *Supply Chain Management Review,* Winter, 36–49.

Handfield, R., and McCormack, K. (2005), "What You Need to Know about Sourcing in China," *Supply Chain Management Review,* 9(5), 56–62.

Monczka, R., and Trent, R. J. (1991), "Evolving Sourcing Strategies for the 1990s," *International Journal of Physical Distribution and Logistics Management,* 21(5), 4–12.

Monczka, R., and Trent, R. J. (1995), *Supply Management and Sourcing Strategy: Trends and Implications,* Tempe, AZ: Center for Advanced Supply Management Studies.

Porter, M. E. (1985), *Competitive Advantage: Creating and Sustaining Superior Performance,* New York: Free Press.

ENDNOTES

1. "A Global Study of Supply Chain Leadership and Its Impact on Business Performance," Accenture and INSEAD, white paper, 2003.

2. Developed jointly with Atlanta-based UPS Consulting, the survey titled "CFOs and the Supply Chain" was carried out by CFO Research Services. Reported in "Paying Attention: Chief Financial Officers Get Involved in Managing More Supply Chains," *Traffic World,* September 2, 2003.

3. Monczka, R., Trent, R., and Handfield, R. (2002), *Purchasing and Supply Chain Management* (2nd ed.), Cincinnati: South-Western.

4. Interview with Dave Nelson, North Carolina State University research study on design for order fulfillment, March 2007.

5. Dobler, D., Lee, L., and Burt, D. (1990), *Purchasing and Materials Management,* Homewood, IL: Irwin.

6. Waxer, C. (2001), "E-Negotiations Are In, Price-Only e-Auctions Are Out," *iSource,* June, pp. 73–76.

7. Hendricks, K., and Singhal, V. (2003), "The Effect of Supply Chain Glitches on Shareholder Wealth," *Journal of Operations Management,* 21(5), 501–522.

8. Hendricks, K., and Singhal, V. (2005), "An Empirical Analysis of the Effect of Supply Chain Disruptions on Long Run Stock Price Performance and Equity Risk of the Firm," *Production and Operations Management,* 14(1), 35–52.

9. Interview with senior executive, North Carolina State research study on global supply chain risk, October 2004.

Chapter 7

SUPPLIER EVALUATION AND SELECTION

Learning Objectives

After completing this chapter, you should be able to

- Recognize the seven-step supplier selection process as an enabler to world-class supplier selection
- Appreciate the many areas that supply professionals consider when evaluating potential suppliers
- Understand the importance of supplier visits
- Identify key criteria to narrow the supplier pool
- Learn about the resources available to identify suppliers
- Understand the importance of supplier financial analysis
- Comprehend the various factors that constitute a supplier performance evaluation
- Identify ways to reduce the time associated with supplier evaluation and selection

Chapter Outline

Selecting U.S.-Based Suppliers at Toyota Industrial Equipment Manufacturing

The need to evaluate and select suppliers comes about in many ways. During the development of purchasing strategies, selecting the right supplier is central to success. The following example shows that Toyota's supplier selection philosophy and its commitment to using U.S.-based suppliers is a central part of its supplier selection strategy.

Toyota Industrial Equipment Manufacturing (TIEM) is committed to building lift trucks in the United States and to purchasing materials and components from domestic suppliers. TIEM is the largest manufacturer of material-handling equipment in the world. Most of the products it builds for the U.S. market are made in Columbus, IN, a facility that opened in 1990 and underwent an $11 million expansion in 2005. In May, the plant celebrated the production of its 250,000th forklift truck.

These American-made lift trucks are manufactured of steel, plastic parts, and other components produced mainly by suppliers located in the United States. Roughly 60% of the Columbus plant's supply base now is domestic. TIEM's parent company in Japan, Toyota Industries Corporation (TICO), still provides some critical components such as engines, which it makes in large volumes for plants in Asia, Europe, and the United States. Sixteen years ago when the Columbus facility opened, the ratio was reversed: Local suppliers provided TIEM with 40% of the materials that went into the lift trucks made in the United States.

According to Bruce Nolting, vice president of purchasing, production control, and logistics, purchasing manages about 65 key suppliers in the United States, which provide 75% of the materials and components that go into the lift trucks built in Columbus. These key suppliers provide TIEM with critical parts, make daily deliveries or "milk runs" to the plant, and are on the kanban system, which is key to meeting the just-in-time (JIT) requirements of the Toyota production system in place at the facility.

This transition to increased purchasing through U.S. suppliers is part of TICO's overall procurement policy to buy from domestic suppliers as a way to help keep local economies healthy. In Columbus, TIEM puts these words into action; purchasing and quality assurance work closely together to qualify and develop key suppliers.

Working together, purchasing and quality assurance look for suppliers that can provide materials and components at a lower price to TIEM with as good or better quality, and the capability to provide deliveries to the plant daily or multiple times per day. They use a formula that takes into account such criteria as piece price, inventory carrying costs, and freight.

SUPPLIER QUALIFICATION AND DEVELOPMENT

Nolting's purchasing team consists of six purchasing specialists who manage categories of related materials or components, such as steel and steel products. These specialists are responsible for supplier selection, evaluation and development, and working with quality assurance, as well as cost reduction activities. Steve Pride, TIEM's purchasing manager, oversees their efforts.

Pride serves on a Toyota Material Handling Group global purchasing committee that consists of representatives of facilities in Europe and Asia. He and his team also are in daily contact with colleagues in Japan via videoconferencing and e-mail during model changes.

Looking to keep the supply base a manageable size, TIEM's purchasing and quality assurance department approach a domestic supplier that manufactures similar parts to determine whether it has the capacity to provide the plant with additional components.

"We are looking at a small supply base that supports us in 100% of our needs on a particular part," says Nolting. "Very rarely do we purchase one part number from dual sources. Our idea is to keep the number of suppliers small, but support them and make sure we feed them accurate forecast information to ensure they have ample capacity to meet our requirements." If the supplier needs assistance with equipment or tooling to take on the additional requirements, TIEM provides the resources.

To qualify a domestic supplier, purchasing and quality assurance visit the supplier's plant and conduct a thorough audit that includes a survey consisting of 130 questions, such as: How do you manage your process? How do you evaluate internal quality? Do you have standardized work in your process? The audit team also queries the supplier on its financial health.

Once a supplier is selected, the team works with suppliers on continuous improvement activities. Purchasing and quality assurance evaluate the supplier's performance using quality, cost, and delivery metrics. They issue a report card monthly and recognize top performers with an annual supplier award. Purchasing specialists work with suppliers to resolve any issues that may arise.

"I feel very committed to the suppliers we select," says Nolting. "Once we make a commitment, we do everything possible to get the supplier to the level of our expectation. We don't make many changes in our supply base."

Twice each year, purchasing and quality assurance work with a small group of suppliers on process improvements that ensure they are providing the plant with good-quality parts. The group consists of suppliers that may have had a number of rejects during a specific time period, or another quality issue.

Recently, a group of five suppliers met with purchasing and quality assurance in Columbus to resolve some recurring problems. Three of the suppliers were providing components that were causing issues in the field. The other two were providing parts that the company was rejecting at the plant.

"We ask the supplier to identify the issue and by using a format we provide, let us know how they plan to resolve it," says Nolting. "We do this in an open forum with representatives of all five suppliers meeting with our management in one room. It's proven very effective."

Key domestic suppliers provide laser- and gas-cut plate steel used to make frames and masts, tubing components that go into lift cylinders, chrome-plated rods, plastic parts, metal stampings, tires, and wheels. (MRO tool crib items bring the total number of domestic suppliers to a little more than 200.) Nolting declined to disclose the plant's annual spend.

Even so, the move to domestic suppliers hasn't been 100% successful, Nolting says. In a few cases, the company has had to move purchasing of certain components back to Japan because of quality or delivery issues.

TIEM's success with supplier development—and manufacturing in the United States—goes back to the selection process, a joint effort between purchasing and quality assurance. "We know what questions to ask," says Nolting. "We know what to look for in a supplier. We don't make many changes to our supply base. We are willing to make a commitment. I think our record really proves that we are here for the long run. A supplier hooks its wagon to this group and it can be a long, prosperous ride down the trail, so to speak."

Source: Adapted from S. Avery, "Toyota Commits to Suppliers in the U.S.," *Purchasing,* November 16, 2006.

One of the most important processes that organizations perform is the evaluation, selection, and continuous measurement of suppliers. Traditionally, competitive bidding was the primary method for awarding purchase contracts. In the past, it was sufficient to obtain three bids and award the contract to the supplier offering the lowest price. Enlightened purchasers now commit major resources to evaluating a supplier's performance and capability across many different areas. The supplier selection process has become so important that teams of cross-functional personnel are often responsible for visiting and evaluating suppliers. A sound selection decision can reduce or prevent a host of problems.

Supplier evaluation and selection decisions are taking on increased importance today. If a firm has reduced its supply base to a much smaller level, and if remaining suppliers usually receive longer-term agreements, the willingness or ability to switch suppliers is diminished. This makes selecting the right suppliers an important business decision.

This chapter focuses on different topics and issues pertaining to the evaluation and selection of suppliers. The first section provides an overview of the evaluation and selection process. The next sections present the various performance categories that a purchaser can include within the evaluation and selection process. The third section focuses on an approach for developing a tool or instrument for use during supplier evaluations. We next highlight the critical issues that confront a purchaser during the selection process. The chapter concludes with ways to reduce the time required for selection decisions.

The Supplier Evaluation and Selection Process

Most purchasing experts will agree that there is no one best way to evaluate and select suppliers, and organizations use a variety of different approaches. Regardless of the approach employed, the overall objective of the evaluation process should be to reduce purchase risk and maximize overall value to the purchaser.

An organization must select suppliers it can do business with over an extended period. The degree of effort associated with the selection relates to the importance of the required good or service. Depending on the supplier evaluation approach used, the process can be an intensive effort requiring a major commitment of resources (such as time and travel). This section addresses the many issues and decisions involved in effectively and efficiently evaluating and selecting suppliers to be part of the purchaser's supply base. Exhibit 7.1 highlights the critical steps involved in the supplier evaluation and selection process.

Recognize the Need for Supplier Selection

The first step of the evaluation and selection process usually involves recognizing that there is a requirement to evaluate and select a supplier for an item or service. A purchasing manager might begin the supplier evaluation process in anticipation of a future purchase requirement. Purchasing may have early insight into new-product development plans through participation on a product development team. In this case, engineering personnel may provide some preliminary specifications on the type of materials, service, or processes required, but will not yet have specific details. This

Exhibit 7.1 Supplier Evaluation and Selection Process

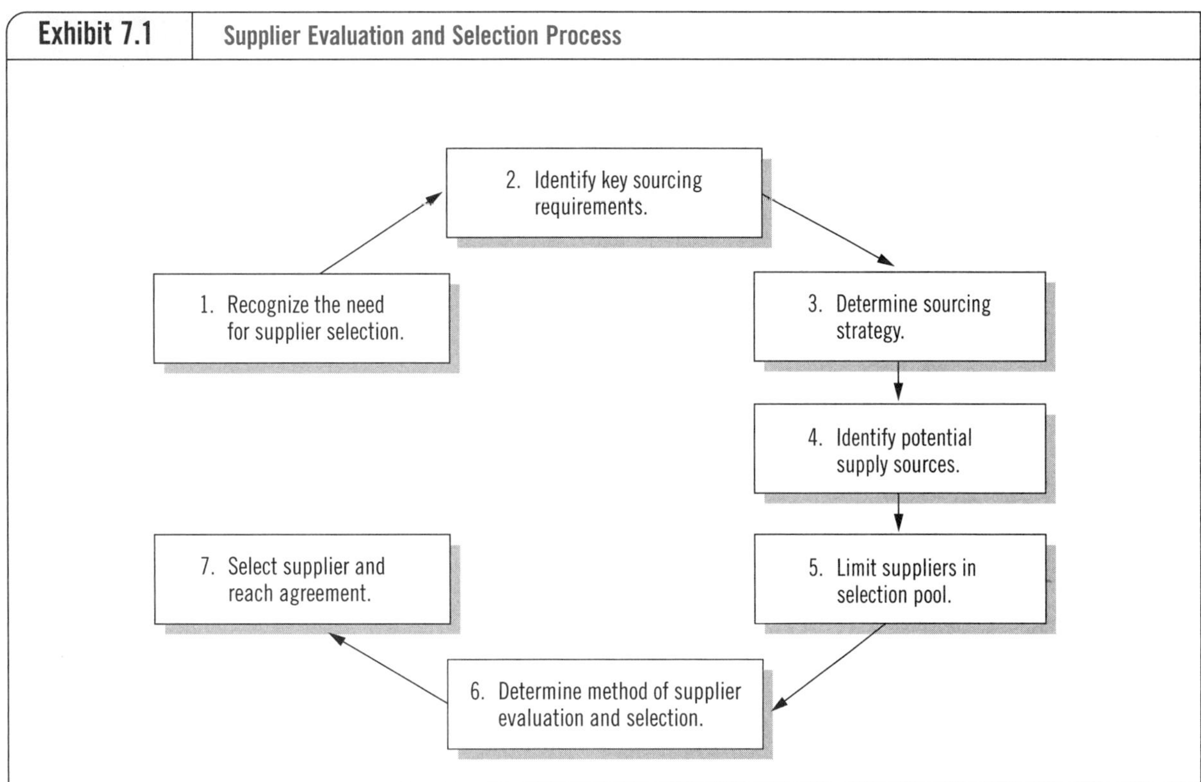

preliminary information may be enough to justify beginning an initial evaluation of potential sources of supply.

The recognition that a need exists to evaluate suppliers can come about in many different ways. Exhibit 7.2 on p. 238 identifies the most common ways that result in a need to evaluate sources of supply. Progressive purchasing groups increasingly anticipate rather than react to supplier selection needs. The complexity and value of a required purchase will influence the extent to which a buyer evaluates potential supply sources.

Identify Key Sourcing Requirements

Throughout the supplier evaluation and selection process, it is important to understand the requirements that are important to that purchase. These requirements, often determined by internal and external customers within the value chain, can differ widely from item to item. A later section discusses the various supplier performance areas where a purchaser should determine its critical sourcing requirements. Although different requirements may exist for each evaluation, certain categories—supplier quality, cost, and delivery performance—are usually included in the evaluation.

Determine Sourcing Strategy

No single sourcing strategy approach will satisfy the requirements of all purchases. Because of this, the purchasing strategy adopted for a particular item or service will influence the approach taken during the supplier evaluation and selection process. In this chapter, we will not go into detail on the processes used to develop a commodity

Exhibit 7.2	When Do Supplier Evaluation and Selection Decisions Arise?
	During new product development
	Due to poor internal or external supplier performance
	At the end of a contract
	When buying new equipment
	When expanding into new markets or product lines
	When internal users submit requisitions for goods or services
	When performing market tests
	When faced with countertrade requirements
	During outsourcing analyses
	When consolidating volumes across a business
	When conducting a reverse auction
	When current suppliers have insufficient capacity
	When reducing the size of the supply base

strategy. Chapter 6 covers this subject in detail. There are many decisions that a purchaser initially makes when developing a sourcing strategy. However, these often change as a result of market conditions, user preferences, and corporate objectives. The considerations developed during the strategy phase need to be re-evaluated during the selection process. The strategy options selected will greatly influence the supplier selection and evaluation process.

These key decisions include the following:

- Single versus multiple supply sources
- Short-term versus long-term purchase contracts
- Selecting suppliers that provide design support versus those that lack design capability
- Full-service versus non-full-service suppliers
- Domestic versus foreign suppliers
- Expectation of a close working relationship versus arm's-length purchasing

Identify Potential Supply Sources

Purchasers rely on various sources of information when identifying potential sources of supply. The degree to which a buyer must search for information or the effort put forth toward the search is a function of several variables, including how well existing suppliers can satisfy cost, quality, or other performance variables. The strategic importance or technical complexity of the purchase requirement also influences the intensity of the search. The following offers some guidelines regarding the effort and intensity of search required during supplier evaluation:

- High capability of current suppliers + High strategic importance of requirement = **Minor to moderate information search**

- High capability of current suppliers + Low strategic importance of requirement = **Minor information search**
- Low capability of current suppliers + High strategic importance of requirement = **Major information search**
- Low capability of current suppliers + Low strategic importance of requirement = **Minor to moderate information search**

The following sections discuss various resources that may be good sources of information when seeking to identify potential supply sources.

Current Suppliers

A major source of information is current or existing suppliers. Buyers often look to existing suppliers to satisfy a new purchase requirement. The advantage of this approach is that the purchaser does not have to add and maintain an additional supplier. Also, the buyer can do business with an already familiar supplier, which may limit the time and resources required to evaluate a new supplier's capabilities.

On the negative side, using existing suppliers, although perhaps easier and quicker, may not always be the best long-term approach. A purchasing manager may never know if better suppliers are available without information on other sources. For this reason, most organizations are continuously seeking new sources of supply and are expanding this search to include suppliers from around the world.

Selecting an existing supplier for a new purchase requirement may be an attractive option if a list of preferred suppliers is maintained. Designation as a **preferred supplier** means that a supplier consistently satisfies the performance and service standards defined by the buyer. A preferred supplier status conveys immediate information about the supplier's overall performance and competency. However, the buyer must still determine if a preferred supplier is capable of providing a particular purchase requirement.

Sales Representatives

All purchasers receive sales and marketing information from sales representatives. These contacts can prove to be a valuable source of information about potential sources. Even if an immediate need does not exist for a supplier's services, the buyer can file the information for future reference. A visit to a purchasing manager's office would probably reveal a set of cabinets or drawers that contain sales and marketing information.

Information Databases

Some companies maintain databases of suppliers that are capable of supporting an industry or product line. NCR, for example, maintains data on about 30,000 companies serving the computer industry. The company searches trade journals and financial newspapers for information about potential suppliers. The use of an automated database or data warehouse can quickly identify suppliers potentially qualified to support a requirement.

Maintaining a supplier database is particularly important in industries where technology changes rapidly. The database may contain information on current products, the supplier's future technology roadmap, process capability ratios, and past performance.

Databases of potential supply sources are also available for purchase from external parties. These can be especially valuable when searching for foreign sources of supply.

Experience

Experienced purchasing personnel usually have strong knowledge about potential suppliers. A buyer may have worked within an industry over many years and may be familiar with the suppliers, perhaps including international suppliers. One argument against rotating buyers too frequently between product lines or types of purchases is that a buyer may lose the expertise built up over the years. Experience and knowledge become valuable because few purchasing organizations have developed an intelligence database about suppliers.

Trade Journals

Most industries have a group or council that publishes a trade journal or magazine that routinely presents articles about different companies. These articles often focus on a company's technical or innovative development of a material, component, product, process, or service. Suppliers also use trade journals to advertise their products or services. Most buyers follow (or should follow) trade journals closely.

Trade Directories

Almost all industries publish directories of companies that produce items or provide services within an industry. Such directories can be a valuable source of initial information for a buyer who is not familiar with an industry or its suppliers. Chapter 10 provides some examples of international supplier directories. A very popular directory for domestic buyers is the *Thomas Register of American Manufacturers.* This directory can be located at www.thomasnet.com.

Trade Shows

Trade shows may be an effective way to gain exposure to a large number of suppliers at one time. Groups such as the Chemical Manufacturers Association and the American Society of Automotive Suppliers often sponsor trade shows. The National Machine Tool Builders Show in Chicago is one of the largest trade shows held in the United States. Buyers attending trade shows can gather information about potential suppliers while also evaluating the latest technological developments. Many contacts are initiated between industrial buyers and sellers at trade shows.

Second-Party or Indirect Information

This source of information includes a wide range of contacts not directly part of the purchaser's organization. A buyer can gather information from other suppliers, such as knowledge about a noncompetitor that might be valuable. Other buyers are another second-party information source. Attendees at meetings of the Institute for Supply Management can develop informal networks that provide information about potential supply sources. Other professional groups include the American Production and Inventory Control Society, the Council for Supply Chain Management Professionals, the American Manufacturing Engineering Association, and the American Society for Quality Control.

Some purchasers publicly recognize their best suppliers. Recognition may come in the form of a newspaper advertisement that highlights the achievement of superior suppliers. Ford Motor Corporation, for example, periodically purchases a full-page advertisement in the *Wall Street Journal* expressing appreciation and recognition of its best suppliers. In the advertisement, Ford lists each supplier by name and why it is being recognized. Because of Ford's approach to recognizing its best suppliers, a buyer gains visibility to a group of blue-chip suppliers.

Internal Sources

Many larger companies divide the organization into units, each with a separate purchasing operation. Sharing information across units can occur through informal meetings, strategy development sessions, purchasing newsletters, or the development of a comprehensive database containing information about potential supply sources. Internal sources, even those from diverse business units, can provide a great deal of information about potential supply sources.

Internet Searches

Buyers are increasingly using the Internet to help locate potential sources that might qualify for further evaluation. Sellers are increasingly using the Internet as an important part of their direct marketing efforts.

After collecting information about potential supply sources, the purchasing manager must begin to sift through and consolidate the information. This can be a huge task, depending on the number of suppliers and the information obtained. During its search for global suppliers for an item, Mack Trucks (part of Volvo) may collect or request information from 500 suppliers. It categorizes this information and puts it into a worldwide database for current and future reference. At some point, companies must eliminate suppliers that do not have a good fit with the buyer.

Sourcing Snapshot

Chemical Distributors Select Global Suppliers with a Customer Focus

Chemical distributors are expanding their global sourcing. International sourcing must be a win-win; their customers need to ensure that what they buy—and where they buy it from—is on their customers' wish list. Buyers at chemical distributors emphasize thorough supplier evaluation and product testing in their global supplier selection process.

Tom Corcoran is vice president of sales and sourcing at Brenntag North America, a Reading, PA–based subsidiary of the German chemical distributor that sources from and sells into a variety of overseas markets. "We don't simply look at global sourcing as leverage for better pricing, but rather we look at it as a way to expand the sourcing options for our customers," he says. That philosophy is embodied in Corcoran's unique title, which includes both sales and sourcing. As a distributor, Brenntag is, in effect, selling its suppliers to its customers, and therefore, its buyers are more closely tied to the customer side than in a typical manufacturing environment.

"Our customers clearly have an impact on where and who we source from and influence which suppliers we use in various global markets," Corcoran says. "And without the suppliers' commitment we'd have nothing to sell. Our suppliers are as important as our customers."

Corcoran says he has an advantage in global sourcing because his company is a subsidiary of the global distributor. Corcoran has counterparts in various other global regions, including Latin America and Europe, which provide leads and assistance in uncovering new suppliers on a case-by-case basis.

Also, Brenntag North America inherited a sourcing office in China when it acquired Los Angeles Chemical, which it has found it to be an extremely useful asset in its efforts to source more from China. The four sourcing employees there work to ensure that the suppliers Brenntag recruits from that market meet its needs in terms of quality and reliability. Brenntag has an office in Shanghai, and his manager there spends time interacting with suppliers and customers looking for information on how to go to market in China and extract the value out of those markets.

Beyond those regions, Corcoran says he is investigating India very closely as a potential source for new suppliers. "We have some suppliers in India now," he says, "but more and more that is becoming a strategic marketplace for us."

Shondra Garrigus is vice president of purchasing at Seattle-based TRInternational (TRI) and says the company's experience in exporting products to various global markets (most notably Europe) has helped the purchasing organization streamline its global sourcing efforts. "For a company our size—we're on the small side—to survive in the chemical industry, we have to be a little bit more innovative about how we source," Garrigus says. In the past, the company has sourced up to 75% of its products from outside the United States, but today that amount has been pared back to about 60%, due mostly to recent currency fluctuations in Europe.

Like many purchasing executives, Garrigus is focused on China. "We've gotten some materials like citric acid from China for a while, but we're rapidly expanding the list of chemicals we source from China," Garrigus says. "In the past year, we've been expanding the breadth of products coming out of China." The biggest challenge in global sourcing, she says, is educating suppliers in new regions about how to export efficiently to the U.S. market. For example, in China there are fewer regulations on the types of packaging or drums that chemicals can be shipped in.

SUPPLIER EVALUATION

As important as supplier evaluation is for manufacturers in global sourcing, it's even more important for distributors. If a manufacturer finds it has been working with a less-than-reputable supplier, it's a problem, but often the problem can be rectified before the end customer is impacted. However, poor supplier selection in distribution can have a direct impact on customer satisfaction in the distribution business.

"The same parameters we'd hold for our domestic suppliers, we hold for all of our foreign suppliers as well," says Corcoran. "That's because the customers' requirements don't change based on the supplier's location." But when it comes to global sourcing, learning by mistake is sometimes the only way.

"Anyone who has been doing this a long time has been burned on more than one occasion," says Garrigus. "It comes with the territory. But we can learn from those experiences. Beyond cost, it's most important to us to make sure we have a secure supply line for our customers.

We have to make sure the suppliers we're working with are reputable and will be around for a long time."

Both Brenntag and TRI receive requests from customers specifying that nothing they buy can be sourced from outside the United States, especially for application-specific and specialty products. Other customers prefer products from certain regions or countries.

"Sometimes customers have a valid reason, but we can sometimes break their biases by providing the right materials," says Garrigus. "We can show them that while this might not be the same supplier they are used to, this is a quality product and can save them money."

Source: Adapted from D. Hanson, "Distributors Take On Global Sourcing with a Customer Focus," *Purchasing,* March 1, 2007.

Sourcing Alternatives

Once the list of potential and current suppliers is put into a database, it is further refined considering the type of supplier a firm may wish to deal with based on the initial sourcing strategy. Major sourcing alternatives include whether to purchase from a (1) manufacturer or distributor; (2) local or national or international source; (3) small or large supplier; and (4) multiple or single supplier for the item, commodity, or service.

Manufacturer vs. Distributor

The choice of buying directly versus from a distributor is usually based on four criteria: (1) the size of the purchase; (2) the manufacturer's policies regarding direct sales; (3) the storage space available at the purchaser's facility; and (4) the extent of services required.

Economically speaking, if all else is equal, the lowest unit price will be available from the OEM. The distributor buys from the OEM and resells, therefore incurring a transaction cost, and it must make a profit. Despite the exchange cost, recent trends have increased the role of distributors in providing the purchaser a low-cost solution. First, many OEMs can't handle or choose not to handle the large volume of transactions required to sell directly. Second, buyers are requiring more services from their suppliers and distributors have stepped in to fill this need. **Vendor Managed Inventory** is a program that distributors market to manage their customer's inventory for them. Several organizations are using **integrated supply**, where a distributor is awarded a longer-term contract. Integrated suppliers are given access to the purchaser's demand data and are expected to maintain certain levels of inventory and customer service on the contracted items.

Local or National or International Suppliers

International and national suppliers may be able to offer the best price and superior technical service. Alternatively, local suppliers are more responsive to the buying firm's changing needs and can economically make frequent smaller deliveries. The popularity of JIT and quick-replenishment systems favor using more local suppliers. Local suppliers also allow the buying firm to build a degree of community goodwill through enhancing local economic activity (see the Toyota case at the beginning of this chapter). International suppliers provide opportunities to attain dramatic price savings. These savings must be evaluated against the additional inventory, communication, and logistics costs (see Chapter 10 for a complete discussion).

Large or Small Suppliers

All suppliers were at one time small suppliers. Growth over time is due to providing superior price, quality, and service compared to their competitors. Many purchasers prefer to focus on "capability to do the job" regardless of size. Size does become a factor when one firm decides to leverage its purchases from one or a few suppliers. This leveraging means that the supplier must have wide variety in its product or service offerings as well as the ability to service multiple geographic locations (in some cases worldwide locations).

Often the buying firm does not want the seller to become dependent on its business. Thus the purchaser would make sure that its purchases do not represent more than a certain percentage (e.g., 35–45%) of the supplier's total business. Finally, supply departments that are building diversity into the supply base will often deal with an increased number of small suppliers.

Multiple or Single Sourcing

Once the number of suppliers is reduced to those qualified, a decision on the optimal number of suppliers in the supply base needs to be made. Certainly there is a trend to reduce the number of suppliers. Although single sourcing provides optimum leverage and power over the supplier, multiple sourcing provides improved assurance of supply.

Limit Suppliers in Selection Pool

The result of this information gathering is that, depending upon the item under consideration, a purchaser may have many potential sources from which to choose. Unfortunately, the performance capabilities of suppliers vary widely. Limited resources also preclude an in-depth evaluation of all potential supply sources. Purchasers often perform a first cut or preliminary evaluation of potential suppliers to narrow the list before conducting an in-depth formal evaluation. Several criteria may support the narrowing of the supplier list.

Financial Risk Analysis

Most purchasers perform at least a cursory financial analysis of prospective suppliers. Although financial condition is not the only criterion upon which to evaluate a supplier, poor financial condition can indicate serious problems. A financial analysis performed during this phase of the process is much less comprehensive than the one performed during final supplier evaluation. During this phase, a purchaser is trying to get a feel for the overall financial health of the supplier. Buyers often consult external sources of information such as Dun & Bradstreet (D&B) reports to support the evaluation.

Evaluation of Supplier Performance

A prospective supplier may have an established performance record with a purchaser. A purchaser may have used a supplier for a previous purchase requirement, or a supplier may currently provide material to another part of the organization. A supplier may also have provided other types of commodities or services to the purchaser than those under consideration. Based on prior experience, a purchasing manager may consider that supplier for a different type of commodity or service.

Evaluation of Supplier-Provided Information

Buyers often request specific information directly from potential suppliers. Requests for information involve sending a preliminary survey to suppliers. The buyer uses this information to screen each supplier and to determine if the buyer's requirements appear to match the supplier's capabilities. Buyers can request information on a supplier's cost structure, process technology, market share data, quality performance, or any other area important to the purchase decision.

A major U.S. chemical producer mandates that suppliers complete requests for information (which it calls presurvey questionnaires) before conducting more detailed supplier surveys. Besides ownership, financial information, and type of business, this company attempts to determine how sophisticated the supplier's current practices are and how far along it is toward achieving total quality.

Before committing time to evaluate a supplier further, suppliers should satisfy certain entry qualifiers. **Entry qualifiers** are the basic components that suppliers must possess before they proceed to the next phase of the evaluation and selection process. One researcher identifies five qualifiers that suppliers must satisfy: financial strength, appropriate business strategy, strong supportive management, proven manufacturing capability, and design capability.[1] The time and cost associated with evaluating suppliers makes it necessary to limit suppliers in the selection pool that meet these qualifiers.

Determine the Method of Supplier Evaluation and Selection

Once an initial cut has eliminated suppliers that are not capable, the buyer or commodity team must decide how to evaluate the remaining suppliers, which may appear to be equally qualified. This requires a finer level of evaluation detail than that used in the initial process. There are a number of ways to evaluate and select suppliers from the remaining companies in the pool. These include evaluating supplier-provided information, conducting supplier visits, and using preferred supplier lists.

Evaluation from Supplier-Provided Information

Buyers often receive and evaluate detailed information directly from potential suppliers for the purpose of awarding a purchase contract. This information may come from requests for quotes or requests for proposals. Not too long ago buyers made almost all purchase decisions using this method. In recent years, however, many organizations have adopted a more direct and in-depth approach to evaluating potential suppliers. Increasingly, companies are also requesting that suppliers provide a detailed cost breakdown of their quoted price in the response to a request for quote, including details on labor, materials, overhead, and profit.

Supplier Visits

A team of cross-functional experts may visit potential suppliers. The next section discusses the criteria often used by cross-functional teams during supplier visits. Although many sources exist to discover information about a potential supplier, visiting the actual facility provides the most complete way to ensure an accurate assessment

Exhibit 7.3 Key Evaluation Criteria to Be Noted During a Supplier Visit

- ✓ Management capability
- ✓ Total quality management
- ✓ Technical capability
- ✓ Operations and scheduling capability
- ✓ Financial strength
- ✓ Personnel relations
- ✓ E-systems capabilities
- ✓ Technological sophistication and efficiency of the equipment
- ✓ ISO certifications
- ✓ Caliber of the supervision and inspection personnel
- ✓ Evidence of good management and housekeeping practices
- ✓ Types of inventory systems
- ✓ Nature of the receiving, storeroom, and shipping areas
- ✓ Quality control philosophy
- ✓ Environmental practices
- ✓ Representation of white and blue collar staffs
- ✓ Employee contract expiration dates
- ✓ Names and contact information of key decision makers

of the supplier. Site visits are expensive and require buyer time in travel and information collection. The purchaser needs to be alert and gather all necessary information while being sensitive to the supplier's limitations on restricted information. Exhibit 7.3 provides a checklist of the key evaluation criteria that should be noted during the site visit. Key personal contacts in management, operations, and marketing may be useful resources in the later stages of the selection process.

Regardless of whether the supplier is a potential or existing supplier, the purchaser should compile this data into a report that is maintained in a data warehouse or on file for easy retrieval by members of the cross-functional team. Evaluation criteria are covered in detail in the next section.

The use of teams for supplier evaluation and selection is increasing, particularly among larger organizations that have the resources to commit to this approach. The advantage to the team approach is that each team member contributes unique insight into the overall supplier evaluation. Members may have expertise in quality, engineering capabilities, or manufacturing techniques, and they may be qualified to assess suppliers in these areas.

Use of Preferred Suppliers

Increasingly, purchasers are rewarding their best suppliers by creating preferred supplier lists, which can simplify the supplier evaluation and selection process. A preferred supplier is one that consistently meets stringent performance criteria. A buyer can refer to the purchasing database to determine if there is a current supplier that can satisfy the purchase requirement. This eliminates the need to perform a time-consuming evaluation. Buyers can also use a preferred supplier list as an incentive to improve the performance of existing suppliers. Only the best suppliers should receive placement on a preferred supplier list.

Sourcing Snapshot

D&B Makes Supplier Evaluation Data Available through the Web

Imagine this scenario: You work for a small organization that simply does not have the financial or human resources to qualify suppliers. Or perhaps you have a minor purchase requirement that does not justify a major search. Do you simply hope for the best when making your selection? Will you be reluctant to try new suppliers for fear that the risk of the unknown is simply too great? For many organizations and purchase situations, supplier evaluation is a luxury when it should be a necessity.

What can you do when faced with these situations? One option is to use an external party to collect and disseminate supplier performance data. Dun & Bradstreet (D&B), a supplier of business information and receivables management services, offers its Supplier Qualifier Report over the Internet. Users around the world can now purchase with a credit card the supplier evaluation report for any of the 80 million businesses worldwide contained in D&B's database.

Designed for purchasing professionals, qualifier reports provide an objective, third-party view of suppliers. These reports provide a wide range of information about suppliers, including a business overview, history and operations, payment information, risk assessment, financial information, and public filings. The reports also indicate if a supplier is ISO 9000 registered or a minority- or women-owned business. D&B maintains that the report is a tremendous resource for companies that want to confidently do business with suppliers.

Source: From www.dnb.com, 2003.

External or Third-Party Information

Mattel Corporation's recent problem with lead paint in toys has resulted in other firms asking for third-party quality audits during the evaluation phase.[2] Sourcing Snapshot: D&B Makes Supplier Evaluation Data Available through the Web highlights another approach for securing reliable third-party information. Using third-party information can be a timely and effective way to gain insight into potential suppliers.

Select Supplier and Reach Agreement

The final step of the evaluation and selection process is to select the supplier(s) and reach a contract agreement. The activities associated with this step can vary widely depending on the purchase item under consideration. For routine items, this may simply require notifying and awarding a basic purchase contract to a supplier. For a major purchase, the process can become more complex. The buyer and seller may have to conduct detailed negotiations to agree upon the specific details of a purchase agreement.

Sourcing Snapshot

Good Ideas When Evaluating IT Suppliers

Buyers of information technology (IT) know that choosing the wrong supplier can create problems that last for many years. The rate of technological change can make the perfect supplier obsolete within months. Unfortunately, it is usually next to impossible to switch to a new IT supplier quickly. For this reason, the selection process takes on added importance. IT experts offer some sound suggestions when making supplier selection decisions:

- Do not rely on only one supplier. Too many companies try to complete all of their computer technology buying using one or two big suppliers. Try to build a supply network that includes some smaller suppliers that have promising emerging technologies.
- Make sure you and the supplier are moving down the same road. Evaluate each supplier's technology and product roadmaps. Are both organizations working toward platforms, capabilities, features, and functions that are compatible?
- Build your portfolio with the best. Choose suppliers that add strength to your ability to add value to your end customer. Do not select suppliers simply because they offer a good purchase price.
- Be a big fish in a little pond. Sourcing from the biggest supplier might bring a good purchase price but limits your ability to leverage. A smaller supplier may be more motivated to innovate in your direction.
- Know the supplier's Internet strategy. Understand how your suppliers are using the Internet to add value to what they develop, manufacture, service, or distribute.

Because information technology has become increasingly important to supply chain management, making the right IT supplier selection decision can mean the difference between success and failure.

Source: Adapted from "Tips on Supplier Evaluation," *InfoWorld,* October 26, 1998, p. 72.

Key Supplier Evaluation Criteria

Purchasers usually evaluate potential suppliers across multiple categories using their own selection criteria with assigned weights. Purchasers that need consistent delivery performance with short lead times to support a just-in-time production system might emphasize a supplier's scheduling and production systems. A high-technology buyer might emphasize a supplier's process and technological capabilities or commitment to research and development. The selection process for a distributor or service provider will emphasize a different set of criteria.

Most evaluations rate suppliers on three primary criteria: (1) cost or price, (2) quality, and (3) delivery. These three elements of performance are generally the most obvious and most critical areas that affect the purchaser. For critical items needing an in-depth analysis of the supplier's capabilities, a more detailed supplier evaluation study is required. The following presents the wide range of criteria that a purchaser might consider during supplier evaluation and selection.

Management Capability

It is important for a buyer to evaluate a supplier's management capability. After all, management runs the business and makes the decisions that affect the competitiveness of the supplier. A buyer should ask many questions when evaluating a supplier's management capability:

- Does management practice long-range planning?
- Has management committed the supplier to total quality management (TQM) and continuous improvement?
- Is turnover high among managers?
- What are the professional experience and educational backgrounds of the key managers?
- Is there a vision about the future direction of the company?
- Is management customer focused?
- What is the history of labor/management relations?
- Is management making the investments that are necessary to sustain and grow the business?
- Has management prepared the company to face future competitive challenges, including providing employee training and development?
- Does management understand the importance of strategic sourcing?

It may be a challenge to identify the true state of affairs during a brief visit or using a questionnaire. Nevertheless, asking these questions can help the purchasing manager to develop a feeling for the professional capabilities of the managers in the supplying organization. When interviewing managers, it is important to attempt to meet with as many people as possible in order to paint a true picture.

Employee Capabilities

This part of the evaluation process requires an assessment of non-management personnel. Do not underestimate the benefit that a highly trained, stable, and motivated workforce provides, particularly during periods of labor shortages. A purchaser should consider these points:

- The degree to which employees are committed to quality and continuous improvement
- The overall skills and abilities of the workforce
- Employee-management relations
- Worker flexibility
- Employee morale
- Workforce turnover
- Willingness of employees to contribute to improved operations

A buyer should also gather information about the history of strikes and labor disputes. This can result in a general idea of how dedicated the supplier's employees are to producing products or services that will meet or exceed the buyer's expectations.

Sourcing Snapshot

H.B. Fuller Uses Supplier Visits to Narrow the Supply Base

H.B. Fuller Corporation illustrates how first-hand information gained through supplier visits plays a large part in narrowing the supply base.

Latin America sourcing manager Roy Calderón of H.B. Fuller narrows down his list of suppliers by obtaining first-hand information. Whenever possible, that means touring supplier plants and interacting with the supplier's staff.

"I have a technical and manufacturing background, so I first try to understand the logistical and manufacturing capabilities of a supplier, as well as their quality assurance process and systems," says Calderón. What he sees at a supplier's plant helps him determine how much H.B. Fuller, headquartered in St. Paul, MN, can expect from that supplier in the way of consistent quality.

Calderón scrutinizes the plant's infrastructure as well as its production staff. "Morale and work environment is hard to put into hard numbers or dollars, but it needs to be part of a supplier's intelligence profile," he says. Though he can't visit every single one of his suppliers, he makes a point to visit at least the top 10 suppliers in his region.

When visiting a supplier, Calderón looks for any signs in the facilities that might signal future supply problems. For example, if a machine looks like it might wear out or if the plant seems like it's falling apart, he takes notice. He also inspects production line pacing as another indicator of a supplier's health. If a supplier is too busy and overloaded, it might not be responsive enough to any order changes. If it is too relaxed, it might not be economically viable for much longer. Neither extreme is encouraging, Calderón says.

Another crucial component of supplier health is the attitude of employees on the plant floor. Calderón wants to see if they seem motivated or happy. He'll speak with employees about non-technical topics, even just to ask them how they're doing, and gauge their reaction. If the workers seem to be proud of their work, it's more likely that supplier will provide a consistently high-quality product.

Although some suppliers might want to keep Calderón in the board room offices, he insists on the broader picture. "If all I see are fancy offices and the suppliers aren't willing to show me their manufacturing process and let me talk to their employees, that's a big question mark," he says.

Source: Adapted from M. Varmazis, "How to Narrow Your Supply List," *Purchasing*, July 17, 2007.

Cost Structure

Evaluating a supplier's cost structure requires an in-depth understanding of a supplier's total costs, including direct labor costs, indirect labor costs, material costs, manufacturing or process operating costs, and general overhead costs. Understanding a supplier's cost structure helps a buyer determine how efficiently a supplier can produce an item. A cost analysis also helps identify potential areas of cost improvement.

Collecting this information can be a challenge. A supplier may not have a detailed understanding of its costs. Many suppliers do not have a sophisticated cost accounting system and are unable to assign overhead costs to products or processes. Furthermore, some suppliers view cost data as highly proprietary. They may fear that the release of cost information will undermine its pricing strategy or that competitors will gain access to its cost data, which could provide insight into a supplier's competitive advantage. Because of these concerns, buyers will often develop reverse pricing models that provide estimates of the supplier's cost structure during the initial supplier evaluation.

Total Quality Performance, Systems, and Philosophy

A major part of the evaluation process addresses a supplier's quality management processes, systems, and philosophy. Buyers evaluate not only the obvious topics associated with supplier quality (management commitment, statistical process control, defects) but also safety, training, and facilities and equipment maintenance. Alcoa defines its supplier quality requirements in four broad areas: management, quality measurement, safety and training, and facilities. Many purchasers are expecting potential suppliers to have adopted quality systems based on the Malcolm Baldrige National Quality Award (MBNQA) or International Organization for Standardization (ISO) 9000 criteria. The wide distribution of these guidelines has exposed many suppliers to the Baldrige and ISO definitions of quality.

Process and Technological Capability

Supplier evaluation teams often include a member from the engineering or technical staff to evaluate a supplier's process and technological capability. Process consists of the technology, design, methods, and equipment used to manufacture a product or deliver a service. A supplier's selection of a production process helps define its required technology, human resource skills, and capital equipment requirements.

The evaluation should include both the supplier's current and future process and technological capabilities. Assessing a supplier's future process and technological capability involves reviewing capital equipment plans and strategy. In addition, a purchaser should evaluate the resources that a supplier is committing to research and development.

A purchaser may also assess a supplier's design capability. One way to reduce the time required to develop new products involves using qualified suppliers that are able to support product design activities. The trend toward the increased use of supplier design capabilities makes this area an integral part of the supplier evaluation and selection process.

Environmental Regulation Compliance

The 1990s brought about a renewed awareness of the impact that industry has on the environment. The Clean Air Act of 1990, for example, imposes large fines on producers of ozone-depleting substances and foul-smelling gases. Recycling of industrial materials is also an issue. Purchasers certainly do not want to be associated with known environmental polluters from a public relations or potential liability standpoint.

The most common environmental performance criteria used when evaluating a supplier's performance include the following:

- Disclosure of environmental infractions
- Hazardous and toxic waste management

- Recycling management
- ISO 14000 certification
- Control of ozone-depleting substances

Herman Miller, a manufacturer of office furniture, makes environmental concerns part of the supplier evaluation and selection process. For instance, Herman Miller includes supplier packaging as an evaluation criterion. Standardized, reusable shipping containers are favored over disposable ones. Such containers also support just-in-time deliveries. Herman Miller also requires its suppliers to label the chemical composition of its plastic procured items so that recyclers will know the exact content of the plastic found in the parts.[3] DuPont's environmental program began with cutting greenhouse gas emissions at its factories by 72% since 1990, an initiative that saved $3 billion in energy costs. Now DuPont views the environmental movement as a key to increasing revenue.[4]

Financial Stability

An assessment of a potential supplier's financial condition should occur during the initial evaluation process. Some purchasers view the financial assessment as a screening process or preliminary condition that the supplier must pass before a detailed evaluation can begin. An organization may use a financial rating service to help analyze a supplier's financial condition.

Selecting a supplier in poor financial condition presents a number of risks. First, there is the risk that the supplier will go out of business. Second, suppliers that are in poor financial condition may not have the resources to invest in plant, equipment, or research that is necessary for longer-term technological or other performance improvements. Third, the supplier may become too financially dependent on the purchaser. A final risk is that financial weakness is usually an indication of underlying problems. Is the weakness a result of poor quality or delivery performance? Is it a result of wasteful spending by management? Has the supplier assumed too much debt?

There may be circumstances that support selecting a supplier in a weaker financial condition. A supplier may be developing but has not yet marketed a leading-edge technology that can provide an advantage to the purchaser. A supplier may also be in a weaker financial condition because of uncontrollable or nonrepeating circumstances.

If the supplier is publicly traded, specific financial ratios can be obtained from a variety of websites providing detailed financial ratios and industry averages to compare these ratios against. Some common ratios used to assess supplier financial health appear in Exhibit 7.4.

Some websites available to obtain such information include the following:

- Yahoo! Financial section (http://www.biz.yahoo.com)
- Morningstar (http://www.morningstar.net)
- Marketwatch (http://www.marketwatch.com)
- 411Stocks (http://www.411stocks.com)
- The Street (http://www.thestreet.com)
- Dun & Bradstreet (http://www.dnb.com)

Procurement specialists should become familiar with financial ratios because they can provide quick and valuable insights into a supplier's financial health. Moreover,

Exhibit 7.4 Interpreting Key Financial Ratios

RATIOS	INTERPRETATION
LIQUIDITY	
Current ratio = Current assets/Current liabilities	Should be over 1.0, but look at industry average; high—may mean poor asset management.
Quick ratio = (Cash + Receivables)/Current liabilities	At least 0.8 if supplier sells on credit; low—may mean cash flow problems; high—may mean poor asset management.
Note: Calculation includes marketable securities	
ACTIVITY	
Inventory turnover = Costs of goods sold/Inventory	Compare industry average; low—problems with slow inventory, which may hurt cash flow.
Fixed asset turnover = Sales/Fixed assets	Compare industry average; too low may mean supplier is not using fixed assets efficiently or effectively.
Total asset turnover = Sales/Total assets	Compare industry average; too low may mean supplier is not using its total assets efficiently or effectively.
Days sales outstanding = (Receivables × 365)/Sales	Compare industry average, or a value of 45–50 if company sells on net 30; too high hurts cash flow; too low may mean credit policies to customers are too restrictive.
PROFITABILITY	
Net profit margin = Profit after taxes/Sales	Represents after-tax return; compare industry average.
Return on assets = Profit after taxes/Total assets	Compare industry average; represents the return the company earns on everything it owns.
Return on equity = Profit after taxes/Equity	The higher the better; the return on the shareholders' investment in the business.
DEBT	
Debt to equity = Total liabilities/Equity	Compare industry average; over 3 means highly leveraged.
Current debt to equity = Current liabilities/Equity	Over 1 is risky unless industry average is over 1; when ratio is high, supplier may be unable to pay lenders.
Interest coverage = (Pretax Inc. + Int. Exp.)/Int. Exp.	Should be over 3; higher is better; low may mean supplier is having difficulty paying creditors.

purchasing managers should track such ratios for possible red flags that may signify potential financial difficulty.

Production Scheduling and Control Systems

Production scheduling includes those systems that release, schedule, and control a supplier's production process. Does the supplier use material requirements planning (MRP) to ensure the availability of required components? Does the supplier track material and production cycle time and compare this against a performance objective or standard? Does the supplier's production scheduling system support a purchaser's just-in-time requirements? What lead time does the supplier's production scheduling and control system require? What is the supplier's on-time delivery performance history? The purpose behind evaluating the production scheduling and control system is to identify the degree of control the supplier has over its scheduling and production process.

Suppliers can formally claim to have a Class A production system once they have undergone a formal review of their system by a professional external reviewer who has verified that the requisite criteria are satisfied. Companies that are considering sourcing high volumes of product with a supplier will also want to consider whether the supplier has adequate capacity.

E-Commerce Capability

The ability to communicate electronically between a buyer and seller is fast becoming a requirement during supplier selection. In the past, many considered electronic data interchange (EDI) a primary condition for doing business. However, more and more companies are moving to web-based business to business (B2B) platforms for their transactions. In early 2000, relatively few companies had implemented B2B electronic commerce platforms, but the rate of technology change in this area has now escalated rapidly.

IBM now states that the majority of its purchases (by dollar spent) occur via the Internet. However, such statements entail that suppliers have the required ability to adopt an e-commerce approach. In contrast to EDI, electronic commerce requires a relatively low investment on the part of suppliers. Besides the efficiencies that B2B e-commerce provides, these systems support closer relationships and the exchange of all kinds of information.

Purchasing managers should also evaluate other dimensions of the supplier's information technology (IT). Does the supplier have computer-aided design (CAD) capability? Does the supplier have bar coding capability or the ability to use radio frequency identification tags? Can the supplier send advance-shipping notices or accept payment by electronic funds transfer? Is the supplier able to communicate via e-mail? Evidence that the supplier is using these technologies can provide reasonable assurance that the supplier is current with e-commerce technologies.

Supplier's Sourcing Strategies, Policies, and Techniques

The concept of understanding a supplier's suppliers is part of integrated supply chain management. Unfortunately, organizations do not have the resources or personnel to investigate all of the suppliers within their supply chain. However, there are ways to obtain information on the performance capabilities of Tier 2 and even Tier 3 suppliers.

It is possible for a purchaser to develop an understanding of the purchasing approaches and techniques of suppliers that are three tiers or levels from the primary buyer. Assume that during the supplier selection process, a purchaser evaluates the sourcing strategies, approaches, and techniques of its first-tier supplier. Through discussions with the purchasing department of the first-tier supplier, the purchaser can gain insight about its second-tier suppliers. If the first-tier supplier also evaluates the sourcing strategies, approaches, and techniques of its first-tier suppliers (second-tier suppliers to the purchaser), then this can provide information about third-tier suppliers. Evaluating a potential supplier's sourcing strategies, approaches, and techniques is one way to gain greater insight and understanding of the supply chain. Because few purchasers understand their second- and third-tier suppliers, those that do can gain an important advantage over competitors.

Longer-Term Relationship Potential

A supplier's willingness to move beyond a traditional purchasing relationship should be part of the evaluation process for items and services where a longer-term relationship might be beneficial. Robert Spekman presented a number of questions that a buyer should ask when evaluating the potential of a longer-term relationship.[5] He argued that approaches emphasizing supplier efficiency, quality, price, and delivery are sometimes incomplete. Although these areas are important, they do not necessarily cover the issues upon which to base a longer-term relationship. Consider the following questions when evaluating the longer-term relationship potential of a prospective supplier:

- Has the supplier indicated a willingness or commitment to a longer-term relationship?
- Is the supplier willing to commit resources specific to this relationship?
- How early in the product design stage is the supplier willing or able to participate?
- What does the supplier bring that is unique?
- Does the supplier have an interest in joint problem solving and improvement efforts?
- Will there be free and open exchange of information across the two companies?
- How much future planning is the supplier willing to share?
- Is the need for confidential treatment of information taken seriously?
- What is the general level of comfort between the two parties?
- How well does the supplier know our industry and business?
- Will the supplier share cost data?
- Is the supplier willing to come to us first with innovations?
- Is the supplier willing to commit capacity exclusively to our needs?
- What will be the supplier's commitment to understanding our problems and concerns?

Although this is not a complete list of questions when evaluating the possibility of a longer-term relationship, it does provide a framework regarding the types of issues that are important. It is relatively straightforward to create a numerical scale to assess these questions as part of the supplier evaluation and selection process.

Developing a Supplier Evaluation and Selection Survey

Supplier evaluation often follows a rigorous, structured approach using formal surveys. An effective supplier survey should have certain characteristics. First, the survey should be comprehensive and include the performance categories considered important to the evaluation and selection process. Second, the survey process should be as objective as possible. This requires the use of a scoring system that defines the meaning of each value on a measurement scale.

A third characteristic is that the items and the measurement scales are reliable. This refers to the degree to which different individuals or groups reviewing the same items and measurement scales will arrive at the same conclusion. Reliable evaluations require well-defined measures and well-understood items.

A fourth characteristic of a sound supplier survey is flexibility. Although an organization should maintain a structure to its supplier survey, the format of the evaluation should provide some flexibility across different types of purchase requirements. The easiest way to make the process flexible is to adjust the performance categories and weights assigned to each category. The most important categories will receive a higher weight within the total evaluation score.

A final characteristic of an effective survey is that it is mathematically straightforward. The use of weights and points should be simple enough that each individual involved in the evaluation understands the mechanics of the scoring and selection process. To ensure that a supplier survey has the right characteristics, we recommend the use of a step-by-step process when creating this tool. Exhibit 7.5 presents the steps to follow when developing such a system. The following section discusses this framework and develops a sample evaluation survey.

Step 1: Identify Supplier Evaluation Categories

Perhaps the first step when developing a supplier survey is deciding the categories to include. As discussed earlier, there are many evaluation categories. For illustrative purposes, assume that a purchaser selects quality, management capability, financial condition, supplier cost structure, expected delivery performance, technological capability, systems capability, and a general category of miscellaneous performance factors as the categories to include in the evaluation. These categories would reveal the performance areas that the purchaser considers most important.

Exhibit 7.5 Supplier Evaluation and Selection Survey Development

Step 1	Identify supplier evaluation categories.	Develop the Survey
Step 2	Assign a weight to each evaluation category.	Develop the Survey
Step 3	Identify and weigh subcategories.	Develop the Survey
Step 4	Define scoring system for categories and subcategories.	Develop the Survey
Step 5	Evaluate supplier directly.	Assess and Select Supplier
Step 6	Review evaluation results and make selection decision.	Assess and Select Supplier
Step 7	Review and improve supplier performance continuously.	Review Performance

Step 2: Assign a Weight to Each Evaluation Category

The performance categories usually receive a weight that reflects the relative importance of that category. The assigned weights reflect the relative importance of each category. The total of the combined weights must equal 1.0.

Exhibit 7.6 shows the weight assigned to each selected performance category in our sample survey. Notice that the quality systems category receives 20% of the total evaluation, whereas systems capability receives 5%; this simply reflects the difference in relative importance to the purchaser between the two performance categories. Recall that an important characteristic of an effective evaluation system is flexibility. One way that management achieves this flexibility is by assigning different weights or adding or deleting performance categories as required.

Exhibit 7.6 Initial Supplier Evaluation

CATEGORY	WEIGHT	SUBWEIGHT	SCORE (5 PT. SCALE)	WEIGHTED SCORE	
Supplier: Advanced Micro Systems					
1. Quality Systems	20				
Process control systems		5	4	4.0	
Total quality commitment		8	4	6.4	
Parts-per-million defect performance		7	5	7.0	
					17.4
2. Management Capability	10				
Management/labor relations		5	4	4.0	
Management capability		5	4	4.0	
					8.0
3. Financial Condition	10				
Debt structure		5	3	3.0	
Turnover ratios		5	4	4.0	
					7.0
4. Cost Structure	15				
Costs relative to industry		5	5	5.0	
Understanding of costs		5	4	4.0	
Cost control/reduction efforts		5	5	5.0	
					14.0
5. Delivery Performance	15				
Performance to promise		5	3	3.0	
Lead-time requirements		5	3	3.0	
Responsiveness		5	3	3.0	
					9.0
6. Technical/Process Capability	15				
Product innovation		5	4	4.0	
Process innovation		5	5	5.0	
Research and development		5	5	5.0	
					14.0
7. Information Systems Capability	5				
EDI capability		3	5	3.0	
CAD/CAM		2	0	0	
					3.0
8. General	10				
Support of minority suppliers		2	3	1.2	
Environmental compliance		3	5	3.0	
Supplier's supply base management		5	4	4.0	
					8.2
			Total Weighted Score		80.6

Step 3: Identify and Weigh Subcategories

Step 2 specified broad performance categories included within our sample evaluation. Step 3 of this process requires identifying any performance subcategories, if they exist, within each broader performance category. For example, the quality systems category may require the identification of separate subcategories (such as those described in the Malcolm Baldrige Award criteria). If this is the case, the supplier evaluation should include any subcategories or items that make up the quality systems category.

Equally important, the purchaser must decide how to weigh each subcategory within the broader performance evaluation category. In Exhibit 7.6, the quality category includes an evaluation of a supplier's process control systems, total quality commitment, and parts per million (ppm) defects performance. The sum of the subcategory weights must equal the total weight of the performance category. Furthermore, the purchaser must clearly define the scoring system used within each category. This becomes the focus of Step 4.

Step 4: Define a Scoring System for Categories and Subcategories

Step 4 defines each score within a performance category. If an evaluation uses a 5-point scale to assess a performance category, then a purchaser must clearly define the difference between a score of 5, 4, 3, and so on. One important point is to develop a scale that clearly defines what a specific score means. For example, it is better to use a 4-point scale that is easier to interpret and is based on the language and principles of total quality management than a 10-point scale where 1–2 = poor, 3–4 = weak, 5–6 = marginal, 7–8 = qualified, and 9–10 = outstanding. The scoring values on the 10-point scale do not have descriptive definitions detailing the difference between a 1 and a 2 or a 3 and a 4, for example. A more specific way is shown in the 4-point scale below:

- Major nonconformity (0 points earned): The absence or total breakdown of a system to meet a requirement, or any noncompliance that would result in the probable shipment of a nonconforming product.
- Minor nonconformity (1 point earned): A noncompliance (though not major) that judgment and experience indicate is likely to result in the failure of the quality system or reduce its ability to ensure controlled processes or products.
- Conformity (2 points earned): No major or minor nonconformities were noted during the evaluation.
- Adequacy (3 points earned): Specific supplier performance or documentation meets or exceeds requirements given the scope of the supplier's operations.

A well-defined scoring system takes criteria that may be highly subjective and develops a quantitative scale for measurement. Effective metrics allow different individuals to interpret and score similarly the same performance categories under review. A scoring system that is too broad, ambiguous, or poorly defined increases the probability of arriving at widely different assessments or conclusions.

Step 5: Evaluate Supplier Directly

This step requires that the reviewer visit a supplier's facilities to perform the evaluation. Site visits require at least a day and often several days to complete. When factoring in travel time and postvisit reviews, we begin to realize that an organization must carefully select those suppliers it plans on evaluating. In many cases, a cross-functional team will perform the evaluation, which allows team members with different knowledge to ask different questions.

Purchasers often notify suppliers beforehand of any documentation required during the initial evaluation. For example, if a purchaser has no previous experience with a supplier, the reviewer might require a supplier to provide documentation of performance capability. The supplier will have to present evidence of process capability studies, process control systems, or delivery performance.

The following explains the calculation for the quality category in Exhibit 7.6: Quality Systems Performance Category (Weight = 20% of total evaluation).

Subcategories are the following:

- *Process control systems* (4 points out of 5 possible points equals 80%) or 0.8 × 5 sub-weight = 4.0 points
- *Total quality commitment* (4 points out of 5 possible points) = 0.8 × 8 sub-weight = 6.4 points
- *PPM defect performance* (5 points out of 5 possible points) = 1.0 × 7 sub-weight = 7.0 points
- Total for category = 17.4 points or 87% of total possible points (17.4/20)

As shown in Exhibit 7.6, Advanced Micro Systems received a total overall evaluation of 80.6%. A purchaser can objectively compare the scores of different suppliers competing for the same purchase contract or select one supplier over another based on the evaluation score. It is also possible that a supplier does not qualify at this time for further purchase consideration. Purchasers should have minimum acceptable performance requirements that suppliers must satisfy before they can become part of the supply base. In this example, the supplier performs acceptably in most major categories except delivery performance (9 out of 15 possible points). The reviewer must decide if the shortcomings in this category are correctable or if the supplier simply lacks the ability to perform.

Step 6: Review Evaluation Results and Make Selection Decision

At some point, a reviewer must decide whether to recommend or reject a supplier as a source. A purchaser may review a supplier for consideration for expected future business and not a specific contract. Evaluating suppliers before there is an actual purchase requirement can provide a great deal of flexibility to a purchaser. Once an actual need materializes, the purchaser is in a position to move quickly because it has prequalified the supplier.

It is important to determine the seriousness of any supplier shortcomings noted during the evaluation and assess the degree to which these shortcomings might affect performance. Evaluation scales should differentiate between various degrees of supplier shortcomings. Alcoa, for example, explicitly defines the difference between a performance problem and a deficiency. A **performance problem** is "a discrepancy, nonconformance, or missing requirement that will have a significant negative impact on an important area of concern in an audit statement." A **deficiency** is "a minor departure from an intended level of performance, or a nonconformance that is easily resolved and does not materially affect the required output."[6]

The primary output from this step is a recommendation about whether to accept a supplier for a purchase contract. Exhibit 7.7 illustrates a simple recommendation form issued after a supplier evaluation visit conducted by a commodity team. An important outcome from any evaluation is the identification of improvement opportunities on the part of the supplier.

Exhibit 7.7 Sample Recommendation Form

Type of Supplier: Mfg.

Qualification Survey Summary

Company Name	Foster Industries	Surveyed By:	Manufacturing Commodity Team
Address	PO Box 1256	Accompanied By:	Quality
City, State, Zip	Stroudsburg, PA 18370	Initial Survey (circled)	Resurvey
Phone	570-619-5411	Survey Date:	9/14/2004
Supplier Code	Foster	Contact:	Robert Jones
Supplier Score	80.8	**Minimum Required Score: 65**	

Recommendations

Supplier has potential to become a critical partner. However, limited design/development capability prevents continued growth. Foster will embark on implementing and upgrading design/development function for our business.

ACTION PLAN IS DUE BY: 1/1/2005

Supplier Acknowledgment:

John Weaver

9/15/2004
Date

Source: Adapted from J. Przirembel, *How to Conduct Supplier Surveys and Audits,* West Palm Beach, FL: PT Publications, 1997, p. 76.

A purchaser may evaluate several suppliers that might be competing for the same contract. The initial evaluation provides an objective way to compare suppliers side-by-side before making a final selection decision. A purchaser may decide to use more than one supplier based on the results of the supplier survey.

The authority to decide the final selection varies from organization to organization. The reviewer or team who evaluated the supplier may have the authority to make the supplier selection decision. In other cases, the buyer or team may present or justify the supplier selection decision or findings to a committee or a manager who has final authority.

Step 7: Review and Improve Supplier Performance Continuously

The supplier survey or visit is only the first step of the evaluation process. If a purchaser decides to select a supplier, the supplier must then perform according to the purchaser's requirements. The emphasis shifts from the initial evaluation and selection of suppliers to evidence of continuous performance improvement by suppliers. Chapter 9 addresses the management of a world-class supply base.

Supplier Selection

Some important issues arise during the supplier evaluation and selection process. Each has the potential to affect the final decision.

Critical Issues

Size Relationship

A purchaser may decide to select suppliers over which it has a relative size advantage. A buyer may simply have greater influence when it has a relative size advantage over the supplier or represents a larger share of the supplier's total business. For example, Allen-Edmonds Shoe Corporation, a 71-year-old maker of premium shoes, tried unsuccessfully to implement just-in-time methods to speed production, boost customer satisfaction, and save money. Unfortunately, Allen-Edmonds had difficulty getting suppliers to agree to the just-in-time requirement of matching delivery to production needs. Although domestic suppliers of leather soles agreed to make weekly instead of monthly deliveries, European tanneries supplying calfskin hides refused to cooperate. The reason? Allen-Edmonds was not a large enough customer to wield any leverage with those suppliers.

Use of International Suppliers

The decision to select a foreign supplier can have important implications during the supplier evaluation and selection process. For one, international sourcing is generally more complex than domestic buying. As a result, the evaluation and selection process can take on added complexity. It may be difficult to implement JIT with international suppliers, as lead times are frequently twice or even three times as long as lead times for domestic suppliers.

Competitors as Suppliers

Another important issue is the degree to which a buyer is willing to purchase directly from a competitor. Purchasing from competitors may limit information sharing between the parties. The purchase transaction is usually straightforward and the buyer and seller may not develop a working relationship characterized by mutual commitment and confidential information sharing.

Countertrade Requirements

The need to satisfy countertrade requirements can also affect the supplier selection decision. **Countertrade** is a broad term that refers to all trade where buyer and seller have at least a partial exchange of goods for goods. (See Chapter 10 for additional discussion.)

Boeing, a producer of commercial aircraft, purchases a portion of its production requirements in markets where it hopes to do business. An organization involved in extensive worldwide marketing may have to contend with countertrade requirements before it can sell to international customers, which can have a direct impact on the supplier evaluation and selection process. Chapter 10 addresses international purchasing and countertrade.

Social Objectives

Most purchasers are attempting to increase their business with traditionally disadvantaged suppliers, including suppliers with female, minority, or handicapped owners. Buyers may also want to conduct business with suppliers that commit to the highest environmental standards. The influence of social objectives on purchasing will continue to remain strong.

Reducing Supplier Evaluation and Selection Cycle Time

Across almost all business applications, competitive and customer pressures are forcing reductions in the time it takes to perform a task or carry out a process. These pressures are also affecting the time available to evaluate and select suppliers. Purchasing must increasingly be proactive and anticipate supplier selection requirements rather than react when a need arises.

Although supplier selection decisions come about for different reasons, many important selection decisions come about as part of the product development process. Consider the cycle time changes that the U.S. automotive industry continues to experience. In the middle of the 1980s, GM, Ford, and Chrysler required 60 months to design and bring a new car or truck to market. During the early 1990s, the benchmark for development time (sometimes referred to as concept-to-customer, or CTC, cycle time) became 48 months. By the mid-1990s world-class producers were aiming for development times of 36 months.

From the 1980s to 2003, product development cycle times changed from 60 months to a new target of 18 months, or a reduction of 70%! In many industries, development times are shortening by 30–50% every five years. Processes that support new-product development, such as supplier evaluation and selection, must also shorten accordingly.

Tools and Approaches

Most managers do not even challenge the need to reduce the time it takes to evaluate and select suppliers. The challenge is one of shortening the process while still arriving at effective decisions. Fortunately, supply managers have many tools and approaches available to help them shorten the selection cycle time. Although dozens of activities can help shorten selection time, the following presents a set of powerful ways to reduce selection time.

Map the Current Supplier Evaluation and Selection Process

Process mapping involves the identification of the steps, activities, time, and costs involved in a process. Once we understand the current evaluation and selection process, opportunities for improvement should become evident. Supply managers should measure process cycle times to identify rates of improvement against pre-established performance targets. Process mapping should be the first step in the improvement process.

Integrate with Internal Customers

The need to anticipate rather than react to supplier evaluation and selection decisions requires closer involvement with internal customers, which can be achieved in a variety of ways. Purchasing can co-locate physically with marketing, engineering, and operations to gain early insight into expected supply requirements. Involvement on new-product development teams is also an ideal way to integrate with internal customers. Allowing internal customers to forward their requirements to purchasing, perhaps through an online requisition system, can also be an effective way to integrate with internal customers, particularly for routine purchase requirements.

Data Warehouse with Supplier Information

A data warehouse consists of easy-to-access supplier data and information. The data warehouse can include information about potential suppliers, performance history of current suppliers, details of current contracts, expiration dates of supply contracts, expected forecasts for purchased items, and any other information that supports a faster selection process.

Third-Party Support

The Good Practice Example following this section highlights the use of a third or external party to provide supplier data, which can significantly reduce time and effort. Another third-party source is Dun & Bradstreet, which provides financial ratio data, the business background of supplier management, payment trends, and an overall supplier risk score. The Internet is also a source of third-party supplier information, including online directories of potential suppliers.

New Organizational Design Features

Commodity teams have become a popular way to manage important purchase requirements. These teams are responsible for understanding in depth entire families or groups of purchased goods and services. The teams are usually responsible for achieving improvements within their commodity, which may involve site visits to evaluate suppliers. Some companies also use a lead buyer model as part of their organizational design. An individual at a site or location is responsible for owning and managing a purchased item. The lead buyer usually manages items that are not critical enough for a commodity team to manage.

Preferred Supplier List

Many firms create a list of their highest-performing suppliers. These suppliers earn their place on a preferred supplier list by consistently providing the best services and products to the buyer. A preferred supplier list can provide dramatic reductions in selection time because a buyer already knows the best suppliers to consider.

Electronic Tools

IT providers have developed a host of electronic tools to improve the evaluation and selection process:[7]

- E-Learning Scorecard is a tool to use during first-time visits with suppliers to make a quick "yes or no" decision about the possibility of using the supplier. The tool requires the user to rank various criteria among suppliers.[8]
- Special Edition is a microsite developed by Northern Light Technology. This tool provides current news and information, as well as Internet links to leading supplier information.[9]
- RFP Version 2.0, developed by eBreviate, is a web-based software package that enables companies to develop customized online supplier surveys and proposal requests. A buyer can establish simultaneous communication with multiple potential suppliers, which allows users to evaluate and quantify discussions with potential suppliers in an online auction format.[10]
- Decision Analysis, developed by Kepner-Tregoe of Princeton, NJ, is a widely used supplier evaluation and selection process that uses a weighted-point system. This tool is part of Kepner-Tregoe's "Problem Solving and Decision Making" series.[11]
- SPEX evaluation kits use a four-step process that consists of industry analysis and project formalization, definition of projects, examining responses to key requirements, and evaluation and selection of suppliers.[12]

Predefined Contract Language and Shorter Contracts

Most contracts address areas that are similar. Progressive supply managers work with their legal group to develop pre-established contract language that can be cut and pasted during a supplier negotiation. The role of the legal department is to review and initial any changes from the pre-established language or approve areas the standard language does not cover. Progressive firms are also working to shorten the length of their contracts.

Good Practice Example

Eaton Corporation Wins Purchasing Medal of Excellence through Supplier Management

When Eaton CEO Alexander (Sandy) Cutler thanked the supply chain management staff for winning the Purchasing Medal of Excellence, he emphasized that the goal didn't include price reductions. Instead, he talked about values. "We want to be the most admired company in our markets through supply chain performance," he told the attendees. "Have the right ethics and the right business practices and you'll attract the best people and suppliers who'll produce the best results," Cutler said.

With that ethos as their foundation, Eaton's vice president for supply chain management Rick Jacobs and the 3,500-strong supply chain team examine suppliers' ethics and business practices as closely as they look at their product quality, core competencies, and potential for value creation. The company has an ombudsman for ethics whom employees or anyone else can confer with. And Eaton doesn't hesitate to stop doing business with suppliers whose business practices aren't up to its own high standards, regardless of their quality or prices. Eaton believes in working collaboratively with the key suppliers that make the cut and are selected for business. Eaton's supply chain team has given birth to a variety of strategic initiatives that support its supply selection and management process. Among the initiatives are the following:

- A supply chain data warehouse that integrates data from the company's myriad ERP systems to create a single repository of critical data for decision making. Its genesis was a shared service center that the supply chain organization initiated with the company's finance group. "But it only contained financial data, and we knew we needed much more, such as information on quality, logistics, non-purchase-order data, and other items so we could more effectively manage spend and monitor suppliers," Jacobs said.
- Significant progress toward the corporate goal of reducing the supply base by 50% by 2010.
- A 50% reduction in the number of incoming parts defects over the last three years, in part by eliminating poor-performing suppliers.
- Major savings and improved cross-functional communication from the work of special hub-and-spoke commodity teams composed of supply chain representatives from each of Eaton's business groups. Each team develops commodity strategies that integrate supply chain and business strategies. On each team, the hub is the business group with the highest dollar purchases in the commodity. The spokes are the remaining businesses. The electronics team, for one, reduced its supplier base from 127 to just 5 key distributors and has achieved 12% annualized savings so far.
- A 10% per-year savings in North American small-package logistics from moving 95% of shipments through a single provider. Partnering with five lead logistics suppliers across the globe for raw materials and finished goods shipments has led to 6% savings per year since 2005.
- Globalization of the indirect buy, including MRO, capital equipment, energy, information technology, telecom, and fleet services.
- Development of special software tools for improving communication with suppliers and other Eaton functional business groups. One, Worldwide Interactive Supplier Performance Evaluation Resource (WISPER), helps the supply chain team manage and evaluate suppliers. Another, Supplier Visualization, gives suppliers visibility into purchase orders, forecasts, and inventory so they can appropriately manage Eaton's inventory.
- Development and implementation of a state-of-the-art training initiative—called the Supply Chain Functional Excellence Program—that helps supply chain staff improve their knowledge and skills and prepare for advancement within the company.

EXHAUSTIVE SUPPLIER QUALIFICATION AND COORDINATION

All those and other successes begin with Eaton's rigorous process to find suppliers whose business practices match their own. For an idea of how rigorously Eaton analyzes the quality, fitness, and potential of prospective suppliers, talk to Jon Barfield, CEO and president of the Bartech Group. The Livonia, MI–based minority supplier finds and manages all of the company's temporary help. "We had discussions and did testing for the better part of a year before they decided to go with us," says Barfield, who calls his company's relationship with Eaton one of the best of all his customers.

Or talk to Gregg Hammer, national accounts manager for Pratt Industries in Conyers, GA, a supplier of corrugated containers. "They are very meticulous about analyzing suppliers' business practices, more so than most others," says Hammer. "Environmentalism is one of their big pushes, and they talked with us about that and our own views on ethics." In fact, Hammer believes Pratt's "green" practices—the fact that their products are 100% recyclable—was a big reason that Eaton increased its business with them.

Sourcing teams develop a single commodity strategy that integrates supply chain and business strategy. Among other things, the teams act as clearinghouses for information and communication, and for resolving supplier problems. For example, two business units located in the United Kingdom and the Netherlands were using the same supplier for custom electronics and electrical assemblies. The supplier was producing these assemblies at several of its plants in Hungary and Bulgaria.

Because of timing differences at the two Eaton business units, the production ramp-up started at an earlier date for the U.K. sites than for those in the Netherlands. As a result, the individual business units signed separate supplier agreements that included differing performance parameters for the relationship. That, of course, inevitably led to different performance expectations and communication issues. Because both business units were part of the electronics hub-and-spoke team, they eventually found a way to jointly set performance parameters by completing a single supply agreement with the supplier and standardizing on communication and performance. Supplier performance improved and the team agreed to consider giving more business to the supplier.

Eaton's hub-and-spoke commodities teams integrate commodity and business strategies. Here are some of the savings the teams have realized:

- Electronics team: Consolidated 127 suppliers into 5 key distributor partners. Annualized cost savings of 12%.
- Plastics team: Consolidated the resin-distribution base from 10 suppliers to 1 supplier. Savings of 5%.
- Packaging team: Consolidated 175 suppliers to 1 supplier. Savings of 12%.
- Raw materials team: Leveraged low spend ($5 million) in one group and $100 million in another group. For a similar product, saved more than 10% on the low-spend portion.

COLLABORATION IS KEY

Besides ethics, quality, and environmentally sound practices, the willingness to collaborate is critical in Eaton's evaluation of suppliers. Within the company's own walls, Jacobs and his team collaborate with virtually every function in the company, including finance, information technology, human resources, legal, and ethics, boosting the supply chain organization's image and influence internally, as well as its value. For example, representatives from product engineering, accounting, and other functions brainstorm strategies with supply chain personnel on the hub-and-spoke commodity teams. Additionally, supply chain staff are working closely with finance and information technology to develop a system to completely digitize invoicing.

Externally, the supply chain team facilitates collaboration between Eaton's engineering staff and its customers to solve design problems. Case in point: the Eaton Automotive Division's work on a supercharger for the Cadillac Northstar. Superchargers are positive-displacement devices that add power and efficiency to car engines. But they have to fit within a very tight space, and the design envelope often changes. Despite the changes, Eaton's task was to hold to its quote.

"We could only get our costs down so much through negotiations," says Jeff Place, director of supply chain management for the Automotive Group. So, Place and his team sat Eaton engineers down with the customer's engineers and the suppliers of the various components of the supercharger. Together, they identified the individual cost drivers for each component, considered the possibility of unnecessary tolerances, and identified opportunities to cut costs. "We took a product-centric view," Place says, "and collaborated with the suppliers to find the lowest cost."

In another case, the supply chain worked with suppliers of a DC motor to get the cost down. Again, the supply chain formed a team with members from engineering, staff from manufacturing, and representatives of the suppliers to identify the key cost drivers. Result: They achieved double-digit cost reductions.

THE SEARCH FOR INNOVATION

And you can't be successful without innovation. Like most progressive manufacturers, Eaton encourages—indeed, expects—its suppliers to be innovative. "That often requires bringing them in at the earliest stages of the design process so they'll understand the product better," says Mike Bungo, vice president of supply chain and operational excellence. And the supply chain team will help suppliers succeed, he says, even if it requires bringing in a master scheduler to adjust delivery dates, or posting Eaton quality engineers and technicians to strategic-supplier sites for extended periods to guide the suppliers' quality efforts.

Source: Adapted from P. E. Teague, "Eaton Wins Purchasing's Medal of Professional Excellence," *Purchasing*, September 13, 2007.

CONCLUSION

This chapter discussed one of the most important functions of business—the evaluation and selection of suppliers. When a purchaser performs these activities well, it establishes the foundation upon which to further develop and improve supplier performance. In his book *Purchasing in the 21st Century,* John Schorr maintains that a buyer should look for certain characteristics when evaluating and selecting suppliers. A good supplier does the following:

- Builds quality into the product, aiming for zero-defect production.
- Makes delivery performance a priority, including a willingness to make short and frequent deliveries to point-of-use areas at a purchaser's facility.
- Demonstrates responsiveness to a purchaser's needs by ensuring that qualified and accessible people are in charge of servicing the purchaser's account.
- Works with a purchaser to reduce lead times as much as possible. Long lead times make it difficult to plan and drive up supply chain costs.
- Provides a purchaser with information regarding capability and workload.
- Creates the future rather than fears the future.
- Reinvests part of its profits in R&D, takes a long-term view, and is willing to spend for tomorrow.
- Meets the stringent financial stability criteria used when evaluating potential new customers for credit.

A focus on selecting only the best suppliers possible will make a major contribution to the competitiveness of the entire organization. The ability to make this contribution requires careful evaluation and selection of the suppliers that provide the goods and services that help satisfy the needs of an organization's final customers.

KEY TERMS

countertrade, 262
deficiency, 260
entry qualifiers, 245
integrated supply, 243
performance problem, 259
preferred supplier, 239
Vendor Managed Inventory, 243

DISCUSSION QUESTIONS

1. Why do organizations commit the resources and time to evaluate suppliers before making a supplier selection decision?
2. Discuss the possible ways that purchasing becomes aware of the need to evaluate and select a supplier.
3. Discuss the sources of information available to a buyer when seeking information about potential sources of supply. When do you think it is appropriate to use different sources?
4. What are various methods for evaluating and selecting suppliers?
5. What are some possible indicators on a supplier visit that might cause you to question whether the managers in the company are forward-looking or whether the company is capable of becoming a best-in-class supplier?

6. Discuss the reasons why suppliers are sometimes reluctant to share cost information with buyers, particularly during the early part of a buyer-seller relationship.
7. Discuss the logic behind a purchaser trying to understand its total supply chain (i.e., the need to understand its supplier's suppliers).
8. What are the issues or questions purchasing needs to address when evaluating whether a supplier is a candidate for a longer-term relationship?
9. Define and discuss the characteristics included in an effective supplier survey.
10. How can a purchaser build flexibility into a supplier survey?
11. What are the advantages of assigning numerical scores to the categories and subcategories included in a supplier survey?
12. Why is it important to discuss promptly the results of a supplier visit or survey with the supplier? If a supplier has a weak area, under what conditions would supplier development be appropriate?
13. Discuss a situation in which a purchaser might select a supplier that is having financial difficulties.
14. Discuss the following statement: If a purchaser decides to select a supplier based on the results of the initial evaluation, the supplier must then meet the purchaser's continuous performance requirements.
15. Why must the time it takes to evaluate and select suppliers decrease? What three ways would you select to have the largest impact on reducing supplier selection time?

ADDITIONAL READINGS

Carbone, J. (1999), "Evaluation Programs Determine Top Suppliers," *Purchasing,* 127(8), 31–35.

Carter, R. (1995), "The Seven C's of Effective Supplier Evaluation," *Purchasing and Supply Management,* 44–46.

Choi, T. Y., and Hartley, J. L. (1996), "An Exploration of Supplier Selection Practices across the Supply Chain," *Journal of Operations Management,* 14, 333–343.

Dwyer, R. F., Schurr, P. H., and Oh, S. (1987), "Developing Buyer-Seller Relationships," *Journal of Marketing,* 51, 11–25.

Ellram, L. M. (1991), "A Managerial Guideline for the Development and Implementation of Purchasing Partnerships," *International Journal of Purchasing and Materials Management,* 27(3), 2–9.

Gottfredson, M., Puryear, R., and Phillips, S. (2005), "Strategic Sourcing: From Periphery to the Core," *Harvard Business Review,* 83(2), 132–139.

Gustin, C. M., Daugherty, P. J., and Ellinger, A. E. (1997), "Supplier Selection Decisions in Systems/Software Purchases," *Journal of Supply Chain Management,* 33(4), 41–46.

Przirembel, J. L. (1997), *How to Conduct Supplier Surveys and Audits,* West Palm Beach, FL: PT Publications.

Schorr, J. (1998), *Purchasing in the 21st Century,* New York: John Wiley & Sons.

Woods, J. A. (Ed.) (2000), *The Purchasing and Supply Yearbook: 2000 Edition,* New York: McGraw-Hill.

ENDNOTES

1. Howard, A. (1998), "Valued Judgments," *Supply Management,* 17, 37–38.

2. Casey, N., Zamiska, N., and Pasztor, A. (2007), "Mattel Seeks to Placate China with Apology on Toys," *Wall Street Journal,* September 22, 23, pp. A1, A7.

3. Seegers, L., Handfield, R., and Melynk, S. (1995), "Environmental Best Practices in the Office Furniture Industry," *Proceedings of the National Decision Science Institute Conference.*

4. Seegers, L., Handfield, R., and Melynk, S. (2007), "Green Movement Turns Mainstream for Corporate America," *Environmental Leader,* environmentalleader.com.

5. Spekman, R. E. (1988), "Strategic Supplier Selection: Understanding Long-Term Buyer Relationships," *Business Horizons,* pp. 80–81.

6. From Alcoa's Supplier Certification Guidelines.

7. From an in-depth literature search and summary of "Supplier Evaluation and Selection" performed by Tara Lewis and Vincent Sedlmyer, Lehigh University, 2001.

8. D. Hartley, (2000), "Looking for a Supplier? Use the E-Learning Scorecard," *Training and Development,* 54, 26.

9. "Northern Lights Simplifies the Supplier Selection Process" (2001), *Business Wire,* p. 2.

10. "eBreviate Unveils Web-Based RFP Version 2.0" (2001), *PR Newswire,* September, p. 2.

11. O'Donnell, D. (1998), "The Evaluation Effect," *Software Magazine,* June, pp. 72–78.

12. O'Donnell, pp. 72–78.

Chapter 8

SUPPLIER QUALITY MANAGEMENT

Learning Objectives

After completing this chapter, you should be able to

- Provide a working definition of supplier quality management
- Recognize the factors that influence supply management's role in managing supplier quality
- Link the principles of total quality management to supply management practices
- Understand the basic principles of Six Sigma quality
- Understand how the Malcolm Baldrige National Quality Award, ISO 9000:2000, and ISO 14000 can help assess and improve supply quality systems and performance

Chapter Outline

Quality Problems Are Not Child's Play

In the fall of 2007, Mattel and other toy manufacturers and distributors were faced with a monumental challenge and a public relations nightmare. A number of the toys purchased from low-cost Chinese manufacturers were contaminated with lead paint, a product that had long since been banned in the United States because of its potential to poison the children who played with them, possibly leading to learning or behavioral problems. Mattel identified about 20 million toys worldwide, in three separate recalls, believed to be contaminated with lead paint or perhaps containing other possible hazards such as small magnets that could easily be removed and swallowed by a child.

Like many companies in other industries, these companies had outsourced much of their manufacturing requirements to lower-cost offshore suppliers. *USA Today* reported that some of the suspect Mattel toys had lead content calculated at 110,000 parts per million, or 180 times the U.S. legal level. In Mattel's case, its long-term Hong Kong–based supplier had subcontracted to another company, which did not use Mattel-approved paint.

Toymakers report that approximately 80% of their imported toys are now made in China, which makes it difficult for consumers to find other alternatives. Due to the public outcry, the Consumer Product Safety Commission, a U.S. federal agency, expanded its investigation of lead-based paints in toys to include other imported products, such as ceramic dishes and cookware from both China and Mexico, as well as various polyvinyl chloride plastic products.

The results of these incidents are both substantial and far reaching. The owner of one of the Chinese manufacturing facilities involved committed suicide. Mattel named a senior executive to head its newly founded corporate responsibility unit, which was tasked with overseeing an internal investigation. The U.S. government negotiated a new trade agreement with the Chinese government that banned future use of lead-based paint and strengthened Chinese regulatory authority (however, local governments within China have a lengthy history of avoiding national policies when they negatively impact local economies). Additional monitoring from Chinese and U.S. agencies will be needed to ensure that these new laws are complied with. The Walt Disney Company announced that it would begin testing toys featuring its various Disney-branded characters. Other companies have now started to market home lead test kits for worried parents. Companies outsourcing a variety of products from China have begun to co-locate their employees on-site at offshore manufacturing firms instead of relying solely on periodic third-party audits.

If we really think about it, were the quality-related problems in this story solely the fault of Mattel or other companies whose brand names were on the final product? Invariably, the buyers and ultimate users of these unsafe products will blame the final producer and distributor because, from their perspective, both the producer and distributor share ultimate responsibility for the safety and usability of the products made and distributed. To be sure, these problems may be due to poor oversight of suppliers by the distributors. However, external suppliers in China provided the toys and other components that were contaminated with lead paint or had other defects, resulting in multiple recalls and highly negative public perception, a lose-lose proposition for all concerned.

Are these defects part of a broader challenge to how Mattel and others manage their far-flung global supply chains? The more dispersed the global supply chain is, the more buying companies must strive to ensure that quality, safety, and labor standards are upheld. Can supplier quality, which many firms too often take for granted, affect the customer's perception of finished products? For Mattel and others, the negative effects are significant. A similar question is whether Ford Motor Company is a stronger or weaker company now because of its past problems with Firestone, a (former) long-term supplier of automotive tires.

The distributors of these unsafe toys focused, perhaps too much, on the design, assembly, and cost of the finished products. Is it possible that these companies should have directed more attention to how they managed supplier quality? If we ask typical parents who purchased one or more of these toys, they will quickly share strong feelings about their negative experiences and the company they hold responsible. And to the detriment of these toy manufacturers and distributors, disgruntled customers will quickly share their feelings, as most dissatisfied customers will, with anyone else who will listen!

Regardless of what happens within a producer's own four walls, it is very difficult, if not virtually impossible, to offer a quality product or service to customers when the inputs received from its suppliers are flawed. Today's consumers demand products and services that are provided on time, at the right quality, with the right features, and at the lowest total cost. Producers receive minimal forgiveness when they fail to satisfy demanding customer requirements, regardless of the source of the defects.

In situations where externally sourced components and subassemblies affect cost, quality, and product performance, or where suppliers provide value-added activities through design, engineering, and testing, effective management of supplier quality is a strategic competitive necessity. Furthermore, any company that is serious about implementing total quality management (TQM) cannot ignore the important relationship between supplier quality and product quality.

Source: Adapted from a sampling of *Wall Street Journal*, *New York Times*, and *USA Today* articles published in August and September 2007.

This chapter approaches supplier quality from several perspectives. The first section presents a broad overview of supplier quality management. The second section investigates the various factors that affect supply management's role in managing supplier quality. Next, we present the principles of total quality management and relate them to supplier quality management. Fourth, we define Six Sigma quality and discuss how it relates to purchasing and supply chain management. The chapter concludes with a discussion of International Organization for Standardization (ISO) 9000:2000, ISO 14000, and the Malcolm Baldrige National Quality Award (MBNQA) criteria and how they can be used to more effectively manage supplier quality.

Overview of Supplier Quality Management

What Is Supplier Quality?

Before discussing supplier quality, we should define the generic term "quality." One renowned quality expert, Armand Feigenbaum, defines **quality** as the total composite of product and service characteristics of marketing, engineering, manufacturing, and maintenance through which the product or service in use will meet or exceed the expectations of the customer.[1] This definition differs from other popular definitions that typically view quality as primarily conforming to customer requirements. Joseph Juran, perhaps the foremost expert on quality, defined quality simply as fitness for use. Philip Crosby, another well-known total quality expert, defined quality as conformance to requirements. In recent years, the concept of quality has changed radically from meeting customer requirements or expectations to exceeding them.

Customer expectations are dynamic and constantly shifting. Not surprisingly, many actions taken by a firm's competitors can change the user's quality expectations. For example, a customer may be satisfied with three-day package delivery service until another company offers two-day service with guaranteed delivery at a competitive cost. Changes due to competition can quickly and dramatically redefine the requirements that customers accept as their standard of performance. This scenario actually occurred as UPS announced it was reducing by one day the time it takes to deliver a package to certain parts of the United States. Its competitors had to adapt their delivery systems and processes to offer comparable services. The challenge with customer expectations is the company's ability to specifically define them and then translate those expectations upstream throughout its supply chain.

From these quality perspectives, we can begin to define what we mean by supplier quality. **Supplier quality** represents the ability to meet or exceed current and future customer (i.e., buyer and eventually end customer) expectations or requirements within critical performance areas on a consistent basis. There are three major parts to this definition:

1. Ability to meet or exceed. This means that suppliers satisfy or exceed buyer expectations or requirements each and every time. Inconsistent supplier performance, whether in physical product quality or on-time delivery, is not a characteristic of a quality supplier.
2. Current and future customer expectations or requirements. Suppliers must meet or exceed today's demanding requirements while also possessing the ability to anticipate and satisfy future customer requirements. Suppliers must be capable of demonstrating continuous performance improvement. A supplier that can satisfy today's requirements but cannot keep pace with future requirements is not a quality supplier.
3. Within critical performance areas on a consistent basis. Supplier quality does not apply only to the physical attributes of a product. Quality suppliers satisfy a buyer's expectations or requirements in many areas, including product or service delivery, product or service conformance, after-sale support, current technology and features, and total cost management.

Within supply chains, supply management does not merely buy parts or services from suppliers—it buys (and sometimes must help manage) supplier capabilities that result in quality products and services. Buyers should focus not only on a supplier's physical output (the end result), but also on the supporting systems and processes that create that output. This includes the supplier's expertise and capabilities in logistics, engineering, and managing its own supply chain.

Part of supply management's role in supplier quality management involves being a good customer to its suppliers. It is difficult to maintain a trusting and collaborative relationship and receive quality goods and services when suppliers do not enjoy doing business with the buying company. For this reason, supplier quality performance requires that a buyer learn how to become a preferred customer by understanding what suppliers appreciate in a buyer-seller relationship.

Some of the expectations that suppliers have within a supply chain relationship include minimizing product design changes once production begins, providing visibility to future purchase volume requirements, and sharing early access and visibility to new product requirements. Suppliers also value adequate production lead time, ethical treatment from the buyer, and accurate and timely payment of invoices. Buyers should also strive for negligible changes in purchase orders after sending material releases to suppliers to alleviate supply disruptions.

A buyer cannot expect the highest levels of supplier performance when the supplier must respond to frequent or short-lead-time changes. Stability allows a supplier to minimize its costs and effectively plan on the basis of timely and consistent buyer information. Frequent changes limit a supplier's ability to meet the buyer's expectations, including quality requirements, in a timely and consistent manner, as well as increasing the supplier's costs. Supply management plays a central role in ensuring that its suppliers perform in a defect-free manner.

Why Be Concerned with Supplier Quality?

Lapses in managing supplier quality can tarnish the reputation of even the world's best brands. As the opening vignette made clear, any firm that does not effectively manage quality throughout its supply chain is risking long-term customer dissatisfaction, reduced market share, and increased costs, as well as negative public relations.

Research continues to reveal that supply managers rate supplier delivery and supplier product and service quality, two important quality indicators, as just above average (5.09 and 5.13, respectively, where 1 = poor, 4 = average, and 7 = excellent). In fact, the perception that supply managers have of supplier quality performance has not changed over the last 10 years.[2] Most firms have grown to rely on their suppliers; the vulnerability that many firms feel toward them, particularly for supplier-designed product and process technology, makes supplier performance critically important. It is a competitive necessity to assess actual supplier performance to make sure it aligns with expected supplier performance.[3]

Supplier Impact on Quality

The late quality expert Philip Crosby estimated that suppliers are responsible for 50% of a firm's product-related quality problems. Furthermore, the average manufacturing firm spends more than 55% of its sales dollar on purchased goods and services; some manufacturers spend even more, with figures approaching 100%. A firm that focuses only on its own internal quality issues will usually fail to recognize and take appropriate action on the true underlying root causes of many quality-related problems. Poor supplier quality can quickly undermine a firm's total quality improvement effort.

Continuous-Improvement Requirements

Most firms plan to achieve continuous quality improvements in all aspects of their business. One way to do this is through the effective management of supplier quality. Quality improvement requirements are a function of a company's industry along with how well its performance compares to that of its competitors. Companies in high-technology industries, such as Chrysler, Boeing, Intel, and Texas Instruments, face intense competitive pressure to achieve quality levels that approach perfection. Other industries, such as furniture making, typically experience a slower and less dramatic rate of change. Regardless, all industries experience at least some pressure from customers to achieve continuous quality improvement.

Sourcing Snapshot — *Supplier Quality Matters on the Ground—and in the Air!*

In 2004, a British Airways Boeing B-777 aircraft taking off from Houston's George Bush Intercontinental Airport experienced an in-flight emergency when an engine manufactured by General Electric caught fire. According to GE and National Transportation Safety Board (NTSB) documents, the cause of the malfunction was traced to a fatigue crack in a high-pressure turbine blade. The failed blade caused a severe vibration in the engine, which ultimately damaged an oil seal, allowing engine oil to enter air lines. Subsequently, the plane's cockpit and passenger cabin were filled with smoke and fumes. The flight crew then declared an emergency and made an immediate landing back at Bush Intercontinental.

The raw material casting for the turbine blade had been misidentified with an incorrect part number. Because of this mistake, the turbine blade remained in service far beyond its specified limits, allowing the fatigue crack to occur. In addition, in-plant inspections designed to prevent such an error were judged inadequate. GE's internal investigation showed that its employees had failed to identify the error when they processed the part and cleared it for installation. The error ultimately cost GE $8 million and subjected it to an NTSB investigation.

Source: Adapted from "GE Errors Linked to Plane Fire," *Cincinnati Inquirer,* December 14, 2004; and A. Wolfson, "Madisonville GE Plant's Mistake Linked to Jet Fire," *Courier-Journal,* December 13, 2004.

Outsourcing of Purchase Requirements

Reliance on a firm's suppliers for raw materials, components, subassemblies, and even finished products is steadily increasing. It is no longer an advantage in some industries to make most of the components of a product or to provide their own services. Therefore, progressive buyers are relying on suppliers that demonstrate significant design and build capabilities, even for highly technical or complex part requirements. For example, Dell Computer is primarily an assembly operation that purchases most of its PC componentry (monitor, hard drive, keyboard, microprocessors, power unit, and so on) from external suppliers. The larger the proportion of the final product that suppliers provide, the greater the impact they will have on overall product cost and quality.

Factors Affecting Supply Management's Role in Managing Supplier Quality

Supply management must assume primary organizational leadership for managing quality with its external suppliers. A number of factors influence how much attention supply management should commit to managing supplier quality:

- The ability of a supplier to affect a buyer's total quality. Certain suppliers will provide items that are highly critical to a firm's success. Supply management must manage the suppliers of these critical items more intently than those providing lower-value, standardized, or easy-to-obtain items or commodities.

- The resources available to support supplier quality management and improvement. Firms with limited resources and minimal expertise in quality management and supplier improvement must carefully select where to budget their resources. Resource availability will greatly influence the overall scope of the firm's quality management efforts. These resources typically include personnel, budget, time, and information technology.
- The ability of a buying firm to practice world-class quality. A buying firm can help its suppliers understand the use and application of quality concepts, tools, and techniques only after the buying firm itself understands and correctly applies these concepts and tools internally.
- A supplier's willingness to work jointly to improve quality. Not all suppliers are willing to work closely and collaboratively with a buying firm. Instead, some suppliers may prefer a traditional purchase arrangement characterized by limited buyer involvement and a more hand's-off or laissez-faire management style. Others will enthusiastically embrace a long-term, collaborative partnership.
- A supplier's current quality levels. A supplier's current performance level influences the amount and type of attention required from a buying firm.

Sourcing Snapshot

Intel Knows the Importance of Supplier Quality

When Intel thinks about supplier quality, it knows that any slips go right to the company's bottom line. "If you take a look at what Intel's revenues are, any kind of problem from a supplier, such as a delivery or quality issue, has an enormous potentially negative revenue impact on Intel. It's much more than any other semiconductor company in the world," says Intel's materials quality systems manager. Intel relies extensively on suppliers for process equipment to run its chip-making facilities. "If we have a problem with a supplier," the quality manager says, "it could mean a billion dollars to us. There aren't too many other semiconductor manufacturers that face a billion-dollar jeopardy if there is a supplier problem."

The need for total supplier quality is one reason Intel developed its Supplier Continuous Quality Improvement (SCQI) program. To win Intel's SCQI award, suppliers must adhere to rigorous quality standards set forth by three high-level requirements. These are a supplier report card score, a Standard Supplier Quality Assessment, and a SCQI plan that measures how well the supplier meets its improvement goals. A vice president at an Intel supplier maintains, "In terms of customer requirements, Intel's quality systems and other special requirements are more stringent and are a higher level of requirements than the typical customer we have."

Intel's SCQI program focuses on the weak-link-in-the-supply-chain theory. This theory states that a supply chain is only as good as its weakest performer. "If we can make our supply base a stronger link, that will make Intel a stronger link in its supply chain to its own customers. We look at a program like SCQI and try to drive improved performance among our suppliers," explains Intel's materials quality systems manager.

Source: Adapted from G. Roos, "Intel Looks for World's Best," *Purchasing,* November 16, 2000, pp. 92–96.

World-class suppliers will require less attention, whereas suppliers providing less-than-desirable quality will require even greater attention.

- A buyer's ability to collect and analyze quality-related data. Supply management must utilize an effective monitoring system and collect the proper metrics to track how well a supplier is meeting quality performance expectations. For most firms, this means developing and employing a research and tracking system that collects and distributes supplier-related quality data on a timely basis.

Supplier Quality Management Using a Total Quality Management Perspective

Supply management professionals at all organizational levels must fully understand and commit themselves to the principles of total quality management if they expect to create upstream value in the supply chain that benefits downstream customers. Applying these principles to supplier quality management becomes critical if firms want to avoid embarrassing and costly errors like those shown in the opening chapter vignette.

The principles that comprise TQM make up perhaps the most robust and powerful business philosophy ever developed. Unfortunately, merely reciting these principles is far easier than embracing and practicing them on a day-to-day basis. Although external suppliers provide more than half the inputs required within a typical supply chain, a bona fide commitment to TQM is often lacking. If supplier quality is so important, why do many supply management departments lack the necessary measurement systems that provide timely and objective information about supplier performance? Why do many buyers make critical supplier selection decisions without analyzing and understanding a supplier's production processes?

Exhibit 8.1 presents an integrated set of quality principles based on the thinking of W. Edwards Deming, Philip Crosby, and Joseph Juran.[4] The following sections present each principle along with a selected (but certainly not comprehensive) set of

Exhibit 8.1 **Eight Key Principles of Total Quality Management**

Define quality in terms of customers and their requirements.

Pursue quality at the source.

Stress objective rather than subjective analysis.

Emphasize prevention rather than detection of defects.

Focus on process rather than output.

Strive for zero defects.

Establish continuous improvement as a way of life.

Make quality everyone's responsibility.

Source: Adapted from R. J. Trent, "Linking TQM to SCM," *Supply Chain Management Review*, 2001, 5(3), 71.

activities that, if fully put into place, will help ensure that firms truly practice TQM in their pursuit of superior supplier quality.

Defining Quality in Terms of Customers and Their Requirements

In a buyer-seller relationship, the buyer is the supplier's direct customer in the supply chain. One of the primary causes of nonconforming supplier quality involves inconsistent communication and the resulting misunderstanding of specifications, expectations, and requirements between supply chain members. Supply managers, working closely with engineers and other internal customers, must provide clear specifications and unambiguous performance requirements regarding the design and operation of a product, as well as any other relevant information that will ultimately affect the quality or delivery of a purchased input. Another important form of buyer communication is sharing of final product requirements, which at times may be broad or incomplete. In this case, the process for determining final requirements must be established and mutually agreed upon between buyer and supplier.

Keki Bhote, a leading quality expert, argues that the incomplete or inaccurate development and communication of specifications has a disproportionate effect on supplier quality.

> *At least half or even more of the quality problems between customer [i.e., the buyer] and supplier are caused by* poor specifications, *for which the customer company is largely responsible. Most specifications are vague or arbitrary. They are generally determined unilaterally by engineering, which lifts them from some boiler-plate document and embellishes them with factors of safety to protect its hide. When bids go out to suppliers, the latter are seldom consulted on specifications, and most suppliers are afraid to challenge specifications for fear of losing the bid. . . . So the first cure for poor supplier quality is to eliminate the tyranny of capricious specifications.*[5]

Developing a clear understanding of a buyer's expectations and requirements has two dimensions. The first is the ability of the buying company to succinctly identify, clearly define, quantify, or specify its technical and sourcing requirements. The second dimension is the buyer's ability to effectively communicate these requirements, which means that both parties completely understand the requirements. Buyers (i.e., customers) must take the initiative and clearly communicate their requirements through detailed requests for proposals, the contract negotiation process, and regular performance feedback sessions, using measurement systems that quantify performance expectations and requirements.

The ability of a supplier to fulfill requirements is partly a function of the buyer's explicitly informing the supplier about what the buyer expects. Exhibit 8.2 on p. 280 provides an example of effectively communicating a purchaser's requirements or expectations to a supplier.

Deming's 14 Points

Dr. W. Edwards Deming, widely considered to be the father of the modern quality movement, developed a comprehensive 14-point management philosophy as the basis for his views on achieving performance excellence in the modern organization,

Exhibit 8.2 Statement of Responsibility

The following details specific responsibilities of XYZ Company project team and ABC supplier during the design and development of light truck J300.

RESPONSIBILITY	XYZ PROJECT TEAM	SUPPLIER
• Agree on performance targets for product cost, weight, quality, and improvement.	X	X
• Work directly with XYZ project team to meet product performance target levels.	X	X
• Provide design support for component requirements.		X
• Develop total project timing requirements.	X	
• Provide build schedules as needed.	X	
• Support vehicle launch at assembly plant.	X	X
• Report project status to executive steering committee.	X	
• Attain manufacturing feasibility sign-off.	X	
• Provide technical/engineering project support.	X	X
• Develop final product concept.	X	
• Provide prototype parts according to agreed-upon schedule.		X
• Identify critical and significant product characteristics.	X	X
• Prepare final detail drawings and transmit to XYZ.		X
• Provide material and product test results.	X	X

which is applicable to manufacturing and service industries alike, as well as government and education. However, Deming's quality philosophy has often been criticized because it does not prescribe specific actions and programs for management to follow. One of the unique features of the Deming philosophy, as outlined in Exhibit 8.3, is that these 14 points are not an a la carte menu of quality improvement activities, from which a company can pick and choose only those with which they agree.

Exhibit 8.3 Unique Features of Deming's Philosophy

- Variation is the primary source of quality nonconformance.
- To reduce variation, the search for improved quality is a never-ending cycle of design, production, and delivery, followed by surveying customers—then starting all over again.
- Although quality is everyone's responsibility, senior management has the ultimate responsibility for quality improvement.
- Interacting parts of a system must be managed together as a whole, not separately.
- Psychology helps managers understand their employees and customers, as well as interactions between people.
- Intrinsic motivation is more powerful than extrinsic motivation.
- Predictions must be grounded in theory that helps to understand cause-and-effect relationships.

Source: Adapted from J. R. Evans and W. M. Lindsay, *Managing for Quality and Performance Excellence* (7th ed.), Mason, OH: South-Western, 2008, pp. 92–100.

His philosophy dictates that all 14 are complementary and necessary to successfully implement a TQM culture.[6]

Point 1: Create a Vision and Demonstrate Commitment

The top managers and executives in an organization are responsible for delineating its future strategic direction: mission, vision, and values. Not only do businesses exist to make a profit for their shareholders and owners, but they must also consider and be good stewards of the overall social and physical environment in which they operate. This requires a long-term view and commitment of sufficient resources by the organization: time, money, and effort.

Point 2: Learn the New Philosophy

Quality must be learned (and relearned continually) by everyone in the organization, which then serves as the pervasive thread that is woven throughout everything the organization does. The focal point of the Deming philosophy is that the entire organization should be focused on satisfying customer needs, whether the customer is internal or external. Quality is no longer just for manufacturing.

Point 3: Understand Inspection

Inspecting for defects has been the traditional method of controlling quality since the Industrial Revolution. The underlying consideration has been that an organization recognizes that defects are inevitable and therefore must be inspected out of the process. Deming indicates that the proper way to deal with defects is to design and operate the process such that defects never occur. This point requires that everyone, from the production line worker all the way through the executive suite, understands the concept of process variation and how it affects every production process. Rework and disposal efforts (also known as the "hidden factory") increase cost and decrease productivity.

Point 4: Stop Making Decisions Purely on the Basis of Price

The lowest purchase price of an item may be good in the short run for the supply management department but may cause increased costs somewhere else in the production system over the long run: scrap, defects, warranty claims, and so on. Modern supply management has embraced this point through its supply base optimization and rationalization initiatives. The focus should be on reducing total system costs, not just purchase price. Working with fewer suppliers allows the supply manager to concentrate on building trusting, collaborative relationships and supplier loyalty while improving quality in purchased goods and services. Communication between buyer and supplier is also enhanced.

Point 5: Improve Constantly and Forever

The quality-oriented organization must intimately understand its customers' needs and wants as they evolve. If the firm remains static in its quality performance, its competition will eventually improve and bypass it. Continuous improvement, or **kaizen**, must be built into every single process in the organization. There is always room for improvement whether the organization is a market leader or not. In addition to maintaining continuous communication with its customers, the TQM organization must also look at reducing process variation and seeking innovation in both product and process.

Point 6: Institute Training

It is very important that management provide its employees and suppliers with the necessary knowledge, skills, and tools to do their jobs efficiently and effectively. Well-developed and specifically targeted training and development can enhance quality and worker productivity, as well as improve morale. Quality-wise, training should address diagnostic and analytic tools, decision making, and problem-solving skills.

Point 7: Institute Leadership

There is a significant gap between leadership and what we traditionally think of as management or supervision. Managers and supervisors are more involved in the day-to-day oversight and direction of workers. Leadership goes well beyond management and supervision by guiding and coaching employees to improve their skills and abilities with an eye to becoming more productive and delivering higher quality.

Point 8: Drive Out Fear

In the workplace, fear is obvious in a variety of ways. Employees may be fearful of making a mistake and being reprimanded for it. Most people have a fear of failure, so they don't want to try anything new or different. They are also creatures of habit and don't like to make changes to their routines. Managers may be fearful of letting go of their traditional control-based power. Departments may not want to collaborate with other departments. Fear-free organizations are rare; it takes a long time to develop a culture that promotes risk taking and change. Eliminating fear encourages employee and supplier trial-and-error experimentation, which can lead to greater productivity and higher-quality processes.

Point 9: Optimize the Efforts of Teams

Teams are becoming more and more a part of day-to-day organizational life. When implemented and operated correctly, teams can be useful in eliminating cross-functional barriers by taking people from different departments and having them work together on a common task or project. Dysfunctional teams can have the opposite effect; they may actually create additional barriers and reinforce existing ones. One of the greatest barriers in Western companies that restricts the potential effectiveness of teams is the mutual distrust between unions and management.

Point 10: Eliminate Exhortations

Slogans, signs, and posters are meant to change people's behavior. However, they are seldom effective because they assume that most, if not all, quality problems are due to human behavior. "Do it right the first time" and "Zero defects" are catchy motivational sayings, but they don't help workers know what to do or how to do it better. Most quality deficiencies are based on the innate design and operation of the systems that create goods and services, not on worker motivation. Designed-in systemic variation is a managerial concern, not a labor issue.

Point 11: Eliminate Numerical Quotas and Measurement by Objective

Workers may circumvent the system to make their production and output goals. These goals do not provide the necessary incentives for workers or suppliers to improve quality. Output standards short-circuit TQM improvements and other quality initiatives. Why would workers stop to fix or adjust a piece of equipment if it meant that they would not make their production quota? In addition, many numerically based goals and objectives are often arbitrary and beyond the control of the worker. Goals should be developed in conjunction with the skills and means to achieve them. Lastly, goals are often short-term in their focus, whereas quality improvement, by design, must take a longer-term perspective.

Point 12: Remove Barriers to Pride in Workmanship

Too often, workers are treated as a commodity—simply interchangeable with each other with no uniqueness or consideration. Managers are often treated in the same manner when they are required to routinely work longer hours without overtime compensation. The performance appraisal systems that most organizations utilize create barriers to pride in workmanship in that they promote competitive behavior and quantity over quality. When given the proper climate in which to work, most people want to do a good job. Unfortunately, the evaluation and reward systems in many companies do not stimulate the right kind of culture to allow the workers to take pride in their efforts. For example, we assign people to work in teams but appraise and pay them as individuals.

Point 13: Encourage Education and Self-Improvement

Unlike training, which is geared primarily toward learning specific task-related skills, education and self-improvement are much broader in nature and focus on improving the quality of life for individuals by teaching them new skills and building higher levels of self-worth. Organizations that invest in education and self-improvement initiatives often find that their employees are more highly motivated and bring additional benefits to both the organization and the individual in terms of productivity and quality.

Point 14: Take Action

Top management must initiate and invest in those activities that result in improved quality, productivity, and quality of work life. A grassroots TQM effort that emanates from the lower levels of the organization is doomed to failure without active and visible top management commitment and support. Appropriate support may include time and monetary investments in process design, education, and training; new evaluation, reward, and compensation systems; and a changed organization culture. The key for success is to maintain the momentum over the long term.

Pursuing Quality at the Source

Quality at the source occurs whenever value is added to a product or service as it moves through the supply chain. The value-adding points or activities in a process represent potential defect originations that require careful management and attention to detail. Perhaps more than any other group, supply management has the ability to affect quality at the source because of its ability to determine and manage the external source for many supply chain inputs.

Because suppliers themselves are a major source of supply chain quality, it makes intuitive sense that the firm's supplier selection process would be a primary vehicle through which to operationalize this principle. Although the cost of making international supplier site visits is quite substantial, the cost of making a poor supplier selection decision can be significantly higher. Skilled and experienced cross-functional teams (CFTs) should visit and evaluate a potential supplier to determine its financial condition, global capacity, logistical networks, supply management practices, process capability, willingness to work with the buyer, and technology innovation before making a strategic sourcing selection decision. See Chapter 7 for a more in-depth discussion of supplier evaluation and selection.

A second major area that defines supplier quality is product and process design. Progressive companies involve suppliers in both product and process development at a much earlier stage than has traditionally been the case. Allowing a supplier to apply its experience and expertise in a development project, known as early supplier design involvement (ESDI), often leads to better quality and product design because the knowledge and experience of the supplier is involved during the initial development of the customer's requirements well before final specifications and cost structure are locked in. Suppliers can provide suggestions about how to simplify a product or process, anticipate and begin preproduction work, and collaborate with the buyer's design engineers to establish reasonable tolerances that more closely match the supplier's capabilities and improve product quality and manufacturability.

Although the logic behind ESDI is relatively straightforward, making it work effectively on a day-to-day basis is often difficult. Many firms continue to struggle with sharing proprietary information with outside entities. In addition, some firms simply do not know how to manage this delicate and sensitive process. The mere presence of such constraints, however, does not mean that firms should not actively pursue early involvement with carefully selected suppliers. Both the buyer and supplier will be better off by working together collaboratively in the design phase of new-product development or through value analysis and value engineering initiatives.

Stressing Objective Rather Than Subjective Measurement and Analysis

An executive responsible for coordinating Xerox's successful drive for the Malcolm Baldrige National Quality Award once stated that one of the keys to achieving total quality is recognizing that facts, rather than subjective judgment, must predominate.[7] Hence, if facts must drive decision making, the need for fact-based measurement becomes evident.

However, many organizations, large and small, have not sufficiently developed objective or rigorous supplier measurement systems, during either supplier selection or postselection measurement and evaluation. Although there are many reasons for this, a primary one is that executives have historically not perceived the importance of external suppliers. Even today, there are wide differences in the quality and capability of supply chain performance measurement.

A survey by *Purchasing* magazine revealed that 51% of responding firms lacked an adequate system for measuring supplier performance. Furthermore, only 1 in 10 respondents claimed to be satisfied with existing supplier measurement systems. Of those firms that did measure supplier quality on a regular basis, almost 70% said their supplier measurement system had noticeably improved the performance of measured suppliers.[8] A Council of Logistics Management study revealed that, although a majority of firms measured some aspect of supply chain performance, most of their measurement systems focused on monitoring internal supply chain activities or functions rather than tracking the end-to-end performance of supply chain processes.[9]

Why is measurement so important to supplier quality? Performance data allow supply managers to develop a preferred supplier list for awarding future business, identify continuous performance improvement opportunities, provide feedback that supports corrective action or future development, and track the results from improvement initiatives. Effective supplier performance measurement systems are also an excellent way to communicate a buyer's quality and performance expectations.

Emphasizing Prevention Rather Than Detection of Defects

Prevention is the avoidance of nonconformance in products and services by not allowing errors or defects to occur in the first place. Although preventive activities take many forms, each stresses the need for consistency and reduced variation in the process. A thorough emphasis on defect prevention reduces reliance on appraisal, inspection, and other detection activities. A rigorous and structured approach to supplier evaluation and selection, for example, is an ideal way to ensure that selected suppliers have the requisite systems, processes, and methods in place to prevent defects.

A supplier certification program, another prime way to prevent defects, is the formal process of verifying, usually through an intensive cross-functional site audit, that a supplier's processes and methods produce consistent and conforming quality. Certification demands that suppliers demonstrate process capability, use of statistical process control, and conformance to other accepted TQM practices. The objective of supplier certification is to ensure that nonconforming items do not leave a supplier's facility. Supplier certification usually applies only to a specific part, process, or site rather than an entire company or product. The Good Practice Example at the end of the chapter presents one company's approach to supplier certification.

The extensive use of corrective action requests also supports prevention of nonconforming defects. For example, FedEx, a Baldrige Award winner, uses a corrective action request system to protect the physical appearance of its brand. When FedEx or a supplier discovers a critical defect with printed shipping forms, the supplier must immediately investigate and remove the source of the error to prevent future defects. The supplier is also required to sort and inspect its current production, remove all defective units, and examine 10 boxes of stock below and 10 boxes above the discovered defect. Finally, the supplier must submit a full written explanation and corrective plan to FedEx for resolving the defect (root cause analysis) along with a continuous-improvement plan.[10] Although corrective action requests do not prevent the initial problem (they are forwarded to suppliers in response to an identified problem), their timely use helps prevent further problems. Exhibit 8.4 on p. 286 presents a sample corrective action form.

Focusing on Process Rather Than Output

Perhaps the most dramatic difference between traditional methods and total quality management thinking involves a shift from a product orientation to a process orientation. Total quality management puts the focus on the processes that create output

Exhibit 8.4 Supplier Corrective Action Form

Supplier Corrective Action Request

Section A: To be completed by buyer

Corrective action request log #:

Date:

To:

From:

Subject:

Type of defect / nonconformance:

Description of defect / nonconformance:

Estimated total cost of defect / nonconformance:

Charge to supplier? ☐ Yes ☐ No

If yes, indicate amount: ____________

Section B: To be completed by supplier

Supplier corrective action response: (Please use back of page if additional space is required.)

Date corrective action response will be fully implemented:

Buyer sign-off: ____________ Supplier sign-off: ____________

Date: ____________ Date: ____________

rather than the output itself. Because quality processes create quality output, a logical focus is on the process of creation rather than the result. It is far less expensive and more efficient in the long run to avoid the defect than it is to inspect for it once it is created.

Assume that an organization evaluates and awards business primarily on the basis of competitive bids and supplier samples. At best, suppliers will provide one or two samples to the buyer for detailed analysis and acceptance. The following questions highlight the risk of focusing strictly on inspected output rather than the underlying process:

- What supplier would knowingly submit a poor sample?
- How many parts did the supplier produce to get an acceptable sample?
- Are the samples representative of the process operating under normal conditions?
- Did the supplier use the same process, methods, and materials that it will use during normal production, or was the sample made under controlled laboratory conditions?
- Did the supplier actually produce the sample, or did a subcontractor?
- Do samples tell the buyer enough about the supplier's capacity or process capability?

An emphasis on process rather than finished product demands that a supplier provide evidence of its process capability (addressed in the next section) to buyers on an ongoing, regular basis. Furthermore, every time a supplier modifies a process, a new capability study is required. Focusing on process means minimizing over-reliance on samples unless there is a timely and comprehensive method of validating sample conformance.

Perhaps the best way to maintain a process focus involves developing a structured companywide supplier evaluation and selection system, which itself represents a process. A well-defined supplier selection process supports the development of best practices, reduces duplication across units, supports the transfer of knowledge across teams or units, and recognizes the critical link between the selection decision and supply chain quality. Leading-edge firms make their selection process, along with any supporting tools and templates, available through their company's intranet for easy access and widespread availability.

Basics of Process Capability

Process capability is the ability of a process to generate outputs that meet engineering specifications or customer requirements. To be considered capable, the outputs from a process must fall between upper and lower specification limits. We assume that the distribution of output from the process is normally distributed. One property of normally distributed data is that 99.73% of all possible observations of process output are within three standard deviations of the process mean. A process that is stable and in control can be expected to produce virtually of its output within these natural tolerance limits. If the natural tolerance limits fall within the product's engineering specifications, the process is deemed to be capable.

Two process capability indices are used to measure a process's capability: C_p and C_{pk}. In order to calculate these indices, the process under study must be in statistical control with only common causes of variation being present. The C_p process capability index quantifies the relationship between the process's natural tolerance limits and the product's specifications using a two-sided approach. It is calculated by subtracting the lower specification limit from the upper specification limit and dividing by six standard deviations. Many quality practitioners suggest a relatively safe C_p index value of 1.5 or higher. Many customer companies require an even higher C_p value of 1.66 for added assurance that process output will conform to product specifications.[11]

However, the C_p index does not account for situations where the process is not centered on the nominal specification target value. For situations where the natural process mean is not centered, the C_{pk} index must be used. The C_{pk} index provides a conservative adjustment to the C_p index that takes into account how far the process mean is from the target value. Hence, the C_{pk} value is always smaller than the C_p index.[12]

A process capability study is designed to provide information about the performance of the process under stable operating conditions, that is, when no special causes of variation are present. The process capability study can provide information to address the following:

1. Determine the operating baseline of a process
2. Prioritize potential quality improvement projects
3. Provide evidence of process performance to a customer

Striving for Zero Defects

Philip Crosby argued that the only performance standard that defines total quality is **zero defects**, which he defined as conformance to requirements. Genichi Taguchi further argued that any deviation from a target value carries with it some level of opportunity loss due to scrap, rework, and customer dissatisfaction.[13] We can operationalize the pursuit of zero defects, however defined, in several important ways. Each method recognizes the importance of eliminating product and process variability.

As mentioned, a well-designed and rigorous supplier evaluation and selection process is one way to identify and do business only with suppliers that strive for zero defects. Measurement systems using key metrics also help identify improvement opportunities and progress. Another major approach, and one of the fastest and most effective ways to improve supply chain quality, is supply base rationalization.

Supply base rationalization or **optimization**, presented in detail in Chapter 9, is the process of determining the right mix and number of suppliers to maintain for a given purchase category or commodity. Almost half of the companies participating in a recent survey reduced their supply bases by 20%, and nearly 15% reduced their supply bases between 20 and 60%. Furthermore, three quarters of the firms indicated that they now commit 80% of their total purchase dollars with fewer than 100 suppliers.[14] Optimization is a continuous activity.

The supply base rationalization and optimization process is critical to improving supplier quality. More advanced strategic sourcing approaches, such as early supplier design involvement and supply chain alliances, demand a reduced supply base. Furthermore, if a firm rationalizes and optimizes its supply base properly, the remaining suppliers should be only those that are the most capable of providing consistent goods and services. Inconsistency is the enemy of total quality. Few supply managers knowingly eliminate their best suppliers. By definition, average supplier quality will increase as lower performers are eliminated.

Cost of Quality[15]

Quality has two impacts on the costs of a company: the costs due to nonconforming quality and the costs related to improving quality. Because the language of management is quantified in dollars, it is important to measure and track how funds are spent in regard to quality. Within this broader viewpoint, the cost of quality can be subcategorized into three classifications: appraisal, failure, and prevention.

Appraisal costs include the direct costs of measuring quality, specifically checking for defects. Areas of appraisal-related expense include laboratory testing of samples, inspection activities during production, supplier quality audits, incoming material inspections, and other forms of monitoring.

Failure costs are further divided into internal and external elements. Internal failure costs occur before the product or service is provided, whereas external failure costs are incurred following production or after the customer takes possession. Examples of internal failure costs include troubleshooting, reinspection following detection of a defect, production downtime caused by defects, scrap, and process waste. Examples of external failure costs include warranty costs, replacement of defective products to customers, lawsuits, and loss of customers.

Prevention costs are costs incurred when production processes are designed or modified to prevent defects from occurring in the first place. Examples include quality planning, equipment calibration, quality training, and maintenance of a quality management system.

Many traditional cost accounting systems are notorious for their failure to provide clear and concise information on just where funds are spent on quality-related expenses. These expenses are often incurred in various departments and not under the control of personnel with quality responsibilities. In addition, many quality-related costs, such as training, are somewhat subjective in nature and not easily identified.

Establishing Continuous Improvement as a Way of Life

The pressure for continuous improvement is severe and relentless. Fortunately, there are a variety of ways to make supplier improvement part of the prevailing organizational culture. One approach involves using a supplier measurement system to shift performance targets. The upward shifting of performance targets takes effect once a supplier demonstrates that it can achieve current performance expectations and is willing to improve. Ideally, supplier performance improves at a rate faster than what the buyer's competitors are realizing from their suppliers.

Value analysis/value engineering (VA/VE), presented in Chapter 12, is another approach for pursuing continuous improvement. VA/VE is the organized and systematic study of every element of cost in a part, material, process, or service to ensure that it fulfills its design function at the lowest possible total cost. Suppliers that are an active part of the VA/VE process actively review customer specifications, submit ideas on materials and process improvements, and work with the buyer to identify and remove nonconformance costs. This approach represents one of the better ways of institutionalizing continuous improvement in the supply base.

Exhibit 8.5 Providing Incentives for Supplier Quality Improvement

Award longer-term purchase contracts.

Offer a greater share of the purchaser's total volume to superior performers.

Publicly recognize superior suppliers, including "supplier of the year" awards.

Share the cost savings resulting from supplier-initiated improvements.

Provide suppliers with access to new technology.

Provide early insight into new business opportunities and product development plans.

Invite suppliers to participate early in new-product and process development projects.

Allow suppliers to use the purchaser's supply agreements to obtain favorable pricing.

Invite suppliers to participate in executive buyer-supplier councils.

Create a preferred list of suppliers that are offered first opportunity for new business.

Source: Adapted from R. J. Trent, "Linking TQM to SCM," *Supply Chain Management Review,* 2001, 5(3), 73.

Perhaps one of the most substantial changes over the last several years involves an increased willingness by larger firms to help develop supplier performance capabilities, a major topic in Chapter 9. Many activities can qualify as supplier development initiatives. Buyers, for example, are increasingly willing to offer Six Sigma quality training to suppliers. These buyers expect their Tier 1 suppliers to support the quality efforts of Tier 2 suppliers, and so on back through the supply chain.

If a firm has streamlined its supply base to a manageable level, and if remaining suppliers receive longer-term, higher-volume contracts, then it becomes clear that switching suppliers will be increasingly difficult and costly. Once a firm fully rationalizes its supply base, improvement will occur primarily by developing the capabilities of current suppliers rather than by switching suppliers on a large scale.

A buyer can also offer rewards to encourage a supplier's continuous-improvement efforts. In fact, most supply managers have at their disposal some very powerful incentives and rewards to positively influence supplier behavior. Offering performance-related rewards to suppliers recognizes that there is a direct link between reward and performance improvement. Traditionally, buyers demanded supplier improvement but were reluctant to share the resulting benefit, which encouraged self-promoting behavior by suppliers. Exhibit 8.5 highlights the various rewards that are available to encourage continuous supplier improvement. Sourcing Snapshot: Do Cost Reduction Pressures Affect Supplier Quality? provides additional discussion on this topic.

Making Quality Everyone's Responsibility

This principle requires that buyers and suppliers assume ownership for total quality across the supply chain. The issue becomes how buyers can align their vision of and need for supplier quality improvement.

Physically co-locating with suppliers is a powerful way to make quality everyone's responsibility and improve buyer-supplier communication. There are a number of ways

Sourcing Snapshot

Do Cost Reduction Pressures Affect Supplier Quality?

In 2001, a survey reported that automotive suppliers were cutting corners in response to OEM demands for price reductions. Only 20% of 261 reporting suppliers indicated that they were improving quality. Unfortunately, tragedies, such as the widespread failure of Firestone tires installed on Ford Explorers, provide substantial evidence that something is awry. The resulting charges and countercharges between the two companies raised serious concerns about the quality and safety of two of America's oldest brands.

Cost reductions alone do not necessarily signify lower quality. According to *Industry Week*'s 2000 census of manufacturers, which surveyed 3,000 companies, manufacturers that were able to reduce their scrap and waste showed more improvement in quality than those whose costs increased. Although taking out waste is good, trimming into the bone is not. When buyers demand deep price cuts from suppliers that are already operating with razor-thin margins, it should come as no surprise that attention to quality might suffer as a result. The rampant cost cutting over the last two decades has caused some producers to question what level of durability and material quality they are willing to design into their products.

Some companies truly understand how to effectively manage cost reductions while achieving continuous quality improvements. Toyota, for example, expects a 3% reduction in costs each year from its suppliers. Even with these year-after-year price reductions from suppliers, how does Toyota maintain its reputation for product quality? The company's willingness to work collaboratively with suppliers to identify ways to jointly reduce costs is in stark contrast to simply mandating reductions, reductions that could lead to decreases in product quality and safety.

Source: Adapted from R. D. Reid, "Purchaser and Supplier Quality," *Quality Progress,* August 2002; and D. Bartholomew, "Cost vs. Quality," *Industry Week,* 250(12), September 1, 2001, pp. 34–36, 40–41.

to create physical coexistence with suppliers. For example, Johnson Controls shares a 225,000-square-foot facility with its plastic mold supplier, Becker Group L.L.C.[16] Plastic door panels produced by the supplier flow directly into Johnson Control's assembly process, allowing immediate quality feedback and eliminating the possibility of in-transit damage. Likewise, Volkswagen built a truck assembly plant in Brazil with seven suppliers located within the assembly facility. These suppliers produce components and subassemblies in the VW facility using their own equipment, with their own labor assembling those items into finished trucks and buses.

Progressive organizations are forming executive-level buyer-supplier councils as a means of aligning and creating a partnership with carefully selected suppliers. As discussed in Chapter 5, these councils meet on a regular basis to coordinate longer-term product, process, and technology requirements; identify projects that buyers and suppliers can work on jointly; and promote closer and more collaborative supply chain relationships. Making quality each participant's responsibility is essential for total supply chain quality.

Pursuing Six Sigma Supplier Quality

The total quality principles just discussed work only if firms are able to operationalize them and demonstrate tangible results. When total quality first was popularized in the 1980s, too many firms educated their employees in the principles of TQM without committing the resources or time necessary to change a culture that believed "close enough is good enough." It is not surprising that many firms failed to achieve the kinds of performance improvement that they envisioned from total quality efforts. As a result, many participants became cynical about all total quality efforts, calling total quality "the management program of the month." "If we just wait another month," many said, "management will move on to another fad." In addition, few buying organizations extended their internal total quality efforts out to their suppliers.

The fact that many firms became disillusioned with their total quality programs does not eliminate the competitive need to seek total quality improvement. Six Sigma is today's version of total quality management. Thomas Pyzdek, a noted Six Sigma author and consultant, explained the importance of Six Sigma this way:

> *Six Sigma is a rigorous, focused and highly effective implementation of proven quality principles and techniques. Incorporating elements from the work of many quality pioneers, Six Sigma aims for virtually error-free business performance. Sigma, σ, is a letter in the Greek alphabet used by statisticians to measure the variability in any process. A company's performance is measured by the sigma level of their business processes. Traditionally companies accepted three or four sigma performance levels as the norm, despite the fact that these processes created between 6,200 and 67,000 problems per million opportunities! The Six Sigma standard of 3.4 problems per million opportunities is a response to the increasing expectations of customers and the increased complexity of modern products and processes.*
>
> *Six Sigma focuses on improving quality (i.e., reduce waste) by helping organizations produce products and services better, faster and cheaper. In more traditional terms, Six Sigma focuses on defect prevention, cycle time reduction, and cost savings. Unlike mindless cost-cutting programs which reduce value and quality, Six Sigma identifies and eliminates costs which provide no value to customers' waste costs.*[17]

Six Sigma reduces much of the complexity that characterized early TQM efforts. One expert estimated that TQM includes more than 400 different tools and techniques. Six Sigma relies on a smaller set of proven methods and trains individuals known as Six Sigma Black Belts to apply these sometimes sophisticated quality management tools and approaches.[18] Design of experiments is an example of a quality improvement approach applied by Black Belts to find and eliminate defects before the final design is specified.

Many observers credit Motorola with coining the term "Six Sigma" and relating it to 3.4 defects per million opportunities (DPMOs). Technically, **Six Sigma** quality means that output will conform to desired specifications 99.9999998% of the time, or 2 defects per billion opportunities. Why, then, are references to Six Sigma phrased in terms of 3.4 DPMO? Did someone mix up the statistical tables?

The area under the normal curve beyond 6 sigmas relates to 2 parts per billion defects. Six Sigma presumes, over the long term, that processes will naturally drift by as much as 1.5 standard deviations. Hence, the defect rate that equates with 6 sigmas (meaning the output conforms 99.9999998% of the time) and 1.5 sigmas of process drift is 3.4 DPMO. As a process shifts to the left or right due to natural variation, the likelihood increases that output will exceed a design specification limit. Because all processes are subject to natural variation and shifting, which can move a process slightly toward its upper or lower design specification limits, the 2 parts per billion rate effectively becomes 3.4 parts per million.

Six Sigma quality relates to supply management in several ways. First, suppliers that operate at 3 and 4 sigma quality levels typically spend between 25 and 40% of their revenues fixing problems. In an era of relentless cost-reduction pressures, this level of quality does not support longer-term competitive success. Suppliers that operate at 6 sigma levels, on the other hand, typically spend less than 5% of their revenues fixing problems.[19] Second, quality management is not only about managing internal quality. Market success demands that firms identify waste upstream through their Tier 1, Tier 2, and even Tier 3 suppliers. Many supplier development programs use experts from the buying company to help smaller suppliers achieve Six Sigma quality, as well as other productivity and cost improvements.

One aspect of helping suppliers improve involves educating them on the Six Sigma performance improvement model. Suppliers that apply this model should accelerate their rate of quality improvement as compared to those that do not. They should also make quality improvement a systematic part of their operations.

Exhibit 8.6 Six Sigma Performance Improvement Model

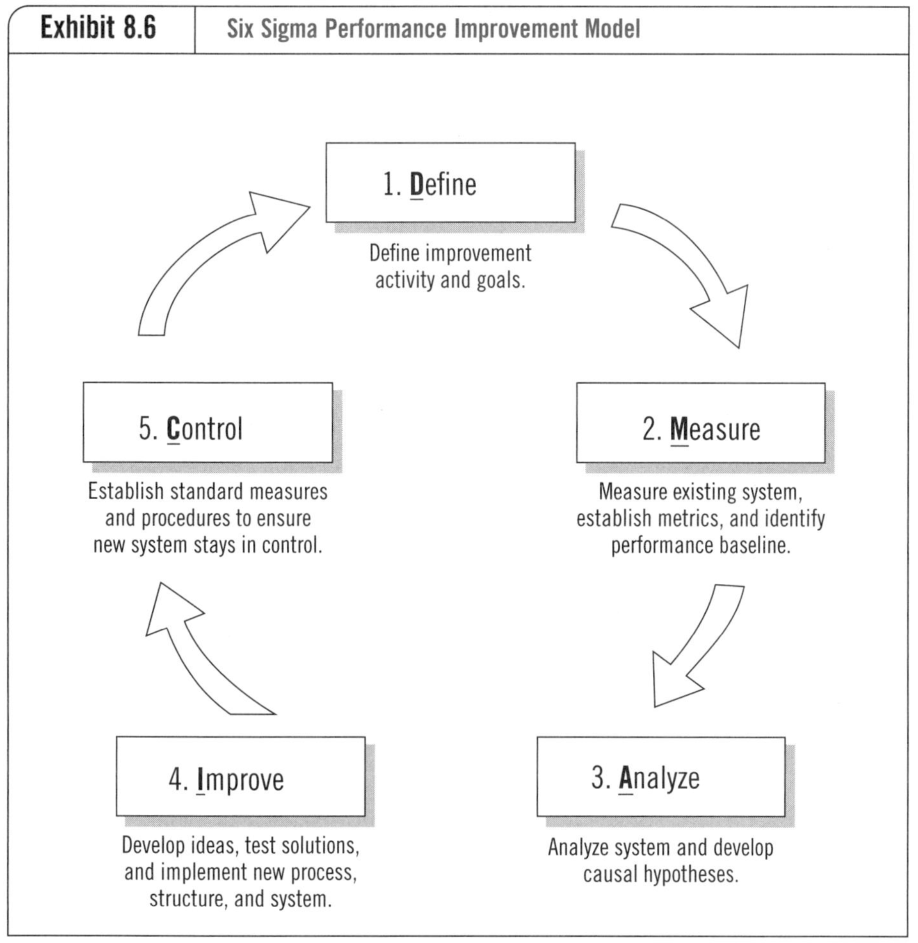
1. Define
Define improvement activity and goals.
2. Measure
Measure existing system, establish metrics, and identify performance baseline.
3. Analyze
Analyze system and develop causal hypotheses.
4. Improve
Develop ideas, test solutions, and implement new process, structure, and system.
5. Control
Establish standard measures and procedures to ensure new system stays in control.

Exhibit 8.6 on p. 293 outlines the features of this model, also known as DMAIC: the D(efine), M(easure), A(nalyze), I(mprove), and C(ontrol) model.

Using ISO Standards and MBNQA Criteria to Assess Supplier Quality Systems

Within the United States, relatively few companies have applied a uniform set of quality standards to their supplier certification process, resulting in duplication of effort and other operating inefficiencies. When measuring and assessing their suppliers' quality management systems, supply managers are increasingly turning to established quality auditing and measurement systems to drive supplier performance improvement.

Three widely accepted quality management frameworks are ISO 9000:2000, ISO 14000, and the Malcolm Baldrige National Quality Award. Companies that are unable to commit the necessary resources to assess or certify supplier quality on their own will often accept ISO 9001 registration as proxy evidence of a supplier's quality capability. Other companies have used ISO 9000, ISO 14000, and MBNQA criteria to develop their own assessment or certification processes. For these reasons, it is important to have a basic understanding of all three programs.

ISO 9000:2000 Registration

A quality management process gaining widespread acceptance throughout the world is ISO 9000:2000. Developed in 1987 to standardize quality requirements in the European Common Market, ISO 9000 originally consisted of a series of process quality standards—not product standards—recognizing that product quality is a direct result of a quality process. Meeting these standards, not an easy task, is often portrayed as a minimum requirement for competing globally.

In December 2000, the International Organization for Standardization released its most recent version of ISO 9000 standards. The revised ISO 9000 document, now called ISO 9000:2000, minimally resembles the previous standards, which were last updated in 1994. Although companies use ISO 9000:2000 standards for guidance and clarification of vocabulary terms, the actual registration that a company earns is ISO 9001:2000. The language in the new standard is less complex; the text follows an outline format rather than paragraphs; and ISO 9002 and ISO 9003 registrations no longer exist. ISO 9004:2000 remains a document that offers guidelines for performance improvements above the basic requirements of ISO 9001:2000.[20] To remain current, registration must be accomplished every three years.

Eight quality management principles influenced the revised ISO 9000 standards, which are described in Sourcing Snapshot: ISO 9000 Undergoes Radical Change. ISO 9000:2000 follows a process-based approach to quality management that stresses planning, acting, analyzing results, and making improvements. The previous version more closely resembled a random list of procedures.

It is in the best interests of suppliers to pursue ISO 9000:2000 quality registration, particularly if their customers (i.e., buyers) value the process. In addition, suppliers receive many benefits from pursuing third-party ISO registration. For example, buyers

Sourcing Snapshot — *ISO 9000 Undergoes Radical Change*

Jack West, lead U.S. delegate to the ISO committee that revised the ISO 9000 family of standards, stated that "people should have quality systems that reflect the way they really operate, rather than some arbitrary structure of 20 sections in a manual." In 2000, sentiments like this resulted in an ISO Technical Committee revising the ISO 9000 standards that were previously revised in 1994. The new ISO quality standards, now referred to as ISO 9000:2000, ISO 9001:2000, and ISO 9004:2000, reflect eight underlying principles.

Principle 1: Customer Focus. Organizations should understand current and future needs and strive to exceed customer expectations.

Principle 2: Leadership. Leaders establish purpose and direction. They should create an internal environment where people can help achieve the organization's objectives.

Principle 3: Involvement of People. Full involvement of employees at all levels will benefit an organization.

Principle 4: Process Approach. Attention to processes rather than simply output will help achieve desired results.

Principle 5: System Approach to Management. Identifying, understanding, and managing interrelated processes as a system contributes to effectiveness and efficiency.

Principle 6: Continual Improvement. Continual performance improvement should become a permanent organizational objective.

Principle 7: Factual Approach to Decision Making. Objective rather than subjective analysis and decisions should lead to effective decision making.

Principle 8: Mutually Beneficial Supplier Relationships. An organization and its suppliers are interdependent. This interdependency enhances the ability to create value.

Source: Adapted from D. Drickhamer, "Standards Shake-Up," *Industry Week,* March 5, 2001, p. 38.

have immediate confirmation that a supplier has achieved registration according to internationally accepted quality process standards. Furthermore, buyers may be willing to recognize ISO 9000:2000 registration in place of individual certification programs, resulting in lower costs for the buyer and supplier.

Each supplier that earns ISO 9000:2000 registration is included on a master list of companies satisfying the ISO standard. Inclusion on this list may lead to interest from other potential customers wanting to do business with ISO-registered companies. Suppliers that earn ISO registration will also be in a better position to satisfy corresponding U.S. ANSI standards as well.

Buying firms also benefit from suppliers achieving ISO 9000:2000 registration. First, few buying firms have the size or resources to independently develop and conduct comprehensive supplier certification audits. Registration may provide insight into a supplier's quality system conformance that a buyer may otherwise lack. The buying firm receives the benefit of a supplier quality certification without actually having to conduct its own quality certification audits.

Another potential benefit for buyers is that the supplier assumes responsibility for meeting the ISO standards and paying its own registration fees. With individual supplier certification programs, the buying firm assumes most, if not all, of the expenses related to certification. ISO registration requires suppliers to contract with a recognized independent registrar that is certified to perform ISO 9000:2000 audits.

Perhaps most importantly, suppliers that earn ISO 9001:2000 registration demonstrate higher quality than those suppliers that do not. The buyer may have higher confidence in the supplier's ability to meet or exceed quality requirements.

ISO 14000 Standards

The ISO 14000 standards, established in 1993, are designed to promote environmental protection and pollution prevention. They are an excellent way to analyze and document an organization's ability to proactively manage its environmental impact. The standards cover a broad perspective of environmental disciplines, ranging from the organization's environmental management system (EMS) to addressing auditing, labeling, and product standards. Benefits achieved through ISO 14000 certification include fewer pollutants generated, reduced liability, improved regulatory compliance, better public and community relations, and lowered insurance premiums.[21]

Another primary result of pursuing ISO 14000 certification is enhanced profitability through improved resource management and reduced waste generation. ISO 14000 is a set of voluntary standards and consists of two general classifications: process-oriented and product-oriented standards. It does not build upon existing governmental regulations, establish emissions and pollution levels, or detail any specific testing methods.[22]

Many buying firms now require their suppliers to become ISO 14000 certified. These suppliers must publish an organizational environmental policy, develop a comprehensive EMS, implement an internal auditing system, and use corrective action plans to address unfavorable audit results.

The Malcolm Baldrige National Quality Award

In 1987, President Ronald Reagan signed the Malcolm Baldrige National Quality Improvement Act, which established a national award to recognize quality improvement among manufacturing, service, and small businesses in the United States. A group of recognized quality professionals, including Dr. Joseph M. Juran, developed the initial award criteria. Since then, the criteria have become a de facto definition of TQM, and the wide dissemination of the application guidelines has exposed many managers to the Baldrige definition of TQM. For example, many companies use the MBNQA criteria as a template for a comprehensive quality management system, and one of the more important outputs of the award has been the creation and dissemination of useful TQM practices.

Some managers believe the MBNQA provides a more comprehensive set of quality-related criteria for North American–based firms than does ISO 9000:2000. The MBNQA is a competition and implies that an organization excels not only in quality management but also in quality achievement. The application for the MBNQA provides a broad framework for implementing a quality program and establishes benchmarks suitable for monitoring quality progress. Although the federal government has distributed thousands of MBNQA award applications over the years, the number of companies actively pursuing the award has actually decreased. Much of the current

Exhibit 8.7 Malcolm Baldrige National Quality Award

Score Summary Worksheet — Business Criteria

Examiner Name ______________________ Application Number ______________________

Summary of Criteria Items	Total Points Possible **A**		Percent Score 0–100% (Stage 1–10% Units) **B**	Score (A × B) **C**
1 Leadership				
1.1 Organizational leadership	85		______ %	______
1.2 Public responsibility and citizenship	40		______ %	______
Category Total		125		SUM C
2 Strategic Planning				
2.1 Strategy development	40		______ %	______
2.2 Strategy deployment	45		______ %	______
Category Total		85		______ SUM C
3 Customer and Market Focus				
3.1 Customer and market knowledge	40		______ %	______
3.2 Customer satisfaction and relationships	45		______ %	______
Category Total		85		______ SUM C
4 Information and Analysis				
4.1 Measurement of organizational performance	40		______ %	______
4.2 Analysis of organizational performance	45		______ %	______
Category Total		85		______ SUM C
5 Human Resource Focus				
5.1 Work systems	35		______ %	______
5.2 Employee education, training, and development	25		______ %	______
5.3 Employee well-being and satisfaction	25		______ %	______
Category Total		85		______ SUM C
6 Process Management				
6.1 Product and service processes	55		______ %	______
6.2 Support processes	15		______ %	______
6.3 Supplier and partnering processes	15		______ %	______
Category Total		85		______ SUM C
7 Business Results				
7.1 Customer-focused results	115		______ %	______
7.2 Financial and market results	115		______ %	______
7.3 Human resource results	80		______ %	______
7.4 Supplier and partner results	25		______ %	______
7.5 Organizational effectiveness results	115		______ %	______
Category Total		450		______ SUM C
GRAND TOTAL (D)		1000		______ D

Source: U.S. Department of Commerce, National Institute of Standards and Technology (http://www.quality.NIST.gov).

application of the MBNQA is for internal use as a quality management tool and not for award purposes.

It can take a company 8 to 10 years to develop a quality system that is competitive for the award.[23] The MBNQA is composed of seven weighted categories, together worth a total of 1,000 points: leadership, strategic planning, customer and market focus, information and analysis, human resource focus, process management, and business results. These categories are outlined in Exhibit 8.7 on p. 297. Higher-performing companies, with scores of 700 or more, demonstrate balanced and outstanding performance across each of these categories.

Continuous improvement is the most basic and important tenet of the MBNQA criteria. In each of the major categories, companies must demonstrate how they plan to improve in that area. The MBNQA criteria are both process and results oriented, addressing operations, processes, strategies, and requirements.

Just what does the MBNQA have to do with supplier quality? Many leading companies are now using MBNQA criteria when designing internal assessment systems for supplier quality performance. Companies such as Cummins Engine, Motorola, Pacific Bell, Alcatel, and Honeywell all use modified versions of MBNQA criteria to conduct in-depth studies of their major suppliers' quality management systems. They use a similar scoring system, and trained assessors typically spend several days visiting the supplier's facilities to rate their continuous-improvement efforts. Progressive companies fully understand the logic behind applying well-established quality principles and guidelines to their total supply chain quality efforts.

Good Practice Example — *Supplier Certification at Alcoa*

Alcoa, a world leader in the production of aluminum and related products, has developed a comprehensive audit system to certify that its suppliers satisfy the company's quality expectations. A primary objective of the audit, besides resulting in a decision about supplier quality certification, is to encourage and assist Alcoa suppliers to achieve continuous quality improvement. One way this happens is by identifying specific supplier deficiencies that provide opportunities for improvement.

Alcoa's certification process, like most certification systems, evaluates supplier quality systems and locations rather than individual products. Furthermore, the company involves its suppliers directly in the quality improvement process. The process also helps these suppliers make substantial and meaningful quality improvements (with Alcoa providing support as required), measures supplier quality improvement progress, and formally recognizes supplier quality achievement.

Alcoa's supplier certification process has several important features. First, the process applies to both internal and external suppliers. An internal supplier is defined as an Alcoa facility that supplies another Alcoa facility. Including internal suppliers credibly demonstrates that Alcoa practices and follows its own quality prescriptions. Second, a trial audit of the supplier's facility occurs before the official quality audit. This trial audit minimizes the possibility of surprise and gives the supplier a fair opportunity to prepare and improve (where necessary) before the official audit. Third, Alcoa relies on a skilled cross-functional team to perform these supplier audits. These CFTs provide a level of expertise that a single individual cannot provide. Finally, suppliers receive a quantified numerical rating after the official audit. This provides immediate visibility about how the team rates a supplier's quality systems and helps to compare data between audits.

Alcoa divides its quality improvement process into a series of steps. Each step represents a progression toward Alcoa's final objective—a supply base capable of world-class quality and continuous improvement. Exhibit 8.8 on p. 301 presents an overview of Alcoa's supplier quality improvement process.

STEP 1: MEET AND PLAN

Once Alcoa identifies the suppliers that it plans to evaluate and consider for certification, the company conducts one-day overview meetings with the suppliers' management team. A representative from Alcoa then meets with each targeted supplier to plan a schedule of initial contact.

STEP 2: THE SUPPLIER SELF-SURVEY

Each supplier has an opportunity to perform a self-survey. The self-survey covers the same four sections as the formal audit (Step 5): quality management, quality measurement, safety and training, and facilities. The supplier rates itself on each survey item on a scale of 0 to 10. During the self-survey, suppliers become aware of Alcoa's specific quality requirements.

STEP 3: STRATEGY PLANNING

Alcoa and the supplier then use the results of the supplier's self-survey to identify specific strengths and weaknesses. Where necessary, Alcoa assigns an employee to work directly with the supplier to assist in developing an improvement strategy. This individual lends personal support and guidance where required.

The supplier must commit to improving itself and not relying on Alcoa personnel over the long run to achieve necessary changes. The supplier initiates the necessary improvements to correct deficiencies during this phase of the process.

STEP 4: THE TRIAL AUDIT

The support person assigned by Alcoa conducts the trial audit once it appears that the supplier has improved in each previously identified deficiency area. The trial audit serves two purposes. First, it reveals the status of the supplier's improvement efforts. Second, it prepares the supplier for the formal audit that will be conducted later by a cross-functional audit team.

STEP 5: THE FORMAL AUDIT

The formal review process includes information from two separate sources. First, each Alcoa location that has direct contact with a supplier evaluates the supplier's performance on a 10-point scale. Internal users evaluate the supplier for material quality, delivery, paperwork, nonconformance resolution (i.e., how the supplier resolves problems), and sales and marketing service.

The user evaluation applies only to a specific supplier location. An Alcoa location that receives material from multiple supplier locations must evaluate each of the suppliers' locations individually. The most comprehensive part of the certification process is the formal supplier audit. If the results of the trial audit indicate that a supplier is likely to achieve the minimum required for certification, then Alcoa schedules a formal audit. The company tries to conduct the formal audit within 90 days of the trial audit.

To make the audit as objective as possible, the audit team uses a corporate supplier quality survey. This survey includes items that relate to quality management, quality measurement, safety and training, and facilities. The audit document defines, as precisely and concisely as possible, the meaning of each value so the audit team can accurately and fairly evaluate a supplier. The scoring system for each item includes a minimum score that a supplier must achieve to qualify for certification.

The team records its score for each audit statement, adds all the item scores together, notes whether the supplier meets all minimum scoring requirements, and makes a certification recommendation. The audit team makes one of three possible recommendations: certification, certification after corrective action, or no certification. Furthermore, a supplier that does not receive certification must have a full reaudit before any future certification is attempted.

STEP 6: RECOMMENDATION REVIEW

An audit review committee evaluates the certification recommendation of the audit team before reaching a final decision. The committee also reviews the user evaluations completed during the review process. The review committee weighs the formal audit team's score as 80% of the total rating and the user evaluation as the remaining 20%.

Supplier certification occurs at three levels. The initial level is a Certified Supplier, the middle level is a Preferred Supplier, and the top level is a Supplier of Excellence. Each level receives different forms of Alcoa recognition and rewards.

Alcoa maintains the information from all audits and user evaluations in a database, which allows the company to assess supplier progress, particularly in areas of initial deficiency. The formal audit and certification are not the end of the quality process. Rather, these activities represent only part of the effort to strengthen the relationship between Alcoa and its suppliers. As Alcoa works with its suppliers to improve quality, a mutual trust and respect can develop that further enhance improvement efforts.

Alcoa's highly effective supplier quality certification and improvement process illustrates the effort put forth as part of its quest for total quality. Although supplier certification requires a major resource commitment on the part of both parties, the longer-term benefits that can result from consistently high supplier quality are worth the effort—both to Alcoa and to the supplier.

Exhibit 8.8 Alcoa Supplier Quality Improvement Process

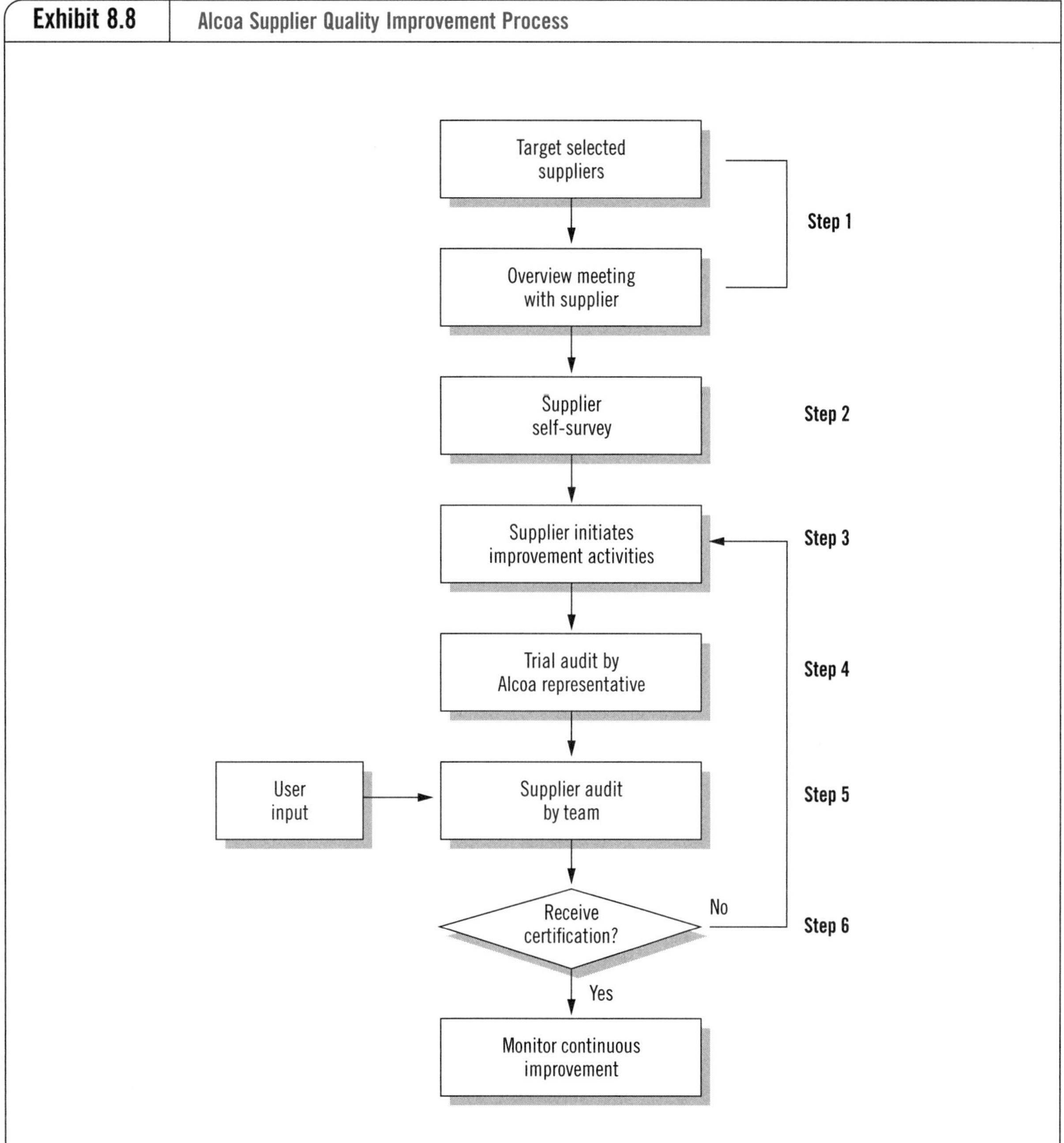

Source: Adapted from a public presentation at the Executive Purchasing and Supply Chain Management Seminar, Michigan State University, East Lansing, MI, 1993.

CONCLUSION

The battleground for global competitive advantage has entered the domain of supply chain management. Although other competitive factors, such as mass customization and flexibility, will increasingly become order-winning market characteristics, the ability to design, produce, and sell high-quality products and services will always remain a primary market qualifier. Without TQM, however, a producer should not expect serious consideration from potential customers.

Improving supplier quality involves much more than providing clear specifications and maintaining open communication. Supply management, pursuing the principles of TQM, can effectively improve supplier quality practices and set a standard for excellence. Supplier quality excellence can be achieved by being a good customer to suppliers, routinely measuring supplier performance and eliminating poor performers, providing timely and accurate feedback, certifying and rewarding Six Sigma supplier performance, and helping suppliers reach joint continuous-improvement goals. To achieve total quality, supply management must have people who understand the principles and tools of TQM, including Six Sigma, and can work effectively with suppliers to ensure that zero defects is the norm rather than the exception.

KEY TERMS

kaizen, 281

prevention, 285

process capability, 287

quality, 273

Six Sigma, 292

supplier quality, 274

supply base rationalization or optimization, 288

zero defects, 288

DISCUSSION QUESTIONS

1. Why should a buyer be concerned with supplier quality performance?
2. Discuss the following statement: Supply management not only buys parts or services from suppliers—it buys a supplier's performance capability.
3. Do suppliers have an equal impact on product quality? Discuss the conditions under which one supplier may have a greater impact on a firm's final product quality as compared with another supplier.
4. Why is it important for a buyer to be a good customer? How can a buyer be a good customer to a supplier?
5. How can early supplier design involvement contribute to higher levels of product quality?
6. Discuss the benefits to a supplier of achieving ISO 9000:2000 registration.
7. Some supply management experts argue that suppliers should not receive rewards for doing something that is already expected (e.g., continuously improving quality). Do you agree with this position? What are some examples of rewards that a supplier can receive?
8. Discuss the benefits to a buying company of certifying its suppliers. Describe the benefits to a supplier of being certified.
9. Why did many total quality management efforts in North America not succeed as expected during the 1980s?

10. What are the differences between TQM and Six Sigma quality approaches?
11. What principles of TQM does a well-developed supplier evaluation and selection process satisfy?
12. What principles of total quality management do supplier measurement systems satisfy?
13. Discuss the role of Deming's 14 points in managing supplier quality.
14. Describe the various classifications of the cost of quality.
15. How can a buyer utilize ISO 14000 to improve supplier environmental performance?
16. How can a buyer utilize MBNQA criteria as a basis for improving supplier quality?

ADDITIONAL READINGS

Carton, T. J., and Jacoby, D. J. (1997), *A Review of Managing Quality and a Primer for the Certified Quality Manager Exam,* Milwaukee, WI: ASQ Quality Press.

Columbus, L. (2007), "Quality Partnerships with Your Customers," *Quality Digest,* pp. 44–48.

Dasgupta, T. (2003), "Using the Six-Sigma Metric to Improve the Performance of a Supply Chain," *Total Quality Management and Business Excellence,* 14(3), 355–366.

Duncan, W. L. (1995), *Total Quality: Key Terms and Concepts,* New York: AMACOM.

Evans, J. R., and Lindsay, W. M. (2008), *Managing for Quality and Performance Excellence* (7th ed.), Mason, OH: South-Western.

Fernandez, R. R. (1995), *Total Quality in Purchasing and Supplier Management,* Delray Beach, FL: St. Lucie Press.

Foster, S. T. (2007), *Managing Quality: Integrating the Supply Chain* (3rd ed.), Upper Saddle River, NJ: Pearson.

Garvin, D. A. (1988), *Managing Quality: The Strategic and Competitive Edge,* New York: Free Press.

Gould, R. A., Arter, D. R., Ball-Brown, P., Creinin, D., Howe Garriz, L., Schoenfelt, T. I., and Van Arsdale, T. (2006), "Quality Management," in *The Supply Management Handbook,* J. L. Cavinato, A. E. Flynn, and R. G. Kauffman (Eds.), New York: McGraw-Hill, pp. 565–586.

Ishikawa, K. (translated by David J. Lu) (1985), *What Is Total Quality Control? The Japanese Way,* Englewood Cliffs, NJ: Prentice Hall.

Juran, J. M. (1988), *Juran on Planning for Quality,* New York: Free Press.

Juran, J. M. (Ed.) (1999), *Juran's Quality Handbook* (5th ed.), New York: McGraw-Hill.

Maass, R., Brown, J. O., and Bossert, J. L. (1999), *Supplier Certification: A Continuous Improvement Strategy,* Milwaukee, WI: ASQ Quality Press.

Merrill, P. (1997), *Do It Right the Second Time: Benchmarking Best Practices in the Quality Change Process,* Portland, OR: Productivity Press.

Minahan, T. (1998), "Purchasing Needs to Do More Than Measure," *Purchasing,* 124(1), 59–61.

Nelson, D., Mayo, R., and Moody, P. E. (1998), *Powered by Honda: Developing Excellence in the Global Enterprise,* New York: John Wiley & Sons.

Newman, R. G. (1988), "Insuring Quality: Purchasing's Role," *International Journal of Purchasing and Materials Management,* 24(3), 14–21.

Pande, P. S., Neuman, R. P., and Cavanaugh, R. R. (2000), *The Six Sigma Way: How GE, Motorola, and Other Top Companies Are Honing Their Performance,* New York: McGraw-Hill.

Reid, D. R. (2002), "Purchaser and Supplier Quality," *Quality Progress,* 35(8), 81–85.

Smith, B. (2003), "Lean and Six Sigma—A One-Two Punch," *Quality Progress,* 36(4), 37–42.

Smith, G. F. (1995), *Quality Problem Solving,* Milwaukee, WI: ASQ Quality Press.

Smith, L. (2006), "Quality around the World," *Quality Digest,* June, pp. 41–47.

Stundza, T. (2007), "Assured Quality Critical in Global Sourcing," *Purchasing,* 136(11), 32.

Trent, R. J. (1999), "Achieving World-Class Supplier Quality," *Total Quality Management,* 10(6), 927–939.

Wesner, J. W., Hiatt, J. M., and Trimble, D. C. (1995), *Winning with Quality: Applying Quality Principles in Product Development,* Reading, MA: Addison-Wesley.

Zhu, K., Zhang, R. Q., and Tsung, F. (2007), "Pushing Quality Improvement along Supply Chains," *Management Science,* 53(3), 421–436.

ENDNOTES

1. Feigenbaum, A. V. (1983), *Total Quality Control* (3rd ed.), New York: McGraw-Hill, p. 7.

2. Trent, R. J., and Monczka, R. M. (1998), "Purchasing and Supply Management: Trends and Changes throughout the 1990s," *International Journal of Purchasing and Materials Management,* 2–11; and The Executive Purchasing and Supply Chain Management Seminar, Michigan State University, Adapted from Robert M. Monczka (Director).

3. Trent and Monczka, pp. 2–11.

4. For a more complete discussion of Deming, Crosby, and Juran, see Walton, M. (1990), *Deming Management at Work,* New York: Putnam; Crosby, P. B. (1996), *Quality Is Still Free: Making Quality Certain in Uncertain Times,* New York: McGraw-Hill; and Juran, J. M. (1992), *Juran on Quality by Design: The New Steps for Planning Quality into Goods and Services,* New York: Free Press.

5. Bhote, K. (1987), *Supply Management: How to Make U.S. Suppliers Competitive,* New York: American Management Association, p. 87.

6. Evans, J. R., and Lindsay, W. M. (2008), *Managing for Quality and Performance Excellence* (7th ed.), Mason, OH: South-Western, pp. 101–107.

7. From a presentation made by Jim Sierk at the Michigan State University Purchasing and Supply Chain Management Executive Seminar during the mid-1990s.

8. Porter, A. M. (1999), "Raising the Bar," *Purchasing,* 127(1), 44–50.

9. Keebler, J. S., Manrodt, K. B., Durtsche, D. A., and Ledyard, D. M. (1999), *Keeping Score: Measuring the Business Value of Logistics in the Supply Chain,* Oak Brook, IL: Council of Logistics Management, pp. 1–10.

10. Used with permission from FedEx Quality Assurance. The five key performance attributes for printed forms are (1) dimension of label, (2) position of the die cut, (3) clarity of print, (4) test line of direct strike, and (5) color quality. A sixth category, called "other," allows additional requirements for specific items.

11. Evans and Lindsay, p. 635.

12. Evans and Lindsay, pp. 633–635.

13. Taguchi, G., and Clausing, D. (1995), "Robust Quality," *Harvard Business Review,* January–February 1990, appearing in *Manufacturing Renaissance,* Cambridge, MA: Harvard Business Review Books, pp. 173–188.

14. Reese, A. (2000), "eProcurement Takes on the Untamed Supply Chain," *iSource,* November, p. 108.

15. Foster, S. T. (2007), *Managing Quality: Integrating the Supply Chain* (3rd ed.), Upper Saddle River, NJ: Pearson Prentice Hall, pp. 115–116.

16. "Johnson Controls to Share New Plant with Becker Group" (2000), *Crain's Detroit Business*, June, p. 2.

17. Pyzdek, T. (2000), "The Six Sigma Revolution," http://www.pyzdek.com/six-sigma-revolution.htm.

18. Pyzdek, p. 2.

19. Pyzdek, p. 1.

20. Drickhamer, D. (2001), "Standards Shake-Up," *Industry Week,* March 5, pp. 37–40.

21. Swift, J. A., Ross, J. E., and Omachonu, V. K. (1998), *Principles of Total Quality* (2nd ed.), Boca Raton, FL: St. Lucie Press, pp. 369–373.

22. Summers, D. C. S. (2003), *Quality* (3rd ed.), Upper Saddle River, NJ: Prentice Hall, pp. 612–614.

23. Handfield, R., and Ghosh, S. (1994), "Creating a Total Quality Culture through Organizational Change: A Case Analysis," *Journal of International Marketing,* 2(4), 15–30.

Chapter 9

SUPPLIER MANAGEMENT AND DEVELOPMENT: CREATING A WORLD-CLASS SUPPLY BASE

Learning Objectives

After completing this chapter, you should be able to

- Recognize that supplier management and development includes a variety of activities intended to improve supplier performance
- Appreciate the relationship between supplier measurement and supplier management
- Understand how to develop different types of supplier measurement tools
- Understand the importance of a manageable supply base in terms of size and quality
- Know when and how to apply supplier development tools, techniques, and approaches

Chapter Outline

Managing Suppliers Is a Priority at Honda of America Manufacturing

Honda of America Manufacturing (HAM), with several production and assembly locations in Ohio, strongly commits to longer-term relationships and supplier development with its suppliers. Long-term supplier viability is critical to Honda's profitability. First, the company fully commits to its suppliers for life. When Honda signs a sourcing contract with a supplier, it expects to maintain that relationship for 25 to 50 years. Second, the company buys 80% of the cost of every car from outside suppliers—the most of any automotive producer. Honda, therefore, commits a significant amount of its resources toward managing and developing local suppliers to ensure Honda has access to capable suppliers that can continuously meet the company's stringent performance standards.

Supplier development and improvement has one primary objective at Honda—to create and maintain a dedicated supply base that supports Honda's U.S. requirements. Pursuit of this objective requires a substantial commitment of resources to support and develop its suppliers:

- Two full-time employees help suppliers develop their employee involvement programs.
- Forty full-time engineers in the supply management department work with suppliers to improve productivity and quality.
- Over 100 engineers in the quality control department deal with incoming parts and supplier quality issues.
- Honda provides technical support to suppliers in a number of technical areas, including plastics technology, welding, stamping, and aluminum die casting.
- Honda forms special teams to help suppliers on an ad hoc basis. One supplier, for example, experienced problems resulting from rapid growth. Honda formed a four-person team that moved to the supplier's town for nine months to help correct the problems.
- A "Quality-Up" program targets suppliers with lower quality. Honda works directly with the supplier's top management team to ensure that the supplier produces a 100% quality product.
- Honda has a loaned-executive program where it sends various executives to work at the supplier's location. This supports greater understanding and communication between Honda and its suppliers, as well as creating long-term commitment and loyalty.

However, most companies are not willing to provide this level of attention and dedication to supplier management and development. A company that maintains either a laissez-faire or a reactive approach to supply base management is probably not willing to provide the necessary resources to support ongoing supplier development. Furthermore, some suppliers are not willing to expose themselves to the level of scrutiny required by Honda. Honda, for example, conducts minimal price negotiation. Instead, the company identifies a target cost and then works with a supplier to jointly meet that cost. Such detailed cost sharing can be difficult or traumatic for many independent suppliers.

This example outlines several key points about supplier management and development. First, suppliers play a critical role in the success of most organizations. Therefore, it makes sense to pay attention to a supplier's performance improvement needs. Second, a supply base that is too large and complex usually prohibits providing adequate supplier development support. There simply are not enough resources available to support and develop a large supply base. Finally, supplier development requires more than slogans and demands for better performance. It means actually committing the joint resources to make the process successful.

Although the Honda approach may seem extreme to some, few can argue with the company's demonstrated success. Automobiles produced at its Ohio assembly plants have consistently been among the highest-quality and best-selling in the United States. The success of Honda's supplier development and improvement effort is one reason the company enjoys such loyal customers.

Source: Adapted from Krause, D., and Handfield, R. (1999), *Developing a World-Class Supply Base,* Tempe, AZ: Center for Advanced Purchasing Studies, p. 102; Harrington, L. H. (1997), "Buying Better," *Industry Week,* July 21, p. 75; Fitzgerald, K. R. (1995), "For Superb Supplier Development, Honda Wins!" *Purchasing,* 21, 32; and Nelson, D., Moody, P. E., and Stegner, J. (2001), *The Purchasing Machine,* New York: Free Press. Also adapted from interviews with various company managers and other public sources.

As the opening vignette illustrates, progressive firms take the need to improve supplier performance quite seriously. Gone are the days when vertically integrated companies mass-produced products with long product life cycles. With increased global competition, companies increasingly rely on an ever-expanding network of dedicated suppliers to meet their business objectives. Businesses across every industry are beginning to realize that success requires them to organize and manage resources and processes across a network of supply chain partners put together on purpose, not haphazardly.[1]

Effective supplier management and development includes a broad array of actions taken to manage and improve a worldwide network of carefully screened and selected supply chain partners or suppliers. The primary objective of these future-oriented management and development processes is the continuous improvement of supplier capabilities. Supplier performance that is good enough today will not suffice in the marketplace of tomorrow. History shows that, unless companies are able to bring supply base performance to world-class levels, they will be at the mercy of competitors that have taken supplier performance improvement more seriously.

This chapter focuses on various ways organizations manage their supply chains. Although a number of supplier management approaches exist, most fall into the broad activities described in this chapter. The first section discusses the important relationship between supplier measurement and effective supplier management. The next section discusses supply base rationalization and optimization, the process of identifying the proper mix and number of suppliers. The third section discusses supplier development as a strategy for improvement. In the final section, we present some of the barriers faced by organizations as they attempt to improve supplier performance through supplier development. Finally, we conclude with a Good Practice Example of supplier measurement at FedEx.

Supplier Performance Measurement

An important part of supplier management involves the continuous measurement, evaluation, and analysis of supplier performance. An organization must have the tools to measure, manage, and develop the performance of its supply base. Without an effective measurement system to record and evaluate supply base performance, how do buyers really know how well their suppliers are satisfying their contractual obligations? Supplier performance measurement includes the methods and systems to collect and provide information to measure, rate, or rank supplier performance on a continuous basis. The supplier measurement system is a critical part of the sourcing process—essentially serving as a supplier's report card. Note that supplier performance measurement differs from the process used to initially evaluate and select a supplier. It is a continuous process as opposed to a unique, one-time event.

Supplier Measurement Decisions

Organizations face several key decisions when developing a supplier measurement system that are critical to the final design, implementation, and effectiveness of the system.

What to Measure

Central to the design of all supplier measurement systems is the decision about what to measure and how to weigh various performance categories. An organization must decide which performance criteria are objective (quantitative) and which are subjective (qualitative), as the metrics will be different between the two. Most of the objective, quantitative variables lie within the following three categories:

- *Delivery performance:* Purchase orders or material releases sent to a supplier have a quantity and a materials due date. A buyer can assess how well a supplier satisfies its quantity and due-date commitments. Quantity, lead time requirements, and due-date compliance also define a supplier's overall delivery performance.
- *Quality performance:* Almost all supplier measurement systems include quality performance as a critical component. Review Chapter 8 for a more in-depth discussion of supplier quality management. A buyer can evaluate a supplier's quality performance against previously specified objectives, track trends and improvement rates, and compare similar suppliers. A well-designed measurement system also helps define a buyer's quality requirements and effectively communicates them to its suppliers.
- *Cost reduction:* Buyers frequently rely on suppliers for cost-reduction assistance, which can be measured in a number of ways. One common method is to track a supplier's real cost after adjustment for inflation. Other accepted techniques involve comparing a supplier's cost against other suppliers within the same industry or against a baseline or target price. Some leading companies use the last price paid in a year as the baseline price for comparisons during the next year.

Buyers can also use a number of qualitative factors to assess supplier performance. Exhibit 9.1 on p. 310 details some of the qualitative service factors available to buyers. Although these factors are largely subjective, a buyer can still assign a score or rating to each factor. A buyer might evaluate five different qualitative factors (assume equal weighting for simplicity) along a five-point scale. The system adds the five scores and divides by the total possible points to arrive at a percentage of total points, so that a buyer can rank suppliers by the percentage of total possible points earned.

Measurement and Reporting Frequency

Two important issues relate to the regularity of measurement: reporting frequency to the buyer and reporting frequency to the supplier. A buyer (or someone responsible for the day-to-day management of suppliers) should receive a daily report sum-

Exhibit 9.1 Qualitative Service Factors

FACTOR	DESCRIPTION
Problem resolution ability	Supplier's attentiveness to problem resolution
Technical ability	Supplier's manufacturing ability compared with other industry suppliers
Ongoing progress reporting	Supplier's ongoing reporting of existing problems or recognizing and communicating a potential problem
Corrective action response	Supplier's solutions and timely response to requests for corrective actions, including a supplier's response to engineering change requests
Supplier cost-reduction ideas	Supplier's willingness to help find ways to reduce purchase cost
Supplier new-product support	Supplier's ability to help reduce new-product development cycle time or to help with product design
Buyer/seller compatibility	Subjective rating concerning how well a buying firm and a supplier work together

marizing the previous day's activities. This report allows the buyer to scan incoming receipt activity and should highlight past-due supplier receipts. A buyer should receive additional reports summarizing supplier performance on a weekly, monthly, quarterly, and annual basis.

Routine reporting of supplier performance relative to goal should happen monthly or quarterly. Buyers should also meet with suppliers on at least an annual basis to review actual performance results and identify improvement opportunities. However, a buyer should never delay reporting a supplier's poor performance, particularly when it adversely affects day-to-day operations. Poor performance must be addressed as soon as it is recognized to avoid financial or operational repercussions.

Uses of Measurement Data

A buyer can use the data gathered from its measurement system in a number of ways. The data can help identify those suppliers that are incapable of performing at expected levels so that remedial action will be taken to get performance back to acceptable levels or to find a new supplier. A measurement system also helps identify those highly capable suppliers that may qualify for longer-term partnerships or designation as preferred suppliers because of exemplary performance.

Measurement data also support supply base rationalization and optimization efforts. If suppliers do not improve performance to minimum acceptable levels, they are not likely to remain part of the supply base over the long term. Another use of supplier performance data includes determining a supplier's future purchase volume based on its past performance rating. Some companies adjust their purchase volumes periodically and reward better-performing suppliers with a higher share of purchase requirements. Adjusting volumes between suppliers provides a financial incentive for a supplier to meet or exceed the buyer's performance expectations.

A major benefit from supplier measurement is that performance data allow the buying organization to identify those areas requiring improvement. Buyers can also use the data when making sourcing decisions. These become clearer when a buyer has a reliable measurement system that rates and ranks a supplier's performance against other suppliers or other established performance standards.

Types of Supplier Measurement Techniques

All supplier measurement systems have some element of subjectivity. Even the implementation of a computerized measurement system will require subjective judgment. What data to analyze, what metrics to use, what performance categories to include, how to weight different categories, how often to generate performance reports, and how to use the performance data are all subjective to some degree. Moreover, there are no hard rules regarding the specific categories to include in supplier measurement systems; the choice will depend on what is strategically important to the buyer.

Organizations typically use one of three common measurement techniques or systems when evaluating supplier performance. Each system differs in its ease of use, level of decision subjectivity, required system resources, and implementation cost. Exhibit 9.2 compares the advantages and disadvantages of these three systems.

Categorical System

A categorical system is the easiest and most basic measurement system to put in place, but it is also the most subjective as far as measuring supplier performance. This system requires the assignment of a rating evaluation for each selected performance category. Examples of ratings typically include: excellent, good, fair, and poor. These subjective evaluations can be completed by the buyer, other internal users, or some combination of both.

The categorical approach is commonly used by smaller organizations because it is both easy and relatively inexpensive to implement. Although the categorical approach provides some structure to the measurement process, it does not provide sufficiently detailed insight into a supplier's true performance. Furthermore, because categorical systems often rely on manually collected data, an organization generates supplier

Exhibit 9.2 Comparison of Supplier Measurement and Evaluation Systems

SYSTEM	ADVANTAGES	DISADVANTAGES	USERS
Categorical	Easy to implement Requires minimal data Different personnel contribute Good for firms with limited resources Low-cost system	Least reliable Less frequent generation of evaluations Most subjective Usually manual	Smaller firms Firms in the process of developing an evaluation system
Weighted-Point	Flexible system Supplier ranking allowed Moderate implementation costs Quantitative and qualitative factors combined into a single system	Tends to focus on unit price Requires some computer support	Most firms can use this approach
Cost-Based	Total cost approach Specific areas of supplier nonperformance identified Objective supplier ranking Greatest potential for long-range improvement	Cost accounting system required Most complex so implementation costs high Computer resources required	Larger firms Firms with a large supply base

performance reports less frequently than if an automated system existed. The reliability of the categorical method is the lowest of the three measurement systems discussed here, which limits the value of this approach when assessing supplier performance. There is often significant variance in the subjective ratings.

Weighted-Point System

This approach overcomes some of the subjectivity of the categorical system. A weighted-point system weighs and quantifies scores across different performance categories. This approach usually features higher reliability and moderate implementation costs.

Weighted-point systems are also flexible—users can change the weights assigned to each performance category or the performance categories themselves, depending on what is most important to the buying organization. For example, the performance categories and weights for an MRO distributor will likely differ from those for a supplier furnishing production components.

Several important issues must be understood regarding the use of weighted-point systems. First, users must carefully select the key performance categories to measure. Second, an organization must decide how to weight each performance category. Although assigning weights is subjective, an organization can reach consensus about how to weigh the performance categories through careful planning and involvement from different functions. Third, a set of decision rules must be in place to compare a

Exhibit 9.3 **Weighted-Point Supplier Measurement and Evaluation of Davis Industries for Third Quarter 2004**

PERFORMANCE CATEGORY	WEIGHT	SCORE	WEIGHTED SCORE
Delivery			
On time	.10	4	.4
Quantity	.10	3	.3
Quality			
Inbound shipment quality	.25	4	1.0
Quality improvement	.10	4	.4
Cost Competitiveness			
Comparison with other suppliers	.15	2	.3
Cost-reduction ideas submitted	.10	3	.3
Service Factors			
Problem resolution ability	.05	4	.2
Technical ability	.05	5	.25
Corrective action response	.05	3	.15
New-product development support	.05	5	.25
Total Rating			**3.55**

1 = Poor, 3 = Average, 5 = Excellent

supplier's performance against a predetermined objective to provide a score for each category.

Exhibit 9.3 illustrates a sample weighted-point system based on a five-point scale, where five is the highest possible score. The weighted-point plan should provide a higher level of objectivity for most performance categories and evaluate supplier performance in more detail compared with the categorical approach. Note that actual rating scales will be much more detailed than the one presented in this exhibit.

Cost-Based System

The most thorough and least subjective of the three measurement systems is the cost-based system. This approach seeks to quantify the total cost of doing business with a supplier, as the lowest purchase price is not always the lowest total cost for an item or service.

Most companies with information system capability can readily implement a cost-based supplier measurement system. The major challenge involves identifying and recording appropriate costs that result whenever a supplier fails to perform as expected. To use such a system, an organization must estimate or calculate the additional costs that result whenever a supplier underperforms. The basic logic of the system is the calculation of a supplier performance index (SPI). This index, with a base value of 1.0 that represents satisfactory performance, is a total cost index calculated for each item or commodity provided by a supplier:

$$\text{SPI} = (\text{Total Purchases} + \text{Nonperformance Costs})/\text{Total Purchases}$$

Exhibit 9.4 illustrates a total cost–based approach for supplier measurement. The cost-based approach can also include an assessment of qualitative service factors to provide a more complete picture of supplier performance. This exhibit compares the

Exhibit 9.4 Supplier Performance Comparison through First Quarter 2005

COMMODITY: INTEGRATED CIRCUIT

PART NUMBER	SUPPLIER	UNIT PRICE	SPI	TOTAL COST
04279884	Advanced Systems	$3.12	1.20	$3.74*
	BC Techtronics	$3.01	1.45	$4.36
	Micro Circuit	$3.10	1.30	$4.03
04341998	Advanced Systems	$5.75	1.20	$6.90*
	BC Techtronics	$5.40	1.45	$7.83
	Micro Circuit	$5.55	1.30	$7.21

Service Factor Ratings:

Advanced Systems	78%
BC Techtronics	76%
Micro Circuit	87%

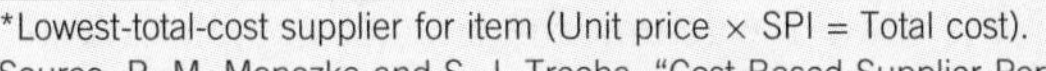

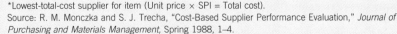

*Lowest-total-cost supplier for item (Unit price × SPI = Total cost).
Source: R. M. Monczka and S. J. Trecha, "Cost-Based Supplier Performance Evaluation," *Journal of Purchasing and Materials Management,* Spring 1988, 1–4.

Exhibit 9.5 Supplier Performance Report for First Quarter 2005

Supplier: Advanced Systems
Commodity: Integrated circuit
Total part numbers in commodity: 2

A. Total purchase dollars this quarter: $5,231.67

NONPERFORMANCE COSTS

EVENT	NUMBER OF OCCURRENCES	AVERAGE COST PER OCCURRENCE	EXTENDED COST
Late delivery	5	$150	$750
Return to supplier	2	$ 45	$ 90
Scrap labor costs	3	$ 30	$ 90
Material rework cost	1	$100	$100
B. Total nonperformance costs			$1,030
C. Purchase + nonperformance cost	(Line A + B)		$6,261.67
D. Supplier performance index	(Line C/A)		1.20
E. Service factor rating			78%

total cost of ownership (TCO) for each supplier for the two items in the integrated circuit category. It also compares suppliers on the basis of their service factor ratings. Note that the lowest-price supplier, BC Techtronics, is not the lowest-total-cost supplier when the costs of nonperformance are included. BC Techtronics also has a lower service rating score as compared with the other two suppliers.

Exhibit 9.5 summarizes supplier performance for a group of items comprising a single commodity. It details the total number of nonperformance occurrences, the cost of each event as identified by the buyer, and the total nonperformance cost for the quarter. Lines C and D include the figures required for the SPI calculation. Line E is the ratio of points earned to the total possible points for the qualitative or service factors.

In many cases, the actual cost per nonperformance event may be difficult to estimate or calculate, as the traditional cost accounting system is not designed to identify and capture such data. For instance, the average cost of a late delivery may vary widely, depending on its impact to the customer, potential lost sales, line shutdown costs, and so on. Therefore, many organizations get around this limitation by assigning a standard charge each time a nonperformance event occurs.

The SPI sometimes provides an incomplete or misleading assessment of supplier performance. For example, consider a supplier that delivers $100,000 of material, with one late delivery charged at $5,000. That supplier will have an SPI of ($100,000 + $5,000)/$100,000, or 1.05. This SPI appears more favorable than that of a supplier that delivers only $30,000 of material and has one late delivery, and that also charged at $5,000. The second supplier has an SPI of ($30,000 + $5,000)/$30,000, or 1.17. Although both suppliers committed the same infraction, the smaller supplier received a

Exhibit 9.6 Supplier Performance Index Calculation with Q Adjustment Factor

Q is a normalization factor that eliminates high-dollar lot biases.

Q = (Average cost of a lot of material for an individual supplier)/(Average cost of a lot of material for all suppliers)

Consider the following information for Suppliers A, B, and C, each with a single late delivery nonconformance calculated at $4,000.

Assume the average cost of all lots for suppliers of this commodity is $2,500.

	SUPPLIER A	SUPPLIER B	SUPPLIER C
3rd quarter shipments	20 lots @ $500 each	20 lots @ 1,000 each	20 lots @ $10,000
Total value of shipments	$10,000	$20,000	$200,000
Average lot cost	$500	$1,000	$10,000
Nonconformance charges	Late delivery $4,000	Late delivery $4,000	Late delivery $4,000
3rd Quarter SPI	**($10,000 + $4,000)/ $10,000 = 1.40**	**($20,000 + $4,000)/ $20,000 = 1.20**	**($200,000 + $4,000)/ $200,000 = 1.02**
Average cost of a lot from all suppliers	$2,500	$2,500	$2,500
Q calculation	$500/$2,500 = .2	$1,000/$2,500 = .4	$10,000/$2,500 = 4

Notice how different the SPI values are for the three suppliers, even though they each committed the same nonconformance. Supplier C, due to the high lot bias, has the lowest SPI.

SPI calculation with Q adjustment = Cost of material + (Nonconformance costs × Q factor)/Cost of material

Supplier A: $10,000 + ($4,000 × .2)/$10,000 = 1.08

Supplier B: $20,000 + ($4,000 × .4)/$20,000 = 1.08

Supplier C: $200,000 + ($4,000 × 4)/$200,000 = 1.08

The Q adjustment now allows a fair comparison.

comparatively more severe penalty relative to purchase volume. A normalization adjustment (Q) is required to eliminate a bias that favors higher-dollar-volume suppliers. Exhibit 9.6 illustrates how to calculate an SPI with the Q adjustment factor, which allows an "apples-to-apples" comparison between suppliers.

Management has many uses for the data derived from a comprehensive cost-based supplier measurement system. Such a system provides necessary information that a buyer may need to justify buying from a preferred supplier despite a higher unit price. The system also allows a buyer to communicate the cost of specific nonperformance occurrences to a supplier, which then helps identify improvement opportunities. Quantifying nonperformance costs can also result in a chargeback to the offending supplier for unplanned costs. Finally, a buyer can use this data to identify longer-term sources of supply based on a supplier's total cost performance history.

Each of the three types of measurement approaches featured in this chapter, although differing in their complexity and scope of use, raises a buyer's awareness about supply base performance. Supplier measurement is a powerful tool for managing and increasing the capabilities of the supply base.

Sourcing Snapshot

McDonald's Takes Supplier Measurement Seriously

To measure supplier performance, McDonald's (Oak Brook, IL) recently employed a supplier relationship management (SRM) process to its global technology buy. According to Joseph Youssef, McDonald's SRM strategy "requires dedicated supply managers, effective processes to create standardized best practices, and tools to track and evaluate the results." Youssef also indicates that an organization must manage its supply base through effective performance measurement and then make supplier-related decisions using the outputs of those measurements. He outlines four prime measurements that organizations should consider in their supplier performance management systems. The first area includes day-to-day tactical measurements such as quality, service, responsiveness, and delivery performance. The second measurement focuses on contract management: making sure that previously agreed-to contractual arrangements are followed. The third area measured is financial management. Measurements in this area track to see that accurate invoices are submitted in a timely manner and for the agreed-upon products and services. Lastly, the fourth measurement centers on the buyer-supplier relationship and the level of two-way communication between the parties.

Source: Adapted from W. Forrest, "McDonald's Applies SRM Strategy to Global Technology Buy," *Purchasing,* September 7, 2006, p. 16.

Rationalization and Optimization: Creating a Manageable Supply Base

Effective supplier management and development begins by determining an optimal number of suppliers that an organization should maintain. Supply base rationalization is the process of identifying how many and which suppliers a buyer will maintain. Supply base optimization involves an analysis of the supply base to ensure that only the most capable suppliers are kept in the supply base as it is rationalized. It often involves eliminating those suppliers that are unwilling or incapable of achieving supply management performance objectives, either currently or expected in the near future.

Supply base rationalization and optimization should be a continuous process. The elimination of both marginal and small-purchase-volume suppliers is usually the first phase of the rationalization process. Subsequent optimization requires the replacement of good suppliers with better-performing suppliers or initiating supplier development projects with existing suppliers to improve performance. Organizations must develop supplier evaluation and measurement systems to identify the best-performing suppliers and then develop stronger business relationships with those suppliers. Oftentimes, companies must search worldwide for the best suppliers.

During the early phases of supply base rationalization and optimization, the process usually results in an absolute reduction in the total number of suppliers. Reduction, however, may not always be the result for every family or group of purchased items. The key is to determine the right number of suppliers, not just arbitrarily cut down on the number. For example, a truck assembly plant in Michigan received tires and wheels from separate suppliers. OEM employees mounted and balanced the tires on the wheels inside the assembly plant in a labor- and space-intensive operation. The buyer established a new supplier near the assembly plant that then received both the tires and wheels, and assembled, balanced, and stored the wheel assemblies until shipping them to the assembly plant on a just-in-time basis. Although the company added an additional supplier to its supply base, overall system efficiency increased, and total cost declined. In this example, the optimization process resulted in the net addition of a supplier.

Advantages of a Rationalized and Optimized Supply Base

Supply base rationalization and optimization should result in real improvements in cost, quality, delivery, and information sharing between buyer and supplier. Because the process identifies the best suppliers in terms of number and quality, the remaining suppliers are often capable of performing additional tasks that improve performance or add value to the buyer-supplier relationship. Suppliers in an optimized supply base often develop longer-term relationships with buyers, which can lead to further joint improvement efforts.

Buying from World-Class Suppliers

Because of the correlation between supplier performance and supply chain success, it is not difficult to see why choosing and maintaining only the best suppliers supports higher performance throughout the supply chain. Instead of being responsible for literally hundreds or thousands of suppliers, supply management can concentrate on developing closer relationships with a smaller core group of qualified suppliers. The benefits of doing business with world-class suppliers include fewer quality and delivery problems, access to leading-edge technology, opportunities to develop collaborative relationships, and a lower product cost as supply management and engineering gain key supplier input during new-product development.

Use of Full-Service Suppliers

The remaining suppliers in a rationalized and optimized supply base are often larger on average and highly capable of offering a broad range of value-adding services. When a buyer uses full-service suppliers, it expects to reap substantial benefits in the form of access to the supplier's engineering, research and development, design, testing, production, service, and tooling capabilities. The full-service supplier approach places a greater burden on a supplier to manage an entire system of components, activities, and services, as well as to effectively manage its own supply base. The full-service supplier can also perform complete design and build work instead of the buyer performing the work internally or using several different suppliers in an uncoordinated effort.

The automobile industry provides many examples of how full-service suppliers can provide these benefits. For example, all vehicles have extensive electrical wiring systems. Traditionally, automobile manufacturers designed each individual wiring harness internally and sent the design specifications to suppliers through a competitive bidding process. It was not uncommon to have 10 different suppliers working on wiring systems for final assembly into a vehicle. Now, a single supplier, or only a few suppliers, might design and produce the entire wiring system for a new vehicle throughout the entire model life cycle. The result is lower cost, improved quality, and reduced product development time. Because of its expertise, a supplier can design the wiring systems concurrently with the overall design of the car, reducing concept-to-customer cycle time.

Reduction of Supply Base Risk

At first glance, it seems illogical that using fewer suppliers can result in reduced supply base risk. **Risk** can be defined as the magnitude of exposure to financial loss or operational disruption and stems from uncertainty. What if the single or sole source for a critical item goes on strike or has a fire at its production facility, disrupting its production process and ability to maintain an uninterrupted flow of materials? Historically, the risk of supply disruption has been the primary argument against supply base reduction or single-sourcing of purchased items.

Many buyers have now concluded that, if they select suppliers carefully and develop close and collaborative working relationships with fewer suppliers, supply risk can actually decrease. Risk does not only include supply disruption. Other supply risks include poor supplier quality, poor delivery performance, or overpaying for items due to a noncompetitive sourcing situation. However, maintaining multiple suppliers for each item can actually increase the probability and level of risk. Having more suppliers for individual items creates the opportunity for increased product variability or inconsistent quality across the supply chain.

Lower Supply Base Administrative Costs

Buyers interact with their suppliers in many ways. Examples include contacting suppliers about design and material specifications, communicating quality and other performance requirements, negotiating purchase contracts, visiting and evaluating supplier facilities and processes, providing feedback about supplier performance, collaborating with suppliers when problems occur, requesting supplier input about product design, contacting suppliers regarding engineering change orders, and transmitting material releases. These activities all have associated costs in terms of time, effort, and potential for miscommunication. For example, the administrative cost of maintaining 5,000 suppliers will be dramatically higher than the cost of maintaining a core group of 500 highly qualified suppliers. Furthermore, highly qualified suppliers require fewer problem-related interactions with the buyer. The best contacts between a buyer and seller are those that add value to the relationship rather than merely resolve problems.

Lower Total Product Cost

During the 1980s, buyers recognized the real cost of maintaining multiple suppliers for each sourced item. Acquisition and operating costs increased as a result of greater variability in product quality and delivery and smaller production volumes offered to each supplier, which did nothing to spread out the supplier's fixed costs over higher output levels. Short-term purchase contracts that award small volumes of business to multiple suppliers only increase production costs and provide no incentive for investments in process improvement. It became evident that, if fewer suppliers received larger-volume contracts, the resulting economies of scale would lower production and distribution costs. Supply base rationalization and optimization provides the opportunity to achieve lower total product costs by awarding larger volumes to fewer suppliers.

Ability to Pursue Complex Supply Management Strategies

Implementing complex supply management strategies requires a rationalized and optimized supply base. The need for more complicated activities with suppliers requires a reduced supply base due to higher levels of two-way interactions between a buyer and seller. Examples of complex supply management strategies include supplier development, early supplier design involvement, just-in-time sourcing, and the development of cost-based pricing agreements with suppliers.

Possible Risks of Maintaining Fewer Suppliers

Few supply management executives would argue in favor of maintaining multiple suppliers for every purchased item. Currently, the debate centers on maintaining a limited number of qualified suppliers for major items versus using a single source. Some organizations believe using several suppliers for a purchased item promotes and maintains a healthy level of competition between suppliers. Others, however, believe that a single source can still deliver cost and quality improvements over the life of a contract if a buyer manages that supplier appropriately. Although most buyers recognize the benefits of supply base rationalization and optimization, there are still potential risks from relying on a smaller supply base.

Supplier Dependency

Some buyers fear that a supplier can become too dependent on the buyer for its economic survival. This situation can easily occur if a buyer combines its total purchase volumes for an item with a single supplier. A smaller supplier with limited capacity may need to eliminate some existing customers in order to meet the increased requirements of its larger customer. As a result, the supplier may become too dependent on a buyer for its financial well-being. If, for some reason, the buyer no longer requires a particular item, the overly dependent supplier may no longer be financially viable. Although supply base optimization can lead to a beneficial mutual commitment between buyer and seller, it can also result in an unhealthy dependence of one party on the other.

Absence of Competition

By relying on only one or a limited number of suppliers, some buyers fear losing the advantages of a competitive marketplace. A supplier may hold the buyer hostage by unduly raising its prices or becoming too complacent. The more difficult and expensive it is to change suppliers (e.g., higher switching costs), the more likely this scenario becomes. However, organizations with substantial supply base optimization experience argue that careful supplier selection and the development of equitable contracts that address continuous improvement requirements should prevent an over-reliance on suppliers that try to take advantage of a single-source situation.

Supply Disruption

Supply disruption is a potential risk when sourcing from a single-location supplier. In 1999, a major earthquake in Taiwan disrupted the supply of computer chips in the global semiconductor industry. Chip fabrication plants were shut down for several days, and the normal level of output was curtailed for several weeks. Customers reacted by hoarding chip inventories and reducing their production of finished goods. Suppliers not affected by the quake increased their prices, resulting in a ripple effect throughout the electronics industry.[2] Likewise, labor strikes, fires, acts of nature, production or quality problems, or disruption within the supplier's own supply base can disrupt the smooth flow of materials through a supply chain. Buyers can minimize this risk by sourcing from a single supplier with multiple production facilities. For example, Dell Computer utilizes multiple sourcing for many of the key components that go into its notebook computers manufactured in Asia. If a disruption or lack of capacity occurs at one supplier's facility, Dell can quickly shift its sourcing to another facility from the same supplier or to a different supplier.[3]

Another method for minimizing supply disruption risk is to select suppliers with multiple capabilities—the practice of cross-sourcing. Here, a buyer selects or develops suppliers with multiple or redundant capabilities. If problems occur with a primary source of supply for an item, the secondary supplier, which is the supplier for another purchased item, then assumes ownership of the sourcing process. This approach requires identifying suppliers capable of producing different items or performing multiple functions throughout the production process.

Overaggressive Supply Reduction

However, buyers can move too aggressively when reducing the supply base. If this occurs, the remaining suppliers may not have adequate capacity to meet purchase requirements if demand increases substantially. This happened when a major producer of hand tools developed a wide array of products that used rechargeable nickel-cadmium batteries. The supplier found that it did not have adequate manufacturing capacity to support new-product requirements for these batteries. In this case, supply base optimization required the company to qualify new sources rather quickly. As part of the supply base optimization process, the buyer must ensure that it carefully evaluates the remaining suppliers' capacity to produce larger volumes or develop other suppliers to cover the increased volumes.

Formal Approaches to Supply Base Rationalization

In his discussion of strategic supply management, Keki Bhote offers several possible supply base reduction methods.[4] Bhote's framework contains three primary elements: (1) phasing out current suppliers, (2) selection of finalist suppliers, and (3) selection of partnership suppliers. This section focuses on several methods commonly used to rationalize the supply base.

Twenty/Eighty Rule

This approach identifies those 20% of suppliers receiving the bulk of purchase spend or that minority of suppliers that cause the most quality problems. Purchase spend and supplier quality are two possible decision criteria used to identify suppliers for elimination. Organizations often use this approach when they require a rapid reduction in the number of suppliers. A disadvantage to the 20/80 approach is the possible elimination of otherwise capable suppliers simply because they received fewer purchase dollars. This approach assumes the best suppliers receive the majority of the purchase dollars, which may not necessarily be true. In addition, the buyer may exclude suppliers with needed capabilities that are not currently utilized.

Exhibit 9.7 Supply Base Optimization and Development

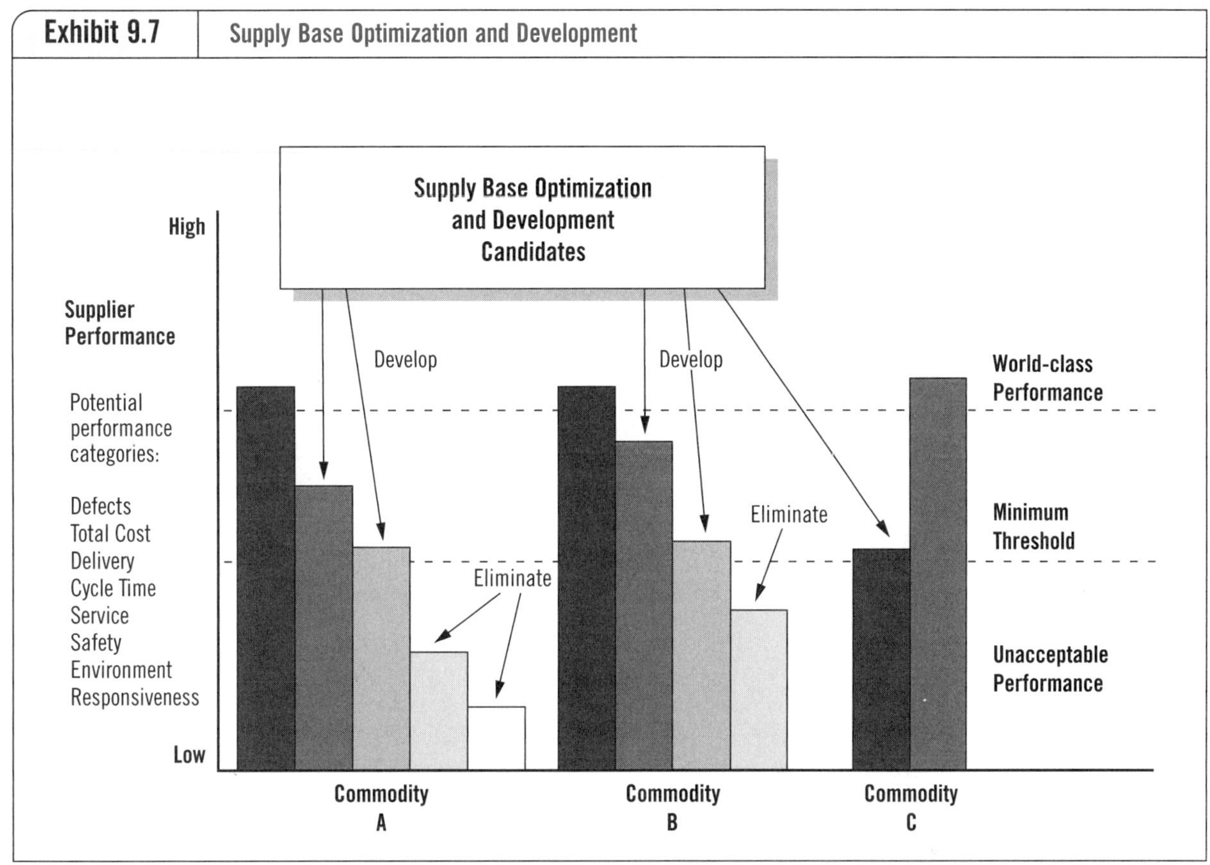

"Improve or Else" Approach

This approach provides all suppliers, regardless of their performance history, a chance to remain in the supply base. It involves notifying suppliers that they have a specified period of time in which to meet new performance requirements—from improved quality levels and delivery performance to lead time and cost reductions, or any other key performance indicator. Suppliers that fall short of expectations may soon become ex-suppliers. Although this approach has the potential for driving rapid performance improvement in the supply base, it can also be a heavy-handed way of dealing with suppliers. For example, this was the approach that General Motors' chief purchasing officer, J. Ignacio Lopez de Arriortua, used in 1992 by demanding that GM's suppliers reduce their prices by 3 to 22% or risk losing their existing supply contracts.[5]

Triage Approach

This approach requires the systematic evaluation of the performance of individual suppliers and placement into one of three categories. The first category, and most likely the largest, includes those suppliers that are marginal performers or otherwise incapable of meeting purchase performance requirements, now or in the future. The buyer targets these suppliers for immediate removal from the supply base. The second category includes those suppliers that do not consistently meet purchase requirements in all areas but demonstrate sufficient improvement potential. The most promising of these suppliers are often targets for supplier assistance and development. The third category includes those high-quality, capable suppliers requiring no improvement assistance. These suppliers are candidates for more collaborative buyer-seller relationships, which may include offering longer-term contracts in exchange for continuous improvement, as well as being considered for an alliance. The distribution of suppliers across these categories may vary across industries.

Exhibit 9.7 on p. 321 illustrates one company's triage approach to supplier reduction. This company compares suppliers against various performance criteria and segments the supply base into three groups: unacceptable performers, suppliers that meet minimum requirements but are not world class, and world-class performers worthy of closer relationships.

Competency Staircase Approach

This method requires suppliers to successfully navigate a succession of performance milestones or hurdles in order to remain in the supply base. First, all suppliers must meet a buyer's basic quality standards for consideration as potential suppliers. Suppliers must then pass a series of hurdles analogous to climbing a staircase. Each hurdle brings the supplier one step closer to its ultimate goal of remaining in the buyer's supply base.

The next hurdle may be a supplier's ability to meet a buyer's technical specifications and product performance requirements. Subsequent hurdles can include demonstrating sustained production competency, delivery capability (such as just-in-time requirements), willingness to share information, supplier size, and physical proximity to the buyer. Note that different purchase requirements will present varying sets of hurdles. Each hurdle results in fewer and fewer suppliers remaining in the supply base. The result is a strong and flexible supply base comprised of highly capable and motivated suppliers.

Summary of Supplier Rationalization and Optimization

Several conclusions about supplier rationalization and optimization can now be made. First, there are a variety of approaches to supply base rationalization and optimization. This chapter provides only a select sample of those approaches. Furthermore, an organization can combine more than one approach to meet its supply base reduction goals. Second, we do not have to limit our evaluation only to suppliers currently in the supply base. A buyer should always be open to the possibility of adding new suppliers if their use makes good business sense. Third, the benefits of supply base rationalization and optimization are real, whereas the potential drawbacks are manageable.

Supply base rationalization and optimization constitutes a critical first step toward the effective management and development of the supply base. It is difficult to manage many suppliers as efficiently as a small core group of suppliers, just as it is challenging to pursue progressive supply management strategies with too many suppliers. A large supply base also means the duplication of a wide range of supply management activities, adding to acquisition cost without a corresponding increase in value added. Finally, supplier rationalization and optimization is a continuing activity. Almost half of the companies participating in a 2000 survey reduced their supply base by 20%, and almost 15% reduced their supply base between 20 and 60% over the last

Sourcing Snapshot

Raytheon Relies on Supplier Development as a Strategic Initiative

Assuming responsibility for supply chain management at Raytheon, one of the country's largest industrial companies, Shelley Stewart Jr. brought to the job a wealth of experience in strategic sourcing, electronic commerce, and supplier diversity activities. The initiatives that he introduced or expanded at Raytheon include the following:

- Introduction of a single process for strategic sourcing for use across all Raytheon businesses
- Companywide deployment of a process for sourcing indirect materials using teams and consortiums
- Application of Raytheon's Six Sigma quality initiative to the company's supplier development effort
- Companywide adoption of the aerospace and defense industries' e-procurement exchange, Exostar, as well as FreeMarkets' reverse auction process
- Creation of a leadership development program
- Enhancement of the company's supplier diversity programs

In keeping with Raytheon's corporate goals, Stewart's organization is applying Six Sigma quality approaches to the company's supplier development activities. He has also assembled a network of Raytheon Six Sigma champions to work directly with suppliers. The Raytheon process for supplier development has six steps:

1. Identify supplier candidates for projects.
2. Define objectives and resources.
3. Baseline the opportunities and rank.
4. Analyze selected opportunities.
5. Implement projects.
6. Document and realize improvements.

When identifying suppliers, Stewart says he does not want his organization to select only suppliers "that are broken. We think we can work Six Sigma with suppliers at the higher end as well as the low end. On the other hand, I don't want suppliers to think we are using it just to attack the small and mid-size suppliers. We are going to use it across the supplier base. Six Sigma is a continuous-improvement or problem-solving tool, and all relationships have problems." Stewart says he is looking to identify not only the right suppliers for the process but also the right projects within those suppliers.

Another area where Raytheon is committed to improvement is its use of disadvantaged suppliers, some of whom are ideal candidates for supplier development. As a company, Raytheon has a series of comprehensive goals for small, women- and minority-owned supplier businesses.

For women owners of small businesses, the company held a Women's Business Forum that linked women business owners with female executives within Raytheon. Through the initiative, "we developed corporate relationships through which our executives mentored the women small business leaders. As we rationalize our supplier base, we don't want to leave some of these businesses behind," says Stewart. "So, we are bringing them along with us." To this end, his supply chain organization has a good record of creating opportunity for small businesses.

Source: Adapted from S. Avery, "Linking Supply Chains Saves Raytheon $400 Million," *Purchasing,* August 23, 2001, p. 27.

several years. Furthermore, three quarters of firms indicate they now commit 80% of their total purchase dollars with fewer than 100 suppliers.[6]

Supplier Development: A Strategy for Improvement

The first documented applications of supplier development came from Toyota, Nissan, and Honda, some as early as 1939. Toyota's *1939 Purchasing Rules* discussed the need to treat its suppliers as an integral part of Toyota and to work together to improve their collective performance. Nissan implemented its first supplier development efforts in 1963, with Honda joining the club as a result of the first Arab oil embargo in 1973.[7] However, the rest of the world has been slow to take up the supplier development banner.[8] Even the United Nations has recognized the need for supplier development; its *Guide to Supplier Development* is designed to improve the skills, capacities, and competitiveness of global industrial subcontracting and partnership exchanges.[9]

Although the concept was mentioned in several early purchasing books, early North American writings on supplier development began in earnest with researcher Michiel Leenders.[10] As broadly defined by a number of authors, supplier development is any activity undertaken by a buyer to improve a supplier's performance or capabilities to meet the buyer's short- and long-term supply needs. Organizations rely on a variety of activities to improve supplier performance, including sharing technology, providing incentives to suppliers for improved performance, promoting

Exhibit 9.8 Process for Implementation of Supplier Development Strategy

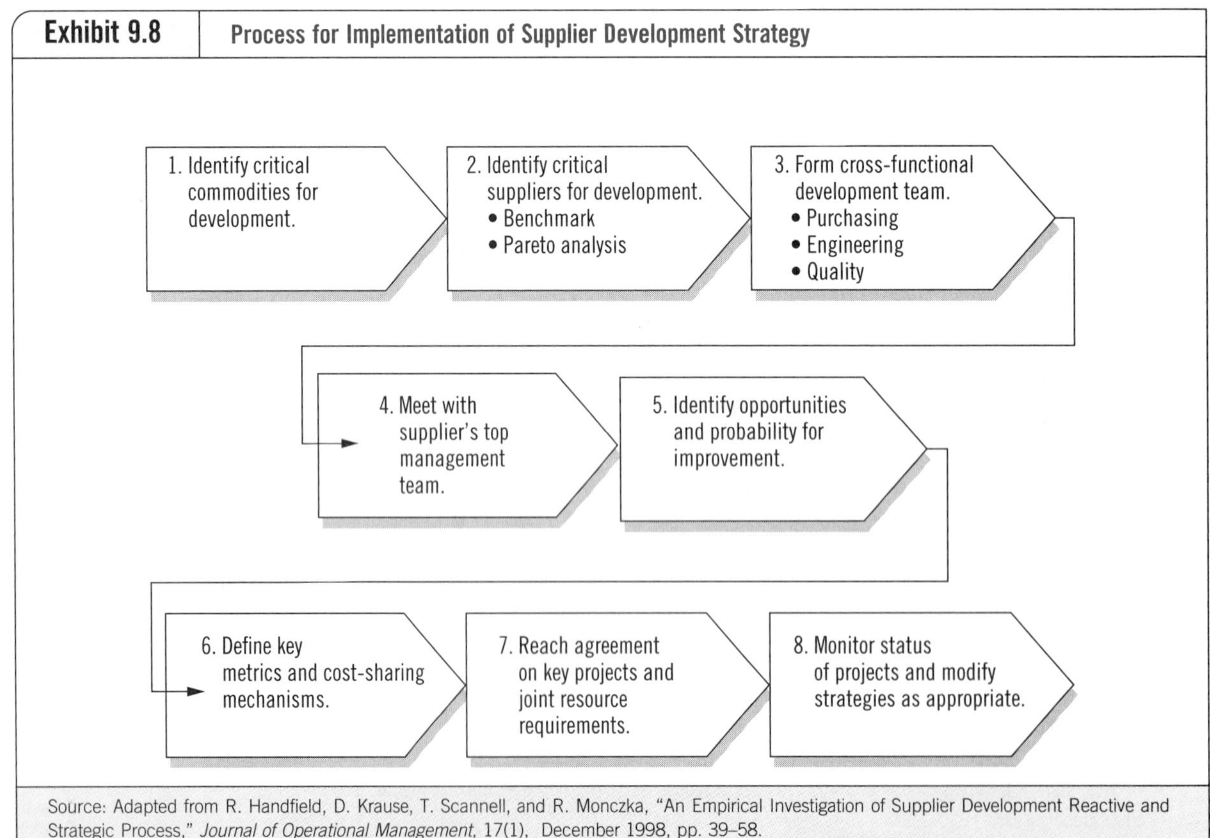

Source: Adapted from R. Handfield, D. Krause, T. Scannell, and R. Monczka, "An Empirical Investigation of Supplier Development Reactive and Strategic Process," *Journal of Operational Management,* 17(1), December 1998, pp. 39–58.

competition among suppliers, providing necessary capital, and directly involving its personnel with suppliers through activities such as training and process improvement.[11]

Direct involvement in a supplier's operations by buyer personnel is undoubtedly the most challenging part of any supplier development process. Not only must internal management and employees be convinced that investing scarce company resources in an outside supplier's operation is a worthwhile risk, but the supplier must be convinced it is in its own best interest to accept direction and assistance. Too often, the supplier is convinced that the only reason a buyer wants to engage in supplier development is to pressure the supplier to pass along all of the savings generated by reducing its price. Even if a mutual understanding of the importance of supplier development is reached, there is still the matter of implementation and allocation of needed resources by both parties, as well as ensuring that the implementation is maintained over time. Effective supplier development requires the commitment of financial capital and human resources, skilled personnel, timely and accurate information sharing, and performance measurement.

A Process Map for Supplier Development

After reviewing the strategies for more than 60 organizations, we have developed a generic process map for deploying a supplier development initiative, as shown in Exhibit 9.8.[12] Although many organizations have successfully deployed the first four stages of the process, some have been less successful in implementing the latter four stages.

Step 1—Identify Critical Commodities for Development

Not all organizations must pursue supplier development. An organization may already be sourcing from world-class suppliers due to its existing strategic supplier selection processes, or it may buy external inputs only in a very small proportion to total costs or sales. Therefore, supply managers must analyze their own individual sourcing situations to determine if a particular supplier's level of performance warrants development, and if so, which specific commodities and services will require attention.

Senior supply managers should thoroughly consider the following questions to determine if a given supplier warrants development effort.[13] A "yes" response to a majority of these questions suggests a need for supplier development.

- Do externally purchased products and services account for more than 50% of product or service value?
- Is the supplier an existing or potential source of competitive advantage?
- Do you currently purchase or plan to purchase on the basis of total cost versus initial purchase price?
- Can existing suppliers meet your competitive needs five years from now?
- Do you need suppliers to be more responsive to your needs?
- Are you willing and able to become more responsive to your suppliers' needs?
- Do you plan to treat suppliers as partners in your business?
- Do you plan to develop and maintain open and trusting relations with your suppliers?

A corporate-level executive steering committee should then develop an assessment of the relative importance of all purchased goods and services to identify where to focus any supplier development efforts. The result of this assessment is a portfolio analysis of those critical products or services that are essential for marketplace success. This discussion is an extension of the company's overall corporate-level strategic planning process and must include participants from other critical functions affected by sourcing decisions, including finance, sales and marketing, information technology, accounting, engineering, production, and design.

Step 2—Identify Critical Suppliers for Development

The supply base performance assessment system helps identify those suppliers within a commodity group that would be targeted for development. A common approach involves a routine analysis of current supplier performance. As shown in Exhibit 9.7, leading companies regularly monitor supplier performance on a facility-by-facility basis and rank suppliers from best to worst. Suppliers failing to meet predetermined minimum performance standards in quality, delivery, cycle time, late deliveries, total cost, service, safety, or environmental compliance are potential candidates for elimination from the supply base. If the supplier's product or service is essential, it should be considered for supplier development. Those suppliers that meet minimum requirements but do not provide world-class performance are the most likely candidates for development efforts. Benchmarking and Pareto analysis are two sourcing tools that can assist in the identification of possible supplier development targets.

Step 3—Form Cross-Functional Development Team

Before approaching suppliers and asking for improved performance, it is critical to develop cross-functional consensus and support from within for the initiative. Supply management executives continually emphasize that supply base improvement begins from within through buyer-focused activities—that is, the buying company must have its own house in order before expecting commitment and cooperation from suppliers. Development teams typically include members from engineering, operations, quality, and supply management.

Step 4—Meet with Supplier's Top Management Team

Once the development team's charter is established and an appropriate supplier has been identified for improvement, the team should approach the supplier's top management team and establish three relational building blocks for seeking supplier improvement: strategic alignment, measurement, and professionalism. Strategic alignment requires a business and technology alignment between the companies. It also requires alignment about key customer needs throughout the supply chain. Measurement requires an objective means of accurately assessing development results and progress in a timely manner. By approaching the supplier's top management with a solid and mutually beneficial business case for improvement, the demonstrated professionalism of all parties helps to establish a positive tone, reinforce collaboration, foster two-way communication, and develop mutual trust.

Step 5—Identify Opportunities and Probability for Improvement

At these meetings with the supplier's senior management, supply management executives should identify areas earmarked for improvement. Companies adopting a strategic approach to supply base development can usually agree upon the areas for improvement. In some cases, such areas are driven by final customer requirements and expectations.

Step 6—Define Key Metrics and Cost-Sharing Mechanisms

Development opportunities, although not necessarily specific improvement projects, are evaluated next in terms of project feasibility and potential return on investment. The parties jointly determine if the opportunities for improvement are realistic and achievable and, if so, then establish measures and improvement goals. The buyer and seller must also agree on how to divide or share the costs and benefits from the development project. A common sharing arrangement is 50/50, but the actual cost/benefit sharing must take each party's level of investment into consideration.

Step 7—Reach Agreement on Key Projects and Joint Resource Requirements

After identifying specific improvement projects to pursue, the parties must identify the resources necessary to carry out the project or development effort and make the commitment to employ them. The parties also need to reach agreement regarding the specific measures and metrics that will demonstrate success. These measures may include a defined percentage improvement in cost savings, quality, delivery or cycle time, or any other area relevant to supply chain performance. The most critical component of supplier development is that it must contain realistic and visible milestones and time horizons for improvement. What gets measured is usually what gets accomplished. The agreement should also specify the role of each party, who is responsible for the outcomes of the project, and the manner and timing for deploying already agreed-upon resources.

Step 8—Monitor Status of Projects and Modify Strategies as Appropriate

Progress must be monitored routinely after initiating a development project. Moreover, an ongoing, two-way exchange of information is needed to maintain project momentum. This can be achieved by creating visible milestones for objectives, posting progress, and creating new or revised objectives based on actual progress. Ongoing project management may require modifying the original plan, applying additional resources, developing new information, or refocusing priorities depending on events.

Supplier Development Efforts That Sometimes Don't Work

Evidence indicates that supplier development projects work—at least some of the time. Exhibit 9.9 on p. 328 presents the results of a comprehensive study of supplier development efforts and clearly indicates that, although there is no guarantee that comparable supplier development efforts will be equally successful, on average the development process produces substantial results. This does not mean that there are no barriers and challenges to successful supplier development. In fact, other studies have found these barriers to be very real. The next section describes some of the proven techniques and tools used by leading-edge companies to address the problems or barriers that may contribute to less-than-desired supplier development effectiveness.

Exhibit 9.9 Supplier Development Results

CRITERIA	BEFORE SUPPLIER DEVELOPMENT	AFTER SUPPLIER DEVELOPMENT
Incoming defects	11.65%	5.45%
% on-time delivery	79.85%	91.02%
Cycle time (from order placement to receipt, inclusively)	35.74 days	23.44 days
% orders received complete	85.47%	93.33%

Source: Krause, 1997, Survey of 527 firms.
Respondents: ISM members.

Overcoming the Barriers to Supplier Development

Barriers to supplier development fall into three classifications: (1) buyer-specific barriers, (2) buyer-supplier interface barriers, and (3) supplier-specific barriers. Companies can use a variety of approaches to overcome barriers to supplier development. In general, these approaches fall into one of three categories:

- Direct-involvement activities (hands-on): Companies often send their own personnel in to assist suppliers. These efforts are characterized as hands-on activities, where the buyer's representatives are directly involved in correcting supplier problems and increasing capabilities. An example would be the buyer assigning one of its process engineers to the supplier's facility to assist in physically rearranging its equipment to be more efficient.
- Incentives and rewards (the "carrot"): Companies also use incentives to encourage suppliers to improve, largely by means of their own efforts. For example, a buyer might agree to increase future order volumes if the desired performance improvement takes place within a specific time, or it could hold an annual award ceremony to recognize the best suppliers.
- Warnings and penalties (the "stick"): In some cases, companies may withhold potential future business if a supplier's performance is deemed unacceptable or if a lack of improvement is evident. Buyers may also use a competitive marketplace to provide a viable threat or incentive to a poorly performing supplier.

In many cases, organizations employ a combination of these three strategies to drive supplier improvement as quickly as possible, applying them judiciously in response to a particular supplier's capabilities and needs. The following sections address barriers to supplier development that are internal, external, or interface based, and provide examples of how leading companies overcome these barriers.

Buyer-Specific Barriers

A buying company will not engage in supplier development unless senior management recognizes the need for or the benefits to be gained from an investment in supplier development. Moreover, if supply management personnel have not already rationalized and optimized its supply base as discussed above, the volume of purchases with any particular supplier will likely not justify the joint investment. In addition, there may be a lack of top-level support for financing supplier development efforts in terms of both dollars and time.

Sourcing Snapshot

Guess Who's Getting into Supplier Development? The U.S. Air Force!

In the late 1990s, the Manufacturing Technology Division (ManTech) of the U.S. Air Force convened a meeting of 30 high-level supply management officials from various aerospace and defense organizations to discuss plans for supply base development. The meeting was an early step in a major ManTech initiative (dubbed the SME Initiative) that set a goal for prime and subprime Air Force contractors to foster improvements among the small- or medium-sized enterprises (SMEs) within their supply base. Underpinning the SME Initiative has been research by a ManTech team indicating that up to 80% of production for most weapons systems is now performed by suppliers, many of which are small- or medium-sized companies.

A study by the ManTech team identified a set of practices that better companies employed with their suppliers (listed in order of popularity):

1. Supplier training
2. Supplier rating, certification, and awards
3. Making customer technical expertise available to suppliers
4. Integrated customer/supplier teams to reduce supplier process waste and solve supplier problems
5. Supplier symposia and suggestion programs
6. Supplier continuous improvement programs
7. Supplier access to customer's volume discount rates
8. Structured methodology for problem solving
9. Integrated customer/supplier technology roadmaps
10. Customer development of a supplier's capability prior to outsourcing.

Under the SME Initiative, ManTech identifies critical small suppliers for direct development by either themselves or third-party consultants and incentives for prime contractors and subsystem producers to pursue supplier development policies. The U.S. Air Force knows that supplier development is essential to the success of future weapons programs.

Source: Adapted from "Air Force Pushes Its Supplier Development Program Forward," *Purchasing,* May 6, 1999, pp. 34–37.

Barrier: The Buying Company's Purchase Volume from the Supplier Does Not Justify Development Investment

Solution: Standardization and single-sourcing. Parts standardization across several product lines is a way to increase total order volumes with suppliers, which may justify a development investment. For example, IBM's Networking Hardware Division, which produces customized networking solutions for customers, is constantly striving to increase its parts commonality. Currently, over 50% of purchased components for major hardware projects contain unique items. If IBM personnel believe that using customized components will provide a market advantage, they will continue to use them. However, standardization remains an important way to leverage worldwide purchase volume and shorten new-product development cycles.

Concurrent with component standardization, many supply managers also plan to reduce their supply base, wherever possible, to achieve economies of scope and scale. Daewoo Corporation, for example, uses single-sourcing wherever possible, relying on two or more suppliers only in situations with high potential for labor disputes. Similarly, NCR, Doosan Corporation of Korea, Honda of America Manufacturing, and Rover currently use single-sourcing or are planning to move in that direction.

Barrier: No Immediate Benefit to Supplier Development Is Evident to the Buying Organization

Solution: Pursue small wins. Varity Perkins, a producer of diesel engines used in automotive and construction vehicles, found its initial supplier development efforts to be relatively unsuccessful. This resulted in lowered internal expectations and dampened enthusiasm for future development efforts. However, Varity personnel realized that part of the problem was that they were trying to accomplish too much. Thus, the company focused on a smaller group of suppliers for kaizen (or continuous improvement) efforts to gain a series of small wins and build momentum. Varity's kaizen approach achieved incremental improvements that ultimately gained renewed internal commitment for the supplier development process.

Barrier: Importance of Purchased Item Does Not Justify Development Efforts

Solution: Take a longer-term focus. Solectron, a contract manufacturer in the computer industry, has a competitive strategy that relies heavily on its supply chain management competencies. The company looks beyond the price of purchased inputs and examines how its most important suppliers affect the quality and technology of its products. Solectron expects its suppliers to provide designs offering integrated solutions that Solectron engineers can use in future product designs. Total cost and long-term strategic impact help justify ongoing investment in suppliers.

Barrier: Lack of Executive Support within the Buying Organization for Supplier Development

Solution: Prove the benefits. Support for supplier development is gained when management becomes convinced that the company can improve if supplier performance improves. For companies spending nearly 80% of their cost of goods sold on purchased inputs, such an argument is easy to make. For companies with lower percentages of purchased content, the argument may be more difficult. Proving a direct relationship between supplier improvement and increased profits can be difficult to achieve; someone within the supply management organization must document that outcome. Managers also note that efforts to optimize their companies' supply bases, combined with part standardization, can help free up scarce resources over the long term, making supplier development more palatable to internal skeptics. In addition, the total cost approach to supplier performance measurement should also prove to be an effective communication tool for demonstrating the deleterious effects of poor supplier performance. However, many companies still view supplier development resources simply as additional overhead costs rather than needed investment in supply chain performance.

Buyer-Supplier Interface Barriers

Barriers to supplier development may also originate in the interface between the buyer and supplier in areas such as open communication, alignment of organizational cultures, and trust. A reluctance to share sensitive information about costs and processes on the part of either buyer or supplier is one of the more significant interface barriers.

Barrier: Supplier Is Reluctant to Share Information on Costs or Processes

Solution: Create a supplier ombudsman. Honda of America has supplier ombudsmen who deal with the "soft side" of the business—primarily human resource issues not usually associated with cost, quality, or delivery. Because the supplier ombudsman is not directly involved in sourcing contract negotiations, suppliers are often much more willing to talk openly and honestly with the ombudsman, who can then act as a liaison between the two companies. One ombudsman emphasized that it takes time to build trust with suppliers, and trust building varies with different suppliers. If a supplier approaches the ombudsman with a problem that is the result of poor communication or misunderstanding between Honda and its supplier, the ombudsman communicates the supplier's perspective to Honda while maintaining as much confidentiality as possible. Over time, suppliers come to trust the ombudsman and appear to be more willing to share proprietary information with the company.

Barrier: Confidentiality Inhibits Information Sharing

Solution: Establish confidentiality agreements. Perhaps one of the biggest challenges in developing suppliers is sharing confidential information, especially when dealing with high-tech suppliers. Thus, many companies require nondisclosure or exclusivity agreements (i.e., the supplier provides a specific product to only one buyer) in development efforts, especially when dealing with technologically advanced products that contribute significantly to the buyer's competitiveness. However, nondisclosure agreements can benefit both parties. Ethical behavior on the part of the buyer will also support more open sharing of information with suppliers.

Barrier: Supplier Does Not Trust the Buying Organization

Solution: Spell it out. The driving forces behind kaizen events at Varity Perkins indicate that the company will not run an event without a properly executed written agreement between the parties. Although some supply management personnel at Varity Perkins prefer a "gentlemen's agreement," kaizen leaders believe the only way to gain a supplier's trust is to have the terms specifically written out and signed, especially when conducting the first supplier development event at a supplier. In one instance, it took Varity Perkins eight months to convince a supplier to consider a kaizen workshop because the supplier felt that a similar event with a different company previously failed to yield any improvements. The trust problem was compounded further because of Varity Perkins' previous reputation for arm's-length relationships with suppliers, manifested by frequent switching of suppliers based solely on price. The company has moved aggressively to reverse this perception by implementing and publicizing a new supply management philosophy emphasizing collaborative relationships with its suppliers.

Barrier: Organizational Cultures Are Poorly Aligned

Solution: Adapt a new approach to local conditions. When setting up its U.S. auto assembly plant in South Carolina, BMW quickly realized it would have to change its supplier development approach to conform to the North American supply market. BMW uses a process consulting approach to supplier development in Germany, which involves analyzing suppliers' processes and telling them what is wrong. This approach works well in a mature supplier relationship, where the supplier intuitively understands what the customer wants because the parties have worked together over time. In the United States, however, it became obvious that a very different approach was required because those long-term relationships did not exist.

When BMW started production, its U.S. suppliers frequently had difficulty understanding what was required in terms of quality and continuous improvement, resulting in strained relationships. Consequently, BMW spent a great deal of time explaining and communicating its expectations to suppliers. Eventually, BMW published a *Supplier Partnership Manual* that clearly delineated supplier responsibilities and its own expectations. The company also held supplier seminars to present its "Roadmap to Quality." These efforts have helped align buyer-supplier expectations and create a shared culture toward improvement.

Barrier: Not Enough Inducements to Participate Are Provided to the Supplier

Solution: Designed-in motivation. Although Solectron is now generally able to offer large order volumes to suppliers, that was not always the case. To gain supplier cooperation in the low-volume years, Solectron emphasized that a supplier could become designed into its products and thus have a greater potential for future business.

Solution: Financial incentives. Hyundai Motor Company uses financial incentives as one motivational tool for supplier improvement. The company rates supplier performance from 1 (highest) to 4 (lowest). Class 1 suppliers receive cash immediately on their invoices; Class 2 suppliers receive payment in 30 days; Class 3 suppliers receive payment in 60 days; and Class 4 suppliers receive no new business. Because all suppliers know how Hyundai evaluates their performance, they can take the steps necessary to ensure higher levels of performance.

Supplier-Specific Barriers

Just as buyers sometimes fail to recognize the potential benefits accruing from supplier development, a lack of recognition by the supplier may also keep its top management from fully committing to the joint effort. This lack of commitment may result in a failure to implement improvement ideas or to provide the technical and human resources necessary to support the development process. In addition, appropriate supplier follow-up may not take place once the development project has been completed, and the supplier's performance may revert back to its previous level.

Barrier: Lack of Commitment on the Part of Supplier's Management

Solution: Implement after commitment. Deere and Company's supplier development managers state that they will not engage in a supplier development project with a supplier unless the supplier's management demonstrates full commitment to the process. This involves a joint examination of the proposed improvement project and determination of the potential costs and benefits. To do so, a supply manager from

Deere arranges an initial contact meeting with the supplier's top local management to obtain its commitment and involvement. To secure this, Deere's supplier development engineers educate the supplier's management about the scope and impact of the desired improvement efforts. Once the supplier's senior management agrees to participate in principle, the supplier development engineer conducts process mapping, establishes the base case, and delineates the expected benefits hand in hand with corresponding supplier personnel. Once Deere and the supplier agree to the goals and objectives of the intended project, the next step is to determine how to share the costs and benefits. Deere typically allows the supplier to recover up front any capital-related costs required to implement the project and then splits the resulting savings 50/50 with the supplier, generally through a price decrease on future volume. By equitably sharing the resulting savings with the supplier, the supplier is more willing to engage in future development projects. In addition, success stories are shared with other possible supplier development targets to demonstrate the viability of the development process.

Barrier: Supplier's Management Agrees to Improvements but Fails to Implement the Proposals

Solution: Supplier champions. JCI Corporation, a first-tier supplier to the automotive industry, has instituted a Supplier Champions Program (SCP) designed to ensure suppliers are proficient in areas that are important to JCI's customers. The program was initiated because many of the suppliers that had attended JCI's training sessions failed to implement the tools and techniques that JCI provided. The SCP identifies what supplier personnel need to implement after they return from training. The program designates a Supplier Champion, a key supplier employee who understands JCI's expectations and demonstrates a high level of competence. The certification process requires that the Supplier Champion submit those actions to JCI that the supplier has identified for improvement. Such actions might include process mapping, failure mode effects analysis, quality control planning, best-practices benchmarking, and process auditing.

Barrier: Supplier Lacks Engineering Resources to Implement Solutions

Solution: Direct support. Honda of America Manufacturing has invested a significant amount of resources in its supplier support infrastructure, which was highlighted in the chapter opening. Of the more than 300 people then in HAM's supply management department, 50 were supplier development engineers who worked exclusively with suppliers. In one case, a small supplier did not have the capacity to keep up with requested volume, resulting in quality deterioration. HAM stationed four of its personnel at the supplier for 10 months at no charge, with additional services offered on an as-needed basis. As a result, the supplier improved its performance and now is a well-established Honda supplier.

Barrier: Supplier Lacks Required Information Systems

Solution: Direct electronic data interchange (EDI) support. At NCR Corporation, a manufacturer of ATMs, managers note that access to timely and accurate information is critical to decision making and ultimately to improved performance. An important focus of NCR's supplier development program has been to get its suppliers to invest in EDI. NCR also provides direct assistance to those suppliers producing lower-level components that do not have sufficient resources to get online. In addition, NCR provides training for suppliers and recommendations on hardware and software purchases.

Barrier: Suppliers Are Not Convinced Development Will Provide Benefits to Them

Solution: Let suppliers know where they stand. Varity Perkins revamped its supplier evaluation system to show suppliers areas of potential improvement. Previously, the company sent a quarterly report to suppliers assessing quality, delivery, and price competitiveness performance. Perkins did not use the data in any manner, and as a result, suppliers did not take the assessments seriously. When revamping the system, the measures were changed to capture the impact of supplier performance on daily operations.

Varity Perkins measured supplier delivery performance using a weekly time bucket, and on-time performance averaged 90 to 95%. With a daily time bucket, on-time performance dropped to 26% on time. Since the new measure has been in place, daily on-time delivery has improved to 90%. The supplier's history, its performance relative to Varity's other suppliers, and deviation from the mean in each evaluated area also appear on the modified report. The report also uses more graphics to make the data more meaningful.

This measurement system has become the foundation for the company's supplier development program. By allowing suppliers to view their performance relative to competitors, the company expects that suppliers will see the potential benefits of participating in supplier development activities as discussed earlier in the chapter.

Barrier: Supplier Lacks Employee Skill Base to Implement Solutions

Solution: Establish training centers. JCI Corporation realized that some suppliers, particularly smaller ones, lacked the internal skills required to implement improvement ideas. With this in mind, JCI built a facility dedicated to providing training to internal stakeholders, suppliers, and customers. Hyundai also established a domestic training center to provide supplier personnel with training in key performance areas, such as specialized welding. The suppliers and Hyundai share this cost. The South Korean government also supports this training center by providing tax benefits for building costs and making the joint training costs tax-deductible.

Solution: Provide human resource support. Hyundai Corporation recognizes that smaller suppliers with limited resources cannot consistently recruit and retain highly skilled engineers and other critical employees. Therefore, the majority of Hyundai's improvement efforts focus on smaller suppliers. Hyundai selects engineers from its own shops to spend time at supplier facilities. The engineers are co-located with their supplier counterparts, performing time/motion studies, teaching layout design, and improving productivity. Suppliers are consistently encouraged to learn, apply, and eventually teach the transferred knowledge to themselves and second-tier suppliers, a train-the-trainer approach.

Lessons Learned from Supplier Development

An underlying theme from these examples is that many of the barriers to supplier development are interrelated. It appears that, as companies work toward solving one barrier, they make concurrent progress toward solving others. Therefore, we can discern several lessons from studying supplier development successes and failures.

1. Managerial attitudes are a common and difficult barrier to overcome. A supply management executive at Honda of America noted that, although quality problems always have a solution, the attitudes of supplier management must be right before a problem can be truly resolved. Suppliers are sometimes not willing to accept outside help in the form of supplier development, either because they are too proud to accept help or because they do not see the value in improving quality or delivery performance. Management attitudes significantly affect the success of supplier development efforts. Oftentimes, suppliers feel that the resources required for improvement come at the expense of other needs. The savings must be real and readily achievable in order to get the supplier to sign on.
2. Realizing a competitive advantage from the supply chain requires a strategic orientation toward supply chain management and the alignment of supply management objectives with business unit goals. Supplier development plays a major role in helping create sustainable competitive advantage while aligning supply management and business goals. A strong supply management mission statement helps promote this strategic emphasis and alignment. Consider the following supply management mission statement from an auto parts manufacturer in the U.K.:

   > *We are committed to procure goods and services in a way that delivers our aims and objectives of becoming the most successful auto parts business in the world.*

   The company pursues this mission through (1) development of a world-class supplier base; (2) obtaining the highest-quality, most cost-effective goods and services in a timely manner; and (3) establishing long-term relationships with suppliers that strive for continuous improvement in all areas.
3. Relationship management is critical to supplier development success. Buyers can strengthen relationships with suppliers through focused supplier development activities. Besides developing mutual trust, the participants within a supply chain can begin to truly understand each other's needs and requirements, thereby making the entire supply chain stronger and more competitive. Ideally, supplier development will lead to the recognition that there is a strong co-destiny between buyer and supplier. Successful supplier development requires a strong, collaborative relationship and mutual commitment between the parties.

Pursuing supplier development activities directly with suppliers is neither quick nor easy. It requires vision, commitment, open communication, and equitable sharing of costs and benefits to work effectively. The long-term objective, of course, is to transform suppliers in such a way that continuous improvement becomes an integral part of each supplier's culture and DNA. Such joint accomplishments are achieved longitudinally and only by those companies that are patient and tenacious enough to make supplier development an important part of their supplier management processes.

Good Practice Example

Supplier Measurement Helps FedEx Manage a Worldwide Supply Base

FedEx, a worldwide leader in package delivery and logistics services, has built a solid reputation for reliable, on-time service. Throughout its history (founded in 1971), FedEx has focused on operational excellence and the ability to consistently pick up, sort, and deliver packages on time to their final destination.

Over the last 10 years, the package delivery industry has become highly competitive. Besides FedEx, customers can select UPS, DHL, or the U.S. Postal Service to deliver their packages. Even electronic mail is a source of new competition—senders simply attach large files with their electronic messages instead of sending paper copies via the overnight letter pack. FedEx must provide new services to customers, expand into new markets worldwide, and control costs if it expects to meet its growth targets.

FedEx purchases billions of dollars of goods and services annually, making supply management a major value-adding activity at the company. Furthermore, FedEx realizes that its suppliers greatly affect total costs and the ability of FedEx to serve its shippers. For example, if a supplier of aircraft replacement parts misses a delivery or ships defective parts, this affects FedEx's ability to keep its planes flying safely and on time. To help in its supply chain management efforts, the company has created a detailed supplier scorecard to evaluate supplier performance for goods, services, and fuel.

The FedEx supplier scorecard, available internally and to suppliers through the company intranet, establishes a level of uniformity among the many diverse supply management groups at FedEx. Buyers or supply chain specialists maintain scorecards for the suppliers for which they have responsibility. Completed scorecards are forwarded to a central database so they can be reviewed for procedural compliance and maintenance. The database allows supply chain specialists to perform a variety of analyses. For example, a supply manager can quickly identify those suppliers failing to meet minimum delivery requirements. The ability to perform this analysis greatly supports FedEx's supplier development and improvement efforts.

Exhibit 9.10 on p. 338 is an example of the supplier scorecard template that FedEx uses for products. The original scorecard system also featured templates with separate scoring guidelines for service and fuel suppliers. These three categories are now combined into a single robust template. The scorecard system allows the individual responsible for managing the supplier to adjust weights within the performance categories to meet the unique needs of a purchase requirement. Besides adjusting the weights, users can also determine which categories and subitems within a category to include.

Although the system offers the user substantial flexibility in selecting categories and weights, several scorecard rules apply. First, the performance category titled Diverse Supplier Development must be included in each evaluation per corporate requirements. Second, the selected performance category weights must sum to 100. Third, all subitems within a category must be scored on a 0–5 scale, which are added together and divided by the number of subitems for an average category score. This average score is then multiplied by the category weight to yield the total score for that category. When all selected categories are scored, the category totals are added to arrive at a performance level ranging from 0 to 500 points, resulting in one of the following designations:

500–450	Platinum
449–400	Gold
399–350	Silver
349–300	Bronze
<300	Requires special attention

A detailed user's manual provides guidance for subitem scoring. For example, the first performance category listed in Exhibit 9.10 is on-time delivery performance. The score is based on the number of deliveries that arrived on time divided by the total number of deliveries. The following scale determines the delivery performance score:

ON-TIME DELIVERY %	SCORE
100–95	5
94–90	4
89–80	3
79–70	2
69–60	1
<60	0

Buyers or supply chain specialists must communicate with internal customers to get additional insight into each supplier's performance history. Ideally, feedback from internal customers is incorporated into the scorecard so results can be shared with suppliers on a regular basis. Because most supplier scorecards include some qualitative assessments or judgments, suppliers may question or even disagree with parts of their score. This is not a major drawback to the system. In fact, disagreements can be positive because they open channels of communication between FedEx and its suppliers.

Users now have the ability to weight the subitems within a category rather than providing a single weight for the entire category. FedEx also expects to expand scorecard use to include a greater number of suppliers. Supply chain managers at FedEx realize that something as important as supplier management requires a rigorous measurement system that supports the attainment of supply objectives.

Exhibit 9.10 FedEx Strategic Sourcing Supplier Scorecard

Supplier Number ______ Eval. Period: From ______
FSC Code ______ To ______

Supplier Name ______ Date: ______
Address ______ FedEx Rep: ______
______ Manager: ______
Representative ______ Department: ______

CATEGORY	6 mths	3 mths	1 mth	Weight	Score	Total
1. On-Time Delivery Performance				25		
No. of on-time deliveries	___	___	___			
Total deliveries	___	___	___			
Pct. On-Time	___	___	___			
(100–95% = 5 // 94–90 = 4 // 89–80 = 3 // 79–70 = 2 // 69–60 = 1 // less than 60 = 0)						
2. Cycle Time Improvement (Yes / No)				5		
3. Quality				10		
A. Discrepancy rate						
No. of problem receipts	___	___	___			
Total receipts	___	___	___			
Discrepancy rate (rec.)	___	___	___			
No. of problem invoices	___	___	___			
Total invoices	___	___	___			
Discrepancy rate (inv.)	___	___	___			
Total discrepancy rate	___	___	___			
(0–1% = 5 //2–3 = 4 // 4–6 = 3 // 7–9 = 2 // 10–12 = 1 // greater than 12 = 0)						
B. MTBF						
C. Bad from stock						
D. No. of customer / quality complaints						
E. No. of warranty claims						
F. Turn time on warranty claims						
G. Certification (yes / no)						
(Average score for quality)						
4. Service				15		
A. Flexibility						
B. Customer service responsiveness						
C. Operational compatibility / coverage / accessibility						
D. Sales person product knowledge						
E. Sales person knowledge of FedEx						
F. Post sales support						
G. Technology upgrades / enhancements						
(Average score for service)						
5. Financial Stability (measured by D&B)				5		
6. Cost				20		
A. Price competitiveness						
B. Cost trends						
C. Add-ons						
D. Frequency / value of cost-reduction ideas						
E. Supplier savings sharing						
F. Gratis service (no incremental costs)						
G. FedEx cost of quality (or benefit)						
(Average score for cost)						
7. Diverse Supplier Development (DSD) — contact DSD for scoring				10		
A. Direct reporting						
B. Indirect tier reporting (completed by DSD & Prime)						
C. Use of local suppliers						
(Average score for DSD)						
8. Optional or Supplier / Product specific				10		
A.						
B.						
C.						
(Average score for optional)						
9. TOTAL SCORE				100		

Scoring Scale: 5 = Excellent // 4 = Above average // 3 = Average // 2 = Below average // 1 = Poor // 0 = Unacceptable
Performance Level: 500–450 = Platinum // 449–400 = Gold // 399–350 = Silver // 349–300 = Bronze // <300

CONCLUSION

Effectively managing and improving supplier performance is a primary supply management and business function. Supplier management and development constitute the new model of supply management. No longer does a buyer simply purchase parts from the lowest-priced source. The activities that best describe today's enlightened buyer include planning, coordinating, managing, developing, and improving performance capabilities throughout the supply base. For many items, buyers no longer just buy parts from suppliers; they manage supplier relationships and capabilities.

Therefore, supply management must carefully select and manage a proper mix of suppliers. To accomplish this, the buying organization must invest the requisite resources for effective supplier management, including a broad-based supplier performance measurement system, contracts with preferred or certified suppliers, and a wide range of supplier development tools and techniques. An effective supplier management program helps maximize the contribution received from suppliers, lowering costs, increasing quality, and developing future capabilities.

KEY TERMS

risk, 318

DISCUSSION QUESTIONS

1. Provide reasons why most firms do not have an adequate supplier measurement system.
2. Your manager at the medium-sized company where you work has just called you in and asked you to explain why the company should spend its scarce financial resources to develop a supplier measurement system. What do you tell her?
3. Why is it critical to have a smaller supply base before committing to a supplier management and development program?
4. Discuss the advantages and disadvantages of an optimized supply base. How can a buyer overcome the disadvantages?
5. Discuss the logic behind maintaining multiple suppliers for each purchased item.
6. Discuss the logic behind maintaining a reduced number of suppliers for each item.
7. What is a full-service supplier? What are the benefits of using full-service suppliers?
8. Why is the Honda approach to supplier development and improvement not widespread among U.S. firms?
9. Many companies are now using the World Wide Web to share performance information with suppliers, thereby allowing suppliers to compare their performance to other suppliers within the buying company's supply base. Discuss the benefits of this strategy to both buyers and suppliers.
10. Discuss the different types of supplier development and support that a firm can offer. Which are the most common? Why?

11. Research has revealed that no single approach to supplier development is effective in achieving performance goals. Rather, a mix of the carrot, stick, and hands-on approaches seems to work best. Explain why you think this is the case.
12. A common statement made in some supply management organizations is, "We can't be spending money on supplier development—we're not in business to train suppliers and do their job for them!" What type of barrier does this statement represent? How would you respond to such a statement?
13. Of the barriers to supplier development mentioned in this chapter, which ones, in your opinion, are the most difficult to overcome?
14. A Chrysler executive once made the following statement: "Only about one in five supplier development efforts are truly 100% successful." Why do you think this is the case? What makes supplier development such a challenging effort?
15. Discuss the reasons why top-management commitment is essential to the success of supplier management and development.
16. What are the advantages of calculating a Supplier Performance Index? What are the challenges associated with developing a measurement system that uses SPI?
17. What is the role of the Q adjustment factor in the SPI calculation?

ADDITIONAL READINGS

Bolstorff, P., and Rosenbaum, R. (2007), *Supply Chain Excellence: A Handbook for Dramatic Improvement Using the SCOR Model* (2nd ed.), New York: AMACOM.

Butterfield, B. (2000), "Mentoring for Advantage," *Purchasing Today,* 11(3), 14.

Davenport, T. H., and Harris, J. G. (2007), *Competing on Analytics: The New Science of Winning,* Boston: Harvard Business School Press.

de Crombrugghe, A., and Le Coq, G. (2003), *Guide to Supplier Development: For Programmes to Be Implemented by Industrial Subcontracting and Partnership Exchanges (SPXs),* Vienna: United Nations Industrial Development Organization.

Desai, M. P. (1996), "Implementing a Supplier Scorecard Program," *Quality Progress,* 29(2), 73–76.

Dunn, S. C., and Young, R. R. (2004), "Supplier Assistance within Supplier Development Initiatives," *Journal of Supply Chain Management,* 40(3), 19–29.

Fitzgerald, K. R. (1995), "For Superb Supplier Development, Honda Wins!" *Purchasing,* 21, 32.

Forker, L. B., Ruch, W. A., and Hershauer, J. C. (1999), "Examining Supplier Improvement Efforts from Both Sides," *Journal of Supply Chain Management,* 35(3), 40–50.

Forrest, W. (2006), "McDonald's Applies SRM Strategy to Global Technology Buy," *Purchasing,* 135(12), 16–17.

Galt, Major J. D. A., and Dale, B. G. (1991), "Supplier Development: A British Case Study," *International Journal of Purchasing and Materials Management,* 27, 16–22.

Giunipero, L. C. (1990), "Motivating and Monitoring JIT Supplier Performance," *Journal of Purchasing and Materials Management,* 26, 19–24.

Hahn, C. K., Watts, C. A., and Kim, K. Y. (1990), "The Supplier Development Program: A Conceptual Model," *International Journal of Purchasing and Materials Management,* 26, 2–7.

Handfield, R., and Krause, D. (1999), "Think Globally, Source Locally," *Supply Chain Management Review,* Winter, 36–49.

Handfield, R. B., Krause, D. R., Scannell, T. V., and Monczka, R. M. (2000), "Avoid the Pitfalls in Supplier Development," *Sloan Management Review,* 41(2), 37–49.

Hartley, J., and Choi, T. (1996), "Supplier Development: Customers as a Catalyst of Process Change," *Business Horizons,* July–August, pp. 37–44.

Hartley, J., and Jones, G. (1997), "Process Oriented Supplier Development: Building the Capability for Change," *International Journal of Purchasing and Materials Management,* 33(3), 24–29.

Hines, P. (1994), *Creating World-Class Suppliers: Unlocking Mutual Competitive Advantage,* London: Pitman.

Humphreys, P. K., Li, W. L., and Chan, L. Y. (2004), "The Impact of Supplier Development on Buyer-Supplier Performance," *Omega: The International Journal of Management Science,* 32(2), 131–143.

Kerr, J. (2006), "The Changing Complexion of Supplier Diversity," *Supply Chain Management Review,* 10(2), 38–45.

Krause, D. R. (1997), "Supplier Development: Current Practices and Outcomes," *International Journal of Purchasing and Materials Management,* 33(2), 12–19.

Krause, D. R., and Ellram, L. M. (1997), "Critical Elements of Supplier Development: The Buying Firm Perspective," *European Journal of Purchasing and Supply Management,* 3(1), 21–31.

Krause, D. R., and Ellram, L. M. (1997), "Success Factors in Supplier Development," *International Journal of Physical Distribution and Logistics Management,* 27(1), 39–52.

Krause, D. R., Handfield, R. B., and Tyler, B. B. (2007), "The Relationship between Supplier Development, Commitment, Social Capital Accumulation and Performance Improvement," *Journal of Operations Management,* 25(2), 528–545.

Krause, D. R., and Scannell, T. V. (2002), "Supplier Development Practices: Product and Service Based Industry Comparisons," *Journal of Supply Chain Management,* 38(2), 13–22.

Lamming, R. (1993), *Beyond Partnership: Strategies for Innovation and Lean Supply,* Hertfordshire, U.K.: Prentice Hall International.

Leenders, M. R. (1965), *Improving Purchasing Effectiveness through Supplier Development,* Boston: Harvard University Press.

Li, W.-L., Humphreys, P., Chan, L. Y., and Kumaraswamy, M. (2003), "Predicting Purchasing Performance: The Role of Supplier Development Programs," *Journal of Materials Processing Technology,* 138(1–3), 243–249.

Liker, J. K., and Choi, T. Y. (2004), "Building Deep Supplier Relationships," *Harvard Business Review,* 83(1), 104–113.

Nelson, D., Moody, P. E., and Stegner, J. R. (2005), *The Incredible Payback: Innovative Solutions That Deliver Extraordinary Results,* New York: AMACOM.

Nix, N. W., Lusch, R. F., Zacharia, Z. G., and Bridges, W. (2007), "The Hand That Feeds You: What Makes Some Collaborations with Suppliers Succeed, When So Many Fail?" *Wall Street Journal,* October 27–28, p. R8.

Patterson, J. L., and Nelson, J. D. (1999), "OEM Cycle Time Reduction through Supplier Development," *Practix: Best Practices in Purchasing and Supply Chain Management,* 2(3), 1–5.

"Performance Measurement: Why It's Important to Measure Suppliers Well" (2000), *Purchasing,* 128(7), 36–39.

Prokopets, L., and Tabibzadeh, R. (2006), *Supplier Relationship Management: Maximizing the Value of Your Supply Base,* Stamford, CT: Archstone Consulting.

Robitaille, D. (2007), *Managing Supplier-Related Processes,* Chico, CA: Paton Professional.

Rogers, P. A. (2005), "Optimising Supplier Management and Why Co-Dependency Equals Mutual Success," *Journal of Facilities Management,* 4(1), 40–50.

Sako, M. (2004), "Supplier Development at Honda, Nissan and Toyota: Comparative Case Studies of Organizational Capability Enhancement," *Industrial and Corporate Change,* 13(2), 281–308.

Sánchez-Rodríguez, C., Hemsworth, D., and Martínez-Lorente, A. R. (2005), "The Effect of Supplier Development Initiatives on Purchasing Performance: A Structural Model," *Supply Chain Management,* 10(3–4), 289–301.

Teague, P. E. (2007), "How to Improve Supplier Performance," *Purchasing,* 136(4), 31–32.

Theodorakioglou, Y., Gotzamani, K., and Tsiolvas, G. (2006), "Supplier Management and Its Relationship to Buyers' Quality Management," *Supply Chain Management,* 11(2), 148–159.

Wagner, S. M. (2006), "Supplier Development Practices: An Exploratory Study," *European Journal of Marketing,* 40(5–6), 554–571.

Watts, C. A., and Hahn, C. K. (1993), "Supplier Development Programs: An Empirical Analysis," *International Journal of Purchasing and Materials Management,* 29(2), 11–17.

ENDNOTES

1. Minahan, T., and Vigoroso, M. (2002), "The Supplier Performance Measurement Benchmarking Report," http://www.aberdeen.com; accessed January 2, 2008.
2. Robinson, S. (1999), "Taiwan's Chip Plants Left Idle by Earthquake," *New York Times,* September 22.
3. Friedman, T. L. (2006), *The World Is Flat, Release 2.0,* New York: Farrar, Straus, and Giroux, p. 517.
4. Bhote, K. R. (1989), *Strategic Supply Management: A Blueprint for Revitalizing the Manufacturer-Supplier Partnership,* New York: AMACOM, pp. 75–78.
5. Greenwald, J. (1992), "What Went Wrong? Everything at Once," *Time,* http://www.time.com/time/magazine/article/0,9171,976990-6,00.html; accessed April 16, 2008.
6. Reese, A. (2000), "E-Procurement Takes On the Untamed Supply Chain," *iSource,* November, p. 108.
7. Sako, M. (2004), "Supplier Development at Honda, Nissan and Toyota: Comparative Case Studies of Organizational Capability Enhancement," *Industrial and Corporate Change,* 13(2), 281–308.
8. Lamming, R. (1993), *Beyond Partnership: Strategies for Innovation and Lean Supply,* Hertfordshire, U.K.: Prentice Hall International, pp. 215–216.
9. de Crombrugghe, A., and Le Coq, G. (2003), *Guide to Supplier Development,* Vienna: United Nations Industrial Development Organization.
10. See Leenders, M. R. (1965), *Improving Purchasing Effectiveness through Supplier Development,* Boston: Harvard University Press; and Leenders, M. R., and Blenkhorn, D. L. (1988), *Reverse Marketing: The New Buyer-Supplier Relationship,* New York: Free Press.
11. Krause and Handfield, p. 7.
12. Handfield, R., Krause, D., Scannell, T., and Monczka, R. (1998), "An Empirical Investigation of Supplier Development: Reactive and Strategic Processes," *Journal of Operations Management,* 17(1), 39–58.
13. Hahn, C. K., Watts, C. A., and Kim, K. Y. (1990), "The Supplier Development Program: A Conceptual Model," *International Journal of Purchasing and Materials Management,* 26(2), 2–7.

Chapter 10

WORLDWIDE SOURCING

Learning Objectives

After completing this chapter, you should be able to

- Identify the differences between international purchasing and global sourcing
- Understand the reasons why firms pursue international purchasing
- Identify the total costs associated with international purchasing
- Become familiar with the problems and obstacles hindering global sourcing efforts
- Understand the key factors needed for successful global sourcing efforts

Chapter Outline

Worldwide Sourcing at Selex

Selex, a U.S.-based electronics company with $2 billion in annual sales, is a company in transition. The early 1990s, which began the longest period of industrial expansion in U.S. history, were not rewarding for the company. Selex experienced eroding profit margins due to intense global competition and mature product lines (with some of its products being 20 to 25 years old), making it vulnerable to cost-reduction pressure and lower profit margins.

The company suffered through several costly product failures during the 1990s and lost market share as new competitors and technologies encroached on core markets. And, with some difficulty, the company was forced to change its culture to respond to the demands of a new marketplace. Selex has had to change from being a technology-driven company to a flexible, market-focused company.

Selex organizes supply management into three distinct groups: indirect purchasing, raw materials purchasing (any material that is required for production), and contract or finished goods purchasing (outsourced finished goods). Each group has pursued innovative approaches to worldwide sourcing.

INDIRECT PURCHASING

Previous efforts at managing indirect purchases were U.S. focused, even though Selex has a manufacturing presence in the United Kingdom, Mexico, the United States, Japan, and China. A major corporate initiative at Selex has involved the development of a global sourcing process called Sourcing Vision. Using this process, project teams systematically review Selex's worldwide indirect spend with the goal of achieving cost savings of 7 to 15% annually.

An executive steering committee oversees the Sourcing Vision process. This committee consists of the vice president of research, the vice president of supply chain management, the vice president of marketing and sales, the vice president of information technology, and the corporate controller. Each member resides at the executive vice president level, and each champions a specific global project.

Cross-functional project teams are an integral part of Sourcing Vision. Project teams engage in the following activities:

- Analyzing the industry and identifying buyer and seller strengths and weaknesses
- Defining improvement goals
- Identifying potential suppliers
- Forwarding and analyzing supplier proposals
- Determining the criteria for supplier selection
- Developing a sourcing strategy
- Making supplier selection decisions

RAW MATERIALS PURCHASING

The second major procurement group is raw materials purchasing (which most companies call direct materials). As part of its global procurement strategy, the raw materials group has focused on (1) identifying and qualifying sources worldwide and (2) aggregating volumes with leveraged agreements. This group also has responsibility for finished goods planning (which includes aggregate product planning).

A major change in raw materials procurement involved technical personnel, operations, and procurement working together worldwide to refine component materials. This cross-functional approach, which is coordinated at the corporate level, examines systems tradeoffs to arrive at an expected lowest total component cost. A second major change emphasized a commodity approach to global strategy development, with leadership roles assumed by personnel from different sites. Selex has also established lead buyers at sites for items that are not part of the coordinated commodity approach. One individual at each plant is responsible for a procurement area and becomes Selex's resident expert.

CONTRACT PURCHASING

The global outsourcing of finished products at Selex is a result of the realization that vertical integration could not support 20 to 40 new-product launches a year. Most Selex products use self-contained electronic components, which the company refers to as media. The physical housing of the product is the hardware. Selex insources media and outsources hardware because most of the innovation that customers value occurs within media rather than hardware.

Approximately seven years ago, Selex formed a contract manufacturing organization with primary responsibility for hardware outsourcing. This group now has responsibility for identifying and qualifying outsource partners, assessing product quality, and working with contract manufacturers during new-product development. As part of the contract manufacturing organization, the outsourcing director also has responsibility for two international purchasing offices (IPOs). The IPOs identify potential contract manufacturers or identify available suppliers for a specific application. The IPOs also support the indirect and raw materials purchasing groups discussed earlier.

Selex illustrates how a major corporation, faced with new competitive threats and declining markets, transformed itself from a slow, functionally driven organization into a responsive, market-driven, cross-functional enterprise. It also illustrates how three procurement groups, each taking very different approaches, have endorsed worldwide sourcing as a way to help achieve corporate objectives.

Source: Interviews with company managers. The company name was changed at the request of the company.

Globalization is dramatically changing interactions among the world's economies through increasing interdependencies. Included in several definitions of **globalization** are the terms "interdependence," "connectivity," and "integration of economies" in social, technical, and political spheres. This trend toward seamless boundaries is explored in depth by Thomas Friedman in his best seller *The World Is Flat.*[1] Information now circles the globe with such ease that 245,000 Indians housed in call centers are scheduling airline flights, soliciting credit card customers, and answering questions about mortgages and insurance policies.[2] When asked to indicate what business drivers were likely to have the most influence on their company's purchasing strategies in the next 10 years, 49% of 359 responding executives stated it would be globalization.[3]

Globalization in developing economies such as China and India represents opportunities for cost savings on the buying side and new markets on the selling side. On the selling side more affluent consumers are desiring higher-level brands. The well-known French cosmetics firm L'Oréal failed to make a profit competing in India's low-priced shampoo market. However, when it shifted its focus and advertising to the emerging middle class, with products selling for 3 to 20 times the price of those of its rivals, profits followed. The 200-million-person Indian middle class desires many foreign brands, from Tommy Hilfiger jeans to Absolut vodka.[4]

On the supply side, the cost/price benefits associated with sourcing in developing countries are a significant motivation for remaining competitive in an increasingly global environment. Several studies have indicated that cost/price savings are the number one reason for global sourcing. Other important benefits realized are availability, quality, and (to a lesser extent) innovation. Once a firm establishes sourcing roots in these countries, it facilitates entry to marketing and selling opportunities. Many larger multinationals take a more global perspective by seeking to supply their worldwide operations with common sources of supply at the lowest worldwide cost, and they are developing centralized and globally coordinated supply organizations to support these efforts.

One indicator of this increased international sourcing is the large U.S. merchandise trade deficit, which in 2006 was more than $700 billion. Much of the focus on the increasing deficit is directed toward China. The U.S. government has stepped up pressure on China to both open its markets and allow its currency to float freely. This pressure is justified; looking at the top U.S. trading partners reveals that Canada leads with China second, followed by Mexico, Japan, Germany, U.K., South Korea, France, Taiwan, and Malaysia. As is shown in Exhibit 10.1, the first four partners account for 75% of total trade. Second, two of the four largest trading partners are part of the North American Free Trade Agreement. Finally, because services such as call centers are not captured by the data, India is not listed as a top 10 trading partner. Outsourcing and offshoring of services are a large part of global sourcing strategies for the 21st-century supply manager.

Globalization is also changing the structure of many marketplaces as global companies extend their reach into all markets. Often the acquiring firm is not a U.S.-based firm. In the aluminum industry, Rio Tinto of Australia acquired Canada's Alcan Aluminum. In obtaining Alcan, Rio Tinto bested U.S.-based Alcoa's bid.[5] In the global steel industry, Germany's Thyssen Krupp is building a $2.7 billion mill outside of Mobile, AL. Scheduled for opening in 2010, the mill is the largest to be built in the United States in over 40 years. Indian steel maker Essar Global announced plans to build an integrated mill outside of Duluth, MN.[6]

Exhibit 10.1 U.S. Trading Partners, 2006

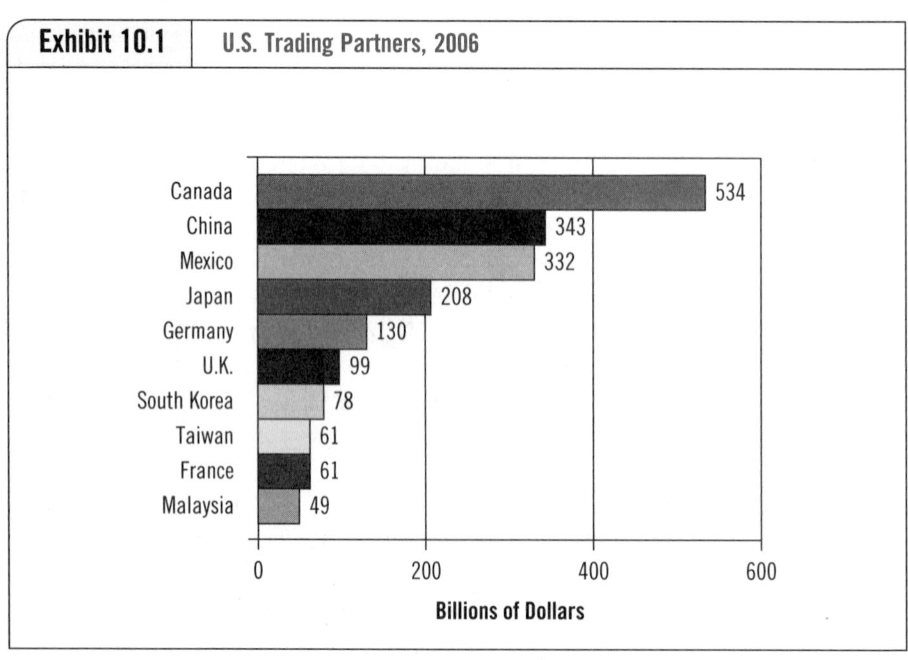

This chapter focuses on how supply managers can capture the benefits of globalization through international purchasing and global sourcing. **International purchasing** relates to a commercial purchase transaction between a buyer and a supplier located in different countries. This type of purchase is typically more complex than a domestic purchase. Organizations must contend with lengthened lead times, increased rules and regulations, currency fluctuations, customs requirements, and a host of other variables such as language and time differences.

Global sourcing, which differs from international purchasing in scope and complexity, involves proactively integrating and coordinating common items and materials, processes, designs, technologies, and suppliers across worldwide purchasing, engineering, and operating locations. Because of the differences between international buying and global sourcing, we will use the term **worldwide sourcing** for general discussions of the process of purchasing from other countries.

This chapter contains three major sections. The first section presents an overview of worldwide sourcing, including the most common reasons why companies source worldwide. The second section identifies the areas that make international purchasing more complex than domestic sourcing. The final section presents those factors that separate successful from less-successful global sourcing efforts.

Worldwide Sourcing Overview

The number of U.S. companies that practice worldwide sourcing has increased dramatically over the past three decades.[7] Between 1973 and 1975, the percentage of companies purchasing internationally more than doubled, from 21 to 45%. The oil embargo of the 1970s, coupled with shortages of other basic materials, forced purchasing to search overseas for suppliers. Many foreign producers were also becoming quality and cost leaders across a number of industries. The foreign items most sought after by U.S. companies in 1975, for example, were production machinery and equipment, followed by chemicals and mechanical and electrical components.

The percentage of U.S. companies engaged in worldwide sourcing increased from 45 to 56% from 1975 to 1982. This increase reflected the continuing inability of domestic suppliers and manufacturers to compete in terms of price, quality, and even delivery. Foreign suppliers could often provide higher-quality parts at a lower total cost. For some, survival against foreign competitors required sourcing from the same suppliers that supported the competition.

The period from 1982 through 1987 saw a sharp rise in the number of companies looking internationally for their purchase requirements—from 56 to 71%. During this time the value of the U.S. dollar increased dramatically against other currencies. U.S. imports became less expensive while U.S. firms found it difficult to export and compete in world markets. The huge trade imbalances of the 1980s reflected the strength of the U.S. dollar in world currency markets along with a continued lack of competitiveness of many U.S. companies.

Since 1987 the level of international purchasing and trade has accelerated rapidly. The end of the Cold War led to the opening of trade with emerging markets in Russia, Eastern Europe, and China, which in turn has led to the development of new markets and new sources of supply. Furthermore, import and export restrictions are lessening, partly as a function of the GATT agreement on free trade signed in

Sourcing Snapshot *Thinking Globally and Buying Locally at Sony*

Countless organizations today face a similar scenario. They are expanding production facilities or distribution networks in a new country, and they must often develop local sources of supply to meet domestic content regulations or to minimize transportation costs. At Sony, its global procurement strategy has been to procure local parts whenever possible and to produce in those countries where the company's products are sold. In Europe, Sony sources approximately 90% of the company's product value locally; in Asia, Sony obtains 30 to 50% of product content locally. When production shifts to a new area, local suppliers are developed whenever possible. As a backup, Sony often negotiates with Japanese suppliers to ship parts to the new production facilities. If no suitable local supplier exists, purchasing may negotiate with a Japanese supplier to set up local production in the new country of operation. Although Sony does not contribute capital to suppliers to set up production facilities, it will help with training of personnel at new locations. Thus, Sony's policy is to produce as many parts as possible locally at each location.

Source: Adapted from R. Handfield and D. Krause, "Think Globally, Source Locally," *Supply Chain Management Review,* Winter 1999, pp. 36–49.

Uruguay. The North American Free Trade Agreement, passed in 1993, has also resulted in a dramatic increase in trade between the United States, Canada, and Mexico. Trade talks between the United States and other countries, such as Japan and China, also reduced trade restrictions.

The average amount of total purchases from non-U.S. sources by larger firms has increased from 9% of total purchases in 1993 to over 25% in 2000. One study indicated that 38% of the firms surveyed forecasted they would source at least 60% of their purchases on a global basis by 2010. This was up from 18% in 2000.[8] The trend toward increased international purchasing activity is clear. The growth in worldwide sourcing is likely to continue rather than decrease. As indicated earlier, business drivers most likely to have an influence on the company purchasing strategies in the next 10 years are globalization and cost leadership.[9] Besides lowest cost, there are many possible reasons why firms will continue to purchase internationally.

Why Source Worldwide?

Although the previous discussion provided some reasons for purchasing internationally, let's discuss formally the more important reasons why companies pursue worldwide sourcing.

Cost/Price Benefits

After considering all the costs associated with international purchasing, savings of 20 to 30% may be available. Cost differentials between countries arise because of

- Lower labor rates
- Different productivity levels
- Possible willingness to accept a lower profit margin

- Exchange rate differences
- Lower-cost inputs for materials
- Government subsidies

Purchasing should consider only suppliers that are capable of meeting rigid quality and delivery standards, although far too often price differentials become the primary criterion behind a foreign sourcing decision. It is important to note that in assessing the cost benefits of sourcing internationally, purchasers should include all of the relevant costs associated with sourcing items beyond piece price, which a later section discusses.

Access to Product and Process Technology

The United States is no longer the undisputed product and process technology leader in the world. Other countries have developed leading-edge technologies in a number of areas, such as electronic components. Purchasers that require these components know that Asian suppliers are technology leaders. Gaining access to the most current technology leaves many companies with little choice except to pursue worldwide sourcing.

Quality

Some countries, such as Japan and Germany, are obsessed with product quality. Producers in these countries have been able to capture an increasing share of world markets across a range of industries. U.S. purchasers stuck with domestic suppliers that produce poor quality often begin to source foreign components with the hope of improving end-product quality. The combination of consistently high quality and lower overall price has been a major contributor to the growth of U.S. companies buying internationally.

Access to the Only Source Available

Economic recessions, mergers, and government environmental regulations often result in suppliers exiting certain lines of business due to higher costs, loss of business volume, or both. This capacity reduction makes it increasingly difficult for U.S. buyers to source domestically. Although copper producers today are enjoying the benefits of high prices and tight capacity, this was not always the case. During the early and mid-1980s, U.S. copper producers closed many mines because of low copper prices and inefficient process technology. Some copper buyers turned to overseas producers to meet their requirements. A loss of supplier capability and availability in the automotive, machine tool, and electronics industries often left domestic buyers with no viable supply alternative except international sources.

Introduce Competition to Domestic Suppliers

Companies that rely on competitive forces to maintain price and service levels within their industry sometimes use worldwide sourcing to introduce competition to the domestic supply base. In industries characterized by limited domestic competition, this can diminish a supplier's power and break certain practices unfavorable to purchasers. Selex, featured at the beginning of this chapter, historically sourced many chemical products with a single large U.S. supplier. However, Selex is now qualifying suppliers in emerging countries as a way to counteract the domestic supplier's pricing power. A more competitive supply market will shift power away from U.S. suppliers as well as shift power from sellers to buyers.

React to Buying Patterns of Competitors

This is probably the least-mentioned reason for worldwide sourcing, because most firms do not want to admit that they are reacting to the practices of competitors. Imitating the action of competitors is the "fashion and fear" motive. A purchaser may try to duplicate the factors that provide an advantage to a competitor, which may mean sourcing from the same suppliers or regions of the world that a competitor uses. There may be a belief that not sourcing in the same region(s) may create a competitive disadvantage. This is especially true today with many firms believing they must source in China or risk being at a cost disadvantage.

Establish a Presence in a Foreign Market

Virtually the whole world is a potential market for goods and services from the United States, so it makes good economic and political sense to buy in those markets when planning to sell there. One way to develop goodwill in the country to assist in gaining product or service acceptance is through business relationships that will help support an expanded marketing presence.

In order to gain access to the lowest costs, cutting-edge technology, and best capabilities, organizations must scan the global landscape in search of the best suppliers. By aligning technology roadmaps with leading-edge suppliers, designers can ensure that their products and services will truly be world class, not just the best in the region. Although the exact reasons each company sources internationally will vary, they surely include some of those discussed here. Without access to worldwide sources of supply, companies may not remain competitive. A domestic company that purchases a portion of its material requirements worldwide is better than a domestic company that is no longer in business as a result of its inability to meet global competition.

Barriers to Worldwide Sourcing

Companies with little or no international experience often face obstacles or barriers when beginning worldwide sourcing. These barriers include (1) lack of knowledge and skills concerning global sourcing; (2) resistance to change; (3) longer lead times; (4) different business customs, language, and culture; and (5) currency fluctuations.

The lack of knowledge and skills pertaining to the intricacies of global sourcing inhibits a company from considering global sources. These shortcomings include a basic lack of knowledge about potential sources of supply or a lack of familiarity with the additional documentation required for international purchasing. International documentation requirements include

- Letters of credit
- Multiple bills of lading
- Dock receipts
- Import licenses
- Certificates of origin
- Inspection certificates

- Certificates of insurance coverage
- Packing lists
- Commercial invoices

Resistance to change from an established, routine procedure or shifting from a long-standing supplier are also major barriers. It is natural to resist changes that represent a radical departure from existing ways of doing business. Domestic market nationalism has also sometimes presented itself as a barrier. Buyers are sometimes reluctant to shift business from domestic sources to unknown foreign sources. Home market nationalism, although not the obstacle it was years ago, can still be an issue.

Another barrier involves managing longer lead times and extended material pipelines. With longer lead times, accurate materials forecasts over extended periods become critical. Buyers must manage delivery dates closely because of the possibility of transit or customs delays. International sourcing also introduces an additional degree of logistical, political, and financial risk.

Other barriers relate to a lack of knowledge about foreign business practices, language, and culture. Negotiations with foreign suppliers can be more difficult, and simple engineering or delivery change requests can become frustrating experiences. Meetings and negotiations with international suppliers require knowledge of the customs and culture associated with the particular country. Lack of understanding of customs can lead to serious problems in making significant progress in negotiations and in building relationships with the supplier.

Currency fluctuations can have a significant impact on the price paid for the item. Major currencies fluctuate daily, and therefore it is important for the buyer to understand the options to minimize this significant risk. Specific currency fluctuation strategies are discussed later in this chapter.

The most common method for overcoming these barriers involves education and training, which can generate support for the process as well as help overcome the anxiety associated with change. Publicizing success stories can also show the performance benefits that worldwide purchasing provides. Globally linked computer-aided design systems, electronic mail, and bar code systems that help track material through international pipelines have helped reduce the communication barriers surrounding worldwide sourcing. Some companies also insist on only working with those foreign suppliers that have U.S.-based support personnel.

Measurement and reward systems can encourage sourcing from the best suppliers worldwide. These firms measure and reward buyers on the basis of their ability to realize performance benefits from the selected use of international sources. The use of third-party or external agents can also help overcome barriers to international purchasing, particularly when first starting out. The use of brokers can be an efficient way to get your feet wet in worldwide sourcing.

Regardless of the technique used to overcome worldwide sourcing barriers, the effort will fail unless top management demonstrates its support for worldwide sourcing. Management must send the message that going international is a means to remain competitive by using the most competitive suppliers and does not represent an effort to force domestic suppliers out of business.

Sourcing Snapshot

The Balancing Act: Low Price versus Safety in Chinese Sourcing

Recent events in the food and toy industries have shown that although cost and price advantages are major factors driving global sourcing, they need to be balanced against the total cost. Mattel recalled more than 1 million lead-contaminated toys that were made in China. The recall involved 83 types of toys from the firm's Fisher-Price unit. The toys contained excessive levels of lead paint despite lead-paint regulations in both China and the United States. Experts estimate that 80% of the toys imported into the United States come from China, so the lead-paint problem is extensive. Supply managers have contract provisions limiting lead paint; however, enforcement is a problem. Using lead additives in paint is inexpensive and allows paint to dry more quickly; it also prevents corrosion of painted parts. These advantages help suppliers meet relentless cost pressures from customers.

Mattel had a 15-year trusted relationship with the supplier, so it allowed the supplier to do the product testing. Mattel's periodic quality audits also didn't catch the problem. Lack of proper testing has heightened the call for independent third-party testing. Tragically, weeks after the Mattel recall, Cheung Shu-Hung, the owner of the Chinese toy factory, reportedly committed suicide. A combination of pressure from the customer to ensure that such events would not happen again and the loss of face in government-business circles created a huge sense of shame for the owner. Mattel now must deal with the cost of recalled toys and multiple lawsuits from parents of children exposed to the lead paint. One of the classes of these suits involves medical monitoring, which allows families to sue toy makers and others before their children show any kind of injury. Should these types of lawsuits be allowed, a significant amount of Mattel's resources would be tied up for the immediate future.

Another toy company, Toys "R" Us, voluntarily recalled 128,700 military toys sold under the Elite Operations brand. According to the company the toys originally passed two tests, the first before they were put into production and the second after first shipment. Subsequent periodic tests conducted by a third party discovered the lead. As a result of the recall, the firm set up a cross-functional team that meets monthly to discuss safety issues.

McDonald's Corporation, another of the world's largest toy buyers, has found the Chinese lead-paint problem to be so pervasive that it has started managing deep into the supply chain. The firm monitors its Chinese toy manufacturers' paint sources back to the paint manufacturers. It requires its Chinese toy makers to use only these approved sources.

Supply managers must take a proactive and hands-on approach to any potential safety risks and factor the costs into the sourcing process. Wal-Mart Corporation worked with its shrimp supplier Rubicon, LLC, to upgrade its 150 Thai shrimp farms. By the end of 2007 these farms must meet a set of environmental and social standards backed by Wal-Mart, Darden Restaurants, and other large shrimp buyers. Wal-Mart is the largest U.S. buyer of shrimp, importing 20,000 tons annually or 3.4% of U.S. total shrimp imports. The Global Aquaculture Alliance will develop similar standards for farming of tilapia, catfish, and salmon. The problem is that many small family-run operations don't have the resources to make the investments or lack the power to recover their investments with higher prices. These small producers feel the procedures merely replicate their country standards and result in higher costs. The net impact may be a consolidation of Wal-Mart's supply base to fewer, stronger suppliers that exert control over the entire shrimp-farming supply chain.

Source: Adapted from a series of articles on Chinese operating practices: J. Spencer and N. Casey, "Toy Recall Adds to Fear of Goods Made in China," *Wall Street Journal,* August 3, 2007, pp. A1, A5; N. Zamiska and N. Casey, "Owner of Chinese Factory Kills Himself," *Wall Street Journal,* August 14, 2007, p. A2; K. Hudson and W. Watcharasakwet, "The New Wal-Mart Effect: Cleaner Thai Shrimp Farms," *Wall Street Journal,* July 24, 2007, pp. B1, B2.

Progressing from Domestic Buying to International Purchasing

An organization progresses (usually reactively) from domestic buying to international purchasing because it confronts a situation for which no suitable domestic supplier exists, or because competitors are gaining an advantage due to international purchasing. First-level firms may also find themselves driven toward international purchasing because of triggering events in the supply market. Such events could be a supply disruption, rapidly changing currency exchange rates, a declining domestic supply base, inflation within the home market, or the sudden emergence of worldwide competitors. Whatever the reason, many issues now become part of the international purchasing process that were not part of the domestic sourcing decision, or are now even more important than when sourcing was done domestically.

Information about Worldwide Sources

After identifying items to purchase internationally, a firm must gather and evaluate information on potential suppliers or identify intermediaries capable of that task. This can prove challenging if a company is inexperienced or has limited outside contacts or sources of information. The following resources can provide valuable leads when identifying potential suppliers or trade intermediaries.

International Industrial Directories

Industrial directories, which are increasingly available through the Internet, are a major source of information about suppliers by industry or region of the world. Hundreds of directories are available that identify potential international contacts. Here are some examples:

- The *World Marketing Directory* covers 50,000 major businesses in all lines having high sales volume and at least an interest in foreign trade; it is published by Dun & Bradstreet. Entries include the company's line of business and industry code.
- *Marconi's International Register* details 45,000 firms worldwide conducting business internationally; it lists products geographically under 3,500 product headings.
- *ABC Europe Production* covers 130,000 European manufacturers that export their products.
- *Business Directory of Hong Kong* details Hong Kong firms, including manufacturers; importers; exporters; banks; and construction, transportation, and service companies.

These directories, and many more, are usually available on CD-ROM or accessible through the Internet.

Trade Shows

Trade shows are often one of the best ways to gather information on many suppliers at one time. These industrial shows occur throughout the world for practically every industry. Most business libraries have a directory that lists worldwide trade shows. Internet searches will also reveal the time and place of industrial trade shows, including how to register. Examples include the International Manufacturing Technology Show; manufacturing industry professionals from the United States and 119 countries attend this show held every two years. It is estimated that over 90,000 buyers and sellers combine with over 1,200 exhibitors to meet and display the latest manufacturing technology. With a minimal amount of research, purchasers can identify trade shows related directly to their purchasing needs.

Trading Companies

Trading companies offer a full range of services to assist purchasers. These companies will issue letters of credit and pay brokers, customs charges, dock fees, insurance, and ocean carrier and inland freight bills. Clients usually receive one itemized invoice for the total services performed. One U.S.-based trading company offers more than 20 services, including

- Finding qualified sources
- Performing product quality audits
- Evaluating suppliers
- Negotiating contracts
- Managing logistics
- Inspecting shipments
- Expediting
- Performing duty classifications

The use of a full-service trading company may actually result in a lower total cost for international purchases compared with performing each activity individually. Countries such as Japan and South Korea have trading companies located in major U.S. cities. KOTRA, a Korean-based trading company, is committed to promoting mutual prosperity between Korea and its trading partners through international commerce and investment (www.kotradallas.com). Foreign trading companies offer one-stop shopping for buyers interested in the goods and services of a particular country. They will locate the sources, quote the prices, insure quality, and handle all the export and import documentation.

Third-Party Support

Experts are available to provide international sourcing assistance. Independent agents, working on commission, will act as purchasing representatives in a foreign country. They locate sources of supply, evaluate the source, and handle the required paperwork and documentation. Some agents also provide or can arrange for full-service capability.

Agents and brokers are an option when a company lacks foreign expertise or a presence in a foreign market. They help locate foreign suppliers and act as intermediaries between the buyer and seller. Direct manufacturer's representatives or sales representatives can also be a source of valuable information. Such individuals work directly for sellers as their representatives in a country. Finally, different state and federal agencies encourage and promote international trade. Services provided by these agencies are usually reasonable in cost.

Trade Consulates

Purchasers can contact foreign trade consulates located in major cities across the United States for information. Almost all consulates have trade experts who are eager to do business with American buyers. Purchasers can also contact U.S. embassies located overseas to inquire about suppliers located in a particular country. The U.S. Department of Commerce also has offices staffed by trade specialists that offer several good services at a nominal fee.

The amount and type of information required is partly a function of how a purchaser chooses to handle the foreign purchase. Purchasers that use intermediaries, such as trading companies and external agents, must search for information that identifies the best intermediaries. Purchasers that control the buying process must obtain information about suppliers from trade directories, trade shows, embassies, supplier representatives, and other sources of international information.

Supplier Selection Issues

Whether the purchaser or an external agent coordinates the international purchase, foreign suppliers must be subject to the same, or in some cases more rigorous, performance evaluation and standards as domestic suppliers. Never assume a foreign company can automatically satisfy a buyer's performance requirements or expectations. Here are some questions to ask when evaluating foreign sources:

- Does a significant total cost difference exist between the domestic and the foreign source after factoring in additional cost elements?
- Will the foreign supplier maintain any price differences over time?
- What is the effect of longer material pipelines and increased average inventory levels?
- What are the supplier's technical and quality capabilities?
- Can the supplier assist with new designs?
- What is the supplier's quality performance? What types of quality systems does it have in place?
- Is the supplier capable of consistent delivery schedules?
- How much lead time does the supplier require?
- Can we develop a longer-term relationship with this supplier?
- Are patents and proprietary technology safe with this supplier? Is the supplier trustworthy? What legal system does the supplier expect to follow?
- What are the supplier's payment terms?
- How does the supplier manage currency exchange issues?

At times buyers use trial orders to evaluate foreign sources. Purchasers may initially not be willing to rely on a foreign source for an entire purchase requirement. A buyer can use smaller or trial orders to begin to establish a supplier's performance record.

Cultural Understanding

Perhaps one of the biggest barriers to international sourcing involves the cultural differences that arise when doing business with other countries. **Culture** is the sum of the understandings that govern human interaction in a society. Culture is a multidimensional concept composed of several elements, including: (1) language, (2) religion, (3) values and attitudes, (4) customs, (5) social institutions, and (6) education. Two very important differences in culture that can affect the supply manager are values and behavior. **Values** are shared beliefs or group norms that are internalized; they affect the way people think. **Behavior** is based on values and attitudes; it affects the way people act. Understanding cultural differences will improve a purchaser's comfort and effectiveness when conducting business internationally. A major complaint about Americans is our ignorance of other cultures.

Cultural differences between countries can result in some unwelcome surprises when buying internationally. For instance, the standard procedures for negotiation and contracting are distinctly different in Asia, Europe, and the United States. Dealing with these issues requires purchasing personnel and organizations to manage different beliefs about contracting. Beliefs in developing countries about ethical issues, such as bribery, differ widely from U.S. practices. What is an illegal activity in the United States (providing bribes) is often an accepted business practice in many regions.

Language and Communication Differences

A major part of the supply manager's role is communicating requirements clearly and effectively to suppliers. Language differences can sometimes interfere with the effective communication of requirements. Not everyone understands English, and Americans will likely not understand the seller's native language.

The largest differences in communication styles across countries are message speed and level of content. Americans tend to give fast messages with the conclusions expressed first. This style is not appropriate in many countries, particularly in Europe.[10]

Dick Locke, a procurement manager who has handled buying operations in Tokyo, Europe, Mexico, and the Middle East, offers this advice about language and communication:[11]

- If a supplier is using English as a second language, the buyer should be responsible for preventing communication problems.
- To aid in communication, speak slowly, use more communication graphics, and eliminate jargon, slang, and sports and military metaphors from your language.
- Bring an interpreter to all but the most informal meetings. Allow an extra day to educate interpreters on your issues and vocabulary.
- Document, in writing, the conclusions and decisions made in a meeting before adjourning.

Logistical Issues

Buyers should not underestimate the potential effects of extended pipelines on their ability to plan and manage a worldwide supply chain. Although advanced industrial countries have a developed infrastructure, many foreign countries do not, making shipping delays a real possibility. China, for example, has 25 kilometers of paved roads, 6.5 kilometers of railways, and 17 kilometers of runways per 1,000 square kilometers of land. In comparison, the United States has 612 kilometers of paved roads, 22.7 kilometers of railways, and 189 kilometers of runways per 1,000 square kilometers.[12]

Fewer railroads, paved roads, and airports often leads to higher logistics costs and less reliable deliveries. In the United States, the ratio of logistics costs to total gross domestic product is about 10%. In developing countries, this ratio can be as high as 25% of total gross domestic product.[13] This becomes a factor when calculating the total landed cost for foreign goods. One study estimated that it takes as much as 50% more to transport goods in China than in the United States or Europe. The density of land transportation is 22% of that in the United States and 5% of that in Japan, and many roads are unpaved or in poor condition, slowing down transit times. This is further complicated by China's lack of a cross-country carrier and the small size of the average Chinese trucker's fleet (two vehicles). Additional regulations between different provinces require frequent changes of trucks when crossing province boundaries.[14]

All international shipments move by a standard set of terms. **Incoterms** are internationally recognized standard definitions that describe the responsibilities of a buyer and seller in a commercial transaction. They are used in conjunction with a sales agreement or other method of transacting the sale. The buyer and seller have an array of terms from which to choose, depending on the extent to which each party wants to be involved with the transportation and insurance. One of the complications is the modes by which an international shipment will move. Typically there will be more than one mode of transportation involved.

Modes of Transportation

EXW, CPT, CIP, DAF, DDU, and DDP are commonly used for any mode of transportation. FAS, FOB, CFR, CIF, DES, and DEQ are used for sea and inland waterway. Exhibit 10.2 on p. 358 highlights the 13 standard Incoterms.

Legal Issues

Legal systems differ from country to country. The United States uses common or case law, which often results in longer and more detailed contracts compared with countries that use code or civil law. Before IBM redesigned its purchasing process in the late 1990s, it was common for purchase contracts to be more than 40 pages in length. A redesign effort reduced this to around six pages. Many foreign countries do not like to deal with the U.S. legal system and long contracts.

Advanced industrial countries have legal systems that provide the buyer protection and fair treatment. This may not be true in developing countries. Many countries offer no effective protection against the piracy of intellectual property. It is necessary, therefore, to perform a thorough check of prospective suppliers before releasing designs or other proprietary information.

Exhibit 10.2 Incoterms 2000

Incoterms 2000 are internationally accepted commercial terms that define the respective roles of the buyer and seller in the arrangement of transportation and other responsibilities and clarify when the ownership of the merchandise takes place. They are used in conjunction with a sales agreement or other method of transacting the sale.

SERVICE	EXW EX WORKS	FCA FREE CARRIER	FAS FREE ALONGSIDE SHIP	FOB FREE ONBOARD VESSEL	CFR COST AND FREIGHT	CIF COST INSURANCE AND FREIGHT	CPT CARRIAGE PAID TO	CIP CARRIAGE INSURANCE PAID TO	DAF DELIVERED AT FRONTIER	DES DELIVERED EX SHIP	DEQ DELIVERED EX QUAY DUTY UNPAID	DDU DELIVERED DUTY UNPAID	DDP DELIV-ERED DUTY PAID
Warehouse storage	Seller	Seller	Seller	Seller	Seller	Seller	Seller	Seller	Seller	Seller	Seller	Seller	Seller
Warehouse labor	Seller	Seller	Seller	Seller	Seller	Seller	Seller	Seller	Seller	Seller	Seller	Seller	Seller
Export packing	Seller	Seller	Seller	Seller	Seller	Seller	Seller	Seller	Seller	Seller	Seller	Seller	Seller
Loading charges	Buyer	Seller	Seller	Seller	Seller	Seller	Seller	Seller	Seller	Seller	Seller	Seller	Seller
Inland freight	Buyer	Buyer/ Seller*	Seller	Seller	Seller	Seller	Seller	Seller	Seller	Seller	Seller	Seller	Seller
Terminal charges	Buyer	Buyer	Seller	Seller	Seller	Seller	Seller	Seller	Seller	Seller	Seller	Seller	Seller
Forwarder's fees	Buyer	Buyer	Buyer	Buyer	Seller	Seller	Seller	Seller	Seller	Seller	Seller	Seller	Seller
Loading on vessel	Buyer	Buyer	Buyer	Seller	Seller	Seller	Seller	Seller	Seller	Seller	Seller	Seller	Seller
Ocean/air freight	Buyer	Buyer	Buyer	Buyer	Seller	Seller	Seller	Seller	Seller	Seller	Seller	Seller	Seller
Charges on arrival at destination	Buyer	Buyer	Buyer	Buyer	Buyer	Buyer	Seller	Seller	Buyer	Buyer	Seller	Seller	Seller
Duty, taxes, and customs clearance	Buyer	Buyer	Buyer	Buyer	Buyer	Buyer	Buyer	Buyer	Buyer	Buyer	Buyer	Buyer	Seller
Delivery to destination	Buyer	Buyer	Buyer	Buyer	Buyer	Buyer	Buyer	Buyer	Buyer	Buyer	Buyer	Seller	Seller

*There are actually two FCA terms: FCA Seller's Premises, where the seller is *only* responsible for loading the goods and *not* responsible for inland freight; and FCA Named Place (International Carrier), where the seller *is* responsible for inland freight.

Source: www.i-b-.net/incoterms.html.

Sourcing Snapshot

Managing Risk: The Hidden Costs of Sourcing in China

The race by firms in the United States and other countries to source goods and services in China shows no indication of slowing down. Through experience many firms are also learning that the cost savings they initially projected may be reduced by hidden costs. Data from a study of more than 150 executives with general management (including supply chain and operations) highlights some important lessons to consider before jumping into China. Three out of four (75%) of these executives were already outsourcing at least one function in China. The most cited outsourced function was manufacturing, but respondents were outsourcing other functions such as research and development or IT support.

Some of the management issues these executives say are important to keep in mind are cultural and extend into Chinese business practices. Cultural norms are different from those in the United States, and therefore it is important to study Chinese culture and norms before entering any serious negotiations. Not doing this is a recipe for failure or much higher costs. For example, it is important to determine the nature of the relationship that will be developed. This could range from a simple agreement for standard items to a very involved partnership for a critical item. Relationships are often coupled with reciprocal obligations. For example, after one U.S. firm reached agreement on one item with a Chinese supplier, they were questioned and cajoled into agreeing that future items would be awarded to them or a supplier that they recommended.

If the firm is outsourcing operations (manufacturing) to China, the current process should be stable and operating at a competitive level. It is not a good idea to outsource a problem process, because China is a developing country and currently has a shortage of high-skilled workers as well as management expertise. Thus there will be some training required on the part of the outsourcer. Outsourcing a stable process will allow the outsourcer to train and measure the Chinese supplier. Most of the respondents in the survey indicated that the transition involves a commitment of both people and time. Most estimated it would take twice as long as originally estimated to reach a steady state of production. One key to reducing the time to steady state is to look at implementation frameworks from other firms that have had successful experiences in China.

Regarding specific outsourcing issues, don't be penny wise and pound foolish. This means visiting the site where the product is to be made. Verify the skill, quality, and turnover rate of the employees. Indications from this sample are that hidden costs can add 15–24% to the unit price when sourcing in China. These hidden costs include higher shipping costs (10–15%), warranty costs (4–7%), and travel/coordination costs (1–3%). By one estimate, 10,000 containers from China annually fall overboard. Additionally, intellectual property laws are not consistently enforced and discussions must address how intellectual property will be protected. Finally, labor rates vary widely and are increasing due to demand for Chinese goods.

In summary, any entry into China needs to be made with a clear strategy that includes a budget for travel, an understanding of the culture, calculation of the expected hidden costs, and site visits to clearly communicate expectations and process improvement plans. Extending a supply chain by 7,000 miles clearly has its challenges, and managers are now beginning to realize this and adjust savings to include these hidden costs.

Source: Adapted from a presentation by Brad Householder, "The Challenges and Hidden Costs of Outsourcing," PRTM Group, Waltham, MA, November 2005.

International contracts can be used if the country the buyer is doing business with follows the **United Nations Convention on Contracts for the International Sale of Goods (CISG)**. The CISG took effect on January 1, 1988. The purpose was to facilitate international trade by removing legal barriers. Unless the parties have specified to the contrary, the CISG applies to sales of goods contracts between parties with places of business in the "Contracting States." Contracting States are those countries that have ratified the CISG.

Countries that are part of the World Trade Organization are expected to follow certain international trade practices and protect intellectual property. Buyers and sellers doing business across boundaries should agree, preferably in a contract, about what laws will cover the business transaction.

U.S. buyers employed by domestic or foreign-based firms must also be mindful of their conduct in dealings with foreign government officials. The Foreign Corrupt Practices Act (FCPA) was passed by Congress in 1977 to prevent companies from making questionable or illegal payments to foreign government officials, politicians, and political parties. The law prohibits U.S. citizens or their agents from making payments to foreign officials to secure or retain business, and it requires accurate record keeping and adequate controls for company transactions. Since 1998, these practices apply to foreign firms and persons who make such corrupt payments while in the United States. There is no dollar threshold on the act, making it illegal to offer even a dollar as a bribe. Enforcement focuses on the intent of the bribery more than the amount.

In 2004 Lucent Technologies fired four top executives from its China operations for making bribes. The deficiencies in China were uncovered during the company's FCPA compliance audits stemming from an investigation into its practices in Saudi Arabia.[15]

Exhibit 10.3 Role of International Purchasing Offices

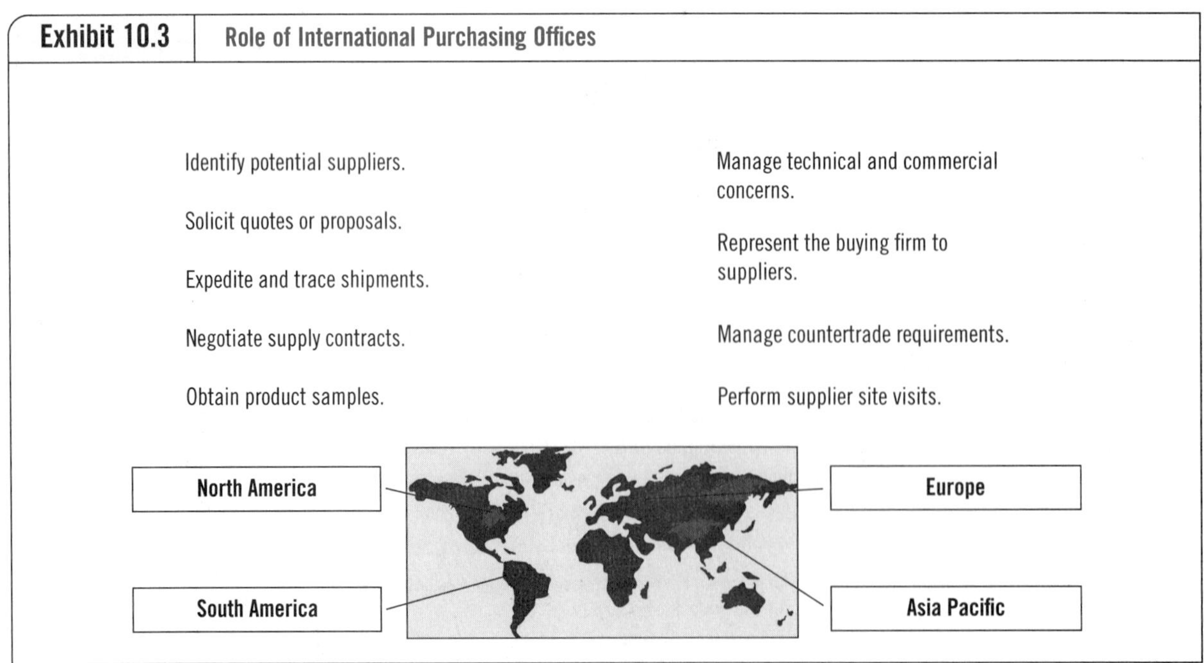

Identify potential suppliers.
Solicit quotes or proposals.
Expedite and trace shipments.
Negotiate supply contracts.
Obtain product samples.
Manage technical and commercial concerns.
Represent the buying firm to suppliers.
Manage countertrade requirements.
Perform supplier site visits.
North America
South America
Europe
Asia Pacific

Organizational Issues

Chapter 5 provides a broad discussion of organizational issues. A logical approach when trying to meet a company's growing worldwide sourcing requirements has been the establishment of international purchasing offices (IPOs) in selected areas around the world. Foreign nationals, who usually report directly to a centralized corporate procurement office, staff the IPO. IPOs can support the sourcing needs of the entire organization, not just a single division or buying unit. Larger firms are more likely than smaller ones to have international purchasing offices. IPOs have several major functions, which Exhibit 10.3 identifies.

A 2006 study on global sourcing indicated that the growth in IPOs over the past five years corresponded to an increase in higher-level global sourcing. Firms were using their IPOs to provide operational support from the development phase through contract management of the global agreement. Specific IPO activities included facilitating import and export requirements, resolving quality and delivery performance problems, and measuring supplier performance.[16]

Another organizational issue is how to structure the overall global sourcing efforts. Recent research stated that maintaining central control and leadership over the strategic elements of a global sourcing program enhances the probability of achieving

Exhibit 10.4 Decentralized Purchasing with Centralized International Purchasing

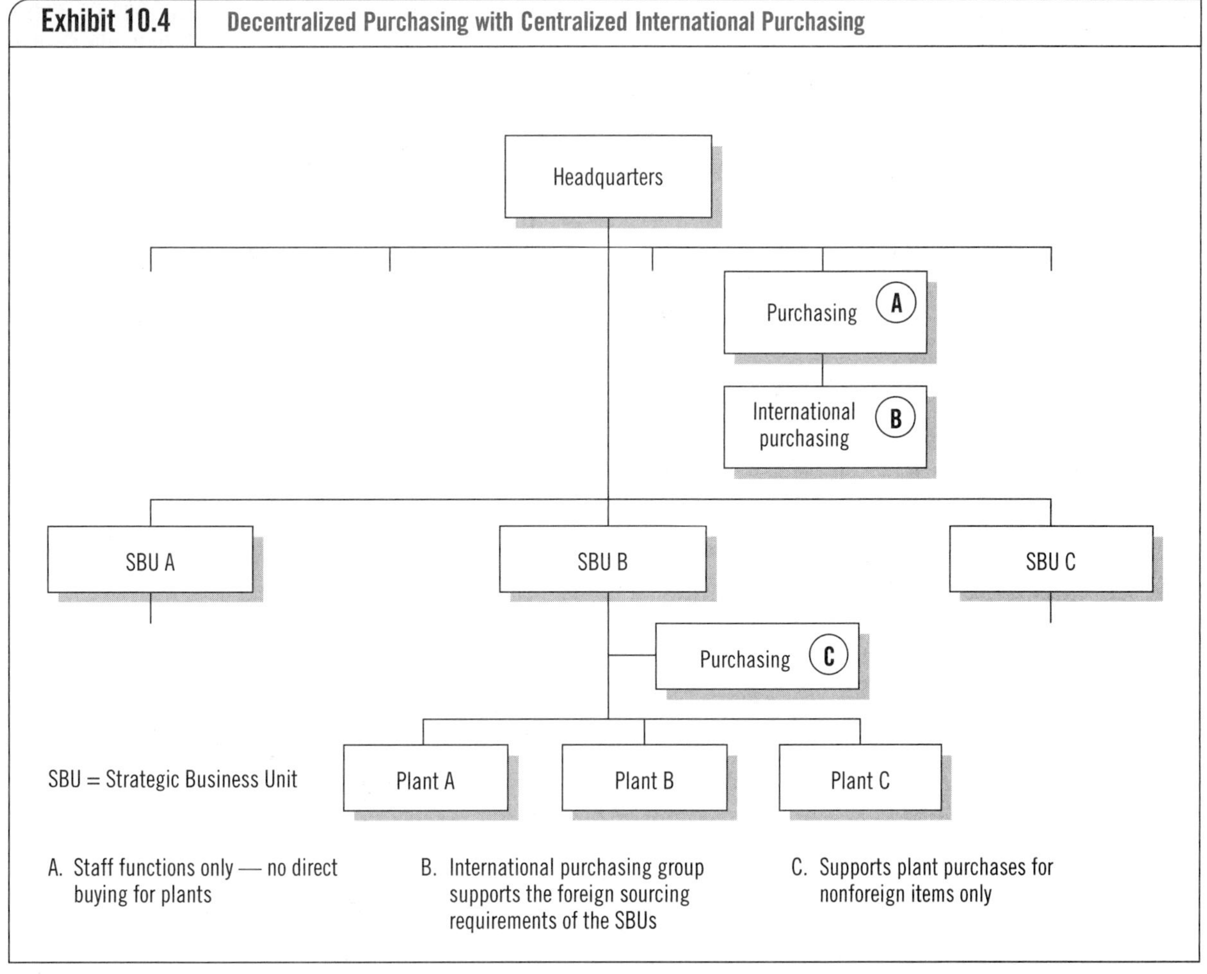

improved sourcing process outcomes.[17] This can occur even though firms may also decentralize operational activities. Exhibit 10.4 on p. 361 presents a structure that contains elements of centralized and decentralized decision making. Decentralized purchasing at the divisional or business unit level supports domestic sourcing, whereas a centralized international purchasing office supports the international requirements of the different business units.

Countertrade Requirements

A specialized form of international trade that has increased over the last 25 years is **countertrade**. This broad term refers to all international and domestic trade where buyer and seller have at least a partial exchange of goods for goods. This exchange can involve a complete trade of goods for goods or involve some partial payment to a firm in cash.

Although many companies have established a countertrade office or department, purchasing is sometimes involved in negotiating and managing countertrade agreements, including determining the market or sales value of countertrade deals or selecting appropriate products to fulfill countertrade requirements.

A country imposes countertrade demands for a number of reasons. First, some countries simply lack the hard currency to purchase imported goods. Developing nations often require Western multinationals to accept goods as at least partial payment for sales within their country. Another reason for countertrade requirements is that countertrade provides a means of selling products in markets to which a company may have otherwise lacked access. A country wishing to sell its products or services in global markets may rely upon the marketing expertise of multinational companies to market or arrange for marketing of the country's products through intermediaries.

Countertrade demands often arise when several factors are present. Items involving large dollar amounts, such as military contracts, are prime candidates for countertrade. Companies can also expect countertrade demands from a country when that country's goods have a low or nondifferentiated perception in the world marketplace. This may include items that are available from many sources, commodity-type items, or items not perceived as technologically superior or having higher quality compared with other available products. Highly valued items or those sought after by the buying country are less susceptible to countertrade demands.

Types of Countertrade

As firms have strived to meet countertrade requirements, several different forms have evolved. The five predominant types of countertrade arrangements are (1) barter, (2) counterpurchase, (3) offset, (4) buy-back, and (5) switch trading.

Barter

The oldest and most basic form of trading is **barter**, a process that involves the straight exchange of goods for goods with no exchange of currency. It requires trading parties to enter into a single contract to fulfill trading requirements. Despite its apparent simplicity, barter is one of the least-practiced forms of countertrade today.

Barter differs from other forms of countertrade in several ways. Barter involves no exchange of money between parties. Next, a single contract formalizes a barter transaction whereas other forms of countertrade require two or more contracts. Finally, barter arrangements usually relate to a specific transaction and cover a period of time shorter than that covered by other arrangements.

Counterpurchase

Counterpurchase requires a selling firm to purchase a specified amount of goods from the country that purchased its products. The amount to counterpurchase is a percentage of the amount of the original sale. This requirement usually ranges from 5 to 80% of the total value of the transaction but can actually exceed 100% under some circumstances.

This form of countertrade requires a company to fulfill its countertrade requirement by purchasing products within a country unrelated to its primary business. The countertrading company identifies a list of possible purchase items that will fulfill the countertrade requirement. The purchaser must market the unrelated goods or use a third party to assume those duties, which introduces increased complexity and cost into the transaction.

Offset

Offset agreements, which are closely related to counterpurchase, also require the seller to purchase some agreed-upon percentage of goods from a country over a specified period. However, offset agreements allow a company to fulfill its countertrade requirement with any company or industry in the country. The selling firm can purchase items related directly to its business requirements, which offers the purchaser greater flexibility. An example of an offset purchase is a U.S. aircraft manufacturer that obtains a contract to sell planes in Spain and agrees to purchase products worth 100% of the contract value in Spain.

Buy-Back

Some countertrade authorities also refer to this type of countertrade as **compensation trading**. **Buy-back** occurs when a firm physically builds a plant in another country or provides a service, equipment, or technology to support the plant. The firm then agrees to take a portion of the plant's output as payment. Countries lacking foreign exchange for payment but rich in natural resources can benefit from this type of countertrade arrangement. Opportunities exist for Western companies to provide the plant, equipment, and expertise to bring resources to market.

Switch Trading

This form of countertrade involves the use of a third-party trader to sell earned counterpurchase credits. **Switch trading** occurs when a selling company agrees to accept goods from the buying country as partial payment. If the selling company does not want the goods from the country, it can sell, at a discount, the credits for these goods to a third-party trader, which sells or markets the goods. The trader charges a fee for handling the transaction. The original selling company must consider the discount and third-party fee when evaluating the total cost of a countertrade arrangement with a country.

Purchasing's role in countertrade will not be as visible as marketing's role. Purchasing is usually a reactive participant that must identify supply sources that will help satisfy any countertrade requirements that a company has incurred through the sale of its product.

Costs Associated with International Purchasing

Purchasers must examine the additional costs associated with international purchasing. Whether the purchase transaction is with a domestic or foreign producer, there are certain common costs. The difference between domestic and foreign purchasing, however, is that foreign purchasing must include the additional costs associated with conducting overseas transactions. If price is a major factor, then a buyer must compare the total cost of the foreign purchase to the total cost of the domestic purchase. Exhibit 10.5 summarizes the various charges often associated with international purchasing and logistics.

Common Costs

Certain costs are common between domestic and foreign purchasing. These include the unit purchase price quoted by a supplier, tooling charges, and transportation from the supplier (common cost does not mean the costs are equal). Unit price evaluation must consider the effect of quantity discounts, minimum buys necessary

Exhibit 10.5 Elements of Total Cost for Worldwide Sourcing

Base Price

- Ascertain quantity breaks, minimum buys for shipping efficiency, and any surcharges.
- Determine price for rush shipments of smaller-than-planned quantities, which are often more.

Tooling

- Ideally, the purchaser should own the tooling and pay for it only once.
- Consider shipping tooling from a domestic source if transferable.

Packaging

- This is a hidden cost (may be expensive for long distances and multiple handlings).
- Consult a packaging supplier or internal engineer for methods to minimize cost on international shipments.

Escalation

- Determine for how long the quoted price is firm.
- Determine components of escalation (i.e., ensure that price increases are not hidden in other costs).

Transportation

- Obtain assistance from logistics personnel who have expertise in international transportation.
- Consider consolidation of shipments with other corporations from the same geographical area.
- Use multinational carriers or freight brokers to manage shipments and cost where required.
- Consult the foreign supplier as a source of information regarding freight sources.

Customs Duty

- Duties paid any time a shipment crosses international lines—can vary widely over range of goods, and often change on short notice.
- Provided by U.S. Published Tariff Schedules.
- Items may fall into more than one classification.
- May be best to discuss this with a customs agent/broker.

Insurance Premiums

- Not typically included in an ocean shipment price (need marine insurance).
- Don't pay for extra coverage that your company may already carry for international transactions.

Exhibit 10.5 Elements of Total Cost for Worldwide Sourcing (Continued)

Payment Terms

- Foreign suppliers often grant longer payment terms such as net 60.
- If dealing with intermediaries, the payment may be requested upon shipment.

Additional Fees and Commissions

- Ask supplier, customs broker, and transportation personnel if other costs may be incurred, and who is responsible for these costs.
- If your shipment is held at the port of entry due to a lack of documentation and customs officials place it in storage, a storage fee will be billed to the customer. (Who will pay for this?)

Port Terminal and Handling Fees

- U.S. port and handling charges (unloading cargo, administrative services of port personnel, and use of port).

Customs Broker Fees

- Flat charge per transaction.

Taxes

- Consider any additional taxes that may be paid.

Communication Costs

- Higher phone, travel, mailing, telex, fax, e-mail charges.

Payment and Currency Fees

- Bank transfers, bills of exchange, hedging and forward contracts.

Inventory Carrying Costs

- Higher levels of inventory will have to be held because of longer lead times.
- Costs include the interest rate forgone by investing funds, insurance, property taxes, storage and obsolescence (check with controller).

Source: Adapted from R. M. Monczka and L. C. Giunipero, *Purchasing Internationally: Concepts and Principles,* Chelsea, MI: Bookcrafters, 1990.

for shipping efficiency, the effect on price due to expedited shipments, and any supplier-specified surcharges or extras.

Transportation costs also require critical evaluation. For example, what is the effect on transportation costs if the purchaser controls a shipment directly from the supplier instead of having the supplier arrange shipment? What is the effect on transportation costs due to longer distances? International transportation often requires assistance from personnel with special expertise. A transportation group can review carrier quotations, evaluate shipping alternatives, and recommend the most efficient course of action, which may include combining international shipments with those of other purchasers to obtain favorable freight rates.

International Transaction Costs

International purchasing creates additional costs that are not part of domestic purchasing. Failure to include these costs in a total cost analysis can lead to a miscalculation of the total cost of the purchase.

For a first-time purchase, the seller may request a **letter of credit**. Letters of credit are issued by the purchaser's bank in conjunction with an affiliate bank in the seller's country. It assures the seller that the funds are in the bank. The supplier can draw against the letter of credit upon presentation of the required documents. There are two basic types of letters of credit: revocable and irrevocable. The revocable type can be changed or canceled at any time by the buyer without the seller's consent and therefore is seldom used. The irrevocable type can only be changed or canceled upon agreement of all parties.

Packaging requirements and costs are usually higher with foreign purchases because of the longer distances traveled and increased handling of shipments. Each item entering a country is also subject to a customs duty or tariff. Duty rates vary widely over seemingly small differences between items. A knowledgeable customs broker may lower duty costs as well as expedite the shipment through customs. Total cost analysis must include duty and broker fees incurred during the international transaction.

International shipments often require insurance protection. This issue is important, because unlike domestic transportation, oceangoing carrier liability is generally limited. Insurance is usually required when a third party is financing the inventory or shipment, and is provided by large firms such as Lloyd's of London.

Sourcing Snapshot

Bose Combines International Purchasing and Supply Chain Management

Companies have different experiences and approaches when developing their worldwide sourcing strategies. Bose Corporation, a manufacturer of some of the world's best-known high-fidelity speakers, is committed to just-in-time manufacturing, although it has suppliers located in North America, the Far East, and Europe. The company must blend its desire for low inventory with the need to buy from distant sources.

Controlling transportation is a central to Bose's international purchasing strategy. Bose controls its inbound and outbound transportation by taking control of shipments when the supplier turns goods over to a carrier and then relinquishing control only when finished goods are delivered to Bose's customer.

Managing a worldwide supply chain requires Bose to rely on a limited number of transportation suppliers, with whom it has developed mutually beneficial partnership agreements. Bose has a contract with PIE Nationwide, a national less-than-truckload carrier based in Jacksonville, FL, to handle North American transportation requirements. W.N. Proctor Company, a Boston-based freight forwarder and customs broker, plays a central role in Bose's critical international shipping. Bose has also established an extensive EDI system called Shipmaster, which allows the company to contact every one of PIE's 230 terminals. If Bose must expedite a shipment, Bose forwards a message directly to PIE's freight terminal.

What Shipmaster does for domestic freight, ProctorLink does for international cargo. When a shipment goes onto a plane or a ship, it goes into the Proctor system. All of the specifications—the ship, customs clearance, and so on—are included, providing the information needed to control the inventory. Proctor also provides hands-on service to Bose, such as selecting overseas agents who help move goods from the Far East to the United States.

Source: Adapted from Bose Corporation sources and public information.

Other costs include port terminal and handling fees. Depending on the exact terms of the purchase contract, a purchaser can expect charges for unloading of cargo, administrative services of port authority personnel, and general use of the port; these are U.S. port terminal and handling charges. Even if a purchaser uses a third party to manage this part of the process and receives a single invoice, these cost elements are still part of the single involved charge. Someone had to pay these charges.

A critical factor during international purchasing is keeping to a minimum the surprises that affect total cost and customer service. For example, if a shipment arrives in Long Beach, CA, without proper documentation, customs will place the shipment in warehouse storage awaiting documentation. Whether the buyer or the seller pays the storage charges should be clear in the event this issue arises.

Currency Risk

A major concern with international purchasing is managing the risk associated with international currency fluctuations. Because of this risk, companies often take steps to reduce the uncertainty associated with fluctuating currencies.

The following example illustrates the principle of currency fluctuation and risk. Suppose a U.S. company purchased a machine from Canada in June. The purchase is denominated in Canadian dollars at $100,000 paid upon delivery in November. For simplicity, assume the exchange rate in June is $1 U.S. equals $1 Canadian. By November, however, the Canadian dollar has strengthened to the point where $1 U.S. equals $0.90 Canadian (it now takes less than one Canadian dollar to purchase a U.S. dollar; the Canadian currency has appreciated vis-à-vis the U.S. dollar). Now, $100,000 U.S. only equals $90,000 Canadian. This U.S. firm needs $100,000 Canadian to pay for the machine, or $100,000 U.S./0.9 exchange rate = $111,111 U.S. If the purchaser does not protect itself from fluctuating currencies, the machine would cost $11,111 more than originally planned. On the other hand, if the U.S. dollar strengthened against the Canadian dollar during this period, the purchase would require fewer U.S. dollars in November to buy $100,000 Canadian dollars.

Companies use a variety of measures to address the risk associated with currency fluctuations. These range from very basic measures to the sophisticated management of international currencies involving the corporate finance department.

Purchase in U.S. Dollars

Buyers who prefer to pay for international purchases in U.S. dollars are attempting to eliminate currency fluctuations as a source of risk by shifting the risk to the seller. Although this appears to be an easy method of risk management, it is not always the best or most feasible approach. The foreign supplier, which is also aware of currency risks, may be unwilling to accept the risk of currency fluctuations by itself. Also, many foreign suppliers anticipate exchange rate fluctuations by incorporating a risk factor into their price. A purchaser willing to accept some of the risk may obtain a favorable price.

Sharing Currency Fluctuation Risk

Equal sharing of risk permits a selling firm to price its product without having to factor in the acceptance of risk costs. Sharing of risk requires equal division of a change in an agreed-upon price due to currency fluctuation. In the Canadian machine example, the U.S. firm realized over $11,000 in additional costs due to currency fluctuations. With equal risk sharing, the Canadian and U.S. firms would evenly divide the additional cost. This technique works best on items that have a set delivery date, such as capital equipment.

Currency Adjustment Contract Clauses

With currency adjustment clauses, both parties agree that payment occurs as long as exchange rates do not fluctuate outside an agreed-upon range or band. If exchange rates move outside the agreed-upon range, the parties can renegotiate or review the contract. This provides a mutual degree of protection because firms do not know with certainty in which direction exchange rates will fluctuate.

Purchase contracts often contain one of two types of currency adjustment clauses: delivery-triggered clauses and time-triggered clauses. Delivery-triggered clauses stipulate that the parties will review an exchange before delivery to verify that the rate is still within the agreed-upon range. If the rate falls outside the range, the buyer or seller can ask to renegotiate the contract price. Time-triggered clauses stipulate that both parties will review a contract at specified time intervals to evaluate the impact of fluctuating exchange rates. The parties review the exchange rate at scheduled intervals, and a new contract is established if the rate falls outside the agreed-upon range.

Currency Hedging

Hedging involves the simultaneous purchase and sale of currency contracts in two markets. The expected result is that a gain realized on one contract will be offset by a loss on the other. Hedging is a form of risk insurance that can protect both parties from currency fluctuations. The motivation for using hedging is risk aversion, not monetary gain. If the purpose of buying currency contracts is to realize a net gain, then the purchaser is speculating and not hedging.

Buyers and sellers trade futures exchange contracts (also referred to as "futures contracts") on commodity exchanges open to anyone needing to hedge or with speculative risk capital. In fact, the exchanges encourage speculation because speculators help create markets for buyers and sellers of futures contracts. Traders sell futures contracts in fixed currency amounts with fixed contract lengths.

Forward exchange contracts have a different focus than futures exchange contracts. Issued by major banks, these contracts are agreements by which a purchaser pays a pre-established rate for a currency in the future (as well as a fee to the bank). Trading participants include banks, brokers, and multinational companies. The use of forward exchange contracts discourages speculation. Forward exchange contracts meet the needs of an individual purchaser in terms of dollar amount and time limit.

Finance Department Expertise

Companies with extensive international experience usually have a finance or treasury department that can support international currency requirements. Finance can identify the currency a firm should use for payment based on projections of currency fluctuations. The finance department can also provide advice about hedging and currency forecasts, and whether to seek a new contract or renegotiate an existing one due to currency changes; it can also act as a clearinghouse for foreign currencies to make payment for foreign purchases.

Tracking Currency Movements

Purchasing managers should track the movement of currencies against the dollar over time to identify longer-term changes and sourcing opportunities due to changing economics. The weakening of the U.S. dollar against the euro during 2006 made exports more attractive to European countries. Purchases from Japan became more expensive to U.S. buyers in the early to mid-1990s as the Japanese yen strengthened in value from 200 yen to 100 yen per dollar. As a result, there was a financial incentive to source domestically or from countries where exchange rates were more favorable. In 2007, the yen stayed in a range between 110 and 120 yen per dollar and has not depreciated to the high 100s or the 200s of the mid-1990s.

Progressing from International Purchasing to Global Sourcing

At some point, many companies determine that moving beyond basic international purchasing might yield new and untapped benefits. Exhibit 10.6 presents international purchasing and global sourcing as a series of evolving levels or steps along a continuum. An internationalization of the sourcing process takes place as firms evolve or progress first from domestic purchasing to international purchasing, and then to the global coordination and integration of common items, processes, designs, technologies, and suppliers across worldwide locations. Level I includes those firms that only purchase domestically. Sourcing domestically could result in purchases from international suppliers that have facilities in the United States.

Referring to Exhibit 10.6, Level II represents basic international purchasing that is usually reactive and uncoordinated between buying locations or units. Moving forward, strategies and approaches developed in Level III begin to recognize that a properly executed worldwide sourcing strategy can result in major improvements.

Exhibit 10.6 International Purchasing and Global Sourcing Levels

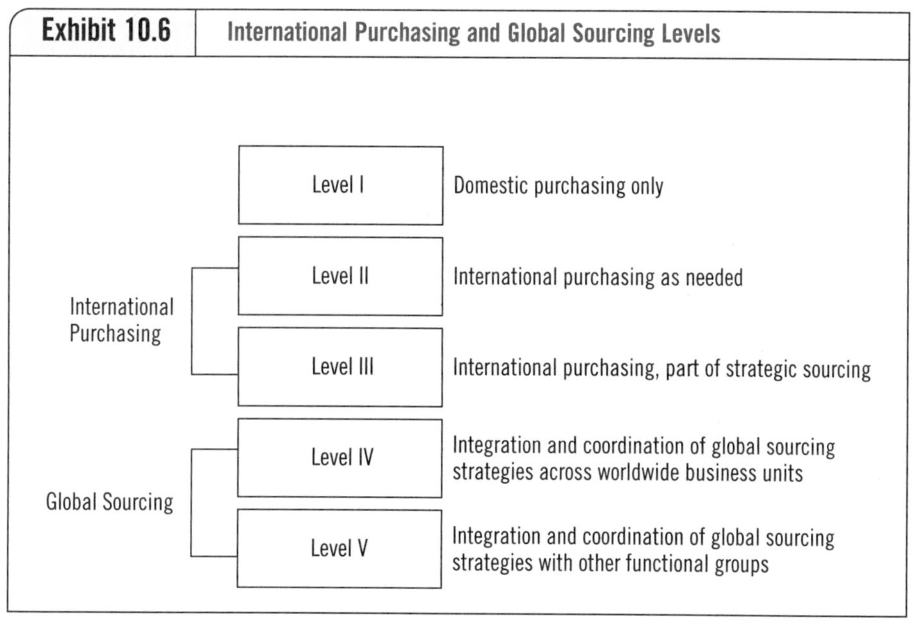

However, strategies at this level are not well coordinated across worldwide buying locations, operating centers, functional groups, or business units.

Level IV, which represents the integration and coordination of sourcing strategies across worldwide buying locations, represents a sophisticated level of strategy development. Operating at this level requires

- Worldwide information systems
- Personnel with sophisticated knowledge and skills
- Extensive coordination and communication mechanisms
- An organizational structure that promotes central coordination of global activities
- Leadership that endorses a global approach to sourcing

Although worldwide integration occurs in Level IV, which is not the case with Level III, the integration is primarily cross-locational rather than cross-functional.

Organizations that operate at Level V have achieved the cross-locational integration that firms operating at the fourth level have achieved. The primary distinction is that Level V participants integrate and coordinate common items, processes, designs, technologies, and suppliers across worldwide purchasing centers and with other functional groups, particularly engineering. This integration occurs during new-product development as well as during the sourcing of items or services to fulfill continuous demand or aftermarket requirements.

Only those firms that have worldwide design, development, production, logistics, and procurement capabilities can progress to this level. Although many firms expect to advance to Level V, the reality is that many lack the understanding or the willingness to achieve this level of sophistication.

Factors Separating Successful from Less-Successful Global Sourcing Efforts

A major research project on global sourcing, with 167 companies, identified a set of factors that drove global sourcing performance. These factors were (1) a defined process to support global sourcing, (2) centrally coordinated and centrally led decision making, (3) site-based control of operational activities, (4) real-time communication tools, (5) information sharing with suppliers, (6) availability of critical resources, (7) sourcing and contracting systems, and (8) international purchasing office support.[18] Exhibit 10.7 highlights these success factors, which are explained in more detail in the following section.

Defined Process to Support Global Sourcing

The development of a rigorous and well-defined approach or process is critical to global sourcing success. Some organizations have taken their commodity or regional strategy process and adapted it for global sourcing. When this occurs, the global process will likely weight certain factors differently (for example, more emphasis placed on risk factors and total landed cost) compared with a regional commodity development process.

A defined process helps overcome many of the differences inherent in global sourcing. Social culture and laws, personnel skills and abilities, and business culture are

Exhibit 10.7 Global Sourcing Success Factors

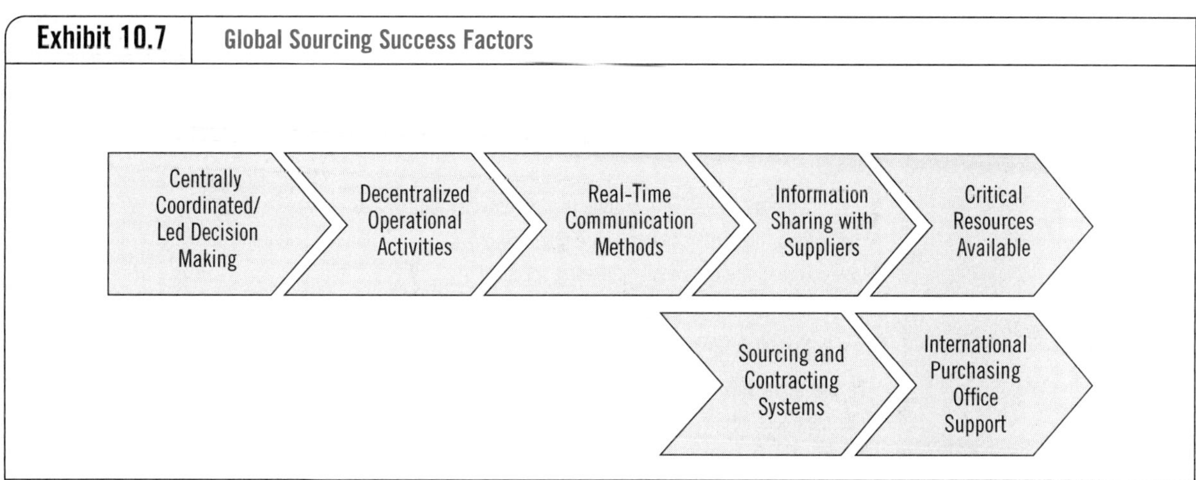

three areas where differences are the greatest across different geographic units. A global sourcing process helps align very different participants and practices around the globe. Exhibit 10.8 on p. 372 outlines the global sourcing process at a chemical company with worldwide operations.

Centrally Coordinated and Centrally Led Decision Making

Maintaining central control and leadership over activities that are strategic in nature enhances the probability of achieving a range of improved sourcing process outcomes. These benefits include

- Improved standardization or consistency of the sourcing process
- Early supplier involvement
- Supplier relationships
- Client, stakeholder, and executive satisfaction with sourcing

Site-Based and Decentralized Control of Operational Activities

Firms that also decentralize operational activities during global sourcing are likely to realize lower total cost of ownership, better inventory management, and improved performance to external customers. Operational activities at a decentralized level include

- Issuing material releases to suppliers
- Expediting orders when necessary
- Resolving performance problems
- Planning inventory levels
- Developing logistics plans

Real-Time Communication Tools

Communication complexity makes global sourcing more complex compared with domestic or regional sourcing. Global sourcing participants are often located around the world, making real-time and face-to-face communication difficult. Furthermore,

Exhibit 10.8 | **A U.S. Chemical Company's Global Sourcing Process**

Step 1: Identify Global Sourcing Opportunities

When identifying specific opportunities, an executive steering committee and globalization manager consider:

- What business units require the largest cost reductions?
- What does the company currently buy?
- How is the commodity currently specified?
- How much effort will it take to create a worldwide set of specifications?

Step 2: Establish Global Sourcing Development Teams

The executive steering committee forms cross-functional/cross-locational (CF/CL) teams with worldwide members to pursue global opportunities.

Step 3: Propose Global Strategy

A team charter provides project teams with responsibility for proposing a global strategy. Teams validate the original assumptions underlying the project, verify current volumes and expected savings, determine if global suppliers exist, evaluate the current set of specifications between design centers, and propose a global strategy.

Step 4: Develop Request for Proposal (RFP) Specifications

Teams are responsible for developing the request for proposal (RFP) that suppliers receive. This step consumes a large portion of the global sourcing process time.

Step 5: Release RFPs to Suppliers

On average, six suppliers receive an RFP during a global project. Project teams are responsible for following up with suppliers and answering any questions.

Step 6: Evaluate Bids or Proposals

A commercial and technical evaluation of supplier proposals occurs. Project teams will ask suppliers for their best and final offer and conduct site visits as required. Face-to-face negotiation occurs after analyzing the RFPs returned from suppliers.

Step 7: Negotiate with Suppliers

A smaller team negotiates with suppliers to finalize contract details. All negotiations are conducted at the buying company's U.S. headquarters and can last up to three days. The negotiation process lengthens if the buying company does not achieve its price and service targets.

Step 8: Award Contract(s)

Information concerning the awarded contract is communicated throughout the company via e-mail. The steering committee calculates expected savings and maintains the agreements in a corporate database.

Step 9: Implement Contract and Manage Supplier(s)

This step involves loading global agreements into the appropriate corporate systems. It also involves managing the transition to new suppliers and/or part numbers.

participants may speak several languages while adhering to different business practices, social cultures, and laws.

Many communication and coordination approaches support global sourcing efforts. Examples include regular review meetings, joint training sessions involving worldwide team members, regularly reported project updates through an intranet, and co-location of functional personnel. A common approach for coordinating work efforts is to rely on audio conferencing with a scheduled time for conference calls, usually on a weekly basis. Participants should take advantage of evolving web-based communication tools, including NetMeeting, Centra, and web-based cameras. One conclusion is clear: Successful global sourcing efforts feature well-established communication methods to help overcome the inherent complexities of the process.

It is hard to imagine a successful global sourcing effort without access to reliable and timely information. Examples of such information include a listing of existing contracts and suppliers, reports on supplier capabilities and performance, worldwide volumes by purchase type and location, and information about potential new suppliers. The ability to provide the data and information that global sourcing requires demands the development of global information technology systems and data warehouses.

Although access to a common coding system and real-time data is a major facilitator, the reality is that many firms lack essential IT capabilities. Many companies have historically grouped their procurement and engineering centers by region, whereas other companies that are the result of mergers and acquisitions usually feature different legacy systems, processes, and part numbers across locations. This forces firms to spend time and money to standardize and commonize their systems and coding schemes. Part number and commodity coding schemes have the second-lowest level of similarity from a list of 20 items when looking across all companywide locations.

Information Sharing with Suppliers

Successful global sourcing requires both access to a range of critical information and the willingness to share that information with important suppliers on a worldwide basis. Firms that share performance information with their most important worldwide suppliers realize lower purchase price and cost. Shared performance information includes details about supplier quality, delivery, cycle time, and flexibility. A second type of information sharing relates to broader outcomes. This includes assessment of the supplier's technological sophistication, future capital plans, and product variety data.

Availability of Critical Resources

Resources that affect global success include budget support for travel, access to qualified personnel, time for personnel to develop global strategies, and the availability of required information and data. The availability of time was correlated highly with team effectiveness. Teams that had the time to pursue their agenda were more effective than those that did not have the time. This is very important given the fact that most organizations use teams to coordinate their global efforts.

Sourcing and Contracting Systems

The most important way to ensure access to information is to develop technology systems that make critical information available on a worldwide basis. Firms that have systems that provide access to relevant information are more likely to report lower total costs of ownership and improved sourcing process outcomes from global sourcing. Examples of these features and the information they provide include a worldwide database of purchased goods and services; common part coding schemes;

contract management modules; and systems for measuring contract compliance, worldwide goods and services usage by location, and purchase price paid by location.

International Purchasing Office Support

As previously mentioned, IPOs support a higher level of global sourcing through greater access to product and process technology, reduced cycle times, and increased responsiveness. Additionally, the IPOs have the capabilities to provide operational support from initial negotiations through the contract management phase of the supplier selection cycle. The increasing movement to global sourcing has been enhanced by the growth of IPOs over the past five years.

Global Sourcing Benefits

Perhaps one of the most revealing and interesting differences between the international purchasing and global sourcing segments is the perception each has regarding the benefits they realize from their worldwide efforts. Exhibit 10.9 presents the top-rated benefits for each group. Although this exhibit presents only 10 benefit areas, firms that engage in global sourcing indicate they realize 16 total benefits at a statistically higher level than firms that engage in international purchasing. In fact, the average rating across all benefit areas is 30% higher for global sourcing firms compared with the overall average for international purchasing firms.

Exhibit 10.9 A. International Purchasing Benefits

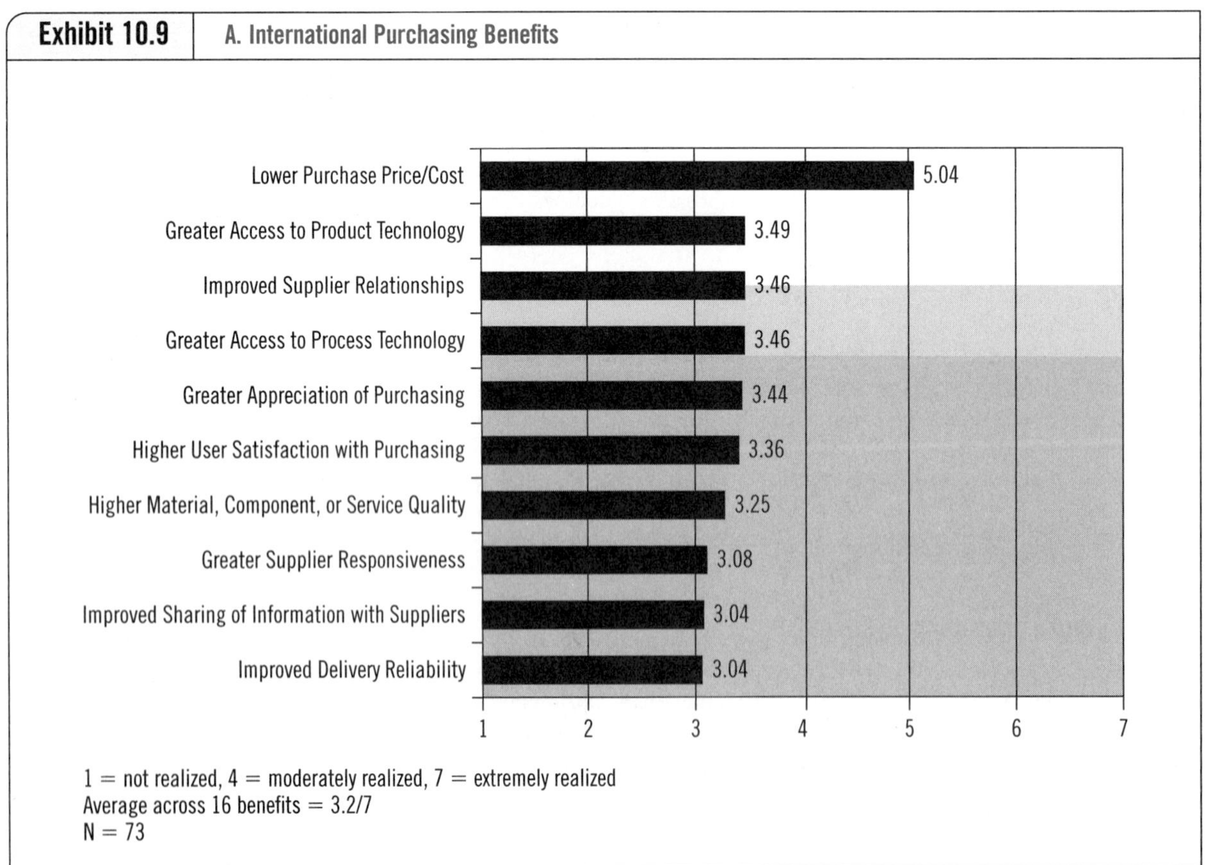

1 = not realized, 4 = moderately realized, 7 = extremely realized
Average across 16 benefits = 3.2/7
N = 73

Exhibit 10.9 B. Global Sourcing Benefits

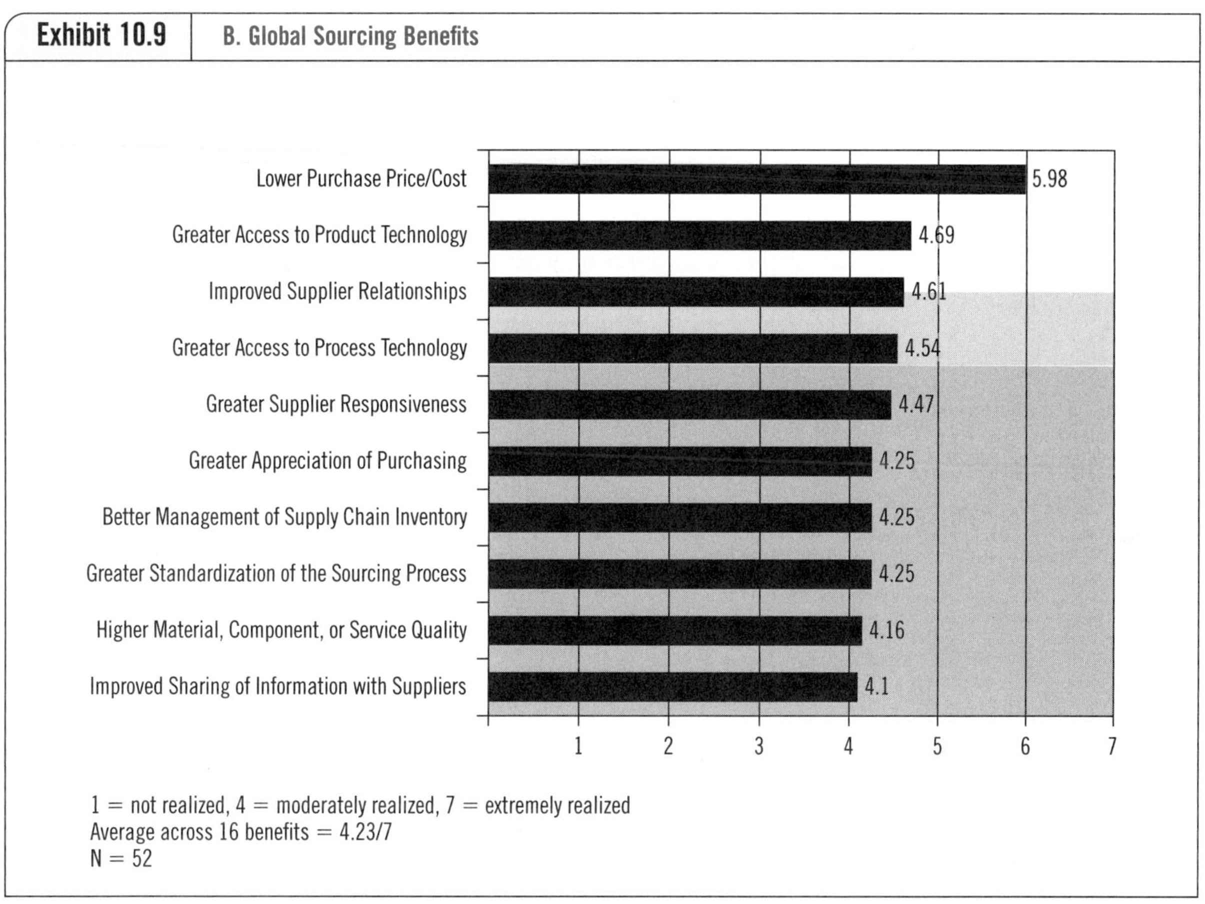

One benefit that both segments rate highly is the ability to achieve a lower purchase price or cost through worldwide sourcing. The initial benefits from international purchasing are usually price focused and are often available from basic international purchasing activities. However, firms realize many nonprice benefits only after they have taken steps to evolve toward higher sourcing levels. In particular, this includes greater access to product and process technology, an outcome that is particularly critical given the more dynamic technology changes that global sourcing firms face. Better management of supply chain inventory is also a benefit that global sourcing firms enjoy at higher levels. This is critical given the emphasis that many firms place on managing costs and inventory investment across the supply chain.

Other important benefits more readily available from global sourcing include greater supplier responsiveness, greater sourcing process consistency, improved supplier relationships, and improved sharing of information with suppliers. The benefits realized between the two groups help explain why so many firms that pursue international purchasing want to evolve toward global sourcing.

Future Global Sourcing Trends

Globalization is a continuous journey of development and improvement. Foremost in this journey is the need to develop or obtain supply management skill sets that encourage evaluating the supply network from a worldwide perspective. Other developments include the need to agree on global performance measures and to establish integrated systems between worldwide units and with suppliers. Doing this requires the continued development and refinement of integrated and coordinated global sourcing strategies across the functional organization. Greater integration between marketing, engineering, and sourcing groups should occur as firms evolve toward higher globalization levels.

We also expect a trend toward doing business with suppliers that have global capabilities. In addition, the focus of global sourcing will shift from part (i.e., component) sourcing to subsystems, systems, and services. Cost reduction pressures will also result in continued sourcing in low-cost emerging supply markets, such as China and Eastern Europe. Although very attractive from a price standpoint, these markets have hidden costs that must be identified. The ability to manage these changes will begin to separate leading companies from average firms.

Companies that produce and sell worldwide should no longer view global sourcing as an emerging approach to sourcing. The pursuit of a competitive advantage requires the development of global processes and strategies that become an integral part of a firm's supply management efforts. Understanding the critical differences between international purchasing and integrated global sourcing is essential before managers can begin to realize the benefits that this complex approach to sourcing potentially offers.

Good Practice Example

Air Products Manages Worldwide Sourcing

One company that has actively pursued integrated global sourcing is Air Products and Chemicals, a U.S.-based company that designs and operates industrial gas and chemical facilities worldwide. In 1999, company executives were surprised when an internal study concluded that the company would have to lower operating costs by 30% to remain competitive globally. Low-cost competitors had emerged in Asia and the Pacific, and industrial buyers were increasingly viewing the company's products as commodity items, factors that together created extensive downward pricing pressures.

Company managers concluded that one way to improve performance was global sourcing. Historically, the company operated in an engineer-to-order environment, using regional design and procurement centers. The result was highly customized design and procurement for each new project. Further, there was a lack of coordination between the company's North American and European units.

These new competitive pressures compelled the company to coordinate design and sourcing activities across its worldwide locations. Accomplishing this resulted in the development of a global engineering and procurement process. The design of each new facility now involves an extensive analysis between U.S. and European centers to identify areas of commonality, standardization, and synergy in procurement and design. Cross-functional teams, with members from the United States and Europe working jointly, develop common design specifications and contracts that satisfy each center's needs while supporting future replacement and maintenance requirements.

After five years of global sourcing experience and with more than 100 global agreements in place, Air Products is averaging 20% in cost savings compared with the regional sourcing and design practices. Furthermore, worldwide design and procurement centers have better aligned their sourcing philosophies and strategies among the centers and with the company's business strategy. Procurement managers now work with marketing to include expected savings from in-process global sourcing projects when responding to customer proposals. Integrated global sourcing is providing a new source of competitiveness to a company that operates in a mature industry.

Source: Adapted from R. M. Monczka, R. J. Trent, and K. J. Peterson, "Effective Global Sourcing and Supply for Superior Results," CAPS Research, 2006, pp. 20–21.

CONCLUSION

International purchases for raw materials, components, finished goods, and services will continue to increase. Because of this, supply management personnel at all levels must become familiar with the nuances of worldwide sourcing. Although most organizations would prefer to purchase from suppliers that are geographically close, this is not always possible. Firms operating in competitive industries must purchase from the best available sources worldwide. Developing these sources requires continual monitoring of both supply market and country trends. Currently the hot spots for sourcing are China and India. Less publicized but just as important is the low-cost-country sourcing occurring in Eastern Europe. Globalization will continue to be a major force that needs to be assessed on a company-by-company basis. Once the assessment is made, then supply management must respond with an effective global strategy.

KEY TERMS

barter, 362
behavior, 356
buy-back, 363
compensation trading, 363
counterpurchase, 363
countertrade, 362
culture, 356
forward exchange contracts, 368
global sourcing, 347
globalization, 345
hedging, 368
Incoterms, 357
international purchasing, 347
letter of credit, 365
offset, 363
switch trading, 363
United Nations Convention on Contracts for the International Sale of Goods (CISG), 360
values, 356
worldwide sourcing, 347

DISCUSSION QUESTIONS

1. Discuss whether globalization and the subsequent growth in worldwide sourcing will have a positive or negative effect over the long run in the United States. Why? What are the alternatives to worldwide sourcing?
2. China, India, and other developing countries are sourcing hot spots. Explain why and also discuss any problems you see in sourcing from these low-cost countries.
3. What are the most important reasons for pursuing worldwide sourcing today?
4. Discuss what the following statement means: Leading-edge companies must develop personnel who have global perspectives. Should personnel from organizations of all sizes have a global perspective? Why?
5. What are the advantages of establishing an international purchasing office? What services do these offices provide?
6. How does the international part-sourcing process differ from the domestic sourcing process?
7. Discuss the reasons why a firm would use a third-party external agent for worldwide sourcing.
8. Discuss some of the sources of information a buyer can use to identify potential foreign sources of supply.
9. How do international purchasing and global sourcing differ? Do you think the differences are meaningful? Why?

10. What is the difference between outsourcing and offshoring? What functions does a firm choose to offshore and why?
11. During the 1980s, many U.S. firms pursued worldwide sourcing on a reactive basis. What does this mean? What might cause a firm to shift from reactive worldwide sourcing to a proactive approach to worldwide sourcing?
12. What are the factors that separate successful from less-successful global sourcing efforts?
13. Refer to the barriers to worldwide sourcing that many firms confront. For each barrier, discuss one or more ways that a company can overcome the barrier.
14. What form of countertrade appears to offer the most purchase flexibility? Why?
15. Some purchasing managers regard countertrade as an infringement of purchasing's authority. Why might some purchasing personnel not view countertrade favorably?

ADDITIONAL READINGS

Alguire, M. S., Frear, C. R., and Metcalf, L. E. (1994), "An Examination of the Determinants of Global Sourcing," *Journal of Business and Industrial Marketing,* 9(2), 62–74.

Bozarth, C., Handfield, R., and Das, A. (1998), "Stages of Global Sourcing Evolution: An Exploratory Study," *Journal of Operations Management,* 16, 241–255.

Das, A., and Handfield, R. B. (1997), "Just-in-Time and Logistics in Global Sourcing: An Empirical Study," *International Journal of Physical Distribution and Logistics Management,* 27(3–4), 244–259.

Fraering, M., and Prasad, S. (1999), "International Sourcing and Logistics: An Integrated Model," *Logistics Information Management,* 12(6), 451.

Giunipero, L., and Monczka, R. M. (1997), "Organizational Approaches to Managing International Sourcing," *International Journal of Physical Distribution and Logistics Management,* 27(5–6), 321–336.

Kaufmann, L., and Carter, C. R. (2006), "International Supply Relationships and Non-Financial Performance: A Comparison of U.S. and German Practices," *Journal of Operations Management,* 24, 653–675.

Kotabe, M. (1994), "Global Sourcing Strategy: R&D, Manufacturing, and Marketing Interfaces," *Journal of Global Marketing,* 7(3), 157.

Locke, D. (1996), *Global Supply Management,* Boston: McGraw-Hill.

Murray, J. Y. (2001), "Strategic Alliance–Based Global Sourcing Strategy for Competitive Advantage: A Conceptual Framework and Research Propositions," *Journal of International Marketing,* 9(4), 30–58.

Petersen, K. J., Frayer, D. J., and Scannel, T. V. (2006), "An Empirical Investigation of Global Sourcing Strategy Effectiveness," *Journal of Supply Chain Management,* 36(2), 29–38.

Rexha, N., and Miyamoto, T. (2000), "International Sourcing: An Australian Perspective," *Journal of Supply Chain Management,* 36(1), 27–34.

Samli, A. C., Browning, J. M., and Busbia, C. (1998), "The Status of Global Sourcing as a Critical Tool of Strategic Planning," *Journal of Business Research,* 43(3), 177–187.

Trent, R. J., and Monczka, R. M. (2007), "Achieving Excellence in Global Sourcing," *Sloan Management Review,* Fall, 24–32.

ENDNOTES

1. Friedman, T. L. (2005), *The World Is Flat,* New York: Farrar, Straus and Giroux.
2. Friedman, pp. 24, 25.

3. Jacoby, D. (2006), "Purchasing 2015: A Global Survey by SAP and the Global Economic Intelligence Unit," Presentation.

4. Passariello, C. (2007), "Behind L'Oréal's Makeover in India: Going Upscale," *Wall Street Journal,* July 13, pp. A1, A4.

5. Glader, P. (2007), "Rio-Alcan Deal Pressures Alcoa," *Wall Street Journal,* July 13, p. A3.

6. Matthews, R. G. (2007), "Foreign Firms Build U.S. Presence," *Wall Street Journal,* August 14, p. A10.

7. The information in this section comes from a variety of sources, including data collected at the Executive Purchasing and Supply Chain Management Seminar, Michigan State University, East Lansing, 1990, 1993, 1997, 1999; "International Buying—The Facts and Foolishness" (1987), *Purchasing,* June; and "MAPI Survey on Global Sourcing as a Corporate Strategy—An Update" (1986), Machinery and Allied Products Institute, February.

8. Monczka, R. M., Trent, R. J., and Peterson, K. J. (2006), "Effective Global Sourcing and Supply for Superior Results," Tempe, AZ: CAPS Research, p. 13.

9. Jacoby.

10. Locke, D. (1996), *Global Supply Management,* Boston: McGraw-Hill, p. 46.

11. Locke, p. 51.

12. Hickey, K. (2003), "Chinese Puzzle," *Traffic World,* September 15, p. 16.

13. Hickey, p. 16.

14. Moradian, R. (2004), "The Logistics of Doing Business in China," *Inbound Logistics,* July, http://www.inboundlogistics.com/articles/3plline/3plline0704.shtml.

15. Taub, S. (2004), "Lucent Fires Four on Bribery Suspicions," *CFO.com*, April 7.

16. Monczka et al., p. 26.

17. Monczka et al., p. 24.

18. Monczka et al., pp. 24–26.

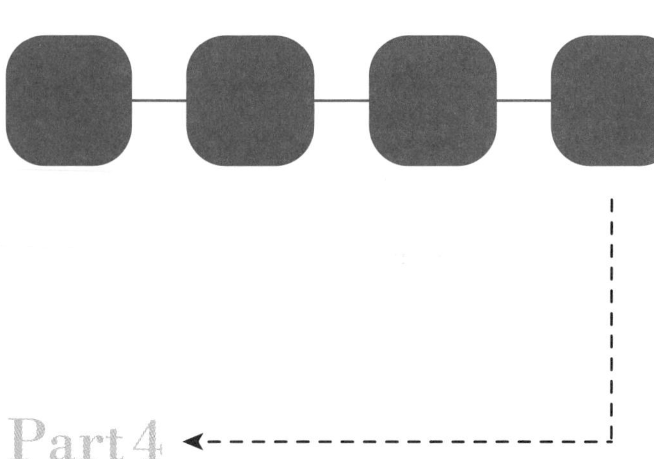

Part 4

Strategic Sourcing Process

Chapter 11

STRATEGIC COST MANAGEMENT

Learning Objectives

After completing this chapter, you should be able to

- Understand the impact of cost management on the supply chain
- Understand the fundamental approaches to price management
- Understand approaches for reducing supplier costs of production and delivery
- Understand the concept of total cost of ownership
- Identify collaborative approaches to cost management

Chapter Outline

Southwest Shrugs Off Oil Prices

The surge in oil prices in 2007 has impacted many industries, not least of which is the airline industry. Fuel costs make up a significant portion of airline operating costs. One airline, Southwest, has used this fact to its advantage in the current high-fuel-cost environment. Although Southwest has for many years dominated the industry because of better service and happier and more productive workers, the reason for Southwest's rapidly increasing advantage in recent years is that it simply loaded up years ago on hedges against higher fuel prices. With oil trading above $90 a barrel, most of the rest of the airline industry is facing a huge run-up in costs. Southwest, however, owns long-term contracts to buy most of its fuel through 2009 for what it would cost if oil were $51 a barrel. The value of these hedges soared as oil raced above $90 a barrel, and they are now worth more than $2 billion. These gains will be mostly realized over the next two years. Other airlines passed on buying all but the shortest-term insurance against high fuel prices, such that they could start reporting losses as early as 2008, unless they are able to rapidly raise fares. At American Airlines, annual fuel costs rise $80 million for every dollar increase in a barrel of oil, said their CFO, Thomas Horton.

In January 2007, other airlines were enjoying the prospect of Southwest's misery as oil dipped down to about $52 a barrel. Southwest's hedges cap most of its fuel needs at about $51 a barrel, so they were of little use at that point. Southwest also has the highest labor rates in the industry, because they have not demanded deep wage concessions from workers. Southwest's hedges used during the first nine months of 2007, which included options that allowed—but did not require—it to buy energy products at certain prices, cost $42 million. This is a small sum in retrospect, but was not so easily spent when higher oil prices were only a possibility. Now, the other airlines are kicking themselves for not having hedged fuel costs. "We all wish we were Southwest," said Tim Walker, a JetBlue officer who manages its fuel contracts. "Southwest was just gorgeous with what they did years ago. They put their foot down." To compensate, other airlines have had six industry fare increases in the third quarter, whereas Southwest's average ticket price was only 62 cents higher than a year earlier. The question for Southwest is whether it can turn yet another huge temporary advantage into a long-term edge. Its revenue-raising ideas are relatively modest, but it faces labor negotiations with its main worker groups, none of whom want to make concessions. Gary Kelly, the chief executive, noted that "this cycle could and should be another one of those times we can prevail." Southwest generally expects high fuel prices to prevail, and if it sees what it thinks is a short-term decline in oil prices, the carrier would consider adding to its hedges for years beyond 2009. In hindsight, executives at Southwest feel that they should have picked up even more when prices were lower.

HEDGED, PRICE CAP (PER BARREL)

	2007 4TH QUARTER	2008	2009	2010
Alaska	50%, $72	32%, $64	5%, $68	0
American	40%, $69	14%, n.a.	0	0
Continental	30%, $93	10%, $93	0	0
Delta	20%, $99	0	0	0
JetBlue	47%, $83	0	0	0
Northwest	50%, $73	10%, $84	0	0
Southwest	90%, $51	70%, $51	55%, $51	25%, $63
United	18%, $93	0	0	0
US Airways	56%, $73	15%, $73	0	0

The table on p. 383 shows the percentage of each airline's fuel needs that is hedged against higher fuel prices.

Source: J. Bailey, "An Airline Shrugs at Oil Prices," *New York Times*, November 29, 2007, p. C1.

In today's economy, the driving force behind global competition can be summarized in a single equation:

$$\text{Value} = (\text{Quality} + \text{Technology} + \text{Service} + \text{Cycle Time})/\text{Price}$$

Although purchasing has a major impact on all of the variables in the numerator in this equation, this chapter focuses on the denominator: price, and its primary driver, cost. A major responsibility of purchasing is to ensure that the price paid for an item is fair and reasonable. The price paid for purchased products and services will have a direct impact on the end customer's perception of value provided by the organization, thereby leading to a competitive advantage in the marketplace. By delivering value through continued progress in reducing costs, and thereby improving profit margins and return on assets for enterprises, purchasing is truly becoming a force of its own within the executive boardroom.

Evaluation of a supplier's actual cost to provide the product or service, versus the actual purchase price paid, is an ongoing challenge within all industries. In many situations, the need to control costs requires a focus on the costs associated with producing an item or service, versus simply analyzing final price. In these cases, innovative pricing approaches involve cost identification as a process leading to agreement on a final price. In other cases, however, purchasing may not need to spend much effort understanding costs, and will focus instead on whether the price is fair given competitive market conditions.

Purchasing and supply chain specialists must understand the principles of price and cost analysis. **Price analysis** refers to the process of comparing supplier prices against external price benchmarks, without direct knowledge of the supplier's costs. Price analysis focuses simply on a seller's price with little or no consideration given to the actual cost of production. In contrast, **cost analysis** is the process of analyzing each individual cost element (i.e., material, labor hours and rates, overhead, general and administrative costs, and profit) that together add up to the final price. Ideally, this analysis identifies the actual cost to produce an item so the parties to a contract can determine a fair and reasonable price and develop plans to achieve future cost reductions. Finally, **total cost analysis** applies the price/cost equation across multiple processes that span two or more organizations across a supply chain. For example, the total cost of shipping a good manufactured from China into the United States may include shipping, tariffs, inventory, quality, and other costs that are over and above the actual price paid to the Chinese manufacturer.

This chapter presents a traditional discussion of price and cost fundamentals along with a number of innovative price and cost management tools that can be applied using available information on the Internet and simple spreadsheet analysis. Some of these tools are price analysis, reverse price analysis, and total cost analysis. By applying such tools, purchasers can evolve toward a system of strategic cost management that seeks to reduce costs across the entire supply chain. Although not all of these tools are appropriate for every situation, supply managers must learn to recognize when and how such tools can be applied.

A Structured Approach to Cost Reduction

Managers are increasingly considering the implications of price and cost management from a total supply chain perspective, as shown in Exhibit 11.1. In the past, many companies focused their cost efforts on internal cost management initiatives. These included approaches such as value analysis, process improvements, standardization, improvements in efficiency by utilizing technology, and others. Although these approaches are still relevant, the impact that they have on the majority of costs is not as great as in the past. Why? With the increased amount of outsourcing occurring in every global company today, the majority of the cost of goods sold is driven by suppliers, which are outside of the four walls of an organization. In this environment, organizations wanting to fully capture the benefits of cost-reduction initiatives must implement approaches that include both upstream and downstream members of their supply chains. Such a change requires a fundamental shift in thinking in the minds of managers and employees.

This new generation of cost management initiatives requires that purchasing and logistics executives adopt a series of new initiatives that can deliver results to the bottom line. As shown in Exhibit 11.2 on p. 386, strategic cost management approaches typically involve at least two supply chain partners working together to identify process improvements that reduce costs across the supply chain. Examples include team-based value-engineering efforts, supplier development and kaizen events, cross-enterprise cost-reduction projects, joint brainstorming efforts on new products, supplier suggestion programs, and supply chain redesign efforts. These types of efforts require that both parties commit to achieving cost-reduction strategies that go beyond simple haggling over prices.

Strategic cost management approaches will vary according to the stage of the product life cycle. As shown in Exhibit 11.3 on p. 387, various approaches are appropriate at different product life cycle stages. In the initial concept and development stage, purchasing will often act proactively to establish cost targets. Target costing/target

Exhibit 11.1 Cost Management Approaches

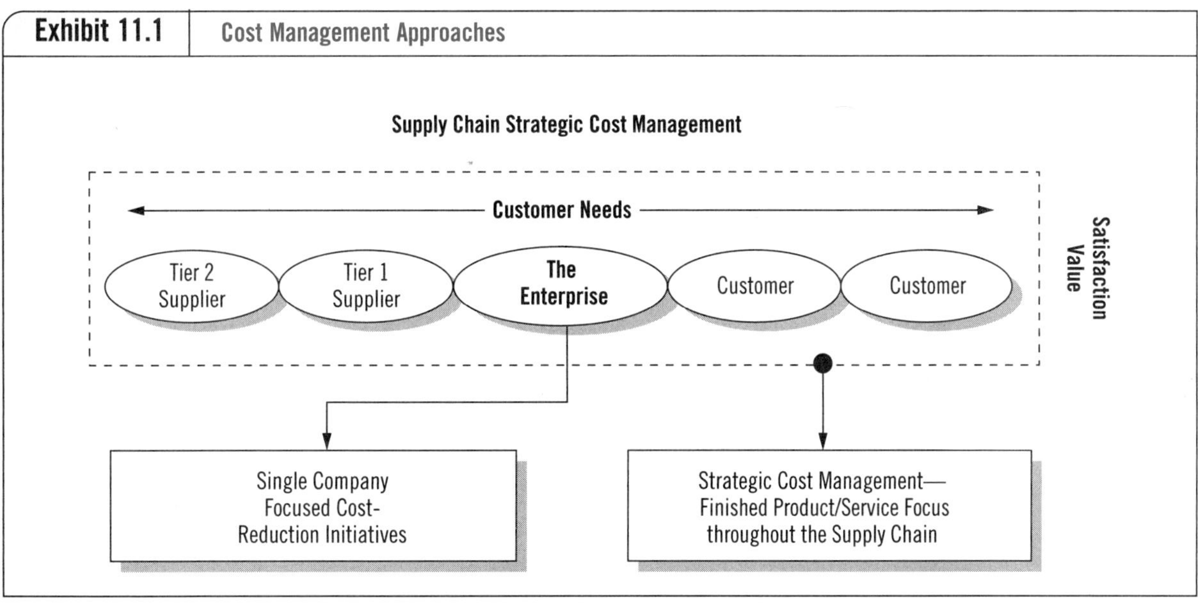

Exhibit 11.2 Supply Chain Strategic Cost Management Processes

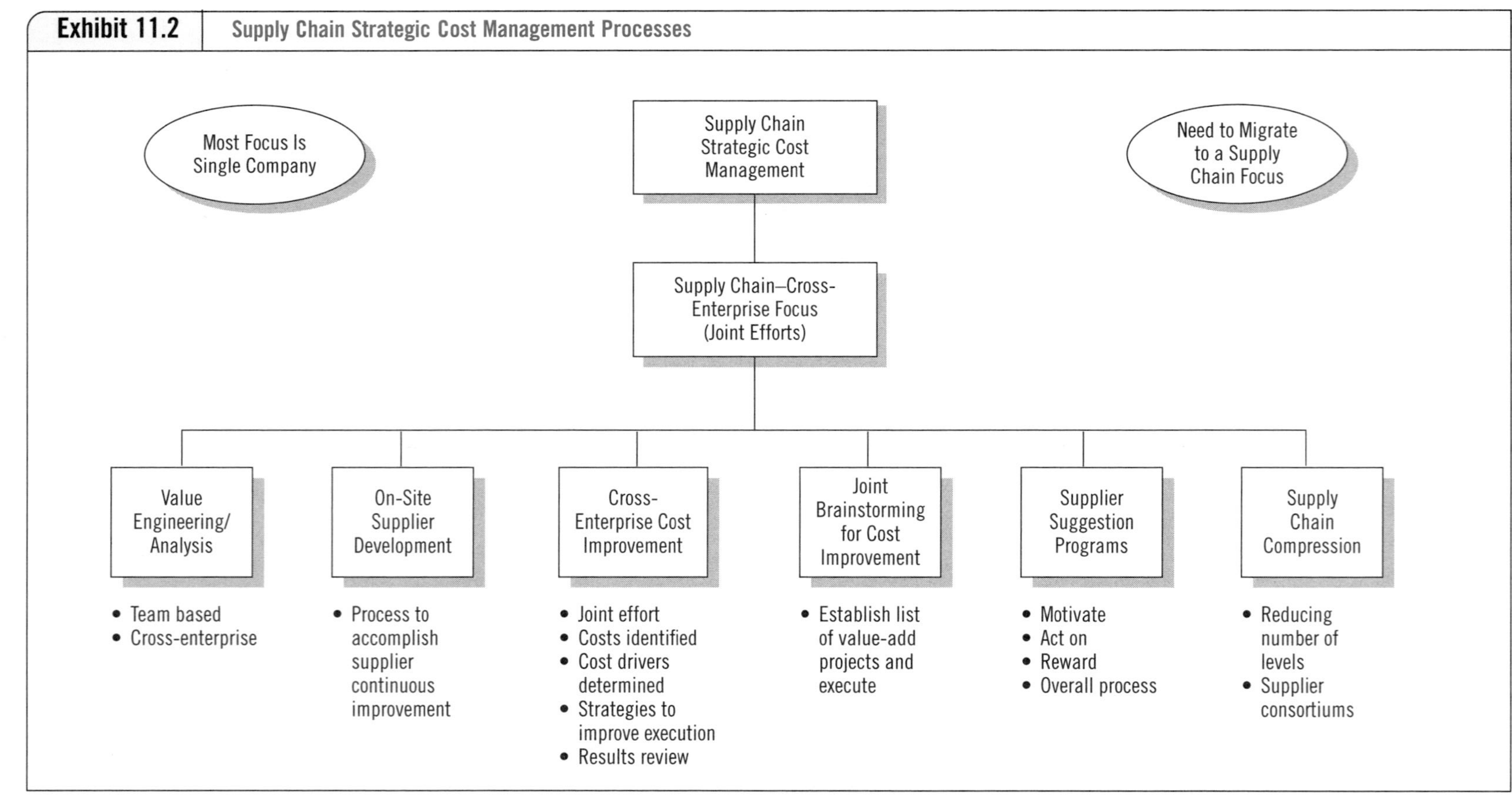

pricing is a technique developed originally in Japanese organizations in the 1980s to combat the inflation of the yen against other currencies. Target pricing, quality function deployment, and technology sharing are all effective approaches for cost reduction used at this stage.

As a product or service enters the design and launch stages, supplier integration, standardization, value engineering, and design for manufacturing can improve the opportunity to use standard parts and techniques, leverage volumes, and create opportunities for cost savings. During the product or service launch, purchasing will adopt more traditional cost-reduction approaches, including competitive bidding, negotiation, value analysis, volume leveraging, service contracts focusing on savings, and linking longer-term pricing to extended contracts. As a product reaches its end of life, purchasing cannot ignore the potential value of environmental initiatives to remanufacture, recycle, or refurbish products that are becoming obsolete. As an example of this, print cartridge manufacturers such as Xerox and Hewlett-Packard have developed innovative technologies that allow customers to recycle laser toner cartridges, which are subsequently refurbished and used again, eliminating landfill costs.

The major benefits from cost-reduction efforts occur when purchasing is involved early in the new-product/service development cycle. When sourcing decisions are made early in the product life cycle, the full effects of a sourcing decision over the product's life can be considered. When purchasing is involved later in the product development cycle, efforts to reduce costs have a minimal impact because the major decisions regarding types of materials, labor rates, and choice of suppliers have already been made. A manager in a major automotive company described this situation as follows: "In the past, we allowed engineering to determine the specifications, the materials, and the supplier. In fact, the supplier already produced the first prototype! That's when they decided to call in purchasing to develop the contract. How

Exhibit 11.3 Managing Life Cycle Costs

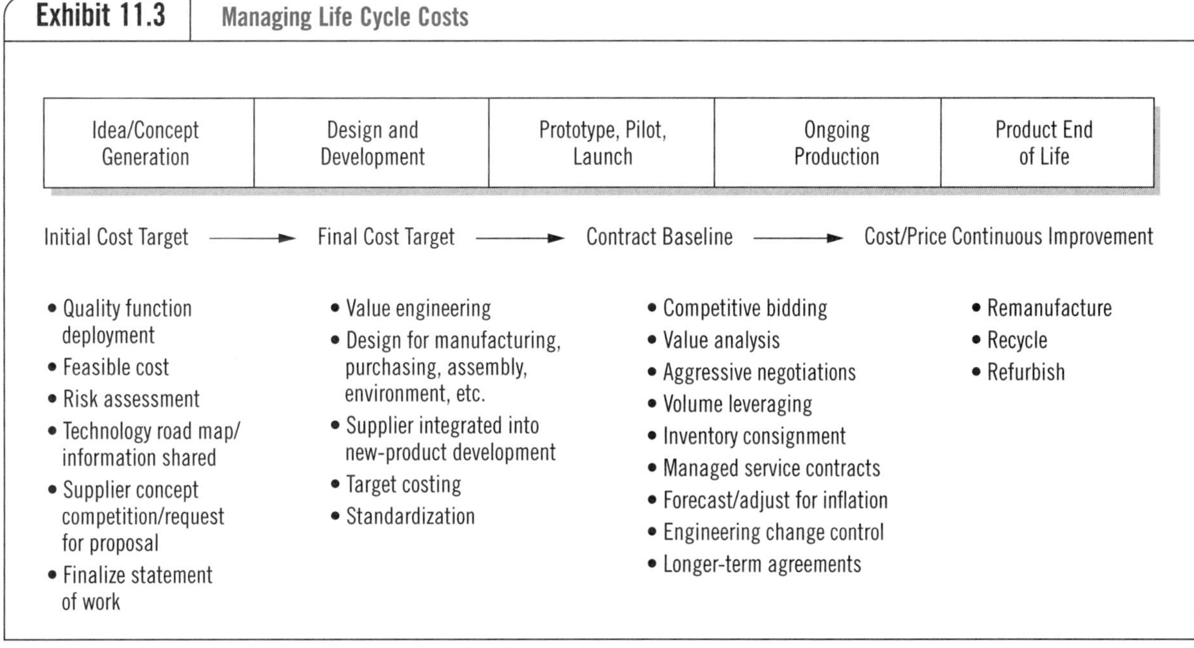

much leverage do you have in convincing the supplier to reduce costs when the supplier already knows they are guaranteed the business, and they have already sunk money into a fixed design and tooling for the product?"[1]

When prioritizing efforts to reduce costs, companies often apply a structured framework for cost reduction similar to the one illustrated in Exhibit 11.4. This framework is consistent with the portfolio analysis framework developed in Chapter 6 and should be integrated into an organization's commodity strategy development process. As shown in Exhibit 11.4, each approach requires a different strategic focus in terms of price versus cost. In general, low-value generics in which a competitive market with many potential suppliers exists should emphasize total delivered price. There is no need to spend time conducting a detailed cost analysis for low-value items that do not produce significant returns. Greater returns can be obtained by having users order these products or services directly through supplier catalogs, procurement cards, or other e-procurement technologies. Commodities are high-value products or services that also have a competitive market situation; for example, computers and technology are certainly in this category (as discussed in the opening vignette). These types of products and services can be sourced through traditional bidding approaches that require price analysis using market forces to do the work and identify what is a competitive price. With greater standardization being introduced in many industries, products once considered as critical are being moved into the commodities quadrant.

Unique products present a different challenge: Companies must strive to reduce costs for products with few available suppliers, yet that are still low value. Examples include suppliers of unique fasteners, specialty papers, and specialty MRO items. For such items, purchasers will want to identify suppliers that are charging too high a price. Further analysis of their pricing through a technique known as "reverse price analysis" (discussed later in the chapter) may identify price discrepancies that can be reduced through greater standardization of user requirements or ongoing negotiations

Exhibit 11.4 Framework for Strategic Cost Management

VALUE	Low (Number of Available Suppliers)	High (Number of Available Suppliers)
High	**Commodities** Strategies: • Leverage preferred suppliers • Price analysis using market forces	**Critical Products** Strategies: • Cost analysis • Collaborative cost-reduction efforts focused on total cost
Low	**Unique Products** Strategies: • Cost analysis — reverse pricing • Standardize requirements	**Generics** Strategies: • Total delivered cost • Automate to reduce purchasing involvement

NUMBER OF AVAILABLE SUPPLIERS

Sourcing Snapshot — *Global Commodity Markets Shifting*

In 2007, the latest demand boom for base metals is in its third year and has elevated nonferrous metals pricing to record highs. Steel prices are reflecting iron ore, scrap, ferroalloy, and energy costs—rather than demand trends—probably for the first time.

"Pricing cycles for commodities are shrinking," says the global procurement manager at a Detroit-area auto parts company. "The steel cycle used to be 7 to 10 years in length from peak to valley in prices. Nowadays, it's more like 18 months due to the rapid change in delivery of information."

Atop all that, says Peter Connelly, CPO at diversified manufacturer Leggett & Platt, "supplier consolidation and pricing volatility is making forecasting difficult and, actually, past a 90-day window, very inaccurate." Rather than being a sign of the top for commodity prices, analysts worry that the deal-making could help put a lid on supply and put even more pressure on a host of commodity prices.

This view is supported by research director Anirvan Banerji at the Economic Cycle Research Institute in New York. Most forecasters have a dismal record of predicting the timing of cyclical turns in economic growth, jobs, and inflation, he writes, "because most people and forecasting models expect recent patterns to persist in the near future." This is "a sure recipe for being surprised on prices by the next turn in the global industrial cycle."

And then, there is nature. The late-summer hurricanes of 2005 taught energy and petrochemical buyers just how fast supply can be disrupted and prices can explode.

"It's all about energy and raw materials these days," says Dan DiMicco, CEO of Nucor Corp., the Charlotte, NC–based steelmaker. "With the volatility in and high level of materials pricing nowadays, nobody wants to carry inventory—whether it's in the raw materials at my mills or the finished products we ship to our customers."

Stating that "in a commodity market today, intelligence is king," DiMicco told a recent steel industry conference that "to run as efficiently as we can, mills and service centers will have to start at the customer—and talk to buyers about what they really need and what they expect they will be paying. Only then can we take some volatility out of the metals market—and come to some equitable long-term arrangements on price and supply."

So, the foundation for any successful commodity-forecasting program must be based on detailed market knowledge that can smooth out current volatility and help ensure against disrupted flow of raw materials, says Mike Burns, global business director for polyethylene at supply chain consultancy Resin Technology Inc. in Fort Worth, Texas.

Burns insists that buyers "emerge from their comfortable silos" and get knowledgeable about global economics, supply, demand, and sourcing alternatives—"whatever they need to know to become expert about their company, their industry, and their regional and global supply chain." Solid market facts are needed to develop effective buying plans, and that includes accurate price forecasting, says Burns.

Source: T. Stundza, "Commodities Forecasting: It's All in Your Head," *Purchasing* magazine online, May 14, 2007.

with problematic suppliers. In effect, this may mean transitioning a product or service from the unique quadrant to the generics quadrant. Many of the commodities previously thought to belong in the generics quadrant are shifting to strategic, based on global capacity and demand forecasts for 2008 onwards (see Sourcing Snapshot: Global Commodity Markets Shifting).

The major focus of a purchaser's efforts to reduce costs should be on critical products where relatively few suppliers exist but the items are higher value. Managers should commit time to exploring opportunities for value analysis/engineering, cost-savings sharing, collaborative efforts focused on identifying cost drivers, and supplier integration early in the product development cycle. Cost analysis involves breaking down a supplier's price into its cost elements to uncover potential cost savings and, hence, price reductions.

The remainder of this chapter presents a discussion of price analysis (commodities and generics quadrants), cost analysis (unique and critical quadrants), and total cost analysis (all four quadrants) that can be applied to help control the costs associated with these different purchased goods and services.

Price Analysis

In order to understand the factors affecting pricing levels in a given market, it is crucial to employ a market analysis—an analytical tool that identifies the primary external forces that are causing prices to either increase or decrease. As shown in Exhibit 11.5, prices are driven to a large extent by the degree of competition in a market, as well as by conditions of supply and demand. The resulting market prices are indicated by a heavier line, depending on the volume of supply in a given situation.

When demand exceeds supply, a seller's market exists, and prices generally increase. The reverse situation, a buyer's market, occurs when supply exceeds demand,

Exhibit 11.5 Market-Based Pricing

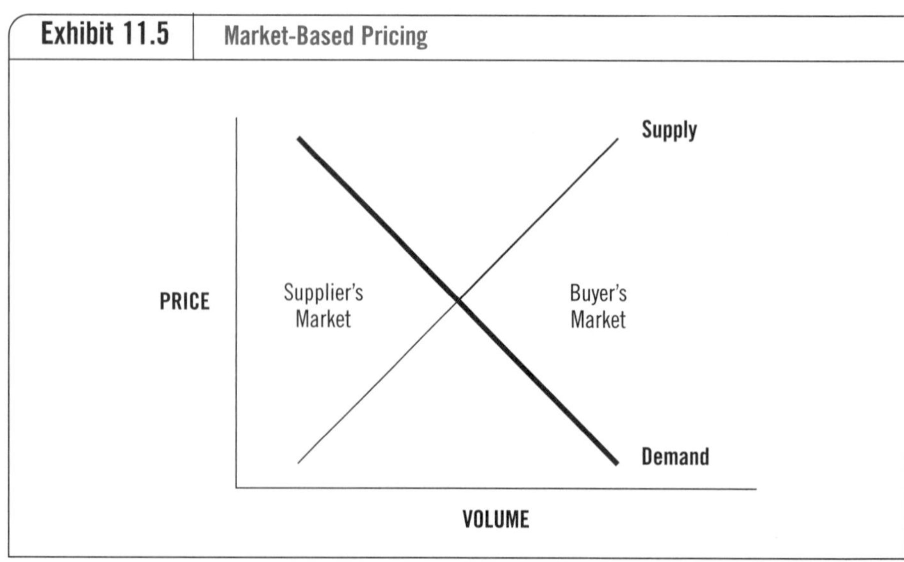

and prices generally move downward. There should be an appreciation for the variety of variables that directly and indirectly influence an item's price.

Market Structure

Although it is clear that the supplier's market condition has a major influence on price, the factors affecting market conditions are not always easy to predict. Market environment is often driven by the number of competitors in an industry, the relative similarity (or lack thereof) of their products, and any existing barriers to entry for new competitors. At one end of the scale, there may exist a monopoly, where only one supplier can provide a given product or service. A good example of this condition exists in the pharmaceutical industry, where the company first to market with a new patented drug has exclusive rights to sell the product for seven years. (At the end of this period, generics, which copy the drug's formulation, enter the market, thereby driving down the cost of the drug.)

At the other end of the spectrum is perfect competition, in which there exist identical products with minimal barriers for new suppliers to enter the market. Price is solely a function of the forces of supply and demand. No single seller or producer controls enough of the market to affect the market price. Of course, a seller could reduce its price with the hope of selling additional products. In the long run, however, this simply results in lost revenue.

An industry with only a few large competitors is classified as oligopolistic. The market and pricing strategies of one competitor directly influence others within the industry. Examples of oligopolies in the United States historically include the steel, automobile, and appliance industries. Within an oligopolistic industry, a firm may assume the role of a price leader and raise or lower prices, which can result in all other firms changing their prices or choosing to maintain existing price levels. If others do not follow, the initiating firm might be forced to reverse the change. The growth of international trade and competition has created additional choices in many industries, shifting market power away from the producer and toward the purchaser.

Economic Conditions

Economic conditions often determine whether a market is favorable to the seller or to the purchaser. When capacity utilization at producers is high (supply is tight) and demand for output is strong, supply and demand factors combine to create pricing conditions favorable to the seller. When this occurs, buyers often attempt to keep prices or price increases below the industry average. When an industry is in a decline, purchasers can take advantage of this to negotiate favorable supply arrangements.

The macroeconomy influences prices; for example, interest rate levels influence the internal rate of return at a supplier—the overall cost of capital, which drives productive investment. Even the level of the dollar in relation to other currencies influences price, particularly for international purchasing. Also, tight labor markets can create cost increases, resulting in higher purchase prices.

Knowledge of economic conditions is helpful when identifying the market factors affecting the supply and demand for a product or commodity. Awareness of current and forecasted economic conditions assists in the development of purchase budgets and material forecasts, and also provides valuable insights when developing future price negotiating strategies. One good source of information is the website for the Institute for Supply Management, www.ism.ws, which presents key data on pricing trends for a variety of commodities. Other sources of pricing trends in commodity markets can be found in industry-specific trade associations, such as Pulp and Paper World (for prices on different grades of pulp and paper: www.paperloop.com), or Textile World (for prices on Texas, Memphis, and California cotton: www.textileworld.com).

Pricing Strategy of the Seller

Sellers pursue different strategies or approaches that affect the pricing of their products or services. Some sellers rely on a detailed analysis of internal cost structures to establish price, whereas others simply price at a level comparable to the competition.

The pricing strategy of the seller has a direct impact on quoted prices. In order to remain in business, suppliers must cover their costs and earn an overall profit to provide for meeting their corporate objectives. In many cases, however, the price charged by a seller may have little or no relationship to actual costs. As strange as this seems, pricing strategies are often based on other factors that are important to the seller. A seller may quote an unusually low price to secure a purchase contract, with the intention of raising the price once it drives competition from the marketplace. In other cases, the seller may exploit its position when it senses it has the purchaser over a barrel by charging an excessive price. In still other cases, the seller may simply not understand its own costs.

Several questions should be asked when analyzing a seller's pricing strategy. These include the following:

- Does the seller have a long-term pricing strategy, or is it short-term in nature?
- Is the seller a price leader (sets new pricing levels in the market), or a price follower (only matches price increases/decreases when the competition does so)?
- Is the seller attempting to establish entry barriers to other competitors by establishing a low price initially, then preparing to raise prices in the future?
- Is the seller using a cost-based pricing approach, which develops price as a function of true costs, or a market-based pricing approach? If a market-based pricing approach is being used, there may be little need for conducting a detailed cost analysis, as the price charged may be unrelated to any elements of cost.

The elements that make up the price charged by a supplier are shown in Exhibit 11.6. Essentially, the supplier's costs include materials and labor (which together make up manufacturing cost), plus overhead and sales, general and administrative expenses (which cumulatively establish the supplier's total cost), plus margin, which then equates to the price charged. Based on the interplay between these different elements, which may vary depending on the supplier's pricing model, the price charged to a buyer can vary significantly. Seller pricing strategies can be grouped into two categories: market-driven models and cost-based models. As we noted earlier, price analysis involves having the supply manager gauge the pricing strategy used by the supplier, without going into the details of how its detailed cost elements are established. We will cover market-driven pricing models first, then cover cost analysis techniques later in the chapter.

Exhibit 11.6 Elements of Price and Associated Cost Drivers

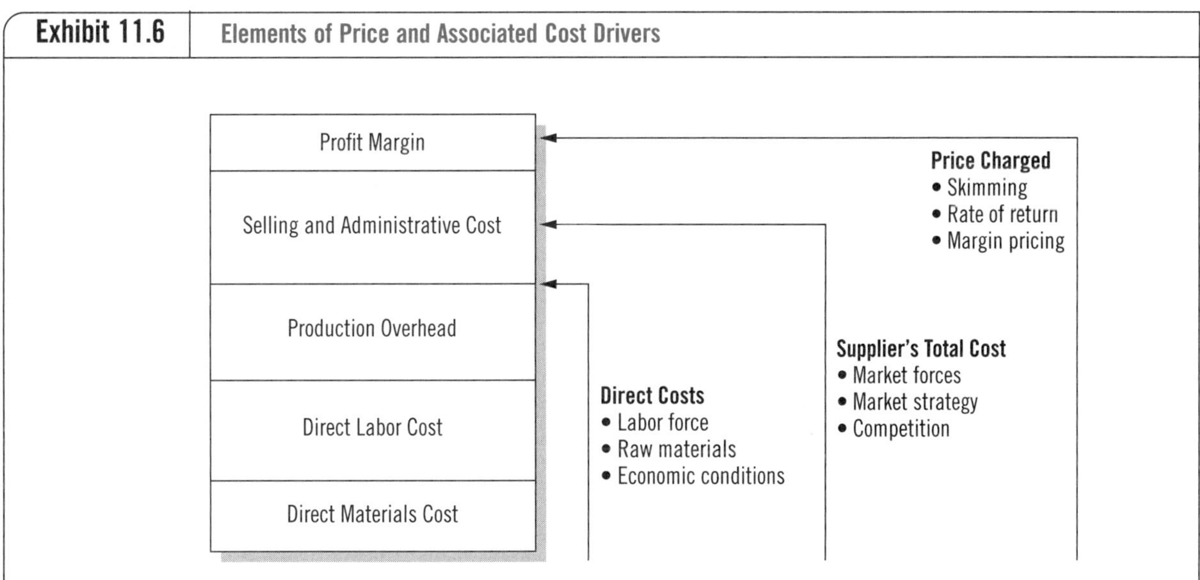

Market-Driven Pricing Models[2]

Price Volume Model

In the price volume model, the supplier analyzes the market to find the combination of price per unit and quantity of sales that maximizes its profit on the assumption that (1) lowering the price will result in more units being sold, and (2) greater volume will spread the indirect cost over more units, therefore maintaining or even increasing the profit as it relates to the price. The most basic example of this model is the supplier's offering quantity price breaks to induce the buyer to purchase in larger quantities (a core approach adopted by Sam's Club and Costco stores). Strategic sourcing initiatives should always engage a thorough analysis of the relationship between price and quantity in different marketplaces.

Combining purchase requirements across separate operating units can yield savings in tooling, setup, and operating efficiencies. A major benefit of reduced or single sourcing is a lower price that results from the higher volumes offered to a supplier. In return for a purchase contract with higher volumes, a buyer expects favorable pricing because a supplier should realize lower per-unit costs. The willingness of a supplier to offer quantity discounts also affects the final selling price.

Although a quantity discount has a positive effect on the purchase price, a purchaser must be cautious about the net impact on the total cost of the item. Buying in larger-than-normal quantities requires additional storage of purchased goods. At a time when most firms are reducing or even eliminating inventory, the additional inventory-carrying costs must be evaluated against the benefit of the quantity discount.

Market-Share Model

In the market-share model, pricing is based on the assumption that long-run profitability depends on the market share obtained by the supplier. This approach, also referred to as "penetration pricing," is an aggressive pricing approach for efficient

Sourcing Snapshot — *Higher Pipeline Costs Forecast*

Across the board, one of the biggest challenges facing the pipeline supply market today is human resources. Indeed, the issue of available personnel was one of the primary topics of discussion at the *Pipeline and Gas Journal*'s third annual Pipeline Opportunities[3] Conference held in March 2007. Many operators and service providers expressed concerns about an aging workforce and the lack of younger people moving into the industry. Senior executives expressed concern that the personnel crisis could have some severe impacts on future pipeline development. As one executive noted, "We in the pipeline industry have been successful with the pipeline contractors in placing in service a number of large projects on time and on budget. At the same time we have another slate of projects where we haven't been as successful. They were either delayed or had significant cost overruns."

There are several reasons for this recent phenomenon.

One of the root causes is that much of the existing infrastructure in pipelines has outlived its useful life. A significant amount of existing pipe in the United States was put in the ground in the 1930s and 1940s, and was designed to have a lifetime of 40 years. Today, 70 years down the path, much of this pipeline now has to be replaced. This has not gone unnoticed by the Department of Transportation, which regulates 85–90% of pipeline activity. Two years ago, new regulations on the nation's pipelines dictated that anyone that was moving liquids had to inspect all of these pipelines by 2007 (by 2009 for gas pipelines). The unfortunate fact is that much of the infrastructure has not been inspected in years, and most oil and gas companies have never inspected them for corrosion.

To cope with this situation, oil and gas companies, and engineering, procurement, and construction companies are running smart gauges through the infrastructure (magnetic calipers that run through the pipe). These companies are realizing that in general much of the pipe is in awful shape. To repair the pipe, maintenance crews have to expose it, identify the extent to which the corrosion exists, and decide whether to keep it or not. If not, the pipe must be replaced. As a result, there has been a huge boom in inspection, maintenance, and replacement of the existing pipelines, which has drawn significantly on the labor resources for pipeline engineering and tank maintenance crews.

Certain Western regions such as the Barnett Shale area in Texas, new finds in Colorado, as well as discoveries in the other lower 48 states will drive new demand, as these geographies have no infrastructure and are being developed. As a result there is a rush to develop new pipelines as well—another draw on resources.

Another draw is the vast number of other major projects under way globally. For example, a new LNG program in Louisiana uses the same labor classifications. The energy industry in the Gulf Coast region is undergoing an impressive expansion with projects worth about $260 billion under development. Contributing to this outstanding growth is the simultaneous peaking of all three sectors of the industry—upstream, midstream, and downstream—happening for the first time in many years. Strong global oil demand growth, fueled primarily by the emergence of China and India as new world economic powerhouses, and availability of reliable low-cost feedstock in the Gulf Coast have provided an ideal opportunity for the region's energy industry to move up the value chain and add refining and petrochemical capacity. This euphoria has contributed to a glut of projects, amounting to 3 million barrels per day of refining capacity and 32 million tonnes per annum of petrochemical plants, under development in the region. This is also drawing on this labor pool.

Source: R. Handfield, "The Pipeline Engineering Labor Market," white paper, Supply Chain Resource Cooperative, October 2007.

producers because price is a direct function of cost. Penetration pricing can lead to faster market penetration for a product because of the lower profit margins a seller is willing to accept. Generally speaking, the seller is willing to take a lower price because of the potential mass market appeal of the product, resulting in substantially higher sales volumes. In the initial stages of this model, the supplier may even accept losses, but as its volume increases, the cost per unit decreases and long-term profits are achieved. A word of caution is in order here: Purchasers should question whether the seller is the most efficient producer willing to accept lower margins to win market share, or is the real intention to drive competition from the marketplace and later raise prices to exorbitant levels?

Market Skimming Model

In the market skimming model, prices are set to achieve a high profit on each unit by selling to supply managers who are willing to pay a higher price because of a lack of purchasing sophistication or who are willing to pay for products or services of perceived higher value. An example of the application of this model is frequently seen by supply managers in the use of backdoor selling to non-purchasing professionals in the firm. Supply managers should always seek to reduce the potential negative impact of this pricing model by cost, price, or value analysis to ensure that the higher price for the product or service is justified by the reported additional benefits. A good example of this situation is shown in Sourcing Snapshot: Higher Pipeline Costs Forecast, where the pipeline engineering industry is faced by so much demand for projects that it is literally in a supplier's market and can charge higher-than-normal prices for their services.

Revenue Pricing Model

When downturns in market demand occur, suppliers often must resort to a current revenue pricing model. The emphasis of this model is on obtaining sufficient current revenue to pay for operating cost rather than on profit. Suppliers using this strategy are typically concerned about capacity utilization, covering fixed costs, and retaining skilled labor during market slowdowns, when they are willing to reduce their prices until market conditions change. However, supply managers should be on guard for negative impacts on quality and service resulting from cost cutting on the part of the supplier.

Promotional Pricing Model

The promotional pricing model presents pricing for individual products and services that is set to enhance the sales of the overall product line rather than to ensure the profitability of each product. Current examples of this are the sale of cell phones at below cost in order to induce consumers to buy the annual service contract, or the use of extremely low prices for printers that require the use of the supplier's highly

Exhibit 11.7 Example of Iron Castings PPI Data

SERIES ID: PCU3321#4 (N)
INDUSTRY: GRAY IRON FOUNDRIES
PRODUCT: OTHER GRAY IRON CASTINGS
BASE DATE: 8606

YEAR	JAN	FEB	MAR	APR	MAY	JUN	JUL	AUG	SEP	OCT	NOV	DEC	ANNUAL
1993	111.1	111.5	111.5	111.6	111.8	111.7	111.8	111.6	111.4	111.4	112.0	112.3	111.6
1994	112.4	112.5	112.7	113.2	113.5	113.7	113.8	114.0	115.1	115.2	115.6	115.7	114.0
1995	116.8	118.5	118.7	118.7	118.7	118.7	119.4	120.6	120.8	121.2	121.3	121.6	119.6
1996	122.5	122.8	122.9	122.9	122.8	122.9	122.9	123.1	122.5	123.3	123.4	123.3	122.9
1997	123.3	123.1	123.2	123.1	123.2	123.2	123.3	123.0	123.5	123.5	123.1	123.2	123.2
1998	123.3	123.6	123.5	123.6	123.6	123.7	123.7	123.7	124.3	124.2	123.9	124.7	123.8
1999	124.6	124.7	124.7	124.6	124.7	124.7	124.7	124.8	124.8	124.8	124.4	124.4	124.7
2000	126.0	126.0	126.1	126.1	126.3	126.4	126.3	126.2	126.3	126.2	126.1	126.1	126.2
2001	126.0	125.9	126.0	126.0	126.0	126.0	126.0	126.0	126.2	126.1	126.2	126.1	126.0
2002	126.1	126.1	126.2	126.4	126.7	126.7	126.8	126.8	127.3	127.4	127.2	127.2	126.7
2003	127.1	127.2	**127.2**	126.8	126.8	**127.5**	127.7(P)	127.6(P)	127.6(P)	127.7(P)			

N: NAICS replaces SIC with PPI data for January 2004. See http://www.bls.gov/ppi/ppinaics.htm. P: Preliminary. All indexes are subject to revision four months after original publication.

profitable ink cartridges. Total cost of ownership (TCO) analysis (discussed later in the chapter) should be used to avoid surprising and unfavorable financial impacts that can result from dealings with suppliers using this model.

Competition Pricing Model

The competition pricing model focuses on pricing actions or reactions to pricing proposals offered or expected to be offered by the supplier's competitors. The pricing strategy is based on determining the highest price that can be offered to the supply manager that will still be lower than the price offered by competitors. An excellent example of this model is the reverse auction process.

Cash Discounts

The practice in most industries is to offer incentives to pay invoices promptly. One way to encourage this is to offer cash discounts for payment within a certain period of time. For example, a seller may offer a discount of 2% for invoice payment within 10 days of receipt. The seller usually expects full payment within 30 days. (This is often expressed as "2% 10/net 30.")

Unlike quantity discounts, it is usually worthwhile to take advantage of cash discounts. Purchasers can rarely earn the equivalent return within a 10-day period of transactions offered with a cash discount. The opportunity cost of not taking the discount is almost always higher than the opportunity cost of taking the discount. Well-managed firms take advantage of cash discounts and arrange payment within the specified time frame.

Understanding the pricing model used by suppliers can provide supply managers with significant insights into the strategies needed to generate cost savings for their firm.

Using the Producer Price Index to Manage Price

As noted earlier, price analysis is appropriate for certain types of commodities. Specifically, monitoring price instead of cost is appropriate for market-based products where pricing is largely a function of supply and demand. Examples include steel, paper, plastic, and other types of bulk commodities. When assessing whether the price charged is fair compared with the market, managers can compare price changes for a purchase family to an external index. An important factor when conducting a price analysis is the Producer Price Index (PPI), which is maintained by the U.S. Bureau of Labor Statistics.

This information can easily be downloaded from the Bureau of Labor Statistics web page (www.bls.gov). The index tracks material price movements from quarter to quarter. It is scaled to a base year (1988) and tracks the percentage increase in material commodity prices based on a sample of industrial purchasers. By converting price increases paid from quarter to quarter into a percentage increase, and comparing the changes to the PPI for a similar type of material, the purchaser can determine whether the price increases paid to the supplier of that material are reasonable.

To use this tool, users will first need to identify the supplier's standard industrial code (SIC). This can be found at www.FreeEDGAR.com. Next, look at the price index for the SIC and product that you are interested in. Consider the following example for iron castings. The PPI for iron castings is shown in Exhibit 11.7.

Price paid to supplier on March 30, 2008: \$52.50/unit

Price paid to supplier on June 30, 2008: \$53.20/unit

Percentage price increase = (\$53.20 – \$52.50)/\$52.50 = 1.33%

Steel castings PPI (March 30, 2008) = 127.2

Steel castings PPI (June 30, 2008) = 127.5

Percentage inflation for steel castings = (127.5 – 127.2)/127.2 = 0.2%

In this case, the price increase paid by the purchaser is over five times as much as the increase in the PPI for iron castings—surely an unreasonable increase! The purchaser should definitely question the supplier about this recent price increase, and negotiate a better price!

In addition to PPI data, the Bureau of Labor Statistics website also contains information on labor rates in different regions of the country, and updates on pricing and market conditions. Information on employment cost data is also available in *Purchasing* magazine's "Buying Strategy Forecast," a semimonthly newsletter, and the Direct-ICE report prepared by Thinking Cap Solutions (www.ice-alert.com). Other sources of commodity price information are the "Pink Sheets" published by the World Bank (www.worldbank.org/prospects).

Some companies set an objective of consistently bettering price inflation with suppliers. That is, they expect that performance should be better than the market.

As shown in Exhibit 11.8, this can provide the company with a relative competitive advantage in terms of pricing. Caution should be used when applying PPI data that match the commodity being purchased. The buyer should carefully study the history of the index to ensure that it has a strong correlation with the price history of the commodity being purchased. Several questions should be asked in this situation:

Exhibit 11.8 Actual Price Change vs. Market Index Change—Graphical View

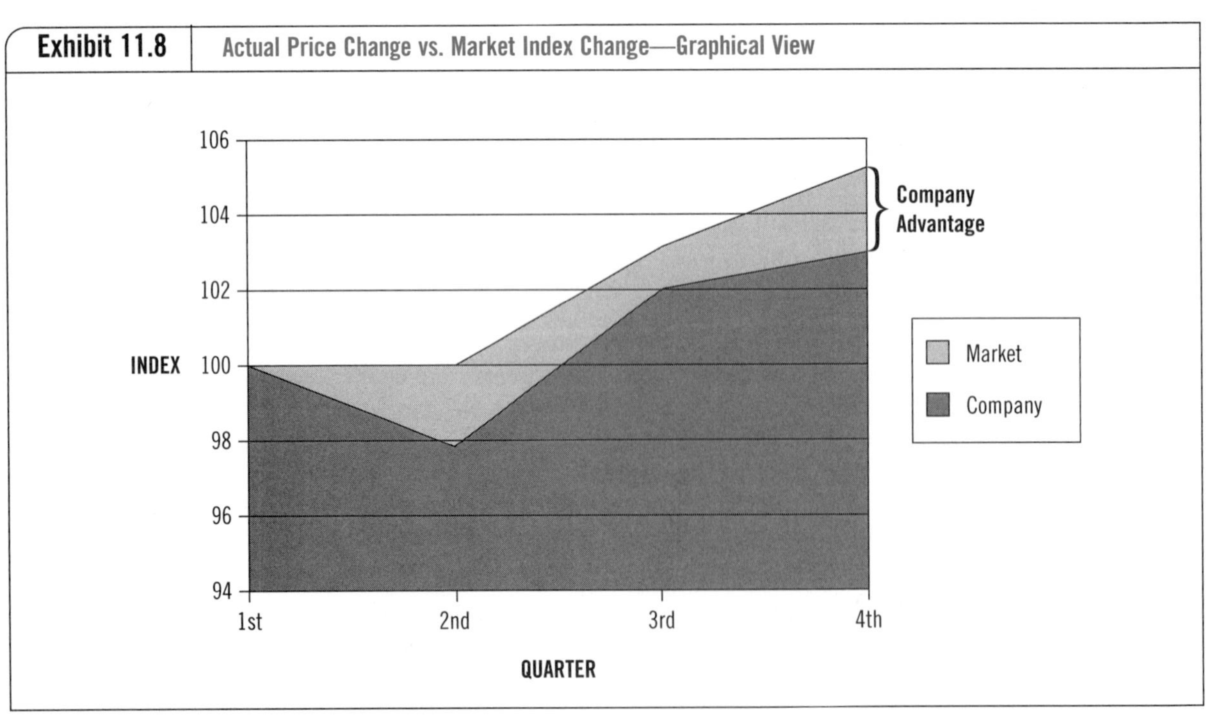

Exhibit 11.9 Actual to PPI Comparison

	PPI 9/02	PPI 9/03	% CHANGE	ACTUAL 9/02	ACTUAL 9/03	% CHANGE
Gasoline	90.3	109.9	21.7	100.0	115.0	15.0
Lumber	169.9	184.5	8.6	100.0	110.0	10.0
Paper	186.8	190.7	2.0	100.0	102.0	2.0

Source: PPI data from U.S. Bureau of Labor Statistics, http://stats.bls.gov/ppihome.htm.

- How did the purchasing situation affect the price fairness and reasonableness at the time?
- How have conditions (e.g., delivery requirements) changed?
- What is the effect on price of changes in the quantity of a material or service purchased?
- Was the purchasing situation a sole source or competitive source?
- Are the index comparisons driving purchasing strategies?

A real benefit of using this price analysis approach is to track price changes across different commodities and compare performance. For example, consider the following.

Three sourcing teams are discussing their cost results for the past year:

Gasoline team: 15% cost increase

Lumber team: 10% cost increase

Paper team: 2% cost increase

Which team has been most effective at managing costs for the year?

At first glance, it would appear that the paper team is doing the best because they have the lowest cost increases (2%). However, in comparing the results with the PPI data shown in Exhibit 11.9, the picture is markedly different. The lumber team has failed to capture savings in a market that has seen prices increase by only 8.6%, while the paper team has limited price increases to 2%, which is only par for the course in terms of what is happening in the market. The gasoline team, however, has been able to contain price increases to 15% in the face of a market that has seen gas prices increase by more than 21%, largely due to speculation associated with the Iraq war during this period. This analysis can help identify different price changes in markets where a fair and open market is present.

Cost Analysis Techniques

As noted earlier, more and more organizations are shifting their attention away from price management and toward cost management. In so doing, there may be opportunities to reduce costs that are not available when the discussion focuses only on price. In cost analysis, the supply manager performs a detailed analysis of the different elements of costs shown earlier in Exhibit 11.6 and identifies what is driving the different elements.

Cost-Based Pricing Models[4]

Cost Markup Pricing Model

In this model, the supplier simply takes its estimate of costs and adds a markup percentage to obtain the desired profit. This markup percentage could be added to the product cost only (usually direct materials plus direct labor plus production overhead), in which case the markup would have to provide for profit, plus all other indirect costs of operating the business. However, if the markup is applied to the total cost (product cost plus general, administrative, and sales expenses), then the markup is solely profit to the supplier. For example, a supplier that wanted a 20% markup over its total cost of \$50 would quote a price of \$60 (\$50 + (20% of \$50) = \$60), which would leave a profit of \$10.

Margin Pricing Model

In the margin pricing model, the supplier is still attempting to obtain a profit related to its costs, but instead of adding a markup to cost, the supplier establishes a price that will provide a profit margin that is a predetermined percentage of the quoted price (i.e., not a percentage of cost, as in markup pricing). For example, the supplier discovered that last year its margin as a percentage of sales was 1%, and this year the supplier would like it to be 20%. Using the same total cost of \$50 as above would result in the supplier quoting a price of \$62.50 in order to obtain the margin of 20%. This is calculated using the new equation for margin pricing:

$$\text{Cost} + (\text{Margin Rate} \times \text{Unit Selling Price}) = \text{Unit Selling Price}$$

Using simple algebra, solving the equation for unit selling price results in the formula:

$$\text{Cost}/(1 - \text{Margin Rate}) = \text{Unit Selling Price}$$

or

$$(\$50)/(1 - 20\%) = \$62.50$$

As in cost markup pricing, the supply manager must be aware if the margin pricing is based on product cost only or if it's based on total cost.

Rate-of-Return Pricing Model

A third common model in the cost-based category is the rate-of-return pricing model, wherein the desired profit is added to the estimated cost. In this model, the supplier bases the profit on the objective of a specific desired return on the financial investment, rather than on the estimated cost. For example, if the supplier wanted a 20% return on its investment of \$300,000 (which might include R&D, equipment, engineering, or other elements), to make 4,000 parts with a total cost of \$50 each, the quoted price would be \$65, using the following approach:

$$\text{Unit Cost} + \text{Unit Profit} = \text{Unit Selling Price}$$

$$\$50 + ((20\% \times 300{,}000)/4{,}000) = \$65$$

Product Specifications

Whether they realize it or not, purchasers impact price at the time they set the specifications for the product or service. Specifying products or services requiring custom design and tooling affects a seller's price, which is one of the reasons purchasers try to specify industry-standard parts whenever possible. Cost (and hence price) becomes higher as firms increase the value-added requirements for an item through design, tooling, or engineering requirements. Purchasers should specify industry-accepted standard parts for as much of their component requirements as possible and rely on customized items when they provide a competitive product advantage or help differentiate a product in the marketplace.

The ability to perform a cost analysis is a direct function of the quality and availability of information. If a purchaser and seller maintain a distant relationship, cost data will be more difficult to identify due to the lack of support from the seller. An obvious approach that can help in obtaining necessary cost data is to require a detailed production cost breakdown when a seller submits a purchase quotation. The reliability of self-reported cost data must be considered. Another approach or option involves the joint sharing of cost information. A cross-functional team composed of engineers and manufacturing personnel from both companies may meet to identify potential areas of the supplier's process (or the purchaser's requirements) that can potentially reduce costs. One of the benefits of developing closer relations with key suppliers is the increased visibility of supplier cost data. The following section details some techniques that focus on cost.

Estimating Supplier Costs Using Reverse Price Analysis

Often suppliers will not be forthcoming in sharing cost data. In these situations, the purchaser must resort to a different type of analytical approach called "reverse price analysis" (also known as "should cost" analysis). A seller's cost structure affects price because, in the long run, the seller must price at a level that covers all variable costs of production, contributes to some portion of fixed costs, and contributes to some level of profit. As discussed later in the chapter, many suppliers are reluctant to share internal cost information. This information, however, is valuable to a purchaser, particularly when evaluating whether a supplier's price is justifiable and reasonable. In the absence of specific cost data, a supplier's overall cost structure must be estimated using a cost analysis—meaning that if the supplier is assigning costs in an appropriate manner, what should the product cost based on these calculations?

Information about a specific product or product line is often difficult to identify. A purchaser may have to use internal engineering estimates about what it costs to produce an item, rely on historical experience and judgment to estimate costs, or review public financial documents to identify key cost data about the seller. The latter approach works best with publicly traded small suppliers producing limited product lines. Financial documents allow estimation of a supplier's overall cost structure. The drawback is that these documents do not provide much information about a specific breakdown of cost by product or product line. Also, if a supplier is a privately held company, cost data become difficult to obtain or estimate.

Despite these difficulties, there are tools available that can be used to estimate a supplier's cost using some publicly available information. When evaluating a supplier's costs, the major determinants of a supplier's total cost structure must be taken into consideration. Let's assume a purchasing manager is buying a product or service for the first time without experience of what fair pricing might be. Because they don't have the tools at hand, or because they're too busy, many purchasers' usual technique is to go with their gut feel or to evaluate competitive bids. It may be worth the time and effort, however, to perform some additional research using data from an income statement or from Internet sites. In doing so, the purchaser may perform a

Exhibit 11.10 **Data Sources**

- Labor: *Annual Survey of Manufacturers*—total direct labor and material for SIC codes
- Overhead: 150% for labor intensive, as high as 600% for capital intensive
- Materials and Profit: Robert Morris Associates data broken out by SICs including the following:
  - Income sources
  - Gross profit margins
  - Percentages for operating expenses
  - Percentages for all other expenses
  - Before-tax profit percentages

Other Sources of Data

Financial reports (profit and SGA estimates):

- Ward's Industrial Directory Census of Manufacturers
- Yahoo! financial section (biz.yahoo.com)
- Morningstar (www.morningstar.com)
- Marketwatch (cbs.marketwatch.com)
- 411Stocks (www.411stocks.com)
- The Street (www.thestreet.com)
- Thinking Cap Solutions (www.ice-alert.com)

reverse price analysis—which essentially means breaking down the price into its components of material, labor, overhead, and profit.

Let's start the process with a supplier-provided price of $20 per unit. The first component to consider is the price contribution toward profit, and sales, general, and administrative (SGA) expenses. For publicly traded companies, this can be estimated by looking at a variety of websites that provide information on financial reports, including balance sheets, income statements, cash flow statements, and annual reports shown in Exhibit 11.10 under the "Financial Reports" section.

Exhibit 11.10 provides a list of available data sources for other components of cost. For this example, assume the purchaser determined that the supplier is a privately held company. This is still not a problem, assuming the buyer can look up the supplier's SIC code (www.FreeEDGAR.com). Another useful resource is Robert Morris Association (www.rmahq.org), which publishes the gross profit margin for this SIC overall, as well as before-tax profit percentages. Although this is a rough estimate, it does offer a good starting point. In Exhibit 11.11, the gross profit and SGA expense percentage for this supplier's SIC code is 15%. Thus on a price of $20 the estimated profit is $3. Next, the purchaser will need to understand the labor and material cost components of price.

Material costs can often be estimated by consulting with internal engineers. Using an estimate of required material, as well as external information on current pricing of these materials (as shown in the previous section), a rough estimate can be made of the amount of material in the product. In our example, we discovered that an approximation of the amount of material included is 20% of the price, or $4.

To find out how much labor is included, the best place to look is the *Annual Survey of Manufacturers,* published by the U.S. Department of Commerce and available

Exhibit 11.11 Reverse Price Analysis

Hypothetical price	$20
Profit/SG&A allowance (15%)	−$ 3
Subtotal	$17
Direct material	−$ 4
Subtotal	$13
Direct labor	−$ 3
Manufacturing burden	=$10

at www.census.gov/prod/www/abs/industry.html. This site allows the purchaser to download information on total direct-labor costs and total material costs for any SIC number. This information allows the purchaser to calculate a materials-to-labor ratio. For the analysis shown in Exhibit 11.11, suppose that the purchaser discovered that the ratio of materials to labor based on the SIC code was 1.333. Thus, if material costs were previously estimated at $4, then direct-labor costs should be approximately $3 (4/1.333).

After subtracting the estimates for profit/SGA, materials, and labor from the price, the remaining portion of cost is considered manufacturing burden or overhead. At this point, the purchaser must determine whether $10 per unit paid on a price of $20 per unit is a reasonable amount for overhead costs. Typically, overhead is expressed as a percentage of labor costs. For labor-intensive industries, the ratio could be as low as 150%. For capital-intensive industries, it could be as high as 600%. In our example, the overhead rate is 333% of labor ($10/$3). Using other data from Robert Morris Associates, the purchaser can also estimate the percentages for operating expenses and for all other expenses. With this cost estimate in hand, the purchaser should now be able to approach the supplier in a negotiation and initiate a discussion that addresses price and cost. Although these estimates may not be 100% accurate, they provide a baseline for discussion of the supplier's cost structure.

Labor cost will be an increasing factor in many cost estimates. The period from 2007 to 2015 will see the next impact of the baby boomer population on society. This impact will be in terms of a large number of people from this group retiring and leaving the work force. The number of retirees from multiple industries is expected to reach levels that have never been seen previously.

At the same time, the U.S. economy will continue to grow, and the demand for labor will escalate proportionately. Given the movement toward the service economy, the need for labor in selected industries is expected to grow significantly. Experts believe that services will be most affected, with a 29% growth rate. Transportation, retail trade, construction, and wholesale trade labor demand will also increase by double digits during this period. In construction alone, demand for drilling, specialty trades, and refining positions will increase by 17 to 18% during this period.

In discussing the supplier's cost structure with the supplier and how it applies to the price paid, the purchaser should attempt to initiate discussion in the following areas to discover opportunities for cost reductions.

- *Plant utilization.* The cost impact of additional business on the operating efficiency of a supplier should be evaluated. Is a supplier currently operating at capacity? Will additional volume actually create higher costs through overtime? Or will a supplier be able to reduce its cost structure through additional volume? The utilization rate of productive assets contributes directly to a supplier's cost structure.

- *Process capability.* The purchaser should also consider if projected volume requirements match a supplier's process capability. It may be inefficient to source smaller lot sizes with a supplier that requires long runs to minimize costs. On the other hand, suppliers specializing in smaller batches cannot efficiently accommodate volumes requiring longer production runs. A supplier's production processes should match a purchaser's production requirements. Purchasing should also evaluate production processes to determine if they are state-of-the-art or rely on outdated technology. Production and process capability influences operating efficiencies, quality, and the overall cost structure of a seller.
- *Learning-curve effect.* Learning-curve analysis indicates whether a seller can lower its cost as a result of the repetitive production of an item.
- *The supplier's workforce.* A supplier's labor force affects the cost structure. Issues such as unionized versus nonunionized, motivated versus unmotivated, and the quality awareness and commitment of employees all combine to add another component to the cost structure. When visiting a supplier's facility, representatives from the purchaser should take the time to talk with employees about quality and other work-related items. Meeting with employees provides valuable insight about a supplier's operation. In recent years, the cost of labor in the workforce has gone up dramatically (see Sourcing Snapshot: The Rising Cost of Welders).
- *Management capability.* Management affects costs by directing the workforce in the most efficient manner, committing resources for longer-term productivity improvements, defining a firm's quality requirements, managing technology, and assigning financial resources in an optimal manner. Management efficiency and capability have both a tangible and intangible impact on a firm's cost structure. In the end, every cost component is a direct result of management action taken at some point in time.
- *Purchasing efficiency.* How well suppliers purchase their goods and services has a direct impact on purchase price. Suppliers face many of the same uncertainties and forces in their supply markets that purchasers face. Supplier visits and evaluations should evaluate the tools and techniques suppliers use to meet their material requirements.

Break-Even Analysis

Break-even analysis includes both cost and revenue data for an item to identify the point where revenue equals cost, and the expected profit or loss at different production volumes.

Firms perform break-even analysis at different organizational levels. At the highest levels, top management uses this technique as a strategic planning tool. For example, an automobile manufacturer can use the tool to estimate expected profit or loss over a range of automobile sales. If the analysis indicates that the break-even point in units has risen over previous estimates, cost-cutting strategies can be put in place. Divisions or business units can use the technique to estimate the break-even point for a new product line.

Sourcing Snapshot — *The Rising Cost of Welders*

There is a chronic shortage of young people who are seeking a career in welding or as electricians, boilermakers, pipefitters, or other trade-school craft labor positions. Let's focus for a moment on welders as a case study that is representative of this problem. With estimates that nearly half of the skilled welders available today are nearing retirement, the recruitment of younger people into the welding industry has become an important issue. The American Welding Society (AWS) has estimated that there will be a shortage of more than 200,000 skilled welders by 2010 in the United States, and the U.S. Department of Labor reports that the number of welders employed in the United States declined about 10% to 576,000 in 2005—the last full year for which data is available—from 594,000 in 2000.[5]

"One of the welding industry's biggest challenges is attracting young talent, which is attributable in large part to its tarnished image," said Dennis Klingman, AWS Education Committee chairman. "Many people still associate welding with black-and-white photos of tired welders covered in scuffmarks and dressed in soiled clothing. But the welding industry has undergone dramatic changes with the advancement of technology, and is no longer confined to the dark and dirty setting reminiscent of the last century's industrial era. Despite this, there continues to be an image problem, and parents, instructors, and counselors have been hesitant to introduce students to the industry."

In a recent interview, an expert noted the following:

> We need to reach out to 17 and 18 year olds, who currently don't understand that you can do very well in these roles. The skilled labor part of the world—engineers, mechanics, and electricians—in building our infrastructure—will cause us to struggle, when people are leaving the workforce. In some of these trades this is a narrow window. You can only be a productive welder for 15–20 years, and it is hard work, dirty work. What are the demographics for welders? I would suspect that most last until they are 30–40 and most don't do it into their 50s. It is backbreaking labor. We are going to be in for an eye-opening experience.

There has also been a huge draw on the demand for new infrastructure. The nation's infrastructure has not been upgraded in a very long time. In addition, there are multiple geographical areas undergoing significant development, which will put additional pressure on demand for labor.

Source: R. Handfield, "The Human Talent Factor in the Supply Chain," white paper, Supply Chain Resource Cooperative, December 2007.

Purchasing and supply chain specialists use break-even analysis to develop the following insights:

- Identify if a target purchase price provides a reasonable profit to a supplier given the supplier's cost structure.
- Analyze a supplier's cost structure. Break-even analysis requires detailed analysis or estimation of the costs to produce an item.
- Perform sensitivity (what-if) analysis by evaluating the impact on a supplier of different mixes of purchase volumes and target purchase prices.

- Prepare for negotiation. Break-even analysis allows a purchaser to anticipate a seller's pricing strategy during negotiations. Research indicates that a direct relationship exists between preparation and negotiating effectiveness.

Break-even analysis requires the purchaser to identify the important costs and revenues associated with a product or product line. Graphing the data presents a visual representation of the expected loss or profit at various production levels. Cost equations also express the expected relationship between cost, volume, and profit. When using break-even analysis, certain common assumptions are typically used:[6]

1. Fixed costs remain constant over the period and volumes considered.
2. Variable costs fluctuate in a linear fashion, although this may not always be the case.
3. Revenues vary directly with volume. This is represented graphically by an upward-sloping total revenue line beginning at the origin.
4. The fixed and variable costs include the semivariable costs. Thus no semivariable cost line exists.
5. Break-even analysis considers total costs rather than average costs. However, the technique often uses the average selling price for an item to calculate the total revenue line.
6. Significant joint (i.e., shared) costs among departments or products limits the use of this technique if these costs cannot be reasonably apportioned among users. If shared costs cannot be apportioned, then break-even analysis is best suited for the entire operation versus individual departments, products, or product lines.
7. This technique considers only quantitative factors. If qualitative factors are important, management must consider these before making any decisions based on the break-even analysis.

Break-Even Analysis Example

The following example assumes that fixed costs, variable costs, and target purchase price for a single item are reasonably accurate. The construction of a break-even graph requires these three pieces of information.

Exhibit 11.12 shows the required cost and volume data along with the break-even graph for this example. Because a buyer is estimating the break-even analysis for a supplier, the price is a target purchase price established by the purchaser. A range of prices can be analyzed to estimate a supplier's expected profit or loss given the fixed and variable costs.

In this example, the purchaser wants to determine if the anticipated volume of 9,000 units provides an adequate profit for the supplier at the target purchase price.

Exhibit 11.12 indicates that the supplier requires at least 7,500 units to avoid a loss with this cost structure and target purchase price. The following equation identifies the profit or loss associated with a given volume:

$$\text{Net Income or Loss} = (P)(X) - (VC)(X) - (FC)$$

where P = average purchase price, X = units produced, VC = variable cost per unit of production, and FC = fixed cost of production for an item.

Exhibit 11.12 Break-Even Analysis for Supplier XYZ

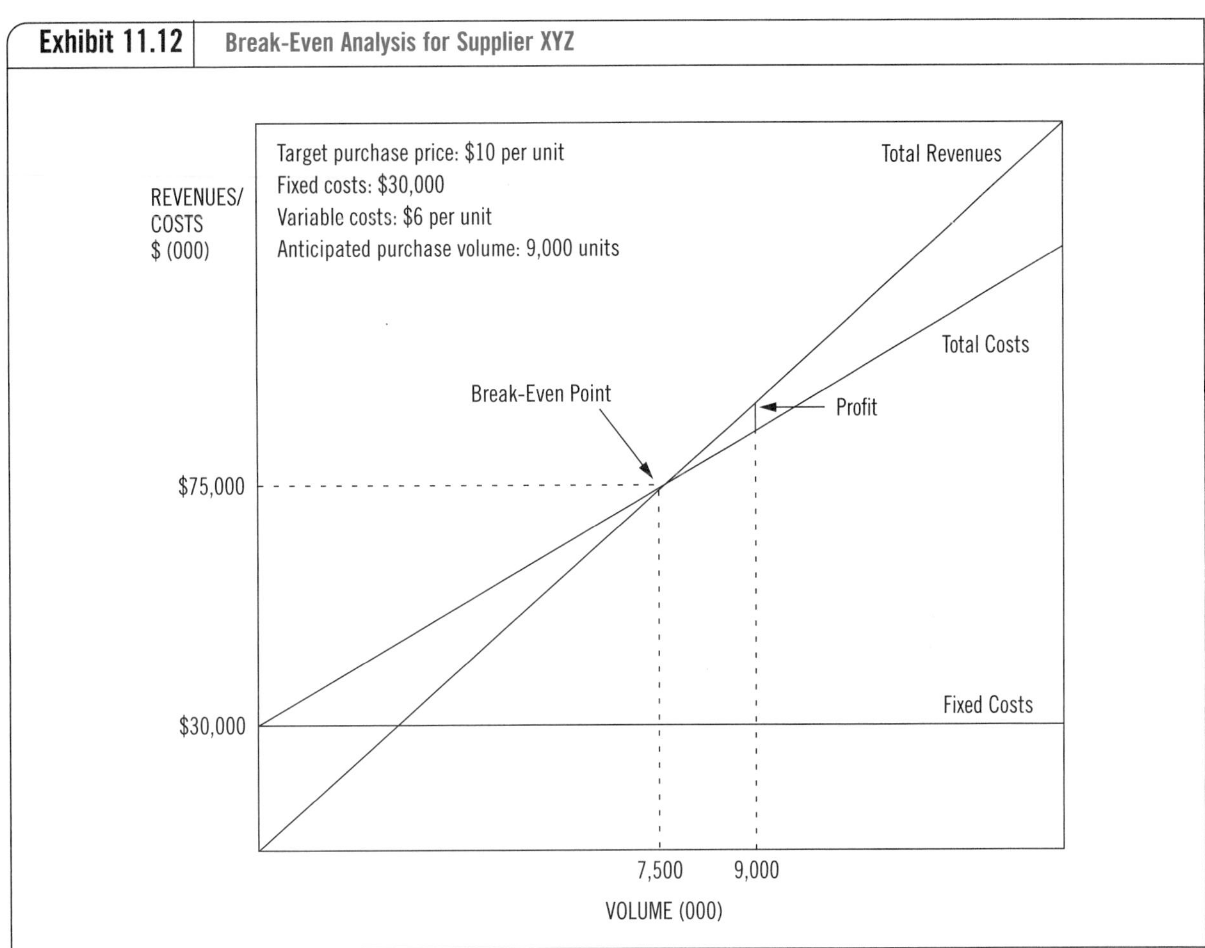

The supplier's expected profit for the anticipated 9,000 units is calculated as follows, using $10 per unit as the average purchase price:

$$\begin{aligned} \text{Net Income} &= (\$10)(9{,}000) - (\$6)(9{,}000) - (\$30{,}000) \\ &= \$60{,}000 \text{ Profit} \end{aligned}$$

We can also calculate the number of units the supplier needs to produce to break even (i.e., cover fixed costs). This is calculated as follows:

$$\begin{aligned} \text{Total Revenue} &= \text{Variable Cost} + \text{Fixed Cost} \\ \$10(X) &= \$6(X) + \$30{,}000 \\ \$4(X) &= \$30{,}000 \\ X &= 75{,}000 \text{ units} \end{aligned}$$

If the cost data are accurate, then the anticipated purchase volume provides a profit to the supplier, because it exceeds 7,500 units. Whether this is an acceptable profit level given the cost structure is an issue both parties may have to negotiate. If the analysis indicates that the purchase volume results in an expected loss to the seller, then a purchaser must consider several important questions:

- Is the target purchase price too optimistic given the supplier's cost structure?

- Are the supplier's production costs reasonable compared with other producers in the industry?
- Are the cost and volume estimates accurate?
- If the cost, volume, and target price are reasonable, is this the right supplier to produce this item?
- Will direct assistance help reduce costs at the supplier?

This method allows an evaluation of a supplier's expected profit over a range of costs, volumes, and target purchase prices. The break-even technique, however, often provides only broad insight into a purchase decision.

Total Cost of Ownership

Total cost of ownership requires a purchaser to identify and measure costs beyond the standard unit price, transportation, and tooling when evaluating purchase proposals or supplier performance. Formally, **total cost of ownership** is defined as the present value of all costs associated with a product, service, or capital equipment that are incurred over its expected life.

Most large firms base purchase decisions and evaluate suppliers on cost elements beyond unit price, transportation, and tooling. Research indicates, however, that companies differ widely about what cost components to include in a total cost analysis.

Typically these costs can be broken into four broad categories:[7]

- *Purchase price.* The amount paid to the supplier for the product, service, or capital equipment.
- *Acquisition costs.* All costs associated with bringing the product, service, or capital equipment to the customer's location. Examples of acquisition costs are sourcing, administration, freight, and taxes.
- *Usage costs.* In the case of a product, all costs associated with converting the purchased part/material into the finished product and supporting it through its usable life. In the case of a service, all costs associated with the performance of the service that are not included in the purchase price. In the case of capital equipment, all costs associated with operating the equipment through its life. Examples of usage costs are inventory, conversion, scrap, warranty, installation, training, downtime, and opportunity costs.
- *End-of-life costs.* All costs incurred when a product, service, or capital equipment reaches the end of its usable life, net of amounts received from the sale of remaining product or the equipment (salvage value) as the case may be. Examples of end-of-life costs are obsolescence, disposal, clean-up, and project termination costs.

Building a Total Cost of Ownership Model

Building a TCO model is not an easy task. It requires input from different parts of the organization and a thorough understanding of the process through the entire life cycle. The following steps must be taken to ensure that all costs are captured correctly:

Step 1. Map the process and develop TCO categories. Construct a process map from the time a need for the product, service, or capital equipment is identified all the way through the life cycle. The activities that you identify will help to develop broad TCO categories.

Step 2. Determine cost elements for each category. Using the process map as a guide, identify the subcost elements that make up each TCO category.

Step 3. Determine how each cost element is to be measured. This is a critical step. The metrics must be determined to quantify each of the cost elements identified in Step 2. For example, to quantify the costs of sourcing labor, the hourly rate of the individuals performing the sourcing activity and the amount of time they spend or will spend doing it will need to be known.

Step 4. Gather data and quantify costs. This is the most difficult and time-consuming step. In this step gather data for each of the metrics identified in Step 3 and quantify the respective costs. This requires information from various sources including interviews, surveys, the A/P system, and other internal databases. If information from internal databases is used, make sure to validate the numbers. Input errors can sometimes cause the numbers generated by these databases to be significantly inaccurate.

Step 5. Develop a cost timeline. Construct a cost timeline for the length of the life cycle. Place each cost element quantified in Step 4 in the appropriate time period. Then calculate totals for each time period as shown in the example.

Step 6. Bring costs to present value. Computing the present value allows decisions to be made based on present dollars. This is important because a dollar spent one year from now is not worth the same as a dollar spent now. The value of money spent anytime in the future will depend on the organization's cost of capital. To calculate the present value, therefore, obtain the organization's cost of capital from its finance department. Then calculate the present value of each total in the cost time line by using a present value table or a financial calculator. The sum of present values for each time period represents the total cost of ownership.

The Importance of Opportunity Costs

When considering usage costs, make sure to identify opportunity costs, if any. An **opportunity cost** is defined as the cost of the next best alternative. Typical opportunity costs include lost sales, lost productivity, and downtime. The absence of these costs in an analysis could lead to an entirely different decision and, possibly, a wrong one, as illustrated below.

A supply manager looking to purchase a machine was evaluating two alternatives. Alternative A was priced at $100,000, and B was priced at $125,000. The delivery lead time for Machine A was 90 days, and Machine B was 30 days. When determining usage costs for A it was important to add the lost revenue that would have been generated during the 60 days (90 – 30 = 60) had machine B been installed. By including the cost of lost revenue, B became the better alternative even though it was priced higher.

In another case, a supply manager made the decision, based primarily on price, to purchase Machine Y instead of Machine X. His analysis, however, omitted the opportunity cost from the difference in production capacity between the two machines. Machine X was capable of producing 10% more units than Machine Y. In a market

Sourcing Snapshot — *Maytag Sources Globally to Compete*

Maytag dishwashers have Chinese motors and Mexican wiring, and are put together in a sprawling American factory in Jackson, Tennessee. Some refer to this three-tiered approach to manufacturing as a triad strategy. Maytag calls it trying to keep ahead of imports. For a long time, bulky appliances like washing machines and refrigerators largely were insulated from competition with cheap imports because of their cavernous size. "Big boxes of air are expensive to ship across the ocean," says Maytag Corp.'s Jim Starkweather.

Over time, though, sharply lower labor and production costs in Asia have offset high freight costs, enabling some imported appliances (such as China's Haier and Korea's LG Electronics) to be sold in the United States at lower prices. With the arrival of low-priced imports, Maytag had to radically rethink how and where it builds refrigerators, washing machines, and dishwashers; it found the triad strategy works best for now. "It's a logical progression for us," says Art Learmonth, senior vice president of supply chain, noting that Maytag wants to avoid a wholesale shift of production out of the United States. The company says it wants to stay as close as possible to its end market and avoid shedding American jobs wherever possible.

In the case of dishwashers, Maytag buys motors in China—from a plant owned by GE—because the design is standardized and stable and China offers the lowest price. Maytag makes wire harnesses for dishwashers in Mexico because those harnesses tend to be different in each dishwasher model, so sudden shifts in demand could make it difficult to supply from farther away. How was this decision made? By "dissecting" competitors' appliances to determine the cost of every component. Whenever a competitor introduces a new dishwasher, for example, Maytag buys one and brings it to Jackson to dismantle it. Engineers examine rival appliances' O-rings, steel tubes, and other elements and estimate what it costs to make the appliance in the United States—and what it would cost to make it in Mexico.

Not everything goes away permanently, though. Subassembly work for dishwashers, essentially putting pumps and motors together in one piece with cables and connectors, was done in Reynosa, Mexico, and shipped to Tennessee. But eventually it grew more cost-effective to do the work in Tennessee: A simpler design was introduced, reducing labor, and it used less-expensive motors from China rather than Mexico. Still, Maytag says it wouldn't build certain items in China. Maytag teamed with a German supplier to develop a "turbidity sensor" that scans water coming out of a dishwasher to determine how clean the dishes are. As long as it detects the tiniest bit of food, the dishes are deemed dirty and the machine keeps churning. Learmonth says the company wouldn't try to have the sensors built in China, because the Chinese "aren't as protective of new technology" and so such proprietary technology is at greater risk of being stolen.

In some cases, though, Maytag decides it simply can't compete with imports. For example, profit margins on refrigerators with the freezer on top, rather than alongside or on the bottom, were so measly due to cheap imports that Maytag decided to quit making them. Instead, it pays Daewoo Electronics in Korea to produce those models and ship them to the United States to be sold under the Maytag name.

Source: T. Aeppel, "Three Countries, One Dishwasher," *Wall Street Journal,* October 6, 2003, p. B1.

upswing, sales potential increased by 10%. Machine Y was unable to handle the increase and a new machine had to be purchased. Had the supply manager selected Machine X, the purchase of a new machine could have been deferred, thereby saving hundreds of thousands of dollars. Mistakes like this can easily be avoided by ensuring that all costs, especially opportunity costs, are captured in the TCO.

Important Factors to Consider When Building a TCO Model

- Building a TCO can be a costly and time-intensive activity. Use it for evaluating larger purchases.
- Make sure to obtain senior management buy-in before embarking on a full-fledged TCO. It will make data gathering much easier, especially if several people from different parts of the organization have to be interviewed.
- Work in a team. This will greatly reduce the time required for data collection activities, which can be distributed among team members.
- Focus on the big costs first. Spending extended periods of time quantifying small cost elements will only delay the decision, which in most cases will not be impacted by them.
- Make sure to obtain a realistic estimate of the life cycle. A life cycle that is too short or too long could result in a wrong decision.
- Whether evaluating a purchase option or making an outsourcing decision, a TCO model will ensure that the right decision is made, at least from a cost perspective.

Exhibit 11.13 TCO Calculation for One Purchase Option

COST ELEMENTS	COST MEASURES
Purchase Price (Step 1):	
• Equipment (Step 2)	Supplier quote: $1,200 per PC (Steps 3 and 4)
• Software License A	Supplier quote: $300 per PC
• Software License B	Supplier quote: $100 per PC
• Software License C	Supplier quote: $50 per PC
Acquisition Cost:	
• Sourcing	2 FTE @ $85K and $170K for 2 months
• Administration	1 PO @ $150, 12 invoices @ $40 each
Usage Costs:	
• Installation	$700 per PC (PC move, install, network)
• Equipment Support	$120 per month per PC—supplier quote
• Network Support	$100 per month—supplier quote
• Warranty	$120 per PC for a 3-year warranty
• Opportunity Cost—Lost Productivity	Downtime 15 hours per PC per year @ $30 per hour
End of Life:	
• Salvage Value	$36 per PC

Exhibit 11.14 Total Cost of Ownership Calculation

COST ELEMENTS	PRESENT	YEAR 1 (STEP 5)	YEAR 2	YEAR 3
Purchase Price:				
Equipment	$1,200,000			
Software License A	$ 300,000			
Software License B	$ 100,000			
Software License C	$ 50,000			
Acquisition Cost:				
Sourcing	$ 42,500			
Administration	$ 150	$ 480	$ 480	$ 480
Usage Costs:				
Opportunity Cost—Lost Productivity		$ 450,000	$ 450,000	$ 450,000
Installation	$ 700,000			
Equipment Support		$1,440,000	$1,440,000	$1,440,000
Network Support		$1,200,000	$1,200,000	$1,200,000
Warranty	$ 120,000			
End of Life Costs:				
Salvage Value				($36,000)
TOTAL	$2,512,650	$3,090,480	$3,090,480	$3,054,480
Present Values @ 12%	$2,512,650	$2,759,799	$2,463,113 (Step 6)	$2,174,790

- When considering global sourcing, consider all of the relevant labor, quality, logistics, and import costs associated with the total supply chain. A good example of this model in action is shown in Sourcing Snapshot: Maytag Sources Globally to Compete.

Example of a TCO Model

Supply manager Joe Smith was considering the purchase of 1,000 desktop PCs for his organization. The life cycle was 3 years and the organization's cost of capital was 12%. He calculated the TCO for one of the purchase options as shown in Exhibit 11.13 on p. 411.

Using these elements, the total cost of ownership for each of these decisions was calculated as shown in Exhibit 11.14.

On the basis of this model, the supply manager should explore the possibilities of reducing service costs such as equipment support and network support—these appear to be the highest value, and contribute most to costs. This is also typically the most profitable area for the supplier, as services are often not audited.

Collaborative Approaches to Cost Management

Progressive purchasing departments across multiple industries such as automotive, electronics, and pharmaceutical have learned the hard way that the most effective way to reduce costs for strategic commodities is not through price haggling, but through effective collaboration. When supply management, engineering, and suppliers put their heads together to find innovative ways to reduce costs, the outcome is generally mutually beneficial for both parties: The buying company gets a lower price, and in many cases, the supplier benefits from a higher margin and a guarantee of future business. Two of the most common approaches to collaborative cost management include target pricing and cost-savings sharing.

Target Pricing Defined

Target pricing is an innovative approach used in the initial stages of the new-product development (NPD) cycle to establish a contract price between a buyer and seller. Japanese manufacturers, in an effort to motivate engineers to select designs that could be produced at a low cost, originally developed target pricing methodologies during the 1980s to battle the rising yen versus the U.S. dollar. These innovators came up with a simple concept to apply in new-product development: The cost of a new product is no longer an outcome of the product design process; rather, it is an input to the process. The challenge is to design a product with the required functionality and quality at a cost that provides a reasonable profit. In a new car, for example, the development team may work with marketing to determine the target price of the vehicle for the product's market segment. Using final price as a basis, the product is disaggregated into major systems, such as the engine and powertrain. Each major system has a target cost. At the component level (which represents a further disaggregation from the system level), the target cost is the price that a purchaser hopes to attain from a supplier (if the item is externally sourced).

With target pricing, a product's allowable cost is strictly a function of what a market segment is willing to pay less the profit goals for the product. Under traditional pricing approaches, however, product cost + profit = selling price. Using a target pricing approach, the selling price − profit = the allowable product cost. Generally speaking, the target cost is not always achievable by the supplier in early negotiations. Moreover, the supplier's current price to provide a product or service today is probably greater than the target price set forth by the buying company.

The difference between the supplier's price and the target cost becomes the strategic cost-reduction objective. This gap must be reduced by both parties in a collaborative effort through such methods as value engineering, quality function deployment, design for manufacturing/assembly, and standardization. Setting product-level target costs that are too aggressive may result in unachievable target costs. Setting too low a strategic cost-reduction challenge leads to easily achieved target costs but a loss of competitive position. In setting target prices and target costs, the new-product development team should bear in mind the cardinal rule of target costing: The target cost can never be violated. Moreover, even if engineers find a way to improve the functionality of the product, they cannot make the improvement unless they can offset the additional cost.

One of the pioneers and industry leaders in target pricing is Honda of America Manufacturing. The company breaks product costs down to the component level. Suppliers are asked to provide a detailed breakdown of their costs, including raw materials, labor, tooling, and required packaging as well as delivery, administrative, and other expenses. The breakdown of costs is helpful in suggesting ways that suppliers can seek to improve and thereby reduce costs. Cost tables are jointly developed with suppliers and used to find differences (line by line) across all elements of cost. A potential area of disagreement involves the supplier's profits and overhead. A fair profit is required but may be dependent on the level of investment. No fixed profit level is used in negotiations. Purchasing must then aggregate the parts costs and compare them with the target costs. If total costs exceed target costs, the design must change or costs must be reduced. Although the supplier's profit margins might be an easy place to look for cost savings, Honda realizes that doing so would squander the trust it worked hard to develop with suppliers.[8]

Once a purchaser has established a target price with a supplier for the first year of a contract, additional cost reductions over the life of the product can be made through an ongoing effort to drive down costs year over year. This can be achieved through a technique known as cost-savings sharing.

Cost-Savings Sharing Pricing Defined

Cost-savings sharing differs from traditional market-based pricing in several ways. First, cost-sharing approaches require joint identification of the full cost to produce an item, which is not the case with market-based pricing (where the buyer has little or no knowledge of the supplier's costs). Second, profit is a function of the productive investment committed to the purchased item and a supplier's asset return requirements (i.e., return on investment). Profit is not a direct function of cost (which is usually the practice with market-driven prices). The cost-based approach provides a supplier with incentives to pursue continuous performance improvement to realize shared cost savings and invest in productive assets. A later example illustrates these concepts.

An important feature of cost-savings sharing is the financial incentives offered to a seller for performance improvements above and beyond the improvements agreed to in the purchase contract. This differs from the traditional market-based pricing approach where one party (usually the purchaser) seeks to capture all cost savings resulting from a supplier's improvement effort. Traditional pricing practices have been a deterrent to cooperative efforts to make design, product, and process improvements. A cost-savings sharing approach recognizes the need to provide financial incentives to a supplier while enhancing closer relationships.

Prerequisites for Successful Target and Cost-Based Pricing

In order for target and cost-based pricing to occur, there must be joint agreement on a supplier's full cost to produce an item. Identification of all costs provides the basis for establishing joint improvement targets. The total cost to produce an item includes labor; materials; other direct costs; any costs due to start-up and production; and administrative, selling, and other related expenses.

Besides total cost components, the parties must jointly identify and agree upon product volumes, target product costs at various points in time, and quantifiable productivity and quality improvement projections. Each firm must also agree on the asset base and return requirement at the supplier that determines an item's profit.

There must also be agreement on the point in time when mutual sharing of cost savings takes place, as well as the formula used to share the rewards. Mutual sharing of rewards usually occurs for savings above and beyond the performance improvement targets agreed to in the purchase contract, and savings on any items incidental to joint performance improvement targets.

This approach requires a high degree of trust, information sharing, and joint problem solving. This process will fail if one firm takes advantage of the other or violates confidentiality of information sharing. There must also be a willingness to provide the resources necessary to resolve problems affecting overall success.

The ability to manage the risks associated with target pricing is another key prerequisite. Perhaps the main risk concerns volume variability. Because volume affects cost levels, both parties must carefully consider and manage the impact of changes from planned volume projections. Higher-than-projected volumes will result in a supplier achieving greater economies and lower per-unit costs. These lower costs, however, are not the result of a supplier's performance improvement. Conversely, lower-than-projected volumes may raise a supplier's average costs. Contractually, the parties must determine how to manage changes from the buying plan.

When to Use Collaborative Cost Management Approaches

A cost-based approach to determining price is clearly not appropriate for all purchased items. Many items do not warrant cost analysis, or the marketplace determines price. Based on the cost management portfolio matrix discussed earlier in the chapter, it is obvious that products that are readily available from multiple sources, standardized instead of customized, and heavily influenced by the market forces of supply and demand do not fit the profile of items appropriate for cost-based pricing.

What types of items are feasible for a cost-based cooperative approach? A cost-based approach is feasible when the seller contributes high added value to an item through direct or indirect labor and specialized expertise. This approach is particularly appropriate for complex items customized to specific requirements. Also, products requiring a conversion from raw material through value-added designs at a supplier are possible candidates. Examples of such items include a specially designed

Exhibit 11.15 Key Data for the Cost-Based Pricing Example

First-Year Target Price: $61.00

Negotiated/Analyzed Cost Structure

Material	$20 per unit
Labor rate	$8.50 per unit
Burden rate*	200% of direct labor
Scrap rate	10%
Selling, general, and administrative expense rate	10% of manufacturing cost
Effective volume range	125,000 units per year ± 10%
Projected product life	2 years
Return on investment agreed to	30%

	YEAR 1	YEAR 2
Supplier investment	$3 million	$2 million
Total supplier investment	$5 million	
Supplier improvement commitment		
Direct labor	10% reduction annually	
Scrap rate	50% reduction annually	

Improvements incidental to agreed-upon performance improvements: Shared 50/50

*"Burden" is a term used in accounting to describe costs of manufacture or production not directly identifiable with an exact product or unit of production. They are indirect or apportionable costs.

antilock brake system or a dashboard for an automobile. These items require a high value-added conversion from raw materials into a semifinished product. The supplier also likely contributes design and engineering support.

An Example of Target Pricing and Cost-Savings Sharing

Although actual target and cost-savings sharing agreements can be lengthy and complex, the following example demonstrates the fundamental principles of this strategic cost management approach. This example is based on an actual situation that occurred between an automotive OEM and a first-tier supplier.

A purchaser seeks to purchase a designed component that is part of a final end product. The final selling price of the product has been determined through discussions with marketing, and this figure has been rolled down (or disaggregated) to the component level. As such, both parties have agreed to target a purchase (or selling) price of $61 for the component for the first year. The purchaser has targeted this price as one that will support meeting the overall target price of the final end product.

Cost-savings sharing assumes that the buyer and seller will collaborate to identify the most efficient processes to produce a product as the basis for the cost structure. This approach does not reward inefficient processes or practices, and also assumes that engineers at the buying organization are flexible and willing to modify product specifications to align with the supplier's processes. Throughout this example the supplier's costs and return requirements serve as the basis for determining a fair and competitive price. Both parties agree to a negotiated cost-based approach because the parties have developed a close working relationship, supporting the sharing of detailed cost data, and because the supplier's cost structure is relatively efficient.

Exhibit 11.15 on p. 415 details the costs and investment data needed to develop a cost-based purchase contract.

Both firms must identify the costs and supplier investment associated with the purchased component, identify and agree on the supplier's asset return requirements, and identify supplier commitments to annual performance improvement targets.

These exhibits provide the basis for evaluating cost and price throughout the life of the contract.

Exhibit 11.16 details the cost breakdown and subsequent price of the component for each year of this contract. Data for year 1 include the negotiated/analyzed information presented in Exhibit 11.15. During the first year, the following events affected the selling price at the start of year 2:

- Overall material costs rise by 4% due to raw material cost increases.
- A joint value analysis team identifies a substitute material that reduces material costs by $1.50 per unit.
- Labor rates increase by 3% per unit due to a scheduled contractual increase at the supplier.
- The supplier meets the agreed productivity improvement targets for reduced scrap and improved labor productivity.

Year 2 data include these events.

- The supplier receives 50% of the $1.50 material reduction identified by the value analysis team.

Exhibit 11.16 Cost and Profit Breakdown for the Cost-Based Pricing Example

	YEAR 1	YEAR 2	
Materials	$20.00	$19.24	Materials reduction of $1.50 plus an overall materials increase of 4% (($20.00 – $1.50) × 1.04)
Labor	8.50	7.88	Reduction of 10% – Contractual target improvement plus 3% increase ($8.50 × .9 × 1.03)
Burden (200% × labor)	17.00	15.76	
Total materials, labor, burden	$45.50	$42.88	
Scrap (10%)	4.55	2.14	Scrap reduced from 10% to 5% – Contractual target ($42.88 × .05)
Manufacturing cost	$50.05	45.02	
Selling and administrative expenses (10%)	5.00	4.50	
Total cost	$55.05	$49.52	
Profit*	6.00	6.75	Includes $.75 share for joint material reduction ($6 + ($1.50/2))
Selling price	$61.50	$56.27	New selling price after year 1 events

*Profit is based on the 30% return on the investment figure agreed to between buyer and seller.

Profit = ($5 million total two-year investment × .3)/250,000 total units

= $6.00 profit per unit

- The profit figure for year 2 includes the supplier's share of the material reduction.
- The selling price at the start of year 2 becomes $56.27.

By focusing on joint and continuous performance improvement, the purchase price was reduced at a time when material and labor costs actually increased. This example illustrates the potential for improvement that can occur through joint price/cost analysis.

Establishing agreement on cost and price early in design and development supports the reduction of material costs through cooperative efforts. The use of cost-savings sharing can induce both parties to work together to achieve mutual goals. The purchaser reduces its cost curve for purchased items and also establishes a basis for continuous cost-improvement initiatives. The supplier benefits from longer-term contracts, a fair profit based on its asset investment, and increased competitiveness due to improvements occurring because of the purchaser's insights and contributions.

Good Practice Example

A Computer Manufacturer Brings in the Voice of the Customer and the Voice of the Factory

Best-in-class companies recognize that cost is designed into the product from the outset, especially the total cost of managing the product over its life cycle. This was an important component for a best-in-class product design at a large computer manufacturer, which recognized the significance of order fulfillment impact as an explicit outcome of the product design decision. This meant developing a process for product design decisions that implicitly involved the voice of the factory (VOF) and the voice of the supplier in product design decisions:

> We were involved in the negotiation of features that marketing wanted. Most of the requests they wanted had to be justified and brought in front of the team. The Voice of the Factory rep typically fought against any decisions that would add complexity to the producibility of the product from an order fulfillment perspective. The VOF team design was an upper management decision that drove this individual into the team structure. However, the specific ways that people went about communicating would typically vary by product and by team. It was, however, part of the mission statement of each NPD team.
>
> Most of the people on the VOF team had physically been to a factory in order to understand what people in the factories were facing day to day, especially in preproduction factory build tests. The factory would tell the VOF reps what the problems encountered in assembly were, and request that these issues be brought forward to the design team. The VOF teams were therefore able to put forth educated arguments to the NPD team. VOF teams also had weekly conference calls to update status and identify issue closure, and were tied to the NPD team from start to finish.

The teams emphasized the need for meaningful involvement of different business functions in the idea generation phase, but also noted that this was a rarity, not a common occurrence in their organizations. A target cost process was established early on to provide targets for the various groups on achieving the target cost for a unit. It quickly aligned marketing and design with supply chain team members on how to achieve those costs at the component and manufacturing level. On the component side the key driver was target cost—and responsibility was placed on all the groups that brought in that part or component. The four major groups (R&D, marketing, operations, and supply) agreed to the final target price. R&D looked at it from a best-case theoretical perspective, and some engineering teams did value engineering to come up with a projected target cost. Supply chain, dealing with the real world, would assess who could do it out there—and how close they could come to target price—based on the size of the product and the part of the country (labor rates).

> Platform manufacturing capability and equipment was brought into the NPD process—and we saved a lot. Proliferation of part numbers was an issue—so we required people to carry over old parts into new products on amortized tooling, which prevented proliferation of part numbers with minor changes made only because engineers would design from the ground up. There were design guidelines and rules calling for 40% carryover for new product. Then R&D and engineering and SCM would get together to decide on which ones would be carried over. First R&D would make recommendations, and then procurement would check to see if tooling and equipment could sustain another four years of production, and what the investment would be.

The importance of establishing impact on customer needs, while weighing the feasibility of introducing new technologies and parts, must be explicitly considered. For example, the manufacturer noted the following:

> If there were specific marketing features that were put forward to an individual team, the decision went one of two ways. If a senior vice president insisted that the product had to have this feature, no one would say no, even if

> the core team did not like it. On the other hand, if marketing put forward a feature such as an additional keyboard option, the representative had to put together a business case, which identified how many extra will be sold, the incremental margin derived, and so on.

This same individual also emphasized that procurement could be playing a more significant role in defining the technology roadmap for the product through its supply market intelligence and knowledge of supplier roadmaps and evolving technologies:

> There is a real missed opportunity by not having the core NPD team involved in the roadmap, which is published two years prior to roll-out. The upper management team makes changes or additions at that level, and there is typically no time to provide input into that process. The NPD VOF and procurement reps could better plan for capacity and align supplier planning processes earlier to better prepare. Typically, however, the team will wait until the product is kicked off before putting together the core team, as some products are killed, and people do not want to put in effort on a product that is not definitely going to go into the pipeline.

Questions

1. What are the typical arguments put forth by marketing for increasing complexity of a product line by adding additional features and options?
2. What are the typical arguments put forward by the supply chain and the Voice of the Factory operations leader in simplifying the product line?
3. Discuss the key elements that are required to build a decision support tool to create a business case to resolve this issue. Where would the data for building this decision support tool come from?

Source: R. Handfield, C. Bozarth, J. McCreery, and S. Edwards, "Design for Order Fulfillment Best Practices," white paper, Supply Chain Resource Cooperative, July 2007.

CONCLUSION

An awareness of cost fundamentals, cost analysis techniques, and innovative approaches to product costing is simply another area for the purchasing and supply chain professional to master. Buyers and supply chain specialists involved with nonstandard, technically complex items must have the ability to evaluate a supplier's cost structure and match supplier capabilities and product requirements from a cost perspective.

The ability to practice price and cost analysis techniques, such as those outlined in this chapter, can make the difference between creating value and creating waste.

KEY TERMS

cost analysis, 384
opportunity cost, 409
price analysis, 384
total cost analysis, 384
total cost of ownership, 408

DISCUSSION QUESTIONS

1. Why should a purchaser evaluate the cost of making an item instead of simply evaluating the purchase price? Is this true for all types of products? Why or why not?
2. List some of the reasons suppliers are reluctant to share detailed cost information. What can purchasers do to convince suppliers that shared cost data will not be exploited?
3. Is global sourcing always the lowest-cost option on account of the low labor rates? What other types of data have to go into this decision?
4. What is the difference between a fixed cost, a semivariable cost, and a variable cost?
5. Discuss the different pricing strategies a seller can use along with the key features of each. Provide examples of current marketplaces where these types of pricing arrangements are shifting dramatically.
6. Can you provide examples of suppliers or industries that are currently utilizing a price volume model, market share model, competition pricing model, and revenue pricing model?
7. What types of cost information are available on the Internet? What types of price information are available on the Internet? Is this information reliable?
8. Under what conditions does a buyer have the most purchasing leverage over a seller?
9. When does a seller have the most leverage over a buyer?
10. What is the total cost of ownership concept? What are some of the challenges that must be overcome when implementing a total cost measurement system?
11. What are the benefits from measuring the total cost of ownership for a purchased item? Are there any potential disadvantages of this approach? If so, what are they?
12. How is the price of an item established in a target pricing contract? What makes target pricing attractive to a buyer and seller?

13. Can a company use a target pricing model without a follow-on cost-savings sharing agreement? Why or why not?

14. If a buyer and seller do not have a close working relationship, how can a buyer obtain cost data to perform a cost analysis for a supplier before awarding a purchase contract?

15. What happens if a supplier cannot meet a purchaser's initial target price? How is this issue resolved?

ADDITIONAL READINGS

Bendorf, R. (2002), "Supplier Pricing Models," *Inside Supply Management,* May, pp. 18–19.

Degraeve, Z., and Roodhooft, F. (1999), "Effectively Selecting Suppliers Using Total Cost of Ownership," *Journal of Supply Chain Management,* 35(1), 5.

Dubois, A. (2003), *Strategic Cost Management across Boundaries of Firms,* Industrial Marketing Management.

Ellram, L. (1993), *Total Cost of Ownership,* Tempe, AZ: Center for Advanced Purchasing Studies.

Ellram, L. (1996), "A Structured Method for Applying Purchasing Cost Management Tools," *International Journal of Purchasing and Materials Management,* 32(1), 11–19.

Ellram, L. (2002), *Strategic Cost Management,* Tempe, AZ: Center for Advanced Purchasing Studies.

Ellram, L. (2002), "Supply Management's Involvement in the Target Costing Process," *European Journal of Purchasing and Supply Management,* 8(4), 235–244.

Ferrin, B., and Plank, R. E. (2002), "Total Cost of Ownership Models: An Exploration Study," *Journal of Supply Chain Management,* 38(3), 18–12.

Lamm, D. V., and Vose, L. C. (1988), "Seller Pricing Strategies: A Buyer's Perspective," *International Journal of Purchasing and Materials Management,* 24(3), 9–13.

Lockamy, A., III, and Smith, W. I. (2000), "Target Costing for Supply Chain Management: Criteria and Selection," *Industrial Management and Data Systems,* 100(5), 210–218.

Monczka, R., and Trecha, S. (1988), "Cost-Based Supplier Performance Evaluation," *International Journal of Purchasing and Materials Management,* 45, 12–18.

Newman, R., and McKeller, J. R. (1995), "Target Pricing: A Challenge for Purchasing," *International Journal of Purchasing and Materials Management,* 31(3), 3, 12–20.

Shank, J. K. (1999), "Case Study: Target Costing as a Strategic Tool," *Sloan Management Review,* 41(1), 73–83.

Shank, J., and Govindarajan, V. (1993), *Strategic Cost Management: The New Tool for Competitive Advantage,* New York: Free Press.

Stundza, T. (2000), "Focus Is on Total Cost of Ownership," *Purchasing,* March 2, p. 34.

"Understanding Total Cost of Ownership" (2000), *NAPM InfoEdge,* 5(3), 22.

ENDNOTES

1. Personal interview by Robert Handfield with John Calabrese, vice president of advanced purchasing, General Motors, August 16, 2000.

2. Based on Bendorf, R. (2002), "Supplier Pricing Models," *Inside Supply Management,* May, pp. 18–19.

3. Tubb, R. (2007), "The Nation's Changing Landscape," *Pipeline and Gas Journal,* March.

4. Based on Bendorf.

5. "AWS District 10 and Local Businesses to Address Shortage of Welders" (2007), *Welding Magazine,* April 26.

6. Schmidgall, R. S. (1986), *Managerial Accounting,* East Lansing, MI: Educational Institute, pp. 271–272.

7. This section is based on Menezes, S. (2001), *Purchasing Today,* January, pp. 28–32.

8. Adapted from Krause, D., and Handfield, R. (1999), *Developing a World Class Supply Base,* Tempe, AZ: Center for Advanced Purchasing Studies.

Chapter 12

PURCHASING AND SUPPLY CHAIN ANALYSIS: TOOLS AND TECHNIQUES

Learning Objectives

After completing this chapter, you should be able to

- Understand fundamentals of project management tools
- Understand how to calculate the effect of learning curves on supplier costs
- Develop a basic understanding of the value analysis process
- Develop basic skills in process mapping of supply chain applications

Chapter Outline

Project Management Does It Better, Faster, and Cheaper

According to a seasoned pro, project managers must constantly clarify the requirements in the faster-cheaper-better mandate, and negotiate their relative importance to the project. The following example highlights some of the tradeoffs that project managers face in building a home, as well as the contradictions. A supply manager working on real-world projects will find this exercise to be a useful tool in helping to meet project expectations.

Initial Project Scope Statement: *Build a 2,000-square-foot, three-bedroom, two-bathroom house.*

The Initial Project Scope doesn't address many parameters of the project. What is the most important criterion for this project? Faster? Cheaper? Better? What does this say about the quality of the house? What does the owner want to be better? We all know you can spend whatever you want on a house, regardless of the size and number of rooms. Materials make a huge difference. Quality would certainly be a factor. Both of those parameters would create conflicts with faster and cheaper. It takes time and money to get the finest materials and the best workers. That's where the blueprints and a list of materials come into play. Those certainly help to specify exactly what shape the house should take and the types of materials to be used but typically would not specify the cost or timeline. That's what a building contract is for and where project management becomes important. Let's look at some other issues that would expand the current scope statement to make it clearer.

Faster is dependent on lots of things. The weather is a factor. Worker availability is a factor, with the right skills at the right time to complete every phase of the project. Building permits can be a factor, as can financing and material delivery. There are literally hundreds of things that can slow down or stop this project. How important is faster? Are you living in a one-bedroom apartment with your family of four, ready to have a mental breakdown if you don't get some space soon? Or do you have time and want to build the house well at a reasonable cost, without concern about common delays? Perhaps there is a threshold for delay that is not tolerable under any circumstances. This would be true if you have sold your existing home and must be out by a certain date and don't want to move twice. Faster can usually be attained with sacrifices to cheaper or better .

Cheaper would be a large factor in most home-building projects because most people live on a limited income. There is only so much house you can afford before the quality of life is affected in other areas. Some people are so passionate about their homes, they are willing to live "house-poor." Mortgage companies use a rule of thumb that your monthly house expenses (mortgage, taxes, utilities, maintenance) should not exceed 28% of your monthly gross income. Some people will sacrifice equity (e.g., 30-year mortgage vs. 15-year mortgage) so they can get a better house, but they are trading off cheaper. The interest difference between those two finance deals is significant. Others are willing to shop for months or years to find the perfect house or the perfect deal. Faster is sacrificed for better or cheaper. Answers to these critical issues will be reflected in your expanded scope statement to clarify your preferences.

There is a documentary about a competition between builders in San Diego, California. The rules were simple. Build a 1,500-square-foot, three-bedroom, two-bath home that must pass code and meet design specifications, *as fast as you can.* This home had to be complete in every way you would expect it to be before moving in. There were no limits on the amount of resources that could be applied to the project. They were given as much time as they needed to plan every detail needed to execute the build. The ultimate project management job was started.

How much time do you think the winning team took to build the house? Weeks? Days? The name of the documentary is "Four-Hour House." The winning team actually built the home, to code and specifications, in a little more than three hours. Each team brought more than 300 workers to the site and every kind of equipment you could imagine to speed up the process. The project plan was down to the minute, with many tasks being performed simultaneously. For example, the holes were being drilled in walls for electrical wire while the walls were being built. The roof was being built off to the side of the house so it could be craned into place when the structure was ready. The foundation used chemicals to quick-cure the cement so building could occur immediately after pouring the cement. It was amazing to watch the coordination and enthusiasm of the teams as they performed what most would consider impossible. They had decided that faster was more important than better or cheaper. Now some would argue they wouldn't want to live in those houses, but they did meet quality standards. The homes were more expensive to build, but not radically. It just depends on what you want from the project. It also demonstrated that months of planning were required to execute a project like this in a day.

After taking preferences into account, our final Revised Project Scope Statement reads: *Within six months, and within a budget of $250,000, build a 2,000-square-foot, two-story home to the attached design specifications. The owner must approve in writing any changes to materials, costs, or building schedule.*

Source: Adapted from D. Cretsinger, "Faster, Cheaper, Better," December 14, 2006, http://www.projectsatwork.com/content/articles/234376.cfm.

Having the right tools and applying the right techniques is an essential part of supply chain management. As the opening vignette illustrates, the skills needed to build a quality house on time and within budget include the ability to (1) manage projects; (2) assess costs associated with work to be done by subcontractors; (3) realize that learning-curve principles will affect time and labor costs; (4) apply value engineering (VE) to the design and construction of the home; (5) ensure the contractor purchases materials in the appropriate quantities for maximum discounts; and (6) process map the actual times required for the subactivities.

To effectively accomplish their assignments, supply managers must be project managers. They must be skilled in managing team assignments involving multiple tasks and team members. Buyers must understand how to analyze competitive bids or negotiate favorable prices due to learning improvements that occur at a supplier or subcontractor. Process mapping helps identify and eliminate waste throughout the supply chain. Value analysis (VA) supports continuous quality improvement. All of these tools are important for purchasers to be effective in driving competitive success for their organization.

This chapter presents a set of tools and techniques that support effective purchasing and supply chain management. The tools discussed include project management, learning-curve analysis, value engineering/value analysis, quantity discount analysis (QDA), and process mapping.

Project Management

Project management is a valuable skill for supply chain managers to have because more and more work is being structured as projects. Projects have certain characteristics that make them unique compared with other forms of work. A **project** is a series of tasks that requires the completion of specific objectives within a certain time frame; has defined start and stop dates; consumes resources, particularly time, personnel, and budget; and operates with limited resources. Examples of projects involving purchasing and supply chain personnel include developing new products, developing new management information systems, implementing value analysis recommendations, developing sourcing strategy, and initiating performance improvement plans at a supplier. Project management can be crucial in applications that span several organizations—from implementing enterprise resource planning systems and construction projects to developing a marketing plan and creating a website.

Defining Project Success

Because projects usually have a defined scope with agreed-upon tasks and responsibilities, it is often easier to measure project success as compared with other types of work.

Did a supplier quality improvement project improve supplier quality by the intended amount? Was a new product developed within the time and budget constraints? Did the new product achieve its initial sales goals? In general, several criteria define whether a project was successfully completed. These include whether the project was completed within the following constraints:

- Within the allocated time period and budget
- At the proper performance or specification level as determined by the stated goals and objectives of the project
- At a level accepted by the customer, user, or management
- With minimal or only mutually agreed-upon changes
- Without disturbing the main work flow of the organization

Before initiating a project, supply managers should consider the following points:[1]

- Make sure the objectives and outcomes are championed by senior executive management
- Place the program under the leadership of people with skill, credentials, and credibility
- Establish an effective governance process with a cross-functional team
- Maintain active participation from team members (e.g., use their talents)
- Break down the project into phased deliverables
- Manage expectations continuously and consistently
- Measure objectively
- Ensure rapid problem escalation and resolution

Project Phases

Projects move through various phases from conception to completion. Exhibit 12.1 summarizes six phases along with the characteristics defining the activities comprising each phase. The phases become increasingly detailed as projects progress from concept through completion.

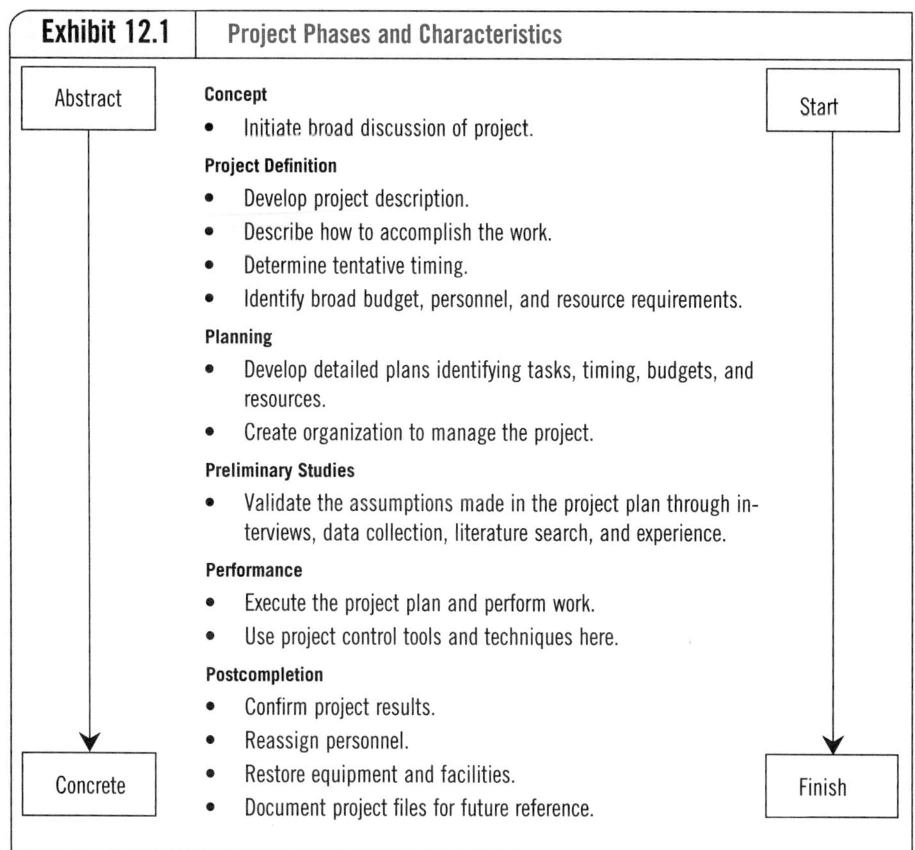

Exhibit 12.1
Project Phases and Characteristics
Abstract
Concrete
Start
Finish
Concept
• Initiate broad discussion of project.
Project Definition
• Develop project description.
• Describe how to accomplish the work.
• Determine tentative timing.
• Identify broad budget, personnel, and resource requirements.
Planning
• Develop detailed plans identifying tasks, timing, budgets, and resources.
• Create organization to manage the project.
Preliminary Studies
• Validate the assumptions made in the project plan through interviews, data collection, literature search, and experience.
Performance
• Execute the project plan and perform work.
• Use project control tools and techniques here.
Postcompletion
• Confirm project results.
• Reassign personnel.
• Restore equipment and facilities.
• Document project files for future reference.

Concept

Early in the project management process, project planners must develop a broad concept or definition of the project. A broad project objective may include developing a new product for a certain market within a specified time and budget. Project planners also identify any broad constraints facing the project. Budget estimates made during the concept phase are usually accurate to within approximately 30% compared with final budget targets.

Project Definition

If a project is initially feasible, it proceeds to the definition phase. This phase requires the development of a project description that provides greater detail than the concept phase. The project description identifies how to accomplish the work, how to organize for the project, the personnel required to support the project, tentative timing schedules, and tentative budget requirements. Budget estimates begin to become more exact, with a target of approximately 5 to 10% of the actual final budget.

Planning

Planning involves preparing detailed plans that identify the tasks, timing milestones, budgets, and resources required to support each task. This phase also includes creating the organization that will carry out the project, often through the use of project teams. The planning phase is particularly critical because there is a strong correlation between effective planning and successful project outcomes.

The project plan developed during the concept or project definition phase is usually not detailed enough to provide guidance during project implementation. Detailed planning provides an opportunity for discussing each person's role and responsibilities throughout the project. An organization must also define how the different tasks and activities comprising the project will come together to complete the project.

Preliminary Studies

A final phase before actually executing the project involves verifying the assumptions in the project plan, including performing literature searches, conducting field interviews, and gathering any required data. This phase confirms the planning work performed (or not performed) to date. Once the project manager or team confirms the assumptions made during detailed planning, then the actual performance of the project begins.

Performance

The performance phase involves carrying out the project's plan and reporting the work results on a continuous basis to management or customers. Effective planning increases the likelihood that actual performance outcomes will meet expectations. Project managers play a particularly important role here in coordinating and directing the work effort. Depending on the type of project, this may be the longest of the six phases in terms of time and resources consumed.

Sourcing Snapshot — *China: Calling All Project Managers*

The economic growth in China has created a need for talented project managers. Greg Balestrero, CEO of the Project Management Institute (PMI), the world's leading provider of project management training and standards, discusses why and how the need for project management professionals has grown.

Q: Projects have been around since the Pyramids; why are project managers so important now?

A: There is the issue of assurance of repeatable success in projects, being able to predict a result and repeat it. This is particularly the case when you're talking about short life cycles, for example, fourth- or fifth-generation products that have a life cycle of less than 12 months. Aligning project skills with product development skills is one of the most important things. Then there is an obsessive demand for return on value earlier and earlier. Even if you're not in product delivery but putting in an IT system in a new facility, the era of the five-year project is long gone. Companies need the IT installation now, and within 12 months it needs to be generating the value that it was set out to do. So there is this increase in shortness.

Q: What has been the impact of globalization on the challenges involved in project management?

A: Nowadays, when we talk about the project manager we are really talking about the global project manager. Globalization—for good, bad, or however you look at it—has created a demand for multicultural projects. Look at the Airbus A380: It required 1,500 suppliers and

2,400 projects across 30 countries. That is pretty complex. When it first came out, the BMW Z4 was seen as a very simple car; everyone thought it was pure German. But only about 18% of the products in that car are manufactured in Germany; 82% are manufactured in 30 other countries. When you are managing projects across cultural lines and national borders, you must put in place a standard that is a common language, a common approach, so everyone can answer the question "Is it on budget?" I don't care if it's 1,500 suppliers working in 27 different currencies, you need an answer that is accurate and understandable to everyone. We promote a global standard which we call the project management body of knowledge. . . . It's like an operating system for projects.

Q: Is there a shortage of people who can manage projects, be it middle managers, line managers, or those who bring a project together?

A: There's a shortage of project managers worldwide. And we are working 24/7 to provide education and certification worldwide. There is no lack of demand for certified professionals in project management. And if you add complex projects, be they the Three Gorges Dam, the Beijing Olympics infrastructure, or space projects, there is a drought of people, so those that are there can command good salaries worldwide.

Q: How are you approaching the market for training project management professionals in China?

A: Our real focus in China is ensuring professionals recognize that our standards and our certification are the two most important things to them. Since 2001 we've had 22,000 certified professionals here in China—we call them Project Management Professionals—and the growth rate is getting close to 50–60% a year. Without a doubt, China is seeing the fastest growth in management professionals, and it's a demand for excellence in project management.

Q: Is China's education platform sufficient? How many project managers does the country need?

A: There was an independent UN study that predicted they would need more than 100,000 trained, certified, qualified project managers over the next five years. These are not just bodies that can go in and manage the projects but people who have been recognized as having the skills and knowledge of standards as well as the right approach to get things done. And that was in 2003; since then it has accelerated. The 11th Five-Year Plan has shown the need to move infrastructure out into central China and—whether it's power generation, roads, transportation, fresh drinking water, health care, education—it's all project-related. This is then magnified by the scope and size of China.

Q: How has the demand in China translated into growth for PMI?

A: We have 225,000 members in 160 countries; in 1996, we had 12,000 members, mostly in the United States. We are growing at a rate of 45% outside of North America, and when you look at the Asia Pacific region, with half the world's population, that's where we are growing in leaps and bounds.

Source: Adapted from "China: Calling All Project Managers," *BusinessWeek* Online, April 18, 2007, http://www.businessweek.com/globalbiz/content/apr2007/gb20070418_435349.htm.

Postcompletion

Project managers or teams perform several important tasks during the postcompletion phase:

- Confirm that the final project meets the expectations of management or customers. This usually involves a comparison of the project performance outcome compared with the expected outcome established during earlier planning.
- Conduct a post-implementation meeting to discuss the strengths and weaknesses of the project. An effective organization learns from the experiences of its project teams. Any lessons learned should be communicated to other project teams.
- Reassign project personnel to other positions or other projects. One of the primary characteristics of projects as a form of work is the movement of personnel from project to project.
- Restore any equipment or facilities used to their original status. Also, make sure all files are in good order and are available for future reference.

Project Planning and Control Techniques

Various tools and techniques are available to plan, control, and coordinate work activities. These tools allow a project manager to track what requires completion, by whom, and by when as specified in the project plan. These tools also allow performance tracking over time, particularly in the areas of time and budget. Two popular planning and control techniques are Gantt charts and project networking tools such as Critical Path Method (CPM) and Program Evaluation and Review Technique (PERT).

Gantt Charts

A **Gantt chart** visually displays the tasks and times associated with a project. Named after Henry Gantt, the chart is a horizontal bar chart with activities listed vertically and times or dates displayed horizontally. The advantage of Gantt charts is that they are relatively inexpensive to develop and use and can convey a great deal of information. The primary disadvantage is that for larger projects, they become increasingly difficult to use or to keep up to date. In such cases, project management techniques such as CPM and PERT are recommended. Exhibit 12.2 illustrates a Gantt chart for a project involving the transfer of equipment to a supplier during an outsourcing project.

CPM/PERT

Critical Path Method (CPM) and **Program Evaluation and Review Technique (PERT)** are two popular project control techniques, particularly for projects that are complex or involve many activities or tasks. These techniques require the user to identify the activities or tasks that make up a project and to determine the sequence of those activities.

Users apply CPM to projects where there is a single known time (referred to as a deterministic time) for each activity with no variance. PERT applies to projects where time estimates are variable or uncertain. Each activity in PERT has three time estimates: (1) most likely, (2) pessimistic, and (3) optimistic. Project managers combine these estimates to arrive at a single estimate of the expected activity time for each activity within the network.

Exhibit 12.2 Gantt Chart for a Supplier Development Technology Transfer Project

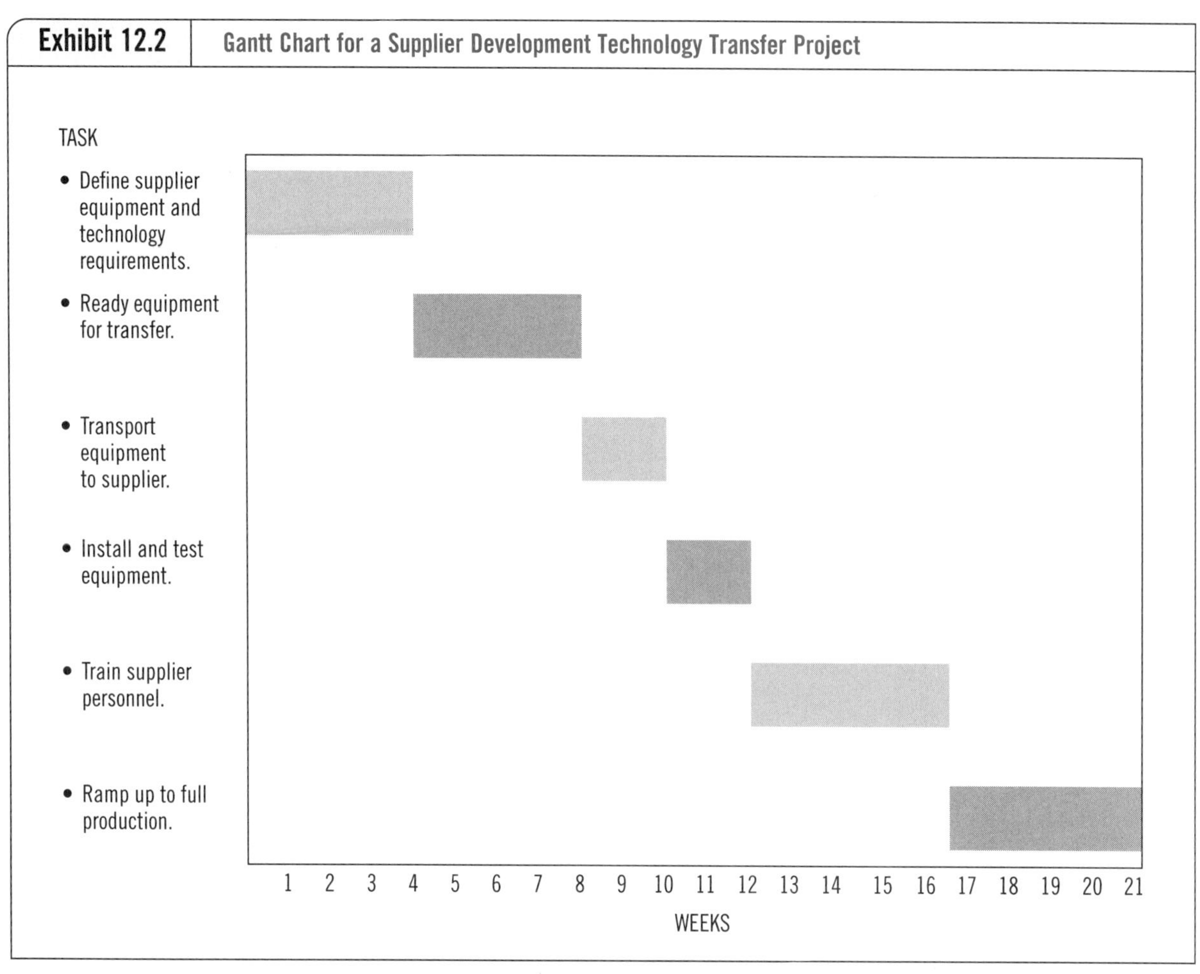

Project control techniques allow project managers to monitor progress over time while managing costs across all activities. Users can also determine the probability of completing projects by certain target dates using normal distribution statistics.

Readers requiring in-depth detail of probability analysis or time/cost tradeoffs are urged to consult an operations research or project management textbook.

Rules for Constructing a Project Management Network

A graphical network can be used to represent each PERT or CPM project. A network is a graphical representation that shows how each individual activity relates in time and sequence to all other activities. Network illustrations are powerful because they show how separate activities come together to form an entire project. The construction of CPM and PERT project networks follows generally accepted rules or conventions, shown in Exhibit 12.3 on pp. 432–433.

Later in this section we will use a purchasing project example to demonstrate the use of these rules, which apply only to constructing the network and do not yet involve the use of time estimates.

Exhibit 12.3 Network Rules

1. Identify each unique activity within a project by a capital letter that corresponds only to that activity.
2. A unique branch or arrow represents each activity in the project. Circles or nodes represent events. For example:

This is the branch for activity A. Sometimes we also number the events, which represent points in time. The events associated with this activity (the circles) represent the start and completion of this activity.

3. This diagram means only that B cannot start until A is complete. Branches show only the relationships between different activities; the length of the branches has no significance.

The sequence of the branches, however, is important.

4. Branch direction indicates the general progression in time from left to right.
5. When a number of activities end at one event, no activity starting at that event may begin before all activities ending at that event are complete.

Activity D can start only after all activities preceding it in the network are complete. In this example, activities B and C must both be complete before beginning D. Activities B and C are predecessors of D (activities that must be complete before work on D can begin).

6. Two or more activities cannot share graphically the same beginning and ending events.

Not allowed:

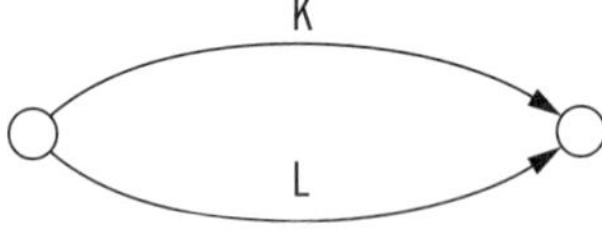

Allowed:

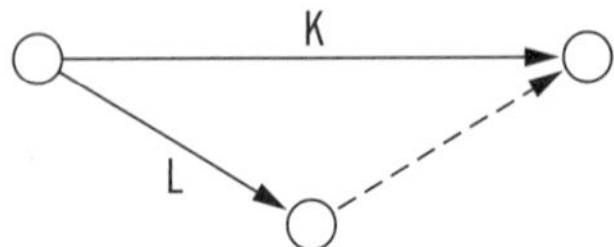

This rule may require the use of a dummy activity, which is simply an extension of the activity that precedes it. In this case, the dummy activity is an extension of activity L. Dummy activities have no expected activity time—they simply carry forward the time from the preceding activity.

7. Networks start and finish at only a single event.

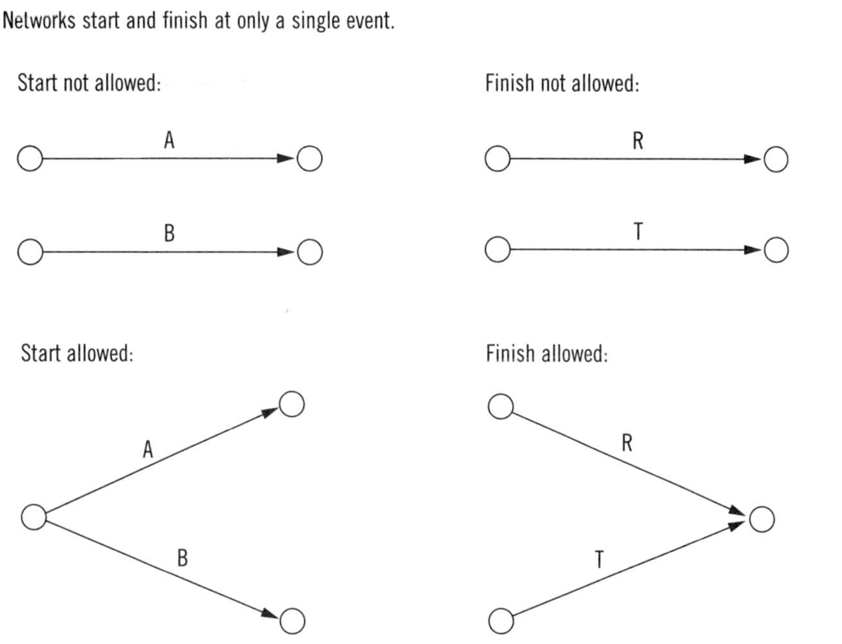

In this example, the project starts and ends with two activities (A and B at the start and R and T at the end). This rule requires each network to start and stop on a single event. There is no limit to the number of activities that can begin or end at a single event.

Project Management Example: Sourcing Strategy

A cross-functional team is responsible for developing a sourcing strategy, which will involve selecting a supplier follow-on systems development. The project has three primary objectives: (1) develop a set of performance criteria along with the evaluation system to assess potential supplier performance; (2) identify, evaluate, and select suppliers for a critical commodity; and (3) develop an information technology system that will evaluate the performance of selected suppliers on a continuous basis.

The project manager has identified the following unique tasks that are required to meet the primary objectives of this project. (The letters refer to the sequence of activities shown in Exhibit 12.4 on p. 434.)

Exhibit 12.4 illustrates the network for this project. There are three paths of activities through this project: A–B–E–F–G–K; A–C–D–F–G–K; and A–H–I–J. (A path is a continuous or connected flow of activities from project start to finish.) The project manager must evaluate the progress of all three paths to ensure meeting the original project objectives. After reviewing Exhibit 12.3, one of the primary benefits of networking should become clear: the ability to see the relationships among all the tasks in a project.

Exhibit 12.4 Project Network Illustration for the Supplier Selection Project

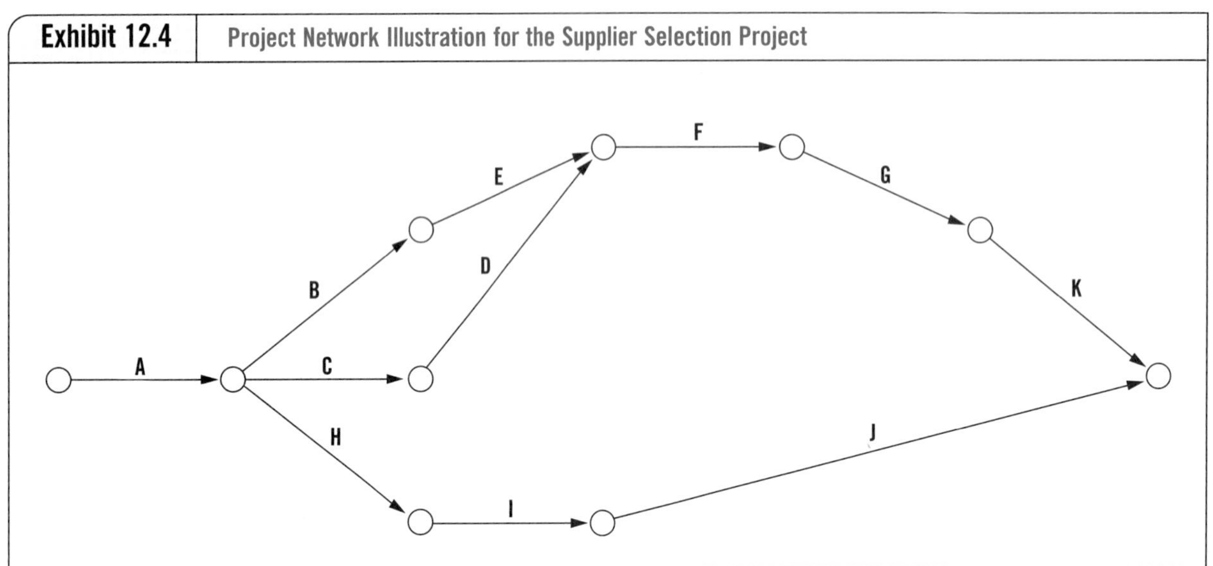

ACTIVITY	DESIGNATION	PRECEDING ACTIVITY
Assemble project team	A	
Identify potential commodity suppliers	B	A
Develop supplier evaluation criteria	C	A
Develop supplier audit form	D	C
Perform preliminary supplier financial analysis	E	B
Conduct supplier site visits	F	E, D
Compile results from site visits	G	F
Identify requirements for computerized supplier performance system	H	A
Perform detailed systems analysis and programming	I	H
Test computerized system	J	I
Select final suppliers	K	G

Three observations are important at this point. First, the project manager has not identified the time associated with each task, only the tasks and their sequence. The manager does not yet know which set of activities will make up the longest path (the critical path) within the project. Second, projects continuously change over time. As the project team progresses on its assignments, it must update the network to reflect that progress. The network only looks like it does in Exhibit 12.4 at the beginning of the project. PERT and CPM require regular updating with the most current information available. Third, computer software, such as Microsoft Project, is available that will construct the network and allow the user to perform various analyses. The most challenging part of project management is defining the activities that make up a project, the relationship between those activities, and the time and budget required for completing the activities.

Project Management with Time Estimates

The following steps describe how to develop a PERT network with variable time estimates.

1. Identify each activity requiring completion during the project and the relationship between those activities. This is a critical step. The activities should not be too broad or too narrow in scope. They must be definable tasks with a start and stop point whose completion supports the objectives of the project.
2. Construct the network reflecting the proper precedence relationships using the rules discussed earlier.
3. Determine the three time estimates for each activity (optimistic = a, pessimistic = b, and most likely = m). The optimistic and pessimistic estimates should reflect the end points on the time estimate continuum. These times should have only a 10 to 20% chance of actually occurring. Accurate time estimates are critical. Inaccurate time estimates or those with a great deal of variability will lessen the validity of the control process.
4. Calculate the expected activity time for each activity using the following formula:

   $$\text{Expected Activity Time} = (a + 4m + b)/6$$

   If activity G has an optimistic time of 5 weeks, a most-likely time of 6 weeks, and a pessimistic time of 13 weeks, then its expected activity time is (5 + 24 + 13)/6 = 7.

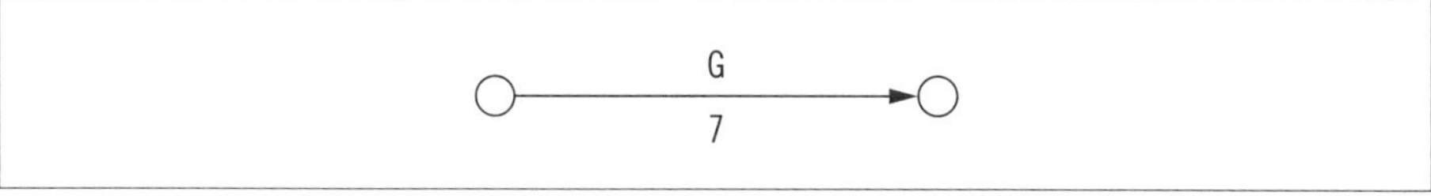

5. Place the expected activity times on the network under their respective activity branches and identify the critical path. The critical path is the longest (in time) path of continuous activities through the network. Any delay for activities on the critical path will delay the entire project. There can be more than one critical path in a project.
6. Identify the early start (ES), late start (LS), early finish (EF), and late finish (LF) times. These times also appear on the activity branch and provide a great deal of information to the project manager:

ES EF
LS LF

- *Early start.* The earliest point in time an activity can begin.
- *Late start.* The latest point in time an activity can begin without delaying the entire project.
- *Early finish.* The earliest time a project can finish given the expected activity time. Early finish time equals ES + expected activity time.
- *Late finish.* The latest time an activity can finish without delaying the entire project. Latest finish time equals LS + expected activity time.

Project Management Example with Time Estimates

Using the project presented earlier, we can now include time estimates (in weeks) and calculate the expected time for each activity. Project planners calculate these estimates during the planning phase of project management.

TASK	OPTIMISTIC	MOST LIKELY	PESSIMISTIC	EXPECTED ACTIVITY TIME
Assemble project team (A)	1	2	3	2
Identify potential commodity suppliers (B)	3	6	9	6
Develop supplier evaluation criteria (C)	2	4	5	3.8
Develop supplier audit form (D)	2	3	4	3
Perform preliminary supplier financial analysis (E)	1	2	4	2.2
Conduct supplier site visits (F)	4	8	12	8
Compile results from site visits (G)	2	5	8	5
Identify requirements for computerized supplier performance system (H)	2	4	8	4.3
Perform detailed systems analysis and programming (I)	8	10	16	10.7
Test computerized system (J)	2	3	5	3.2
Select final suppliers (K)	1	2	3	2

Exhibit 12.5 shows this project with all times displayed. When calculating times, the user always completes the early start (ES) and early finish (EF) times, moving left to right across the top of the network. Next, complete the bottom half of the network, which includes the late finish (LF) and late start (LS) times, by moving right to left through the network. Notice that all projects start at time 0, and not time 1.

Activities E and D converge at the same event, which means that activity F, in this case, requires the completion of both E and D before it can begin. It is common for two or more activities to conclude at the same event. When this happens, the early start (ES) time for the next activity (activity F) is the larger of the early finish (EF) times for the preceding activities. This makes sense because the subsequent activity cannot start until all preceding activities are complete. Working right to left to arrive at the late finish and late start times on the bottom half of the network, we notice that three activities (B, C, and H) originate from the same event. In this case, the smaller of the late start (LS) times becomes the late finish (LF) time for activity A. In this case, two weeks is the late finish time for activity A.

The longest path (in time) through the network is the critical path. It is also the path on which the connected activities each have no slack. In our example, the critical path of this project consists of activities A–B–E–F–G–K. Any delay beyond the estimated times for each activity will result in a delay to the entire project. Project managers must always be aware of the status of critical path activities because they have no time slack.

The difference between the late start and early start (LS – ES) or the late finish and early finish (LF – EF) times is slack—the maximum amount of leeway in an activity that will not delay the entire project. Activities without any slack (activities A, B, E, F, G, and K) are by definition on the critical path. Activities not on the critical path will have slack.

Exhibit 12.5 Project Network Illustration for the Supplier Selection Project with All Times Displayed

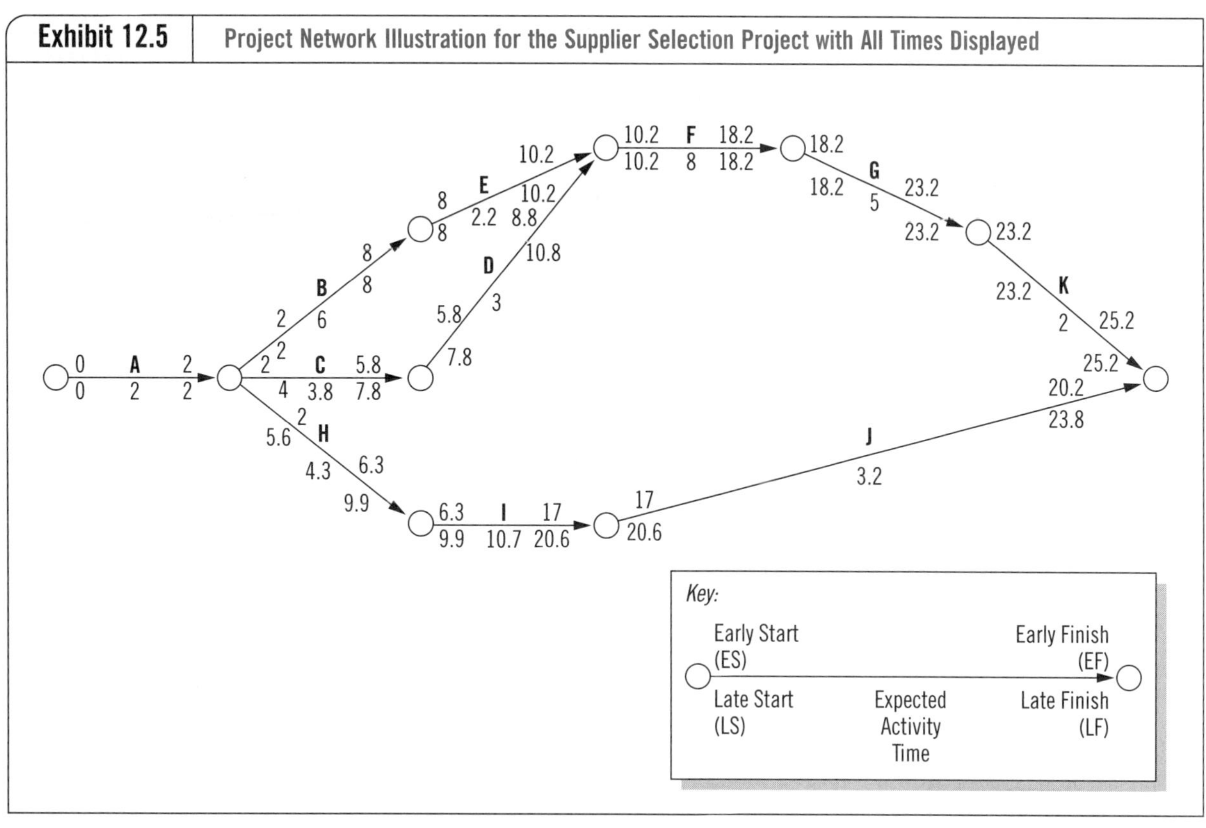

Of special interest to project managers is a project's path slack—the amount of time that activities along the path can be delayed without delaying the entire project.

Notice in our example there are three continuous paths throughout the project. Exhibit 12.5 details the paths and their total time. Of the three paths, A–B–E–F–G–K is the longest path at 25.2 weeks. None of the activities on this path have any slack.

The length of the path equals the sum of the expected activity times for each activity on that particular path. Note that the length of path A–C–D–F–G–K is 23.8 weeks. We must further notice that the slack for this path resides in only two activities—C and D each have two weeks of slack. However, this does not mean there are a total of four weeks of slack. There are only two weeks between the two activities. If activity C finishes at week 7.8 instead of 5.8, then activity D no longer has any slack because it now cannot start until week 7.8.

Project management tools are critical when managing large-scale projects, such as the example discussed in the opening vignette. Purchasing professionals are managing an increasing number of projects involving more than one functional area and large amounts of resources. To do this effectively, they must have an understanding of project management control tools and techniques.

Learning-Curve Analysis

Learning curves establish the rate of improvement due to learning as producers realize direct-labor cost improvements as production volumes increase. When referring to learning improvement, the learning rate represents a reduction in the cumulative average number of labor hours as production doubles from a previous level. For example, with an 85% learning rate, the average amount of direct labor required to produce a single unit declines by 15% each time production doubles.

With a 90% rate, direct-labor requirements decrease by 10% each time production doubles. The fundamental principle of the learning curve is that as production doubles, direct-labor requirements decline by an observed and predictable rate. The rate of improvement varies from situation to situation.

Why should purchasers be concerned with learning curves? If learning occurs at a supplier during the performance of a purchase contract and the buyer does not take that into account, then the supplier will reap the financial benefits that result from learning. If learning occurs, the benefits must go somewhere—either into the supplier's profit line, or to the buyer's cost savings budget! In collaborative relationships, buyers and suppliers can work together to mutually share the benefits of learning curves and productivity improvements.

Learning curves apply to the average direct labor required to produce a unit of output. The labor component is usually the easiest data to gather because companies assign direct-labor hours to specific items or projects. Historically, the term "learning curve" refers to the reduced direct-labor requirement per unit of output due to the effects of learning. This empirically derived concept was first noted by Boeing Corporation, which noticed that the amount of time required to build the same model aircraft decreased over time. The term "experience curve" refers to the longer-term factors of production that systematically reduce production costs. These factors include the shorter-term labor component along with longer-term product and process modifications.

Components of the Learning or Experience Curve

What drives the expected cost reductions, which are the basis of the learning curve and the broader experience curve? Different factors combine to produce a learning effect. The first factor is the workforce. This includes the ability of the worker on the job to learn and improve through repetitive effort and increased efficiency, and the effort by management to pursue productivity gains.

The next factor includes modifications to the production process. Because labor improvements quickly reach the point of smaller and smaller returns, management often relies on process changes to realize continuous improvement. Management may introduce new production methods, substitute increased automation for labor, or pursue vertical integration that results in greater cost control. Some firms also update their process technology during the life of a product to take advantage of improvements offered with newer equipment. Offering a supplier a longer-term contract with guaranteed volumes, for example, encourages investment in equipment that results in lower production costs.

When to Use the Learning Curve

Not all processes or items benefit from or exhibit improvement from learning. In fact, when used incorrectly, this approach can result in a significant underestimation of true production costs. The learning-curve approach applies when certain operating conditions are present.

Learning-curve analysis is appropriate when a supplier uses a new production process or produces an item for the first time. Production efficiency usually increases as a supplier's workforce become familiar with a new process. The learning curve is also appropriate when a supplier produces a technically complex item for the first time. The approach is also appropriate when an item has high direct-labor content.

The human factors present at the beginning of production must remain fairly constant over time to apply the learning curve. If an organization experiences high turnover, then the workforce may not demonstrate the anticipated rate of learning. For

Sourcing Snapshot — *Accelerating the Learning Curve in an Online World*

In the 1980s Japanese manufacturing techniques were in vogue. You could hardly read the business press without encountering mention of "lean manufacturing," "just-in-time inventory systems," and "total quality management."

You don't hear much about these ideas anymore, but not because they are no longer in fashion. Quite the reverse is true: The practices have become so widely adopted that they are no longer newsworthy.

Nowadays, it is American executives—especially those from high-tech industries—who are lecturing the rest of the world on the wonders of Web 2.0 and the latest new new thing emanating from Silicon Valley.

It is therefore a paradox that one of the most important drivers of online business success is taken directly from the pages of Japanese management techniques. I am referring to kaizen, the practice of continuous improvement.

Kaizen doesn't just mean a business should keep trying new things. Rather, it refers to a disciplined process of systematic exploration, controlled experimentation, and then painstaking adoption of the new procedures. In the original formulation, kaizen was applied to manufacturing, where experimentation could determine whether a new process resulted in quality improvements or cost savings in a matter of months.

It is much more difficult to apply kaizen to product design, because it can easily take years to design and market a new product. To take a recent example, the iPhone has been two and a half years in the making.

Product development can cost hundreds of millions of dollars, making it almost impossible to run a controlled experiment with a product introduction.

But it is simple to run a controlled experiment with a web page. Amazon can show a different page layout to every hundredth visitor and determine in a few days whether the new design increases sales.

Similarly, a search engine can run a controlled experiment to try out a new tweak to its search algorithm and discover in a few hours whether users find it an improvement on the old algorithm. On the web, continuous improvement really is continuous.

The cycle of exploration, experimentation, and adoption is drastically shortened for web-based applications. This isn't just the old atoms and bits distinction. Vista, Microsoft's new operating system, has also taken years to develop and only time will tell how successful it will be.

What's the difference between Vista and Google? There is no feasible way for Microsoft to experiment with Vista in real time; but it is very easy for Google to conduct controlled experiments and do so more or less continuously.

Given a performance measure, be it clicks, revenue, or something entirely different, a disciplined process of experimentation and evaluation can lead to rapid improvement. The easier it is to experiment and the larger the number of users, the quicker this process can work.

The most successful online businesses are built on kaizen, though few of those who carry out the testing would recognize the term, because many of those who created these online businesses were in grade school in the 1980s.

Old media just do not understand online kaizen. Their perceptions are tied to the print world, where design changes are costly. The *Wall Street Journal* spent years planning its recent redesign of the print edition and millions of dollars rolling it out. Yet it will be months before it becomes clear how successful these changes were.

By contrast, small tweaks in the page layout of online content can be very effective in improving user satisfaction and ad clicks. Controlled experiments can be used to determine the impact of these changes in days rather than months.

Yet how many mainstream publishers have web page software that allows for such controlled experimentation? In most cases, there is but one layout, and experimentation is difficult if not impossible. You can't manage what you can't measure—and if you can't easily experiment with what you are doing, management is seriously handicapped.

Kaizen means that the companies currently in an industry have an inherent advantage over new entrants. Entrants have to guess what will work; the companies that are already operating can experiment and find out.

This information advantage doesn't preclude new entries; it just makes it more costly because the learning curve is steeper.

Amazon has some worthy competition in online department stores. But how likely is it that a new entrant will emerge from nowhere and successfully compete in this area? The experience that existing online retailers like Amazon, Buy.com, and eBay have built up is hard to duplicate. A new entrant, even one as strong as Wal-Mart, finds the online world rough going.

This is not to say that new entry is impossible. As the old saying goes, "You can always tell the pioneers, they're the ones with the arrows in their backs."

New entrants have the advantage of avoiding earlier mistakes. They can copy successful operations and, in many cases, improve on them. Newer, faster, and more flexible information systems can sometimes confer a competitive advantage on new entrants over the pioneers stuck with the last generation of computing infrastructure.

But the ability to experiment easily is a critical factor for web-based applications. The online world is never static. There is a constant flow of new users, new products, and new technologies. Being able to figure out quickly what works and what doesn't can mean the difference between survival and extinction.

Source: Adapted from H. R. Varian, *New York Times,* February 8, 2007, p. C3.

example, in the 1960s the Douglas Aircraft Company experienced high turnover due to a tight labor market during the initial production of its DC-9. The company was unable to realize the labor efficiencies it had factored into the sales price of the aircraft. The resulting higher-than-planned costs created a financial strain on the company.

Learning curves require the accurate collection of cost and labor data, particularly during the early stages of production. A buyer must have confidence that learning occurs at a uniform rate and that any improvements result from employee learning. Initial production data often provide the basis for negotiation regarding expected improvement rates and scheduled price reductions.

Learning Curve Illustrated

Exhibit 12.6 provides direct-labor data for a purchased item over increasing levels of output. Learning-curve examples can become quite complex, especially when using logarithmic scales to show the relationship between units produced and labor requirements.

This simple example illustrates the effect on the average labor requirement due to a fairly consistent rate of learning.

Each column in Exhibit 12.6 provides data needed to estimate the cumulative learning rate for this supplier:

- Column A: The total units produced over a period of time. In this example, a total of 64 units were produced.
- Column B: The cumulative total labor hours (TLH) required to produce a given level of units. This supplier used 288 total labor hours to produce 32 total units but only 493 total labor hours to double production to 64 total units.
- Column C: The total labor hours for a given level of output divided by the units produced. The figure represents the cumulative average labor per unit of output.
- Column D: The associated learning rate for each doubling of production. The learning rate from one to two units of production equals (20 LH/unit – 17 LH/unit)/(20 LH/unit) = 0.15 or 15%. Note that LH/unit is the average

Exhibit 12.6 Supplier Learning-Curve Data

(A) UNITS	(B) TOTAL LABOR HOURS	(C) AVERAGE LABOR HOURS PER UNIT	(D) LEARNING RATE
1	20	20.0	—
2	34	17.0	15.0%
4	58	14.5	14.7%
8	100	12.5	14.8%
16	168	10.5	16.0%
32	288	9.0	14.3%
64	493	7.7	14.4%

Average improvement rate: 15% or 85% learning curve

labor hours per unit and is calculated by dividing the total labor hours (column B) by the number of units (column A). The learning rate from two to four units equals

$$(17\ \text{LH/unit} - 14.5\ \text{LH/unit})/(17\ \text{LH/unit}) = 0.147 \text{ or } 14.7\%$$

Each level can be calculated in a similar way.

This analysis reveals that the supplier has an approximately 85% learning curve for this item, which means that as production doubles, the direct labor required to produce a unit should decrease 15% on average. A producer realizes the most dramatic learning improvements over early volumes when the effect from learning is the greatest.

The successful use of the learning curve requires knowing when and how to apply the technique. A buyer's objective must be to use the tool to identify anticipated labor costs for increasingly larger production volumes. An analyst often cannot identify a learning rate until some preliminary production data are available. If data are not available, one approach is to rely on historical learning rates or previously observed rates at a supplier.

Learning-Curve Problem

A buyer does business with a supplier that uses a production process that historically demonstrates an 80% learning curve; that is, as production rates double, there is a 20% reduction in the average direct-labor hours required to produce a unit. Given this learning rate, a buyer hopes to capture this reduced labor requirement through a lower purchase price.

Exhibit 12.7 outlines one use of the learning curve in purchasing. In this example, the buyer expects the per-unit price on a 600-unit order to lower from \$228 to \$170 due to learning. Whether the buyer actually receives a \$170 unit price will probably be subject to negotiation. The supplier may argue that overhead did not change since the original order and should remain at \$50 per unit. The supplier's profit is affected as both direct and overhead costs decline and profit remains at 20% of total costs. The buyer may counter that material costs should decline due to larger volumes. The key point is that the buyer now has a price range for negotiation with the supplier.

Learning-curve analysis highlights a key reason why many purchasers consolidate purchase volumes with fewer suppliers. Astute buyers know that an even lower purchase price may be obtained if the buyer correctly factors in the effects of learning as production volumes increase.

Value Analysis/Value Engineering

Value analysis involves examining all elements of a component, assembly, end product, or service to make sure it fulfills its intended function at the lowest total cost. Value analysis techniques are primarily applied to existing products and services. In contrast, **value engineering** is the application of value principles during product or service design. VE is a much more proactive approach to embracing value concepts. Larry Miles is said to have started using the technique at General Electric in the late 1940s and is considered the father of VA/VE.

Exhibit 12.7 Learning-Curve Problem

XYZ Corporation is buying a new item produced by a process that historically demonstrates an 80% learning curve. A buyer has placed an order for 200 pieces and receives a quote of $228 per unit. The buyer has accumulated the following per-unit cost data:

Material	$ 90	
Direct labor	$ 50	(Five hours on average per unit at $10 per hour)
Overhead	$ 50	(Assume 100% of direct labor)
Total costs	$190	
Profit	$ 38	(Difference between per-unit price and total costs, which equals 20% of total costs)
Total per unit	$228	(Quoted price)

The buyer wants to place a second order for an additional 600 pieces, or a combined total order of 800. How much should the buyer expect to pay per unit *given the expected benefit of the learning curve* (which affects direct-labor requirements)?

1. Calculate the average labor hours for the entire combined order of 800 units:
   From the first order, 200 units required an average of 5 hours labor per unit. Therefore, 400 units should require only 80% as much as the original 200, or an average of 4 hours of labor per unit, given an 80% learning rate. 800 units should require an average of 3.2 hours of labor per unit (80% of 4 hours is 3.2 hours). One of the guidelines of learning curve is that labor costs decrease by a predictable rate each time production doubles.
2. Calculate the hours required for the total combined order of 800 units less the labor incurred for the original 200-piece order:

   800 units × 3.2 average hours/unit = 2,560 total hours

   Less:

   200 units × 5 average hours per unit = 1,000 (direct labor required for original 200-piece order)
   1,560 total labor hours required for the next 600 units
3. Calculate the additional total and per-unit labor cost for the additional 600-unit order:

   1,560 hours × $10 per direct-labor hour = $15,600 total additional labor cost
   $15,600/600 units = $26 per unit
4. Calculate the expected new per-unit price for the additional 600-piece order:

   Additional 600 pieces per-unit cost

Material	$ 90	(Remains unchanged, although higher quantities may reduce the per-unit material cost)
Direct labor	$ 26	
Overhead	$ 26	(Assume 100% of direct labor)
Total costs	$142	
Profit (20%) of total costs	$ 28.40	
Total per unit	$170.40	

The basic component of VA and VE is value—the lowest total cost at which an item, product, or service achieves its primary function while satisfying the time, place, and quality requirements of customers. Although value analysis traditionally applies to tangible products, there is no reason that companies cannot apply VA techniques to services.

The primary objective of value analysis is to increase the value of an item or service at the lowest cost without sacrificing quality. In equation form, value is the relationship between the function of a product or service and its cost:

$$\text{Value} = \text{Function}/\text{Cost}$$

There are many variations of function and cost that will increase the value of a product or service. The most obvious ways to increase value include increasing the functionality or use of a product or service while holding cost constant, reducing cost while not reducing functionality, and increasing functionality more than increasing cost. For example, offering a five-year warranty versus a two-year warranty with no price increase raises the value of a product to the customer.

Value analysis is a way to achieve continuous performance improvement in an item, product, or service. It is not a technique for cheapening a product or service by lowering quality or other performance attributes below what customers expect. Many firms realize that VA is a powerful technique that can help a firm achieve its continuous cost and quality improvement targets.

Who Is Involved in Value Analysis?

Value analysis, certainly not exclusively a purchasing tool, involves many organizational functions. However, because most products and services require major inputs from suppliers, purchasing should take an active role in coordinating value analysis activities. A common approach for using value analysis involves creating a VA team composed of professionals with knowledge about a product or service. Many functional groups can contribute to the value analysis team:

- *Executive management.* Executive management provides overall guidance and support for the VA process and allocates the time, budget, and personnel to work actively on VA projects.
- *Suppliers.* Because much of what value analysis examines involves the cost and design of component parts, it is logical to request input from suppliers, a group that can propose alternative materials, provide insights into what other firms are doing, and identify lower-cost production methods.
- *Purchasing.* Purchasing often takes a primary role in organizing the VA effort by coordinating and disseminating relevant information.
- *Design engineering.* Design engineers evaluate any proposed changes to the design of an item. They also help define product function, establish quality and engineering standards, and evaluate the effect of VA changes on other parts within the product.
- *Marketing.* The marketing group provides insight about the impact that VA changes may have on customers.
- *Production.* The production group has the responsibility of producing final items or products, and it can also propose better ways to produce an item or service to achieve higher quality or lower total cost. It is essential that this group be informed about any changes proposed by other functional groups.
- *Industrial/process engineering.* This group can contribute extensively, particularly when discussing methods of producing and delivering a product or service. Industrial/process engineers can evaluate proposed manufacturing methods, material handling and flow, the effect of alternative materials on the production process, and packaging requirements.
- *Quality control.* Quality control can evaluate the impact on quality that proposed changes may have. Quality control can also establish how and where to evaluate quality performance levels for a proposed production method.

This group can also work with purchasing to support quality control efforts at suppliers.

Tests for Determining Value in a Product or Service

Value analysis teams ask a number of questions to determine if opportunities exist for item, product, or service improvement:

1. Does the use of this product contribute value to our customers?
2. Is the cost of the final product proportionate to its usefulness?
3. Are there additional uses for this product?
4. Does the product need all its features or internal parts?
5. Are product weight reductions possible?
6. Is there anything else available to our customers given the intended use of the product?
7. Is there a better production method to produce the item or product?
8. Can a lower-cost standard part replace a customized part?
9. Are we using the proper tooling considering the quantities required?
10. Will another dependable supplier provide material, components, or subassemblies for less?
11. Is anyone currently purchasing required materials, components, or subassemblies for less?
12. Are there equally effective but lower-cost materials available?
13. Do material, labor, overhead, and profit equal the product's cost?
14. Are packaging cost reductions possible?
15. Is the item properly classified for shipping purposes to receive the lowest transportation rates?
16. Are design or quality specifications too tight given customer requirements?
17. If we are making an item now, can we buy it for less (and vice versa)?

The most likely VA improvement areas include modifying product design and material specifications, using standardized components in place of custom components, substituting lower-cost for higher-cost materials, reducing the number of parts that a product contains, and developing better production or assembly methods.

The Value Analysis Process

Value analysis projects follow a systematic approach consisting of five stages:

1. Gather information
2. Speculate
3. Analyze
4. Recommend and execute
5. Summarize and follow up

These stages occur after identifying an item or product as a VA candidate.

Gather Information

The first stage for any value analysis project requires agreement about an item or product's primary and secondary functions for customers. VA participants should ask, "What does this product do for the customer?" and "Why does a customer buy this product?" It is important to understand a product's primary and secondary functions. Value analysis experts recommend naming each function of an item or product with two words—a verb and a noun. After this is complete, the team must agree on which functions are primary versus secondary. For example, the primary function of an industrial pump may be to move fluids at a rate required by the customer. A secondary function may be to minimize noise in the customer's facility. In this case, the VA team must recognize that moving fluids is the primary function of the industrial pump. Minimizing noise, a secondary consideration for industrial pumps, still must receive attention during analysis.

During this stage, detailed information about the item or product is collected. This includes sales trends, supplier performance data, costs to make and sell, design drawings, quantity estimates, and production method analyses.

Speculate

This stage calls for wide-open or creative thinking on the part of the VA team. Brainstorming is ideal as the team evaluates an item or product against the various tests or questions presented earlier. The primary objective of this phase is to develop as many improvement ideas as possible while withholding judgment on any one alternative. A VA team moves to the analysis stage after it exhausts its ideas about how to improve a particular item or product.

Analyze

This stage critically evaluates the different ideas put forth during the speculation phase. Analysis can include cost/benefit calculations or assessment of the feasibility of implementing an idea. The result is a set of ideas that satisfy the original goals and objectives of the VA effort. This phase is very specific and no longer involves generalities.

Recommend and Execute

Up to this point the VA process has generated only a prioritized list of ideas. The team may have to present its proposals to executive management for approval. Moving an idea from the team to the organization requires the ability to motivate others, creativity, good communication skills, the ability to think analytically, solid product knowledge, commitment, and salesmanship.

Once a team receives approval, it must implement its ideas. Some ideas will be quite simple to carry out, whereas others will be more complex. The team must develop a project plan with timings, budget requirements, and responsibilities. The team often has to generate support outside the team for its proposals and help during implementation.

Summarize and Follow Up

This step is common during the implementation of any idea or plan. It may be the responsibility of the VA team or group to follow up and track implementation progress. The team may also track the gains achieved by the VA effort.

Quantity Discount Analysis

Quantity discount analysis is a technique used to examine the incremental changes in cost between quantities within a supplier's price quotation. This tool allows the user to verify that quantity discounts are reasonable. Using this technique, a buyer may be able to negotiate price improvements through a better understanding of incremental unit costs.

There are two primary types of quantity discount analyses. The first involves prices at specific quantities, whereas the second examines discounts over quantity ranges.

Quantity Discount Analysis Illustrated

Exhibit 12.8 on p. 448 demonstrates how to use QDA when a buyer has price breaks at specific quantities. Exhibit 12.9 on pp. 449–450 illustrates how to use QDA when a buyer has price breaks in ranges of quantities. The exhibits explain how to perform the appropriate calculations.

When using quantity discount analysis, the key calculation is the incremental cost of each additional unit at different quantity levels. In Exhibit 12.8, even though the original quote at the three quantity levels moves lower on a per-unit basis, the incremental cost for units 7–10 ($67.50) is actually higher than for units 4–6 ($60). The same type of situation occurs in Exhibit 12.9. A buyer faced with this quote would want to know why incremental unit costs increase rather than decrease. Often, the supplier is unaware why the incremental costs are higher.

QDA provides the buyer with information for questioning and negotiating improvements in the discount schedule. The analysis often reveals an up-and-down roller-coaster effect between incremental price differences. Questions asked because of a QDA often produce additional discounts and a better understanding of the quotation by the buyer and seller. The buyer should not accept a quote that features higher incremental costs as volumes increase unless the supplier can provide a valid explanation.

Process Mapping

Process mapping is a tool that reduces processes to their component parts or activities and helps identify and then eliminate non-value-added activities (waste) or delays within a process. Process mapping is valuable in purchasing, for example, when attempting to streamline the flow of material or information between suppliers and a purchaser.

Organizations have many processes that, when taken together, define the organization's primary work. A process is essentially an outcome composed of a set of tasks, activities, or steps. How well an organization performs these tasks determines how efficient and effective it is at that process. The following supply chain processes are among those that most businesses perform:

- Supplier evaluation and selection
- Supply-base management
- New-product design and development
- Accounts receivable/accounts payable

Exhibit 12.8 Quantity Discount Analysis (Price Breaks at Specific Quantities)

1. Quotation from Avco at Specific Quantities

1 unit @ $85 each

3 units @ $80 each

6 units @ $70 each

10 units @ $69 each

2. Instructions

Line 1: Place specific quantities from the quotation on line 1 in the appropriate column. Each column represents a specific quantity. Assume that ordering 0 is an option. This will support the quantity discount calculation.

Line 2: Place the quoted price from the supplier for each specific quantity on line 2 in the appropriate column.

Line 3: Multiply line 1 by line 2 for each column to arrive at a total price per order.

Line 4: Take the difference between the total price per order (line 3) and each successive order. For column A, it is the difference between $85 and ordering zero pieces, or $0.00. For column B, it is the difference between column B/line 3 and column A/ line 3, or $240 – $85 = $155.

Line 5: This is the difference between each quantity break specified on line 1.

Line 6: This equals line 4 divided by line 5 for each column.

3. Price Breaks at Specific Quantities

Supplier Avco Part Name & No. Compressor 04273999 Date 10/24/07

		A	B	C	D	E	F	G	H
1. Number of units per order	0	1	3	6	10				
2. Price per unit (quoted price)	0	85	80	70	69				
3. Total price per order	0	85	240	420	690				
4. Price difference between orders		85	155	180	270				
5. Quantity difference between orders		1	2	3	4				
6. Price per unit per order quantity difference		$85	$77.50	$60	$67.50				

4. Quantity Discount Analysis

QUANTITY	TOTAL COST	INCREMENTAL QUANTITY	INCREMENTAL COST
1	$ 85	1	$85
		2	$77.50
3	$240	3	$77.50
		4	$60
		5	$60
6	$420	6	$60
		7	$67.50
		8	$67.50
		9	$67.50
10	$690	10	$67.50

Exhibit 12.9 Quantity Discount Analysis (Price Breaks in Ranges of Quantities)

1. Quotation from Dynamic Industries at Ranges of Quantities

RANGE	PRICE PER UNIT IN RANGE	RANGE	PRICE PER UNIT IN RANGE
1–5	$10.00 each	21–100	$7.60 each
6–10	$ 8.00 each	101–499	$7.00 each
11–20	$ 7.80 each	500+	$6.90 each

2. Instructions

Line 1: Place specific quantity ranges from the supplier quotation on line 1 in the appropriate column. Each column represents a specific quantity range provided by the supplier.

Line 2: Place the price per unit within each quantity range in the appropriate column. This is information provided by the supplier on the quote.

Line 3: "Total price per order" equals the lowest quantity in a range from line 1 times the "Price per unit" in line 2 for each column. For example, for column C (quantity range 11–20), "Total price per order" equals 11 × $7.80 = $85.80.

Line 4: Take the "Total price per order" from the next-highest quantity range (line 3) and divide this by "Price per unit" for the column being calculated. For example, for column A, the maximum units to order equals 48/10 equals 4.8. For column B, the maximum units to order equals 85.80/8 = 10.7, and so on. Round down to the nearest whole number.

Line 5: This equals line 2 times line 4 for each column.

Line 6: Calculate the difference between the "Total price maximum order" for successive quantity ranges. For example, the "Total price per maximum order" for column B (6–10 quantity range) is $80, while the "Total price per order" for column A (1–5 quantity range) is $40. The difference is $40, which appears in column A on line 6. Calculate all other columns on line 6 accordingly.

Line 7: This is the difference between line 4 and the preceding column value on line 4. It is the difference between the maximum units to order from one quantity range to the next.

Line 8: This equals line 6 divided by line 7 for each column. It represents the incremental cost for each unit within that quantity range.

3. Price Breaks in Ranges of Quantities

Supplier Dynamic Industries Part Name & No. Wedge 04336280 Date 9/14/07

		A	B	C	D	E	F	G	H
1. Number of units per order	0	1–5	6–10	11–20	21–100	101–500	500+		
2. Price per unit (quoted price)	0	10	8	7.80	7.60	7.00	6.90		
3. Total price per order (use minimum quantity)	0	10	48	85.80	159.60	707	3,450		
4. Maximum units to order	0	4	10	20	93	492	—		
5. Total price per maximum order		40	80	156	706.80	3,444	—		
6. Price difference between maximum order		40	40	76	550.80	2,737.20	—		
7. Quantity difference between maximum units to order		4	6	10	73	399	—		
8. Price per unit per order quantity difference		$10	$6.67	$7.60	$7.54	$6.86			

Exhibit 12.9 Quantity Discount Analysis (Price Breaks in Ranges of Quantities) (Continued)

4. Quantity Discount Analysis

QUANTITY	QUOTED PRICE	QUANTITY RANGE	INCREMENTAL COST
1–5	$10.00	First 5 units	$10.00 each
6–10	$ 8.00	Next 5 units	$ 6.67 each
11–20	$ 7.80	Next 10 units	$ 7.60 each
21–100	$ 7.60	Next 80 units	$ 7.54 each
101–500	$ 7.00	Next 400 units	$ 6.86 each
500+	$ 6.90	—	—

- Inventory control and management
- Customer service support
- Training and education
- Inbound logistics
- Outbound logistics and physical distribution
- Research and development
- Customer order fulfillment

Most processes cross more than one functional boundary. When this happens, there is a risk that no one actually owns or takes responsibility for the entire process. In fact, some departments may actually have goals that are in conflict with one another. A transportation department evaluated on cost may use the least expensive method possible, such as rail. Customer service, on the other hand, may want to make material available to customers as soon as possible, which implies speed. Rapid delivery will likely increase transportation costs. These two groups may thus have goals that conflict.

Organizations use process mapping to redesign or re-engineer processes. There are two basic types of processes: sequential and concurrent. **Sequential processes** are those in which the set of steps or activities comprising the activity occur one after the other. As shown in the following diagram, Activity B does not begin until A is complete, whereas C does not begin until B is complete. When mapping processes, we may place time estimates of the activity along with the sequence of the activities. A primary goal of process mapping is to eliminate waste from a process. Activity times are important to this goal.

Sequential Process

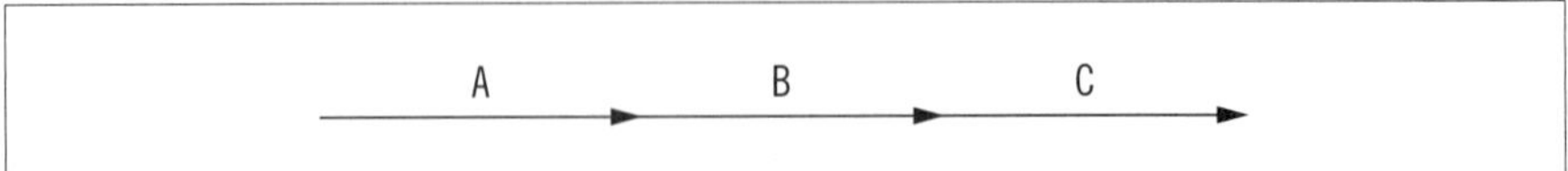

Concurrent processes consist of activities or steps performed concurrently during the main flow of work. For example, many organizations are attempting to develop new products concurrently rather than sequentially, which not only saves time and money but also allows agreement on major issues early in the process.

Sourcing Snapshot — *A Day in the Life of a Procurement Project Manager*

Carlton W. Bradshaw, C.P.M., a procurement project manager for Eaton Corp., arrives at the office between 7:00 and 8:00 a.m. and prepares for the day checking e-mail, voice mail, faxes, and so forth. Big question: Just how unusual or normal will today be?

It can be said that the day in the life of a project manager is never really typical and for many that's what makes this specialized career exciting. Meetings, check-up on progress, evaluation of project by key players, checking future needs for upcoming critical events, and much more—these elements keep project managers hopping. And here's what it looks like.

8:30 a.m.: It's Wednesday and time for the "core teams" meeting—the people who are functional representatives of a project team. The meeting lasts an hour and a half, and several issues are reviewed. Each team member takes information back to his or her respective function.

10:00 a.m.: Next comes a meeting with Susan Whalen, engineering process development manager, whose responsibilities include engineering processes. Bradshaw and Whalen discuss how procurement will support engineering on various projects, and Bradshaw identifies any special needs that might arise. All this takes place on a high process level.

11:00 a.m.: Back in the office, Bradshaw does follow up and department management tasks.

1:00 p.m.: A subproject team that supports larger project teams in connection with materials in the pipeline and cost reduction meets. This is a detail-oriented working meeting. Engineering could have from 15 to 30 miniprojects going under the umbrella of a larger one, and this subteam works out the details of these aspects. A weekly meeting establishing engineering priority also takes place. This focuses on the larger horizon of engineering marketing—where are the markets going further out? Bradshaw represents procurement at these meetings. They are typically two hours long and focus on three market segments, one per meeting.

3:00 p.m.: A weekly supplier-driven cost-reduction program meeting is held. Bradshaw leads a small team on this one. Ideas from suppliers are evaluated and fed to engineering.

4:45 p.m.: Bradshaw meets with staff within the procurement function of procurement project leaders to get caught up.

Source: Adapted from M. Lester, "Purchasing and Supply Meet Project Management," *Purchasing Today,* December 1998, 9(12), pp. 30–36.

Cross-functional teams often use process mapping. Because most processes move across functional boundaries, it is logical to have those groups connected with the process involved with mapping and improving the process. This involvement will help generate buy-in from different groups concerning any proposed changes while keeping all impacted groups informed of those changes.

Process Mapping Illustrated

Perhaps the best way to describe process mapping is with an example. Exhibit 12.10 on p. 452, taken from the automobile industry, describes the receiving process at a physical distribution facility. This process is critical because the speed at which a

Exhibit 12.10 Physical Receipt of Purchased Material as a Sequential Process

Step Description and Average Time Required per Trailer

- Employee 1 physically places trailer at receiving dock (*15 minutes*).
- Employee 2 unloads the trailer with material handling equipment (*30 minutes*).
- Employee 3 checks load quantity from the trailer against shipping documents for accuracy* (*30 minutes*).
- Employee 4 acknowledges receipt of the material on the computer and prints control tickets to move material to required warehouse locations (*60 minutes*).
- Employee 5 attaches control tickets to individual loads (*20 minutes*).
- Employee 6 inspects inbound material* (*30 minutes*).
- Employee 7 moves material to required warehouse location, freeing up the receipt line for another trailer (*30 minutes*).
- Employee 4 files copy of shipping documents and forwards copies to Accounts Payable at the end of the day. This does not impact the physical movement of material (*15 minutes*).

Total inbound trailer processing times: 215 minutes (excludes Step 8), or 3 hours and 35 minutes

*Non-Value-Added Activity: As purchasing works with suppliers to improve material and delivery quality, it is not necessary to check each inbound load.

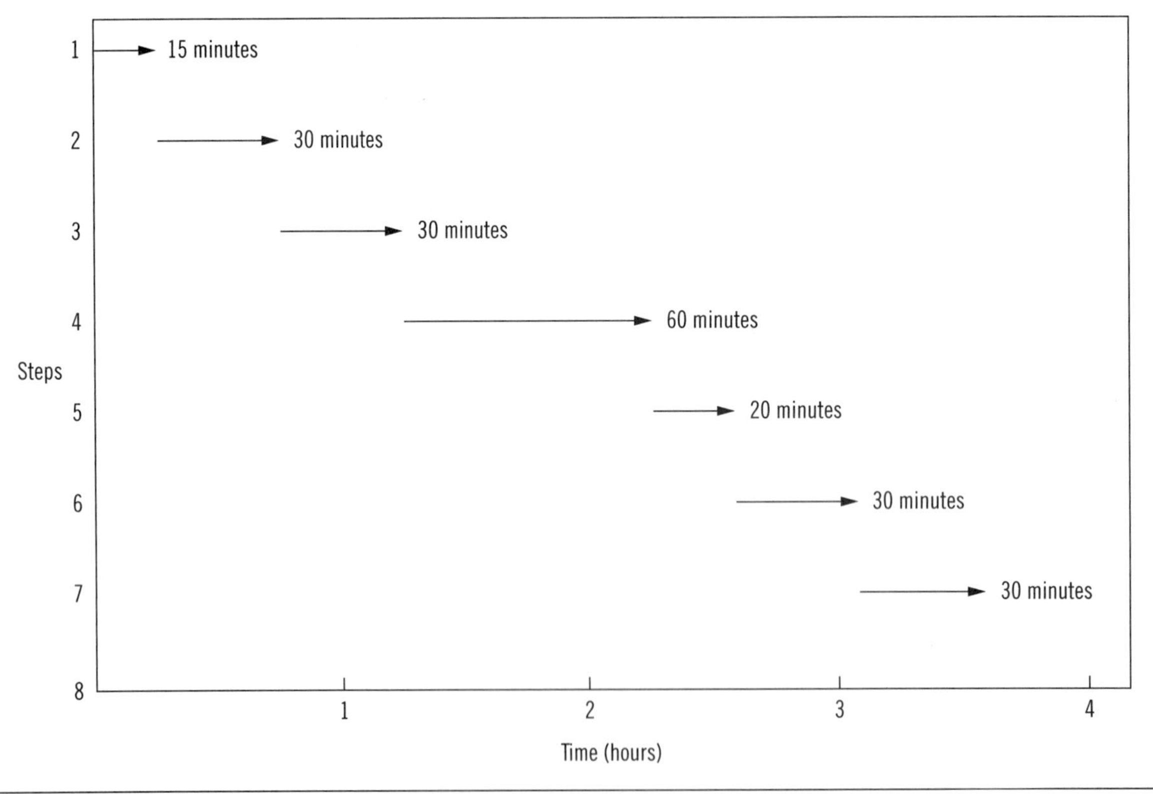

facility receives and moves material defines the flow for downstream work centers. If the receiving process is slow, it can create a bottleneck affecting the entire facility as well as other facilities requiring material from that location. The process itself may also contain non-value-adding tasks or waste.

Exhibit 12.10 reveals that seven different employees take part in the physical receipt and movement of material. The average time to unload, process, and move material from a truck is 215 minutes, which means that, on average, each receiving line can process and move two trailerloads of material a day. With eight receiving lines, this process averages 16 truckloads per eight-hour shift.

As volumes at this company increased, the company faced two options: add a second shift or improve the receiving process to make it more efficient. In the short run it added a second shift as a fix to the receiving capacity problem. A longer-term solution required a total revamping of the process, which Exhibit 12.11 illustrates. The new system combined physical system changes with information technology.

The redesigned system generates move-control tickets automatically once the front gate of the plant acknowledges the arrival of a truck. Furthermore, the new process operates concurrently rather than sequentially. The employee unloading the trailer now has expanded duties. The employee not only unloads the material but also hangs control tickets and resolves receiving discrepancies, which illustrates the benefit of flexibility versus specialization. These changes reduced the time required to process an inbound trailer by

Exhibit 12.11 Physical Receipt of Purchased Material, Revised Process

Step Description and Average Required Time

- Employee 1 physically places trailer at receiving dock. Move-control tickets are printed concurrently and automatically as facility guard acknowledges the arrival of the trailer electronically at the front gate (*15 minutes*).
- Employee 2 picks up printed control tickets for the trailer, unloads the trailer with material handling equipment, performs a cursory check of the loads as they are unloaded, and hangs load tickets as material comes off the truck (*60 minutes*).
- Employee 3 physically moves material to required warehouse location, freeing up the receipt line for another trailer (*30 minutes*).
- Receipt information stored electronically with information forwarded to Accounts Payable (*0 minutes*).

Total inbound trailer processing times: 105 minutes, or 1 hour and 45 minutes

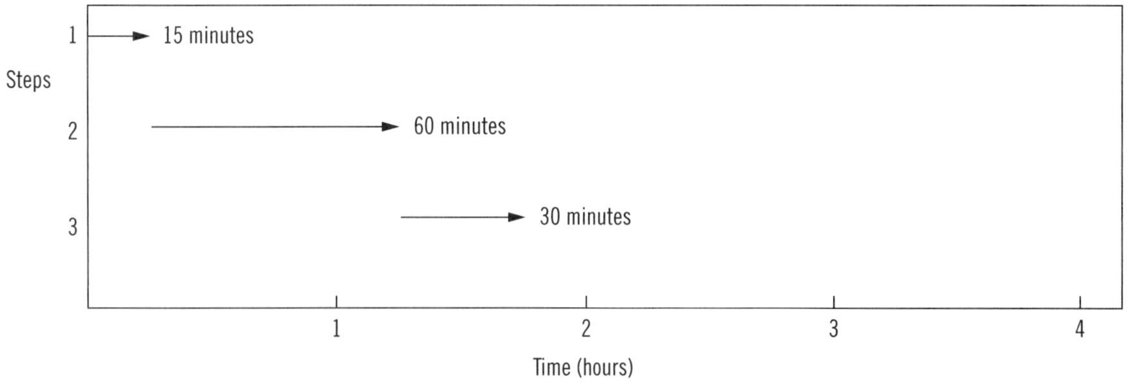

over 50%, which means that a single shift can now process over twice as many trailers a day. Material moves faster and the process requires fewer total resources. Until an organization maps its processes, it cannot realize major improvements.

The following steps are critical to process mapping:

- Search for better ways and methods to perform the tasks comprising a process, which often involves using information technology to automate transactions within the process.
- Replace sequential activities with concurrent activities wherever possible.
- Identify those activities that contribute to waste or add minimal value to the process and target those for elimination.
- Identify the time associated with each part of a process and identify how much of that time is waste.
- Involve the functional groups that impact a process.
- Represent graphically the process so those involved have a clear understanding of the process steps.

Good Practice Example — *Lean Takes Off at Cessna*

Facing a $9 billion backlog, Cessna Aircraft Co. is turning to its supply chain for help filling the orders. Demand for Cessna's business jets is strong. In 2006, the company delivered more than 1,200 aircraft and reported revenues of about $4.2 billion, up from $3.5 billion in 2005.

The company is growing; it employs more than 13,000 people, versus 8,000 just four years ago. But, in an effort to be more efficient and competitive around the world, it's also changing its business model and expanding its lean initiatives. (Lean techniques involve using and applying a set of tools that assist in the identification and elimination of waste anywhere in the supply chain. Lean programs have a goal of improving productivity and quality while reducing costs.) Cessna, which historically was vertically integrated, is purchasing more parts and larger assemblies today than in the past.

In 2003, buyers were sourcing 48,000 part numbers. Today, this figure is more than 62,000, with many part numbers representing large assemblies such as an entire tail section of an airplane. The company buys these parts from 791 suppliers and has long-term agreements with 280 of them, representing 95% of its $1.8 billion annual spend on direct materials.

Although Cessna's supply base performs very well, many of the company's suppliers are not accustomed to providing some of the parts or larger assemblies that the aircraft maker requires, says Brent Edmisten, director of strategic sourcing and integrated supply chain (ISC) strategies at Cessna in Wichita, Kansas. "So we are approaching suppliers we know are able," Edmisten says, "and we're going to their facilities to help them develop that capability."

Cessna Aircraft Co. is a Textron Inc. company. Cessna operates using the Textron Production System, which is based on the Toyota Production System and other principles, and focuses on reducing lead time and assets and improving flexibility and customer responsiveness by eliminating waste. To do this, a supplier participates in value-stream mapping and improvement workshops. These efforts help simplify processes and improve productivity. The ISC operation (which is the melding of the supply chain and operations functions) has developed a process for selecting suppliers for development, based on business complexity, risk, and opportunity.

Many Cessna suppliers do not fit the model for supplier development. This does not mean that ISC takes them off the radar screen. For these suppliers, they developed a supplier value improvement process (SVIP). Through SVIP, Cessna and its suppliers collaborate to solve quality, delivery, reliability, or cost issues. In essence, these suppliers are performing well; ISC works with them to take them to the next level.

Of those suppliers critical to Cessna's ISC strategy—suppliers with high business complexity, high risk, and high opportunity—the company selects a group of four to six suppliers for its development process.

For Cessna, supplier development is all about knowledge transfer. That is, a commodity team and others spend time at the supplier's facility to train its personnel on use of such tools as lean, Six Sigma, and purchasing best practices. With what it's learned, the supplier, in turn, then works to improve its capabilities on its own.

"We teach them to be an extension of our company," says Teresa Kirkendoll, director of supplier integration at Cessna. "A key success factor in our supplier development process is the relationship. It's important that there be trust between us—before we even get started."

One such supplier is PZL Swidnik, a provider of welded seat assemblies and engine mounts based in Poland. Before Cessna selected the supplier, it had been doing this work internally.

Prior to working with the aircraft maker, PZL Swidnik struggled for years with on-time delivery and quality performance. Cessna's development efforts "had a huge impact on its ability to take on more work, and to handle the work," says Kirkendoll, adding that ISC helped the supplier with its processes for building seat frames. Based on success with the parts, the supplier applied what it learned to its processes for engine mounts.

"As a company in the former Eastern bloc, PZL Swidnik was not used to producing for performance," she says. "We spent time on culture, the layout of their facility, and developing their people. It was the first time they looked at building parts for flow and optimizing for productivity and profit."

One area that Cessna and PZL Swidnik worked to improve: scheduling. In fact, Cessna learned that some issues the supplier was having were due to the aircraft company sending a schedule for different amounts of parts each month. Now, it provides a consistent order schedule, a simple improvement achieved by replacing discrete orders with a level load process.

Cessna also worked with the supplier on ways to reduce inventory. "We got them together with one of our other suppliers, a distributor that helped manage their inventory and is now delivering raw material cut to size when they need it," says Edmisten. "It was a huge improvement for their overall business, beyond what they do for Cessna."

Cessna's lean philosophy is passed down to their suppliers' suppliers. For example, one supplier, Rockwell Collins, was recognized for outstanding supplier performance in 2005. Rockwell provides Cessna with avionics components. Rockwell practices lean and has passed these practices on to FTG, Inc., one of its top suppliers. Rockwell Collins' human interface (displays and keyboards) commodity team, as well as representatives of the company's lean supply team, traveled to FTG's facility in Toronto to help the supplier reduce its cycle time and create more flow in its factory. They used such lean tools as 5S events and value stream mapping as well as kanban supermarkets—a system of locating parts at individual workstations rather than a central storeroom—to get more inventory to the point of use for the company.

One technique Rockwell Collins used is a spaghetti flow diagram, which essentially follows a part through the manufacturing process to determine the distance that it travels. The team re-laid out the process, and, by using the kanban supermarkets, was able to reduce the total distance traveled by 39% as well as the time it takes to go from one process to another by 24%.

"To have Rockwell Collins volunteer to provide a facilitator to run us through a lean program, and train our people, was a huge benefit to us as a smaller company," says Kerry Scrase, director of corporate operations for FTG.

These lean efforts throughout the supply chain have paid off. Cessna's efforts have led to improvements in on-time delivery, from 42% to 97%; quality, from 37,732 parts per million (ppm) to 1,257 ppm; and cost reductions of $1.5 million.

Source: Adapted from S. Avery, "Lean Takes Off at Cessna," *Purchasing,* June 14, 2007, http://www.purchasing.com/article/CA6450825.html?q=process+mapping+2007.

CONCLUSION

Purchasers and supply chain specialists rely on various tools and techniques to support and improve the purchasing and sourcing process. The need to routinely apply the techniques and tools presented in this chapter is critical to world-class purchasing and supply chain management. Wherever possible, decisions should be based on quantitative analysis rather than qualitative information.

KEY TERMS

concurrent processes, 450

Critical Path Method (CPM), 430

Gantt chart, 430

learning curves, 438

process mapping, 447

Program Evaluation and Review Technique (PERT), 430

project, 425

quantity discount analysis, 447

sequential processes, 450

value engineering, 442

DISCUSSION QUESTIONS

1. Why does the learning curve apply mainly to direct rather than indirect labor?
2. If each time production volume doubled and cumulative average direct-labor requirements decreased by 5%, what would be the appropriate learning rate?
3. Discuss why it is important for buyers to have knowledge of a supplier's learning rate when preparing to negotiate a purchase contract.
4. What are the major differences in working on projects, as opposed to general work in most purchasing environments?
5. Describe the concept of value as it relates to value analysis. Provide examples of how an organization can increase value to itself or to its customers.
6. Why do progressive firms actively practice value analysis?
7. Discuss why different functional groups often work together when value analyzing a product or service.
8. Assume you are the leader of a value analysis team. Discuss how you would go about identifying value analysis opportunities.
9. In general, do you believe the demands and responsibilities placed on project managers are making them more valuable to organizations? Why or why not?
10. When are users most likely to use Gantt charts for project management? When are they likely to use CPM or PERT?
11. What does it mean for a path to have three weeks of slack? Does each activity necessarily have three weeks of slack? Why or why not?
12. Discuss the information gained from flowcharting a process.

ADDITIONAL READINGS

Campbell, P., and Pollard, W. (2002), "Applying Project Management Principles to Supplier Management," *Inside Supply Management,* June, pp. 48–52.

Geiger, H. (2003), *Project Management Fundamentals,* New York: Element K.

Hartley, J. (2000), "Collaborative Value Analysis: Experiences from the Automotive Industry," *Journal of Supply Chain Management,* 36(4), 27–32.

King, D., and Wright, D. (2002), "Back to Basics: Use Process Mapping," *Logistics and Transport Focus,* 4(3), 42.

Miles, L. (1972), *Techniques of Value Analysis,* New York: McGraw-Hill.

Moore, J. (2002), "Project Management for Supply Management," *Inside Supply Management,* February, pp. 16–18.

Muller, M. (2002), *Essentials of Inventory Management,* New York: AMACOM.

Sinclair, G. (1999), "Purchasing and the Learning Curve: A Case Study of a Specialty Chemicals Business Unit," *Journal of Supply Chain Management,* 35(2), 44–49.

Westney, R. (Ed.) (1997), *The Engineer's Cost Handbook: Tools for Managing Project Costs,* New York: Dekker.

Westney, R. (Ed.) (2004), *A Guide to the Project Management Body of Knowledge,* Newtown Square, PA: Project Management Institute.

ENDNOTES

1. Campbell, P., and Pollard, W. (2002), "Applying Project Management Principles to Supplier Management," *Inside Supply Management,* June, pp. 48–52.

Chapter 13

NEGOTIATION

Learning Objectives

After completing this chapter, you should be able to

- Understand when and why a buyer enters into a sourcing negotiation
- Recognize the importance of planning within the negotiation process
- Appreciate the different sources of power that are present during negotiations
- Understand the characteristics of effective negotiators
- Appreciate the role of concessions during negotiation
- Recognize the subtleties and complexities involved with global negotiation

Chapter Outline

Creating New Value through Negotiation

Wayne Delaney is a relative newcomer to the railroad business. That has not stopped him, however, from using the knowledge and skills gained from his many years at General Electric to improve the performance of the subsidiary railroads at a major steel producer. So how did he do it?

Executive management at the parent steel company directed all operating units (including the railroads) to concentrate on return on net assets (RONA) as an important performance indicator. Improving RONA forced different functional groups at the railroads to search, both individually and collectively, for creative ways to increase earnings while simultaneously reducing assets and other current liabilities. The purchasing group, representing the interests of five separate railroads, focused on reducing the assets required by the railroads to maintain track, equipment, and facilities. Inventory makes up a large part of the denominator of the return on net assets equation.

The purchasing group's approach to higher asset return relies on negotiated longer-term contracts featuring consignment inventory from suppliers. Inventory consignment involves deferring payment for an item until an internal customer physically uses it. Previously, each railroad purchased its own requirements using short-term purchase orders.

Although the five railroads operate as separate entities, Wayne works directly with each railroad to develop and negotiate systemwide contracts. Purchasing identifies potential items for long-term contracts, identifies and analyzes potential suppliers, creates benchmark prices to compare final prices against, calculates annual demand requirements, and represents the interests of each railroad during negotiations with suppliers.

Each railroad has an opportunity to present its specific needs before purchasing enters a negotiation. Internal customers at each site electronically receive a generic contract before a supplier negotiation. The railroads have an opportunity to identify the contractual options they prefer, and users can expand the contract by listing any items they would like to see addressed in final negotiations.

Has Wayne's approach to contracting and negotiation been successful? Over a three-year period, current inventory maintained by the railroads has decreased by over 50%. Longer-term agreements have also allowed for some downsizing at the railroads because suppliers have assumed responsibilities previously performed by the railroads, such as delivering and placing physical inventory in storage. Furthermore, the railroads have realized price reductions due to the combining of common purchase requirements. Overall, the railroads now achieve a 35% return on net assets, prompting some at the railroad to joke that perhaps the railroad should divest itself of the parent steel company, which has failed to achieve its own operating goals.

The opening vignette highlights how a supply management professional, using negotiation and contracting practices transferred from an unrelated industry, has created new value that has enhanced his company's competitiveness. The ability to improve return on net assets was possible only through extensive planning, negotiation, and the use of longer-term contracts that combined the requirements of geographically diverse operating units. Negotiation is a skill that is essential to all purchasing and supply managers.

Everyone negotiates something every day, ranging from dealing with other drivers at a four-way stop sign all the way to merging with or acquiring another company. As such, negotiation is generally a highly complex and dynamic process, and many books and articles have been written on how to effectively negotiate in a variety of situations. This chapter highlights important topics that are typically part of any negotiation, especially those between buyers and suppliers. We begin this chapter by broadly defining the concept of negotiation. The second section presents negotiation as a five-phase process. Next, perhaps the most important part of any negotiation process—planning—appears in detail. The following sections present common sources of negotiation power, the effective use of concessions, negotiation strategies and tactics, and the important topics of win-win negotiation, international negotiation, and the effect of the Internet on the future of negotiation.

What Is Negotiation?

One of the most important activities performed by supply managers involves negotiating agreements or contracts with their suppliers. Although supply management is certainly not the only group in an organization that negotiates, negotiation is a vital part of every sourcing process. Negotiation is an ideal way to implement the supply management strategies and plans that a business unit develops. It is also often an ideal way to convey the buyer's specific sourcing requirements and specifications to

Sourcing Snapshot — *American Airlines Knows the Importance of Negotiation*

In a previous era, the sign of a good purchase negotiator was someone who could get a rock-bottom price from suppliers. Today, experienced negotiators realize that not all negotiations require a price focus or the same set of skills. "Low-level negotiations," says John MacLean, vice president of purchasing with American Airlines, "involve products or services that are competitive in the marketplace but are not strategically important to American Airlines." He points out that getting the best price is a good indicator of effectiveness for these types of items. MacLean also knows the importance of strategic negotiations when obtaining critical items and services. "Win/win negotiations," says MacLean, "are conducted in long-term relationships with suppliers. In these cases it is important that the supplier and American Airlines feel they are getting a good deal because the plan is to work together for a long while." At the most advanced level, the strategic compatibility of the companies involved may determine the success of a negotiation. Says MacLean, "Principle-based negotiating is used in a single-source situation or alliance where the two parties begin the negotiation by agreeing to certain principles, such as how the companies plan to grow together." American Airlines recognizes two important principles about negotiation. First, not all negotiations are equal in importance or require the same skill set. Second, negotiation is a fundamental part of the company's strategic supply plans.

Source: Adapted from A. Ciancarelli, "Strategic Negotiating Goes Far beyond Best Price," *Purchasing,* March 25, 1999, 126, 4.

its supply base. See Sourcing Snapshot: American Airlines Knows the Importance of Negotiation for a discussion of the importance of negotiation for American Airlines.

Negotiation has been defined in a variety of ways: "A negotiation is an interactive communication process that may take place whenever we want something from someone else or another person wants something from us."[1] "Negotiation is the process of communicating back and forth for the purpose of reaching a joint agreement about differing needs or ideas."[2] "Negotiation is a decision-making process by which two or more people agree how to allocate scarce resources."[3] "Negotiating is the end game of the sales process."[4]

For our purposes, we define negotiation as a process of formal communication, either face-to-face or via electronic means, where two or more people come together to seek mutual agreement about an issue or issues. The negotiation process involves the management of time, information, and power between individuals and organizations who are interdependent. Each party has a need for something that the other party has, yet recognizes that an interactive process of compromise or concession is often required to satisfy that need.

An important part of negotiation is realizing that the process involves relationships between people, not just organizations. A central part of negotiation involves each party trying to persuade the other party to do something that is in its best interest. The process involves skills that individuals, with the proper training and experience, can learn and improve upon. Good negotiators are not born; they hone these necessary skills through planning and practice.

There are a number of terms with which all negotiators should be familiar: BATNA, positions, interests, needs, and wants. A negotiator's best alternative to a negotiated agreement (BATNA) is also known as the negotiator's bottom line or reservation point, that is, that point in the negotiation where it is most advantageous for the negotiator to walk away from the table and implement his or her next-best option.[5] A negotiator should take extra caution to ensure that his or her reservation point or BATNA is never revealed to the other party because the final settlement is unlikely to vary much from that point.[6] In addition, all negotiation settlements must ultimately be judged in light of the other viable alternatives that existed at the time of the agreement.

A negotiator's **position** can be defined as his or her opening offer, which represents the optimistic (or ideal) value of the issue being negotiated. A position is the stated demand that is placed on the table by a negotiator. In contrast, the negotiator's **interest** is the unspoken motivation or reason that underlies any given negotiation position. In many negotiation scenarios, the negotiator's underlying interests are unlikely to be expressly stated or acknowledged, oftentimes because they may not be directly germane to the stated position or may be personal in nature. Sharing the underlying interests behind a position may cause a negotiator's power to shift toward the other party, resulting in a less-than-desired outcome. The negotiator must, in effect, play detective to try and discern the other party's interests through a series of open-ended, probing questions. In order to reach a negotiated agreement using principled negotiation, a negotiator should always attempt to focus on the other party's underlying interests, not his or her stated position.[7]

The astute negotiator must also be able to distinguish between the other party's needs and wants. **Needs** are considered to be those negotiated outcomes that the negotiator must have in order to reach a successful outcome to the negotiation. **Wants**, on the other hand, refer to those negotiated outcomes that a negotiator would like to have as opposed to those outcomes that must be achieved. Wants can also be exchanged as concessions to the other party during a negotiation because they are not as critical to achieving a successful conclusion to the negotiation. When a negotiator is planning an upcoming negotiation, it is imperative to prioritize all of the potential issues to be negotiated into needs and wants, thereby knowing what must be achieved and what can be exchanged for something else of value.

A simple negotiation planning tool, called "Triangle Talk," can help the negotiator begin the initial preparation for an upcoming negotiation. This planning process, shown in Exhibit 13.1, consists of the following three steps: (1) know exactly what you want; (2) find out what they want and make them feel heard; and (3) propose action in such a way that they can accept it.[8]

Step 1 in Triangle Talk is determining and formalizing the negotiator's specific goals and objectives for the upcoming negotiation. Being specific with one's expectations and writing them down helps the negotiator to remain focused on his or her predetermined priorities during the negotiation. Having them written down also allows the negotiator to refer back to them during the course of the negotiation, when it is often easy to be distracted by the other negotiator's tactics and the pace of the give-and-take process. The more clearly a negotiator can define his or her priorities, the more likely he or she is to obtain them in the final agreement.

Step 2 involves trying to discern what the negotiator's counterpart is likely to need or want from the negotiation. It is difficult to develop common ground in the negotiation without knowing what the other party is seeking. Ask specifically, "What does the other party need or want?" Delve into the other party's likely positions and try to

Exhibit 13.1 Triangle Talk

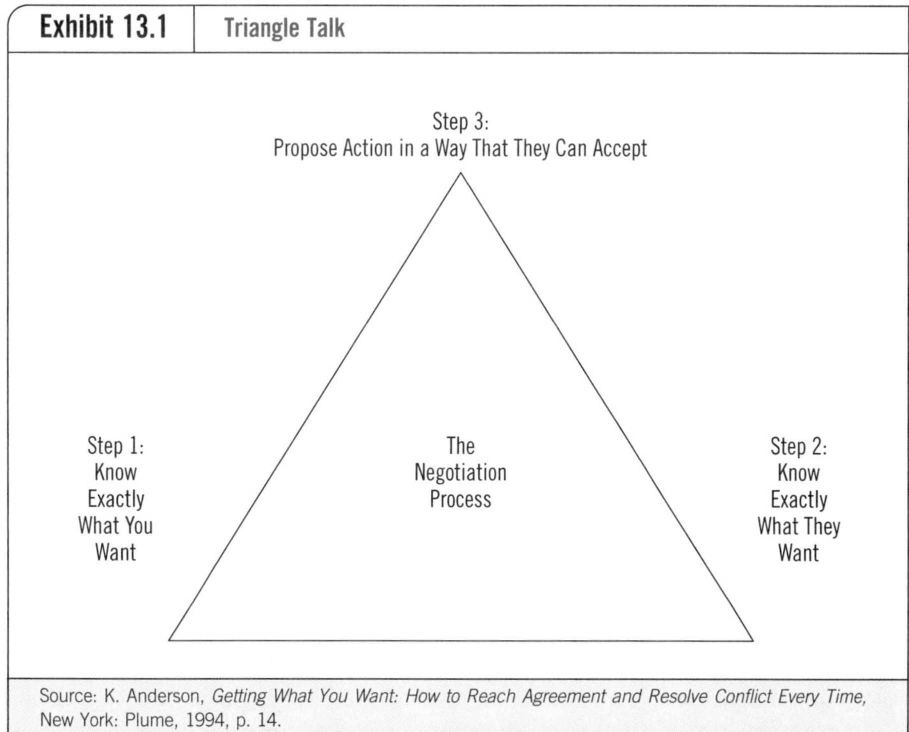
Step 3:
Propose Action in a Way That They Can Accept
Step 1:
Know
Exactly
What You
Want
The
Negotiation
Process
Step 2:
Know
Exactly
What They
Want

Source: K. Anderson, *Getting What You Want: How to Reach Agreement and Resolve Conflict Every Time*, New York: Plume, 1994, p. 14.

estimate what the underlying interests are behind the positions. However, a negotiator cannot automatically assume that the other party thinks the same way he or she does. During the negotiation, the negotiator can ask open-ended, probing questions to verify his or her preliminary analysis of the other party's needs and wants. In addition, the negotiator should develop a strategy and accompanying tactics that will make the other party feel heard. This will allow the third step in Triangle Talk to take place.

Step 3 involves the consideration and analysis of the negotiator's own needs and wants and the needs and wants of the other party. This way, proposals and counterproposals can be offered that take both sets of needs and wants into account and are framed in such a way as to make it easy for the other party to say "Yes." It is important to remain flexible, fair, and reasonable so that the parties can work out an agreement in which they are both better off. In addition to acknowledging (but not necessarily agreeing with) the other party's concerns, the negotiator can accomplish this by speaking to those needs first when framing his or her proposals.

Negotiation Framework

Perhaps the best way to approach a buyer-supplier negotiation is by presenting it as an interactive, give-and-take process involving five major phases:

1. Identify or anticipate a purchase requirement
2. Determine if negotiation is required
3. Plan for the negotiation
4. Conduct the negotiation
5. Execute the agreement

Exhibit 13.2 summarizes this general negotiation process.

Identify or Anticipate a Purchase Requirement

The purchasing cycle begins with identifying or anticipating a purchase requirement. Chapter 2 addresses how firms identify or anticipate purchase requirements, or what we typically call the purchasing process. The purchasing cycle begins with identifying (or anticipating) a material need or requirement for a component, raw material, subassembly, service, piece of equipment, or finished product. Often, supply management can identify new requirements during new-product development in collaboration with its various internal customers within the buying organization, such as marketing, operations, design, and research and development. For many existing items, there may not be a need to identify a supplier because an existing sourcing agreement may already be in place. New sourcing requirements, however, often require supply management to identify, evaluate, and qualify new potential suppliers.

Determine If Negotiation Is Required

Not all purchase requirements will require buyers and sellers to conduct a thorough and detailed negotiation. For many items, the competitive bidding process will satisfy a buyer's purchase requirements, as may be the case for items that are low value, are widely available commodities, or have pre-existing standards. Negotiation is often appropriate when other issues besides price are important or when competi-

Exhibit 13.2 Five-Phase Negotiation Process

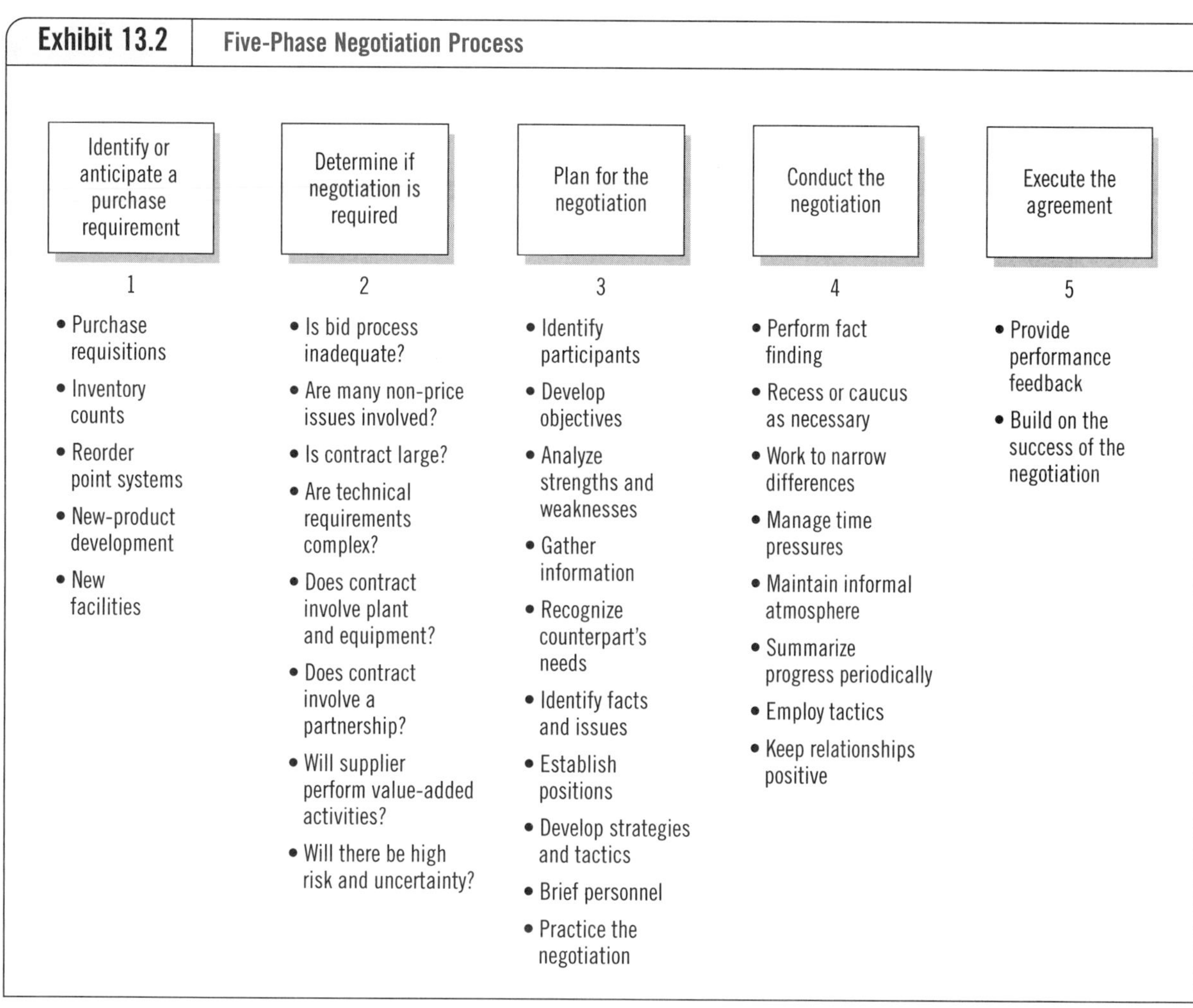
Identify or anticipate a purchase requirement
Determine if negotiation is required
Plan for the negotiation
Conduct the negotiation
Execute the agreement
1
2
3
4
5
• Purchase requisitions
• Inventory counts
• Reorder point systems
• New-product development
• New facilities
• Is bid process inadequate?
• Are many non-price issues involved?
• Is contract large?
• Are technical requirements complex?
• Does contract involve plant and equipment?
• Does contract involve a partnership?
• Will supplier perform value-added activities?
• Will there be high risk and uncertainty?
• Identify participants
• Develop objectives
• Analyze strengths and weaknesses
• Gather information
• Recognize counterpart's needs
• Identify facts and issues
• Establish positions
• Develop strategies and tactics
• Brief personnel
• Practice the negotiation
• Perform fact finding
• Recess or caucus as necessary
• Work to narrow differences
• Manage time pressures
• Maintain informal atmosphere
• Summarize progress periodically
• Employ tactics
• Keep relationships positive
• Provide performance feedback
• Build on the success of the negotiation

tive bidding will not satisfy the buyer's purchase requirements on various issues. However, a buyer can still use a competitive bidding process to identify several potential sources of supply. After identifying a potential supplier through bidding, the buyer may need to negotiate with the preferred supplier to resolve other non-price issues affecting the sourcing agreement.

The following areas or issues may require supply management to negotiate with its suppliers:

- Identification of and agreement on a supplier's allowable costs
- Delivery schedules and lead time requirements
- Expected product and service quality levels
- Performance metrics and how information is to be gathered and shared
- Technological support and assistance
- Contract volumes
- Special packaging and shipping requirements
- Liability for loss and damage

- Payment terms and currency issues
- Progress payment schedules
- Mode of transportation and responsibility for selecting carriers, as well as filing freight claims
- Warranties and replacements
- Capacity commitments
- Material lead times
- Nonperformance penalties or performance incentives
- Contract length and renewal mechanism
- Protection of proprietary information
- Ownership of intellectual property
- Resources related to developing closer relationships
- Improvement requirements in quality, delivery performance, lead time, cost, and so on
- Resolution mechanisms for contract disputes
- Spare parts, after-sales service, and operator or maintenance training support

This list, although lengthy, is not exhaustive and represents only a portion of the topics that negotiators can address. Besides the need to agree on non-price issues, other reasons exist for negotiating with suppliers:

- *The total contract value or volume is large.* It is not unusual for supply managers to negotiate contracts worth millions of dollars. Nonperformance on large contracts can cause unusually severe problems, such as an interruption in continuity of supply. The buyer may want to negotiate special safeguards to make sure the supplier recognizes the importance of performing exactly as required.
- *The purchase involves complex technical requirements, perhaps even product and process requirements and specifications that are still evolving.* Under this condition, it is difficult for the parties to reach definitive agreement on a purchase requirement. However, a buyer may want the supplier to begin work even if final product requirements and specifications have not yet been established.
- *The purchase involves capital-intensive plant and equipment.* Suppliers often customize or dedicate capital-intensive plant and equipment to meet a buyer's specific needs.
- *The agreement involves a special or collaborative relationship.* Special or collaborative relationships must address issues beyond a traditional or conventional purchase agreement. For example, the two parties may discuss the joint development of technology featuring the sharing or co-location of technical personnel.
- *The supplier will perform important value-added activities.* Increasingly, buyers are asking suppliers to perform activities such as product design, testing, or inventory management. These additional activities often require substantial discussion and negotiation to determine appropriate compensation and how performance is to be measured.

An important question for the supply manager today is how much will the development of information technology systems, such as Internet-based reverse auctions and use of electronic-based communication media, change the need to negotiate or have face-to-face interaction with suppliers? The use of reverse auctions has likely reduced the need for face-to-face interaction or negotiation between buyers and sellers. However, it also likely that the type of items and services obtained through reverse auctions (e.g., standard commodities with a moderate total dollar spend) do not warrant higher-level negotiations in the first place. For items that are critical to the buyer or involve many non-price issues, the likelihood that buyers and sellers will no longer engage in face-to-face negotiation is small. See Sourcing Snapshot: Will E-Procurement Change Negotiation? for a discussion on how electronic communication media can affect negotiations conducted at a distance.

Plan for the Negotiation

Negotiation planning involves a series of steps that prepare the parties for a forthcoming negotiation. Many buyer-supplier negotiations are relatively straightforward and may require only basic preparation and planning. Other negotiations may be highly complex and require months of thorough and detailed preparation. Regardless, supply managers who take the time necessary to plan and prepare for a negotiation will usually experience better outcomes than those negotiators who do not adequately plan and prepare. Planning is so crucial to achieving desired negotiation outcomes that a later section addresses this topic in greater detail.

New electronic communications technology may make face-to face buyer-supplier negotiation, both for domestic and international requirements, far less necessary.

Sourcing Snapshot — *Will E-Procurement Change Negotiation?*

As the number of people buying online continues to grow, certain changes are in store for supply management professionals who have traditionally prided themselves on their face-to-face people skills. Kevin Rohan, a purchasing specialist at JP Cannon Associates in New York, believes being a strong negotiator is not enough in today's market. Candidates need to continue to develop their skills and be familiar with the latest technology such as how to use the Internet, identify market changes, and perform strategic planning. However, the chances that e-procurement will completely replace one-on-one negotiation in the near future are slim. Emery J. Zobro, president of the John Michael Personnel Group in Chattanooga, TN, is confident that, while the characteristics of a successful supply management professional might change over time, certain qualities will survive e-procurement's infiltration of the industry. "In five years a person who hasn't established a track record with e-commerce and e-procurement will definitely be left behind," Zobro says. Nevertheless, he remains firm in the assessment that "buying things over the computer will never take the place of one-on-one negotiations."

Source: Adapted from D. Francis, "The Decline of the Negotiator?" *Purchasing,* August 24, 2000, 129(3), 160.

This can be a very attractive alternative to expensive and time-consuming international travel as more organizations engage in global supply management, which creates a host of new negotiation challenges. It will also substantially change how a supply manager plans for and conducts the negotiation.

More advanced online communication tools are becoming readily available that feature the ability to negotiate issues beyond price with multiple suppliers, regardless of their physical location. With these tools, e-procurement managers no longer have to spend hours in face-to-face meetings arguing over details with suppliers. A buyer simply fills out a predetermined request for proposal (RFP) or request for quotation (RFQ) template and then forwards the document electronically to a select group of its qualified suppliers.[9] Suppliers can then easily and quickly respond electronically with detailed online proposals outlining price, payment terms, shipping methods, or any other issue that is relevant to the buyer. It is also much easier to make changes as the negotiation process progresses. These tools enable a buyer to negotiate simultaneously with more than one supplier during this process, which leads to greater bidding efficiencies and lower prices through increased competition (similar to reverse auctions).

Conduct the Negotiation

Negotiations with a supplier should occur only when a buyer feels confident about the level of planning and preparation put forth. However, planning is not an open-ended process; buyers must usually meet deadlines that satisfy the needs of internal customers within the buyer's organization. Thus, the buyer faces pressure to initiate, conduct, and conclude the negotiation within a reasonable time. Effective planning also requires hard work on the following points:

- Defining the issues
- Assembling issues and defining the bargaining mix
- Defining interests
- Defining one's own objectives (targets) and opening bids (where to begin)
- Assessing constituents and the social context in which the negotiation will occur
- Analyzing the other party
- Planning the issue presentation and defense
- Defining protocols: where and when the negotiation will occur, who will be there, what the agenda will be, and so on[10]

Deciding where to negotiate can be an important part of the planning process. A home location can provide a substantial advantage to a negotiator, particularly during international negotiations. Advances in telecommunication technology now allow some negotiations to occur electronically rather than face-to-face. Most experts agree that the atmosphere surrounding a negotiation should be less formal wherever possible to build trusting relationships and long-term commitment.

Excessive formality can effectively constrain the parties and restrict the free exchange of ideas and solutions. It is also a good idea to summarize positions and points of agreement throughout the negotiation, which helps reduce misunderstanding while helping track progress against the negotiation agenda. It may also help to have a dedicated note taker or scribe throughout the negotiation whose primary responsibility is to record what was said, who said it, what the other party's reaction was, and what the areas of agreement were.

It is during the negotiation that the parties play out their strategy with **tactics**—the skill of employing available means to accomplish or achieve a desired end. Tactics are the action plans designed to help achieve a desired result. A later section reviews various common tactics that negotiators may employ or should be prepared for.

A sequence of four phases often characterizes face-to-face negotiation sessions. The first consists of fact finding and information sharing between the parties. This part of the process helps clarify and confirm information provided by the buyer and seller. During the second phase, the parties often take a recess after fact finding. This allows each party the opportunity to reassess relative strengths and weaknesses, review and revise objectives and positions if necessary, and organize the negotiation agenda. Next, the negotiating parties meet face-to-face in an attempt to narrow their differences on the specific issues. This phase typically includes the offering of proposals and counterproposals and exchanging concessions. Finally, the parties seek an agreement and conclusion to the negotiation, plus establish any agreed-upon follow-on activities.

Effective negotiators typically display certain behaviors or characteristics when conducting a negotiation. They may be willing to compromise or revise their goals, particularly when new information effectively challenges their predetermined position. Effective negotiators may also view issues independently, without linking them in any particular sequence. Linking issues risks undermining an entire negotiation if the parties reach an impasse on a single issue within the negotiation package. Effective negotiators should also establish lower and upper ranges for each major issue, as opposed to a single, rigid position that may limit the number of viable options available and be more likely to create an impasse.

Highly effective or skilled negotiators explore more options per issue than do average negotiators. Furthermore, effective negotiators also make more comments about the common ground between the parties (rather than the differences) than do average negotiators. Finally, when compared with average negotiators, effective or skilled negotiators make fewer irritating comments about the other party, give fewer reasons for arguments they advance (too many supporting reasons can dilute an argument), and make fewer counterproposals. Effective negotiators are willing to make counterproposals, though not as many as an average negotiator. A willingness to make too many counterproposals means the negotiator is probably compromising too much or offering too many concessions. It may also indicate a lack of adequate planning and preparation or a sign of vulnerability.

Execute the Agreement

Reaching agreement is not the end of the negotiation process by any means. Rather, an agreement merely represents the beginning of the contract's performance for the item, service, or activity covered by the agreement. An important part of executing and following through on a negotiated agreement is loading the agreement into a corporate contract system so others throughout the organization have visibility of the agreement.

During the life of an agreement, a buyer must let a supplier know if the supplier is not meeting its contractual requirements. Conversely, it is the supplier's responsibility to let the buyer know if the buyer is not meeting its responsibilities within the negotiated agreement. Both parties should work to build upon the success of a negotiation. Carrying out the agreement as agreed upon should reaffirm the commitment of the parties to work together in the future.

Negotiation Planning

Experts on negotiation generally agree that planning is perhaps the single most important part of the negotiation process. Unfortunately, many negotiators fail to prepare properly before entering into a formal negotiation. A **plan** is a method or scheme devised for making or doing something to achieve a desired end. **Planning**, therefore, is the process of devising methods to achieve a desired end. Once negotiators develop their plan and an overall guiding strategy, they can begin to develop the specific actions and tactics necessary to carry out that plan. Negotiators frequently fall short of their goals or reach an impasse because they neglect the other party's problems, focus too much on price, focus on positions instead of interests, focus too much on common ground, neglect their BATNAs, or overadjust their perceptions during the actual negotiation.[11]

At least 90% of the successful outcomes of any negotiation are determined by effective planning. Preparing at the last minute just prior to a negotiation is a sure recipe for disaster, especially when negotiating against someone who is far more prepared. Therefore, being quick and clever while thinking on one's feet is simply insufficient to ensure a successful negotiation outcome. Successful negotiation planning is proactive, not reactive, and consists of the following nine steps, none of which should be passed over.

Develop Specific Objectives

The first step of the negotiation planning process involves developing specific goals and objectives desired from the negotiation. An **objective** is an aspiration or vision to work toward in the future. For example, an obvious objective in a sourcing negotiation would be to reach an agreement that covers the purchase of a good or service. Neither a buyer nor a seller would commit scarce resources if the goal were to see a negotiation fail. Before actual negotiations begin, the parties need to believe they can reach an agreement. If the parties believed otherwise, they would not put forth the requisite time and effort to prepare for and conduct a successful negotiation.

An important objective during a sourcing negotiation is to reach agreement on a fair and reasonable price between a buyer and seller. Examples of buyer objectives could include achieving an acceptable unit price, required delivery lead time, or improved supplier quality in terms of defect levels. The buyer may also want to persuade the supplier to collaborate with the buyer at a level higher than other competing buyers would receive. Not all objectives are equally important, so the buyer must begin to identify the importance of each one and prioritize them depending on the negotiation at hand. One leading company separates its objectives into "must have" and "would like to have" categories. This begins to differentiate the importance of each objective.

Analyze Each Party's Strengths and Weaknesses

Knowledgeable negotiators strive to understand their counterparts through research and experience. This means understanding what is important to the other company along with understanding the personality and history of the negotiator's opposite number. For example, when buyers negotiate with a supplier for the first time, they must often commit substantial time and energy to additional research in order to more fully understand that particular supplier and its needs, wants, and priorities.

Analyzing the other party requires a thorough assessment of the relative strengths and weaknesses of the parties, as well as each individual issue to be negotiated. This due diligence process can greatly influence the effectiveness of the strategy and tactics employed at the bargaining table. Buyers cannot assume that they have power or influence over the supplier or vice versa. Many times a supplier holds a power position over the buyer because of its financial size, or perhaps because the supplier does not have a great need for the contract. A later section details various sources of power that are part of the negotiation process.

Gather Relevant Information

The ability to analyze yourself and your negotiating counterpart requires sufficient, timely, and accurate information. This process need not be complex, particularly if the buyer and seller have previously negotiated together. When this is the case, the buyer may have already answered a number of important questions. What happened between the parties? Were we satisfied with the previous outcome of the negotiation? Are we negotiating with the same people or different negotiators? What are the important issues to this supplier? To us? What were the areas of disagreement? Is there anything about the rules of the negotiation we would like to change?

Where does a buyer, who has no experience with a supplier, gather the required information? One possible source may be contacting others who have experience with that supplier. Published sources of information may also be available. These sources include trade journals, other business publications, trade association data, government reports, annual reports, financial evaluations (such as Dun & Bradstreet reports), commercial databases, inquiries directly to personnel at the supplier, and information derived through the Internet.

Recognize Your Counterpart's Needs

The buyer and seller in a sourcing negotiation are, in many ways, mirror images of each other. Each side wants to reach an agreement that is favorable to its longer-term success. As a buyer gathers information about a supplier, it is important to identify those key issues that are particularly critical to the supplier. For example, a supplier may want to maintain or grow its market share and volume in its industry. Therefore, receiving the entire purchase contract, rather than only a portion, may be an important objective to that supplier.

The issues that are most critical to a supplier are not likely to be those most critical to a buyer. When one party has an issue or requirement that is relatively unimportant to the other, then the parties are more likely to reach agreement. For example, a supplier's production scheduling system may require the supplier to produce a buyer's requirement late in the day with delivery during the evening. If a buyer has an evening work crew that can easily receive late deliveries, the buyer can satisfy the supplier's requirement for later deliveries. In return, the buyer may now expect the supplier to be more accommodating on one or more issues that are important to the buyer. Give and take is essential to negotiation, and each party should not expect to prevail on all issues. This is why it is important for buyers to do their homework before the negotiation begins by identifying ranges of acceptable outcomes for each and every issue and setting priorities in the event that concessions or tradeoffs are required.

Identify Facts and Issues

Negotiation planning requires differentiating between facts and issues. The two parties will want to reach agreement early concerning what constitutes a fact versus an issue. A **fact** is a reality or truth that the parties can easily state and verify or prove. In negotiation, facts are not open to debate. For example, a buyer wants to purchase a piece of capital equipment. There is no negotiating with a supplier on whether the buyer actually needs that particular piece of equipment (although the specific type of equipment may be an unanswered question requiring interactive discussion).

Issues, on the other hand, are items or topics to be resolved during the negotiation. Issues that might require resolution include purchase price and delivery date. The parties to a negotiation can discuss and resolve many issues besides price, including quality, delivery, service, metrics, and performance improvement. Part of the planning process requires identifying all of the critical issues and outcomes that each party seeks to resolve through the negotiation. As discussed earlier, the Triangle Talk technique can help negotiators determine not only the issues involved but the range of acceptable outcomes for each issue.

Establish a Position on Each Issue

The parties to a negotiation should establish positions that offer flexibility. Negotiators should therefore develop a range of positions—typically, a minimum acceptable position (or BATNA), a maximum or ideal outcome, and a most likely position. If the issue is price, a seller may have a target price for which it wants to sell a product. Of course, the seller will take a higher price if the buyer is willing to offer one. The critical part of the range will be based on the seller's minimum acceptable price or resistance point. This is the lowest price at which the seller is willing to sell to a buyer. Any price lower than the minimum will result in no deal or an unacceptable outcome to the supplier. The area of overlapping positions among issues, when there is one, is termed the **bargaining** or **settlement zone.**[12] The bargaining zone represents the heart of the negotiation process, as any proposal offered outside of this range is likely to be rejected by the other party because it is less than what he or she is willing to settle for.

Exhibit 13.3 demonstrates a settlement zone for a typical purchase price–based negotiation. Looking at example A, the parties will probably not reach agreement unless one or both parties modify their original price range or position. The minimum selling position of the seller is far above the buyer's maximum position, with no overlap. In example B, there is an overlap between the two positions that should lead to an agreement. The buyer is willing to pay up to $11.45 per unit. The supplier is willing to sell as low as $11.15 per unit. The two parties will likely reach an agreement somewhere between those two figures. As a bargaining tactic, the buyer may open with an offer to purchase at something less than $11.00 (that is, start out very low). However, if the seller remains with its original plan, the negotiation will likely conclude within the overlap range.

Several factors influence whether a party modifies or even abandons its original position. These include the desire for the contract, the revelation of new or improved

Exhibit 13.3 Developing Negotiating Ranges for a Purchase Price

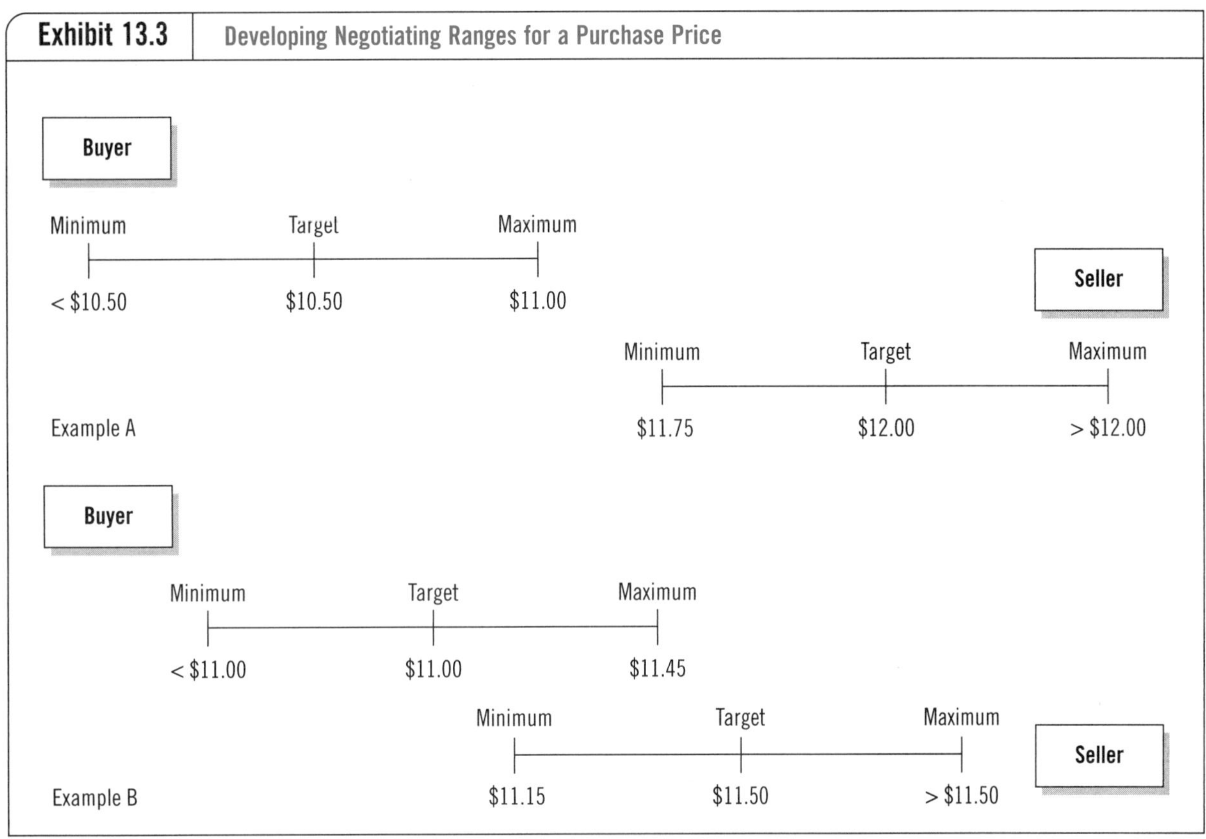

information that challenges the accuracy and credibility of the party's original position, or a major concession that leads the other party to modify its position on another issue for the sake of reciprocation.

Develop the Negotiation Strategy and Accompanying Tactics

Negotiation **strategy** refers to the overall approach used to reach a mutually beneficial agreement with a supplier that holds different points of view from the buyer. A major part of the strategic planning process involves the application of tactics—the art or skill of employing available means to accomplish an end, objective, or strategy. They include the current set of action plans and activities adopted to achieve the negotiation objectives and strategy. A later section discusses the effective use of tactics in greater detail.

Strategic negotiation issues involve the broader questions regarding who, what, where, when, and how to negotiate. We can think of strategy and tactics as two dimensions of the same negotiation process. The ideal situation is to have a well-developed negotiation strategy with appropriate and ethical tactics that support that strategy. As an analogy, consider a military battle. The best-developed strategy will fail unless a commander has the tactics and the resources to implement that strategy in the field.

Brief Other Personnel

A purchase negotiation usually affects other parties throughout the organization. The individual or team conducting the negotiation should adequately brief these internal stakeholders to ensure that they are aware of and in agreement with the desired objectives for the negotiation. This briefing should also address the major issues of the negotiation and the organization's positions on these issues. Briefing personnel before a negotiation helps eliminate unwanted surprises during and following face-to-face negotiation. Oftentimes, it is important to garner stakeholder buy-in to the negotiation through this briefing process to ensure that the negotiation outcomes are implemented as agreed upon at the bargaining table.

Practice the Negotiation

Experienced negotiators often practice or rehearse before commencing a formal negotiation, especially if the negotiation involves a large dollar amount or is highly critical to the success of the organization. One way to do this is to hold a mock or simulated negotiation. For instance, a marketing representative or salesperson might represent the supplier. The counterpart in a practice negotiation session may be able to raise questions and issues that the buyer had not originally considered. When using simulation, it is important for each party to play its role as realistically as possible.

Another effective way to conduct a mock negotiation is for the buyer to role-play the supplier's side. This allows the buyer to empathize with the supplier and more fully understand how the supplier might approach the negotiation; it also could provide valuable insight into the supplier's expected needs and wants. Here again, the use of Triangle Talk can play a valuable role in this key planning process.

Effective planning means that buyers achieve an agreement that is more creative and valuable than one that might be available to their competitors. It also means managing the buyer-supplier relationships that support future negotiation and cooperative interaction between the parties.

Power in Negotiation

An important part of the negotiation process involves the recognition and analysis of the relative power relationship that exists between parties. **Power** is the ability to influence another person or organization. "A" has power over "B" if "A" can get "B" to do something that directly benefits "A." Throughout human history, we have seen both positive and negative uses of power. As such, power, in and of itself, possesses neither a positive nor a negative connotation; it is how that relative power is used that gives it a particular perception. Within negotiation, the use of power employed by the parties can dramatically influence the actual outcome of a negotiation or even result in a stalemate.

Both individuals and organizations bring different sources of power to the negotiation table, and the consideration of power should be a part of any negotiation strategy. Some types of power are detrimental to a continued relationship, whereas others are the result of expertise or access to information. Therefore, negotiators must understand the advantages and disadvantages of using each source of power. They must also understand the possible effects that using a particular source of power will have on the relationship between the parties.

Sources of Negotiation Power

Researchers have identified six general types of power exercised by individuals or organizations: (1) informational, (2) reward, (3) coercive, (4) legitimate, (5) expert, and (6) referent.[13]

Informational Power

Ready access to relevant and useful information is typically the most common application of power found in a negotiation. It relies on influencing the other party through the presentation of facts, data, and persuasive arguments to support one's own positions and to mitigate or challenge the other party's positions. However, the effective use of information in a negotiation does not necessarily mean open and complete sharing. For example, one party may present only favorable information that supports its position, whereas the other side may present only negative information to refute a position. One party often manipulates information, as a source of power, to control or constrain the options available to the other party.[14]

Reward Power

Reward power means that one party is able to offer something of perceived value to the other party, such as a purchase contract or access to a new source of technology. Using rewards represents a direct attempt to exert control over the negotiation, particularly when compared with the use of informational power, which relies more on persuasion. The basis of reward power is the belief that individuals respond and behave accordingly when valued rewards are available. An important risk of reward power is that a negotiation counterpart may eventually learn to respond positively only when offered rewards.

Coercive Power

Coercive and reward power are somewhat related; they are two sides of the same negotiation coin. If one party can give the other party something of value (reward power), then that party can also take it away (coercive power). Therefore, coercive power includes the ability to punish the other party—financially, physically, or mentally. Note that repeated use of coercive power can have damaging effects on longer-term relationships. There is also a strong likelihood that retaliation or escalation can occur if the power structure shifts unfavorably in the future. For example, when supply markets begin to tighten during an economic recovery, suppliers may retaliate against the buyer by pursuing large price increases, not providing excellent service to certain buyers, or even disrupting continuity of supply to the offending buyer.

Legitimate Power

The job position that an individual holds, rather than the individual him- or herself, is the basis of legitimate power. Parents, pastors, managers, and political officeholders are examples of individuals possessing legitimate power. In sourcing, a buyer may have legitimate power simply because he or she legally represents a prominent company and has the authority to buy. It is not necessarily the case that individuals with legitimate power have reward or coercive power (e.g., a church pastor).

Expert Power

Expert power is a related and special form of informational power. Successful application of informational and expert power involves the development and retention of a body of knowledge. Informational power exists when someone has thoroughly researched and prepared for a negotiation. An expert is recognized as having accumulated and mastered vast knowledge about a particular subject, often with verifiable credentials to document that mastery. Expert power can influence others in a negotiation by reducing the likelihood that another party will be able to successfully refute the expert's position. Furthermore, nonexperts are less likely to challenge an expert because of the expert's perceived depth of knowledge. However, the other party must value the expertise in order for it to be effective.

Referent Power

This source of power comes from attraction based on socially acceptable personal qualities and attributes of an individual, such as one's personality. These qualities could be physical but likely include individual characteristics such as honesty, charisma, friendliness, and sensitivity. In this source of power, the power holder—the referent—has some attributes or personal qualities that attract the other party or make him or her want to be like or respect the power holder. The basis of referent power is that the nonreferent wants the referent to look favorably upon him or her. Referent power is most successful in negotiation when the referents are aware that a counterpart identifies with or has an attraction to them.

Parties holding power will likely apply all available types of power to their advantage during a negotiation. Negotiators must be careful not to abuse their power, or they risk damaging relationships, inviting retaliation, or diminishing the value of that power. In most negotiations, the sources of power that are usually the most effective are legitimate, informational, and expert. They are usually the sources of power that allow the parties to maintain a positive relationship after reaching agreement. However, referent power can also synergistically interact with the other sources of power, making them stronger or more effective in the influence process.

Concessions

A fundamental part of every negotiation process involves the offering and exchange of concessions—movements away from a negotiating position that offer something of value to the other party. For example, a buyer's willingness to offer $8.50 per unit instead of $8.25 is a concession that favors the supplier. Effective negotiators quickly learn to offer concessions that have little value to themselves in exchange for concessions by the other party that do have perceived value. To make the negotiation process work, each party must recognize that the give and take of concessions is a normal and necessary part of any negotiation. Buyers, however, will still want to minimize how much they concede on each point by getting corresponding value in return. Do not give away any concession without getting something of equal or greater value in return.

Without an effective concession strategy, most negotiations will result in deadlock or a failure to agree. However, a deadlock does not necessarily mean that the negotiation failed. The parties to a negotiation could be so far apart in their positions that an agreement is not likely. In such cases, it may actually be better not to agree than to accept a poor agreement. This is why it is very important for the negotiator to have adequately prepared and established a thoughtful BATNA before the negotiation begins. The negotiator must be aware of available options and understand that no deal may be better than a bad deal.

The manner in which a negotiator approaches concession making is an important part of every negotiation strategy. A buyer who opens the negotiation with a low initial offer (on price, for example) followed by a relatively small concession is signaling a reluctance to be flexible. Conversely, a cooperative opening position or moderate offer followed by a relatively strong concession signals a willingness to be flexible and to reach mutual agreement.

Exhibit 13.4 illustrates how the pattern of concession making might influence the other party's response. If a seller continues to offer concessions during a negotiation, the buyer is likely to continue to ask for further concessions. Examine Exhibit 13.4, and ask yourself if you would continue to another round of negotiation given the pattern of concessions presented. How negotiators position their concessions will often affect the length and cost of the negotiation. It also affects the other party's expectations of the possible outcomes.

Hendon, Roy, and Ahmed offered the following 12 guidelines for making successful concessions:[15]

- Give yourself enough room to make concessions.
- Try to get the other party to start revealing his or her needs and objectives first.
- Be the first to concede on a minor issue but not the first to concede on a major issue.

Exhibit 13.4 Offering Concessions

SUPPLIER	Round 1	Round 2	Round 3	Round 4	Continue to Round 5?
1	$50	$50	$50	$50	________
2	$110	$75	$0	$15	________
3	$35	$45	$55	$65	________
4	$200	$0	$0	$0	________
5	$0	$0	$0	$200	________
6	$80	$60	$40	$20	________

CONCESSIONS RECEIVED PER NEGOTIATION ROUND

- Make unimportant concessions and portray them as more valuable than they are.
- Make the other party work hard for every concession you make.
- Use tradeoffs to obtain something for every concession you make.
- Generally, concede slowly and give a little with each concession.
- Do not reveal your deadline to the other party.
- Occasionally say "no" to the other negotiator.
- Be careful trying to take back concessions, even in tentative negotiations.
- Keep a record of concessions made in the negotiation and try to identify a pattern.
- Do not concede too often, too soon, or too much.

Suppliers or buyers who open with their best and final offers with no concessions are practicing **Boulwarism**—a negotiating style named after Lemuel R. Boulware, the former CEO of General Electric. This approach usually creates an unrealistic expectation because negotiators expect more concessions to follow. When concessions fail to come about as expected, the other side often becomes angry or believes that its counterpart is not bargaining in good faith. In fact, Boulwarism is now generally defined as bad-faith or no-concession bargaining.[16] Negotiations featuring Boulwarism are more likely to end in deadlock or no agreement.

Although concessions are an important part of the negotiation process, a willingness to offer large concessions is usually not in the best interests of a buyer. The level of planning and the relative power of each party will influence how much, how often, and when each party concedes its positions during a negotiation.

Negotiation Tactics: Trying to Reach Agreement

Negotiation tactics are the short-term plans and actions employed to execute a strategy, cause a conscious change in a counterpart's position, or influence others to achieve negotiation objectives. Negotiators develop tactics to ethically persuade their counterparts to endorse a certain position or agree to a preferred outcome. Furthermore, a negotiator must learn to recognize and understand the type of tactics a counterpart is using. An awareness of a counterpart's tactics usually mitigates the effectiveness of those tactics.

Some tactics used by buyers and sellers are actually ploys or tricks to get the other party to agree to an issue or contract without question. However, this does not diminish the fact that there are many legitimate and ethical tactics that a buyer or seller can use to persuade the other party to endorse a particular perspective. The following represents only a small sample of negotiation tactics that the astute and adequately prepared negotiator should be aware of and prepare for:

- *Low Ball.* This tactic involves one party, often the seller, offering an unusually low price to receive a buyer's business (getting one's foot in the door). Suppliers know that, once a buyer makes a commitment to a seller, it is often difficult for that buyer to switch to another supplier due to the consistency principle.
- *Honesty and Openness.* Parties with a close working relationship often have a level of mutual trust that promotes free and open sharing of information.

The objective of this tactic is to make each party aware of the relevant information needed to create a mutually acceptable agreement.

- *Questions.* Open-ended questions serve a dual purpose as a negotiation tactic. First, insightful questions can result in revealing new information about the interests underlying the other party's stated position. Second, questions provide a period of relief or reflection as the other party takes time to consider an answer. Questions seeking only a "yes or no" answer do not provide much additional information.
- *Caucus.* This tactic involves taking a time-out; negotiators might need to process new information, take a needed break, or take a recess if the negotiation is going poorly; negotiators might feel they are making too many concessions and need to break the pattern.
- *Trial Balloon.* A negotiator using this tactic might ask, "What if I can persuade my manager to endorse this option? Would you go along?" Trial balloons are tests of acceptability. The other party's on-the-spot reaction to the idea influences whether the parties should pursue the idea further.
- *Price Increase.* Sellers sometimes argue that, if a buyer does not agree to a certain price or condition, the price will soon increase. A well-informed and adequately prepared negotiator can tell the difference between a real price change and a tactic used by the seller merely to make the sale.
- *High Ball.* This tactic involves taking an abnormally high initial position on an issue. For example, the seller may put forth an extremely high selling price. The underlying logic is that, once a party actually makes a concession from the extreme position, the new position may appear more acceptable to the other party. It also attempts to shift the bargaining zone in one's favor.
- *Best and Final Offer.* This tactic often signals the end of a negotiation on a given issue. The caveat to this tactic is that the person making the best and final offer must be prepared to actually end the discussion if the other party does not accept the offer. If a party rapidly amends a best and final offer, this tactic quickly loses its effectiveness, and the negotiator loses credibility when the bluff is called.
- *Silence.* This tactic involves not immediately responding when the other party makes an offer in the hope that an awkward silence will encourage further offers or concessions. We often show the tendency to fill in the gaps when a discussion encounters silence so as to not offend the other party. Also, when the counterpart makes a point that weakens our position, it may be better to remain silent than to admit the other party is correct. The other party may actually back away from its earlier position.
- *Planned Concessions.* This tactic uses concessions to influence the other party's behavior. The use of planned concessions signals that it is now the other party's turn to reciprocate and make a concession on an important issue. There is a natural tendency for an individual to respond in kind when receiving a concession.
- *Venue.* Some negotiators insist on negotiating in a location that is more favorable to them. One party may have to travel a great distance, face the sun, or sit in an uncomfortable chair in an effort to create stress. Also, the choice of venue can affect whether or not a negotiator can get up and leave the negotiation at a critical time.

According to Robert Cialdini, an expert on the psychology of negotiation and conflict resolution, we can cluster the hundreds of negotiation tactics that exist into six general categories, which represent fundamental social psychology principles that guide human behavior.[17]

- *Reciprocation.* Virtually every human society adheres to the principle of reciprocation, which means that we feel an obligation to give something back of equal or greater value to someone after we have received something from them. In negotiation, this principle creates an obligation to return something in kind when the other party offers a concession. Effective negotiators understand the influence that reciprocity has on most individuals. Negotiations have a definite pattern in the concession exchange process and can strongly influence the level of concession offered by each party. However, it is often unnecessary to respond to a concession at the same or higher level of value if the concession requested is important to you.
- *Consistency.* This principle says that we prefer to be consistent in our beliefs and actions. In a negotiation, if we can get others to agree to something, then not following through on their part would be inconsistent and irrational, a behavior to be avoided. Also, skilled negotiators also understand that, after someone agrees to something, he or she feels better about that decision than before he or she agreed. Furthermore, once a small commitment is in place, it becomes easier to request larger commitments later. The consistency trap is a very powerful tactic and can be difficult to back away from.
- *Social Proof.* According to this principle, we look to the behavior of others to determine what is desirable, appropriate, and correct.[18] This principle often works against us in negotiations if we look to others to determine our behavior. For example, a seller may state that a well-respected company uses its product, thereby providing social proof of the value of the purchase to the buyer.
- *Liking.* This principle states that we work well and are more agreeable with people we like or who are like us. Effective negotiators, therefore, should take sufficient time to get to know their counterparts, knowing that desired concessions are more likely when a favorable level of familiarity exists.
- *Authority.* This principle states that we are more likely to accept the positions, arguments, and direction from recognized authority figures, not unlike the impact of legitimate power described above. In a negotiation, a senior sales executive may be able to substantially influence an inexperienced buyer, simply because of his or her implied authority or formal position in the organization.
- *Scarcity.* Sellers learn early in their career the powerful influence that scarcity, or even the perception of potential scarcity, can have on a buyer. Who wants to close a plant because supply will be short next month (unless the buyer acts now)? The same argument applies to price increases. If the product will be scarce at the new price, then the implication is that the buyer needs to act before the price increase takes effect.

A tactic used during one negotiation may not be successful or applicable to another negotiation, even with the same counterpart. When conducting a negotiation, effective negotiators must be willing to modify tactics that are not effective and prepare for responses to tactics that are likely to be used against them. Tactics are most effective when the other party is unprepared, stressed, under severe time deadlines, inexperienced, fatigued, or disinterested. Be prepared, and don't react off the cuff without analyzing the tactic and its real effects.

Win-Win Negotiation

Many traditional supply managers believe that the primary objective of negotiation is to win at the expense of suppliers. We call this win-lose negotiation (also called competitive or distributive bargaining). **Win-lose negotiation** means that two or more parties are competing over a fixed value with the winner taking the larger share. It is also known as a zero-sum, or fixed-sum, game—if one party gains, it is only at the expense of the other party. Every increase in the purchase price benefits only the seller, and every decrease in price benefits only the buyer. There are no other possible outcomes. The level of competition in a win-lose purchase negotiation rarely makes a supplier anxious to cooperate with a buyer to provide advantages that are not available to other customers. There is no inherent advantage for the supplier to do so.

Win-win negotiation (also called integrative bargaining) seeks to expand the value or resources available to all participants through collaborative negotiation. The parties still negotiate, but they do so to determine how to equitably divide a bigger and expanded value pie through the use of creative proposals. For example, increased value to the buyer may mean receiving a more favorable purchase price than a competitor, a shorter order cycle time from the supplier, joint efforts to reduce duplication or waste between the parties, or assistance in developing new technology or product designs. On the supplier's side, increasing value may mean additional sales volume, preferential treatment for future business, or technical assistance provided by the buyer to help reduce its operating costs. Exhibit 13.5 contrasts the characteristics of win-lose and win-win negotiation.

The fundamental question of win-win negotiation is how the buyer and seller, through a collaborative negotiation process, can pursue integrative bargaining and expand the pie available to both parties. Previous research has identified five different methods for pursuing integrative (win-win) agreements.[19]

- *Expand the Pie.* Working closely together, the parties identify creative ways to expand available resources or generate new value obtained through a negotiated agreement. For example, the seller that offers a buyer early access to new technology for inclusion in its own new products can help create new

Exhibit 13.5 Characteristics of Win-Lose and Win-Win Negotiations

CHARACTERISTICS OF WIN-LOSE NEGOTIATION (DISTRIBUTIVE BARGAINING)	CHARACTERISTICS OF WIN-WIN NEGOTIATION (INTEGRATIVE BARGAINING)
• Assume rigid negotiating positions.	• Understand each other's needs and wants.
• Compete over a fixed amount of value.	• Focus on common rather than personal interests.
• Practice strict use of power by one party over another.	• Conduct joint efforts to solve problems and develop creative solutions that provide *additional* value.
• Pursue adversarial relationships.	• Engage in open sharing of information.

value. If the market embraces the new product, presumably sales will increase, and the supplier will receive larger purchase orders. Both parties become better off.

- *Logroll.* Successful logrolling requires the parties to identify more than one issue where disagreement exists. The parties agree to trade off these issues so each party has a top-priority issue satisfied. This is a form of compromise in which each party gets more in those issues that are most important to him or her while giving up more on those issues that are less critical yet are important to the other party.
- *Use Nonspecific Compensation.* With this approach, one party achieves his or her objective on an issue while the other receives something of value as a reward for going along. This approach works only when the compensating party knows what is valuable to the other party and makes a reasonable offer to make the other party whole for agreeing.
- *Cut the Costs for Compliance.* With cost cutting, one party (usually the buyer) gets a lower price as the parties work jointly to reduce the seller's costs or the transaction costs of doing business together. The buyer satisfies his or her objective of a obtaining a competitive price while the seller becomes more competitive in the marketplace due to a reduced cost structure.
- *Find a Bridge Solution.* Bridging involves inventing new options that satisfy each party's needs. Although bridging solutions will likely not totally satisfy each party, they are usually satisfactory to each side. As in the third point of Triangle Talk (propose action in such a way that they can accept it), the negotiators seek to jointly create solutions that satisfy the interests and needs of both parties.

A win-win negotiation approach works best for items or services that are important to the buyer's products or business or when the item involves high-dollar items or services where cost control is critical. It is also appropriate when the supplier adds a high level of value to the product or service. When variables such as technology, cycle time, quality, and price/cost are important, win-win negotiating may also be the best approach.

Good Practice Example

Mack Trucks Uses Negotiation to Rev Up Its Sourcing Process

Mack Trucks, which is part of a newly consolidated operation comprising the truck-making units of Volvo, Renault, and Mack, is facing intense pricing pressure from customers and competitors. The ability to meet its financial targets has presented a major challenge for the company. With limited ability to raise truck prices and declining demand, the alternatives facing Mack were to manage material costs better or absorb price increases through lower profit margins and profitability.

Even before Volvo assumed ownership of Mack Trucks and Renault, Mack and Renault sought to leverage the commonality between them on a global basis. Mack Trucks had concluded that procurement offered excellent opportunities for global synergy across Europe and North America. Mack Trucks, working jointly with Renault, had implemented a global sourcing process designed to leverage the volumes available through the combined truck units. Volvo Truck is now part of that process. A central part of this process features negotiation to help the three combined companies carry out their vision of global procurement.

MACK TRUCK'S GLOBAL SOURCING PROCESS

The global sourcing process at Volvo/Renault/Mack Trucks, originally developed by Mack, consists of nine steps. Part of the benefit from this process is the discipline built into each step concerning the completion of tasks. Cross-functional sourcing teams are responsible for following this process as they develop and negotiate global procurement contracts. The company uses the nine-step process even for contracts that the sourcing teams determine are regional rather than global.

Exhibit 13.6 describes the Volvo/Renault/Mack Trucks' nine-step global sourcing process. Steps 0–4 of the process involve strategy development, whereas Steps 5–8 involve strategy implementation.

STEP 0: SELECT GLOBAL SOURCING PROJECTS

An executive steering committee is responsible for selecting sourcing projects and identifying the cost savings expected from each project. The steering committee plays a vital role in maintaining the intensity of the global sourcing process. Step 0 is continuous because the agreements established early in the global process eventually come up for periodic review and/or renewal.

STEP 1: LAUNCH THE PROJECT

Perhaps the most important task associated with Step 1 is the formation of sourcing teams. The executive team selects team members based on their familiarity with the items under review. A formal team leader works with the team to develop time schedules, a list of deliverables, and expected milestones.

In Step 1, the teams validate the sourcing opportunity by collecting and analyzing data. Various tools are available to support each team's analysis. For example, the teams use a portfolio analysis approach with suggested tactics and strategies depending on the characteristics of the purchase requirement. This tool helps the team develop a sourcing strategy that best matches the actual purchasing need.

STEP 2: DEVELOP THE SOURCING PROJECT

Some managers believe this step to be the most critical, as the sourcing teams identify potential worldwide suppliers. From a list of potential suppliers, the teams sends a request for information, which is a generic questionnaire that asks about sales, production capacity, quality certification (such as ISO 9000), familiarity with the truck business, and major customers.

Exhibit 13.6 Nine-Step Global Sourcing Process

Step 0:	Select Global Sourcing Projects
Step 1:	Launch the Project
Step 2:	Develop the Sourcing Project
Step 3:	Develop Requests for Proposals
Step 4:	Recommend Strategy and Negotiate with Suppliers
Step 5:	Certify Suppliers
Step 6:	Formalize the Sourcing Contract
Step 7:	Sample Testing and Approval
Step 8:	Production Readiness

Step 2 requires a major work effort on the part of engineering. Engineers will examine drawings in an effort to standardize part specifications among Volvo, Renault, and Mack Trucks. Although a team may conclude that there is no global supplier, they may be able to standardize design specifications across the companies.

STEP 3: DEVELOP REQUESTS FOR PROPOSALS

Step 3 features the development, sending, and analysis of formal proposals to suppliers identified in Step 2. Suppliers typically require six weeks to analyze and return the RFPs. The sourcing teams are responsible for analyzing the details of the returned RFPs. The teams are empowered to determine the criteria and the evaluation weights used to analyze each supplier, but members must reach consensus in their choices about which suppliers to recommend.

A negotiation workshop occurs during this step at the Renault Learning Center in France. The purpose of this workshop is to review the tools that are necessary to support the global process and to improve negotiation skills. The first half of the meeting is committed to overall training. The second half helps individual teams develop their negotiation strategy. The teams will also select a negotiation leader. The decision of who should be the negotiation leader is based on discussion and consensus rather than voting. Of the first 27 global projects, fully one third of the negotiation leaders were selected from outside the sourcing team.

STEP 4: RECOMMEND STRATEGY AND NEGOTIATE WITH SUPPLIERS

Each sourcing team makes a strategy recommendation to an executive committee comprising the vice president of purchasing and the vice president of engineering from each of the three companies. Team recommendations include the selected supplier(s) to use with expected savings and timings identified.

All negotiation that occurs in Step 4 is face-to-face with suppliers. To date, half of the negotiations have occurred in the United States and half in Europe at company-owned sites. When suppliers arrive for a negotiation, they review the global sourcing process so they are aware that this step will only produce a recommendation.

Before suppliers arrive for negotiations, they receive feedback concerning their competitiveness, which allows them to revise their proposal before negotiations commence. A team may disqualify a supplier if the supplier is not competitive and chooses not to revise its proposal. The negotiation also serves as an opportunity to verify that new suppliers can meet technical or commercial requirements.

Once the lead negotiator takes over, the team leader's role begins to diminish (unless the team leader is the lead negotiator). The team leader usually remains part of the negotiating team. Negotiation sessions generally last three hours. Although the team's objective is to achieve cost savings, the negotiations can discuss many kinds of issues.

STEP 5: CERTIFY SUPPLIERS

During Step 5, the purchasing and engineering groups receive the global sourcing team's recommendation and results from the negotiation. Functional directors will begin budgeting expected savings in their financial plans. The output from Step 5 is a certification from affected functional groups of the recommended supplier. Step 5 represents a hand-off of a proposed and negotiated sourcing strategy from the global sourcing team to the purchasing, engineering, and quality groups.

STEP 6: FORMALIZE THE SOURCING CONTRACT

This step involves formalizing what transpired during contract negotiations. The negotiation leader remains with the process until the contract is complete. The legal department is also involved, but a buyer writes the contract using a predetermined template.

Global contracts, which are typically two to three years in duration, differ from traditional contracts. The global agreements include productivity improvement requirements to offset material cost increases and encourage technical advancements by the supplier. And, in a somewhat significant departure from previous contracting practices, incentives such as 50/50 improvement sharing are starting to appear.

STEP 7: SAMPLE TESTING AND APPROVAL

This step assesses the samples provided by the selected supplier. The production facilities develop initial sample inspection reports, and the negotiation leader develops a production rollout plan.

STEP 8: PRODUCTION READINESS

Step 8 is the pilot production stage. The selected supplier may send a day's worth or a week's worth of supply for use and testing in actual production.

The Good Practice Example illustrates how a company uses negotiation to add value to its sourcing process. Without highly skilled and well-trained negotiators, the development of global sourcing strategies, such as the one illustrated here, would not be possible. The magnitude and complexity of global agreements, which are usually longer term in length and address many non-price issues, demand face-to-face negotiation.

International Negotiation

With the burgeoning growth in international business, especially in outsourcing and global sourcing activities over the last 20 years, the need to effectively and efficiently negotiate across cultures has increased exponentially. Thomas Friedman gave us an example of a truly global supply chain in his recent book, *The World Is Flat,* in which he describes how Dell sources components for and builds its notebook computers.[20] In a truly global supply chain, Dell utilizes multiple suppliers located in a variety of countries for different parts and components. If a given Dell supplier is unable to meet current demand, then Dell can shift its sourcing to another supplier with available capacity regardless of location. For example, Dell can shift its sourcing of Intel microprocessors from factories located in the Philippines, Costa Rica, Malaysia, or China. Therefore, different negotiation strategies are needed to negotiate purchase agreements in such diverse cultures as Costa Rica and Malaysia.

Negotiations with suppliers located literally anywhere on the globe take on added complexity and challenge when the parties have different languages, customs, laws, and cultures. When preparing for a negotiation with a supplier located in another country, companies must invest in substantial extra time and effort in planning for the negotiation to accommodate new translation, travel, and other foreign business requirements. One of the more important considerations in negotiating a global sourcing agreement is culture shock.[21] Culture shock occurs as a result of negotiators being immersed in a place in which their established norms have been confronted and may no longer be applicable. The negotiator's pre-existing values, beliefs, rules, and schema may not apply in the new situation. Emotions run higher, and they may initially encounter substantial anxiety, disorientation, and confusion, thereby reducing the likelihood of achieving their desired negotiation outcomes.

Various barriers may dramatically affect the conduct of international negotiations.[22] In order of importance, major obstacles to effective international negotiation include miscommunication due to language, time limitations, cultural differences, and limited authority of the international negotiator. Effective international negotiators also demonstrate certain personal characteristics that can help overcome these obstacles. These characteristics include patience, knowledge of the contract agreement, an honest and polite attitude, and familiarity with foreign cultures and customs. See Sourcing Snapshot: FedEx Expert Shares His International Negotiating Insights for a look at how one company effectively considers the nuances and differences between cultures to more effectively negotiate.

Beyond the natural barriers of language differences, it is still possible to fail to understand and be understood. What we consider as generally accepted words may have substantially different meanings in other countries, even between countries that speak the same language, because culture plays such a significant role in communication. For example, during international negotiation, an interpreter might verbally communicate yet not fully convey the significance of unspoken actions, signals, and customs that are invisible to the foreign or non-native negotiator.

Sourcing Snapshot

FedEx Expert Shares His International Negotiating Insights

Mike Babineaux, senior business specialist at FedEx's Strategic Sourcing and Supply Center of Excellence, offers good advice for any American who negotiates internationally. "Every person who negotiates with other cultures must be aware of the serious and costly mistakes and misunderstandings in business practices that are caused by cultural differences," warns Babineaux. Although nations, on the surface, are changing every day in many ways, the fundamentals of culture evolve at a much slower pace.

In the area of communication, Babineaux says, "Americans tend to speak directly and openly. We want the truth, and we want it now. We are suspicious when we think someone is being evasive." Unfortunately, the American who proceeds in the direct American style in a negotiation will not be particularly effective in some countries. "He or she will be on a different wavelength than the foreigner because our style of communication is very different from others," he explains. An open person may be seen as weak, directness may come across as abrupt, and written contracts may imply that a person's word is not good. In the end, Babineaux explains, "Negotiators who have the greatest success in doing business around the world are those who have learned to have credible appreciation and understanding of those with whom they do business."

Source: Adapted from J. Mazel, "5 Negotiation Experts Reveal Their Secrets to *Supplier Management,*" *Supplier Selection and Management Report,* March 1, 2000, available at http://www.ioma.com.

International negotiation requires additional planning and preparation to be successful. Not only must buyers perform their normal supplier analysis and fact finding, they must also strive to more fully understand the customs and traditions of their counterpart. As buying and selling increases between organizations located in different countries, the need for higher-level global negotiation skills will also increase.

Selected Countries

The following presents a sample of national characteristics when negotiating, admittedly from an American perspective. However, understanding these profiles can prove beneficial when developing negotiation strategies and tactics.[23] A negotiator must be aware, however, that there is a danger in stereotyping or oversimplifying characteristics of different cultures. There is always substantial interpersonal variation to consider within a single culture. However, there are certain tendencies within the culture of which to be aware.

The following discussion outlines very general observations and guidelines for several popular business cultures (shown in alphabetical order) in which a supply manager is likely to negotiate.

Brazil

Although Brazilians are receptive to discussing most subjects, home and family are private, personal matters and are not appropriate topics for casual acquaintances. Avoid conversations involving religion or politics. You may speak English or use an interpreter unless you are conversant in Portuguese. They are generally more analytical than other Latin American cultures and will look at the particulars of each situation rather than referring to rules or laws for guidance. They like to bargain and concede little by little. During negotiations, Brazilians tend to approach problems indirectly, allowing their feelings, passion, and enthusiasm to influence their decisions. Although the presentation of facts during a negotiation is acceptable, these facts usually will not overrule underlying subjective feelings. The image of the macho male is still prevalent, although to a lesser extent than in Mexico, for example, and Brazilian men expect women to be subordinate. There are also large numbers of German and Japanese descendents in Brazil, which may complicate the negotiation somewhat.

China

When negotiating with the Chinese, it is important to avoid slang or jargon and to use short, simple sentences with pauses to ensure your words are understood exactly. Never do anything that might embarrass your Chinese counterpart. A negotiator should expect to make presentations to many groups at various organizational levels. Because U.S. managers have a reputation for impatience, the Chinese will extend negotiations beyond the deadline to gain an advantage. Do not exaggerate your ability to deliver on your promises. Your counterparts will hold you to your commitments. They may even try to renegotiate previously agreed-upon issues on the last day, and they will continue to try for a better deal even after signing the agreement. However, you must be patient in your dealings with Chinese negotiators, who also prefer to deal with groups, not individuals. Use an interpreter, even if your Chinese counterpart speaks excellent English.

France

Given their highly formal and reserved nature, a casual attitude during business may alienate the French. Allow for sufficient time to conduct the negotiation, as decisions are made slowly and deliberately. During negotiations, arguments are made from a critical perspective with elegant wit and logic. The French enjoy engaging in debate, striving for effect rather than detail and facts. You should consider using a local agent to assist with the process. Although the French will accept information for the purpose of debate and may even change their minds, a desire to maintain a strong cultural heritage often prohibits them from accepting anything that is contrary to their cultural norm. Because the French are strongly individualistic with a centralized authority structure, negotiating with the proper individual can lead to quick decisions. Dress conservatively in well-made clothing.

Germany

Germans are not openly receptive to outside information. Their strict hierarchies and separation of units often prohibit the sharing of information even across the same organization. These hierarchies can also slow the making of business decisions. Germans rarely engage in humor during business activities. During a negotiation, objective facts form the basis of truth rather than subjective feelings, and Germans are highly analytical. Nowhere is punctuality more important than in Germany. Arriving just two or three minutes late to a negotiation can be insulting. During negotiations, Germans tend to be unemotional because of a high need for social and personal order. German contracts are often more detailed and specific than in the United States, and documentation and clarity are both very important.

India

English is widely spoken in India among businesspeople and government officials; therefore, it is less necessary to obtain an interpreter or translate one's business cards. Be sensitive of the need to avoid personal questions and talking about religion, poverty, or politics. It is important to speak with the highest-ranking person possible, as decisions are made at the highest levels of the organization. Organizations in India tend to be very hierarchical and autocratic. In addition, Indian bureaucracy is very burdensome, while the pace of business tends to be leisurely. As a result, delays in the negotiation are to be expected. Vegetarian diets are typical, and business negotiations often occur in prominent hotels, not in restaurants. Titles are highly valued, so always address your counterparts by their official titles.

Japan

Japanese culture is vastly different from American culture. Despite such differences, the extra effort needed to develop mutually satisfying negotiations can result in an excellent relationship—Japanese firms are dependable and loyal suppliers. They will treat their customers like valuable family members. The negotiation process with Japanese companies is unique. For example, the Japanese are comfortable with extended silence, which is not true with Americans. As members of a collectivist society, they are loyal team players concerned with the well-being of their country and firm rather than themselves as individuals. Politeness is valued above all else. Instead of saying "No," the Japanese often say "Hai," which does not indicate agreement but merely that they hear or understand. The Japanese don't like surprises, and they typically reach decisions through a consensus process, which can often extend negotiations. When negotiating, keep in mind that it is necessary to convince the whole group rather than a single individual. Also, avoid placing the Japanese in a position in which they must admit failure or lose face. The Japanese do not like the appearance of having to make forced concessions. There is a strong emphasis on interpersonal relationships and less on formal contracts. Therefore, connections with intermediaries are important. Choose them wisely.

Mexico

As in Brazil, subjectivity is often the basis for decision making. Mexican negotiators enjoy the process of bargaining and exchange. The pace of business activity will be much slower than what Americans are used to. It is important to develop and maintain close personal friendships with the right people. Individual dignity is important, so be polite and avoid anything that might embarrass your Mexican counterpart. The foreign negotiator should emphasize the benefits of a proposal to the individual, his or her family, and pride. Financing is often an issue, so you need to be creative in offering financial solutions. It is customary for the oldest person to pick up the tab for a group meal, although it is typical to haggle over the check. It is important to recognize a person's title and position.

Russia

Russian negotiators are very patient, as compromise is considered a sign of weakness. However, they tend to make very extreme initial demands and wait for the foreign negotiator to concede. Final offers are seldom final during the initial stages of negotiation. Long-term interpersonal relationships are less important than in many other cultures. They expect you to walk away from the table and threaten that you cannot reach agreement with them. However, Russian negotiators often have limited authority to make decisions at the table and will refer to absentee third-party decision makers. You need to be aware that some negotiations are designed only to generate information, not make a deal. End-of-negotiation demands are typical, even though you may assume that the deal is complete. Because of the inconvertibility of the ruble, financing may be difficult and require creative solutions such as countertrade or third-party financing.

Saudi Arabia

Saudi negotiators are considered astute and perceptive. They may stand very close to you and place a hand on your shoulder. Concession making is ritualistic and stems from extreme opening proposals. Decisions take time to materialize from extensive deliberation. Deadlines are made to be ignored. As in many other cultures, developing and maintaining a strong interpersonal relationship with your counterpart is important. Social life usually takes place during the day, as there is no nightlife as we might expect at home. Saudi negotiators rely heavily on their religious beliefs to make decisions. Also, plan your trip so as not to conflict with religious holidays. "Yes" generally means "maybe."

Vietnam

You will need to be patient and wait until your Vietnamese counterpart initiates the business discussion. Answers to many questions will be broad and not very specific. A nodding head does not mean "yes," merely that you are being heard or even that they disagree with you. Patience is very important and is often used to wear down the foreign negotiator into making unreciprocated concessions. Use of a skilled interpreter is vital as there are various nuances to the words chosen and gestures made. Speak to the other party, not to the interpreter. Vietnamese typically negotiate in a group setting, not individually.

The Impact of the Internet on Negotiations

Use of information technology, particularly the Internet, e-mail, and instant messaging, can dramatically change the nature of a negotiation. Electronic means of negotiation tend to equalize the interactions between the parties because normal visual cues and sources of power are not as evident.[24] Status differences are not as visible, and social norms and behaviors are more difficult to discern. Voice inflections, which often provide substantial meaning to the words used to communicate, do not exist electronically. The use of such devices as emoticons attempts to provide context but is not as effective as nonverbal communication, which is missing from electronic negotiations. In addition, the negotiator at the other end of the electronic connection is relatively anonymous. Is the person you think you are negotiating with actually doing the negotiating?

Research indicates that negotiators communicating by electronic means often a different persona than they do face-to-face. They engage in more risky behaviors and are more aggressive in their demands than their face-to-face counterparts. E-negotiators make more aggressive demands, threats, and take-it-or-leave-it ultimatums. Information richness, usually obtained from nonverbal clues, context, and informal communication, is lost electronically. In addition, active listening and effective feedback are more difficult to conduct when not negotiating face-to-face.

E-negotiators tend to engage in behaviors that indicate that they are communicating in real time even when they are not. The normal give-and-take in a face-to-face negotiation is not present, and the e-negotiators ask fewer questions and tend to make more assumptions during the negotiation. For example, what does silence mean when the negotiators are communicating electronically? Also, e-negotiators often feel less accountable for the outcomes because of a perceived disconnect with their counterparts in a different locale. They also tend to take on a more adversarial, "us-versus-them," mentality. The bottom line is that negotiators who interact face-to-face are more likely to reach agreement and avoid impasse than their electronic counterparts.

Considering all of the challenges in negotiating electronically, it remains a business reality that some negotiations, particularly global negotiations, must be accomplished at a distance because of timing constraints and substantial travel costs. One way to mitigate the negative effects of a distance-challenged negotiation is to conduct an initial face-to-face meeting prior to e-negotiations. This face-to-face meeting helps to foster greater trust and reduce uncertainty in future interactions that are conducted electronically. Many long-term sourcing agreements can be facilitated effectively in this manner, that is, an initial physical meeting followed by electronic-facilitated communication. If a face-to-face meeting is impractical, some of the same positive effects can be accomplished initially through the use of a telephone call or videoconference between the parties, allowing for an informal period of sharing and getting to know your counterpart as a person.

Good Practice Example

Texas Instruments Provides Its Procurement Professionals with Comprehensive Global Negotiation Skills and Enhanced Cultural Understanding[25]

Many U.S.-based companies have successfully demonstrated their negotiation and relationship skills in dealing with domestic suppliers. However, those same levels of negotiation skills and relationship management experience often prove inadequate when dealing with an increasingly global supply base. There are substantial caveats and challenges involved in negotiating with foreign suppliers, particularly in the initial stages of negotiating a sourcing contract. In 2003, Texas Instruments (TI) developed and implemented a comprehensive professional development program to more effectively prepare its procurement professionals and others within the company to comprehend, value, and appropriately act in response to those cultural differences they will face in foreign cultures where they conduct business.

TI introduced this cultural awareness program in response to a corporate strategy that focused on finding and utilizing suppliers in low-cost countries and regions, such as Eastern Europe and Asia. The program allows TI's procurement professionals to develop higher-level negotiation and relationship skills with suppliers located in these cultures. These professional development programs are delivered by internal personnel and can be tailored to TI employees operating throughout the world. Training can be specifically adapted to cultural differences encountered and for different industries, companies, and products.

Program deliverables include the ability to challenge personal expectations and assumptions from both the buyer and supplier perspectives, describe the buyer's expectations in clear and understandable terms, scrutinize and cultivate understanding of the supplier's assumptions, and bridge the differences encountered in the exchange process. The overall program objective is to prevent, preclude, or mitigate the difficulties and disruptions that would typically be encountered when negotiating with people from other cultures.

One of the prime benefits from this has been the ability of negotiators to understand why previous negotiations may not have gone as well as expected. Building on this expanded knowledge and cultural awareness, the outcomes from more recent negotiations have been more in line with company expectations. Those who have completed this training have been able to effectively break down negotiation and relationship barriers. It has proven important to understand the supplier's perspectives and values and take them into active consideration when planning and conducting a sourcing negotiation. The TI courses have also conditioned participants to be better prepared to deal with the extended time frames typically involved in negotiating with global suppliers due to the need for protracted relationship building. One additional benefit that doesn't relate to global negotiations is that the same skills have been applied to improving the performance of TI's global work teams.

CONCLUSION

An organization's commercial success is partly due to the skill of its negotiators, from both its buying and selling activities. Regardless of the industry, skilled negotiators share some common traits. They realize that they are not born with the requisite negotiation knowledge and skills. Therefore, they must study, practice, and train to become more effective negotiators. Research shows that skilled negotiators also have higher aspirations and pursue more aggressive goals than their less-effective counterparts, which they generally achieve. Finally, individuals who are skilled at negotiation are destined to be among an organization's most valued professionals.

Professional supply managers must become more effective negotiators by participating in training, simulations, and workshops that develop these critical negotiation skills. The difference between a good sourcing agreement and an excellent one is often more a function of the level of preparation and interpersonal and relationship-building skills of the negotiator or negotiating team.

KEY TERMS

bargaining, 472
Boulwarism, 478
fact, 472
interest, 462
issues, 472
needs, 462
negotiation, 462
objective, 470
plan, 470
planning, 470
position, 462
power, 474
settlement zone, 472
strategy, 473
tactics, 469
wants, 462
win-lose negotiation, 481
win-win negotiation, 481

DISCUSSION QUESTIONS

1. Why is negotiation such an important part of the purchasing process?
2. Discuss the resources necessary to support effective negotiation planning and execution.
3. The parties to a sourcing negotiation can discuss many issues besides price. Select five non-price issues over which a buyer and seller can reach agreement, and explain why each issue might be important to the buyer or seller.
4. Will electronic purchasing through the Internet increase or decrease the need for negotiation between buyers and sellers? Why?
5. Develop a profile of a skilled or effective negotiator.
6. Contrast a win-win negotiator with a win-lose negotiator.
7. Discuss different strengths and weaknesses that a buyer and seller might bring to the negotiating table.
8. What information should a buyer gather about a supplier before entering a negotiation?
9. What are likely to be the most important sources of power in a buyer-seller negotiation?
10. Why are concessions important during a sourcing negotiation? How do the parties to a negotiation demonstrate their willingness to compromise?

11. What is the risk of relying too heavily on the typical profiles of international negotiators? Is there a benefit to using these profiles?
12. Why does a negotiator who practices Boulwarism risk sending a negotiation into deadlock?
13. Give examples of tactics practiced by a buyer or seller that might be considered unethical.
14. Discuss the concept of BATNA and explain how a negotiator can effectively use it to plan a negotiation.
15. Describe the technique of using Triangle Talk to plan a sourcing negotiation.

ADDITIONAL READINGS

Acuff, R. L. (1997), *How to Negotiate Anything with Anyone Anywhere around the World,* New York: AMACOM.

Anderson, K. (1994), *Getting What You Want: How to Reach Agreement and Resolve Conflict Every Time,* New York: Plume.

Bazerman, M. H., and Neale, M. A. (1992), *Negotiating Rationally,* New York: Free Press.

Burr, A. M. (2001), "Ethics in Negotiation: Does Getting to Yes Require Candor?" *Dispute Resolution Journal,* 56(2), 8–15.

Cialdini, R. B. (2001), *Influence: Science and Practice* (4th ed.), Boston: Allyn and Bacon.

Corvette, B. A. B. (2007), *Conflict Management: A Practical Guide to Developing Negotiation Strategies,* Upper Saddle River, NJ: Pearson Prentice Hall.

Fells, R. (1989), "Managing Deadlocks in Negotiation," *Management Decision,* 27(4), 135–141.

Fisher, R., and Ury, W., with Bruce Patton (Ed.) (1991), *Getting to Yes: Negotiating Agreement without Giving In,* New York: Penguin Books.

Fogg, R. W. (1985), "Dealing with Conflict: A Repertoire of Creative, Peaceful Approaches," *Journal of Conflict Resolution,* 29(2), 330–358.

Gelfand, M. J., and Brett, J. M. (Eds.) (2004), *The Handbook of Negotiation and Culture,* Palo Alto, CA: Stanford University Press.

Ghauri, P. N., and Usunier, J.-C. (Eds.) (1996), *International Business Negotiations,* Tarrytown, NY: Pergamon.

Hendon, D. W., Hendon, R. A., and Herbig, P. (1998), "Negotiating across Cultures," *Security Management,* 42(11), 25–28.

Hunt, P. (2000), "Making a Good Deal," *Supply Management,* October 5, pp. 37–39.

Kublin, M. (1995), *International Negotiation: A Primer for American Business Professionals,* New York: International Business Press.

Lewicki, R. J., Saunders, D. M., and Barry, B. (2006), *Negotiation* (5th ed.), New York: McGraw-Hill Irwin.

Lewicki, R. J., Saunders, D. M., Minton, J. W., and Barry, B. (2003), *Negotiation: Readings, Exercises, and Cases* (4th ed.), New York: McGraw-Hill Irwin.

Lytle, A. L., Brett, J. M., and Shapiro, D. L. (1999), "The Strategic Use of Interests, Rights, and Power to Resolve Disputes," *Negotiation Journal,* 15(1), 31–51.

McCormack, M. H. (1995), *On Negotiating,* Los Angeles: Dove Books.

McRae, B. (1998), *Negotiating and Influencing Skills: The Art of Creating and Claiming Value,* Thousand Oaks, CA: Sage.

Miller, P., and Kelle, P. (1998), "Quantitative Support for Buyer-Supplier Negotiation in Just-in-Time Purchasing," *International Journal of Purchasing and Materials Management,* 34(2), 25–31.

Mintu-Wimsatt, A. (2002), "Personality and Negotiation Style: The Moderating Effects of Cultural Content," *Thunderbird International Business Review,* 44(6), 729–748.

Moran, R. T. (1991), *Dynamics of Successful International Negotiations,* Houston: Gulf Publishing.

Morrison, T., Conaway, W. A., and Borden, G. A. (1994), *Kiss, Bow, or Shake Hands: How to Do Business in Sixty Countries,* Holbrooke, MA: Adams Media Corporation.

Mortensen, K. W. (2004), *Maximum Influence: The 12 Universal Laws of Power Persuasion,* New York: AMACOM.

Shell, G. R. (2006), *Bargaining for Advantage: Negotiation Strategies for Reasonable People* (2nd ed.), New York: Penguin Books.

Thompson, L. (2005), *The Mind and Heart of the Negotiator* (3rd ed.), Upper Saddle River, NJ: Pearson.

Watkins, M. (2002), *Breakthrough Business Negotiations: A Toolbox for Managers,* San Francisco: Jossey-Bass.

ENDNOTES

1. Shell, G. R. (2006), *Bargaining for Advantage: Negotiation Strategies for Reasonable People* (2nd ed.), New York: Penguin Books, p. 6.

2. Acuff, R. L. (1997), *How to Negotiate Anything with Anyone Anywhere Around the World,* New York: AMACOM, p. 18.

3. Thompson, L. (2005), *The Mind and Heart of the Negotiator* (3rd ed.), Upper Saddle River, NJ: Pearson, p. 2.

4. McCormack, M. H. (1995), *On Negotiating,* Los Angeles: Dove Books, p. 7.

5. Fisher, R., and Ury, W., with Bruce Patton (Ed.) (1991), *Getting to Yes: Negotiating Agreement without Giving In,* New York: Penguin Books, p. 100.

6. Thompson, p. 46.

7. Fisher and Ury, pp. 10–11.

8. Anderson, K. (1994), *Getting What You Want: How to Reach Agreement and Resolve Conflict Every Time,* New York: Plume, pp. 10–15.

9. Waxer, C. (2001), "E-Negotiations Are In, Price-Only E-Auctions Are Out," *iSource,* June, pp. 73–76.

10. Lewicki, R. J., Saunders, D. M., and Barry, B. (2006), *Negotiation* (5th ed.), New York: McGraw-Hill Irwin, p. 113.

11. Lewicki et al., p. 447.

12. Lewicki et al., p. 35.

13. Thompson, citing original work by French and Raven, *The Bases of Social Power,* in *Studies in Social Power,* Ann Arbor: University of Michigan Press, 1959.

14. Lewicki et al., pp. 188–191.

15. Lewicki et al., p. 51, citing original work by D. W. Hendon, M. H. Roy, and Z. U. Ahmed, "Negotiation Concession Patterns: A Multicountry, Multiperiod Study," *American Business Review,* 2003, 21, 75–83.

16. Lewicki et al., p. 51.

17. Cialdini, R. B. (2001), *Influence: Science and Practice* (4th ed.), Boston: Allyn and Bacon.

18. Thompson, pp. 164–165.

19. Lewicki et al., pp. 83–86.

20. Friedman, T. L. (2006), *The World Is Flat: A Brief History of the Twenty-First Century, Release 2.0,* New York: Farrar, Straus and Giroux, pp. 515–520.

21. Martin, D., Mayfield, J., Mayfield, M., and Herbig, P. (2003), "International Negotiations: An Entirely Different Animal," in R. J. Lewicki, D. M. Saunders, J. W. Minton, and B. Barry (Eds.), *Negotiation: Readings, Exercises, and Cases* (4th ed.), New York: McGraw-Hill Irwin, pp. 340–343.

22. Min, H., and Galle, W. (1993), "International Negotiation Strategies of U.S. Purchasing Professionals," *International Journal of Purchasing and Materials Management,* 29(3), 46.

23. Morrison, T., Conaway, W. A., and Borden, G. A. (1994), *Kiss, Bow, or Shake Hands: How to Do Business in Sixty Countries,* Holbrooke, MA: Adams Media Corporation; and Acuff.

24. Thompson, pp. 304–316.

25. Atkinson, W. (2007), "Texas Instruments Trains Buyers on Global Negotiating Skills," *Purchasing,* August 16, 16–17.

Chapter 14

CONTRACT MANAGEMENT

Learning Objectives

After completing this chapter, you should be able to

- Understand the different types of contracts that exist
- Develop knowledge of long-term contracts and when they should be used
- Understand different types of contracts for nontraditional areas of spending
- Understand legal alternatives to contractual disputes that work

Chapter Outline

The Journey to Contracting Transformation at Roche Diagnostics

Back in 2003, David Barnes and his small team of contracts professionals at Roche Diagnostics knew that their process was under pressure. Contract management was a tactical, largely administrative activity, struggling to keep pace with their growth and the increasing complexity of industry pricing schemes. Resources were deployed to fill gaps as they arose, resulting in a fragmented organization, spread between different business groups and with significant role variations. Short-term technical "fixes" were no longer sufficient.

As vice president for finance, Barnes could see that the current organization was full of inefficiencies. The transactional nature of the contracts work limited sharing of information, resulting in very little replication and no consolidation of data to understand trends, issues, or opportunities to improve. His instincts for quality told him that this was an area that could yield significant benefits, so his team set to work.

Initially, they focused on software. Clearly, this problem was not unique, so there must be an application to address it. Solutions were identified, but they certainly were not cheap. And during the voyage of discovery, the team came to realize that they lacked experts and had no real sense of contracting "best practices."

BUILDING CONSENSUS

Analysis soon revealed a range of negative consequences that arose from a manually intensive, decentralized organization with no overall contracts strategy. These included a heavy administrative burden on Sales as well as on their customers' procurement groups, and time-consuming financial and billing reconciliations. It was also clear that contracting policies and practices were being applied inconsistently.

The team recognized that change would not be easy; an effective contracting strategy and consistent process would require the support and agreement of many internal stakeholders: Marketing, Legal, Pricing, Regulatory, Sales, Credit, and HR were among them. "Executive support was critical to our success," Barnes comments. "We knew that we had a mountain to climb, so we established an Executive Steering Committee."

Strategy, process, people, and technology—these were the four areas that the project had to address. Having gained agreement on the need for a center of excellence (CoE), the team defined its mission: "Roche Diagnostics' Contracting CoE will deliver industry-leading contract life cycle management that creates a competitive advantage and ensures quality, driving sustainable market share, sales, and profitability."

It was in 2004 that Roche became aware of IACCM and invited a visit to review their work and discuss best practices. Later that year, IACCM issued its best practices benchmark study, detailing the top 10 areas requiring focus. "At last this gave us something tangible against which we could assess our plans and monitor our progress," Barnes explains. "We found we had recognized many of the items on their list, but were tackling only some of them. That was OK—we knew we must prioritize."

MONITORING PROGRESS

In the early phases, the Sales groups were reluctant to agree on any centralization or rationalization, for fear that this would damage flexibility and responsiveness to customer needs. It was important to demonstrate that centralization did not equate to increased bureaucracy or a rigid, rules-based mentality. The question of ownership was inevitably sensitive and highly political. So rather than dictate an answer, the question was posed to the cross-functional project team: Where should this report? They produced a helpful matrix of pros and cons.

The Reporting Line Challenge

	FINANCE (CFO)	SALES	LEGAL	OPERATIONS
Pro	Knowledge of the broad picture	Understands creating deals	Strong audit ties	Neutral party
	Understands price/ margin	Understands customer needs	Sarbanes-Oxley	Close to product supply/logistics
		Great prep to become a commercial leader	Understands risk	Close to credit
		Customer facing		
Con	Not close to customer; may not understand specific needs	Lacks knowledge of the entire process and system capabilities	Focus on a narrow scope	Not close to customer needs; may not understand specific needs
	"Go/No Go" mentality	Volume philosophy versus margin	Not close to customer needs; may not understand specific needs	Product knowledge
		"Fox watching the hen house"		

"In the end," Barnes says, "the team agreed on Finance because of our process focus and our ability to understand risk and opportunity tradeoffs."

Today, the re-engineering has resulted in substantial progress on five of the IACCM top ten. These include close alignment with product life cycle management; development of an electronic contracting strategy; proactive change management; and strategically aligned measurements and reporting.

"Having external benchmarks definitely assisted our progress," Barnes says. "It motivated the team and confirmed we were on the right track. It also gave management a sense of confidence that we were doing the right things, that investment made sense."

But in the end, the project depended on visible results to obtain continued support and funding. "Good results continue to get funded," Barnes says, "but you need evidence." To ensure that quality and continuous improvement were built into the process, the team established a Contracting Strategy Board and obtained a seat for Contracts at key meetings; they built robust monitoring processes, including strong feedback loops from the field, the market, and customers. "Proactive people are key," Barnes comments. "You must hire people who want to make a difference—and are not afraid to be held accountable."

THE JOURNEY CONTINUES

Nearly three years on, we asked Barnes to define the tangible results and benefits from the journey. He highlighted seven.

1. Earlier realization of business benefits
2. Improved or advanced cash flow
3. More efficient operations
4. More effective control environment (SOX)
5. Improved customer/partner relationships
6. Better communication/information flow
7. Improved employee morale: satisfaction in doing it right!

"Make no mistake," he comments. "We still have a way to go in achieving our contracting CoE vision—there are many benefits yet to be realized! To get there we will continue to leverage the resources of IACCM including their training programs, their interest groups, their best practices, and their good counsel."

Source: www.iaccm.com.

Introduction

In global commerce, people make risky deals—and make promises they can't keep. They sign a contract without reading it, and one they do not understand. They make risky assumptions, without noticing it, and make or accept unreasonable demands with or without knowing it. They assume that the terms of one market are acceptable in another, and do not recognize cultural or legal landmines. All of these are major pitfalls in the current global economic environment.

The area of managing contracts in a global environment continues to be a major source of problems, misunderstanding, and poor execution for companies we interviewed. Moreover, companies often fail to be able to bring the required resources to bear in contractual discussions that fall outside of "normal" contractual guidelines that are traditionally accepted in Western settings. As noted earlier, this is particularly true in Asia Pacific and Latin America, where there are significant differences in the perception of how to view and manage contractual relationships, and the importance of legislative action versus ongoing commitment and relationship management as an element that supersedes contractual terminology. Many executives in international settings recognize that seeking legislative retribution for contract noncompliance is often a nonproductive outlet, especially given the uncertain and risk-laden environment for many judicial disputes. As such, many companies seek to resolve issues through a process known as "preventive contracting," which involves spending more time in the initial contracting stages to fully understand stakeholder requirements, expectations, and repeated communication of expectations, in order to gain a full understanding of elements. Another important element was the need for flexibility in contractual terms and clauses, in order to facilitate mutual benefit for the sustenance of the relationship, given highly volatile market input factors and uncertain factor demands.

These issues were reflected in a recent study[1] in which a number of interviews with key individuals discussed some of the challenges they had experienced in global contracting environments:

> *Our global corporate culture demands ultimate flexibility from the supplier. We will give you no demand forecast, and we expect you to do it. We can also terminate at will and will retain all of the IP rights—so all the flexibility is on our side. Strangely enough, suppliers see this as unreasonable. So when they see that, they will of course assign costs to this requirement. We are blind, as we force them to give us all the flexibility, as if there is NO COST to doing so! We need to have some flexibility in establishing price redetermination clauses, and have the ability to tie it into quantity discounts. However, we are unable to stick to any forecast or*

production curve, which presents a huge risk in the marketplace. We cannot give suppliers a forecast that they can depend on.

What we need to do is to be able to break the contract into three key chunks: (a) standard T's and C's with basic housekeeping elements, which we know we can get right, (b) commercial terms for this specific deal around quality and price determination, and (c) actual pricing structures which reflect the changes in the marketplace. This is the biggest challenge for us on a global contractual basis.

In considering the challenges around contracts, Louis Brown, the father of preventive law, who wrote the now-famous *Manual of Preventive Law,*[2] noted the following:

> *It usually costs less to avoid getting into trouble than to pay for getting out of trouble.*

What this means is that contracts are a critical juncture for determining the success or failure of a commercial relationship. It is better to spend the time up front to discuss expectations, define specific language and terminology, and ensure 100% communication of potential contingencies than fight a lawsuit later on when things go wrong! Despite the obvious simplicity of this statement, firms continue to fight lawsuits at an escalating rate, and firms continue to expend extraordinary funds on legal dispute resolution and lawsuits. One executive noted the following:

> *We have a legal counsel to avoid litigation. We will do everything possible to stay out of the court systems—because it always costs money to do so. We do not want to be involved in appearances of the big bad Fortune 100 company versus the little supplier. Ethically we seek to do the right thing. We will settle and go to extremes to stay out of the press. Disagreements around labor contracts with consultants and manpower people are one of our biggest headaches. Suppliers who are supplying IT labor to us seem to cause a big problem. We buy $12 billion of labor annually and a lot of this is with smaller companies. We have been proactive in leveraging of labor spend. We appear to use global suppliers, but in reality they will outsource and tier down to a second- or third-tier supplier. Unfortunately, if we push down to a supplier in their first year, $5 million worth of business, and they have no credit line, many are not able to handle the business, and default with their second-tier suppliers. We want to deal only with first tier from a leveraged standpoint, but the complaints still bubble up. And we end up having to resolve the conflicts and try to keep it out of court and out of the press.*

Because supply professionals buy products and services as a career, it is not surprising that they deal regularly with contracts and complicated Tier 1 and Tier 2 supplier contracts. It is therefore critical for supply managers to understand the underlying legal aspects of business transactions and develop the skills to manage those contracts and agreements on a day-to-day basis. Once a contract has been negotiated and signed, the real work begins. From the moment of signing, it is the supply manager's responsibility to ensure that all of the terms and conditions of the agreement are fulfilled. If the terms and conditions of a contract are breached, purchasing is also responsible for resolving the conflict. In a perfect world, there would be no need for a contract, and all deals would be sealed with a handshake. However, contracts are an important part of managing buyer-supplier relationships, as they explicitly define the roles and responsibilities of both parties, as well as how conflicts will be resolved if they occur (which they almost always do!).

The importance of understanding contracts is even greater in the Internet age. President Clinton signed the Electronic Signatures in Global and National Commerce Act in early 2000, which recognizes electronic signatures as equivalent to hard copies, but there are important exceptions for noncommercial contracts such as divorce settlements, wills, and many other types of contracts where electronic signatures do not have legal parity with written signatures. This law facilitates the full integration of business transactions via the Internet and was a major stepping-stone to future developments in electronic commerce. However, the importance of understanding contracts and "reading the fine print" should not be overshadowed by this event. In fact, it makes the role of contracts even more important in e-business.

This chapter addresses contracting from several perspectives. The first sections address the core elements of a contract and how purchasing managers go about writing a contract. Then, the different types of contracts available to purchasing managers are described. The next section deals with an important type of contract being used more in purchasing scenarios: long-term contracts and alliance agreements. In the following section, we discuss a number of unique contracts, involving information systems deployment, minority business contracts, consulting, and construction. In the final section, we conclude with an important element: how to settle contractual disputes in a buyer-supplier relationship when they arise.

Elements of a Contract

Although there are significant differences in the specific wording and details of contracts employed by supply managers for sourcing products, processes, and services, the structures of contracts used in purchasing products and services are fairly standard and have a number of common attributes. In general, these attributes are established by a firm's legal counsel and then are modified for different types of suppliers, products, and services. The important point to remember is that contracts establish the terms and conditions by which two parties agree to conduct business. They define the type of relationship and pave the way for ensuring that both parties come away with mutual benefits. As such, it is always better to spend more time in negotiations to ensure that the right terminology, measures, and requirements are spelled out in detail and agreed to. If both parties are clear about their understanding of how they will work together, the likelihood that there will be problems and misunderstandings is reduced significantly. It is much more difficult to go back and negotiate what contractual terms actually mean once the contract has been signed and a period of time has passed! In this regard, contracts are sometimes compared to human relationships and nuptial vows; you'd better define your understanding of what the expectations will be early on, rather than try to define expectations after the marriage has taken place!

A contract typically begins with an introduction of the parties who will be engaged in the contract. For example, it might begin with the following:

THIS AGREEMENT IS MADE this ________ day of ________ 2008

BETWEEN

1. ABC COMPANY LIMITED, a company registered in England and having its registered office at 44 Downing Street, London (the "Buyer") and
2. XYZ, INC., a corporation duly organized under the laws of the State of Illinois and having its principal place of business at 123 Ridge Road, Chicago, Illinois 60014, U.S.A. (the "Supplier").

Following the introduction, there are several numbered sections (called "clauses") that describe the different sets of conditions that the parties agree to follow in their conduct of their business relationship. These clauses in the first part of the contract may also refer to a series of "schedules" that provide specific details behind the clauses. These schedules may provide additional information on the method of manufacture, the statement of work, how to calculate specific measures, heath and safety requirements, pricing schedules, and other important details. The schedules (which are typically contained in the appendices at the end of the contract) are where the real "meat" of the negotiations has often taken place. The following example of a specific contract between two companies (a large Fortune 500 company and a mid-sized service supplier) is used to illustrate typical contract structures with clauses and schedules. Bear in mind that there will be major variations in the details of a contract, but the contract structure that follows is fairly representative of what most supply management students will use in contract negotiations.

1. *Definitions.* This section defines all of the important terms contained within the contract and is important so everyone understands exactly what each term means. It is better to get this clear up front, to avoid confusion later on. Some of the typical terms might include the product or service definition and terms such as raw materials, purchase orders (POs), on-time delivery, and price. Although these might seem obvious to some people, if it is in writing, it is clear!
2. *Scope of Agreement.* This section defines what is in and out of scope. This might include the geographical limitations, the validity or invalidity of prior contracts, preferential treatment by the supplier, or other elements.
3. *Purchase Orders.* This section outlines the relationship between the Agreement and any other purchase orders issued by the company to the supplier. For example, it might state that "any Purchase Order for Products submitted by a Buyer affiliate during the term of this Agreement shall be deemed to be on the terms and conditions set out in this Agreement." This also stipulates what happens if a purchase order is cancelled and what happens if terms conflict between the PO and the Agreement, and which document supersedes which.
4. *Supply and Delivery.* This clause specifies the terms for supply and delivery of the product or service. For instance, if there is a 10-day lead time stipulated between order placement and delivery, what happens if the supplier does not deliver in time? This clause may also reference an appendix that provides additional details on how delivery is measured, what is considered on-time delivery, what are the penalties for late delivery, and other details.
5. *Specifications, Quality, and Health, Safety, Environment.* This clause describes method of manufacture and quality requirements, and may include language specific to terms of quality (e.g., "The Products delivered under this Agreement shall be manufactured in conformity with any mandatory requirements of applicable law in the country of origin or supply and any international standards relevant to such Products."). Charges for delivery of off-specification products or services may also be identified in the appendix. For services, a

Statement of Work contained in the appendix will provide details of the exact scope of work to be performed and the service quality expectations. Finally, elements associated with safety, health, and environmental standards are identified in terms of expectations from the supplier.

6. *Payment.* This section may specify terms such as "current price," "prior price," and other criteria that determine how or if prices will be adjusted over the course of the contract. Again, details of how often prices will change and any indices associated with pricing change agreements or related to cost-savings sharing are identified in a schedule in the appendix.
7. *Liability.* This can sometimes be a contentious clause and may often contain language such as "The Supplier shall assume entire responsibility for and shall defend, indemnify and hold Buyer and Buyer's Affiliates harmless against all losses, liabilities, costs and expenses arising directly or indirectly out of or in connection with this Agreement or any Purchase Order and arising from injury or damage to the property of the Supplier." The clause generally specifies who is responsible if there are injuries or damage, over the course of the contract, and any damages to be paid. This may also include insurance requirements and subsupplier issues as they arise.
8. *Force Majeure.* This clause describes the course of events that occurs if there are unforeseen events such as earthquakes or hurricanes that prevent a supplier from fulfilling its obligations to the buyer. Generally, this clause includes language such as "The party whose performance of this Agreement is so affected shall notify the other party as soon as is reasonably practicable giving the full relevant particulars and shall use its reasonable efforts to remedy the situation immediately."
9. *Effective Date and Termination.* This clause states when the contract becomes effective, when it terminates, and any agreements relating to conditions when the contract can be extended beyond the termination date. It also stipulates whether either party has the ability to terminate the contract at any time, and how much advance notice must be given.
10. *Intellectual Property.* This clause specifies conditions regarding who owns any intellectual property (IP) that comes out of the agreement, and who owns what IP going into the agreement. If an innovation comes out of the agreement, there may also be stipulations as to who owns the "residuals" of that IP.
11. *Assignment and Contracting.* This clause stipulates whether the supplier can assign its rights described in the agreement to another party, and whether subcontracting is permissible.
12. *Technology Improvements.* If the buyer becomes aware of any technology or cost improvements of other products in the market, this section may specify whether they can share this information with the supplier, and how the supplier should act on this information.
13. *Most Favored Customer.* This clause states whether the buyer can expect to receive preferential status over the supplier's other customers. This is not only difficult to measure, but also difficult to enforce, so it is not always used in practice.
14. *Confidentiality.* This clause ensures that all information, technology, and so on shared between the parties remains confidential and is not shared with other customers or suppliers.

15. *Statistics.* This clause provides guidelines regarding what type of reporting statistics and measures the supplier must provide to the buyer on a regular basis, defined clearly. Additional details may be in a schedule in the appendix.
16. *Key Performance Indicators and Compensation.* This clause provides specific details on how the supplier's performance will be measured and if any compensation will be awarded by the supplier to the buyer if these defined levels of performance are not maintained. For example, if delivery falls below 90%, there may be a penalty the supplier will need to pay.
17. *Notices.* This clause establishes where bills, invoices, notices, and other documents should be sent, as well as the key contact person at the buying and supplying company to whom to direct all questions and issues concerning the relationship.
18. *Severability.* This clause describes how an issue will be addressed if a portion of the agreement is void or unenforceable, and which court of law will resolve the difference.
19. *Third-Party Rights.* This clause stipulates that any benefits attributed to a third party (other than the buyer and supplier) identified in the contract must be enforced. For example, if there is a bank that handles transactions between the two and charges a fee, this fee must be paid by the parties according to the agreement.
20. *Free Trade Areas.* This clause identifies any free trade issues and benefits, and how to share the benefits.
21. *Minority- or Women-Owned Business Enterprises.* This clause stipulates that the supplier agrees to use its best efforts to support MWBE (Minority- and Women-Owned Business Enterprises) purchasing or that a certain percentage of its business must be awarded to MWBE enterprises.
22. *General.* Any other general business principles.
23. *Governing Law.* This clause stipulates the court of law where any disputes will be settled. This clause contains language such as "Mandatory application of local law or a statement to the contrary in the relevant Purchase Order, which is agreed to by the Supplier, shall be exclusively governed by the laws of England." This clause may also stipulate the use of arbitration or other forms of conflict resolution (described later in this chapter).
24. *Signatures*

IN WITNESS WHEREOF this Agreement has been duly executed by the parties hereto, the day and year first above written.

ABC COMPANY LIMITED

By: ____________________

Name: ____________________

Title: ____________________

XYZ, INC.

By: ____________________

Name: ____________________

Title: ____________________

An example of schedules that may be used in the appendices include the following:

Schedule 1: Product/process/service specifications, statement of work, or scope of work

Schedule 2: Prices and price adjustment mechanisms

Schedule 3: Health, safety, and environment guidelines and requirements

Schedule 4: Packaging materials

Schedule 5: Approved method of manufacture, delivery, or service deployment

Schedule 6: Delivery targets and lead times

Schedule 7: Supplier's hours of operation

Schedule 8: Storage and inventory control

Sourcing Snapshot

Services Contracts at Intuit Share Risk and Reward with Suppliers

Intuit, a premier provider of small business and personal finance software such as Quicken and QuickBooks, decided in 2004 that to better serve the overall organization, every contract written must go through procurement. The four contract managers who managed contact centers procurement were assigned to specific business units to provide continuity and a single point of contact. To provide consistency and ensure the coverage of all key issues, Intuit developed a standardized Master Service Agreement (MSA) that is used for all call center contracts. The MSA contains all of the terms of the agreement including potential risks and opportunities. Pricing, technology, and performance expectations are created to clearly define both supplier and Intuit responsibilities, as well as the terms for non-conformance to the specifications. Key elements of the MSA include (1) Services, generic services to be performed by the supplier with reference to the statement of work, (2) Intuit's Obligations, which provides the supplier with training and licenses to software they will support during the provision of services and other obligations, (3) Business Turndown/Upturn and Disaster Recovery, which sets up expectations when there is a significant turn in business and sets up planning in case there is a disaster, (4) Compensation and Payment Terms, including early payment discount, process for disputed invoices, and maintaining financial records, (5) Quality Control/Gain Share Opportunities, supplier requirements for QC, (6) Term/Termination, events required to terminate the agreement prior to the term, and (7) Ownership, which outlines the property rights of all software, works from the agreement, and other materials. Other terms include Confidential Information, Representation and Warranties, Indemnification, Insurance, Limitation of Liability, Dispute Resolution, and General. Attachments to the MSA will generally include the Statement of Work, Privacy Requirements, Security Requirements, Reimbursement/Expendable Items, and Amendments to the Statement of Work. The Risk and Reward clause is a unique aspect and identifies specific performance metrics as part of the contract to be used as a baseline. If suppliers exceed expectations on key performance parameters, they may receive additional payments, or conversely their payments may be adjusted if they fall short of the baseline. This is used to motivate the supplier to meet or exceed contractual service levels and encourage continuous improvement.

Source: L. Ellram and W. Tate, "Managing and Controlling the Services Supply Chain at Intuit," *Practix*, CAPS Research, August 2004; www.capsresearch.org/Research/Practix.aspx.

Schedule 9: Quality assurance manual

Schedule 10: Loss allowance calculations and throughput allowances

An example of how one company, Intuit, structured its contract master service agreements is shown in Sourcing Snapshot: Services Contracts at Intuit Share Risk and Reward with Suppliers. Notice that the flow of the contract provides greater and greater detail around the expectations. Next, we describe how such contracts are developed.

How to Write a Contract

Most commonly used contracts are developed from earlier contracts that are subsequently modified to fit the situation at hand. Although this procedure minimizes the amount of administrative effort required each time a purchase contract is written, there is a danger in blindly assuming that all past contracts will be appropriate, particularly in dynamic environments where technology changes occur rapidly or where there are few legal precedents. Purchasing managers should keep a contract file and refer to portions of previous contracts to create a contract that uniquely fits the situation at hand.

The most appropriate method of drafting a new contract is to start with a general form (or forms) and samples of past contracts for similar situations. Purchasing managers will often get advice from the legal department or appropriate counsel and create several different general forms for the various types of purchase situations that may be routinely encountered. Verifying the following information will help ensure that the contract is appropriate:[3]

- The contract identifies clearly what is being bought and the cost.
- The contract specifies how the purchased item is going to be shipped and delivered.
- The contract covers the question of how the items are to be installed (if installation is to be a part of the contract).
- The contract includes an acceptance provision detailing exactly how and when the purchaser will accept the products.
- The contract addresses the appropriate warranties.
- The contract spells out remedies including liquidated damages and clauses specifying the consequences for late performance.
- The contract does a good job on the "boilerplate," which includes the standard terms and conditions common to all contracts and purchase agreements. It is common among these clauses to include a force majeure clause that identifies the conditions under which performance is excused. Common items included in a force majeure clause are war, embargo, and changes in the law.

The purchasing manager should consider arbitration or other dispute resolution mechanisms for inclusion in the contract. The advantages of arbitration are important: Arbitration is fast and confidential, with less variance in outcome or damage awards, and it is not appealable. It is always a good idea to double-check all attachments to the contract, because many of the technical details are included there.

Technical sections of the contract are typically the greatest source of misinterpretation of terms and conditions. For instance, if the contract contains a clause that says, "This is the entire agreement," remember that this means exactly what it says; there are no other additions or modifications to the agreement that are enforceable. This is called an "integration clause" and should be located near the end of the contract.

In developing international contracts, purchasing managers should pay particular attention to the following details:[4]

- *Forum selection.* In the event of a dispute, where would the arbitration forum for resolving the dispute take place?
- *Choice of law.* The parties to an international contract should agree on the contract law that will govern the contract in the event of a dispute.
- *Payment.* What currency will be used to make payments under the contract?
- *Language.* The contract should specify the official language to be used in the contract, as translations are not exact.
- *Force majeure.* It is common in international contracts to excuse performance when events take place that make performance as called for in the contract impossible. Force majeure clauses typically excuse performance when war, natural disasters, or political upheaval occurs.

Types of Contracts

Purchasing contracts can be classified into different categories based on their characteristics and purpose. Almost all purchasing contracts are based on some form of pricing mechanism and can be categorized as a variation on two basic types: fixed-price and cost-based contracts. As described earlier, the general description of the type of price/cost mechanism is contained in the "Payment" clause, but the actual details describing the specific nature of the pricing formula, cost elements, pricing index, or other elements is typically described in a schedule in the appendices. If a specific formula-based pricing or costing model is going to be used, it is also a good idea to include an example in the schedule that shows how the price or cost should be calculated given the data that is available, so everyone clearly understands how the calculation occurs. The major types of contracts are shown in Exhibit 14.1 on p. 508.

Fixed-Price Contracts

Firm Fixed Price

The most basic contractual pricing mechanism is called a firm fixed price. In this type of purchase contract, the price stated in the agreement does not change, regardless of fluctuations in general overall economic conditions, industry competition, levels of supply, market prices, or other environmental changes. This contract price can be obtained through any number of pricing mechanisms: price quotations, supplier responses to the buying organization's requests for proposal, negotiations, or any other method. Fixed-price contracts are the simplest and easiest for purchasing to manage because there is no need for extensive auditing or additional input from the purchasing side.

If market prices for a purchased good or service rise above the stated contract price, the seller bears the brunt of the financial loss. However, if the market price falls

Exhibit 14.1 Types of Contracts

TYPE OF CONTRACT	DESCRIPTION	BUYER RISK	SUPPLIER RISK
Firm fixed price	Price stated in the agreement does not change, regardless of any type of environmental change.	Low	High
Fixed price with escalation/ de-escalation	Base prices can increase or decrease based on specific identifiable changes in material prices.	↑	↑
Fixed price with redetermination	Initial target price based on best-guess estimates of labor and materials, then renegotiated once a specific level or volume of production is reached.	│	│
Fixed price with incentives	Initial target price based on best-guess estimates of labor and materials, then cost savings due to supplier initiatives are shared at a predetermined rate for a designated time period.	│	│
Cost plus incentive fee	Base price is based on allowable supplier costs, and any cost savings are shared between the buyer and supplier based on a predetermined rate for a designated time period.	│	│
Cost sharing	Actual allowable costs are shared between parties on a predetermined percentage basis and may include cost productivity improvement goals.	↓	↓
Time and materials contract	Supplier is paid for all labor and materials according to a specified labor, overhead, profit, and material rate.		
Cost plus fixed fee	Supplier receives reimbursement for all allowable costs up to a predetermined amount, plus a fixed fee, which is a percentage of the targeted cost of the good or service.	High	Low

below the stated contract price due to outside factors such as competition, changes in technology, or raw material prices, the purchaser assumes the risk or financial loss. If there is a high level of uncertainty from the supplying organization's point of view regarding its ability to make a reasonable profit under competitive fixed-price conditions, then the supplier may add to its price to cover potential increases in component, raw material, or labor prices. If the supplier increases its contract price in anticipation of rising costs, and the anticipated conditions do not occur, then the purchaser has paid too high a price for the good or service. For this reason, it is very important for the purchasing organization to adequately understand existing market conditions prior to signing a fixed-price contract to prevent contingency pricing from adversely affecting the total cost of the purchase over the life of the contract.

Fixed-Price Contract with Escalation

There are a number of variations on the basic firm fixed-price contract. If the item being purchased is to be supplied over a longer time period and there is a high probability that costs will increase, then the parties may choose to negotiate an escalation clause into the basic contract, resulting in a fixed-price contract with escalation. Escalation clauses allow either increases or decreases in the base price depending on the circumstances. A greater degree of price protection is therefore provided for the supplier, while the purchaser enjoys potential price reductions. All price changes should be keyed to a third-party price index, preferably to a well-established, widely published index (such as the Producer Price Index for a specific material).

Fixed-Price Contract with Redetermination

In cases where the parties cannot accurately predict labor or material costs and quantities to be used prior to the execution of the purchase agreement (e.g., an unproven technology), a fixed-price contract with redetermination may be more appropriate. In this scenario, the buying and selling parties negotiate an initial target price based on best-guess estimates of the labor and materials to be used in manufacturing a new product. Once a contractually agreed-upon volume of production has been reached, the two parties review the production process and redetermine a revised firm price. Depending on the circumstances surrounding the contract, the redetermined price may be applied only to production following the redetermination, or it may be applied to all or part of the units previously produced. Care should be taken, though, because a contract that calls for an agreement to agree in the future is not enforceable.

Fixed-Price Contract with Incentives

A final type of fixed-price contract is the fixed-price contract with incentives. This contract is similar to the fixed-price contract with redetermination except that the terms and conditions of the contract allow cost-savings sharing with the supplier. As in the redetermination contract, it is difficult for the buying and selling parties to arrive at a firm price prior to actual production.

If the supplier can demonstrate actual cost savings through production efficiencies or substitution of materials, the resulting savings from the initial price targets are shared between the supplier and the purchaser at a predetermined rate. This type of purchase contract is typically utilized under conditions of high unit cost and relatively long lead times. The sharing of cost savings may be 50/50 (or some other split may be a negotiated part of the contract).

Cost-Based Contracts

Cost-based contracts are appropriate for situations in which there is a risk that a large contingency fee might be included using a fixed-price contract. Cost-based contracts typically represent a lower level of risk of economic loss for suppliers, but they can also result in lower overall costs to the purchaser through careful contract management. It is important for the purchaser to include contractual terms and conditions that require the supplier to carefully monitor and control costs. The two parties to the agreement must agree what costs are to be included in the calculation of the price of the goods or services procured.

Cost-based contracts are generally applicable when the goods or services procured are expensive, complex, and important to the purchasing party or when there is a high degree of uncertainty regarding labor and material costs. Cost-based contracts are generally less favorable to the purchasing party because the threat of financial risk is transferred from the seller to the buyer. There is also a low incentive for the supplier to strive to improve its operations and lower costs (and hence price) to the purchaser. In fact, there is an incentive, at least in the short run, for suppliers to be inefficient in cost-based contracts because they are rewarded with higher prices.

Cost Plus Incentive Fee

Another cost-based contract is the cost plus incentive fee contract. This contract is similar to the fixed-price plus incentive fee contract except that the base price depends on allowable supplier costs rather than on a fixed-price basis.

As before, if the supplier is able to improve efficiency or material usage as compared with the initial target cost, then the buying and selling parties will share any cost savings at a predetermined rate. This type of contract is appropriate for cases where both parties are relatively certain about the accuracy of the initial target cost estimates.

Cost-Sharing Contract

With pure cost-sharing contracts, allowable costs are shared between the parties on a predetermined percentage basis. The key to successful negotiation is the identification of a firm set of operating guidelines, goals, and objectives for the contract. When in doubt, the two parties to a cost-sharing contract need to spell out their expectations in as much detail as possible to avoid confusion and misunderstanding regarding their respective roles and responsibilities. Cost-sharing contracts are especially important during a period when raw material prices are increasing. The contract schedule detailing how both parties can share the expense of increasing input costs can prevent major problems and may also ensure that the supplier does not go bankrupt because of its inability to produce the product at a fixed price when the cost of materials is going up. Sourcing Snapshot: Pricing Dispute Leads a Ford Supplier to Stop Production provides a very good example of what can happen if a strong buyer (in this case, Ford) does not work with the supplier (in this case, Collins & Aikman) to restructure a fixed-price contract in the face of escalating raw material costs.

Time and Materials Contract

Another cost-based contract is the time and materials contract. This type of contract is generally used in plant and equipment maintenance agreements, where the supplier cannot determine accurate costs prior to the repair service. The contract

Sourcing Snapshot — *Pricing Dispute Leads a Ford Supplier to Stop Production*

In a sign of the heightened tensions over sharing the financial misery in the U.S. auto industry, parts maker Collins & Aikman Corp. (C&A) took the rare step of cutting off deliveries to Ford Motor Co., a move that caused Ford to temporarily shut down production at an assembly plant in Mexico.

Collins & Aikman's showdown with the nation's No. 2 automaker came in a pricing dispute over instrument panels, carpeting, and other interior plastic parts in which several million dollars were at stake, according to a person familiar with the dispute. People interviewed said that as a result of Collins & Aikman's action, Ford will no longer consider it for future business but won't pull its existing business, at least for now.

This type of contractual disagreement is not surprising, given the current environment for U.S. automotive manufacturers. For years, Detroit's Big Three automakers have squeezed their suppliers in an effort to protect their own profit margins and—more recently—to stanch heavy losses. Ford, General Motors Corp., and Chrysler Group have wrested deep price cuts from their supply networks and have also pushed suppliers to relocate operations to low-cost countries like China.

"The relationship has been irreparably harmed," says Ford spokesman Paul Wood. "We're very disappointed C&A would choose this course of action over a commercial disagreement." The flare-up between Ford and Collins & Aikman, based in Southfield, Michigan, is the latest indication that battered suppliers are fighting harder to get price increases from the Big Three.

Ford, which accounts for 25% of Collins & Aikman's North American sales and is its third-largest customer, made 400 fewer cars than it had intended to build as a result of the production shutdown, according to the people familiar with the dispute.

All three of the nation's big automakers are struggling to make money in North America, and their loss of market share over the past several years has taken a heavy toll on suppliers. Over the past year or so, parts makers have also been hurt by rising prices for commodities such as plastic and steel, and for the most part have been unable to get the Big Three to cover those higher costs. Contractual disputes arising from the inability to factor in pricing agreements tied to raw material costs are largely at the root of this problem.

Now, a half dozen or so of the parts industry's biggest companies, including Collins & Aikman, Delphi Corp., and Tower Automotive, are operating under Chapter 11 protection and are using the bankruptcy courts to push for better terms from the automakers, renegotiating contracts for more money, exiting existing contracts, or demanding financial help from their Big Three customers.

In some cases, parts makers are taking a harder line with Detroit at the urging of hedge funds that have invested millions in distressed automotive suppliers, betting the companies can regain some of their pricing power.

Automotive suppliers occasionally threaten not to deliver parts, but rarely follow through. The few that do are typically very small suppliers that are close to going under. "That's a very rare move and very serious one. It shows there is so much tension and financial stress between automakers and suppliers," says James Gillette, director of supplier analysis for CSM Worldwide, an auto-research firm.

Source: J. McCracken, "Ford Gets Cut Off by a Top Supplier as Detroit Squeezes Parts Makers," *Wall Street Journal,* October 18, 2006, p. A3.

should spell out the appropriate labor rate (generally computed on a per-hour basis), plus an overhead and profit percentage, resulting in a "not-to-exceed" total price. With these terms and conditions, the purchaser has little control over the estimated maximum price. Thus labor hours spent should be carefully audited over the life of the contract.

Cost Plus Fixed-Fee Contract

In a cost plus fixed-fee contract, the supplier receives reimbursement for all of its allowable costs up to a predetermined amount plus a fixed fee, which typically represents a percentage of the targeted cost of the good or service being procured. Although the supplier is guaranteed at least a minimal profit above its allowable costs, there is little motivation for the supplier to dramatically improve its costs over the life of the contract. The U.S. military has been highly criticized for using such contracts on a routine basis with suppliers, which are making above-normal profits for commonly used goods and services at the expense of taxpayers.

To be most effective, cost-based contracts should include cost productivity improvements in order to drive continuous cost reduction over the life of the contract.

Considerations When Selecting Contract Types

Among the more important factors to consider when negotiating with a supplier over contract type are the following (see Exhibit 14.2):

1. Component market uncertainty
2. Long-term agreements
3. Degree of trust between buyer and seller
4. Process or technology uncertainty
5. Supplier's ability to impact costs
6. Total dollar value of the purchase

The first of these factors, component market uncertainty, refers to the volatility of pricing conditions for major elements of the product, such as raw materials, purchased components, and labor. The more unstable the underlying factor market prices, either upward or downward, the less appropriate a fixed-price contract will be for the two parties. Increasing factor market prices will place more risk on the supplying organization, while decreasing such prices will shift the contract economic risk to the purchasing party. (This condition also applies in the case of unstable currency exchange rates in contracts with international suppliers.)

The length of the purchase agreement can also have a significant impact on the desirability of different contract types. The longer the term of the purchase agreement, the less likely firm fixed-price contracts will be acceptable to the supplier. For ongoing purchase arrangements, suppliers will generally prefer to employ fixed price with escalation or any of the cost-based contracts, because they incur less economic risk for the selling party. Purchasing managers must therefore evaluate the economic risk of the different contract types and make a decision as to the acceptability of each type for the entire length of the agreement. For most short-term contracts and in conditions of stable component factor markets, firm fixed and fixed-price with redetermination contracts can safely be applied. The choice of contract type is also dependent on the nature of the buyer-seller relationship.

Exhibit 14.2 Desirability of Using Contracts under Different Conditions

ENVIRONMENTAL CONDITION	FIXED-PRICE CONTRACT	INCENTIVE CONTRACT	COST-BASED CONTRACT
High component market uncertainty	Low	Desirability of use ←——→	High
Long-term agreements	Low	←——→	High
High degree of trust between buyer and seller	Low	←——→	High
High process/technology uncertainty	Low	←——→	High
Supplier's ability to affect costs	Low	←——→	High
High dollar value purchase	Low	←——→	High

If the relationship has been mutually beneficial in the past and has existed for a considerable period of time, a greater degree of trust may have developed between buying and selling parties. In such cases, both buyer and supplier are more likely to cooperate in the determination of allowable costs, thereby preferring cost-based purchase agreements.

For products and services characterized by high process or technological uncertainty, fixed-price contracts are less desirable for the seller. However, if the purchaser has a reasonable estimate of the supplier's cost structure, then cost-based contracts may be preferable because they allow the price to be adjusted either upward or downward depending on the efforts of the supplier. If the supplier can potentially reduce costs through continuous improvement, then an incentive-type contract may prove beneficial to both contracting parties.

As the total dollar value/unit cost of the contract increases, purchasers must spend more effort creating effective pricing mechanisms. The contracting parties must consider each of the factors in Exhibit 14.2 in detail, as well as the total impact of the contract over the lifetime of the agreement. It is important to remember that both parties in a contract must benefit (although not necessarily in the same proportion).

Long-Term Contracts in Alliances and Partnerships

A common method of classifying industrial buying contracts is based on the length of the contract term. **Spot contracts** are defined as those purchases that are made on a nonrecurring or limited basis with little or no intention of developing an ongoing relationship with the supplier. **Short-term contracts** are defined as contract purchases that are routinely made over a relatively limited time horizon, typically one year or less. **Long-term contracts** are contract purchases that are made on a continuing basis for a specified or indefinite period of time, typically exceeding one year. Because long-term contracts involve greater commitments into the future, the contractual terms and conditions must be carefully developed. In this section we focus primarily on long-term contracts, but a number of the considerations covered may apply to shorter-term agreements as well.

Benefits of Long-Term Contracts

Regardless of the terminology used, almost all buyer-seller relationships have a contract (even if it is implied) that governs them. Even when there is no contract, most transactions are covered by a "gap filler" known as the Uniform Commercial Code (UCC), covered in the next chapter. The contract itself is a formal symbol indicating that these joint responsibilities and expectations exist. Effective long-term contracts (with a duration of more than one year) generally have specific and measurable objectives clearly stated in them, including pricing mechanisms, delivery terms, quality standards and improvements, productivity improvements, cost-savings sharing, evergreen clauses, risk sharing, conflict and dispute resolution, and termination of the relationship. Because long-term contracts are increasingly being used in industry, it is worthwhile to discuss the attributes, advantages, and risks of this approach in detail.

Exhibit 14.3 Advantages and Disadvantages of Long-Term Contracts

POTENTIAL ADVANTAGES	POTENTIAL DISADVANTAGES
Assurance of supply	Supplier opportunism
Access to supplier technology	Selecting the wrong supplier
Access to cost/price information	Supplier volume uncertainty
Volume leveraging	Supplier forgoes other business
Supplier receives better information for planning	Buyer is unreasonable

Why would a buying organization consider a long-term contract with a supplier? In a general sense, the buyer usually expects a greater level of commitment from a supplier involved in a long-term contract. Long-term contracts can also result in an opportunity for creating joint value between the contracting parties. Joint value can be enhanced through the sharing of information, risk, schedules, costs, needs, and even resources. In addition, a long-term contract serves as a blueprint or guide for the relationship between the buyer and the supplier. It typically delineates initial price, mechanisms for price adjustments, cost-reduction expectations, intellectual properties such as patents and copyrights, and currency adjustment procedures, as well as any other responsibilities.

There are many reasons why both buyers and suppliers would want to consider a long-term contract (see Exhibit 14.3). These are discussed in more detail here.

Assurance of Supply

Perhaps the most compelling reason to consider a long-term contract, from the buyer's perspective, is that such contracts may reduce the level of risk incurred if shorter-term contracts are employed. By committing to a clearly defined, concise, and mutually beneficial long-term agreement, buyers can reasonably assure themselves of a continued source of supply, particularly important if the material, product, part, or component being procured is subject to potentially severe supply disruptions or extreme variations in quality, price, availability, or delivery. "Most Favored Customer" clauses are especially important when committing to these types of agreements.

Access to Supplier Technology

Long-term contracts can help the buyer to gain exclusive access to proprietary supplier technology. Blocking competitor access to this supplier technology through a long-term exclusivity contract can result in at least a short-term competitive advantage for the buyer. Tying up a supplier in the initial introductory stage of a new or dramatically improved technology product life cycle either forces competitors to spend valuable time and effort searching for a comparable technology elsewhere or means they have to develop it internally. The buying firm therefore can reach the marketplace first and establish a "first mover" advantage. The potential risk here is that the buyer must be forward-looking enough to choose suppliers with the most promising or most marketable technology, at the peril of locking themselves into the wrong technology and losing their expected competitive advantage.

Access to Cost/Price Information

Agreeing to a long-term contract frequently allows the buyer to have access to more detailed cost and price information from the supplier in exchange for the extended contract term. Longer-term contracts create greater incentives for suppliers to improve or expand their processes through capital improvements because they are able to spread their fixed costs over a larger volume. Long-term contracts should be written to include incentive or cost-sharing arrangements (written into a schedule) that reward the supplier for making improvements in its processes while passing some of the cost savings along to the buyer. This additional supplier investment can also result in higher product quality as well as lower costs. Joint buyer-seller teams may work together to improve the supplier's process and divide the resulting savings. The cost-savings sharing terms should be explicitly negotiated and written into the contract (do not assume that the savings will automatically be divided 50/50).

Volume Leveraging

A final benefit of developing a long-term contract is that the buyer can leverage his or her enhanced position to drive the supplier toward a higher rate of performance improvement. Using the added leverage of a long-term, multiyear agreement with the supplier, the buyer can require the supplier to increase its rate of progress up the learning curve and pass along the savings to the buyer at an accelerated rate. This performance improvement can be driven by additional capital investment as described earlier, an accelerated learning curve effect, and a higher level of commitment on behalf of the supplier. Long-term contracts with incentives are based on the notion that as purchase volumes increase, cost structures change. Long-term agreements in cases of increasing volumes should establish productivity improvement goals and cost-savings sharing, where both buyer and seller share in cost reductions achieved. If suppliers are not forthcoming with labor and material cost data, cost models can be developed to improve the buyer's negotiating position using material/labor ratios available from industry databases (see Chapter 11).

Supplier Receives Better Information for Planning

A supplier may have several reasons for preferring a long-term contract. First, the supplier receives better scheduling information, which in turn helps the supplier's production area improve efficiency and materials planning. With less uncertainty in production schedules, the supplier's purchasing departments can buy material in larger quantities, thereby obtaining volume discounts. Second, detailed projections of volumes and delivery dates allow the supplier to better budget the flow of funds and investment stemming from the expectation of continued future volume. In turn, the supplier's organization lowers unit costs, because fixed costs are spread out over a larger number of units. Third, the supplier can realize lower administrative costs over the term of the contract. Less effort is required to seek out and develop replacement volume on an ongoing basis.

Risks of Long-Term Contracts

A buyer or seller must consider a number of risks when evaluating whether a long-term contract is necessary or even desirable. Three primary questions must be asked when developing a long-term contract and considering the risks:

1. What is the potential for opportunism? In other words, how likely is the supplier to take advantage of the purchaser (or vice versa)?
2. Is this the right supplier to engage in a long-term contract?
3. Is there a fair distribution of risk and gains between the parties involved?

Supplier Opportunism

From the buyer's perspective, there is a major risk that the supplier will become too complacent and lose motivation to maintain or improve performance as the contract progresses. Performance deterioration can be observed in a variety of ways: higher price, deteriorating quality and delivery, lagging technology, and increased cycle times. It is important for buyers to build appropriate incentive clauses into their long-term agreements that serve to motivate suppliers to adequately perform as expected over the term of the agreement.

Selecting the Wrong Supplier

An additional risk associated with long-term contracts is the possibility that the best available supplier may not be recognized or chosen to participate in the long-term agreement. It is the buyer's responsibility to conduct adequate research that documents the supplier's past performance, capabilities, financial health and stability, technology roadmap, and commitment to the relationship.

Once a long-term agreement with a given supplier has been executed, it is much more difficult (and expensive) to switch suppliers. In order to ensure a successful future relationship, sufficient time and effort must be invested prior to signing a long-term contract.

Supplier Volume Uncertainty

To be successful, a good long-term contract considers the needs of both parties. The buyer must consider a number of issues from the supplier's perspective. The first and foremost is volume uncertainty, particularly when dealing with a new product or a new customer. Although the prospective buyer may indicate to the supplier that a certain purchased volume level may be expected, there are many reasons why that volume might never be achieved. Possible reasons include overforecasting of requirements, lack of marketability of the end item, intense competition in the marketplace, and other environmental considerations such as government regulation. A related reason is that the item being supplied may be in the mature or decline phase of the product life cycle. A long-term contract that indicates volume growth under these circumstances is unlikely ever to be fully realized.

Supplier Forgoes Other Business

Agreeing to a long-term contract that limits the supplier's ability to service the buyer's competitors might lock the supplier out of several profitable business opportunities. Also, when companies agree to supply a particular customer's needs, this precludes them from taking on more profitable business with other customers later on due to a lack of available capacity. This is particularly true in industries that are approaching full capacity.

Buyer Is Unreasonable

Another risk that the supplier must consider is the likelihood of the buyer making extraordinary demands once the contract has been executed. Unforeseen customer demands typically result in higher costs that the supplier may or may not be able to recover under the terms of the agreement.

Contingency Elements of Long-Term Contracts

Effective long-term contracts contain a number of elements that allow for contingencies that may arise during the course of the contract.

Initial Price

A buyer must focus intently on determining an acceptable initial price because over the course of a long-term contract the price adjustment mechanism will use the initial price as the base for future adjustments. An initial price that is too high will cause all following prices to be too high. A buyer needs to be aware that some suppliers often front-load their initial price by including excess profits, which inflates all future prices. Likewise, if the initial price is too low, then the supplier may not be motivated to perform as expected because all future prices will be too low and unprofitable. In a long-term contract the relationship between the parties is immaterial unless both parties gain something during the course of the exchange.

Price-Adjustment Mechanisms

Selecting an appropriate price-adjustment mechanism is also a key consideration in a long-term contract. If future price adjustments are linked to an outside index or the price of a related product, then care should be exercised in selecting which index or related product is to be used. Choice of the wrong index or related product can also result in higher prices over the term of the agreement.

Supplier Performance Improvements

Buyers should use long-term agreements to obtain specific supplier performance improvements over time. Again, this compels the buyer to conduct extensive research regarding the supplier's capabilities and past performance, as well as determining the types and levels of risk that might be associated with a particular long-term supply contract. Managers must decide whether the contract should be written for a specific period such as three or five years, or whether the contract should be a series of rolling contracts with an evergreen clause, which renews the agreement at the end of every period.

Evergreen, Penalty, and Escape Clauses

An evergreen clause assumes the contract will be renewed every year unless the supplier is otherwise notified that this is not the case. An effective evergreen clause should be based on a periodic joint review period, typically one year or shorter, and should incorporate a point system that rewards the supplier for acceptable performance. In cases when expectations are not met, the purchasing manager may request specific corrective action and may even charge back lost time and expenses to the supplier.

Associated with the evergreen clause is an escape clause, which allows the buyer (and possibly the supplier) to terminate the contract if either side fails to live up to contractual requirements. However, a long-term contract will usually contain terms and conditions that call for a corrective action process if the supplier continually fails to meet its contractual performance requirements. In such a scenario, the buyer must first notify the supplier within a particular time period if the supplier's performance has not met expectations. The supplier will have a specific time period to take corrective action to bring quality, delivery, and responsiveness to acceptable levels. If the supplier has not achieved contractually acceptable levels of performance within the specified time period, then the buyer can terminate the contract without recourse. Long-term contracts should also contain appropriate clauses covering conflict resolution, termination of the agreement, and handling of unanticipated requirements. Such contingency planning may prolong the contract negotiation period up front but may prove to be invaluable later on down the line should problems occur.

Nontraditional Contracting

In addition to long-term contracts, companies must also create special types of contracts with information systems providers, consultants, minority business owners, and service providers. All of these purchases require unique contractual approaches.

IT Systems Contracts

Systems contracts, also known as systems outsourcing, are designed to provide access to expensive computer networks and software that single companies are unable to afford on their own. Examples of systems contractors include SAP, Oracle, IBM, and EDS.

Subcontracting information technology (IT) requirements to an outside service provider is a major contractual issue for companies. Both legal and purchasing executives from the company should bring their expertise to the table on issues that represent a major cost and commitment for the enterprise. Unfortunately, IT departments often enter into such agreements on the basis of technical evaluation without the benefit of input from purchasing or legal, and later pay in the form of higher costs or poor service requirements contained in the "fine print." Prior to committing to an outsourcing contract with such a service provider, a systems outsourcing team should consider the length of the proposed agreement, the role of company growth or downsizing, service provider defaults or contract amendments, data security, control of outsourcing costs, and control of information systems operations. A number of other issues pertain to IT systems contracting.

Systems Contracting Risks

One of the leading causes for failure of systems contracts is that purchasers become locked into price structures that do not adequately reflect changes occurring since the agreement was originally signed. Examples of such changes include dramatic shifts in user demand patterns, dramatically reduced costs for services provided, and quantum leaps in software and hardware technology.

Level of Service

The extent that a systems supplier becomes involved in the buying firm's operation is determined by three basic levels of service: (1) turnkey, (2) modular, and (3) shared. In the turnkey approach, the client company essentially turns over the entire outsourced service at a given point in time. The outsource service provider performs 100% of that function for the buying organization. In the modular approach, the outsource service provider takes on only two or three small functions from the client, using a stepping-stone approach. As the service provider and the client company become more at ease with each other and a higher level of trust develops, additional services are shifted from the client to the service provider. In the shared approach, the service provider and the client company share resources and operational control over the outsourced service. Under the best of conditions, outsourcing systems contracts remains a risky proposition due to the nature of uncertainty associated with the transaction. Purchaser negotiations should focus on price, performance, and procedures.

Price

Purchasers should consider negotiating a fixed, all-inclusive fee instead of relying on a flexible pricing system that may or may not accurately reflect changing business conditions. If future changes are anticipated, then the purchaser should carefully think how contract prices should be set to reflect those changes. Critical pricing issues include the payment method and timing, scheduling of workloads, and reporting. There should also be an auditing process to ensure that the work carried out was billed at the appropriate rate and that the right personnel associated with a work rate actually completed the work.

Performance Criteria

Performance considerations for a systems contract should, at a minimum, include specification of the overall business requirements required by the service provider. The acceptance test criteria should be specified before issuing the contract so that both parties completely understand how the outsourcing system is expected to perform. A primary concern for the purchaser is the development of a measurement system for evaluating the service provider over the course of system development.

A major concern with many outsourced system contracts today is that much of this work is going overseas to countries such as India. Programming, call centers, and software design are increasingly being performed by lower-cost workers in these countries. To ensure that the work is performed according to specific criteria, many enterprises are adopting the Software Capability Maturity Model developed by the Software Development Institute and Carnegie Mellon University. This model ensures that the provider complies with specific criteria measuring elements of software development performance.

The more specific the purchaser can be in providing clear goals and objectives for the service provider to meet, the less likely it is that misunderstandings and conflicts will result.

Procedures

In addition to acceptance criteria, systems contracts should also provide a complete conversion plan that details the steps to be taken in converting from an inhouse system to the outsourced system. Again, the more specific the purchaser can be in providing this information, the less likely it is that serious problems will occur later. Also, the purchaser should be careful in specifying how to handle technological changes. Updates to the system may often be excessive, so language in the contract needs to be included that specifies the cost of such updates. It is the joint responsibility of the purchasing manager and the supplier to ensure that the technology provided remains current with future needs. Various types of information requirements planning techniques can be beneficial in the earliest systems-planning stages to make sure that the system will actually meet user needs.[5]

Other Service Outsourcing Contracts

The use of outsourcing contracts is not limited strictly to information processing. Other potential applications include the following:

- Facility management services
- Research and development
- Logistics and distribution
- Order entry and customer service operations
- Accounting and audit services

Minority- and Women-Owned Business Enterprise Contracts

There have been programs to stimulate growth of minority-owned businesses in the United States since the late 1960s. The term "minority-owned suppliers" is used by the U.S. federal government to describe a company that is at least 51% owned by minorities such as African Americans, Hispanic Americans, Native Americans, or Asian-Pacific Americans (at one time that status also applied to enterprises that were more than 50% owned by women).

Women-owned businesses and firms that are owned by physically disabled people are separate classes of firms with unique designations. The following federal actions were carried out to promote minority-owned businesses:

- Executive Order 11485 (1969): Established by the U.S. Office of Minority Business Enterprise within the Department of Commerce for the purpose of mobilizing federal resources to aid minorities in business.
- Executive Order 11625 (1971): Gives the secretary of commerce the authority to implement federal policy in support of minority business enterprise programs, to provide technical and management assistance to disadvantaged businesses, and to coordinate activities between all federal departments to aid in increasing minority business development.
- Executive Order 11246 (1965): Requires that all contractors that do more than $50,000 worth of business with the federal government must have affirmative action programs for each job category that is under-represented by minorities. "Under-representation" is defined by the 4/5ths Rule, which is the ratio of minority job incumbents relative to their population in the relevant labor market relative to the ratio of nonminorities relative to their population, for each job category. If that ratio falls below 0.8 (4/5ths), then the company must report to the government its plans for remedying the under-representation.

Consulting Contracts

A knowledgeable consultant can often provide an objective point of view and contribute to an analysis of a situation that is not biased in favor of a predetermined solution. An important factor to consider when hiring an outside consultant to perform contract services for a company is that such a person is the purchasing company's agent, not its employee. The distinction is critical because as an agent, the consultant will often maintain ownership of any intellectual properties developed during the consultation. As such, language must be specified in the contract that the intellectual property shared remains with the buyer. Another important element of discussion is regarding "residuals." A residual is new intellectual property (such as tools, methodologies, and knowledge) developed as the result of the interaction between the enterprise and the consulting company. Some companies (such as the Bank of America and others) have specific language in the contract that requires that any residuals created through the contract remain the property of the buyer. This prevents the consultant from taking this knowledge and selling it to a competitor, thereby eliminating the competitive advantage. Further information on best practices for structuring consulting contracts from a recent study is shown in Sourcing Snapshot: Best Practices in Consulting Contracts.

There is an automatic determination of copyright ownership unless the consultant and the client company execute an agreement specifically assigning the copyright to the client company. If the consultant were considered an employee, then the firm—

Sourcing Snapshot — *Best Practices in Consulting Contracts*

A benchmarking study of how different companies manage professional services and consulting contracts was performed by a team of students and faculty at the Supply Chain Resource Cooperative (scrc.ncsu.edu). The study found that 66% of the participating companies used some sort of standardized contractual agreement/form/policy/process for the procurement of professional services. Of those companies that use a standardized contractual agreement/form/policy/process for the procurement of professional services, all of the companies indicated that every element of the agreement/form/policy/process is useful. Another similarity in the data is that none of the participating companies use a different agreement/form/policy/process when procuring professional services for the first time. Furthermore, 66% of the survey respondents indicate that their company's procurement agreement/form/policy/process does not change when urgency becomes an issue (e.g., the company uses a unique process when acquiring immediate services versus those services that are not required until some time in the future). Moreover, 66% of the survey respondents have incentives available to ensure compliance with their company's formal agreement/form/policy/process (e.g., incentive to use preferred suppliers). Finally, 66% of the participating companies use a formal pricing method (e.g., job-specific price list, price scale, or hourly rate) for the procurement of professional services. When responding to the question "What percentage of professional services are purchased from this predetermined/prenegotiated list?" 33% indicated 80%, 33% indicated less than 40%, and none applied for the rest of the respondents.

Source: Supply Chain Resource Cooperative, "Procuring Professional Services," 2003; scm.ncsu.edu.

not the individual, because of the "works made for hire" concept under U.S. copyright law—would own the copyright. One of the legal means to distinguish an independent contractor consultant from an employee is the presence of a written contract that describes the consultant's expected services and the ability to produce the results of the consultation. Also, if the company does not withhold income taxes, the consultant will normally be viewed as an independent contractor, not an employee.

Consultants will typically consider the following six goals when negotiating a consulting contract for their services:[6]

- Avoidance of misunderstanding
- Maintenance of working independence and freedom
- Assurance of work
- Assurance of payment
- Avoidance of liability
- Prevention of litigation

Perhaps the most important clause of a consulting contract is the assurance of payment.

Typical consulting contracts will demand a large down payment, perhaps as much as one third of the total amount. There are a range of options for payment of the balance due, including percentage of work accomplished and time elapsed. Due to the extensive litigative climate in the business world, contracts written by the consultant will seek to minimize the consultant's exposure to liability and subsequent potential litigation. Language in this section of the contract should spell out exactly what the consultant is and is not liable for. Consultants will try to identify those circumstances that may cause the project to fail and for which they will disavow any responsibility.

There are two general causes for litigation arising from a principal-client relationship. The first concerns belief on the purchaser's part that the consulting work was not completed in full, within a reasonable time, or properly. The second concern is when the consultant fails to receive the entire fee that he or she believes was due and proper. Consultants will typically avoid litigation whenever possible to avoid negative public relations. Payment clauses, down payments, and installment payments usually include the following terms and conditions:

- Payment on delivery of the final report
- Late-payment penalties
- A negotiable promissory note or a collateralized promissory note
- The inclusion of an arbitration agreement, so that disputes can be resolved quickly and expertly. Arbitrators are specialized, and a contract can call for selection of arbitrators among specialists. Arbitration agreements generally call for confidentiality and for rapid, nonappealable decisions, which can sometimes salvage a business relationship between the client-business and the consultant, whereas such a relationship is unlikely to survive protracted court litigation.

To summarize, it is critical that purchasing develop a standard contract template/format for all consulting/professional services and ensure that users comply with the use of this template. Adoption of a standard contract template provides visibility regarding a company's policy to all potential consultants. Some companies have an online format that can be downloaded from the company intranet, which ensures that all service-level agreements are built-in. The entire scope of the project should be defined at this level, with emphasis on the various elements of the scope as independent clauses in the contract. These should include deliverables, deadlines, budget, and so on. If a company utilizes an incentive system to reward or penalize suppliers, it should also be built into the contract. Finally, the contract should allow for renegotiation in case of major scope changes.

Construction Contracts

Many construction contracts involve the owner/purchaser seeking bids from approximately four or five contractors. A typical sequence of events starts with the owner/purchaser determining a base of preferred contractor bidders. The bidders are then contacted prior to distribution of the bid package to ascertain if they are interested in preparing a competitive bid for the proposed construction project. Following the distribution of the bid requests, the purchaser usually holds a prebid meeting with interested bidders to answer any questions that they may have regarding the initial bid documents. All future questions are then submitted to the purchaser in writing to prevent any misunderstanding.

All final bid submissions should consider the stated completion period. The purchaser should require that all bid submissions break the total price into different costs by type, phase, or area. The purchaser should also provide guidance to the bidders regarding how the bidders' indirect costs are to be applied. Contractor overhead costs can be segregated into several categories based on the chosen method of cost allocation or recovery. The following are the most common categories:

- Payroll taxes and insurance premiums
- Field project overhead
- Home office overhead

Construction safety requirements are an important aspect of any construction contract. In selecting from a group of bidders who have already qualified because of past safety performance for the project, the following guidelines should be followed:[7]

1. Make a thorough review of each bidder's written construction safety plan.
2. Before the final selection is made, refer to each bidder's previous injury experience to determine if it is current and if any areas need improvement because of an excessive number of one type of injury from the same hazard. Check with government sources such as OSHA to see if there have been any recent citations of the bidder and what corrective measures are required. Calls to the state worker compensation authorities may be a good check to determine if there are any claims that have been filed against the contractor for failure to complete work in a timely manner.
3. Make a site visit to current projects on which bidders are working to see first-hand the day-to-day quality and functioning of each bidder's construction safety program. References from past clients should also be researched in detail.

In all of these cases, the purchaser is seeking to determine whether senior managers in the firm have established an accountability system under which supervisors at all levels are held accountable for their subordinates' accidents. Previous research about the effect of top management on safety in construction has found that safety had to be a goal of top management in order for others in the firm to take it seriously. A buyer of construction services who maintains a "hands-off" policy through the use of "hold-harmless" clauses is in for a surprise if an accident occurs; the only way to guarantee reduced liability for accidents is to ensure that fewer accidents occur.[8]

Once a construction contract has been completed, a monthly job cost summary can be used to identify the contractor's total costs. An actual cost system records the amounts actually expended, while a standard cost system estimates what the cost should be based on known parameters. Any claims presented by the contractor must be carefully scrutinized, as the claimed costs may not actually be incurred costs.

Contractors must be able to substantiate their costs by producing records consistently maintained in the normal course of business.

Purchasers can minimize the likelihood of contractor claims through a number of actions. The first is the presence of a realistic timetable that takes into account foreseeable delays due to factors beyond the control of either the contractor or the purchaser. A second action involves setting clear specifications that define exactly what is to be constructed. Last, the design documents created by the architect should be complete and up-to-date, reflecting any and all changes as they occur. If the contractor presents a claim against the purchaser, the purchaser should insist on the following information, at a minimum, to help determine the accuracy and appropriateness of the contractor's actual costs in the claim:

- A breakdown of the claim by dollar amounts into the greatest possible number of components
- A detailed outline of the derivation of all hourly rates, equipment costs, overhead, and profit
- The underlying assumptions on which the claim is based to help ensure that the claim is not inflated

Contract administrators for construction projects may also wish to employ penalty clauses to avoid prolonged delays in the construction schedule. Technically, penalty clauses are called "liquidated damages clauses." If they are labeled "penalty" clauses, there is a long line of cases that says they are not enforceable. For instance, a liquidated damages fee of $100 to $1,000 per day for every day late can provide strong incentives to the construction firm to meet schedules.

Other Types of Contracts

Some of the other types of contracts that may be encountered by purchasers include the following.

Purchasing Agreements

Agreements that group similar items together for procurement help to reduce the amount of paperwork for numerous and repetitive small orders. Purchasing agreements also increase the buyer's negotiating clout with the supplier by leveraging its volume of business. There are a number of variations of purchasing agreements:

- Annual contracts: Generally run for a 12-month period and may or may not come up for renewal at the end of the year.

- National contracts: Specify that the purchaser will buy a certain amount of goods and services for the duration of the agreement.
- Corporate agreements: Specify that business units within a corporate organization must buy from specific suppliers during the term of the agreement.
- National buying agreements: Nonbinding on either the purchaser or the supplier; typically provide discounts to corporate buyers based on total volume for the corporation as a whole, not for any subunits individually.
- Blanket orders: Typically cover many different items that can be purchased under the same purchase order number, thereby minimizing repetitive paperwork in the purchasing department for relatively low-cost items (e.g., office supplies).
- Pricing agreements: Occur in situations in which a buyer is allowed to automatically discount the published purchase price by a negotiated percentage for all purchases from a given price list or catalog during the contract period.
- Open-ended orders: Similar to blanket orders but allow the addition of items not originally included in the blanket order; may also allow the original purchase order to be extended for a longer term.

Online Catalogs and E-Commerce Contracts

Coupled with the growing trend toward longer-term agreements and consolidated purchasing agreements, many firms have turned to electronic commerce in order to further reduce their administrative overhead. The use of automated online catalogs by major suppliers of MRO items such as Staples, Grainger, and OfficeMax allows users to buy directly from blanket orders and national contracts from their desktop. Such transactions are facilitated by operating resource management systems such as Ariba and Commerce One.

Despite the recent laws validating electronic signatures on contracts, many firms are wary of using electronic contracts and related documents because of a perceived lack of control regarding who is authorized to represent the firm. There are four major issues that buyers and sellers need to be aware of with respect to e-commerce contract:[9]

1. Parity between electronic and paper records. Unless online agreements are enforced, little e-commerce will take place. The prospect of treating electronic records the same as paper records is opposed by many groups. "Record" is the legal term now used to replace "document" or "writing."
2. Enforceability of shrinkwrap, clickwrap, and boxtop agreements and licenses. In many situations, buyers are bound by agreements that are appended to the basic transaction (purchases of goods or transfers of computer software) that have significant legal effects that are not apparent to purchasers at the time of purchase.
3. Attribution procedures. With electronic (mouse-click) purchases, a vendor needs secure mechanisms to be assured that an order received is legitimate. The vendor also wants a procedure that legally points to an individual so that individual's credit card can be debited by the vendor. Accompanying concerns revolve around the conditions under which a vendor can sue a person for an order received online from a website visitor.

4. Digital signatures. With standard paper contracts, signatures have operated to uniquely identify parties to a contract. Recent legislation by Congress attempts to provide several acceptable substitutes for traditional signatures in electronic commerce, but not without some remaining concerns. Article 2 of the UCC is being revised to accommodate e-commerce issues.

Settling Contractual Disputes

All contracts, no matter how carefully worded and prepared, can be subject to some form of dispute or disagreement. It is virtually impossible to negotiate a contract that anticipates every potential source of disagreement between buyer and seller.

Generally speaking, the more complex the nature of the contract and the greater the dollar amounts involved, the more likely it is that a future dispute over interpretation of the terms and conditions will occur. Purchasing managers must therefore attempt to envision the potential for such conflicts and prepare appropriate conflict-resolution mechanisms to deal with such problems should they arise (see Exhibit 14.4). Sourcing Snapshot: Online Dispute Resolution also describes a more recent application of e-commerce technology, where companies are beginning to use online dispute resolution websites to manage contractual conflicts.

The traditional mechanism for resolving contract disputes is grounded in commercial law, which provides a legal jurisdiction in which an impartial judge can hear the facts of the case at hand and render a decision in favor of one party or the other.

Due to the uncertainty, cost, and length of time required to settle a dispute in the U.S. legal system, most buyers and sellers prefer to avoid the problems associated with litigation and deal with the situation in other ways. Taking a dispute into the jurisprudence system should be viewed as a last resort, not an automatic step in resolving contractual disputes.

Legal Alternatives

New methods of settling buyer-seller disputes have evolved in the last several years. These techniques, although diverse in form and nature, have a number of similar characteristics:[10]

Exhibit 14.4 Means of Settling Contractual Disputes

ACTION	DESCRIPTION
Legal action	File a lawsuit in a federal/state/local court
Nonlegal actions	
Arbitration	Use of an impartial third party to settle a contractual dispute
Mediation	Intervention by a third party to promote settlement, reconciliation, or compromise between parties involved in a contractual dispute
Minitrial	An exchange of information between managers in each organization, followed by negotiation between executives from each organization
Rent-a-judge	A neutral party conducts a "trial" between the parties and is responsible for the final judgment
Dispute prevention	A progressive schedule of negotiation, mediation, arbitration, and legal proceedings agreed to in the contract

Sourcing Snapshot — *Online Dispute Resolution*

As with other aspects of the Internet, innovation in online dispute resolution (ODR) has been rapid. Cybersettle.com is an online mechanism for settling disputes, particularly those that involve insurance companies. Not surprisingly, there are other online vendors offering both mediation and arbitration services. For mediation, there is Online Mediation (www.onlineresolution.com) and MediationNow (www.mediationnow.com). Online arbitration services include Online Resolution—Arbitration (www.onlinesolution.com/index-ow.cfm). According to the latter's website, "Online Arbitration is similar to traditional arbitration, except that all communications take place online. The Online Arbitrator appointed for your case will be an experienced professional, who knows the subject area of your dispute." One advantage of ODR is that through use of the computer, rather than personal appearances, the costs of "attending" negotiations, mediation, and arbitration proceedings are lower. However, it is important to bear in mind that most mechanisms for resolving disputes online are unfamiliar to many businesses. For ODR to serve as an effective mechanism, both parties must agree to use ODR, even though parties unfamiliar with the process will be cautious in trying such a "new" procedure. In order for them to be enforceable, courts must accept ODR results. In at least one case, a federal district court refused to be bound by the results of a proceeding.

Source: D. L. Baumer and J. C. Poindexter, *Legal Environment of Business in the Information Age*, New York: McGraw-Hill/Irwin, 2004.

- They exist somewhere between the polar alternatives of doing nothing and escalating conflict.
- They are less formal and generally more private than ritualized court battles.
- They permit people with disputes to have more active participation and more control over the processes for solving their own problems than traditional methods of dealing with conflict.
- Almost all of the new methods have been developed in the private sector, although courts and administrative agencies have begun to borrow and adapt some of the more successful techniques.

Perhaps the simplest method of resolving a contractual disagreement involves straightforward, face-to-face negotiation between the two parties involved. Frequently, there are other factors surrounding the dispute that can be brought into consideration by the parties, even though these factors are not directly involved in the dispute at hand. For example, if the buying and selling parties to a contract disagree on the interpretation of the contract's terms and conditions regarding delivery, then perhaps they might be able to collaborate on other terms and conditions such as price or scheduling.

When this alternative is exhausted, both parties may become aware of the fact that it is infeasible to agree on suitable alternatives. In such cases, it may be virtually impossible for the parties to negotiate an acceptable resolution of the dispute on a good-faith basis without additional assistance from outside parties.

Arbitration

The use of an outside arbitrator, or third party, to help settle contractual disputes is the fastest-growing method of conflict resolution among contracting parties, both in the United States and overseas. Because of the parties' inability to reach a negotiated settlement, emotional reactions to the problem (frustration, disappointment, and anger) may prevent rational examination of the true underlying causes of the source of disagreement.

The only solution in such cases may be **arbitration**, which is defined as "the submission of a disagreement to one or more impartial persons with the understanding that the parties will abide by the arbitrator's decision."[11] If set up and handled properly, arbitration can serve to protect the interests of both parties to the dispute because it is relatively inexpensive, less time consuming, private, and typically a reasonable solution for all involved.

When writing and negotiating purchase contracts, many purchasing managers include an arbitration clause in the boilerplate terms and conditions. Such a clause typically spells out how the disputing parties will choose an appropriate arbitrator and the types of disputes for which arbitration will be considered. A good source for commercial arbitrators is the American Arbitration Association, which can also handle the administrative burden of the entire process from an impartial point of view. It is important to ensure that the arbitrator's opinion will be binding on both parties to the dispute. A key point to remember here is that adequate advance planning for potential disputes can prevent significant problems later should an unforeseen conflict arise. Also, it is a good idea to spell out the location and method of conducting the arbitration hearings, particularly if the dispute involves companies or individuals from different states or countries.

When preparing the purchase contract or purchase order, contract managers should consider two factors (in conjunction with the organization's legal counsel), to ensure that the ruling of an arbitrator will be legally binding:

- State statutes must be reviewed to determine whether the state or states in question do in fact have such legal provisions allowing arbitration.
- Wording of the arbitration clause should be developed carefully in accordance with state law, federal law (the Federal Arbitration Act), and the guidelines published by the American Arbitration Association.

Purchasing managers wishing to take advantage of the process in their dealings with suppliers should understand several caveats regarding binding arbitration.

Purchasers cannot rely on an arbitration clause contained in their forms, particularly if the supplier's forms do not contain such a clause. If the supplier's forms contain an arbitration clause that is not in the buyer's forms, and the buyer does not want to follow it, the supplier cannot rely on the presence of such a clause. Finally, if both the buying and selling organizations' forms contain arbitration clauses, arbitration will become an enforceable part of the overall agreement.

Other Forms of Conflict Resolution

Along with the rising popularity of arbitration between buyers and sellers, a number of different forms of conflict resolution have been introduced. When people think of the arbitration process, the process that generally comes to mind is mediation—an intervention between conflicting parties to promote reconciliation, settlement, or compromise.

The mediator's responsibilities include listening to the facts presented by both parties, ruling on the appropriateness of documents and other evidence, and rendering judgment on a solution that reconciles the legitimate interests of both disputing parties. Mediation varies from arbitration in that arbitration is binding on the parties. In the mediation process, however, the disputing parties preserve their right of final decision on the solution proffered by the mediator.

The second type of dispute resolution mechanism is called a minitrial, which is not actually a trial at all. The minitrial is a form of presentation, involving an exchange of information between managers from each organization involved in the dispute.

Once the executives hear both sides of the presentation, they then attempt to resolve the dispute through negotiation with their executive counterparts. Because minitrials are generally more complicated than other forms of negotiation, they are typically used when the dispute between the parties is significant and highly complex. One of the benefits of such a process is that it turns a potential legal conflict into a business decision and promotes a continuing relationship between the parties.

Another related conflict-resolution mechanism is the "rent-a-judge," which is a popular name given to the process by which a court refers a lawsuit pending between the parties to a private, neutral party. The neutral party (often a retired judge) conducts a "trial" as though it were conducted in a real court. If one or both of the parties is dissatisfied with the outcome of the rent-a-judge decision, then the verdict can be appealed through normal appellate channels. In this process, the parties agree to hire a private referee to hear the dispute. Unlike the binding arbitration process, rent-a-judge hearings are subject to legal precedents and rules of evidence.

A final alternative to dispute litigation and dispute resolution that is gaining popularity is dispute prevention, a key factor in the concept of collaborative business relationships such as long-term contracting, partnering, and strategic alliances. When contracting parties initially agree to dispute-prevention processes, a progressive schedule of negotiation, mediation, and arbitration followed by litigation as a last resort can be defined and delineated in the agreement. The "baring of souls" involved in this type of close, collaborative relationship dictates that the two parties fully recognize and agree upon the mechanisms for dispute resolution that are to be utilized under certain conditions.

There are a number of factors to consider when deciding which dispute-resolution mechanism to use. The first, and perhaps foremost, consideration is the status of the relationship between the parties in the dispute. In cases where the relationship between the parties is ongoing and expected to continue for the foreseeable future, the disagreeing parties will prefer to resolve the contract dispute through means that hopefully will preserve the relationship.

The choice of mechanism should also be based on the type of outcome desired by the purchaser. There may be a need to establish an appropriate precedent to govern the purchaser's actions in future disputes as well as the one at hand. Another consideration is whether the disputing parties need to be directly involved in generating the outcome or resolution. The presence of the disputing parties is important to successfully resolving disputes using techniques such as negotiation, arbitration, mediation, minitrials, and rent-a-judge proceedings. Active participation by all parties involved in a dispute generally results in a more equitable and harmonious resolution (as opposed to having third parties such as attorneys involved).

The level of emotion displayed by the principals is another important consideration. If emotions such as anger and frustration are high, the total cost of litigation, in terms of time, money, and management effort, may be more significant than originally anticipated. For example, the situation shown in Sourcing Snapshot: Leaking Capacitors Create Problems for PC Manufacturers has many different parties involved, with a lot of "finger-pointing," and may well indeed require the use of an international mediator to sort out the source of responsibility for the problem at hand.

Sourcing Snapshot — *Leaking Capacitors Create Problems for PC Manufacturers*

It has all the elements of a good thriller: a stolen secret formula, bungled corporate espionage, untraceable goods, and lone wolves saving the little guy from the misdeeds of multinational corporations. In this case, a mistake in the stolen formulation of the electrolyte in a capacitor has wrecked hundreds of PCs and may wreck still more in what is an industrywide problem.

Aluminum electrolytic capacitors with a low equivalent series resistance (ESR) are high-capacitance components that generally serve to smooth out the power supply to chips. Throughout 2002, they were breaking open and failing in certain desktop PCs. Motherboard and PC makers stopped using the faulty parts, but because the parts can fail over a period of several months, more such failures are expected.

It is clear now that a faulty electrolyte is to blame for the burst capacitors. The mystery is: Where did it come from and which manufacturers used it? Citing Japanese sources, initial reports claimed that major Taiwanese capacitor firms, including the island's market leaders, Lelon Electronics Corp. and Luxon Electronics Corp., had turned out faulty products. But both companies have denied the accusations.

Most of the leaking capacitors pulled from bad boards in the United States, according to repair people, were labeled Tayeh, not a brand affiliated with known capacitor makers. Many others were unmarked. Some, however, did bear the trademarks of Taiwanese passive components firms such as Jackcon Capacitor Electronics Co. (Taipei). Jackcon claims that it has been out of the motherboard market for two years but received some complaints from U.S. consumers in 2002. Jackcon blames the motherboard design and remains confident in the quality of Jackcon products. According to Jackcon executives, the company's low-ESR capacitors passed quality tests at the Industrial Technology Research Institute, a nonprofit R&D organization partly funded by the Ministry of Economic Affairs (Taipei), which is also often the source of Taiwanese firms' electrolyte formulas.

The origins of the motherboard malaise seem to provide a lesson in how not to commit corporate espionage. According to a source in Taiwan, a scientist stole the formula for an electrolyte from his employer in Japan and began using it himself at the Chinese branch of a Taiwanese electrolyte manufacturer. He or his colleagues then sold the formula to an electrolyte maker in Taiwan, which began producing it for Taiwanese and possibly other capacitor firms. Unfortunately, the formula as sold was incomplete.

"It didn't have the right additives," says Dennis Zogbi, publisher of *Passive Component Industry* magazine (Cary, North Carolina), which broke the story in the fall of 2004. According to Zogbi's sources, the capacitors made from the formula become unstable when charged, generating hydrogen gas, bursting, and letting the electrolyte leak onto the circuit board. Zogbi cites tests by Japanese manufacturers that indicate the capacitor's lifetimes are half or less of the 4,000 hours of continuous ripple current they are rated for.

Electronics makers are ordinarily very careful about capacitor quality. "The large volumes of passive content in any electronic device means that you have that many more chances for a product to fail," says Zogbi, who also runs The Paumanok Group (Cary, North Carolina), a market analysis firm focused on the passive components industry. Electronics firms generally supply their manufacturers with a list of parts and materials they can use from suppliers whose quality they trust. Zogbi suspects that, in an effort to cut costs, contract manufacturers used dodgy component sources that were not on the approved list. This action was in default of their contractual terms. Major Taiwanese capacitor makers have vigorously denied having made any bad components, but the crisis had a chilling effect on the island's whole industry, which produces 30% of the world's aluminum electrolytic capacitors.

Taiwanese suppliers says that Japanese customers who stopped buying from their company even showed the firm internal documents written in Japanese that state that any relationship with Lien Yan would lead to boycotts on the part of the Japanese firm's customers.

While Taiwanese passives makers are trying to shore up relations with their customers, some of the computer firms affected are doing the same.

Carey Holzman, as a builder of custom PCs, has been trying to raise awareness about the defects. He thinks manufacturers should be more public about the problem and issue a recall. "Main board replacement is a big job. It's a huge amount of downtime for the user," he says. Failures can also occur after the warranty has expired, he points out. "The manufacturers should do the right thing."

Source: *IEEE Spectrum News and Analysis,* www.spectrum.ieee.org/WEBONLY/resource/feb03/ncap.html.

The harsh experience of a prolonged court battle has convinced more than one set of potential litigants to consider less costly and more timely dispute-resolution alternatives.

The importance of speed in obtaining a resolution can be a factor determining whether to litigate, mediate, or arbitrate. In many instances the alternatives to court adjudication are quicker than litigation. Time pressures may force the disputing parties to be more creative and understanding in reaching an appropriate resolution short of meeting in court. There is a direct relationship between the time involved in settling a dispute and the cost involved. Quicker resolution is generally cheaper.

The information required to reach a settlement may dictate the mechanism preferred. The closer the parties come to having the courts settle their dispute, the more formal the information requirements. Strict rules of evidence in the courtroom may not be desirable to parties because of publicity. Companies involved in the dispute may not be willing to spread out their dirty linen or trade secrets in public. In addition, the credibility of experts and other witnesses may be more difficult to achieve or maintain in a trial. All of the conflict-resolution mechanisms or settlement options presented here allow a greater degree of privacy to the parties involved than that which can be attained in a court.

Good Practice Example

The Top Ten Most Frequently Negotiated Terms Reveal Continued Focus on Failure

Each year, the International Association of Commercial and Contract Managers (IACCM) collects data from more than 500 international companies and organizations, representing several thousand contract negotiators. Their CEO, Tim Cummins, asks members which terms and conditions they negotiate most frequently. The data tells us where time is spent; it reflects changing issues and concerns; and it also reveals much about the ways companies behave and the value they place on their trading relationships. After completing the most recent survey for 2006, Mr. Cummins communicated his disappointment with the results in his weekly blog, which follows:

> Once again, the results for 2006 indicate many opportunities for rethinking the role of contracting in shaping relationships, supporting brand image and as tools for sophisticated risk management—as opposed to blunt instruments for risk allocation. This report highlights the results and suggests new approaches that could result in significant business benefits.
>
> Leading consultants and business gurus have emphasized the growing importance of the "quality of interactions" in determining a company's market image and reputation. Over the last year, there have been signs that corporate executives understand the direct link between commitment management and business success, how a company negotiates, the commitment terms it offers, and market perceptions of how easy (and "fair") they are to do business with.
>
> For all the talk about a changing environment, this year's Top Ten Frequently Negotiated Terms shows no sign that it has affected the behavior or attitudes of those charged with responsibility for setting policy or leading negotiations. True, most corporations continue to issue very mixed messages. They declare a strategic intent to differentiate, to partner, to add value. But at the same time, they send internal messages about control, cost reduction, standardization, and risk avoidance. They highlight the need to be flexible, adaptive, and agile, yet they introduce software tools and measurement systems that enforce compliance and inhibit change. And in their trading relationships, they offer the promise of a match made in heaven—until they introduce the prenuptial agreement and its administrators.
>
> And so we end another year with value-reduction terms heading the list: limitations of liability, levels of indemnity, control of intellectual property, rights to terminate, liquidated damages for performance failure. . . . These are often called "value reduction" terms because they contribute little or nothing to the quality of the relationship, nor the likelihood of its success. They distract from value-add relationships or eliminate the possibility for discussions that can lead to more productive relationships. And they tackle risk in only a very narrow sense—most of these terms are about allocating the consequences of

failure. By undermining the framework for collaboration, they often increase the probability that failure will occur.

To suggest that today's "Frequently Negotiated Terms" represent good governance is misleading. At present, there are few signs of change. Companies continue to invest in resources and software systems that focus on control and compliance. Internal measurements are either insufficient or lacking when it comes to the quality or outputs of the contracting process; they do not encourage or prompt change or improvement. They do not require the custodians of terms and conditions to become more innovative or creative in their thinking, or to focus on wider issues of company performance and risk.

What changes might we have hoped for? How would the list change if we were indeed moving towards a more collaborative framework for business relationships?

With the right focus, measurements, and incentives, I believe that the discussion would switch to ensuring the methods and mechanisms for building and measuring success. Certainly this would involve topics like Service Levels (relatively static at #11) because these set agreed parameters for performance. But it should also focus attention on governance topics such as Change Management (not in the Top 30), Business Continuity (down from #19 to #22) and Project/Relationship Reviews (also not in the Top 30). The only clause that is arguably part of the "good governance" portfolio to have made significant progress (from #35 last year to #17 this year) is Dispute Resolution.

I would also expect that those charged with better governance (or those seeking a route to higher value and status within the organization) might spare a few minutes to question their traditional adherence to the methods by which contracts and disputes are managed. For example, as international trade mushrooms, we all know that the legal system is ill equipped to manage trading relationships. Arguments over governing law and jurisdiction are common. Recent U.S. research has shown that even in a sophisticated and well-developed market like the United States, the courts are weighted against foreign litigants. So why would any right-thinking businessperson want to lose the advantage of home turf? To reduce the contentious debate, one may move to alternative dispute resolution mechanisms such as arbitration or mediation—and institute different (nonjudicial) forms of incentives for proper performance and sanctions for specific failures.

Another example where we waste so much time is in the area of liquidated damages. Recent IACCM research illustrated the frequency with which we negotiate such terms—and then either have no mechanism to monitor performance or consistently elect not to enforce the term because "it would damage our relationship."

Superior companies that truly focus on customer value will also peruse the list and identify ways that terms and conditions might offer differentiation. Performance Undertakings, Security, Most Favored Customer clauses, Disaster Recovery, and Benchmarking are among the examples where creative thinking and innovative approaches can add value through reducing customer risk and increasing relationship loyalty.

IACCM Top 10 Frequently Negotiated Terms 2006

	TERM	2005	2004	2003	2002
1	Limitation of Liability	1	1	1	1
2	Indemnification	2	4	10	3
3	Intellectual Property	3	5	3	2
4	Price/Charge/Price Changes	6	3	5	7
5	Termination (Cause/Convenience)	7	7	7	5
6	Warranty	5	2	2	6
7	Confidential Information/Data Protection	8	10	14	15
8	Delivery/Acceptance	9	8	12	13
9	Payment	4	6	4	11
10	Liquidated Damages	12	9	13	19
11	Service Levels	10	13		
12	Insurance	15	11		
13	Performance Bonds/Guarantees/ Undertakings	13	23		
14	Applicable Law/Jurisdiction	14	12		
15	Rights of Use	—	16		
16	Assignment/Transfer	16	17		
17	Dispute Resolution	—	—		
18	Audits/Benchmarking	17	18		
19	Invoices/Late Payment	—			
20	Most Favored Client	18			
21	Freight/Shipping	22	19		
22	Business Continuity/Disaster Recovery	19			
23	Entirety of Agreement	21			
24	Security	24			
25	Enterprise Definition/Future Acquisitions/Divestiture	11			
26	Nonsolicitation of Employees	—			
27	Force Majeure	20	24		
28	Export/Import Regulations	23			
29	Product Substitution				
30	Escrow	25			

Source: www.iaccm.com.

Questions

1. Do you agree with the comment that Limitation of Liability, Indemnification, and Intellectual Property clauses are "value reduction" clauses and provide little in the way of promoting collaboration between buyers and suppliers?
2. What are the implications if negotiations focus primarily on these terms, given that there is never enough time to discuss all terms in a contract?
3. What is the role of legal staff in driving these negotiations and contracts? Does corporate counsel become too involved in contract negotiations in your opinion?

CONCLUSION

This chapter provides an overview of the types of contracts used by purchasers, administration procedures applied, and methods of resolving contractual disputes.

Although it is impossible to cover all potential situations where a specific contract should be applied, the rules of thumb developed here should provide a reasonable set of guidelines. As a final point, it is interesting to note that many organizations are eliminating contracts altogether and are choosing to do business with suppliers on an informal basis. This type of arrangement requires the development of excellent supplier relationships and trust between the parties. It is highly unlikely, however, that contracts between buyers and sellers will ever disappear.

KEY TERMS

arbitration, 528

long-term contracts, 513

short-term contracts, 513

spot contracts, 513

DISCUSSION QUESTIONS

1. Where do you believe buyers spend most of their time in negotiations: on the up-front clauses or on the attached schedules?
2. What are some examples of price indices that might be used to track commodity prices such as steel or copper, and how should they be included in the schedule to minimize risk to both parties?
3. What are the risks to buyers associated with each of the different types of contracts (fixed-price, incentive, and cost-based contracts)?
4. What are the risks to suppliers associated with each of the different types of contracts (fixed-price, incentive, and cost-based contracts)?
5. Which types of firms are most suited to using turnkey systems contracts for their information system development?
6. Suppose you are a purchase manager who is the contract administrator for a major consulting firm installing a major enterprise resource planning system such as SAP or Oracle. What are some of the key elements that you would wish to include in the contract with the consulting company implementing this system?
7. Why do consultants typically want to avoid including detailed outcomes in their contracts? Is this ethical?
8. Under what conditions are short-term contracts preferable to long-term contracts?
9. Certain industries, such as the computer industry, are faced with constantly changing technologies, short product life cycles, many small-component suppliers, and demanding customers. Under these conditions, what type of contract would you recommend for a critical component supplier? What other measures would you include in this contract?
10. What are the implications for contract writing as a result of electronic signatures now being enforceable by law?

11. What are the dangers associated with taking an old contract and merely changing the name of the supplier for use in a new three-year contract with a different supplier?
12. Why do many firms attempt to avoid litigation in settling contract disputes?
13. What are the different venues available for arbitration settlements?
14. What are the implications of e-commerce on enforcing contracts? Where do you think the venue for resolution should be if a conflict arises?

ADDITIONAL READINGS

Alston, F. M., Worthington, M. M., and Goldsman, L. P. (1992), *Contracting with the Federal Government,* New York: John Wiley & Sons.

Baumer, D. L., and Poindexter, J. C. (2004), *Legal Environment of Business in the Information Age,* New York: McGraw-Hill/Irwin.

Behn, R. D. (1999), "Strategies for Avoiding Pitfalls of Performance Contracting," *Public Productivity and Management Review,* June, 470–490.

Buvik, A. (1998), "The Effect of Manufacturing Technology on Purchase Contracts," *International Journal of Purchasing and Materials Management,* Fall, 21–28.

Carbonneau, T. E. (1989), *Alternative Dispute Resolution: Melting the Lances and Dismounting the Steeds,* Urbana: University of Illinois Press.

Coulson, R. (1982), *Business Arbitration: What You Need to Know* (2nd ed.), New York: American Arbitration Association.

Cummins, T. (2007), *Contracting Excellence, November 2007,* www.iaccm.com/contracting excellence.php?id=67.

Ellram, L., and Tate, W. (2004), "Managing and Controlling the Services Supply Chain at Intuit," *Practix,* CAPS Research, August, http://www.capsresearch.org/Research/Practix.aspx.

Emiliani, M. L., and Stec, D. J. (2001). "Online Reverse Auction Purchasing Contracts," *Supply Chain Management,* 6(3–4), 101–105.

Fisher, R. X. (2000), "Checklist for a Good Contract for IT Purchases," *Health Management Technology,* March, 14–17.

Gordon, S. B. (1998), "Performance Incentive Contracting: Using the Purchasing Process to Find Money Rather Than Spend It," *Government Finance Review,* August, 33–37.

Hancock, W. A. (Ed.) (1987), *The Law of Purchasing* (2nd ed.), Chesterland, OH: Business Laws.

MacCollum, D. V. (1990), *Construction Safety Planning,* New York: Van Nostrand Reinhold.

Maughan, A. (2003), "Crash-Proof Contracts," *Supply Management,* 8(1), 37.

Murray, J. (2001), "Contract Modifications Can Lead to Problems," *Purchasing,* 130(5), 20–22.

Rohleder, S. (1999), "Contracting for the Best Results," *Government Executive,* September, 72.

Seide, K. (Ed.) (1970), *A Dictionary of Arbitration and Its Terms,* Dobbs Ferry, NY: Oceana Publishing.

Shenson, H. L. (1990), *The Contract and Fee-Setting Guide for Consultants and Professionals,* New York: John Wiley & Sons.

Singer, L. R. (1990), *Settling Disputes: Conflict Resolution in Business, Families, and the Legal System,* Boulder, CO: Westview Press.

Tepedino, F. J. (1991), *Contract Claims and Litigation Avoidance,* San Diego: Condor Group.

Tuttle, A. (2001), "Becoming a Single Source," *Industrial Distribution,* 90(9), 47–49.

Werner, C. (1998), "Contract Compliance: A Double-Edged Sword for Most Suppliers," *Health Industry Today,* May, 1–2.

ENDNOTES

1. Handfield, R. B. (2005), "Legal and Regulatory Requirements in the Emergent Global Supply Chain," white paper, Supply Chain Resource Cooperative, http://scm.ncsu.edu.

2. Brown, L. (1950), *Manual of Preventive Law,* New York: Prentice Hall.

3. Hancock, W. A. (Ed.) (1987), *The Law of Purchasing* (2nd ed.), Chesterland, OH: Business Laws, p. 68.02.

4. Baumer, D. L., and Poindexter, J. C. (2004), *Legal Environment of Business in the Information Age,* New York: McGraw-Hill/Irwin.

5. Wetherbe, J. C. (1991), "Executive Information Requirements: Getting It Right," *MIS Quarterly,* 15(1), 51–65.

6. Shenson, H. L. (1990), *The Contract and Fee-Setting Guide for Consultants and Professionals,* New York: John Wiley & Sons, pp. 131–134.

7. MacCollum, D. V. (1990), *Construction Safety Planning,* New York: Van Nostrand Reinhold.

8. Samelson, N. M., and Levitt, R. E. (1982), "Owner's Guidelines for Selecting Safe Contractors," *ASCE National Spring Convention Proceedings,* April 26–30, pp. 617–623.

9. Baumer and Poindexter.

10. Singer, L. R. (1990), *Settling Disputes: Conflict Resolution in Business, Families, and the Legal System,* Boulder, CO: Westview Press, p. 5; Baumer and Poindexter.

11. Coulson, R. (1982), *Business Arbitration: What You Need to Know* (2nd ed.), New York: American Arbitration Association, p. 5.

Chapter 15

PURCHASING LAW AND ETHICS

Learning Objectives

After completing this chapter, you should be able to

- Understand the liability of the purchasing manager from a legal standpoint
- Understand the essential elements of contract law in purchasing
- Understand the role of the Uniform Commercial Code
- Identify other laws that may impact purchasing
- Understand why it is so important for purchasing to act in an ethical manner, and identify the risks of unethical behavior
- Recognize the increased corporate awareness of social responsibility

Chapter Outline

Iraqi Food Probe Uncovers Trail of Potential Ethical Conflicts

A probe of the supply chain that provides food to U.S. forces in Iraq is the subject of a continuing investigation into alleged wrongdoings by several members of the supply chain and was the reason for the apparent suicide of an Army officer. This officer was responsible for operations in Camp Arifjan, a large logistics and food staging facility in Kuwait. The ongoing investigation reveals potential ethical issues in the complex web of transactions that ultimately provides daily meals to U.S. troops located in Iraq and Kuwait.

The entire investigation started when U.S. Army Lieutenant Colonel Marshall Gutierrez "blew the whistle" on a Kuwaiti firm, Public Warehousing Company. Lieutenant Colonel Gutierrez felt he had discovered rampant overcharging by the firm. Two examples of this overcharging were (1) $95 for five-gallon bags of Coca-Cola syrup, which were selling for around $40 from Kuwait City merchants, and (2) $8 a pound for green beans. Public Warehousing, in its defense, claims that it was charging a total price that must consider not only the cost of the food it supplies but other costs including those associated with storing, handling, and delivering it to multiple locations. It also cited that more than 30 of its employees have been killed on the job. Regarding the green beans, it claims the military required a hard-to-find style of green beans.

Public Warehousing is one of the world's largest transport companies and is designated as the "prime vendor" for virtually all food served to some 150,000 U.S. troops in Iraq and Kuwait. However, Lieutenant Colonel Gutierrez's allegations spawned a larger inquiry into the practices of the entire supply chain extending back through Public Warehousing's suppliers. The following illustration highlights the flow of the food supply chain.

Food Supply Chain to U.S. Troops in Iraq

U.S. Food Manufacturers

⇩

American Grocers, Inc.

⇩

Sultan Center Kuwait

⇩

Public Warehousing, Kuwait

⇩

U.S. Military, Iraq, Kuwait

Potential conflicts have been cited at various points in the chain. American Grocers is the primary supplier to Sultan Center, which in turn supplies more than $200 million of food items annually to Public Warehousing. Members of the powerful Sultan merchant family of Kuwait are large stockholders in both Sultan Center and Public Warehousing. Sultan Center owns 31% of the firm National Real Estate Company WLL, which owns 24% of Public Warehousing. Evidence has indicated that Sultan Center, after receiving payment for goods it supplied, returned 10% of the amount to Public Warehousing. If the two firms were related and not negotiating at "arm's length," then the discounts should have been passed directly to the U.S. government. Government contracts pay a supplier costs plus a certain profit margin. It is generally not legal to pass goods among a series of related entities to inflate the price of those goods. Records show that Sultan Center acted as a middleman, supplying Public Warehousing with American food products such as peanut butter, pepperoni, calzones, and potato wedges from American Grocers. It is unclear why American Grocers couldn't ship these directly to Public Warehousing.

Meanwhile American Grocers, which is run by a Lebanese immigrant (Samir Itani), has been charged with 46 criminal counts of conspiring to defraud the United States and making false claims with at least $1.9 million of allegedly bogus invoices. Charges claim that American Grocers inflated its bills for food by putting costs on its invoices that were never incurred, such as trucking charges. These charges were then passed along to Public Warehousing, which then passed them on to the U.S. government. Mr. Itani of American Grocers has pleaded not guilty and his lawyer claims he did not engage in any intentional wrongdoing.

The investigation is also extending back to U.S. food producers. Records indicate that Sara Lee Corporation paid 5% of the purchase price back to Public Warehousing for meat and bakery products. The agreement was negotiated by a Sara Lee executive in charge of military sales, who had previously served as a chief warrant officer in the Army. In an April 2007 letter to the Pentagon, a lawyer for Tyson Foods complained that "elements within the military" were providing sole-source contracts "to certain companies employing former military personnel." Further, Tyson's attorney stated that "it appears the process for specifying brand-named merchandise may have been inappropriate." Since 2003 the Army Center for Excellence Subsistence has issued guidelines directing that chicken breast, turkey breast, ham, and sausage consumed by U.S. forces in Iraq and Kuwait be supplied by Sara Lee.

Meanwhile, the events leading to the death of whistleblower Lieutenant Colonel Gutierrez in Kuwait took another twist. He was accused of asking for a cash payment from a Public Warehousing sales executive. He also solicited help from Tamimi Global, Public Warehousing's chief competitor, in assisting with the overpricing investigation. Then in May of 2006, Lieutenant Colonel Gutierrez requested that an order for some $21 million of vegetables, dairy, and baked goods be placed with Tamimi Global. His contact at Tamimi Global was Shabbir Khan, who was already under investigation for fraud and bribery at the U.S. base in Kuwait. Tamimi Global allegedly had a "party house" on the Arifjan base, regularly visited by contractors and contracting officers. According to a sworn statement in July 2006, a former Army officer admitted taking $8,000 in gifts and bribes from a Tamimi executive and $50,000 from another catering firm. He further admitted to seeing at least five other Army officers taking bribes during a dozen parties at the Tamimi house.

Lieutenant Colonel Gutierrez was then charged with bribery and mishandling of secret information and accepting illegal gifts. Records show that he also had married an 18-year-old Kuwaiti woman, while his wife of 22 years was in the States attending to a sick relative. After five days of detention, Colonel Gutierrez was released and transferred to another camp to await court-martial proceedings. On September 4, 2007, his body was found in camp quarters, and no note was found. Two autopsies concluded that he had died of poisoning from ethylene glycol, an active ingredient in anti-freeze. The Army ruled his death a suicide. Following his original arrest in late August, Army investigators searched Lieutenant Colonel Gutierrez's home; they found $27,000 in U.S. and Kuwaiti currency, a two-week-old Kuwaiti marriage certificate, alcohol, and a magazine it termed pornography. Both of the latter two items are illegal in Kuwait.

Many issues remain in the ongoing investigation into the Army's food procurement system. Of prime importance is, how pervasive are fraud and corruption in the food procurement supply chain? The amount in dispute in the Public Warehouse investigation is at least $100 million. Additionally, many questions remain about Lieutenant Colonel Gutierrez. How did he meet his second wife and why did they decide to marry? What was the nature of Lieutenant Colonel Gutierrez's relationship with the Tamimi executive later convicted of bribery? In his defense,

Mrs. Brenda Gutierrez, Lieutenant Colonel Gutierrez's first wife, refuses to believe that he was corrupt. "None of this stuff fits his character at all," she said.

Source: Adapted from G. R. Simpson, "Inside the Greed Zone," *Wall Street Journal,* October 20–21, 2007, pp. A1, A6; G. R. Simpson, "Food Companies Face U.S. Probe over Iraq Deals," *Wall Street Journal,* October 17, 2007, pp. A1, A14; G. R. Simpson, "Houston Businessman Is Key Figure in U.S. Probe of Iraq Food Contracts," *Wall Street Journal,* October 18, 2007, pp. A1, A13.

As illustrated in the Army's food investigation, today's global business environment has made it more important than ever for purchasing managers to understand the changing nature of law at the international, federal, state, and regional levels. Purchasing's daily activities are essentially concerned with the laws regarding contracts and the laws regarding agency. The majority of purchasing law is derived primarily from the laws regarding contracts.

Contract law essentially determines the nature of agreements that are enforceable and create legal rights between the parties. The characteristics of offer and acceptance, satisfaction, and nonperformance have all been clearly established by the law. Contracts between two or more parties allow the shifting of risk between the entities and constitute the foundation and fabric for every type of supply chain relationship.

Agency law, on the other hand, deals with the role of managers as individual representatives acting on behalf of their organization. It is important that purchasing managers understand the role they play as agents of their organization, so that they do not exceed the responsibilities bestowed upon them in this role. As agents of their organization, purchasing managers also wield a great deal of power in allocating the business of the company to their suppliers. They must also be aware of the potential for ethical abuses of this power that may be encountered.

Although we cannot provide a comprehensive treatment of these issues here, this chapter will introduce some of the basic legal concerns that purchasing managers must be aware of in their profession. Specifically, we begin with a discussion of the roles and responsibilities of purchasing managers as individuals representing their organization and then discuss the major features of the Uniform Commercial Code (UCC). The major features of contract law are reviewed as well as the important area of patents and intellectual property. Antitrust laws that affect purchasing are discussed next, followed by an overview of purchasing ethics and social responsibility.

Legal Authority and Personal Liability of the Purchasing Manager

Laws of Agency

The laws regarding agency are concerned with governing the relationship of principals and agents. An **agent** is a person or entity who has been authorized to act on behalf of some other person or entity. A principal, on the other hand, is the corresponding person or entity for whom agents carry out their authority. The purchasing manager/buyer is typically considered to be a general agent for the buying firm (the principal). That means that a supplier dealing with this manager/buyer has a right to rely on the individual's statements, both in written form and verbally. Conversely, the sales representative can also be considered to be an agent of the selling firm (also a principal). In most cases, the sales representative is a special agent who can only solicit orders but not change prices, terms, or conditions. Meanwhile, the purchasing agent is a general agent with broad authority to change prices, terms, and conditions.

Legal Authority

Purchasing managers generally have final authority over purchasing decisions within their firms. However, this final decision may be reached through the input provided by a cross-functional sourcing team. In the end, however, someone has to sign the contract, so the purchasing manager is most often considered as the general agent. (A general agent role merely implies that the guidelines provided by the employer for this individual are quite broad and general in nature.) Because purchasing managers are responsible for a significant amount of expenditures, the employer's instructions to its purchasing managers should be expressed clearly and succinctly. The purchasing agency relationship is created between the employer and employee when the company hires an individual to perform the purchasing job. Typically, a job description provides the basis for an agreement between the employing firm and purchasing agent/manager regarding actual scope of authority.

Purchasing managers have the right to require clear and unequivocal instructions from their employers regarding the scope of their day-to-day job performance expectations. From a legal perspective, purchasing managers have a fiduciary obligation to act in the best interests of their employer. This means that if they carry out their duties in a faithful, ethical, and conscientious manner, then their obligations to the employers are fulfilled. However, in agreeing to perform the purchasing duties for the employer, purchasing managers do not imply that they will never make mistakes.

Personal Liability

Certain individuals in many organizations have interpreted the statement "acting in the best interests of the employer" in radically different ways. There are a number of ways in which purchasing managers can be held personally liable in the conduct of their day-to-day activities, even if they were supposedly following these guidelines. Depending on the issue at hand, this personal liability can take the form of either a civil or criminal suit. The concept of "apparent versus actual authority" is the determining factor in such cases.

Actual authority stems from the instructions and granting of authority to the purchasing manager via the job description provided by the employer. These documents typically define the limits and parameters under which the purchasing manager is expected to operate. Apparent authority, on the other hand, is that level of authority perceived by the seller to be available to the purchasing manager. In most instances, apparent authority can be defined as the scope of authority possessed by other purchasing managers with similar positions in other organizations within the same industry.

If a purchasing manager, in carrying out normal procurement responsibilities, exceeds his or her actual but not apparent authority, then the employer is still responsible for performance of the resulting contract but could seek legal action against the purchasing manager personally. Exceeding both actual and apparent authority can

Exhibit 15.1 Laws of Agency

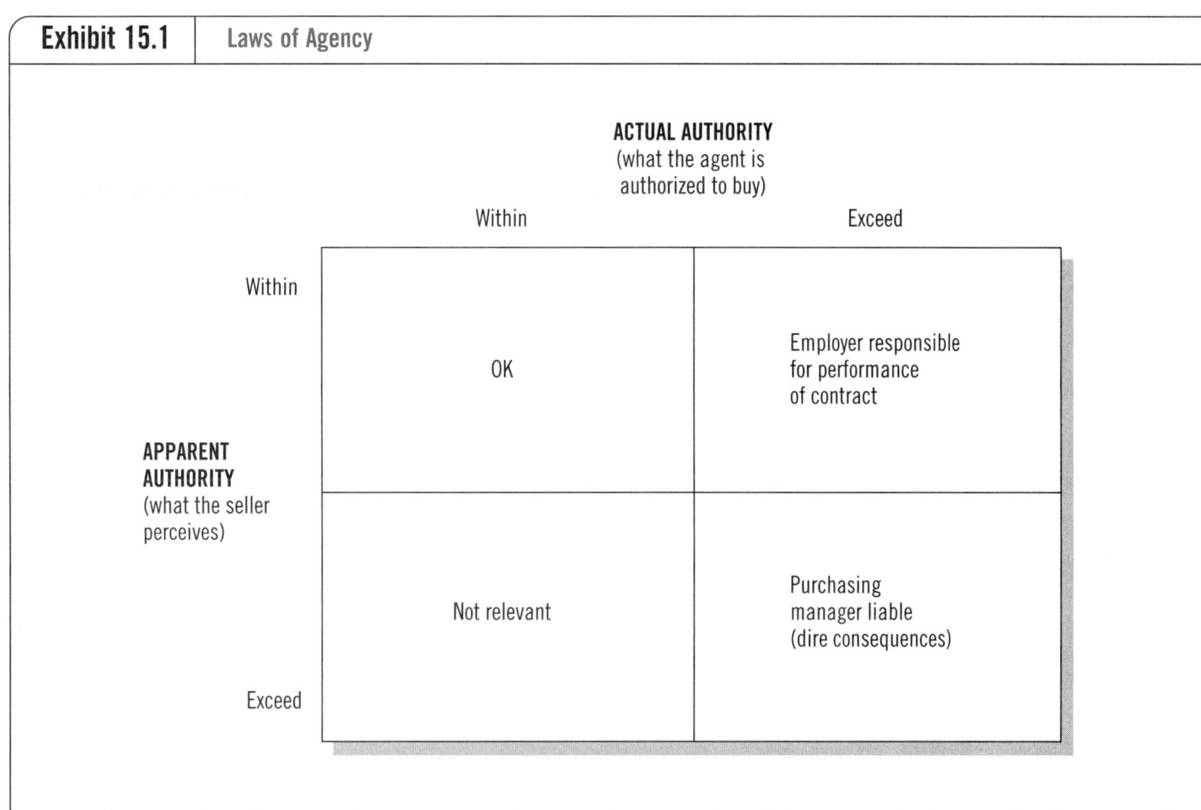

have dire consequences; an individual may be held directly liable by the supplier or other third party (see Exhibit 15.1).

ACTUAL AUTHORITY
(what the agent is authorized to buy)
Within
Exceed
Within
OK
Employer responsible for performance of contract
APPARENT AUTHORITY
(what the seller perceives)
Not relevant
Purchasing manager liable (dire consequences)
Exceed

It is in the purchasing manager's own self-interest to ensure that all suppliers or other third parties are aware that his or her actions are on behalf of the employing firm. All contracts should be signed in a manner that demonstrates the agency relationship. The following language might be used in a contract:[1]

> *[your name] on behalf of [your company] or [your company name] by [your name]*

Purchasing managers can be held personally liable for their damaging and illegal activities if they perform them without the authority of their firm. This personal liability may occur even if the purchasing manager believes (incorrectly) that he or she actually possesses the authority. Any damaging acts performed outside of the manager's scope of authority (whether actual or apparent) can lead to personal liability even though such acts were intended to benefit the employer. In essence, any act that causes damage to any other person could cause a legal liability to the purchasing manager who performs such an act.

Other areas of activity for the purchasing manager that could lead to personal liability include the following:[2]

- Deception for personal gain while acting as an agent for the principal firm (includes taking bribes)
- Violating the lawful protection of items owned by others, such as patent infringement

- (Mis)use of proprietary information
- Violation of antitrust laws
- Unlawful transportation of hazardous materials and toxic waste

These activities are related to another important aspect of purchasing law: ethical behavior. A good rule of thumb is to remember that purchasers must always act in the best interests of their employer. This includes maintaining loyalty, respecting confidential information, and avoiding compromising relationships that may lead to a conflict of interest, which will be discussed later in the Purchasing Ethics section. Understanding contract law is one way to ensure that purchasers will legally protect their employer's best interests.

Contract Law

Essential Elements of a Contract

Commercial law is defined as that "body of [the] law that refers to how business firms (parties) enter into contracts with each other, execute contracts, and remedy problems that arise in the process."[3] There are two major topical areas of commercial law that are of day-to-day interest to the purchasing professional: the laws regarding agency and the laws regarding contracts. We have already discussed agency law to some extent earlier in the chapter. Thus, we will turn our attention to the laws regarding contracts.

In its most basic form, a contract can be defined as an agreement between two or more parties that can be legally enforced. Note that people make agreements every day, but not every agreement can be considered a contract. A contract is an agreement between two or more people to do specified things in exchange for other specified things. For example:

> *Shirley wants to go to the store to buy some potato chips but she doesn't have a car. She says to Rich, "I will pay you a dollar to take me to the store to buy some potato chips." Rich agrees and takes Shirley to the store.*

The above statement can be characterized as a contract. Shirley agreed to do a specified thing (pay Rich a dollar) in exchange for another specified thing (take Shirley to the store). In legal thinking a contract has three essential elements:

- Offer
- Acceptance
- Consideration

If any one of these elements is lacking, then an enforceable contract does not exist. Let's take a closer look at these three elements.

Offer

An **offer** is a proposal or expression by one person that he or she is willing to do something for certain terms. For example:

Betsy goes into Mimi's Wholesale Video Store and says to Mimi, "I want to buy 1,000 DVDs of the Harry Potter movie from you. I will pay you $15 for each DVD."

Betsy has made a specific offer—to purchase a specific movie—in specific volumes (1,000)—at a specific price ($15,000). This constitutes a valid offer. Somewhat different is a conditional offer, which includes additional criteria for completion of the agreement.

For example:

Betsy goes into Mimi's Wholesale Video Store and says to Mimi, "I want to buy 1,000 DVDs of the Harry Potter movie from you. I will pay you $15 for each DVD IF you deliver them to my place of business on February 1, 2008."

In this case, a deadline has been added to the offer. The offer is valid if the conditions are met.

Acceptance

The second important part of the contract is the acceptance. Legally, a contract does not exist until the offer is formally accepted, either verbally or in written form. The offer and acceptance should generally match. However, this is not always the case. Under the Uniform Commercial Code (discussed later in the chapter), the offer and acceptance need not always match. An acceptance can have additional terms, which will become part of the contract unless the offeror objects within a reasonable amount of time.

Assuming the offer and acceptance match, there is an agreement leading up to a contract. If they don't, it's more like a negotiation: an offer, to which someone responds with a counteroffer rather than an acceptance, must be restated. This continues until both sides reach an agreement, or a so-called meeting of the minds. It is important to note that a contract exists only when there is an agreement resulting from both an offer and an acceptance. The agreement doesn't exist until the supplier accepts the offer, and a meeting of the minds occurs. An acceptance, as recognized by the Uniform Commercial Code, can be in "any manner and by any medium reasonable to the circumstances." In other words, the manner and medium of acceptance by the supplier can be met either through the promise of an acceptance or by the supplier's performance of the terms and conditions of the contract—that is, the actual delivery of the requested goods or services without prior verbal advance notice.

Many customer purchase orders typically contain a written copy that outlines the procedures for acknowledgment or acceptance by suppliers. However, suppliers frequently accept or acknowledge customer orders on their own form, which may contain language and terms different from the customer's original purchase order. When this occurs, the supplier's terms will automatically be incorporated into the final contract unless one of the following conditions is present:

1. The supplier's terms substantially or materially alter the original intent of the offer (purchase order).
2. The buyer objects to the supplier's acceptance terms in writing.
3. The purchase order explicitly states that no alteration of terms is acceptable.

When the terms of the buyer's purchase order and the supplier's acceptance or acknowledgment conflict, and none of the conditions listed above are present, all of the terms of both the purchase order and the acceptance become part of the resulting contract except the conflicting terms and conditions. In effect, the conflicting terms and conditions are simply disregarded. The purchasing manager must therefore ensure that the terms and conditions of all supplier acceptance forms are carefully reviewed.

If the buyer wants to avoid any dispute over the terms and conditions of the contract, the purchase order should include a statement to the effect that "absolutely no deviation from the terms and conditions contained herein is permitted."

Consideration

The third element of a contract is difficult to define. Consideration, which has nothing to do with being considerate or nice to people, is rather a form of "mutual obligation"—with each party bound to perform at certain levels and agreeing to carry out his or her responsibilities. **Consideration** is something of value in the formation of the contract that gives it legal validity. Consideration takes place when the offeree incurs a legal detriment in response to the offeror's offer. The offeree indicates a willingness to give up something of value to the offeror or a designated third party or give up something of value to him- or herself. In the business world, mutual promises in a contract of sale, whether express or implied, are generally sufficient consideration. For example, in the previous example, Betsy made an offer that Mimi accepted. There has also been consideration. Betsy's consideration is express: She promised to pay $15 per tape. Mimi's consideration is implied: By saying "OK," she implied that she promised to sell Betsy 1,000 tapes for $15 apiece.

Two other elements are important to consider in contract law: competent parties/mutual assent and legal subject matter.

Competent Parties / Mutual Assent

The parties to a legally enforceable contract must have full contractual capacity through being either principals or qualified agents as described earlier. In addition, both the buyer and the seller must not have engaged in any fraudulent activities when formulating the agreement. The use of force or coercion to reach an agreement is not acceptable in signing a contract because both parties must enter into the agreement of their own free will. Both parties must indicate a willingness to enter into the agreement and be bound by its terms.

Legal Subject Matter

If an agreement has been made regarding a purpose that is illegal, then the resulting contract is null and void. The performance of a party in regard to the contract must not be an unlawful act if the agreement is to be enforceable. However, if the primary purpose of a contract is legal, but some terms contained within the agreement are not, then the contract may or may not itself be illegal depending on the seriousness of the illegal terms and the degree to which the legal and illegal terms can be separated.

The Purchase Order—Is It a Contract?

In most instances, the contracting parties participate in a series of negotiation deliberations through which the various terms and conditions of the contract are discussed, outlined, and agreed upon. As shown in Exhibit 15.2, a process takes place before the purchase order develops. This is initiated by the request for quotation (RFQ), sent by the buyer to the supplier. The RFQ contains the following:

- Standard terms and conditions of the transaction
- Quantity/conditions of delivery
- Description, specifications, and end use of the item
- If customized, reviewed by legal counsel before the RFQ is submitted
- If a competitive bid, description of the manner and time period in which the bids will be evaluated
- Services

The RFQ is not an offer but a request for price and availability. The supplier will generally respond to the RFQ with a quote (an offer to sell), which may then initiate further discussion and negotiation between the purchasing commodity team and the supplier's team. Eventually, this leads to a contract, which documents all of the different offers and counteroffers. Most commercial contracts are comprised of similar sets of general terms and conditions. With the exception of a description of the parties involved, a description of the basic subject of the contract and statement of work including dates, and a clearly definable or determinable quantity, the UCC can be relied upon to supply all other terms.

A purchase order can be an offer, acceptance, or counteroffer, depending on the circumstances. It is an offer if it is sent without a quote or other conversation with the seller concerning terms of the order. It would be a counteroffer if it is sent in response to a quote but changes one or more of the terms of the quote (e.g., delivery

Exhibit 15.2 The Contracting Process

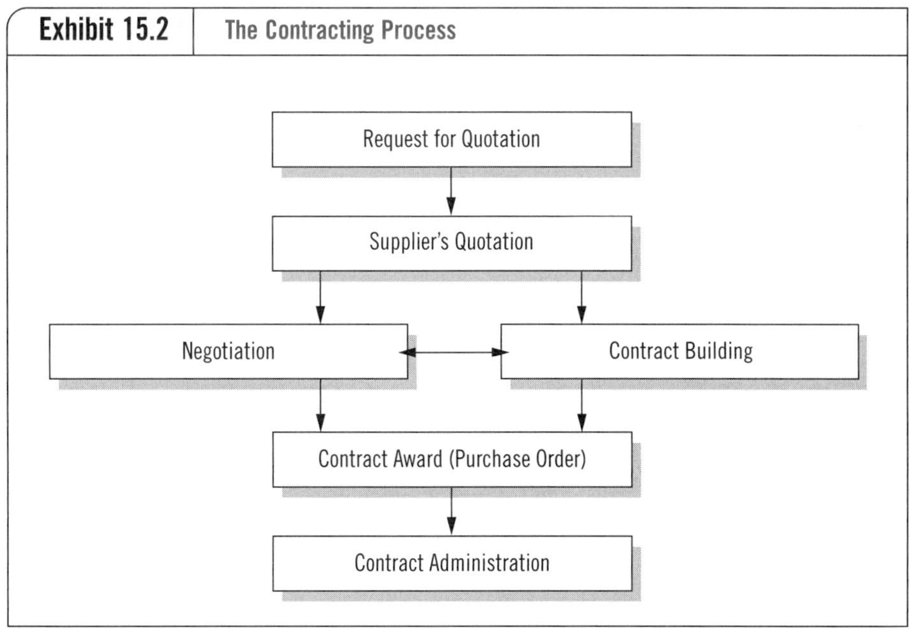

quantity or packaging). It would be an acceptance if it mirrors the seller's quote. Once accepted, a purchase order becomes a contract. The major parts of a purchase order include the following:

- Fixed prices and quantities (including taxes)
- Buyer's right of inspection and rejection
- Right to make specification/design changes
- Holding buyer harmless, patent infringement
- Supplier's right to assign contract to a third party
- Instructions regarding risk of loss
- Statement of credit and payment terms
- Identification
- Packing and preparation
- Statements of warranty
- Shipment quantities/dates
- Assignment of seller's rights
- Arbitration clause
- Right to cancel unshipped portion

Price

Of the terms listed above, the price term is perhaps the single most important element of the entire contract. Section 2-305 of the UCC, entitled "Open Price Term," indicates explicitly that the parties do not necessarily need to reach agreement on a price in order to have an enforceable contract. Although the UCC allows for open price terms, quantity must be specified so that there is a reasonably certain basis for determining damages in the event of a breach of contract. Although the "open price term" clause promotes flexibility in setting prices, the possibility of being charged an unacceptable price increases. If the contract indicates that the price is to be determined at some point in the future or by some other mechanism, two basic requirements must be satisfied per Section 2-305 of the UCC. First, both parties must intend to make a binding contract even though the price remains open. Second, there must be some reasonably certain basis for giving relief (or determining value). A purchasing manager who is in doubt as to whether an enforceable contract might have been reached without agreeing upon a price should indicate in correspondence with the supplier that no contract or agreement exists unless there is agreement on a specific price.

Boilerplate Contract Terms and Conditions

In addition to the negotiated terms of price determination, description of the goods, delivery, and quantity, a number of other standard terms and conditions (often referred to as "boilerplate") are typically included in most commercial contracts and purchase order agreements. Usually preprinted on the back of forms used by the purchaser (and the seller), these terms and conditions are intended to provide a measure of protection for the purchaser against undesirable actions by a supplier and require the supplier to conform to certain business practices and procedures.

Because boilerplate language and the wording of other preprinted purchase order and sales documents may often conflict, it is important to communicate clearly with suppliers exactly which terms are in effect. (If in doubt, don't sign it and assume that things can be worked out later!) Many purchase orders are placed over the telephone, in person, and increasingly, through the Internet; purchasing managers must thus be aware of the potential pitfalls of oral contracts. It is important to remember that a contract is a relationship—not a physical entity—between the parties involved.

When the contract is reduced to writing, the written document is not the actual contract but simply hard evidence of the existence of the underlying contractual relationship. Also, whenever a contract is reduced to writing, the written document supersedes all previous oral evidence. It is therefore important to ensure that all relevant negotiated data and warranty-related oral statements deemed to be part of the agreement are also reduced to writing in the contract. The UCC under Section 2-201 specifies the following:[4]

- In order for a contract to exist, there must normally be some written (and signed) notation if the value of the order for the sale of goods is $500 or more. (The most recent revision of the UCC increases the triggering point for the UCC Statute of Frauds to $5,000, but currently no U.S. state has adopted revised Section 201.) Exceptions where a verbal contract would be valid on orders over $500 are when the following conditions are met:
  - The goods are made specifically for the buyer.
  - There is proof to show the parties behaved as if a contract existed.
  - The parties have always done business on a verbal basis.
- If the supplier provides a written confirmation memorandum that is not in accordance with the purchaser's understanding of an oral order, the purchaser must give a notice of objection to the supplier within 10 days of receipt of the memorandum.

A good example of this situation is when you are shopping for a used vehicle. The salesperson may exaggerate the virtues of a particular car while walking around the lot, yet when you sit down to review the contract, you may find that many of the "promises" are no longer in writing. In order to determine the true conditions of the sale, you should write down exactly what you have been told, and ask for the salesperson's written signature underneath your notes while still out on the lot.

Cancellation of Orders and Breach of Contract

A good contract will protect the interests and rights of both buyer and seller. As a result, contractual obligations are equally binding upon both parties to the agreement.

People cannot go around arbitrarily canceling or defaulting on their contracts. In some instances, however, one of the parties to a contractual arrangement may seek to cancel the agreement after it has been made. In other cases, the supplier may simply fail to perform in the manner agreed to in the contract. Under these conditions, the buyer will always go back to the original contract to determine what the potential remedies are to these situations. If they are not spelled out in detail, the UCC once again provides some help.

Cancellation of Orders

Contract cancellations can generally be classified into three categories: (1) cancellation for default, (2) cancellation for convenience of the purchaser ("anticipatory breach"), or (3) cancellation by mutual consent.

Cancellation for default can be defined as failure of one of the parties to live up to the terms and conditions of the contract. Supplier actions that can result in this type of breach of contract include late deliveries, failing to meet product specifications, or otherwise failing to perform in accordance with contract provisions. The types of damages that might be awarded include production cost penalties, additional overtime, or expedited transportation costs. In actual practice, more effective settlements can be reached through negotiation with the supplier rather than through the litigation process.

Cancellation for the convenience of the purchaser, or anticipatory breach, makes the purchaser liable for any resulting injury to the supplier. A general rule here is that the supplier should not be called upon to incur any loss due to the purchaser's default.

Generally speaking, purchasers should stay away from this term altogether in their purchase contracts. The term is highly interpretable in court and can result in any number of negative actions.

Cancellation by mutual consent indicates that cancellation of a previously agreed-upon contract does not automatically lead to legal action. If both parties mutually agree to terminate the agreement, then they have, in effect, created another contract with the intent of nullifying the first agreement. If there is no potential loss, the supplier will often accept a purchaser's cancellation in good faith as a normal risk of doing business. Even when suppliers have purchased special components or materials in anticipation of fulfilling their responsibilities under the agreement, the parties can usually reach a mutually agreeable resolution through the process of negotiation rather than through litigation.

Breach of Contract

Under a commercial contract, the supplier is obligated to deliver the goods according to the contract's terms and conditions, and the purchaser is likewise obligated to accept and tender payment for the goods according to the terms of the agreement. A **breach of contract** occurs when either party fails to perform the obligations due under the contract (without a valid or legal justification). A breach may entitle the offended party to certain remedies or damages (discussed in greater detail in the next section).

For example:

> *Mimi's Wholesale Video Store and Betsy now have a valid contract. Betsy has promised to buy 1,000 DVDs for $15 apiece, and Mimi has promised to deliver them to Betsy's place of business on February 1. However, Mimi never shows up with the delivery.*

Mimi may indeed be liable for breach of contract. However, one of the basic rules of the UCC is that each party to a contract must give the other party the total time agreed upon to complete his or her obligations under the contract.

Buyers should avoid the practice of routinely tolerating suppliers that breach purchase contracts. Doing so may result in the buyer forfeiting the right to legal action. If you, as the purchaser, have systematically accepted late deliveries from a supplier in the past and continue to accept late deliveries even though you must expedite late shipments, then you may have waived your right to pursue legal action for damages caused by the late shipments. For example:

> *A buyer and a supplier have been doing business for several years. During the past year, approximately one third of the shipments from the supplier arrived a week or so late, but the buyer accepted them without serious complaints. In the eyes of the law, these acceptances by the buyer may well have set a precedent that waives the buyer's rights to timely delivery on future contracts.*

To regain his or her legal rights, the buyer must give explicit written notice to the supplier and provide the supplier a reasonable period of time to gear up to meet the new delivery requirements. The new contract should also include the minimal lead time required for design changes, and so on.

In major contracts, it is often apparent that a breach of contract may create major headaches for either the buyer or supplier; the level of damages in such cases is difficult to determine. To avoid this confusion, many organizations include an up-front termination or liquidated damages provision in the contract at the time of negotiation.

This type of provision stipulates the mechanism to be used in determining any costs and damages to the injured party in the event of a breach of contract. Once again, spelling it out in the contract helps avoid confusion later on.

Damages

The concept of damages in the UCC is based on the remedy of a party being "made whole." In other words, a purchaser who is damaged by a breach of contract must receive damages that bring the purchaser back to the position where he or she would have been if the breach had not occurred. Damages include either actual damages (which include losses that are real or known, or can be reasonably estimated), as well as punitive damages (extra money over and above as "punishment" for the defendant's bad behavior). The UCC is quite clear on the point that punitive damages are not allowed, even if such a provision is contained in the contract. There are essentially three types of damages available to the purchaser:

- *Restitution.* Money the plaintiff actually paid to the defendant in connection with the contract.
- *Reliance.* Money the plaintiff lost because he or she was relying on the contract, depending on the defendant to live up to his or her obligations under the contract.
- *Expectancy.* Money the plaintiff was hoping to gain from the contract.

Back at Mimi's Wholesale Video Store, Mimi and Betsy had a valid contract. Betsy promised to buy 1,000 DVDs for $15 apiece, and Mimi promised to deliver them to Betsy's place of business. Betsy gave Mimi $2,000 as a down payment on the delivery. Betsy also spent $5,000 building new shelves in her retail video store to display and store the DVDs. Finally, Betsy expected to make a profit of $20,000 after expenses from selling or renting the DVDs to her customers. However, Mimi never delivers the DVDs, and Betsy sues for breach of contract. What damages is she entitled to?

Betsy can sue for $2,000 in restitution damages for loss of the down payment, $5,000 in reliance damages for the shelves, and $20,000 in expectancy damages for the $20,000 in profits she expected to make (for a total of $27,000).

It should be noted by the reader that in order for a firm to recover lost profits, the firm must produce credible evidence that it would have made such profits. In the above example, in real life it would indeed be rare for a party to recover $27,000 in a contract where the other damages are $7000. Why? Because the plaintiff in such a case could be asked, "Why didn't you go out on the market and cover?" meaning that the plaintiff would have an obligation to purchase alternative supplies and continue operations. The plaintiff cannot just lie back in the event of breach and reap profits without effort.

There are various methods of calculating damages. General damages are equal to the difference between the value of the purchased goods at the time of delivery and the goods' value at the time of specified delivery. Incidental damages include expenses reasonably incurred in inspection, receipt, transportation, and the care and custody of goods appropriately rejected by the purchaser.

Consequential damages are those expenses incurred by the purchaser because the goods were not delivered when expected or as specified. Liquidated damages are those that result if the terms of the contract are not fulfilled and, as discussed above under remedies, are typically defined prior to the breach under the terms of the contract.

It should be noted that even though the UCC calls for full compensation for a party that is a victim of breach of contract, attorney fees are not recoverable. Also, speculative damages and lost time of executives are not generally recoverable. The bottom line is that a breach of contract lawsuit will rarely make the nonbreaching party completely whole again.

Acceptance and Rejection of Goods

The UCC allows the purchaser to accept part of the shipment and reject the remainder for cause, or to accept or reject the entire shipment. After the point of acceptance, the supplier's rights increase and the purchaser's rights decrease. Once the purchaser accepts the goods, there is only one recourse—to make a claim against the supplier.

The UCC specifies that the purchaser does not have the legal right to withhold payment from the supplier once acceptance has been made. The purchaser also does not have the right at this point to send the goods back unless the supplier consents to this action.

The legal concept of acceptance is closely related to the concept of inspection. Purchasers have a legitimate right to inspect contracted goods before accepting or rejecting them. The law is quite explicit when it states that the purchaser accept the goods within a reasonable time whether or not the goods are physically inspected.

Obvious defects must be discovered and rejected within this reasonable time frame, or the purchaser has no recourse against the seller. "Latent" defects are those that could not have been easily discovered during an inspection and do not fall under this rule. In certain limited situations, the purchaser is able to revoke an acceptance of delivered goods. A purchaser may revoke a prior acceptance if a problem is discovered that substantially impairs the value of the goods. Also, a purchaser can revoke a prior acceptance when a prior inspection could not take place for reasons not related to negligence on the part of the purchaser.

When the goods delivered by the supplier are actually rejected by the purchaser due to nonconformance, the purchaser must provide notice to the supplier within a reasonable period of time. The purchaser should be specific in notifying the supplier that he or she is in breach of contract. General statements about the problems at hand without stating that the supplier is considered in breach of contract are not adequate notification. The exact terms "breach of contract" must be used, or the purchaser stands to lose his or her right to recourse from the supplier.

Once goods are accepted, there are two obligations that the purchaser must meet in order to recover his or her rights. First, the purchaser must carry the burden of proof that the goods did not conform to the terms and conditions of the contract. Second, the purchaser must, within a reasonable time after the breach is discovered, notify the supplier of that breach or lose the chance for remedy.

Acceptance of the contracted goods by the purchaser means that ownership of the goods has been transferred. There are no rituals or formalities required to make the transfer of ownership. Any words or acts by the purchaser that provide an indication of the purchaser's intention to transfer ownership are enough to effect the transfer.

Even though the goods may have been formally rejected by the purchaser, actions typifying ownership may indicate that acceptance has instead been accomplished. In order to prevent or mitigate problems arising from the acceptance or rejection of goods, a number of steps to manage the acceptance process can be implemented by the purchaser:[5]

- The receiving department should stamp all receipts of goods with a statement something to the effect of "Received subject to inspection, count, and testing."
- A thorough set of purchase order terms and conditions should indicate that all receipts from suppliers are subject to inspection, count, and testing.
- All delivered goods should be inspected as quickly as possible, and ideally, immediately upon delivery.
- If goods are not inspected until they are used, it is a good idea to maintain a stock rotation system to ensure that older quantities of goods are used first.
- In some cases, purchasers may want to consider putting language in their purchase order terms and conditions that defines the reasonable time for inspection and acceptance.
- An internal reporting system should be set up to ensure that defects encountered in the organization are reported to the purchasing department within a reasonable time so that remedies can be pursued.
- Contracts for such items as production equipment should contain a clause stating that acceptance will not be made until the equipment has been installed and run satisfactorily for a certain period of time.
- For hardware- and software-related contracts, the purchaser should carefully define the acceptance criteria and notify the supplier of the specific process that this equipment and software will be subjected to.

Honest Mistakes

Sometimes, in spite of the best efforts of the purchaser and the supplier, honest mistakes occur when parties draw up a purchase agreement. In such instances, careful consideration of all the circumstances is necessary to determine whether the resulting contract is valid or invalid. Generally, honest mistakes by a single party to the contract will not void the contract. If the other party was truly unaware of the mistake, then the contract is still intact. Note that mistakes made by both parties also do not necessarily affect the validity of the contract.

Mistakes are not covered under the UCC. The parties must rely on traditional contract law to solve any dispute resulting from a mistake. "As a general rule, a party will not be given relief against a mistake induced by his own negligence. But the rule is not inflexible and in many cases relief may be granted although the mistake involved some element of negligence, particularly when the other party has been in no way prejudiced."[6] The rules for determining whether or not a contract exists after a mistake has been made are the basic fairness rules. The judicial system will more than likely allow a supplier to be absolved from the contract due to a mistake if the supplier gave the purchaser notification of the mistake before the purchaser relied on the bid. Buyers should therefore attempt to minimize the occurrence of contractual mistakes.

The Uniform Commercial Code

Purchasing Law before the UCC

In today's society, we take for granted that there is a certain level of fairness and predictability in the legal system. This was not always the case. Laws differed from nation to nation, state to state, and city to city. In the United States, every state had, and still does have, the power to enact is own laws concerning business transactions.

Beginning in the 1950s, a national editorial board of legal scholars drafted the body of laws concerning business transactions, which was intended to make business transactions regular and predictable. The goal was to reduce the number of state-by-state variations. The resulting code was the federal Uniform Commercial Code. In 1952, all of the states (with the exception of Louisiana) adopted the UCC.

It is important to note that the UCC does not apply in international contracts. In such cases, it makes sense to specify the substantive law that applies to the contract in the contract, enforcing the precaution of "buyer beware."

A number of subsequent revisions to the UCC have kept its provisions more responsive to changing business conditions. The UCC that is in use today consists of the following 10 articles:

1. General introductory provisions
2. Sales of goods and products
3. Transactions in commercial paper (bank checks, liability for endorsements)
4. Bank deposits and collections
5. Letters of credit (financial instruments issued by banks and other institutions)
6. Bank transfers
7. Warehouse receipts, bills of lading, and other documents of title to goods
8. Transfers in investment securities
9. Secured transactions
10. Technical matters

It is important to understand that the established common law of contracts discussed in the previous section may often be at odds with actual commercial practices that were favored by contracting parties for the flexibility and efficiency they offered. As such, the Uniform Commercial Code is not actually "the law" of commercial contracts. For the most part, the UCC is a "gap-filler" and is only pertinent if the parties themselves do not supply a contract term, or the term is left open. For example, if nothing is said in a sales contract about delivery, then under the UCC, the goods are considered delivered to the buyer when they are given to the buyer at the seller's establishment. In like fashion, under the UCC if nothing different is said in a sales contract, payment is due at the time of delivery of goods. In general, the "standard terms" as dictated by the UCC are applicable unless the parties agree to something else, which they generally do.[7]

The primary portion of the Uniform Commercial Code that concerns purchasing is Article 2, which deals with sales contracts. The UCC provides benefits to the buying firm in four ways:

1. If a seller makes an offer in writing, the seller has to live up to it for the period of time stated.
2. Verbal agreements, when confirmed in writing and if no objection is made, are valid.
3. The conflict between a buyer's purchase order terms and a seller's acknowledgment terms will generally be resolved according to the two firms' prior conduct. Specifically, a course of dealing (prior conduct) between parties and any usage of trade in the vocation or trade in which they are engaged give particular meaning or qualify terms of an agreement.
4. As far as warranties are concerned, the purchasing manager can legally rely on the supplier to provide the item needed to do the job.

The real effect of Article 2 is to support the buying firm's position in its commercial dealings with its suppliers. The UCC, as opposed to other laws such as the Uniform Sales Act, establishes each party's rights and obligations based on the concepts of fairness and reasonableness, which are founded on accepted business practices.

It should also be noted that the sale of services is not outlined but is covered under common law (system of jurisprudence). In cases where either the common law or the UCC may apply, the prevailing condition is the location where the bulk of funds is expended. One can also agree in a contract to override parts of the UCC—so it is important to read the fine print on contracts, being aware of the words "unless otherwise agreed." Because the UCC does not apply outside the boundaries of the United States—international law may have a wide range of agreements related to business transactions—the rule of thumb is "buyer beware." The most basic elements of Article 2 within the UCC involve the following four issues:

- Warranties
- Transportation terms and risk of loss
- Seller's rights
- Buyer's rights

Sourcing Snapshot — *Contract Rights in a Declining Market*

The decrease in market price of an item was the cause of a dispute involving an electronic manufacturing service (EMS) that supplied the subassemblies to a major military contractor. The EMS purchased the components from a distributor of electronic components for a contract it had received on a major satellite project.

After receiving the subcontract on the satellite project, the EMS sent out bids on a number of components. The distributor was awarded a contract to supply integrated circuits (ICs) and other items on an "as needed" basis. In essence the EMS agreed to buy all of the integrated circuits needed during the contract period from the distributor.

After nine months the distributor noticed that the quantities of ICs had dropped dramatically. An e-mail was sent to the supply manager indicating that hardly any ICs had been purchased during the past six weeks. The supply manager's e-mail reply was that "a competitor is supplying us ICs to the same specification at less than half of the price you charged us. If you can meet the price, fine. Otherwise we no longer need ICs from your firm." In her reply the distributor agreed that a new technology and lower demand had triggered lower market prices. However, the EMS had agreed to purchase all the ICs at a higher price earlier in the year. Subsequent meetings failed to produce a satisfactory agreement and the parties agreed to binding arbitration.

In its arguments to the arbitrator the EMS contended that the contract merely represented its agreement to purchase as few or as many ICs as it desired and that the distributor was obligated to supply the ICs as needed. Because the EMS was well stocked with ICs from the distributor's competitor it didn't require additional ICs. The distributor argued that the EMS was committed to buying all ICs from it at the agreed-upon price. Any purchases from an outside source violated the spirit and terms of the contract.

ARBITRATOR'S RULING

The arbitrator ruled that a mere price drop was not a reason to circumvent the terms of the contract. First, the contract was voluntarily made by competent parties. There was no indication of undue pressure or that one of the parties was made to accept the terms. Thus the contract was not "unconscionable." Second, a needs contract should be given its literal interpretation. In this case the EMS must purchase any ICs it needs from the distributor named in the contract. Clearly it needed the ICs it purchased from the competitor. It is unfortunate for the buyer that the market price for the ICs dropped. However, if the price had risen, the distributor would have had to furnish the ICs at the lower price. These are hazards of the marketplace that are faced by both buyers and sellers. The EMS was directed to purchase the entire quantity of the ICs it had contracted for from the distributor and all future requirements needed over the remainder of the contract period.

Source: Adapted from G. H. Friedman, "Contract Challenge," *Electronic Buyer News,* August 1992.

Warranties

Warranties ensure that a buyer can legally rely on a supplier to provide the item needed to do a job. In its most basic form, a warranty is defined as "a promise or representation made by the seller, which, if necessary, can be legally enforced."[8] There are two major types of warranties: express and implied.

Express Warranty

The UCC definition of an **express warranty** is, "Any affirmation of fact or promise made by the seller to the buyer which relates to the goods and becomes part of the basis of the bargain creates an express warranty that the goods shall conform to the affirmation or promise." Section 2-313 of the UCC indicates that use of a sample or a description of a good, which could include advertising, can create an express warranty. Warranties can be created in a variety of ways without being a written part of the contract.

Buyers must be aware that the legal system in the United States has repeatedly ruled that suppliers' sales representatives (i.e., special agents) have a natural tendency to promote the capabilities and performance of their products and services for the sole purpose of making a sale. In other words, it is not illegal for sellers to exaggerate the merits of their product during their sales pitch. Because sales personnel are considered special (not "general") agents, it is not illegal for them to exaggerate the merits of their product. In general, sellers are bound by representations of sales agents unless they indicate in the contract that they are not bound.

For example, consider the following:

> *Mike's Bakery needs flour, so Mike goes to Billy Bob's Flour Power Mill. Billy Bob says that he has a shipment of Grade A flour ready to sell. Billy Bob says that the shipment is all Grade A flour, and he gives a sample of the flour to Mike to inspect and provides a written statement describing the composition of the "Grade A flour." The sample of flour that Mike inspects meets the requirements for Grade A flour.*

Mike buys the flour, pursuant to a contract of sale for "Grade A flour." However, when the shipment arrives at the bakery, it is not Grade A flour; it is spoiled and full of worms.

There is no doubt that Mike can sue Billy Bob for breach of an express warranty that the flour was Grade A flour. The contract said the shipment would be Grade A flour, and Billy Bob made an affirmation of fact when he told Mike that the shipment was Grade A flour and more importantly provided a written statement describing the composition of Grade A flour. Further, the sample of flour was an express warranty that the rest of the flour would be as good as the sample.

Implied Warranties

The other form of warranty is the **implied warranty**, which deals with the concept of fitness for use and merchantability. These are also part of the contract even though they are not written, unless they are specifically disclaimed. The implied warranty of fitness for use (particular purpose) means when the seller at the time of contracting has reason to know of any particular purpose for which the goods are required, and the buyer is relying on the seller's skill or judgment to select or furnish suitable goods, there is (unless excluded or modified) an implied warranty that the goods shall be fit for such purpose. For example:

> *Mike goes to buy an industrial air-conditioning unit for his bakery. He goes to Joe's Air-Conditioning Supply Company. Mike describes the size of his bakery, the amount of heat produced by the machinery, how cool he wants to keep the facility, and so on. Joe recommends the NotSoHot 1000,*

and Mike buys it. The machinery turns out to be inadequate: It can't keep the bakery cool, and it blows out after a few days.

In this case, Mike can sue Joe for breach of the implied warranty of fitness for a particular purpose, because Joe had reason to know that Mike was buying an air conditioner for a particular purpose and that Mike relied on Joe's skill and judgment to select a suitable machine. A warranty of merchantability means that the good being exchanged meets the standards of the trade and its quality is appropriate for ordinary use. This means that people who are in the business of selling certain products imply to their customers that the products are of "fair average quality." Another example:

Mike's Bakery sells 10,000 glazed doughnuts to Dot. Dot runs a retail business called Dot's Donut Dollies, which sells coffee, doughnuts, and other breakfast items. The doughnuts turn out to have been mistakenly glazed with salt instead of sugar and, as a result, have a terrible flavor.

Dot can sue Mike for breach of an implied warranty of merchantability, because Mike's Bakery is a merchant with respect to doughnuts, and the doughnuts are not fit for the ordinary uses for which such products are used (i.e., enjoyable eating!).

Warranty of Title and Warranty of Infringement

The purchasing manager in day-to-day activities may occasionally encounter two other types of warranties: warranty of title and warranty of infringement. Warranty of title essentially indicates that the supplier warrants that it has title to the goods and that they are not stolen or subject to any security interest or liens. In our example, Billy Bob warrants that the flour is his to sell to Mike, and that it is not stolen property. When there are doubts as to the legitimacy of the title to the goods, purchasing managers will need to take additional steps to ensure proper transfer of title, and ensure that the supplier has the right to sell the product.

The warranty of infringement refers to the supplier's guarantee that the goods being exchanged do not illegally infringe on another party's patent protection. The costs and penalties for patent infringement are so severe that most standard purchasing agreements contain an appropriate patent indemnification clause. If patent infringement is determined, then the damaged party can sue for an injunction to prevent further use of that item, potentially disrupting a firm's sales of products containing the item in dispute. A simple warranty of infringement in the purchaser's contracts is not enough protection. A broader patent indemnification clause provides a greater level of safety for the buying organization. For example, if a firm provides design specifications that infringe on a third party's patent, the organization as well as the maker of that particular part may be subject to litigation. If the seller warrants that his goods do not infringe and the buyer obtains an indemnification clause, it means that the seller is liable to pay the legal expenses and court damages for a buyer sued by a third party for a patent infringement.

Patent infringement goes both ways and should be adequately protected against.

The following general suggestions can help purchasing managers to protect their organizations against warranty problems:[9]

- Write a good purchase order (and order acceptance form)
- Build a file

- Write letters and save letters
- Use good standard terms and conditions
- Consider calling the seller's attention to the warranties

Transportation Terms and Risk of Loss

Although very important, transportation documentation and delivery terms are frequently overlooked as a significant factor in many purchasing contracts. Transportation documents are used in domestic transportation to govern, direct, control, and provide information about a shipment.[10] Most of the laws governing movement of freight by truck or rail have been transferred to the new National Surface Transportation Board (NSTB).

The bill of lading—perhaps the most common and singularly important shipping document—describes the origin of the shipment, provides specific directions for the carrier, delineates the transportation contract terms, and functions as a receipt for the shipment. In some circumstances, the bill of lading may also serve as a certificate of title for the shipment. The bill of lading contains the following information:

- The name and address of the consignor and consignee
- Routing instructions for the carrier
- A description of the goods being transported
- The number of items with corresponding commodity descriptions
- The freight class or rate for the commodity being shipped

The freight bill serves as the carrier's invoice for the freight charges involved in the movement of a particular shipment. As part of the freight bill, the NSTB regulations require that credit terms be listed to avoid potential price discrimination between shippers. Freight bills may be classified as either prepaid or collect, to determine when the freight bill is to be tendered, regardless of whether the charges are paid in advance or not. On prepaid shipments, the freight bill is presented on the effective date of shipment. On collect shipments, the freight bill is presented on the effective date of delivery. Also, any adverse condition of the shipment should be noted here to facilitate any potential freight claims with the carrier.

Under the UCC, the risk of loss is with the seller until the title passes to the buyer.

However, the following conditions can apply:

- The buyer and seller can agree in their contract as to when in the transaction the risk of loss becomes the buyer's rather than the seller's.
- If the seller is to ship goods by a third-party carrier, but the seller is not required to deliver the goods to a specific place (just to take the goods to the carrier), the risk of loss becomes the buyer's when the goods are delivered to the carrier.
- If the seller is required to ship goods to a specific place, the risk of loss becomes the buyer's when the goods are delivered to the specific place.
- If the goods are held by a third party that is responsible for their storage, such as a commercial warehouse, the risk of loss becomes the buyer's when the buyer receives certain documents of title or the third party acknowledges the buyer's right to take the goods.

- If the goods are defective, the risk of loss does not become the buyer's unless the defects are fixed or the buyer agrees to accept the defective goods.

Delivery terms essentially describe who is responsible for the selection of a carrier and payment of the freight bill, and the method in which the title of goods passes between the purchaser and the supplier. The term "FOB" (free on board) delineates the point at which the supplier is responsible for freight charges and where the purchaser assumes title to the shipment. "FOB shipping point" (or "FOB origin") indicates that the purchaser is responsible for payment of transportation costs and assumes title of the goods at the supplier's shipping dock. "FOB destination" (or "FOB delivered") tells us that the supplier is responsible for transportation, and the purchaser assumes title of the goods at his or her own shipping dock. The FOB term also defines which party is responsible for filing any freight damage claims. Essentially, the party who possesses title to the goods is responsible for filing the claim. The designation "CIF"—similar to FOB but referring to international shipments—stands for "cost, insurance, and freight," so that essentially the contract price includes these costs in addition to the price of the goods. These costs may also include tariffs, customs duties, inspections, and so on, so buyers should be especially careful when agreeing to CIF terms.

In most cases, a loss results in a freight claim being filed with the carrier to recover payment as a result of shipment loss, damage, or delay. Such documents can also be filed with the carrier to recover overcharge premiums. In order to be valid, freight claims must be filed within nine months of the date of actual or reasonable date of delivery.

The carrier must respond with an acknowledgment of receipt of the claim within 30 days and then notify the claimant regarding whether or not the claim will be paid within 120 days. If the claim is not resolved within an additional 120 days, the carrier must notify the claimant of the reasons for not settling the claim each 60 days.

If the carrier has refused to pay the claim, then the claimant has two years from the time the claim was disallowed to file for legal relief in the courts.

It is recommended that purchasing managers clearly specify delivery terms in the purchase contract to ensure that they receive the shipping and freight terms expected.

It is important to signify these terms in as much detail as possible, even to the point of spelling out exact locations including street addresses and dock locations, if applicable.

When in doubt, err on the side of increased detail. Unless otherwise specified in the purchase contract, the UCC recognizes FOB origin as the default delivery term.

Seller's and Buyer's Rights

Seller's Rights

Article 2 of the UCC is very specific about sellers' and buyers' rights. Specifically, sellers have the right to do the following:

- Sue the buyer for the purchase price of the goods if the buyer basically refuses to pay for them.
- Recover reasonable costs and expenses incurred if goods have to be resold.

- Receive compensation for additional costs and expenses incurred by reason of the buyer's wrongful conduct.

The right to sue for the purchase price of goods is basically a breach of contract lawsuit. However, if there are still goods in the seller's possession, the seller may be required to try to resell the goods for a fair price in order to offset what the buyer owes. This becomes especially important in end-of-life strategies. The buyer should let the seller know well in advance if a product is going to be discontinued to allow the seller to deplete existing inventories. If the goods are in the possession of the seller, the buyer cannot resell them.

Buyer's Rights

According to the UCC, a buyer's rights include the right to do the following:

- Reject defective goods that the seller cannot repair within a reasonable time.
- Sue for breach of contract.
- Revoke acceptance of goods if the buyer discovers defects.
- Seek a court order forcing the seller to deliver the goods ("specific performance").
- Recover any extra expense incurred for having to purchase replacement goods from another seller.
- Retain the right to recover costs and expenses caused by a breach of warranty.

According to Article 2 of the UCC, a buyer can reject defective goods, but that right is waived once the buyer accepts the goods after having an opportunity to inspect. However, the buyer has responsibility with respect to seller goods in the buyer's possession. When a buyer accepts delivery of goods from a supplier (including a pickup from the supplier's plant), the buyer is responsible if it does not catch the defects. This is an excellent argument for certifying suppliers' processes and not relying on inspection as a means to ensure quality. In most cases, a supplier will want to remedy the problem to avoid conflict, but not always. If absolutely necessary, a buyer can get a court order to force the seller to deliver the goods. This might occur in a capacity problem and is known as "specific performance." A buyer can also recover costs and expenses caused by a breach of warranty, including inspection costs, storage costs, and return shipment costs.

Patents and Intellectual Property

As suppliers become increasingly integrated into new-product development, intellectual property agreements are becoming the norm. The U.S. Constitution provides the framework for the intellectual property legal system, including patent and copyright law, as we know it today, through Article 1, Section 8, Clause 8, which says that "Congress shall have the Power . . . to promote the Progress of Science and useful Arts, by securing for limited Times to Authors and Inventors the exclusive Right to their respective Writings and Discoveries."[11] There are three kinds of intellectual property in the United States: (1) patents, (2) copyrights, and (3) trade secrets. Patent law has been established in several federal patent statutes including the Patent Act of 1790, 35 U.S.C. Section 1, and companion laws. Copyright law is founded in the federal statutes, particularly in the Copyright Act of 1976. Federal patent and copyright laws overrule any contradictory state statutes. By contrast, trade secret law is grounded in common law and is intended to protect unique ideas that would not otherwise have legal protection under patent and copyright law. Because common law varies by state, there is some variance in actual statutes. However, most states have created laws that are very similar.

Sourcing Snapshot — *You Be the Judge*

SCENARIO 1

The Mark Anthony Pet Shop writes to Cleopatra, stating, "Dear Cleo: A once-in-a-lifetime opportunity for you. We just received a shipment of asps. They are healthy, friendly, love kids and make great watch-snakes. As a preferred customer you can receive one for \$50. The price includes fang removal. Please respond by fax only." Cleo sends a letter of acceptance by regular mail because the UCC allows acceptance by "any reasonable means." Is Cleo's acceptance valid?

SCENARIO 2

The Voyager Ports Steamship Line contracts to buy 50 of the 25-person-capacity lifeboats from Robinson Crusoe's Lifeboat Company. Crusoe ships the 15-person lifeboats instead of the 25-person ones. Could there be a contract under these conditions?

SCENARIO 3

Amanda, a buyer for ABC, orders 100,000 RAM devices for delivery on June 1. On May 10 the seller advises Amanda there will be no shipment on June 1 due to production problems. What are Amanda's alternatives?

ANSWERS

SCENARIO 1

Cleo's acceptance is not valid because Mark Anthony specifically and unambiguously asked for a fax. Although acceptance through any reasonable means is normally valid, offerors can restrict the acceptable means of acceptance as long as they do so unambiguously.

SCENARIO 2

There is a contract only if Voyager Ports Steamship accepts the nonconforming goods. This could occur in the following ways: (1) notifying Crusoe that it will take the boats even though they are nonconforming; (2) failing to inspect them after a reasonable time to do so; and (3) acting inconsistently with Crusoe's ownership (UCC Section 2-606), such as attaching the lifeboats to Voyager's ships.

SCENARIO 3

UCC Section 2-217 states that after a breach the buyer is entitled to cover by going into the market and buying the goods to replace those not forthcoming. The buyer must recover from the seller the difference between the contract price and cover price. The buyer may also recover any incidental and consequential damages less any expenses saved as a result of the cover.

Source: Adapted from "UCC Article 2 Quiz," *Purchasing Management of Silicon Valley Newsletter*, April 1991, p. 4.

In its most basic form, a patent is an agreement between the inventor and the federal government. Successful patentees in the United States are now entitled to exclusive rights (to make, use, or sell) an invention for the life of the patent 20 years from the filing date with the U.S. Patent Office.

Although the inventor has exclusive rights (i.e., a monopoly) to the invention during the patent period, others gain that right to the benefits of the invention following expiration of the protection period, thereby providing public benefit. A U.S. patent is applicable only to the inventor's exclusive use within the borders of the United States. Inventors wishing to expand their patent protection to other countries must file appropriate patent applications in each country in which protection is desired.

Note that in some countries, such as China and India, copyrights and patents may not be recognized at all. In recent years, because of the entry of these countries into the World Trade Organization, both China and India recognize copyrights (at least verbally), but piracy remains a constant problem.

A firm needs to protect itself from inadvertent patent infringement whenever it purchases a product from a supplier. This can best be done by including a patent indemnification clause in all purchasing documents. This clause should consist of three parts:

1. An indemnification, which seeks the supplier's assurances that the goods being contracted for do not infringe on any other party's patents
2. The right to require the supplier to defend any patent infringement suit itself
3. The right to have the purchaser's own attorneys involved in defense of any lawsuit concerning patent infringement

The UCC provides minimal protection for the purchasers in defending themselves against legal actions stemming from patent infringement. Therefore, indemnification agreements should be included in contracts with suppliers whenever possible.

A copyright is designed to afford protection for persons who create original works such as books, software, songs, and films. A copyright on written material is generally good for the life of the author plus 50 years. Copyright law does not require a formal application, as does patent law. In addition, it is not necessary for the copyright originator to place any legend or indication on the protected material indicating that the material is copyrighted. Copyright is automatically assumed. However, most legal experts recommend that some sort of language in the form of a copyright notice be included on any works desired to be protected, along with the copyright symbol: ©. This notice provides evidence that the creator of the article in question intends to maintain copyright privileges in the event of infringement. It should also be noted that registering copyrightable works and providing notice entitles copyright owners to much greater damages in the event of a copyright infringement suit.

A trade secret (also known as confidential information) is a very broad category of intellectual property. Virtually any information believed to be confidential and important to an organization can be deemed to be a trade secret or confidential information.

Resources as diverse as formulas, supplier and customer lists, procedures, and training programs could all be regarded as trade secrets. In order to receive trade secret protection under the law, the organization must take steps to minimize or preclude the distribution of its sensitive information. The information must also be deemed to possess the following three characteristics:

- It is economically valuable.
- It is not generally known.
- It is kept as a secret.

Exhibit 15.3 Nondisclosure Agreement

Supplier's Name
Supplier's Address
City, State, Zip Code

Re: *Nondisclosure Agreement*

In conjunction with recent discussions, our Company has disclosed and it is anticipated in the future that our Company will disclose to your company or your company will observe, or come in contact with, certain confidential information that is the property of our Company. This information will include, without limitation, certain proprietary items related to our Company's know-how, processes, machinery, and manufacturing aspects of our Company's business.

In consideration thereof, it is our understanding that except as hereafter specifically authorized in writing by our Company, your company shall not disclose to any party (a) the fact that it is assisting our Company in this matter; (b) any confidential information heretofore or hereafter disclosed by our Company to your company or that your company observes or comes in contact with, not in the possession of your company prior to the date of such disclosure, observance, or contact; or (c) any marketing, financial, or technical information developed or generated by your company for our Company at our request and direct or indirect expense. Your company shall neither use nor furnish to any party any equipment or material embodying or made by the use of such information, provided, however, that:

1. Should any of the aforesaid information be published or otherwise made available to the public through sources that are entitled to disclose the same, and should your company demonstrate to our Company that it has obtained said information from a source available to the public, then in that event your company shall be free with respect to this understanding to disclose said information to any party;
2. Your company understands that nothing herein shall be construed to grant any right or license under any industrial property rights (patents, trademarks, and copyrights) of our Company.

Will you please indicate your company's concurrence in the foregoing understanding by signing and returning to us the enclosed duplicate of this letter.

Very truly yours,

____

(Name and title)

XXX: xxx

Accepted By: ______________________

Name: ______________________

Title: ______________________

Date: ______________________

Trade secret protection becomes essentially self-serving through the actions of the organization itself. For instance, if information that could otherwise be considered trade secrets is not protected through devices such as limited access or other security precautions, then the courts have ruled that this information is not confidential and, therefore, not entitled to protection. This test of confidential information can also be applied to any information that suppliers provide to the purchasing firm through the normal course of business dealings. As before, however, the supplier must make it known that the information is proprietary and is to be kept confidential. As a precaution, any information provided to a supplier should be accompanied by notification that the information is provided in confidence and should be treated as such by the supplier. This is typically known as a nondisclosure agreement (NDA). See Exhibit 15.3 for an example of a nondisclosure agreement.

Other Laws Affecting Purchasing

Laws Affecting Antitrust and Unfair Trade Practices

A number of federal laws deal with antitrust and competitive practices of interstate commerce. Each law seeks to promote the fair conduct of business and preserve competition in markets. Although most of these laws apply to the conduct of the seller, some provisions apply directly or indirectly to purchasers.

Sherman Antitrust Act (1890)

This law prohibits actions that are "in restraint of trade" or actions that attempt to monopolize a market or create a monopoly. Price fixing, dividing territories among competitors, and agreements that limit the supply of a commodity are violations of the Sherman Act. However, the law also prohibits reciprocity or reciprocal purchase agreements, where the effect of such agreements limits competition.

Federal Trade Commission Act (FTCA, 1914)

This act authorizes the Federal Trade Commission (FTC) to interpret trade legislation, including the provisions of the Sherman Antitrust Act that deal with restraint of trade. The FTCA also addresses unfair competition and unfair or deceptive trade practices. Unfair trade practices include (1) those that allow large firms to gain advantage over smaller rivals; (2) predatory competition; (3) restraint of trade; and (4) misleading or deceptive practices such as false advertising.

Clayton Antitrust Act (1914)

This law, which broadened the Sherman Act, makes price discrimination illegal and prohibits sellers from exclusive arrangements with purchasers or product distributors. One of the most common exclusive agreements is a tying agreement, where a supplier makes the sale of one product contingent upon the sale of another product. Thus suppliers must make unbundled individual products available to buyers. Exclusive agreements are those where the buyer must purchase all requirements from one supplier. Price discrimination between different purchasers is prohibited if such discrimination substantially lessens competition or tends to create a monopoly in any line of commerce.

Robinson-Patman Act (1936)

This law strengthens the Clayton Act by clarifying the issue of price discrimination, particularly as it pertains to limiting the powers of large buyers. It prohibits sellers from offering a discriminatory price where the effect of discrimination may limit competition or create a monopoly. There is also a provision that prohibits purchasers from inducing a discriminatory price. Although a seller may legally lower a price as a concession during negotiations, the purchaser should not mislead or trick the seller, thus resulting in a price that is discriminatory to other buyers in the market. Robinson-Patman violations occur when different prices are charged to different buyers. Thus most sellers develop uniform pricing policies that are subject to quantity discounts as a result of economic scale advantages for producing and selling larger quantities.

The law makes provision for price differences in certain situations. First, as mentioned above, is for differences in costs of manufacturing or sale due to quantities and methods of production and distribution. Second is the good-faith attempt to meet a lower competitive price. Third is if the goods are perishable via deterioration, seasonality, or distress sales under court orders.

Laws Affecting Global Purchasing

Many laws—U.S., foreign, and international—affect global commerce. The following briefly summarizes some of the laws that can affect a purchaser's international business dealings.[12]

The United Nations Convention on Contracts for International Sale of Goods (CISG)

This is an attempt by the United Nations to facilitate international trade by removing legal barriers. Unless the parties have specified to the contrary, the CISG applies to the sale of goods between parties with places of business in the contracting states. Contracting states are countries that have ratified the CISG. As of 2006 there were 70 countries that had ratified the CISG. These 70 countries account for 75% of the world's trade. One of the key provisions to its success is the flexibility to take exception to specified articles of the code on a contract-by-contract basis.

Foreign Corrupt Practices Act

This law prohibits payments (such as bribes) that might benefit a foreign official personally. Although the law usually pertains to sellers, purchasers should understand its provisions so they can recognize situations addressed by the act.

Anti-Boycott Legislation

Various laws address doing business with countries that support the boycott of one nation against another. Examples include the boycott of Israel by Arab countries and the boycott of Taiwan by mainland China. These laws require reporting of any request to participate in a boycott, which purchasers often fail to do.

Export Administration Act

Various laws and regulations govern, and sometimes even restrict, the export of goods, information, and services. Purchasers may not perceive that they are engaged in exporting. However, the law views certain types of drawings, specifications, and prototypes forwarded to a foreign entity as restricted exports of technology. Purchasers are urged to seek the advice of an expert when questions arise in this area.

Customs Laws

This body of law addresses the importation of goods into the United States. Customs brokers who are familiar with customs laws can be quite valuable in understanding the rules and regulations governing importation.

Foreign Laws

In addition to the U.S. laws that apply to foreign transactions, the laws and regulations of other countries involved in a business transaction may also apply. These laws will likely address contract law, export control, currency control, and criminal law. Some transactions could be illegal if structured in a certain manner.

International Laws

Other laws may apply to a business transaction that are not part of any specific country's laws and regulations. Maritime laws are a good example of international laws that affect international commerce. Several international documents are also pertinent to international transactions. These include International Contracting Terms.

The laws governing purchasing are complex and varied. Other laws address environmental and labor issues. This overview simply points out that today's purchaser must be aware of the laws and regulations governing domestic and international purchasing.

A purchaser is urged to discuss with legal counsel any questions that arise during the performance of job responsibilities. Ignorance of the law is not a valid defense.

Purchasing Ethics

Ethics have their basis in the field of philosophy and identify common principles associated with appropriate versus inappropriate actions, moral duty, and obligation. Ethics are the set of moral principles or values guiding our behavior. In a business setting, ethical behavior is the use of recognized social principles involving justice and fairness throughout a business relationship. When interacting with suppliers, an ethical buyer treats them in a just, decent, fair, honest, and fitting manner. Being ethical means following a code viewed as fair by those within the profession as well as the community.[13] A 2004 study on purchasing education and training requirements indicated ethics was the number one knowledge requirement now and forecasted to be five years into the future.[14]

Three rules are understood to be a part of ethical behavior. First, buyers must commit their attention and energies for the organization's benefit rather than personal enrichment at the expense of the organization. Ethical buyers do not accept outside gifts or favors that violate their firm's ethics policy. Ethical buyers are also not tempted or influenced by the unethical practices of salespeople and do not have personal financial arrangements with suppliers. Second, a buyer must act ethically toward suppliers or potential suppliers. This means treating each supplier professionally and with respect. Finally, buyers must uphold the ethical standards set forth by their profession. A code or statement of professional ethics usually formalizes the set of ethical standards.

Purchasing managers, more than any other group within a firm, experience enormous pressure to act in unethical ways. This occurs for several reasons. First, purchasing has direct control over large sums of money. A buyer responsible for a multimillion-dollar contract may find sellers using any means available to secure a favorable position. The very nature of purchasing means that a buyer must come in contact with outside, and occasionally unethical, sellers. A second reason is the pressure placed on many salespeople. A seller that must meet aggressive sales goals might resort to questionable sales practices.

Risks of Unethical Behavior

A buyer who performs an unethical act runs the risk that the act is also illegal. For example, a government buyer who accepts payment from a defense contractor has clearly committed an unethical and illegal act. If this payment becomes known, the buyer risks legal penalty as defined by the law. The buyer's firm also risks a legal penalty. At a minimum, the buyer will probably lose his or her job.

Unethical behavior also presents a personal risk to a buyer's professional reputation.

Sellers quickly become aware of buyers who are open to offers "on the side." Once a buyer earns a reputation within an industry, it is difficult to change it. A buyer also runs a risk that management will discover his or her lack of ethics and terminate employment. A professional reputation is something a buyer carries throughout an entire career. If a buyer is found guilty of accepting a bribe, companies will not only terminate the buyer, but may often pursue litigation as well. Personal financial bankruptcy or even jail sentences can result for buyers who are found guilty of accepting large bribes.

A final risk of unethical behavior is the risk to a firm's reputation. A buyer who makes purchase decisions based on factors other than legitimate business criteria risks the reputation of the entire firm. For example, quality may suffer if a buyer accepts substandard performance from a supplier that offered outside inducements. A buyer's unethical behavior can jeopardize the livelihood of others dependent on a firm's success. World-class suppliers do not have to practice unethical behavior to win contracts.

To summarize the legal perspective, accepting a supplier's outside gifts and favors in exchange for special treatment is a form of corruption. The U.S. business environment does not treat unethical behavior lightly. Buyers who practice unethical behavior subject themselves and their firms to increased risk and diminish the integrity of the purchasing profession. Firms dealing with global sourcing sometimes encounter unethical behavior, particularly in developing countries, where bribery may be viewed as a routine source of extra income. However, global firms are increasingly adopting an unequivocal zero-tolerance stance toward any form of bribery, even if it means sacrificing short-term profitability to maintain a global reputation of integrity and honesty in its dealings with suppliers. Further, the main provisions of the Foreign Corrupt Practices Act (part of the securities laws) make it illegal to bribe government officials in foreign countries and prevent companies from deducting bribes from their federal taxes.

Types of Unethical Purchasing Behavior

Suppose a buyer at Firm XYZ has the highest moral and ethical values—the buyer has strong beliefs about what is proper behavior within the purchasing profession. Conflict can occur if a supervisor asks the buyer to do something the buyer feels is unethical. For example, a manager may ask a buyer to award a contract because of a personal friendship with a supplier. The buyer may feel this is unethical.

Does the buyer simply award the contract in compliance with the manager's instruction, and ignore his or her own personal and moral values? Or does the buyer refuse to award the contract, thereby challenging the authority of a manager and jeopardizing his or her career? Although a professional buyer should know the difference between right and wrong, organizational pressures can force a buyer to behave in ways that conflict with personal values, which creates a difficult situation for the individual. How should a person respond in this situation?

The definition of ethical behavior can differ from buyer to buyer or from firm to firm. Despite these possible differences, most professionals recognize certain behavior or actions as unethical. Most companies have established guidelines that reinforce that these behaviors are unethical and therefore unacceptable. Some of these behaviors are listed below.

Reciprocity

This action involves giving preferential treatment to suppliers that are also customers of the buying organization.[15] In simple terms, it refers to a purchasing arrangement that dictates "I'll buy from you if you buy from me." The Federal Trade Commission has taken an aggressive stance against reciprocal buying arrangements, ruling that it is illegal "to abusively use large buying power to restrict competitive market opportunities." In the early 1970s, many larger firms entered into agreements with the FTC forbidding reciprocal purchasing. These firms also eliminated their internal trade departments established to coordinate these arrangements.[16]

FTC rulings have convinced most firms to prohibit reciprocal purchasing. Most firms do recognize a customer's right for consideration as a potential supplier. A buyer, however, must rely only on legitimate performance criteria to evaluate supplier capability.

Personal Buying

This occurs when a purchasing department purchases material for the personal needs of its employees. Some states have outlawed such practices with statutes called "trade diversion laws." These laws prohibit purchasing from engaging in personal buying for items not required during the normal course of business.

There are some exceptions to these laws. For example, a firm can purchase safety shoes, hats, gloves, or even special tools required by the employee. A purchasing department can use its knowledge to purchase products conforming to specific quality standards. Personal buying is a gray area for some purchasing departments. Some firms view personal buying as a fringe benefit and service to the employee. Other firms flatly prohibit the practice. A buyer confronted with a request for personal buying should determine the legal status of the practice, and then discuss the subject with management.

Accepting Supplier Favors

Accepting gifts and favors from a supplier is the most common ethical infraction involving buyers. These gifts and favors can affect a buyer's judgment to evaluate and select the most capable suppliers. The policy on supplier offerings is often a confusing issue. At what point does a supplier's gift or favor depart from a friendly showing of appreciation for a firm's business to an attempt to influence a buyer's purchase decisions? Accepting free items from potential suppliers is especially questionable. Here, a supplier does not even have a purchase contract. Firms can address this issue in their ethics policy by specifying exactly what a buyer may accept from a supplier.

Sharp Practices

A **sharp practice** is any misrepresentation by a buyer that falls just short of actual fraud.[17] Sharp practice occurs whenever a buyer "plays games" with a supplier and operates in an underhanded manner. The practice includes many different behaviors:

- Willful use of misinformation, when a buyer knowingly deceives a supplier to realize some advantage. For example, requesting quotes on inflated volumes and then placing smaller orders at the reduced price is a willful use of misinformation.
- Exaggerating problems. A buyer who exaggerates the size of a supplier-caused problem to extract a larger penalty or concession from a supplier is using a sharp practice.
- Requesting bids from unqualified suppliers for the sole purpose of driving a qualified supplier's price lower. A buyer should request bids from qualified suppliers only.
- Gaining information unfairly through deception.
- Sharing information on competitive quotations. The integrity of the competitive bid process requires confidentiality. Buyers who share supplier-quoted information violate the ethics of the bid process.
- Not compensating a supplier for design or other work. Buyers often request design and cost-savings assistance from suppliers. A supplier that helps a buyer should receive fair compensation for its efforts.
- Taking unfair advantage of a supplier's financial situation. A buyer who knowingly pressures a financially troubled supplier into providing a lower-than-normal price places the supplier in further financial jeopardy. Taking advantage of a financially susceptible supplier is an unethical business practice.
- Lying or misleading. Any instance of lying or misleading a seller is a sharp practice.

Financial Conflicts of Interest

When a buyer awards business to a supplier because the buyer, the buyer's family, or relatives of the buyer have a direct financial interest in a supplier, this is considered a major unethical practice. This behavior is one reason many companies require employees to detail any investments in outside companies.

Awarding a purchase contract to a company in which a buyer has a significant personal financial interest (versus owning a mutual fund that owns a small amount of stock in the company) is a serious breach of ethics. This action is similar to an executive buying or selling stock because of inside knowledge, which is an illegal act.

Influence and Ethics

Influence and attempts to influence decisions exist at several points in the supply chain. Recently, the Institute for Supply Management's (ISM's) Ethical Standards Committee addressed this important issue. Influence can be defined in several ways. Most frequently, **influence** is defined as the power to sway: "the power that somebody has to affect other people's thinking or actions by means of argument, example, or force of personality." Supply professionals regularly make decisions about what their organization buys, who they buy from, how much they buy, and how they buy it. Often, they also have input into the specifications and requirements surrounding the purchase. Suppliers regularly work to influence the decisions of supply professionals.[18]

Supply professionals must overcome the negative aspects of influence to ensure that they are objective in their decision making and that they are operating in an ethical manner. Influences such as (1) suppliers sharing new ideas, methodologies, and technologies, (2) sharing data when being involved early in design issues, and (3) a cross-functional team being involved in a comparative analysis of competing suppliers are positive and appropriate influences; they add value to decision making, whereas other influences may detract from the quality of decisions. Negative sources of influence conflict with the goal of supply professionals and other leaders to manage their responsibilities according to ethical guidelines set forth by their organizations or ISM. Examples of negative influences include (1) giving personal interests priority over employer interests; (2) inappropriate sharing of confidential or proprietary information with suppliers; and (3) accepting gifts, entertainment, or meals as a reward for a decision that could be made in favor of the supplier. These negative factors can have a negative impact on an organization.[19]

An ethics survey by the ISM's Ethical Standards Committee (see p. 572) showed that influence is a challenge for supply professionals. Survey results related to influence revealed that inappropriate preference for suppliers in sourcing decisions was a concern from 34% of the survey respondents, and politics inappropriately influencing sourcing decisions was a concern to 46% of respondents. Although only 6 to 7% of supply professionals were concerned about gifts, entertainment, and meals influencing sourcing decisions within their function, over 40% of the survey respondents indicated that individuals outside of their function received gifts, entertainment, or meals from suppliers.[20] It is important for supply professionals to be aware of the subtleties of influence so that they can better manage the potential impact on their decisions and behaviors. Regardless of the culture or continent, influence is a reality, and the goal of the supply professional is to appropriately manage it.

ISM Professional Code of Ethics

The Institute for Supply Management is the largest organization representing the purchasing profession. In 1959, the ISM officially adopted its initial Standards of Conduct.

The document serves as a guide for the ISM membership by imposing rules of conduct, particularly when a buyer's own company lacks a policy or statement of ethics.

ISM ETHICS SURVEY: INFLUENCE ISSUES	NO INFLUENCE	INFLUENCE
There are instances where your organization gave inappropriate preference to suppliers in sourcing decisions.	66%	34%
There are examples in your organization where politics inappropriately influenced sourcing decisions.	54%	46%
Gifts or entertainment inappropriately influenced sourcing decisions in your function.	93%	7%
Meals with suppliers influenced sourcing decisions in your function.	94%	6%
Others outside of your function have received gifts or entertainment from suppliers outside of your organization's policy.	55%	45%

Source: 2006 ISM Ethics Survey.

In the words of the code, "It is necessary for all of us to exercise a strict rule of personal conduct to insure that relations of a compromising nature, or even the appearance of such relations, be scrupulously avoided." The document reflects the ISM's commitment to ethical behavior and fair business dealings.

The Standards of Conduct specifies three guiding principles of purchasing practice: (1) loyalty to company, (2) justice to those with whom a buyer deals, and (3) faith in the purchasing profession. From these principles ISM derived its standards of purchasing practice, or Code of Ethics:

1. Consider, first, the interest of your company in all transactions and carry out and believe in its established policies.
2. Be receptive to competent counsel from your colleagues and be guided by such counsel without impairing the dignity and responsibility of your office.
3. Buy without prejudice, seeking to obtain the maximum value for each dollar of expenditure.
4. Strive consistently for knowledge of the materials and processes of manufacture and establish practical methods for the conduct of your office.
5. Subscribe to and work for honesty and truth in buying and selling, and denounce all forms and manifestations of commercial bribery.
6. Accord a prompt and courteous reception, so far as conditions will permit, to all who call on a legitimate business mission.
7. Respect your obligations and require that obligations to you and to your concern be respected, consistent with good business practice.
8. Avoid sharp practice.
9. Counsel and assist fellow purchasing managers in the performance of their duties, whenever the occasion permits.
10. Cooperate with all organizations and individuals engaged in activities designed to enhance the development and standing of purchasing.

These standards often help guide a firm's ethical code of conduct and policy.

The ISM standards specifically state that its members should maintain standards on an even higher plane than those accepted by society—what becomes the "true test of greatness." This is stated as follows in the code:

> *Nothing can undermine respect for the purchasing profession more than improper action on the part of its members with regard to gifts, gratuities, or favors. People engaged in purchasing should not accept from any supplier or prospective supplier any money, gift, or favor that might influence, or be suspected of influencing, their buying decisions. We must decline to accept or must return any such gift or favor offered us or members of our immediate family. The declination of these gifts or favors must be done discreetly and courteously. Possible embarrassment resulting from refusals does not constitute a basis for exception.*

The ISM Standards of Conduct is a powerful document. It holds the purchasing profession to the highest levels of ethical conduct. Companies of all sizes from many industries have used the Code of Ethics as a guide when developing their own ethical policies.

Supporting Ethical Behavior

A firm can take many actions to make sure its employees conduct business in an ethical manner. The following sections summarize the actions a firm can take to enhance the ethical behavior of its purchasing personnel.

Developing a Statement of Ethics

Most research on purchasing ethics concludes that adopting a formal ethics policy helps define and deter potentially unethical purchasing behavior. An earlier study found that firms without formal ethical policies disclosed supplier bid prices to other suppliers at a much higher rate than firms with a formal policy prohibiting this practice.[21] Also, firms without a formal ethics policy were more likely to make discounted purchases for their employees, a questionable practice in some states. A formal ethics policy helps define the boundaries of ethical behavior.

Top-Management Commitment

Executive management sets the ethical code of behavior within a firm. Although the highest executive may not actually write a firm's purchasing or marketing code of ethics, the ethical behavior of top executives sends a message about whether or not unethical behavior is tolerated. Lower-level managers quickly recognize top management's commitment to ethical behavior and imitate the commitment, especially when other managers are fired because of their unethical behavior! (See the Good Practice Example on Eaton Corporation at the end of this chapter.)

Closer Buyer-Seller Relationships

Dealing with a smaller supply base or a single supplier for an item will probably do more for ethical purchasing behavior than any other recent trend or action. Firms are increasingly using buying teams to evaluate potential suppliers across different performance categories. Using a team approach to evaluate a supplier's capabilities limits the opportunity for unethical behavior. Unethical suppliers will find it tougher to influence a team of professionals.

Ethical Training

New buyers, usually at larger firms, often enter a training program before actually assuming their professional duties. One part of the training usually deals with purchasing ethics. Such a program is an opportunity to educate a new buyer about a firm's ethics policy. Firms often use role playing to help buyers learn how to identify different types of unethical behavior and how to confront and deal with these situations. Ethics training reinforces a firm's commitment to the highest ethical standards.

Developing Consistent Behavior

Confusion about proper ethical behavior can arise when marketing and purchasing have separate ethical standards. A firm that prohibits its purchasing personnel from accepting gifts from suppliers but allows its marketing department to distribute gifts to its customers is not acting consistently. When different standards of behavior exist within the same firm, it becomes easier for one group to rationalize or justify unethical behavior. How can it be ethical for one group (marketing) to provide gifts and favors but unethical for another group (purchasing) within the same firm to accept any items?

Internal Reporting of Unethical Behavior

Executive purchasing management should create an atmosphere that supports the reporting of unethical behavior. A buyer should be able to approach management about an ethical impropriety with confidence that management will correct the problem. A firm should also encourage suppliers to report instances of unethical behavior by anyone within the buying firm.

Preventive Measures (Commodity Rotation and Limits of Authority)

One common strategy is to rotate buyers among different items or commodities, which prevents a buyer from becoming too comfortable with any particular group of suppliers. Although a buyer should become familiar with purchased items and suppliers, it is often a good idea to rotate personnel between buying assignments. Rotation usually occurs every several years.

Another preventive measure is to limit a buyer's purchase authority without higher-level approval. For example, a firm's policy may limit a buyer's authority for awarding purchase contracts to amounts of $10,000 or less. Contracts greater than $10,000 then require a manager's signature. A buyer must justify the selection decision based on sound purchasing criteria before obtaining the final sign-off. This provides a system of checks and balances and reduces the possibility of unethical supplier selection

Although there is a fine line between ethical and legal behavior, we believe that ethics should always come first. However, it is also important that a qualified purchasing manager develop a detailed understanding of purchasing law. Having good working knowledge of legal issues can have a positive impact on daily and long-term actions in the profession.

Corporate Social Responsibility

Corporate social responsibility is the idea that organizations and institutions have an obligation to society that extends beyond compliance with regulations in considering the broader effects of their actions. Social responsibility is becoming more accepted in 21st-century corporations. ISM has developed a guide to assist supply managers in developing their socially responsible practices. The areas covered in the policy are (1) community; (2) diversity; (3) environment; (4) ethics; (5) financial responsibility; (6) human rights; and (7) safety. Many of these topics are covered in Chapters 7 and 8 on supplier strategies and selection. This chapter has discussed ethics and to a lesser extent community issues. We will focus on the environmental issues in the remainder of this chapter; ISM's Principles of Social Responsibility encourage buyers to be proactive with suppliers and customers in creating a culture of environmental responsibility (see Exhibit 15.4 on p. 576).

The environment under the green movement is becoming a large initiative, as several major corporations have become aware of the need to reduce their impact on the environment. For example, G.E.'s chairman, Jeffrey Immelt, has made a big push toward making G.E. a corporate leader in addressing climate change. Immelt has stated he "doesn't want to change the economic flow of the company." Thus, G.E. still sells coal-fired steam turbines and is delving deeper into oil and gas production. However, its campaign dubbed "eco-imagination" was expected to sell $14 billion of environmentally friendly products in 2007 and is forecasted to grow another 10% in 2008. The firm also claims it has reduced its gas emissions by 4% in the past two years.[22]

General Motors has announced plans to invest in researching environmentally friendly technologies for the Chinese market. GM's investment will be part of a $250 million corporate campus and will involve collaboration with its local joint venture partners, the Chinese government and academia. Research will focus on several green technologies, such as hybrid vehicles, electric vehicles, alternative fuels, and new engine technologies.[23]

In addition, firms are asking supply managers to press their suppliers on increasing environmental efforts. A group of firms called the Supply Chain Leadership Council has partnered with the London-based Carbon Disclosure Project (CDP) to assist in implementing this project. CDP monitors the "carbon footprints" that firms emit. Carbon footprints are estimates of the amount of carbon dioxide emitted by firms in producing and distributing their products. Many firms measure the direct emissions such as the energy consumed in lighting their stores or the gas consumed in transporting it.[24]

Looking upstream produces a more comprehensive footprint because more emissions are involved in making the products. These end-to-end measures are leading firms such as Cadbury Schweppes to calculate the amount of carbon released in making a milk chocolate dairy bar from the farm through the factory and into the store. Future labels could contain a carbon footprint number along with the calories and ingredients.[25]

Wal-Mart has also started asking suppliers about their carbon footprint. Oakhurst Dairy, a major dairy supplier located in Portland, Maine, was asked to measure the carbon footprint of a case of milk. The result is that the company is looking at reducing energy use by converting delivery trucks to biodiesel and installing solar hot-water heaters for washing milk crates, thus reducing the company's carbon footprint.[26]

Finally, going green may be a great source of talent. "Students are looking to work for companies that care about the environment," claims author Lindsey Pollak. "They are almost expecting greenness like they expect work-life balance, ethnic diversity, and globalization." To attract students, corporations are advertising their

Exhibit 15.4 ISM Principles of Social Responsibility

Social responsibility is defined as a framework of measurable corporate policies and procedures and resulting behavior designed to benefit the workplace and, by extension, the individual, the organization, and the community in the following areas (in alphabetical order):

I. Community

1. Provide support and add value to your communities and those in your supply chain.
2. Encourage members of your supply chain to add value in their communities.

II. Diversity

1. Proactively promote purchasing from, and the development of, socially diverse suppliers.
2. Encourage diversity within your own organization.
3. Proactively promote diverse employment practices throughout the supply chain.

III. Environment

1. Encourage your own organization and others to be proactive in examining opportunities to be environmentally responsible within their supply chains either "upstream" or "downstream."
2. Encourage the environmental responsibility of your suppliers.
3. Encourage the development and diffusion of environmentally friendly practices and products throughout your organization.

IV. Ethics

1. Be aware of ISM's Principles and Standards of Ethical Supply Management Conduct.
2. Abide by your organization's code of conduct.

V. Financial Responsibility

1. Become knowledgeable of, and follow, applicable financial standards and requirements.
2. Apply sound financial practices and ensure transparency in financial dealings.
3. Actively promote and practice responsible financial behavior throughout the supply chain.

VI. Human Rights

1. Treat people with dignity and respect.
2. Support and respect the protection of international human rights within the organization's sphere of influence.
3. Encourage your organization and its supply chains to avoid complicity in human or employment rights abuses.

VII. Safety

1. Promote a safe environment for each employee in your organization and supply chain. (Each organization is responsible for defining "safe" within its organization.)
2. Support the continuous development and diffusion of safety practices throughout your organization and the supply chain.

environmental efforts. For example, Merrill Lynch outlines its environmental initiatives on the back of every recruiting brochure. One college student interviewed noticed that the companies he wanted to work for have their environmental policies prominently displayed on their websites.[27]

Good Practice Example

Eaton's CEO Talks Openly about Ethics

When Eaton Corporation Chairman and CEO Alexander M. (Sandy) Cutler addressed the winners of the company's Supplier Excellence Awards, he thanked the winners and explained the company's goals. But the goals he emphasized didn't include price reductions. Instead, he talked about values. "We want to be the most admired company in our markets through supply chain performance," he told the attendees. "Have the right ethics and the right business practices and you'll attract the best people and suppliers who'll produce the best results," Cutler said. The company has an ombudsman for ethics, with whom employees or anyone else can confer. And Eaton doesn't hesitate to stop doing business with suppliers whose business practices aren't up to its own high standards, regardless of the supplier's quality or prices.

Cutler speaks frankly about ethics and ethical issues that have faced Eaton, and how the company has dealt with them. Eaton has published a new ethics guide—translated into 14 languages—that will go to all employees to help them understand Eaton's expectations and their responsibilities. Cutler specifically discussed several examples that arose with respect to ethical issues and globalization:

"We had an issue many years ago where we were doing some advanced product development work for a significant global OEM customer. There were established timetables for development, testing, and shipment, and our customer was expecting the fully tested product to be shipped at the end of a particular quarter. When it came to the end of that quarter, not all of the testing had been accomplished. Two senior operating managers in the United States falsified the test results and thereby misrepresented the product's readiness for shipment. Both signed the reports willingly. Upon investigation, we learned that they felt they should do this in order to meet the targeted shipment timetables, because they thought this was what both Eaton and the customer wanted. Yet clearly this was a violation of Eaton's quality and ethics policies. We terminated the two managers. Both had been high-potential, highly promotable people.

"We learned a lesson from this incident—that integrity can break down at any level, no matter how much you preach and teach ethics. These were respected managers who had performed well for years. But they made a serious, serious mistake in judgment.

"We will not tolerate any compromise of our standards for quality. Nor will we knowingly violate any laws or regulations in any country. At Eaton, we do not practice what I call 'geographic' ethics. We have one set of ethics worldwide. And if the laws and regulations of a given country differ from our own company standards, we comply with whatever requirement represents the higher standard of behavior in that situation.

"It's common knowledge that governments in certain parts of the world demand substantial payments in exchange for the conduct of business. This is unacceptable geographic ethics, which is not tolerated at Eaton. I'll give you an example. Several years ago we had a facility that encountered piracy of our technology, theft of other intellectual property, and the sale of our products into gray markets. Additionally, local businessmen made copycat versions of Eaton products and threatened to label them with Eaton brand names unless we paid them not to. The local government repeatedly approached us for payments, without which it would not pursue or prosecute these matters. It became clear that we were not going to be able to do business in an environment where the ethics of local officials were so different from our own. So we abandoned the facility and our business in that country, at a not-insignificant cost. I believe that operating under a single code of ethics not only strengthens our own organization, but also those organizations that do business with Eaton. When 'a rising tide lifts all boats,' the situation changes. Can one company change the world? No, but it can chart its own ethical destiny.

"In conflict-of-interest situations, I think a company clearly controls its own destiny. Conflicts of interest can arise in any aspect of business life and therefore present multiple opportunities to choose the ethical course. China, for example, is a country where some people may see conflict-of-interest issues differently than these matters are viewed in other countries. We've learned a lot about operating in that region and are very explicit about our expectations. Eaton had a plant manager in China, a Chinese national, who fell afoul of our prohibition against conflicts of interest. Although his actions may have been acceptable to some in that country, they were not acceptable to Eaton. He replaced the supplier that was providing a commodity to our plant with a supplier in which his wife had a financial interest. It was quite clear that his decision had not been based on quality or price issues with the previous supplier. Until then, we had been very pleased with this executive's performance. He was a highly valued employee in whom we'd invested considerable training, including almost four years of cumulative operations experience in the United States and China. Despite our investment in this employee, we had to let him go. We simply could not allow this action to stand or to appear to be endorsed when it was so clearly a violation of our conflict-of-interest standards.

"When a supplier or business partner acts without integrity, we trust that our employees will make it clear that if the unethical action does not stop, the business relationship will. We do not take or use data that has been inappropriately or illegally procured. Yes, we care about results, but not at the expense of integrity."

Questions

1. Do you believe that Eaton is "too tough" in its emphasis on refusing to allow bribery, even in countries where bribery is acceptable?
2. "When in Rome, why not do as the Romans do?" Do you agree or disagree with this sentence as it pertains to Eaton's policies in dealing with international governments?
3. When individuals are found to act unethically, why doesn't Eaton give them a reprimand and a second chance?

Source: S. Cutler, *Eaton Today,* August 2003, Chairman's Column, "One to One," pp. 3–4; P. E. Teague, "Eaton Wins Purchasing's Medal of Professional Excellence," *Purchasing,* September 13, 2007, pp. 18–23.

CONCLUSION

The field of purchasing is dynamic and changing rapidly. When dealing with suppliers in contract negotiations, contract management, breach of contracts, potential damages, and patent or trade secret disputes, purchasing managers must be sure to stipulate the appropriate terms and conditions. Nevertheless, many legal disputes are being handled through discussions with suppliers instead of being referred to legal departments. Both purchasing managers and suppliers also generally prefer using negotiation as an alternative to court decisions. In either case, purchasing managers must be aware of the potential pitfalls implicit in standard legal terminology and must seek to prevent the occurrence of such disputes. An operational rule of thumb is, when in doubt, err on the side of prudence.

KEY TERMS

agent, 541

breach of contract , 550

commercial law , 544

consideration, 546

corporate social responsibility, 574

express warranty, 557

implied warranty, 557

influence, 571

offer, 544

sharp practice, 570

DISCUSSION QUESTIONS

1. Why is it important for purchasing managers to understand legal issues? Isn't that what lawyers are for?
2. What is the relationship among contract law, the UCC, and commercial law?
3. What does the term "agent" mean? Under what conditions can purchasing agents be held personally responsible for abusing their position?
4. Suppose you arrive at a verbal agreement with someone on the price of purchasing his or her vehicle. Under what conditions have you reached an enforceable contract?
5. Suppose you sign a contract with a supplier for $5,000 worth of steel castings. You tell the supplier that you are only authorized to sign contracts for $4,000 without approval from the comptroller of your company, but the supplier agrees anyway. Later, you find out that you only need $2,500 worth of castings. How many dollars worth of castings are you legally bound to purchase from the supplier?
6. A seller verbally tells you that his cleaning product can remove any stain from the surface of a vehicle. You later find out that this is not the case. In fact, you find that the cleaning product does not work very well at all in removing paint stains. Do you have a legal claim against this seller? What types of damages are you entitled to?
7. In the above case, the seller points to the fine print on the product, which states that the product can only be used in temperatures above 40 degrees Fahrenheit. You were using it in temperatures of 35 degrees. Do you have a claim?
8. What are the important items that should be used anytime you decide to enter into a long-term contract (e.g., more than one year) with a supplier?
9. Briefly, what is the Uniform Commercial Code? Is it enforceable in all U.S. states?

10. If you write a contract that contains specific language about transportation requirements, and the supplier agrees to it but later claims that it is not acceptable under the UCC, who in your opinion has the upper hand in this case?
11. Suppose a supplier gives you a price on a contract and then later comes back and claims that he mistakenly wrote down the wrong price. Do you have the right to sue the supplier over breach of contract? What conditions are important here?
12. Discuss the concept of ethics. Why is the purchasing profession particularly sensitive to this topic?
13. What are the different risks associated with unethical behavior?
14. Discuss the reasons why some issues that confront a buyer are often not clear from an ethical perspective.
15. What is the purpose of a professional code of purchasing ethics?
16. Why is it important for a firm to have a written ethics policy? What is the importance of top management's commitment to the policy?
17. Discuss why you would be more interested in working for an organization that supports environmentally friendly policies. Are there any negatives to working in this type of organization?
18. You are a supply manager for a major distributor; the CEO has strongly encouraged that you buy lighting products for the new municipal stadium from a supplier that belongs to the CEO's country club. How would you handle this attempt to influence you?

ADDITIONAL READINGS

Bailey, H. J., III, and Hagedorn, R. B. (1988), *Secured Transactions in a Nutshell* (3rd ed.), St. Paul, MN: West Publishing.

Baumer, D. L., and Poindexter, J. C. (2004), *Legal Environment of Business in the Information Age,* New York: McGraw-Hill/Irwin.

Carter, C. R. (1998), *Ethical Issues in Global Buyer-Supplier Relationship,* Tempe, AZ: Center for Advanced Purchasing Studies.

Cavinato, J. L., Flynn, A., and Kauffman, R. (2006), *The Supply Management Handbook,* New York: McGraw-Hill, pp. 643–675.

Cooper, R. W., Frank, G. L., and Kemp, R. A. (1997), "The Ethical Environment Facing the Profession of Purchasing and Materials Management," *International Journal of Purchasing and Materials Management,* 33(2), 2–11.

Gabriel, H. (1994), *Practitioner's Guide to the Convention on Contracts for the International Sale of Goods (CISG) and the Uniform Commercial Code (UCC),* New York: Oceana Publishing.

Johnston, D. F. (1978), *Copyright Handbook,* New York: R. R. Bowker.

Murray, J. E., Jr. (2003), "When You Get What You Bargained For—But Don't," *Purchasing,* 132(4), 26–27.

Schildhouse, J. (2005), "Corporate Ethics: Taking the High Road," *Inside Supply Management,* March, 30–31.

"The Terrible Twos: How Articles 2, 2A and the Emerging 2B Are Addressing Common Issues" (1997), presented by the Committee on Uniform Commercial Code and Young Lawyers Division, American Bar Association Section of Business Law, Chicago.

Van Den Hendel, J. (1995), "Purchasing Ethics: Strain or Strategy," *Purchasing and Supply Management,* Summer, 50–52.

Woods, J. A. (Ed.) (2000), *The Purchasing and Supply Yearbook,* New York: McGraw-Hill.

ENDNOTES

1. Hancock, W. A. (Ed.) (1989), *The Law of Purchasing* (2nd ed.), Chesterland, OH: Business Laws.

2. Cavinato, J. L. (1984), *Purchasing and Materials Management: Integrative Strategies,* St. Paul, MN: West Publishing, p. 146.

3. Scheuing, E. E. (1989), *Purchasing Management,* Englewood Cliffs, NJ: Prentice Hall, p. 55.

4. Hancock, pp. 10.18–23.18.

5. Hancock, pp. 22.05–22.06.

6. Hancock, pp. 10.18–23.18.

7. Baumer, D. L., and Poindexter, J. C. (2004), *Legal Environment of Business in the Information Age,* New York: McGraw-Hill/Irwin.

8. Stockton, J., and Miller, F. (1992), *Sales and Leases of Goods in a Nutshell* (3rd ed.), St. Paul, MN: West Publishing, pp. 84–87.

9. Hancock.

10. Coyle, J. J., Bardi, E. J., and Langley, C. J., Jr. (1988), *The Management of Business Logistics* (4th ed.), St. Paul, MN: West Publishing, p. 360.

11. Kintner, E. W., and Lahr, J. L. (1975), *An Intellectual Property Law Primer,* New York: Macmillan, p. 6.

12. Cabarra, M. J., and Gabbard, E. (2000), "What's on the Books: Other Laws Affecting Purchasing and Supply," in *The Purchasing and Supply Yearbook,* Woods, J. A. (Ed.), New York: McGraw-Hill, pp. 332–339.

13. Haynes, P. J., and Helms, M. M. (1991), "An Ethical Framework for Purchasing Decisions," *Management Decision,* 29(1), 35; Page, H. (1986), "More on Ethics—Helping Your Buyers," *Purchasing World,* 30(12), 60.

14. Giunipero, L., and Handfield, R. (2004), *Purchasing Education and Training II,* Tempe, AZ: CAPS Research.

15. Haynes and Helms, p. 36.

16. Parker, R. C., Fordyce, G. C., and Graham, K. P. (1982), "Ethics in Purchasing," in *Purchasing Handbook,* L. G. Farrell and L. A. Alijian (Eds.), New York: McGraw-Hill, pp. 7–16.

17. Haynes and Helms, p. 36.

18. Adler, D., Baranowski, J., Kalin, L., Lallatin, C., Smiley, S., Turner, G., and Sturzl, S. (2007), "Ethical Behavior: Boundaries of Influence," 92nd ISM International Conference Proceedings, May.

19. Adler et al.

20. Adler et al.

21. Forker, L. B., and Janson, R. L. (1990), "Ethical Practices in Purchasing," *International Journal of Purchasing and Materials Management,* 26(1), 19–26.

22. Kranhold, K. (2007), "GE's Environment Push Hits Business Realities," *Wall Street Journal,* September 14, pp. A1, A10.

23. Blumenstein, R. (2007). "GM to Invest in Green Technology in China," *Wall Street Journal,* October 30, p. A10.

24. Spencer, J. (2007), "Big Firms Press Suppliers on Climate," *Wall Street Journal,* October 9, p. A7.

25. Ibid.

26. Ibid.

27. Mattoli, D. (2007), "How Going Green Draws Talent, Cuts Costs," *Wall Street Journal,* November 13, p. B10.

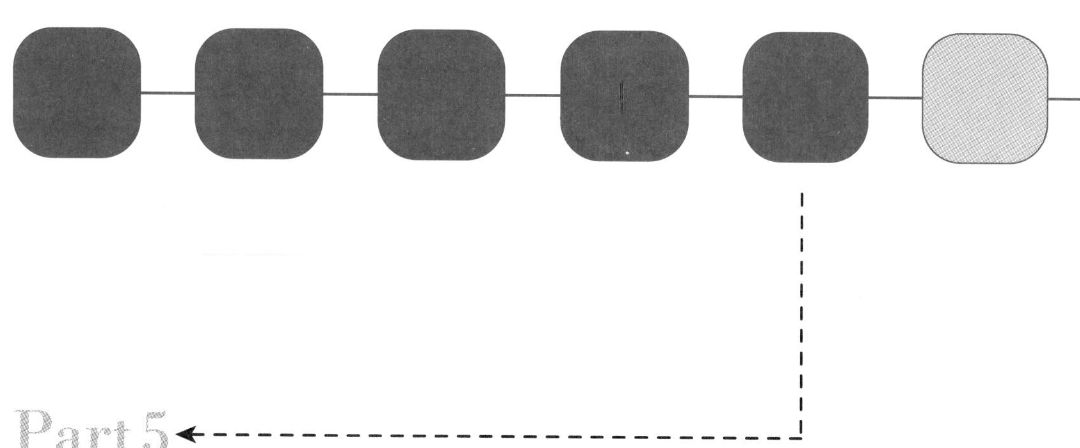

Part 5

Critical Supply Chain Elements

Chapter 16

LEAN SUPPLY CHAIN MANAGEMENT

Learning Objectives

After completing this chapter, you should be able to

- Identify the different categories of inventory
- Identify the various costs associated with maintaining supply chain inventory
- Assess the financial impact of managing inventory more effectively
- Understand the right reasons for maintaining an investment in inventory
- Appreciate the challenges of creating a lean supply chain
- Identify ways to manage and improve inventory investment
- Recognize the important relationship between inventory management and delivering the perfect customer order

Chapter Outline

Managing Hospital Pharmacy Inventory: Cardinal Health's Race to the Bedside

Hospitals are facing mandates from local and federal governments to reduce operating costs, improve patient safety, reduce budgets, and cut Medicare reimbursements. One of the major areas for targeting improvements is in pharmaceutical distribution and inventory, which constitutes a major portion of hospitals' budgets. Hospitals are now applying lean principles to their inventory systems, in an effort to improve efficiency and reduce hospital operating costs. A number of hospitals, such as the Mayo Clinic, the University of San Diego Hospital, University of California (both Davis and San Francisco), Seton Hospital, and University of North Carolina (Chapel Hill), have implemented medical dispensing technologies to improve their pharmaceutical inventory systems. A recent study conducted by the Supply Chain Resource Cooperative (scrc.ncsu.edu) suggests that hospitals engaging in these new medical dispensing technologies will over a five-year period realize significant benefits that will contribute to meeting these mandates.

Although many hospitals have invested in automated pharmacy distribution technologies (e.g., Pyxis Medstations) that automate the distribution, tracking, management, and security of medications, there are several challenges associated with this approach, which include management of inventory expenses, labor involved in refilling stations, station configuration, stocking optimization, reducing stockouts, and most importantly, opportunities to reduce hand-offs, which results in fewer medication errors. Cardinal Health is a major innovator in development of hospital inventory management and replenishment systems, and several years ago it introduced a replenishment system called Cardinal ASSIST. ASSIST is an automated replenishment system for Pyxis Medstation machines, with full functionality in generating reports to optimize inventory levels and minimize stockouts. ASSIST was conceived and developed by hospital pharmacists, who sought a system to manage the size and frequency of replenishments, and truly understood the needs of a hospital pharmacy. Hospital pharmacies that learn to exploit the full functionality of Cardinal ASSIST have seen improved pharmaceutical utilization (percentage of formulary going through the system) and have derived significant benefits.

Specifically, hospital pharmacies using Cardinal ASSIST at mature levels of implementation realized the following:

- Improved inventory turns from 8 (six weeks of stock on hand) to 24 (two weeks of stock on hand)
- Reduced picking of medications from 600 per day to less than 80 per day
- Reduced medication picking errors from 7.0 per day to less than 0.5 per day
- Reduced stockouts from more than 200 per day to less than 30 per month

These benefits have a significant impact on the total cost of patient care (TCPC).

Total cost of patient care is a metric not often considered in discussions, but comprises the hidden costs of mistakes that impact patient care. The elements that make up TCPC include the following items:

- Lost nursing time
- Technician productivity rates
- Missed opportunities for pharmacist clinical intervention
- Nursing turnover costs associated with dissatisfied nurses
- Lengthened hospital stays as a result of slower healing rates attributed to missed doses and drug errors
- Legal costs associated with settling claims for drug errors

- Reduced revenues from dissatisfied patients, or lost revenue from returning patients
- Any other elements that negatively impact the rate at which patients become better while in the facility

Although there is a defined learning curve for pharmacists who introduce Cardinal ASSIST, many of the pharmacists who have successfully deployed the system declare that they would never return to a manual system. Systems such as Assist will be important stepping-stones in the journey towards supply chain excellence in hospital pharmacy distribution.

Source: R. Handfield, "Future Trends in Medical Dispensing Technology: The Race to the Bedside," position paper, Supply Chain Resource Cooperative, North Carolina State University, 2007.

If U.S. companies learned anything over the last 10 years, it is that managing inventory efficiently and effectively is central to remaining competitive. As shown in the opening vignette, this also applies to diverse industries such as health care, not just to manufacturing. Service companies, although they do not produce manufactured products, nevertheless still have to manage significant amounts of inventory. For example, the concluding Best Practice study in this chapter illustrates how a financial services institution, Bank of America, invested significant resources to create a document management system that not only reduced inventory, but created significant operational efficiencies throughout its complex banking network.

Although maintaining high levels of inventory was an accepted practice for many years, it resulted in high carrying costs, reduced profit, and diminished market share. Furthermore, high inventory levels often hid other problems such as poor material quality, inaccurate demand-forecasting systems, and unreliable supplier delivery. To avoid having to deal with these problems, it was often easier to increase safety stock levels or increase the amount ordered from suppliers.

When inventory moves so fast that firms essentially hold zero inventory on hand, they are following a system known as the lean supply chain. John Shook defined **lean** as "a philosophy that seeks to shorten the time between the customer order and the shipment to the customer by eliminating waste."[1] Womack and Jones, in their book *Lean Thinking,* argued that all activities associated with lean attempt to achieve three objectives: flow, pull, and striving for excellence.[2]

Flow means that inventory moves through the supply chain continuously with minimal queuing or non-value-added activity being performed. **Pull** means that customer orders start the work process, which ripples down through the supply chain. An upstream work center or operation will not create output unless a downstream center directly requests (i.e., pulls) that output. The downstream center needs and then consumes the output, leading to no inventory or waste. The third element, **striving for excellence**, means that supply chains must have perfect quality. Anything less than perfect quality leads to waste.

The primary objective of this chapter is to provide an understanding of the importance of managing and controlling supply chain inventory in creating lean supply chains. In the following sections, we present the types and costs of inventory, the right and wrong reasons for maintaining inventory, and the close ties between the concept of the lean supply chain and the just-in-time (JIT) philosophy. We also present powerful ways to manage inventory investment and discuss the concept of the perfect customer order. The chapter concludes with a Good Practice Example of a financial institution's implementation of lean supply chain management, as well as multiple examples of lean thinking from diverse industries and settings.

Understanding Supply Chain Inventory

The best place to start our discussion of lean supply chains is to understand the basic principles of inventory management. This section discusses the different types of inventory, the costs associated with holding inventory, and the changing view of inventory as a financial and operating liability rather than an asset.

Types of Inventory

Inventory represents the largest single investment in assets for most manufacturers, wholesalers, and retailers. The five primary categories of inventory are (1) raw material and semifinished item inventory; (2) work-in-process (WIP) inventory; (3) finished-goods inventory; (4) maintenance, repair, and operating (MRO) supplies inventory; and (5) pipeline/in-transit inventory.

Raw Material and Semifinished Item Inventory

This inventory includes the items purchased from suppliers or produced internally to directly support production requirements. Raw materials include those items purchased in a bulk or unfinished condition. Bulk quantities of chemicals, resins, or petroleum are examples of purchased raw materials. Semifinished inventory includes those items and components used as inputs during the final production process. Every producer relies on some level of raw material or semifinished inventory to support final production requirements. This type of inventory is managed primarily by purchasing, a materials planning group, or supply chain managers.

Work-in-Process Inventory

At any given point in time, work-in-process is the sum total of inventory within all processing centers. Work-in-process is incomplete—it has not yet been transformed to a saleable finished good. This includes materials that are the following:

- Waiting to be moved to another process
- Currently being worked on at a work center
- Lining up at a processing center due to a capacity bottleneck or machine breakdown

If WIP increases over a certain level, this may indicate production bottlenecks or delays. One study found that in most facilities, 36% of WIP inventory is in line waiting for further work or processing. Another 27% is waiting on movement to another work area or center, 4% is in the process of being moved, and only 24% is actually in process.[3] If WIP builds up at a workstation, a scheduler may have to reroute the flow of material to another work center.

Finished-Goods Inventory

Finished-goods inventory includes completed items or products that are available for shipment or future customer orders. A firm that produces items in anticipation of customer orders should monitor its finished-goods inventory closely. A higher-than-anticipated level of finished goods may mean that a decrease in customer demand is occurring. A lower-than-anticipated finished-goods inventory level may indicate that customer demand is increasing. Either condition may also indicate that the forecasts of anticipated customer demand do not match current output levels.

When firms produce goods in anticipation of future customer orders, they are operating in a make-to-stock environment. They expect to hold finished inventory in anticipation of future demand. When firms produce goods in response to a customer order, they are operating in a make-to-order environment. Just-in-time firms usually operate in a make-to-order environment.

Maintenance, Repair, and Operating Supplies Inventory

MRO inventory includes the items used to support production and operations. These items are not physically part of a finished product but are critical for the continuous operation of plant, equipment, and offices. Examples of MRO inventory include office supplies, spare parts, tools, and computers.

Pipeline/In-Transit Inventory

This inventory is in transit to a customer or is located throughout distribution channels. Most consumable-goods inventory is either on trucks or on grocery store shelves. In fact, grocery stores only provide a shelf for the product; they do not own the inventory. The inventory is owned by the supplying company or distributor, which receives payment when the consumer buys the product.

Inventory-Related Costs

One of the drawbacks of holding excessive inventory is the effect this has on a firm's working capital. Working capital represents the funds committed to operating a business, including the purchase and holding of inventory. Excessive inventory consumes or ties up funds that a company could use more productively elsewhere. Ordering and carrying physical inventory involves a number of costs.

Unit Costs

The most basic and the easiest inventory-related cost to quantify and track is unit cost. We can view the calculation of unit costs in several ways. First, each item or good purchased from a supplier or another internal facility has a related unit cost, which is the price a firm pays. Second, a finished product has a unit cost. The calculation of this cost may be more complex. Besides the direct material used to manufacture the finished product, the product also has a labor cost and allocated overhead. Cost accountants are largely responsible for identifying and assigning these costs.

Ordering Costs

Ordering costs are a composite of the costs associated with the release of a material order. These costs may include the cost of generating and sending a material release, transportation costs, and any other cost connected with acquiring a good. If a firm produces an item or good itself, the ordering cost may also include machine setup costs.

Carrying Costs

Carrying costs consist of three separate components: (1) cost of capital; (2) cost of storage; and (3) the costs of obsolescence, deterioration, and loss. The dollar amount invested in physical inventory has an opportunity cost associated with it. Resources committed to inventory are not available for other economic uses. Therefore, committing financial resources to holding physical inventory creates an inventory carrying cost.

The physical storing of inventory creates costs, including any costs related to storage space, insurance costs, or the cost to maintain the inventory (such as performing cycle counts). Carrying costs vary with the level of inventory, which makes these costs variable. Fixed costs are not included as part of carrying costs because inventory levels typically have no effect on a fixed cost, at least in the short run.

Holding inventory also increases the risk of theft, damage, spoilage, and obsolescence. For example, obsolescence is a major issue in the computer industry, where inventory loses about 1.5% of its functionality a week as a result of rapidly changing technology, making the extended holding of any inventory financially risky.

For most industries, inventory costs typically range from 15 to 25% of the value of the inventory, depending on the company's cost of capital. As shown in Exhibit 16.1, a variety of costs makes up the total carrying cost. The calculation of an inventory carrying cost is as follows:

$$\text{Inventory Carrying Cost} = \text{Average Inventory in Units} \times \text{Unit Price} \times \text{Carrying Cost per Year}$$

If a company averages 1,000 units in inventory, for which the unit price is $1.00 per unit, and the annual carrying cost is 25%, the total inventory carrying cost per year for inventory is (1,000 × $1 × 0.25) = $250.

Quality Costs

Quality costs include any cost associated with nonconforming items or goods. The total cost of inventory ownership is more than simply the unit, ordering, and carrying costs. Quantifying the cost of poor quality can help identify the causes of problems. Examples of additional costs due to defective inventory include field failure costs, rework, losses due to poor product yields, inspection, lost production, and warranty costs.

It is often difficult to quantify the total costs associated with ordering and carrying physical inventory. Part of this results from the historical neglect of calculating total

Exhibit 16.1 Inventory Carrying Cost Components

ELEMENT	AVERAGE	RANGES
Capital cost	15.00%	8–40%
Taxes	1.00%	0.5–2%
Insurance	0.05%	0–2%
Obsolescence	1.20%	0.5–2%
Storage	2.00%	0–4%
Total	19.25%	9–50%

Source: D. J. Bowersox and D. J. Closs, *Logistical Management*, New York: McGraw-Hill, 1996, p. 255.

inventory costs along with a lack of systems capable of identifying inventory-related costs. Most cost accounting systems are not capable of identifying and assigning the true costs related to maintaining physical inventory. However, activity-based costing accounting systems are increasingly able to quantify the distinct costs associated with holding inventory. New types of enterprise resource planning systems also help managers more accurately measure the actual level of inventory on hand, as opposed to "guesstimating."

Inventory Investment—Asset or Liability?

The opportunity to improve financial performance through effective inventory management practices is great and, at many firms, largely unrealized. For example, many companies in historically high-margin industries (such as energy, utilities, and pharmaceuticals) pay little attention to inventory, as it was always argued that the savings associated with inventory reduction outweighed the potential risk of a lost customer sale. This view has begun to change, as the full impact of inventory on the balance sheet and financial valuations on Wall Street reflect heightened awareness of inventory turns as a key indicator of financial health.

This has not always been the case. From the financial accounting perspective, inventory has historically been considered a current asset (see Exhibit 16.2). When inventory resides in the same category as cash and marketable securities, one cannot help but get a feeling that there is actually something good associated with holding lots and lots of inventory! For many years, this was precisely how most U.S. managers viewed this special kind of asset. Only recently, financial analysts have begun to weigh in the impact that the funds committed to inventory have on cash flow, working capital requirements, and profitability, and are making stock-buying recommendations based on this factor. All of a sudden, senior leadership at firms are beginning to pay attention to this number in their analyst calls!

Exhibit 16.2 Consolidated Balance Sheet

	JUNE 30	
	2004 (IN THOUSANDS)	2003 (IN THOUSANDS)
Current Assets		
Cash and cash equivalents	$ 647,595	$ 408,378
Marketable securities	242,952	421,111
Receivables	638,974	632,870
Inventories	917,495	771,233
Prepaid expenses	84,588	70,211
Total current assets	2,531,604	2,303,803
Investments and Other Assets		
Investments in and advances to affiliates	205,835	160,455
Long-term marketable securities	770,808	813,631
Other assets	56,735	40,314
	1,033,378	1,014,400
Property, Plant, and Equipment		
Agricultural processing	2,275,016	1,724,460
Transportation	420,609	407,347
	2,695,625	2,131,807
	$6,260,607	$5,450,010

Exhibit 16.3 Linking Inventory Management and Financial Performance

	FIRM A	FIRM B
Sales	$200	$200
Profit Margin	6%	7%*
Assets		
Cash	$ 10	$ 10
Securities	$ 15	$ 15
Receivables	$ 8	$ 8
Inventories	$ 20	$ 10
Plant and equipment	$ 75	$ 75
Total Assets	**$128**	**$118**
Financial Formulas:		
Inventory Turns = Sales/Inventories	$200/$20 = 10 turns/year	$200/$10 = 20 turns/year
Asset Turnover = Sales/Total Assets	$200/$128 = 1.56 turns/year	$200/$118 = 1.69 turns/year
Return on Investment = Profit Margin × Asset Turnover	6% × 1.56 = 9.36%	7% × 1.69 = 11.55%
		Through efficient inventory management, Firm B has an ROI that is 23% higher than that of Firm A.

Note: All figures in millions of dollars.
*Assumes more efficient supply chain operations and less waste.

Any discussion of inventory management should focus on the need to translate the impact that inventory management practices have on financial measures. A CEO of an industrial company is not likely to get overly excited when he or she hears that total inventory turns increased from seven to nine because of better inventory practices. Executive managers have not traditionally been concerned about the same set of key performance indicators as the typical supply chain manager. However, in recent years senior executives have begun to appreciate the importance of effective inventory management, once the relationship between the impact of increased turns on financial indicators has been elevated by Wall Street analysts.

Exhibit 16.3 illustrates one way to translate the impact that improved inventory turns (which is the visible outcome of inventory management practices) has on an important performance indicator, return on investment. The two firms in this exhibit are identical in every way but two—Firm B has half the amount of inventory on its balance sheet as Firm A, and Firm B has a slightly higher profit margin than Firm A. It is reasonable to assume that Firm B will have a higher profit margin due to lower average carrying charges resulting from shorter periods of storage with less handling and reduced inventory maintenance requirements. Margins should also improve due to the elimination of non-value-adding activities.

This exhibit shows how better inventory management can affect return on investment. A doubling of inventory turns, combined with the benefit of lower inventory-related expenses that contribute to a higher profit margin, increases return on investment from 9.36% to 11.55%, an increase of almost 25%.

Identifying the impact of inventory management activities on return on investment is not the only way to demonstrate the value of such efforts. Supply chain and financial managers should work together to determine the impact of inventory management activities on earnings per share, economic value-add, return on assets, working capital, cash flow, and profit margin. The point here is that effective inventory management is critical for managing assets and controlling expenses. Translating inventory actions into their effect on higher-level performance indicators is essential for capturing executive management's attention. This was indeed the case when Amazon realized its inventory management practices were causing significant ripples on Wall Street, and turned around its inventory system in a matter of two years (see Sourcing Snapshot: Amazon Slashes Its Supply Chain Inventory Levels).

Sourcing Snapshot — *Amazon Slashes Its Supply Chain Inventory Levels*

When they first started appearing in the late 1990s, web-based "e-tailers" such as Amazon.com hoped to replace the "bricks" of traditional retailing with the "clicks" of online ordering via computer keyboards. Rather than opening dozens or even hundreds of stores filled with expensive inventory, an e-tailer runs a single virtual store that serves customers around the globe. The e-tailer business model suggested that inventory could be kept at a few key sites chosen to minimize costs and facilitate quick delivery to customers. In theory, e-tailers were highly scalable businesses that could add new customers with little or no additional investment in inventory or facilities. (Traditional retailers usually need to add stores to gain significant increases in their customer base.)

But how has this actually played out for Amazon.com? Exhibit 16.4 contains sales and inventory figures for Amazon.com for the years 1997 through 2006. The first column reports net sales for each calendar year, whereas the second column contains the amount of inventory on hand at the end of the year. The third column shows inventory turns, which is calculated as (Net Sales/Ending Inventory). Retailers generally want higher inventory turns, indicating that they can support the same level of sales with less inventory.

Graphing these results provides some interesting insights. Consider Exhibit 16.5. In late 1999, Amazon.com learned that managing inventory can be a challenge even for e-tailers. That was the year the company expanded into new product lines, such as electronics and housewares, with which it had little experience. Amazon.com's purchasing managers were faced with the question of how many of these items to hold in inventory—too little, and they risked losing orders and alienating customers; too much, and they could lock up the company's resources in unsold products. Only later, when sales for the 1999 holiday season fell flat and Amazon.com's inventory levels skyrocketed, did they realize they had overstocked. In fact, as the figures show,

Exhibit 16.4 Amazon.com Financial Results, 1997–2006

YEAR	NET SALES (MILLIONS)	INVENTORY (DEC. 31, MILLIONS)	INVENTORY TURNS
1997	$ 148	$ 9	16.4
1998	$ 610	$ 30	20.3
1999	$ 1,640	$221	7.4
2000	$ 2,762	$175	15.8
2001	$ 3,122	$143	21.8
2002	$ 3,933	$202	19.5
2003	$ 5,264	$294	17.9
2004	$ 6,921	$480	14.4
2005	$ 8,490	$566	15.0
2006	$10,711	$877	12.2

Exhibit 16.5 Inventory Turns at Amazon.com, 1997–2006

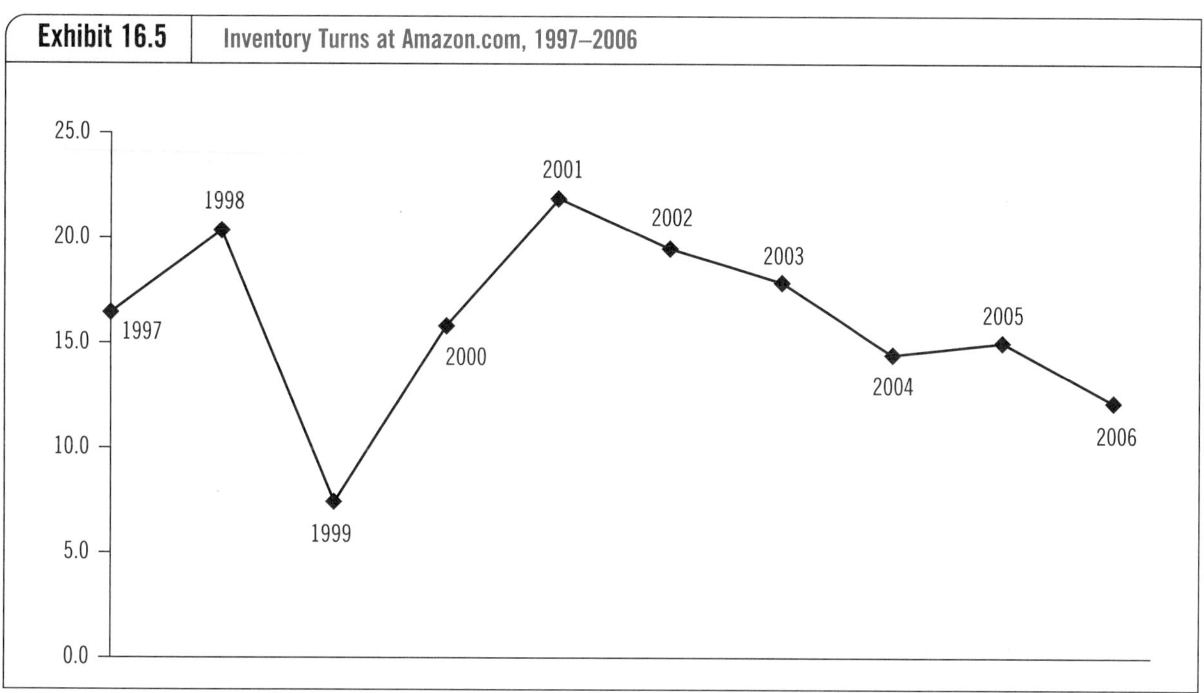

by the end of 1999, Amazon.com's inventory turnover ratio was 7.4—worse than that of the typical bricks-and-mortar retailer.

After 1999, Amazon seemed to learn its lesson. Inventory turns rose to nearly 22 in 2001, but have fallen steadily ever since, to 12.2 turns for 2006. Still, these results are better than the more typical bricks-and-mortar retailers. As a comparison, in 2006, Wal-Mart's consolidated operations generated just 9.7 turns.

Source: Adapted from C. Bozarth and R. Handfield, *Operations and Supply Chain Management* (2nd ed.), Upper Saddle River, NJ: Prentice Hall, 2008.

The Right Reasons for Investing in Inventory

Physical inventory plays an important role in all supply chains. Without inventory companies cannot build products, provide customer service, or run their operations. When deciding whether to maintain an investment in inventory, a broad premise to follow is that inventory should be held only when the benefit of holding inventory exceeds the cost of holding inventory. The following section examines the proper reasons for carrying inventory.

Avoid Disruptions in Operational Performance

A major reason for maintaining an investment in inventory is to support production requirements and avoid any type of supply disruptions. Even in an era of just-in-time production, almost all firms hold some level of preproduction inventory, which may include bulk supplies of raw materials, semifinished goods, or materials to support the packaging and shipping of finished products.

Production inventory consumes a major portion of inventory investment. For this reason, firms emphasize the development of systems designed to control and reduce the amount of production-related inventory maintained at any given time. The reduction of production (particularly work-in-process) inventory results in reduced inventory costs. Although the need to support production requirements will always remain as a primary reason to hold physical inventory, it is not a reason to hold excessive inventory. Supply managers need to strike a delicate balance between avoiding any supply disruptions and holding excessive amounts of inventory that weigh down a firm's or business unit's balance sheet.

Support Operational Requirements

Nearly every organization carries MRO inventory—maintenance, repair, and operating supplies—to support operations. The true cost of MRO inventory often goes unnoticed because firms fail to track these items with the same intensity as production inventory. Multiple or obsolete items may be held in stock, and inventory pilferage can further lead to inventory-shrinking losses if proper tracking systems are not established.

Most firms are trying to control the costs associated with ordering and maintaining MRO items. Some of the techniques used to control MRO costs include the use of a central MRO stores location, online requisitioning systems, and full-service distributors. These distributors are responsible for managing the entire supply and demand for MRO inventory items and may charge an additional fee for their services.

Support Customer Service Requirements

Many products, such as computers, appliances, and automobiles, require service or replacement parts. A lack of adequate spare parts inventory increases the risk of not meeting customer service requirements. To avoid this possibility, companies often maintain a significant inventory of service and replacement parts.

Service and replacement parts can be a major source of inventory waste or customer dissatisfaction if incorrect inventory levels are maintained. Accurate parts forecasts and material control systems are critical for maintaining proper inventory levels for service and replacement parts.

Hedge against Marketplace Uncertainty

Supply chains are sensitive to changes in markets, including changes in the availability of material supply as well as price changes. When purchasers anticipate materials shortages or price increases, they often increase purchase quantities as a hedge against these uncertainties. Material hedging is a common response, for example, when a strike by a supplier appears likely. Another reason to hedge occurs when potential shortages in common commodities (e.g., lumber) appear imminent, with the knowledge that price increases are likely. In these situations, purchasers will carry out forward buys by ordering larger-than-normal quantities.

Increasing inventory levels in response to a legitimate threat of a shortage can be a good reason, at least in the short run, for holding additional material. One of the primary objectives of purchasing and supply chain management is to support continued and uninterrupted operations. If this requires increased inventory to avoid a materials shortage, then a purchaser should consider such an action, assuming that additional

Sourcing Snapshot *Managing Inventory in a Volatile Market*

For anyone wanting to make a cleaner car or sport-utility vehicle, a little-known metal called palladium is a must. Unfortunately, the main exporter of palladium is Russia, which has created chaos on the market by holding up deliveries, including delaying releasing the metal from its huge stockpile. At one point, concerns that political infighting in Moscow could choke supplies drove the price of palladium to nearly $1,000 an ounce, or about 10 times the levels seen in the early 1990s. Although there is less than an ounce of palladium in most vehicles—it is used inside the catalytic converter—that kind of price surge means palladium suddenly is becoming a big-ticket inventory item for auto companies.

In the mid-1990s, automakers agreed to accelerate their adoption of tighter national emission standards as part of a deal to head off separate state-by-state rules, which would have played havoc with manufacturing and distribution. Palladium looked like the best solution, because it began cleaning exhaust sooner after starting up the engine than platinum, then the dominant metal in catalytic converters. The price for little-used palladium had not gone above $200 an ounce in more than a decade, whereas platinum had jumped above $400. Engineers designed palladium into the emission control system. In the process, they created a tremendous amount of demand for a metal having a volatile supply.

Economics dictates that producers should boost output to bring the palladium market into balance in this kind of situation. However, geology makes palladium special. In nature, it occurs mostly with other metals, nickel in Russia and platinum in South Africa, and in both places there is much less palladium per ton of ore than the other metals. Even if palladium prices take off, big producers will not add to output, because that would mean flooding the nickel and platinum markets.

Purchasers responded to the palladium crisis in different ways. General Motors signed a five-year supply deal with the only major palladium producer outside of Russia and South Africa, Stillwater Mining Company in Montana. Ford's purchasing group, on the other hand, secured its supply of palladium by entering into contracts that locked in prices at near-record highs. As the demand for palladium declined due to engineering changes that reduced the amount of palladium required in each vehicle, Ford found itself with massive quantities of overpriced palladium. In 2002, Ford shocked Wall Street by announcing a $1 billion write-off of the value of its palladium stockpile. Ford discovered that managing inventory in a volatile market is a tricky business!

Source: Adapted from G. L. White, "Unruly Element: Russian Maneuvers Are Making Palladium Ever More Precious," *Wall Street Journal,* March 6, 2000, p. A1; G. L. White, "How Ford's Big Batch of Rare Metal Led to $1 Billion Write-Off," *Wall Street Journal,* February 6, 2002, p. A1.

sources of supply are not readily available. However, firms should avoid taking undue and unnecessary hedging risks, as Ford did in the case discussed in Sourcing Snapshot: Managing Inventory in a Volatile Market.

Take Advantage of Order Quantity Discounts

Suppliers often offer quantity discounts to encourage larger orders from purchasers, which Chapter 12 discussed. A purchaser might consider ordering a two-month supply versus a one-month supply, for example, in exchange for a per-unit discount. At one time most companies felt these discounts were worthwhile because they resulted in a lower average price. However, a lower purchase price does not necessarily translate into a lower total cost. Lower total costs result only if the benefit from reduced ordering costs (larger purchase quantities means ordering less frequently) and a lower per-unit price outweigh the cost of holding additional inventory. It sometimes makes economic sense from a total cost perspective to take advantage of the quantity discounts offered by suppliers and to hold larger amounts of inventory.

Each of the reasons presented here can result in holding some level of physical inventory. Regardless of the reason for holding inventory, supply chain managers must be aware of total inventory costs. The key is to minimize inventory investment wherever possible while still meeting competitive and customer requirements.

The Wrong Reasons for Investing in Inventory

Any discussion of inventory must differentiate between the good and bad reasons for carrying inventory. Unnecessary inventory usually results from one thing: uncertainty. Uncertainty results in not being able to adequately plan inventory requirements because of supply chain variability. It may be the consequence of variability in forecasting accuracy or inconsistent logistics, which usually results in greater amounts of safety stock. The following discussion considers the bad reasons for maintaining an investment in inventory. Some of the ideas presented in the later section titled "Approaches for Managing Inventory Investment" address these bad reasons directly.

Poor Quality and Material Yield

Poor quality and material yield have historically been major sources of unnecessary inventory investment. Unfortunately, it is easier to increase a material release by 10% or carry safety stock to cover supplier quality problems than to correct a problem's root cause. It became a routine practice for many companies to order more than required to cover expected supplier inconsistency. A certain level of material defects was an accepted part of the transaction.

Variable material yield also may also contribute to unnecessary levels of inventory. Material yield is a term typically associated with raw materials. A purchaser who specifies a raw material at a particular grade expects to receive a shipment conforming to that specification. Poor quality affects material yields when a portion of the shipment is a lower grade or quality than what was specified, therefore providing less output than expected. When this happens, purchasers must often increase their purchase quantity to guarantee that their receipt yields the proper amount of usable material. This increase in inventory provides nothing of value in return.

Unreliable Supplier Delivery

Suppliers that cannot meet delivery schedules create delivery uncertainty. To compensate for unreliable delivery, supply chain managers usually increase safety stock levels or make ordering lead times longer. Delivery uncertainty is often the result of poor supplier scheduling or production systems and can be a problem when buying from small suppliers that do not have the resources or experience to develop sophisticated scheduling systems. It can also be the result of discrepancies and logistics problems. Missed shipments, delays at international customs points, bad weather, and many other unexpected problems can result in late deliveries.

Purchasers must also accept part of the blame for delivery uncertainty. Suppliers value a stable production schedule with reasonable production lead times. A purchaser who provides suppliers with short notice or requests frequent changes to a schedule increases the probability of delivery uncertainty. A major step toward eliminating delivery uncertainty is a commitment to stable release schedules with realistic (but not overly generous) supplier lead times.

Extended Order-Cycle Times from Global Sourcing

A major business objective today is to reduce the total time between the recognition of a purchase requirement and the physical receipt of material from a supplier—that is, the order-cycle time between purchaser and seller. As order-cycle times lengthen as a result of the extension of supply chains due to global sourcing agreements (which may require six-month lead times), a common practice has been to carry a higher level of inventory to compensate for greater uncertainty. The ability to plan material requirements accurately decreases as order-cycle time lengthens. Much more can happen to disrupt plans over a three-month ordering cycle than over a two-week ordering cycle.

Inaccurate or Uncertain Demand Forecasts

Inaccurate or uncertain demand forecasts are a common source of uncertainty affecting inventory levels, particularly for companies that produce products in anticipation of future orders. Companies often use increased safety stock levels to compensate for demand uncertainty or inaccurate forecasts. Some firms simply have poor forecasting systems.

Consider the case of an East Coast confectioner that forecasts monthly in a make-to-stock environment. The supply chain group at this company recently analyzed finished product forecasting error in its efforts to manage inventory investment more effectively.[4] The company found that its stock-keeping units (SKUs) had an average error of 45% when comparing actual and predicted monthly demand using the mean absolute deviation technique of error assessment. A closer investigation revealed some disturbing findings. Material planners believed that a four-week safety stock for all items would alleviate the impact of poor forecasting, thereby reducing the need to be concerned with forecast accuracy. Furthermore, no single manager or group was accountable for forecast integrity. Marketing, which technically had responsibility for generating monthly forecasts, admitted that forecasting was a "nuisance" and not the best use of their members' time. Finally, an analysis across the company's 900 SKUs found that inventory was sometimes severely misallocated across geographic locations and product lines, creating problems in meeting the delivery dates for key customer orders. As a result, this company has created a cross-functional sales and operations planning group to address product forecasting and finished-goods distribution.

Companies should periodically evaluate the accuracy of their forecasting systems by comparing forecasted demand to actual requirements. Forecasting systems should have a goal of minimizing the difference between a forecasted requirement and an actual requirement to avoid having to carry higher inventory levels as protection.

Specifying Custom Items for Standard Applications

Specifying custom items for standard applications is an area of debate between purchasing and engineering. Purchasers would like to buy industry-standard parts wherever possible while still meeting engineering's quality and design requirements. Specifying customized parts when standardized parts are available adversely affects material inventory because customized parts are usually more expensive. A supplier usually designs and creates specific tooling for each customized item. In addition, a supplier usually produces smaller batches of the item because of its custom specification. The smaller batches result in an increased piece-part cost. Customized parts, because of higher design and production costs, increase total unit and inventory-carrying costs.

Extended Material Pipelines

Long distances between supply chain members can result in higher inventory levels and costs. Distance increases delivery uncertainty, often for reasons outside the control of a supplier or buyer. Overseas shipments can experience a variety of delays at customs. Longer shipping distances also increase the potential for in-transit shipping damage, theft, or obsolescence. Furthermore, someone in the supply chain (the supplier, purchaser, or end customer) owns the inventory as it travels over great distances. This increases the risk and exposure to financial loss, if the inventory is damaged, is stolen, or simply disappears into one of the many "black holes" that exist in the global supply chains at distribution points, ports, shipping terminals, railway nodes, and other locations. Extended material pipelines are a major consideration when comparing the cost of domestic versus international purchasing. Many firms fail to consider the higher cost of inventory when they outsource their supply chain to Asia and do not take into account the impact of longer planning times, inventory obsolescence, and slower customer response associated with long global supply lead times. There are, of course, some exceptions to this rule, as the Sourcing Snapshot: In Year of Disasters, Lean Emergency Materials Management Brings Order to the Chaos of Relief Operations suggests, when global suppliers are able to develop just-in-time capabilities!

Sourcing Snapshot

In Year of Disasters, Lean Emergency Materials Management Brings Order to the Chaos of Relief Operations

Amid the chaos of the huge Kashmir earthquake relief effort that took place in October 2005, an experiment took place in Hangar 14 of the Pakistan Air Force base in Islamabad.

Chris Weeks, an executive on loan from express-shipping company DHL Corp., worked with American soldiers to improvise a method for quickly getting food and shelter to some of the hundreds of thousands of quake survivors camping on remote mountainsides in the Pakistani province, where roads and airports are rare. Their solution: the "speedball."

They stuffed tents, food, and other supplies into red polypropylene bags that DHL has been using for years to move loose cargo, tossed them into Chinook helicopters, and headed for rough landing strips in the hills. In just two weeks, they delivered some 6,000 of the bean-bag-chair-size speedballs, each holding shelter, food, and water to keep seven people alive for

10 days. "They would kick them out the door at landing strips," says U.S. Air Force Colonel Richard Walberg, the officer in charge at the Islamabad base. "That was quite a system."

The bags are one product of an unusual effort by the global cargo industry to try to transform the notoriously inefficient supply chain for disaster relief. A loose-knit collection of companies and executives is seeking to help governments and private aid groups respond more effectively to major disasters such as earthquakes, tsunamis, and hurricanes.

They're applying to emergency-supply chains the nuts-and-bolts inventory management and logistics techniques that helped revolutionize their industry and helped make global giants like Dell and Wal-Mart successful.

Shipping companies like DHL, UPS, and FedEx are experts in integrating technology with an almost militaristic level of organization to squeeze inefficiencies out of supply chains—and better manage inventory in these channels. Most of the industry's expertise is in somewhat mundane areas like parcel tracking, inventory control, jet routing, and cramming lots of material into small spaces. Many improvements are marginal, but the cumulative result is dramatic: the ability to move huge loads across the globe with new speed and precision.

In a year of unprecedented calamities, that expertise is now in high demand. "The most important thing in a sudden disaster is logistics," says Adrian van der Knapp, who coordinates emergency-relief operations for the United Nations and helps DHL get quick government authorization to go into disaster zones. Aid groups and the U.N. are often deluged with donated supplies but struggle to get them where they're needed, he adds. "There is no U.N. fire brigade or standby army that can be called upon in natural disasters."

Enter Weeks, who in Kashmir was responding to his third major disaster since January. The 48-year-old Briton, who is based at DHL's vast hub in Brussels, went to Kashmir within days of his return home from a U.S. Air Force base near Little Rock, Arkansas. There, he had been helping deliver foreign aid to victims of hurricanes Katrina and Rita. Before that, his team of about 35 veteran airport-cargo handlers took charge of aid operations for overwhelmed Sri Lankan authorities at Colombo Airport after the Indian Ocean tsunami. "We were not ready to receive all these flights," says Ari Hewage, the Sri Lankan Secretary to the Ports and Aviation Minister, who nervously gave the corporate experts the go-ahead to take over.

The effort to bring modern shipping methods to disaster relief is largely the inspiration of a San Francisco cargo tycoon named Lynn Fritz. He sold his own company, Fritz Cos., to United Parcel Service Inc. in 2001, banked some $200 million, and started looking for a philanthropic enterprise. He soon became an evangelist for applying logistics techniques to the delivery of disaster relief, eventually founding the Fritz Institute, a nonprofit devoted to the cause. "I did not just want to be a philanthropist that gave to local charities," Fritz says. "The supply chain for the humanitarian emergency is highly unpredictable. . . . We thought we could apply these skills with the help of the private sector."

Source: G. R. Simpson, "In Year of Disasters, Lean Emergency Materials Management Brings Order to the Chaos of Relief Operations," *Wall Street Journal,* November 22, 2005, p. A1.

Inefficient Manufacturing Processes

A producer whose manufacturing system is not efficient must hold higher-than-necessary inventory levels to compensate for poor quality or process yield. One indication of an inefficient scheduling or production system is a large amount of work-in-process inventory located behind each work center. Inefficient scheduling and productions often create congested work areas as inventory accumulates in production centers. This increases total inventory carrying costs because longer production times increase work-in-process inventory. Inefficient production processes also lead to higher costs through poorer yield or quality.

Most inventory waste results from underlying problems that management has failed to correct. When inventory disguises operating inefficiencies, this accepts inefficiencies as part of conducting business. Failure to correct these underlying problems makes the inefficient producer vulnerable to challenges from cost-efficient producers. Whereas balance sheet accounting presents inventory as an asset, experienced supply chain managers recognize it is an asset worth controlling and, when necessary, even eliminating.

Creating the Lean Supply Chain[5]

Lean supply chains have their origin in the just-in-time philosophy, first adopted by many American and European firms in the late 1980s. As the following definition suggests, JIT touches on many of the areas we have dealt with throughout this book.

> *Just-in-Time (JIT) is a philosophy of manufacturing based on planned elimination of all waste and on continuous improvement of productivity. It encompasses the successful execution of all operations activities required to produce a final product, from design engineering to delivery, and includes all stages of conversion from raw material onward. The primary elements of Just-in-Time are to have only the required inventory when needed; to improve quality to zero defects; to reduce lead times by reducing setup times, queue lengths, and lot sizes; to incrementally revise the operations themselves; and to accomplish these activities at minimum cost. In the broad sense, it applies to all forms of production—job shop, process, and repetitive—and to many service industries as well.*

Firms following the JIT philosophy often experience remarkable improvements in their productivity (outputs/inputs), inventory levels, and quality. To understand why JIT made such an impact in the late 1980s, consider some eye-opening statistics from 1986, which compared performance at Toyota's Takaoka facility with that of GM's Framingham plant (Exhibit 16.6). Numbers such as these kicked off the JIT revolution in the American automotive industry during the late 1980s and early 1990s.

Notice how the Toyota plant needed fewer hours and much less inventory to do its job. This ability to do more with less led many people to refer to JIT as lean production. Similarly, the phrase "just-in-time" reflected the idea that the timing and level of inventory and production activities are closely matched to demand. With average inventory levels of only two hours, the Toyota plant was clearly "just" receiving parts and materials before they were needed.

The underlying emphases of JIT—to eliminate all forms of uncertainty and waste—are relevant to all organizations, regardless of the specific planning and control tools that are used. Second, even though some techniques such as kanban are not suitable in certain production and service environments, it is entirely possible that an organization can follow the JIT philosophy. To summarize:

Exhibit 16.6 The Performance Advantage of a JIT Plant, Circa 1986[6]

	GM FRAMINGHAM	TOYOTA TAKAOKA
Assembly hours per vehicle	40.7 hours	16 hours
Defects per 100 vehicles	130 defects	45 defects
Average inventory levels	Two weeks	Two hours

- The JIT philosophy can be applied to a wide range of production and service environments. In fact, one could easily argue that there is no environment that wouldn't benefit from adopting its core principles.
- Companies following the JIT philosophy can and do use a wide range of planning and control techniques, not just kanban.
- JIT is closely aligned with total quality management and supplier management initiatives.

With this background, let's look at the historical roots of JIT, the various forms of waste and uncertainty, the special role of inventory in a JIT environment, and the three core elements of lean supply chains: JIT purchasing, JIT transportation, and JIT kanban systems.

The JIT Perspective on Waste

A key component of the JIT philosophy is a never-ending effort to eliminate **waste**, which is defined as "any activity that does not add value to the good or service in the eyes of the consumer."[7] Starting with Taiichi Ohno, a Toyota engineer, experts have sought to identify the major sources of waste (or "muda," in Japanese). The following eight sources are commonly recognized:[8]

1. Overproduction—caused by inflexible or unreliable processes that cause organizations to produce goods before they are required.
2. Waiting—caused by inefficient layouts or an inability to match demand with output levels.
3. Unnecessary transportation—transporting goods always increases costs and the risk of damage, but it does not necessarily provide value to the final customer.
4. Inappropriate process—using overly complex processes, when simpler, more efficient ones would do.
5. Unnecessary inventory—caused by uncertainty with regard to quality levels, delivery lead times, and the like.
6. Unnecessary/excess motion—caused by poorly designed processes.
7. Defects—not only do defects create uncertainty in the process, they rob production capacity by creating products or services that require rework or must be scrapped.
8. Underutilization of employees—the newest form of waste added to the list. This form of waste recognizes that too often, companies often do not fully utilize the skill and decision-making capability of their employees.

To put these forms of waste in context, suppose it takes an inspector at a manufacturing plant 15 minutes to inspect an incoming batch of material. The traditional perspective would be that inspections like these are a necessary and prudent business expense. But according to JIT, this is a waste of *both* time and personnel caused by defects. Services examples abound as well. If you have to wait even five minutes at the doctor's office before being seen, then waste has occurred. If this definition seems harsh, it is meant to be. The point is to get organizations thinking critically about the business processes they use to provide products and services, as well as the outcomes of these processes. As far as JIT is concerned, if there is any waste at all, there is room for improvement.

The JIT Perspective on Inventory

One hallmark of a JIT environment is the strong emphasis placed on reducing raw material, work-in-process, and finished goods inventories throughout the system. This is because inventory is not only seen as a form of waste in and of itself, but also because inventory can cover up wasteful business practices. Under the JIT philosophy, lowering inventory levels forces firms to address these poor practices.

To illustrate how inventory can hide problems, consider a simple facility consisting of three work centers (A, B, and C), shown in Exhibit 16.7.

The triangles in the diagram represent inventory. In addition, between each work center is plenty of room for inventory. Take one of the work centers, say Center B, and consider what happens if it has an equipment breakdown that reduces its output. The answer is, in the short run, only Center B is affected. Because there is plenty of space for inventory between A and B, then Center A can continue to work. And because inventory exists between Center B and C, Center C can continue to work as long as the inventory lasts. Most importantly, the customer can continue to be served. The same result occurs regardless of the reason for any disruption in Center B, including worker absenteeism, poor quality levels, and so forth. Whatever the problem, inventory hides it (but at a cost).

Now let's take the same facility after a successful JIT program has been put in place. The work centers have been moved closer together, eliminating wasted movement and space where inventory could pile up. Setup times have also been reduced, allowing the work centers to make only what is needed when it is needed. If we assume the program has been in place for a while, we can also assume that the

Exhibit 16.7 Inventory Positioned throughout a Supply Chain

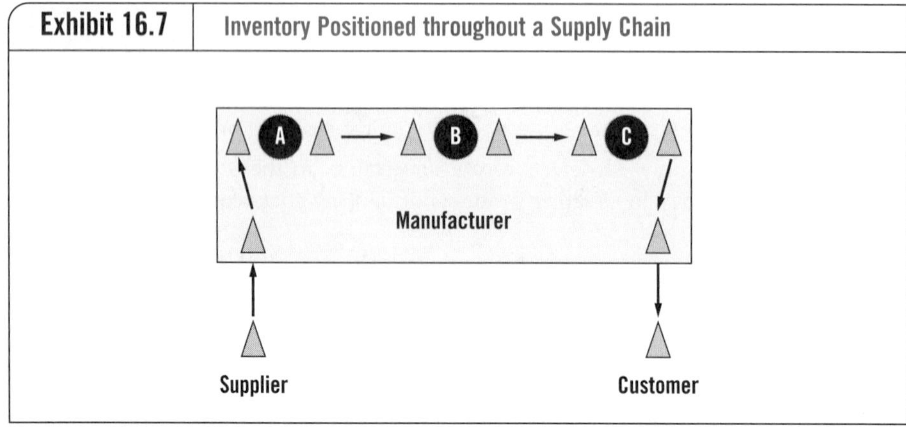

Exhibit 16.8 Supply Chain after the Elimination of Excess Inventories

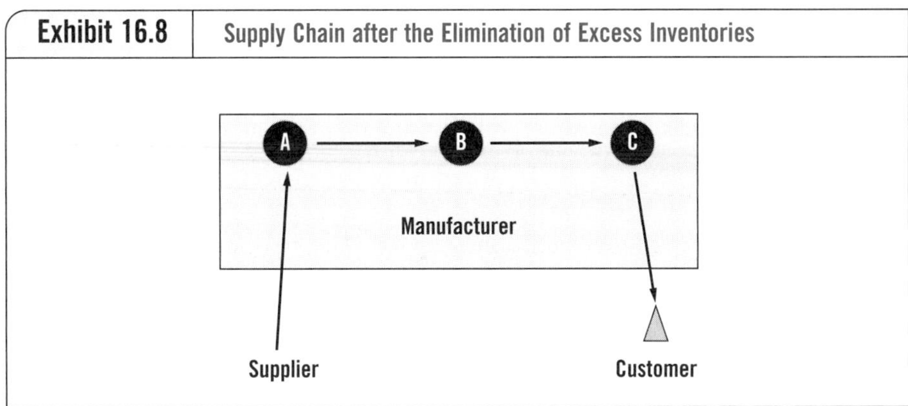

inventory levels have been reduced dramatically, giving us a revised picture of the facility (see Exhibit 16.8).

Now, inventory has been reduced to the point where it shows up only in the customer facility. Under these conditions, what happens in the short run if the equipment at Center B breaks down? The answer this time is that everything stops, including shipments to the customer. Center A has to stop because there is no spot for it to put inventory, nor is there any demand for it. Center C has to stop because there is no inventory on which to work.

Inventory in the supply chain is often compared to water in a river. If the "water" is high enough, it will cover all the "rocks" (quality problems, absenteeism, equipment breakdowns, etc.), and everything will appear to be running smoothly.

Under JIT, the approach is to gradually remove the "water" until the first "rock" is exposed, thereby establishing a priority as to the most important obstacle to work on. After resolving this problem, inventory levels are reduced further until another problem (and opportunity to eliminate waste) appears. This process continues indefinitely, or until all forms of waste and uncertainty have been eliminated (see Exhibit 16.9).

This is not an easy approach to implement. The implication is that every time a process is working smoothly, there may be too much inventory and more should be removed until the organization hits another "rock." That is certainly not a natural

Exhibit 16.9 How Inventory Hides Problems

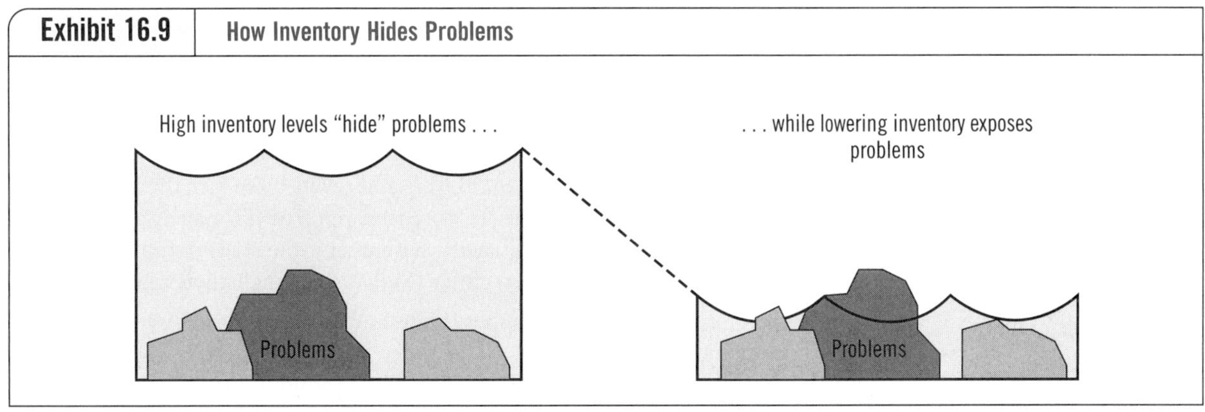

action for most people, and the performance evaluation system needs to be altered to reflect this type of activity.

Next, let's examine three of the primary elements of a lean supply chain: (1) just-in-time purchasing, (2) just-in-time transportation, and (3) just-in-time kanban systems.

Just-in-Time Purchasing

Implementing a just-in-time purchasing system is the first major element of a lean supply chain. A JIT purchasing system receives frequent receipts of material from suppliers to meet immediate requirements. The following features define a JIT purchasing system:

- A commitment to zero defects by the buyer and seller
- Frequent shipment of small lot sizes according to strict quality and delivery performance standards
- Closer, even collaborative, buyer-seller relationships
- Stable production schedules sent to suppliers on a regular basis
- Extensive sharing of electronic information between supply chain members
- Electronic data interchange capability with suppliers

Not simply a series of techniques, a JIT purchasing system is an operating philosophy that does not tolerate high inventory levels, less-than-perfect quality, or other inefficiency and waste between buyer and seller. JIT purchasing also requires permanent changes in how a firm conducts business. It is not a one-time effort or a project but rather a continuous improvement process. A true JIT purchasing system requires cultural and personnel mind-set changes on the part of the purchaser and the suppliers. Perhaps most important, JIT purchasing does not mean pushing inventory back to the supplier. JIT purchasing requires cooperation, coordination, and information sharing to eliminate inventory across the supply chain.

JIT Purchasing Barriers

JIT purchasing between Western companies has been slowed or even prohibited by a variety of barriers that are part of the Western business system and culture, although industries are affected differently. Fortunately, some of these barriers are not as great as they were when JIT first became popular during the early and mid-1980s. Important barriers include the following:

- *Dispersed supply base.* Most purchasers have a geographically dispersed supply base. Because JIT relies on frequent deliveries of smaller quantities from suppliers, it may be difficult to achieve a level of consistent delivery reliability from suppliers located 800 or even 8,000 miles away. The greater the distance between buyer and seller, the greater the variability around delivery times.
- *Historic buyer-seller relationships.* Buyers and sellers often lack the cooperative relationship required to pursue JIT purchasing. A true JIT system requires mutual trust and respect between parties. Historically, the relationship between U.S. buyers and sellers has been closer to adversarial than cooperative.
- *Number of suppliers.* Some supply chains still have too many suppliers to support an efficient JIT system. Like other progressive purchasing strategies, JIT requires a drastically reduced supply base to minimize interaction and

communication costs. It is nearly impossible to develop closer relationships with thousands of suppliers.

- *Supplier quality performance.* Some sellers simply have not achieved the levels of near-perfect quality required for JIT purchasing. A total commitment to product and delivery quality is a prerequisite for a successful JIT system.

The barriers limiting the increased use of JIT purchasing are beginning to break down. A reduction in the number of suppliers is the most obvious change. JIT purchasing has clearly been a major factor behind the supply-base reduction effort of most U.S. companies. Another change includes buyers and sellers developing closer working relationships. The two parties are increasingly willing to share information such as production scheduling and product development plans. Information sharing has contributed to the greater use of electronic systems linking supply chain members.

Just-in-Time Transportation

JIT transportation, the second element of a lean supply chain, refers to the efficient movement of goods between the buyer and seller. This involves frequent deliveries of smaller quantities directly to the point of use at the purchaser. A lean transportation network relies on company-owned or contracted vehicles that pick up and deliver according to a regular and repeatable schedule. This repeatable schedule, also called a closed-loop system, moves goods from supplier to purchaser and then from purchaser back to supplier with return material, such as containers. Long-term dedicated contract carriage replaces commercial carriage as the primary mode of transportation in a closed-loop transportation system.

Exhibit 16.10 on p. 606 compares a traditional delivery system with a just-in-time delivery system. In a traditional system, the supplier and purchaser do not coordinate their material requirements or production schedules. Suppliers produce material and then store that material, awaiting an order from the purchaser. In a JIT system, suppliers coordinate production schedules with customer schedules. Production moves from the supplier's work center to the carrier and directly to the purchaser. Designing a JIT transportation network involves certain steps:

- *Reduce the number of carriers.* Reduce the number of carriers, perhaps even to one per region.
- *Use longer-term contracts.* Negotiate longer-term agreements with carriers that formalize the dedicated transportation network.
- *Establish electric linkages.* Establish electronic/satellite linkages with suppliers and carriers to coordinate and control the movement of material through the network.
- *Implement a closed-loop system.* Pick up all freight from suppliers and deliver on a regular schedule. Use returnable containers to eliminate waste.
- *Efficiently handle material.* Use state-of-the-art material-handling equipment and technology. JIT transportation systems feature certain innovations that can further eliminate supply chain waste. The first includes specialized transportation vehicles that allow easy loading and unloading of smaller quantities. These trucks are smaller, more efficient, and more versatile. The second innovation includes the extensive use of returnable plastic or steel containers. As drivers pick up material from suppliers, they leave empty containers for reuse. A third innovation involves point-of-use doors at production

Exhibit 16.10 JIT Transportation Delivery Systems

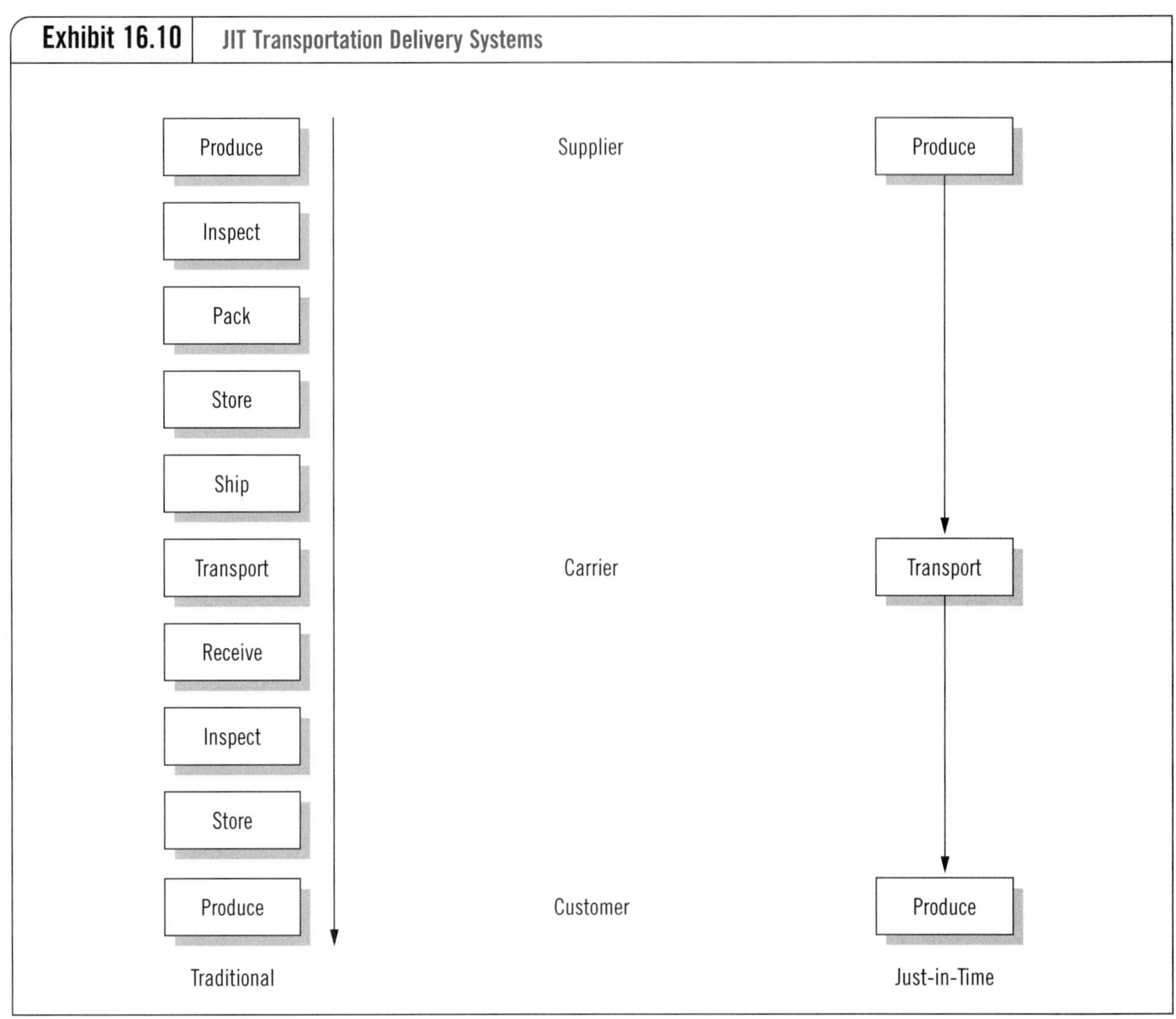

facilities. Because excessive material handling and travel within a facility is wasteful, deliveries occur close to where the material is needed.

Just-in-Time Kanban Systems

Developed along with the JIT movement, a **kanban system** is a production control approach that uses containers, cards, or visual cues to control the production and movement of goods through the supply chain. These systems have several key characteristics:

1. Kanban systems use simple signaling mechanisms such as a card, or even an empty space or container, to indicate when specific items should be produced or moved. Most kanban systems, in fact, do not require computerization.
2. Kanban systems can be used to synchronize activities either within a plant or between different supply chain partners. As such, a kanban system can be an important part of both production activity control and supplier order management systems.

3. Kanban systems are not planning tools. Rather, they are control mechanisms that are designed to pull parts or goods through the supply chain based on downstream demand. As a result, many firms use techniques such as material requirements planning (MRP) to anticipate requirements, but depend on their kanban systems to control the actual execution of production and movement activities.

As we noted before, cards aren't the only signaling method used in a kanban system. Some other methods include the following:

- Single-card systems. The single card is the production card, and the empty container serves as the move signal.
- Color coding of containers.
- Designated storage spaces.
- Computerized bar coding systems.

Approaches for Managing Inventory Investment

The effective management of inventory investment should be a primary objective when searching for ways to manage costs, improve profitability, and enhance shareholder value. How managers view inventory can differ depending on where one resides in the supply chain. Although financial planners view inventory in terms of dollars, as reported on the balance sheet, supply chain planners typically view inventory in terms of units. What is the right viewpoint if we expect to manage this investment? Actually, assuming multiple perspectives about inventory is a worthwhile way to approach this topic.

Companies that are serious about managing inventory must visualize how their practices and approaches will affect the three Vs of inventory management—the volume, velocity, and value of inventory. Exhibit 16.11 on p. 608 highlights the "Three-V Model of Inventory Management," including key objectives, measures, and examples of activities that relate to each dimension.

Volume refers to the amount of inventory that a firm owns at any given time. Volume measures will relate to total units on hand, including safety stock levels. Velocity refers to how quickly raw material and work-in-process inventory transform into finished goods that the customer accepts. As the rate at which inventory moves from suppliers, through operations, and on to customers accelerates, the average amount of inventory on hand at any given time is reduced. Faster velocity requires a lower commitment of working capital and improves cash flow. Velocity measures include material throughput rates, inventory turns, and order-to-cash cycle times. Finally, value refers to the unit cost of the inventory. Key measures include standard costs and the total value of inventory, including raw materials, components, subassemblies, and finished goods.

Although certain actions can predominantly affect a specific variable (velocity, volume, or value), there is often interdependence among these variables. The point here is that organizations must pursue activities and approaches that positively affect the volume, value, and velocity of inventory through and across the supply chain. The following sections present some powerful ways to manage inventory investment.

Exhibit 16.11 Three-V Model of Inventory Management

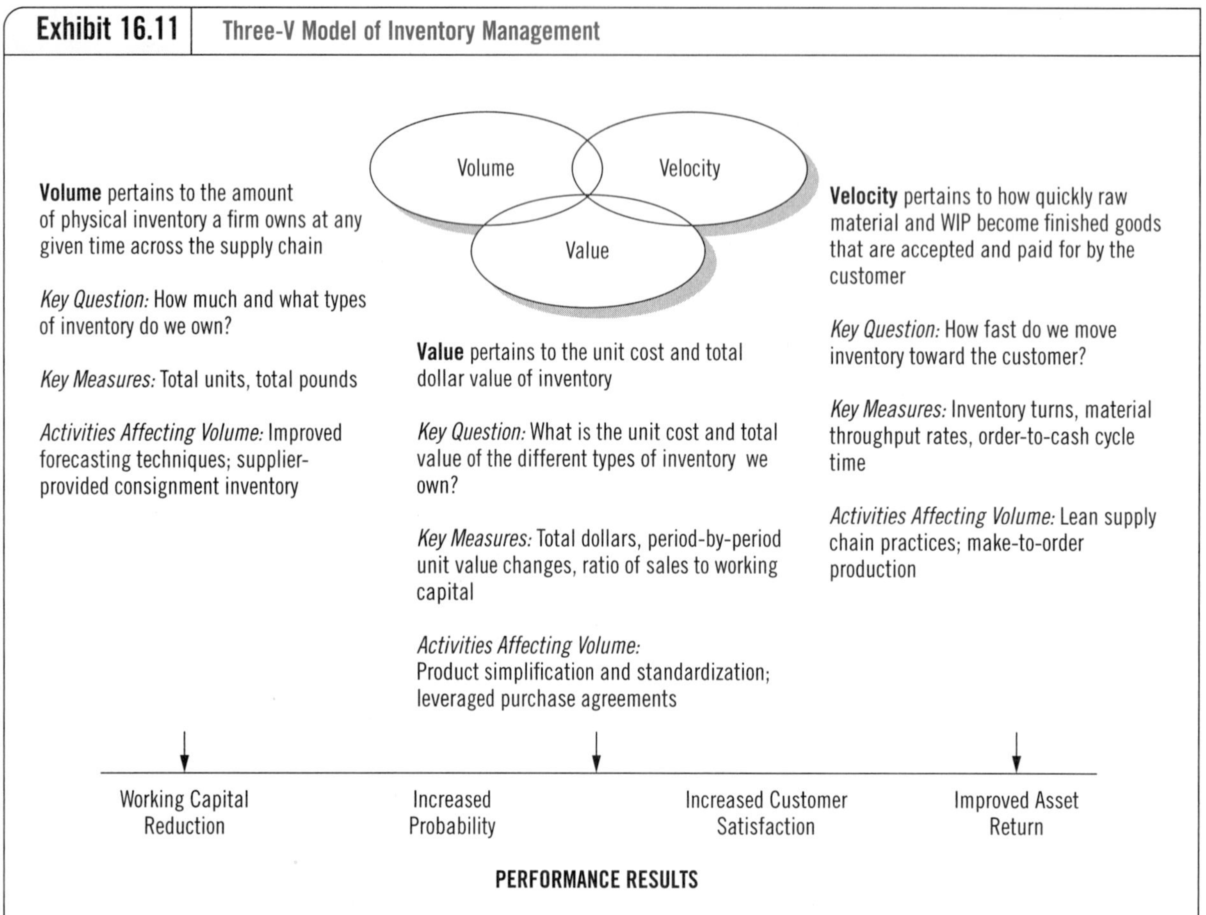

Volume
Velocity
Value
Volume pertains to the amount of physical inventory a firm owns at any given time across the supply chain
Key Question: How much and what types of inventory do we own?
Key Measures: Total units, total pounds
Activities Affecting Volume: Improved forecasting techniques; supplier-provided consignment inventory
Value pertains to the unit cost and total dollar value of inventory
Key Question: What is the unit cost and total value of the different types of inventory we own?
Key Measures: Total dollars, period-by-period unit value changes, ratio of sales to working capital
Activities Affecting Volume: Product simplification and standardization; leveraged purchase agreements
Velocity pertains to how quickly raw material and WIP become finished goods that are accepted and paid for by the customer
Key Question: How fast do we move inventory toward the customer?
Key Measures: Inventory turns, material throughput rates, order-to-cash cycle time
Activities Affecting Volume: Lean supply chain practices; make-to-order production
Working Capital Reduction
Increased Probability
Increased Customer Satisfaction
Improved Asset Return
PERFORMANCE RESULTS

Achieve Perfect Record Integrity

A logical place to begin when managing inventory investment is to make sure there is agreement between physical and electronic inventory. Firms often compensate for error and variability in supply chains with excess inventory, usually in the form of safety stock or safety lead times. This also applies when there is excessive error in record integrity systems. Perfect record integrity must become an important inventory management objective.

Record integrity is the result of various activities and procedures designed to ensure that the amount of physical material on hand (POH) is equal to the computerized record of material on hand (ROH). In short, record integrity exists when the physical inventory on hand equals the electronic record on hand (POH = ROH), regardless of the quantity of inventory. Any difference between POH and ROH represents error. This error can be the result of operationally mismanaging inventory, which affects the physical (POH) side of record integrity. Error can also result from systems-related sources, which affect the computerized side (ROH) of record integrity. Concern over managing the actual volume, velocity, and value of inventory should arise only after we have confidence in the integrity of inventory records.

The effects of poor record integrity on supply chain operations can be severe. When physical inventory exceeds the amount the computerized system believes is available (POH > ROH), the physical inventory cannot be sold or used to satisfy customer demand. When the record on hand is larger than what is physically available (ROH > POH), there is the risk that an item will be scheduled for production or even sold to a customer when in fact it is not available. This inevitably leads to backorder situations and dissatisfied customers.

When record integrity is lacking (i.e., there are discrepancies between physical quantities and electronic records), steps must be taken to identify the sources of error with corrective action expected. This will require asking and answering a range of questions. For example, are record errors displaying a random or systematic pattern across SKUs? How severe are the differences between physical stock and electronic records? Are proper receiving, stockkeeping, and withdrawal procedures and systems in place? Is theft a problem? Are suppliers shipping quantities that match their documentation? Are effective cycle-counting procedures used? Is inventory scrap and obsolescence accounted for correctly? Do employees properly move, handle, and disburse material?

Record integrity is an essential but often overlooked part of inventory management. It is difficult to manage inventory when we lack confidence in knowing what we own or physically have on hand.

Improve Product Forecasting

Perhaps the most important piece of information that moves across a supply chain is the forecast of end customer demand. Unfortunately, many companies fail to recognize the effect that inaccurate forecasting has on the volume and velocity at which inventory moves toward the customer. The downside of poor forecasting includes higher inventory volumes and carrying charges, poor customer service as inventory is misallocated across locations and products, and excessive safety stock levels. For companies that are serious about better inventory management, improving the quality of product forecasts, like improving record integrity, is an ideal place to start.

Longs Drug Stores illustrates the benefits of better forecasting and product placement.[9] This company has improved its ability to identify the best possible combination of when to order prescription drugs, how to ship them, and how much to carry in a retail outlet on any given day. The company worked with a third party to develop a system that pulls data each day from point-of-sale terminals at hundreds of stores. Then, using two years of historical data and a forecasting algorithm that includes 150 variables per product that effectively predicts consumer demand out to 91 days, the company determines finished goods requirements for its retail outlets on a daily basis. The system also determines the amount to order from upstream suppliers (the pharmaceutical companies).

What effect has improved forecasting had on inventory and capital requirements? Longs executives say that the new system has allowed a 26% reduction in systemwide inventory requirements, leading to $30 million in savings. This system has also freed $60 million in working capital, which the company has used to acquire a 20-store drug chain. The results are so encouraging that Longs signed a five-year extension with its third-party forecaster and expects to extend the system to include nonprescription products in the front of its stores. This example illustrates the link between better forecasting, reduced inventory requirements, and improved financial performance.

Standardize and Simplify Product Design

Why be concerned with standardizing and simplifying designs? A simplified design usually requires fewer part numbers, resulting in fewer suppliers, reduced transactions to support the inventory, and lower inventory management costs. The elimination of unnecessary components also reduces product cost, which reduces the value of the inventory required to support customer demand and service requirements. In some cases, this approach to greater standardization may require a major cultural shift in the company and a strategic decision to move in a particular direction. In many cases, the product complexity decision is embedded in the very DNA of the organization and requires a fundamental shift driven by top leadership toward containing complexity and SKU proliferation. For example, a leading truck manufacturer was undergoing a major shift in company philosophy, in which the entire product line and product offering was undergoing a major transformation:

> *We are primarily engineer to order historically—but are moving more towards standardized options. We are making some components standard and are moving from 13 variations to 3 or 4 and are being pushed to do that by senior management. As it stands historically, if the customer wanted it we would put it on. The move towards standardization is a senior management decision. We have some tools to measure complexity versus revenue generated whereby we are able to establish a value for that option. It is easy to determine which parts a customer wants and what we charge for it—and in these cases we can do a pretty good job of passing it on with a nice margin.*[10]

Product design is the right time to consider simplification and standardization, although continuous improvement efforts can later alter existing designs. Many companies use value-engineering techniques during product design to reduce part count and cost. Some of the other policies used to improve design simplification and reduce complexity are as follows.

Establish Premium Pricing for Customization

Many companies are loath to develop premium pricing options. However, this practice can assist in shaping customer demand and can even, in some cases, drive additional margin into the business if required. Many companies are now recognizing that there is a cost to complexity and that customers should be willing to pay more to offset these costs.

Establish Geographic-Specific Options and Standards

Companies are also working to establish regional requirements based on regional customer preferences and designing supply chain configurations around these regional requirements. This approach must be orchestrated carefully with plants and suppliers to ensure success and accommodate appropriate order-to-delivery lead time promises aligned with this design. For example, one manufacturing company noted the following:

> *We are also standardizing certain configurations around certain regions of the country where our plants are. Our plants are from Seattle to Montreal, to the Midwest, Canada, and Mexico to the Southwest and Southeast—and the options are very distinct. Texas truckers like shiny stuff, Midwestern*

> *ones, not so much. So we configure by plant and by region. If someone wants an option in one area they have to go to a different plant. This is managed by our order fulfillment group that allows us to maintain good plant focus for certain options and configurations.*[11]

Maintain a Database of Option Requests

One company has dedicated a formal approach to maintaining complexity and has identified this as a core element, even though it acknowledged the problems associated with managing the business in this manner and the pain inflicted on the supply chain. The order fulfillment manager described the emotional decisions and back-room wars that took place when they were bought out and the buyer sought to standardize components of their product line, considered to be a company trademark:

> *We track active options and custom unpublished options. We track usage, and if we have a group of options that has no usage over time, we will try to eliminate them from the available product offerings and get them out of the maintenance mode. On the other hand, if we have some customized options showing increasing usage, we will promote them to a published standard as it is becoming a popular item. In that case we will look closely at the design to see if it is designed for higher volume, to get some cost out of the process.*[12]

Do Not Eliminate Frequently Requested Options!

The importance of maintaining a company's trademark requirements in product design can be an important counterpoint to the standardization argument. An organization needs to carefully evaluate the standardization decision and ensure it does not design out elements that are critical to its product branding and positioning.

Utilize Business Modeling and TCO Tools to Support Complexity Reduction Decisions

Many companies are developing more formal approaches to managing complexity and have developed business modeling and TCO approaches to developing a business case with tools associated with the decision. For example, Dell Computer utilizes a template of decision criteria against which product design decisions are baselined:

1. Will the item be sole, single, or multisourced?
2. Does the new offering involve a new technology risk item (this could signal a potential quality yield risk)?
3. Who are the manufacturers and who are the integrators for the parts?
4. Where are all the suppliers located and what is the logistics plan?
5. Where are these parts used in the industry today and in future, which could affect overall demand?
6. What are the expected cost takedown rates?
7. What does the product roadmap look like in terms of possible product substitutes?
8. Are there any key alliances that need to be considered from key suppliers/competitors?

9. What is the flexibility to use a particular part in other product lines, or is this part leveraged from another product?
10. Can these parts be sold as aftermarket options or service parts?[13]

Leverage Companywide Purchase Volumes

The consolidation or leveraging of common items and services across buying locations has increased dramatically over the last 10 years, including across worldwide units.[14] This has resulted in major savings as leveraged agreements lead to lower material costs. Lower material costs can significantly reduce the amount of capital committed to inventory over the life of an agreement.

Besides seeking a lower unit cost in leveraged agreements, buyers often pursue other nonprice issues that affect inventory investment. One such issue is **consignment**, which the *APICS Dictionary* defines as the process of a supplier placing goods at a customer location without receiving payment until after the buyer uses the goods. The advantage of consignment to the buyer is the ability to defer ownership and avoid committing working capital and incurring carrying charges. This reduces the average amount of inventory a buyer owns as well as improving velocity.

Use Suppliers for On-Site Inventory Management

Almost all organizations use distributors to provide at least some portion of their inventory requirements, particularly maintenance, repair, and operating supplies. A distributor may stock and sell a full range of items from different manufacturers. If the purchaser has enough volume, then the distributor may be willing to locate an employee at the purchaser's facility to manage the inventory.

Purchasers are increasingly entering partnerships or formal agreements with distributors featuring on-site support. Besides the on-site support, these agreements stipulate that a supplier/distributor will stock a wider range of items and provide agreed-upon service levels. The buyer, in exchange for purchasing solely from the distributor, no longer stocks inventory for items under contract.

The on-site representative orders on an as-needed basis, often directly into the distributor's order-processing system. This reduces the amount of paperwork required to submit an order. A buying firm avoids stocking or managing this inventory, while the distributor benefits from a higher share of a purchaser's total purchase requirements. Not stocking the items relieves the purchaser of carrying inventory.

The purchase of most MRO items is a nuisance because (1) they require a disproportionate amount of a buyer's time and (2) this often involves lower-value items. A formal agreement providing on-site supplier support can reduce the MRO ordering problem. These arrangements offer an opportunity to control a category of inventory that usually does not receive enough attention.

Reduce Supplier-Buyer Cycle Times

Shortening the material pipeline in terms of time between suppliers and a buyer can reduce the average amount of inventory in a system. One area of emphasis will be to support reduced order-cycle times with suppliers. A reduced (and reliable) order-cycle time positively affects inventory investment by allowing frequent orders received in smaller quantities. Planning horizons are also shorter, which reduces the need to carry safety stock.

Several actions support reduced order-cycle time with suppliers:

- *Expanded electronic capability.* The electronic exchange of information in a supply chain supports paperless procurement, faster data movement, and increased information accuracy. Electronic data interchange has the potential to reduce order-cycle times by 15 to 40% from current levels.
- *Supplier development support.* Supplier development means working directly with suppliers to improve performance. This support may include working directly at a supplier's facilities to speed order entry, production, and delivery through the removal of waste.
- *Order-cycle time measurement.* Tracking order-cycle times helps identify areas of improvement. We expect to see greater emphasis on the development of performance measures that are time oriented.
- *Focus on second- and third-tier suppliers.* Total supply chain management requires working with first-, second-, and even third-tier suppliers. The ability of a purchaser to reduce order-cycle time and inventory with its immediate suppliers is partly a function of a supplier being able to work with its suppliers. Suppliers located two and three tiers from the buyer will increasingly capture the interest of supply chain managers.

The activities described here are not the only actions that supply chain managers can or will emphasize to manage inventory investment. This discussion points out, however, that there are creative approaches for the systemwide control and management of inventory investment.

Delivering the Perfect Customer Order

Managing inventory investment is not only important from a financial perspective. If a firm can balance the right supply of inventory with the demand for inventory across a supply chain, it increases the probability that it can deliver the perfect order to customers. Simply put, the perfect customer order is one that is delivered on time, accurately, and in perfect condition. "The perfect order metric is especially valuable because it is a comprehensive measure of demand-fulfillment capability and acts as a lightning rod for all the deficiencies in a company's operations," said Debra Hoffman, a Boston-based consultant.[15] Although most companies measure different elements contained in the perfect order measure, only 40% have a perfect customer order measure.[16]

A number of factors can cause an order not to be perfect, some of which are inventory related. Orders may be late due to supplier delivery problems, stockouts or manufacturing delays, or in-transit or delivery delays to customers. An order that arrives at the customer may not meet specifications because of inaccurate quantities, poor quality of finished goods, damage during transit, or incorrect or missing documentation. Any of these conditions can result in a less-than-perfect order.

The following identifies various planning systems and ways that progressive companies bring all parts of the supply chain together to pursue the perfect customer order.

Material Requirements Planning System

When we discuss systems that forecast future demand for products or services we sell, we are referring to independent demand systems. This means that demand for an item is not directly dependent upon the demand for any other item that we produce. Systems that plan at the independent demand level are critical for achieving the perfect customer order.

A major task of the materials manager, however, is to control the inventory of items whose demand is dependent on the production of other items. A riding lawn mower is an example of an independent demand item. Demand for the final part is independent—expected orders determine the final amount produced. The demand for the steering wheel or tires that go on the mower, for example, are dependent on the demand for the mower. The component or subassembly demand is simply a function of the production schedule for the final part number.

A widely used system that controls dependent demand inventory is the material requirements planning system. An MRP system takes a period-by-period set of master production schedule requirements (anticipated or booked customer orders) and produces a time-phased set of material, component, and subassembly requirements timed to support an expected build schedule. This system relies on production schedules developed for final part numbers in the master production schedule to determine the timing and quantities of materials required for components or subassemblies. If supplier quality and lead times are reliable, planners can time the arrival of components just before production of the final part number.

Component requirements and quantities required to produce or assemble a final part number appear on a bill of material file. The bill of material file details the components or subassemblies and the quantity required to produce a final part number or end item. In some systems, the bill of material also indicates if any components require components themselves. Components that require components are subassemblies of the final part number. An MRP system links directly to the bill of material file and recognizes what components or subassemblies must go into the final item or package. The system will also recognize how many of each part may already be on hand.

Distribution Resource Planning System

Distribution resource planning (DRP) systems attempt to make the most effective use of finished-goods inventories. These systems, which are concerned with inventory that has left the work-in-process status and is working its way through a channel of distribution toward the customer, perform many functions:

- Forecasting finished-goods inventory requirements
- Establishing correct inventory levels at each stocking location
- Determining the timing and replenishment of finished-goods inventories
- Allocating items in short supply
- Transportation planning and vehicle load scheduling

A DRP system, combined with upstream supply chain planning systems such as MRP, can provide a total supply chain perspective.

Supply Chain Inventory Planners

The establishment of a supply chain or logistical planner position responsible for working with supply chain planning and execution systems is gaining popularity as a way to pursue the perfect customer order. A supply chain planner, a position often organized along product lines, manages the flow of inventory and information from suppliers through end customers. This position ties together the requirements of purchasing/materials management, production, inventory control, and product distribution.

The planner coordinates the movement and placement of inventory throughout the supply, production, and distribution channel. This position also acts as the liaison between various groups in the supply chain. Other assignments include developing smooth production schedules, establishing production targets from marketing forecasts, determining inventory deployment at field warehouses, and continuously evaluating inventory safety stock levels. The supply chain planner works closely with purchasing to coordinate material requirements to support production targets and with marketing and sales to meet customer order requirements. The performance of the planner is often measured against his or her ability to ensure that customers receive a perfect order.

Automated Inventory Tracking Systems

Automated inventory control systems involve computerized material and electronic data interchange systems that track the flow of inventory throughout the entire supply chain. This approach electronically connects suppliers, production plants, field distribution centers, and even customers. A customer may be a retail outlet or an independent distributor.

An integrated systems approach relies on new forms of information technology, such as EDI and bar code scanning, to link the entire supply chain electronically. Wal-Mart, for example, has benefited greatly from automated inventory tracking systems, using bar code technology to capture data at the point of sale and sending this up the supply chain to suppliers. Tracking sales allows Wal-Mart to identify what is selling and to replenish shelves quickly. Automated tracking systems present an opportunity for controlling inventory investment throughout the entire supply chain. Increasingly, producers and channel members use radio frequency identification tags to track material movement across the supply chain. Real-time visibility to inventory across the supply chain makes planning for the perfect customer order that much easier.

Good Practice Example

Managing Low-Value Inventory for High-Value Savings at Lockheed

Lockheed Martin Energy Systems (LMES) has taken an aggressive step to control its maintenance, repair, and operating (MRO) suppliers. Confronted by a constant flow of small-dollar purchase requests, thousands of individual MRO suppliers, and difficulty tracking inventory and usage, LMES created its Accelerated Vendor Inventory Delivery (AVID) system. This

Exhibit 16.12 Lockheed Martin Energy Systems AVID System Overview

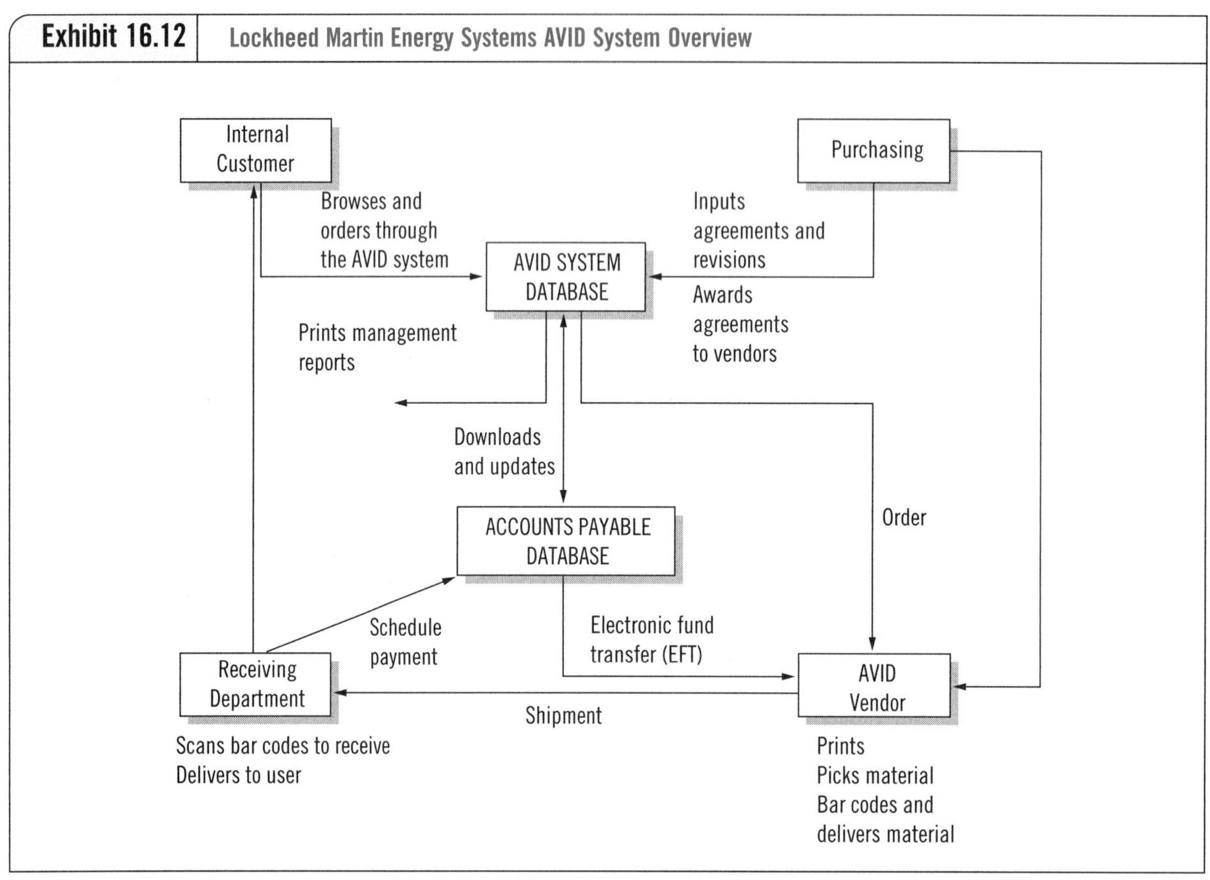

system links LMES electronically with a selected group of MRO distributors and allows users to order online using electronic catalogs. Exhibit 16.12 provides an overview of the AVID system.

Relying extensively on electronic data interchange between the user and suppliers, AVID allows users to control the purchase of low-dollar off-the-shelf items while significantly reducing the transaction costs of processing low-value purchases. Items typically acquired electronically through the system include electrical items, paper, lab supplies, building supplies, personal computers, electronics, and office supplies. The AVID system, which traces its origin back to 1988, allows more than 3,400 users to conduct transactions with 36 suppliers. The system accounts for 225,000 transactions involving $55 million per year.

The company has attained certain benefits from this system, most of which directly affect MRO inventory investment:

- Established a just-in-time delivery system for MRO purchasing
- Increased purchasing power due to larger volumes with fewer suppliers
- Eliminated the need for stocking MRO items at the company's facilities

- Created a streamlined channel of electronic communication between LMES and suppliers
- Reduced the total order-cycle time
- Improved overall quality of MRO items and reduced inventory aging
- Reduced inventory-carrying costs drastically
- Reduced paperwork and improved productivity through bar-coded labels on all receipts
- Improved accountability from both users and suppliers

LMES offers selected suppliers the opportunity to become the company's sole supplier for a wide range of items. In return, the company requires a price reduction on MRO items, 24-hour turnaround on regular replenishment orders, two-hour emergency deliveries, and no paperwork. In addition, suppliers must broaden their own inventory levels and depth to meet company requirements.

When the AVID system was developed, a steering committee was put in place that included representatives from executive management, accounts payable, accounts receivable, procurement, treasury, and business systems. In addition, the company established an AVID project team and an AVID advisory team to monitor the operation of the system and to assume responsibility for the selection of AVID suppliers.

The selection criteria for AVID suppliers include technical and price considerations. The technical criteria include the supplier's warehouse and delivery capabilities, inventory management, financial strength, and the ability to work with the AVID system. Technical criteria during the selection process are weighted 60 percent while price is weighted 40 percent. Quality and time are also critical considerations during selection. For example, can a chosen supplier deliver the correct product in 24 hours?

A Web-based version of AVID now includes current suppliers but also allows LMES to increase the number of electronic catalogs that are part of the system. The AVID system clearly demonstrates that a company can successfully manage low-value inventory to create high-dollar savings.

Source: Interviews with company managers.

CONCLUSION

The dollars committed to inventory represent a major investment. Like any investment, careful management will help ensure the investment provides an adequate return. Lean supply chain management requires the involvement of multiple parties within the organization, including senior leadership, operational executives and line managers, supply chain managers, logistics, transportation, finance, and other key players, all of whom play an important role in the management of inventory investment. The goal of this chapter is to create an awareness of (1) the function of inventory, (2) the operational problems that tempt firms to increase inventory levels, (3) the major approaches used to manage inventory investment, and (4) the role of lean thinking in managing inventory. As firms continue to outsource more of their operational and manufacturing requirements, the inclusion of inventory cost within the total cost of ownership equation will also continue to be a challenge and will cause supply chain executives to continue to update their strategies in light of different requirements for trading off supply chain risk, inventory investment, customer responsiveness, and financial performance.

KEY TERMS

consignment, 612
flow, 586
kanban system, 606
lean, 586
pull, 586
striving for excellence, 586
waste, 601

DISCUSSION QUESTIONS

1. What does it mean to say that higher inventory levels often disguise underlying problems? What types of problems does this indicate?
2. How is purchasing directly and indirectly involved in the control of a firm's inventory investment?
3. What are some of the operational problems that excessive work-in-process inventory might indicate?
4. Discuss several reasons why managers often neglect the true costs of holding physical inventory. What has happened to change our perspective about holding physical inventory?
5. Why is the control of maintenance, repair, and operating inventory typically a difficult task for most companies?
6. What are the benefits of calculating the total cost of ownership associated with carrying physical inventory?
7. Of the following functions of physical inventory, select the one that purchasing is most likely to be directly involved in: (a) support of production requirements, (b) support of operational requirements, or (c) support of customer service requirements. Explain your choice.
8. Describe the actions that purchasing can take to reduce uncertainty associated with (a) supplier quality, (b) supplier delivery, (c) long order-cycle times, (d) extended material pipelines, and (e) inaccurate demand forecasts.

9. What problems does overforecasting demand create within a supply chain? What problems does underforecasting demand create? What can a company do to resolve the problem of forecasting inaccuracy?
10. The chapter presented various approaches for the control of inventory investment. Discuss three additional approaches not included that might involve supply chain managers.
11. What is a lean supply chain? Explain the three primary elements of a lean system.
12. What are the main characteristics of a JIT purchasing system? What are the barriers to a JIT purchasing system?
13. What is a closed-loop transportation system? Why does such a system require dedicated or contracted transportation carriers?
14. When putting in place a JIT purchasing system, what changes typically occur in the ordering and transportation system between buyer and seller?
15. Discuss the advantages of taking a systemwide approach to the control of inventory investment. Are there any disadvantages? If yes, discuss the disadvantages.
16. What is the perfect order? Why do so few companies measure the perfect order?

ADDITIONAL READINGS

Bernard, P. (1999), *Integrated Inventory Management,* New York: John Wiley & Sons.

Bonney, M. C. (1994), "Trends in Inventory Management," *International Journal of Production Economics,* 35(1–3), 107–114.

Briscoe, A., Pancerella, M. B., and Pleskunas, G. (1997), "The Perfect Order Initiative," *Pharmaceutical Executive,* 17(7), 82–85.

Dong, Y., and Xu, K. (2002), "A Supply Chain Model of Vendor Managed Inventory, Transportation Research," *Part E: Logistics and Transportation Review,* 38(2), 75–95.

Fazel, F. (1997), "A Comparative Analysis of Inventory Costs of JIT and EOQ Purchasing," *International Journal of Physical Distribution and Logistics Management,* 27(2), 496.

Germain, R., and Droge, C. (1998), "The Context, Organization, Design, and Performance of JIT Buying versus Non-JIT Buying Firms," *International Journal of Purchasing and Materials Management,* 34(2), 12–18.

Gould, L. (2003), "Automotive Supply Chain Management: As Good as It Gets?" *Automotive Design and Production,* 115(2), 60–62.

Lewis, C. (1998), *Demand Forecasting and Inventory Control: A Computer Aided Learning Approach,* New York: John Wiley & Sons.

Minner, S. (2003), "Multiple-Supplier Inventory Models in Supply Chain Management: A Review," *International Journal of Production Economics,* 81–82, 265–279.

Narasimhan, S. L. (1995), *Production Planning and Inventory Control,* Englewood Cliffs, NJ: Prentice Hall.

Orlicky, J. (1994), *Materials Requirements Planning,* New York: McGraw-Hill.

Silver, E. A. (1998), *Inventory Management and Production Planning and Scheduling,* New York: John Wiley & Sons.

Stundza, T. (2001), "Buyers Save Money with Smart Inventory Programs," *Purchasing,* 130(23), 8B1–8B6.

Wild, T. (1998), *Best Practice in Inventory Management,* New York: John Wiley & Sons.

Witt, C. E. (2003), "Economic Strategies: Inventory Management," *Material Handling Management,* 58(5), 31–40.

Zipkin, P. H. (2000), *Foundations of Inventory Management,* New York: McGraw-Hill.

ENDNOTES

1. John Shook, as quoted in Liker, J. K. (Ed.) (1998), *Becoming Lean,* Portland, OR: Productivity Press.

2. Womack, J. P., and Jones, D. T. (1996), *Lean Thinking,* New York: Simon & Schuster.

3. Handfield, R. (1993), "Distinguishing Attributes of JIT Systems in the Make-to-Order/Assemble-to-Order Environment," *Decision Sciences Journal,* 24(3), 581–602.

4. This example is based directly on interviews with company managers.

5. This section is drawn from Bozarth, C., and Handfield, R. (2008), *Operations and Supply Chain Management* (2nd ed.), Upper Saddle River, NJ: Prentice Hall.

6. From Womack, J., Jones, D., and Roos, D. D. (1991), *The Machine That Changed the World: The Story of Lean Production,* New York: HarperCollins.

7. Cox, J. F., and Blackstone, J. H. (Eds.) (2002), *APICS Dictionary* (10th ed.), Falls Church, VA: APICS.

8. Womack, J., and Jones, D. (2003), *Lean Thinking: Banish Waste and Create Wealth in Your Corporation* (rev. ed.), New York: Free Press.

9. Adapted from Doan, A. (1999), "Vitamin Efficiency," *Forbes,* November 1, pp. 179–186.

10. Handfield, R., Bozarth, C., McCreery, J., and Edwards, S. (2006), "Design for Order Fulfillment," working paper, Supply Chain Resource Cooperative, North Carolina State University, November.

11. Handfield et al.

12. Handfield et al.

13. Handfield et al.

14. Trent, R. J., and Monczka, R. M. (1998), "Purchasing and Supply Management: Trends and Changes throughout the 1990s," *International Journal of Purchasing and Materials Management,* November, pp. 2–9.

15. "The Perfect Order: How Does Your Demand Fulfillment Stack Up?" (2003), *MSI,* November, p. 37.

16. Keebler, J. S., et al. (1999), *Keeping Score: Measuring the Business Value of Logistics in the Supply Chain,* Oak Brook, IL: Council of Logistics Management, p. 59.

Chapter 17

PURCHASING SERVICES

Learning Objectives

After completing this chapter, you should be able to

- Understand the impact of indirect spending on company performance
- Understand the fundamentals of transportation management and third-party logistics providers
- Understand the role of third-party logistics providers in supply chain management
- Discuss best practices in managing indirect spending and purchasing of services

Chapter Outline

Indirect Purchasing at Saab

As part of a major corporate reorganization in the 1990s, Saab decided to centralize and modernize many of its core support functions, including indirect purchasing. This initiative was designed to improve corporate efficiency and increase the firm's profitability. Magnus Strömer, Saab's vice president of corporate sourcing, was tasked with centralizing a historically decentralized purchasing organization. Analysis of the company revealed that Saab had minimal control and visibility of its indirect spend.

Based on the results of an internal purchasing survey, Strömer and his staff decided that more than 80% of indirect material sourcing could be consolidated and leveraged at the corporate level. The survey also indicated that the company suffered from a lack of automation, high levels of maverick spending, and almost no enterprisewide contracts in its indirect spend.

Over the following year and a half, Saab was able to totally revamp its indirect spend by centralizing its staff, utilizing a common strategic sourcing process, and deploying a variety of tools and methods, including e-procurement. More than 4,800 purchase orders per month are now placed using the new e-procurement system. Strömer indicates that this is a continuous, dynamic process.

The next steps for Saab include developing and implementing global corporate contracts with many of its suppliers and evaluating use of the e-procurement tool globally. Initial results indicate far fewer manual transactions and paper invoices. Strömer says, "If we look at our annual spend of SEK 2.6 billion (EUR 290 million), we have saved SEK 230 million, or roughly 10%, of our total spend per year. This is very important as Saab, like every other company, needs to look at costs to be successful on the market."

Part of this implementation process has been focused on the identification and development of "super users," who set the standard for sourcing performance and can help show other users how to effectively use the process to their advantage. Once other users were made aware of the system's benefits, it was easy to get them to accept and adopt the new tool.

Corporate support of the new e-procurement process and tools was demonstrated by widespread acceptance of Saab's top management team. They supported the implementation by developing broad policies and mandates that applied to those who were not prone to accept the system. Other supporting activities included delivering measurable results and storytelling of successes.

Source: A. Eames, "Take-Off for New Procurement," *Efficient Purchasing,* 2007, 5, pp. 38–42.

Indirect spending continues to receive growing attention from top management at large corporations. This spend category can be defined as the sum of all purchased goods and services that are not a direct part of products or services delivered to the customer. It is not uncommon for indirect spend to equal 50% or more of a company's total purchases. Unfortunately, a substantial amount of indirect spend is not purchased using the organization's formal sourcing function or established supply management processes. Many companies, like Saab in the opening vignette, are aggressively measuring and attacking costs of indirect purchasing. Senior management have realized that reducing or eliminating their firm's indirect spend offers an opportunity to substantially reduce a company's costs. Common examples of indirect spend include professional services, consulting, utilities, travel, maintenance, repair, operating supplies, and employee benefits. However, because of industry differences, one company's indirect spend may be considered direct spend for another.

Historically, expenditures for indirect materials and services have not received the same level of management attention as have direct materials. They are typically controlled and spent from outside the supply management hierarchy even though the dollar amount of such expenditures is usually fairly significant as a percentage of total purchases. As such, organizations have overlooked a substantial opportunity to effectively reduce cost in the services supply chain.[1]

A substantial area of indirect spend that does affect customers is the purchase of transportation and logistics services. Companies are increasingly using third-party logistics (3PL) companies to create competitive marketplace advantage from which their customers benefit directly. Without effective transportation sourcing, getting the right product to the right place in the right condition at the right time becomes problematic. Selecting the right transportation and logistics provider can be as critical as any other supplier evaluation and selection decision, perhaps even more so.

In this chapter, we begin by describing the role that supply management plays in managing the organization's indirect spend. We begin by discussing that role in managing transportation, then discuss other areas of indirect spending (such as services) where supply management can have a major impact on the cost structure and performance of organizations today.

Transportation Management

The Council of Supply Chain Management Professionals defines **logistics** management as "that part of supply chain management that plans, implements, and controls the efficient, effective forward and reverse flow and storage of goods, services, and related information between the point of origin and the point of consumption in order to meet customers' requirements."[2] Transportation is a key element of logistics management, and logistics management, in turn, is a key element of supply chain management.[3]

Transportation service providers support the four major linkages throughout a typical supply chain shown in Exhibit 17.1 on p. 624: (1) inbound logistics, (2) intraorganizational movements, (3) outbound logistics, and (4) recovery and recycling (or reverse logistics). The first link includes all inbound shipments moving between supplier and buyer facilities. This element is often included in sourcing negotiations and is a substantial part of the contractual terms discussed earlier.

Companies with multiple production and warehouse locations usually have a second major transportation link—intraorganizational movement. This includes movement of materials between production facilities within the same organization as well as movement into and out of intermediary storage facilities. A storage facility may be located in the same manufacturing complex as the production facility or at some other geographic location, which another company may control. Some companies directly control the movement of goods within this link through the use of company-owned or leased transportation vehicles, for example, its private fleet. Others are

Exhibit 17.1 Types of Logistics/Transportation Links

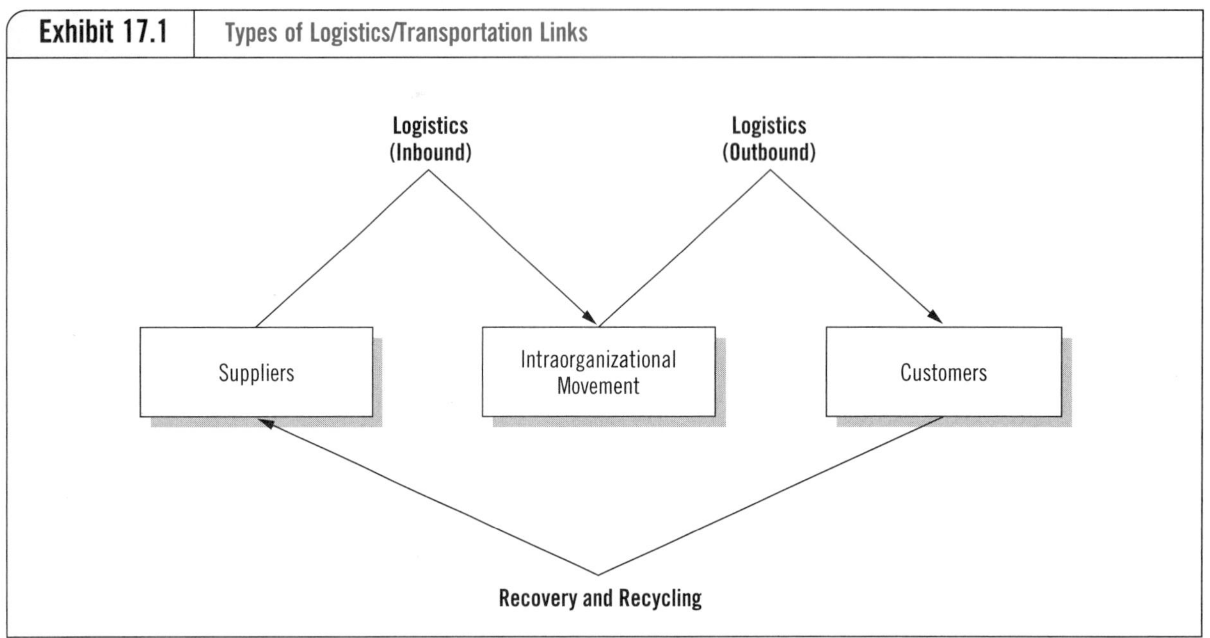

increasingly bypassing this link by producing material only when they have a customer order, which allows direct shipment to the customer and thus reduces the need for multiple handling through costly warehouse and distribution facilities.

The third link—outbound logistics—represents the link between a company and its customers. Historically, this was referred to as physical distribution, where the transportation department controlled the movement of outbound goods while suppliers arranged the movement of inbound freight to the buyer. Since the deregulation of the transportation industry in the early 1980s, supply management's involvement with the control of all three transportation links has increased greatly. The fourth link is one that companies are increasingly becoming concerned with—recovery and recycling of obsolete products and goods. This reverse logistics flow requires companies to find innovative methods of recovering and recycling products to minimize the impact on the environment. This may also include the shipment of repairable items back to maintenance facilities for refurbishment and return to usable condition.

As organizations focus more on their core competencies, they come to recognize that many of these transportation and logistics services can and should be outsourced to companies specializing in transportation and logistics services. When these services are outsourced to third parties, supply management assumes the responsibility of managing these relationships. Without effective and efficient sourcing and management of transportation services, world-class supply chain management can never be readily achieved. In order to describe these processes, we begin by briefly discussing the deregulation of the transportation industry in the United States, followed by supply management's role in sourcing transportation services, and an effective decision-making framework for developing transportation strategy. We will then focus specifically on how to manage third-party logistics providers.

Deregulation of Transportation and Supply Management's New Role

Transportation Deregulation

Legislation passed in the United States during the late 1970s and early 1980s, designed to open up economic competition in transportation, also encouraged supply management's involvement in the procurement and management of transportation services. Congress passed the Air Cargo Deregulation Act in 1977, the Air Passenger Deregulation Act in 1978, and the Negotiated Rates Act in 1993. Shortly after, the Motor Carrier Act of 1980 and the Staggers Rail Act became law. Other major deregulation legislation in the United States includes the Transportation Industry Regulation Reform Act of 1994, the ICC Termination Act of 1995 (creating the Surface Transportation Board), and the Ocean Shipping Reform Act of 1998, which reduced the Federal Maritime Commission's authority.[4]

The primary objective of deregulation in the United States was to make its domestic transportation system more efficient by increasing marketplace competition in the transportation industry and reducing burdensome economic regulation. From the buyer's perspective, these laws offered new opportunities to negotiate lower transportation rates and higher service levels with individual carriers. From the carrier's perspective, these laws took away a comfortable blanket of government protection and significantly reduced profit margins on almost all national contracts. Many carriers had to learn how to compete in a deregulated market and become more cost efficient in the process. Many long-standing carriers in all modes that were not able to do so went out of business or merged with other carriers in order to survive in a new, open, competitive economy.

These carriers now had to compete openly and aggressively against new entrants, existing carriers, and competition from other modes of transportation. They also had to contend with requests for substantial discounts from their published tariff rates, although filing published tariff rates with the federal government is no longer required. These legislative changes vastly reshaped the domestic transportation industry. Both supply and transportation managers discovered they now had the power to influence both transportation cost and corresponding service levels. Buyers became increasingly involved in the buying of transportation services, something that did not frequently occur when transportation was highly regulated economically.

If Congress had not deregulated the transportation industry, it is likely that supply management would not have taken as great an interest in the evaluation, selection, and control of transportation service providers. Although each piece of legislation created some level of uncertainty for both shippers and carriers, the legislation also created opportunities for innovative buyers to add new value through the procurement of transportation services.

Effectively managing transportation services is important for several reasons. First, transportation is a major cost center at most manufacturing companies. On average, transportation costs comprise 10% of a product's total cost. For many firms, logistics expenses are second only to material costs in terms of their impact on the cost of goods sold, and logistics expenditures represent one of the largest costs in international commerce.

Perhaps even more important than cost savings is the direct impact transportation has on operations. Transportation affects production and scheduling systems, inventory levels, carrying costs, and customer order management. Companies that do not effectively manage transportation activities will experience increased waste, higher costs, and reduced competitiveness. Although often taken for granted, transportation can have serious consequences if not managed properly. When managed properly, world-class transportation systems can satisfy end-customer needs faster and at a lower cost.

A New Role for Supply Management

As supply management professionals take a more active role in transportation procurement, what exactly are the duties they assume? Supply management can support the purchase of inbound, outbound, and ancillary transportation services just as it supports the purchase of other products, materials, and services. As supply managers take an active role in transportation decision making, they often become involved with identifying and selecting inbound transportation carriers and service providers, although greater involvement with outbound transportation providers is becoming more common in best-in-class firms.

Supply management can also negotiate long-term freight agreements and evaluate carrier performance similarly to evaluating suppliers of purchased goods. The transportation department, if one still exists, usually involves itself with day-to-day management of the overall transportation system or the development of transportation strategies that need not involve supply management. These non-procurement-related activities may include arranging pickups and deliveries, processing damage and loss claims, tracing and expediting shipments as required, coordinating interplant and outbound movements, auditing freight bills for accuracy, and determining plant and warehouse locations.

Both the supply management and transportation departments need to combine their individual expertise when developing transportation strategies. Transportation-related decisions should not be made in a vacuum.

A Decision-Making Framework for Developing a Transportation Strategy

The development of an effective transportation strategy typically involves a series of decisions. Exhibit 17.2 outlines a general framework of normal decisions and issues that a supply manager faces when helping formulate the organization's transportation strategy. How a transportation network is designed and organized may vary greatly depending on the commodity or material. For example, transporting bulk raw material usually requires rail or barge movement, whereas small, costly, time-sensitive components may use faster but more expensive modes such as airfreight. No single approach or strategy covers the entire transportation needs of a company.

Determine When and Where to Control Transportation

The initial decision regarding transportation requirements involves determining how, when, and where to control shipments. A significant amount of inbound domestic materials, for example, is still shipped FOB destination. This means the supplier retains title to the goods and controls the shipment until it is physically received and off-loaded at the consignee's dock. Unless otherwise negotiated, this also means the supplier is responsible for paying the carrier's freight bill and filing any loss and damage claims against the carrier. In this case, these costs are included in the invoiced unit price to the buying company. Controlling inbound shipment costs usually re-

Exhibit 17.2 Transportation Strategy Development—A Decision-Making Process

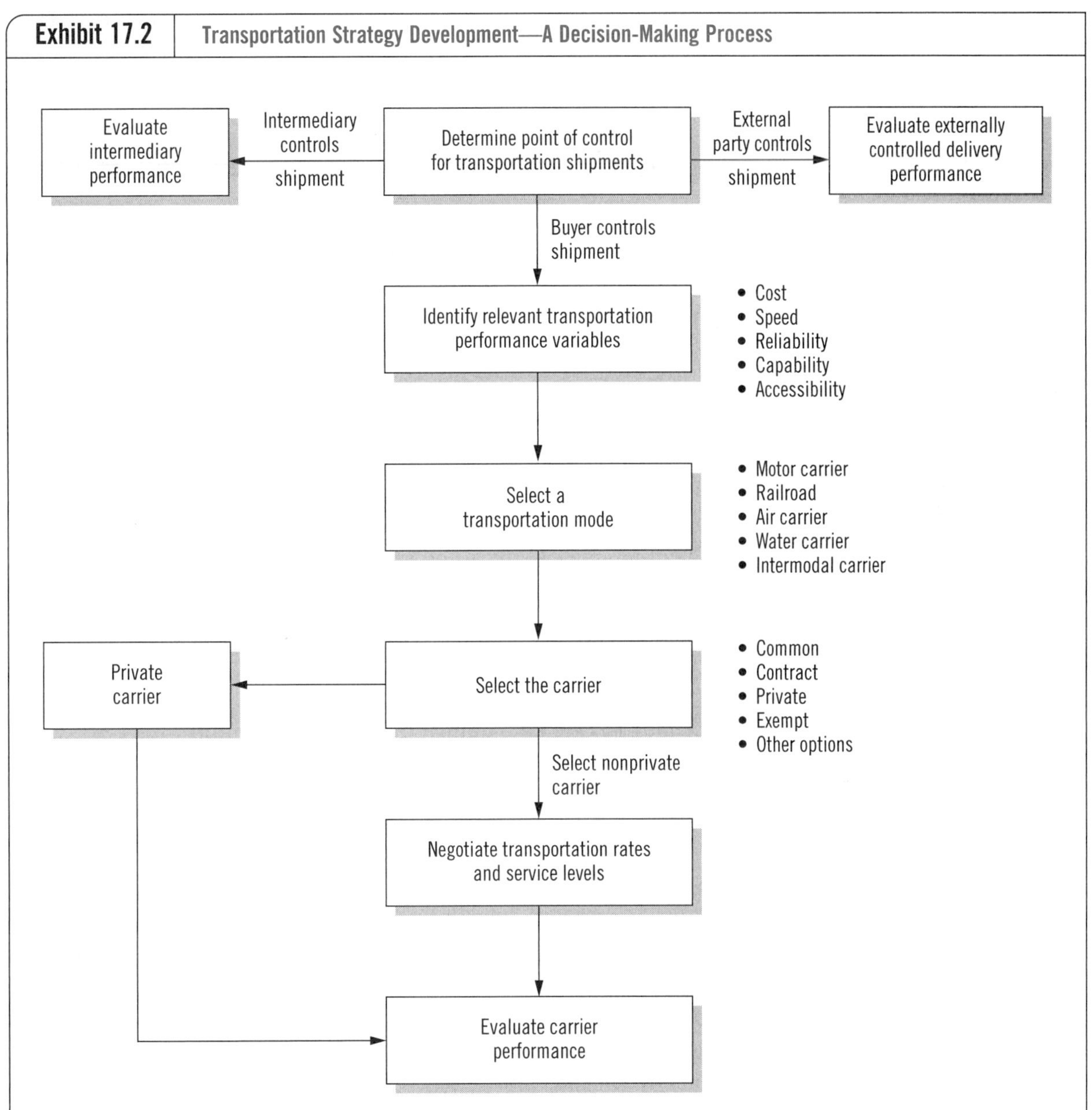

quires purchasing goods under a shipping designation of FOB origin. Here, the buyer or consignee is responsible for selecting the carrier, arranging the movement, paying the freight bill, and filing loss and damage claims. The title of the goods passes when the goods are tendered to the carrier at the loading site. A savvy buyer will want to control these costs internally instead of simply allowing the shipper to pass them along in the form of a delivered price. FOB origin is more complicated than buying goods with a delivered price, but the buyer can more effectively monitor its freight costs and delivery performance.

Whenever a supplier includes transportation charges as part of the unit cost of a good (i.e., FOB destination), the buyer often loses the ability to track or control its

Exhibit 17.3 Defining Domestic Transportation Shipping Terms

CARRIER

SHIPPER'S FACILITY FOB SHIPPING POINT	BUYER'S FACILITY FOB DESTINATION

What does FOB shipping point mean?
• Buyer controls or directs shipment
• Buyer assumes title to goods and risk of loss at seller's shipping point, unless agreed to otherwise (UCC Section 2-401)
• Seller has certain responsibilities (UCC Section 2-504):
  • To put the goods in the possession of the carrier
  • To make a proper contract for the transportation of the goods, taking into consideration the nature of the goods and other circumstances
  • To obtain and promptly deliver to the buyer any documents necessary for the buyer to take possession of the goods
  • To promptly notify the buyer of the shipment
	What does FOB destination mean?
	• Seller is required at own risk and expense to transport goods to that place and there tender delivery (UCC Section 2-319)
	• Seller assumes title to goods and risk of loss until satisfactory delivery to buyer's facility, unless agreed to otherwise (UCC Section 2-401)

inbound transportation expenses. This also artificially increases the value of the buyer's inventory, which may have tax and other financial implications. Even when a supplier assumes responsibility for transportation costs, buyers may require the supplier to identify and list transportation-related costs separately from material costs on the invoice.

Exhibit 17.3 compares these two primary FOB shipping designations as well as the Uniform Commercial Code (UCC) sections that apply to domestic transportation shipments.

The choice of insourcing or outsourcing transportation services is similar to a typical make-or-buy decision. A buyer who chooses to have an external party, such as a supplier or a third-party logistics provider, arrange and control its shipments has abdicated the ability to make further decisions regarding the movement. For some shipments, such as low-volume shipments, a buyer may determine it is not worth spending the time and energy necessary to arrange and manage their own transportation needs. When this is the case, an option is to provide suppliers with a list of preapproved or otherwise acceptable carriers or 3PLs. The buyer may even have a contract in place with the carrier for discounted freight rates based on combined volume. A buyer who relinquishes control of inbound transportation to a supplier or 3PL should still periodically evaluate the delivery performance of externally arranged shipments.

Another option here involves the use of a third-party transportation broker or intermediary, such as a forwarder. Although this also means giving up direct control of shipments, a buyer may realize additional benefits. The preferred broker or intermediary must have the buyer's best interests in mind, as the buyer is the intermediary's immediate customer. The broker or intermediary acts as the buyer's agent when arranging transportation. The intermediary can also consolidate the buyer's shipments with those of other customers to achieve a lower total transportation cost. Intermediaries can also perform other value-added services, such as expediting customs, negotiating rates directly with carriers, providing temporary storage, or performing light assembly. This option is popular for small- to mid-sized organizations lacking the resources or experience to manage their own transportation systems. It is also an appropriate option for small or infrequent shipments.

Identify Key Transportation Performance Variables

Different carrier or 3PL performance variables must be carefully determined and evaluated when developing an effective transportation strategy. Data on the following set of variables should be collected and evaluated when comparing competing transportation modes as well as specific carriers within the same mode. The criteria used to measure transportation performance are shown in Exhibit 17.4.

Total Cost

Total cost plays a major role in the transportation decision-making framework. If cost were unimportant, more shipments would arrive via air carrier instead of by truck or rail. Cost, however, is only one of a number of important variables. Selecting a mode or carrier based solely on the lowest freight cost ignores the total cost and customer service implications of the decision. The lowest-cost mode or carrier may not provide reliable delivery or other value-added services that separate marginal from exceptional service providers. The cost variable, although important, should not be the sole variable used. Furthermore, any cost evaluation should always be in a total cost context, not merely using the price shown on the freight bill. An apparently low-cost carrier may actually end up costing far more than a seemingly higher-cost carrier when the total associated costs are calculated. Note, however, that the typical cost accounting system may not fully delineate where all of the costs are derived. Costs may also change over time (see Sourcing Snapshot: Trucking Costs Rise under New Federal Hours of Service Rules).

Speed

This variable refers to the in-transit time of a mode or carrier. For some items, such as bulk raw materials, speed may not be an important factor. For producers operating in a time-sensitive or just-in-time environment, speed is the critical factor for

Exhibit 17.4 Criteria Used to Measure Transportation Performance

PERFORMANCE MEASURE	DESCRIPTION
Total Cost	In addition to the fee charges, total cost includes the cost of extra inventory, warehousing, buffer stock, and in the case of international shipments, broker fees, customs, etc. Other cost factors such as extra managerial time may also have to be factored in.
Speed	Measured as time from when the shipment is released at the supplier's facility to the time of receipt at the buyer's receiving dock.
Reliability	Sometimes described as *fill rate.* Refers to the ability to deliver on time. Can be measured in different ways, but is typically a window of time when the delivery must be made. The measure is thus the percentage of deliveries made within the specified window.
Capability	Refers to the ability of the carrier to move the material, including special materials, hazardous materials, etc.
Accessibility	Refers to whether the carrier is capable of picking up the shipment and delivering it door to door.

Sourcing Snapshot

Trucking Costs Rise under New Federal Hours of Service Rules

The first major changes in truck driver work hours since 1939 are designed to reduce highway fatalities but will also contribute to the biggest non-fuel-related increase in trucking rates in two decades. These hours of service (HOS) changes, mandated under new sets of federal safety rules that took effect in January 2004 and October 2005, are designed to reduce fatigue among truck drivers, a major cause of motor carrier accidents. The Federal Motor Carrier Safety Administration estimates that between 196 and 585 fatalities occur annually due to driver fatigue. The new HOS rules increase the time that truck drivers must rest in each 24-hour period to 10 hours, up from 8. Thus, the total time a driver can be on duty will fall to 14 hours from 16 hours per day, including a maximum of 11 hours of driving time. Drivers will also be required to include, as work hours, that time spent waiting at loading docks or fueling their rigs.

Wal-Mart, which unsuccessfully opposed the new rules, believes that the more stringent 14-hour rule will reduce its drivers' daily work time by 6% on average and require it to add 275 new drivers and 300 new trucks just to handle the same amount of cargo volume. The giant retailer expects the changes to cost it at least $24 million just for the additional trucks. "The rule will impose serious costs on society, not only on motor carriers but on shippers and receivers as well," the company said in a regulatory filing. Because motor carriers haul so much commerce, accounting for more than 81% of the U.S.'s $571 billion freight-transportation bill last year, the effects could be far-reaching, particularly when coupled with higher fuel costs and a smaller pool of qualified truck drivers.

Some users of truck transportation say higher motor carrier freight rates could lead to a broad-based increase in prices of all goods, from paper to chemicals, diapers to trash cans. During the last few years, the increasing number of failed trucking companies has led to a tight supply of transport capacity, as freight volumes have begun heading higher as the economy improves. The United States has about 585,000 interstate motor carriers, the bulk of which operate 20 or fewer trucks. Truckers and their customers are exploring ways to dodge the higher costs, such as by combining more intermodal shipments with rail carriers. Other initiatives, such as improved handling of trucks and cargo at warehouses and distribution centers, could make truckers more efficient and perhaps offset some of the costs of the new HOS rules. Indeed, freight docks have become a source of massive inefficiency, often holding up trucks and drivers for hours on end. Under these new rules, such delays are very costly because they count as work time for drivers and thus cut into the time they can be on the road.

Source: D. Machalaba, "Costs of Trucking Seen Rising under New Safety Rules," *Wall Street Journal,* November 12, 2003, p. A1; and "New Hours of Service Rules," http://www.thetruckersreport.com/hours/new_hours_of_service_rules_for_truckers.shtml, accessed December 3, 2007.

either inbound shipments from suppliers or outbound shipments to customers. Companies that ship products directly to customers after receiving an order are more likely to be focused on speed as a key performance variable.

Critical items that must arrive as soon as possible from a supplier or reach a customer quickly will require a different mode of transportation from routine items. For example, high-value items, such as pharmaceuticals and semiconductor chips, will often be shipped via high-speed priority carriers. Their value to the buyer is such that tying them up in transit is not economically wise. Certain items will always arrive by the same type of transportation mode simply because of their physical nature. When this is the case, a lack of transportation flexibility concerning the speed variable is something that must be managed by a buyer.

Reliability

A critical performance variable for any mode or carrier is reliability, which refers to the accuracy and on-time consistency of the transportation service, arriving neither late nor early. It also relates to a carrier's ability to deliver a shipment in an undamaged condition.

For example, if a carrier says a shipment will arrive at 9:00 a.m. on Monday morning, the consignee should expect that the shipment will actually arrive at the promised date and time. Note that reliability differs from speed—it is the measure of actual arrivals against planned arrivals. A reliable carrier requiring a longer in-transit time is oftentimes preferable to an unreliable carrier with a faster average in-transit time, particularly from an operational planning perspective. The buyer requires less inventory and safety stock to cover delivery variability from the more reliable carrier.

Capability

This variable refers to a mode or carrier's ability to provide the proper equipment and provide the appropriate services for a given product movement. This variable has several dimensions. First, does the mode or carrier have the physical capability to transport an item? For example, can the carrier safely transport a hazardous material or handle and transport large quantities of bulk products? Second, does the carrier have the proper equipment in the right location to perform the requested movement? Lastly, does the carrier have the equipment and resources to transport multiple, frequent shipments for a specific traffic lane? Capability is important because it affects a mode or carrier's ability to provide consistent transportation service or provide a requested service.

Accessibility

Transportation accessibility refers to a mode or carrier's ability to provide service over a geographic area. A totally accessible mode or carrier is capable of picking up a shipment and delivering it directly to its final destination. Geographic constraints, however, restrict some modes. Inland water carriers, for example, are usually not accessible for most shippers, as lakes, rivers, and canals cannot be moved. Use of this mode often requires another mode for pickup and delivery to and from the waterway. Note that a carrier that cannot offer total accessibility for its customers is not necessarily all bad. However, each time a shipment changes hands, additional handling occurs, and a longer lead time must be accounted for. Also, the risk of greater loss and damage increases.

A carrier may not have the appropriate authority or travel the physical routes necessary to transport goods between two points or to operate in a specific geographic region. Carriers lacking legal authority to move goods directly between two points are considered not highly accessible. Motor carriers sometimes market their services on the basis of their authority to operate in 48 states. Instead of using different carriers for different shipments around the country, one full-service carrier may be capable of meeting an organization's total transportation requirements.

Select a Transportation Mode

There must be a close match between those key transportation performance variables identified in the previous section and the ability of the different modes or carriers to satisfy these variables. For some items, it is not a difficult decision to make. For example, overseas shipments are usually shipped in containers via ocean vessel or, in a limited number of cases, by air carrier. Bulk or liquid commodities, such as coal or chemicals, usually ship via rail. The most common domestic modal decisions involve comparisons and tradeoffs between rail and motor carrier, rail and inland water, or motor and air carrier. The most common modal decision for international shipments is between oceangoing vessels and aircraft.

There are five principal modes of transportation available to users of transportation services: (1) motor carrier, (2) rail, (3) air, (4) water, and (5) pipeline. A summary of the major advantages and disadvantages of each is shown in Exhibit 17.5.

Exhibit 17.5 Advantages and Disadvantages of Transportation Modes

TRANSPORTATION MODE	ADVANTAGES	DISADVANTAGES
Motor Carrier	• High flexibility • Good speed • Good reliability • Good for JIT delivery • Can negotiate rates	• High cost • Limited to domestic or regional transportation • Cannot be used for large volumes
Rail Carrier	• Lower cost • Can handle wide range of items • Piggyback service can increase flexibility • Direct between major cities • Greater intermodal service • Safe for hazardous materials	• Limited access to rail line or spur • Longer in-transit lead times • Less flexible—may not have rails to all locations
Air Carrier	• Quick and reliable • Good for light/small, high-value shipments (e.g., electronics) • Good for expediting/emergency situations	• Very high cost • Location of large airports limits shipping points • Cannot be used for large, bulky, or hazardous shipments
Water Carrier	• Good for bulk commodities (inland) and heavy, large items (international) • Can handle most types of freight • Low cost	• Limited flexibility • Seasonal availability • Very long lead times • Poor reliability (may encounter delays at ports, etc.)
Pipeline	• Good for high-volume liquids and gases • Low cost once installed	• High up-front installation costs • Limited to only certain items

Motor Carriers

The greatest competition between domestic transportation modes involves rail and motor carriers. The availability of modern trucking equipment, the advent of the U.S. interstate highway system after World War II, and the inherent flexibility of motor carriage has resulted in the rapid growth of motor transportation, much at the expense of rail carriers.

It should come as no surprise that over-the-road motor carriers are a popular transportation option. They uniquely provide direct door-to-door service, making it a highly flexible mode of transportation. In addition, motor carriers are ideal for carrying smaller-volume, or less-than-truckload (LTL), shipments, involving multiple shippers and multiple consignees. A well-established motor network exists for the movement of LTL shipments throughout the United States, using a hub-and-spoke arrangement, whereas it is far more difficult for a rail carrier to accommodate less-than-carload shipments. Motor carriers also have an advantage of speed and reliability over the other modes, particularly for full truckload shipments.

The most significant disadvantage of a motor carrier is its relatively higher cost. On average, motor carrier transportation is more expensive than rail on a volume basis and far more expensive than inland water. Also, motor carriers have limited ability to transport bulk commodities as compared to rail, inland water, and pipelines. There are minimal economies of scale in motor carrier; you cannot simply add additional cargo-carrying capacity, because of weight, width, and length constraints.

Motor carriers are characterized by higher variable costs (approximately 70–90% of total cost) due to labor, fuel, maintenance, tolls, operating fees, and other costs resulting from compliance with rules and regulations.[5] A limit to the amount of weight a motor carrier can transport at one time also makes variable costs higher. These limits are often reduced as a result of seasonal weather conditions and the condition of the infrastructure. Furthermore, each trailer, or tandem of trailers, requires a separate power unit (tractor) and operator. A motor carrier does not have the volume flexibility of a rail carrier.

Rail Carriers

A major advantage of a rail carrier is the wide range of items it is capable of hauling. Although most rail freight today consists of bulk commodities, such as coal, ethanol, and agricultural products, a railcar can handle virtually any type of shipment, including manufactured goods. Another advantage of rail, and perhaps its primary one, is its relatively low cost. The ability to move huge amounts of freight over long distances at a per-pound cost that is lower than other transportation modes is the main reason that rail still commands a large share of all intercity ton-mile shipments.

The costs associated with owning and operating equipment, switch yards, and rail line rights-of-way means that rail carriers have comparatively high fixed costs. However, their low variable cost structure allows rail carriers to move freight at a relatively low rate per mile. Additional freight cars can be added to a freight train with only a minimal increase in its total variable cost.

Firms that rely on rail shipments must have access to a rail line or spur unless they are willing to use motor carriers to perform pickup and delivery functions. This constraint limits the use of rail in many instances and highlights perhaps the major disadvantage of rail carriers—limited accessibility. Rail carriers have attempted to overcome this inherent limitation through intermodal shipments involving shipping truck trailers or containers directly on flat cars, which is also referred to as piggyback service, a form of intermodalism.

Another disadvantage of rail carriers, and one that motor carriers have successfully exploited, is long in-transit and handling times. A two-day shipment by truck can often take a week or more by rail. Few trains move as a single unit over long distances. Rail carriers ship loaded cars between cities by attaching them to an outbound train moving in the general direction of the consignee's facility. As such, a cross-country journey may require several switches of a customer's railcar at various switching yards. Each switch increases total shipping and handling time. At the destination city, a local train moving only a few cars at a time makes the final delivery to the consignee.

In recent years, the rail industry has engaged in significant consolidation and merger activity, a process that has eliminated thousands of miles of track from the rail system. In addition, less competitive rail companies have merged together to share infrastructure and improve their operations and financial condition. There has also been an increase in the number of smaller railroads that serve only limited regions and lanes.

Rail carriers will always be the mode of choice for certain commodities. Rail movement is particularly economical for the shipment of agricultural products, output from extractive industries (e.g., coal or chemicals), or products from heavy manufacturing industries, such as steel, agricultural equipment, and automobiles.

Air Carriers

Air carriers haul the least amount of commercial freight because of the high cost of air travel and the limited amount and type of freight a plane can carry. Historically, a major reason for using air freight has been to satisfy emergency requirements. For example, a mining machine breakdown overseas may require a replacement part as soon as possible to get the equipment back into productive use. The buyer is less concerned with the high cost of air freight when an expensive machine is sitting idle because of a broken or defective part. In this case, an air carrier may be the only option capable of meeting the performance variable of speed. Plus, the shape of the aircraft's fuselage limits the size and weight of the containers used.

More firms are evaluating air transportation in relation to their just-in-time inventory and manufacturing systems. Shipping a high-priced component via air may actually be a cost-effective option, particularly if the material does not require much space, because of high inventory carrying costs. Some companies actually ship live lobsters or fresh-cut flowers via air to maintain their freshness. A significant amount of competition for most traffic lanes exists among air carriers today, which supports lower rates and increased service levels.

Higher cost per pound is the primary disadvantage to the increased use of air transportation. Air has a high variable-cost-to-fixed-cost ratio due to the high costs of operating a flight, such as fuel and labor. Because of the need to cover variable costs, airfreight rates are much higher than other modes. Air carriers also suffer from limited capacity and flexibility. The dimensions of the plane itself limit the size and weight of a shipment. In addition, if the airline has to make a decision on whether to carry freight or take on another passenger, the freight will usually be off-loaded for a later flight. Furthermore, the location of larger airports limits the shipping points available to an air carrier, unless a pickup-and-delivery network with motor carriers is utilized. Once an air shipment arrives, a motor carrier almost always makes the final delivery to the consignee.

Water Carrier

This transportation mode includes both inland water (river, canal, and lake) and oceangoing vessels. Inland water carriers typically transport low-value, large-quantity items such as bulk commodities and raw materials (e.g., ores, chemicals, sand, rocks, cement, and agricultural products). For example, it is common to see freighters moving raw materials, such as coke and iron ore required for steel production, from Minnesota to steel mills in northwestern Indiana. This material moves via the Great Lakes inland waterway system. However, this mode is closed down during the winter, requiring large inventories to cover the season or the use of alternative modes.

Inland water carriers rarely transport finished or semifinished products because of the lengthy in-transit time. The main advantage of water transportation is the large volume an inland barge or ship can move at one time, as well as the relatively low cost per pound. The primary disadvantages include limited flexibility of shipping and receiving points, seasonal shipment in some areas of the country, slow speed, and the potential for natural disasters such as oil spills, which can have devastating effects on the natural environment.

Growth in international trade has increased the amount of freight moving on oceangoing vessels. If a buyer purchases from an international supplier, the modal decision is usually straightforward. Most global shipments move across the ocean on

Sourcing Snapshot — *Maritime Supply Chain Security*

Several government and industry initiatives have been introduced to improve the security of the supply chain segment that deals with shipping containers that travel across the waterways of the world. Many of the world's 2,700 container ships travel through the ports of America each day, unloading more than 17,000 shipping containers. These containers carry more than 80% of all U.S. imports.

These shipping containers and ports must be protected to ensure the nation's security. A security attack on a U.S. port would cost the economy several orders of magnitude (in billions of dollars) more than the cost to prevent such an attack. Due to the sheer size and scope of maritime shipping, any attack on the maritime supply chain would effectively suspend international trade, while stopping or slowing shipping interests around the world.

One of the most significant security programs is the Container Security Initiative (CSI). The CSI is a U.S. Customs and Border Protection initiative that encourages foreign governments to inspect and screen container shipments before leaving port to detect possible security problems. This program sets up the exchange of customs officers between countries so that outbound shipments will be inspected by that country's customs officers. The CSI focuses on 20 ports around the world where most imported products originate. The aim is to reduce the risk of security problems on vessels and prevent an explosion or other incident in a port before the vessel can be unloaded. Once a vessel departs the originating port, security initiatives must be in place to prevent tampering with containers while in transit.

In addition, an Automated Targeting System (ATS) is being put in place, whereby U.S. Customs requires shippers to send a detailed description of cargo being loaded on a vessel destined for the United States at least 24 hours in advance of loading. Vessels will not be allowed into U.S. ports without this advance notice. U.S. Customs and Border Protection uses the ATS as an advanced screening tool to determine which potentially suspicious shipments need to be inspected upon arrival.

Finally, to increase security and improve the supply chain, the U.S. government is also encouraging companies to streamline their documentation and materials handling processes through the Customs-Trade Partnership Against Terrorism (C-TPAT) program. The C-TPAT is a program for manufacturers, suppliers, importers, and carriers to analyze their own supply chain security processes. It encourages them to improve supply chain security plans, communicate security plans with their trading partners and suppliers, and monitor and improve security measures on a routine basis. Once these companies are C-TPAT-certified by the U.S. government, their products will be able to proceed through ports and border crossings more quickly. They will also develop a closer working relationship with U.S. Customs and Border Protection and other C-TPAT-certified companies. The U.S. C-TPAT program enables companies to avoid increased transportation costs associated with border delays; reduce inventory needs by having a secure, reliable supply chain; and improve supply chain relationships and communication between suppliers and customers. More than 500 companies have joined the C-TPAT program to improve their supply chain security processes.

Source: R. G. Edmonson, "Beyond Calculation," *Journal of Commerce,* August 25, 2003, pp. 18–22; H. L. Lee and M. Wolfe, "Supply Chain Security without Tears," *Supply Chain Management Review,* January/February 2003, pp. 23–35; M. McGuire, H. Cousineau, and M. Stephanou (2002), "The New Era of International Supply Chain Security," *World Trade,* November 2002; and *Securing the Global Supply Chain,* Washington, D.C.: U.S. Customs and Border Protection, 2004.

deepwater containerships or tankers, and to a lesser extent via air carrier. Ocean carriers are capable of handling virtually any type of freight or raw material. Although mode selection is usually not an issue for international ocean shipments, as in all strategic supplier selection decisions, carrier selection is still paramount. The possibility of encountering customs delays due to increased security inspection and documentation requirements at ocean ports is another looming disadvantage of ocean carriers (see Sourcing Snapshot: Maritime Supply Chain Security).

Pipeline

The use of a pipeline is usually not part of the decision tradeoff between transportation modes. Pipelines primarily transport petroleum products, natural gas, or coal in a slurry condition. Even if a buyer purchases these products, it is not likely the buyer will make the decision to use a pipeline for transportation. Because of the huge quantities involved, deciding on the use of pipeline is rarely something a buyer needs to consider. Individual buyers will buy railcar or truckload quantities of these products from a terminal, not directly from a pipeline. This discussion mentions pipeline only because it is a legitimate mode of transportation.

The total cost structure of pipelines is similar to rail carriers as the equipment, rights-of-way, and physical pipeline have a high fixed cost and a low variable operating cost. Labor and direct operating costs are relatively low for this mode. Although pipeline movement is low cost and reliable, it is extremely slow.

Intermodal Transportation

Oftentimes, a single mode of transportation may prove inadequate for a specific shipment. For example, a typical surface shipment of material from China may require a variety of modes and carriers in order to complete the movement. Once the material is produced in China, it will need to be loaded into a container, which is then transported by either motor carrier or railroad to the port of departure. From there, it will be loaded onto a deepwater containership. Once the containership docks at the U.S. port of arrival, it will be loaded onto another motor carrier's or railroad's equipment to be moved to its final destination. Note that each element in this complex move may be performed by a different carrier.

If the shipper or consignee were to deal individually with each mode and carrier, the administrative cost and effort would be prohibitive and inefficient. To resolve this complexity and provide better service, many global carriers now offer one-stop shopping, where the shipper or consignee contracts with one carrier, which then coordinates and manages the entire intermodal shipment, regardless of carrier or mode, and also provides a single point of contact and unified freight bill. The underlying idea of intermodal transportation is to utilize the inherent advantages of each mode while minimizing their respective disadvantages, resulting in a seamless movement to the customer.

Exhibit 17.6 presents the relative ranking of the different transportation modes against our five performance criteria. Examining the relative rankings from the chart, it is easy to see why the popularity of motor carrier has increased with transportation

Exhibit 17.6 Relative Ranking of Domestic Transportation Modes

	Lowest per-Unit Cost	Speed	Reliability	Capability	Accessibility
Air	5	1	4	3	3
Rail	3	3	3	1	2
Pipeline	1	4	1	5	5
Motor	4	2	2	2	1
Inland Water	2	5	5	4	4

1 = Highest rated compared to other modes
5 = Lowest rated compared to other modes

service buyers. In total, motor carriers hold a real advantage over other modes when taking a systems approach to these performance variables.

Select the Carrier

Once the buyer decides what transportation mode is best suited to move a given item, the next step involves evaluating and selecting the actual service provider. A supply manager has several options available besides simply contacting a for-hire company

Exhibit 17.7 Overview of Interstate Motor Carrier Industry

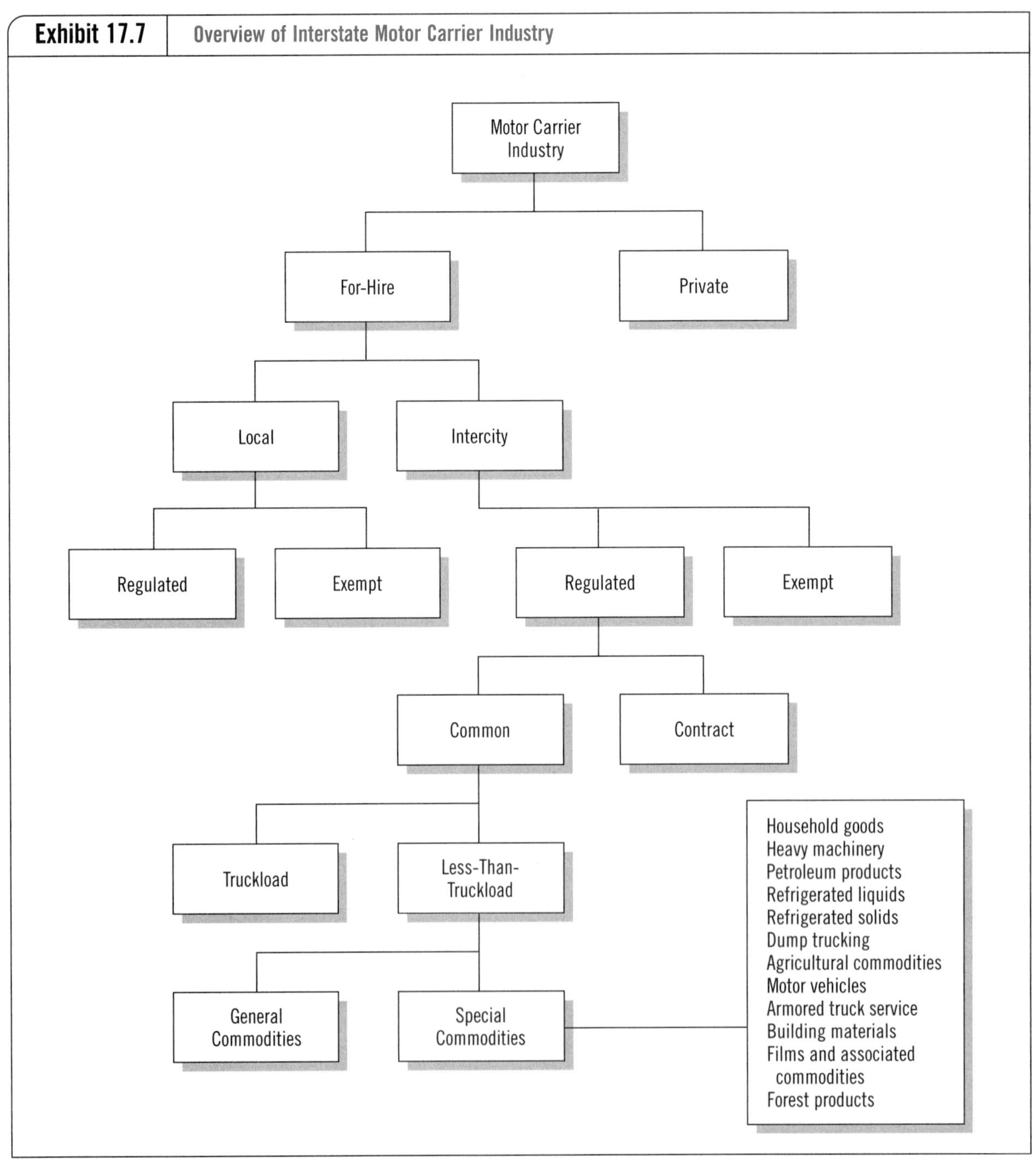

and arranging shipment. Shippers can select a common (or public) carrier, negotiate for services with a contract or exempt carrier, arrange shipments on company-owned vehicles (private carrier), or use a third-party logistics provider to select and manage the carrier. The most common decision is whether to use a common, contract, or exempt carrier (see Exhibit 17.7).

Common Carriers

By law, a common carrier must serve the general public without discrimination based on published rates for specific goods.[6] Part of a common carrier's operating authority comes from its obligation to serve transportation users in a fair and nondiscriminatory manner. Besides its duty not to discriminate against transportation users, a common carrier must offer reasonable rates, although rates are not published in the same manner as they were during the days of economic regulation. A buyer deciding to use a common carrier, particularly a motor carrier, often has a wide choice of carriers within a geographic region. Examples of common carriers include Yellow, J.B. Hunt, and Schneider National (recognized for its bright orange trucks).

Contract Carriers

Shippers that rely heavily on precise and frequent transportation might consider the use of a contract carrier. A contract carrier does not hold itself out to serve the general public, as does a common carrier. The contract carrier serves a shipper (i.e., a buyer) under specific, negotiated contract terms. A contract carrier, sometimes referred to as a dedicated carrier, serves the transportation requirements of the party with which it has a legal agreement and provides only those services that have been negotiated with the shipper.

Contract carriers can offer many benefits to the transportation buyer. Besides negotiating a favorable rate based on frequency and volume, a buyer can usually receive a higher level of service than might otherwise be expected because the carrier and shipper have a continuous contractual relationship.

Private Carriers

A private carrier is a manufacturer or distributor that controls and manages its own transportation equipment, whether owned or leased. Typically, a private carrier moves goods between suppliers, in-house facilities, or customers. Besides offering greater control of its freight, a private carrier can increase the utilization of company-owned assets. Some companies operate their own private fleets to maintain delivery reliability or to more effectively manage those costs that outside carriers incur, making them a better buyer of transportation services. Private carriers may also be utilized to make daily "milk runs," picking up smaller amounts of materials from close-by suppliers to be used in a just-in-time environment.

Perhaps the greatest drawback to using a private fleet for inbound shipments is a lack of dedication to this task. For example, it might be difficult to arrange shipments from a supplier's facility on a regular basis using company-controlled vehicles. Practical experience with a number of firms indicates the use of private carriers for inbound shipments is the exception rather than the rule. When firms use a private carrier for receiving purchased items, it is usually the result of a geographically convenient arrangement between a purchaser and supplier such as the milk runs described earlier. A company operating a private fleet must ensure that it balances the utilization of its equipment for both inbound and outbound shipments. Otherwise, empty miles reduce the cost-effectiveness of operating a private fleet.

Exempt Carriers

Exempt carriers are free of any economic regulation. They gain this status because of the type of commodities they haul and the nature of their operation. These carriers usually transport seasonal agricultural products, newspapers, livestock, or fish. Exempt carriers are primarily local water carriers of bulk items. The presence of exempt carriers ensures a supply of available transportation in markets where only one-way traffic exists (e.g., from an agricultural area during the harvest season). Goods move one way and not the other.

Negotiate Transportation Rates and Service Levels

A buyer with substantial transportation needs across its supply chain will likely negotiate directly with a single carrier or a small number of carriers for dedicated or contracted services. This does not mean that buyers must negotiate only with contract carriers. Negotiation can also occur with a common carrier, particularly regarding transportation rates and service requirements.

A major outcome from transportation economic deregulation has been the shift of pricing information garnered from published tariffs and rate bureaus to the negotiating table. A buyer can negotiate specific services and required service levels, while the carrier can indicate what freight volumes are necessary to support a particular service level or rate. This negotiation process can address a number of topics:[7]

- The carrier's service performance guarantees with penalties and rewards based on actual performance
- The shipper's commitment to ship a minimum amount of volume during the life of the contract
- How the parties handle freight loss and damage claims
- The type and quantity of equipment utilized by the carrier
- Frequency and timing of shipments
- Establishment of information-sharing systems
- Freight rates and discounts
- Creative and innovative joint cost reduction activities

A shipper does not necessarily negotiate a contract with every carrier it uses, particularly if it is considered a small or infrequent shipper. A smart buyer, however, can take advantage of the various opportunities offered in today's transportation environment by consolidating transportation volumes with fewer carriers to achieve shipping economies of scale.

Performance-Based Logistics[8]

Performance-based logistics (PBL) is an emerging collaborative business model that seeks to move away from the traditional transaction-based model toward meeting the mutual interests of both the buyer and logistics service provider. Under the traditional transaction-based model, logistics service providers are typically compensated for each and every transaction conducted, regardless of need. As such, there is little motivation for the logistics service provider to become more efficient, as any operational improvement negatively impacts its revenue stream. This business model generally results in the lowest cost for each transaction but does not promote an efficient, low-total-cost logistics system. Therefore, the underlying interests of the buyer and logistics service provider are at odds with each other. In addition, the onus for any cost and efficiency improvement is placed strictly on the buyer, who must then negotiate those improvements and revised pricing with the logistics service provider.

In comparison, a performance-based logistics system seeks to drive the logistics service provider's performance by clearly delineating the buyer's preferred outcomes, not by transaction, but in terms of provider value added and overall systems cost. In PBL, the logistics service provider is compensated by how well it enables the buyer to achieve these outcomes. Compensation is structured to reward the logistics service provider with longer-term contracts and performance incentives, leading to its increased profitability. In order for PBL to work, both the buyer and logistics service provider must explicitly agree as to what the buyer's desired outcomes, goals, and objectives are and on how the logistics service provider can help meet them.

Following the determination of and agreement to the buyer's goals and objectives, a key factor to consider here is the development of timely, accurate, and cost-effective metrics designed to measure key performance variables (i.e., who measures the logistics service provider's performance, how and where it is measured, and how often it is measured).

Use of PBL is not without its concerns. For example, performance measurement is often difficult to define, let alone accomplish. There can be disagreement regarding the buyer's perception of the logistics service provider's performance and the efficacy of the metrics used to determine its level of performance. Research conducted by the University of Tennessee indicates that total logistics system risk can actually be reduced for both buyer and logistics service provider through the collaboration made possible by PBL.

To date, the single largest proponent of PBL has been the U.S. Department of Defense (DoD), which uses PBL contracts to procure logistics support for its various major weapons systems. Based on its previous successes with PBL, the DoD began mandating its use in all of its major acquisition categories beginning in 2006. Performance-based logistics offers significant promise in the private sector but has not yet been widely adopted.

However, a comparable sourcing strategy, service-level agreements (SLAs), has been used in a number of spend categories, including travel and entertainment, software and technology, and back-office operations. Application of an SLA allows the buyer to specify target or minimum performance and service levels that the supplier is expected to provide. As with PBL, the key is to develop key performance indicators (KPIs) that outline specific performance criteria that a supplier is expected to meet.

An effective PBL system requires the logistics service provider to take a far more proactive role in interacting with the buyer to jointly manage the buyer's supply chain. Requirements for implementing a successful PBL project include the following:

- Commitment to mutual collaboration and alignment of interests
- Creation of a win-win environment for the buyer and logistics service provider, focused on the value added by the logistics service provider

- Development of a sound sourcing strategy, including close alignment of the buyer's goals and objectives with the logistics service provider's compensation and incentive structure
- Application of an effective checks and balances system utilizing timely and accurate data collection and multiple metrics, including a formal reporting and review process[9]

Outsourcing Logistics to Third-Party Logistics Providers

A buyer can initiate various actions to improve transportation service and delivery performance throughout the supply chain. One of the most common actions is to outsource logistics to a third-party logistics provider that is responsible for managing all inbound and outbound transportation, as well as providing other logistics and warehousing services. The use of 3PLs is increasingly becoming an option for smaller shippers and shipments. Third-party logistics providers can furnish convenient, low-cost, and reliable transportation and logistics services, whereas the shipper may not have sufficient volume for economies of scale or available expertise on staff. These service providers also offer linked information systems that provide readily accessible visibility to their services, providing a substantial competitive advantage. For this reason, many distributors and mail-order companies use FedEx and UPS as their primary transportation provider as well as for other logistics services.

Select Providers

Supply managers should be very careful in selecting 3PLs, which may pass themselves off as "integrated global logistics service providers," claiming to offer complete end-to-end supply chain services even when they are not capable of doing so. In a global marketplace, there are many different elements of transportation and logistics that can be managed by a 3PL, including the following:

- Customs brokers
- Freight brokers (both air and surface)
- Warehousing and distribution center operations
- Packaging and export documentation
- Delivery services
- Local sourcing and purchasing
- International trade management
- Global transportation optimization
- Supply chain planning
- Export packaging services

It is rare in practice to find a 3PL company that is capable of providing world-class services in all of these areas simultaneously. Therefore, supply management should be leery of companies that claim that they are world-class providers in all of these areas. To avoid selecting 3PL providers that cannot meet the shipper's requirements, savvy buyers should consider using the following approach:

1. **Plan**
   - Define specific logistics service requirements and how they will be measured and evaluated
   - Confirm the selection process
   - Involve key players to ensure internal buy-in
   - Remove barriers to success
2. **Select**
   - Target best-in-class logistics service providers
   - Select 3PL or contractor
   - Negotiate mutually beneficial agreement
3. **Implement**
   - Share supply chain information to deliver superior value
   - Build relationships
   - Work jointly to resolve start-up issues
4. **Improve**
   - Exchange performance measures to identify improvement opportunities
   - Encourage cross-organization training and project activities
5. **Partner**
   - Develop supply chain alliances to agree on tradeoffs and share risks
   - Involve 3PL partners in joint strategic planning and decision making

Some of the advantages and disadvantages of considering a third-party logistics provider are shown in Exhibit 17.8.

Exhibit 17.8 Third-Party Logistics

Advantages	Disadvantages
• Economies of scale and increased flexibility • Improve service performance levels • Release capital from sale of assets • Release running costs • Concentrate on core business activities	• Relinquish control, ownership, and expertise • Loss of integration between sales and supply • Changeover costs and operational problems • Loss of dedicated in-house managed staff • Sacrifice key business service differentiation

Merchandise	Cross Docking	VMI
Marshalling	Transport	Export Packaging
Postponement	FG Pull Expediting	Spares (Returns and Repairs)
Installation Prefit	Inventory Control	Reverse Flow

Shared Resources or Dedicated Resources?

When selecting qualified 3PLs, buyers should consider the following elements of performance and determine whether a given provider can effectively execute them.

Gain Access to Critical and Timely Data

Access to accurate and timely information represents power to a decision maker. It is difficult to manage material shipments without the ability to collect and analyze critical transportation-related data. Ideally, the following logistics information should be readily available and should be reported by the 3PL to the buyer. An inability to quickly and accurately provide this information in a useable format may indicate that the 3PL is not effectively managing the supply network.

- Number of carriers providing inbound, intraorganizational, and outbound transportation services
- Total transportation expenditures by specific carrier and mode of transportation
- Number of suppliers shipping material (i.e., the number of shipping points)
- Volume and transportation costs associated with shipments by supplier
- Breakdown of volumes by commodity or type of material
- Performance statistics and ratings for individual carriers
- Percentage of shipments arranged by suppliers versus buyers (e.g., FOB destination versus FOB origin)

Develop Systems Visibility to Material Shipments

Up-to-the-minute information concerning the status and location of shipments can provide at least partial visibility that is required for total material control. The need for control supports the development of electronic data and communications systems between carrier and buyer. Third-party logistics companies should be able to provide immediate access to information on shipment status, whether on motor carriers linked electronically with shippers through global positioning systems or on a ship, aircraft, or customs location.

Many 3PLs offer detailed shipment tracking systems to provide current status updates. Several levels of complexity exist in these systems. One-way information systems allow a buyer to gain information about the location of a shipment on a real-time basis. A buyer simply requests data directly from a carrier's information system, now often provided via the carrier's website.

However, many 3PLs now utilize event-based systems. These provide status alerts, via e-mail, fax, pager, and so on, to a buyer or salesperson that a particular shipment has been delayed and that this may affect other entities in the supply chain (e.g., manufacturing plants, warehouse locations, and customers). Even though problematic events cannot always be prevented, early warning signals, using an event-management system, can help sourcing companies deal with the problem in a more timely manner.

Develop Closer Relationships with Fewer Providers

A common theme throughout this book is that buyers and suppliers often benefit from closer, more collaborative relationships. This logic also applies to 3PL relationships. Transportation buyers are increasingly reducing the number of 3PLs they do business with on a companywide basis with the intention of working more collaboratively with the remaining ones. This allows a buyer to realize improved service and greater benefits that otherwise might not be available through a traditional, arm's-length business relationship. For example, a buyer may receive a guarantee that carrier equipment will be available when and where needed. Controlling and managing the movement of goods is easier and more efficient when a buyer selects only the best 3PLs available and develops a closer working relationship with them.

Establish Companywide Contracts

Real and substantial cost and service benefits are possible when transportation volumes between facilities, divisions, or business units are combined for increased purchasing leverage and put under the jurisdiction of a limited number of highly capable 3PLs and/or 4PLs. An example of such a relationship is discussed in Sourcing Snapshot: GM Develops Vector as Its Fourth-Party Logistics Provider.

Sourcing Snapshot

GM Develops Vector as Its Fourth-Party Logistics Provider

To deal with increased complexity in a build-to-order environment, GM sought a fourth-party logistics (4PL) partner within the logistics industry for the following reasons:

- Avoid/defer structural or fixed costs, and drive more costs to variable
- Gain access to specialized logistics resources
- Rapidly develop and deploy cutting-edge IT logistics solutions
- Provide a single point of organizational accountability responsible for managing logistics activities

A 4PL is a distinctive business model that extends outsourcing to new levels as it combines the best capabilities and technologies from logistics companies and other service organizations to deliver value through total supply chain management. Selecting a non-asset-based provider that is neutral with respect to selecting logistics shippers and materials management providers is a must.

GM's supply chains were integrated with logistics processes and IT management controlled by a 4PL, leveraging multiple service providers. Why was it important for GM to go with a 4PL? To reduce the cost of GM's huge logistics network, which includes raw materials providers (such as steel), customs brokers, third-party logistics providers, first- and second-tier component suppliers, freight forwarders, assembly operations, original equipment manufacturers, distribution centers, new vehicle dealers, parts and service dealers, and third-party logistics distributors of aftermarket parts. Looking at this hugely complex network, GM's logistics team realized that nobody can do it all and that GM wasn't capable of managing this network themselves either. To cope with this complexity, GM signed a contract with CNF to form a 4PL joint venture called Vector SCM. GM will be able to do the following:

- Retain strategic planning, benchmarking, and operational competency
- Have board representation and super-majority rights on critical issues
- Reduce logistics costs through a gain share agreement
- Avoid significant IT development costs
- Provide full accountability to GM Global Logistics for all aspects of logistics performance

Vector will do the following:

- Manage GM's current global network of logistics service providers
- Manage GM's global tactical and operational logistics activities
- Enable logistics capabilities (visibility, speed, flexibility, and reliability)
- Provide best-of-breed logistics technology
- Provide people, process, and technology to support GM global logistics operations
- Partner with leaders in the industry to build, buy, or leverage skills and technology

GM and Vector SCM have created common global solutions across logistics networks through the use of regional Logistics Control Centers. Vector assumed the responsibility of managing approximately one third of GM's logistics spend. The gradual transition of responsibility to Vector SCM is well under way, managed through a disciplined business case process, involving discovery of opportunities, business case development, implementation, and business case approval. This has required major changes in the way that GM works and allows it to focus on its core competency of designing and building value for the end customer in the form of new vehicles and services.

Source: Presentation by George Wilkinson, Vice President of Global Logistics, Supply Chain Resource Consortium meeting, North Carolina State University, Raleigh, December 2002.

One clear trend is that many carriers no longer market themselves simply as providers of physical transportation services. For complex freight movements—those movements involving multiple parties or additional handling—many carriers now perform those duties that previously required the use of in-house personnel or third parties. Full-service providers, in addition to picking up and delivering goods, may consolidate shipments, provide simplified billing, ship just-in-time from local storage points, handle complex overseas shipments, coordinate shipments with other carriers or modes, or configure final products for direct shipment to end customers. This allows a transportation buyer to focus on strategy development while the full-service carrier manages the mundane details of the transportation network.

There are many examples of using service providers for more than just transportation. UPS handles all the worldwide aftermarket spare parts business for Allison Engine. Burlington Air Express has reduced a computer company's order-cycle time by warehousing its inventory, configuring PCs with the correct software, and delivering directly to customers. Internet services provided by carriers are expanding as well. Most overnight package delivery companies provide full tracking of packages via software that allows users to arrange for, track, and complete entire shipping transactions over the Internet.

Purchasing Services and Indirect Items[10]

Over the past several years, supply management departments in high-performing, best-in-class companies have made great strides in reducing the price of direct material inputs. Because procurement of direct materials is often associated with distinct strategic business units (SBUs), managing this spend is usually accomplished through centralized commodity groups, with sourcing decisions and contract administration occurring at the SBU level. More companies, however, now realize that, until they can capture the benefits of including indirect spending under the umbrella of their company's overall sourcing strategy, a large percentage of this spend will not be managed effectively.

We can define **indirect spend** as any purchased good or service that does not end up in the product or service delivered to a customer. This component can be a significant percentage of a company's expenditures. Research on Fortune 500 companies found that services spending accounted for 11% of total revenue and 30% of total purchase spend. Indirect spending averaged 9% of revenue and 23% of total purchases. By comparison, direct spending (where the attention of supply management is most often focused) accounted for 18% of total revenue and 44% of total purchase spend. Another important indicator was that participants expected services spend to increase by 13% in the next five years, an indication that the Western world is outsourcing more and more activities to external service organizations. A breakout of the average percentage of total purchasing spending by category is provided in Exhibit 17.9.

With continued growth in outsourcing of non-core capabilities, the expansion of the services sector, and increasing cost pressure, the importance of effectively managing an organization's indirect spend is increasing. However, due to the decentralized nature and wide variety of goods and services in most indirect spend categories, the problem is more complex from a managerial and administrative standpoint. Issues often arise in segmenting or allocating indirect spend across or between different functional and budgetary areas. Another common problem is that indirect spend is often

Exhibit 17.9 Average Services Spend Activity

SERVICES SPEND CATEGORY	PERCENTAGE OF TOTAL PURCHASE SPEND (NORMALIZED)
Manufacturing	20.24
Inventory	7.93
Professional services	7.61
Construction/engineering	6.04
Information technology	5.24
Marketing	5.13
Logistics	4.94
Real estate	4.25
Advertising	3.00
Project-based services	2.81
Human resources	2.04
Telecommunications	2.00
Travel	1.79
Facilities management	1.86
Printing/copying	1.51
Legal	1.45
Administrative services	1.15
Temporary staffing	0.97
Research and development	0.78
Call center	0.76
Accounting services	0.40
Finance	0.29
Warehouse management	0.14
Other	8.49

Source: CAPS Research, 2003.

hidden in the price of direct materials (e.g., FOB destination). For example, if a supplier pays for shipping, the transportation cost (an indirect service) is buried in the cost of the direct material.

The CAPS Research Critical Issues Report referred to above found that companies have begun using two distinct methods to identify, manage, and reduce their indirect spend: internal and external methods. An overview of these results is provided as follows.

Internal Methods of Managing Indirect Spend

Data Collection and Consolidation

In many cases, several units within one organization will unknowingly purchase the same goods and services from different suppliers (or even the same supplier at different prices). For example, John Deere discovered that it was spending $1.4 million annually on work gloves. This total was represented by 425 separate part numbers purchased from 20 different suppliers. In some instances, a single supplier was supplying the same glove to different Deere manufacturing and distribution facilities at disparate prices. Research showed that consolidating and standardizing this indirect purchase alone with a few well-chosen suppliers would result in an annual savings of $500,000.[11] In this situation, Deere encountered higher costs by not leveraging its total volume enterprisewide.

If indirect spend is to be leveraged, supply management must have a clear understanding of exactly what indirect goods and services are being purchased by individual SBUs. As Deere's work glove example above shows, there are many indirect purchases in a typical organization that are not recognized as having volume leverage opportunity. Comprehensive data collection and focused analysis allow companies to maximize leverage in their indirect spend and also recognize comparable goods or services that might be standardized and aggregated.

For example, FedEx contracted with a firm specializing in electricity usage audits to collect billing information from each of its 2,000 facilities and review whether the correct tariff rates were used for each facility. These facilities varied in size from over 10,000 employees to as few as 2 and were located in every state. Based on this approach alone, eliminating overbilling errors from improperly applied utility rates yielded a savings of from 4 to 5% of its energy spend after all consulting fees have been paid. The most important component of this strategy was not the upfront cost savings as much as it was determining the overall pattern and volume of electricity consumption across this network of facilities. Once this pattern of consumption was identified and understood, FedEx could initiate a strategy for rationalizing its energy spend in accordance with varying deregulation patterns across the different states. In addition, FedEx was able to modify business processes at its stations and hubs to improve electricity usage efficiency.[12]

Restructuring to Establish Accountability

Establishing a capable supply management structure and setting up accountability for indirect purchases are closely connected with data collection, consolidation, and analysis. By gaining a clear understanding of who is spending what, where, and when, supply management can implement procedures and safeguards that deter and control maverick spend. **Maverick spend** can be defined as that amount of an organization's

Sourcing Snapshot — *FedEx Uses Elance to Purchase Services*

FedEx Corporation throws all its weight into negotiating prices with the 15 firms that provide it with temporary worker services, telephone customer service representatives, and computer programmers. So it was with some dismay that Edith Kelly Green, FedEx's chief sourcing officer, realized managers were doing end runs around its paper-logged purchasing department, striking independent deals with contractors, in many cases without the discounts that FedEx was supposed to incur. "It's one thing to select suppliers and another to make sure employees actually use them," says Kelly-Green.

To deal with this maverick spending problem, FedEx began using spend management software from Elance to automate the hiring, paying, and discharging of temporary employees. By keeping managers wedded to previously negotiated contracts and reducing paperwork, FedEx expects to save between 10 and 15% of its multibillion-dollar annual services budget. Although services typically account for more than half of a business's purchasing expenditures, fewer than 10% of large companies have installed software to track and manage what they spend on services. The big temporary-employee firms, like Manpower and Kelly Services, offer their own internally developed programs. Also competing with Elance is CascadeWorks, which has partnered with Ariba and White Amber. These firms claim to be able to trim between 2 and 35% off temporary-employee expenditures by tracking time cards, keeping tabs on laptops and other company property that temporary employees receive, and allowing supervisors to evaluate both contract laborers and their agencies.

Source: C. Schoenberger, "At Your Service," *Forbes*, March 3, 2003, p. 90.

total procurement budget that is purchased from unauthorized sources. Here is where the supply management organization's delegation of responsibility for cost saving occurs: A chain of command is established that matches appropriate procurement authority and ensures that the correct protocol is followed (see Sourcing Snapshot: FedEx Uses Elance to Purchase Services).

Automating the Requisition/Sourcing Process

Companies have improved their sourcing process by using electronic requisitioning and automating routing, approvals, and purchase order/release creation. Such automation also facilitates the receiving function by automatically checking receipts against both the supplier's invoice and the buyer's purchase order. Finally, once the supply or service has been delivered or provided and is considered complete, the automated process also authorizes the payment, oftentimes an electronic transfer of funds transaction, which saves both the buyer and supplier time and money. A Miller Brewing executive pointed out, "This allows procurement managers more time to focus on the strategic areas of buying rather than having to worry about the mundane tasks associated with the various buying procedures."

Standardization

Supporting an automated sourcing system with e-catalogs helps to promote item standardization and aggregation of indirect spend. By limiting internal requisitioners to previously approved catalogs of already contracted goods and services from preselected and approved suppliers, volume commitments to approved suppliers can be achieved and maverick spending reduced. Some companies have gone so far as to establish policies that require every indirect goods purchase made off-catalog to be submitted to an executive for review and approval. This visibility is essential in minimizing unauthorized purchases from nonapproved sources.

External Methods of Managing Indirect Spend

Reverse Auctions

The use of reverse auctions is increasing and can greatly impact the indirect buying process. This method of managing indirect spend is projected to increase 10 to 15% per year in the foreseeable future. Among the many reasons for this is that electronic reverse auctions allow buyers and suppliers to easily communicate in real time from anywhere in the world via the Internet. Buyers have indicated they are seeing an average price savings of 10 to 20%. However, many buyers are beginning to question the sustainability of such cost savings over time once the initial reductions are made.

Purchasing Consortia

Another growing trend for improving buyers' leverage is the use of purchasing consortia, which are created by buyers from various businesses to pool their buying power in order to reduce prices. Some companies, such as Raytheon, have been so successful at building and managing their purchasing consortia that they generate revenue by charging other businesses a service fee for using them. However, one of the challenges faced by purchasing consortia is getting the individual members to agree on exactly what is to be collectively purchased. Because of these coordination difficulties, purchasing consortia are often run by an independent third party, which takes all of the different specifications and develops a joint product list that it feels best matches the needs of all the participants.

Supply Management Outsourcing

Some companies have decided to outsource their indirect spend altogether. For example, Harley-Davidson wanted to better manage its indirect spend, but instead of managing this process internally, it decided to outsource all indirect purchases to three reliable suppliers. To do this, Harley-Davidson's supply management department conducted a lengthy search for those outstanding suppliers thought to be able to handle this responsibility. These three suppliers then became responsible for making sure that all indirect sourcing needs were met, either internally or by procuring externally from another supplier. This saved Harley-Davidson over $4 million in savings in its first year of implementation.

Enabling Tactics and Strategies

The previously mentioned CAPS report notes that several enablers are necessary to successfully implement an indirect spend procurement strategy. These are discussed below.

Zero-Based Budgeting

Tracking and capturing the indirect savings achieved by supply management is very difficult to achieve in most organizations, as responsibility for indirect spend is typically decentralized throughout the organization. In addition, traditional cost accounting systems are not designed to systematically track and consolidate indirect spend across an organization. This approach forces business units to start with and justify the same indirect budget they had in the previous planning cycle. Once this is prepared, supply management examines the spend categories and looks for cost-savings opportunities. If opportunities are found and result in lower-cost purchases, the business unit must write a check to the CFO for the amount of the savings.

Prebudget Savings

Another approach to capturing negotiated savings in the indirect spend is the use of forced budget reductions. Several companies stated that they forced 5 to 10% budget reductions on all indirect items. Business units then had the following option:

- Negotiating price reductions on current volumes
- Aggregating spend within or across business units to gain additional volume-based price concessions
- Decreasing demand for indirect items
- Using a combination of the above methods

Organizational Structure

The debate about centralized, decentralized, and hybrid supply management organizations was discussed earlier in Chapter 5. In many cases, however, it appears that a hybrid organization will allow different regions or business units the flexibility to make their own localized procurement decisions and be a good fit with the indirect sourcing needs of most large organizations.

Sourcing Snapshot — *Bayer Attacks Indirect Spend*

In addressing concerns over its indirect spend, Bayer initiated a program it called the "Money Room." This involved establishing money room centers in plants or administration units that act as control centers for the supply management department. Indirect spend is typically mapped out into 20 to 25 areas (in columns) and linked to days of the month (in rows). All requests for materials are sent daily to these centers, where they are charted. At any given time, money room personnel meet to discuss that day's requisitions. If the requisitions meet that day's target spend and no foreseeable savings can be made, the orders are placed. If the day's requisition exceeds the approved target, control personnel are responsible for finding ways of reducing, mitigating, or eliminating the projected spend. This can be done by consolidating SKUs for more leverage, delaying purchases, or whatever other means seems reasonable. Control personnel are expected to bring costs down to 80% of historical numbers and are rotated every three to four months to bring fresh ideas to the program. At one location, Bayer reports that the money room program has saved more than 46% on indirect spend!

Source: "Money Rooms Attack Bayer's Indirect Spend," *Purchasing*, November 1, 2001, 129(12), pp. 25–26.

Integrating Accounts Payable into Supply Management

Several companies have integrated their accounts payable processes into the supply management organization, addressing one of the more pressing challenges associated with indirect spend, namely contract compliance. This arrangement gives supply management the authority to not pay for indirect items that were bought off-contract. To have the bill paid, the business unit is forced to speak to the CFO, an embarrassing and rarely repeated process, thereby effectively controlling maverick spending.

Power Spenders

This represents those key individuals or units that control substantial indirect spending and that typically have positions of great authority within the organization. Due to their authority and the sheer volume of the indirect spend they control, supply management often has a hard time getting these power spenders to comply with organizationwide supply management policies. Several companies indicate that properly training these power users is key to controlling their indirect spend. Training often includes information on general strategic sourcing strategies, as well as specific information on the strategies and tools employed by supply management for effectively controlling the indirect spend. Once trained, enlightened power spenders are usually more willing to comply with pre-established supply management contracts and play an appropriate role in managing their indirect spending.

Supplier-Managed E-Catalogs

E-catalogs, coupled with automated requisitioning and supply management systems described earlier in the chapter, help organizations ensure greater compliance with existing contracts. However, most companies indicate that creating and maintaining current in-house e-catalogs can be extremely costly and difficult. In general, suppliers should provide and manage the e-catalogs, as they have a vested interest in doing so to create additional sales volume.

Commodity Coding for Indirect Spend

Assigning and maintaining accurate and representative commodity codes for indirect goods and services across an enterprise can prove extremely difficult. Indirect goods can often be logically coded into different expense categories, leading to inconsistent coding across units, individual purchases, or perhaps even no coding at all (e.g., indirect expenses are put into a generic catch-all account such as Freight In). Supplier coding is also a challenge. Suppliers of multiple indirect items can often have multiple ship-to and bill-to addresses, resulting in multiple codes being assigned to the same supplier for the same item. Many suppliers will simply code these disparate purchases with the same accounting information, effectively masking them from detailed analysis and effective cost management by the indirect buyer. This also disguises the total indirect spend with a given supplier and hinders the buyer from fully leveraging its volume. To help counter these problems, companies should limit their commodity coding system to a few levels of detail, which makes it easier for the end user to properly identify commodity purchases and reduce the time for determining the perfect code.

One Commodity Team Assigned to Large Suppliers

There can be many challenges when sourcing from large suppliers with a broad and diverse product offering. These include commodity coding as well as standardizing products, pricing, terms, and conditions. One effective solution is to assign a designated commodity team to work with each large supplier. When another buyer is considering using this supplier, a commodity team member already assigned to this supplier is consulted to ensure that existing contracts with the appropriate standardized products, pricing, terms, and conditions are used. This collaborative approach helps the buying company counter the common divide-and-conquer strategy often used by large suppliers.

Outsourcing Indirect Sourcing

Although outsourcing any part of a supply management organization can be controversial, it can often return significant benefits. For example, one company decided to outsource its nonstrategic indirect spend. This bold move had a number of benefits. The first benefit was the development of an up-to-date e-catalog that was implemented quickly. The second was tighter control of the organization's indirect spend accompanied by real-time data. The third was a substantial reduction in the cost of indirect goods and services. And lastly, the company was able to reduce its headcount.

Sourcing Professional Services[13]

In this section, we will review best practices in an area of service procurement facing increasing scrutiny: the sourcing of professional services, including consultants and software development. In buying professional services, incorporating such basic steps as rationalizing and optimizing the supply base, working hand in hand with key suppliers, leveraging volume across business units, implementing better control systems, and developing cost savings ideas can save companies a substantial amount of money.[14]

Although implementation of these strategies can prove crucial in any typical sourcing scenario, its significance in the cost-effective procurement of professional services is further enhanced by the fact that professional services are often used quite differently among departments or business units. Like many other areas of supply management, the first step should be to perform an internal audit to establish a baseline of just how much the company is currently spending on professional services and where those funds are actually spent. An effective audit process should examine expenditure records to get an approximate estimate of the total value of these services. The audit team should then reclassify these expenditures by description, supplier, and internal user. It should also review the recent procurement history for previously contracted professional services.[15] This determines the current state of the professional services sourcing process and allows the company to decide if it requires change. In addition, the following steps are recommended for buying professional services, such as outside consulting.

Have a Clearly Defined Scope

Every project must have a scope that succinctly defines the project to help avoid misunderstandings between the buyer and the service provider. At a minimum, the scope should provide detailed guidance to the service provider, including project deliverables, milestones and deadlines, and budget. The scope should also include whether rewards and penalties are appropriate and how risk is to be distributed between the parties as well as instructions describing how major scope changes are to be handled to ensure that what was contracted for actually gets accomplished and to avoid scope creep. In some cases, it may be advisable to renegotiate the agreement if the desired changes are too substantial and materially alter the intent of the original agreement. The scope also needs to include nondisclosure statements to protect the buying company's interest. The buyer may want to insert language that specifies the actual persons who are supposed to do the work. Finally, the scope needs to include statements as to who has operational control over both internal and external project personnel once the contract is signed.

It is a good idea that, when using a new professional services supplier, the buyer should develop a very detailed project scope. However, if the buyer is using a previously established or preferred supplier, the scope of the new project may be more limited because the buyer already has a long-term relationship with the service provider. This relationship allows for work to be released with only a phone call or e-mail message. However, even with an established service provider, it is always important to follow up with a written confirmation outlining the understanding of the project, although a highly detailed document may not be necessary.

Move to a Centralized Procurement Structure

Moving to a centralized process for procuring professional services allows the buying company to leverage its corporate buying power to ensure they are sourcing the highest-quality service at the most cost-effective price.[16] According to Anne Millen Porter, "Cost reduction is, hands down, the main reason for bringing sizeable purchasing power to bear in the market place."[17] For example, Dial saved $100 million over five years, including $10 million in 2001, by moving to centralized sourcing.[18] After San Diego Gas and Electric centralized its procurement process, it found many positive results including greater objectivity, improved negotiation, and better pricing.[19]

Centralization of professional service procurement can also increase the accountability of outside consultants to the buyer by increasing the monitoring and auditing of services provided. Centralized procurement often leads to the ability to reduce the number of professional service providers, thus gaining additional pricing leverage with each. Additionally, centralization can also reduce service provider redundancy and reduce likelihood of unnecessary charges.[20] Another advantage of centralized procurement for professional services is that it reduces the risk of business units purchasing duplicated services.

Although utilizing a centralized procurement process has all of the advantages discussed above, it does have disadvantages. One major disadvantage is that no single consultant is likely to be the expert in a variety of consulting projects, so having a decentralized approach can help tailor the sourcing of professional services to better fit specific needs. Therefore, many companies feel that decentralized procurement of professional services is better for highly diversified companies with many business units.

Develop a Professional Services Database

In order for a professional services database solution to be effective, it should include the following two databases.

A Cumulative Knowledge Database

A cumulative knowledge database is vital in preventing the sourcing of duplicate or redundant professional services by different departments or business units. In general, this database should contain an organized listing of results obtained from past projects, including but not be limited to user satisfaction level, timely project completion, work quality, accuracy of work delivered, and affordability. This database is useful because it allows employees to search past projects to see if a similar solution has already been delivered. If a similar solution is available on the database, redundant services may not be needed, unless conditions have changed significantly. This increased project record keeping will ultimately save the company a significant amount in professional service expenditures.

A Preferred Supplier List Database

This database, including supplier performance records and related user comments, can be extremely useful for companies considering multiple professional service providers. By having access to a list of preferred suppliers, employees know which professional service providers the company recommends. These recommendations can be determined by user satisfaction ratings, the existence of long-term contracts, or price discounts. In any event, the preferred supplier list must be easily accessible by employees when they search for suppliers on new projects.

The database should also be set up to generate a list of preferred suppliers based on previous project performance criteria. For example, the Intelli-Gage system at Merrill Lynch is designed so that hiring managers can select desired skills from a comprehensive menu of options. Once a search request is completed, the database then provides a prioritized list of appropriate or preferred candidates. The system should also display the supplier's most recent hourly rate and fee structure, as well as other useful information such as performance ratings and previous project user comments. According to Merrill Lynch, "The ability to track the consultant's performance is an enormous benefit for companies with multiple locations and multiple information technology organizations around the globe. In addition, the system's ability to track individual supplier performance, as well as overall supplier performance, allows us to prevent hiring poor performers who leave one supplier company only to resurface under a different corporate umbrella."[21]

As long as the preferred supplier database is meticulously maintained, and employees are encouraged to use the preferred supplier list, companies should see improvements in their procured services. Moreover, as new and refined search criteria come along, it is important that these criteria be added to the database. This will allow sourcing managers to easily walk through menus to populate future supplier searches. Performance records, supplier evaluations, and project comments will also need to be continually updated in a timely manner for the database to remain effective. Together, these IT elements should enhance the organization and efficiency of the supply management department.

Develop a Sound Procedure for Evaluation and Selection of Consultants

One of the most important functions in procurement is the initial evaluation and selection of consultants and other professional service providers. As such, buyers often commit major resources to perform initial supplier evaluations. Although there are different requirements for each performance area, it is typical to evaluate such areas as supplier quality, cost competitiveness, potential delivery performance, and technological capability. To help avoid potential bias, it is essential that a cross-functional team carry out this analysis. Companies report cost savings in the range of 15–25% by utilizing a cross-functional team.

Optimize the Supply Base

Once the first cut has eliminated those professional service providers that are not capable of performing the desired work, the buyer must decide how to evaluate the remaining suppliers, some of which may appear equally capable on the surface. This procedure includes an evaluation drawn from supplier interviews and conversations, as well as the use of a preferred supplier list as discussed before. A preferred supplier list can designate whether a professional service provider's capabilities and quality meet the highest performance and service standards as defined by the users. This list may also take into account any price discount or volume-leveraging opportunities offered by the supplier. Such a list helps to monitor the performance of selected suppliers closely, facilitates organizational visibility in the long run, and avoids duplication of efforts to re-evaluate the supplier. This information is a key input in the knowledge database. The buyer and supplier should conduct detailed negotiations to agree upon the specific details of the agreement that can be included in the scope of work.

Although it is important to develop a rationalized supply base so that buying power can be appropriately leveraged, a single-source strategy rarely maximizes the value of professional services. Often the addition of a single new supplier will greatly enhance the performance of the others because of the added competition. Using multiple sources for products encourages professional service providers to act more competitively. Although no single supplier should be considered an expert in all areas, using a variety of sources allows managers to find and tap specific expertise for a given project. Use of multiple sources also increases the flow of new ideas and information and reduces the dependence on any single supplier. Additionally, all efforts should be taken to avoid one-stop shopping; most service companies are second rate outside their core businesses. Use professional service providers for their core expertise only.

Develop a Standardized Contract

It is critical for supply managers to develop skills and abilities to understand and manage professional service contracts on a regular basis. It is also important for a standard contract template/format to be developed in association with the organization's legal department. Some companies have created an online contract template where all the standard professional service clauses are built in. The entire scope of the project should be clearly and succinctly defined at this level, with emphasis on the various sections of the project scope as additional clauses in the contract. These should include project deliverables, deadlines and milestones, and budget. If a company utilizes an incentive system to reward or penalize its professional service providers, this should also become part of the final agreement. Finally, the contract should contain a clause that allows for renegotiation in case of major scope changes.

Monitor Results

The company should have a predetermined methodology to gauge the performance of its professional service providers at various stages of their projects. The parameters on which the supplier is evaluated should include, but not be limited to, quality, cost management, delivery, technical support, and wavelength. **Wavelength** can be defined as how easy the professional service provider is to do business with.

The results of service provider performance evaluations should be entered into the knowledge database in a timely manner, enabling retrieval both at the time of supplier evaluation and after supplier selection.

The internal customers of any contracted professional service (i.e., the users who are directly impacted), should have an active role in the sourcing and evaluation process. Their participation in defining the detailed scope of the project and providing relevant feedback on services rendered by the service provider should be consistently updated in the knowledge database throughout the life cycle of the project. Finally, the company should monitor its expenses, utilizing an information systems tool where available.

Develop Policy Compliance

For the execution of best practices into a systematic professional services procurement process, the prerequisites are mentioned above. The degree of success for implementation and ongoing management of this process will depend not only upon how comprehensive and exhaustive these practices and policies are for a given company but also on whether adequate buy-in has been obtained from affected employees and internal stakeholders. Top management should consider this completely before defining the final scope of the procurement project. Because the maintenance of best practices is a highly dynamic process, the organization's information systems and knowledge databases should be checked for the most recent updates.

The Procurement Governance Team at Allstate reduced the number of suppliers for one type of professional service from 300 to 11, resulting in a 20% cost reduction. The procurement team handles the complete sourcing process from beginning to end, allowing employees to concentrate on their core responsibilities. This also permits the organization to operate more efficiently and receive a greater benefit. According to the vice president and head of procurement governance, effective demand management of professional services depends on establishing clear usage policies, then monitoring and reporting compliance with these policies. Realizing actual savings requires compliance throughout the entire company.[22]

Service Supply Chain Challenges

Research indicates that effectively managing an organization's services supply chain is fraught with challenges.[23] Many service sourcing agreements are characterized by imprecise and unclear specifications. Without clear and concise specifications, it is unlikely that a buyer can properly determine whether a service has been performed to the satisfaction of the internal customer. Not having a well-thought-out and thoroughly defined set of performance and outcome expectations can lead to reduced customer satisfaction with the user. Secondly, in trying to write out specific service requirements, many buyers and users find out that clear and accurate service specifications are very difficult to delineate; for example, what determines satisfactory progress on the development of a software program?

Likewise, service providers can often take advantage of unsuspecting buyers when service performance specifications are unclear or ill-defined. More than one service provider has been able to expand the scope of a contract (and its corresponding fees) through change orders. Without exception, scope creep unfairly favors the service provider, not the buyer. Completion of the service provided is oftentimes also difficult to clearly define. What constitutes "completion" or "level of effort"?

Good Practice Example — *Bank of America's Document Management Services*

Bank of America (BoA) is one of the world's leading financial services companies. BoA serves 28 million customers and clients from its 4,200 banking centers. These centers are located in more communities across the country than any other U.S. bank. Bank of America also provides corporate financial services to more than 90% of U.S. Fortune 500 companies through offices in 30 countries around the world.

Bank of America chose a unique approach to documents and created a Document Management department charged with oversight for the entire document life cycle, from conception to end-of-life functions, including archiving, recycling, and confidential destruction. This group approached reducing the end-to-end cost of documents with a methodology that began with capturing the document in a digital library that was tied to a relational database that stored the pertinent approval and production specifications of that document. Around that dual database, the Document Management group developed a disciplined change control process that mandated a review of compliance issues and opportunities to reduce the end-to-end cost of delivery. They then categorized all potential delivery channels, including document production and distribution, through warehousing, print-on-demand, distribute and print-on-demand, desktop delivery through multifunctional devices, desktop printers, reprographic networks, fax machines, and Internet delivery. Distribution expense contributed an ever larger percentage to the end-to-end cost, so there was an increased focus on distribution cost, freight, expedited delivery, postal expense, and interoffice mail costs.

This approach had some significant implications for the culture and ways that people performed their jobs. By digitizing all documents at their origins, the bank shifted a good portion of document delivery from the traditional hard-copy print methodology to electronic delivery at the desktop, which created a need to fully understand the cost of delivering documents to the desktop.

While contrasting the cost of these channels, it became apparent that there was a gap in understanding the desktop delivery environment. Although the bank had a tight control on the cost of faxing and the cost of impressions on multifunctional devices, it discovered two elements of concern. Bank of America owned one of the largest fleets of multifunctional copiers of any organization in the world (more than 5,000 units). A multifunctional copier is one capable of copying, faxing, printing, and scanning documents.

Several major problems emerged in the discovery process initiated by the sourcing team. First, it was noted that only 5% of copiers were connected to computers or similar devices; the remaining 95% were used solely for manual copying, which failed to fully exploit their inherent multifunctional capabilities. Second, because there was no active management of the desktop printer environment, the bank was actually pushing print from a traditional method to an even more expensive channel, the unregulated desktop printer. Finally, there were no metrics in place to understand the total cost of ownership at the desktop level. The total amount spent on copying and printers was unknown but was estimated in the $90 million range.

To make matters worse, there was no single group responsible for managing desktop printers, no demand management, and no understanding of the total cost of ownership. As such, the bank had no idea how many desktop printers were currently in use. All of these factors made the task of managing the desktop environment, or even understanding the cost of that environment, virtually impossible.

THE SOLUTION: PRINTSMART

Faced with this situation, Document Management developed a program known as PrintSmart that was aimed at controlling the desktop environment. The team began by centralizing all responsibility for the desktop environment under a single group. This organization created a demand management function designed to drive impressions to the lowest-cost option appropriate for workflow needs, with a target of concentrating impressions on connected multifunctional devices. Desktop printers were now required to be networked where feasible, and contracts were converted to cost-per-impression, using a total cost of ownership arrangement. A three-year technology upgrade cycle was also built in.

The Document Management team recognized that the best way to control document cost would be to create a digital library of literally every document created. Once a document was stored in the digital library, only then could supply management control how each piece was printed. This approached was extended further. A senior vice president noted, "If it was printed or in use, we wanted it in the library!" This included everything from checks, deposit tickets, magnetic integrated character recognition documents, and marketing pieces, to every other type of bank document imaginable. The library had to capture, image, and upload data on the use of every document, including usage patterns that included the volume data but also indicated geographies, cost centers, lines of business, and so on. This required the creation of a very large relational database.

The senior vice president also noted, "Once the digital library was established, a number of things started to happen. The team began to (1) consolidate suppliers and leverage pricing; (2) move a considerable amount of inventory to print-on-demand; and (3) standardize documents and consolidate documents. The bank went from 45,000 forms to 6,000 through this process. The print library has effectively reduced print cost by over 20% year over year. This did not include the added advantages of reduced obsolescence and reduced time to market."

RESULTS

To control the cost of document handling and printing, the Document Management team initiated the PrintSmart strategy, with excellent results. This was accomplished through two approaches: demand management and facility re-engineering. Demand management, in the context of document management, involves having supply management redirect all requisitions originally targeted for desktop printers to multifunctional devices or shared networked printers in its building. In only very rare circumstances, such as when someone works from home or is traveling, Document Management will approve the purchase of a black-and-white, standalone printer. These are purchased from an preapproved printer manufacturer with whom a negotiated contract exists. This supplier provides a total cost of ownership lease on printers, which is about a quarter of standard print costs, allowing Document Management to more effectively monitor the network and track the volume of hard copies made.

The second approach was to re-engineer every Bank of America facility across the country. Early pilot program results were promising: The program reduced print cost by an additional 15 to 20%. The bank has now rolled facility re-engineering out to two cities, or 11 buildings. To date, Document Management has increased connectivity for multifunctional devices from

5% to over 35%. About 7% of cost is still driven by people printing from old desktop printers, now about 55% of total print volume.

The senior vice president notes, "Previously, we had two to three associates per print device —and in a PrintSmart-ed environment, we moved to one machine serving an average of seven employees. All of the multifunctional copier/printers were leased, and we paid only for the number of impressions. We are exploring an application that will allow us to track who is making the impressions and how many per floor, allowing us to replenish paper and toner based on consumption of equipment. We could then begin to track impressions per floor versus cut sheet volumes purchased—which allows us to do three things: (1) reduce the investment of paper held on-site; (2) improve predictive maintenance schedules; and (3) track missing paper inventory."

PrintSmart is a process that must interface with all other desktop groups within the bank, including the help desk, which is outsourced to Compaq. The PrintSmart solution also had to consider the impact of pushing increased digital traffic through the bank's networks and the effects on bandwidth limitations that might exist across the bank's multiple locations. This limitation required that Document Management work closely with the desktop group located in the technology and operations organization group at the bank. Prior to implementing PrintSmart, the team ensured that the desktop technology team was 100% on board. The initiative required that the senior vice president meet frequently with the corporate real estate team, the networking team, and other key facilities and technology groups that would be affected by the re-engineering of facilities to accommodate PrintSmart technology.

Several problems soon became apparent. A typical issue was that there might be an inadequate number of print servers in a given city. The team also discovered that it was simpler to centralize printer types on individual servers to enhance diagnostic capabilities. The team also set up a device labeling methodology that mirrored the mail code system. Associates can log on to the LAN in a re-engineered building, search devices by mail code, and discover the networked devices that they can access locally.

PrintSmart is a major initiative that will take several years to implement—and will clearly entail a major culture change. The biggest change is for administrative staff, who now complain about having to walk 20-plus feet to the printer ("It ruins my workflow."). The groundswell level of discontent cannot be underestimated. The senior vice president noted, "At one point we were worried if, politically, PrintSmart could survive this onslaught of protest. A program that requires behavioral changes from almost every associate requires an unusual level of support from the higher echelons. But at Bank of America, the executive sponsors have supported the program 1000%."

The Document Management team also made a point of implementing PrintSmart at the bank's corporate offices in Charlotte, North Carolina first after the five pilot buildings were re-engineered. Why? "We felt that if we were going to drive change into the company, we would begin by changing Rome first," the senior vice president says. "That way, people couldn't point to us and complain that corporate wasn't taking its own medicine!"

Source: R. Handfield, "Improving the Total Cost of Ownership of Document Management at Bank of America," *Practix,* October 2003, pp. 1–6.

CONCLUSION

In studying the best practices used in the procurement of transportation and logistics services, indirect spending, and other professional services, several common themes pervade the discussion. These include the following:

- Link transportation, logistics, and other service activities directly to corporate strategy.
- Organize transportation, logistics, and indirect spending activities under a single executive-level position if possible, utilizing a hybrid procurement structure if the indirect spend is spread across several diverse business units.
- Expand and use the power of information and information-processing technology to capture spending behaviors, costs associated with procuring transportation and services, and maverick spending.
- Establish buy-in from senior executive management to the strategy, particularly from the chief financial officer, who is key in overseeing compliance with the strategy.
- Tie cost savings directly to actual spending in business units and be sure to capture the savings either through a zero-based budget or through other appropriate means.
- Form partnerships or alliances with a fewer number of service, transportation, and logistics providers to improve collaboration and cost-savings opportunities, while leveraging the indirect spend volume of the organization.
- Measure transportation, logistics, and service provider performance to drive and sustain superior performance.
- Establish benchmarks against which suppliers and providers are expected to perform and regularly review supplier performance against predetermined goals.
- Establish project scope up front, and follow up routinely to ensure that it is met in a reasonable and cost-effective manner.
- Review and re-evaluate indirect procurement strategies periodically to ensure that user requirements and expectations are being met, along with cost targets.

Supply management's involvement in transportation and services, although fairly recent, is expected to continue to grow. Excellent opportunities exist for the supply management professional to make major contributions in this important, but often overlooked, area. Supply management professionals tasked with sourcing indirect materials and services must strive to become experts in these categories in order to manage and control them effectively. In addition, it is imperative for supply management professionals to take into account user needs and tailor the sourcing process to adequately accommodate them. A recent joint research paper by CAPS Research and A. T. Kearney, Inc., sums up the importance of procuring services best: "As companies seek to outsource additional non-strategic, non-core activities, outsourcers will have to learn how to serve and add value in addition to landing initial contracts."[24]

KEY TERMS

indirect spend, 647

logistics, 623

maverick spend, 648

wavelength, 656

DISCUSSION QUESTIONS

1. Discuss the business and legislative changes that resulted in an increased awareness of the sourcing of transportation and logistics activities.
2. What are the benefits associated with maintaining control and visibility of transportation shipments?
3. What are some of the key items you should plan on reviewing with a transportation or logistics service provider during a negotiation?
4. Give a definition of a third-party logistics provider. What function does it serve?
5. Discuss the conditions under which a buyer might prefer that a third-party logistics provider arrange and control the transportation and storage of purchased items.
6. Compare and contrast the relative costs and service advantages and disadvantages of air, motor, water, pipeline, and rail carriers.
7. What are the major differences between a common and a contract carrier? Can a buyer negotiate with a common carrier? Why or why not?
8. How can an indirect buyer effectively use performance-based logistics or service-level agreements to control the costs of procuring services?
9. What are the different types of performance metrics used to measure transportation providers? Could this same list be used for a third-party logistics provider? Why or why not?
10. One of the benefits often cited by third-party logistics providers is their ability to provide access to critical performance and operating data. Explain what is meant by this statement.
11. Provide some examples of spending that would fall under the category of services versus indirect spending. What is the different between the two?
12. One of the biggest problems cited by supply management executives in managing their indirect spend is identifying where and how the spending is taking place. Why do you think this is the case? How can an indirect buyer collect and use this data?
13. Why is it so important to have senior executive support when implementing an indirect spend procurement strategy?
14. Discuss the importance of defining expectations and using standardized contracts when sourcing professional services. Why is this different from sourcing direct materials and components?
15. Can you provide some examples of power spenders of indirect spending and services? How can training help to deploy an indirect spending strategy?

ADDITIONAL READINGS

Ballou, R. H. (2004), *Business Logistics/Supply Chain Management: Planning, Organizing, and Controlling the Supply Chain* (5th ed.), Upper Saddle River, NJ: Pearson Prentice Hall.

Bowersox, D. J., Closs, D. J., and Cooper, M. B. (2007), *Supply Chain Logistics Management* (2nd ed.), New York: McGraw-Hill Irwin.

Carter, P., Beall, S., Rossetti, C., and Leduc, E. (2003), *Indirect Spend,* Tempe, AZ: CAPS Research.

Carter, P. L., Carter, J. R., Monczka, R. M., Blascovich, J. D., Slaight, T. H., and Markham, W. J. (2007), *Succeeding in a Dynamic World: Supply Management in the Decades Ahead,* Tempe, AZ: CAPS Research.

Coyle, J. J., Bardi, E. J., and Langley, C. J. (2003), *Management of Business Logistics: A Supply Chain Perspective* (7th ed.), Mason, OH: Thomson South-Western.

Coyle, J. J., Bardi, E. J., and Novak, R. A. (2006), *Transportation* (6th ed.), Mason, OH: Thomson South-Western.

Ellram, L. M., Tate, W. L., and Billington, C. (2004), "Understanding and Managing the Services Supply Chain," *Journal of Supply Chain Management,* 40(3), 17–32.

Frazell, E. H. (2002), *World-Class Warehousing and Material Handling,* New York: McGraw-Hill.

Handfield, R. (2004), "The Impact of Energy Deregulation on Sourcing Strategy," *Journal of Supply Chain Management,* 40(2), 38–48.

Kasilingam, R. G. (1998), *Logistics and Transportation: Designs and Planning,* Boston: Kluwer Academic Publishers, 1998.

Lee, H. L., and Wolfe, M. (2003), "Supply Chain Security without Tears," *Supply Chain Management Review,* 1, 18–34.

Perry, C. (1998), *Purchasing Transportation,* West Palm Beach, FL: PT Publications.

Reilly, C. (2002), "Central Sourcing Strategy Saves Dial $100M," *Purchasing Online,* January 17.

Stock, J. R., and Lambert, D. M. (2001), *Strategic Logistics Management* (4th ed.), New York: McGraw-Hill.

Vitasek, K., and Geary, S. (2007), "Performance-Based Logistics: The Next Big Thing?" *ProLogis Supply Chain Review,* Summer, 1–12.

Wade, D. S. (2003), *Managing Your "Services Spend" in Today's Services Economy,* Tempe, AZ: CAPS Research.

Waters, D. (Ed.) (2003), *Global Logistics and Distribution Planning: Strategies for Management* (4th ed.), London: Kogan Page.

ENDNOTES

1. Ellram, L. M., Tate, W. L., and Billington, C. (2004), "Understanding and Managing the Services Supply Chain," *Journal of Supply Chain Management,* 40(3), 20.
2. http://cscmp.org/aboutcscmp/about.asp, June 2008.
3. A complete discussion of transportation and logistics is beyond the scope of this book. For a more complete discussion of the topic, see Bowersox, D. J., Closs, D. J., and Cooper, M. B. (2007), *Supply Chain Logistics Management* (2nd ed.), New York: McGraw-Hill Irwin; Stock, J. R., and Lambert, D. M. (2001), *Strategic Logistics Management* (4th ed.), New York: McGraw-Hill; or Coyle, J. J., Bardi, E. J., and Novak, R. A. (2006), *Transportation* (6th ed.), Mason, OH: Thomson South-Western.
4. Coyle et al., p. 59; and Bowersox et al., pp. 174–176.
5. Coyle et al., p. 112.
6. Coyle et al., p. 29.
7. Dillon, T. F. (1988), "Trends Facing Transportation Buyers/Carriers," *Purchasing World,* September, pp. 32–34.
8. Adapted from Vitasek, K., and Geary, S. (2007), "Performance-Based Logistics: The Next Big Thing?" *ProLogis Supply Chain Review,* Summer, 1–12.
9. Vitasek and Geary, pp. 5–7.

10. Based on the following reports: Carter, P., Beall, S., Rossetti, C., and Leduc, E. (2003), *Indirect Spend,* Tempe, AZ: CAPS Research, www.capsresearch.org; and Wade, D. S. (2003), Managing Your "Services Spend" in *Today's Services Economy,* Tempe, AZ: CAPS Research.

11. Patterson, J. L. (2000), "Glove Story at John Deere," in *Case Book: Supply Management Cases,* Tempe, AZ: National Association of Purchasing Management, pp. 43–49.

12. Handfield, R. (2004), "The Impact of Energy Deregulation on Sourcing Strategy," *Journal of Supply Chain Management,* 40(2), 38–48.

13. Based on a best practices report by the Supply Chain Resource Consortium, North Carolina State University, Raleigh, August 2002.

14. Reilly, C. (2002), "Central Sourcing Strategy Saves Dial $100M," *Purchasing Online,* January 17.

15. The Global Procurement and Supply Chain Benchmark Institute (1998).

16. Avery, S. (2000), "Allstate Leverages Sourcing to Better Serve Customers," *Purchasing,* 128(2), 12–14.

17. Porter, A. M. (2001), "Big Companies Struggle to Act Their Size," *Purchasing,* 130(21), 24–25.

18. Reilly.

19. "Using Purchasing to Procure Professional Services" (1988), *Purchasing World.*

20. Baker, W. E., and Faulkner, R. R. (2003), *Strategies for Managing Suppliers of Professional Services,* Tempe, AZ: CAPS Research.

21. Porter, A. M. (2000), "How One Firm Automated Its Professional Services Buy," *Purchasing,* 129(5), S52.

22. Avery.

23. Ellram et al., pp. 27–29.

24. Carter, P. L., Carter, J. R., Monczka, R. M., Blascovich, J. D., Slaight, T. H., and Markham, W. J. (2007), *Succeeding in a Dynamic World: Supply Management in the Decades Ahead,* Tempe, AZ: CAPS Research and A. T. Kearney, pp. 107–108.

Chapter 18

SUPPLY CHAIN INFORMATION SYSTEMS AND ELECTRONIC SOURCING

Learning Objectives

After completing this chapter, you should be able to

- Understand how e-supply chain systems have evolved over time
- Identify the key types of information required in purchasing and supply chains
- Develop a broad knowledge of the different types of systems in use
- Understand the drivers underlying increased use of systems in supply chain management
- Understand the primary elements of enterprise resource planning, purchasing databases, and electronic communication between buyers and sellers
- Understand the benefits and limitations of e-sourcing suites
- Understand the future requirements of e-supply chain systems that will enable information visibility across the supply chain

Chapter Outline

Rolls-Royce Managing Critical Material Inputs

When we think about Rolls-Royce, we most likely envision a wealthy person driving up to a castle. Certainly the Rolls-Royce name is associated with luxury cars. Lesser known are its high-quality jet engines. The company recently developed a new line of jet engines that have superior fuel efficiency. These engines are based on advances in materials, manufacturing technologies, and design.

Delivering the finished product is dependent on suppliers and their ability to secure critical raw materials such as titanium and nickel alloys. This problem is complicated by the fact that titanium and nickel alloys are in short supply. Further, some of the critical suppliers are smaller specialty parts suppliers that don't have volume to develop any priority with alloy providers. If the suppliers can't secure the raw materials, then Roll-Royce customers such as Boeing and Airbus don't receive engines when needed.

In 2003 Rolls-Royce, with the assistance of Newview Technologies, began building the critical raw material supply chain planning capabilities to meet the demands of aerospace manufacturers. The e-sourcing tool, called Material Specification Management, was rolled out in 2006 and enables aerospace manufacturers to manage the risk of acquiring critical raw materials.

Benefits include the ability to understand the total value chain's material needs, the capabilities to publish coordinating schedules for sub-tier suppliers, the ability to help control material and part source decisions, and the management of cost exposure to material price volatility. Below is a discussion of the various modules embedded in the software and their benefits to Rolls-Royce.

The forecasting module allows Rolls-Royce to estimate the amount of material required to produce every part for every engine on the production plan. In cases where data does not exist, inputs are derived on the basis of benchmarks for similar parts. Historically, Rolls-Royce only had a rough idea of how much material its suppliers needed to meet part demand.

By managing the critical supply chain node, demand plans can be developed that permit visibility of part origination and location in the supply chain. Highly engineered parts such as shafts, rings, disks, and rotative parts and blades often go through multiple-step processes, and activities occur at different suppliers.

Managing price volatility provides the ability to forecast the impact of material price changes across the organization for individual engine models at any part level or part category level. Historically, Rolls-Royce did not have a firm understanding of the total supply chain material spend and therefore had a difficult time managing price volatility with hedging tools. Improvements made through cost reductions on parts were offset by material price increases. For example, if a buying team was able to reduce the part cost because of increased volume, leverage, or process improvements, it was often offset by key material price increases.

Controlling material and sourcing decisions in the supply chain permits Rolls-Royce to provide its suppliers with electronic part and material catalogs. Rolls-Royce then specifies which products are preferred for suppliers to purchase. Rolls-Royce can also capture the supplier's purchasing history and track the degree to which the supplier adhered to its recommendations. This allows Rolls-Royce to control the design-related material decisions at its suppliers, ensuring that its critical quality requirements will be met.

Managing bills of resources allows Rolls-Royce to initiate and manage information requests to suppliers. Now the company can understand what material and supplier dependencies it has, and where the critical bottlenecks reside within the extended supply chain, and it has the ability to manage around these constraints. This capability gives Rolls-Royce new visibility into its suppliers, the materials they use, and the process steps performed in the extended supply chain.

Demand aggregation and managing sourcing decisions allow Rolls-Royce to publish the material characteristics and specifications for all materials to sub-tier suppliers. It can also communicate the material specifications and suppliers that it prefers its parts suppliers to utilize. This allows Rolls-Royce to further leverage its purchases of critical materials and provide important input into contract negotiations. It can also help identify potential supply bottlenecks in the supply chain.

Source: Adapted from "Securing the Future at Rolls-Royce," Case Study, 2007, www.newview.com.

The electronic revolution continues to affect the supply chain. As can be seen from the chapter opening vignette and throughout this chapter, there are several exciting new software tools emerging that will help supply managers in the future. This contrasts sharply with a few years ago when many organizations became pessimistic about the opportunities to utilize web-based supply chain (e-SCM) solutions after the dot bust era of 2001–2003. What actually happened was a change in market emphasis and focus. Weaker firms touting business models that did not provide value in the supply chain were washed out of the market and became roadkill for the stronger, market-focused firms. Mergers and consolidations reduced the number of value players even further.

Thus, by early 2004 the market carnages had eliminated the market excesses, built during the dot boom era, and left the remaining market players in a better position to offer value in SCM solutions. Meanwhile, on the buying side, organizations were becoming much more focused and sophisticated in making decisions involving investments in e-SCM systems. Business cases had to provide solid justifications that supported a need for these systems. Given that there were fewer software providers, possessing increased capabilities, the cycle times from system design to implementation were shortened. Finally, in this market providers were giving their customers better pricing and terms, making justification of e-SCM systems even more likely. Contrary to doom-and-gloom experts, e-SCM software uses are growing in application and sophistication.

This chapter is not a technical presentation of computerized information systems. Instead, it focuses on a host of issues that managers in the supply chain must be aware of to appreciate the role of information systems (IS) within purchasing. Many purchasers will at some point become involved in the development of different types of purchasing information systems, and knowledge of information systems applications is necessary in order for future managers to realize purchasing performance objectives.

We will begin the chapter with a discussion of the evolution of e-SCM systems, provide an overview of supply chain information systems, and then discuss the business drivers for implementing these systems and applications. We will then describe enterprise systems in more detail, followed by the fundamental elements of purchasing databases and data warehouses. Next we will discuss the elements of electronic data interchange (EDI) as a precursor to the new era of e-sourcing and supply tools, including web-based systems, supply chain applications, and full integrated systems. There are also discussions on ERP supplier relationship management and integrating ERP systems into e-sourcing.

Evolution of E-SCM Systems

Today supply managers expect powerful solutions to their business problems. However, organizations did not always have sophisticated systems at their disposal. Exhibit 18.1 traces the evolution of e-SCM systems. Early uses of information systems were in the accounting and financial areas. However, beginning in the 1970s more IT resources and software solutions were allocated to purchasing, operations, and distribution. Organizations installed systems such as material requirements planning (MRP) and distribution requirements planning (DRP). These systems were used to improve the planning and control of inventory in manufacturing (MRP) and distribution (DRP).

Because MRP and DRP systems were primarily internal, an electronic linkage to suppliers and customers was needed. Led by efforts of the railroad and retail sectors, electronic data interchange was developed as a solution to transfer customer and supplier information in the 1980s.

Although these early efforts provided efficiencies in the supply chain, intense competition in the final two decades of the 20th century forced firms to re-engineer their business processes to become even leaner. During this period, almost every major Fortune 500 company went through some form of restructuring, as thousands of workers and managers were shed in an effort to increase productivity and reduce costs. In conjunction with this change, organizations further increased their information systems to perform tasks previously done by these workers. Thus enterprise resource planning (ERP) systems became the rage of the 1990s and they continue today. The goal of ERP systems is to integrate all business function planning and processing, and to avoid data interruption in order to make better business decisions and run the business more effectively and efficiently. Ideally, all the different functions in the organization have access to and are working with the same data. Supply managers were at the center of this trend and were challenged to develop accurate databases to improve their decision making.

Exhibit 18.1 The Evolution of E-SCM Systems

SOLUTION	TIME PERIOD	FOCUS	PRIMARY USE OF SYSTEM
MRP-DRP	1970s	Internal/managing inventory	Inventory planning, inventory control, and distribution efficiencies
EDI	1980s	External	Electronic transmission of purchase orders
ERP	1990s	Internal	Integration of all business functions for processing and reporting
SRM and CRM	2000s	External	Managing and controlling the interface between buyers, suppliers, and customers
Collaboration	2000s	External-internal	CPFR systems permit constant communication within the supply chain via RFID and point of sale systems
Advanced sourcing analytics	2010 and beyond	External-internal	Sourcing analytics and computerized negotiations

The next era in electronic commerce broadcast different applications on the World Wide Web. Similar to the events that occurred 20 years earlier, ERP systems were primarily internal and lacked the linkage to suppliers and customers. The Internet provided the bridge; because of its low cost, lead software providers developed systems that could link customers and suppliers into the ERP system. These systems are popularly termed "supplier relationship management (SRM)" and "customer relationship management (CRM)" systems.

As we move further into the 21st century, software solutions are aimed at collaboration among supply chain partners through point of sale systems, RFID, and other information-sharing systems. Lastly, there are newer applications such as product life cycle software, bid optimization, and computerized negotiation models that will be available to the purchasers of the future. These increasingly powerful tools will be linked to an e-mobile environment with smaller laptop computers, personal digital assistants (e.g., Blackberry), and increasingly powerful cell phones (e.g., Apple's I-phone), allowing supply managers to have data access on a 24/7 basis irrespective of geographic location.

An Overview of the E-Supply Chain[1]

In this section we present an overview of the e-supply chain and describe some of the leading software providers in this fast-changing marketplace. Although the players in this industry have changed and will continue to change over time, the areas of functionality and linkages will not.

Supply Chain Information Flows

Supply chain information flows (and the information systems that embody them) serve six major functions:

- Record and retrieve critical data
- Execute and control physical and monetary flows
- Automate routine decisions
- Support planning activities
- Support higher-level tactical and strategic decision making
- Move and share information across firms and between users

Levels of Functionality

Note from the list above how information flows cover everything from relatively low-level functionality (record and retrieve data) to sophisticated analytical support tools. In addition, some of these information flows take place with little or no human intervention, whereas others provide more of a support role to higher-level planning and decision making.

At the most basic level, information flows record and retrieve critical data, and execute and control physical and monetary flows. This is sometimes referred to as **transaction processing**. For example, your credit card company has a record including your address, credit limit, payment history, and most recent balance. As time goes on and you pay (or don't pay!) your monthly bills, these records are updated automatically. Another example of transaction processing would be a bar code system to track the actual location of a package in the distribution network.

At a somewhat higher level of functionality, information systems are often used to support **routine decision making**. In many cases, these decisions are automated, with exceptions dealt with manually. Suppose, for example, you are a retailer with 60,000 items to manage. Do you want to manually forecast, calculate the correct order quantities, establish reorder points for all these items, and kick off an order when needed? Of course not. In cases like this, companies often depend on automated inventory management systems to make the decisions for them. Of course, companies can always override the information system's decisions when the situation warrants.

Beyond these transactions and routine decisions, information systems also play a critical role in supply chain planning and strategic decision making in sourcing and supply. As an example of the former, a company will decide on the technologies that may be required for the next generation of products or services, and identify the requirements in terms of the supply base, forecasted demand, production decisions, and projected cash flows. The strategic planning systems can provide critical information and provide it in a way that is meaningful to marketing, operations, purchasing, and finance personnel.

In such cases, information systems can support **strategic decision making**. Here, sophisticated analytical tools are often used to search for patterns or relationships in the data. Examples include customer segment analysis, product life cycle forecasting, and what-if analyses regarding long-term product or capacity decisions. These information systems have to be highly flexible in how they manipulate and present the data because the strategic question of interest may change from one situation to the next. Such information systems are generally referred to as **decision support systems (DSSs)**. The name emphasizes the fact that these systems support, but do not make, the decision.

Directions of Linkage

To fully understand the role of information flows in a supply chain, we have to consider not only the level of functionality, but also the direction of the linkages. For example, there are information flows that link a firm with its customers, broadly referred to as customer relationship management flows, and those that link a firm with its suppliers, known as supplier relationship management flows (Exhibit 18.2). There are also flows that link higher-level planning and decision making with lower-level activities within the firm (dubbed internal supply chain management by Chopra and Meindl[2]). Later we will describe some of the specific IS applications found in the CRM and SRM areas.

A Map of SCM Systems

The map of SCM systems was first laid out in 1999 by Steven Kahl,[3] then a software industry analyst at Piper Jaffray. Kahl's map was later refined by Chopra and Meindl,[4] who applied the labels "customer relationship management," "supplier relationship management," and "internal supply chain management" to various areas of the map.

Our map (Exhibit 18.3) distinguishes the various applications by the level of functionality (strategic, planning/tactical, and execution) and the direction of linkages (suppliers, internal supply chain, and customers). Here we add an additional column labeled "Logistics." Logistics applications deal with warehousing and transportation issues, such as determining warehouse locations, optimizing transportation systems, and controlling the movement of materials between supply chain partners. Most businesses

Exhibit 18.2 Decision Making

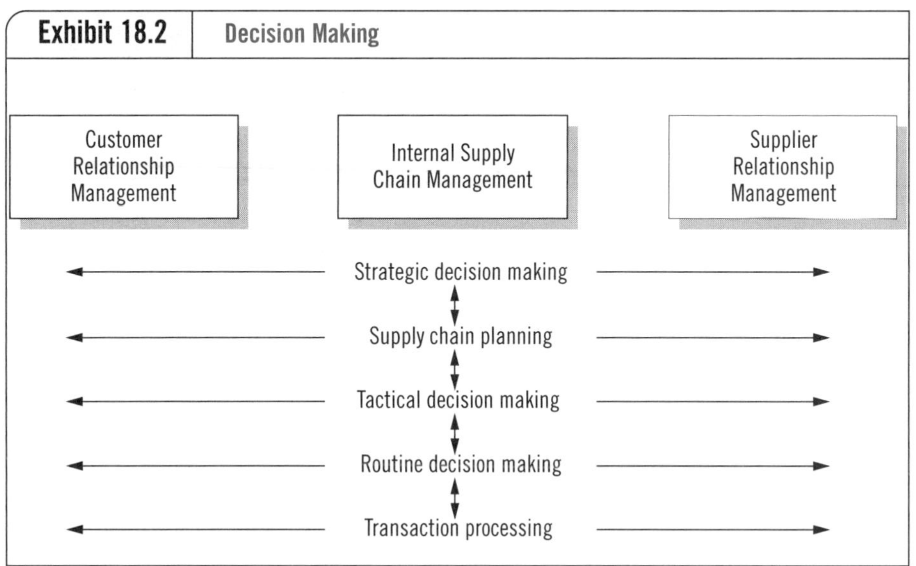

do not do a good job of integrating these applications with the other applications. We will return to this point later in the chapter.

Enterprise resource planning systems are large, integrated business transaction processing and reporting systems. The primary advantage of ERP systems is that they pull together all of the classic business functions such as accounting, finance, sales, and operations, to name a few, into a single, tightly integrated package that uses a common database (Exhibit 18.4 on p. 673).

Exhibit 18.3 SCM Systems

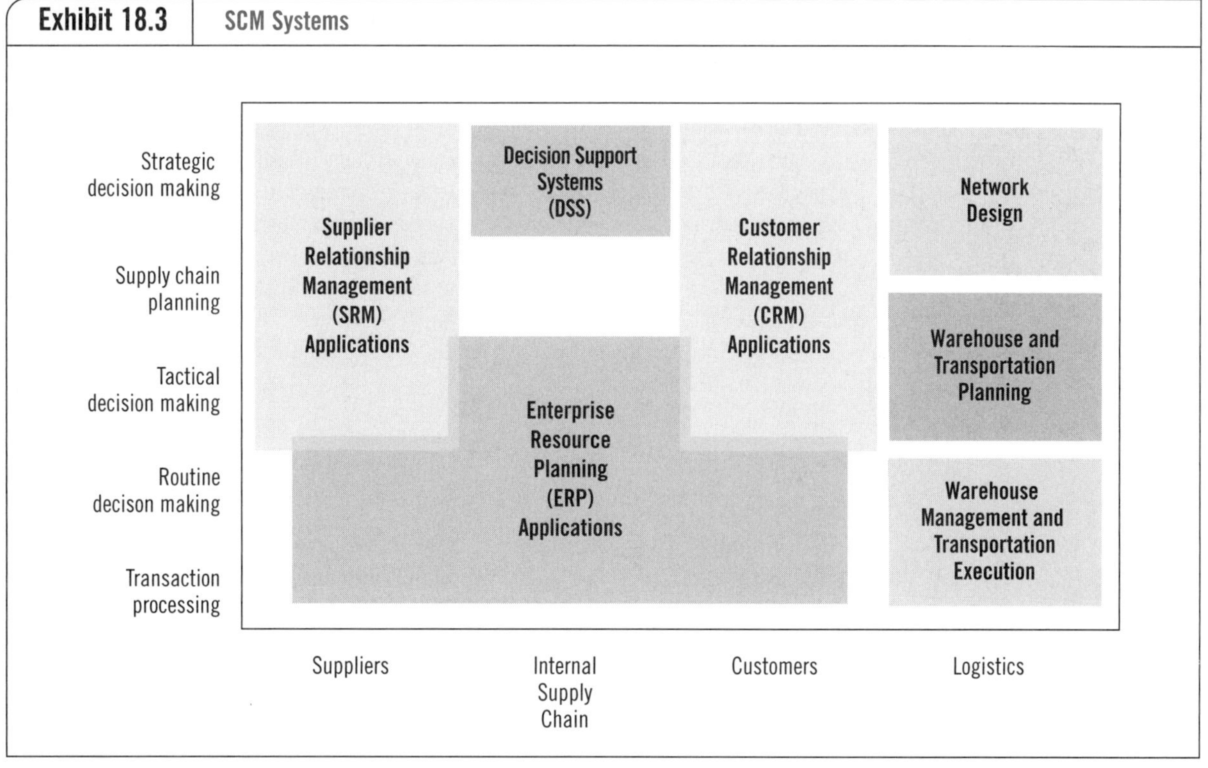

Sourcing Snapshot

Invisible Supplier Has Penney's Shirts All Buttoned Up

On a Saturday afternoon in August 2003, Carolyn Thurmond walked into a JC Penney store in Atlanta and bought a white Stafford wrinkle-free dress shirt for her husband, size 17 neck, 34/35 sleeve. On Monday morning a computer technician in Hong Kong downloaded a record of the sale. By Wednesday afternoon, a factory worker in Taiwan had packed an identical replacement shirt into a bundle to be shipped back to the Atlanta store. The speedy process, part of a streamlined supply chain and production system for dress shirts that was years in the making, has put Penney at the forefront of the continuing revolution in U.S. retailing. In an industry where the goal is speedy turnaround of merchandise, Penney stores now hold almost no extra inventory of house-brand dress shirts. Less than a decade ago, Penney would have had thousands of them warehoused across the United States, tying up capital and slowly going out of style. The entire program is designed and operated by TAL Apparel Ltd., a closely held Hong Kong shirtmaker. TAL collects point-of-sale data for Penney's shirts directly from its stores in North America, then runs the numbers through a computer model it designed. The Hong Kong company then decides how many shirts to make, and in what styles, colors, and sizes. The manufacturer sends the shirts directly to each Penney store, bypassing the retailer's warehouses—and no corporate decision makers. Penney and other retailers such as Brooks Brothers and Lands' End have been willing to turn over these decisions because TAL can do them better and more cheaply. With decisions made at the factory, TAL can respond instantly to changes in consumer demand, stepping up production if there is a spike in sales or dialing it down if there's a slump. The system "directly links the manufacturer to the customer," says Rod Birkins, vice president for sourcing of JC Penney Private Brands Inc. To develop this system, TAL designed a computer model to estimate an ideal inventory of house-brand shirts for each of Penney's 1,040 North American stores, by style, color, and size. Penney provided TAL with goals for how often a store's inventory should be replenished, then stepped back and let it do the rest. TAL's computer model began to outpace the Penney system still used for the retailer's other merchandise. For some shirt models, stores could not keep half as much in stock as they had previously. The system hasn't been flawless, though. On a few occasions, TAL underestimated Penney's needs significantly, and the factory had to sacrifice other customers to rush out Penney's order first, sending some shirts by air freight to be sure they arrived on time. Costing 10 times as much as ocean shipping, sending shirts by air was "a painful decision," admits Ming Chen, a manager at TAL's factory. "But sometimes you have to decide which customers you're going to take care of."

Source: G. Kahn, "Invisible Supplier Has Penney's Shirts All Buttoned Up," *Wall Street Journal,* September 11, 2003, p. A1.

To understand why this is such a big deal, we have to consider what things looked like in the old days. First, every functional area had its own set of software applications, often running on completely different systems. Sharing information (such as forecasts or customer information) between systems was a nightmare. To make matters worse, the same information often was entered multiple times in different ways. ERP pulled all of these disparate systems into one place.

Exhibit 18.4 Enterprise Systems

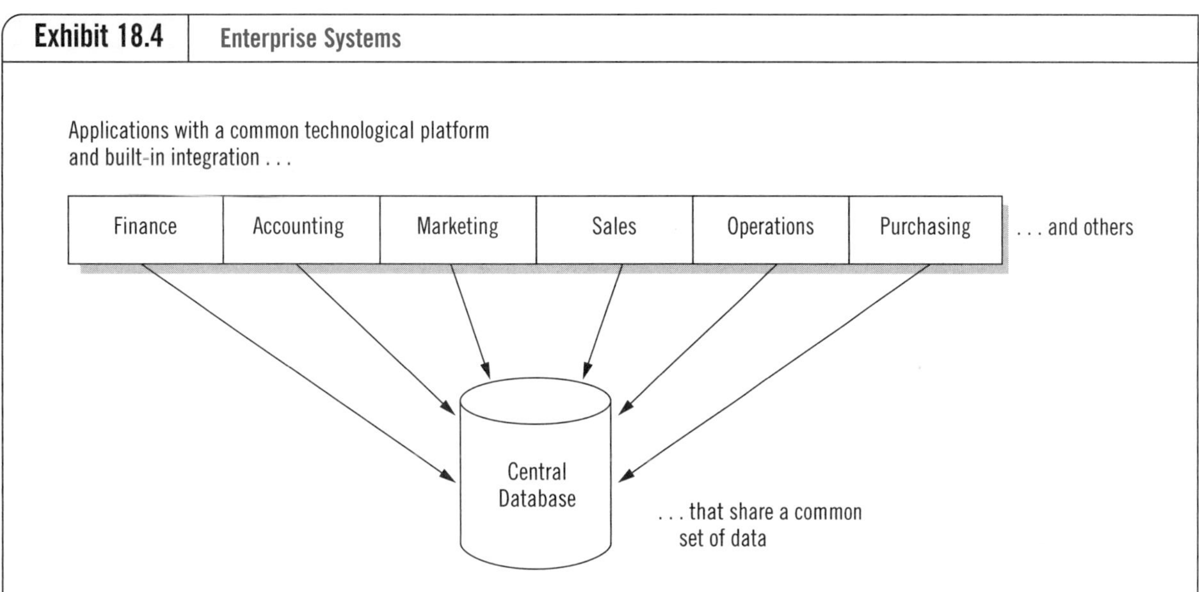

As Exhibit 18.4 suggests, ERP's traditional strengths lie in routine decision making and transaction processing. To the extent that ERP systems support higher-level planning and decision making, these systems tend to focus primarily on internal operations. ERP systems also capture much of the raw data needed to support higher-level decision support systems aimed at strategic decision making.

SRM and CRM applications, in contrast, are directly focused on planning and managing the firm's external linkages. Exhibit 18.5 shows how Chopra and Meindl give examples of the types of functionality provided by these applications.

Currently, vendors specializing in CRM and SRM tend to provide higher levels of functionality in their chosen areas than do the ERP vendors. As a result, many firms choose a standard ERP package for routine decision making and transaction processing, and use bolt-on CRM and SRM applications to manage external relationships.

However, this situation is changing as the major ERP vendors, such as SAP and Oracle, look for ways to increase the CRM and SRM functionality of their own systems. Whether the specialized CRM and SRM vendors can maintain enough of a functionality lead to justify a separate system remains to be seen.

The last set of supply chain IS applications we will discuss are those dealing directly with logistics decisions. These applications can be divided into three main cate-

Exhibit 18.5 SRM/CRM Applications

SRM APPLICATIONS	CRM APPLICATIONS
Design collaboration	Market analysis
Sourcing decisions	Sell process
Negotiations	Order management
Buy process	Call/service center management
Supply collaboration	

gories: network design applications, transportation and warehouse planning systems, and execution systems.

Network design applications address such long-term, strategic questions as where should we locate warehouses, and how large should our transportation fleet be? These applications often make use of simulation and optimization modeling.

Transportation and warehouse planning systems attempt to allocate fixed logistics capacity in the best possible way, given business requirements. For example, such a system could help you decide how many units to ship from each warehouse to each demand point. To find the optimal answer, the system would allow you to build an optimization model that used data on warehouse capacities, demand levels, and shipping costs to generate the lowest-cost solution.

Execution systems kick off and control the movement of materials between supply chain partners. Within a warehouse, for example, sophisticated execution systems tell workers where to store items, where to go to pick them up, and how many to pick. Similarly, bar code systems and global positioning systems have dramatically changed the ability of businesses to manage actual movements in the distribution system. Fifteen years ago, the only thing a trucking firm could tell you was that your shipment was "on the way" and "should be there in a day or two." Now, trucking firms can tell their customers the exact location of a shipment and the arrival time within hours, if not minutes.

As important as these logistics applications are, the level of integration between these applications and those in the other areas of the map is astonishingly weak at present. But what does this mean? For one thing, it means that many supply chain decisions, such as when to order materials and when to ship customer orders, are often made without considering the impact on logistics. Let's look at the experience of an actual firm.

Buyers were ordering materials from suppliers whenever they needed them, without regard to the shipping costs. The result was many small, expensive shipments. Although inventory costs were low, transportation costs were going through the roof. The company determined that by batching up orders over several days, they could place bigger orders with the suppliers. The suppliers, in turn, could make larger, cheaper shipments, and shipping costs were cut by nearly 70%. An unexpected benefit was that the firm also had fewer invoices to deal with, because the supplier would send one invoice with each shipment, whether there were 10 items or 100 items listed.

Increasing the level of integration between logistics and other SCM applications presents firms with both technical and organizational hurdles. On the technical side, efforts to integrate decisions across sales, operations, and distribution increase the complexity of the optimization and simulation models currently used by logistics managers. On the organizational side, firms have to get used to involving logistics personnel earlier in the decision-making process, rather than just calling on them when it is time to make a shipment.

Drivers of New Supply Chain Systems and Applications

As organizations continue to face increasing cost pressure, they are relying more on systems to do the work of people, which in turn increases the productivity of these workers. Productivity is a critical metric of performance that is driving companies to integrate new information systems. As mentioned previously, unlike with the previous generation of dot-com companies, executives are now very careful to develop a solid business case and justify the benefits and payback of investments in new supply chain systems. The primary drivers of these new e-SCM systems include (1) internal and external integration, (2) globalization and communications, (3) data information management, (4) new business processes, (5) replacement of legacy or obsolete systems, and (6) strategic cost management.

Internal and External Strategic Integration

As supply chain members increasingly work together, integration must occur between different functions that are internal to the organization (purchasing, engineering, manufacturing, marketing, logistics, accounting, and so on), as well as between parties that are external to the organization (end customers, third-party logistics firms, retailers, distributors, warehouses, transportation providers, suppliers, agents, financial institutions, and so on). Both types of integration present their own set of challenges. Internal strategic integration requires that all members within a company use the same information system that spans across business sites and functions. This is most often accomplished through a companywide enterprise resource planning system that links these internal groups together via a single integrated set of master records. We will discuss the challenges of ERP later in the chapter. External integration refers to the systems that link external suppliers, distributors, and final customers to the focal company. This integration is needed to forecast demand and balance the levels of supply and demand at different points in the supply chain. Systems used to integrate supply chain members include Internet linkages, network communications, and e-sourcing applications.

Globalization and Communication

Although the notion of a global market is easy to envision, carrying out business in different cultures and geographies is an extremely challenging proposition. Companies require systems that enable them to manage suppliers and customers in all corners of the world, calculate total global logistics costs, increase leverage and component standardization worldwide, and improve communication of strategies across global business units and supply chain partners.

Data Information Management

New forms of servers, telecommunication and wireless applications, and software are enabling companies to do things that were once thought impossible. These systems raise the accuracy, frequency, and speed of communication between suppliers and customers, as well as for internal users. Information systems must be able to effectively filter, analyze, and mine an abundance of data to enable effective decision making. Users must be able to extract from databases the information they need to make better supply chain decisions. This is often achieved through data warehouse systems (described later in the chapter) and associated decision support systems.

New Business Processes

Business processes are constantly being changed in response to a rapidly shifting external environment. Such processes—which include supplier evaluation and selection, negotiation, contracting, co-design efforts, and inventory management—are being mapped, studied, and changed in order to reduce redundancies, delays, and waste. In so doing, organizations can create a rapid response capability that allows them to quickly adapt to their customers' changing needs and control costs whenever possible.

Information systems such as computer networks and ERP are enabling companies to link these processes in a more effective manner.

Replacement of Legacy Systems

As companies adopted systems over time, people became familiar with the new procedures. In so doing, however, companies often adopted a piecemeal approach to system usage, such that each function (accounting, purchasing, engineering) used its own system, which was not linked to other functional systems. These obsolete systems (often called **legacy systems**) have now been integrated into a single enterprise-wide system used by everyone in the supply chain. Promising to solve hardware incompatibilities that existed before and to reduce excessive maintenance and programming costs, the systems are also being adopted to exploit the new hardware technologies emerging in the areas of computer networking, telecommunications, and web-based applications.

Strategic Cost Management

Throughout the complete supply chain cycle, from order fulfillment back to purchasing and order payment, millions of transactions take place between different parties. In the past, these transactions were all done on paper. In order to determine specific cost drivers behind different business processes, companies often estimated costs based on outdated cost accounting systems. New systems promise to automate data capture throughout supply chain systems, thereby automating the transactions that occur in the traditional procurement cycle. Not only will this reduce the costs of operating purchasing and logistics departments, but it will also enable the effective allocation of resources and result in immense reductions in inventory held in warehouses and stockrooms throughout the entire supply chain.

In the remainder of the chapter, we discuss the four primary types of information systems used in managing supply chains: (1) enterprise resource planning, (2) purchasing databases and data warehouses, (3) electronic data interchange, and (4) e-sourcing applications. Although we cannot hope to do justice to the breadth of these topics in one chapter, this is meant as an introduction to them, with the understanding that continual learning and evolution of user needs in these systems is required.

Enterprise Resource Planning Systems

An enterprise resource planning system is an integrated transaction processing and reporting system. The different software applications and forms of ERP support the re-engineering of business processes. Expressed in simpler terms, **ERP systems** provide the means for tracking organizational resources, including people, processes, and technology. The system serves as the backbone to the organization in terms of providing the information and support required for making decisions.

ERP systems add a process logic to an organizational information system and create a fundamental discipline in business processes. Whereas in the past managers and staff were free to make decisions independent of other functional areas, ERP systems effectively force people to interact together in a single system, even if they would prefer not to! As shown in Exhibit 18.6, ERP systems also create a process logic between the closely related areas of customer order management, manufacturing planning and execution, purchasing processes, and financial management and accounting.

In effect, ERP systems enable people in these very different parts of the business to communicate with one another. In an ideal case of moving information across the supply chain, sales representatives enter customer orders directly into a company's ERP via a laptop and modem. The sales reps access the sales order planning and master production schedule. Once the orders are input in the system, the sales reps can provide an available-to-promise report and can inform customers when they can expect order delivery. The master production schedule drives the material requirements system, which automatically generates purchase orders to ensure that suppliers deliver parts, components, and services in time to produce the customer's order.

The material requirements planning module converts material requirements into purchase requisitions that purchasing places with selected suppliers. When the supplier delivers the components, this information is passed through to the scheduling system, which ensures that the components are linked to the specific production order on the shop floor. Once production begins, the salesperson in the field also

Exhibit 18.6 Enterprise Resource Planning Systems

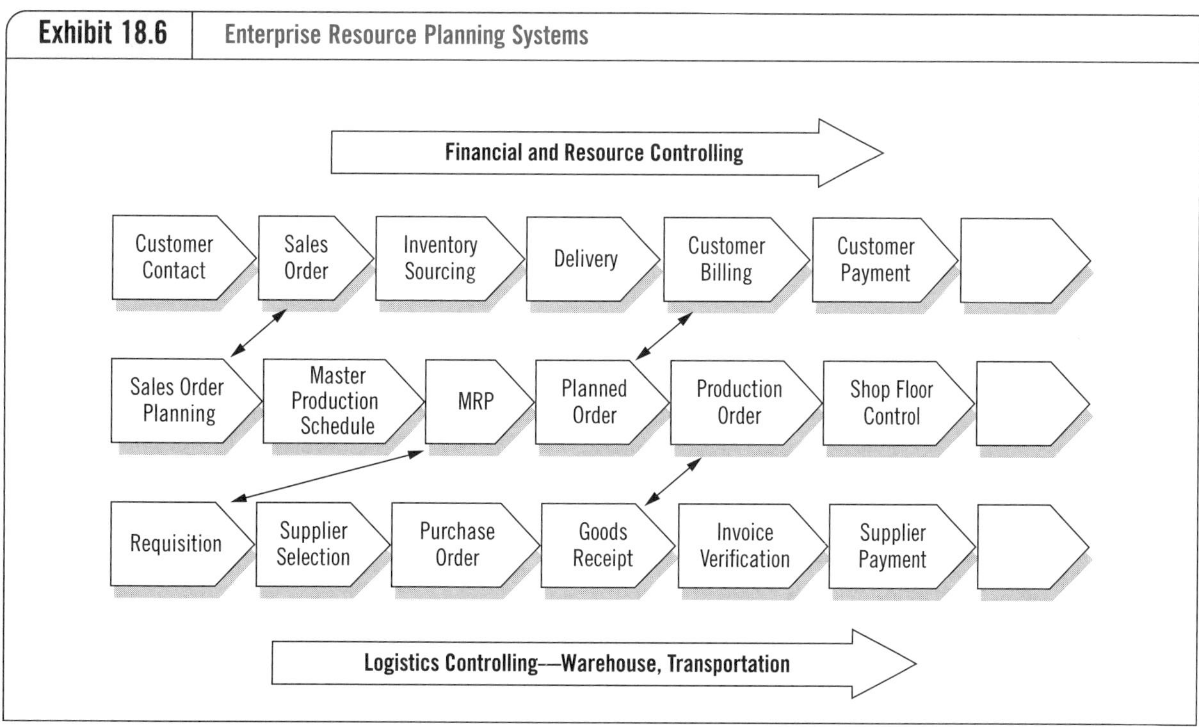

knows that the order will soon be delivered to the customer. Once delivered, customer billing and payment are also automatically generated by the ERP system.

The idea of having a single information system that links sales, production, transportation, warehousing, and purchasing appears to be an inherently obvious way to manage these different business processes. Historically, individual systems were able to fulfill the informational requirements of sales, purchasing, production, and so on, but they were not linked to one another in any way. Most importantly, different legacy systems did not communicate with accounting or financial reporting systems. This made it difficult, if not impossible, to be able to extract cost data to allocate overhead costs to different parts of the business.

A typical ERP system is designed around four primary business processes (see Exhibit 18.6):

1. *Selling a product or service.* Customer order management process
2. *Making a product.* Production planning and execution process
3. *Buying a product.* Procurement process
4. *Costing, paying the bills, collecting.* Financial/management accounting and reporting process (integrated across the prior three processes)

ERP systems facilitate the integration of these processes by adopting a single customer, product, and supplier database. One master record is used for the enterprise with multiple views. All processes use a common database, and information is captured only once, essentially eliminating the possibility of inaccurate data entering the database. Information is rolled down to the affected business process in real time, eliminating delays of information sharing. Visibility of specific transactions taking place in each business process is accessible to everyone in the organization; theoretically, anyone wanting to find out information, such as where an order is in the process or whether a supplier has been paid, can obtain the latest updates by going through the system (instead of making phone calls). In addition, all business processes are linked with the work flow through the use of templates for entering information about transactions at every step.

The actual process of implementing a new ERP system in an environment where people have grown accustomed to using their single, familiar legacy system has proved to be a monumental task in many organizations. Many implementation efforts have turned into multimillion-dollar projects involving consultants residing onsite for months and even years. Why is the task of ERP implementation proving to be so difficult and expensive?

Implementing ERP Systems

When businesses implement an ERP system, they must by definition adhere to a more rigorous set of business processes. Chapter 12 discusses process mapping as a tool to identify what exactly happens within any given business process. Before organizations actually implement ERP, they must first create a process map for every process shown in Exhibit 18.6. When companies actually map what they believe a process looks like, they discover that the actual process is quite different from what they thought it should look like. In some cases, no formal process exists, because everyone in the functional organization has done it his or her own unique way. When it comes time to create an information system around business processes, many companies discover that they must also re-engineer or change their business processes before they can build an information system around them. In some cases, changing these business processes requires a major organizational and cultural shift. Although ERP consultants can effectively create a system around a well-defined business process, they cannot create a system around a business process that has not been well defined or explained to them by employees.

In order to effectively implement an ERP system, a company must go through four steps to ensure that the business processes are effectively re-engineered and improved:

1. Define the current process as is. An ERP implementation team of subject-matter experts document what the current process looks like.
2. Define what the best-in-class business process should be. At this point, the team must have a clear understanding of what the final objective of the process is. Further, they must understand what the ERP system will replace and how the benefits are likely to occur.
3. Develop the system. This is an iterative process in which consultants work in conjunction with those managers who are most familiar with the business processes in question.
4. Work through all final bugs and then flip the switch. A danger that often exists when flipping the switch—switching over from the old system to the new system—is that the company may not be ready for the change, or the system may not be completely configured to handle the specific activities that keep the business running.

Sourcing Snapshot: A Consultant's Views on Navigating ERP Implementations provides a detailed implementation strategy from the perspective of one ERP consulting firm. The seven-stage process provides the basis for implementing these complex systems.

Sourcing Snapshot

A Consultant's Views on Navigating ERP Implementations

Abide Consulting, a Florida-based consulting firm, has worked with several organizations to assist in the transition from disparate legacy-based systems to an integrated ERP system. Currently, Premier International is working with a consumer products organization to coordinate the worldwide implementation of an ERP system. What follows is a detailed look at one strategy for ERP implementation.

The typical life cycle of an ERP implementation utilizes a seven-stage process. The cycle involves the following phases: (1) discovery; (2) design; (3) system build-out; (4) testing; (5) end user training; (6) cutover; and (7) post-cutover support. The stages are shown in Exhibit 18.7 on p. 680.

In the *discovery phase,* a core team is assembled consisting of both internal and external subject-matter experts. Teams are typically grouped into work streams of the functional areas being implemented in the ERP system (e.g., operations, inventory management, finance, sourcing). Training sessions bring the team up to speed on strategic objectives of the project, time lines, project organization and process, new software functionality, and so on. The team then begins a detailed analysis and review of the existing business processes.

Exhibit 18.7 ERP Implementation Life Cycle

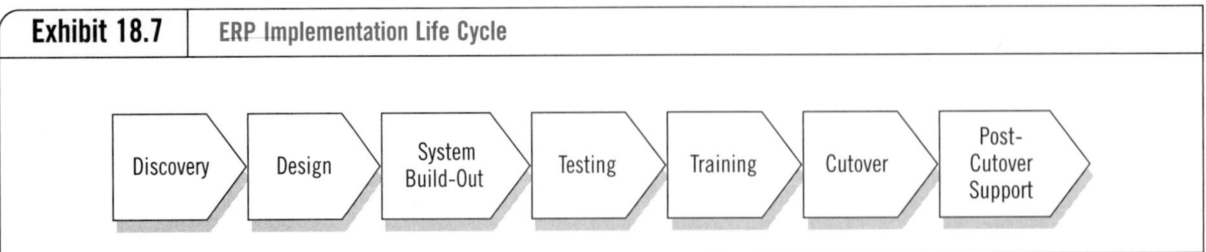

On larger, more complex ERP implementations, it is also recommended that significant attention be focused on the data and data delivery processes. Data integrity (consistency of data within or across systems) and data quality (accuracy and completeness of data) are critical components of an ERP implementation and can often be overlooked. For example, at a previous client, it was discovered the first day live on the new ERP system that the finished product weight data were inaccurate and in many cases missing altogether. Weights for shipping manifests could not be calculated. The situation brought outbound shipping to a standstill. Trucks and product sat idle in the shipping docks for days until the issue was resolved.

Next, in the *design phase,* the new processes "to be" required to support the ERP system are developed and process flow mappings are created. Any process requiring IT involvement is documented in a functional specification. These include reports, integrations, conversions, and enhancements (RICE elements). Next a fit/gap analysis is conducted, which involves finding out the difference between the existing systems and the new ERP design. Finally, once the core team has identified and resolved the fit/gaps, it is able to define and document the detail scope of the ERP solution required for the business.

The third step is the *build phase.* In this phase, the IT team begins to take a larger role in the implementation. The ERP system is configured with functional parameters and customized business data (company branch plants, financial chart of accounts, and so on) The IT team completes the initial development of the RICE elements that were defined in the design phase.

A typical *testing phase* will involve several iterations of testing business processes and RICE elements associated with the new ERP system. Unit testing and conference room pilots (CRPs) involve executing scripts isolated to a specific business process or RICE element. If the tests are successful then an integrated conference room pilot (iCRP) is performed. The iCRP involves executing end-to-end scripts across business processes and work streams (e.g., plan to make, make to deliver). Finally, key users of the system are given access to test their business process in the new system (referred to as user acceptance testing). Key users involve many functional departments along the supply chain including sourcing, inventory control, production planning, and customer service.

End user *training* can be performed exclusively by outside consultants, a mix of external and internal personnel, or strictly internally within the organization. The deciding factor as to the method is the extent of ERP implementations at other business units and whether there are internal personnel willing to conduct the training. Oftentimes, to bridge this gap, consultants will perform a train-the-trainers program to initialize the training and build a cadre of trainers within the organization.

During the *cutover phase,* the organization begins to take greater ownership of the ERP system. Throughout the implementation, the organization must have internal champions, who are experts that have the backing of top management to drive the implementation. As with any other change initiative, ERP involves changing people's behavior, and this requires management support. In the cutover phase, both customers and suppliers are contacted to ensure that any and all outstanding issues have been addressed.

All too often, unplanned issues surface internally or at the supplier and customer end immediately after the cutover. Precautionary steps can be taken well in advance of the actual cutover in order to limit risk to business processes. Suppliers, customers, and business partners are notified of the activity to prepare them for any issues or changes. Safety stocks of components and ingredients can be increased. Additionally, some organizations choose to execute a prebuild of finished stock, where production is ramped up over normal demand.

Data integrity issues also provide unplanned surprises.

In the last phase (*post-cutover support*), the core implementation team resolves post-implementation problems and software failures, and conducts process upgrades. It is important that the organization discuss the expected role of the consultants and the software provider in the post-cutover phase during contract negotiations.

In summary, successful ERP implementation is a journey, not a destination. There are several key issues that will enhance the experience of the journey and reduce both costs and risks. These include the following:

- Develop a good understanding of the existing business process
- Develop improved future business process designs
- Identify inconsistencies and poor quality in existing data
- Ensure that business processes conform to ERP system parameters
- Insist that users replace redundant legacy systems
- Stagger implementations of ERP systems across regions and business locations
- Schedule cutover during off-peak seasons
- Determine how much additional safety stock is necessary
- Develop and train a core team of internal personnel as resources
- Execute rigorous and structured testing cycles

Source: Interview with Matthew Giunipero, Senior Manager, Abide Consulting, and Karina Jarzec, Demand Planning Specialist, July 2007.

Purchasing Databases and Data Warehouses

A prerequisite needed before introducing any type of ERP system that manipulates data is the development of a reliable **database**—an integrated collection of computer files capable of storing operational data essential for managing a department.

Databases are highly efficient in the storage and retrieval of data because there is minimal overlapping of information between the files. Reduced redundancy of information between files allows different systems to cross-reference and efficiently use the data contained in all files.[5] In the past, different user groups could share data from the files as needed but gain access only to the data necessary to support their system needs. The new forms of ERP systems are allowing more users from functional groups other than purchasing to access these files.

Although definitions vary, a **data warehouse** is generally thought of as a decision support tool for collecting information from multiple sources and making that information available to end users in a consolidated, consistent manner. Rather than trying to develop one unified system or linking all systems in terms of processing, a data warehouse provides the means to combine the data in one place and make it available to all of the systems.

In most cases, a data warehouse is a consolidated database maintained separately from an organization's production system databases. Many organizations have multiple databases, often containing duplicate data. A data warehouse, in theory, is organized around informational subjects rather than specific business processes. The data warehouse stores, in a format that is readily accessible by end users, data fed to it from multiple production databases. Data held in data warehouses are time-dependent, historical data; they may also be aggregated. For example, separate production systems may track sales and coupon mailings. Combining data from these different systems may yield insights into the effectiveness of coupon sales promotions that would not be immediately evident from the output data of either system alone. Integrated within a data warehouse, however, such information could be easily extracted.

Purchasing processes require a variety of information maintained on different databases, which make data warehouses very useful. The purchasing system must be able to pull data from and store data into the host data file. If a proposed purchasing system requires nonexistent data, then a new database must collect and store the information.

A basic purchasing system requires, at a minimum, access to a number of databases or files. A file may be a collection of specific data, sorted in alphanumeric order or by criteria chosen by the user. Examples of some of these files include the following:

- *Part file.* Records the part numbers or stockkeeping units (SKUs) that all firms rely on to identify the thousands of unique purchased entities within a system. The actual content of the part file is a function of a firm's specific informational requirements. The time required to capture information on part numbers and enter them into a database can be significant.
- *Supplier name and address file.* Contains the names and addresses (including e-mail addresses) of every supplier with which a firm does business.
- *Historical usage file.* Stores historical usage by part number and using location. This information supports inventory analysis and updating of material forecasts with actual historical data.
- *Open-order and past-due file.* Maintains the status of open material releases and stores an order as pending until a firm physically receives the scheduled release. Any orders not received by their due date become past due. This file provides data that a buyer or material planner requires to maintain visibility and control of the material pipeline.
- *Bill of material file.* Details the component requirements of a part number. It is an integral part of the material requirements planning system. If the material system generates a release for an end-item or subassembly part number, then the system must also generate releases for all components as well. This file also provides visibility about sourcing requirements for new parts with components.
- *Engineering requirements file.* Provides visibility to the specific engineering requirements and specifications for a part number. May also include updates

or engineering change orders detailing changes to specific SKUs or requirements over time.

- *Forecasted demand file.* Calculates anticipated demand requirements for each part number in the part file. It relies on the historical usage file to update and calculate projected future requirements.

These databases support the development of both basic and sophisticated purchasing and material information systems. Although purchasing is not responsible for directly maintaining all of the data on these files, it must have access to the data to support its operating requirements.

Technology for Electronic Communication between Buyers and Sellers

Up until now, we have discussed elements of purchasing information and data flows that reside primarily within the enterprise. Clearly, however, purchasing must communicate effectively with external suppliers to be able to share information, forecasts, and updates, and to make payments and so on. Traditional information flows between buyers and suppliers often necessitate a lengthy sequential process composed of multiple steps required to support the servicing as well as the fulfillment of the order. Examples of these information flows include:

- Transmission of the product specifications from buyer to supplier
- Submission of a bid
- Acceptance of the contract
- Inspection and receipt of documents associated with the shipment
- Accounting audits
- Submission of payment

Some of the problems that occur within these traditional information flows include increased transaction time, low accuracy due to data-handling errors, high utilization of staff time and resources, and increased uncertainty in the form of both mailing and processing delays. Although many companies rely on e-mail as a tried-and-true communication method, there are a number of other technologies that allow purchasing to communicate effectively with external suppliers.

Electronic Data Interchange

An early approach to facilitating transactions electronically was electronic data interchange—a communications standard that supports interorganizational electronic exchange of common business documents and information. First implemented in the 1980s, EDI represented a cooperative effort between buyer and seller to become more competitive by streamlining the communication process through eliminating many of the steps involved in traditional information flows. The basic components of an EDI system include the following:

1. *A standard form (EDI standards).* Includes the basic rules of formatting and syntax agreed upon by the users in the network. The American National

Standards Institute ACS X12 series of EDI standards was one of the first adopted by many companies.

2. *A translation capability (EDI software).* Translates the company-specific database information into EDI standard format for transmission.
3. *A mail service (EDI network).* Responsible for the transmission of the document, usually in the form of a direct network or through a third-party provider. Such a value-added network (VAN) serves as an intermediary post office for the systems.

The process that occurs when buyer and supplier go through an EDI transaction ideally progresses in the following manner:

1. The computer in the buying company monitors the real-time inventory status of the item purchased using technologies such as bar code scanners.
2. When it is determined, according to a predefined reorder criterion, that there is a need to order more of the item, the application program notifies the translation software.
3. An EDI purchase order is created and released against a prenegotiated blanket amount, and the purchase order is sent to the supplier.
4. The supplier's computer receives the order and the EDI software translates the order into the supplier's format.
5. A functional acknowledgment, which indicates receipt of the order, is automatically generated and transmitted back to the buyer.
6. When the original EDI purchase order is created, a number of additional electronic transactions may occur. Bridging software transmits the relevant data to the buyer's accounts payable application, to the buyer's receiving file, to the supplier's warehouse or factory file, and to the supplier's invoicing file.
7. Once the order is filled from the supplier's warehouse or factory, a shipping notice is created and transmitted to the buyer. This shipping notice may require some manual data entry by the shipper. However, this is the first time that any manual keystrokes are required in the entire process.
8. Upon receipt of the goods, a shipping notice is electronically entered into the receiving file. Although additional keying may be required, technology often eliminates this step as well.
9. The receipt notice is transmitted through bridging software to the accounts payable application and to the supplier's invoicing application, whereupon an invoice is electronically generated and transmitted to the buyer.
10. Once the invoice is received by the buyer's computer, it is translated into the buyer's format and the invoice, receiving notice, and purchase order are electronically reconciled (eliminating the need for an accounting audit).
11. A payment authorization is electronically created and transmitted to accounts payable, the receivables application is updated to indicate an open receivable, and payment is transmitted electronically from the buyer's bank to the supplier's bank.
12. An electronic remittance advice is transmitted to the supplier, and upon receipt, this information is translated into accounts receivable and the buyer is given credit for payment.

Within this process, there are only three instances of manual data entry. In traditional information flows, each step would require that paperwork be completed and filed by clerical staff. Thus EDI saves a great deal of time and paperwork—as well as allowing fewer opportunities for errors, no mailing or physical transmission delays, and lower clerical costs.

EDI and the Internet

Despite the promise of greater diffusion of EDI via value-added networks, EDI remained a technology that required significant investment by companies to implement. EDI technology required investment in application-specific hardware that could not be used for other purposes. Because there are service fees associated with VANs, they may be more expensive to use than direct networks. Smaller suppliers in particular found it difficult to justify the investment in EDI technology and struggled with the demands placed on them from different companies to adopt differing EDI systems. Finally, EDI was never considered an interactive mode of communication. Each time a transmission was sent, it implied that a decision had been made: an order for a fixed amount placed, a forecast of future demand fixed, a lead time for delivery specified. There was never any means for the buying and supplying parties to actually interact, collaborate, and reach a decision through joint, bilateral communication. In the last five years, however, Internet technology emerged that has changed business-to-business (B2B) information systems.

As shown in Exhibit 18.8 on p. 686, the Internet facilitates collaboration between parties in the supply chain through a virtual private network. A virtual private network is similar to a VAN, but is hosted on a third party's website and server, and does not require any significant investment on the part of either buyer or supplier. Instead of having to invest in a significant amount of hard technology, a supplier can be connected to a large customer through EDI simply by having a computer, a modem, and software. In other cases, a T1 line may be used to transmit higher volumes of data. A T1 line is a high-speed optical network line that enables quicker response time when a user goes online. Ford, for example, has offered to connect their suppliers to the Internet for as little as $8 a month, which they recover in improved communication with their supply base.

Let's look at an example to see the way this system works. Suppose a supplier wishes to notify a customer that it is shipping an order. First, a local Internet service provider creates a virtual private tunnel using tunneling protocols—essentially the alphabet and rules of grammar that allow different systems to work together—including PPTP, L@F, L2TP, and others, which may be clustered around different industry groups. For example, many high-tech companies have adopted rosettanet (http://www.rosettanet.org), whereas U.S. automotive companies are adopting protocols established by the Automotive Industry Action Group (http://www.aiag.org). Using this protocol, data are transferred over the Internet from the supplier to the customer's router at its headquarters. The router at headquarters strips off the tunneling protocols and forwards transmission to a local area network and then to the right individuals. When the customer wishes to place an order with the supplier, the reverse process takes place.

Internet EDI is certainly an important application providing numerous benefits. This approach is typically much less expensive than a traditional, hard-wired EDI system and presents fewer standards issues, but it also typically requires a common

Exhibit 18.8 Internet EDI with Virtual Private Networks (VPNs)

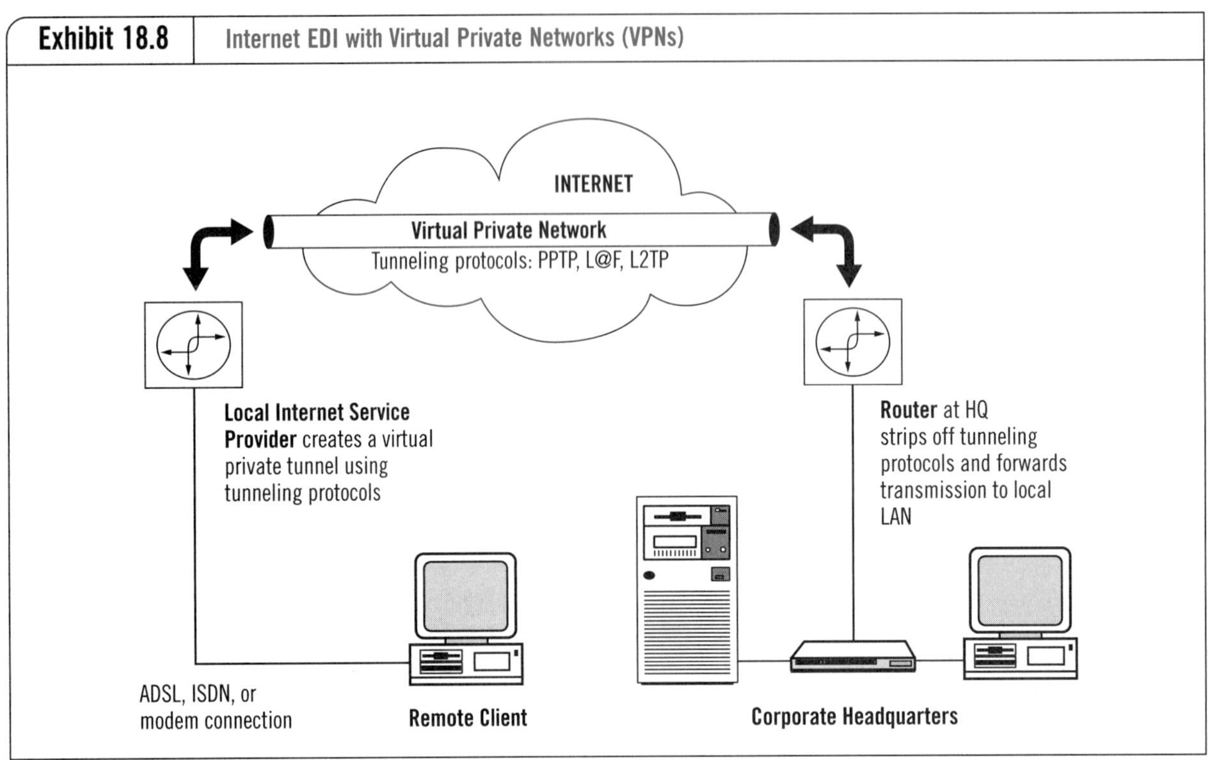

platform on either end (e.g., common ERP systems). The tunneling protocol used helps to address security concerns that users may have when relying on the Internet to transmit data. However, the true benefits of the Internet go far beyond this. In fact, the Internet enables buyers and suppliers to achieve a level of collaboration that extends far beyond EDI technology as it was originally conceived.

E-Sourcing Suites

E-tools used by purchasers can be used to communicate within and outside the organization. As we have studied in previous chapters, a major goal of purchasing is to communicate effectively with external suppliers to be able to source items; share information, forecasts, and updates; make payments; and so on. Traditional information flows between buyers and suppliers often necessitate a lengthy sequential process composed of multiple steps required to service as well as fulfill the order. Examples of these information flows include transmission of the product specifications from buyer to supplier, submission of a bid, acceptance of the contract, inspection and receiving documents associated with the shipment, accounting audits, and submission of payment. Some of the problems that occur within these traditional information flows include increased transaction time, low accuracy due to data-handling errors, high utilization of staff time and resources, and increased uncertainty in the form of both mailing and processing delays. **E-sourcing tools** are defined as a set of tools employed by supply managers to streamline processes and leverage technology in order to meet the needs of the organization.[6] Supplier relationship management tools are e-sourcing tools that allow the purchaser to manage the external linkage with suppliers. Although earlier versions of e-sourcing tools were directed more toward process efficiencies (streamlining the purchase order process), SRM tools are focused on managing the entire purchasing cycle from recognition of need through contract management and supplier evaluation. Prior to discussing SRM tools, we will cover some of the basic e-sourcing tools.

E-Sourcing Basics

E-Sourcing Models

There are basically three major types of e-sourcing business models: (1) sell-side systems, (2) buy-side systems, and (3) third-party marketplaces. A brief explanation of each is presented in the following paragraphs.

Sell-side systems contain the products or services of one or more suppliers. Registration on sell-side sites is usually free and the supplier guarantees the security of the site.[7] Most suppliers today have a web presence and many offer the ability to place orders on their sites. Sell-side systems have the advantages of no investment by the buyer, ease of access, and the availability of many suppliers. Drawbacks include the inability to track or control spending by the buying organization and varying degrees of security.[8] A much-used sell-side site in the MRO area is www.grainger.com.

Buy-side systems are controlled by buyers and are tied into their intranets and extranets. These buy-side systems can be self-developed or acquired through third-party software providers of e-sourcing suites.[9] Buy-side systems allow the supply manager to manage the sourcing cycle, track spend, and exert control over contract management, in a secure environment. They do require an investment by the buying organization and need periodic updating as well as training for users. They are the dominant form of e-sourcing systems used by organizations today.

Third-party marketplaces are independent firms that neither buy nor sell goods but seek to facilitate the electronic purchasing process through value enhancement. These organizations proliferated during the dot boom era of 1999–2001. Essentially, they sought to be an electronic marketplace for the needs of organizational purchasers. Their idea was to bring buyers and sellers together in cyberspace the way Amazon.com did in the consumer world. One group specialized in a commodity such as chemicals or steel; they were termed **vertical portals.** The other group provided a broad category of services, e.g., office supplies or MRO items; they were called **horizontal portals.** The value of most of these horizontal portal models faded as traditional business firms developed a web presence through sell-side sites (e.g., officedepot.com and mcmastercarr.com). Some specialized vertical portals survived and evolved and provide value through their superior market knowledge. One example is http://www.paperexchange.com.pk/, a firm that serves the worldwide market for pulp and paper. Others such as newview.com, formerly esteel.com, have survived by developing and marketing software to the industries they formerly served.

Supplier Relationship Management

SRM systems are typically organized around specific modules that interact with different elements of the purchasing database, elements of the enterprise resource system, and integration of data obtained through external EDI or Internet-based communications with suppliers or customers. Although ERP systems such as SAP and Oracle generally manage the internal transactions that take place in processing invoices and purchase orders (as described in Chapter 2), e-sourcing systems are focused on decision support around a broader group of transactions that are specific to certain business processes.

SRM systems have capabilities to allow purchasers to make improved decisions. Decision support systems use both data and structured mathematical models to support the decision-making process. A set of SRM sourcing modules act as an interactive system designed to support purchasing managers in making effective decisions concerning supplier selection, contract management, contract compliance, and so on.

This section describes some typical characteristics of SRM systems, which may nevertheless be used by all functions in the organization. We have classified the primary forms of e-sourcing/supply systems as follows:

- Spend analysis
- Sourcing
  - Request for quotation processing
  - Reverse auctions (R/As)
  - Bid optimization
  - Negotiation and total cost support
  - Purchase order issuance
  - Receiving and inspection
- Contract management and compliance
- Supplier performance measurement and control
- Total cost reporting
  - Price forecasting

Spend Analysis

Spend analysis is the determination of the dollar amount and volume of expenditures that an organization makes to provide its products and services and support its operations. The goal of spend analysis is to determine what goods and services are purchased, what suppliers they are purchased from, and where the demand for the items originates in the organization. Once a baseline of spending is established, the organization can effectively look at opportunities to reduce spending. Such spending reduction occurs through multiple strategies such as (1) consolidation of similar purchases; (2) reduction in the number of suppliers; (3) reduction of maverick spend; (4) reduction of spend by other departments such as human resources, marketing, and finance; (5) increased use of more efficient contracting methods; and (6) the development of contracting methods to reduce risk and increase supply assurance.

Spend analysis data is usually derived from a combination of existing purchase orders and accounts payables records. Typically, organizations (1) collect at least one year of spend data, (2) develop similar categories of spend, (3) assign spend to the categories, and (4) develop various strategies. Once collected, these data are entered into the spend analysis module and can be analyzed in an unlimited number of ways.

Sourcing

Sourcing modules usually contain several phases of the sourcing process, including the request for quotation (RFQ), reverse auctions, e-bid optimization, e-purchase order issuance, and receiving and inspection.

Request for Quotation

The request for quotation module is the direct responsibility of purchasing. Most software providers call this process the eRFx module. The eRFx module includes a request for information, request for proposal, and request for quotation. Because different organizations have alternate uses for these terms, we will use "RFQ" as our term for the quotation module.

An **RFQ** is a request to submit a proposal based on a set of specifications provided by a buyer. This module assists in identifying qualified suppliers to receive RFQ requests.

This module automatically generates, issues, and tracks the progress of the RFQs throughout the system. Usually the buyer has a strategy underlying the RFQ that will be facilitated by the software.

E-Bid Optimization

E-bid optimization is a software tool that extends the traditional bid process to permit suppliers to configure their bids in any number of alternative ways. The flexible bidding process is often termed **expressive bidding** because suppliers can bid in ways that emphasize their strengths. Traditionally, suppliers have had to quote per the buyer's request or the bid would be ruled nonresponsive. E-bid optimization is an advanced sourcing solution that provides a tool for buyers to increase their analytical capabilities in reviewing bids and in realizing more optimal solutions. This software module uses a basic set of mathematical algorithms to assist a buyer when evaluating different supply and cost scenarios.

For additional information on this emerging technology, readers are encouraged to visit the websites of CombineNet (www.combinenet.com), Emptoris (www.emptoris.com), and Iasta (www.iasta.com).

Reverse Auctions

Of all the technologies that have impacted e-sourcing, none are more publicized or controversial than **reverse auctions**. Suppliers claim that buyers evaluate them solely on price and forget all the other nonprice benefits they have provided over time. This need not be the case; Sourcing Snapshot: Reverse Auctions and Buyer-Seller Relationships summarizes research that shows that buyers can use reverse auctions and have relationships with suppliers. Reverse auctions are electronic processes where multiple sellers of a product are vying for the business of a single buyer, resulting in the price being driven down. Bidding continues until a pre-established bidding period ends or until no seller is willing to bid any lower, whichever comes first. In a **regular reverse auction**, prices are revealed to all sellers; however, the identity of the competitors remains anonymous. In a **rank reverse auction**, sellers are only told their relative rank and thus are not aware of their competitors' prices.

It is widely acknowledged by buyers that reverse auctions have led to significant cost savings for various buying requirements. The reverse auction tool inexpensively connects buyers and sellers worldwide and supports competitive bidding while driving the price of the item to its true market value.

It is very critical that the reverse auction tool be well integrated with the strategic sourcing process to harness its full potential. The procurement process should be robust to adapt to any changes, incorporate financial controls, drive down costs, and eliminate waste. A successful e-auction requires the development of a preauction

Sourcing Snapshot — *Reverse Auctions and Buyer-Seller Relationships*

Reverse auctions (R/As) have been used in the sourcing process since the mid-1990s, bursting onto the scene led by a new Pittsburgh-based venture appropriately named Free Markets. Suddenly, buyers had a new tool to establish prices during the bidding cycle.

Essentially, a reverse auction is a buyer-initiated bidding event utilizing electronic software that permits price or rank visibility to sellers. The process is conducted in a secure, online environment within a specified time frame with the goal of obtaining a rational market price for the commodity or service being procured. The reverse auction has been touted as a means of reducing the time associated with the supplier selection and award process. One of the major benefits of the time savings associated with reverse auction use is the ability of the supply management professional to devote more effort to strategic sourcing activities. Some of these activities include making in- and outsourcing decisions, strategic cost management, benchmarking, and supplier development. In addition, it is commonly held that the use of reverse auctions results in a reduction in prices paid for products and services.

Despite the proposed benefits associated with reverse auction technology, managers and academicians alike have expressed concern regarding how its use impacts, and is impacted by, buyer-supplier relationships. Some fear the use of reverse auctions tells suppliers that the buying firm is simply looking to extract price reductions without regard to existing or future business relationships, thereby breeding mistrust and lack of cooperation.

Research with 142 experienced purchasing managers (averaging 12 years of experience) was recently conducted to assess the impact of R/As on relationships. The respondents' annual sales ranged from $4.5 million to $45 billion. Total annual purchase expenditures ranged from $1 million to $17 billion. Respondents reported more than 30 different lines of business. Forty-one percent of the sample were managers, which is indicative of their experience level; 59% of the sample were nonmanagers. All had experience with reverse auction use, averaging 22 reverse auctions. Respondents used reverse auctions fairly consistently for both standardized direct materials and indirects (MRO, services, and so on).

The research provided some positive results related to a major concern that reverse auctions threaten buyer-supplier relationships. The results suggest that firms that place higher levels of strategic importance on the relationships with their suppliers opt for relational-type structures to govern the subsequent contract. This supports previous writings that indicate that the offer and execution stages of the reverse auction process should be independent.

In the offer phase of the reverse auction process, explaining the rules accurately to the parties, prior to conducting the actual R/A event, increases the chances of a successful reverse auction. Once the R/A has been completed, the selection of the appropriate form of contract to govern the relationship becomes an independent decision. Thus, purchasers must evaluate the strategic importance of their existing supplier relationship prior to using a reverse auction, clearly explain the rules of the engagement, and establish the appropriate contract form after completing the R/A and selecting the desired supplier.

Price should be a very important element of the R/A selection process but not the only one. The research supports a relational approach when using reverse auctions for relationships that are strategically important.

Supplier cooperation was significantly related to a relational type of contract structure when using reverse auctions. It appears that the supplier's level of cooperation is contingent, at least in part, upon its expectation of continued interaction with the buying firm. When both parties involved in a business relationship expected it to last for an extended period of time, the relationship was characterized by a pattern of cooperation.

Price is the most controversial element of the reverse auction phenomenon. The research strongly supported the view that relational contract structures are negatively related to purchase price reduction. Organizations pursuing a more market-based (bid-and-buy) approach will realize greater savings using reverse auctions than those looking to develop or maintain relationships. Consequently, firms must assess the tradeoff between obtaining lower prices (that may or may not be sustainable) and the opportunity cost of not choosing suppliers that can provide assistance in vital non-price-related areas (e.g., product design) when designing the appropriate R/A structure.

The use of reverse auctions will provide the buyer time savings, which could be used to pursue higher value-added or more strategic activities. However, these additional time savings will be mitigated by the increased time required to build and maintain relationships. Given the need to perform more value-added duties, purchasers must carefully select suppliers with whom they enter into relational governance. What the purchaser chooses to do with the time savings realized by reverse auction use is important because employing a relational form of governance structure is time consuming. Consequently, not all suppliers can be managed using a relational approach. Many reverse auctions will continue to be conducted for the sole purpose of obtaining lower prices and will be governed in an arm's-length manner.

Overall, the research model has demonstrated that purchasers can implement relational governance mechanisms and still use reverse auctions. These relational governance mechanisms will ensure increased levels of supplier cooperation. However, this increased cooperation comes at a cost to the buyer: lower purchase price savings and time savings. If the time savings attributed to reverse auction use is dedicated to building improved relationships, which ultimately lead to lower costs, better service, and higher quality, then both parties win.

Conversely, if the purchaser uses reverse auctions to pursue a more market-based bid-and-buy strategy, firms will benefit from increased purchase price savings and realize greater time savings, but this will be at the expense of supplier cooperation. Hence, much of this time savings may be used to monitor the supplier's performance to ensure that the actual savings attributed to reduced purchases prices are realized. Overall, much of the interest in reverse auctions is due to their ability to result in price reductions for the buying firm; the model indicates there are relational benefits that may outweigh temporary reductions in purchase price.

Source: D. Pearcy, L. Giunipero, and A. Wilson, "A Model of Relational Governance in Reverse Auctions," *Journal of Supply Chain Management,* Winter 2007, pp. 4–15.

strategy, which sets goals, targets specific potential partners, and clearly lays out the applicable rules to be followed throughout. The process normally follows these loose steps:[10]

1. The purchasing company decides which contracts (products, materials, services) would benefit from reverse auction procurement.
2. Suppliers are initially evaluated and invited to participate in the bidding process. The list of suppliers contains companies formally accepted through quality and performance criteria, along with potential suppliers that have been

researched and approved. Oftentimes the market research is conducted by the website hosting the reverse auction.

3. The company writes the request for quotation and sends it through e-mail to all qualified suppliers. Accompanying the RFQ is other pertinent information such as when and where the bidding will take place and auctioning rules and etiquette.
4. The bidding process begins at a certain time and usually lasts no more than 30 minutes. This portion can be open, where all competitors can see other bids, or it can be closed, where buyers are not able to see other bids. The supplier identities are always kept confidential during bidding.
5. The company then analyzes the auction and awards the business to the chosen supplier. This supplier is not necessarily the lowest bidder.

Reverse auction technology is readily available today from a number of sources. It can be self-service, where the technology is downloaded from the software provider; the buying organization trains the suppliers, sets up the auction, and conducts it by itself. A software provider full-service model is also available. In this model the software provider helps the organization with selection of the commodity, assists in qualifying suppliers, conducts training, and runs the reverse auction for the firm. The relative level of experience with reverse auctions is the single most important factor in whether to use a self-service or full-service model.

Negotiation and Total Cost Support Models

Different e-sourcing systems can aid purchasers to estimate the total cost of ownership for products and services. These models incorporate shipping, freight, duty, imports and tariffs, inventory costs, and quality costs.

Purchase Order Issuance

This module supports the generation of purchase orders, which involves the automatic assignment of purchase order numbers for selected items along with the transfer of purchase order information to the proper database(s). This module provides purchasing with visibility to current purchase orders on file.

Receiving and Inspection

The receiving and inspection module updates system records upon receipt of an item. Most systems hold a received item in a protected state (unavailable for use) until all inbound processing is complete. Sophisticated systems are able to do this via a bar code reader that automatically transmits all necessary information to the database. This processing includes tasks such as inspection (if required), material transfer, and stockkeeping. Systems can also send alerts to key stakeholders when there are potential stockouts or imminent shortages.

Contract Management and Compliance

Contract management and compliance provides oversight of the back end of the sourcing process. Once a source is selected and the contract terms negotiated, there is a need to manage the contract to ensure that suppliers and users are in compliance with established contract terms. Other challenges faced with manual contract management systems are pricing compliance; changes in terms, volume discount thresholds, payment schedules, and due dates; and contingencies for nonperformance. Reliable contract management systems provide the ability to keep these issues current with real-time data collection capabilities. These real-time capabilities ensure that the buying organization will realize the full potential of the negotiated terms of the contract.

Software provider Emptoris describes its contract management tool as combining powerful contract authoring, negotiation, and approval processes with contract administration, enterprise reporting, and proven controls, in an easy-to use interface. It enables companies to optimize contract management processes while managing payment obligations and capitalizing on profit opportunities to ensure that supplier management strategies are achieving their full potential.[11]

Supplier Performance Measurement and Control

This module provides visibility to open-item status, and measures and analyzes supplier performance. Electronic supplier scorecards may also be updated electronically. The key features include automatic inquiry of item status, monitoring of order due dates, and analysis of supplier performance. This module should have the capability to monitor planned receipts against due dates, provide immediate visibility to past-due items, and flag those items likely to become past due. The system should generate summary reports of supplier performance compared against predetermined performance criteria, which may include due-date compliance, quality ratings, price variances, quantity discrepancies, and total transportation charges.

Key performance indicators are developed that can highlight hidden additional costs created by poor quality, delivery, and service issues. Supplier performance modules provide several benefits including (1) input into supplier selection considering total costs, not just price; (2) isolating supplier process inefficiencies; (3) improving total cycle times; and (4) providing suppliers with reliable feedback on their historical performance.

Total Cost Reporting

A well-designed e-sourcing system has the ability to generate timely management reports, providing visibility to the entire materials process. In creating these total cost reports, more and more companies are turning to data warehouses (described earlier).

Most systems have the capability to generate new reports, assuming data are available or can be generated by using other data. Another capability of a well-designed system is that the frequency of data reporting and system updating matches a user's operational needs. A system that operates in a real-time environment provides the most current data. **Real-time updating** is a process in which all data files that include a specific address are automatically updated within the system. In contrast to real-time updating is the **data bucket**—a process of storing each transaction in a temporary file and updating the system at scheduled times throughout the day or on a weekly basis. **Batch updating** refers to the process of downloading all data buckets into the main system on a regularly scheduled basis.

Price Forecasting

Price forecasting requires the construction of a model to identify the variables affecting an item's price, including the length of an item's product life cycle, the life cycle stage the item is in, and the item's price history. Life cycle cost curves can forecast expected price performance through time. Purchasing can use these projections to develop budget projections.

E-Sourcing and Supply: Fully Integrated Systems[12]

Although we discussed ERP systems and e-sourcing systems separately in this chapter, it would be a mistake for readers to think that these systems are already integrated. ERP systems often work independently of decisions made by managers using the web to order materials and transmit forecasts. In the future, we will see a change, with increased integration between standalone ERP systems, the systems used to make decisions on sourcing strategies, and the systems that communicate information along the supply chain between customers and the buying organization and its suppliers. We are likely to witness a convergence of customer-focused applications that link suppliers with internal production schedules and production schedules between different plants in a single enterprise.

Requirements between plants will be consolidated and communicated to suppliers via a supply chain planning module, and these schedules will be linked forward to customers. Sales representatives in the field will be able to promise exact delivery dates to customers using an available-to-promise module, a system that allows salespeople to access plant schedules and determine if enough capacity is available to produce the product for the customer by a certain date, and also whether suppliers will be able to deliver the materials in time to produce it.

In addition, we may see other modules facilitate transactions between buyers and suppliers. A distribution planning module will help identify the transportation requirements and distribution center inventory levels in time to meet customers' delivery requirements. A demand planning module will help identify whether long-term capacity requirements will be sufficient to meet the demand for new products coming onstream. Finally, a supplier collaboration module will help ensure that future supplier capacity requirements will be in place to meet future demand requirements for new products and services. In effect, these linked systems will enable a single view of the entire supply chain. Managers can analyze the factory and the supply chain simultaneously, and synchronize demand and supply. Distribution centers will act as a shock absorber for customer demand variability and will help to facilitate stable production schedules at the plants, thereby collapsing the cycles. These types of systems are only now beginning to emerge. Sourcing Snapshot: The Top 10 Emerging Technologies in Supply Management discusses some of the exciting new emerging technologies that will begin to be available to sourcing professionals in the coming years.

One of the most important elements that will lead to the success of e-supply chain applications is the concept of information visibility. We will discuss the types of systems that enable supply chain information visibility in the remainder of the chapter.

What Is Information Visibility?

Information visibility within the supply chain is the process of sharing critical data required to manage the flow of products, services, and information in real time between suppliers and customers. If information is available but cannot be accessed by the parties most able to react to a given situation, its value degrades exponentially.

Sourcing Snapshot

The Top 10 Emerging Technologies in Supply Management

Pierre Mitchell of the Hackett Group, in a recent presentation, highlighted 10 emerging technologies for supply management. His top 10 are listed below:

- CRM for procurement
- Guided buying
- Advanced supply planning
- Win-win sourcing optimization
- Design for supply
- Content-enabled analytics
- Portfolio management
- Knowledge networking
- Open systems
- Software as a service

CRM for procurement is a process and set of tools to help supply managers better serve their internal customers. It includes tools such as project planning and scheduling, customer self-service and training, service-level agreements, and customer satisfaction measurement tools. These tools will help supply managers align themselves around the originators of the spend rather than just the supply markets. Users get exactly what they need from suppliers and the supply organization itself.

Guided buying is an e-tool that combines ERP and e-purchasing systems with virtual catalogs, search engines, and web agents to help guide employees to preferred sources of supply and to preferred sourcing processes and personnel. This almost Google-like technology will contain elements of artificial intelligence (AI) and will become smarter over time.

Advanced supply planning tools provide a linkage from sales and operations plans to supply planning and back again. This includes translating demand (volumes and variability) upstream across multiple tiers of the supply chain and improves risk analysis, decisions on hedging tactics, and other supply tradeoff analyses (e.g., make vs. buy, transportation, inventory). It would also identify bottleneck items and their potential impact on revenue and profits (i.e., not just costs).

Win-win sourcing optimization techniques and supporting tools allow suppliers to better match their capabilities with those of the buying firm and create more win-win scenarios and fewer win-lose ones. Rather than using a winner-take-all bidding process geared toward price or cost, or having the buyer guess which lots to create for different suppliers, it allows buyers to open up their market baskets to suppliers that can then do their own demand management to flexibly bid (i.e., choose the multivariate line items that they can best compete on) in order to harness their best capabilities and put their best foot forward, passing on their optimized cost structures to the buyers. This allows true capability discovery versus just forced price discovery in traditional closed bidding or reverse auction formats. (Note: Expressive bidding is covered in this chapter under e-bidding optimization.)

Design for supply is an extension of the product life cycle management process and provides a set of decision support tools to evaluate and manage the early design and sourcing cycles. It allows better reuse of existing designs, evaluation of new or alternative designs, and the ability to assess the cost and feasibility of those designs with respect to the upstream manufacturing and logistics capabilities of internal and external suppliers.

Content-enabled analytics are decision support tools that marry internal supply planning processes with external supplier or market data. These tools would allow the supply manager to do predictive analyses such as price or cost forecasting, profitability planning, and supplier or market risk analysis.

Portfolio management is the process of periodically assessing the software tools and packages that the supply organization possesses. An assessment is then made of the usefulness, degree of use, and capacity of the current systems. Older software packages and those no longer being used will be discontinued. Future needs and newer tools will be evaluated for potential acquisition.

Knowledge networking is the process of using Internet-based collaboration tools and services to better capture and disseminate supply knowledge both internally and externally. It supports the capture and sharing of commodity knowledge or supply best practices in an internal community of experts, an external community of peers, or a buyers' supply chain (i.e., sharing best practices with and among suppliers).

Open systems e-tools allow internal and external technology providers to provide supply managers with quickly developed customized applications that interoperate with software application suites from independent software vendors (ISVs) like SAP and Oracle. The tools themselves can be open-source products (e.g., Coupa is an open-source e-procurement vendor), software that is hosted as a service to provide a certain specific function (e.g., providing a list of potential suppliers based on a commodity code and region), or products that utilize standardized integration over the Internet to harness the specific functionality from applications developed by the ISVs or by the buying firm.

Software as a service is broader term that includes on-demand software that is provided as a hosted Internet service rather than software code shipped on a CD. It is being driven by customers' needs for cheaper and more quickly upgradeable applications. It is putting competitive pressures on large independent software vendors to provide more cost-effective and modularized solutions.

Source: Adapted from "Top 10 Emerging Technologies in Procurement," 2007 Conference Board Procurement Technologies Conference, presented by Pierre Mitchell, Director of Procurement Executive Advisory Program, the Hackett Group.

Increasing information visibility among supply chain participants can help all parties reach their overall goal of increased stockholder value through revenue growth, asset utilization, and cost reduction. To improve responsiveness across their supply chains, companies are exploring the use of collaborative models that share information across multiple tiers of participants in the supply chain: from their supplier's supplier to their customer's customer. These trading partners need to share forecasts, manage inventories, schedule labor, and optimize deliveries, and in so doing they reduce costs, improve productivity, and create greater value for the final customer in the chain. Software programs for business process optimization and for collaborative planning, forecasting, and replenishment are evolving to help companies forecast and plan among partners, manage customer relations, and improve product life cycles and maintenance. Traditional supply chains are rapidly evolving into "dynamic trading networks"[13] comprised of groups of independent business units that share planning and execution information to satisfy demand with an immediate, coordinated response.

Some of the considerations that must be planned for in implementing an information visibility system include the size of the supply base and customer base with which to share information, the criteria for implementation, the content of information shared, and the technology used to share it. Clarifying these issues will help to ensure that all participants have access to the information required to effectively control the flow of materials, manage the level of inventory, fulfill service-level agreements, and meet quality standards as agreed upon in the relationship performance metrics.

Dell's Information Visibility System: The Benchmark

Perhaps no other company has been as successful in implementing information visibility as a competitive strategy as Dell Computer. Dell has fulfilled its commitments to customers through the company's direct model, in which it holds only hours of inventory yet promises customers lead times of five days. Component suppliers that wish to do business with Dell have to hold some level of inventory, because their cycle times are typically much longer than Dell's.[14] For example, if a supplier has a lead time of 45 days and Dell is promising online customers a lead time of 5 days from order placement to delivery, the supplier must have real-time information to meet Dell's strict demands.

Dell has developed a business model that features a lean, build-to-order manufacturing operation. By utilizing the Web, Dell provides its supplier with forecasting information and receives information about the supplier's ability to meet the forecasts. Dell uses i2 Technologies products for demand-fulfillment operations and products from Agile Software for engineering change orders and bill-of-materials management. Communication about engineering changes, component availability, and capacity (in addition to forecasting and inventory data) flows both ways between Dell and its suppliers.

Dell is also able to review suppliers and place web-based orders in their factories in hours. After outsourcing to third-party contract manufacturers, Dell executives realized that many of these manufacturers did not have adequate visibility of customer orders. This was a major driver in the initiative to increase visibility of orders. Dell's build-to-order web-based customer model has become the benchmark for other industries, and organizations such as General Motors, Ford, and General Electric are seeking to create build-to-order models using the Web as the platform for taking customer orders.

Benefits of Information Visibility

Information regarding forecasts, changes in production schedule levels, and ongoing supply chain performance metrics needs to be conveyed by customers to suppliers on a regular basis. Information flows from suppliers to customers can include current order lead times, capacity levels, order status, and inventory levels. There are many benefits of having parties receive this information. Receiving and conveying the correct information will ensure that the suppliers are aware of what needs to be produced while, at the same time, the buying firm is sure that it is possible to receive ordered quantities on time, every time.

The most important benefit of a visibility system is not that the system is able to correct a supply chain problem, but that it allows people to become aware of problems earlier and thus take corrective actions more quickly than they would otherwise. The benefits of information visibility include reduced lead times, improved constraint management, better decision making, lower costs, and increased profits. Although problems such as shortages, changes in customer orders, engineering changes, obsolete inventory, and equipment failures can still occur with a visibility system in place, the effects of these problems are less than if the participants in the supply chain were not made aware of these problems until a later date. In other words, without visibility systems, a $5,000 problem could turn into a $500,000 problem.

When implemented properly, a visibility solution results in the following additional benefits that promote improved supply chain performance:

- Breaks organizational barriers and enables sharing of mission-critical information about business activities and interaction on a near-real-time basis across the supply chain.
- Builds visibility into the supply chain and provides people with a real-time snapshot of supply chain performance metrics.
- Manages by metrics, aligns performance metrics with cross-organizational business processes, and assigns ownership of processes and metrics to specific individuals.
- Reduces the decision cycle process and allows an upstream or downstream participant to respond to market or customer demand in hours or days, not weeks or months.
- Encourages decision-making collaboration and facilitates the ability to make decisions collaboratively on the Internet, bringing relevant internal and external stakeholders into the process.
- Reduces opportunity and problem resolution latency, and measures and monitors supply chain activities iteratively, allowing people to quickly respond to events as they occur.

Conversely, the dangers of poor execution of supply chain processes include increased lead and cycle times, higher costs, and less informed decision making. For example, in the semiconductor industry, a lack of visibility across the supply chain, coupled with inaccurate supply-and-demand forecasting, is hurting the industry's ability to promptly deliver products, efficiently spend capital, and properly manage inventory.[15]

Good Practice Example

Deploying Information Visibility Systems at a Tier 1 Automotive Company[16]

The following is a case example addressing the deployment of an information visibility system, as described by a large first-tier U.S. supplier to the automotive industry.

MOTIVATION FOR INVESTMENT

In the words of the project manager responsible for implementing this system: "We were looking for a tool that gets our company and its supply chain connected via the Internet. We needed to align our supply chain with a simple tool to get our feet wet and start to prepare for the new automotive supply chain: the 10-day car. Information will need to be shared quickly to establish a supply chain to support a one-piece flow. The initial tool is expected to do the following:

- Provide a view of the same information to suppliers and the company
- Display inventory status, schedules, history of transactions
- Provide a reporting capability
- Display alerts to exceptions

- Communicate replenishment triggers
- Rate suppliers
- Support the next generation for EDI
- Display logistics information

Some of the benefits they hoped to achieve by implementing the system included the following:

- Increased customer satisfaction through the supply chain
- Supply chain flexibility
- Decreased inventory
- Decreased number of expediting activities
- Decreased production interruptions or changes
- Increased focus on collaboration and proactive activities

IMPLEMENTATION

Implementing the process required a series of stages. Several software vendors were initially reviewed. The company chose to pilot with one, and then a second. The possibility of developing the software internally was also considered. The criteria used to select the vendor involved several issues. First, purchasing was looking for a provider that wanted to have a relationship. In the words of the purchasing project manager, "We want to use our knowledge of supply chain management to improve the product to benefit us as well as other participants across the supply chain. As a result, cost is a major factor in determining the level of our relationship with our knowledge and their product. We always perform a pilot to let the provider and us test the product and its value proposition. Another key area for us to consider is the service level that is provided. We now look at application services providers as a viable option to lessen the load of our internal IT staff. Finally, we decided to proceed with the pilot. We piloted six sites and about 50 suppliers. After a month, we added three other sites with the same suppliers. Our second pilot used the same plants with some new suppliers and some in common with the original pilot."

PILOT PROGRAM

The project manager described the pilot program as follows:

"In our pilot, we implemented the system in two to four weeks, but it really takes a month or so to get the business processes adjusted and the users familiar with the software. The amount of training required varied at each location. We utilized centralized training sessions where it was applicable. Otherwise, we used site training sessions, and some one-on-one sessions. It was a requirement to have hands-on training with all of the individual users in every situation. The outcome of doing so is that everyone in the organization saw the value of information visibility in its simplest form. We realized that a tool is only as good as the business process execution in the plant and the standardization and acceptance of the process across plants. We also learned that one replenishment method would not work in all situations. Rather, it is better to have several different methods that are executed the same way across the organization. We also recognized that there were entrenched manual processes (e.g., releases and ship schedules) in the suppliers' business processes and that would be difficult to change. The system operates effectively in real time as our system is updated."

BARRIERS AND SOLUTIONS

Several barriers and solutions were encountered along the way, but purchasing was able to overcome them in the following manner:

- *Barrier:* Lack of technical expertise in suppliers. *Solution:* The pilot system was fairly simple, and the provider as well as the company's IT resources provided assistance.
- *Barrier:* Internal resistance. *Solution:* Internal resistance was addressed by saying, "This is a pilot and we want to learn about the software, but also want to determine where our business processes are out of line." In addition, participants were given the opportunity to have input into the system requirements up front.
- *Barrier:* Lack of internal resources. *Solution:* Lack of internal resources was addressed by trying to prove with the pilot that with this new business process, fewer resources would be required. However, this is a constant battle; lack of resources will be a huge issue when looking down the road at full implementation of the system.
- *Barrier:* Lack of top management support and understanding. *Solution:* The company had to do several knowledge-sharing events with its leadership group and some one-on-one sessions as well. It also provides frequent updates on the status. This helps to keep executives up to speed on the progress and prevents problems from occurring.
- *Barrier:* Lack of standards in the technology. *Solution:* The company does not use a common platform. This is in process, but not complete for the pilot. The biggest challenge was the different business processes used across plant locations and within the plants. Training helped to solve this problem.

LESSONS LEARNED

Lessons learned from this pilot implementation included the following:

- Top-down support is absolutely critical. People will not participate initially unless they are told to do so.
- Involvement from all levels of the organization will also help people to participate (functional, business unit leadership, plant leadership).
- Current system transaction processes are not adequate; the company needed to develop new ones.
- Business process execution must be in place. Without a good business process that is executed in a consistent manner, the best system in the world will not solve your problems.

Questions

1. What were the major problems encountered by this company in implementing an IT information visibility system? Were they technical problems or related to dealing with change?
2. What are some of the important lessons learned by this company in terms of change management and implementing new technology?

CONCLUSION

Supply managers must expand their use of information technology to increase both individual and functional performance. The use of web-based applications, ERP systems, and e-sourcing systems can help professional buyers shift attention from routine to strategic tasks. For example, systems that support the making of better supplier selection decisions—one of a firm's most strategic tasks—can reduce or eliminate future supply-base problems. Also, a system that monitors supplier performance can provide timely visibility concerning potential supply problems.

Ordering and implementing new ERP systems requires systematic planning coupled with process and behavioral changes. The final decision about any system usually represents a long-term commitment to the selected features and equipment. Supply managers have access to a very broad range of e-sourcing solutions and must extensively research available tools and software providers and build case studies to support justification for acquiring these systems. It is important to identify systems that not only meet current operating requirements but also have capabilities to meet future needs.

Emerging technologies are supplementing and in some cases replacing current technologies. Many of the strategies being pursued within supply chain organizations will rely on end-to-end supply chain solutions that

- Integrate suppliers and distributors
- Share information
- Link ERP systems to sales personnel in the field
- Outsource manufacturing and logistics systems
- Facilitate supplier, on-site engineering, and maintenance activities

These strategies will require new e-business applications to enable information sharing and, most importantly, provide an effective order fulfillment process with rapid delivery. Although many solutions providers promise these capabilities, in fact they are extremely difficult to deploy. Moreover, many companies lack the fundamental supply chain infrastructure required to be able to apply these technologies across multiple tiers of customers and suppliers.

To learn to crawl before learning to walk and then run, organizations must address the current flawed designs of their existing supply chains and only then build these applications around their re-engineered networks. An e-sourcing application cannot fix the problems associated with an unmanaged or poorly performing supply base, characterized by adversarial relationships, lack of trust, and an unwillingness to share information. Success in e-sourcing requires management commitment, supply management skills that foster strategic sourcing capabilities, key relationship management, and changes to outdated processes that have been embedded in the organizational culture.

Progressive supply managers should always be looking five years ahead to identify system trends, operating requirements, and systems applications. For purchasing to contribute to a firm's performance objectives, it must have the resources and ability to develop world-class information systems supported by leading-edge technology.

KEY TERMS

batch updating, 693
buy-side systems, 687
data bucket, 693
data warehouse, 682
database, 681
decision support systems (DSSs), 670
ERP systems, 676
e-sourcing tools, 686
expressive bidding, 689
horizontal portals, 687
legacy systems, 676
rank reverse auction, 689
real-time updating, 693
regular reverse auction, 689
reverse auctions, 689
RFQ, 689
routine decision making, 670
sell-side systems, 687
strategic decision making, 670
third-party marketplaces, 687
transaction processing, 669
vertical portals, 687

DISCUSSION QUESTIONS

1. Why do you believe there has been such an emphasis on information systems in purchasing transactions in the last 20 years?
2. In your opinion, what was the primary reason why the concept of online exchanges and B2B technology did not take off? In other words, if one of the main assumptions underlying them was incorrect, what was it?
3. Why are ERP systems not typically considered a means to improve external integration?
4. Discuss the seven-stage ERP implementation model. What are some of the barriers that would hinder or lengthen actual ERP implementation time?
5. One executive noted that "ERP systems take too long to implement and are not worth the cost." Do you agree or disagree with this statement? Explain why.
6. Another executive made this comment: "Many of our suppliers are too small to implement ERP systems." Do you think that this situation may change in the future?
7. Why do you believe that reverse auctions are so controversial? Why would you participate in one as a seller? Why would you organize one as a buyer?
8. What is the difference between e-procurement tools discussed in Chapter 2 and e-sourcing tools discussed in this chapter? What is the objective of each type of system?
9. Discuss the major emerging e-sourcing tools and the impact they will have on the supply management function in the future.
10. Discuss the pros and cons associated with the major e-sourcing tools discussed in this chapter.
11. Why should supply management professionals have an understanding of the role of information systems? What is the danger of not keeping up with emerging technology in this area?
12. Imagine walking into the purchasing office of the future. How might you go about completing your tasks for the day using future information technologies?
13. What are the primary benefits associated with information visibility systems and the major barriers associated with implementing them?

ADDITIONAL READINGS

Angeles, R. (2003), "Electronic Supply Chain Partnership: Reconsidering Relationship Attributes in Customer-Supplier Dyads," *Information Resources Management Journal,* 16(3), 59–84.

Antonette, G., Sawchuk, C., and Giunipero, L. (2002), *ePurchasingPlus* (2nd ed.), Goshen, NY: JGC Enterprises.

"Auto Supplier Moves to New Quote Management System" (2002), *Purchasing,* 131(5), S12–S14.

Beall, S., Carter, C., Carter, P., Germer, T., Hendrick, T., Jap, S., Kaufmann, R., Maciejewski, D., Monczka, R., and Peterson, K. (2003), *The Role of Reverse Auctions in Strategic Sourcing,* Tempe, AZ: CAPS Research.

Handfield, R., and Straight, S. (2003), "What Sourcing Channel Is Right for You?" *Supply Chain Management Review,* July/August, 62–68.

Hope-Ross, D., Eschinger, C., and Kyte, A. (2003), "Strategic Sourcing Applications Magic Quadrant," 1Q03, Research Note, Gartner Group.

Kaplan, S., and Sawhney, M. (2000), "E-Hubs: The New B2B Marketplaces," *Harvard Business Review,* May–June, 97–103.

Morton, R. (2007), "Software on Demand," *Logistics Today,* February, pp. 22–23.

Neef, D. (2001), *E-Procurement: From Strategy to Implementation,* Saddle River, NJ: Prentice Hall.

Pearcy, D., Giunipero, L., and Wilson, A. (2007), "A Model of Relational Governance in Reverse Auctions," *Journal of Supply Chain Management,* Winter, 4–15.

Teague, P. E. (2007), "PLM Gets Buyers under the Hood," *Purchasing,* March 1, http://www.purchasing.com/article/CA6419151.html.

Turner, N. (2001), "Choosing the Most Appropriate Warehouse Management System," *Corby,* 3(7), 30–33.

"What Purchasing Needs to Know before Selecting an ERP System" (1999), *Purchasing,* 127(6), 76.

ENDNOTES

1. Bozarth, C., and Handfield, R. (2004), *Operations and Supply Chain Management,* Upper Saddle River, NJ: Prentice Hall.
2. Chopra, S., and Meindl, P. (2004), "Information Technology and the Supply Chain," in *Supply Chain Management: Strategy, Planning and Operation,* Upper Saddle River, NJ: Prentice Hall, Chapter 16.
3. Kahl, S. (1999), "What's the 'Value' of Supply Chain Software?" *Supply Chain Management Review,* 2(4), 59–67.
4. Chopra and Meindl.
5. Bradley, J. (1987), *Introduction to Data Base Management,* New York: Holt, Rinehart and Winston, p. 7.
6. Antonette, G., Giunipero, L., and Sawchuk, C. (2002), *ePurchasingPlus,* Goshen NY: JGC Enterprises, p. 86.
7. Antonette et al., p. 56.
8. Antonette et al., p. 57.
9. Antonette et al., p. 58.
10. Handfield, R., Straight, S., and Sterling, W. (2002), "Reverse Auctions: How Do Suppliers Really Feel about Them?" *Inside Supply Management,* November, pp. 28–32.
11. http://www.emptoris.com/solutions/procurement_contracts.asp.

12. This section is based on a benchmarking report developed by Steven Edwards, Meenakshi Lakshman, members of the Supply Chain Resource Consortium, and a number of undergraduate students at North Carolina State University.

13. Cole, S. J., Woodring, S. D., Chun, H., and Gatoff, J. (1999), "Dynamic Trading Networks," *The Forrester Report,* January.

14. Lewis, N. (2001), "Dell Portal Adds 'Value': valuechain.dell.com Provides Pipeline to Info Exchange," CMP Media Inc., www.my-esm.com/showArticle?articleID=2911571.

15. Lewis.

16. Handfield, R., and Nichols, E. L. (2003), *Supply Chain Redesign,* Upper Saddle River, NJ: Prentice Hall.

Chapter 19

PERFORMANCE MEASUREMENT AND EVALUATION

Learning Objectives

After completing this chapter, you should be able to

- Introduce a purchasing and supply measurement framework
- Review and provide insight into key purchasing and supply measurements
- Review benchmarking and its importance
- Identify key characteristics of effective measurement systems

Chapter Outline

Measuring Purchasing and Supply Performance at a Global Automotive Parts Manufacturer

OVERVIEW

This multibillion-dollar diversified manufacturer of electrical and electromechanical components and systems has worldwide operations, markets, and suppliers. Purchasing is done at the corporate, division/business, and regional levels. Global coordination is achieved through the corporate headquarters in the United States. Major operating locations are in North America, Europe, Asia/Pacific, and South America.

Purchasing is organized with companywide product and nonproduct purchasing directors reporting to the vice president of global purchasing. Global commodity directors and business unit leaders also report to the vice president or to the product/nonproduct purchasing directors. Also at corporate headquarters are purchasing staff groups, including lean operations, organization and employee development, supplier development, supplier quality, minority supplier development, strategic planning, finance, communications, e-systems, strategy and process, and risk management.

Staff number in the hundreds and are located worldwide. Annual spend is in the billions of dollars. The vice president of global purchasing reports to an executive vice president. The overall strategic intent of global purchasing is to provide the corporation with a competitive advantage through achieving extended supply chain performance excellence. Achieving this extended supply chain excellence on a worldwide basis requires vertical and horizontal integration, detailed business plans, and an integrated set of metrics to drive and measure behaviors.

The measurement system is aligned vertically and horizontally with corporate goals and other functions and business units through the strategic global purchasing plan. The plan is integrated with the critical competitive requirements through the company's executive committee. Critical drivers are cost, quality, and availability. In addition, minority purchasing spend, effective product launches, and a competitive supply base are also important.

The global purchasing plan is structured around the strategic intent of global purchasing, and key contributing elements include supplier development, cost, sourcing strategically, quality, e-systems, people, supplier relations, and accelerated change. Horizontal linkage is achieved by establishing a multiyear strategy and annual business plans. The strategy and business plans focus on the current and desired state and link together the corporate, commodity, regional, and business unit strategies and plans.

This strategy and planning process clearly provides for effective communication, project planning, and horizontal and vertical alignment with goals and resulting measurements. An extensive set of integrated financial and nonfinancial measures are in place to guide behavior and review performance. The most significant are discussed here.

COST MANAGEMENT

Two measures are most critical: (1) year-over-year price performance based on contract prices for the same or similar items, and (2) material cost improvement that can be achieved through various approaches such as design change, process improvement, packaging, and so forth.

In addition, the company's overall financial plan includes cost-reduction levels that need to be achieved by purchasing. Revenues of the firm, as they increase or decrease, influence the purchasing cost-reduction target because of the need to protect margin. The finance group makes final judgments regarding validation of purchasing cost savings.

Other important measures in use include the following:

- Quality and quality improvement based on parts per million (PPM) defective determination
- On-time delivery and availability
- Flawless on-time launch of new products
- Minority supplier spend targets
- "Rightsizing" the supply base based on an objective measurement of the appropriate number of suppliers
- Supplier relationships and development via scorecards
- People development based on number of hours of training per year
- Cost management models
- E-system applications
- Lean project

This company regularly reviews all measures above. Goals and specific targets are modified regularly, based on business needs. Examples include enhanced cost improvement and flawlessly launching new products to ensure timely introduction to the market.

Targets can be reset at any time the business requires a change. Reviews are at least monthly. There is a heavy emphasis on cost improvement. Targets are aggressive in nature, going beyond what has normally been achieved, and are in place at all purchasing levels and business units.

The purchasing performance measures are organized around the eight contributing key elements identified earlier as part of the global purchasing plan. The strategies by strategy areas and metrics are in place for the current and future states. The global purchasing business plan forces a linkage across the key elements of the corporation, including divisions, commodity teams, and regional purchasing groups.

Measured performance is regularly reported to all appropriate personnel companywide. Owners of performance across the company are established at all levels with project plans in place with appropriate metrics. For example, supplier development may include project steps and metrics for cost savings, developing supplier engineers, and implementing a supplier council.

Personal business priorities, which drive performance, are based primarily on team recognition rather than personal rewards. However, appraisals are done at the individual level and people are expected to perform at stretch levels to gain the most significant financial and nonfinancial rewards. Incentive compensation is based on overall achievement of the company's business plan and is primarily awarded at the executive level.

Significant resources are committed to the global purchasing business planning process and related measurements. Strategy and process personnel at corporate have lead roles in the planning process.

Purchasing personnel across the organization have execution responsibility, with specific personnel assigned to measurement systems input, data integrity, and enhanced systems development. Finance staff work to ensure the accuracy and validity of cost savings. Cost management personnel are developing cost models against which to evaluate purchasing and supplier performance.

Current systems provide significant support for the measurements. Cost and cost improvement are tracked and reported at all organizational levels and by division and product in considerable detail. Finance validates cost-reduction and purchasing performance to the financial plan for both direct and indirect procurement. Various other metrics are provided by SAP and internal systems models for performance monitoring.

In addition, e-systems are being enhanced and will include advanced supplier profiling and scorecards, a supplier suggestion system, and cost management.

The performance of purchasing (both direct and indirect) is critical to the financial success of the company. Top executives regularly review the performance of purchasing and the supply base, with a keen focus on cost, quality, availability, and launch. Companywide and purchasing executives drive the measurement system and critical metrics, using them to guide behavior and to reward performance.

Source: "Strategic Performance Measurement for Purchasing and Supply," CAPS Research, 2005, pp. 42–44.

Note: This case discusses an extensive purchasing and supply measurement system. It is organized around key principles of measurement.

This chapter begins with a basic overview of performance measurement and evaluation, including the reasons to measure performance and the problems associated with measurement and evaluation. Next, there is a discussion of the most common purchasing and supply chain measurement categories, with specific examples of performance measures presented. The third section discusses the development of a performance measurement and evaluation system. The fourth section discusses performance benchmarking, which is a process involving comparisons against leading firms to establish performance plans and objectives. The next section discusses the balanced scorecard. The chapter concludes with observations about performance measurement and evaluation.

Purchasing and Supply Chain Performance Measurement and Evaluation

A purchasing and supply chain performance evaluation system represents a formal, systematic approach to monitor and evaluate purchasing performance. Although this sounds easy, it is often difficult to develop measures that direct behavior or activity exactly as intended. Some firms still rely on measures that could be harmful, depending on performance objectives, rather than supporting long-term performance. For example, the ability to win significant price concessions from a supplier is still a major objective for certain price/cost performance measures. However, if a purchaser continually squeezes short-term price reductions from a supplier, will that supplier have the financial resources or the commitment to invest in longer-term performance improvements?

Modern purchasing and supply chain performance measurement and evaluation systems contain a variety of measures. Most of these measures fall into two broad categories: effectiveness measures and efficiency measures. **Effectiveness** refers to the extent to which, by choosing a certain course of action, management can meet a previously established goal or standard. **Efficiency** refers to the relationship between planned and actual sacrifices made to realize a previously agreed-upon goal.[1] Efficiency measures usually relate some input to a performance output.

Almost all measures include a standard or target against which to evaluate performance results or outcomes. It is incomplete to say, for example, that a measure will track improvement in supplier quality. We still need to compare actual improvement against a pre-established target or objective. Meeting this target, which is presumably based on world-class performance levels, will bring value to an organization. Each performance measure should include actual performance levels and a targeted performance level.

Why Measure Performance?

There are a number of reasons for measuring and evaluating purchasing and supply chain activity and performance.

Support Better Decision Making

Measurement can lead to better decisions by making performance and results visible. It is difficult to develop performance improvement plans without understanding the areas in which performance falls short. Measurement provides a track record of purchasing performance over time and directly supports decision-making activity by management.

Support Better Communication

Performance measurement can result in better communication across the supply chain, including within purchasing, between departments, with suppliers, and with executive management. For example, a purchaser must clearly communicate performance expectations to suppliers. The measures that quantify supplier performance reflect a purchaser's expectations.

Provide Performance Feedback

Measurement provides the opportunity for performance feedback, which supports the prevention or correction of problems identified during the performance measurement process. Feedback also provides insight into how well a buyer, department, team, or supplier is meeting its performance objectives over time.

Motivate and Direct Behavior

Measurement motivates and directs behavior toward desired end results. A measurement system can accomplish this in several ways. First, the selection of performance categories and objectives indicates to purchasing personnel those activities that an organization considers critical. Second, management can motivate and influence behavior by linking the attainment of performance objectives to organizational rewards, such as pay increases.

Problems with Purchasing and Supply Chain Measurement and Evaluation

Measuring and evaluating performance, including purchasing and supply chain performance, historically has had certain problems and limitations. Mark Brown, an expert on performance measurement, argued that most managers and professionals today are like a pilot trying to fly a plane with only half the instruments needed and many additional instruments that measure irrelevant data.[2] He states that practically every organization has some type of problem with its measurement system.

Too Much Data and Wrong Data

Having too much data is the most common problem an organization has with its measurement system. A second and more serious problem is that the data that managers pay attention to are often the wrong data. The metrics are selected because of history or a feeling that the measure is related to success, which may not be the case at all. In fact, measures that managers follow may sometimes be in conflict with measures used in other units or functional areas. As a general rule, employees should monitor no more than a dozen measures, with half of those being the most critical.

Measures That Are Short-Term Focused

Many small- and medium-sized organizations have a problem of relying on measures and data that are short-term focused. Typically the only data they collect are financial and operating data. In purchasing, this would mean a short-term focus on workload and supply chain activities, while ignoring the longer-range or strategic measures.

Lack of Detail

At times the data that are reported are summarized so much as to make the information meaningless. A measure that reports on a single measure of monthly supplier quality probably lacks detail. A supply manager will want to know what are the specific types of defects the supplier is experiencing, what the defects cost the buyer's company, and the supplier's quality performance over time.

An operations manager at a major automotive regional parts distribution facility receives a monthly measure of the facility's quality as measured by claims made by customers. However, he also receives reports that detail the following:

- The type of errors that are occurring (wrong part picked, damage, shortages, missed shipments, and so on)
- Which customers are making the quality claims
- Which employees are responsible for the quality errors
- The total cost of the quality claims against the facility
- The part numbers that have quality claims against them

With this information the manager can take action that will attack the root causes of the quality problems at his facility.

Drive the Wrong Performance

Unfortunately, many measures drive behavior that is not what was intended or needed. If buyers are measured on the number of purchase orders written, then they will make sure to split orders between suppliers to generate as many purchase orders as possible. Part of this is due to the fact that measuring intellectual work is difficult. However, organizations still want to look for factors that can be measured and reported. These factors may not, however, always be the right factors.

Measures of Behavior versus Accomplishments

The problem with measuring behavior is there is no guarantee the behavior will lead to desired results. A behavioral measure that tracks the amount of purchase volume covered by corporatewide contracts, for example, is becoming increasingly common. A better measure, however, is one that tracks the total savings due to the use of corporatewide contracts.

Another example of a behavioral measure is one that measures the number of meetings held by a commodity team each quarter. A better set of measures will track the performance results that occurred because of the team's actions. Although some set of behavioral measures will always be present, measures that capture accomplishments are the ones that really matter.

Purchasing and Supply Chain Performance Measurement Categories

As part of a company-focused purchasing and supply chain measurement approach, firms should follow a systematic process to maximize results and achieve vertical and horizontal alignment of purpose. Exhibit 19.1 on p. 712 illustrates the process. As indicated, company objectives drive specific company strategies such as being the low-cost producer or technology leader. These company strategies should then drive appropriate and prioritized purchasing and supply chain objectives and specific strategies.

Alignment of strategies, measures, and actions will bring together top-down direction and bottom-up targeting to produce positive contributions. In a single enterprise, this could deliver competitive advantage. Integrated purchasing and supply chain management can also produce competitive advantage for the end-to-end supply chain level, improving effectiveness and reducing overhead.

There are hundreds of purchasing and supply chain measures. Perhaps the best way to summarize the vast number of separate measures is by developing performance measurement categories as shown in Exhibit 19.1. Within each category, many separate measures relate to each general category. Most purchasing and supply chain measures fall into one of the following categories:

- Price performance
- Cost-effectiveness
- Revenue
- Quality
- Time/delivery/responsiveness
- Technology or innovation
- Physical environment and safety
- Asset and integrated supply chain management
- Administration and efficiency
- Government and social
- Internal customer satisfaction
- Supplier performance
- Strategic performance

The following sections discuss each of these categories.

Exhibit 19.1 Integrated Company/Purchasing Measurement Process

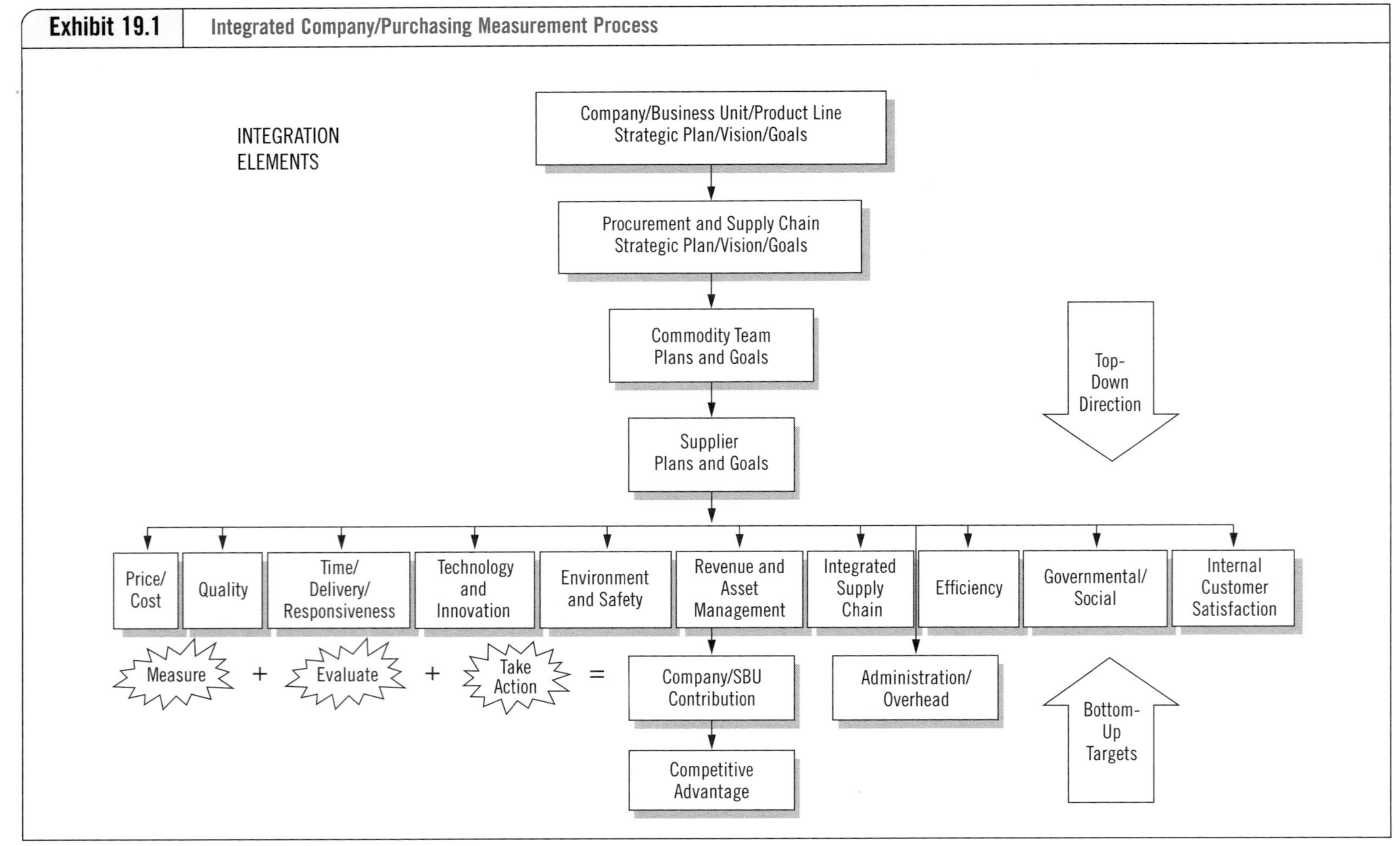

Price Performance Measures

Purchasing uses various indicators to evaluate price performance measures—in other words, how effectively it spends purchase dollars. The most common price performance measures include actual purchase price versus planned purchase price comparisons, actual purchase price(s) compared to a market index, comparisons of actual to actual purchase prices for individual and aggregated items between operating plants or divisions within an organization, and target prices achieved. Two price performance measures that are gaining importance are target prices achieved and price to market index comparisons.

Actual Price Compared to Plan

A common price performance measure is the difference between actual and planned purchase prices. Measurement of planned purchase price variance can occur at different organizational levels. One level includes actual versus planned purchases for the total material budget; this is an aggregated price performance measure. Other levels show comparisons that provide greater detail.

For example, purchasing may calculate actual versus planned price variances for each individual purchased item. Exhibit 19.2 presents various methods for calculating purchase price variance from a plan.

Actual Prices versus Market Index

Purchase price versus market index measures provide information about the relationship between actual prices and published market prices. These measures are most appropriate for market-based products where pricing is primarily a function of supply and demand. This also applies to standard and readily available products. Index

Exhibit 19.2 Purchase Price Variance from Plan

Various Formats for Measuring Purchase Price Variance

1. Purchase price variance = Actual price − Planned price
2. Purchase price variance percentage = Actual price/Planned price
3. Total purchase price variance = (Actual price − Planned price) × Purchase quantity or estimated annual volume
4. Current year dollar impact of purchase price variance = (Actual price − Planned price) × (Estimated annual volume × Percentage of requirements remaining)

Units of Measure

Dollars or percentages

Performance Reported by

Purchase item

Commodity or family group

End product

Project

Buying location or department

Buyer

Management group

Supplier

measures take into account the difference between a published index number over a designated period (such as a quarter) and the change in the actual price paid. The following illustrates this concept:

1a. Market-based index for Item X	March 31, 2007	= 125
1b. Market-based index for Item X	June 30, 2007	= 128
1c. Market index change	= (128 – 125)/125	= 2.4% increase
2a. Actual price paid for Item X	March 31, 2007	= $150
2b. Actual price paid for Item X	June 30, 2007	= $152
2c. Price paid change rate	= ($152 – $150)/$150	= 1.3% increase
3. Comparison to market	2.4% – 1.3%	= Better by 1.1%

Price Comparisons between Operations

Actual prices for similar items are also compared between plants, divisions, or business units. These comparisons provide an opportunity to identify purchase price differences within a firm. This provides visibility as to which unit is negotiating or securing the best purchase price. The comparison activity can also help identify commonly purchased items between units for purchase consolidation. A number of firms also attempt actual-to-actual price comparisons between companies to determine true price competitiveness.

Although firms are increasingly focusing on cost versus price, price performance measures are still popular, especially with firms that lack detailed cost data. Price

Sourcing Snapshot — *The Tight Squeeze at Chrysler*

Sales representatives from Detroit-area auto suppliers have been complaining about the cost-cutting pressure coming from the U.S. unit of DaimlerChrysler, which is hurting the cooperative relationships that existed between suppliers and the automotive manufacturer. During the 1990s, Chrysler extensively measured the savings generated from supplier-provided ideas. Now, facing lower sales, high rebate costs, and the cost of launching new vehicles, DaimlerChrysler announced a $600 million quarterly loss at its Chrysler unit. The red ink will likely increase the pressure at Chrysler to cut more than $2 billion as part of a $5.7 billion corporate belt-tightening. A supplier doing $300 million in business with Chrysler will now have to find an extra $3 million, and many suppliers are already struggling with razor-thin margins. Premerger Chrysler was renowned for working closely with its suppliers and received an enthusiastic response as new products were jointly developed that helped reduce Chrysler's manufacturing costs. By 1998, this strategy had helped Chrysler measure up as one of the lowest-cost producers in the world, with the highest profits per vehicle.

One supplier, complaining about the shift in performance metrics, suggested that his company may market its best technology to other automakers if the trend continues.

And that is a cost that Chrysler can ill afford.

Source: J. Green, "The Tight Squeeze at Chrysler," *Business Week,* October 9, 2000, pp. 33–34.

performance measures are also commonly used when purchasing raw materials, other commodity or standard-type items, components, systems, and contract services.

Target Prices Achieved

Target pricing is the process of determining what the external customer is willing to pay for a product or service and then assigning specific cost targets to the components, assemblies, and systems that make up the product or service. Target costing uses the following formula to determine allowable costs:

$$\text{Target Price} - \text{Profit Target} = \text{Allowable Cost}$$

Allowable cost is then allocated to various elements that make up the final product or service.

Cost-Effectiveness Measures

The measures in this category focus attention on efforts to reduce purchase costs. Cost-effectiveness measures fall into two general categories: cost changes and cost avoidance. The use of cost-effectiveness measures requires a word of caution. The method used to achieve cost reductions is critical. A cost reduction based on mutual cooperation is the same, on paper, as a cost reduction resulting from heavy-handed pressure on a supplier. Although the end result (i.e., a cost reduction) appears to be the same, the process used to achieve that result can have longer-term implications. Cooperation may reduce costs through joint improvement, whereas heavy-handed cost pressure may force a supplier to cut corners, resulting in poor quality.

Cost Changes

A cost-change measure compares the actual cost of an item or family of items over a period of time. A cost change is the increase or decrease in cost resulting from a change in purchasing strategy or practice brought about by an individual or a group.

The primary measure of concern to companies is cost reduction achieved, which is calculated by taking (New price − Prior price) × Estimated volume. For example, if the new price was $9/unit and the prior price was $10/unit with an estimated volume of 10,000 units for the next budget period, there would be a projected cost reduction of $10,000. Actual usage would determine the final cost reduction achieved.

Cost Avoidance

Cost avoidance represents the difference between a price paid and a potentially higher price (which might have occurred if purchasing had not obtained the lower price through a specific effort or action). For example, assume that purchasing paid $5.00 per unit for an item in the past, but the supplier has now quoted a price of $5.50 per unit. If the buyer negotiates a price of $5.25 per unit, then he or she has achieved a cost avoidance of $0.25 per unit, even though the price was still $0.25 higher than the prior price. Unfortunately, finance often argues that cost-avoidance savings rarely show up on a firm's profit line.

Cost-change and cost-avoidance measures differ significantly. Cost change represents an actual change from a prior-period price, whereas cost avoidance refers to the amount that would have been paid minus the amount actually paid. Purchasing departments that require tangible cost improvement should focus more on the cost-change approach. This represents actual changes that can impact a firm's overall profitability.

Cost-avoidance figures almost always require manual calculation and are sometimes subject to exaggeration. As a result, some observers have described cost-avoidance measures and figures as "soft," "funny money," and "easy to manipulate."

Revenue Measures

Revenue measures demonstrate the impact of purchasing and supply strategies and actions on revenues of the firm. For example, purchasing and supply may uncover new supplier technologies before others in the industry do and gain exclusive access, resulting in new product applications with favorable pricing and volume growth.

In addition, firms have achieved revenue growth due to royalty agreements negotiated with suppliers that have sold jointly developed technologies to other customers. Revenue from royalty generated from licensing patents and other technologies may be measured and reported.

Meeting new-product introduction dates with perfect supplier performance, enabling a first-to-market position with premium pricing, was also linked to revenue growth. Perfect-launch revenue is critical at many firms and is influenced by supplier performance.

Revenue measures for purchasing and supply are important because they link purchasing and supply strategies to the revenue elements of economic value-add. However, relatively few revenue measures are in use. Apparently, firms have not fully recognized the contribution to revenue generation that purchasing and supply can make. This is the case for direct goods and even more true on the indirect side, where the linkage of purchasing and supply strategy to revenues is less obvious or, perhaps, nonexistent.

Revenue Measure Examples

- Royalty revenues generated from supplier- or buyer-developed technology and patents initiated by purchasing or sourcing
- Supplier contribution as a reason for new business, e.g., new business development, unique technology found by purchasing, flexibility in shifting output product or service mix to meet higher profit or revenue, generating customer demand
- Return on licensing technology driven by purchasing or sourcing
- Number of patents that have led to royalties
- Number of invention disclosure forms filed
- Number of patents granted
- Value of free samples from suppliers

Quality Measures

Parts per Million

This measure expresses a maximum number (in absolute or percentage terms) of level of defects allowable for any particular product, assembly, or service. It may be expressed by using one of the following specific definitions or could be the mean time between failures for a plant or equipment item. When applied to products, components, assemblies, or systems, the traditional metric has been parts per million failing to conform to specification. As quality control has improved and the ability to manufacture to tighter tolerances has increased, this metric may also be tightened. In determining the PPM result, there is a need to measure (by factual inspection, testing, or statistically reliable sampling) the incidence of defective or nonconforming parts. The measure demands a reference point such as production, receipt, incoming inspection, or shipment. In addition, quality measures are also being developed and being used for services.

Customer Defects per Supplier

This is a measure of the number of defects from individual suppliers to indicate comparative quality performance among competing suppliers. It is also used as an absolute target for suppliers in total to attain and surpass, often as part of an assessment, certification, and reward approach. Measurement is calculated by inspecting or sampling the number of acceptable components, assemblies, or systems delivered as a proportion of the total number of those parts delivered by that supplier.

It is possible to aggregate this measure across all the different items supplied by any one supplier to arrive at an average number of defects for that supplier. However, the strategic criticality of items is not taken into account.

Field Failure Rates by Purchase Item and by Supplier

This measures the incidence of failures of components, assemblies, and systems or services when actually incorporated into the final product or service and supplied to external customers. As a measure, it indicates failures after sale, and organizations will tend to aim for a zero incidence of such failures. However, in some industries (e.g., equipment rental) this measure becomes a key measure of customer satisfaction.

The metric is calculated by developing a ratio of failures against total installed population. It is used to monitor product performance after sale, manage after-sales support costs, and provide input to supplier improvement, product design improvement, and replacement design by tracking failure rates and their root causes.

Time/Delivery/Responsiveness Measures

Time-to-Market Targets, New Products/Services

This measure is the amount of time (in weeks or months) from concept to first shipment or provision of a product or service to the external customer. The objective is continuous reduction so as to reduce the amount of time it takes to achieve break-even of investment and also to be first to market with the product or service.

On-Time Delivery/Responsiveness

These measures indicate the degree to which suppliers are able to meet customer schedule requirements. Key elements for such measures include the following:

- Due dates, scheduled or promised
- Delivery windows
- Acceptable early or late arrivals to due dates (e.g., minus two days or no days late)

The metrics are typically calculated as the percentage of shipments, services, or individual items on time or late (occasionally early). These measures can be applied in service or manufacturing businesses. Supplier and procurement performance can be measured through indices based on the above measures. These metrics can be further organized by commodity or purchase family. Percentages are calculated by company total on-time to total deliveries, and then further reported by purchase family and supplier.

Achieving New-Product Introduction Ramp-Up Schedules and Introduction Dates

These measures indicate whether procurement and supply chain management and strategic processes and suppliers are achieving necessary available volume goals at milestones and at market introduction dates for the product or service.

Cycle Time Reductions: Order Entry, Manufacturing/Operations, Distribution, and Logistics

These measures should identify total cycle time and its key components. Measures focus on reduction through elimination of delays and delivering continuous improvement to target times. Examples include supplier manufacturing cycle times, order entry, internal operations, transportation, and so forth.

Responsiveness to Schedule Changes, Mix Changes, and Design or Service Changes

These measures indicate how quickly suppliers can respond to demand or use changes, for example, the ability to adjust schedule by 50% within two weeks of scheduled delivery. Another measure could be time to achieve design changes to allowable targets. These measures recognize the need for flexibility.

Technology or Innovation Measures

First Insight/Production Outputs of New Supplier Technology

This measure would typically link to a contractual agreement whereby, for new technologies, your firm may get insight, some period of time before new technology developments are shared with other organizations. This may be an important focus in dealings with selected key technology suppliers to your firm. A specific metric can be the number of such agreements with key suppliers for critical technologies. Any target would be firm specific. A potential drawback with this measure is that no account is taken of the success or failure arising from such technology insights.

Standardization and Use of Industry Standards

These measures focus on achieving standardization of components, systems, and services and application of currently used purchased items or the use of industry-standard versus -unique items. Specific measures include reduction of different items used, percentage of new products or services made up of currently purchased items, and number of industry-unique items utilized in a new product or service. Your firm would then establish these and similar measures for product- or service-specific goals.

Physical Environment and Safety Measures

Companies are tracking the achievement of environmental and safety goals and costs associated with compliance, both voluntary compliance and where legislation enforces compliance. The objective is to drive performance improvement to achieve self-imposed or regulatory goals.

Asset and Integrated Supply Chain Management Measures

The measurement of inventory as an asset for a single enterprise may include a number of typical unit or aggregate inventory measures such as the following:

- Dollar value of inventory investment (following appropriate accounting rules)
- Inventory turnover
- Days/weeks/months of supply of inventory

The objective is to reduce inventory cost by increasing the velocity of throughput or reducing inventory carrying cost. A unique use of this measure is its application across inventory throughout various stages within a firm's supply chain and, more importantly, across firms in the aggregate supply chain (external to your firm) with specified future targets.

In addition, it is common to have additional measures that track different aspects of a firm's inventory investment. Examples include percentage of active versus inactive part numbers, total number of part numbers, working capital savings, and inventory investment by type of purchased item (for example, production items, maintenance items, and packaging materials).

It is also common to have measures that track the speed or velocity of inventory as it moves through different elements of the supply chain. This includes raw material, work-in-process, and finished-goods inventory turns. The amount of inventory maintained as safety stock is also a common measure. The accuracy of computer records that are part of the inventory location system is also closely tracked.

Transportation Cost Reduction

Transportation measures include tracking actual transportation costs against some pre-established objective, demurrage and detention costs, and premium transportation. Transportation carrier quality, delivery performance levels, and transportation lead time can also be measured.

Cost-reduction measures focus on the total transportation costs incurred per planning period to conduct business and those premium transportation costs incurred where expediting requires a nonstandard transportation method to meet internal or external requirements, for example, using air shipments when trucking is the preferred shipping mode.

Transportation costs can be measured in total dollars and as a percentage of cost of goods sold or sales revenue. Premium transportation can be measured in dollars or percentage of overall transportation costs. These costs can be measured inbound, intracompany, and outbound.

Customer Orders

These measures evaluate how well an organization is satisfying its commitment to downstream customers. Various measures include the percentage of on-time delivery, total time from customer order to customer delivery, returned orders, and warranty claims. Although we have focused primarily on purchasing and upstream supply chain activities, purchasing and materials planners are increasingly responsible for managing inventory from a total supply chain perspective. This may also include downstream activities.

E-Transactions (Number and Percentage of Suppliers/Dollars/Orders)

These measures show some degree of cross-enterprise linkage. The magnitude of use of electronic data interchange or web-based systems that link buyers and suppliers can, for example, be measured by the following:

- Absolute number of suppliers
- Percentage of suppliers
- Dollar value and percentage of orders
- Percentage of advance shipping notices
- Electronic funds transfer
- Meeting customer requirements
- Inventory throughout the supply chain
- Other

Pull Systems/Shared Schedules/Supplier Managed Inventory (SMI)

These measures establish the number (or percentage) of suppliers that are sharing schedules and operating in a pull system environment. They may also measure percentages of suppliers that are sharing schedules against those that should be. SMI measures establish the number of suppliers and magnitude of inventory being managed by suppliers for which they have financial responsibility.

Administration and Efficiency Measures

Management uses administration and efficiency measures to plan purchasing's annual administrative budget and to help control administrative expenses during a budget period. Budgeted expense items commonly include salaries, travel and living expenses, training expenses, office supplies, and other miscellaneous expenses. Salaries traditionally take the largest share of the purchasing administrative budget. The two most common methods to establish the purchasing administrative budget are the current budget plus adjustment and the use of control ratios.

Current Budget Plus Adjustment

The most common method of establishing a budget uses the current administrative budget as a starting point. Management then adjusts the budget for the next period (usually the next fiscal year) upward or downward depending on expected business conditions or other departmental requirements. Budget adjustments reflect management's view about projected purchasing workload and a firm's profitability. Decreasing workload or profits can result in a budget reduction. Conversely, increasing workload or profits may justify a budget increase.

Sourcing Snapshot *The Perfect Order at Procter and Gamble*

The **perfect order** represents the ability of the supply chain to provide 100% availability in a timely, error-free manner. Procter and Gamble (P&G), a manufacturer and distributor of consumer products, defines the perfect order metric as on time to the buyer's requested delivery date, shipped complete, invoiced correctly, and not damaged in transit. In 1992, P&G began to measure its perfect orders. Initially, managers were shocked to discover that the number of perfect orders was only around 75%. Since that time, substantial improvements have been made. In 1995, 82% of orders were perfect; and by 1998, 88% were perfect. This has been achieved through continuous replenishment, having customer service representatives work closely with major customers, and improved information systems. Procter and Gamble estimates that every imperfect order costs approximately $200 as a result of redelivery, lost revenue, damage, warehouse and shipping costs, deductions, and backorders. P&G knows that continuous supply chain improvement requires measuring what is really important to the customer. And to the customer, the perfect order is important.

Source: Presentation by Ralph Drayer, Eli Broad Graduate School of Management, Michigan State University, East Lansing, December 1998.

Control Ratios

With the control ratio approach, the purchasing administrative budget is a percentage of another measure that reflects purchasing's workload. Planned dollar expenditure for direct material is often the selected workload measure.

The historical control ratio as well as negotiation between purchasing and higher management often determines the control ratio percentage used during calculation of the administrative budget. A projection of direct material purchase requirements for the next period then affects the administrative budget. Purchasing workload is assumed to be proportional to planned dollar expenditures for direct material. The purchasing administrative budget becomes the following:

$$\text{Purchasing Budget} = \text{Estimated Expenditures for Direct Materials} \times \text{Control Ratio}$$

Purchasing managers use the total budget figure to allocate resources among different departmental uses. Management must determine how many buyers are required, the size of the clerical support staff, and other budget-related issues.

Other Approaches

Current budget plus adjustment and control ratios are not the only methods used to arrive at a purchasing administrative budget or efficiency. Purchasing workload such as purchase orders processed, line items processed, and headcount may also be used to measure efficiency. Again, we must warn against emphasizing purchasing efficiency over purchasing effectiveness as a strict indicator of performance.

Governmental and Social Measures

Minority, Women, and Small Business Enterprise Objectives

In the United States there are social, state, and federal requirements that public and private organizations place a percentage of their business with minority- and women-owned business enterprises (MWBEs). These expenditures are regularly targeted at specific performance levels, tracked, and reported; they are used to drive purchasing strategy. Small-business purchases may also be included. Specific measures may include the following:

- Percentage of spend (the proportion of purchase spend from MWBE suppliers as a percentage of total annual purchase spend), calculated as follows:

$$\frac{\text{Annual Purchase (\$) from MWBE Suppliers}}{\text{Total Annual External Purchases (\$)}} = \%$$

- Number of suppliers in each MWBE category
- Growth of MWBE spend

Internal Customer Satisfaction Measures

Companies are also applying measures that indicate the degree of satisfaction with purchasing's value-add contribution. This is typically done by surveying internal customers and asking them to indicate their satisfaction with purchasing by responding to a series of check-off and open-ended questions. Supplier satisfaction surveys and measures are also used.

Supplier Performance Measures

Supplier performance measurement is an area in which many firms have made great progress. Supplier scorecards frequently contain many of the measures discussed above. Purchasers generally track supplier quality, cost, and delivery along with other performance areas. Furthermore, firms are beginning to quantify the cost associated with supplier nonperformance. The resulting cost figure represents the total cost of doing business with a supplier. Supplier total-cost measures allow direct comparisons between suppliers.

Hewlett-Packard developed a supplier performance evaluation model that evaluates supplier performance (and the teams that manage those suppliers) in the areas of T (technology contribution), Q (quality), R (supplier responsiveness), D (delivery performance), C (cost), and E (environmental performance). The FedEx supplier scorecard featured in Chapter 9 provides additional details about supplier performance measurement systems. These supplier scorecards are increasingly important in selecting, motivating, and developing suppliers.

Strategic Performance Measures

Purchasing requires measures that reflect its ability to support overall corporate and functional goals, which means a reduced emphasis on pure efficiency measures (e.g., the cost to issue a purchase order or current workload status) and greater emphasis on effectiveness measures (those that reflect purchasing's strategic contribution). Examples of the latter include tracking early supplier involvement in product design, performance gains resulting from direct supplier development efforts, and supplier-provided improvement suggestions. Within most industries, purchasing must shift from measuring itself as an administrative support function to measuring how well it provides strategic value.

Exhibit 19.3 provides examples of key strategic purchasing measures. Notice that these measures are a combination of activity- and results-oriented measures. Emphasis shifts from strict indicators of personnel performance or efficiency to how well the purchasing function supports strategic supply-base management goals and objectives. To shift from an operational to a strategic perspective, the purchasing measurement and evaluation system must also shift.

The performance indicators in Exhibit 19.3 are more strategically and externally focused than traditional performance indicators. They are also specified in terms of broader purchasing goals rather than specific activity. For example, a buyer may be responsible for a performance objective stating that 75% of the buyer's suppliers will be quality certified by the third quarter of 2007. This differs from a measure that states a buyer must process 10 requests for quotation per day on average.

Exhibit 19.3 Examples of Strategic Purchasing Measurement Indicators

- Percentage of purchasing's operating budget committed to on-site supplier visits
- Proportion of quality-certified suppliers to total suppliers
- Percentage of receipts free of inspection and material defects
- Total number of suppliers
- Proportion of suppliers participating in early product design or other joint value-added activities
- Revenue increase as a result of supplier-provided technology that differentiates end products to customers
- Percentage of operating budget allocated to supplier development and training
- Total cost supplier selection and evaluation measures
- Supplier lead-time indicators
- Purchasing's contribution to return on assets, return on investment, and economic value-added corporate measures
- Purchasing success with achieving cost reductions with Tier 2 and Tier 3 suppliers
- Percentage of purchase dollars committed to longer-term contracts
- Savings achieved from the use of companywide agreements
- Purchasing's contribution to product development cycle time reduction
- Percentage/dollar value of items purchased from single sources
- Percentage of purchase dollars committed to highest-performing suppliers
- Percentage of purchase transactions through electronic data interchange (EDI) or web-based systems
- Percentage of total receipts on a just-in-time basis
- Supplier quality levels, cost performance, and delivery performance compared with world-class performance targets
- Supplier development costs and benefits
- Continuous supplier performance improvement measures
- Reductions in working capital due to purchasing and supply chain efforts
- Contribution to return on investment and assets realized from strategic outsourcing efforts
- Savings achieved from part number reduction efforts
- Savings achieved from part standardization efforts

Developing a Performance Measurement and Evaluation System

The development of a measurement and evaluation system requires the leadership, support, and commitment of executive management, who must commit the financial resources necessary for system development. Management must also require all purchasing locations to use the same system structure, which can reduce duplication of effort and save development and training costs. This does not mean that each location must use the same performance objectives or performance criteria. It only means that the system's basic design should be similar. Executive management support also sends a message about the seriousness of tracking and improving performance.

Development of an effective measurement and evaluation system follows a general sequence of activities. These include determining which performance categories to measure, developing specific performance measures, establishing performance standards for each measure, finalizing system details, and implementing and reviewing the system and each performance measure. Exhibit 19.4 presents an overview of the development of a purchasing and supply chain performance measurement system.

Determine Which Performance Categories to Measure

A previous section discussed various performance measurement categories. The first step of the development process requires identifying which measurement categories to emphasize. Also, a firm can weight its performance measures and categories differently.

Management does not concern itself with specific performance measures during this phase of system development. The selected performance categories must relate broadly to organizational and purchasing and supply chain goals and objectives.

Selecting the performance measure categories is a critical step prior to developing specific performance measures.

Develop Specific Performance Measures

Developing specific performance measures begins once management identifies the measurement categories it will emphasize. Certain features characterize successful purchasing and supply chain performance measures.

Objectivity

Each measure should be as objective as possible. The measurement system should rely on quantitative data instead of qualitative feelings and assessments. Subjective evaluation can create disagreement between the rater and the individual or group responsible for the performance objective.

Clarity

Personnel must understand a performance measure's requirements in order to direct performance toward the desired outcome and minimize misunderstandings. All parties must be clear about what each performance measure means, agree on the

Exhibit 19.4 Developing a Purchasing and Supply Chain Performance Measurement and Evaluation System

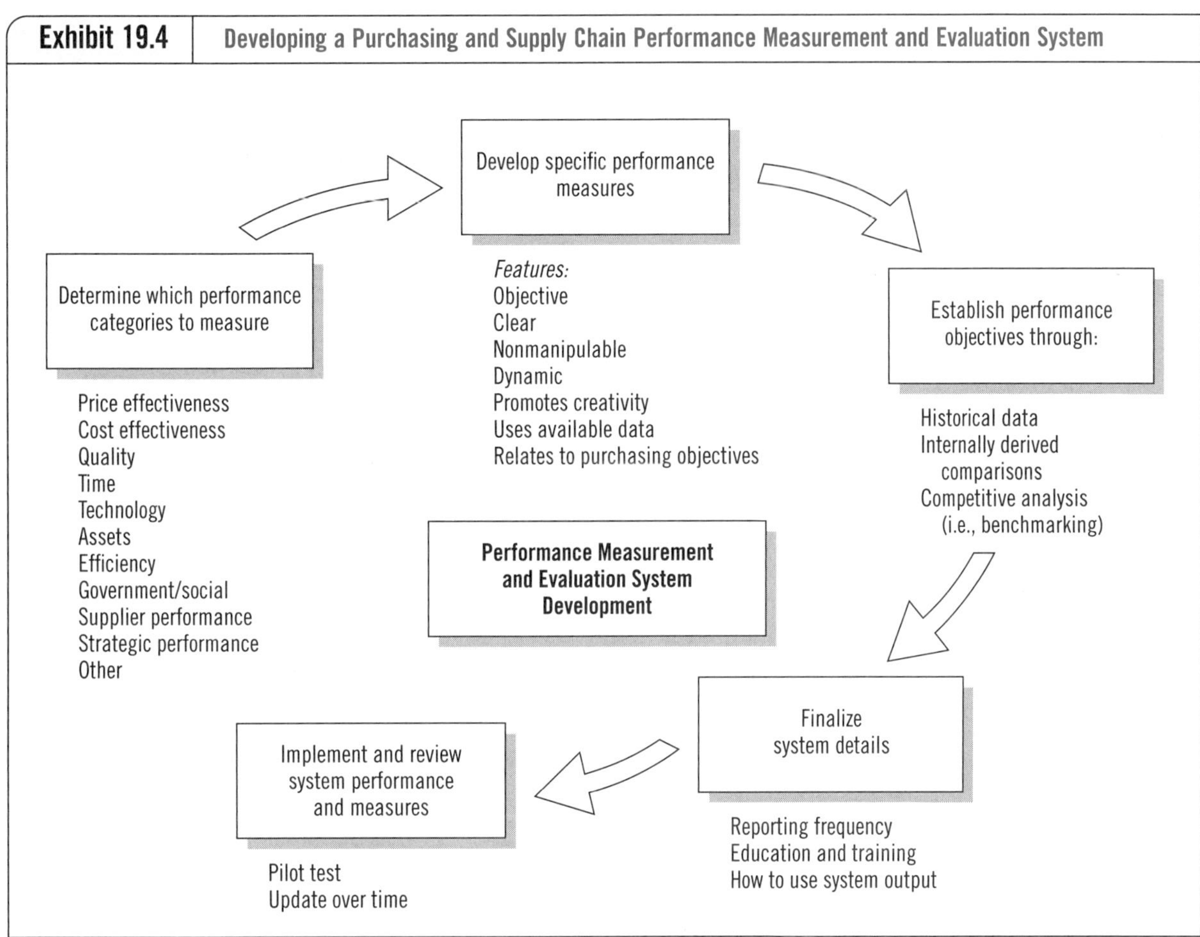

performance objectives associated with the measure, and understand what it takes to accomplish the measure. Well-understood measures are straightforward and unambiguous.

Use of Accurate and Available Data

Well-defined measures use data that are available and accurate. If a measure requires data that are difficult to generate or unreliable, the probability of using the measure on a consistent basis declines. The cost of generating and collecting the required data should not outweigh the potential benefit of using the performance measure.

Creativity

A common misconception is that a performance evaluation system should measure every possible activity. When this occurs, the measures can stifle individual creativity. The measures control behavior so tightly that the system eliminates room for personal initiative. A successful system measures only what is important while still promoting individual initiative and creativity, which may mean focusing on 5 or 6 important, clearly defined measures instead of 25 vague measures.

Directly Related to Organizational Objectives

Exhibit 19.5 illustrates how corporate goals and objectives influence purchasing goals and objectives. Other functional objectives also can influence purchasing. For example, manufacturing's goals can have a direct impact on purchasing because purchasing supports the manufacturing process. To meet its goals and objectives, purchasing executives develop strategies and action plans. Finally, management develops measures that evaluate the output or performance from the activities required to accomplish purchasing's strategies and plans. The measures serve as indicators of purchasing's progress.

Joint Participation

Joint participation means that the personnel responsible for each measure participate in developing the measure or establishing the measure's performance objective. Joint participation can go a long way toward getting the support of the personnel responsible for achieving the measure.

Dynamic over Time

A dynamic system is one that management reviews periodically, to determine whether existing measures still support purchasing's goals and objectives, if there is a need for new measures, or if performance standards or objectives require updating.

Exhibit 19.5 Linking Purchasing Measures and Corporate Objectives

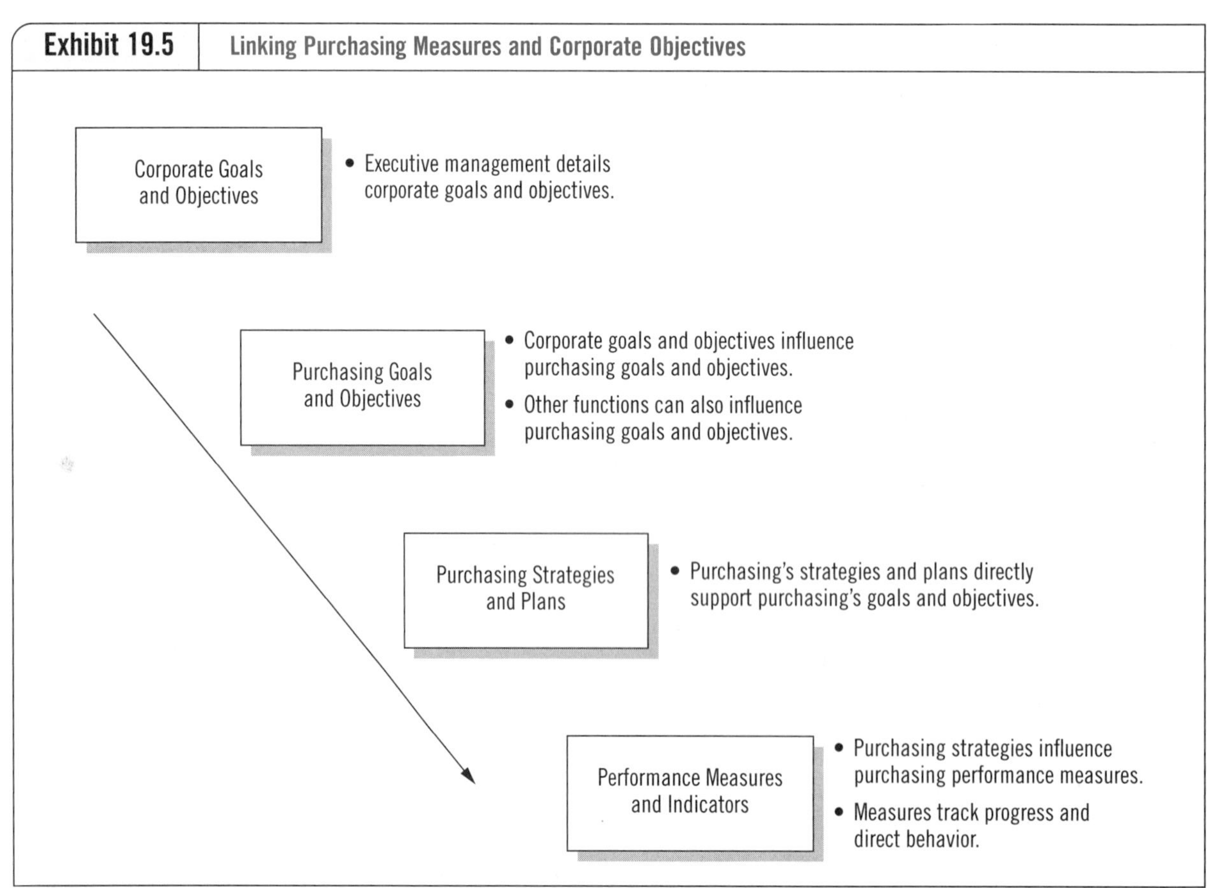
Corporate Goals and Objectives
• Executive management details corporate goals and objectives.
Purchasing Goals and Objectives
• Corporate goals and objectives influence purchasing goals and objectives.
• Other functions can also influence purchasing goals and objectives.
Purchasing Strategies and Plans
• Purchasing's strategies and plans directly support purchasing's goals and objectives.
Performance Measures and Indicators
• Purchasing strategies influence purchasing performance measures.
• Measures track progress and direct behavior.

Nonmanipulable

A nonmanipulable measure is one that personnel cannot inappropriately influence the results of (i.e., the measure is cheat-proof). Ideally, the individual(s) responsible for the measure should not be responsible for supplying the data to the reporting system. This becomes an issue of accountability and integrity. The measure's output should be a true reflection of actual activity or performance results. Systems receiving their input from automated or computerized systems are generally less susceptible to data manipulation.

Establish Performance Objectives for Each Measure

Establishing an objective for each performance measure is critical. Objectives quantify the desired performance target or goal. Management must not specify objectives that are too easy. The too-easy objective can become an accepted performance standard within a department.

Performance standards or objectives must be realistic, which means the measure should be challenging yet achievable through a solid effort. An objective should not be so easy that it requires minimal effort. It should not be so difficult that it discourages personnel from even attempting to achieve the objective. The objective must also reflect the realities of a firm's competitive environment. An objective that is challenging internally yet does not reflect the competitive environment is not part of a well-defined measure.

Firms commonly use three methods when establishing performance measure objectives: (1) historical data, (2) internal comparisons, and (3) external analysis.

Historical Data

This method uses past data about an activity as the basis for establishing a formal performance objective. Historical performance is often modified with a performance improvement factor to arrive at a current objective. Purchasing and supply chain managers often use the historical approach with efficiency-related measures.

Relying on historical data can create some problems. The possibility exists that past performance was less than optimal. By establishing an objective based on suboptimal performance, even with an improvement factor, a firm risks continuing suboptimal performance. Also, historical data provide no insight about the performance capabilities of competitors or other leading firms. In addition, the firm's goals, strategies, and financial objectives will drive purchasing and supply goals. Purchasing cannot be a value contributor without contributing to firm success through goal achievement.

Internal Comparisons

A firm can perform internal comparisons between departments or business units. The best internal performance level can become the basis for a companywide performance objective. Firms with multiple business units often compare and rank performance internally across different performance categories.

This approach, which offers some advantages over the historical approach, also has disadvantages. A firm that stresses comparisons between internal units can lose sight of its external competition. Unhealthy rivalry can also develop between internal business units or departments. Furthermore, there is no guarantee that the best-performing internal unit matches the best-performing unit of a direct competitor.

External Analysis

This approach requires examination of the practices and performance objectives of competitors or other leading firms. The advantage of this approach is that it requires an external assessment at very specific levels of detail. A later section discusses benchmarking as a competitive-analysis approach for establishing performance objectives.

Finalize System Details

The next phase of implementation requires management to consider issues such as the frequency of performance reporting, the education and training of system users, and the final determination of how to use system output.

Performance-Reporting Frequency

A sound measurement and evaluation system provides regular reporting of performance results. The actual reporting frequency can differ from measure to measure. Management must determine what frequency supports the most effective use of each measure. A measure that tracks the status of inbound transportation shipments, for example, must be available on a frequent (daily or real-time) basis. A summary measure evaluating overall supplier performance may require only weekly or monthly reporting.

Education and Training

A firm must train its personnel and suppliers to use the performance measurement and evaluation system. Each participant must understand his or her accountability and responsibility under the system and how to use the system's output to improve performance. The measurement and evaluation system is a tool, and like all tools, it requires proper education and training in its use.

Using System Output

Managers use the output of a performance measurement and evaluation system in a number of ways. Some managers rely on the output to directly evaluate the performance of purchasing personnel or suppliers. Managers may use the system to track the effectiveness of individual buyers. System output may also identify better-performing suppliers that deserve future purchase contracts.

Managers must give careful thought to how best to use system output.

Implement and Review System Performance and Measures

All systems have an implementation phase, which may include pilot or trial runs to make sure the system performs as planned. The measurement and evaluation system, along with each performance measure, must be subject to periodic review. Having a system that contains obsolete or inappropriate measures can be more damaging than having no formal system at all.

Performance Benchmarking: Comparing Against the Best

An ongoing approach for establishing performance standards, processes, measurements, and objectives is benchmarking, a process that is not exclusively a purchasing or supply chain practice or approach per se. Rather, it is an approach used by corporate- and functional-level executives and managers. Benchmarking has definite applications, however, when establishing purchasing and supply chain management performance objectives and action plans. Before discussing specific benchmarking applications, we must first gain an understanding of the benchmarking process.

Benchmarking Overview

Benchmarking is the continuous measuring of products, services, processes, activities, and practices against a firm's best competitors or those companies recognized as industry or functional leaders.[3] Formally, the benchmarking process or activity requires measuring performance against that of best-in-class companies, determining how the best-in-class achieve their performance levels, and using that information as the basis for establishing a company's performance targets, strategies, and action plans.[4]

Benchmarking does not always involve comparisons against competitors. Firms often rely on comparisons with noncompetitors as a source of information, especially when benchmarking a process or functional activity common to firms across different industries (for example, supply chain management). It is usually easier to obtain benchmarking data and information from a cooperative noncompetitor.

Benchmarking is necessary for firms that are not industry leaders. Unfortunately, many U.S. firms did not recognize the need for performance benchmarking until after foreign competitors captured worldwide market share. Industry leaders should also practice performance benchmarking on a regular basis. A firm may not retain market leadership if it is unaware of the actions and capabilities of its competitors.

Types of Benchmarking

There are three basic types of performance benchmarking.[5] The first type is **strategic benchmarking**, which involves a comparison of one firm's market strategies against those of another. Strategic benchmarking usually involves comparisons against leading competitors, allowing a firm to gain an in-depth understanding of their market strategies.[6] With this knowledge, a firm can develop strategies and plans to counter or pre-empt the competition.

The second type of benchmarking is **operational benchmarking**, a process that the purchasing function follows when it performs benchmarking comparisons. Operational benchmarking focuses on different aspects of functional activity and identifies methods to achieve best-in-class performance. Selecting the function and the activities within that function to benchmark are critical to the success of operational benchmarking. Firms should benchmark functional activities that provide the greatest return over time.

The third type of benchmarking is **support-activity benchmarking**. During this process, support functions within an organization demonstrate their cost-effectiveness against external providers of the same support service or activity. Firms are increasingly using support-activity benchmarking as a way of controlling internal overhead and rising costs.

Benchmarking Benefits

There are a number of ways that a company hopes to benefit from actively pursuing performance benchmarking.[7] The benchmarking process helps identify the best business or functional practices to include in a firm's business plans, which can lead directly to performance improvement. Benchmarking can also break down a reluctance to change. Managers begin to see what it takes to maintain corporate or functional leadership by viewing the outside world. Benchmarking can also serve as a source of market intelligence. For example, competitive benchmarking may uncover a previously unrecognized technological breakthrough. Finally, valuable professional contacts between firms can result from the benchmarking process.

Benchmarking Critical Success Factors

Certain factors are critical to benchmarking success. Performance benchmarking must become an accepted process within a firm or function and not simply another fashionable program or fad. Personnel must view performance benchmarking as a permanent part of a system that establishes goals, objectives, and competitive strategies. Executive management support for the process is critical.

A firm must also be willing to commit the necessary legwork to data gathering. A firm must identify which company is the best-in-class for an activity, identify why that company is best, and quantify the benchmarked performance measure. The success of the benchmarking process depends on detailed and accurate benchmarked data and information that becomes part of a firm's action plans and performance objectives.

Managers must view benchmarking as a way to learn from outside companies and improve internal operations on a continuous basis.[8] Some individuals resist the benchmarking process because of a reluctance to recognize the value of a competitor's way of doing business—the "not invented here" syndrome. One way around this syndrome is to benchmark a noncompetitor's activities and performance wherever possible. Obviously, strategic benchmarking requires comparisons against direct competitors. For functional activities, however, a firm can study the performance and methods of noncompetitors.

Information and Data Sources

A solid source of benchmarking data includes trade journals, other business library resources, and the World Wide Web. Trade journals and other industry publications often feature firms that have distinguished themselves in some way. If this is not adequate, a firm can contact a benchmark target directly to request further information.

Industrywide conferences and professional seminars are also good sources of information, particularly at a functional level. These meetings often serve as a forum for the exchange of ideas about different topics. Leading firms often make presentations at industry trade meetings. These meetings can provide clues about which firms are the most highly regarded in a particular business area or practice.

Suppliers are another source of information. Purchasers can ask suppliers to identify the firms they believe are the best for each benchmark performance area. A firm can also rely on a professional consultant or other industry experts to identify benchmarking candidates.

An ongoing major purchasing benchmarking initiative conducted by CAPS Research (jointly sponsored by the Institute of Supply Management and W. P. Carey School of Business at Arizona State University) is another important source of information.

This effort includes specific industry-by-industry performance benchmarks and an ongoing study of leading-edge supply strategies. The CAPS Strategic Sourcing and Excellence Model provides the framework for the supply strategy and practice research. Data are collected via focus group visioning sessions, field research, and Internet-based surveys and assessments. Research findings about industry benchmarks and current and future supply chain strategies and practices are available at Knowledge Central, an online database sponsored by CAPS Research (http://www.capsresearch.org).

The Benchmarking Process

Robert Camp noted that there are five distinct steps or phases before a firm fully receives the benefits of the performance benchmarking process.[9] Exhibit 19.6 on p. 732 graphically presents these five phases.

Planning

During this initial phase of the benchmarking process, a firm addresses issues such as which products or functions to benchmark, which companies to select as benchmarking targets (competitors, noncompetitors, or both), and how to identify data and information sources. Benchmarking plans should focus on process and methods rather than simply on quantitative performance results. The process and methods cause the quantitative end results.

Analysis

Data and information collection and analysis occur during the second phase. A firm must determine how and why the benchmarked firm is better. A variety of questions should be asked:

- In what product or functional areas is the benchmarked company better?
- Why is the benchmarked company better?
- How large is the gap between the benchmarked company and our company?
- Can we include the benchmarked company's best practices directly in our operating plans?
- Can we project future performance levels and rates of change?

This phase is critical because it requires management to interpret and understand the benchmarked company's processes, methods, and activities.

Integration

Integration is the process of communicating and gaining acceptance of the benchmarking findings throughout an organization. During this phase, management begins to establish operational targets and functional goals based on the benchmarking findings.

Exhibit 19.6 Benchmarking Implementation Phases

Phase		*Characteristics:*
Phase 1	Planning	• Determine which products, processes, or functions to benchmark • Identify benchmark target • Determine data and information requirements
Phase 2	Analysis	• Determine how and why benchmark target is better • Determine how to include benchmark company's best practices • Identify future trends and performance levels
Phase 3	Integration	• Communicate benchmark findings to key personnel • Establish operational targets and functional goals based on benchmarking findings
Phase 4	Action	• Include personnel responsible for carrying out plans during formulation of action plans • Develop a schedule for review and updating of goals and plans • Develop system to communicate benchmarking progress
Phase 5	Maturity	• Continuous use of benchmarking at all organizational levels • Continuous performance improvement resulting from the benchmarking process

Action

The action phase requires translating the benchmark findings into detailed action plans. Critical items during this phase include having personnel directly responsible for carrying out the plans involved with formulation of the plans, developing a schedule for updating plans and objectives over time, and developing a reporting system to communicate progress toward benchmarking goals.

Maturity

A firm reaches maturity when benchmarking becomes an accepted process for establishing performance plans and objectives. Another indicator of benchmarking maturity occurs when a firm realizes continuous performance improvement as a direct result of performance benchmarking.

A formal process, such as benchmarking, is essential for establishing performance targets and action plans that are externally focused. Without external comparisons, most organizations run the risk of losing sight of what defines best practices or what the competition is doing. Purchasing and supply chain managers must endorse this practice when attempting to establish plans, measures, and objectives that represent best-in-class performance.

Balanced Scorecard for Purchasing and Supply

The balanced scorecard was first presented by Robert S. Kaplan and David P. Norton in 1992. The original premise was that a total reliance on financial measures was leading organizations to make poor decisions. Kaplan and Norton argued that firms must go beyond financial measures, which are lagging indicators, and utilize measures that are leading indicators of performance.

They further suggested that the most appropriate measures that would cause organizations to do the right things would be those metrics that measure the strategy of the firm, its functional activities, and processes.

According to Kaplan and Norton, the balanced scorecard included four key linked performance measurement areas:

1. How do customers see us? (customer satisfaction perspective)
2. What must we excel at? (operational excellence perspective)
3. Can we continue to improve and create value? (innovation perspective)
4. How do we look to shareholders? (financial perspective)

In addition, Kaplan and Norton stressed that measurement itself is not the objective. Measurement and specific metrics provide clarity to general statements and a strategy focus around which to provide performance recognition and rewards.

The balanced scorecard and its related ideas have been adapted by numerous companies and applied to purchasing and supply.

Exhibit 19.7 on p. 734 is one example of a balanced scorecard for purchasing and supply. Included are measures related to the following questions:

1. How do we look to shareholders? (financial perspective)
2. How do our customers see us? (internal and external perspectives)
3. What must we excel at? (operational excellence perspective)
4. What do we need to do to improve? (innovation perspective)

Based on the company's purchasing and supply strategies, the balanced scorecard would then be connected to a specific set of appropriate performance measurements. The result will be a scorecard by department or people with specific key performance indicators.

A Summary of Purchasing Measurement and Evaluation Characteristics

A review of purchasing and supply chain performance and measurement systems supports a number of conclusions. These fall into two categories: system characteristics and human resource characteristics.

Exhibit 19.7 Case Example of Strategic Performance Measures—Semiconductor Manufacturer

Financial

- Revenue
  - Revenue from suppliers based on process improvements
  - Royalty revenue from patents
- Cost
  - Cost for direct material, indirect spend, and capital spend
  - Bill of material cost versus target
  - Savings on direct materials used by contract manufacturers
  - Administrative costs per headcount
  - Maverick spend

Customer Satisfaction

- Internal
  - Number of plant shutdowns
  - Single-source risk mitigation
  - Internal stakeholder survey
  - Factory quality incidents
  - Supplier business continuity
  - Tool performance
  - On-time delivery
  - Ramp-up readiness
  - Percentage of spend with preferred suppliers
- External
  - Customer quality incidents

Operational Excellence

- Contract price enforcement
- Audit results and severity of errors
- Payment terms in contracts
- Most favored customer clauses in contracts
- Not to exceed pricing in contracts
- Keeping pricing current in ERP database
- Strategic sourcing plans in place

Innovation

- New-product development
  - Performance versus data milestones in the new-product innovation (NPI) process
  - Current estimated cost against target in NPI process
  - Cost savings initiated by purchasing/supply in the NPI process
- People development
  - Training hours
  - Leadership development pipeline
  - Employee morale

System Characteristics

1. Measurement is not free. An evaluation system must compare the costs associated with measurement against the benefits. Furthermore, increased measurement does not necessarily mean improved performance. The amount and type of measurement should be enough to achieve the intended result but not cause negative or dysfunctional behavior.
2. Not all aspects of performance lend themselves to quantitative measurement. Negotiating skill and obtaining supplier cooperation are two examples of performance categories that are difficult to quantify.
3. Purchasing and supply chain managers are better served by a few precisely defined and thoroughly understood measures than by many poorly defined measures.
4. An effective measurement system requires a database that provides consistent and reliable data. All personnel must have access to the same data when calculating and reporting purchasing performance indicators.
5. Periodic review of the purchasing and supply chain measurement system should occur to eliminate unimportant or unnecessary performance measures, add new measures as required, and re-evaluate performance measure objectives or targets.

6. There is no best way to measure performance. Performance measures differ from firm to firm and industry to industry. No established industry purchasing performance standards have yet emerged. However, the movement toward performance benchmarking does support the development of performance indicators common to more than one firm.
7. Measurement-reporting requirements and content vary by position and level within the organization. Careful planning helps guarantee effective use of the system at each organizational level.
8. A single, overall productivity measure representing purchasing and supply chain performance is not feasible.
9. Many industries need to shift from operational measures focusing on activity to strategic measures assessing a desired end result (for example, increased participation by suppliers during new-product development).
10. The strategies and plans used to produce a performance measure's result are probably more important than the end performance result itself.
11. A balanced scorecard approach is an effective method of measurement and evaluation for purchasing and supply.

Human Resource Characteristics

1. A measurement and evaluation system is not a substitute for effective management. The system is a tool that can be used to assist in the efficient and effective operation of the purchasing and supply chain function.
2. An effective system requires communication. Responsible personnel must clearly understand the performance measure, its performance expectation, and the role of the measure during the performance evaluation process.
3. Measures must reinforce positive behavior and be positively linked to an organization's reward system and not serve as punitive tools. If management uses the measures solely as a means to identify nonperforming individuals, negative, dysfunctional, or beat-the-system behavior may result.

Good Practice Example

Using Measurement to Drive Continuous Supply Chain Improvement at Accent Industries

Accent Industries, a U.S.-based consumer goods company, manufactures products for direct shipment to retailers worldwide. This company's strategy is to excel across various operational aspects of service by being the industry leader in price, service, and convenience. Accent has developed a set of organizational objectives that it believes are critical to worldwide success. These objectives include being a low-cost producer; providing the highest quality to customers; and offering the best customer service, delivery, and responsiveness in the industry. The company has also developed a set of purchasing and supply chain performance measures that it believes directly supports its organizational directives.

When implementing its purchasing and supply chain measurement system, Accent followed a series of defined steps:

Step 1: Conduct cross-functional discussions and benchmarking to establish measures, measurement objectives, and performance targets.

Step 2: Formalize measurement objectives into written policy and procedures.

Step 3: Formally communicate measures and objectives to the supply base.

Step 4: Receive feedback from suppliers.

Step 5: Modify, if necessary, performance measures and their objectives.

Step 6: Implement final distribution of the measurement objective and process.

Step 7: Collect and maintain performance data.

Accent relies on a wide range of purchasing and supply chain measures that relate directly to the company's corporate objectives. A sample of the more critical measures include the following:

QUALITY

- Supplier defects in parts per million
- Internal manufacturing defects in parts per million
- Internal process capability
- Damage
- Number and cost of warranty claims

PRICE/COST

- Actual price to market price comparisons
- Price/cost reductions
- Tooling cost management
- Transportation cost management

CYCLE TIMES

- New-product development cycle time

DELIVERY AND SERVICE

- Supplier on-time delivery

INVENTORY/FORECASTING

- Total inventory dollar value over time
- Raw material, work-in-process, and finished-goods inventory turns
- Forecast accuracy

Supplier quality performance is determined during on-site supplier visits and statistical inferences from product receipts. The frequency of calculation varies with each supplier's current quality levels. Suppliers with known quality problems or higher levels of defects are targeted for more frequent measurement.

Accent uses its performance measurement system to establish and convey performance objectives, track progress, and promote continuous improvement.

Each supplier is provided clear, comprehensive goals and timely feedback. Factors that are critical to effective measurement include a process for establishing aggressive but attainable goals, supplier consensus that the goals are achievable, senior management support, and accurate measurement with regular feedback.

In the future the company plans to expand its use of total cost of ownership models for supplier evaluation and selection. In addition, Accent wants to pursue the open measurement and sharing of cost elements with its suppliers.

Source: Based on interviews with company managers. Company name has been changed at the request of the company.

CONCLUSION

A purchasing and supply chain performance measurement and management system should directly support corporate goals and objectives. A measurement system that directs behavior and activity away from those goals and objectives is counterproductive and can cause greater harm than good.

There is a need to create measurement systems that are responsive to change. Firms will also increasingly require measures that focus on end results rather than on specific activities. Emphasis will increasingly shift from efficiency measures to effectiveness measures. In addition, executive management must have the ability to distinguish between good and poor purchasing practices and results. A well-developed performance measurement and evaluation system can help provide this distinction. The balanced scorecard is a useful approach to purchasing and supply measurement.

KEY TERMS

benchmarking, 729

effectiveness, 708

efficiency, 708

operational benchmarking, 729

strategic benchmarking, 729

support-activity benchmarking, 729

DISCUSSION QUESTIONS

1. What is a purchasing performance measurement and evaluation system? Why would a firm want to measure purchasing performance?
2. Why would a firm want to measure supplier performance? Describe the kinds of measures that can be used to measure supplier performance.
3. What is performance benchmarking? Why is it increasingly being used when establishing purchasing performance goals and objectives?
4. What are the three types of performance benchmarking? Which type is most commonly used by the purchasing function?
5. What is the difference between effectiveness and efficiency measures? When should a firm focus on purchasing effectiveness measures? When should a firm focus on purchasing efficiency measures?
6. Discuss the reasons why measuring and evaluating purchasing performance has historically had certain problems or limitations. Do you think the purchasing function should increase or decrease its effort to measure performance? Why or why not?
7. Consider the following statement: Some firms still rely on measures that harm rather than support purchasing's long-term performance objectives. What does this mean? Provide examples of performance measures that might actually result in a negative longer-term effect on purchasing performance.
8. What is the benefit of developing performance measures that focus on cost versus purchase price?
9. Discuss the major difference between cost-reduction and cost-avoidance measures. Why have some described the reported savings in cost-avoidance measures as "soft," "funny money," and "easy to manipulate"? When can purchasing take credit for a legitimate cost reduction or cost avoidance?

10. Assume you are responsible for developing a benchmarking program. Describe how you would go about establishing the benchmarking process. Be sure to discuss the critical issues you must address.
11. Discuss what is meant by each of the following statements:
    a. Purchasing measurement is not free.
    b. There is no best way to measure purchasing performance.
    c. Many industries need to shift from operational measures focusing on buyer activity to strategic measures focusing on a desired end result.
    d. A purchasing measurement and evaluation system is not a substitute for solid management.
12. Why is it sometimes advantageous to benchmark performance against a noncompetitor?
13. Effective performance measurement systems have certain characteristics. Select three characteristics and discuss why a measure should possess that characteristic.
14. Discuss the different uses a manager has for purchasing and supply chain performance data.
15. What is required to establish a balanced scorecard to measure purchasing and supply performance?

ADDITIONAL READINGS

Avery, S. (2006), "GM Strives for Consistent Metrics," *Purchasing,* October 5.

Brown, M. G. (1996), *Keeping Score: Using the Right Metrics to Drive World-Class Performance,* New York: American Management Association, pp. 15–26.

Carter, P. L., Monczka, R. M., and Mosconi, T. (2005), "Strategic Performance Measurement for Purchasing and Supply," CAPS Research.

Cooper, R., and Kaplan, R. (1988), "Measure Costs Right: Make the Right Decisions," *Harvard Business Review,* September–October, 23–28.

D'Avanzo, R., et al. (2003), "The Link between Supply Chain and Financial Performance," *Supply Chain Management Review,* November–December, 6–7.

Eccles, R. G. (1991), "The Performance Measurement Manifesto," *Harvard Business Review,* January–February, 131–137.

"Inside Purchasing: Four Pillars of Supply Strategy" (1995), *Purchasing,* 118(10), 13.

Kaplan, R. S., and Norton, D. P. (1992), "The Balanced Scorecard—Measures That Drive Performance," *Harvard Business Review,* January–February, 71–79.

Sharman, P. (1995), "How to Implement Performance Measurement in Your Organization," *CMA Magazine,* May, pp. 33–38.

Smeltzer, L. R., and Manship, J. A. (2003), "How Good Are Your Cost Reduction Measures?" *Supply Chain Management Review,* May–June, 3–7.

Timme, S., and Williams-Timme, W. (2000), "The Financial-SCM Connection," *Supply Chain Management Review,* May–June, 33–40.

Trunick, P. A. (2007), "What You Do, Start Measuring," *Logistics Today,* August 22–24.

Vitale, R., and Mavrinac, S. C. (1995), "How Effective Is Your Performance Measurement System?" *Management Accounting,* August, 43–47.

ENDNOTES

1. van Wheele, A. J. (1984), "Purchasing Performance Measurement and Evaluation," *International Journal of Purchasing and Materials Management,* Fall, 18–19.

2. Brown, M. G. (1996), *Keeping Score: Using the Right Metrics to Drive World-Class Performance,* New York: American Management Association, pp. 15–26.

3. Camp, R. C. (1989), "Benchmarking: The Search for Best Practices That Lead to Superior Performance: Part I," *Quality Progress,* January, 66.

4. Pryor, L. S. (1989), "Benchmarking: A Self-Improvement Strategy," *Journal of Business Strategy,* November–December, 28.

5. Pryor, pp. 29–30.

6. Pryor, p. 29.

7. Camp, R. C. (1989), "Benchmarking: The Search for Industry Best Practices That Lead to Superior Performance: Part III," *Quality Progress,* March, 77–80.

8. Furey, T. R. (1987), "Benchmarking: The Key to Developing Competitive Advantage," *Planning Review,* September–October, 32.

9. Camp, R. C. (1989), "Benchmarking: The Search for Best Practices That Lead to Superior Performance: Part II," *Quality Progress,* February, 71.

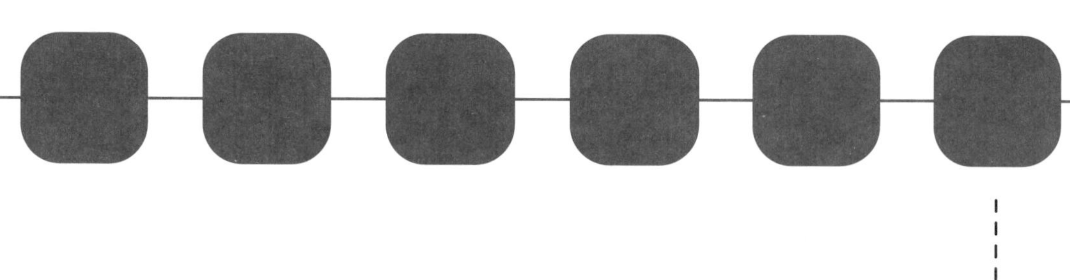

Part 6

Future Directions

Chapter 20

PURCHASING AND SUPPLY STRATEGY TRENDS

Learning Objectives

After completing this chapter, you should be able to

- Understand key purchasing and supply strategy directions
- Recognize high-impact strategy areas
- Understand critical characteristics of key strategies

Chapter Outline

Supply Chain Integration Becomes a Reality

Customer-focused supply chains that can better align and link the various firms making up the supply chain are increasingly likely to gain competitive advantage. This can be exemplified by Wal-Mart, Dell, and IBM examples. Supply chain integration with agreement on goals, business strategies, and information transparency can have significant impacts on capacity investment, inventories, design, responsiveness, and support of a firm's worldwide product/service development, operations/manufacturing, and sourcing footprints.

An example, discussed here in more detail, is the Motorola supply chain integration. In 2005, Motorola undertook the task of linking the various elements that make up its supply chains worldwide. The objectives were cost, cash, and customer service. Cost competitiveness would enable competitive pricing, cash would enable business investment, and customer service would enable the retention of customers.

The challenge was significant, as Motorola operates worldwide. Sales spanned all regions of the globe and purchases came from suppliers in 47 countries (as of 2004), and in the past the six business units generally did little sharing of resources or facilities.

To achieve transformation to an integrated supply chain, the focus was to align and link product design, procurement, manufacturing, logistics, and customer service. In addition, the following six key steps provide a high-level process approach to implement the change:

1. Identify best-in-class processes for duplication throughout the company
2. Develop a supply base that has been right-sized and improve working relationships with key suppliers
3. Establish clear-cut supplier quality expectations and provide performance feedback via a performance scorecard
4. Establish most effective and efficient manufacturing and logistics operations
5. Focus information technology improvement projects to maximize the impact across all business units
6. Create an action-oriented and results-driven culture

The results of the transformation by 2007 were dramatic. Examples are the following:

- Various teams identified best-in-class practices and the highest-priority practices were implemented worldwide.
- Business units work collaboratively to solicit quotes and award business.
- Suppliers were required to develop "quality renewal plans" to continue to do work with Motorola, and Motorola provided performance data to suppliers.
- Motorola's manufacturing and distribution operations square footage was reduced by 40% by examining its worldwide footprint and consolidating facilities.
- Ninety percent of Motorola's information technology spend is now on systems that are common and help all business units—not just one.
- In addition, a number of achievements as of year-end 2006 include reduced ppm defects from suppliers by 50%; achieved customer on-time deliveries of 85 to 92% at some business units (up from 30 to 40%); improved material expenses, product quality, and manufacturing efficiency by 40%; and achieved an 18% improvement in inventory turns.

Overall, this example suggests that a focused effort on integrating the vertical or functional silos into a more integrated supply chain(s) can produce performance results. This supply chain integration is a major ongoing challenge and will be the focus of future efforts.

Source: Adapted from J. A. Cook, "Metamorphosis of a Supply Chain," *CSCMP Supply Chain Quarterly*, 2007, pp. 34–38.

A common theme throughout this book is that the functional area called purchasing, along with the activities that support supply chain management, are experiencing dramatic change. Once regarded as a reactive and administrative activity capable only of neutral or negative contribution, purchasing and supply chain leaders and managers must today be at the forefront of responding to and creating change. As a vice president of a large manufacturing firm in the transportation industry commented, "Over 60% of our revenue is spent with external suppliers, and effective purchasing and world-class suppliers are absolutely required for us to be successful in the future."[1]

This chapter outlines the real and projected changes and trends that have affected and will continue to affect purchasing and supply chain professionals. These changes and trends appear within eight areas and are based on a joint research initiative of CAPS Research, the Institute for Supply Management (ISM), and A.T. Kearney, Inc.[2] These areas are (1) expanding the mission, goals, and performance expectations of purchasing and supply; (2) developing category strategies; (3) developing and managing suppliers; (4) designing and operating multiple supply networks; (5) leveraging technology enablers; (6) collaborating internally and externally; (7) attracting and retaining supply management talent; and (8) managing and enabling the future supply management organization and measurement systems. Much of the discussion in this chapter is drawn from this recent and detailed study. In closing, a series of high-impact strategies are presented.[3]

Expanding the Mission, Goals, and Performance Expectations

Over the past five years and going forward, the mission, goals, and performance contributions required of purchasing and supply by company executives have been increasing and will continue to do so. Increasing contributions in cost reduction, effective asset management, and revenue generation are being required by firms worldwide.

In addition, external forces are continuously changing and will likely impact purchasing and supply management's role and required contributions to a firm's success. These forces include the following:

1. Global competition
2. Mergers, acquisitions, and supply market consolidation
3. Increased governmental regulation
4. Technology advances
5. Customer and channel dynamics
6. Increased product/service variety and shorter life cycles
7. Social responsibilities
8. Environmental responsibilities such as sustainability

Each of these factors individually and in combination will influence change in purchasing and supply strategies and practices, and increase complexity. The rate of future business model and purchasing and supply transformations will also likely quicken and impact purchasing and supply mission and goals.

Overall, future purchasing and supply mission and goals will be broader and more aligned with the strategic objectives of the firm. The future focus will be on several supply chain performance areas including the following:

1. Accelerating and obtaining more innovation from suppliers.
2. Leveraging supplier capabilities and know-how to establish new sources of revenue: e.g., leverage jointly developed technologies with suppliers for internal use or for sale to other customers.
3. Identifying and mitigating supply risks of any kind to ensure business continuity: e.g., price volatility, potential supply disruptions, financially troubled suppliers, negative impacts on sustainability and the environment, protection of intellectual properties, and so forth.
4. Expanding the breadth and depth of cost management efforts in areas such as outsourcing/insourcing, non-traditional purchases, and purchase item standardization and complexity reduction.

Innovation driving change in products, services, and processes will provide increasing competitive advantage in the future. For example, the use of composites in the Boeing 787; the iPod from Apple; and side-by-side, front-loading, and colorful washers and dryers on a platform by Whirlpool all provide marketplace advantage. In addition, firms recognize that innovation cannot be totally achieved utilizing internal resources alone, but must also tap supplier expertise in developing innovations.

Purchasing and supply will also be expected to play a growing role in the sustainability efforts of firms, many of which closely involve suppliers. For example, Tyler Elm, vice president and senior director of corporate strategy and business sustainability at Wal-Mart, recognized that in contrast to early campaigns, their new sustainability strategy would need to be deeply embedded in Wal-Mart's operations and supply chain management to meet the ambitious goals set in 2005. Elm put it this way: "We recognized early on that we had to look at the entire value chain. If we had focused on just our own operations, we would have limited ourselves to 10% of our effect on the environment and eliminated 90% of the opportunity that's out there."[4] Purchasers will have to fully understand sustainability issues and make appropriate decisions based on sustainability considerations, which are growing in importance.

However, the broadening role of supply management will not reduce the need to continue to contribute to other important purchasing objectives, such as the following:

- **Continuous improvement in purchase unit cost, quality, and delivery performance.**

A CAPS Research project[5] provides insight into the degree of supply performance achievements across various important performance areas in 2007 based on responses from 110 companies for the assessment question shown in Exhibit 20.1 on p. 746. The primary focus was cost, quality, and delivery.

Providing ongoing purchase price and cost reduction, combined with quality and delivery performance improvement, is the minimum contribution expected of purchasing and supply. Positive results in these areas are required in order to compete.

- **The reduction of time, particularly during product and process development.**

Although high quality, delivery, and low cost will always be important, time-related capabilities have driven and will continue to drive the next generation of order winners in the eyes of the customer. In particular, product and service support and best customer service with short lead times and the ability to bring new products

Exhibit 20.1 2007 Purchasing Supply Performance Achievements

Assessment Question: "For your most important purchases (80/20 rule) over the past twelve (12) months, indicate the magnitude of measurable performance improvements and/or business unit contribution achieved through sourcing and supply chain strategies at your business unit."

PERFORMANCE AREA	AVERAGE IMPROVEMENT RESULTS
Unit purchase price	4.1% (↑20% ↓18%)
Transportation and logistics costs	2.6% (↑6% ↓20%)
Total cost of ownership	3.5% (↑16% ↓20%)
Overall inventory investment costs	2.0% (↑10% ↓30%)
Supplier quality	3.3%
Supplier on-time delivery	3.6%
Supplier responsiveness/flexibility	2.3%
Supplier diversity	3.1%
Operating earnings	7.6% (↑30% ↓10%)
Fixed asset utilization	2.6% (↑16% ↓8%)

Note: ↑ = improved, ↓ = worsened (range).

Source: R. M. Monczka and K. J. Petersen, *Supply Strategy Implementation: Current State and Future Opportunities,* Tempe, AZ: CAPS Research, 2007.

from concept to customer in the shortest time rival cost and quality as critical market attributes.

Most managers agree that reduced cycle times are essential for market success. Competition is no longer between big and small but rather between fast and agile firms and slow firms. Purchasing plays an important role in time-based competition because of its ability to affect time-related processes and activities. For example, reducing material delivery cycle times with suppliers can also help reduce internal manufacturing cycle times.

Faster supplier responsiveness supports faster responsiveness to end customer requirements, particularly as planning horizons become shorter and less certain. Although beyond the scope of this discussion, material ordering cycle time has four components that supply chain practices affect directly: (1) transmission of requirements to suppliers, (2) suppliers' ordering and manufacturing cycle time, (3) delivery from suppliers, and (4) incoming receiving and inspection.

Perhaps the most obvious area where firms are concentrating their time-reduction efforts is during product and process development. Major changes have occurred in the methods and time required for developing products and processes over the past decade, such as the use of product development teams, rapid prototyping technologies, and computer-aided design systems shared with suppliers. As a result, average product development cycle time has declined and is viewed as significantly important by executive management.

Developing Category Strategies Will Become Broader and More Complex

This second of the eight strategy areas critical to future success focuses on category strategy development.

In the decade ahead, companies will think differently about category strategies. The purpose of a category strategy is to maximize value by leveraging external resources and capabilities. In the future, changes in business models, degree of outsourcing, industry structures, technologies, customer demands, environmental regulations, and other factors will change both how value is defined and how external resources can help deliver it.

"Until the mid-1990s, many companies took a conservative approach to category strategy development by buying the same components, products, and services that they had always bought from the same markets and suppliers. The supply management function was charged primarily with securing the 'best' price and ensuring supply.

In addition, companies traditionally bought goods and services from the same markets and suppliers. Today, companies are taking the next step by looking globally for new suppliers, and defining strategies for new categories. For example, when considering to outsource business processes and activities to reduce costs, new categories like contract manufacturing, facilities management, and logistics are established."

Companies are going even further by seeking suppliers with discrete capabilities that can add new types of value and they are leveraging untapped competencies and knowledge already in the supply base for an existing category. "For example, a food manufacturer utilized a flavoring supplier's knowledge and expertise to rationalize its own ingredient base into flavor and additive 'modules' that provide specific taste or texture. Significant savings for the manufacturer and additional sales for the supplier were achieved, also providing for time-to-market reductions, which was critical to business success in their competitive space."

Companies will increasingly use value-based sourcing approaches to evaluate how a supplier or group of suppliers may be utilized to gain competitive advantage for categories with high business impact.

A robust category strategy will include multiple and concurrent initiatives, including low-cost-country sourcing, design specification changes, switching suppliers to

Sourcing Snapshot — *Global Sourcing for Worldwide Competitiveness*

Firms are increasing their global footprint in search of suppliers in worldwide markets for goods and services. Manitowoc Company, a large maker of cranes, is searching the world for goods: industrial tires in China, bearings from the Midwest, and important chassis parts from suppliers in Poland. At Manitowoc, purchasing and supply has been given executive-level status, with an executive who can lead and manage complex outsourcing and global sourcing decisions, who can establish global supplier relationships, and who is knowledgeable about various foreign cultures. The company recognized that it had to establish a purchasing executive to be in charge of purchasing for its 41 facilities in 14 countries across three divisions. Maximizing opportunities to leverage company spend and ensure dependable supply required worldwide sourcing and organizational and personnel transformations, all in support of globalization, which will continue into the future.

Source: Adapted from T. Aeppel, "Global Scramble for Goods Gives Corporate Buyers a Lift," *Wall Street Journal*, October 2, 2007.

Sourcing Snapshot *China Sourcing*

General Motors Corporation is increasing the China purchasing staff, which is expected to develop suppliers in China. The purchasing staff will increase from the 200 working with suppliers in Shanghai and the office staff will also increase in Beijing and Guangzhou. GM currently has 198 suppliers in China and is working with over 300 China suppliers to assist them in becoming global suppliers to GM.

Source: Adapted from "GM's on the Hunt for China Suppliers," *Automotive News,* December 17, 2007, p. 45.

increase product innovation, and supplier development. "Value" will become better defined and definitions accepted worldwide, and the application of sourcing total cost and value-decision tools will increase.

The breadth and scope of category strategies will also increase. Supply base reduction and global sourcing, especially from emerging markets, will continue to play an important role. However, in the next decade, strategies will increasingly focus on total cost and value creation related to supply and supplier contributions through product/service design and complexity reduction, supplier improvement initiatives, design for supply chain effectiveness, and enhanced collaboration between suppliers to improve performance and achieve sustainability. Category strategy time horizons will be expanded to three to five years.

Strategy Formulation and Selection

"A supply network focus (versus an individual supplier focus) for category strategy development will be increasingly applied. Supply networks, many of which will be in competition with other networks, will require that leading companies develop strategies that leverage the capabilities of all suppliers that make up specific supply networks supporting end-customer demand for goods and services. Category strategies

Sourcing Snapshot *Parts Standardization*

Bosch is asking for parts standardization because of significant investment demands being placed on automakers and parts suppliers. Bosch further pointed out that the company made 44 different heads for the ABS speed sensor, as one example of many. The functionality of all of the sensors is basically the same and the variation could be significantly reduced, yielding economies of scale and possible cost reductions. If there were parts standardization, cost reduction of 5 to 10%, and possibly up to 30%, could be achieved for certain products. Teamwork between OEMs and suppliers, required to cut costs, is an important consideration. How effective purchasing is in working collaboratively with suppliers in the future will be a competitive differentiator.

Source: Adapted from R. Shreifkin, "Bosch Standardized Parts Can Cut Costs," *Automotive News,* January 28, 2008.

in the fast-changing future that align, link, and achieve collaborative efforts by companies throughout the supply network will strongly influence future success."

Outsourcing of Non–Core Competencies

A focus on core competencies and capabilities has influenced the strategic planning process and category strategy development at most firms, and will continue to do so in the decade ahead. There will always be debate about which activities or operations should be performed internally and which should be outsourced. Because purchasing deals extensively with external sources, it becomes involved with the insourcing/outsourcing process. The trend toward outsourcing should continue, although firms have to be careful about being too aggressive with their outsourcing strategy or relying on outsourcing partners that do not fulfill their performance promises. There are a number of reasons why an emphasis on outsourcing will continue:

- As mentioned earlier, the pressure to reduce costs is severe and will only increase.
- Cost-reduction pressures are forcing organizations to use their productive resources more efficiently. As a result, executive management will increasingly rely on insourcing/outsourcing decisions to provide a way to effectively manage costs.
- Firms are continuing to become more highly specialized in product and process technology. Increased specialization implies focused investment in a process or technology, which contributes to greater cost differentials among firms.
- Firms will increasingly focus more on what they excel at while outsourcing areas of nonexpertise. Some organizations are formally defining their core competencies to help guide the insourcing/outsourcing effort. This has affected decisions concerning what businesses a firm should engage in.
- The need for responsiveness in the marketplace is increasingly affecting insourcing/outsourcing decisions. Shorter cycle times, for example, encourage greater outsourcing with less vertical integration. The time to develop a production capability or capacity may exceed the window available to enter a new market.
- Wall Street recognizes and rewards firms that achieve higher return on investment. Because insourcing usually requires an assumption of fixed assets (and increased human capital), financial pressures are causing managers to closely examine sourcing decisions. Avoidance of increased fixed costs is motivating many firms to rely on external rather than internal assets.
- Improved computer simulation tools and forecasting software enable firms to perform insourcing/outsourcing comparisons with greater precision. These tools allow the user to perform sensitivity (what-if) analysis that permits comparisons of different sourcing possibilities.
- Globalization and finding lower-cost sources in emerging countries continue to promote outsourcing.

Concluding Observations

Category strategies are required to define the supply base (internal and external), sourcing allocations, contracting approaches, supplier development, product/service designs, and physical supply chain considerations and are developed from the bottom up by category teams to meet business objectives and customer requirements. These strategies do and will go far beyond volume aggregation or a unit price reduction focus. In the future, value elements will strongly influence category strategies, the development of which will become an increasingly important part of the company strategy. More effective teams with improved personnel and truly global, cross-functional representation will be required.

Category strategies will become more complex and require both internal functional and executive engagement across enterprises. Category strategies will be more agile because they will have to be quickly reconfigured as conditions change. Strategy development will include approaches to influence supply markets and supply networks. Category strategies will increasingly aim to block competition, and early warning or predictive approaches will be used as part of an improved approach to risk within the strategies.

Developing and Managing Suppliers as a Truly Extended Part of the Organization

"In the decade ahead, the development of a competitive worldwide supply base and suppliers that collaboratively help to create value in support of the buying company's business models will become the norm. This focus will be driven by global competition, continuous outsourcing, and the need to develop supply chains for innovative products and services to meet unique customer requirements worldwide." Leading sustainability efforts with suppliers will increase in importance.

Sourcing Snapshot — *Sustainability and Leadership*

Leading sustainability efforts internally and with suppliers will require significant purchasing and supply transformation in the future to ensure competitiveness. Customer buying decisions may become increasingly concerned about how "green" their supplier is. S.C. Johnson's approach provides one example of this transformation.

The company works to improve the environmental impact of the raw materials it purchases. Suppliers and S.C. Johnson work to improve the environment by producing more environmentally friendly ingredients and also improving raw material choices to produce green products.

To support the green efforts, S.C. Johnson developed "Greenlist," an environmental classification system that rates ingredients on four to seven criteria such as biodegradability and aquatic toxicity. Scoring ranges from 3 (best) to 0 (indicates that the material is only used with special permission, and that a substitute for the raw material must be found).

The results of this effort internally and with suppliers have been very successful. Examples include the following:

- Increased the use of better and best materials significantly by more than 13 million kilograms
- Eliminated millions of kilograms of 0-rated materials
- Phased out chlorine-based external packaging materials worldwide
- Phased out the use of bleached paperboard, which uses elemental chlorine as the bleaching agent

The beneficiary of environmentally favorable philosophies and principles laid down throughout 12 decades of business, S.C. Johnson believes it must still work closely with many organizations that have varying agendas and priorities. However, what is found among a disparate supplier community is widespread and common acceptance of Greenlist and its objectives—and a genuine enthusiasm for helping meet those objectives. The recent scale of successes at S.C. Johnson would not have been possible without the active collaboration of suppliers—and without a clear process to guide collaboration.

Source: Adapted from S. Johnson and D. Long, "The Greening of the Supply Chain," *Supply Chain Management Review,* May–June 2006, pp. 36–40.

"In addition, based on the increasing availability of information about the forces affecting industry supply and demand, cost structures, and supplier capabilities, including financial conditions and product/service costs, we may be entering into an era more characterized by companies looking for ways to strategically leverage key supplier/buyer capabilities for innovation and 'enlarging the pie' rather than playing the zero-sum game whereby one company's gain may be at the expense of the other. The importance of strategic partners, both buyers and sellers, will likely increase."

"These factors will affect which supply networks a supplier will choose to join. The buying company at the heart of a given supply network will need to develop philosophies, attitudes, and practices that will give suppliers the opportunities to jointly achieve financial and other benefits. Emphasis will be placed on more cooperative versus adversarial approaches, including selective information transparency between strategically aligned buyers and sellers—and among the suppliers in a network."

In the decade ahead, companies will put significant effort into strategically structuring their supply bases to support the business model and category strategies. As worldwide outsourcing continues, combined with the need for value creation and innovation from suppliers, establishing the best suppliers globally grows in importance.

"In the future, companies will more carefully and strategically answer the following questions to most effectively structure the supply base for each of their purchase category families.

- How many suppliers do we want for this category (and in the supply base) and what role should each play?
- What current and future capabilities are required and where in the world should the supplier(s) be located?
- Which suppliers should we work with and why?
- Do we want to lead and/or manage supplier networks at the Tier 2 and 3 levels?
- Which suppliers do we want to collaborate with, or have them collaborate with other suppliers, and why?"

Improving Supplier Relationships

Making significant improvements in working relationships with key suppliers will be increasingly critical to gain supplier innovation and preferential customer treatment in the years ahead. Companies will have to more effectively structure their supply base by category and identify those suppliers that are truly strategic and capable of providing innovation. Attitudes about the approaches to be used when working with these most important suppliers will have to be further developed and move from purely adversarial to more collaborative.

To enhance future working relationships with important suppliers, the following elements must be in place:

- Supplier segmentation
- Supplier scorecards and feedback
- Supplier capability matrices
- Rewards to best performers
- Joint executive meetings
- Supplier councils and conferences
- Process improvement and innovation workshops
- Two-way performance evaluations and satisfaction surveys
- Supplier suggestion systems
- Risk/reward sharing
- Executive engagement
- Trust

The future requirement is the holistic implementation of all of the above, not just two or three elements. Today, many firms are limited in their implementation of the above elements.

Concluding Observations about Supply Base Management

Three dominant themes emerge for the future. First, the purchasing management function will have to clearly determine company needs and align with suppliers that have the necessary current and future capabilities to meet typical performance objectives, provide innovation, and help create value to support company business model(s)

Sourcing Snapshot — *Ford Aligned Business Framework*

In 2005, Ford Motor Company established the Aligned Business Framework, an attempt to improve Ford's supplier relations. The plan included reducing the number of suppliers by half and providing longer-term business to those that remained together with early access to new-product programs.

However, at the same time, the financial condition of the firm deteriorated and much of the purchasing focus was on price reductions. Even though the degree of cooperation that was desired was not fully achieved and supplier relations remained combative, respondents to a supplier survey say that the Aligned Business Framework program has met or exceeded expectations. Access to Ford's senior management has improved, and purchasers and engineers are starting to collaborate. This progress is significant.

Source: Adapted from "Ford Suppliers Plan Is Still Just a Work in Progress," *Automotive News*, September 10, 2007.

and competitiveness. Second, working relationships between buying and selling companies, strategically important to each other, must improve to unlock value-creating potential. Third, the future will require more bilateral (or multilateral) and collaborative approaches as opposed to dictatorial and price-dominated approaches in companies that want to achieve value creation through the supply base.

Designing and Operating Multiple Supply Networks to Meet Customer Requirements

Supply chains that are seamless and driven by end user or customer needs will be required. Revenues will flow to companies that can get the correct product or service bundles to customers at the lowest landed and total costs. Supply chain innovation and different supply chains to meet different customer segments will be key to future revenue and market share growth, for example, having different supply chains for short product life cycle cell phones versus mature and longer product life cycle televisions at a consumer electronics firm.

In addition, companies like Dell and Wal-Mart raised the bar with supply chains that operate effectively on cost, quality, and responsiveness measures while adding a new dimension: the ability to identify and respond to change in a timely manner, providing advantage over less agile competitors.

In tomorrow's world, the ability to respond to change will be the price of admission to compete. "Competitive advantage will require agility, while supply chain excellence will be defined by the ability to:

- Anticipate changes worldwide in customer requirements, product offerings, supply conditions, regulations, and competitor actions
- Adapt to the changes by reconfiguring existing supply chains or creatively assembling new ones
- Accelerate implementation of the transformed supply chain to capture the new opportunities ahead of the competition

"Make-to-order or assemble-to-order product/service bundles that fill distinct and possibly numerous market niches will quite obviously require the management of several supply chains simultaneously on a global scale—only multiple supply chains will be able to make a company this flexible." Purchasing and supply and suppliers at Tiers 1, 2, and even 3 will play a key role in supply chain success. Lack of availability or a quality problem at a Tier 2 supplier can create significant end customer performance problems.

Concluding Observations

Many supply chain design strategies, approaches, and solutions are available to assist companies. Significant amounts of information provide concepts and ideas about how to meet market and customer needs. Almost all companies, market niches, and customers have different needs. However, a supply chain design that works at one organization will not necessarily work for others. Companies that do not carefully tailor their supply chains will find their efforts resulting in poor performance or broken supply chains. To achieve success, supply chains will have to be segmented and customer focused within an organization, with strong supplier networks.

Sourcing Snapshot — *Engaging Suppliers Earlier in Product/Service Design and Standardization*

Chrysler LLC believed that its interiors lacked refinement in recent years. To change this situation, Chrysler began to bring suppliers into the design process much earlier, some at least two years before the design freeze. The objective was to try more variations and choose the correct materials. It was believed that in the past, suppliers were chosen too late to fully evaluate design options. Now management can make better design decisions and decide what materials to spend money on. This transformation to truly implement the extended enterprise will require that purchasing and supply find innovative suppliers and construct business deals to accelerate supplier innovation for the benefit of the buying company.

Source: Adapted from B. Wernie, "To Aid Interiors, Chrysler Brings in Suppliers Earlier," *Automotive News*, September 17, 2007.

Leveraging Technology Enablers Takes on Additional Focus

There will be continuing improvements to supply management e-system applications over the next decade, coupled with technological advances integrating applications and data to enhance people's personal effectiveness and collaboration. We will have continued refinements of technologies already introduced.

Spend management will continue to increase its flexibility for analytics and will be more easily implemented—companies will be less challenged by the need to perform setup data cleansing. Spend management will also become more closely aligned with specific contract provisions. Purchasing will more fully move to a digitized and paperless world and tactical activities will become more automated.

"Optimization will continue to expand features to e-sourcing as the discipline becomes more sophisticated. Contract management software will become more integrated with spend management, particularly in terms of compliance. Collaboration software will also enhance the ability to streamline the contract management process. Performance monitoring and capability mapping will continue to expand supply management's potential. The flexibility provided by user definition and role-based access will enrich the potential for added supply management. E-systems will increasingly provide cross-enterprise visibility and transparency and link to companywide enterprise resource planning systems."

Linking Collaboration Tools to Product Life Cycle Management

By linking collaboration tools to product life cycle management technologies, the influence and visibility that supply management has over interactions with engineering and operations, both internally and with suppliers, will be extended.

"For example, Toyota leads the automotive industry in profitability and time to market because it is the leader in design commonality and parts reuse. Collaboration tools play a critical role in achieving these goals; through the use of these tools the company's suppliers actively share and collaborate with Toyota."

"Today, other industries are adopting collaboration tools. For example, Procter & Gamble uses the same tools as GM to facilitate its brand management and product development processes from idea generation through production. The tools offer data integration capabilities to help manage product formulations, packaging design and artwork, and labeling regulations. As a result, P&G reduced its new-product launch time by 50% and has an almost error-free process for producing artwork and labels. P&G plans to look at Tier 2 and 3 suppliers for innovation as well as for supply assurance."

For supply management executives, the information provided by collaboration tools will play a critical role in improving the effectiveness and efficiency of sourcing initiatives. The data from these tools will help supply executives understand spend by item number, purchase item, and supplier. The level of specification information provided will make discussions with suppliers much more productive and also allow engineering and supply management to work more effectively together.

Sourcing Snapshot

Sourcing E-Tools at Harris

Harris has focused much of its recent transformation attention on the information it needs to determine which suppliers can provide the best-suited products at the lowest overall cost. The company has established a companywide database infrastructure to capture and store data, processes, and e-system applications.

The e-system transformation took two to three years to somewhat fully develop. Harris now has the ability to view the entire business and drive collaborative decision making with the capabilities in place.

Harris has implemented numerous buying tools, including an internally developed program called EXPO. This is an enterprisewide portal that connects Harris's four divisions, the ERP programs, and company engineers. The system provides for internal collaboration and billing and enables direct e-system communications with suppliers. EXPO enables Harris to determine parts quality performance, assess whether a part is environmentally safe, view inventory records, identify the type of supplier to which the purchase item is sourced, and so forth.

In addition, Harris uses Oracle's Agile product life cycle management software to help manage product life cycle decisions throughout the company. Harris also uses Indecka's search engine technology to help product development engineers locate parts to meet specific technical requirements. This enables engineers to specify parts that are early in their product life cycle and that meet Harris's cost targets. Harris also uses Dun & Bradstreet's financial alerts to determine the financial status of a supplier and other profile information.

Source: Adapted from W. Forest, "Center-Led Collaboration Powers Harris Sourcing Initiatives," *Purchasing,* 137(3), March 2008, pp. 14–16.

Exhibit 20.2 Technology Tools Will Evolve Even Further

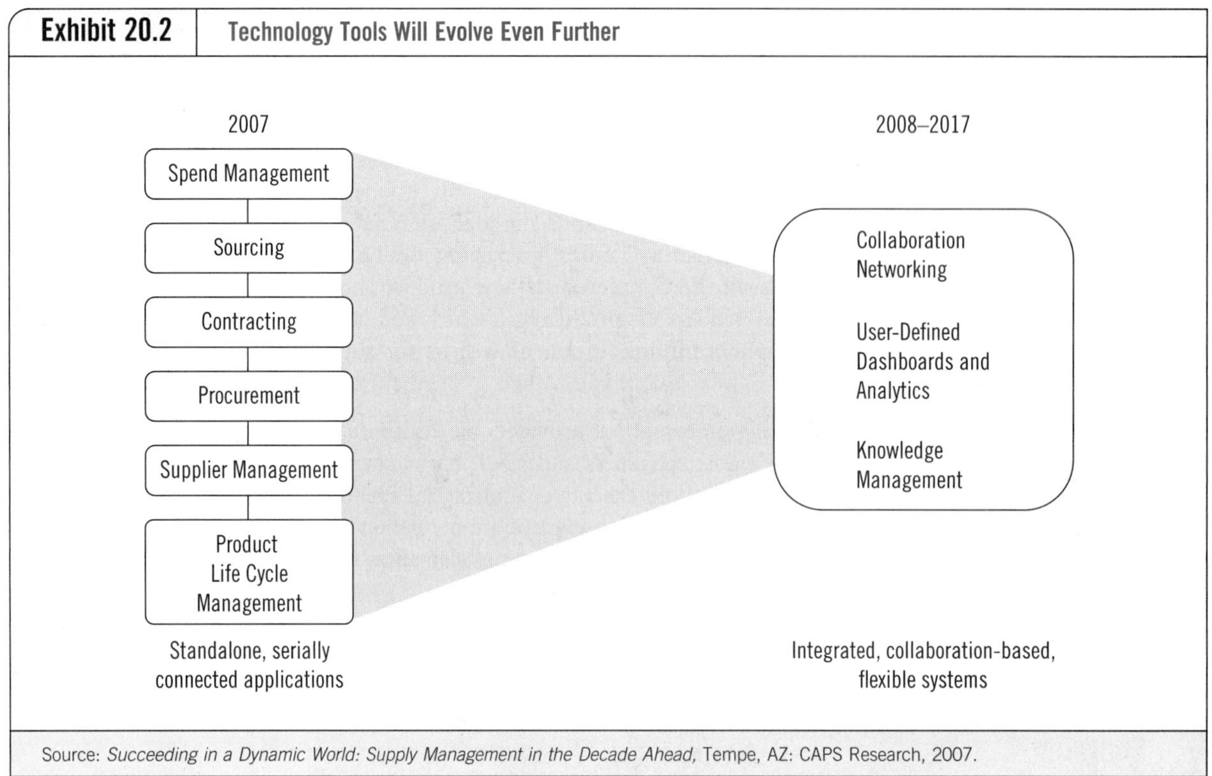

Source: *Succeeding in a Dynamic World: Supply Management in the Decade Ahead,* Tempe, AZ: CAPS Research, 2007.

Concluding Observations

Overall, technology will move from standalone, serially connected application to integrated, collaboration-based, flexible systems emphasizing collaboration, user-defined analysis, and knowledge management, as shown in Exhibit 20.2. Reporting will be on-demand, and the purchasing function will become more digitized and paperless. Cross-enterprise transparency will increase, as will collaboration enabled by technology.

Collaborating Internally and Externally Will Grow in Strategic Importance

Collaboration with suppliers is quite frequently identified as an important success factor in achieving competitiveness. However, supplier collaboration may not easily fit in with the traditional view of supply management's role in many organizations. Four main themes around collaboration were established for the decade ahead by the CAPS, ISM, and AT Kearney study:

1. Internal collaboration and integration will be enhanced to meet future company needs.
2. External collaboration will signal a shift from pure competition to cooperation for some segments of a company's supply base.

3. Technology is required to enable an increase in collaboration—providing for both internal and external information transparency.
4. Management risk and protecting intellectual property may limit collaboration with suppliers.

Purchasing and supply management, combined with other functional leadership and company executives, will have to establish the company strategy and policies governing collaborative efforts with suppliers (and customers). Significant changes in attitudes, strategies, practices, and working relationships will be required.

Obtaining Innovation

"In the future, companies will need to use collaboration to keep their innovation pipeline filled. For some, this may be as simple as having purchasing interface with their own product development organization as well as their suppliers." More complex collaboration will enable companies to link internal technological advances to demands of external customers.

Linking customer needs to supplier capabilities will continue to be complex, requiring enhancements of approaches to and attitudes about collaboration.

Concluding Observations

In the past, supply management has focused on establishing a competitive environment for purchasing—a practice enhanced through cross-functional category sourcing teams working to achieve competitive advantage. In the future, there will be an increased need for systematic approaches for creating and operating collaboratively with strategic suppliers. Collaboration will be enhanced by technology linked to product life cycle management software along with access to networks that ease internal collaboration and working with external suppliers. In addition, suppliers and supply personnel must be convinced that the openness and trust needed in a genuinely collaborative environment will generate positive performance results.

Attracting, Developing, and Retaining Supply Management Talent Will Become a Key Differentiator for Success

"A great deal will be expected of tomorrow's purchasing and supply management professionals, as they will be charged with developing and executing value acquisition strategies that find new value in the supply base, deliver value as quickly as possible within the cost parameters defined by the demand market, and maximize the return to the company. To do so, they will need to find and leverage external sources of innovation, contribute to revenue generation, expand efforts to manage costs, and ensure business continuity and sustainability."

To achieve all of these requirements, supply management professionals will need the skills and capabilities to understand and interpret supply market dynamics, analyze complex supply options and risks, and develop innovative value acquisition strategies that integrate with and support business and functional strategies. Supply leaders will also be asked to create and manage collaborative supplier relationships and lead

Exhibit 20.3 Future Skills and Capabilities for Supply Management Professionals

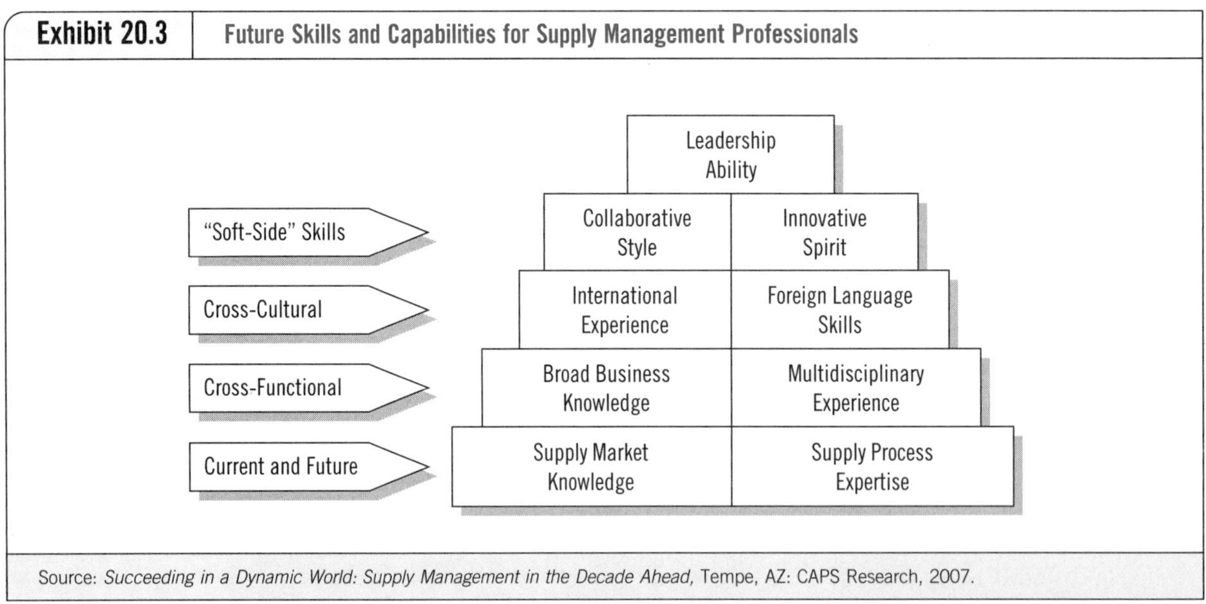

Source: *Succeeding in a Dynamic World: Supply Management in the Decade Ahead,* Tempe, AZ: CAPS Research, 2007.

cross-functional and cross-organizational teams on a global basis." Exhibit 20.3 presents an overview of the many skills and capabilities that supply management professionals will need to succeed.

Current and Future Supply Management Skills

The foundational skills for supply will continue to center upon a combination of supply market knowledge and supply process expertise, including competitive market structure and price and cost models. Also required will be awareness of the future forces at work on the industry (e.g., emerging supply markets sustainability, merger and acquisition activity, potential new entrants, and technology trends). "Requirements for supply will include the ability to develop robust forward-looking strategies, to conduct a rigorous sourcing effort using data collection and analysis tools, to carry out negotiations and contracting, and to drive supplier development/operational improvement programs (including applying tools such as lean and Six Sigma)."

Cross-Functional Skills and Teaming

"Supply management professionals will increasingly need both broader general business knowledge and multidiscipline skills. A working knowledge of business fundamentals including finance, accounting, and business law, and project management skills, as well as exposure to/experience in operations, engineering, product and service development, marketing and sales, and business planning, will help supply professionals to work effectively across functional and organizational boundaries. Understanding how their own business and key suppliers operate and compete will also be key. Understanding will help enhance overall value received, reduce costs, and ensure business continuity."

The use of cross-functional teams will be an important supply management strategy because they provide a broader base of knowledge for decision making and can lead to decisions that take into account the needs of all the major stakeholders in the organization. Including internal users on sourcing teams acknowledges their expertise in their particular areas and leads to much better cooperation, which in turn leads to better supplier agreements, in which internal users have a vested interest. Cross-functional teams will be used in particular for category and supplier strategy development and implementation.

Cross-functional teams focused on and for process and system improvement processes will also be critical in the future. Companies will develop global systems capability and functional processes to align their global systems. However, problems will arise when global processes are not supported by cross-functional teams. Companies may have best-in-class financial, operational, and supply chain processes, but there may still be significant "white space" or disconnects between the functional processes. Cross-functional teams will be used to help fill this organizational white space and connect the disparate systems.

Sourcing Snapshot

Teamwork and Cooperation Come Slowly between Functions

Companies are taking steps to get different departments to work together effectively, but they're still falling short of the goal. And although most purchasing professionals agree that teamwork and cooperation are the best mechanisms for getting different corporate functions to work together, they also point out that neither attribute exists naturally in a corporate setting.

The results of a recent survey indicate that although there are good signs of cooperation between corporate departments, many companies are not doing enough to foster cooperation between purchasing and other functions. Even worse, many such efforts are actually counterproductive. "There's too much competition among departments," says Ronald Blizzard, materials administrator for Massachusetts-based Guilford Rail System. His response was typical of many purchasers who say that long-standing rivalries between groups do not die easily or quickly.

Most of the survey participants say their companies are not taking the most effective approach to the problem of promoting teamwork and cooperation.

Some survey respondents say that employees themselves are the root of the problem, that staff members simply refuse to play along or work well with others. But the majority of survey respondents lay the responsibility at the feet of management. They say whatever process is adopted, it must receive the blessing and support of upper management. Too often, the departments of production, planning, design, quality, and purchasing have different leaders to answer to. Those who have watched this process work well report that their purchasing departments were successfully linked with operations management, logistics and planning, materials, and warehouse receiving/shipping departments.

Management must continually reinforce the common goal of teamwork, reminding employees that they are part of a company, not only a department.

Source: Adapted from B. Milligan, "Despite Attempts to Break Them, Functional Silos Live On," *Purchasing,* November 4, 1999, pp. 24–26. See also S. Avery, "Rockwell Collins Takes Off," *Purchasing,* February 20, 2003, pp. 25–28.

Cross-Cultural Skills

The ability to work cross-culturally, with foreign-language skills, will increase in importance as companies further expand around the world and continue to outsource globally and pursue suppliers in emerging markets. Individuals with international experience bring a broader perspective and understanding of how to be effective in different cultures.

"Soft-Side" Skills

Strong "soft-side" skills will be a key determinant of success. Soft skills of importance include a collaborative working style, an innovative spirit that challenges current approaches and seeks innovative solutions to problems, and having leadership abilities. In the future, the ability to lead virtual, geographically dispersed teams will be critical, driven by cross-functional and cross-organizational initiatives, more globalization, and a shortage of talent, and enabled by the application of collaboration technology.

Concluding Observations

Companies that are able to attract, develop, and retain people with the above knowledge and skills will likely be the most competitive. To gain this differential advantage in talent, broader and worldwide hiring practices will have to be enhanced. Development programs will also be required, enabling people to work independently, on-demand, to meet development goals, as well as in groups. Retention of the best

Sourcing Snapshot — *Measuring Future Purchasing Skill Requirements*

As the purchaser's job has evolved, so have the skills needed to handle both day-to-day and strategic tasks. What's lacking, however, is a corporate understanding of how to evaluate those skills and define expectations for higher-level procurement positions, according to Larry Giunipero, who authored the study *A Skills-Based Analysis of the World-Class Purchaser* for the Center for Advanced Purchasing Studies.

According to Giunipero's report, companies that will show the way in this area must continually assess the skills and knowledge of their purchasers, measure those skills against an ideal, make training convenient and readily available to their purchasers, understand the importance of having suppliers involved in the training process, and establish quantifiable metrics that can be converted into measurable training goals.

To get to the next level, companies should consider devising a weighted skill matrix, a technique that defines the skills required by individuals for a particular position and uses a rating scale where each number represents proficiency in a particular skill set. Before setting up the matrix, however, companies must define what skills are needed for the position today and in the future. From there, companies can evaluate the level of skills currently demonstrated and identify the gaps between an ideal skill set and what an employee possesses. Once those gaps are defined, top management and the purchasing department can establish a plan to foster the future growth of skills.

Source: Adapted from L. Giunipero, *A Skills-Based Analysis of the World-Class Purchaser*, Tempe, AZ: Center for Advanced Purchasing Studies, 2000.

professionals will also grow in importance and require that the company be viewed as a "best" or "interesting" or "exciting" place to work in supply.

Managing and Enabling the Future Supply Management Organization and Measurement Systems

The currently dominant center-led model for supply management will continue to be a key strategy over the next decade, and will likely be the norm. This is especially true as organizations better develop the balance between companywide advantages from scale and expertise and product/service, business unit needs such as continuity of supply, and fast product/service development with perfect launch. Decentralized supply strategies will not dominate.

However, a significant issue is how to integrate purchasing and supply management with the rest of the organization. The most likely scenarios are shown in Exhibit 20.4.

In one scenario, purchasing/supply will become part of a larger supply chain function, which would have responsibility for all functions on both the demand and supply sides of the firm, required to meet customer needs. Specific activities on the demand side that virtually touch the customer would not generally be included.

"In the second likely scenario, supply management will take on a leading role to manage both external and internal supply. The top supply management role will closely resemble today's chief operating officer's job description." In this organizational structure,

Exhibit 20.4 Organization Alternatives

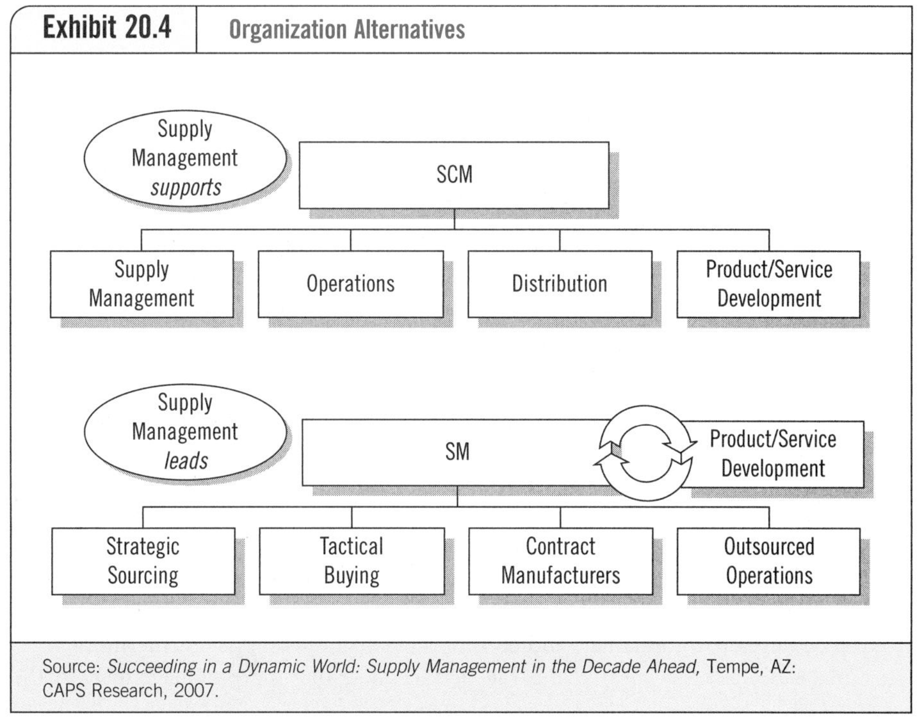

Source: *Succeeding in a Dynamic World: Supply Management in the Decade Ahead,* Tempe, AZ: CAPS Research, 2007.

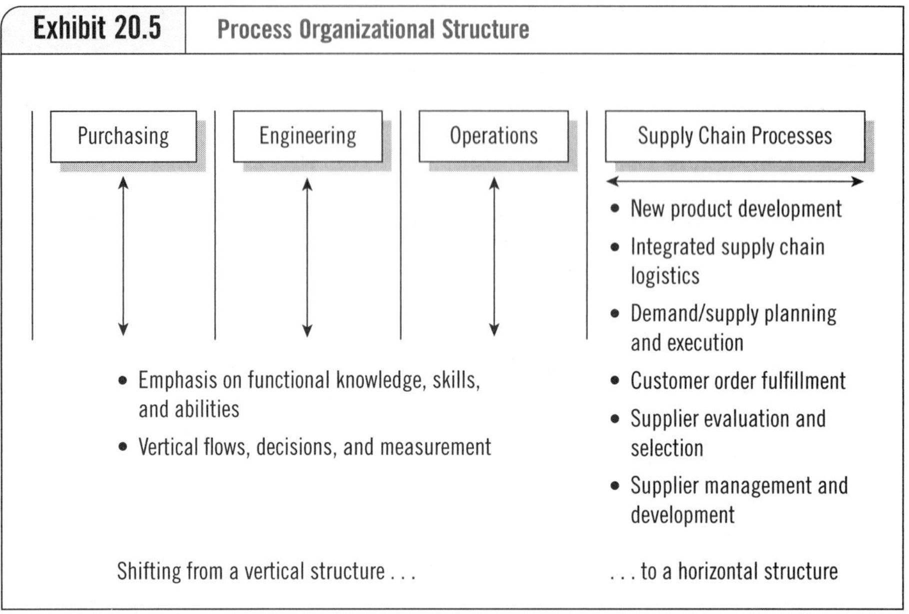

supply will manage all of the external supply base. Doing so will require a tight integration with operations, engineering, and internal customers to help ensure the proper management of new-product introductions and continuous improvement in legacy products and processes.

"Under this model, supply management will have near-complete responsibility for the management of all expenditures in the corporation. The supply management leader would act as the chief cost management officer."

Exhibit 20.5 further illustrates the increasing focus on horizontal structures integrating various functions. To be competitive in the decade ahead, more cross-functional and customer-focused integration will be necessary.

Measuring Supply Management Performance

"Today, supply managers think that they have good alignment between measures of supply performance and linkage with corporate measures and that this linkage will become more important in the decade ahead. Not surprisingly, they also think they currently have good operational measures for supply management and that it will be highly important to maintain these measures over the next decade."

In addition to the importance of internal metrics, supply managers feel that common metrics across trading partners in the supply chain will be an important strategy going forward and believe improvement is needed. Supply measures will increasingly become customer centric. For example, measuring the ability of the firm to meet significant customer schedule or demand shifts, product redesign and reliability of performance will be linked back to purchasing and supply. Also, as companies become larger and spread more widely across the globe, relevant and effective metrics will be developed to manage and control the global operations. Furthermore, metrics will be needed that clearly link the performance of supply management to the strategic performance of the organization. Measurement systems linking purchasing and supply more directly to a firm's economic value-add or return on invested capital will be utilized. A balanced scorecard approach to measuring the contribution of supply management to the success of the company will be in common use.

Concluding Observations

The traditional view has held that only a centralist model provides companies the ability to leverage the category, supply, and talent strategies discussed. However, given the global nature of some businesses, the need for a local focus and information technologies suggests the need to better balance the scale benefits of center-led approaches with agility in meeting business unit needs. Strategic business units (SBUs) or regional organizations may become the highest organizational level around which supply activities are managed in the largest organizations. However, the center-led model will predominate at either the company or SBU level.

In addition, purchasing and supply will become more integrated with other company functions such as engineering, operations, and finance. Performance measures will become more customer focused within a balanced scorecard and tightly coupled to a firm's financial performance.

Twelve High-Impact Sourcing and Supply Chain Strategies for 2009–2015

The Project 10X Executive Assessment conducted by CAPS Research,[6] combined with *Succeeding in a Dynamic World: Supply Management in the Decade Ahead,* have identified 12 key purchasing and supply strategies that firms need to focus on to achieve competitive success in the future. These strategies, which build on our prior discussions, provide a very focused approach to achieving excellence for leading companies:

1. Continuous outsourcing determination and globalization of supply with greater focus on risk management with key suppliers.
2. Enhanced supply chain integration and collaboration with strategic suppliers.
3. Increased information sharing and transparency internally and with suppliers.
4. Sourcing becoming more integrated with other functions, processes, and customers including external customer-facing activities.
5. Enhancing the quality, number, and execution of written purchase family/supplier category strategies with a focus on value, including the total supply network.
6. Selectively ensuring the adequacy of sourcing and supply strategies as a means to accelerate and obtain innovation from suppliers.
7. Requiring suppliers to take a greater cost management role by providing value-adding services in research and development, manufacturing/operations, customer order fulfillment, and system integration.
8. Providing common customer-focused measurements and metrics across the supply chain.
9. Developing an e-sourcing and supply applications portfolio including digitized and paperless supplier invoicing, e-sourcing (with the Internet and

global data warehouses providing the backbone), and knowledge management systems, combined with internal applications focused on analytics.

10. Supply taking a leading role in sustainability with suppliers.
11. Strategic sourcing and supply chain activities primarily center-led, with appropriate activities being located at sites worldwide, and with decentralized execution on a global basis.
12. Human resources strategies and dedicated personnel focusing on identifying, hiring, and developing highly talented, flexible, and globally oriented personnel, who can immediately contribute—a critical success factor.

Good Practice Example

Cessna Transforms to Achieve Leading-Edge Sourcing and Supply Status

Charles B. Johnson, president and COO of Cessna, pointed out, "As our supply chain processes house the majority of our cost, it was necessary to create a more strategically aligned supply chain that yielded the most competitive quality, delivery, flexibility, and value." This was a major driver underlying the transformation process at Cessna. Under the leadership of Michael R. Katzorke, supply chain management senior vice president, supply chain management at Cessna has created a long-range strategic plan and cross-functional commodity teams. The purpose was to rationalize the company's supplier base. In addition, Cessna developed a Maturity Path Development tool that aligned suppliers and Cessna strategy. They also revised the company's sales, inventory, and operations plan (SIOP), aimed at improving performance to customer expectations and reducing inventory turns. Malcolm Baldrige National Quality Award criteria and Six Sigma quality tools were used to drive improvement in supplier performance. A value analysis/value engineering process was also introduced, encouraging supplier involvement in removing cost from the supply chain.

Katzorke and the supply chain management team have involved suppliers in supporting Cessna's corporate "High Five" objectives of total customer satisfaction, world quality standards for aviation, breakthrough operating performance, top 10 company to work for, and superior financial results. Clearly Cessna's sourcing and supply strategy transformation is aimed at contributing to overall company objectives.

"Perhaps the biggest achievement of Katzorke and his team," says Johnson, "has been the engagement of the organization in the Cessna supply chain transformation process from a transactional purchasing organization to an integrated full supply chain process."

Katzorke has stated: "For breakthrough change, we needed the vision, skills, incentives, resources, and action plan fully linked across the entire business."

One of the key transformation elements in achieving an integrated supply chain is the use of cross-functional commodity teams. These teams include representatives of supply chain management, manufacturing engineering, quality engineering, product design engineering, reliability engineering, product support, and finance. The teams work to drive supplier improvement and integration of suppliers into Cessna's design and manufacturing process, thereby integrating critical components of the supply chain. There are six commodity teams for direct materials and one for indirect materials and services. Each team has a strategic plan linked to the CEO's strategic objectives, which are updated annually.

One key task of the commodity teams was to rationalize the supply base, which they did, resulting in a reduction from 3,000 to 132 suppliers. Remaining suppliers were then classified into growth suppliers, where Cessna's business will grow; provisional suppliers, whose future prospects are uncertain; and phase-out suppliers, whose business with Cessna is about to end. The teams then formed long-term partnerships with the growth suppliers, aligning the supply base contractually in terms of objectives, strategies, processes and data, and supply chain integration. Today, growth suppliers receive 77% of Cessna's business. The teams are also further integrating suppliers into Cessna's design, manufacturing, and other key processes so that they become fully integrated with and part of Cessna's business.

Cessna also developed a new process that included demand and SIOP processes. Suppliers have clear visibility to production plans and capacity planning interfaces, focusing on end-customer demand. This high-level review of Cessna illustrates the magnitude and company emphasis being placed on developing leading-edge purchasing and supply strategies and processes that contribute to financial performance of the firm.

Source: Adapted from S. Avery, "Cessna Soars," *Purchasing,* September 4, 2003, pp. 25–35.

CONCLUSION

This chapter—as well as this book—presents purchasing and supply chain management as a dynamic field of study. Surviving in an era of rapid change and intense competition requires a commitment to (1) develop the skills of purchasing professionals, (2) actively use information technology across the supply chain, (3) pursue activities and practices that capture the full benefit of a world-class supply base, (4) create responsive new organizational structures, and (5) establish the most effective purchasing and supply chain measurement system. Competing today requires purchasing and supply chain managers to play an active role in helping achieve an organization's cost, quality, time, technology, innovation, and sustainability goals—or risk losing market share to competitors that are benefiting from world-class supply chain management.

DISCUSSION QUESTIONS

1. Given the trends described in this chapter, what do you think the future purchasing organization will look like?
2. What are some of the primary skills that purchasing and supply chain managers will need to be successful in the future?
3. What will the role of the Internet and e-systems be in supporting purchasing and supply chain management activities?
4. Why will there be an increase in using suppliers for product and process technology?
5. Why will the development of global databases increase? What kind of information should a global database provide?
6. Why will global sourcing increase?
7. Do you believe the total number of suppliers within a typical firm's supply bases will increase or decrease? Why?
8. The need to reduce cycle time is important. How can purchasing help in this process?
9. What will an integrated supply chain look like in terms of key elements?
10. How can more innovation from suppliers be achieved? What is required?
11. What is the possible role of purchasing in leading sustainability efforts?

ADDITIONAL READINGS

Billington, C., and Jager, F. (2008), "Procurement: The Missing Link in Innovation," *Supply Chain Management Review,* January.

Carter, P. L., Carter, J. R., Monczka, R. M., Blascovich, J. D., Slaight, T. H., and Markham, W. J. (2007), *Succeeding in a Dynamic World: Supply Management in the Decade Ahead,* Tempe, AZ: CAPS Research.

Hirsch, C., and Barbalho, M. (2003), "Toward World Class Procurement," *Supply Chain Management Review,* 5(6), 75.

Katzorke, M. (2000), "Cessna Charts a Supply Chain Flight Strategy," *Purchasing,* 129(4), 42.

Monczka, R. M., Markham, W. J., Carter, J. R., Blascovich, J. D., and Slaight, T. H. (2005), *Outsourcing Strategically for Sustainable Competitive Advantage,* Tempe, AZ: CAPS Research.

Monczka, R. M., and Petersen, K. J. (2007), *Supply Strategy Implementation: Current State and Future Opportunities,* Tempe, AZ: CAPS Research.

Monczka, R. M., Petersen, K. J., and Trent, R. J. (2006), *Effective Global Sourcing and Supply for Superior Results,* Tempe, AZ: CAPS Research.

Monczka, R. M., Trent, R. J., and Petersen, K. J. (2008), "Getting on Track to Better Global Sourcing," *Supply Chain Management Review,* March.

"One on One: An Interview with Edith Kelly-Green—A Leading Purchasing and Supply Management Professional Shares Her Views on Technology and Trends" (2000), *Journal of Supply Chain Management,* 36(2), 2.

"One on One: An Interview with Gene Richter—A Leading Purchasing and Supply Management Professional Shares His Views on Technology and Trends" (2000), *Journal of Supply Chain Management,* 36(1), 2.

Rudzki, R. A. (2008), "Supply Management Transformation: A Leader's Guide," *Supply Chain Management Review,* March.

Slone, R. E., Mentzer, J. T., and Dittmann, P. J. (2007), "Are You the Weakest Link in Your Company's Supply Chain?" *Harvard Business Review,* September.

Smock, D. A., Rudzki, R. A., and Rogers, S. C. (2007), "Sourcing Strategy—The Brains behind the Game," *Supply Chain Management Review,* May.

ENDNOTES

1. Interview with R. M. Monczka, 2003.
2. Carter, P. L., Carter, J. R., Monczka, R. M., Blascovich, J. D., Slaight, T. H., and Markham, W. J. (2007), *Succeeding in a Dynamic World: Supply Management in the Decade Ahead,* Tempe, AZ: CAPS Research.
3. Quotation marks have been placed around the passages taken directly from Carter et al.
4. Plambeck, E. L. (2007), "The Greening of Wal-Mart's Supply Chain," *Supply Chain Management Review,* July–August, 19.
5. Monczka, R. M., and Petersen, K. J. (2007), *Supply Strategy Implementation: Current State and Future Opportunities,* Tempe, AZ: CAPS Research.
6. Monczka and Petersen.

Cases

1 Avion, Inc.

Susan Dey and Bill Mifflin, procurement managers at Avion, Inc., sat across from each other and reviewed a troubling performance report concerning a key supplier, Foster Technologies. The report detailed the deteriorating performance of Foster Technologies in the areas of material quality and on-time delivery.

Susan: I don't believe what I am seeing. This supplier was clearly a star when we performed our supplier visits before awarding the contract for the new Amrod product line.

Bill: I'm not pleased. I was on the team that performed the audit and site visit. Foster's management was so smooth—they indicated they could meet all our requirements. I feel like we've been misled by this supplier.

Susan: Didn't you look at their processes and quality systems?

Bill: Sure we did. Everything checked out fine. But now every other shipment has some problem, and the delays are hurting our ability to get our product to our customers. What really struck us about this supplier was how innovative they were. Foster's biggest drawback was their size—they lacked some depth at key manufacturing engineering positions. Maybe that's why they are having problems. It could be that someone has left the company.

Susan: We are going to have to address these problems quickly.

Bill: I'll tell you what I am going to recommend. We should begin immediately to look for another supplier. I never was a fan of these single-source contracts. They leave us open to too much risk.

Susan: But won't that take a long time?

Bill: Sure. We'll have to perform another supplier search with team visits. New tooling could really cost, too. This could take months.

Susan: Has anyone talked with the supplier about these problems?

Bill: Kevin went over personally today and talked with the production manager. He didn't have much time to explain, but he indicated on the phone that Foster's production manager said we should accept responsibility for a good part of the problems that are occurring!

Susan: Why should we? I think they are just trying to shift the blame for their poor performance.

At this point, Kevin O'Donnell, another procurement manager, entered the room.

Bill: Kevin, glad you're here. We were just discussing how Foster is trying to blame us for their problems. I think we should dump them fast!

Kevin: Yeah, well, I've got news for you two. I think Foster's production manager is correct. I think I would be frustrated with us, too!

Susan: What are you talking about?

Kevin: I spent a good part of the day over at Foster and learned some interesting things. For example, do either of you remember what we told Foster the monthly volume requirements for the product would be?

Bill: I remember exactly. The volumes were projected to be 2,500 units a month. So what's the problem?

Kevin: We need to talk with our production group more often. The monthly volumes are now over 4,000 units a month! And not only that, our production group now wants material within 10 days of a material release rather than two weeks. We have also been changing the final material release quantities right up to the last minute before delivery.

Bill: Uh oh. I remember on our site visit that the most their production system could handle was 3,500 units a month. And a two-week lead time was about as low as they could go.

Susan: But why didn't they inform us that these changes were causing problems? They still have some explaining to do.

Kevin: Apparently they tried. What did your team tell this supplier about communicating with us after you finished negotiating the contract?

Bill: We said that any operational problems or issues have to go through our materials management people. The team was responsible for evaluating and selecting the supplier, and then negotiating the agreement.

Kevin: Foster's production manager produced a log detailing seven memos and letters outlining the impact of our production and scheduling changes on their operation. He also called us several times with no response. Each of these inquiries received little attention on the part of our materials group. I'm not sure how fond Foster is of us as a customer. I think they are anxious for this contract to wind down so they can dump us!

Susan: What do we do now?

ASSIGNMENT

1. What parts of the supply chain are most closely involved with the situation in this case? What is the responsibility of each part in order to maintain a smooth flow of material?
2. What initially appears to be the problem? What really is the problem(s) in this case?
3. How easy is it to switch suppliers? What could complicate a firm's ability to switch to a new supplier?
4. What does it mean to get to the root cause of a problem?
5. What does it mean to be a good *customer?* Why does a buying firm want to be perceived by a supplier as a good customer? Provide specific examples of what a firm must do to be a good supply chain customer.
6. Explain the role of performance measurement in managing supply chain activities.
7. Why can changes within a supply chain disrupt the normal flow of goods and services within a supply chain?

8. Why might Avion want to reduce the lead times on its purchased materials and components?
9. Why do firms single-source contracts?
10. Develop an action plan for Avion that addresses the issues presented in this case. Be prepared to fully explain your recommendations.

2 The Global Sourcing Wire Harness Decision

Sheila Austin, a buyer at Autolink, a Detroit-based producer of subassemblies for the automotive market, has sent out requests for quotations for a wiring harness to four prospective suppliers. Only two of the four suppliers indicated an interest in quoting the business: Original Wire (Auburn Hills, MI) and Happy Lucky Assemblies (HLA) of Guangdong Province, China. The estimated demand for the harnesses is 5,000 units a month. Both suppliers will incur some costs to retool for this particular harness. The harnesses will be prepackaged in 24 × 12 × 6-inch cartons. Each packaged unit weighs approximately 10 pounds.

Quote 1

The first quote received is from Original Wire. Auburn Hills is about 20 miles from Autolink's corporate headquarters, so the quote was delivered in person. When Sheila went down to the lobby, she was greeted by the sales agent and an engineering representative. After the quote was handed over, the sales agent noted that engineering would be happy to work closely with Autolink in developing the unit and would also be interested in future business that might involve finding ways to reduce costs. The sales agent also noted that they were hungry for business, as they were losing a lot of customers to companies from China. The quote included unit price, tooling, and packaging. The quoted unit price does not include shipping costs. Original Wire requires no special warehousing of inventory, and daily deliveries from its manufacturing site directly to Autolink's assembly operations are possible.

Original Wire Quote:

- Unit price = $30
- Packing costs = $0.75 per unit
- Tooling = $6,000 one-time fixed charge
- Freight cost = $5.20 per hundred pounds

Quote 2

The second quote received is from Happy Lucky Assemblies of Guangdong Province, China. The supplier must pack the harnesses in a container and ship via inland transportation to the port of Shanghai in China, have the shipment transferred to a container ship, ship material to Seattle, and then have material transported inland to Detroit. The quoted unit price does not include international shipping costs, which the buyer will assume.

HLA Quote:

- Unit price = $19.50
- Shipping lead time = Eight weeks
- Tooling = $3,000

In addition to the supplier's quote, Sheila must consider additional costs and information before preparing a comparison of the Chinese supplier's quotation:

- Each monthly shipment requires three 40-foot containers.
- Packing costs for containerization = $2 per unit.
- Cost of inland transportation to port of export = $200 per container.
- Freight forwarder's fee = $100 per shipment (letter of credit, documentation, etc.).
- Cost of ocean transport = $4,000 per container. This has risen significantly in recent years due to a shortage of ocean freight capacity.
- Marine insurance = $0.50 per $100 of shipment.
- U.S. port handling charges = $1,200 per container. This fee has also risen considerably this year, due to increased security. Ports have also been complaining that the charges may increase in the future.
- Customs duty = 5% of unit cost.
- Customs broker fees per shipment = $300.
- Transportation from Seattle to Detroit = $18.60 per hundred pounds.
- Need to warehouse at least four weeks of inventory in Detroit at a warehousing cost of $1.00 per cubic foot per month, to compensate for lead time uncertainty.

Sheila must also figure the costs associated with committing corporate capital for holding inventory. She has spoken to some accountants, who typically use a corporate cost of capital rate of 15%.

- Cost of hedging currency—broker fees = $400 per shipment
- Additional administrative time due to international shipping = 4 hours per shipment × $25 per hour (estimated)
- At least two five-day visits per year to travel to China to meet with supplier and provide updates on performance and shipping = $20,000 per year (estimated)

The additional costs associated with international purchasing are estimated but are nevertheless present. If Sheila does not assume these costs directly, then both suppliers have agreed to either pay them and invoice Sheila later, or build the costs into a revised unit price. Sheila feels that the U.S. supplier is probably less expensive, even though it quoted a higher price. Sheila also knows that this is a standard technology that is unlikely to change during the next three years, but which could be a contract that extends multiple years out. There is also a lot of "hall talk" amongst the engineers on her floor about next-generation automotive electronics, which will completely eliminate the need for wire harnesses, which will be replaced by electronic components that are smaller, lighter, and more reliable. She is unsure about how to calculate the total costs for each option, and she is even more unsure about how to factor these other variables into the decision.

ASSIGNMENT

1. Calculate the total cost per unit of purchasing from Original Wire.
2. Calculate the total cost per unit of purchasing from Happy Lucky Assemblies.

3. Based on the total cost per unit, which supplier should Sheila recommend?
4. Are there any other issues besides cost that Sheila should evaluate?
5. Based on this case, do you think international purchasing is more or less complex than domestic purchasing? Why? Is it worth the additional effort?

3 Managing Supplier Quality: Integrated Devices

Bill Edwards is a quality engineer assigned to the Injected Molding Commodity Team at Integrated Devices. The commodity team is responsible for evaluating, selecting, and negotiating agreements with plastic-injected molding suppliers to be used throughout Integrated Devices. The team is also responsible for improving service quality and material that Integrated Devices receives from its suppliers. Bill's role after supplier selection involves working directly with suppliers that require training or technical assistance concerning quality control and quality improvement.

The company spends about 70% of each sales dollar on purchased goods and services, so suppliers have a major impact on product quality.

Bill just received a call concerning a recurring manufacturing problem at Integrated Devices' Plant No. 3. The plant buyer said the plant is experiencing some quality variability problems with a key plastic-injected molding component supplied by Trexler Plastics. The component is sometimes too short or too long to fit properly with other components within the finished product. On occasion, the bracket snaps, causing end-product failure. Although the unit cost of the plastic-injected molding component is only $1.55, these quality issues (length variability and snapping) are creating production problems that far exceed the component's purchase price.

The local buyer announced he was having difficulty resolving the problem and asked for support from the corporate commodity team. The buyer said, "You corporate guys selected this supplier that we all have to use. The least you can do is to help us out of the jam your supplier choice is causing." The buyer's comment surprised Bill, although Bill would soon come to understand that plant personnel resented not being able to select their own suppliers.

After investigating the problem during a tension-filled meeting with Plant No. 3 personnel, Bill determined he would have to visit the supplier directly. He would work with Trexler's process engineers to address the manufacturing variability caused by the nonconforming component. Bill went back and reviewed his team's actions when selecting a single supplier to provide an entire family of plastic-injected moldings.

Trexler had quoted the lowest price of all competing suppliers and had provided samples that passed Integrated Devices' engineering tests.

Upon his arrival at the supplier, Bill learned that Trexler did not have a dedicated process engineer. One engineer, Steve Smith, was responsible for plant layout, process, quality, and industrial engineering. This individual, who was hired only two months previously, was still becoming familiar with Trexler's procedures. When Bill asked to review the supplier's quality control procedures, Steve had to ask several people before he could locate Trexler's procedures manual.

Bill decided that his first step should be to understand the process responsible for producing the defective component. At an afternoon meeting, Bill asked Steve for actual output data from Trexler's process. Steve explained they did not collect data for process capability studies or for statistical control charting of continuous production. However, he did say that sometimes, "things don't seem to be operating well" with the equipment that produces the component. Trexler uses an inspector to examine every finished item to determine if it should be shipped to the customer.

After explaining the basics of process capability to Steve, Bill asked him to collect data from the process that produced the bracket component. Bill requested that Steve take exact measurements periodically from the process so they could draw statistical conclusions. Bill said he would return in three days to examine the data.

Upon his return three days later, Steve shared with Bill the details of the data collection effort (see Exhibit 1).

Exhibit 1 **Process Output Data Part #03217666**

4.01	4.02	4.00	3.99	3.98	4.00	4.00	4.03
4.04	4.02	4.07	3.95	3.98	4.01	4.03	4.00
4.00	3.96	3.94	3.98	3.99	4.02	4.01	4.00
4.05	3.98	3.97	4.03	4.07	4.04	4.02	4.01
3.99	3.96	4.00	4.00	4.01	4.02	4.02	4.01
3.98	3.99	3.94	3.93	4.00	4.02	4.00	3.97
3.99	4.02	4.04	4.00	3.96	3.97	4.00	4.01

Component: #03217666

Description: Bracket

Design specification: 4 ± 0.06 inches

Once Bill calculated a preliminary process capability from this data and examined the training and quality control procedures at Trexler, he realized he had some serious work ahead of him.

ASSIGNMENT

1. Calculate the C_p and C_{pk} of the process that produces the component purchased by Integrated Devices. Remember—Process width = 6 times the standard deviation of the sample. Can the process at Trexler satisfy design requirements? What should be a target C_{pk} level?
2. Why is it important to prove that a process is proven capable before developing statistical control limits (i.e., SPC charts)?
3. Is Integrated Devices being reactive or proactive when it comes to managing supplier quality? Why?
4. Discuss the possible advantages of negotiating quality requirements directly into supplier contracts.
5. What is the risk of relying on product samples when selecting suppliers? What is the risk of relying too heavily on unit cost when making the selection decision?
6. Why was it so important for Bill to work with Plant No. 3 personnel before visiting Trexler?

7. The local buyer at Integrated Devices did not seem pleased that a corporate team selected the supplier that the local plants must use. Why do firms use corporate commodity teams to select suppliers? How can firms get support from plant personnel for companywide suppliers?
8. Is quality a major emphasis at this supplier? Why or why not?
9. What are the possible effects if Trexler's inspector approves components for shipment that should be rejected due to nonconformance (Type II error)? What are the possible effects if Trexler's inspector rejects components for shipment that are in conformance with specifications (Type I error)? How can we control error of measurement?
10. When evaluating supplier quality, why is it important to focus on the process that produces the material or service rather than on the material or service itself? What did Integrated Devices rely on?
11. Discuss the likelihood that Bill will resolve the problem(s) with this component.
12. If Integrated Devices decides to continue using Trexler as a supplier, what must both companies do to begin improving Trexler's component quality?
13. Design a supplier quality management process for Integrated Devices that focuses on the prevention of supplier defects. (Hint: Activities performed during supplier evaluation and selection should be part of this process. Process capability analysis may also be part of your supplier quality management process.)

4 Negotiation—Porto

Due to competitive pressures, firms in the computer industry are constantly looking to reduce costs. Computer manufacturers compete fiercely for contracts based on meeting the technology, quality, and price requirements of customers. Profit margins and return-on-investment targets are almost always under pressure. Dell Computer recently saw its operating margins slip to a slim 7%.

Most computer manufacturers have programs designed to improve quality and reduce the costs associated with their products. One strategy that many producers use is to contract only with high-quality suppliers and develop longer-term buyer-seller relationships. One major computer company, Porto, also initiated a program requesting suppliers to continually improve productivity, which should lead to cost reductions.

The objective of the program was to reduce purchase costs over the foreseeable future. Porto also expects its suppliers to contribute cost-saving ideas whenever possible.

The high-technology industry features high fixed costs due to large investments in plant and equipment. These companies also commit large expenditures to research and development.

Porto currently has a requirement for an electronic component termed "New Prod," which is part of a recently designed product. The estimated volume requirement of New Prod is 200,000 units with additional follow-on orders likely. For the New Prod component, Porto felt there were five to eight highly competitive suppliers capable of producing the item. These suppliers are located primarily along the East and West Coasts of the United States. After a request for quote and preliminary analysis, the buyer for Porto decided to pursue further discussions with Technotronics.

Negotiation Session Requirements

Each negotiator must plan and prepare before conducting the negotiation. The group leader has information packets for the buyer and the seller that provide additional information and assignments required for conducting the negotiation. Buyers and sellers can share as little or as much of the information with each other as they desire during the actual negotiation.

Your negotiation strategy should be developed prior to the negotiation session. If working in groups, all group members should participate in the research planning as well as the actual negotiation. Remember, price is not the only variable subject to negotiation. In highly volatile industries like the computer industry, for example, capacity guarantees from suppliers are often critical. Be creative when crafting your purchase agreement.

5 Purchasing Ethics

Scenario 1

Bryan Janz was just arriving back from lunch when his office phone rang. It was his wife, Nina, calling from home. Nina told Bryan that FedEx had just delivered a package addressed to her. The package contained a beautiful clock, now sitting over the fireplace. In fact, Nina said, "the clock looks absolutely beautiful on our living room fireplace." Thinking the clock was from a family member, Bryan asked who sent the present. She said she did not recognize the name—the clock was from Mr. James McEnroe. Bryan immediately told Nina that she had to repack the clock because it was from a supplier who had been trying to win business from Bryan's company. They definitely could not accept the clock. Nina was very upset and responded that the clock was perfect for the room and, besides, the clock came to their home, not to Bryan's office. Because of Nina's attachment to the clock, Bryan was unsure about what to do.

ASSIGNMENT

1. What should Bryan do about the clock?
2. What does the Institute of Supply Management (ISM) code of ethics say about accepting supplier favors and gifts?
3. Why do you think the supplier sent the clock to Bryan's home and addressed it to his wife?
4. Does the mere act of sending the clock to Bryan mean that Mr. McEnroe is an unethical salesperson?

Scenario 2

Lisa Jennings thought that at long last, her company, Assurance Technologies, was about to win a major contract from Sealgood Instruments. Sealgood, a maker of precision measuring instruments, was sourcing a large contract for component subassemblies. The contract that Assurance Technologies was bidding on was worth at least $2.5 million annually, a significant amount given Assurance's annual sales of $30 million. Her team had spent hundreds of hours preparing the quotation and felt they could meet Sealgood's requirements in quality, cost, delivery, part standardization, and simplification. In fact, Lisa had never been more confident about a quote meeting the demanding requirements of a potential customer.

Troy Smyrna, the buyer at Sealgood Instruments responsible for awarding this contract, called Lisa and asked to meet with her at his office to discuss the specifics of the contract. When she arrived, Lisa soon realized that the conversation was not going exactly as she had expected. Troy informed Lisa that Assurance Technologies had indeed prepared a solid quotation for the contract. However, when he visited Assurance's facility earlier on a prequalifying visit, he was disturbed to see a significant amount of a competitor's product being used by Assurance. Troy explained his uneasiness with releasing part plans and designs to a company that clearly had involvement with a competitor. When Lisa asked what Assurance could do to minimize his uneasiness, Troy replied that he would be more comfortable if Assurance no longer used the competitor's equipment and used Sealgood's equipment instead. Lisa responded that this would mean replacing several hundred thousand dollars worth of equipment. Unfazed, Troy simply asked her whether or not she wanted the business. Lisa responded that she needed some time to think and that she would get back to Troy in a day or so.

ASSIGNMENT

1. Do you think the buyer at Sealgood Instruments, Troy Smyrna, is practicing unethical behavior? First, what is the term for this behavior, and defend why you think it is ethical or unethical behavior.
2. What should Lisa do in this situation? Formulate a response.

Scenario 3

Ben Gibson, the purchasing manager at Coastal Products, was reviewing purchasing expenditures for packaging materials with Jeff Joyner. Ben was particularly disturbed about the amount spent on corrugated boxes purchased from Southeastern Corrugated. Ben said, "I don't like the salesman from that company. He comes around here acting like he owns the place. He loves to tell us about his fancy car, house, and vacations. It seems to me he must be making too much money off of us!" Jeff responded that he heard Southeastern Corrugated was going to ask for a price increase to cover the rising costs of raw material paper stock. Jeff further stated that Southeastern would probably ask for more than what was justified simply from rising paper stock costs.

After the meeting, Ben decided he had heard enough. After all, he prided himself on being a results-oriented manager. There was no way he was going to allow that salesman to keep taking advantage of Coastal Products. Ben called Jeff and told him it was time to rebid the corrugated contract before Southeastern came in with a price increase request. Who did Jeff know that might be interested in the business? Jeff replied he had several companies in mind to include in the bidding process. These companies would surely come in at a lower price, partly because they used lower-grade boxes that would probably work well enough in Coastal Products' process. Jeff also explained that these suppliers were not serious contenders for the business. Their purpose was to create competition with the bids. Ben told Jeff to make sure that Southeastern was well aware that these new suppliers were bidding on the contract. He also said to make sure the suppliers knew that price was going to be the determining factor in this quote, because he considered corrugated boxes to be a standard industry item.

ASSIGNMENT

1. Is Ben Gibson acting legally? Is he acting ethically? Why or why not?
2. As the Marketing Manager for Southeastern Corrugated what would you do upon receiving the request for quotation from Coastal Products?

Scenario 4

Sharon Gillespie, a new buyer at Visionex, Inc., was reviewing quotations for a tooling contract submitted by four suppliers. She was evaluating the quotes based on price, target quality levels, and delivery lead time promises. As she was working, her manager, Dave Cox, entered her office. He asked how everything was progressing and if she needed any help. She mentioned she was reviewing quotations from suppliers for a tooling contract. Dave asked who the interested suppliers were and if she had made a decision. Sharon indicated that one supplier, Apex, appeared to fit exactly the requirements Visionex had specified in the proposal. Dave told her to keep up the good work.

Later that day Dave again visited Sharon's office. He stated that he had done some research on the suppliers and felt that another supplier, Micron, appeared to have the best track record with Visionex. He pointed out that Sharon's first choice was a new supplier to Visionex and there was some risk involved with that choice. Dave indicated that it would please him greatly if she selected Micron for the contract.

The next day Sharon was having lunch with another buyer, Mark Smith. She mentioned the conversation with Dave and said she honestly felt that Apex was the best choice. When Mark asked Sharon who Dave preferred, she answered, "Micron." At that point Mark rolled his eyes and shook his head. Sharon asked what the body language was all about. Mark replied, "Look, I know you're new but you should know this. I heard last week that Dave's brother-in-law is a new part owner of Micron. I was wondering how soon it would be before he started steering business to that company. He is not the straightest character." Sharon was shocked. After a few moments, she announced that her original choice was still the best selection. At that point Mark reminded Sharon that she was replacing a terminated buyer who did not go along with one of Dave's previous preferred suppliers.

ASSIGNMENT

1. What does the Institute of Supply Management code of ethics say about financial conflicts of interest?
2. Ethical decisions that affect a buyer's ethical perspective usually involve the organizational environment, cultural environment, personal environment, and industry environment. Analyze this scenario using these four variables.
3. What should Sharon do in this situation?

6 Insourcing/Outsourcing: The FlexCon Piston Decision

This case addresses many issues that affect insourcing/outsourcing decisions. A complex and important topic facing businesses today is whether to produce a component, assembly, or service internally (insourcing) or purchase that same component, assembly, or service from an external supplier (outsourcing).

Because of the important relationship between insourcing/outsourcing and competitiveness, organizations must consider many variables when considering an insourcing/outsourcing decision. This may include a detailed examination of a firm's competency and costs, along with quality, delivery, technology, responsiveness, and continuous improvement requirements. Because of the critical nature of many insourcing/outsourcing decisions, cross-functional teams often assume responsibility for managing the decision-making process. A single functional group usually does not have the data, insight, or knowledge required to make effective strategic insourcing/outsourcing decisions.

FlexCon's Insourcing/Outsourcing of Pistons

FlexCon, a $3 billion maker of small industrial engines, is undergoing a major internal review to decide where the company should focus its product development efforts and strategic investment. Executive management is arguing that too much capacity and talent are being committed to producing simple, commodity-type items that provide small differentiation within the marketplace. FlexCon concluded that in its attempts to preserve jobs, it has insourced parts that are easy to manufacture, while outsourcing those that are complex or challenging. Producing commodity-like components with mature technologies is adding little to what FlexCon's customers consider important. The company has become increasingly dependent on suppliers for critical components and subassemblies that make a major difference in the performance and cost of finished products.

Part of FlexCon's effort at redefining itself involves creating an understanding of insourcing/outsourcing among managers and employees. The company has sponsored workshops and presentations to convey executive management's vision and goals, including educating those who are directly involved in making detailed insourcing/outsourcing recommendations.

One presentation given by an expert in strategic sourcing focused on the changes in the marketplace that are encouraging outsourcing. The expert noted six key trends and changes that influence insourcing/outsourcing decisions:

1. *The pressure for cost reduction is severe and will continue to increase.* Cost reduction pressures are forcing organizations to use their production resources more efficiently. A recent study found that over 70% of firms surveyed expect stable or increasing purchased material costs through 2010. As a result,

executive management will increasingly rely on insourcing/outsourcing decisions as a way to manage costs.

2. *Firms are continuing to become more highly specialized in product and process technology.* Increased specialization implies focused investment in a process or technology, which contributes to greater cost differentials between firms.
3. *Firms will increasingly focus on what they excel at while outsourcing areas of nonexpertise.* Some organizations are formally defining their core competencies to help guide the insourcing/outsourcing effort. This has affected decisions concerning what businesses a firm should engage.
4. *The need for responsiveness in the marketplace is increasingly affecting insourcing/outsourcing decisions.* Shorter cycle times, for example, encourage greater outsourcing with less vertical integration. The time to develop a production capability or capacity may exceed the window available to enter a new market.
5. *Wall Street recognizes and rewards firms with higher ROI/ROA.* Because insourcing usually requires an assumption of fixed assets (and increased human capital), financial pressures are causing managers to closely examine sourcing decisions. Avoidance of fixed costs and assets is motivating many firms to rely on supplier assets.
6. *Improved computer simulation tools and forecasting software enable firms to perform insourcing/outsourcing comparisons with greater precision.* These tools allow the user to perform sensitivity analysis (what-if analysis) that permits comparison of different sourcing possibilities.

One topic that interested FlexCon managers was a discussion of how core competencies relate to outsourcing decisions. FlexCon management commonly accepted that a core competency was something the company "was good at." This view, however, is not correct. A core competency refers to skills, processes, or resources *that distinguish a company,* are hard to duplicate, and make that firm unique compared to other firms. Core competencies begin to define a firm's long-run, strategic ability to build a dominant set of technologies or skills that enable it to adapt quickly to changing market opportunities. The presenter argued that three key points relate to the idea of core competence and its relationship to insourcing/outsourcing decisions:

1. A firm should concentrate internally on those components, assemblies, systems, or services that are critical to the finished product and where the firm possesses a distinctive (i.e., unique) advantage valued by the customer.
2. Consider outsourcing components, assemblies, systems, or services when suppliers have an advantage. Supplier advantages may occur because of economies of scale, process-specific investment, higher quality, familiarity with a technology, or a favorable cost structure.
3. Recognize that once a firm outsources an item or service, it usually loses the ability to bring that production capability or technology in-house without committing a significant investment.

The manager or team responsible for making an insourcing/outsourcing decision must develop a true sense of what the core competency of the organization is and whether the product or service under consideration is an integral part of that core competency.

The workshops and presentations have given most participants a greater appreciation of the need to consider factors besides cost when assessing insourcing/

Exhibit 1 | **Key Factors Supporting Insourcing/Outsourcing Decisions**

FACTORS SUPPORT INSOURCING:	FACTORS SUPPORT OUTSOURCING:
1. Cost considerations favor the buyer.	1. Cost considerations favor the supplier.
2. A need or desire exists to integrate internal plant operations.	2. Supplier has specialized research and know-how, which creates differentials in cost and quality.
3. Excess plant capacity is available that can absorb fixed overhead.	3. Buying firm lacks the technical ability to build an item.
4. A need exists to exert direct control over production and quality.	4. Buyer has small volume requirements.
5. Product design secrecy is an important issue.	5. Buying firm has capacity constraints while the seller does not.
6. A lack of reliable suppliers characterizes the supply market.	6. Buyer does not want to add permanent workers.
7. Firm desires to maintain a stable workforce in a declining market.	7. Future volume requirements are uncertain—buyer wants to transfer risk to the supplier.
8. Item or service is directly part of a firm's core competency, or links directly to the strategic plans of the organization.	8. Item or service is routine and available from many competitive sources.
9. Item or technology behind making the item is strategic to the firm. The item adds to the qualities customers consider important.	9. Short cycle time requirements discourage new investment by the buyer—using existing supplier assets is logical.
10. Union or other restrictions discourage or even prohibit outsourcing.	10. Adding capacity at the buyer requires high capital start-up costs.
11. Outsourcing may create or encourage a new competitor.	11. Process technology is mature with minimal likelihood of providing a future competitive advantage to the purchaser.

outsourcing opportunities. One breakout work session focused exclusively on developing a list of the key factors that may affect the insourcing/outsourcing analysis at FlexCon, which appears in Exhibit 1.

The Piston Insourcing/Outsourcing Decision

FlexCon is considering outsourcing production of all pistons that are part of the company's "R" series of engines. FlexCon has machined various versions of these pistons for as long as anyone at the company can remember. In fact, the company started fifty years ago as a producer of high-quality pistons. The company grew as customers requested that FlexCon produce a broader line of products. This outsourcing analysis has generated a great deal of interest and emotion among FlexCon engineers, managers, and employees.

FlexCon produces pistons in three separate work cells, which differ according to the type of piston produced. Each cell has six numerically controlled machines in a U-shape layout, with a supervisor, a process engineer, a material handler, and 12 employees assigned across the three cells. Employees, who are cross-trained to perform each job within their cell, work in teams of four. FlexCon experienced a 30% gain in quality and a 20% gain in productivity after shifting from a process layout, where equipment was grouped by similar capabilities, to work cells, where equipment was grouped to support a specific family of products. If FlexCon decides to outsource the pistons, the company will likely dedicate the floor space currently occupied by the work cells to a new product or expansion of an existing product. FlexCon will apply the work cell equipment for other applications, so the outsourcing analysis will not consider equipment write-offs beyond normal depreciation.

Although there are different opinions regarding outsourcing the pistons, FlexCon engineers agreed that the process technology used to produce this family of components is mature. Gaining future competitive advantages from new technology was probably not as great as other process applications within FlexCon's production process. This did not mean, however, that FlexCon could avoid making new investments in process technology if the pistons remained in-house, or that some level of process innovation is not possible.

Differences over outsourcing a component that is critical to the performance of FlexCon's final product threatens to affect the insourcing/outsourcing decision. One engineer threatened to quit if FlexCon outsourced a component that could "bring down" the entire engine in case of quality failure. He also maintained, "Our pistons are known in the industry as first-rate." Another engineer suggested that FlexCon's supply management group, if given support from the engineers, could adequately manage any risk of poor supplier quality. However, a third engineer noted, "Opportunistic suppliers will exploit FlexCon if given the chance—we've seen it before!" This engineer warned the group about suppliers "buying in" to the piston business only to coercively raise prices. Several experienced engineers voiced the opinion that they could not imagine FlexCon outsourcing a component that was responsible for making FlexCon the company it is today. Several newer members of the engineering group suggested they should wait until the outsourcing cost analysis was complete before rendering final judgment.

Management has created a cross-functional team composed of a process engineer, a cost analyst, a quality engineer, a procurement specialist, a supervisor, and a machine cell employee to conduct the outsourcing analysis. A major issue confronting this team involves determining which internal costs to apply to the analysis. Including total variable costs is straightforward because these costs are readily identifiable and vary directly with production levels. Examples of variable costs include materials, direct labor, and transportation.

The team is struggling with whether (or at what level) to include total factory and administrative costs (i.e., fixed costs and the fixed portion of semivariable costs). Factory and administrative costs include utilities, indirect labor, process engineering support, depreciation, corporate office administration, maintenance, and product design charges. Proper allocation of overhead is a difficult, and sometimes subjective, task. The assumptions the team makes about how to allocate total factory and operating costs can dramatically alter the results of the analysis.

Exhibit 2 Aggregated Two-Year Piston Demand

	YEAR 1 EXPECTED DEMAND	YEAR 2 EXPECTED DEMAND
January	30,000	34,000
February	30,000	34,000
March	30,000	34,000
April	27,000	31,000
May	25,000	28,000
June	25,000	28,000
July	23,000	27,000
August	21,000	25,000
September	22,000	25,000
October	23,000	27,000
November	23,000	27,000
December	21,000	25,000
Total	300,000	345,000

The aggregated volume for pistons over the next several years is critical to this analysis. Exhibit 2 provides a monthly forecast of expected piston volumes over the next two years. Total forecasted volume is 300,000 units in Year 1 and 345,000 units in Year 2. The team arrived at the forecast by determining the forecast for FlexCon "R" series engines, which is an independent demand item. Pistons are a dependent demand item (i.e., dependent on the demand for the final product).

Although this is a long-term decision likely to extend beyond ten years, the team has confidence in its projections (including supplier pricing) only through two years. Although maintaining piston production internally would require some level of process investment in Years 3 through 10, the team believes any projections past Year 2 contain too much uncertainty. (Conducting a net present value for expected savings from outsourcing, if they exist, is beyond the scope of this assignment.)

Insourcing Costs

The team has decided that a comprehensive total cost analysis should include all direct and indirect costs incurred to support piston production. FlexCon tracks its materials and labor by completing production worksheets for each job. The team collected data for the previous year, which revealed that the three work cells produced 288,369 pistons.

Direct Materials

FlexCon machines the pistons from a semifinished steel alloy purchased directly from a steel foundry. The foundry ships the alloy to FlexCon in 50 lb. blocks, which cost $195 per block. Each piston requires, on average, 1.1 lb. of semifinished raw material for each finished piston. This figure includes scrap and waste.

The team expects the semifinished raw material price to remain constant over the next two years. Although FlexCon expects greater piston volumes in Years 1 and 2 compared with current demand, the team does not believe additional material economies are available.

FlexCon spent $225,000 last year on other miscellaneous direct materials required to produce the pistons. The team expects to use this figure as a basis for calculating expected Year 1 and 2 costs for miscellaneous direct material requirements.

Direct Work Cell Labor

The direct labor in the three work cells worked a total of 27,000 hours last year. Total payroll for direct labor was $472,500, which includes overtime pay. The average direct labor rate is $17.50 per hour ($472,500 / 27,000 total hours = $17.50 per hour). As a rule of thumb, the team expects to add 40% to direct labor costs to account for benefits (health, dental, pension, etc.). The team also expects direct labor rates to increase 3% a year for the next two years. The team does not expect per-hour production rates to change significantly. The process is well established, and FlexCon has already captured any learning curve benefits.

Work cell employees are responsible for machine setup, so the team decided not to include machine setup as a separate cost category.

Indirect Work Cell Labor

FlexCon assigns a supervisor, material handler, and engineer full-time to the three work cells. Last year, the supervisor earned $52,000, the material handler earned $37,000, and the engineer earned $63,000 in salary. Again, the team expects to apply an additional 40% to these figures to reflect fringe benefits. The team expects these salaries to increase 3% each year.

Factory Overhead and Administrative Costs

This category of costs is, without doubt, the most difficult category of cost to allocate. For example, should the team prorate part of the plant manager's salary to the piston work cells? One team member argued that these costs are present with or without piston production and, therefore, should not be part of the insourcing calculation. Another member maintained that factory overhead supports the factory, and the three work cells are a major part of the factory. Not including these costs would distort the insourcing calculation. She noted that the supplier is most assuredly considering these costs when quoting the piston contract. Another member suggested performing two analyses of insourcing costs. One would include factory overhead and administrative costs, and the other would exclude these costs.

The team divided the factory into six "zones" based on the functions performed throughout the plant. The piston work cells account for 25% of the factory's floor space, 28% of total direct labor hours, and 23% of plant volume. From this analysis, the team has decided to allocate 25% of the factory's overhead and administrative costs to the piston work cells for the analysis that includes these costs. Exhibit 3 presents relevant cost data for the previous year. The team expects these costs to increase 3% each year.

Preventive Maintenance Costs

FlexCon spent $40,250 on preventive maintenance activities on the 18 machines in the three cells last year and expects this to increase by 10% in each of the next two years (due to the increasing age of the equipment).

Machine Repair Costs

An examination of maintenance work orders reveals that the 18 work cell machines, which are each five to seven years old, required total unplanned repair expenses of $37,000 last year. The maintenance supervisor expects this figure to increase by 8% in Year 1 and 12% in Year 2 of the analysis due to increasing age and volumes.

Exhibit 3 Total Factory Overhead and Administrative Costs

COST CATEGORY	PREVIOUS YEAR EXPENSE/COST
Administrative staff	$1,200,000
Staff engineering	$ 900,000
Taxes	$ 120,000
Utilities	$1,500,000
Insurance	$ 500,000
Plant Maintenance	$ 800,000
Total	$5,020,000

Ordering Costs

Although FlexCon produces pistons in-house, the company still incurs ordering costs for direct materials. The team estimates that each monthly order to the foundry and other suppliers costs FlexCon $1,500 in direct and transaction-related costs.

Semifinished Raw Material Inventory Carrying Costs

FlexCon typically maintains one month of semifinished raw material inventory as safety and buffer stock. The carrying charge assigned to this inventory is 18% annually.

Inbound Transportation

FlexCon receives a monthly shipment of semifinished alloy that the work cells use to machine the pistons. Total transportation costs for the previous year amounted to $31,500 (which resulted in 288,369 pistons produced).

The team expects transportation charges for other direct materials used in production to be $0.01 per unit in Years 1 and 2 of the analysis.

Consumable Tooling Costs

The machines in the work cell are notorious for "going through tooling." Given the consumable tooling costs realized during the previous year, the team estimates additional tooling expenses of $56,000 in Year 1, and $65,000 in Year 2.

Depreciation

The team has decided to include in its cost calculation normal depreciation expenses for the 18 work cell machines. The depreciation expense for the equipment is $150,000 per year.

Finished Piston Carrying Costs

Because FlexCon coordinates the production of pistons with the production of "R" series engines, any inventory carrying charges for finished pistons are part of the cost of the finished engine and are not considered relevant to this calculation.

Opportunity Costs

The team recognizes that opportunities may exist for achieving a better return on the space and equipment committed to piston production. Unfortunately, the team does not know with any certainty what management's plans may be for the floor space or equipment if FlexCon outsources piston production. The team is confident, however, that management will find a use for the space. If the facility no longer engages in piston production, then FlexCon must allocate fixed factory and overhead costs across a lower base of production. This will increase the average costs of the remaining items produced in the plant, possibly making them uncompetitive compared with external suppliers.

Outsourcing Costs

The following provides relevant information collected by the team as it relates to outsourcing the family of pistons to an external supplier. Although it is beyond the scope of this case, the team has already performed a rigorous assessment of the supply market and has reached consensus on the external supplier in the event the team recommends outsourcing. This was necessary to obtain reliable outsourcing cost data.

Unit Price

The most obvious cost in an outsourcing analysis is the unit price quoted by the supplier. In many respects, outsourcing is an exercise in supplier evaluation and selection. Insourcing/outsourcing requires the evaluation of several suppliers in depth—the internal supplier (FlexCon) and external suppliers (in the marketplace). The supplier that the team favors if FlexCon outsources the pistons quoted an average unit price of $12.20 per piston (recall that this outsourcing decision involves different piston part numbers). The team believes that negotiation will occur if FlexCon elects to outsource, perhaps resulting in a lower quoted price. Because the team does not yet know the final negotiated price, some members argued that several outsourcing analyses are required to reflect different possible unit prices. Quoted terms are 2/10, net 30. The supplier says it will maintain the negotiated price over the next two years.

Safety Stock Requirements

If the team decides to outsource, FlexCon will hold physical stock from the supplier equivalent to one month's average demand. This results in an inventory carrying charge, which the team must calculate and include in the total cost analysis. Although FlexCon likely will rely on or draw down safety stock levels during the next two years, for purposes of costing the inventory the team has decided not to estimate when this might occur. Inventory carrying charges include working capital committed to financing the inventory, plus charges for material handling, warehousing, insurance and taxes, and risk of obsolescence and damage. FlexCon's inventory carrying charge is 18% annually.

Administrative Support Costs

FlexCon expects to commit the equivalent of one third of a buyer's total time to supporting the commercial issues related to the outsourced family of pistons. The team estimates the buyer's salary at $54,000, with 40% for fringe benefits. The team expects the buyer's compensation to increase by 3% each year.

Ordering Costs

The team expects that FlexCon will order monthly, or twelve material releases a year. Unfortunately, suppliers in this industry have not been responsive to shipping on a just-in-time basis or using electronic data interchange. Although FlexCon would like to pursue a JIT purchasing model, the team feels that assuming lower volume shipments on a frequently scheduled basis is not appropriate. The company expects the supplier to deliver one month of inventory at the beginning of each month. The team estimates the cost to release and receive an order to be $1,500 per order.

Quality-Related Costs

The team has decided to include quality-related costs in its outsourcing calculations. During the investigation of the supplier, a team member collected data on the process that would likely produce FlexCon's pistons. The team estimates that the supplier's defect level, based on process measurement data, will be 1,500 ppm. FlexCon's quality assurance department estimates that each supplier defect will cost the company an average of $250 in nonconformance costs.

Inventory Carrying Charges

FlexCon must assume inventory carrying charges for pistons received at the start of each month and then consumed at a steady rate during the month. For purposes of calculating inventory-carrying costs for finished pistons provided by the supplier, the team expects to use the average inventory method. The formula for determining the average number of units in inventory each month is the following:

$$((\text{Beginning Inventory at the Start of Each Month} + \text{Ending Inventory at the End of Each Month})/2) \times \text{Carrying Cost per Month}$$

For calculation purposes, the team assumes that ending inventory each month is zero units (excluding safety stock, which requires a separate calculation). The team expects production to use all the pistons received at the beginning of each month. The carrying charge applied to inventory on an annual basis is 14% of the unit value of the inventory.[1] Appendixes 1 and 2 on pp. 791 and 792 will help in the calculation of monthly carrying charges associated with holding supplier-provided piston inventory.

Transportation Charges

Although it is FlexCon's policy to have suppliers ship goods F.O.B. shipping point, the company does not accept title or ownership of goods until receipt at the buyer's dock. However, the company assumes all transportation-related charges. The team estimates that transportation charges for pistons will average $2,100 per truckload, with fourteen truckloads expected in Year 1 and sixteen truckloads expected in Year 2. The outsourcing supplier is in the United States, which means the team does not have to consider additional costs related to international purchasing.

Tooling Charges

The supplier said that new tooling charges to satisfy FlexCon's production requirements would be $300,000. The team has decided to depreciate tooling charges over two years, or $150,000 per year.

Appendix 1 Year 1 Inventory Carrying Charges Outsourcing Option

	BEGINNING INVENTORY	ENDING INVENTORY	AVERAGE INVENTORY	INVENTORY CARRYING COSTS
January	30,000	0		$
February	30,000	0		$
March	30,000	0		$
April	27,000	0		$
May	25,000	0		$
June	25,000	0		$
July	23,000	0		$
August	21,000	0		$
September	22,000	0		$
October	23,000	0		$
November	23,000	0		$
December	21,000	0		$
			Total Inventory Carrying Costs	

Appendix 2	Year 2 Inventory Carrying Charges Outsourcing Option			
	BEGINNING INVENTORY	ENDING INVENTORY	AVERAGE INVENTORY	INVENTORY CARRYING COSTS
January	34,000	0		$
February	34,000	0		$
March	34,000	0		$
April	31,000	0		$
May	28,000	0		$
June	28,000	0		$
July	27,000	0		$
August	25,000	0		$
September	25,000	0		$
October	27,000	0		$
November	27,000	0		$
December	25,000	0		$
			Total Inventory Carrying Costs	

Supplier Capacity

The team has concluded that the supplier has available capacity to satisfy Flex-Con's total piston requirements.

Appendix 3 provides a worksheet to help in the insourcing/outsourcing cost analysis.

Appendix 3	Insourcing/Outsourcing Cost Factors Worksheet				
INSOURCING COSTS PER UNIT	YEAR 1	YEAR 2	OUTSOURCING COSTS PER UNIT	YEAR 1	YEAR 2
Direct materials			Purchase cost		
Semifinished					
Other					
Direct labor			Transportation		
Indirect labor			New tooling		
Factory overhead and administrative			Administrative support		
Preventive maintenance			Inventory carrying		
Machine repair			Safety stock		
Ordering			Quality-related costs		
Depreciation			Ordering		
Inventory carrying			Other costs		
Inbound transportation			**Total Outsourcing Costs per Unit**		
Consumable tooling			Total savings (1)		
Other costs			Less: Taxes on savings (40%)		
Total Insourcing Cost per Unit			**Net Outsourcing Savings**		

Total Savings = (Total Insourcing Costs – Total Outsourcing Costs) × (Total Volume).
Note that the total savings could be negative if the analysis shows that outsourcing costs are greater than insourcing costs.

ASSIGNMENT

1. Perform a quantitative insourcing/outsourcing analysis using the data provided. What qualitative issues might affect your final decision? Identify any costs or issues that are not part of your analysis that might affect your decision. What is your recommendation regarding what FlexCon should do with its family of pistons? Support your arguments with evidence gathered during your analysis.
2. Assume your group decided to outsource the pistons to the external supplier. Identify a plan that would enable FlexCon to carry out this recommendation. Be as thorough as possible.
3. Discuss the primary reasons when and why insourcing/outsourcing decisions occur.
4. A major challenge with an insourcing/outsourcing analysis involves gathering reliable data. Discuss the various groups that should be involved when conducting an insourcing/outsourcing analysis such as the one presented in this case. What information can each of these groups provide?
5. Discuss the major issues associated with an insourcing/outsourcing analysis and decision.

ENDNOTES

1. The 14% figure is less than the 18% figure applied to safety stock carrying charges. The supplier does not receive payment until at least four weeks after FlexCon receives the pistons. This makes FlexCon's working capital committed to financing production inventory somewhat less than the capital committed to financing safety stock.

Index

Page numbers in italics refer to exhibits.

F

J

K

L

P

Q

R

S

T